Communicating in Spanish

Communicating in Spanish

Level One

Enrique E. Lamadrid
University of New Mexico at Albuquerque

William E. Bull

Laurel A. Briscoe
University of Texas at Austin

Houghton Mifflin Company · Boston
Atlanta   Dallas   Geneva, Illinois
Hopewell, New Jersey   Palo Alto   London

Acknowledgments

We are grateful for the suggestions many friends and colleagues have made in the preparation of these materials. We are especially grateful to Margaret Brown of UCLA for coming to our aid when there was insufficient time to accomplish all the tasks that remained to be done, and to Carl Dellaccio of the Tacoma, Washington Public Schools whose advice and criticism over the past several years have been of great value in the development of these materials.

The Visual Grammar of Spanish posters are reprinted by permission of Houghton Mifflin Company and The Regents of the University of California. Copyright © 1972 by Houghton Mifflin Company. Copyright © The Regents of the University of California, and produced under contract between The Regents of the University of California and the United States Office of Education, Department of Health, Education, and Welfare.

Library of Congress Catalog Card Number: 73-8444

ISBN: 0-395-17529-1

Portions of this work first appeared in *Spanish for Communication*, Level One and Level Two, copyright © 1972 by Houghton Mifflin Company.

Introduction to the Student

COMMUNICATING IN SPANISH (CIS) is an entirely new program for learning Spanish. It takes into account the most recent developments in learning theory, applied linguistics, methods of teaching foreign languages, and classroom teaching techniques. The following is a brief description of the materials which make up the program, a brief statement of the philosophy behind CIS, and a list of suggested study procedures to increase your chances of success.

Description of Materials

Student Text: The student text is divided into two sections: Assignments and Ejercicios (Exercises). The Ejercicios are done in class with your instructor, so that you need not spend any time working on them outside of class. There are 110 Assignments, divided into six phases called Etapas, for you to complete outside of class. Each Etapa is preceded by a list of Performance Objectives for that phase of instruction. The Performance Objectives simply state what it is you should be able to do after completing a given Etapa that you couldn't do before. Each Assignment usually consists of: one or more "programs" which are set up as a series of numbered frames that give bits of information and provide a problem for you to solve, followed by the answer to each problem; a Summary of the information in the programs; self-correcting exercises that test your mastery of the Assignment; and a list of new vocabulary.

Each Assignment should be studied prior to each class meeting. To derive full benefit from this program, it is very important that you study each Assignment when it is assigned. (Please see pages vi and vii for additional information on the importance of pre-class preparation in the CIS program.) In each class meeting, your instructor will lead you through a series of activities co-ordinated with the Assignment you read before class. These activities are designed to help you master the use of the concepts and information presented in the student text.

Workbook of Optional Assignments: The Workbook contains 110 Optional Assignments designed to do the following: 1) to give you a different presentation of each major language problem in case you learn more effectively from a style of learning other than that provided in the regular Assignments and in class, 2) to make readily available all important information in case you are absent from class, 3) to provide additional reviews and self-correcting practice in preparation for tests or in an area in which you feel weak, and 4) to enable you to achieve a higher level of mastery (if you wish to and if you have time) than that attainable with the regular materials.

Recorded Materials: A complete recorded program is provided which parallels your class work and the material in the student text. Some selections are designed to improve listening comprehension of spoken Spanish and may be used in class by your instructor. All recorded material is suitable for laboratory work on a self-instructional basis. You will increase your listening and speaking proficiency if you arrange time to use the recorded material regularly.

The "Why's" of CIS

In every foreign language program designed for classroom instruction, there are three active participants: the teacher, the student, and the author of the text. COMMUNICATING IN SPANISH is based on the obvious facts that to achieve the objectives of any program, there is a specific number of tasks and operations which have to be performed, and that these tasks must be assigned to the participant who can carry them out most effectively and with a minimal expenditure of time and energy.

CIS acknowledges a fundamental difference between imparting knowledge or information and teaching language skills. To say to you, for example, that the English verb has two parts—a stem and a suffix—while in contrast the Spanish verb has three parts—a stem and two suffixes—is not really teaching. The speaker merely serves as an information source, and you either store that information in your memory for future reference or forget it.

There is no basic difference between imparting facts of this kind and saying that water is composed of two parts hydrogen and one of oxygen. In contrast, teaching you to generate a Spanish p sound automatically, requires the presentation of information (unlike English, it is made without a puff), and supervised practice. The instructor, in reality, serves as a coach who observes your efforts, makes suggestions for improvement, and signals you when you have unconsciously made a mistake.

CIS is based on research which indicates that when the students are literate, it is inefficient for the instructor to spend class time presenting the factual information needed to learn to communicate in a foreign language. There are three basic reasons for this. First, there is very little communication if the instructor speaks at a rate over 150 words per minute, or if the amount of information needed is so large that the course becomes a lecture about the language. This is a great waste of time when you can read the same information at the rate of three or four hundred words per minute.

Second, since the instructor presents the information from memory, essential steps in learning may be skipped, the sequence of presenting the facts may be wrong, and key words may not be understood. However, when the same information is presented in writing, the authors can spend whatever time is needed to polish the presentation, to test it on students, and to re-write until the majority of readers achieve the desired objectives.

Third, there is incontrovertible evidence that different individuals accept, process, and store information at different speeds. There are, in fact, geniuses who are very slow in doing this. It is obvious that the instructor who has more than one student in his class cannot be the most efficient medium for transmitting knowledge. The input rate is the speed at which the instructor speaks, and there is no time for the students to stop and think over a point before going on to the next step. Therefore, with only minor exceptions, all information to be learned in CIS is initially presented in the written Assignments. This permits you, the student, to select the rate of input which is most comfortable and efficient.

CIS is *not* designed to teach for mastery the first time through. When something is introduced in a given class, it is re-entered in subsequent classes as many times as needed to assure that a majority of the students have achieved mastery of the particular point. This distributed practice procedure requires class strategies in which only a few minutes are devoted to an activity, and many items are practiced in each class hour. The length of each activity is not determined by how long it takes the class to master the item, but by how long the average class can profit from it.

After the first few classes, each meeting will provide practice in some things you do quite well, some you can do slowly, and others that you are just beginning to practice. You should not request that your instructor extend the practice time on an item just because you feel insecure on a given day. What you are worrying about today will be re-entered in the Assignment and in class tomorrow, and at carefully planned intervals on subsequent days.

How To Be Successful with CIS

No two people learn in exactly the same way. Your inherited potential and past life experiences make your learning style unique. Fully aware of this, the authors of CIS have built into the program a variety of learning opportunities, as well as instructions on how to study efficiently and effectively. For the most part, the programs in each Assignment use a "guided discovery" approach to learning. The presentation is verbal with some diagrams and charts. If you learn more readily through pictures, there are visuals which present a grammatical concept in pictorial form. Should you be the kind of learner who prefers to see a set of rules followed by examples before you are given practice problems, you will find this approach in the Workbook. If you use all three presentations, each will tend to strengthen the other and should provide the means for you to be as successful as possible.

The following are suggestions that will help you to be an outstanding student in learning to communicate in Spanish:

1 Attend class regularly and participate in all class activities.

2   Respond to every problem your instructor poses in class, no matter who is called on to answer. You can respond mentally and then check your accuracy when the answer is given. If you do this regularly, you will have hundreds more practice opportunities than if you merely sit and wait your turn.

3   Complete every Assignment on time. The programs in many Assignments are designed to prepare you specifically for the class session that follows.

4   Experiment to discover how you learn best. You may do the Assignment first and use the Summary to review and check on what you have learned. In reverse, you may study the Summary first and use the Assignment to find out whether you understand the details.

5   Keep a vocabulary list and study it for two to four minutes every day. Suggestions on how to do this are given in the Assignments.

6   Read aloud in Spanish for two or three minutes every day to improve your pronunciation and fluency.

7   From the very beginning of the course, think and talk to yourself in Spanish, using whatever Spanish you have learned. This can be done at any time when you do not need to use your mind for other things, *e.g.*, while brushing your teeth, waiting for a bus, eating alone.

8   Read the objectives at the beginning of each Etapa, and re-read them regularly. Research shows that students who know what their learning objectives are for an instructional sequence learn far more than students who do not.

9   Repeat the self-correcting exercises in each Assignment until your responses are nearly automatic.

Neither your instructor nor this program can teach you Spanish. They can only provide the information needed and the exercises necessary for practice. But you have to do the learning. Thus, your instructor can tell you that the Spanish for "town" is *pueblo*, but you have to store *pueblo* in your memory and learn to retrieve it on demand. CIS defines your learning tasks very carefully. If you are faithful in performing them, the program will achieve its goal of teaching you to communicate in Spanish, and to better understand the world as a Spanish speaker sees it.

Contents

ETAPA TRES

ETAPA CUATRO

ETAPA CINCO

ETAPA SEIS

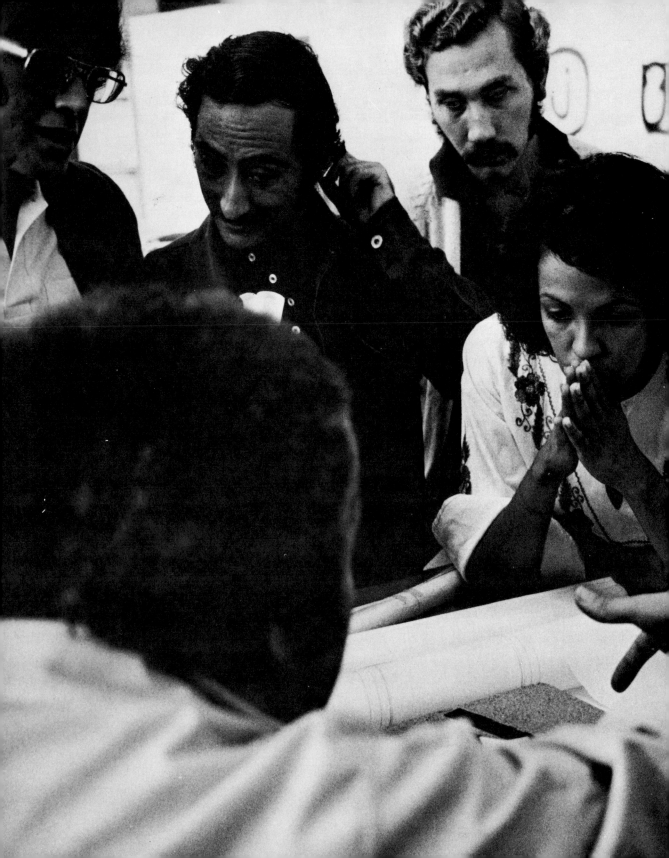

ETAPA UNO

Performance Objectives
for Assignments 1–17

Recent investigations overwhelmingly substantiate the hypothesis that a student's learning increases in proportion to his <u>awareness</u> of the learning goals toward which he is striving.

Until you see the final examination in some of your courses, you may have only faint notions as to what learning objectives your instuctor has in mind for you. Frequently students use considerable mental energy in an effort to "psych out" the instructor's goals. Some instructors pride themselves on making a course as difficult as possible for students. Such instructors may, on the final examination, include problems for which little—if any—previous preparation has been provided.

That will <u>not</u> be the case with this Spanish course. At the beginning of each of the six phases of learning (six *Etapas*), the objectives (along with illustrative test items) are stated in terms of specific bits of information to be learned and skills to be mastered. So that you may be continually informed of the goals toward which you are working, read the objectives carefully as you <u>begin</u> each *Etapa*, and refer back to them regularly.

It is not the intent of the authors of CIS to provide "trick" test problems nor to build a reputation that Spanish is a difficult language to learn, but rather to provide the most efficient and effective way possible for you to learn to communicate in Spanish. To this end these objectives are provided.

You will be prepared to continue your study of Spanish successfully if by Assignment 17 you have achieved the following objectives:

Listening Comprehension

1   Given an oral statement in Spanish based on vocabulary through Assignment 17 and an English question about the statement, you write the correct answer in English at least seven times out of ten.

You hear: *Estudian en la oficina.* What do they do in the office?
You write: They study.

2   At least four out of five times you write the numerical equivalent of arithmetical problems presented orally in Spanish.

You hear: *Diez y cinco son quince.*
You write: $10 + 5 = 15$.

Listening and Reading Comprehension

3   From three written responses to an oral statement or question you select the most logical one at least seven times out of ten.

You hear: *¿Cuántos son siete menos tres?*
You select *c* from the three alternatives:

a   Son cinco.
b   Son dos.
c   Son cuatro.

Reading Comprehension

4   Given in Spanish a sentence fragment or question and three possible completions or responses containing vocabulary studied through Assignment 17, you choose the most logical completion or answer at least two times out of three.

You see the following problem and select *b* as the appropriate answer:

Hoy es miércoles y . . .
a   mañana es domingo.
b   mañana es jueves.
c   mañana es martes.

Vocabulary

5   You match correctly at least seven of nine Spanish words with their nearest English equivalents.

You see:
1 *día* ( )   (a) pencil
2 *lápiz* ( )   (b) ten
                                          (c) day

You write *c* in the first parentheses and *a* in the second.

Pronunciation and Spelling

6   (Evaluated following Assignment 7) You write from dictation with correct spelling at least sixteen out of twenty Spanish words containing any of the five vowels, *p, t, m, n, f, l,* or *d*.

You hear and write: *mano, pata, etc.*

7   (Evaluated following Assignment 12) You write from dictation with correct spelling at least nineteen out of 23 familiar Spanish words.

You hear and write: *Hasta mañana.*

8   You identify correctly at least nine times out of twelve [r], [rr], and the allophones of /d/ and /b/.

You see:

```
        1              2             3          4    5    6
L a s   d o s   s e ñ o r i t a s   n u e v a s   s o n   d e   R o m b a l s a.
```

And you are told to circle the numbered instances of [r] and the stop allophones of /d/ and /b/, and to underline [rr] and the fricative allophones of /d/ and /b/. You circle 2, 4, and 6; and you underline 1, 3, and 5.

Morphology and Usage

9   (Evaluated following Assignment 12) Given orally six Spanish nouns, you write the correct matching form of the indefinite article for at least five.

You hear: *pupitre.*
You write: *un*

10 (Evaluated following Assignment 12) Given orally nine Spanish nouns you write the correct matching form of the definite article for at least seven.

You hear: *alumnas.*
You write: *las*

11 Given ten English sentences each containing an indicated adjective you write the appropriate Spanish translation for at least seven of the adjectives.

You see: They are **good** students. *Ellas son alumnas . . .*
You write: *buenas.*

12 Given twelve sentences, each with an indicated verb and followed by a new subject, you write correctly at least nine of the verb forms that match the new subject.

You see: *Tú **eres** de Perú. Tú y él . . .*
You write: *son.*

13 Given twelve English sentences whose verb is a form of "to be," you choose correctly at least nine times *hay, es, or está* as the appropriate translation.

You see: Mr. Smith **is** in New Mexico.
You write: *está.*

Assignment 1

Learning with Programed Assignments

The assignments for this course may be radically different in function and design from assignments you have had in other courses. Their *function* is to prepare you for participation in the activities of the following class session. It is essential, consequently, that the assignment be completed *before* class if you are to receive maximum benefit from the course.

The *design* of the first section of each assignment is called *programing*. This section is made up of a number of *frames* each consisting of two parts: the first part asks you to do something, and the second part gives you the correct answer for what you were asked to do. Here is how you work with this type of learning material: Use a blank sheet of paper to cover the remaining portion of this page. Slowly slide the sheet down the page until it uncovers the line containing the first black triangle. Immediately below each triangle on the right side of the page are given the answer frames.

Solve each problem and write your response *before* looking at the answer frame.

1 The Spanish word for "flower" is *flor*. The name of one of the southern states comes from and begins with *flor*. This state is _____. ▲

    Florida (*Florida* describes a place that has many flowers.) If you missed this, circle the number 1 and go on.

2 The Spanish verb *nevar* translates "to snow." One of our western states was described by the early Spaniards as "a place covered with snow." The name of this state is *Neva* _____. ▲

    Did you write number 2 and *da* on your answer sheet?

3 The Spanish word for "color" is *color*. The name of what state begins with *Color* _____? ▲

    Colorado (Colorado has many red rocks. In Spanish *colorado* may mean "red.")

4 *Florida, Nevada* and *Colorado* are words borrowed from Spanish. Many English and Spanish words come from Latin. English "student" and Spanish *estudiante* both came from Latin. These look-alikes are called **cognates**. The Spanish cognate of "mountain" is the name of one of our western states. This state is _____. ▲

    Montana (Spanish *montaña* means "mountain.")

The following frames will present some facts about learning a new language. Write number 5 on your work sheet and position your cover sheet.

5 There are two ways of sending messages by using words. One way is by speaking, the other is by _____. ▲

    writing (We speak words and we write words.)

6 Speech and writing are not alike. The front part of a ship is called its *bow*. Say *bow* like *how*. You shoot an arrow with a *bow*. Now, say *bow* and *arrow* aloud. Does the written word, by itself, tell us how to say *bow*? ▲

    no

7   The capital of Spain is written *Madrid*. Is it likely that the spelling *Madrid* suggests one pronunciation to a Spanish speaker and another to you?   ▲

8   The following words are all Spanish words: *general, rodeo, metal, gas*. Can   yes the same letters, arranged in the same order, stand for the different sounds of two different languages?   ▲

yes (What you see in writing or print does not always tell you what language the words belong to.)

9   A female deer is called a *doe*. Bread is made out of *dough*. Does what you hear always tell you what to write?   ▲

10   One learns to spell *dough* from (a) hearing the word (b) seeing it written.   ▲   no

seeing it written or hearing it spelled aloud (When you hear *dough*, all by itself, you do not know whether to write *dough* or *doe*.)

11   The Spanish word for "foot" is *pie*, and the Spanish word for "bread" is *pan*. Can you tell from what is written (*pie, pan*) how the Spanish speaker says these words?   ▲

no (To speakers of English *pan* is a dish in which one bakes a *pie*.)

12   If you see a Spanish word before you hear it, will you pronounce it (a) like a Spanish speaker? (b) like a speaker of English?   ▲

like a speaker of English

13   To learn to speak a new language, one must first (a) see the written words (b) hear the spoken words.   ▲

hear the spoken words (Hearing must come before speaking.)

Summary

Learning to deal with the Spanish vocabulary requires the recognition of three sets of words:

1   English words borrowed from Spanish: *rodeo, Florida, Nevada, etc.*

2   Identical cognates: *general, metal, gas, etc.*

3   Identical spelling with very different meaning and pronunciation in each language:

New Vocabulary

señor	Mr., sir, man, gentleman	**número**	number
señora	Mrs., madam, lady, wife	**cero**	zero
señorita	Miss, young lady	**uno**	one
profesor (male)	teacher, professor	**dos**	two

profesora (female)	teacher, professor	**tres**	three
Buenos días.	Good morning.	**cuatro**	four
Buenas tardes.	Good afternoon.	**cinco**	five
Buenas noches.	Good night (evening).	**seis**	six
Adiós.	Good-by.	**siete**	seven
Hasta mañana.	Until tomorrow.	**ocho**	eight
Me llamo . . .	My name is . . . (I call myself . . .)	**nueve**	nine
¿Cómo se llama usted?	What is your name?	**diez**	ten

Diálogo Uno: Tomás y Luisa

T: ¡Hola, Luisa! ¿Qué tal?
L: Bastante bien. Y tú, ¿cómo estás?
T: Estoy muy bien, gracias.

Dialog One: Tom and Louise

T: Hi, Louise! How goes it?
L: Pretty well. And how are you?
T: I'm very well, thanks.

Adiós

Hold hand at almost shoulder height, palm upward; move fingers toward you and back several times as if beckoning a person to come.

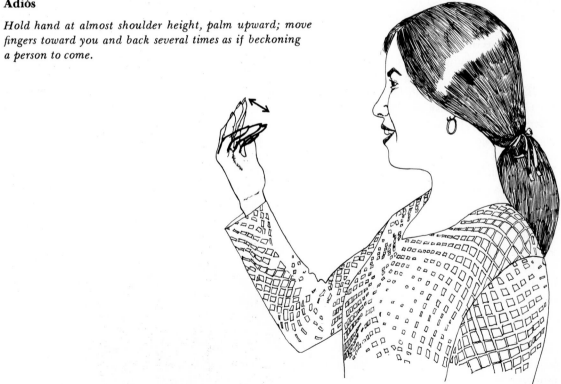

Assignment 2

Some Facts about Speech Sounds

It is necessary to know the meaning of certain marks used in writing about sounds and letters. To keep from confusing a letter of the alphabet with the sound represented by that letter in actual speech, the letter is always printed in italics. So you will see: "In our written alphabet *b* is the second letter." In contrast, when a statement is made about the sound made in speech, the letter appears in brackets. So you will see things like this: The [b] of *boy* is very much like the Spanish [b].

1   Cut a piece of thin paper into a strip about an inch wide and three inches long. Grasp one end of the strip and hold the flat side of the other end about one-half inch from your lips. Now say *pay* quite loudly and watch the strip. Did the strip (a) stay still? (b) jump?   ▲

> jump (The [p] of *pay* is followed by a sharp puff. This makes the paper jump.)

2   Now watch the strip of paper and say English *pie* and *spy* quite loudly several times. The paper jumps when you say (a) pie (b) spy.   ▲

> pie (Linguists say this [p] is *aspirated*—made *with* a puff.)

3   Hold the strip of paper before your lips again and say the following pairs of words together. Watch the paper carefully: *pin-spin, pat-spat, pot-spot*. The paper does not jump when [p] comes right after the sound _____.   ▲

> [s] ([p] has no puff after [s]. It is *unaspirated*—made *without* a puff. The letter *p*, in English, stands for two slightly different sounds, one *with* a puff and

4   There is no Spanish word in which the sound [p] is ever made with a puff. one *without* a puff.)
The Spanish [p] is always (a) unaspirated (b) aspirated.   ▲

5   There is no [p] with a puff in any Spanish word. However, you have been   unaspirated
making this puff sound at the beginning of words starting with *p* all your life. This English habit has to be broken or you will have an accent in Spanish.

In the experiments you just tried, you found that *p* stands for two sounds in English. Most speakers of English do not hear this difference because we are trained to "tune out" sound differences which do not change meaning. To learn Spanish, you must learn to "tune in" sounds you do not listen to in English. It is a lot easier to do this when you know something about how sounds are made.

The sounds we make in speaking are made by forcing air out of our lungs up through the throat and out through either the mouth or nose. Here is a way to prove this. Say *hum* rather loudly and hold the [m] sound for a second. Say *hum* again and watch what you are doing with your lips. Are they (a) closed? (b) open?   ▲

> closed (You cannot say the sound [m] with your mouth open.)

6   Say *hum* again, hold the [m] sound, and while you are doing this, pinch your nose tightly closed with your fingers. Did the sound (a) stop? (b) go on?   ▲

> the sound stopped (Your lips were closed and the air was coming out your nose. With your nose closed, you cannot say the [m] sound.)

7 Hold your nose closed and say *ah*. The air comes out (a) your nose (b) your mouth. ▲

8 Say the name for the letter *e* and the sound *ah*. Say *e-ah* several times. Watch what your jaws are doing. When you go from the sound of *e* to *ah*, do you (a) open your mouth wider? (b) close your mouth more? ▲

> your mouth

> open your mouth wider

9 Here is another way of making sounds different. Cup your hands and hold them tightly over your ears. Say *fuzz* and *fuss* real loud. Try this again and hold the last sound of each word for a second. Which word makes a buzzing sound? ▲

10 Take a tight hold of your Adam's apple. Now say the [ss] of *fuss* and the [zz] of *fuzz*, hold the sounds, and feel the difference. Which sound makes your throat vibrate? ▲

> fuzz

> [zz] (When you say *fuzz* the edges of two muscles in your throat—the vocal cords—vibrate to make the buzzing sound.)

11 A sound made with the vocal cords vibrating is said to be *voiced*. A sound made without the vocal cords vibrating is said to be *unvoiced*. Say *resin, resident,* and *president* aloud until you make the same sound for the *s* in all three. Is this sound (a) voiced? (b) unvoiced? ▲

> It is voiced. (The vocal cords vibrate.)

12 In English you may answer roll call by saying *present*. Say *present* aloud several times and listen to the [s] sound. Is it (a) unvoiced? (no buzz) (b) voiced? ▲

13 The equivalent answer in Spanish is *presente*. The second syllable starts like English "sent." Say *sente* and *presente* aloud several times. Is the [s] for *sente* (a) voiced? (b) unvoiced? ▲

> voiced

> unvoiced: no buzz (Spanish, unlike English, never has a voiced [s] sound before a vowel.)

14 Say *hat* aloud several times, and each time hold the tip of your tongue in the position it has when you finish saying the sound [t]. When you say the sound [t], the tip of your tongue touches (a) the back of your upper front teeth (b) the gum ridge right above the back of your upper front teeth. ▲

> the gum ridge (When a Spanish speaker makes a [t] sound, his tongue always touches the back of his upper front teeth, not the gum ridge. *"Dent*ists" work on teeth. The Spanish [t] is said to be "dental" because the tongue tip touches the teeth.)

A Difference Between English and Spanish Sounds: The English Sound "Schwa"

1 Most spoken words are made up of a series of different sounds which are represented, in writing, by the letters of the alphabet. These sounds are grouped together in syllables. When a word has two or more syllables, one of them is always spoken a little louder than the others. In the word *mention*, the syllable *men* is louder than the syllable *tion*. This louder syllable is said to be (a) stressed (b) unstressed. ▲

> stressed

2 Say the following words aloud, copy them, and underline the stressed syllable in each: gen-er-al, pen-cil, im-por-tant. ▲

gen-er-al, **pen**-cil, im-**por**-tant

3 Copy the following words and underline the unstressed syllable in each: pen-cil, pis-tol, to-tal, fruit-ful, can-cel. ▲

pen-**cil**, pis-**tol**, to-**tal**, fruit-**ful**, can-**cel**

4 The two unstressed syllables in *im-por-tant* are _____. ▲

5 Say "It's not important" aloud several times. Try to say this in a way that says you really don't care. Listen carefully to see if you can hear how you pronounce the *a* of *tant*. Is the sound of *a* in *tant* more like (a) the *a* of *tan* or (b) the *u* of *tun*? ▲

im-por-**tant**

the *u* of *tun*

6 Say *fruitful* and *total* aloud several times, one after the other. The sound of *al* in *total* is (a) very much like the *ul* of *fruitful* (b) very different from the *ul* of *fruitful*. ▲

al is very much like *ul*

7 Say *total*, *pencil*, *cancel*, and *pistol* aloud several times. In these words, the sounds of *al*, *il*, *el*, and *ol* are (a) alike (b) very different. ▲

For most speakers of English, these sounds are alike.

8 Look at these words. The unstressed syllable is indicated: pen-**cil**, to-**tal**, can-**cel**, pis-**tol**. The letters standing for the vowels in the unstressed syllables are _____. ▲

9 The last two sounds of *to-tal*, *pen-cil*, *can-cel*, and *pis-tol* are in an unstressed syllable. Say these words aloud again and listen to what you do with *al*, *il*, *el*, and *ol*. In these words, the letters *a*, *i*, *e*, and *o*, stand for sounds which are (a) alike (b) different. ▲

i, a, e, o

alike (In some unstressed syllables *a, e, i, o,* and *u* may stand for the same sound. This sound is called *schwa*. We represent it by this symbol: [ə].)

10 The following words are divided into syllables. Say them aloud, copy them, and underline the letter which may stand for the schwa sound in each. Remember, it must be in the unstressed syllable: trail-er, sail-or, cri-sis, mi-nus, dol-lar, at-las. ▲

trail-**e**r, sail-**o**r, cri-s**i**s, mi-n**u**s, dol-l**a**r, at-l**a**s

11 In spelling, the difference between *pistol* and *total* is shown in two ways. The first syllables are different, *pis* and *to*. In the second syllable, *tol* and *tal*, there is a contrast between *o* and *a* in spelling. However, the difference between the *o* of *tol* and the *a* of *tal* is lost in speech. In speech the vowel of the second (unstressed) syllable is schwa in both words. So the difference, in speech, between the two words is marked only by the stressed syllables _____. ▲

12 In English speech, the vowels in unstressed syllables are frequently not used to mark a difference between words. Spanish is very different from English. The two following Spanish words are divided into syllables. The stressed syllable of each is indicated: **ca**-sa (house), **co**-sa (thing). In both English and Spanish, the difference between two words may be marked by a contrast between vowels in (a) a stressed syllable (b) an unstressed syllable. ▲

pis; to

13 These Spanish words are divided into syllables. The unstressed syllables are indicated: ca-**sa** (house), ca-**si** (almost). In Spanish, unlike English, the differ-

stressed syllable

ence between two words may be marked by a contrast between vowels in (a)
stressed syllables (b) unstressed syllables. ▲

14 If Spanish speakers pronounced *casa* and *casi* with the schwa sound in the   unstressed syllables
unstressed syllables *sa* and *si*, would they be able to tell the difference between
these two words? ▲

no (They would sound exactly alike.)

15 The difference between *cosa* (thing) and *casa* (house) is marked by *o* and *a*
in the stressed syllables **co**-sa and **ca**-sa. The difference between *caso* (case)
and *casa* (house) is also shown by *o* and *a*, but in the unstressed syllables ca-**so**
and ca-**sa**. The vowels *o* and *a* mark a difference in meaning (a) in both stressed
and unstressed syllables (b) only in unstressed syllables. ▲

in both stressed and unstressed syllables

16 Since *o* and *a*, in Spanish, show a difference in meaning in either stressed or
unstressed syllables, must each be pronounced the same all the time? ▲

yes (Spanish vowel sounds are the same in either stressed or unstressed
syllables. *Spanish has no schwa sound.*)

As a speaker of English, you have the habit of using the schwa sound in many
unstressed syllables. To speak Spanish properly, you must now break this habit.

Summary

1   In print *b* stands for the letter; [b] stands for the spoken sound.

2   The Spanish [p] is *not* made with a puff; that is, it is *not* aspirated.

3   Spanish has no [z] sound before a following vowel.

4   There is no schwa in Spanish.

5   Spanish [t] is dental and unaspirated.

New Vocabulary

libro	book	**once**	eleven
cuaderno	notebook	**doce**	twelve
lápiz	pencil	**trece**	thirteen
reloj	clock, watch	**catorce**	fourteen
papel	paper	**quince**	fifteen
pupitre	desk (student)		
Un momentito.	Just a moment.		
Un poquito.	A little bit.		

Dialog One (*continued*)

L: ¿A dónde vas, Tomás? ¿A clase?   L: Where are you going, Tom? To class?
T: No, voy a la oficina.   T: No, I'm going to the office.

Un momentito

Hold hand in front with thumb and index finger about one-half inch apart as if showing the thickness of a book.

Assignment 3

Tú *versus* usted: *A Spanish Social Custom*

In every highly structured culture there are elaborate rules which govern how people are to interact with each other. Some of these rules are categorized under the heading *etiquette* and may even be codified in books on the subject. In very special cases there are codified rules on how people are to address each other: lawyers address a judge in court as *Your honor*, and diplomats have handbooks on how to address foreign dignitaries, *etc*. Very little attention, however, is given to the fact that there are hundreds of subtle features in ordinary speech which clearly mark different kinds of social and personal relationships between people speaking to each other.

There are some religious groups which still use the old English forms *thou*, *thee*, and *ye* when talking to members of their family or to members of their church. These same people usually use *you* when speaking to strangers or people who are not members of their in-group. It is obvious, then, that the choice between *thou* or *you* is determined, even at times dictated, by the social or personal relationship between the speaker and the person spoken to.

All speakers of modern Spanish are required to choose between *tú* (thou) and *usted* (you) when addressing a person.

The cues for making this choice are virtually identical in both cultures. The difference between English and Spanish lies only in the fact that English etiquette or social custom no longer requires the use of *thou*. The following frames identify the social and psychological signals which you have learned to ignore as signals for linguistic choices.

1 When a child speaks to its mother, which is more formal: *Mom, Mother?* ▲

Mother

2 Most children do not address their parents or teachers by their first names. Is it improper or disrespectful for parents or teachers to call children by their first names? ▲

no (It is considered proper for older people to call children by their first names.)

3 Is it disrespectful for you to call your brother or sister by his or her first name? ▲

no (It is generally proper for equals to call each other by their first names.)

4 The president of a large corporation, Peter R. Hollister, addresses his private secretary as *Betty*. She should call him (a) Pete (b) Peter (c) Mr. Hollister. ▲

Mr. Hollister

5 When a private in the Army answers a general, he says: (a) Yup (b) Yeah (c) Yes (d) Yes, sir. ▲

Yes, sir. (The words *sir* and *mister* are most often used in speaking to persons of higher rank.)

6 Which of the following shows the greatest respect? (a) Kathy (b) Kathleen (c) Kathleen Durand (d) Mrs. Durand ▲

Mrs. Durand (A title of address is a mark of respect.)

7 A child is being naughty. Which of the following, spoken by his mother, is more stern and authoritative? (a) Johnnie, come here! (b) John Harrington Smith, come here! ▲

John Harrington Smith, come here! (The full name is more formal than a nickname.)

8 Which form is more likely to be used by a very close friend? (a) Maggie (b) Margaret ▲

Maggie

9 Titles are not generally used with nicknames. Which is the proper way to address a letter? (a) Mr. Bill Hammond (b) Mr. William Hammond ▲

Mr. William Hammond

10 When one small child asks another his name, the second may reply, "My name's Billy." Is it proper for a lawyer in court to answer the judge by saying, "My name's Billy"? ▲

no (Adults do not usually introduce themselves with their nicknames, and especially in a very formal situation. They give their first and last name.)

11 A judge and a lawyer are very close friends. When they go fishing together they call each other *Ed* and *Walt*. When the lawyer is before the court, how does he address the judge? (a) Walt (b) Your honor ▲

Your honor (The formality of a situation determines the form of address.)

12 Your father may call your mother *honey* or *sweetheart*. Is it common for people who have just met to use these terms to address each other? ▲

no (Terms of endearment are usually used only between persons who are very intimate.)

13 When English was still using *thou* and *ye* in contrast with *you*, it was possible to indicate different social relationships or different degrees of formality by choosing between these forms. Today all second persons are addressed as *you*, but differences in rank, degrees of intimacy, familiarity, or formality are still shown by differences in the use of many other words.

Modern Spanish, like old English, still uses pronouns and verb forms which reveal the speaker's social relationship to the person spoken to. The modern Spanish form which is like old English "thou" is *tú*.

The pronoun *usted*, which also translates "you," is a contraction of an older form *vuestra merced*, which meant "your grace." *Vuestra merced* was used as a title of respect in speaking to noblemen. In modern Spanish *señor*, *señora*, *señorita*, *doctor*, *etc.* are still titles of respect. When a Spanish speaker uses a title in speaking to a person, he also uses *usted*. (The abbreviated forms of *usted*, *ustedes* are *Ud.*, *Uds.*, or *Vd.*, *Vds.* COMMUNICATING IN SPANISH will use *Vd.*, *Vds.* most frequently.)

14 Which form, *tú* (thou) or *usted* (your grace) indicates the greatest respect and the highest degree of formality? ▲

usted

15 The kinds of social relationships which exist between Spanish speakers are basically the same as those between speakers of English. The difference between the two cultures lies in the fact that Spanish must use pronouns and verb forms to indicate these relationships.

From what you now know about *tú* and *usted* and about English and Spanish social customs, can you decide which form will be used in the following situations? You are speaking to your teacher. (a) *tú* (b) *usted* ▲

usted (You show respect by using *usted*. *Tú* would be insulting.)

16 You are in grade or high school. Your teacher addresses you. (a) *tú* (b) *usted* ▲

tú (Older persons regularly speak to young people in *tú*. College professors, however, address their students with *usted*. You will probably use *tú* with your fellow students except when directed to do otherwise in class practice.)

17 You are speaking to a person of higher rank, greater authority, or more social prestige. (a) *tú* (b) *usted* ▲

18 You address a person using Mr., Mrs., or Miss and his or her last name. (a) *tú* (b) *usted* ▲

usted

usted

19 You are talking to a dog or cat. (a) *tú* (b) *usted* ▲

usted

tú (Animals have a lower rank than people and are addressed with *tú*.)

20 You are at home talking to a brother, sister, cousin. (a) *tú* (b) *usted* ▲

21 A man addresses a girl friend as *Lolita*, the nickname for Dolores. ▲

tú

tú (People rarely use nicknames unless they are intimate enough to use *tú*.)

22 You are speaking to a clergyman. ▲

23 You are asking a police officer for information. ▲

usted

24 Two intimate friends are members of a government committee discussing diplomatic problems. They speak to each other as part of the proceedings. ▲

usted

usted (The situation is very formal. It is improper to let personal relationships show.)

25 Two people are in love. ▲

tú (People in love talk to each other in *tú*.)

26 A Christian is praying to God or to some Saint. (This one will catch you if you don't watch it.) ▲

tú (Christians feel very close to their God and their Saints. The Lord's Prayer addresses God in the familiar: Who art, Thy will be done, *etc.*)

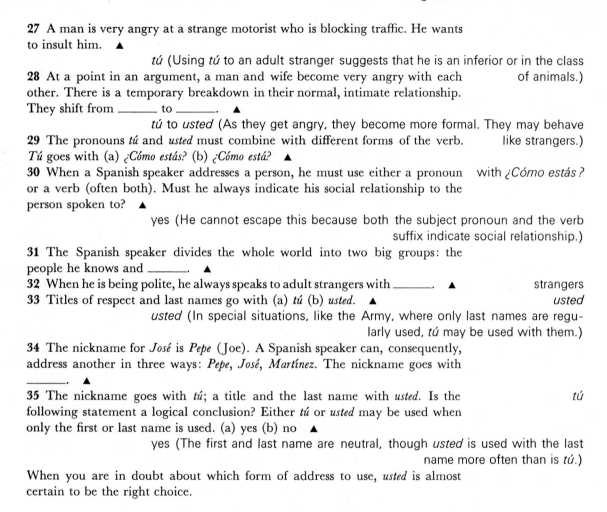

27 A man is very angry at a strange motorist who is blocking traffic. He wants to insult him. ▲

> *tú* (Using *tú* to an adult stranger suggests that he is an inferior or in the class of animals.)

28 At a point in an argument, a man and wife become very angry with each other. There is a temporary breakdown in their normal, intimate relationship. They shift from _____ to _____. ▲

> *tú* to *usted* (As they get angry, they become more formal. They may behave like strangers.)

29 The pronouns *tú* and *usted* must combine with different forms of the verb. *Tú* goes with (a) *¿Cómo estás?* (b) *¿Cómo está?* ▲

> with *¿Cómo estás?*

30 When a Spanish speaker addresses a person, he must use either a pronoun or a verb (often both). Must he always indicate his social relationship to the person spoken to? ▲

> yes (He cannot escape this because both the subject pronoun and the verb suffix indicate social relationship.)

31 The Spanish speaker divides the whole world into two big groups: the people he knows and _____. ▲

32 When he is being polite, he always speaks to adult strangers with _____. ▲

> strangers

33 Titles of respect and last names go with (a) *tú* (b) *usted*. ▲

> usted

> *usted* (In special situations, like the Army, where only last names are regularly used, *tú* may be used with them.)

34 The nickname for *José* is *Pepe* (Joe). A Spanish speaker can, consequently, address another in three ways: *Pepe, José, Martínez.* The nickname goes with _____. ▲

35 The nickname goes with *tú*; a title and the last name with *usted*. Is the following statement a logical conclusion? Either *tú* or *usted* may be used when only the first or last name is used. (a) yes (b) no ▲

> *tú*

> yes (The first and last name are neutral, though *usted* is used with the last name more often than is *tú*.)

When you are in doubt about which form of address to use, *usted* is almost certain to be the right choice.

The Pieces and Parts of Words: Morphology

You already know that, in speaking, words are made up of sounds which, in writing, are represented by letters. You also know that words can be broken up into syllables. There are two syllables in the word *Spanish: Span-ish.* Together they have meaning. Separately they do not. There are two syllables in the word *untie: un-tie.* In this word each syllable has a meaning of its own. The syllable *un* in *under*, however, does not have a meaning apart from the whole word. The *un* of *untie*, like *dis* of *disappear* and *mis* of *misjudge* are called prefixes. They are not words but may be put in front of words to change the meaning.

Compare *act, actor,* and *actress.* The *or* and *ress* are suffixes which, when added to *act*, tell us that the person acting is male or female.

1 There are many kinds of suffixes. There is, believe it or not, a suffix in the word *this.* Here is how you can prove it. Compare *this book* and *that book.* If you are speaking and also pointing to one of the two books, which is closer to you? (a) this book (b) that book ▲

2 What part of *this* and *that* is the same? ▲

this book

th (This part, the *th*, tells us we are pointing something out. For this reason words like "this" and "that" are called *demonstratives*, from the verb *demon-*

3 The *th* is the same in both *this* and *that*. *This book*, however, is closer to *strate,—to show.*)
the speaker than *that book*. What part of *this* must say "close"? (a) *th* (b) *is* ▲

is (Remember: the *th* is the pointing-out part: the demonstrative.)

4 The demonstrative *that* points something out and says that it is not close:
that book over there. What part of *that* says "not close"? ▲

5 How many syllables are there in *this* or *that*? ▲

at

one (The demonstratives *this* and *that* have only one syllable each, but both have two meaningful parts. The *th* points something out. The *is* says that it is close. The *at* says it is farther away.)

6 May a word have more meaningful parts than syllables? ▲

yes (The meaningful parts of a word may be the same as syllables; *un-tie*, *re-tread*, *mal-formed*. The meaningful parts of a word may also be pieces of the same syllable: *this, that*.)

7 What part of *this* and *these* is the same? ▲

th (The *th* is called the *stem*.)

8 The part of a word which is added to the end of a stem is called a "suffix."
Copy the suffixes of *this, these, that, those*. ▲

9 The demonstrative *this* combines with *dog: this dog*. It is not proper to say is, ese, at, ose
this dogs. When you have the plural form *dogs*, you change *this* to _____. ▲

these (*This dog* becomes *these dogs*.)

10 The suffix *ese* of *these* matches the *s* of *dogs*. It is (a) singular (b) plural. ▲

11 The demonstrative *that* has a stem, *th*, and a singular suffix *at: that dog*. plural
To make the plural form which combines with *dogs*, the suffix *at* must be
replaced by _____. ▲

ose (*That dog* becomes *those dogs*.)

12 The suffix of *these* says "close" and "plural." (a) true (b) false ▲

13 Now be careful, and remember that *these* is a demonstrative. It points out true
something. How many pieces of information does the whole word *these* give
you? 1, 2, 3 ▲

3 (It <u>points out</u> something that is <u>close</u> and <u>plural</u>.)

14 Compare *dog, dogs*. How many pieces of information are there in *dogs*? ▲

15 Both *dogs* and *these* have two parts: a stem and a plural suffix. The stems two
are _____. ▲

16 May a stem be a word by itself? ▲ dog; th

17 Are all stems words? ▲ yes

no (Stems like *th* must be a part of a word. They are used only when a suffix

18 The *dis* of *displease* and the *im* of *impossible* are like *not*. They are negating is added.)
prefixes. What does the *re* of *remake* or *redo* tell you? (a) not (b) again ▲

to make or do again

19 Can you really understand the meaning of *remake* if you do not pay attention
to the meaning of both parts, the prefix and the stem? ▲

no (If you wrote "yes," think of the difference between *remake* and *unmake*.)

The study of the pieces and parts of words is called *morphology*. The *morph* part of *morphology* comes from the Greek meaning "shape" or "form." The parts of words which have meaning (prefixes, stems, suffixes) are also called *morphemes* (meaningful forms).

Summary

Tú versus *usted*

1 The singular "you" is translated by either *tú* or *usted*, which comes from *vuestra merced* (your grace).

2 *Tú*, and its matching verb form, is used to speak to:
a God, saints, small children, animals, immediate members of the family, and intimate friends.
b strangers, to be insulting, or to show contempt.

3 *Usted* is used to speak to:
a adults in all very formal situations (court proceedings, diplomatic conferences, *etc.*)
b adult strangers, casual acquaintances.
c superiors, persons of authority, anyone treated with deference or special respect.
d anyone normally addressed as *tú*, to show anger, annoyance, to be stern, or to indicate a breakdown of former friendly relations.

Morphology

1 Words are made up of three elements: sounds, syllables, and meaningful parts.

2 There are three kinds of meaningful parts or morphemes: stems (**dog**-s, **th**-ese, **act**-ress), prefixes (**un**-tie, **mis**-judge, **dis**-appear), and suffixes (dog-**s**, act-**or**, th-**ose**).

3 A syllable may contain more than one morpheme (dog-s, th-is) and a morpheme may be split between two syllables (ac-tor).

4 The meaning of a word cannot be understood without reacting to the meaning of each morpheme.

New Vocabulary

pluma	pen	**dieciséis**	sixteen
silla	chair	**diecisiete**	seventeen
mesa	table	**dieciocho**	eighteen
ventana	window	**diecinueve**	nineteen
puerta	door	**veinte**	twenty
el, la	the	**¿Dónde está . . . ?**	Where is . . . ?
un, una	a (an)	**¿Qué es . . . ?**	What is . . . ?

Dialog One (*continued*)

L: Bueno, adiós. Hasta luego. Well, good-by. I'll see you later.
T: Adiós, Luisa. Hasta pronto. Good-by, Louise. See you soon.

¡Ojo!

Touch index finger of right hand to cheek directly below right eye pointing up toward it.

Assignment 4

Forms of the Articles and Plurals

1 All English words must begin either with a vowel or a consonant sound. This tells us when we must use *a* or *an*, the two forms of the indefinite article. We say "a pen" and "a book" but "an apple" and "an eagle." The indefinite article form *a* precedes words which begin with a _____ sound; *an* precedes words which begin with a _____ sound. ▲

a goes with consonant sounds; *an* with vowel sounds. (When a consonant letter is not spoken, you use *an*: an hour.)

2 Do *a* and *an*, in *a pen* and *an apple*, have different meanings? ▲

no (Two forms having the same function may have the same meaning.)

3 Spanish, like English, has two forms of the indefinite article: *un* and *una*.

But Spanish is just the opposite of English. The <u>last</u> sound of a word (with very few exceptions) tells the Spanish speaker when to use *un* or *una*. English has only one form of the definite article: "the." Spanish has four forms. You have already learned two of them: *el* and *la*.

Look at the form of the two articles and the last sound of the word with which they combine.

un libro	una mesa
el libro	la mesa
un rodeo	una silla
el rodeo	la silla

The forms *un* and *el* combine with words ending in the vowel _____; the forms *una* and *la* combine with words ending in the vowel _____. ▲

un and *el* with *o; una* and *la* with *a*

4 Spanish, like English, has only two common forms of the plural suffix: *s* and *es*. The difference between vowels and consonants, at the end of words, tells the Spanish speaker when to use *s* or *es*. Look at each of the following words and notice the sound (vowel or consonant) that comes right <u>before</u> the plural suffix *s* or *es; libros, mesas, papeles, señores*. The plural suffix *s* follows a _____; the plural suffix *es* follows a _____. ▲

s after a vowel; *es* after a consonant (The few exceptions have to be memorized.)

5 You have already learned that the demonstratives *these* and *those* carry three pieces of information. *These* and *those* are used when you point to more than one thing. They are *plural. This* and *that* are *singular.* Which word, *this* or *these*, goes with each of the following: churches, cat, cats? ▲

these churches, this cat, these cats

6 The plural suffix of *these* (ese) matches the plural suffix of *cats* (s), and *churches* (es). This matching is called *agreement.*

The demonstratives (this, that, these, those) are the only English adjectives whose suffixes match the suffixes of the nouns they go with. In Spanish all adjectives agree with (match) their nouns in number (singular or plural). As a result, to make *la mesa* plural, the Spanish speaker must add the plural suffix _____ to both *la* and *mesa.* ▲

7 What is the plural of *la silla?* ▲

s : las mesas las sillas

8 The singular form *el* changes to *lo* when the plural suffix *s* is added. So the singular *el papel* becomes the plural *los papeles.* The plural of *el rodeo* is _____. ▲

9 The indefinite article *un* and the definite article *el* combine with words ending in *o; un libro, el libro.* They also go with *papel: un papel, el papel. Un* and *el* may combine with words which end in the consonant _____. ▲

los rodeos

l

More on Speech Sounds: Stop versus Fricative

1 Say *boy* and *bat* several times. At the start of these words are your lips (a) tightly closed? (b) open? ▲

tightly closed (Because your closed lips stop the air from coming out, these sounds are said to be *stops.* The [b] sound of *boy* is a "stop [b].")

2 Say *bun* and *fun*. When you say the first sound of *fun*, are your lips (a) closed tightly? (b) opened a little? ▲

> opened a little (Some consonants are made by closing the air passageway until the air comes out with a little friction noise. For this reason, these sounds are called *fricatives*.)

3 Say *dough* and *though* several times. Which of these two words starts with a fricative sound? (a) dough (b) though ▲

4 Say *Buenos días* (Good morning) aloud and pay attention to what your   though
tongue is doing when you say the [d] sound. The [d] sound is more like the *th*
of "though" than the *d* of "dough." Say *dos* aloud and note that your tongue
touches the back of your upper front teeth when you say the sound [d] and the
tongue blocks the air passage for a split second. When you say *dos* by itself, is the
sound [d] (a) a stop? (b) a fricative? ▲

> a stop (All stops are made by blocking the air passage in some way.)

5 In *Buenos días* the [d] is a fricative. However, when you say *días* all by itself,
the [d] is a stop. The Spanish *d* stands for two sounds just as English *p* stands
for two sounds. *Días*, said with a fricative [d], has the same meaning as *días*
said with a stop [d].

There must be some signal that tells the Spanish speaker when to say *días*
with a stop or fricative [d]. Before you try to find out, let's first look at similar
signals in English: You say "an apple," but "a man" in English. What signals
you to choose *an* or *a*: the sound that (a) precedes? (b) follows? ▲

> follows (*An* before vowels; *a* before consonants.)

6 The plural of *pat* is *pats*. Say *pats* aloud and listen to the sound [s]. Is it
like the (a) [ss] of *miss*? (b) [zz] of *fuzz*? ▲

> the [ss] of *miss* (It is unvoiced; the vocal cords do not vibrate.)

7 The plural of *pad* is *pads*. Say *pads* aloud and listen to the sound [s]. Is it
like the (a) [ss] of *miss*? (b) [zz] of *buzz*? ▲

> the [zz] of *buzz* (It is voiced; the vocal cords vibrate.)

8 The plural suffix *s* stands for two different sounds in English: [ss] after [t]
which is unvoiced and [zz] after [d] which is voiced. What tells you when the
plural suffix *s* is to be said like [ss] or [zz]? (a) the sound that follows it (b) the
sound that precedes it ▲

> the sound that precedes it

9 The sound that follows either the stop or fricative [d] of *días* is always the
same. It is the vowel [i]. What, then, must tell the Spanish speaker when to
say the stop or the fricative: (a) what follows [d]? (b) what comes before [d]? ▲

> what comes before

Review of Dialog One

When you make the English [t] sound, the tip of your tongue touches the gum
ridge above the upper front teeth; when you make the Spanish [t], the tip of
your tongue should touch the back of the upper front teeth. In addition

English [t] is frequently aspirated while Spanish [t] is always unaspirated, made without a puff of air.

1   These dialog words have the [t] sound. Say them aloud carefully with the Spanish dental [t]: **t**al, bastante, **t**ú, estás, estoy, **T**omás, hasta, pronto.

2   Say these same words a second time as fast as you can: pronto, **t**al, hasta, bastante, **t**ú, **T**omás, estás, estoy.

3   There is no schwa sound in Spanish. Speakers of English often substitute a schwa for the indicated unstressed vowels in the following dialog words. Say them aloud carefully avoiding the schwa: hol**a**, L**u**isa, b**a**stante, graci**a**s, dond**e**, clas**e**, of**i**cina, hast**a**.

4   Now say them again faster but start with the last word.

5   In Spanish the letter *d* can stand for two sounds: a fricative, very similar to the [th] in "though"; and a stop, as the [d] in "dough". In the dialog phrase *¿A dónde vas?*, does the first *d* stand for a stop, or a fricative sound?   ▲

fricative (It is preceded by a vowel.)

6   Does the second *d* in *¿A dónde vas?* stand for a stop, or a fricative?   ▲

stop (It is preceded by the nasal [n].)

7   Say *¿A dónde vas, Tomás?* and *Adiós, Luisa* several times. Only the second *d* in *dónde* stands for a stop, the rest are fricatives.

8   In the English words "honor" and "hour", *h* does not represent any sound. Knowing that *h* never represents any sound in Spanish, say aloud *hola* and *hasta* several times.

9   Keep in mind how you learned the dialog in class. Do you say *¿A dónde vas?* (a) with a brief pause between each word? (b) as though all three words were run together in one long word?   ▲

as though all three words were run together in one long word: *¿Adóndevas?*

10 Here are all the phrases in the dialog which are spoken as though they were one long word. In the left column is what you see in writing or print. In the right column is what you say in speech. Practice saying the right column aloud several times.

¿Qué tal?	¿Quétal?
Bastante bien.	Bastantebien.
Y tú . . .	Ytú . . .
¿Cómo estás?	¿Cómoestás?
Estoy muy bien.	Estoymuybien.
¿A dónde vas?	¿Adóndevas?
¿A clase?	¿Aclase?
Hasta luego.	Hastaluego.
Hasta pronto.	Hastapronto.

11 Recite the whole dialog from memory several times until you can say it in about 15 seconds without allowing your English habits of pronunciation to interfere with the Spanish. If you have a tape recorder, you will find it fun to tape yourself and hear how you are doing. If you need to see it, see p. 24.

Learning to Write Spanish and to Read It Aloud: I

Sounds and Spelling

Before you can learn to write what you hear in Spanish and to say aloud what you see, you must first understand that the relationship between speech sounds and the letters of the alphabet is not exactly the same in English and Spanish. Here are some examples that show this difference. English "baseball" is spelled *béisbol* in Spanish. A "homerun" is *jonrón*. "Philadelphia" is *Filadelfia*. Let's turn, now, to the more precise differences between English and Spanish.

1   The letter *h* stands for a sound in *has* and *happy* but not in *honor*, *honest*, or *hour*. Does *h* ever stand for a sound in Spanish?   ▲

> no (So you have to write it in when you do not hear it, but you do not pronounce it when you see it in reading aloud.)

2   There is no Spanish word that has the spelling sequence *th* in it. When you hear a Spanish sound like [th], as in "though," you must write _____ in Spanish.   ▲

> *d* (Spanish uses *d* to spell both the stop and fricative /d/.)

3   The Spanish speaker may say *días* with a stop [d], or *buenos días* with a fricative [d]. Does *días* mean "days" no matter how you say it?   ▲

4   These same two sounds appear in "dough" (stop) and "though" (fricative) in English. Do these words have the same meaning?   ▲   yes

> no (For you these sounds are different in English; they mark a contrast in meaning. For the Spanish speaker, however, they are the same: they mark no contrast in meaning.)

5   Say the English name for the letter *a*. Now say *pa*, *pe* in Spanish. Stop and think. If you asked a Spanish speaker (who knew no English) to write the letter for the sound of the name for *a*, would he write *a* or *e*?   ▲

6   Say the English name for the letter *e*. Now say the Spanish *pe*, *pi*. When   *e* (As in *de* or *pe*.)
you say English [e], the Spanish speaker thinks you are saying Spanish _____.   ▲

7   Say "pot" and "hot" in English and *pa* in Spanish. Listen to the vowel   [i] (As in *si* or *ti*.)
sound. Can the English letter *o* and the Spanish *a* stand for essentially the same vowel sound?   ▲

8   When you hear a schwa in a word in English, you must choose, in writing,   yes
between six letters (*a, e, i, o, u, y*) in order to spell the word correctly. Spanish has no schwa, and each vowel is clearly pronounced. When you have learned the Spanish system of spelling, will the Spanish vowel sounds always tell you what letter to write?   ▲

9   There is a [w] sound in Spanish, but Spanish uses the letter *w* only in words   yes
of foreign origin. Say [bweno] aloud. The Spanish speaker writes _____ when he says the [w] sound.   ▲

> *u* (*bueno, luego, etc.* Spanish also uses *u* for the vowel sound [u].)

10   Here is a new use of *u*. When you say *¿Qué tal?*, the first word sounds very much like the English name for *k*. One does not say [kue] or [kwe]. Does the *u* of *qué* stand for a vowel sound?   ▲

> no (Spanish uses the letter *k* only in words borrowed from other languages,

such as *kilo, kilómetro, etc.* In native words, the [k] sound is spelled *qu* before
11 Spanish, like English, has another way of writing the [k] sound. Look at   *e* or *i*: *que, qui*.)
"cent, cinder" and "sent, sinner." English can write the [s] sound before *e* or *i*
either with a *c* or an *s*. When *c* comes before *a* (can), *o* (control), or *u* (cunning),
it almost always stands for the [k] sound. Spanish also uses *c* for the [k] sound
before *a, o,* or *u.* So the translation of "how" in "How are you?" is written
¿_____ estás? ▲

12 Say this word aloud in Spanish: *ate.* Do you make a sound for both vowel   *Cómo*
letters? ▲

13 Now, say "ate" in English. Do you make a sound for the *e?* ▲   yes
no (Spanish, with just one exception, does not write a vowel letter unless it
stands for a spoken sound.)

14 Let's look at this problem in another way. Say *sa-le* in Spanish and "sail"
in English. Now say "sale" in English. Do "sail" and "sale" sound exactly
alike in English? ▲

yes (English may write the same vowel sounds in two ways. Spanish is neater.
A difference in spelling almost always shows some difference in pronunciation
of vowel sounds.)

Reading Aloud What Is Written

Compare these two questions: "Where are you going, Thomas?" and *¿A dónde
vas, Tomás?* You will notice that both English and Spanish end a question with
the same punctuation mark (?), but only Spanish tells you right at the beginning of the written question that you are to use an interrogative intonation by
using the upside down or inverted question mark (¿).

1 Here is another way that Spanish is different from English in punctuation.
Look at this sentence from Dialog 1: *Y tú, ¿cómo estás?* The inverted question
mark comes (a) before the whole sentence (b) before just the part which is
the question. ▲

just before the question part

2 Spanish also has an inverted exclamation mark (¡) which tells you right at
the beginning of the sentence what intonation pattern to use. Write the translation of "Hi, Louise!" ▲

3 The comma (,) and period (.) in Spanish tell you almost the same thing   *¡Hola, Luisa!*
about reading aloud as they do in English. The period marks the end of an
utterance. The comma signals a pause within the utterance. Do these two
sentences say the same thing? (1) Can you see George? (2) Can you see,
George? ▲

no (In the first sentence, George is the person to be seen. In the second,
George is the person trying to see. The pause and a change in intonation,
marked by the comma, tell you how to say the second sentence so it does
not have the same meaning as the first.)

4 In Spanish *No voy a la oficina* says "I'm not going to the office." In contrast,
No, voy a la oficina translates _____. ▲

No, I'm going to the office.

5 The accent mark is a feature of word spelling in Spanish and, from the Spanish speaker's point of view, leaving off an accent mark is a spelling error. You will learn later what the accent mark tells you to do in reading aloud. For the moment let's see what you have observed. The Spanish accent mark is written (a) like this (`) (b) like this (´). ▲

like this (´) (As in *tú*.)

6 Copy and add the accent marks to the following: *Y tu, ¿como estas?* ▲

7 The accent mark is written only over (a) vowels (b) consonants. ▲

Y tú, ¿cómo estás?
only over vowels

8 Here is the dialog between *Tomás* and *Luisa*. Read it aloud.

Tomás: ¡Hola, Luisa! ¿Qué tal?
Luisa: Bastante bien. Y tú, ¿cómo estás?
Tomás: Estoy muy bien, gracias.
Luisa: ¿A dónde vas, Tomás? ¿A clase?
Tomás: No, voy a la oficina.
Luisa: Bueno, adiós. Hasta luego.
Tomás: Adiós, Luisa. Hasta pronto.

9 You probably have read the dialog correctly. Did you do so because (a) you truly understand what all the printed marks signal you to do? (b) you memorized the dialog by imitating your instructor *before* you saw it in print? ▲

because you have the dialog memorized (You still do not really know how to read Spanish aloud. You have not been taught enough as yet to do this.)

10 Here is something else you probably have not observed. The first letters of *Bastante bien* and *Voy a la oficina* are *B* and *V* but both stand for exactly the same sound. Let's see, now, whether you can discover two more letters in the phrases above, which also stand for the same sound. Don't look at the answer until you have tried hard. These two letters are _____. ▲

The *s* of *bastante* and the *c* of *oficina* both stand for an unvoiced [s] sound. Up until now these letters have not been really telling you what sounds to make when reading aloud. You have made the right sounds because you learned, by imitation, to say the dialog before you tried to read it aloud.

When you try to read aloud something you have never heard before, you have to know exactly what the letters, the accent marks, and the punctuation tell you to say. These facts are not hard to learn, but it will take a while to tell you all about them and more class practice before you can read aloud the way you do in English.

Summary

Forms of the Articles and Plurals

1 The indefinite article has two forms: *un* and *una*. *Un* combines with nouns whose singular form ends in *o*; *una* with those ending in *a*: *un libro, una mesa*.

2 The definite article has four forms. Two are singular: *el* and *la*. Two are plural: *los* and *las*. The form *el* matches *o*-nouns; *la* matches *a*-nouns. The plural forms match their plural equivalents:

el libro   la mesa

los libros   las mesas

3 Nouns are made plural by adding *s* to vowels and *es* to consonants: *mesa, mesas; papel, papeles.*

Stop and Fricative [d]

1 The letter *d* stands for two sounds. One is a stop, as in *dough*, and the other is a fricative, as in *though*.

2 These variant sounds do not mark a difference in meaning. Depending on what precedes, the same word may be said with either sound:

stop [d]: *el día*

fricative [d]: *mi día*

Sounds and Spelling

The following are some of the ways Spanish differs from English:

1 *h* never stands for a sound in Spanish.
2 English [th] (as in "this") is written *d*.
3 The [o] of "pot" or "hot" is almost the same as the [a] of *papa*.
4 Except for foreign words, [w] is written *u*.
5 [k] before [e] or [i] is written *qu*.

New Vocabulary

Begin a section in your notebook entitled *Vocabulary*. Draw a line down the middle of the page. On the left half of the page, write all the words and phrases listed at the end of the first four Assignments; on corresponding lines on the right half of the page, write the English equivalents. Always add the new words and phrases at the end of each Assignment to your vocabulary list from now on.

The amount of vocabulary that is being presented to you is increasing at a pace that will make it difficult for you to learn all new words and phrases unless you study them regularly. Most students can learn vocabulary thoroughly by studying their list for about four minutes per day. Cover the Spanish column, look at the English equivalents and see if you can remember the Spanish. Make a light check mark opposite the words that you don't remember. Return to them several times during the four minutes until they are learned well. Study regularly your own vocabulary list using the procedure just described.

pizarra	blackboard	**ejercicio**	exercise
regla	ruler	**español (el)**	Spanish, Spaniard
luz (la)	light	**¡Ojo!**	Watch out!, Be careful! (eye)
tiza	chalk		

tú	you (familiar)	**quién**	who
usted (Vd., Ud.)	you (formal)	**allí**	there
ustedes (Uds., Uds.)	you (plural)	**luego**	then, later

Assignment 5

Learning to Write Spanish and to Read It Aloud: II

Sounds and Spelling

You will learn to read and write Spanish more easily and efficiently if you first understand more about what you really have to do. A Spanish baby has to learn *how* to make *every* Spanish sound. You do not have to go through the same process because many English and Spanish sounds are exactly alike.

1 The [s] of *clase* is exactly like the [s] of English "say". However, the [s] of *presente* is not like the [s] of "present". In *presente*, *s* stands for a sound that is (a) voiced (vocal cords vibrate) (b) unvoiced. ▲

> unvoiced (You do not have to learn to say the Spanish unvoiced [s], as in "sent". You only have to learn to use this sound where English uses the voiced sound.)

2 Spanish [p] is not aspirated in any position. This does not mean that you have to learn how to make an unaspirated [p] for it occurs in English after [s], as in "spot". You have the English habit of starting a word with a [p] sound that is (a) aspirated (b) unaspirated (no puff of air). ▲

> aspirated (This means that you now have to learn to make an unaspirated [p] in a different place and that you must realize that English has an extra [p] sound which you cannot use in Spanish.)

3 When two languages have the same two sounds, but between, before, or after different sounds in words, linguists say the sounds have a different *distribution*. It is most important, consequently, for you to know whether you are practicing a different distribution of a sound you can already make or whether you are trying to learn a sound you do not have in English.

Look at the first *t* of "estate" and the *t* of *estás*. Do these *t*'s have the same distribution? ▲

> yes (They are preceded and followed by the same sounds.)

4 The [t] sounds of Spanish and English, however, are not exactly alike. Spanish [t] is dental, the tip of the tongue touches the back of the upper front teeth. In order to learn to say a proper Spanish [t], you must practice saying [t] with your tongue (a) in the same position as in English (b) in a different position. ▲

> in a different position

5 Compare English "ban" and "van". Do *b* and *v* in English stand for the same sound? ▲

no (You have been trained, in English, to make two different sounds when you see *b* and *v*.)

6 The first syllable of *bastante* and the verb form *vas* sound exactly alike when each word is said by itself. (a) true (b) false. ▲

true (Since *b* and *v* may stand for the same sound in Spanish, when you are reading aloud, you must inhibit the tendency to assign different sounds to these letters.)

7 In Spanish both *b* and *v* may stand for a stop (lips closed) or a fricative (lips open just enough to cause friction as the air escapes) depending on what (a) precedes (b) follows. ▲

precedes (Stop after a pause or a nasal sound, *n* or *m*; fricative everywhere else.)

8 To say the *v* in *¿A dónde vas, Tomas?* you have to learn how to make a sound you do not use in English. You do this in just the same way you learned how to change an English [t] into a Spanish [t], only this time you change an English stop [b] into a Spanish fricative [b]. When you make a fricative [b], the lips are (a) closed (b) opened just enough to cause friction as the air escapes. ▲

open to cause friction

9 When you change a stop [b] to a fricative [b], have you made a totally different sound? ▲

no (The basic sound is the same. It is just made in a slightly different way.)

10 You have discovered, now, that you have one kind of problem when you imitate spoken Spanish and another when you read aloud. You will have a third when you try to write down what you hear. What tells you to write *hola* and *hasta* with an *h*? (a) what you have heard (b) what you have seen ▲

only what you have seen (Just as in English, you must learn which words can be spelled "by ear" and which ones must be spelled "by eye." Remember: sale, sail; there, their; to, two, too.)

11 Will what you hear tell you whether to write *b* or *v* in Spanish? ▲

no (You must learn to spell all words having these letters by seeing them. Spanish speakers have the same problem, and when they hear a new word, they may ask if it is spelled with *b de burro* (burro) or *v de vaca* (cow). When they ask, they say *b* and *v* exactly alike.)

12 Learning to write what you hear is going to be a lot easier if you divide all the Spanish sounds into two classes: the ones that always or almost always tell you what letter to write, and those that tell you the choice must be learned from looking at the written word.

Say these vowel sounds aloud in Spanish: *a, e, i, o, u.* Does each sound tell the Spanish speaker what letter to write? ▲

yes (When there is only one vowel in a syllable you can spell by ear. But notice this single exception: the translation of "and" is **y**.)

13 There are two [d] sounds in Spanish, a stop and a fricative. Will either one tell you to write *d*? ▲

yes (One letter stands for both sounds. So your ear will tell you what to write, but your eye will not tell you what to say.)

14 In English you write the [f] sound several ways: **Ph**il, fill, **off**er, laug**h**.

Except for foreign words, Spanish uses only *f* for this sound. The cognate of "office" is _____. ▲

> *oficina* (With one *f*. Spanish rarely writes double letters unless both stand for a sound.)

15 Say *clase* and *gracias* aloud. Do the *s* of *clase* and the *c* of *gracias* stand for the same sound? ▲

> yes (The letters *s* and *c* stand for the same sound before *e* and *i*.)

16 Will the [k] sound, by itself, tell you what letter to write?

> no (You write *qu* in *¿Qué tal?*, but *c* in *¿Cómo estás?*)

17 Spanish uses *w* only in foreign words. When you hear a [w] sound, you write _____. ▲

> *u* (As in *bueno, luego, puerta*.)

18 Say this aloud: *¡Hola, Luisa! ¿Qué tal?* Will your ear tell you to write *e* in *qué*? ▲

> yes (You can always trust the [e] sound to tell you what to write.)

19 Unlike English, the Spanish [t] sound is a dental. Does this change the spelling? ▲

> no (The [t] sound is always spelled with *t*.)

20 You hear the question word *dónde*. Will what you hear tell you how to write the word? ▲

> no (Hearing does not tell you the word has a written accent. When the word is not used in a question it is spelled *donde*.)

The Accent Mark and Reading Aloud

The accent mark tells the Spanish speaker what syllable to stress when he reads a word aloud.

1 The words *estás* and *Tomás* have two syllables: *es-tás, To-más*. Say them aloud. Which syllable is stressed (spoken louder)? (a) the first (b) the last ▲

> the last (The one with the accent mark.)

2 The word *gracias* also has two syllables: *gra-cias*. Say it aloud. Which syllable is stressed? (a) the first (b) the last ▲

3 *Gracias* has two syllables and ends in *s*. It has no accent. The stressed syllable in *gra-cias* is _____. ▲   the first

> *gra* (When the last syllable of a word ends in *s*, but has no written mark, the stress falls on the syllable before last: **gra**cias, not gra**cias**.)

4 The verb form *estás* has two syllables, ends in *s*, and has an accent mark. Which syllable is stressed? (a) *es* (b) *tás* ▲

> *tás* (When the last syllable of a word ends in *s* and has an accent mark, this syllable is stressed.)

5 Copy each word, say it aloud, and be careful to stress the proper syllable: *Tomás, gracias, estás, buenas tardes*.

Writing Practice

1 The accent mark is put only over vowels. Copy these words and add the accent mark: *¿que?, tu, ¿donde?, Tomas, ¿como?, estas, adios*. ▲

> *¿qué?, tú, ¿dónde?, Tomás, ¿cómo?, estás, adiós*

2 Say these words aloud: *hola, bastante, bueno, vas, gracias, voy, hasta.* You have to see these words in order to learn to spell them. Cover each one with your finger and write it from memory.

3 Copy the following phrases from the dialog and add all needed punctuation as well as the marks not used in English: *Hola Luisa   Que tal   Y tu   como estas* ▲

¡Hola, Luisa!, ¿Qué tal?, Y tú, ¿cómo estás?

4 The Spanish question word for "where" is _____. ▲

¿dónde? (Question words require the accent mark.)

5 Copy this word and correct the error: *tomás.* ▲

Tomás (Spanish proper names are capitalized as in English.)

Summary

1 Keep these facts in mind when you read aloud in Spanish:

a do not say [z] as in "zinc" when you see *z* or *s; s, z,* and *c* before *e* or *i* are said with an unvoiced [s], as in "sink": *seis, lápiz, cero, oficina.* You will learn some exceptions later.

b *p* is not said with a puff of air (aspiration); watch particularly the beginning of words: *papel, profesora.*

c *t* is said with the tip of the tongue against the back of the upper teeth, not the gum ridge, and without a puff of air: *tú.*

d avoid saying [v] as in "vivid"; *v* and *b* represent a stop sound after a pause or after *n* or *m*, and a fricative sound elsewhere.

e *h* does not represent any sound; compare with "honor" and "hot."

f depending on the sounds that precede it, *d* is said as a stop (**d**ough) or as a fricative (**th**ough).

g an accent mark over a vowel tells you which syllable to stress: *Tomás,* not *Tomás.*

h unlike English, at the beginning of questions and exclamations the inverted marks *¿* and *¡* signal the reader to use appropriate intonation.

2 Keep the following facts in mind when you write in Spanish.
Some sounds you can spell by ear; that is, what you hear tells you what to write:

a all the vowel sounds are spelled *a, e, i, o, u;* only exception is [i] which is written *y,* the equivalent of "and".

b both the stop as in "**d**ough" and the fricative as in "**th**ough" are spelled with *d; th* is never used.

c [t] is always spelled *t,* not *th* or *tt: tiza, Tomás.*

d [f] is always spelled *f,* not *ff, ph,* or *gh: oficina, profesor.*

Other sounds you must learn to spell by looking at the written word or remembering rules. What you hear does not tell you what letters to write:

a [k] is spelled *qu* before *e* and *i,* and *c* elsewhere: *catorce, Cuba, Colombia, qué, quince.*

b [w] is spelled *u: cuaderno, buenas.*

c　stop and fricative [b] are spelled either *b* or *v: vas, **b**astante, nue**v**e, muy **b**ien.*

d　[s] is spelled *s, z,* or *c* before *e* or *i: clase, **s**illa, **z**eta, on**c**e, **c**inco.*

e　you have to remember all the words spelled with *h: **h**ola.*

f　question words require an accent mark: *¿**Qué** tal?, ¿**Có**mo se llama?*

g　proper names are capitalized as in English: *Lui**s**a, Tomá**s**.*

Doers and Their Actions: Subject Pronouns and Verb Forms

When people talk, in any language, they have to talk about something. They talk about other people, animals, things like cars, dolls, or law, religion, and democracy. Almost anything we talk about can be thought of as a doer. A doer is somebody or something that acts or does something. In the sentence, *Dogs bark,* the word which tells what the doer does is *bark.* The subject (doer) is *dogs* and the verb (action) is *bark.*

1　Compare *bark* and *barks.* Which verb form has two parts?　▲

> barks (*Bark* is the stem; *s* is the suffix.)

2　Copy the suffix in each verb form: *burns, burned, burning.*　▲

3　The pronouns *he, she,* and *it* go with (a) burn easily (b) burns easily.　▲　　　s, ed, ing

> he burns, she burns, it burns easily

4　The subject pronouns *I, we, you,* and *they* combine with (a) burns easily (b) burn easily.　▲

> I burn, we burn, you burn, they burn easily

5　In *I see you,* who is the speaker? The person spoken to?　▲

> *I* is the speaker; *you* is the person spoken to

6　Who does *they* stand for in *They are home?* (a) the speaker (b) the persons spoken to (c) the persons spoken about　▲

> the persons spoken about

7　When we have a conversation, the speaker is called "first person." The person spoken to is "second person," and the person or thing spoken about is "third person." In the following sentence there are three pronouns: *I* see *you* have *it.* Copy the pronouns, and write either 1, 2, or 3 after each to show which is first, second, and third person.　▲

8　In *I want a ginger ale,* the speaker is one person (singular). A speaker may　I—1, you—2, it—3 talk for several persons. When this happens, *I* is replaced by _____.　▲

> we (We want a ginger ale.)

9　In *We want a ginger ale, we* is first person plural. What person and number is *they* in *They want a ginger ale?*　▲

10　The singular of *they* may be *he* or *she.* What person and number is *she* in　third person plural *She wants a new car?*　▲

> third person singular

11　Here are all the regularly used subject pronouns in English. Copy those which are third person, *I, they, we, she, you, he, it.*　▲

> they, she, he, it

12 The third person singular pronouns are *she, he, it*. There is only one English third person plural pronoun. It is _____. ▲

they (You will soon learn that there are two in Spanish.)

13 Which subject pronoun, *she* or *they*, goes with each of the following? (1) _____ talk a lot. (2) _____ talks a lot. ▲

They talk a lot; *She* talks a lot. (This is another kind of "agreement." The *s* of *talks* goes with *he, she*, and *it*, but not with *I, we, you*, or *they*. In English and Spanish the subject matches or agrees with the verb suffix.)

14 The verb form *talks* has a stem (*talk*) and a suffix (*s*). The form *talk* has no suffix. Another way of saying this is that *talk* has a *zero suffix*. The zero suffix of *talk* tells us as much about agreement as the *s* suffix of *talks*. Copy the pronouns which match a zero suffix. As a guide for choosing, say each pronoun with _____ *talk too much: I, he, we, it, you, she, they.* ▲

I, we, you, they *talk* too much. (But he, she, it *talks* too much.)

15 All third person pronouns may stand for or be used in place of a noun. *They* may stand for *dogs*. Will *they* and *dogs* agree with the same verb suffix? ▲

yes (*Dogs bark* too much; *They bark* too much.)

16 *They* may stand for proper names, for example, *Linda and Paul*. Which of the following is standard English? (a) Linda and Paul works after school. (b) Linda and Paul work after school. ▲

Linda and Paul work after school.

17 Nouns can only be replaced by the subject pronouns *he, she, it*, or *they*. What person must all subject nouns be? (a) first (b) second (c) third ▲

18 The subject pronouns in both English and Spanish agree with the verb suffix and tell us the person of the subject (first, second, third). In both languages they also give us some special information. For example, *he* refers to a male, *she* to a female. Does *they* indicate sex? ▲

third

no (It just says third person plural.)

19 Modern English has only one second person subject pronoun. It is "you." This pronoun can be used to speak either to one or to several persons. The Spanish words for "you" always indicate whether the subject is singular or plural. The formal form *usted* is singular. It is made plural by adding (a) *s* (b) *es* ▲

es (*Ustedes* is like *papeles* or *señores*.)

20 The Spanish word for "she" is *ella*. It is made plural by adding _____. ▲

s (*Ellas* is like *plumas* or *sillas* and it means "they" (all females).)

21 Compared to English "they," Spanish *ellas* gives us (a) less information (b) more information. ▲

more information (English "they" does not tell us the sex of the subject.)

22 When you ask, in Spanish, *¿Cómo está usted?*, you are speaking to one person. The subject, *usted*, and the verb, *está*, are singular. Look carefully at the two indicated verb forms in these two questions:

> *¿Cómo **está** usted?*   How **are** you?
> *¿Cómo **están** ustedes?*   How **are** you?

What has been added to the second Spanish verb form to make it agree with the plural *ustedes*? ▲

n (*n* is a mark of the plural when added to a verb form.)

23 Look carefully at the indicated suffixes of both the verb forms and the pronouns in:

> *¿Cómo están ustedes?*   How are you?
> *¿Cómo están ellas?*   How are they?

The plural suffix *n* agrees with the suffix of *ustedes* and *ellas*.

Think about this carefully: *ustedes* is second person; *ellas* is third person. Both are plural. Both combine with *están*. What does the *n* of *están* tell us? (a) the person of the subject (first, second, third) (b) just that the subject is plural. ▲

> just that the subject is plural (*n* goes with either second person, *ustedes*, or third person, *ellas*.)

24 Look carefully at the indicated verb forms in both Spanish and English in Frame 22. In which language does the verb form carry the most information? ▲

> Spanish ("Are" does not tell whether the subject is singular or plural.)

What's Your Name?

1 Everyone in our culture has several names: a regular name like *Mark* or *Mary* and several pronoun names used in conversations. What's your pronoun name in English when you are the speaker? (The doer and subject of a sentence.) ▲

2 What's your pronoun name when you are spoken to? ▲   I (*I am speaking.*)

3 You are a girl. What's your pronoun name when someone talks *about* you? _____ *has a new dress.* ▲   you

4 You are a man. What's your name when someone talks *to* you? *About* you? ▲   She

5 You are the speaker for a group. What's the name for all of you? ▲   you; he

6 Someone talks to you and all your group at once. What's your name? ▲   we

7 You are outside a friend's house making a noise. The people inside do not know what is making the noise: a person, an animal, the wind. Fill in your name. _____ *is making a noise again.* ▲   you

8 You already know that when you are talked to in Spanish you may have two different pronoun names. They are _____. ▲   It

> *tú; usted* (You will soon discover that you are going to have more pronoun names in Spanish than in English.)

Summary

1 The doer of an action and the subject of a verb may be labeled by a noun or a pronoun. A noun subject may be replaced by *he, she, it,* or *they.* The other subject pronouns are the labels for the people actually engaged in a conversation: *I, we* (the speakers) and *you* (the listener).

2   The person and number of the subject cues the choice of the verb form that is used with it: Third person singular: *John (he, she, it)* **talks**.

The third person plural and all other subjects combine with *talk*, which has a zero suffix: *The boys (they, I, you, we)* **talk**.

The form *talk*, unlike *talks*, does not indicate person and number.

3   All Spanish tense forms have a suffix which marks the number (singular or plural) of the subject. Some forms do not indicate the person. Thus the plural marker *n* combines with either *ustedes* or *ellos* and a zero suffix may combine with *usted, él,* or *ella.* Compare:

¿Cómo **está** *usted?*	How **are** you?	*¿Cómo* **están** *Vds.?*	How **are** you?
¿Cómo **está** *él?*	How **is** he?	*¿Cómo* **están** *ellos?*	How **are** they?

4   The subject pronouns actually label the role that an individual plays in a conversation: the speaker *(I, we)*, the listener *(you)*, and the person talked about *(he, she, they)*. The same individual may be cast in all three roles.

Self-Correcting Exercises

First, read each phrase incorrectly, pronouncing the indicated parts with schwa; then read each phrase as it should be without any schwa sounds. Do this three times.

1	Hol*a*, Luis*a*.		**5**	Sí, profesor*a*, c*a*torce.
2	Es un*a* mes*a*.		**6**	Buen*a*s noch*e*s.
3	Buen*o*s dí*a*s, señor*a*.		**7**	Hast*a* mañan*a*.
4	Much*a*s graci*a*s.		**8**	La señorit*a* se llam*a* Lol*a*.

New Vocabulary

Add these words and phrases which are mostly from Dialog One to the vocabulary list in your notebook. Then study them using the procedure described in the preceding Assignment.

muchacha	girl, young woman	**o**	or
muchacho	boy, young man	**a**	to, at
oficina	office	**hasta**	until; even
clase (la)	class (room)	**hola**	hello, hi
las, los	the (plural)	**gracias**	thanks
bastante	enough, quite, fairly	**¿Qué tal?**	How goes it?, How's everything?
bien	well	**¿Cómo está Vd.?**	How are you? (polite)
bueno	good, O.K.	**¿Cómo estás?**	How are you? (familiar)
muy	very	**¿A dónde va Vd.?**	Where are you going? (polite)
no	no, not	**¿A dónde vas?**	Where are you going? (familiar)
sí	yes	**¿Cómo se dice . . .?**	How do you say . . .?
y	and, plus	**¿Verdad?**	Right? (truth)

No

Wave index finger of either hand from left to right just below shoulder height, pivoting at the elbow and/or wrist.

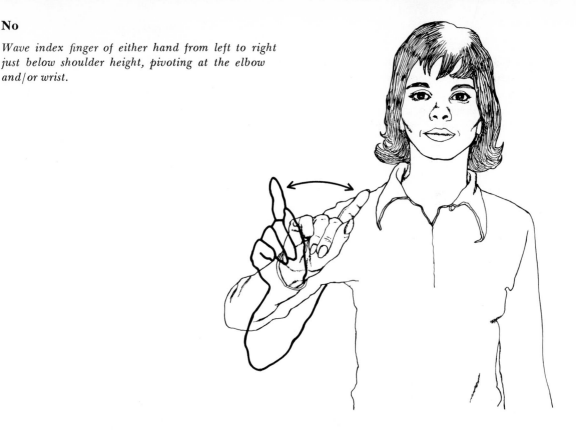

Assignment 6

The Difference Between Speech and Writing: Learning to Spell

1 Here is a perfectly good English sentence which is made up of four clauses: *Ifurightwriteriteukanreedhwatuwrightbuttifuritewrightrongukanknot* Can you read it aloud? Do you know what it means? Why can't you read it aloud? (a) because there are no punctuation marks (b) because the words are not spelled correctly (c) because there are no spaces between the words ▲

You probably decided that the reason you cannot read the sentence is because there are no spaces between the words. Let's see how important this really is.

2 Here is the same sentence with spaces between the "words." Look at it, but do not *say* the words aloud or to yourself:

If u right write rite u kan reed hwat u wright butt if u rite wright rong u kan knot. You now have the spaces between the words but the sentence is still hard to understand.

Here is the sentence with all the proper punctuation marks. This time read all the "words" aloud, one after the other, and listen carefully to what you are saying. Remember to pause just a little at each punctuation mark:

If u right "write" rite, u kan reed hwat u wright: butt if u rite "wright" rong, u kan knot.

Now, read the sentence aloud again and, then, write what you think the spoken words should be in standard spelling. ▲

> With the exception of "rite" and "wright," you should have written: *If you write "rite" right, you can read what you write; but if you write "wright" wrong, you cannot.*

3 This experiment proves that speech and writing are very different. What told you what to write? (a) what *you saw* (b) what *you* actually *said* ▲

> what you actually said

4 The experiment has shown that what you say can be written in several different ways. Do you always say *reed* and *read* exactly alike? ▲

> no (If you wrote "yes," you will see why you are wrong in the next frame.)

5 Say this question aloud: *Did you read what you wrote?* Now this answer. *Yes, I read it.* In which sentence must *read* be spoken like "red"? (a) first (b) second ▲

> the second: *Yes I read it.* (You are talking about the past and what you say is like "Yes, I red it.")

6 Say this question aloud: *Do you read Spanish?* Now this answer: *Yes, I read it.* This time you said *read* like "reed," not like "red." What tells you to say *read* in two different ways? (a) spelling (b) meaning ▲

> meaning

7 Say these words aloud: *right, write, rite, wright.* They are exactly alike when spoken. What tells us how to spell words like this? (a) the sounds they stand for (b) their meaning. ▲

> their meaning (To learn to spell them, you also have to see them. This is "eye" spelling.)

8 We can write things we cannot say. We can also say things we cannot write. These three words in English are spoken exactly alike: *to, two, too.* Can you fill in the space in this sentence? *There are three _____ s in English.* ▲

> no (You can say it, but you cannot write it.)

9 You have now learned the following facts: (1) You can write what you say in different ways (*doe, dough*). (2) You can say what you write in different ways (*read*). (3) You can write things you cannot say (*rite, right*). (4) You can say things you cannot write. Is writing an accurate way of representing what we actually say? ▲

10 We write most words in just one way, but there are many words which we say in several different ways. For example, the form *going* is made up of the stem *go* and the suffix *ing*. Say the suffix *ing* aloud and, then, say *going* very carefully. Do this until you can hear precisely what you are saying. (a) Did you say the last [g] sound of *going*? (b) Did you leave it off? ▲

> no

> You said the last [g] sound if you pronounced *going* carefully. (When a word is said all by itself it is called a *citation form*.)

11 Read this sentence aloud very carefully: *I am going to Madrid.* Did you say the last [g] sound of *going*? Did you pronounce *to* with a schwa? ▲

> You said the last [g] and you did not use the schwa.

12 Which of the following pairs do you say in an ordinary conversation with a friend? You can't be sure until you say them aloud.

I'm going to Madrid.   I'm gointuh Madrid.

I'm going to make it.   I'm gonna maykit.

(a) the first pair (b) the second pair ▲

> the second pair (All educated speakers of American English, even teachers of English, regularly say the second pair in relaxed conversation.)

13 We do not pronounce the same word in the same way when we give a citation form, read aloud, or just talk. How many different ways may we pronounce *going*: (a) one (b) two (c) three? (If you are uncertain, look at Frame 12 again.) ▲

> three (We say *going*, with the last [g] sound, *goin*, without the last [g] sound, and *gon*, as in *gonna*.)

14 What we write does not always represent what we say. Let's prove this once more. We say this very frequently: *Shur, aikinduit.* Say it aloud and, then, rewrite it with standard spelling and word spacing. ▲

15 You have seen that there are different ways of saying many words. What is standard spelling most like? (a) the pronunciation of citation forms (words spoken by themselves) (b) the reading pronunciation (c) the way we talk ▲   Sure, I can do it.

> the pronunciation of citation forms

16 The difference between plain talk, reading aloud, and writing is just about the same in Spanish as in English. The word which the Spanish speaker says for clock is [reló] but the word is spelled *reloj*.

Sent and *cent* are pronounced exactly alike. The letter *c* stands for the same sound in *cent* and *cinder* but not in *can't*.

Look at the vowel which follows *c* in these sets of words and say them aloud: **c**at, **c**ot, **c**ut, **c**enter, **c**inder, **c**ent. The *c* stands for a [k] sound when it is followed by the vowels _____; the *c* stands for an unvoiced [s] sound when it is followed by _____. ▲

> *c* for [k] before *a*, *o*, and *u; c* for [s] before *i* and *e* (with a few minor exceptions)

17 In Spanish the letter *c* stands for the [k] sound before *a, o, u* and the unvoiced [s] sound before *e* and *i* just as in English. Which *c* of *cinco* stands for the [k] sound? (a) *ci* (b) *co* ▲

> *co* (You are really saying [sinko].)

18 Which *c* of *catorce* stands for the unvoiced [s] sound? (a) *ca* (b) *ce* ▲

> *ce* (You say [katorse].)

19 What sound does the *c* of *oficina* stand for, [k] or [s]? ▲

20 Copy each word carefully and underline every letter that stands for an unvoiced [s] sound. Say each word aloud before you decide: *mesa, gracias, tiza, lápiz, tres, cinco, luz.* ▲   [s]

> *me**s**a, gra**c**ia**s**, ti**z**a, lápi**z**, tre**s**, **c**inco, lu**z***

21 Spanish (except for the Castilian dialect) has three letters which stand for the unvoiced [s]. They are _____. ▲

22 You can learn to spell Spanish words which have an [s] sound only by seeing and writing them. Here are 10 Spanish words which you know that have an [s] sound in them. Say each aloud and copy it.   *s, c, z*

lápiz	pencil	*tiza*	chalk
silla	chair	*gracias*	thanks
mesa	table	*luz*	light

pizarra	chalkboard	*está*	is, are
oficina	office	*cinco*	five

23 The Spanish letter *r* stands for two sounds: a single [r] and a double [rr]. The *r* stands for a double [rr] sound at the beginning of words. Say these words aloud and copy them: *reloj*, *regla*.

24 The *r* stands for a single [r] sound in these words. Say them aloud and copy them: *cuaderno*, *libro*, *pupitre*, *puerta*. Check your spelling.

25 Say *libro* and *ventana* aloud. Does what you hear tell you when to write *b* or *v*? ▲

> no (You have to see words with *b* and *v* in them to learn how to spell them. You do not, however, write *v* before a consonant in Spanish.)

26 Say *papel* and *pluma* aloud. Does what you hear tell you how to spell these words? ▲

> yes (The sounds of *p*, *l*, *m* and the vowels always tell you what to write.)

Review: tú *and* usted; ustedes *for the familiar plural*

1 When "you" (singular) are spoken to in Spanish you may have two pronoun names: *tú* and *usted*. Add the plural suffix to *usted*. ▲

2 In Spain the plural of *tú* is *vosotros* or *vosotras*. These forms are not used in Latin America, and you will, consequently, only have to learn to read them or understand them when you hear them. Since there is no special plural form for *tú* in common use in Latin America, when you talk, you will have to use _____ as the plural of *tú*. ▲

> *ustedes*

3 When you address your instructor, which subject pronoun do you use? (a) *tú* (b) *usted* ▲

> *ustedes*

4 When adult strangers meet, they speak to each other with (a) *tú* (b) *usted*. ▲

> *usted*

5 Children usually talk to each other with _____. ▲

> *usted*
>
> *tú* (There is even a verb for this: *tutear*, to talk with *tú*.)

6 Which pronoun is used most frequently when you address a person by his or her last name? ▲

7 Very intimate friends usually talk to each other with _____. ▲

> *usted*

8 When you talk to animals, you use _____. ▲

> *tú*
>
> *tú*

Morphemes and the Pieces and Parts of Verbs

1 You already know that words may be divided into either syllables or meaningful parts. The meaningful parts of words are called *morphemes*, pronounced [morefeems]. This word comes from the Greek *morph* (shape), and *eme* (meaningful). How many morphemes (meaningful parts) are there in the verb form *walking*? (a) one (b) two ▲

> two (The stem *walk* and the suffix *ing*.)

2 The two plural suffix forms, *s* of *libros* and *es* of *papeles*, tell the Spanish speaker the same thing as do the *s* of "dogs" and the *es* of "churches." When two forms (parts), like *s* and *es*, have the same meaning, each is called an *allomorph* (other shape) of the same morpheme. So linguists say that in both English and Spanish the *s* and *es* are allomorphs of the plural morpheme. The allomorphs of a morpheme can never be used in the same combination. In Spanish you add the plural allomorph *s* to nouns ending in a vowel (*libros, mesas*). When a noun ends in a consonant, you add the plural allomorph _____.   ▲

es (papeles, señores)

3   Pay special attention to the meaning and the suffix of the indicated words in these sentences: (1) He builds *churches*. (2) He *teaches* Spanish. Does the *es* of *churches* have the same meaning as the *es* of *teaches*?   ▲

no (*Church* stands for a building; *teach* for an action.)

4   When *es* is added to a noun stem like *church*, it indicates plural. When *es* is added to a verb stem like *teach*, it indicates (a) past tense (b) present tense.   ▲

5   Look at the suffixes of the indicated verb forms in these sentences: (1) She   present tense
talks to him in Spanish. (2) She *teaches* him Spanish. Are the *s* of *talks* and the *es* of *teaches* allomorphs of the same morpheme?   ▲

yes (Both indicate present tense.)

6   The difference in meaning of the following sentences is shown by the contrast between just two morphemes: (1) She talks to him in Spanish. (2) She talked to him in Spanish. The two morphemes are _____.   ▲

7   The morpheme in *talked* which tells us the action is past is *ed*. The *s* of   s ; ed
talks and the *es* of *teaches* say the action is present or current. Compare the verb forms of these sentences. (1) They talk to him in Spanish. (2) They talked to him in Spanish. Does the zero suffix of *talk* indicate (a) past action? (b) present action?   ▲

present action (The zero suffix of *talk* and the *s* of *talks* indicate the same tense.)

8   Are the *s* ([s]) of *talks*, the *s* ([z]) of *digs*, and the *es* ([əz]) of *teaches* allomorphs of the same morpheme?   ▲

yes (All are markers of third person singular present tense.)

9   Which form describes an action that may be going on right now? (a) walked (b) walking   ▲

walking (She is *walking* in the park.)

10   The verb form *walking* has two morphemes, a stem and a suffix. Which morpheme says the action may be going on now?   ▲

11   How many morphemes are there in each of these verb forms: calls, called,   ing
calling?   ▲

two (The stem *call* and the suffixes *s, ed, ing.*)

12   The stem (*call*) is the same in *calls*, *called*, and *calling*. Does this stem have the same meaning in all three forms?   ▲

yes (The verb stem always tells us what action is being talked about.)

13   Most English verb forms are made up of just two morphemes: the stem and one suffix. Almost all Spanish verb forms have three morphemes: the stem and two suffixes. The stem of *estoy, estás,* and *están* is the part that is the same in all three forms. It is _____.   ▲

est

14 What immediately follows the stem? (a) a vowel (b) a consonant ▲

a vowel (All regular Spanish verb forms, in all tenses, always have a vowel right after the stem.)

15 The suffix *n* of *están* agrees with the *es* of *ustedes* in *¿Cómo están ustedes?* There are three morphemes in *están*: the stem _____, the first suffix _____, and the second suffix _____. ▲

16 The *n* of *están* agrees with the plural suffix *es* of *ustedes*. Which suffix of *están*, *á* or *n*, tells the Spanish speaker that the form is present tense? ▲

est, á, n

á (The first suffix after the stem indicates tense.)

17 The subject pronoun that goes with *estás* is *tú*. *Tú* stands for one person. The *s* of *estás* agrees with *tú*. The *n* of *están* agrees with *ustedes* (plural). The second suffix of a Spanish verb indicates (a) tense (b) whether the subject is singular or plural. ▲

whether the subject is singular or plural (And sometimes the person.)

18 In Spanish, as in English, there can be three persons in a conversation: first, second and third. The *s* of *estás* agrees in number and person with *tú*. Both *s* and *tú* indicate _____ person. ▲

second (The person spoken to.)

19 In which sentence do both the subject pronoun and the verb have a zero suffix which indicates singular? (a) *¿Cómo está usted?* (b) *¿Cómo están ustedes?* ▲

¿Cómo está usted? (Spanish, like English, uses zero to indicate meaning.)

20 What subject pronoun goes with *estoy* and *voy*? ▲

21 *Están* is plural, but *yo estoy* and *yo voy* are _____. ▲

yo

22 Which person are *estoy* and *voy*? (a) first (b) second (c) third ▲

singular

first (*Yo* stands for the speaker.)

23 The forms *am*, *is*, *are*, *was* and *were* all belong to the same verb in English. There is another form. "Are you going to _____ at home tonight?" ▲

24 When we have to talk about all these forms, we need to pick one as the name of the verb. So we say that *am*, *is*, *are*, *was*, and *were* are all forms of the verb "to _____." ▲

be

25 Forms like *to be*, *to sing*, *to play*, or *to learn* are called *infinitives*. This is the name form for the verb. The infinitive for *found*, as in "He found the money," is _____. ▲

be

26 The mark of all Spanish infinitives is the suffix *r*. The infinitive form of *estoy*, *estás*, or *están* is *estar*. The vowel which follows the stem of *estar* is _____. ▲

to find

27 The vowel between the stem and the *r* mark of the infinitive determines the verb set. So *estar* is said to be an *a*-verb. There are two more verb sets in Spanish: *e*- and *i*-verbs.

a

The Marks Used in Writing Spanish

There are three different kinds of marks used in writing Spanish. Letters of the alphabet stand for sounds. When a word has more than one syllable, the written accent mark tells which syllable to stress. Punctuation indicates the pauses and intonation pattern for a sentence or utterance.

1 When you see a comma, a semi-colon, or a colon in reading aloud, (a) you keep right on going (b) you pause for a split second. ▲

2 Below is a sentence without punctuation marks. Say it aloud as instructed and, then, write the punctuation mark for each example. (a) You are making a statement of fact. *Henry is sick* (b) You want to check what you just heard. *Henry is sick* (c) You are astonished at what you heard. *Henry is sick* ▲

you pause

(a) Henry is sick. (statement) (b) Henry is sick? (question) (c) Henry is sick!

3 Spanish written questions and exclamations, unlike English, must _____ and end with the question or exclamation mark. ▲

(exclamation)

4 The English noun *résumé* (pronounced [rez-zoom-máy]) means "a summary" or "a condensed statement." The verb *resume* (pronounced [re-zoom]) means "to take up again." Are the accent marks necessary to spell *résumé* correctly? ▲

begin

yes (If you leave them off, you get *resume,* a different word.)

5 Do all the letters of Spanish always stand for a speech sound? ▲

no (You hear *ola, asta,* and *reló,* but must write *hola, hasta,* and *reloj.*)

Optional Writing Practice

Here are some Spanish words you have to see and hear in order to learn to spell them. Say each aloud and copy very carefully. The indicated part is the one that may cause errors. Check it carefully.

cuaderno	*notebook*	**pi**zarra	*chalkboard*	**reloj**	*clock*
silla	*chair*	**ve**rdad	*true (really)*	luz	*light*
ventana	*window*	**re**gla	*ruler*	**mesa**	*table*
puerta	*door*	**lá**piz	*pencil*	gracias	*thanks*

Summary

Learning to Spell

1 Writing is an incomplete and often inaccurate representation of speech.
   a The same spoken word may have multiple meanings and different spellings: *right, write, rite, wright* or *to, too, two.*
   b The same spelling may represent two different spoken words: present tense *read* = [reed], past tense *read* = [red].
   c Standard spelling, in both English and Spanish, is more like what is said when a word is spoken by itself (the citation form) or read aloud than like relaxed conversation. Speech: *Shur, aikinduit;* reading: *Sure, I can do it.*
   d Letters do not always represent the sound spoken: *colonel* = [kernel].
   e The same letter may stand for different sounds: *c* spells [s] in *cent,* [k] in *can't.*

2 The Spanish spelling system has similar inadequacies.
   a [k] is written *qu* before *e* and *i* but *c* elsewhere.
   b [s] may be written *c, z,* or *s.*

c [b] is spelled *b* or *v*.

d *r* stands for [rr] at the beginning of words but for [r] between vowels.

Morphemes and the Pieces and Parts of Verbs

1 When a word like *teaches* carries two pieces of information, it must have two meaningful parts or "morphemes": *teach* plus *es*.

2 When two forms, the *es* of *teaches* and the *s* of *talks*, carry the same information (third person, present tense) they are called "other forms" or *allomorphs* of the same morpheme.

3 Most English verb forms have two morphemes. Most Spanish verb forms have three. The stem of *estamos* is *est*. The first suffix, *a*, marks present tense and indicative mode, and *mos* says the subject is *nosotros*.

4 The first suffix of Spanish verbs marks tense and mode; the second suffix always indicates number (singular or plural) and sometimes person.

5 The "name" for a verb is the infinitive, which is marked by *to* in English: *to be, to eat, to live*. The Spanish infinitive mark is a final *r*: *estar, comer, vivir*. The final vowel, *a*, *e*, or *i*, marks the verb set and cues the choice of the forms of the first suffix.

Self-Correcting Exercises

In this and future assignments, there will be many self-correcting exercises. In order for maximum learning to take place, they should be done as follows:

(a) Cover the answers, which will appear either on the right margin or below each item.

(b) Write your responses on a separate sheet of paper.

(c) Immediately after writing each answer, check its accuracy before doing the next problem. It is important that you have immediate knowledge of results, so do not wait until you have finished the entire exercise to find out whether you were right or wrong.

A Using the above procedure, circle each stop [d] and its cue and underline each fricative [ð] and its cue.

1 d u d o   n o   d u d o   d o n d e   d e s d e

    (d)u d o   n o   d u d o   (d)o (n d)e   (d)e s d e

2 d u d a   n o   d u d a   a d o n d e   D o n a l d o

    (d)u d a   n o   d u d a   a d o (n d)e   (D)o n a(l d)o

3 d u d e   n o   d u d e   e s   d e   a   D o n a l d o

    (d)u d e   n o   d u d e   e s   d e   a   D o n a(l d)o

4 ¿D ó n d e   está   D o n a l d o?   ¿Q u é   d í a   es,   L i n d a ?

    (¿D)ó (n d)e   está   D o n a(l d)o ?   ¿Q u é   d í a   es,   L i (n d)a ?

B   Ask and answer these questions aloud trying to sound as much like a native speaker as possible. Do the entire exercise three times.

1	¿Dónde está la pizarra?	La pizarra está allí.
2	¿Dónde están las ventanas?	Las ventanas están allí.
3	Las luces están allí, ¿verdad?	Sí, las luces están allí.
4	El libro está en la mesa, ¿verdad?	No, el libro está en el pupitre.
5	¿Dónde está el cuaderno, en la mesa, o en el pupitre?	El cuaderno está en la mesa.
6	Y la puerta, ¿dónde está?	La puerta está allí.

New Vocabulary

Add these words to your notebook and study the entire vocabulary list for three or four minutes.

día (el)	day		**tarde (la)**	afternoon
noche (la)	night, evening		**menos**	minus, less
mañana	morning, tomorrow		**pronto**	soon, quick, fast

Assignment 7

Review of Subject Pronouns and Verb Forms

1   Most English verb forms have just two parts, a stem and one suffix. The present tense forms of a Spanish verb, in contrast, have three parts, a stem and two suffixes.

   The word *hablamos* may be divided in two ways. To pronounce it properly, we must divide it into syllables. To understand what it means, we divide it into meaningful parts or morphemes: the stem and the two suffixes. Which of the following is divided into syllables? (a) *ha-bla-mos* (b) *habl-a-mos*.   ▲

ha-bla-mos (*Habl-a-mos* shows the three morphemes.)

2   The morpheme in *habl-a-mos* which indicates present tense is _____.   ▲

3   The present tense morpheme of *a*-verbs has two allomorphs. One is *a* as in   *a*
tú habl-a-s or *nosotros habl-a-mos*. The other goes with *yo* and is *habl-*_____.   ▲

o (*Yo hablo inglés.*)

4   The second suffix of a Spanish verb form sometimes indicates person (first, second, third). It always indicates the _____ of the subject.   ▲

5   The subject pronouns *él* (he) and *ella* (she) indicate number (singular),   number
person (third), and sex (male or female). Both combine with the same form, *habla: él habla, ella habla.* No part of *habla*, or any other Spanish verb form, tells you whether the subject is male or female. Spanish subject pronouns give us more information about the number and sex of the subject than English pronouns. To do this they have to have more meaningful parts than English. The

pronouns *ellos* and *ellas* are made up of three parts (morphemes): *ell-o-s* and *ell-a-s*. The stem is _____.   ▲

ell (This says third person.)

6 The final *s* tells us the subject is plural. The *a* of *ellas* says the subject is (a) all males (b) all females.   ▲

7 The translation of *ellas* (all females) is "they." The translation of *ellos* is also "they." Spanish has no other word for "they"; as a result, the form *ellos* may stand for either all males or a group made up of males and females. (a) true (b) false   ▲

all females

true (*Ellas* clearly says "all females" but *ellos,* like English "they," is am-

8 Which form, *nosotros* or *nosotras*, is used when the group is all males?   ▲   biguous.)

9 When a pronoun has two forms, the *o*-form may stand for either all males or _____.   ▲   *nosotros*

10 *Usted* and *ustedes* do not show the difference between male and female.   males and females
They show only singular and plural. *Yo* does not tell whether the speaker is male or female. Either a male or a female may say *Yo hablo inglés*. Here are all the subject pronouns you are going to learn to use. Which ones clearly indicate the subject is female: *yo, nosotros, nosotras, usted, ustedes, él, ellos, ella, ellas, tú?*   ▲

11 Look at these pronouns and translate them: *yo, nosotros, usted, ustedes, él,*   *nosotras, ella, ellas*
ellos, tú. There is only one that clearly says the subject is male. It is _____.   ▲

12 Which of these pronouns tell you the subject is plural: *yo, nosotros, nosotras,*   *él*
usted, ustedes, él, ellos, ella, ellas, tú.   ▲

nosotros, nosotras, ustedes, ellos, ellas

13 The singular form of *ellas* (they) is *ella* (she). The stem is _____.   ▲

14 The *a*-suffix of *ella* says female. When the *a* is dropped, the zero suffix   *ell*
stands for the opposite or male. In modern spelling one *l* of *ell* has been dropped. The form *el* translates "the." To make it stand for "he" in writing, you must add _____.   ▲

15 To make *ella* plural you just add *s* (*ellas*). To make *él* plural, you drop the   an accent mark: *él*
accent mark, change *el* to the stem _____, and add *os*.   ▲

16 "You" in English may be either singular or plural. The Spanish equiv-   *ell* (*él; ellos*)
alents used among strangers are _____ (singular) and _____ (plural).   ▲

17 The plural of the English subject pronoun "I" is _____.   ▲   *usted; ustedes*

18 The plural of Spanish *yo* has two forms based on the stem *nosotr*. Both   we
show sex. They are _____.   ▲

19 When you speak in private to a very close friend, you address that friend   *nosotros; nosotras*
with the subject pronoun _____.   ▲

20 When we talk about a verb and all its forms, we use the name form or   *tú*
infinitive. Thus, we say, "*Spoke* is a form of *to speak*." The Spanish equivalent of the "to" in "to speak" is the last suffix of any Spanish infinitive. It is _____.   ▲

r: hablar (The stem *habl-* labels the action. The first suffix is *a*, the set vowel, and the second suffix, *r*, marks the form as the infinitive.)

21 To make *hablar* agree with *tú*, the *r* is replaced by _____.   ▲

22 To change *hablas* so it agrees with *ustedes*, the *s* is replaced by _____.   ▲   *s*

n

23 Make *ustedes hablan* singular by dropping the plural suffix of both the pronoun and the verb. The result is _____.   ▲

24 Both the subject pronoun and the verb in *ella habla* are singular. To make these forms plural, you add the plural suffixes: *ella* _____ *habla* _____.   ▲

usted habla

25 The second suffix of the singular form *habla* is zero. What suffix must be added to *habla* to make it agree with either *nosotros* or *nosotras*?   ▲

ellas hablan

26 When *yo* is the subject of a regular verb form, the first suffix in the present tense is the vowel _____.   ▲

mos

27 The *s* of *hablas* matches *tú* and gives us the same three pieces of information as the subject pronoun: person, number, and social relationship. Select the right combination for meaning of both *tú* and the suffix *s*: (a) second person, singular, friend (b) second person, plural, stranger (c) second person, plural, friend (d) second person, singular, stranger   ▲

o

second person, singular, friend (Spanish verb forms give more information than English.)

28 To learn all the present tense forms of *hablar*, you must learn first, the stem, *habl*, which gives the meaning of the verb. The first suffix is *a* which marks the verb set and is used in all forms of the present tense except the *yo* form. The second suffix may be zero or an actual form: *mos*, *n*, or *s*. Which suffix goes with these subject pronouns?

| nosotros | habla _____. |
| nosotras | |

| tú | habla _____. |

ustedes	habla _____.
ellos	
ellas	▲

nosotros—*mos*, *tú*—*s*, and *n* matches the plural suffix *es* and *s* of *ustedes*, *ellos*, and *ellas*

29 The present tense of all regular *a*-verbs in Spanish is made up just like *hablar*. To get all the present tense forms of *llamar* you simply replace the stem *habl* with _____.   ▲

llam

What Have You Learned?

1 Here are ten facts about English which have been talked about in your Assignments. Check those which you really knew for sure *before* you began this course:

(1) Most English verb forms are made up of two meaningful parts (morphemes).

(2) The demonstratives *this*, *that*, *these*, and *those* have a stem and a suffix.

(3) The demonstratives agree in number with the nouns they combine with.

(4) The *s* of *talks* indicates present tense.

(5) A zero suffix can have meaning.

(6) The letter *p* stands for two different English sounds.

(7) The air comes out your nose when you say [m].

(8) The first sound of a noun tells us when to say *a* or *an*.

(9) Any English vowel may become schwa in an unstressed syllable.
(10) The *s* of *present* is voiced. ▲

> If you were consciously aware of three or more of these facts before you began this course, you already had unusual training in the nature of English.

2 You learned to talk English without being consciously aware of any of these facts. Yet you do make demonstratives agree with their nouns and you do use *a*, instead of *an*, before a noun that begins with a consonant. When you say *an apple,* (a) do you stop to think about choosing between *a* and *an*? (b) do you just say the right one out of habit? ▲

> You say the right one out of habit without thinking about the choice.

3 When you were learning to write, did someone have to tell you how to make certain letters or to use a capital letter to begin a name? ▲

4 You have two sets of language habits or skills. One set you learned by yourself without being aware of what you were learning. The other set was taught to you. Let's see which way of learning will be the fastest in learning Spanish. Which is the fastest way to learn to swim? (a) by just watching and imitating others (b) by taking lessons in which you are told precisely what to do with your arm and legs ▲

> yes

5 An Olympic champion cannot win if he has to think about what the coach taught him every time he takes a stroke. To become a champion swimmer one must turn consciously learned knowledge into a set of automatic habits. Let's apply this logic to learning Spanish. What is the fastest way for a speaker of English to learn how to say *Buenos días* without using the English *schwa?* (a) by just listening to and imitating a native (b) by first learning that there is a *schwa* in English, but none in Spanish, and, then, practicing how to say *Buenos días* without a schwa ▲

> by taking lessons

> by first learning about the schwa and how to get rid of the English habit

6 Native children take several years to learn when to use *tú* or *usted* correctly. You learned this in one Assignment. However, will you ever learn to speak Spanish well if you have to stop and think about which pronoun to use every time you speak to someone? ▲

> no (What you are now learning to do must become an unconscious habit before you can talk Spanish well.)

7 You first learn the facts about the Spanish language in the Assignments. The purpose of most of the classroom activity is to practice what you already know until it becomes a habit. Does the awareness that English verbs have a stem and a suffix make it easier to deal with and learn the stem and suffixes of Spanish verbs? ▲

> yes (You do not have to learn so much.)

How Much Do You Remember? A Test

1 Look-alike words such as "mountain" and *montaña* are called cognates. Look at the first part of "library" (libr) and think of what you will find on the shelves in a library. The Spanish cognate of "library" that you already know is the noun _____. ▲

> *libro* (Both cognates come from the Latin stem *libr.*)

2 The two standard ways of sending messages (communicating) are
_____. ▲

3 There are four language skills: reading, speaking, writing, and hearing.   speech and writing
You must hear Spanish before you can learn to speak it. You must see some
written Spanish before you start learning how to write it. If you have not seen
hasta and have only heard *asta*, you will not know that what you say and what
you see are the same word. In what order, then, should the four language skills
be learned? (1) _____ (2) _____ (3) _____ (4) _____ ▲

hearing, speaking, reading, writing.

4 When we say that the [p] of English *pie* is aspirated, we mean that the sound
is followed by a little puff of air. All Spanish [p] sounds are (a) aspirated
(b) unaspirated. ▲

5 The [s] sound of "present" is not like the [s] sound of *presente*. The Spanish   unaspirated
[s] before a vowel is (a) voiced (b) unvoiced. ▲

unvoiced (The vocal cords do not vibrate.)

6 When you make a Spanish [t] sound, the tip of the tongue touches _____. ▲

the back of the upper front teeth (The Spanish [t] is dental.)

7 The *h* stands for no sound in *honor* or *hour*. It never stands for a sound in
Spanish. Write one Spanish word having an *h*. ▲

(You know two!) *hola*; *hasta*

8 Spanish can show which syllable of a word is stressed by using _____ in
writing. ▲

the written accent mark (′)

9 The first syllable of English *total* is stressed: ***to**-tal*. Which syllable normally
has a schwa sound? ▲

tal (We normally say something like [totul].)

10 The English schwa appears in unstressed syllables and may be substituted
for any English vowel. As a result, in relaxes speech you do not hear the difference between *vender* and *vendor*. Spanish has no schwa. Can the vowel in unstressed syllables be used in Spanish to show that two words have different
meanings? ▲

yes (Spanish *libro* is "book"; *libre* translates "free.")

11 The meaningful parts of words have a technical name which comes from
the Greek meaning "meaningful shape." This word is _____. ▲

12 Morphemes and syllables are not always identical. (a) true (b) false ▲   morpheme
true (*Ha-bla-mos* shows syllables: *habl-a-mos* shows morphemes.)

13 The suffixes of the four English demonstratives *this, that, these, those* are
_____. ▲

14 Look at the difference between the suffixes of both words in this pair of   is, at, ese, ose
phrases: *this hat: these hats*. English demonstrative adjectives agree in _____
with their nouns. ▲

15 Do most Spanish adjectives agree in number with their nouns? ▲   number
16 Which word has a zero suffix? (a) *mesas* (b) *mesa* ▲   yes
17 The first part of *morpheme* is like the first part of *morphology*. Morphology   *mesa*
is (a) the study of speech sounds (b) the study of the pieces and parts of words,
or morphemes. ▲

the study of the pieces and parts of words

18 *Tú* is used when you address a person with a title of respect (*señor, señorita, etc.*). (a) true (b) false   ▲

false (The use of a title of respect requires usted.)

19 You should always use *usted* when you address a person by his first name. (a) true (b) false   ▲

false (The choice depends on how intimate the speakers are.)

20 When you speak to adult strangers, you use (a) *tú* (b) *usted*.   ▲

21 When sweethearts talk to each other, they use (a) *tú* (b) *usted*.   ▲   usted

22 What tells you to use *a* or *an* with a noun in English? (a) the first sound in the noun (b) the last sound   ▲   tú

the first sound (an egg, but a leg)

23 What tells you to match *la* with *mesa* and *el* with *papel* in Spanish? (a) The first sound in the noun (b) the last sound   ▲

the last (a with a; l with l)

24 When a noun ends in *a*, the form of the Spanish indefinite article to be used is almost always (a) *una* (b) *un*.   ▲

25 If *un* agrees with a noun (*un libro*), the definite article form _____ will also agree with that same noun.   ▲   una

el (un libro; el libro)

26 Spanish has two allomorphs of the plural noun suffix. They are _____.   ▲

27 Which plural suffix follows (a) a consonant? (b) a vowel?   ▲   s; es

es after a consonant; s after a vowel

28 When the air passage is closed in making a sound, that sound is called a _____.   ▲

29 The stops in *¿Dónde?* are _____.   ▲   stop

30 When a sound is made with friction, it is called a _____.   ▲   the two [d]'s

31 Say this aloud: *¿A dónde vas?* The two fricatives are _____.   ▲   fricative

first d of dónde and v

32 What tells you that the first [d] is a stop in *¿Dónde?* but a fricative in *¿A dónde vas?* (a) what comes before (b) what follows   ▲

33 There are spaces between the words of *¿A dónde vas?* Do you say the sentence (a) with a pause for each space? (b) like this: *¿Adóndevas?*   ▲   what comes before

like one, big word (Writing does not represent exactly what we say.)

34 The two Spanish punctuation marks which begin a sentence (or phrase), and are not used in English, are _____.   ▲

35 The precise meaning of *Me llamo Pablo* is not the common translation "My name is Pablo." To the Spanish speaker the meaning is "I _____ myself Pablo."   ▲   ¡ and ¿

36 Copy the six Spanish subject pronouns which indicate sex: *yo, nosotros, nosotras, usted, ustedes, él, ella, ellos, ellas, tú*.   ▲   call

nosotros, nosotras, él, ella, ellos, ellas

37 There are three persons: first, second, and third. Which person is each of the following: *yo* _____, *tú* _____, *ellos* _____?   ▲

yo, first; tú, second; ellos, third

38 English verb forms have _____ parts. Spanish verb forms have _____ parts.   ▲

two; three

39 The infinitive or name form of *hablas* has _____ in place of the final *s*.   ▲

40 Which two morphemes in *ustedes hablan* show agreement?   ▲

41 The second suffix of a Spanish verb form indicates (a) tense (b) person and number.   ▲

42 What part of *estoy* is irregular?   ▲

43 Write *hablas* indicating the morphemes.   ▲

44 The stem *habl* labels the action. The *s* agrees with *tú*. The first suffix *a* gives the verb set and also tells us the verb is _____ tense.   ▲

45 Write *ellas* indicating the morphemes.   ▲

46 Rewrite and make both forms singular: *ustedes hablan*.   ▲

47 The singular of *ellos* is _____.   ▲

r (hablar)

ustedes hablan

person and number

oy

habl-a-s

present

ell-a-s (The *a* marks sex, female, and the *s* is the plural suffix.)

usted habla

él

Study the frames in which you made a mistake.

Self-Correcting Exercises

A   With the answers covered, circle each stop [d] and its cue, and underline each fricative [đ] and its cue. Check the accuracy of your answers, before doing the next problem.

1 ¿D ó n d e   está el   c u a d e r n o?

¿D ó n d e   está el   c u a d e r n o?

2 B u e n o s   d í a s.   Es un   b u e n   d í a.

B u e n o s   d í a s.   Es un   b u e n   d í a.

3 D o n a l d o,   buenas   t a r d e s.

D o n a l d o,   buenas   t a r d e s.

4 ¿A d ó n d e   vas,   D o n a l d o?

¿A d ó n d e   vas,   D o n a l d o?

5 ¿Y   u s t e d?   ¿Q u é   d í a   es?

¿Y   u s t e d?   ¿Q u é   d í a   es?

B   For each verb in parentheses, write the present indicative form that matches the subject. Check each of your responses against the correct answers on the right margin of the page.

1 Usted (hablar) español muy bien.

2 Yo no me (llamar) Antonio.

3 Nosotros (hablar) en la clase.

4 Ellos no (hablar) bien.

5 Ustedes (hablar) inglés y español.

habla

llamo

hablamos

hablan

hablan

6   Ella se (llamar) Nancy Díaz.   llama
7   Él se (llamar) Tomás Dávila.   llama
8   Yo (hablar) mucho en la clase.   hablo
9   Luisa (hablar) italiano.   habla
10 Tú te (llamar) Ché y tú (hablar) inglés, ¿verdad?   llamas, hablas

C   In the next class there will be a dictation quiz. It will cover all vowel sounds
and the sounds represented by *p, t, m, n, f, l,* and *d* which can be spelled by ear.
You will be asked to write from dictation syllables like *fi, to, od, al, etc.* and words
and nonsense combinations like *tapete, minola, dedo, fila, etc.*

New Vocabulary

Add these words to your vocabulary list and study them in the usual manner.

hombre	man	**llamar(se)**	to call (oneself)	**jueves**	Thursday
mujer (la)	woman	**fue**	was	**viernes**	Friday
estudiante	student	**hay**	there is (are)	**sábado**	Saturday
inglés	English	**es**	is	**calendario**	calendar
yo	I	**son**	are	**hoy**	today
nosotros, -as	we	**semana**	week	**ayer**	yesterday
él	he	**domingo**	Sunday	**aquí**	here
ella	she	**lunes**	Monday	**cuánto, -a**	how much
ellos, -as	they	**martes**	Tuesday	**cuántos, -as**	how many
hablar	to speak	**miércoles**	Wednesday	**cuál, -es**	which

Assignment 8

Matching Sounds and Suffixes: Nouns, Adjectives, and Pronouns

1   Matching is possible only when a word has at least two different forms
(a, an) or a stem has at least two different suffixes (th-is, th-ese). The definite
article forms *los* and *las* have a matching sound (*o* or *a*) and a matching plural
suffix (*s*). Copy the following pairs of words and draw a circle around the letter
which comes *right before* the plural suffix of each word: *los papeles, los señores,*
los libros.   ▲

l⊙-s pape l⊙- es, l⊙-s seño r⊙- es, l⊙-s libr⊙-s
(This is the word's *matching sound.*)

2   The *o* of *los* matches the _____ of *papeles,* the _____ of *señores,* and the
_____ of *libros.*   ▲

o matches *l, r, o*

3 The final sound of each singular noun form is its matching sound. The notion of singular is shown by a zero suffix. The *l* of the definite article form *el* matches the final sounds _____ of *papel, señor,* and *libro.* ▲

4 Which allomorph of the indefinite article, *un* or *una,* may replace *el* in *el papel, el señor,* or *el libro?* ▲

> *l, r, o*

> *un* (The *n* is the matching sound of this allomorph. It matches the same sounds as the *o* of *los* and the *l* of *el*: **un** *libro,* **el** *libro,* **los** *libros.*)

5 *Un* does not combine with *mesa, señora,* or *puerta.* It is replaced by *una.* The *a* of *una* matches the *a* of the nouns. The *a* of the definite article forms, _____ and _____, also matches the *a* of the nouns. ▲

> *la* and *las* (The plural suffixes come after the matching sounds.)

6 There are six forms of the articles: *un, una, el, la, los,* and *las.* They are divided into two matching sound sets. Every member of one set has the matching vowel sound _____. ▲

> *a: una, la, las* (This is the *a*-set, and the nouns they combine with are

7 The second set of article forms is made up of _____. ▲ *a*-nouns.)

> *un, el, los* (Because *los* has an *o,* this is called the *o*-set, and the nouns they combine with are called *o*-nouns.)

8 Which set combines with *muchacho* or *libro?* (a) *o*-set (b) *a*-set ▲

> *o*-set (*los muchachos, los libros, un muchacho, un libro, etc.*)

9 Which set combines with *muchacha* or *mesa?* (a) *o*-set (b) *a*-set ▲

> *a*-set (*una muchacha, una mesa, la muchacha, las muchachas*)

10 Which set combines with *señor* and *papel?* (a) *o*-set (b) *a*-set ▲

> *o*-set (*un señor, los papeles, el señor, etc.*)

11 When one member of an article set combines with a matching noun sound, then all other members of that set may also combine with the same noun. (a) true (b) false ▲

> true (If the *n* of *un* matches the *r* of *señor,* you know you can say *el señor* or

12 The articles are also adjectives. There are many other Spanish adjectives *los señores.*) which have two forms and two matching sounds. The matching sound of one of these forms is always *a,* as in *una* or *la.* The most common contrasting sound is *o.* The two forms for "Chilean" are *chilena* and *chileno.* Which form goes with *señora* or *mesa?* ▲

> *chilena* (*a* matches *a.*)

13 The form *chilena* belongs to which set of adjectives? (a) *o*-set (b) *a*-set ▲

> *a*-set (*una chilena, la chilena, las chilenas*)

14 When two or more adjectives combine with a noun, all must be of the same set. Which of the following shows the proper matching of sounds? (a) *una muchacho chileno* (b) *una muchacho chilena* (c) *un muchacho chileno* ▲

> *un muchacho chileno* (All three words belong to the *o*-set.)

15 When the form is plural, there are two kinds of agreement: sound matching and number agreement. Add what is necessary to *chilen* to make it match the noun and its article: *un libro chilen* _____, *los libros chilen* _____. ▲

> *un libro chileno,* **los** *libros chilenos*

16 Once more: *los papeles chilen* _____, *las mesas chilen* _____. ▲

> **los** *papeles chilenos,* **las** *mesas chilenas*

17 Spanish has another kind of agreement. *María* and *Pilar* combine with *muchacha: María es una muchacha; Pilar es una muchacha; María y Pilar son muchachas.* Which is correct? (a) *Pilar es chilena* (Chilean). (b) *Pilar es chileno.* ▲

Pilar es chilena. (Pilar es una muchacha chilena.)

18 If you say, *José es un muchacho,* which is correct? (a) *José es chileno.* (b) *José es chilena.* ▲

José es chileno. (José es un muchacho chileno.)

19 *José y María son muchachos.* Which is correct? (a) *José y María son chilenas.* (b) *José y María son chilenos.* ▲

José y María son chilenos. (Son muchachos chilenos.)

20 Which set of adjectives will combine with *ella* and *ellas?* (a) the *o*-set (b) the *a*-set ▲

21 Write the matching sound. *José es chileno. Él es chilen _____.* ▲   the *a*-set

22 Write the matching sound. *María es chilena. Ella es chilen _____.* ▲   *Él es chilen**o.***

23 Add what is needed to make the adjective agree with the subject pronoun.   *Ella es chilen**a.*** *Ellos son chilen . . . ; Ellas son chilen . . . .* ▲

Ell**os** son chilen**os** ; Ell**as** son chilen**as.**

24 Suppose you are talking to a man. Which question is correct? (a) *¿Es usted chilena?* (b) *¿Es usted chileno?* ▲

25 You are talking to several girls. Which question is correct? (a) *¿Son ustedes chilenos?* (b) *¿Son ustedes chilenas?* ▲   *¿Es usted chileno?*

¿Son ustedes chilenas?

26 Which is correct? (a) *Nosotros somos chilenas.* (b) *Nosotros somos chilenos.* ▲

Nosotr**os** somos chilen**os.** (o matches o. The o of mos does not agree.)

27 You want to say, "I am Chilean." You say, *Soy _____.* ▲

Soy chileno (male); Soy chilena (female).

There are, in all of Spanish, a very few exceptions to the rules of agreement which you have just learned. One that you already know is *Buenos días.* The noun *día* ends in *a,* but it combines, nevertheless, only with the *o*-set of adjectives (*un día, el día, los días*). These exceptions have to be memorized.

More about the Differences between English and Spanish Sounds

1 Spanish [t] and [d], like Spanish [p] are unaspirated. If you hold the back of your hand about one-half inch from your lips and say "too," you will feel a puff of air. If you pull your tongue away from your teeth before air pressure builds up as you say *tú,* you will feel no puff. Practice saying *ta, te, ti, to, tu* and *da, de, di, do, du* until you feel no puff of air.

2 When English speakers say words like *qué* as in *¿Qué tal?,* they have a tendency to say "Kay" instead of [ke]. Say "Kay" and "day" and notice what your jaws do. (a) Do you move your jaws? (b) Do you hold them in the same place? ▲

You closed your jaws slightly. (Some linguists call this a "complex" vowel.
It starts with [e] as in "red" and glides into [ee] as in "reel.")

3 How many vowel sounds are there in *de*? ▲

only one (The jaws do not move. It is a simple or pure vowel.)

4 For English "day" the jaws close slightly. What happens to your jaws when
you say "see"? (a) They open a little. (b) They close a little. ▲

They open a little. (For Spanish *sí* the jaws do not move at all. Keep your
lips very close together and practice until you can say *sí* without moving
your lips or jaws.)

5 Say *noches* aloud. The last syllable of *noches* is *ches*. It is pronounced (a) like
the last syllable of English "notches" (b) like the English word "chess." ▲

like "chess" ("Notches" has a schwa sound in *tches*.)

6 Say "no" in English emphatically. Now say it in Spanish. In which language
is the sound [o] the longest? ▲

English (Spanish cuts the sound short even when emphatic.)

7 Say *bueno* aloud twice. Now say it without the [b] sound: *ueno*. When you
say *ueno*, is the first sound (a) a vowel? (b) a consonant? ▲

A consonant. This one may have trapped you if you looked at *u* instead of
listening to the sound [w]. Spanish uses the letter *w* only in a few foreign
words. Spanish speakers write the sound [w] as *u* before a vowel. Practice
saying these words aloud:

Luisa	*bueno*	*luego*	*muy*	*cuaderno*	*puerta*

Now say them without the first sound and with *w* in place of *u*.

wisa	*weno*	*wego*	*wy*	*waderno*	*werta*

Now put the first sound back and say:

Lwisa	*bweno*	*lwego*	*mwy*	*cwaderno*	*pwerta*

8 A *ventana* is something the wind or air may come through. One English
cognate of *ventana* is the verb "ventilate." Do you say the *ven* of both words in
precisely the same way? ▲

9 Say *ventana* and *la ventana*. Did you say the syllable *ven* the same way both
times? ▲   no

no (When you say *ventana* by itself the *v* represents a stop sound. When you
say *la ventana* it represents a fricative. Linguists call these sounds bilabial
or two-lip sounds.)

10 Say *ventana*, *la ventana*, and English "ventilate" and watch what your lower
lip is doing as you say the [v] sound in each. In which word does your lower lip
touch your upper front teeth as you make the [v] sound? ▲

ventilate (Linguists call this a labiodental (lip-tooth) sound. No sound of
Spanish *v* or *b* is normally made this way.)

11 If you wrote *ventana* as *bentana*, or *la ventana* as *la bentana*, would you pronounce each differently in Spanish? ▲

no (*b* and *v* always stand for the same sounds in standard Spanish.)

12 When the letter *n* is followed by *p*, as in *un pupitre* it does not stand for [n]
but for [m], [umpupitre]. You say [umpokito] but you write _____. ▲

un poquito (Note also that [k] is spelled *qu* before *i*.)

13 Say *señor* aloud and notice how you make the [r] sound. Say English "for"
and *señor* one after the other. Now say "ladder," and notice the sound you

make for *dd*. The [r] of *señor* is (a) like the [r] of "for" (b) like the [dd] of "ladder." ▲

like the [dd] of "ladder"

Summary

Matching Sounds and Suffixes

1 The plural suffixes of *those* and *voters* both carry the same information. The singular suffix of *that* and the zero suffix of *voter* carry the same information. These forms are said to "agree" because their suffixes match each other: *plural + plural* (th**ose** vote**rs**) and *singular + singular* (th**at** vote**r**).

2 *An author* and *a writer* "agree" in a different way. *An* is matched with a following vowel sound; *a* with a consonant sound.

3 Matching or agreement is possible only when a word has two allomorphs (*un, una*) or two suffixes (*el, los; la, las*).

4 Spanish adjectives which have two forms (*bueno, buena; español, española*) match their nouns in two ways:

   a When the noun is singular, the adjective is singular. Both have a zero suffix: *la muchacha española, el rodeo español*. When the noun is plural, the adjective is plural. Both have a plural suffix: *las muchacha**s** española**s**, lo**s** rodeo**s** español**es**.

   b When a singular adjective has two forms, one always ends in *a* (*buena, chilena*) and the other may end in *o* (*bueno*), *n* (*un*), *l* (*el, español*), plus other phonemes to be learned later (*e, r,* and *s*). For the present, memorize these rules:

     Adjectives ending in *a* match nouns ending in *a: cas**a** buen**a**, muchach**as** chilen**as***.

     Adjectives ending in *o, n,* or *l* match nouns ending in the same phonemes: *u**n** libr**o** buen**o**, e**l** libr**o** españo**l**, u**n** hote**l** buen**o***. To simplify memory, *libro* is called an *o*-noun; *casa* is an *a*-noun. *Un, el,* and *bueno* match *o*-nouns; *una, la,* and *buena* match *a*-nouns.

5 Exceptions like *día* (*un día, el día, los días*) have to be memorized.

6 Spanish has another kind of matching. Adjectives are usually matched to the sex of persons labeled by proper nouns or subject pronouns. *O*-adjectives match males: ***Juan** es chilen**o**. **Yo** (male) soy chilen**o***. *A*-adjectives match females: ***María** es chilen**a**. **Tú** (female) eres chilen**a***. However, when both sexes are modified by the same adjective, the *o*-form is used: ***Juan** y **María** son chilen**os***.

Differences between English and Spanish Sounds

1 English may aspirate several consonants: [*p, t, d, k*]. These same sounds in Spanish are unaspirated, or made without a puff.

2 Spanish vowels are only about half as long as their English equivalents and, unlike English, they are made without changing the position of the jaws, tongue, or lips. *Que*, *de*, *sí*, and *no* are said with a shorter vowel and no jaw movement.

3 Spanish uses the letter *w* only in foreign words. The sound [w] is written *u*. You see *bueno* and say [bweno].

4 The letters *b* and *v* stand for the same phoneme in Spanish. It has two allophones: a bilabial (= two lips) stop and a bilabial fricative. The stop is like the [b] of "boy"; the fricative is made the same way except that the lips do not touch.

5 Standard Spanish has no equivalent of the English [v] which is made by touching the upper front teeth with the lower lip. Say "visit"; then in Spanish using a stop [b], say *visitar*.

6 Before *p*, *n* is pronounced [m]: *un poco* is said [umpoco].

7 The sound of *dd* in "ladder" or *tt* in "matter" is made in almost the same way as Spanish [r].

Self-Correcting Exercises

A Refresh your memory on the vocabulary for the days of the week (Assignment 7) and the new words at the end of this Assignment. After doing that, pretending that today is Wednesday, ask and answer each question aloud with your best pronunciation. Check your responses with the answers on the right. Do the entire exercise three times.

1 ¿Qué día es hoy?	Hoy es miércoles.
2 ¿Qué día fue ayer?	Ayer fue martes.
3 ¿Qué día fue anteayer?	Anteayer fue lunes.
4 ¿Qué día es mañana?	Mañana es jueves.
5 Y pasado mañana, ¿qué día es?	Pasado mañana es viernes.

B Read each sentence aloud and then say it again changing it to the singular or the plural, the opposite of what is given. If you don't do it well the first time, repeat the operation. Don't forget to cover the answers.

1 Nosotros hablamos inglés.	Yo hablo inglés.
2 Ustedes hablan inglés.	Usted habla inglés.
3 Ustedes hablan inglés. (another way)	Tú hablas inglés.
4 Ella habla español.	Ellas hablan español.
5 Tú hablas español.	Ustedes hablan español.
6 Yo estudio español.	Nosotros estudiamos español.

C Read the model sentence (*Tú estudias inglés*) aloud. Then say it again with the new subject (*Tú y yo, etc.*) making all the necessary changes. Check the answer after each new sentence.

1 Tú estudias inglés.	
Tú y yo . . .	Tú y yo estudiamos inglés.

2	Yo . . .	Yo estudio inglés.
3	Ellos . . .	Ellos estudian inglés.
4	Usted . . .	Usted estudia inglés.
5	Ellas . . .	Ellas estudian inglés.
6	Paco . . .	Paco estudia inglés.
7	Nosotras . . .	Nosotras estudiamos inglés.

New Vocabulary

estudiar	to study	**anteayer**	day before yesterday
desear	to wish, desire	**pasado mañana**	day after tomorrow

Assignment 9

Numbers and Their Spelling

1   The end of the Spanish number words *once, doce, trece, catorce, quince,* is what is now left from the Latin *decim,* "ten." When you take the *ce* away from these words, you have something left that looks somewhat like the modern Spanish number word that is added to 10. Write the modern Spanish word for each of the above.   ▲

uno, dos, tres, cuatro, cinco

2   *Trece* is actually *tre* (three) plus *ce* (ten). The number *dieciséis* is translated as "sixteen" which actually means six + ten. What is the word-for-word translation of *dieciséis,* which may also be written *diez y seis?*   ▲

ten and six, or 10 + 6

3   Write the Spanish number words for the Arabic numbers from 0 through 10.   ▲

cero, uno, dos, tres, cuatro, cinco, seis, siete, ocho, nueve, diez

4   Write the number words for 11, 12, 13, 14, 15.   ▲

once, doce, trece, catorce, quince

5   Write the number words for 16, 17, 18, 19. The word for "ten," *diez,* is to be written *diec* and the plus word *y* is to be written *i.*   ▲

dieciséis, diecisiete, dieciocho, diecinueve (Check your spelling.)

6   The number word for 20 is *veinte.* Now try to make up the number words from 21 through 29. Add the number words 1–9 to *veinte,* using the plus word *y* just as you did for *dieciséis.* (You drop, however, the final *e* of *veinte.*) The number word for 21 is _____.   ▲

7   Write the number words for 22, 23, 24, 25, 26, 27, 28, 29.   ▲   *veintiuno*

veintidós,   veintitrés,   veinticuatro,   veinticinco,   veintiséis,   veintisiete, veintiocho, veintinueve

8 The order of the vowel letters in certain numbers causes spelling problems. Write the Spanish word for these numbers: 6, 7, 20, 9, 10. ▲

seis, siete, veinte, nueve, diez

Pronouns and Verb Forms

1 Say the plural form for each of the following pronouns: *yo, tú, él, ella, usted.* ▲

nosotros or *nosotras, ustedes, ellos, ellas, ustedes*

2 Say the form of *hablar, desear,* and *estudiar* which goes with *tú, él, nosotros.* ▲

tú hablas, deseas, estudias; él habla, desea, estudia; nosotros hablamos, deseamos, estudiamos

3 There are three different subject pronouns which may combine with the verb form *desean.* They are _____. ▲

ellos, ellas, ustedes

Summary

1 English *thirteen* comes from *three + ten;* Spanish *trece* comes from *tres* plus what is left of Latin *decim* (ten). The words having this pattern are:

uno	dos	tres	cuatro	cinco
once	doce	trece	catorce	quince

2 The number words 16 through 19 are simply 10 + 6, 10 + 7, etc. They may be written two ways:

diez y seis	diez y siete	diez y ocho	diez y nueve
dieciséis	diecisiete	dieciocho	diecinueve

3 The numbers 20, 30, 40, *etc.* are one word: *veinte, treinta, cuarenta,* etc. All numbers in between are like 20 + 1. The numbers 21 to 29 may be written two ways: *veinte y uno, veinte y dos,* etc. or *veintiuno, veintidós, veintitrés, veinticuatro, veinticinco, veintiséis, veintisiete, veintiocho, veintinueve.* Note that those ending in the consonant *s* require an accent mark.

4 The order of the vowels in the following often cause spelling problems: *seis, siete, veinte, nueve, diez.*

Question Words

1 The question word in "What is this?" is "what." The Spanish equivalent of "what" is _____. ▲

qué (With an accent mark.)

2 Write the missing question word: ¿_____ *son siete menos tres?* (It asks for an amount and is plural.) ▲

Cuántos (With capital *C* and accent mark.)

3 When you want a place or destination as an answer, you use the question
word _____. ▲

4 Now look at *qué*, *cuántos*, and *dónde*. What do they all have in common? ▲   *dónde*
an accent mark (When a question word is used in a question, it *always* has an
accent mark in writing.)

5 When you ask about a person's health, the question word is _____. ▲

cómo (¿Cómo está Vd.?)

Everyone knows that the Japanese, Africans, and the Hindus have cultures and ways
of life that are very different from the American. There are, however, so many Hispanic
people living in the United States that it is frequently assumed that the only major
difference between the Spanish speaker and the American is the language that they
speak. There are, in fact, hundreds of different ways in which the two cultures are not
alike and, as a result, great misunderstandings can be created if you and the Spanish
speaker do not realize how and why you are different. To help you understand the
Spanish speaker better, you will find hereafter short descriptions of some significant
difference between Hispanic and American culture. Read these carefully and eventually
you will have a deeper understanding of how you and the Spanish speaker differ. Here
is an example.

The Spanish speaker has a very different attitude towards animals than most
Americans. The American may keep almost any type of animal as a pet. Many people
keep dogs and cats as household companions, and each animal is generally given a name,
the way the human members of the family are. There are, in addition, pet stores, animal
hospitals, pet beauty salons, and even special graveyards for pets. The Spanish speaker,
in sharp contrast, has no word at all for *pet* and frequently does not even give names to
animals. Moreover, he carefully keeps animals and people clearly separated in his mind,
and it is generally considered improper to describe human speech with verbs used to
describe animal noises, such as *growl*, *bellow*, *roar*, and *hiss*. As a result, few words in the
Spanish vocabulary can be used as impolite substitutes for "to say." In the same way
Spanish has two words for "foot," one for people (*pie*) and another for animals (*pata*),
and when a person sticks his nose (*nariz*) into someone else's business the word used is
hocico, the equivalent of "snout." In general it is considered derogatory to use animal
terms to describe people.

More Practice in Writing and Spelling

In writing what you hear, there are three basic things to which you must pay
attention. One is intonation, which helps you know how to punctuate a spoken
sentence. Another is putting spaces between words even though in speech all
the words of a phrase are run together as though they were one long word.
You hear *¿Adóndevas?* but you write *¿A dónde vas?* Finally, you have to spell
each word.

1 There are four different kinds of cues that tell you how to spell what you
hear. One is meaning. When two different words sound exactly alike but have
different spellings, only the meaning tells you what to write. In the sentence,
"She . . . a lot" you write _____, not "ways." ▲

weighs

2 Spanish *el* and *él* sound exactly alike. Which spelling goes in the following blanks? _____ *muchacho está allí;* _____ *está allí.* ▲

El (the definite article); *él* (the subject pronoun)

3 *Papel* does not sound like *tarde*. What you hear tells you what to write. But Spanish, like English, has a lot of tricky words. What you hear only tells you how to spell part of these words. You have to see the other part(s) in print to learn how they are spelled. For example, you hear [yama] in the question [¿*kómo se yama él?*] but you write _____. ▲

4 You hear [senyor], but you write _____. ▲

llama

5 You hear [ke], but you write _____. ▲

señor

6 The four kinds of cues for spelling are (1) meaning, (2) what you hear, (3) what you see in print, and (4) rules. What you hear and rule spelling are the easiest, the other two you must memorize.

que or *qué*

Some words which you will have to practice more in order to learn to spell them correctly are those that have letters or marks not used in English. Copy these words and add the tilde: *espanol, senor, manana, Espana, senorita.* ▲

español, señor, mañana, España, señorita

7 The written accent mark is placed over (a) consonants (b) vowels. ▲

8 When a word has only one syllable, the meaning, not what you hear, tells you that it has an accent mark in writing. Copy these words and add the accent mark: *tu, el, si, que.* ▲

vowels

9 Question words always have an accent mark on the stressed syllable. The following are divided into syllables. Copy them the way they are normally written and add the accent mark. ¿*Co-mo?* ¿*Don-de?* ¿*Cuan-tos?* ▲

tú, él, sí, qué

¿*Cómo?* ¿*Dónde?* ¿*Cuántos?*

10 The accent mark on all other words indicates the syllable to be stressed in speech. Copy the following words the way they are normally written and add the accent mark: *di-as, a-lli, a-dios, a-qui, es-tas, per-don, in-gles, la-piz.* ▲

días, allí, adiós, aquí, estás, perdón, inglés, lápiz

11 What you see below represents what you actually hear. Say these aloud, then spell them correctly: [ay], [oy], [asta], [ola], [ora]. ▲

hay, hoy, hasta, hola, hora

12 When you say the Spanish word for "watch," you say [rreló]. You spell this word *reloj*. It ends in a consonant so its plural is _____. ▲

13 Spanish differs from English in writing the days of the week. Write the Spanish for "Wednesday, Thursday, Friday, Saturday." ▲

relojes

miércoles, jueves, viernes, sábado (Did you remember no capital letter?)

14 Copy and underline the letter(s) that stand(s) for the [k] sound: *aquí, cinco, poquito, escuela, catorce, qué.* ▲

*a***qu***í, cin***c***o, po***qu***ito, es***c***uela, ***c***atorce,* ***que*** (The [k] sound is written *qu* before *i* and *e*, and *c* elsewhere. With this rule you can spell the [k] sound

15 You hear [keso] and [kosa]. You write _____ and _____. ▲   from what you hear.

16 The words for "I" and "call" begin with the same sound in Spanish. Write "I call myself Pancho." ▲

queso, cosa

Yo me llamo Pancho (You must see *yo* and *llamo* to know how to spell the first sound of each.)

17 Learning to spell requires practice in copying words accurately, as well as studying how they may be changed. Copy the following and make them stand for females: *señor, profesor, muchacho, nosotros, alumno.* ▲

señora, profesora, muchacha, nosotras, alumna

18 Copy and make plural: *señor, reloj, mes, usted.* ▲

señores, relojes, meses, ustedes

19 Copy and make plural: *tarde, noche, oficina, tiza, ojo, cuaderno.* ▲

tardes, noches, oficinas, tizas, ojos, cuadernos

20 What is the rule for making words plural? You add *es* to _____ and *s* to _____. ▲

es to consonants; *s* to vowels

21 The noun *lápiz* and all other nouns ending in *z* have a change in spelling when the plural suffix *es* is added to them. The *z* is replaced by *c*. Write the plural for *luz* and *lápiz.* ▲

22 What you see tells you when to write *b* or *v*. In this and the next frame, say   *luces, lápices*
the Spanish for each word aloud, then write it: window, twenty, well, enough. ▲

ventana, veinte, bien, bastante

23 Translate and write the following: Isn't it?, good, I speak. ▲

¿Verdad?, bueno, hablo

24 In this and the next four frames there are some words that contain sounds that are often misspelled. Write the Spanish equivalents and check your spelling very carefully: professor, notebook, school. ▲

profesor, cuaderno, escuela

25 desk, chair, blackboard ▲

26 I am (*ser*), See you later, there ▲   *pupitre, silla, pizarra*
Soy, Hasta luego, allí

Self-Correcting Exercises

A Circle each stop [b] and [d] and underline each fricative [b̸] and [d̸], including in both cases the cue that precedes them. Then read everything aloud with your best pronunciation.

1 t o d o   p a t a   d o t e   t a p a   p u d e

t o̲ d̲ o   p a t a   (d)o t e   t a p a   p u̲ d̲ e

2 P a b l o ,   T o t i   y   L i n d a   e s t á n   e n   E s p a ñ a.

P a̲ b̲ l o ,   T o t i   y   L i (n d)a   e s t á n   e n   E s p a ñ a.

3 A l l í   e s t á n   l a s   v e i n t e   v e n t a n a s ,   ¿v e r d a d?

A l l í   e s t á n   l a̲ s̲ ̲v̲ ̲e̲ ̲i̲ ̲n̲ ̲t̲ ̲e̲   ̲v̲ e n t a n a s ,   (¿v)e r d a̲ d̲?

4 D i l e   b u e n o s   d í a s   a   D o n a l d o.

(D)i l e̲ ̲b̲ u e n o̲ s̲   d í a s   a̲   D o n a (l d)o.

5 ¿A d ó n d e v a s t ú, P a b l o?

¿A d ó n d e v a s t ú, P a b l o?

6 V o y a E s p a ñ a e n v e i n t e d í a s.

V o y a E s p a ñ a e n v e i n t e d í a s.

B Select the form of the definite article (*el, la, los, las*) that goes with each noun.

silla, cuaderno, lápices, luces   la, el, los, las

reloj, regla, ventanas, papeles   el, la, las, los

C Write the form of the verb that would be needed if the indicated subject were replaced by the one in parentheses. Then say the new sentence aloud.

1 *Ustedes* hablan inglés. (Tú)   hablas
2 ¿Habla *usted* español? (ellos)   Hablan
3 *Nosotros* estudiamos bien. (Ella)   estudia
4 *Pancho y tú* estudian mucho. (Tú y yo)   estudiamos
5 ¿Cómo se llama *ella*? (ellas)   llaman

New Vocabulary

alumno, -a	pupil	**nuevo, -a**	new
director, -a	director, principal	**amable**	kind, friendly
escuela	school	**mucho, -a**	much, a lot
país (el)	country (nation)	**poco, -a**	little (quantity)
trabajar	to work	**de nada**	you're welcome
necesitar	to need	**por favor**	please
soy	I am	**¡Perdón!**	Excuse me! (pardon)
tengo	I have	**¡Piensa!**	Think! (gesture p.139)
tiene (Vd.)	you have	**con**	with
tienes que	you have to	**conmigo**	with me

Assignment 10

Learning How to Read for Meaning

1 Here is a sentence you have never seen. It has three words you do not know. Read it aloud in Spanish. *Esas camas cuestan mucho.* This proves an important point about reading. You can read aloud something you do not understand. There is a very great difference between reading aloud and reading for meaning. You do not have to say words aloud when you read for meaning. It is what you *see* that counts, not the sounds. Look at this sentence (do not say the words aloud), copy and underline all the words you have studied so far: *El primer presidente de los Estados Unidos fue Jorge Washington.* ▲

El *primer presidente* **de los** *Estados Unidos* **fue** *Jorge Washington.*

2 The verb *fue* translates "was." Which word in the sentence translates what George Washington was? ▲

3 Remember that in Spanish only proper names are capitalized. Look at the word *Unidos* in *los Estados Unidos.* It has an English cognate. Now translate the following into English: *Jorge Washington fue el presidente de los Estados Unidos.* ▲

presidente

George Washington was the president of the United States.

4 There is now only one word in the original sentence that you do not know. You can probably guess its meaning. The translation of the adjective *primer* is _____. ▲

first (The book used to teach *first* graders to read is called a "primer.")

5 When you read for meaning, you begin with what you know and, then, go on to what you do not know. You can often make out the meaning of words you have never seen before. An unknown word is like a blank which you have to fill in. Select the most logical English word to complete this sentence. *El día veinticinco de diciembre es _____.* ▲

6 Each word in a sentence helps you figure out the meaning of the others. Words combine in a logical fashion, and each one carries signals that tell you what it may combine with. To learn to read for meaning, you must learn to spot these signals and to find out what they are telling you. Let's practice this.

Christmas

Suppose you know the sentence is talking about a person. The unknown words combine with *una: una mujer.* The article *una* tells you the person is (a) a man (b) a woman. ▲

7 The sentence begins with *El muchacho se llama . . .* What is most likely to follow? (a) another verb (b) a name ▲

a woman

a name (*El muchacho se llama Jorge.*)

8 The question word *dónde* asks about a place. When *dónde* combines with *de* (*de dónde*), the question is about (a) where something is (b) where it is from (c) where it is going. ▲

where it is from (*¿De dónde es José?*)

9 When *dónde* combines with *a* (*a dónde*), the question is about (a) where something is (b) where it is from (c) where it is going. ▲

where it is going (*¿A dónde vas?*)

10 When *dónde* is used without a relator in front of it, the question is about (a) where something is (b) where it is going (c) where it is from. ▲

where something is (*¿Dónde está Jóse?*)

11 Is it logical to assume that either *está* or *vas* will combine with *de dónde*? ▲

no (The *de* signals origin, not location or destination.)

12 A word can tell you what will go with it. It can also tell you which meaning another word will have. You see the name of a person, a city, and a country in *José es de Santiago, Chile.* This tells you that *de* means _____. ▲

13 Does *de* have the same meaning in *El señor Moreno es el director de la escuela?* ▲

from

no (Mr. Moreno is the principal *of* the school.)

14 What a word combines with usually signals its meaning. When you say, *Sí, señor*, the word *señor* is a title of respect which is translated as _____. ▲

15 When *señor* combines with a proper name, *Sí, señor Moreno*, it is still a title of respect, but now it is translated by _____. ▲

sir

16 When *señor* is used as a common noun and combines with an article, *Es un señor muy amable*, it has a third meaning. It now stands for a person who is male and is translated _____. ▲

Mister

17 The little words of a sentence almost always carry big signals. Look at this: *En la . . . de la escuela.* The definite article *la* tells you that the blank must be filled with (a) a verb (b) a noun (c) a relator. ▲

man or gentleman

18 The same article, *la*, tells you the noun must be singular. *La* also tells you that the noun is likely to end in the sound of _____. ▲

a noun

a (En la oficina de la escuela.)

19 When you combine *en* and *la oficina*, the verb must describe either an action that can take place <u>in</u> the office (*Trabaja en la oficina.*), or it must say that someone or something _____ <u>in</u> the office. ▲

is; is located (*José está en la oficina.*)

20 A key word may tell you the meaning of its substitute. For example: *María habla dos lenguas, el inglés y el español.* The translation of *lenguas* is _____. ▲

21 *El señor Prieto es de México.* (a) *¿Es mexicano?* (b) *¿Es chileno?*

languages

22 All question words are key words. *Cómo* asks for what in *¿Cómo se llama él?* ▲

Es mexicano.

a name (*Se llama Miguel.*)

23 *Cómo* asks about what in *¿Cómo estás?* ▲

health or state of being (*Estoy bien.*)

24 In your answer to *¿Qué es esto?* you will replace *qué* with what kind of word? ▲

the name for the thing: *tiza, lápiz, etc,* (*Es un lápiz.*)

25 *Qué* asks about what in *¿Qué estudia usted?* ▲

a lesson, a language, some school subject, *etc.* (*Estudio español.*)

26 *Cuánto* and *cuántos* always ask about _____. ▲

amount (how much, how many)

27 If you pay attention to key words, the context, and cognates, you will be surprised at just how much Spanish you are already prepared to read and understand. Look at the following sentence carefully and then translate it mentally: *Cristóbal Colón descubrió las Américas en 1492.* ▲

Christopher Columbus discovered America in 1492.

28 Want to try another? *El presidente Kennedy fue asesinado en Dallas, Tejas.* ▲

President Kennedy was assassinated in Dallas, Texas.

Summary

You can now read aloud many sentences you cannot immediately understand, but you will rarely encounter a sentence from which you cannot abstract some meaning. You can almost always get more meaning by consciously applying certain strategies in an orderly sequence. Here are some useful steps:

1 Begin with the words you already know. If they have suffixes, use these to establish the grammatical class of the unknown words. The plural definite article *los*, for example, carries a lot of information: a noun probably follows, it stands for something countable (marked by the plural suffix), the noun stands for something generally known or previously mentioned.

2 Since all words have a limited combinatory potential, use the ones you know to delimit the potential meaning of the unknown words and to fix their probable meaning. For example, *escribir* can have only predictable subjects and objects.

3 Pay special attention to cognates and *all* their English meanings. The book used to teach *first* graders is a "primer." This provides the clue to the meaning of *primer* in *Jorge Washington fue el primer presidente de los . . .*

4 Treat each unknown word as a blank which, theoretically, can be defined by the context. So the blank above can hardly be filled with anything else than *United States* (*Estados Unidos*). However, be prepared to tolerate some mistakes.

5 Keep in mind that the relators, *a*, *de*, *en*, *con*, etc. have no meaning all by themselves for the native. The meaning is established by what precedes and follows them:

Los hombres **de** España. (*from*)   Está **en** la cocina. (*in*)
Las puertas **de** la oficina. (*of*)   Está **en** la mesa. (*on*)

6 All question words predict what will be used in the answer:

¿a dónde?	where to?	*¿cuántos?*	(how many?) number
¿de dónde?	where from?	*¿cuánto?*	(how much?) amount
¿dónde?	where?		

7 Put everything together and guess intelligently. You can understand:

Cristóbal Colón descubrió las Américas en 1492.
El presidente Kennedy fue asesinado en Dallas, Tejas.

Self-Correcting Exercises

Practice reading these pairs aloud for at least five minutes. The pronunciation of *dd*, *tt*, and *d* in the English examples will make you aware of the position of the tongue for Spanish [r] and [rr].

ladder, better, rudder, muddy, lady, shudder

ere/erre	rosa/zorra	tres/puerta
era/erra	roca/corra	Brasil/árbol
pero/perro	rana/narra	gracias/Vargas
pera/perra	ropa/porra	grande/tarde
caro/carro	rabo/borra	frío/martes
fiero/fierro	reto/torre	trece/catorce

New Vocabulary

veintiuno	twenty-one	**veintiocho**	twenty-eight
veintidós	twenty-two	**veintinueve**	twenty-nine
veintitrés	twenty-three	**treinta**	thirty
veinticuatro	twenty-four	**universidad (la)**	university
veinticinco	twenty-five	**de**	of, from
veintiséis	twenty-six	**en**	in, on
veintisiete	twenty-seven	**España**	Spain

This Assignment is shorter so that you can spend some extra time studying vocabulary.

Assignment 11

The Forms of estar

1 A verb is said to be regular when the stem is the same in all forms and when the morphemes of the first and second suffixes are those used by the vast majority of the verbs of that set. Thus, *hablar*, *estudiar*, and *necesitar* are regular *a*-verbs. The first suffix of the present tense of a regular *a*-verb that agrees with *yo* is _____. ▲

o (yo hablo, yo estudio, yo deseo)

2 The form of *estar* that goes with *yo* is _____. ▲

3 The form *estoy* has the suffix *oy* instead of *o*. The *oy* of *estoy* is the more ob-   *estoy*
vious irregularity in the slot for the first suffix. All the other present tense forms
have the vowel _____ in this slot. ▲

a (estamos, está, están, estás)

4 The present tense of *estar* has another irregularity. Compare the present tense of the regular verb *hablar* and the irregular verb *estar*. The stressed syllables are indicated. In what way is *estar* irregular? ▲

  ha-*blo*, *ha*-**bla**-*mos*, **ha**-*blas*, **ha**-*bla*, **ha**-*blan*

  es-**toy**, *es*-*ta*-*mos*, *es*-**tás**, *es*-**tá**, *es*-**tán**

The stress is on the second syllable of <u>all</u> the *estar* forms.

5 When a word ends in a vowel or *n* or *s*, stress falls on the next-to-last syllable. Which three forms of *estar* are exceptions to this rule? ▲

estás, está, están (The written accent mark tells you they are exceptions.)

6 The other rule about stress says that a word ending in a consonant (except *n* or *s*) has the stress on the last vowel (syllable). The form *estoy* has the stress on *toy*. Does this explain why *estoy* has no written accent mark? ▲

yes (Spanish speakers consider final *y* to be a consonant.)

7 Write the two forms that do not have a written accent mark. ▲

estoy, estamos

Sets and Patterns

1   When you learn any language, you learn patterns. *¿Habla usted español?* is a question pattern. A pattern, like the forms of a verb, is made up of a series of slots. You can keep the pattern, but change the message, by putting different words in each slot. What word do you know that you could put in place of *español* in the question given above?   ▲

inglés (¿Habla usted inglés?)

2   Only words of a certain kind can go in a given slot of a pattern. You cannot say, for instance, *¿Habla usted lápiz?* The noun *español* can be replaced only by the name of another _____.   ▲

language (These names make up a set: *español, francés, italiano, ruso,* etc.)

3   If one member of a set goes in a slot, then all members of the same set may also go in that slot. The action of speaking (*hablar*) belongs to a set which combines with languages. What other action could replace *hablar* in the pattern *¿Habla usted español?* Think of what you are doing right now.   ▲

estudia (Hablar and *estudiar* belong to the same set. *Trabajar* does not.)

4   In the pattern *Usted habla inglés* a noun can replace *usted: El muchacho habla inglés.* But you cannot say *La mesa habla inglés.* To be able to speak or write a language you must know all its basic patterns and the sets that go into each slot. Here is another pattern: *Yo trabajo en la oficina.* Of the following verbs copy those that can logically replace *trabajo: estudio, tengo, necesito, estoy.*   ▲

estudio, estoy (The verb forms *necesito* and *tengo* cannot replace *trabajo* in *Yo trabajo en la oficina* because they have to have an object, something that is acted on. When you say, "I have" or "I need" you have to add something: "I have a book"; "I need a book.")

5   There are three basic ways of changing a pattern to send a different message. First, you may keep all the same stems and just change the suffixes. *Yo tengo* **las plumas** *en la oficina* can be changed to *Yo tengo* **la pluma** *en la oficina.* When the suffix of one word matches the suffix of another word in the pattern, you cannot change one without changing the other. Rewrite the following pattern by changing *habla* to *hablan* and by making whatever other change is needed: *¿Habla usted inglés?*   ▲

¿Hablan ustedes inglés?

6   The second way of changing a pattern is to keep the same suffixes and to replace the stems. Rewrite the following and put the stem of *estudiar* in place of *habl: ¿***Habl***an ustedes inglés?*   ▲

*¿***Estudi***an ustedes inglés?*

7   The third way to change a pattern is to replace whole words. You still have the same basic pattern, but now you may have a very great change in the message. The message of the following pattern deals with movement toward a destination: *¿A dónde* **va** *usted?* Rewrite this and replace the indicated words so that the message deals with the origin of the subject.   ▲

*¿***De** *dónde* **es** *usted?*

You learn a new language by memorizing patterns and the sets of stems, suffixes, and words which can logically go into each slot. The purpose of the pattern drills which you have in class is to teach you to replace parts of the patterns without having to stop to think about the mechanics of the pattern.

More on the Spanish r's

Spanish has three letters in its alphabet which are actually digraphs (*two graphs*): *ch, ll*, and *ñ*. It is helpful to know when a digraph stands for one sound or two. The *ch* stands for the same sound in both English and Spanish (*Chile*, church) and is no problem. The *ll* stands for just one sound [y] in the Spanish American dialects (*silla, llamo*). The *ñ* stands for two sounds: [n] plus [y] as in *señor* [senyor]. The letters *rr* in *pizarra* do not stand for two *different* sounds. They stand for two or more repetitions of the *same* sound. This section of your assignment is designed to help you perfect your pronunciation of the Spanish *r*'s.

1 Say *latter* and *ladder* aloud several times and watch what your tongue is doing when you make the [t] and [d] sounds. When the Spaniard makes the sound for [r] or [rr], his tongue is in almost the same position. Say *feed* and *fear* and watch where your tongue is when you say the [d] and the [r]. The tongue position is (a) the same (b) different. ▲

different (English [r] is not like Spanish [r].)

2 Say *feed* and *fear* again. Your tongue touches the gum ridge above the front teeth when you say (a) the [d] of *feed* (b) the [r] of *fear*. ▲

the [d] of *feed* (This is the tongue position for Spanish [r].)

3 If you say the Spanish adjective *todo* with an English stop [d], you have the right tongue position for Spanish [r] and many natives will mistake *todo* (all) for *toro* (bull). However, they never mistake *de*, said with a stop [d], for *re*. What does this tell you? Stop and think. The tongue positions for [d] of *de* and [r] of *re* are the same. Are these sounds made in exactly the same way? ▲

no (The next frames will tell you more precisely how to learn to say Spanish [r] correctly.)

4 You can say English *hot* in two different ways. Say *hot* and be very careful *to hold the tongue position at the end of the word.* This [t] sound is a stop. (a) It is aspirated (is followed by a puff of air). (b) It is unaspirated (is not followed by a puff of air). ▲

It is unaspirated. (You held your tongue position and no air could escape.)

5 Say, very emphatically, *Boy is it hot!* To be emphatic, you let out a big puff of air at the end of *hot*. Now say, very fast, *hot-hot-hot-hot*. Now watch how long your tongue stays on the gum ridge as you say the [t] of *hot* and the [tt] of *tottle*. Go very fast: *hot-hot-hot-hot; tottle-tottle-tottle-tottle*. In which word does your tongue stay on the gum ridge longer? ▲

hot

6 When you say *tottle* very fast, the tongue tip snaps or flaps very hard against the gum ridge for just a very tiny fraction of a second but is not there long enough to build up enough air pressure to make a real stop sound. Say this nonsense word aloud until you can say it very fast: *poddle*. Say it several times and, then, at the end, leave off the sound of *le*. If you do this right, you are saying the Spanish noun *par* (pair) with a very good Spanish accent.

7 This frame is a test to find out whether you have trained your tongue to make and your ear to hear the Spanish [r] sound. Say English "ear," and Spanish *ir*. Did you flap your tongue against the gum ridge when you said *ir*? ▲

If you did not, you need more practice.

There are still many ways of writing numbers in the world today, but the one used by mathematicians everywhere came to Europe from India after the Arabs conquered most of the Spanish Peninsula in 711 A.D. Since the Arabs introduced their way of writing the Hindu numbers into Europe, we still speak of these numbers as Arabic numbers. Some of the Arab mathematicians tried to make each number have the same number of angles as the number itself. So 3, which originally was the written form ≣ , took the shape of

with three angles as numbered above. To make 7 have seven angles it was necessary to use two bars, one through the middle 7 and another at the bottom 7. Part of this old Arabic symbol is still conserved in Spanish writing today, that is, the seven is still written with a bar: 7 . What Americans write as a seven (7), consequently, is frequently read as a 1 by a Spanish speaker, and great care is needed, for example, when writing checks.

Writing Geographic Names

1 With just two exceptions, the names of the South American countries are spelled the same in both English and Spanish. In English, what is different about *Perú* and *Brasil*? ▲

no accent on Peru; *z* for *s* in Brazil

2 *Juan is a Colombian* is translated *Juan es colombiano*. What are the two spelling differences in the Spanish adjective? ▲

no capital letter; final *o* (Names of countries and cities, however, are capitalized, as in English.)

Vocabulary Review and Practice Reading Aloud

The following dialog contains words which you have studied in recent lessons.
Read each line aloud and then translate it mentally.

1 El nuevo alumno ▲

The New Pupil

2 —Perdón, señorita, ¿habla usted español? ▲

Excuse me, miss, do you speak Spanish?

3 —Sí, un poquito. ¿Qué desea? ▲

Yes, a little. What do you wish?

4 —Tengo que hablar con el director del Centro, por favor. ▲

I have to speak with the director of the Center, please.

5 —¿De dónde es usted? ¿De España? ▲

Where are you from, Spain?

6 —No, soy de Chile. Necesito estudiar inglés. ▲

No, I'm from Chile. I need to study English.

7 —Muy bien. Allí está la oficina. ▲

Very well. There is the office.

8 —Usted es muy amable conmigo. Muchas gracias. ▲

You are very kind to me. Thank you, very much.

9 —De nada, señor. ▲

You're welcome, sir.

10 Here is the entire dialog. Read it aloud twice and apply everything you have learned about pronunciation.

El nuevo alumno

Pablo: Perdón, señorita, ¿habla usted español?
Linda: Sí, un poquito. ¿Qué desea?
Pablo: Tengo que hablar con el director del Centro, por favor.
Linda: ¿De dónde es usted? ¿De España?
Pablo: No, soy de Chile. Necesito estudiar inglés.
Linda: Muy bien. Allí está la oficina.
Pablo: Usted es muy amable conmigo. Muchas gracias.
Linda: De nada, señor.

Summary

The Forms of *estar*

The present tense of *estar* has two features which do not appear in regular *a*-verbs:

1 The first suffix of the *yo* form is *oy: yo estoy*.

2 The stress is on the first suffix of all forms and a written accent is required on three:

yo	est—oy
nosotros	est—a—mos
tú	est—á—s
usted, él, ella	est—á
ustedes, ellos, ellas	est—á—n

More on the Spanish *r's*

1 The letter *r* may stand for [r] or [rr]. These are not two different sounds. The [rr] is simply two or more repetitions of [r].

2 The single flap [r] stands in meaningful contrast with the multiple flap [rr] only between two vowels:

coral (*coral*)	:	corral (*corral*)
pero (*but*)	:	perro (*dog*)
caro (*expensive*)	:	carro (*car*)

3 The multiple flap [rr] may replace [r] in any other sequences to give emphasis to a word. So *puerta* or *mar* may be pronounced [puerrta] and [marr]. However, *r* stands for [rr] at the beginning of words, *regla, rico*, and immediately after *n, s,* or *l: Enrique, Israel, alrededor.*

4 The sound [r] is a very short, voiced stop. The tongue position is the same as that for [d] of English "Tod," which is a voiced stop. Consequently, if you say *todo* with the English stop [d], many natives will mistake it for *toro* (bull).

Self-Correcting Exercises

A Read each pair aloud several times until you feel you have mastered all the sounds.

coro/corro	ida/ira	árbol/Brasil
cero/cerro	todo/toro	Vargas/gracias
caro/carro	cero/cedo	tarde/grande
foro/forro	cara/cada	martes/frío
	vado/varo	
	mido/miro	

B   After reading silently the selection in Ejercicio 11, p.E5 , ask and answer
the following questions aloud.

¿Cómo se llama el muchacho?	Se llama David.
¿De dónde es?	Es de Santiago de Chile.
¿Dónde está?	Está en la oficina del Centro Internacional.
¿Cómo se llama la muchacha?	Se llama Luisa.
¿Dónde trabaja?	Trabaja en la oficina del Centro.
¿Qué estudia?	Estudia español.
¿Quién es la doctora Navarro?	Es la profesora de español.
¿Quién es el señor Moreno?	Es el director del Centro.
¿Habla español el señor Moreno?	Sí, habla español.
¿Dónde estudia él?	Estudia en la Escuela de Medicina.

No new vocabulary. Study the words on your vocabulary list that you have found
difficult to remember and review all the others.

Assignment 12

Some Differences between ser, haber, *and* estar

Location versus Origin: *estar* and *ser*

The translation of *ser*, *estar*, and *haber* into English "to be" does not give cues
for choice. The cues are to be found in the context, that is, in the forms and
meaning of the sentence.

1   Chile, Bogotá, Ecuador, and Chicago belong to a set of words that label
geographic entities (countries or cities). A person or thing may be located <u>in</u> a
country or may be <u>from</u> a country or city. In *Pablo está en Chile*, the relator *en*
tells you Pablo is (a) *in* Chile (b) *from* Chile.   ▲

2   In *Pablo es de Chile*, the relator *de* tells you Pablo is (a) *in* Chile (b) *from*
Chile.   ▲

in Chile

3   Now, compare these sentences: (1) *Pablo está en Chile*. (2) *Pablo es de Chile*.
Here is one rule for choice: when you locate a person <u>in</u> a place, the use of *en*
cues the choice of (a) *ser* (b) *estar*.   ▲

from Chile

4   Here is the second rule for choice: when you say where a person or thing is
<u>from</u>, the use of *de* cues the choice of _____.   ▲

estar

5   Here is a way to summarize this: person + location + *en* = _____ (*ser*, or
estar?); person + origin + *de* = _____ (*ser*, or *estar*?).   ▲

ser

person + location + *en* = *estar;* person + origin + *de* = *ser*

Estar versus *haber* for Locating Count Entities

1 A Spanish speaker chooses between *estar* and *haber* for location according to easily recognized cues. Copy the following questions, compare them word for word, then underline those words which are exactly the same in both: (1) *¿Hay un libro en la mesa?* (2) *¿Está el libro en la mesa?* ▲

(1) *¿Hay un **libro en la mesa**?* (2) *¿Está el **libro en la mesa**?*

2 The parts that are exactly alike will not cue the choice between *hay* (*haber*) and *está* (*estar*). The cues are in the context. These cues are the words _____. ▲

3 Look at these sentences carefully: (1) *¿Hay un libro en la mesa?* (2) *¿Está el libro en la mesa?* Here's the first rule: when something is to be located, the Spanish speaker uses *hay* when the noun combines with _____. ▲

un; el

4 The summary of this rule is: entity + location + *un* cues the use of _____. ▲

un

haber (There is only one present tense form of *haber* for location; it is *hay*.)

5 Here's the second rule: when something is to be located, the Spanish speaker uses *estar* when the noun combines with _____. ▲

6 The summary of this rule is: entity + location + *el* = _____. ▲

el

7 Now, let's expand these two rules. If you can say, *Hay un libro allí,* it is logical to assume that you can also say, *Hay una pluma allí.* The answer to the question *¿Hay una pluma allí?* may be *Sí, hay una allí.* Translate the answer. ▲

estar

Yes, there is one there. (The word *una* has three English translations: "one,"

8 Spanish has three number words for the Arabic numeral 1: they are *un,* *una,* and *uno.* All numbers belong to the same set. Write the missing verb form: _____ *tres plumas allí.* ▲

"a" or "an.")

9 Your expanded rule is now: the indefinite article forms *un* or *una* and all other numbers cue the choice of _____ for location. ▲

Hay

haber (Do not mark this frame wrong if you wrote *hay.*)

10 Numbers like 5, 10, 20, *etc.* are called *public numbers* because they stand for precise amounts understood by everyone. In contrast, words like *some, few, many, a lot, etc.* are called *private numbers* because they stand in place of different public numbers. Each of us may, consequently, have a different answer to "How many is some?"

A person has 10 close friends. Does he have (a) some friends? (b) a few friends? (c) many friends? ▲

It depends entirely on you. To some people 10 is a lot; to others 10 is a few. That is why these words are called private numbers.

11 The plural suffix *s* is like a private number word. Which verb form will you use? (a) *Están* (b) *Hay*—libros en la mesa. ▲

Hay (A private number, like any other, cues the use of *haber* for location.)

12 Here is a summary of the cues for choosing *haber* for location:

*Hay **un** libro en la mesa.*	(Indefinite article = "a" or "one.")
*Hay **diez** libros en la mesa.*	(Public number + plural suffix.)
*Hay **muchos** libros en la mesa.*	(Private number + plural suffix.)
Hay libros en la mesa.	(_____ all by itself.) ▲

plural suffix (*s* or *es*)

13 We now have to expand the rule for choosing *estar* for location. If you can say, *La muchacha está en Quito, Ecuador*, you can also say, *Las muchachas están en Quito, Ecuador.* What other forms of the definite article cue the choice of *estar* for location?　▲

14 The subject pronoun which can replace *la muchacha* is *ella.* You can say, *Ella está en Quito.* All members of the set of subject pronouns cue the choice of *estar* for location.

　　The pronouns *él, ellos, ella,* and *ellas* stand for people. People have names. What kind of an educated guess can you now make? Which form will you use? (a) *Hay* (b) *Está* ¿_____ Pedro en La Paz, Bolivia?　▲

el; los

15 A proper name <u>all by itself</u> cues *estar* for location. Now be very careful. Which form will you use? (a) *Hay* (b) *Está* ¿_____ un Pedro en la clase?　▲

Está

Hay (This is just like *Hay un muchacho en clase.*)

16 Here is a summary of the cues for choosing *estar* for location:

Santiago *está* **en** *Chile.*	(A proper name all by itself.)
Pedro *está* **en** *Chile.*	
Él *está* **en** *Chile.*	(Any subject pronoun.)
Yo *estoy* **en** *Chile.*	
El *libro está* **en** *la mesa.*	
Los *libros están* **en** *la mesa.*	(All forms of the _____ article.)　▲
La *pluma está* **en** *la mesa.*	
Las *plumas están* **en** *la mesa.*	

definite

The Equals Sign in Math and Speech: *ser*

1 When you say $4 + 4 = 8$ or $8 - 4 = 4$ in Spanish the word for $=$ is _____.　▲

son

2 Compare these sentences: (1) *Cuatro y cuatro son ocho.* (2) *Ocho menos cuatro son cuatro.* The words on either side of the verb stand for the same amount. Do *Martínez* and *profesor* stand for the same person in *Martínez es profesor?*　▲

yes

3 When you want to say that two numbers are equal or that two words stand for the same person or thing, you use the verb (a) *haber* (b) *ser* (c) *estar.*　▲

ser

A Test on What You Have Learned

1 Pilar and María *are* girls. Which verb do you use?　▲

ser (Pilar + María = girls. *Pilar y María son muchachas.*)

2 Miguel *is in* Caracas.　▲

estar (Proper name + location: *Miguel está en Caracas.*)

3 The book *is under* the table.　▲

estar (Definite article + location cues *estar: El libro está debajo de la mesa.*)

4 Rosario *is from* Lima, Perú.　▲

ser (Origin or place from cues *ser: Rosario es de Lima, Perú.*)

5 *Near here is a* volcano called Paricutín. ▲

> *haber* (Indefinite article + location cues *haber*.)

6 4 = 4 ▲

> *ser* (The equals sign is *ser*.)

7 What *is* this? ▲

> *ser* (What = this?)

8 *Is* there *a* Mr. Machado *in* this office? ▲

> *haber* (Indefinite article + location cues *haber*.)

9 They *are from* La Paz, Bolivia. ▲

> *ser* (Origin cues *ser*.)

10 They *are in* La Paz, Bolivia. ▲

> *estar* (All subject pronouns cue *estar* for location.)

If you missed two or more frames you need to go through this Assignment again. The verbs *ser*, *estar*, and *haber* are used more frequently than any other verb in Spanish. To use one of these verbs in the wrong place is a glaring mistake much like saying in English "Is you there?"

The Present Tense Forms of *ser*

The Spanish you are learning is a modern dialect of ancient Latin, the language spoken by the Romans who invaded Spain and made it a province of the Roman Empire. While Latin was slowly changing into Spanish, the people got mixed up about the meaning of the Latin verbs *sedere* (to sit) and *esse* (to be). Gradually they came to believe that the different forms of these two verbs actually belonged to the same verb. As a result, the modern verb *ser* has forms which come from both Latin verbs. It is very irregular, and its forms have to be learned one by one. English "to be" is also very irregular: am, are, is, was, were, be.

Here are all the present tense forms of *ser*. Say them aloud twice before starting Frame 1.

yo soy	usted		ustedes	
nosotros somos	él	es	ellos	son
tú eres	ella		ellas	

1 In this and the next eight frames, you are to write the proper form of *ser*.
Nosotros _____ de Asunción, Paraguay. ▲

> *somos* (Like all regular verbs the *nosotros* form ends in the suffix *mos*.)

2 Usted _____ muy amable. ▲

> *es* (*Usted es* means "you is" but is translated "you are.")

3 Tú _____ muy amable. ▲

> *eres* (Notice the suffix *s* which combines with *tú* in regular verb forms.)

4 María y Linda _____ muchachas. ▲

> *son* (*Son* ends with *n* as do all regular verbs.)

5 ¿_____ ustedes de Venezuela? ▲

6 Él _____ profesor. ▲

> *Son*
> *es*

7 José y yo _____ alumnos. ▲
8 Ellas _____ chilenas. ▲   *somos*
9 Yo _____ Pilar. ▲   *son*
                    soy (Soy has the same ending as the *yo* form of *estar, estoy.)*
10 To learn all the present tense forms of *ser*, you really have to learn only
five forms. They are: *es, son,* _____. ▲

                                                                          soy, somos, eres

Ser and Adjectives of Nationality

1 Adjectives of nationality have two forms. The singular forms you have
learned so far end in *o* or *a* as in *chileno, chilena.* Adjectives of nationality, like
all other Spanish adjectives, agree in number with the object or objects being
described. When the singular form of an adjective ends in a vowel, it is made
plural by adding _____. ▲

                                          s (chileno, chilenos; chilena, chilenas)
2 Adjectives which have two forms behave like nouns which have two forms.
What do you say? *José es un muchacho* (a) *argentino* (b) *argentina.* ▲
                            argentino (The *o* of *argentino* matches the *o* of *muchacho.)*
3 What do you say? *Josefa es una* (a) *muchacho argentino* (b) *muchacha argentina.* ▲

                                                                muchacha argentina
4 What do you say? *José y Josefa son* _____ (Argentine children). ▲
                    muchachos argentinos (When you talk of a male and a female, you use the
                            o-form of the noun and the *o*-form of the adjective in the plural.)
5 To learn to use adjectives in Spanish, you have to learn to react to cues to
which you pay no attention in English. For example, you are a woman. What
do you say? (a) *Soy uruguayo.* (b) *Soy uruguaya.* ▲
6 You are a woman and are talking for a group made up of men and women.   *Soy uruguaya.*
What do you say? (a) *Somos paraguayos.* (b) *Somos paraguayas.* ▲
7 You are a man talking to a woman. What do you say? (a) *Pancho y tú son*   *Somos paraguayos.*
chilenas. (b) *Pancho y tú son chilenos.* ▲

                                                          Pancho y tú son chilenos.
8 You are a girl talking to a girl. You must say, (a) *No somos argentinos.*
(b) *No somos argentinas.* ▲

                                                                No somos argentinas.
9 You are a man talking to a woman. You must say, (a) *No somos bolivianos.*
(b) *No somos bolivianas.* ▲

                                                                No somos bolivianos.

10 The pronoun forms *yo, tú, usted,* and *ustedes* do not tell you whether to use
an *o*-form or *a*-form adjective. Only the sex of the person you are speaking to
or about gives you the cue. Write the four plural subject pronouns that do have
an *o* and *a* contrast. ▲

                                                  nosotros, nosotras, ellos, ellas

11 The form *ella* contrasts with _____ to indicate sex. ▲

                                                                                  él

Summary

1 The cues for using *ser* are:
    a **de** + a place name (origin): **Soy** *de los Estados Unidos.*
    b equations (the "equals" sign): *Dos y dos* **son** *cuatro.*
                               Ustedes **son** *estudiantes.*

2 The cues for using *estar* for location are:
    a location + entity + definite article (*el, la, los, las*): *Los libros* **están** *en la mesa.*
    b location + any unmodified proper name that labels an entity (<u>not</u> an event): *José* **está** *en San Francisco. Buenos Aires* **está** *en Argentina.*
    c location + any subject pronoun: *Ella* **está** *en México.*

3 The cues for using *haber (hay)* for location are:
    a location + entity + indefinite article (*un, una*): *Hay* **un** *tigre en el corral.*
    b location + entity + any private or public number: **Hay 30** *alumnos en la clase.* **Hay muchos** *estudiantes aquí.*
    c location + unmodified plural noun (suffixes *s* and *es*): *¿***Hay** *elefantes en el zoológico?*

4 The present tense forms of *ser* are: *soy, somos, eres, es, son.*

5 Adjectives of nationality must match the number, sex, or terminal sound of the noun or subject pronoun:

      Yo (female) *soy american**a**.*   *Los muchach**os** son peruan**os**.*
      Juanito *es argentin**o**.*   *Está en una escuel**a** chilen**a**.*

6 When the adjective of nationality modifies any mixed group of males and females, the *o*-form is used: *Tú* (male) *y yo* (female) *somos colombian**os**.*

Preparing for a Quiz

Unless your instructor indicates otherwise, in your next class session you will have a quiz consisting of three parts.

1 **Part A,** *Dictation*: The instructor will read once only a series of words and short sentences. You are to write what you hear. If you have done well on practice dictations in class, you will probably do well on this. As you review your vocabulary, notice again those words containing eye spelling problems, especially the "silent" *h* and the spellings for /s/ and /b/. Remember also the spelling rules you are learning. How is the sound [k] spelled before *e* and *i*? ▲

2 Write the plural of *luz* and the singular of *lápices.* ▲

qu (que, Quito)
luces, lápiz

3 **Part B,** *Matching Indefinite Articles:* Your instructor will read several singular nouns from words that you should know. You are to write *un* or *una* for each according to the indefinite article that matches them. Do this for the following: *señorita, día, noche, pupitre, libro.* ▲

                                             una *señorita,* **un** *día,* **una** *noche,* **un** *pupitre,* **un** *libro*

4   Part C, *Matching Definite Articles:* Again your instructor will read several nouns (some singular, some plural) that you should know. You are to write *el, la, los* or *las* according to the definite article that matches them. Do this for the following: *luces, oficina, señoras, profesor, tardes, sábados.*   ▲

las luces, **la** oficina, **las** señoras, **el** profesor, **las** tardes, **los** sábados

5   As you review your vocabulary, besides checking on any eye spelling problems, check each noun to be sure that you know whether it is an *o-* or an *a*-noun.

Self-Correcting Exercises

A   Count aloud from memory from 0 to 30. If you forget any numbers, check them in your vocabulary list and study them.

B   Cover the Spanish. Say the following numbers aloud in Spanish. Check each as you proceed.

20	veinte	14	catorce
10	diez	18	dieciocho
30	treinta	22	veintidós
7	siete	12	doce
15	quince	26	veintiséis
11	once	13	trece
9	nueve	0	cero

C   Read these pairs aloud three times. Be sure to give the correct pronunciation to all *b*'s and *v*'s.

va/iba	bien/Estoy bien.
be/ive	bien/Muy bien.
vi/ibi	ventana/una ventana
bo/ivo	ventana/la ventana
vu/ibu	veinte/las veinte ventanas

New Vocabulary

ciudad (la)	city	**foto(grafía) (la)**	picture, photo(graph)
capital (la)	capital (city)	**estar**	to be
mina	mine (noun)	**¡Espera!**	Wait! (gesture p. 170)
corral (e)	corral	**argentino, -a**	Argentinian
jardín (el)	garden	**boliviano, -a**	Bolivian
animal (el)	animal	**chileno, -a**	Chilean
tigre (el)	tiger, cougar	**uruguayo, -a**	Uruguayan
elefante (el)	elephant	**paraguayo, -a**	Paraguayan
cartel (el)	poster	**si**	if

Word Sets and Using a Dictionary

A set of dishes is made up of cups, saucers, plates, bowls, *etc.* All members of this set have one thing in common: they are all used to serve food.

To be a member of a set, a form, a word, or a thing must have something in common with all other members of that set. *Dogs, Chinese, bolts,* and *wars* are members of a set of things that can be counted, but otherwise they have nothing significant in common. In contrast, *oranges, apples, peaches,* and *pears* can be counted and, in addition, are members of the set of fruit that grows on trees.

Every culture organizes all entities, events, *etc.* in sets, and no one can learn a language without discovering the role sets play in communication. You are probably not aware of it, but before you were two years old you had a lot of information in your head about sets and English usage.

In the next few frames you will discover a generalization which really troubles foreigners learning English.

1 You can *count* apples, pigs, cars, and telephones but you *measure* water, dust, and milk. Copy the words which stand for entities which belong to the same set as water, dust, and milk: *hat, mud, ink, pen, flour, butter, boy.* ▲

> mud, ink, flour, butter (These words label *measure* entities.)

2 Which would you say: (a) What are waters? (b) What is water? ▲

3 Do you say, "Pass the butters please."? ▲   What is water?

> no (You have proven that you can identify the members of the set made up of measure entities and that you know their labels do not take a plural suffix without changing the meaning.)

4 You know more about this set. Write the number for the sentences which are *not* proper English answers to the question, *What's that on the table?* (1) It's a bug. (2) It's a milk. (3) It's a pencil. (4) It's a dust. (5) It's a bottle. ▲

> 2, 4 (*Milk* and *dust* are measure entities and the indefinite article *a* is not used with measure entities.)

5 It took you many years to learn to deal with English sets by feel or intuition. You do not have time to learn Spanish in this way. You need to learn to deal with sets consciously, that is, by actually *knowing* what they are and what they can tell you about Spanish usage.

Here is a new example. Compare these two sets of questions and answers:

¿Dónde está el libro?	*El libro está en la mesa.*
	Está en la mesa.
¿Dónde está José?	*José está en clase.*
	Él está en clase.
	Está en clase.

The two subjects, *el libro* and *José*, do not belong to the same set. *José* is a living being and *libro* an inanimate or non-living entity. *José* can be replaced by the subject pronoun *él* but *libro* cannot. Here is a new generalization: No noun standing for an inanimate entity may be replaced by *él*. Spanish has no word to translate "it" when used as subject of a sentence. You use zero and the verb. Now translate: It is on the table.   ▲

6   Spanish also has no word to translate "they" when this subject pronoun stands for inanimate entities. Translate: They are on the table.   ▲

> *Está en la mesa.*

7   Sets are very important in learning the meaning of words. When you meet a new Spanish word you must assign what it stands for to a set. You know, for example, the word *mesa*. The set it belongs to is called _____.   ▲

> *Están en la mesa.*

> furniture (table, chair, desk, stool, *etc.*)

8   There are many words which can stand for things belonging to different sets. Words of this kind have more than one meaning. A Spanish speaker may say, "I bought that ranch up on the *mesa*." *Mesa*, in this sentence, cannot be standing for a piece of furniture. When logic tells you that a word you have learned cannot stand for the set you have assigned it to, you have been signaled that it has another meaning. When a ranch is on a *mesa*, *mesa* must stand for _____.   ▲

> a tableland, a geographic shape, an upland

9   Now, let's turn this around. Suppose you do not know the Spanish word for "magazine." You want to look it up in an English-Spanish dictionary. You will find *revista*, *almacén*, *cámara*, and *santabárbara*. All of these translate "magazine," but each one stands for something belonging to a different set. You cannot decide which one to pick before you decide the set you want "magazine" to stand for.

Suppose you want "magazine" to stand for the set composed of newspapers, pamphlets, periodicals, and reviews. You have a better chance of picking the right translation now. Look for a cognate and copy the word in this list which looks like it might be a cognate of "review": *almacén*, *cámara*, *revista*, *santabárbara*.   ▲

10   You want a different meaning for "magazine." This time you are talking about a gun. Another name for the magazine of a gun is its "chamber." Copy the word which looks like it might be a cognate of "chamber": *almacén*, *cámara*, *revista*, *santabárbara*.   ▲

> *revista*

> *Cámara* is the only one beginning with *c*.

11   A Spanish speaker says, "Our house has a kitchen, dining-room, parlor, two baths, and *tres cámaras*." *Cámara*, in this context, does not logically stand for the magazine of a gun. It stands for _____.   ▲

> bedroom (The set he is talking about is rooms of a house.)

12   People who are interested in hunting, read "magazines" about guns. Which word would you pick for "magazine"? (a) *cámara* (b) *revista*   ▲

> *revista* (People don't "read" bullet chambers.)

13   The verb "read" in "People read magazines about guns" helps you define the set to which "magazine" belongs. Other words in a sentence help you discover the set of an unknown word and, in the process, its meaning. You

have not had the word *cuchara*. What set does it belong to in this sentence?
"He bought a knife, a fork, and *una cuchara*." ▲

silverware (or tableware) (The translation is "spoon.")

14 Here are more examples of the importance of sets in learning Spanish. To choose between *haber* and *estar* for location you must be able to recognize the set of relator words used in locating entities. Copy the words <u>not</u> used in talking about locating something in space: *in, under, over, from, near, on, for.* ▲

15 Question words all belong to the same set. What they have in common *in writing* in Spanish is an _____. ▲

from; for

16 The adjectives of nationality belong to the same set. In writing they differ from English in that they do not begin with a _____. ▲

accent mark

capital letter

Review of Uses of ser, estar, *and* haber

1 When you ask about a person's health, you use _____. ▲

estar (¿Cómo está usted?)

2 The origin of a person or thing cues _____. ▲

ser (¿De dónde es usted? ¿De España?)

3 To state a person's nationality. (He is Bolivian), you use _____. ▲

4 Any one of the four forms of the definite article cues the use of _____ for location. ▲

ser (Es boliviano.)

estar (Los libros están en el pupitre.)

5 To say that two things are equal or the same, you use _____. ▲

ser (Panchito es un elefante.)

6 Any form of the indefinite article or any number (public or private) cues the use of _____ for location. ▲

haber (Hay un tigre en el corral; Hay dos tigres en el corral.)

7 An unmodified plural noun cues the use of _____ for location. ▲

haber (Hay gauchos en el rodeo.)

8 An unmodified proper name cues the use of _____ for location. ▲

estar (Pedro está en Paraguay.)

9 The subject pronouns cue the use of _____ for location. ▲

estar (Ellos están en Bolivia.)

Practice in Writing ser *and* estar, *and Adjectival Agreement*

Treat this section of your Assignment as a self-test to find out what you still have to learn to reach perfection.

1 You have learned, so far, only one form of *haber*. It is _____. ▲

2 Translate the indicated part of each sentence: (1) *There is* a book on the table. (2) *There are* two books on the table. ▲

hay

Hay *un libro en la mesa;* **Hay** *dos libros en la mesa.* (*Hay* does not agree
in number with what is being located.)

3   The cue to say *hay* for location is the indefinite article, any number (public
or private), or _____.   ▲

"zero" before a plural noun (*Hay estudiantes en la oficina.*)

4   Translate the verb form only: Near our house *is* a large tree.   ▲

hay (*Hay* translates "is" and "are" as well as "there is"and "there are.")

5   The *yo* form of *estar* is irregular. It is _____.   ▲

6   The forms *está* and *están* are irregular because they _____.   ▲   *estoy*

have the stress on the first suffix (This is shown by the written accent marks.)

7   Change *estoy* so it will match *nosotros.*   ▲

estamos (*Estoy* and *estamos* are the only present tense forms of *estar* that do
not have a written accent mark.)

8   Make *ellas están* singular.   ▲

9   What form of *estar* goes with *tú?*   ▲   *ella está*

10 The plural of *tú estás* is _____.   ▲   *estás*

ustedes están (There are forms for a plural of *tú: vosotros estáis, etc.* These
are not part of the ordinary speech in Latin America. You will learn to read
and understand these later on.)

11 *Usted, él,* and *ella* combine with *está. Ustedes, ellos,* and *ellas* combine with
_____.   ▲

12 A proper name cues the use of *estar* for location. Translate the indicated   *están*
part: Miguel *is in* Santiago.   ▲

13 The (a) definite (b) indefinite article is the cue to use *estar* for location.   ▲   *está en*

14 Translate: The pen is on the table.   ▲   definite

La pluma está en la mesa.

15 All subject pronouns cue the use of _____ for location.   ▲

16 Translate: We are in the class.   ▲   *estar*

Nosotros estamos en la clase.

17 There are two verbs in Spanish that are used to locate entities in space.
They are _____.   ▲

estar; haber (*Ser* is never used to locate entities.)

18 *Estar* is also used to talk about a person's health or state of being. Translate,
using the *tú* form: How are you?   ▲

19 Translate: I'm fine, thank you.   ▲   *¿Cómo estás?*

20 When the relator *de* combines with the name of a place, it is translated   *Estoy bien, gracias.*
by _____.   ▲

21 Translate: Carlos is from Lima.   ▲   from

22 The origin of a person or thing is indicated by the verb _____ and *de.*   ▲   *Carlos es de Lima.*

23 The equals sign (=) is translated into a word by _____.   ▲   *ser*

24 "We" and "students" stand for the same persons in "We are students."   *ser*
Translate the verb form in "We are students."   ▲

somos (*Ser* is used to say that numbers equal numbers or that words equal
25 In this frame and the next three each sentence translates "You are   words.)
Brazilian." *Tú* (man) _____.   ▲

Tú eres brasileño. (The verb is *ser.* The adjective has no capital letter, it ends
in *o,* it is written with an *s,* and has a tilde over the *ñ.*)

26 *Usted* (woman) _____. ▲

Usted es brasileña. (a for female)

27 *Ustedes* (women) _____. ▲

Ustedes son brasileñas. (son and s for plural; a for females)

28 *Ustedes* (any combination of men and women as: men and women; men and woman; man and women; man and woman) _____. ▲

Ustedes son brasileños. (s for plural; o for men and women or any combination

29 The present tense forms of *ser* are very irregular. The subject pronouns of the two.)
usted, *él*, and *ella* combine with _____. ▲

30 *Ustedes*, *ellos*, and *ellas* combine with _____. ▲

es

31 The forms that go with *yo* and *nosotros* are _____. ▲

son

32 *Tú* combines with _____. ▲

soy; somos

eres

Self-Correcting Exercises

A Do this drill aloud three times. Increase your speed each time. Don't forget to cover the answers and to check each response immediately.

1 Nosotros estamos en la clase.
Yo . . .

Yo estoy en la clase.

2 . . . estudio . . .

Yo estudio en la clase.

3 . . . en la universidad.

Yo estudio en la universidad.

4 Pancho . . .

Pancho estudia en la universidad.

5 . . . trabaja . . .

Pancho trabaja en la universidad.

6 . . . en una mina.

Pancho trabaja en una mina.

7 Ellos . . .

Ellos trabajan en una mina.

8 . . . están . . .

Ellos están en una mina.

9 Tú . . .

Tú estás en una mina.

10 . . . en la oficina.

Tú estás en la oficina.

11 Tú y yo . . .

Tú y yo estamos en la oficina.

12 . . . trabajamos . . .

Tú y yo trabajamos en la oficina.

13 Usted . . .

Usted trabaja en la oficina.

B Read each adjective of nationality aloud. Then say the name of the corresponding country. If you need more practice, reverse the procedure.

1	ecuatoriana	Ecuador	**6**	argentina	Argentina
2	peruana	Perú	**7**	paraguaya	Paraguay
3	colombiana	Colombia	**8**	boliviana	Bolivia
4	venezolana	Venezuela	**9**	uruguaya	Uruguay
5	brasileña	Brasil	**10.**	chilena	Chile

C Do this drill aloud. You will have to note carefully the subject-adjective agreement. You may want to work with a partner. Remember to cover the answers.

1 Si él es de Paraguay, ¿qué es?

Es paraguayo.

2 Si él es de Ecuador, ¿qué es?

Es ecuatoriano.

3	Si él es de Brasil, ¿qué es?	Es brasileño.
4	Si ella es de Chile, ¿qué es?	Es chilena.
5	Si ella es de Perú, ¿qué es?	Es peruana.
6	Si ella es de Bolivia, ¿qué es?	Es boliviana.
7	Si ellos son de Colombia, ¿qué son?	Son colombianos.
8	Si ellos son de Uruguay, ¿qué son?	Son uruguayos.
9	Si ellos son de Brasil, ¿qué son?	Son brasileños.
10	Si ellas son de Bolivia, ¿qué son?	Son bolivianas.
11	Si ellas son de Argentina, ¿qué son?	Son argentinas.
12	Si ellas son de Venezuela, ¿qué son?	Son venezolanas.

New Vocabulary

Hace calor.	It's hot.	**Hace viento.**	It's windy.
Hace frío.	It's cold.	**Hace buen tiempo.**	It's good weather.
Hace fresco.	It's cool.	**Hace mal tiempo.**	It's bad weather.
haber	to be, have	**brasileño, -a**	Brazilian
ser	to be	**colombiano, -a**	Colombian
también	too, also	**ecuatoriano, -a**	Ecuadorian
perfecto, -a	perfect	**peruano, -a**	Peruvian
malo, -a	bad	**venezolano, -a**	Venezuelan

Perfecto

Hold right hand in front of you and bring the thumb and index finger together to form a circle or O. The hand is frequently given a quick shake and, then, brought quickly to a still position.

Assignment 14

A New Verb Form

All regular Spanish verb forms are made up of three morphemes: the *stem* and two *suffixes*. The stem tells *what* the action is, the first suffix tells *when* the action takes place (past or present), and the second suffix tells *who* performs the action.

The three sets of verbs in Spanish are shown by the vowels *a, e, i* which come before the infinitive marker *r*. The forms of the second suffix are the same for the present tense of all verbs.

1 The first suffix of the present tense of *a*-verbs (*trabajar, hablar*) has only two forms. They are the vowels _____. ▲

2 The stem of *leer* (to read) is *le*. To what verb set does *leer* belong? ▲   *o; a*

3 The *yo* form of the present tense of all regular verbs of all sets ends in *o*.   *e*-set
The first suffix of the present tense of *e*-verbs has two forms or morphemes, *o* and *e*. Copy and add the first suffix to these forms: *yo le . . . , usted le . . . , él le . . . .* ▲

           yo leo, usted lee, él lee

4 Copy and add the first and second suffix to these forms: *nosotros le . . . , ustedes le . . . , ellos le . . . , ellas le . . . .* ▲

         nosotros leemos, ustedes leen, ellos leen, ellas leen

5 To know all the forms of a new verb set you only had to learn the meaning of *leer* and *e* for the first suffix for all of the forms except the *yo* form which is *o*, the same as with *a*-verbs. You are now going to learn another *e*-verb, *comer* (to eat). The cognate is "comestible" (edible). Say it aloud: *co-mer*. The stem of *comer* is _____. ▲

6 To change *leemos* (we read) to "we eat" you replace the stem *le* with _____   *com*
and you have _____. ▲

         com and you have *comemos*

7 Change *leen* to "they eat." ▲

       comen (*Ellos* may be omitted in speech when the subject is already known.)

8 Change *leo* to "I eat." ▲

9 You already know that the way a verb is divided into morphemes is not   *como*
the way it is divided into syllables in speech. Here are the present tense forms of *comer* divided into syllables. The indicated syllable is stressed. Say them aloud and, remember, no schwa sound. Notice that the forms in the first column have no second suffix.

yo ***co***-mo	tú ***co***-mes
usted ***co***-me	nosotros co-***me***-mos
él ***co***-me	nosotras co-***me***-mos
ella ***co***-me	ustedes ***co***-men
	ellos ***co***-men
	ellas ***co***-men

Learning by Sets

1 Because all members of a set behave alike, you can now make up the present tense forms for all the regular *e*-verbs in the entire Spanish language. Here is another regular *e*-verb, *vender*, "to sell." Write the forms for "I sell" and "we sell." ▲

2 The verb *temer* is regular and translates "to fear." Write the form that goes with *ustedes*. ▲

vendo; vendemos

3 Change *temen* so it agrees with *tú*. ▲

temen

4 "To drink" is translated by the regular *e*-verb *beber*. Write the form that agrees with *yo*. ▲

temes

5 There are five different forms in the present tense of every regular *e*-verb. If you learn 100 new *e*-verbs and all their forms *one by one*, you must learn 500 separate forms. Obviously it's easier to learn the forms for the whole set than to learn 500 forms one by one. To learn a new *e*-verb you only have to learn the _____ and its meaning. ▲

bebo

6 The stem *corr* describes the action of using one's feet to move very rapidly from one place to another. How do you say "we run" in Spanish? ▲

stem

7 Everything you learn is learned more easily and remembered longer when you know the set to which it belongs. Here is a different kind of set for you to practice on. When we say, "He eats too much," does *too much* describe (a) the *manner* of eating? (b) the *amount* of food eaten? ▲

corremos

the amount of food eaten

8 Look at the indicated parts of these sentences: (1) He eats *too much*. (2) He eats *too rapidly*. Do these two adverbs belong to the same set? ▲

no (*Too much* deals with amount; *too rapidly* describes speed.)

9 The notion of "amount" covers many different degrees of amount. Here are three Spanish words that deal with amount. They are arranged in their degree order, that is, from small to large: *poco, mucho, demasiado*. Match them with: a little, a lot, too much. ▲

a little—*poco*, a lot—*mucho*, too much—*demasiado*

10 Translate: She eats too much. ▲

(*Ella*) *come demasiado.*

11 Which sentence describes a person who does not read a great deal? (a) *Lee demasiado*. (b) *Lee mucho*. (c) *Lee poco*. ▲

12 *Poco* and *mucho* do not belong to the same set as *bien* and *mal*. Which sentence describes the manner in which the action is performed? (a) *José lee poco*. (b) *José lee bien*. ▲

Lee poco.

José lee bien tells you how he reads. *José lee poco* tells you how much he reads.

13 The opposite of *bien* is _____. ▲

14 *Bien* and *mal* stand for degrees on a scale. The adverb *bastante* is used to increase the degree of either *bien* or *mal*. It is put just before these words. Translate: *José* reads quite well. ▲

mal

José lee bastante bien.

15 The opposite of *José lee bastante bien* is *José lee* _____. ▲

16 Every word belongs to two very different kinds of sets. One set deals with what the word stands for. The other set deals with the linguistic class of the word. Copy the words which belong to the set that stands for <u>actions.</u> *José lee bastante bien; Tú comes mucho.* ▲

bastante mal

lee; comes (These two words belong to the linguistic set called "verbs.")

17 The words *leer* and *comer* belong to more than one set. One set deals with reality and actions. The other set deals with the form and function of the word. In addition they belong to a special set of verbs (a sub-set) whose first suffix in the present tense can only be the morphemes (vowels) _____. ▲

o or *e*

Oral Reading

All educated people are able to read aloud the language that they speak. However, there is another important reason for learning to read a foreign language.

So far in this course you have been taught about 235 words and forms. There will never be enough time in class to learn to hear and practice the many thousands of words you need in order to talk about all the things you can talk about in English. When you can say words that you have not heard before (read aloud), as when you look them up in a dictionary, you can add them to your speaking vocabulary.

1 You have never heard or seen this sentence. Read it aloud and then translate it mentally: *Miguel es de Buenos Aires, pero hoy está en Montevideo.* ▲

Miguel is from Buenos Aires, but today he is in Montevideo.

2 There are spaces between the words in the clause *Miguel es de Buenos Aires* but you read it like one long word: *Miguelesdebuenosaires*. This is the way to say *Miguel es de: Mi-**gue**-les-de.* Say it aloud. The *l* of *Miguel* goes with the verb *es*. Read this aloud: *Bue-no-**sai**-res.* The *s* of *Buenos* goes with the *ai* of *aires*. Now practice saying the following until it all comes out as one long word: *Mi-**gue**-les-de-bue-no-**sai**-res.*

3 Say "red ants" in English. Can we run these words together the way Spanish words are run together? Say *redants*. Does this sound like "red ants"? ▲

no (We sometimes run words together; for example, *gonna*.)

4 Say *Whatchaduin?* until you understand it. Then write it out the standard way. ▲

What are you doing?

5 The way words are spaced in writing does not tell you how they are said in speech. Do the letters in the words always tell you what sound to make? ▲

no (If you answered "yes", say this word aloud: [rreló]. It is spelled *reloj*.)

6 Does the letter *r* at the beginning of a word always stand for the sound [rr]? ▲

7 You see the letter *h* in a Spanish word. Do you make a sound for it? ▲   yes

8 The word "honor" is spelled and means the same in both English and   no

Spanish. Say it in English and Spanish. Now say: *hola, hasta, hoy, hora.*

9 You see the letter *d* in a word. Will it tell you, all by itself, what sound to make? ▲

no (If you answered "yes," study the next frames very carefully.)

10 When the difference between *two words* having *two different meanings* is marked only by a contrast between *two sounds*, these contrasting sounds are called *phonemes* (sounds that mark meaning). The two contrasting phonemes of *dos* and *los* are written _____. ▲

11 In "telephone" and "phoneme" the part *phone* is the Greek for "sound."   *d; l*
The *eme* of phon*eme* is the Greek for "meaning." Does the word *dos* have the same meaning for a Spanish speaker in these two utterances? (1) *¡Dos libros!*
(2) *¡Los dos libros!* ▲

12 Is the [d] sound of *¡Dos libros!* a (a) stop or a (b) fricative? ▲   yes

a stop (Because it comes after silence.)

13 Is the [d] sound of *¡Los dos libros!* also a stop? ▲

no (Except after *n* or *l*, it is always a fricative inside a word or phrase.)

14 *Dos*, spoken with a fricative [đ], and *dos*, spoken with a stop [d], signal the same meaning in Spanish. When a phoneme has two different sounds, these sounds are said to be *allophones* (other sounds) of that phoneme. The Spanish phoneme /d/ has two allophones, a stop and a fricative. What letter stands for either allophone? ▲

15 This letter all by itself will not tell you what sound to make when you   *d*
read aloud. What comes _____ the *d* will tell you which allophone to make. ▲

before (When the phoneme /d/ follows silence, [n] or [l], you say the stop
16 Copy and underline the two *fricative* [đ]'s: *Donaldo, ¿cuándo va usted? ¿Los*   allophone.)
domingos? ▲

*Donaldo, ¿cuándo va uste**d**? ¿Los **d**omingos?*

17 The Spanish phoneme /p/ does not have two allophones. Hold the back of your hand near your lips and say "paper." You will feel the puff of the aspirated [p]. Can you say *papel* with no puff at all? Practice until you feel no puff. Spanish [p] is always _____. ▲

18 Do the letters *b* and *v* stand for two different phonemes in Spanish? ▲   unaspirated

no (They stand for the same phoneme in standard Spanish.)

19 Now be careful. Do both *b* and *v* stand for two different sounds in Spanish? ▲

yes (For two allophones of the same phoneme /b/.)

20 Say *ventana* and *Bolivia* aloud. After a pause or silence, either *v* or *b* stands for the same sound. This allophone is (a) a stop (b) a fricative. ▲

21 You say *Bolivia* and *en Bolivia* with a stop [b]. What happens when you say   a stop
de Bolivia or *una ventana?* Both sounds are now _____. ▲

fricatives (When any phoneme, except /n/ or /m/, comes before *b* or *v*, they stand for the fricative allophone.)

22 Speakers of English frequently make two kinds of mistakes in saying Spanish vowels. When the vowel is in an unstressed syllable, they often substitute a sound called _____. ▲

schwa (Say *buenos días* without schwa.)

23 When a vowel is the last sound in a word, as in *de*, English speakers tend to substitute two sounds (a complex vowel) and make *de* sound like English

_____. ▲

24 Say English "to" and Spanish *tú* until you are certain you can hear the   day
difference and can say *tú* with just one vowel sound.

25 You have never read these sentences before. Say them aloud.

> Roberto le dice buenas noches a Pilar.
> El número de días en una semana es siete.
> En un mes hay cuatro semanas.
> Hay veinte sillas en la clase.
> ¿Cuántas horas hay en un día?
> Brasilia y Asunción son ciudades.
> Si yo soy de Chile, ¿qué soy?

Summary

A New Verb Form

1 There are three sets of Spanish verbs.

2 The set is indicated by the vowel *a*, *e*, or *i* before the infinitive marker *r*.

3 The *yo* form of the present tense of *all* regular verbs of *all* sets ends in *o*.

4 The other morpheme of the first suffix for *e*-verbs is *e*.

5 The forms of the second suffix are the same in all present verb forms (zero, *mos*, *s*, *n*).

Learning by Sets

1 Because all members of a set behave alike, knowing the first suffix for one *e*-verb, makes it possible to make up all the present tense forms of all regular *e*-verbs.

2 *Poco, mucho, demasiado* belong to the set of adverbs of amount; *bien* and *mal* are adverbs of manner. The adverb *bastante* is used to increase the degree of either *bien* or *mal*.

3 Every word belongs to two different kinds of sets. One set deals with reality, the other with form and function.

Oral Reading

1 Spanish, unlike English, always runs the words of a phrase or breath group together as one long word.

2 The letter *r* at the beginning of a word always stands for the sound [rr].

3 The letter *h* stands for no sound.

4 The phoneme /d/ has two allophones: stop [d] and fricative [đ]. Both allophones are spelled *d*. Stop [d] follows silence, *n*, or *l*; fricative [đ] follows all other letters.

5 Spanish [p] is unaspirated.

6 After silence and the phonemes /n/ or /m/, either *b* or *v* stands for stop [b]. The same letters stand for fricative [b̶] after all other phonemes.

7 Spanish, unlike English, does *not* have a schwa for the vowel sound in unstressed syllables.

8 English speakers tend to substitute a complex vowel for a simple vowel when speaking Spanish. ("day" for *de*)

Self-Correcting Exercises

A Read the name of each country aloud. Then say the adjective of nationality that would be needed to describe two or more women from that country. If you need more practice, reverse the procedure.

1	Ecuador	ecuatorianas
2	Perú	peruanas
3	Colombia	colombianas
4	Venezuela	venezolanas
5	Brasil	brasileñas
6	Argentina	argentinas
7	Paraguay	paraguayas
8	Bolivia	bolivianas
9	Uruguay	uruguayas
10	Chile	chilenas

B Answer these questions aloud. Note carefully the subject-adjective agreement. You may want to work with a partner.

1	Si él es de Paraguay, ¿qué es?	Es paraguayo.
2	Si ella es de Ecuador, ¿qué es?	Es ecuatoriana.
3	Si ellos son de Brasil, ¿qué son?	Son brasileños.
4	Si ellas son de Chile, ¿qué son?	Son chilenas.
5	Si ella es de Perú, ¿qué es?	Es peruana.
6	Si ellos son de Colombia, ¿qué son?	Son colombianos.
7	Si él es de Bolivia, ¿qué es?	Es boliviano.
8	Si ellas son de Uruguay, ¿qué son?	Son uruguayas.
9	Si ella es de Argentina, ¿qué es?	Es argentina.
10	Si ellos son de Venezuela, ¿qué son?	Son venezolanos.

C Read this drill aloud three times. Be sure to use the correct allophones of /d/ and /b/.

boda/una boda	debe/rumbo
burro/un burro	adobe/ronda
broma/una broma	roba/Dora
duro/un duro	borra/beber
drama/un drama	red/dudar
¿Dónde vive el burro?	Donaldo tiene un cuaderno y un libro.

D On a separate sheet of paper, write the combinations for this visual-graphic drill.

Ejemplo: 71 = Ustedes son paraguayas.

1	María		1	paraguay-
2	Nosotras		2	ecuatorian-
3	Nosotros		3	brasileñ-
4	Ustedes *(male)*		4	venezolan-
5	Tú *(female)*	ser	5	peruan-
6	Yo *(male)*		6	colombian-
7	Ustedes *(female)*			
8	Juan			
9	Yo *(female)*			
10	Tú *(male)*			

1)	94	Yo soy venezolana.
2)	62	Yo soy ecuatoriano.
3)	35	Nosotros somos peruanos.
4)	12	María es ecuatoriana.
5)	101	Tú eres paraguayo.
6)	23	Nosotras somos brasileñas.
7)	76	Ustedes son colombianas.
8)	44	Ustedes son venezolanos.
9)	51	Tú eres paraguaya.
10)	83	Juan es brasileño.

New Vocabulary

comer	to eat	**demasiado bien (mal)**	too well (badly)
leer	to read	**bastante bien (mal)**	pretty (quite) well (bad)
demasiado	too much	**mucho**	a lot, a great deal
bastante	enough; quite	**poco**	a little

Assignment 15

Telling Time in Spanish

In a calendar system each interval of time is a multiple of a smaller interval and, also, a fraction of a larger interval. A day (*día*) is a fraction of a week (*semana*), which in turn is a fraction of a month (*mes*), which is a fraction of a year (*año*).

1 A day, like a month or a year, may be divided into smaller intervals. Three positions of the sun are used to measure these intervals: (1) sunrise, (2) the point at which the sun is highest in the sky, and (3) sunset. The interval between sunset and sunrise is called _____. ▲

> night (*noche*—the dark part of the day)

2 The point at which the sun is highest in the sky is called _____. ▲

> noon (*mediodía*—mid-day)

3 The interval between midnight and noon is called _____. ▲

> morning (*mañana*—This interval is half dark and half light.)

4 The interval between noon and sunset is called _____. ▲

> afternoon (*tarde*—This interval is all light.)

5 The words *morning, afternoon, day, week, month, etc.*, stand for intervals of calendar time, the time between natural events. To make smaller divisions, man had to invent mechanical substitutes for natural events. The most widely used mechanical substitute for natural events is a _____. ▲

> clock (The intervals *hours, minutes,* and *seconds,* do not have special names to indicate their position in a series such as Monday, Tuesday; January, February; 1912, 1960, *etc.*)

6 In the sentence, *It is three o'clock*, the number *three* stands for (a) an interval of time (b) a point in time. ▲

> a point in time (The point at which the hour begins.)

7 We are "lost" in time if we do not know the calendar interval in which we happen to be and the time point at which we are. When we say, *It is three o'clock in the morning*, we use both the clock point (three) and the calendar interval (_____) to locate ourselves in time. ▲

8 We can locate ourselves in terms of a clock point in just three ways. We can say we are *at* a point (It is two o'clock), *before* a point (It is fifteen minutes before two), or *after* a point (It is fifteen minutes after two). Look at these sentences:

> morning

It is fifteen minutes to two.   It is fifteen minutes of two.
It is fifteen minutes before two.   It is one forty-five.

Are they all talking about the same clock point? ▲

9 When we say, *It is one forty-five*, we are adding minutes to the hour. *It is ten minutes to five* subtracts ten from five. How do you say this by adding? ▲

> yes

10 Change *It is three forty* to the subtraction equivalent. ▲

> It is four fifty.

> "It is 20 minutes to four" or "It is 20 minutes before four."

11 The English speaker says, "What time is it?" The Spanish speaker, however, asks, *¿Qué hora es?* The noun *hora* is a cognate of the English word _____. ▲

> hour (So the Spanish speaker asks, "What hour is it?")

12 Spanish *hora* ends in the phoneme /a/. What form of the definite and indefinite article will go with it? ▲

13 The Spanish speaker uses *hora* when he asks, "What time is it?" *¿Qué hora es?* Hundreds of years ago the answer might have been *Es la hora una.* Today the Spanish speaker always drops *hora* in the answer and simply says, *Es la una.* This is translated into English by _____. ▲

> *la; una*

> It is one o'clock.

14 In *Es la una* the verb *ser* is third person singular and the form agrees with *una*, a singular number. The third person plural form of *ser* is _____. ▲

son

15 Look at *Es la una* (It is one o'clock.). If a Spanish speaker wants to say, "It is two o'clock," he must change *una* to _____, *la* to _____, and *es* to _____. ▲

16 *Es la una* translates "It is one o'clock." Translate: It is two o'clock. ▲

dos, las, son

17 Translate: It is ten o'clock. ▲

Son las dos.
Son las diez.

18 As in English, the Spanish speaker adds and subtracts minutes in telling time. The Spanish word for the plus sign ($+$) is *y*. The word for the minus sign ($-$) is the cognate *menos*. Translate: *Es la una y diez.* ▲

"It is 1 + 10" or "It is ten minutes after one." (The plus sign *y* is translated as "after.")

19 In English we subtract ten minutes from the following hour (one) in "It is ten to one." We can give the same time by adding 50 minutes to the previous hour (twelve). This gives "It is twelve fifty." The Spanish speakers also add minutes to the previous hour and subtract minutes from the following hour but, unlike the English, most Spanish speakers add *only up to 30 minutes*. After the half hour they *subtract* from the following hour. As a result, the standard Spanish translation for "It is ten to one, It is twelve fifty" subtracts ten from one. It is _____. ▲

Es la una **menos** *diez.*

20 The two English translations for *Son las ocho menos veinte* are _____. ▲

It is twenty to eight. It is seven forty.

Summary

1 An interval of calendar time has two names, one for its position in a series (*domingo*) and the other for its length (*día*).
2 The numbers on a clock mark points in time; each stands for the point at which the hour begins.
3 If the time is not exactly on the hour, Spanish adds and subtracts minutes using the math words *y* and *menos*. (*Son las cinco y diez, Es la una menos veinte.*)
4 Spanish usually adds only up to 30 minutes to the hour, then subtracts from the next hour.
5 Spanish asks for the "hour," not the "time." *¿Qué hora es?*

Practice with ser, estar, *and* haber

The only form of *haber* that you have had so far is *hay*, a word which comes from Latin meaning "he has there." Spanish verbs agree with their subject, not their object, so *hay* does <u>not</u> agree in number with what is being located. Consequently, *hay* translates both "there is, there are" and "is, are."

1 The _____ article or any _____ cues the use of *hay* for location. ▲

indefinite article, number

2 Translate: There is a book on the table. ▲

Hay un libro en la mesa.

3 Translate: There are books on the table. ▲

Hay libros en la mesa.

4 Translate: On the table are books. ▲

En la mesa hay libros.

5 Translate: On the table is a book. ▲

En la mesa hay un libro.

6 Now translate: The book is on the table. ▲

El libro está en la mesa. (The definite article *el* cues *estar*.)

7 Copy and fill in the blanks with *pluma* and the right cue: *Hay* _____ *en la mesa.* _____ *está en la mesa.* ▲

Hay **una pluma** *en la mesa.* **La pluma** *está en la mesa.*

8 The stress falls on *ha* in *ha-blas*. It falls on _____ in *es-tás*. ▲

9 There are two present tense forms of *estar* that do not have a written accent on the first suffix. They are _____. ▲

tás

10 Write the forms that go with *usted, ellos,* and *tú.* ▲

estoy; estamos
usted está, ellos están, tú estás

11 The present tense of *estar* has two irregularities: the stress on the first suffix and the use of _____ instead of *o* for the *yo* form. ▲

oy (*Soy* from *ser* also takes *oy* for the *yo* form.)

12 When you make up the present tense of *ser*, you add what to *tú er* _____ , *nosotros so* _____ , *ustedes s* _____ ? ▲

*tú er**es**, nosotros so**mos**, ustedes s**on***

13 The present tense form of *ser* that goes with *usted, él,* and *ella* is _____. ▲

14 Copy and fill in the blanks with the proper choice of *ser* or *estar*: *Yo* _____ *en Madrid. Yo* _____ *de Madrid.* ▲

es

Yo **estoy** *en Madrid. Yo* **soy** *de Madrid.*

15 *Estar en* plus a place noun gives the _____ of the subject. ▲

16 Translate: They (females) are in Caracas. ▲

location
Ellas están en Caracas.

17 *Ser de* plus a place noun tells us the _____ of the subject. ▲

18 Translate: We are from Colombia. ▲

origin
Somos de Colombia. (You may omit the *nosotros*.)

19 Write out these equations: *Nosotros = alumnos. Dos y dos = cuatro.* ▲

Nosotros somos alumnos. Dos y dos son cuatro.

20 To say that two words stand for the same thing or that numbers are equal, you use the verb _____. ▲

21 —*Yo (una muchacha) soy de Argentina. ¿Qué soy?* —*Tú eres* _____. ▲

ser

—*Tú eres argentina.* (Adjectives of nationality cue you to use *ser*.)

22 Translate: "What time is it?" ▲

23 When the hour is 1 (1:00 o'clock), you answer _____. ▲

¿Qué hora es?

24 For all other hours you must use the verb form _____. ▲

Es la una.

son (*Son las dos, tres, cuatro,* etc.)

25 In this and the following frames, you will find a statement about cues for choice of *ser, estar,* or *haber* and a sentence to be translated. Write the infinitive and translate the sentence with the proper form of the verb. Any subject pronoun cues the choice of _____ for location: They are in Bogotá. ▲

estar (*Están en Bogotá.*)

26 The relator *de* plus a place name cues the choice of _____ for origin: We are from Lima. ▲

ser (Somos de Lima.)

27 An unmodified plural noun cues the choice of _____ for location: Are there pens on the table? ▲

haber (¿Hay plumas en la mesa?)

28 A proper name, all by itself, cues the choice of _____ for location: Santiago is in Chile. ▲

estar (Santiago está en Chile.)

29 The combination *un señor Abreu* cues the choice of _____ for location: There's a mister Abreu here. ▲

haber (Hay un señor Abreu aquí.)

30 Any kind of equals sign cues the use of _____: She is the professor. ▲

ser (Ella es la profesora.)

31 The definite article cues _____ for location: The girl is here. ▲

estar (La muchacha está aquí.)

32 When an adjective of nationality describes the subject, you use _____: He is Bolivian. ▲

ser (Él es boliviano. (No capital B.))

33 Any number cues the choice of _____ for location: There are ten girls in the class. ▲

haber (Hay diez muchachas en la clase.)

34 In telling time you use _____: What time is it? ▲

ser (¿Qué hora es?)

Self-Correcting Exercises

A Read these sentences aloud twice trying to sound as much as possible like a native speaker of Spanish. Especially be sure to use the correct pronunciation of the indicated letters.

1 **R**obe**r**to le **d**ice **b**uenos **d**ías a **Bárb**ara.
2 —**B**uenos **d**ías—le **d**ice **Bárb**ara a **R**obe**r**to.
3 El nom**br**e **d**e esta señorita es **Bárb**ara **D**elga**d**o.
4 El muchacho se llama **R**obe**r**to **R**amos.
5 Los **d**os son alumnos **d**e una escuela **v**enezolana.
6 **R**obe**r**to es **d**e La Paz, **B**olivia, pero **v**i**v**e en Caracas.
7 Cuan**d**o no hay clases, **R**obe**r**to **v**a a La Paz.
8 **Bárb**ara es **v**enezolana; es **d**e Caracas.
9 Los **d**os alumnos estu**d**ian inglés en su escuela.
10 Es jueves y hace **b**astante calor.
11 En la clase **d**on**d**e estu**d**ian hay treinta y nueve pupit**r**es.
12 En la clase hay nueve **v**entanas y **d**os puertas.
13 La escuela es nueva y el **d**irecto**r** es un señor muy amable.
14 La escuela está en el centro **d**e la capital **d**e **V**enezuela.
15 **R**obe**r**to y **Bárb**ara son muy **b**uenos alumnos. Ha**b**lan inglés **b**astante **b**ien.

B Write each combination on separate paper and check the accuracy of each answer before proceeding to the next problem.

Example: 71 = Usted es boliviana.

1	Paco		1	bolivian-
2	Nosotros		2	argentin-
3	Ustedes (*m*)		3	chilen-
4	Yo	ser	4	uruguay-
5	Ellas		5	ecuatorian-
6	Tú (*m*)		6	venezolan-
7	Usted (*f*)		7	brasileñ-
			8	american-

1)	57	Ellas son brasileñas.
2)	62	Tú eres argentino.
3)	16	Paco es venezolano.
4)	28	Nosotros somos americanos.
5)	74	Usted es uruguaya.
6)	48	Yo soy americana(-o) (*Are you male or female?*)
7)	35	Ustedes son ecuatorianos.
8)	73	Usted es chilena.
9)	61	Tú eres boliviano.
10)	55	Ellas son ecuatorianas.

No new vocabulary. Are you devoting a few minutes per day to vocabulary study and review? You will need to have complete mastery of all the vocabulary listed at the end of these Assignments in order to be successful in the forthcoming major test.

Assignment 16

Regular i-*Verbs and Present of* ir

You already know that there are three morphemes in the present tense forms of Spanish verbs: the stem and two suffixes, and that the second suffix forms (*mos, n, s,* and "zero") are the same for all verbs. To learn the forms for a new verb set, you only have to learn the new stems and the morphemes of the first suffix. The first suffix of regular *i*-verbs has three morphemes in the present tense. They are *o, e,* and *i.*

1 The *o*-suffix of any verb in the present tense always goes with the subject pronoun _____. ▲

2 The infinitive *vivir* is translated by "to live." The stem is *viv*. How do you say "I live in Madrid"? ▲

yo

3 The *i*-suffix appears in only one form, the one that goes with *nosotros*. How do you say "We live in Madrid"? ▲

Yo vivo en Madrid.

(Nosotros) vivimos en Madrid.

4 All other forms are like *e*-verbs and have *e* for the first suffix. The form of *vivir* that goes with *tú* is _____. ▲

5 The form that goes with *él, ella,* and *usted* is _____. ▲

vives

6 The form that goes with *ustedes, ellos,* and *ellas* is _____. ▲

vive

7 You can now make up all the present tense forms of all the regular *i*-verbs in the Spanish language. You must, of course, learn the infinitive and its meaning. Here is an *i*-verb which is an obvious cognate: *admitir*. The stem is

viven

_____. ▲

admit (The Spanish stem is one form of the English verb.)

8 Copy and add the suffixes. Say the forms aloud in Spanish: *yo admit* _____, *nosotros admit* _____, *ustedes admit* _____. ▲

*yo admi**to**, nosotros admit**imos**, ustedes admit**en***

9 The *i*-verb which translates "to go" is very irregular in Spanish. The infinitive is *ir*. It has no stem. Hundreds of years ago, when the ancient Spaniards made up a stem for it, they confused Latin *ire* (to go) and *vadere* (to go quickly), so that today *ir* is treated as though the infinitive were *var* (the stem is *v*). The present tense forms of *ir* are like those of *estar*. The form that goes with *yo* is

_____. ▲

10 All other forms of *ir* are also said to be irregular because they take the same first suffix as *a*-verbs. The form that goes with *nosotros* is _____. ▲

voy

vamos (Like *estamos*.)

11 To make *vamos* agree with *tú* you replace *mos* with _____ and you get *tú* _____. ▲

12 The form that goes with *usted, él,* and *ella* is _____. ▲

s; vas

13 To get the form that goes with *ustedes, ellos,* and *ellas* you add _____ to *va*. ▲

va

14 It does not make much sense to learn to say "go" in Spanish unless you also learn more words for places to which people actually go. The words of this set will replace which word in the answer to the question *¿A dónde vas?* ▲

n (Ustedes van.)

dónde (This is the question word for place. "(To) where are you going ?")

15 One word that will replace *dónde* is *cine*, a shortened form of the cognate "cinema." Most people no longer say that they are going to the cinema. They say, instead, that they are going to the _____. ▲

16 In Assignment 1 you learned that *montaña* gave us the state name "Montana." The common noun English cognate of *montaña* is _____. ▲

movies

17 Translate: "I am going to the mountains" as the answer to *¿A dónde vas?* ▲

mountain

(Yo) voy a las montañas.

18 The cognate of *parque* is _____. ▲

19 Translate: *¿Vas tú al parque?* ▲

park (qu for [k])

Are you going to the park ? or Do you go to the park ?

20 The land area in between cities and towns is called *el campo* in Spanish. The English word for this area is _____. ▲

country (He lives in the country.)

21 Say the following words aloud:

ci-ne (The *c* stands for an [s] sound.)

*mon-**ta**-ña* (You say [ny] for *ñ*: [mon-ta-nya].)

***par**-que* (Flap the [r].)

*cam-**po*** (The [p] has no puff. Two English cognates are "camp" and "campus.")

22 A sandy place at the edge of an ocean, lake, or river is a *playa*. Translate "They are going to the beach" as the answer to *¿A dónde van ellos?* ▲

Van a la playa. (Now say it aloud.)

23 Spanish uses the same word for either "house" or "home"; it is *casa*. They know which is which from the context. Look at these sentences.

I'm going home.	*Voy a casa.*
I'm going to the house.	*Voy a la casa.*

Which word in the context tells you that *casa* has the meaning of "house"? ▲

la (Notice that there is no article before either "home" or *casa*.)

24 The form *voy* all by itself tells you the subject is _____. ▲

yo (So you actually say *yo voy* only when you want to be emphatic or to call special attention to what **you** are doing: *Tú vas a casa, pero* **yo** *voy al parque*.)

25 Which sentence describes what you do regularly or habitually? (a) I am going to the movies. (b) I go to the movies. ▲

I go to the movies. (You could add "regularly" or "very often.")

26 Which sentence is the most likely answer to "What are you doing tomorrow?" (a) I go to the movies tomorrow. (b) I'm going to the movies tomorrow. ▲

I'm going to the movies tomorrow. (This says what you are planning to do.)

27 You are riding a bus. Someone asks, "Where are you going?" Which sentence describes what you are actually in the process of doing? (a) I go to the movies. (b) I am going to the movies. ▲

I am going to the movies.

28 Does "I am going to the movies" have two different meanings in English? ▲

yes (If you missed this, reread Frames 26 and 27.)

29 Spanish is more economical in speech than English. *Voy al cine* is the standard translation for both meanings, "I am going to the movies" and "I go to the movies." Must the Spanish speaker pay more attention to context to get the right meaning every time? ▲

30 You have been practicing reading aloud so you can learn to say new words that you have never heard before. Practice saying the following and begin to learn their meanings:

yes

café (*cafe, restaurant*)	banco (*bank*)
centro (*center, downtown*)	iglesia (*church*)
correo (*post office*)	tienda (*store*)

You already know that the Latin's sense of human dignity does not normally allow him to use words for animal sounds to describe human speech. This same sense of dignity has prevented the development of certain figures of speech which are common in English. As a result, Spanish has no literal equivalents of *buckteeth, frog-voiced, weasle-eyed, bull-necked, bullheaded,* or *dog-tired. Buckteeth* comes out as *dientes salientes* (projecting teeth); *bullheaded* is *obstinado,* and *dog-tired* is *cansadísimo.* What English considers as picturesque speech, Spanish sometimes treats as undignified.

On Using AM and PM, and Learning How to Reason Linguistically

Everyone who has learned one language can also learn another but there is not enough time in any course to learn another language in the way you learned English, just by imitation. You have to be shown short-cuts, and you have to learn to think logically about what you are learning. Experts who are trained to reason linguistically can learn to speak and read a new language in a few months. From now on some Assignments will have a section which will teach you some of the expert's learning tricks.

1 One "trick" is that the meaning or form of one word often tells you something about the meaning or form of another. For example, when the number *dos* stands before a common noun, that noun will end with the _____ suffix. ▲

plural (*s* or *es*)

2 The meaning and form of a word may tell you what something unknown is. The following sentence begins with an abbreviation for a "subject" pronoun: *Vds. son alumnos. Vds.* stands for the full form _____. ▲

ustedes (There is only one subject pronoun that has a *d* in it and ends in the plural *s* that matches *son.*)

3 The abbreviations *Sra.* and *Srta.* stand for the titles of address _____. ▲

4 What is a difference, in writing, between *señora-Sra.* and *señorita-Srta.?* ▲ *señora; señorita*

The abbreviations are capitalized; the long forms are not.

5 The English abbreviations AM and PM are the first letters for the Latin words *ante meridiem* and *post meridiem.* If *ante* means "before" and *post* means "after," then *meridiem* must stand for (a) an interval of time (b) a point in time. ▲

a point in time

6 *Meridiem* came from an earlier Latin combination of an adjective, *medius,* and a noun, *dies.* As Latin became Spanish *medius dies* changed to *mediodía.* The second part of this compound word is the modern Spanish word for

_____. ▲

day (The English translation of *meridiem* and *mediodía* is "noon.")

7 Since there are 24 hours in a day and only 12 numbers on the clock, we need AM and PM because each number stands for two points in the day. "Tomorrow at ten o'clock" can stand for either 10 AM or 10 PM, that is, 10 *before* noon (*ante meridiem*) or 10 *after* noon (*post meridiem*). What part of the day does 10 *after noon* fall in? (a) morning (b) afternoon (c) night ▲

8 The AM hours stop at 12 o'clock noon. When do the PM hours stop? ▲

> night
> at 12 o'clock midnight

9 Now let's see how your linguistic reasoning is getting on. The Spanish cognate of *mid*, as in "mid-night," appears in *mediodía*—"mid-day" or "noon." It is the adjective _____. ▲

10 If "mid-day" in Spanish is *mediodía*, then it is logical that "mid-night" should be _____. ▲

> *medio*

> Did your logic fail you ? Did you remember that *el día* takes *medio* but *la noche* takes *media*? Copy, if you made a mistake: *el mediodía, la medianoche.*

11 Spanish speakers do not use AM and PM when they tell time. They say, rather, that each hour point belongs to <u>two</u> of the <u>three</u> parts of the day (*mañana, tarde, noche*). When the Spanish speaker says, *Son las dos de la tarde* he means (a) it is 2 AM (b) It is 2 PM. ▲

12 In the Spanish speaker's way of organizing the world, the hour point labeled "2" belongs also to another part of the day. When he says "2 AM." this hour point belongs to (a) *la tarde* (b) *la noche* (c) *la mañana.* ▲

> It is 2 PM.

> *la mañana* (2 AM is "2 in the morning": *las dos de la mañana.*)

13 All AM numbers in English fall in the morning and become *mañana* numbers in Spanish. The Spanish speaker says *Son las dos de la mañana* and *Son las once de la mañana.* Now watch your logic. All AM numbers become *mañana* numbers. Will all PM numbers become *tarde* numbers? ▲

> no (PM numbers become either *tarde* or *noche* numbers.)

14 11 PM is a _____ number. ▲

> *noche* (*Son las once de la noche.*)

15 3 PM is a _____ number. ▲

> *tarde* (*Son las tres de la tarde.*)

16 When a Spanish speaker tells time, does *noche* stand for the entire dark part of the day? ▲

> no (Only for the interval between sunset and midnight.)

17 You are now reaching a point in your learning of Spanish where it is impossible to tell you everything which would make learning easier for you. Your instructor does not have enough class time for this and to put everything in your textbooks would require hundreds more pages. As a result, you have to learn some things all by yourself. There may be some things that you might have learned in this Assignment that you did not. Memory experts know that we remember new words better if we tie them to something we already know very well. Say *tarde* aloud. Does it remind you of a word that is used when a child is late for class? The word is _____. ▲

> tardy (*Mañana* is the early part of the day; *tarde* is the late part of the day.)

18 *Tarde* and "tardy" both come from the same Latin word. They are called _____. ▲

> cognates (You recognize them by matching spelling, not by pronunciation.)

19 The number of cognates that you can discover as memory helpers depends, of course, on how many English words you already know. Wild animals that sleep during the day and prowl at night are called "nocturnal" animals. The Spanish cognate of "nocturnal" is _____. ▲

20 Here is something else you could have noticed in this Assignment. In the two sentences, *Son **de** Venezuela* and *Son las diez **de** la noche*, does *de* have the same meaning in both sentences? ▲

noche

no (*Venezuela* and *noche* are not members of the same set. *De* is a relator which describes the relationship between people and places in *Son de Venezuela.* The same relationship cannot exist between *horas* and *noche.*)

21 Look at the translation of *de* in these sentences: (1) Las muchachas son *de* Lima. (from) (2) Son las diez *de* la noche. (at) (3) Son las diez *de* la mañana. (in) Is it logical to suppose that *de* means "from," "at," and "in" to Spanish speakers? ▲

no (We should say that there are several English translations of *de.*)

22   To the Spanish speaker the *de* in *Es la una de la tarde* has the same meaning as the *de* in *Es el director de la escuela.* If English were exactly like Spanish, both would be translated by the relator _____. ▲

23 The only translation of "Pilar's house" is *la casa de Pilar.* Does *de* here have the meaning of "belonging to"? ▲

of

24 So the Spanish speaker says there is an *una* that belongs to the *tarde* (*Es la una de la tarde.*) and another *una* that belongs to (a) *la noche* (b) *la mañana.* ▲

yes

25 You translate an AM number by *de la mañana.* You translate PM in two ways. Before sunset you use *de la* _____. ▲

la mañana

26 After dark you use _____. ▲

tarde

27 You have now observed that there is a great difference between meaning and translation. Let's think about this some more. The common translation of *días* is "days." The common translation of *bueno* is "good." The greeting *Buenos días* is not translated as "Good days," but as _____. ▲

de la noche

Good morning. (The greeting *Buenos días* means something like "may all your days be good.")

28 When we translate from one language to another, we do not translate the individual words, we find equivalent meanings. *Yo me llamo Juan Saucedo* means in Spanish "I call myself Juan Saucedo." The common English equivalent is _____. ▲

My name is Juan Saucedo.

29 Here is a nice example of translating meaning, not words. We say in English, "You can't have your cake and eat it too." The best Spanish translation of this says, "You can't walk in the parade and ring the bell in the church steeple." The Russians say, "You can't take a bath and have a dry skin."

   All of these say the same thing with very different words. Do you really know what they mean? Think about this for a while, then look at the answer. ▲

They all mean that there are some actions which one person cannot perform at the same time. They also mean that the person who tries to do this really wants the impossible.

Summary

Regular *i*-Verbs and Present of *ir*

1 The first suffix morphemes for the *i*-verb are *o* for the *yo* form, *i* for the *nosotros* form, and *e* (like the *e*-set) for all other forms.
2 The second suffix forms are the same for all verbs in the present.
3 The irregular verb *ir* has the stem *v*.
4 The present tense forms of *ir* are like those of *estar* (*voy, vamos, vas, va, van*).

AM and PM, and Reasoning Linguistically

1 Below are two clocks. One represents the dark half of the day; one the light half.

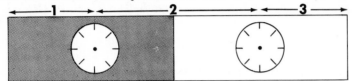

The names for the intervals marked 1, 2, and 3 are *noche, mañana,* and *tarde.*
Spanish says: *Es la una de la mañana.* (2)
                    Es la una de la tarde. (3)
                    Son las once de la mañana. (2)
                    Son las once de la noche. (1)
2 Translation from one language to another means finding equivalent meanings.

Self-Correcting Exercises

A Prepare for the first major test by reviewing the vocabulary presented in the first 15 Assignments.
B Assignments 1 through 15 in the Workbook provide additional practice in preparation for the test.

New Vocabulary

These words will not be included on the major test.

casa	house, home	**montañas**	mountains
cine (el)	movie (theater)	**campo**	country
café (el)	restaurant, cafe (coffee)	**lugar**	place
tienda	store	**hora**	hour, time (of day)
iglesia	church	**cuarto**	quarter
banco	bank	**media, -o**	half
correo	post office	**escribir**	to write
centro	downtown, center	**vivir**	to live
parque (el)	park	**ir**	to go
playa	beach	**al (a + el)**	to the

When the people of two different cultures first come into contact with each other, what each group usually notices first are the differences in customs and attitudes. It frequently happens that a custom which is so common in one culture that it is hardly noticed is considered to be rude, ugly, obscene, or immoral in the other. When a member of the other culture observes this custom he frequently suffers what sociologists and anthropologists call *cultural shock*. You believe, for example, that drinking milk is wholesome and proper. In contrast, for the people of one African tribe this is something filthy because they put cow's milk in the same category as urine. Similarly, most American males think nothing of showing a bit of bare leg between the top of their sock and the bottom of their trousers when they sit down and cross their legs. This is obscene in Indonesia. In the same way, many American business men do not hesitate to sit down on the edge of somebody else's desk. This is considered rude in Latin America. Kissing is a common way for couples in America to show affection. This custom shocks most Japanese and is frowned on in the Hispanic world when done in public.

The culturally sophisticated person quickly recovers from these shocks and rapidly learns to accept the behavior of the natives of each culture in terms of their own standards. At the same time such a person also learns not to do those things which seem natural to him, but shock the other people, when he is in their country as a guest. This is the meaning of the old saying, "When in Rome, do as the Romans do."

Assignment 17
Getting Ready for a Test

A test is not just a means of providing your instructor with a grade. In a programed course of study, tests are designed primarily to help the teacher find out how to make learning less confusing to you. Every major exam in this course actually tests you, your instructor, and the course program. In other words, a test shows (1) how much *you* have learned *by your own efforts*, (2) how well you *are being taught* in the class, and (3) *the efficiency* of the course materials. Since tests are designed to discover what needs to be changed (your study habits, classroom procedures, or the course materials), the test results will be useless if you make mechanical errors, if you fail to understand what you are to do, or if you do not prepare yourself properly for the test.

Do this Assignment carefully. Be sure you do *not* look at the answers *before* you have tried to think of them. If you make a mistake, study the frame carefully.

The test consists of nine sections marked A through I. Here is a preview of *every* type of problem you will find on the test.

1 **Part A** (10 points): On your answer sheet you will find a column of spaces numbered 1 to 10. For each number you will hear a statement in Spanish. For example: *Los gauchos son de Argentina.* You will then be asked a question in English. "Where are gauchos from?" Write your answer, *in English*, in three words or less. You write ———. ▲

> Either "from Argentina" or "Argentina" is correct.

2 Here is another example: *Ayer fue lunes.* What day is today? (You answer with the day after *lunes.*) ▲

3 Part B, *Listening Comprehension, Multiple Choice* (10 points): There are 10 numbers each followed by the letters a, b, and c. These letters will also be on the board. You will hear a statement or a question and then, as the instructor points to the letters, you will hear three possible reactions. You wait until you have heard the entire problem twice and, then, draw a circle around the letter for the best or most logical answer or rejoinder. For example:

> Tuesday

Question: ¿De dónde son los elefantes?
Answers: a   Son de la escuela.
     b   Son de Alaska.
     c   Son de África.

You circle ———. ▲

4 Here is an example of the rejoinder type:

> c

Statement: Deseo hablar con el profesor.
Rejoinders: a   Él trabaja mucho en la oficina.
      b   Hay veinte estudiantes en la clase.
      c   Él no está en la oficina ahora.

You circle ———. ▲

5 Part C, *Listening Comprehension, Numerical Equations* (15 points): There are 5 blank spaces. You will hear an equation twice: *Veinte menos siete son trece.* You write out the whole equation using Arabic numbers and mathematical signs: ———. ▲

> c

> $20 - 7 = 13$ (For addition, the equivalent of plus (+) is *y.*)

6 Part D (10 points) deals with adjective and noun agreement. You will see 10 English sentences and their partial Spanish equivalents. You are to complete the Spanish translation by writing the missing form of the adjective. Examples: She is Venezuelan. *Ella es* ———. ▲

7 You are a very good instructor. *Usted es un profesor muy* ———. ▲

> *venezolana*

> *bueno* (The *o*-form is for males; the *a*-form for females.)

8 American pens are not bad. *Las plumas americanas no son* ———. ▲

> *malas* (In addition to number (singular-plural) agreement, *a*-nouns match the *a*-form of the adjective.)

9 The pencils are very bad. *Los lápices son muy* ———. ▲

> *malos* (The *o*-form of the adjective matches an *o*-noun.)

10 Part E (12 points) deals with the present indicative forms of regular *a*-verbs, *ser,* and *estar.* There are 12 items. You will see a model sentence followed by a new subject: *María **está** en la clase. Los estudiantes* . . . . You write the form of the indicated verb that matches the new subject: ———. ▲

> *están*

11 ¿De dónde **es** usted? . . . ustedes ▲

12 ¿**Trabajan** ellos aquí? . . . tú . . . ▲   *son*

13 Part F (12 points) tests your ability to spot the cues which tell you when to   *Trabajas*
use *ser*, *estar*, and *haber* (*hay*). There are 12 English sentences and you will decide
whether *hay*, *es*, or *está* would be used if the indicated verb were translated to
Spanish. Examples: There **are** 30 students in the class. ▲

14 Where **are** you (polite) from? ▲   *hay*

15 The elephant **is** in the zoo. ▲   *es*

16 Part G (12 points) tests whether you can recognize the written cues which   *está*
tell you when to say [r], [rr], and the proper allophones of /d/ and /b/. It will
be done as follows:

Circle the *r*'s that stand for the single flap [r] and underline those that stand
for the multiple flap [rr] in:

L a   s e ñ o r i t a   R o m e r o   e s   m i   p r o f e s o r a

d e   r u s o. ▲

L a   s e ñ o(r)i t a   R o m e(r)o   e s   m i

p(r)o f e s o(r)a   d e   r u s o.

17 Circle the *b*'s and *v*'s that stand for a stop; underline them if fricative:

V í c t o r   y   R o b e r t o   t r a b a j a n   e n   u n

b a n c o   t a m b i é n   y   v a n   a   l a   o f i c i n a

l o s   v i e r n e s. ▲

(V)í c t o r   y   R o b e r t o   t r a b a j a n   e n   u n

(b)a n c o   t a m(b)i é n   y   v a n   a   l a   o f i c i n a

l o s   v i e r n e s.

18 Circle the *d*'s that represent stops; underline the fricatives. Assume that the
sentence is read without pauses between words:

D a v i d   v a   a   e s t u d i a r   c o n   D a n i e l   e l

s á b a d o   y   e l   d o m i n g o. ▲

(D)a v i d   v a   a   e s t u d i a r   c o n   (D)a n i e l

e l   s á b a d o   y   e l   (d)o m i n g o.

19 Part H (9 points) deals with vocabulary. You will match 9 Spanish words
with their English equivalents, as follows:

1	ventana ( )	a *needs*
2	trece ( )	b *window*
3	necesita ( )	c *thirteen*
		d *three* ▲

1 ventana (b), 2 trece (c), 3 necesita (a)

20 Part I (10 points) tests your ability to read for meaning in 10 multiple choice items. On your answer sheet you will circle the letter corresponding to the most logical completion of each sentence, or reaction to each question or statement. Examples:

En la clase de español hay . . .

  a treinta tigres.

  b muchas montañas.

  c veinticinco alumnos.

  d dos países. ▲

21 ¿Necesita usted un lápiz?   ⓒ

  a Sí, soy de La Paz.

  b Sí, tengo que comer.

  c No, hablo español.

  d Sí, por favor. ▲

22 Tengo que ir a la oficina. ¡Adiós!   ⓓ

  a Buenos días, ¿qué tal?

  b ¿Cómo estás, Luisa?

  c Hasta luego, Tomás.

  d Muchas gracias, profesora. ▲

          ⓒ

Self-Correcting Exercises

A Ask and answer these questions aloud. *Sí* and *no* between parentheses tell you whether to give negative or affirmative answers. Cover the answers and check your response before going to the next question.

1	¿Vas al campo hoy? (no)	No, no voy al campo.
2	¿Va Vd. a la playa mañana? (no)	No, no voy a la playa mañana.
3	¿Van Vds. al cine esta noche? (sí)	Sí, vamos al cine esta noche.
4	¿Voy yo a casa? (sí)	Sí, Vd. va a casa.
5	¿Vamos Paco y yo al parque? (no)	No, Vds. no van al parque.
6	¿Vas a las montañas? (no)	No, no voy a las montañas.

B The Assignments (summaries and exercises) and the *Workbook* (Choose from the first 15 Optional assignments) will provide additional review and practice before the test, if needed.

C As you review vocabulary, check yourself on the proper matching of nouns and articles. Now that you have had a large enough number of words this expanded rule will be helpful: most nouns ending in *n, o, r, s, e, l* (the nonsense word *norsel*), and those labeling males combine with *el* and *un*; most nouns ending in *a, d,* the suffixes *ción* (*sión, xión, tión*), *sis, itis,* and those labeling females combine with *la* and *una.* The exceptions to this rule must be memorized.

Indicate by letter which nouns in each group combine with *el, un,* and *o*-adjectives.

1 (a) papel (b) calor (c) verdad (d) inglés	a, b, d
2 (a) perdón (b) universidad (c) puerta (d) mujer	a
3 (a) hombre (b) ciudad (c) semana (d) pupitre	a, d
4 (a) jardín (b) jueves (c) parque (d) animal	a, b, c, d
5 (a) favor (b) hotel (c) directora (d) profesor	a, b, d
6 (a) bus (b) cuestión (c) crisis (d) corral	a, d

Here are the nouns you have had so far that have to be memorized as exceptions: *el día, el reloj, el lápiz; la tarde, la noche, la clase, la luz,* and *la capital.*

D Devote special attention to the words in your vocabulary list that you have marked as troublesome.

ETAPA DOS

Performance Objectives
for Assignments 18–35/36

You will be prepared to continue your study of Spanish successfully if by Assignment 35/36 you have achieved all previous and the following objectives:

Listening Comprehension

1 For an oral statement or question followed by four possible responses, all based on vocabulary up to Assignment 35/36, you select the most logical response at least nine times out of twelve.

You hear the following and choose *c* as the response:

Hay siete días en la semana.
a Y hay veinticuatro horas en el mes.
b Y hay diecinueve días en el mes.
c Y hay doce meses en el año.
d Y hay cien horas en dos semanas.

Reading Comprehension

2 Given a written sentence fragment, statement or question and four possible completions or responses containing vocabulary through Assignment 35/36, you select the most logical response or completion at least nine times out of twelve.

You see the following and select *b* as the answer:

Aquí en Estados Unidos el Día de Gracias es . . .
a el primer día del año.
b el tercer jueves de noviembre.
c el primero de abril.
d el segundo lunes de mayo.

Writing and Spelling

3 (Evaluated following Assignment 23) You write from dictation with correct spelling at least 23 out of 27 words containing any of the spelling problems practiced through Assignment 23.

You hear and write: *El alumno no es argentino.*

Morphology and Usage

4 (Evaluated following Assignment 29) Cued in English by orally described situations which contain a form of "to be", you correctly select *ser* or *estar* as the appropriate translation at least eight times out of ten.

You hear: The redwood trees that grow in California **are** tall.
You write: *ser.*

5 (Evaluated following Assignment 29) Cued by written situations in Spanish, you correctly choose between the two conjugated forms of *ser* or *estar* given in parentheses.

You see: *Mi hermano . . . en Buenos Aires esta semana. (está, es)*
You write: *está.*

6 Twenty model sentences are presented orally followed by the cue for a new subject. You write the present tense form of the verb in the model sentence that matches the new subject with no more than four errors.

You hear: *Ellos tienen bastante dinero. Yo . . .*   You write: *tengo.*

7 Given sentences with a blank preceding the done-to (direct object), you write or omit *a* according to the requirements of the language with no more than one error out of six.

You see: *Vamos a invitar . . . la señorita López.*   You write: *a.*

8 You choose correctly between the form of *ir* or *venir* given in parentheses as the appropriate verb for each situation in at least five sentences out of seven.

You see: *¿Quieres (ir, venir) aquí a leerme esto?*   You choose: *venir.*

9 Cued by Arabic numerals plus A.M. or P.M., you write a complete sentence in Spanish that tells what time it is with no more than two errors out of eight.

You see: 4:30 P.M.   You write: *Son las cuatro y media de la tarde.*

10 A sentence is given with a slot left blank for a possessive adjective. You write the correct form that matches the subject as possessor with no more than three errors out of ten.

You see: *Yo tengo que estudiar con . . . hermanas esta noche.*   You write: *mis.*

11 Given eight pairs of sequential statements in which the second sentence of each pair contains a redundant direct-object (done-to) noun, you rewrite the second sentence, omitting the redundant noun, and making any other necessary changes with no more than two errors out of eight.

You see: *Aquí tienes las plumas. Pongo las plumas allí.*
You write: *Las pongo allí.*

12 A written sentence containing a subject and predicate adjective is followed by a similar sentence in which a new subject cues a change in the adjectival form. You write the appropriate matching adjectival form with no more than one error out of five.

You see: *Los niños están cansados. Ella está . . .*
You write: *cansada.*

13 In at least eight out of ten written sentences where you are required to fill in the verb, you correctly choose the proper equivalent of "to be" (*hay, es, está, tiene,* or *hace*).

You see: *Ella siempre . . . mucho cuidado cuando . . . con los niños.*
You write: *tiene* and *está.*

Assignment 18

Adjectives of Nationality

1　Men from Argentina are called, in Spanish, _____. ▲

argentinos (No capital letter for adjectives of nationality.)

2　*Los hombres de Chile se llaman chilenos.* The noun *hombres* means _____. ▲

men (Men from Chile call themselves *chilenos*.)

3　All of the adjectives of nationality you have learned so far have two forms. When they describe a male, they end in the phoneme / /; when they describe a female, they end in / /. ▲

/o/ for males; /a/ for females

4　To change *Bolivia*, *Colombia*, and *Chile* into adjectives you use a small letter and add the suffix _____. ▲

5　Copy these three adjective forms: *boliviano, colombiano, chileno.*

no or *na*

6　To convert *Paraguay* and *Uruguay* to adjectives, you add either _____. ▲

7　Change *Perú* into an adjective describing a girl. ▲

o or *a*

peruana (Small letter, no accent mark, and the suffix *ana*.)

8　Change *Brasil* into an adjective describing males. ▲

brasileños (Did you remember the tilde over the *n*?)

9　The *a*-form of one adjective of nationality is spelled almost exactly like the name of the country. This adjective is _____. ▲

argentina (It is not exactly like *Argentina* because it does not begin with a

10　You know two adjectives of nationality whose stem is not spelled exactly like the name of the country. To write the adjective for *Ecuador*, you must change *d* to _____. ▲

capital letter.)

11　Write the *o*-form. ▲

t

12　When you write the adjective for Venezuela, you must change *ue* to _____. ▲

ecuatoriano

13　Write the plural *o*-form. ▲

o

14　Let's learn something about these Spanish spelling changes and the difference between English and Spanish spelling habits. These words are divided into syllables with the stressed syllable indicated: *Ve-ne-zue-la, ve-ne-zo-la-nos.* When Latin *o* was stressed it sometimes changed to _____ in Spanish. ▲

venezolanos

ue (So many related Spanish words have two different spellings.)

Weather

1　When the Spanish speaker describes the weather, as in "It is hot, cold," *etc.*, he uses the verb _____. ▲

2　To describe present weather he uses only one form. It is _____. ▲

hacer

3　The translation of *Hace calor* is "It is hot." *Hace* does not mean "It is" to a Spanish speaker. It means "makes." Both "to make" and *hacer* cannot stand

hace

by themselves. When you make, you must make something. This something
is the object of the verb (the done-to) and the word for it is always a noun.
The Spanish noun which is a cognate of "fresh" is _____. ▲

fresco (Hace fresco.)

4 The Spanish noun which is a cognate of "frigid" is _____. ▲
5 A house that is well "ventilated" has lots of air moving through it. The stem   *frío (Hace frío.)*
vent is like the Spanish cognate _____. ▲

viento (Hace viento.)

6 The Spanish word for "weather" is _____. ▲

tiempo (Our English cognate "tempest" does not mean "weather" but a
7 There are two other forms of *bueno*. They are *buena* and _____. ▲   storm.)
buen (This is the form used directly in front of any noun that also takes *un*.
Uno becomes *un*; *bueno* becomes *buen*.)

8 Translate: It is nice weather. ▲
9 *Bueno* becomes *buen* and *malo* becomes _____. Translate: The weather is   *Hace buen tiempo.*
bad. ▲

mal; Hace mal tiempo.

10 The word that comes after *hace* in all these examples is always a noun: *calor,
viento, tiempo*, etc. The English noun for *calor* is not "hot," but _____. ▲

heat (So *Hace calor* means "Makes heat." The translation is "It is hot.")
11 In English we say "It is very hot, very cold, very windy" because "hot,"
"cold," and "windy" are used as adjectives. The Spanish speaker cannot use
muy in his translation of these weather expressions because *muy* is an adverb
and cannot combine with a noun (*calor, viento, frío*, etc.). He cannot say,
"Makes very heat," he must say, *Hace* _____ *calor*. ▲

Hace mucho calor. (Makes much heat.)
12 What you say in English does not tell you very much about what words and
forms you will use to give the same meaning in Spanish. Will you ever learn to
understand Spanish like a native speaker if you really believe that *Hace mucho
viento* means "It is very windy"? ▲

no (Because, to a Spanish speaker, it means "Makes much wind.")

Adverbs and Adjectives

1 Many words in both English and Spanish have multiple functions. Thus in
"a slow train" the word "slow" is an adjective, but in "go slow" it is an adverb.
The following words may be used either as adjectives or adverbs: *mucho, poco,
mal, demasiado, bastante*. In this and the next frames, give the Spanish and, then,
the English translation. "Makes much wind." ▲

Hace mucho viento. It's very windy.

2 Makes enough wind. ▲

Hace bastante viento. It's quite windy.

3 Makes too much wind. ▲

Hace demasiado viento. It's too windy.

4 Makes little wind. ▲

Hace poco viento. It's not very windy.

5 In this and the next four frames, translate the adverb. *Habla* _____ (too much). *Come* _____ (enough). ▲

Habla demasiado. Come bastante.

6 *Lee* _____ (badly). *Trabaja* _____ (a lot). ▲

Lee mal. Trabaja mucho.

7 *Estudia* _____ (very little). ▲

8 The adjective *bueno* has a companion form which is used only as an adverb.   *Estudia muy poco.*
It is _____. ▲

9 What form is used in *Hace* _____ *tiempo* (good); in *Miguel trabaja* _____   *bien*
(well)? ▲

Hace buen tiempo; Miguel trabaja bien.

Reasoning Linguistically

1 The adjective *todo* is like *bueno* and has four forms. They are _____. ▲

todo, todos, toda, todas

2 These four forms have two meanings and two English translations: "all" and "every." When you say, "All the boys are here" or "Every boy is here," you are talking about several boys. The Spanish for "the boys" is _____. ▲

3 If we say "All the boys are here" we say _____ *están aquí.* ▲   *los muchachos*

Todos los muchachos *están aquí.*

4 Another translation for *Todos los muchachos están aquí* is _____. ▲

Every boy is here. (Spanish has no word for "every.")

5 How do you say "All the girls are here" or "Every girl is here"? ▲

Todas las muchachas están aquí.

6 Compare: "I am here every week" and "I am here all week." The sentence that talks about more than one week is "I am here _____ week. ▲

7 Fill in the missing word: *Estoy aquí* _____ *las semanas.* ▲   every

8 The translation of "I am here all week" is *Estoy aquí* _____ *la semana.* ▲   *todas*

9 Now, how will we say in Spanish "every day" and "all day"? ▲   *toda*

todos los días; todo el día

10 "World" in Spanish is *mundo.* Complete the phrase that means "all the world" and is translated as "everyone" or "everybody." _____ *mundo.* ▲

todo el mundo

Positive and Negative Sentences

Many words mean much more when you know their opposites. In this section you will study several pairs of antonyms, the most common Spanish negative words and their positive opposites, and how they are used. Several frames also will test your linguistic logic.

1 The English opposite of "no" is "yes." The Spanish opposite of *no* is *sí.* You know what these paired words mean. Now let's see how they are used. The negative of "I have some money" is "I have no money." Do *some* and *no* both modify *money*?   ▲

> yes (Both *some* and *no* are adjectives in English.)

2   These two sentences translate each other: "I speak no Spanish." *Yo no hablo español*. In English the "no" modifies the noun "Spanish." In Spanish the *no* modifies the _____.   ▲

3   An important difference between English and Spanish is that English "no" modifies (negates) nouns. Spanish *no* negates _____.   ▲

> verb *hablo*

> verbs (Spanish *no* does not combine with nouns.)

4   Another English way of saying "I speak no Spanish" is: "I do not (don't) speak Spanish." There is only one common Spanish translation for either "I speak no Spanish" or "I do not speak Spanish." It is: *Yo no hablo español*. Does Spanish have an equivalent of "do not"?   ▲

5   Now look at these sentences and their translations:

> no

He speaks Spanish.	*Él habla español.*
Does he speak Spanish?	*¿Habla él español?*
He does not speak Spanish.	*Él no habla español.*

English uses the helping verb "do" in questions and negative statements. Spanish has no helping verb like "do." To make a question, Spanish puts the subject _____ the verb.   ▲

> after (And changes to the question intonation.)

6   To make a negative statement, Spanish puts *no* _____ the verb.   ▲

> before (between the subject and the verb)

7   Do you remember the difference between meaning and translation? Make a literal translation of *Él no habla español* to show its real meaning.   ▲

> He no speaks Spanish. (This is closer to "He speaks no Spanish" than to "He does not speak Spanish.")

8   Have you ever observed something peculiar about the spelling of most negative words? Notice: *negate, negative, never, no, none, not, nothing, nobody*. What do they have in common?   ▲

9   Do these two sentences say the same thing? (1) He never speaks Spanish (2) He does not ever speak Spanish.   ▲

> All begin with *n*.

> yes (Now you have discovered that *never* is a contraction of an old negative prefix (*ne* + *ever*) which becomes *not ever* in modern English.)

10   The opposite of "He *never* speaks Spanish" is "He *always* speaks Spanish." The equivalents in Spanish are: *Él nunca habla español; Él siempre habla español*. Which word translates "always"?   ▲

11   The opposite of *siempre* is _____.   ▲

> *siempre*

> *nunca* (Notice it begins with an *n* also.)

12   Translate: "Pablo reads no Spanish" and "Pablo does not read Spanish." There is only <u>one</u> translation for <u>both</u> sentences.   ▲

> *Pablo no lee español.*

13   Rewrite this sentence with the Spanish for "never."   ▲

> *Pablo nunca lee español.*

14   The opposite of "nothing" is "something." Compare: *No hay nada en la mesa; Hay algo en la mesa*. Which word translates "nothing"?   ▲

> *nada*

15 The translation of *algo* is _____. ▲

16 Compare: *No hay nadie en la oficina; Hay alguien en la oficina.* Which word translates "somebody"? ▲

17 The translation of *nadie* is _____. ▲

something

alguien

nobody (Have you noticed that *nadie* and *nada* begin with an *n*?)

18 You will remember these four new words much better if you say them aloud and write them. Do this: nothing—*nada*; nobody—*nadie*; something—*algo*; somebody—*alguien*. (Say *gu* as [g].)

19 Standard English permits two negative words in a sentence only when they cancel each other and produce a positive. "That is *not im*possible" means "That is possible. Spanish uses the <u>double negative</u> in the same way. *Eso no es imposible* means *Eso es posible.* But Spanish also uses <u>two negative words</u> where standard English permits only one. Translate this sentence word for word: *Pedro nunca lee nada.* ▲

Pedro never reads nothing.

20 In standard English "nothing" is replaced by _____. ▲

anything (Pedro never reads anything.)

21 Write the *meaning* of *Pedro no lee nada.* Then put it into standard English. ▲

Pedro no reads nothing. Pedro does not read anything.

22 When "anything" combines with a negative in English, its Spanish translation is _____. ▲

23 What can you generalize from this? The Spanish equivalent of "anybody" in "I do *not* see *anybody*" is _____. ▲

24 To translate "There isn't anybody in the office," you will use *No hay* _____ *en la oficina.* ▲

25 "Somebody is talking" becomes *Alguien habla* in Spanish. There are two possible opposites. One is like English: *Nadie habla.* The other is like non-standard English: _____. ▲

nada

nadie

nadie

26 Look at these pairs:

No habla nadie.

Pedro *nunca* habla.	Pedro *no* habla *nunca*.
Nadie habla.	*No* habla *nadie*.
Nada hay en la mesa.	*No* hay *nada* en la mesa.

When a negative word <u>follows</u> the verb in Spanish, you must put _____ in front of the verb. ▲

Copy these sentences and make them negative.

no

27 Ella va al banco. Ellos siempre comen algo. ▲

Ella no va al banco. Ellos nunca comen nada.

28 Tengo algo bueno. Aquí vive alguien. ▲

No tengo nada bueno. Aquí no vive nadie.

In most American buildings the first floor is the ground or street floor. In contrast, the *primer piso* (first floor) in Hispanic buildings is regularly the equivalent of the American second floor. The ground floor is the *piso bajo* (low floor), and the top floor is the *piso alto* (high floor).

Summary

Adjectives of Nationality

1 The stems of the adjectives of nationality of the countries of South America are *argentin-*, *chilen-*, *peruan-*, *bolivian-*, *colombian-*, *paraguay-*, *uruguay-*, *brasileñ-*, *ecuatorian-*, and *venezolan-*.

2 When describing a male, *o* is added; when describing a female, *a* is added.

3 The plural suffix is *s*.

4 In some Spanish words stressed Latin *o* changes to *ue*.

Weather

1 Spanish uses *hacer* to talk about the weather.

2 The weather nouns *calor*, *frío*, *fresco*, *viento*, *tiempo* are modified by adjectives.

Adverbs and Adjectives

1 The words *mucho*, *poco*, *mal*, *demasiado*, and *bastante* may be used either as adjectives or adverbs.

Positive and Negative Sentences

1 English "no" negates nouns; Spanish *no* negates verbs.

2 Spanish has no helping verb equivalent of "do."

3 In a question the subject usually follows the verb.

4 In a negative statement *no* or another negative word (*nunca*, *nada*, *nadie*) precedes the verb.

5 Spanish allows *two* negative words in sentences where standard English permits only one.

Self-Correcting Exercises

A   Cover the answers and check yourself as you proceed. In this guided conversation you assume the role of all the individuals involved and say aloud all the questions and responses.

Paco, pregúntale a Lola si come bien.	Lola, ¿comes bien?
Lola, contéstale.	Sí, como bastante bien.
Pregúntame a mí si como mucho.	¿Come usted mucho?
(Como bastante, pero no demasiado.)	
Pregúntale al señor si habla inglés.	Señor, ¿habla usted inglés?
Contéstale que no, que tú no hablas inglés.	No, no hablo inglés.
Pregúntanos a Paco y a mí si escribimos bien.	¿Escriben ustedes bien?
Paco, contéstale que sí, que tú y yo escribimos bien.	Sí, escribimos bien.

B　Read this selection aloud to yourself three times. Make an effort to pronounce accurately and to understand what you read.

Pancho, el boliviano

Me llamo Francisco Ramírez Velasco, pero (*but*) en el pueblo donde vivo me llaman Pancho.

Soy boliviano. Vivo en un lugar muy frío en las montañas de los Andes. En mi pueblo hay muchas minas. Bolivia es un país muy rico (*rich*) en productos minerales. Yo trabajo en una mina toda la semana de lunes a sábado. Soy minero.

Yo no voy a la escuela durante el día con los otros muchachos del pueblo. Yo voy a una clase especial de siete a diez de la noche. En la clase estudiamos español, historia y matemáticas. La profesora es una señora muy amable. Ella es de la capital, pero ahora (*now*) ella vive aquí en el pueblo con nosotros. Hay más de veinte estudiantes en el programa nocturno. Todos son mineros y trabajan en las minas muchas horas durante el día.

Yo vivo con mis padres (*parents*) en una casa de adobe con un jardín muy bonito. En el corral hay muchos animales. Mi papá es boliviano, pero mi mamá es peruana. Ella trabaja mucho en la casa todos los días. Mi padre y yo trabajamos mucho en la mina. Siempre llegamos a casa a las seis y media de la tarde con mucho apetito. Papá come bastante. Yo como mucho también. El trabajo en las minas es demasiado fuerte (*hard*).

New Vocabulary

página	page	**alguien**	somebody	**todo el día**	all day
cantar	to sing	**nadie**	nobody	**todos los días**	every day
siempre	always	**cada**	each	**todo el mundo**	everybody;
nunca	never	**ahora**	now		all the world
algo	something	**todo, -a**	all	**de la mañana**	AM
nada	nothing	**todos, -as**	every, all	**de la tarde (noche)**	PM

Assignment 19

Learning Meaning from Context

1　You have already learned the first three lines of the following dialog. Read the entire dialog aloud and isolate the words that are new to you.

En el apartamento de Roberto

Roberto: ¡Caramba! ¡Qué calor hace!
Miguel: ¡Terrible! Creo que hace más fresco afuera.
Roberto: Es verdad, pero es muy difícil estudiar allí.

Miguel: ¡Caray! Ya son las cinco y media.
Roberto: Todavía es temprano. ¿A qué hora comen en tu casa?
Miguel: A las seis, pero vivo muy lejos de aquí.

There are four new words: the exclamation *caray*, *ya*, *temprano*, and *lejos*. You can figure out their meaning from what you already know and by an analysis of the context.

What is Miguel exclaiming about when he says *¡Caray!*? ▲

The time of day: *Son las cinco y media.*

2 What does Roberto relate this time to? ▲

The dinner hour in Miguel's home: *¿A qué hora comen en tu casa?*

3 Miguel's answer is *A las seis*. So Miguel has 30 minutes to get home and he says, "*pero vivo muy lejos de aquí.*" Would Miguel be surprised at the time or be worried about getting home for dinner on time if he lived close by? ▲

4 So *lejos* must be the opposite of *cerca* and mean _____. ▲   no

5 Miguel lives far away, he looks at the clock, it is 5:30, and (1) later (2) earlier than expected. ▲   far

6 He exclaims, "My gosh. It's _____ five-thirty." ▲   later

7 Roberto counters with *Todavía es temprano*. This must be the opposite of *tarde*. So Roberto is saying "It is still _____." ▲   already

Now that you know the meaning of the dialog, go back to frame 1 and read it aloud until you are satisfied that you can do it well in your next class.   early

Review: Spelling and Vocabulary

1 Except in some of the dialects of Spain, the letters *s*, *z*, and *c* stand for the same sound, [s]. Here are all the words you have had in which *z* and *c* stand for the [s] sound. Say them aloud and copy them carefully: *gracias, cinco, oficina, lápiz, diez, once, tiza, Asunción, La Paz, venezolano, centro, doce, trece, catorce, quince, pizarra, luz, necesitar, ciudad, Venezuela, cine.*

2 The [k] sound is written *c* when it is followed by the three vowels _____ (or a consonant, *clase, creo*, etc.). ▲

3 The [k] sound is written *qu* when it is followed by the two vowels _____. ▲   *a, o, u*

4 Think about the spelling of these words as you copy them: *cuaderno, poquito, aquí, quince, cuarto, cuánto, escuela, Ecuador, parque, qué, quién, cuál, casa, colombiano.*   *e, i*

5 Sounds, like everything else, fall into sets, and the cues for spelling the members of a set are the same. The Spanish [g] sound is the voiced equivalent of the unvoiced [k] sound. The digraph *qu* stands for the [k] sound before the vowels *e* and *i*. The digraph *gu* stands for the [g] sound before *e* and *i*. You will write *g* before the vowels _____. ▲

a, o, u (and before consonants)

6 Copy the following and think about their spelling: *tengo, uruguayo, alguien, algo, guitarra.*

7 Here are some words that need a tilde over the *n*. Copy them and write it in: *manana, Espana, brasilena, senorita.* ▲

mañana, España, brasileña, señorita

8 Here are some words that need a written accent mark. Copy them and write
it in: *frio, sabado, Bogota, Peru, lapiz, estan.* ▲

frío, sábado, Bogotá, Perú, lápiz, están

9 Here are some cognates that are spelled differently in Spanish. Write the
Spanish: present, professor, pardon, minus, Brazil, park, students, university,
class. ▲

presente, profesor, perdón, menos, Brasil, parque, estudiantes, universidad,

clase

A Self-Test

Unless you get almost all of the following right, you are beginning to build up
an unsatisfactory deficit of basic knowledge.

1 The four forms of the definite article are _____. ▲

2 In writing, the infinitive form of a verb always ends in the letter _____. ▲   *el, la, los, las*

3 The plural noun suffix in Spanish has two forms. After a vowel it is _____.   *r*
After a consonant it is _____. ▲

the vowel + *s*; the consonant + *es*

4 The only present tense form of an *i*-verb which has the *i* as the first suffix is
the form that goes with the subject pronoun _____. ▲

5 The definite article, the subject pronouns, and an unmodified proper noun   *nosotros (vivimos)*
cue the choice of the verb _____ for location. ▲

6 When you describe the weather, you use the verb _____. ▲   *estar*

7 The four vowels which appear as the first suffix of present tense forms   *hacer* (Hace)
are _____. ▲

8 In telling time in Spanish, you can add how many minutes to the previous   *o, a, e, i*
hour? ▲

9 When you add or subtract numbers the form of *ser* is _____. ▲   only 30

10 The first suffix of the present tense form for *yo* for all regular verbs is _____   *son*
for all three verb sets. ▲

11 Silence, /n/, or /l/ cue you to use which allophone of /d/? ▲   *o*

12 Why do English "day" and Spanish *de* not sound alike? ▲   the stop

The [e] of *de* is one pure vowel; the *ay* of "day" represents two vowels. (If
you got this general idea, do not mark this frame wrong.)

13 You use *mucho* (the adjective), not *muy* (the adverb), to say *Hace mucho calor*
because *calor* is a _____. ▲

14 The number *dieciséis* is really made up of three words. They are _____. ▲   noun

15 The plural noun *muchachos* stands for all boys or _____. ▲   *diez y seis*

16 The relator *de* plus a place name cues the verb _____ to express origin. ▲   boys and girls

17 If a noun takes *el* or *un*, it will also take adjective forms ending in _____. ▲   *ser*

18 Are the names for the days of the week capitalized in Spanish? ▲   *o*

19 There are five Spanish digraphs. They are: *gu, qu, ñ,* and _____. ▲   no

20 Two punctuation marks and two spelling marks used in Spanish but not in   *ch, ll*
English are _____. ▲

¿, ¡, ˜, ´

Months of the Year

About 2,300 years ago the old Romans had named only ten of the twelve lunar months in the year. The Latin and English names for the last four months in this ancient version of the calendar are the same: *December*, *November*, *October*, and *September*. In all four names the last syllable *ber* comes from Latin *fer*, meaning "to bear" or "to carry", so these were the months that bore the numbers 7, 8, 9, and 10. The old Latin tenth month *December* is now our twelfth month: the stem *decem* means 10.

1 Here are the Spanish equivalents of all the number-bearing months. Notice that they are not capitalized and that the suffix *ber* changed to *bre*. Say them aloud and copy them.

        septiembre   octubre   noviembre   diciembre

2 What Spanish number words are suggested by the part of the name that precedes *bre*? Write them. ▲

       siete, ocho, nueve, diez

3 English "March" and its Spanish equivalent *marzo* are cognates. This month was named after Mars, the Roman god of war and of vegetation. In ancient Rome, warfare and planting were undertaken in this month. One of the days of the week in Spanish also honors Mars. It is _____. ▲

4 In the Roman ten-month calendar there were no names for the two lunar months that preceded March, the first month of their calendar. It was a religious custom in those days to get ready for the new year by performing ceremonies of purification. Gradually the un-named month before the new year came to be called the month of "purification." The Latin verb for "to purify" is *februare* from which came Spanish *febrero*. The English name of this month is

_____. ▲

martes

5 The old Romans now had one un-named lunar month. They named it after the god *Janus*, the god of "beginnings," and because this was the month when new government officers *began* their term of office, in 153 B.C., they changed their calendar and made this month the beginning month of the new year. It became *enero* in Spanish and _____ in English. ▲

February

6 In the spring the buds unfold and the blossoms open up. The Latin verb *aperire* ("to open"; *abrir* in Spanish) describes this and provides the base for Spanish *abril* and English _____. ▲

January

7 Does *b* in *abril* stand for a stop or a fricative sound? (It does not follow silence, *n*, or *m*. Say *abril* aloud.) ▲

April

8 There are two months which got their names so long ago that it is uncertain where they came from. Some scholars believe that one of these may have been dedicated to old people (*maiores*) or to the goddess *Maia*. The Spanish name for this month is *mayo* and its English equivalent is _____. ▲

fricative

9 The other month whose name is in doubt may have been dedicated to the young (*juniors*) or to *Juno*, the wife of Jupiter. It is *junio* in Spanish and _____ in English. ▲

May

June (In Spanish *j* stands for a sound which is similar to that of *h* in "hot."

The first syllable of the Spanish name for this month sounds almost like "who." Say aloud *ju-nio, junio*.)

10 Julius Caesar was born in the month of *Quintilis*, the fifth month, and after his death this name was changed to honor him. The Spanish for "Julius" is *Julio*, but since the names of the months don't have to be capitalized, the equivalent of "July" is written _____ in Spanish. ▲

julio (Both *Julio* and *Julia* are popular names in Spanish; *junio*, however, is not used as a name for a woman.)

11 The first syllable in *junio* and *julio* sounds almost like the English question word _____. ▲

who (Say aloud "who", *junio, julio*. You will be taught to make this sound correctly later in the course.)

12 The sixth month in the old Roman calendar was called *Sextilis* until 8 B.C. when it was renamed to honor the Roman Emperor *Augustus* from which comes Spanish *agosto* and English _____. ▲

13 Copy the Spanish names for the months of the year and practice saying them aloud. Although you have not heard them in class yet, by following the hints given in the preceding frames and applying what has been taught about Spanish sounds you can demonstrate to your instructor in the next class that you can pronounce them without major errors. The stress is indicated.

August

e**ne**ro	**a**bril	**ju**lio	oc**tu**bre
fe**bre**ro	**ma**yo	a**gos**to	no**viem**bre
marzo	**ju**nio	sep**tiem**bre	di**ciem**bre

14 Of the four *b*'s occurring in the names of the last four months, how many stand for a stop sound? ▲

three (*b* always stands for a stop sound after [m])   *Septiembre* can also be spelled and pronounced *setiembre*.

Self-Correcting Exercises

A (Remember *not* to look at the answers until after doing each problem.) Write the combinations in this visual-graphic drill.

Ejemplo: 43 = Paco y Elena están en el campo.

1	Todos los muchachos		1	bien, gracias.
2	Tú y yo		2	venezolan- .
3	Yo	estar	3	en el campo.
4	Paco y Elena	ser	4	aquí ahora.
5	Tú (*f*)		5	brasileñ- .
6	Usted		6	de Caracas.

1) 11

2) 22

3) 33

Todos los muchachos están bien, gracias.

Tú y yo somos venezolanos (-as).

Yo estoy en el campo.

4)	44	Paco y Elena están aquí ahora.
5)	55	Tú eres brasileña.
6)	66	Usted es de Caracas.
7)	12	Todos los muchachos son venezolanos.
8)	23	Tú y yo estamos en el campo.
9)	45	Paco y Elena son brasileños.
10)	56	Tú eres de Caracas.

B Do this multiple substitution drill aloud.

1	Todos van a la playa.	
	Yo . . .	Yo voy a la playa.
2	. . . cine.	Yo voy al cine.
3	Tú . . .	Tú vas al cine.
4	. . . parque.	Tú vas al parque.
5	Tú y él . . .	Tú y él van al parque.
6	. . . iglesia.	Tú y él van a la iglesia.
7	Pepe . . .	Pepe va a la iglesia.
8	. . . montañas.	Pepe va a las montañas.
9	. . . campo.	Pepe va al campo.
10	Ustedes . . .	Ustedes van al campo.
11	. . . tienda.	Ustedes van a la tienda.
12	. . . correo.	Ustedes van al correo.
13	Nosotros . . .	Nosotros vamos al correo.
14	. . . café.	Nosotros vamos al café.

New Vocabulary

Note that about half of these words are cognates.

año	year	**noviembre**	November	**ya**	already
mes	month	**diciembre**	December	**temprano**	early
enero	January	**apartamento**	apartment	**lejos**	far
febrero	February	**padre**	father	**afuera**	outside
marzo	March	**creer**	to believe,	**más**	more
abril	April		think	**pero**	but
mayo	May	**tu**	your	**que**	that
junio	June	**tacaño, -a**	stingy	**cuándo**	when
julio	July	**difícil**	difficult,	**Es verdad.**	It's true ((the)
agosto	August		hard		truth).
se(p)tiembre	September	**terrible**	terrible	**¡Caramba!**	Wow! Gosh!
octubre	October	**todavía**	yet, still	**¡Caray!**	Wow! Gosh!

Tacaño

Bend elbow of left arm until hand is directly below chin. With right hand sharply pat the end of left elbow two or three times.

Assignment 20

More on Dialog II

1 The purpose in memorizing dialogs is not so much to remember what is said but to learn intonation and sentence patterns and some vocabulary in context. A sentence pattern can be treated as a series of slots each of which is filled by words or phrases. Compare the statement *Hace calor* and the exclamation *¡Qué calor hace!* In what way does the exclamation pattern differ from that of the statement? ▲

Word order is reversed. (This is the reverse of English: It is hot; Boy, it is hot!)

2 *Hace calor* is a basic pattern used in describing weather. Which word do you replace when the weather changes? ▲

calor (*Hace frío; hace fresco, etc.*)

3 The same sentence pattern may be used to send a great many messages simply by changing what is in one slot: *Hace frío* ⟶ *Tiene frío*. Which word in *Creo que hace más fresco afuera* can be replaced by the phrase *en el patio?* ▲

afuera (A single adverb can be replaced by an adverbial phrase.)

4 The slots of *Hace mucho calor* can be changed to *Tengo mucha hambre*. The noun *hambre* means "hunger," but the translation of the sentence is _____. ▲

I'm very hungry. (Like "It's very hot.")

5 Here is the entire dialog. The last three lines are new.

En el apartamento de Roberto

Roberto: ¡Caramba! ¡Qué calor hace!
Miguel: ¡Terrible! Creo que hace más fresco afuera.
Roberto: Es verdad, pero es muy difícil estudiar allí.
Miguel: ¡Caray! Ya son las cinco y media.
Roberto: Todavía es temprano. ¿A qué hora comen en tu casa?
Miguel: A las seis, pero vivo muy lejos de aquí.
Roberto: Espera, hombre. Vamos a terminar la lección.
Miguel: No puedo. Estoy cansado de leer.
Roberto: Bueno, yo también. Además, tengo mucha hambre.

The literal translation of the last three lines is:
Wait, man. We go to terminate the lesson.
I cannot. I am tired of to read.
Good, I also. Besides, I have much hunger.
Reread the whole dialog, pay special attention to the situation and the context, and see if you can figure out a more natural translation. Compare it with the one given below. ▲

Wait, man. Let's finish the lesson.
I can't. I'm tired of reading.
O.K. So am I. Besides, I'm very hungry.

Reread the Spanish aloud until you are satisfied with your performance. Use all that you know about pronunciation so as to sound like a native. Learn these new lines before going to the next class.

Writing Dialog II

At this stage in your learning Spanish your prime problem in writing is spelling what you can already say. Below is the dialog. The words that are likely to cause trouble in spelling are in boldface type. Read the dialog silently and try to identify the spelling problem in each indicated word.

En el apartamento de Roberto

Roberto: ¡Caramba! **¡Qué** calor **hace!**
Miguel: ¡Terrible! Creo **que hace más** fresco **afuera.**
Roberto: Es verdad, pero es muy **difícil** estudiar **allí.**
Miguel: **¡Caray!** Ya son las **cinco** y **media.**
Roberto: **Todavía** es temprano. ¿A **qué** hora comen en **tu** casa?
Miguel: A las **seis,** pero **vivo** muy **lejos** de **aquí.**
Roberto: Espera, **hombre. Vamos** a terminar la **lección.**
Miguel: No **puedo. Estoy** cansado de **leer.**
Roberto: **Bueno,** yo **también. Además,** tengo mucha **hambre.**

1 In this and the remaining frames, you can check your analysis of some spelling problems by deciding what spelling problem is exemplified by the word or words given in phonetic script. [ke] ▲

Exclamation *qué*; conjunction *que*

2 [ase] ▲

Eye spelling for both *h* and *c*: *hace*

3 [mas] ▲
4 [ayí] ▲

accent mark: *más*
Eye spelling for *ll*: *allí*

5 [sinko] ▲

Eye spelling for first *c* and rule for second *c*: *cinco*

6 [tu] ▲

No accent mark as an adjective (your). The pronoun is *tú* (you).

7 [pwedo] ▲

[w] is written *u*: *puedo*

8 [leksion] ▲

[k] is *c* as syllable final; eye spelling for second *c*, and accent mark.

9 [estoi] ▲

Only *y* for [i] in word final (with a few rare exceptions)

10 [bibo], [bweno] ▲

Eye spelling for *v* and *b* and [w] = *u*: *vivo, bueno*

11 But [ambre] ▲

Only *b*, never *v*, before another consonant and eye-spelling *h*: *hambre*.

More Practice in Learning to Spell

1 There are many cues in Spanish which tell you how to spell words. The vowels are the best signals. The sound [s] may be spelled *c*, *s*, or *z* only before the vowels _____. ▲

e, i (There are extremely few Spanish words which have *z* before *e* or *i*.)

2 The sound [s] may be spelled *s* or *z*, but not *c*, before the vowels _____. ▲

a, o, u (*C* spells [k] before *a, o, u*.)

3 There are two sets of vowels. One is made up of *i* and *e*; the other of *a, o*, and *u*. Let's see some of the things they tell you about spelling. The sound [k] is a voiceless stop. The only letter, besides *k*, which can stand for [k] before *a, o*, and *u* is *c*. Before *e* and *i* you write [k] with the digraph _____. ▲

4 The sound [g], as in *tengo*, is the voiced equivalent of the voiceless [k]. The only letter that can stand for [g] before *a, o*, and *u* is _____. ▲

qu (que, quien)

g (venga, algo, Paraguay)

5 Now, remember that the only difference between [k] and [g] is the difference between *voiceless* and *voiced*. You write [k] with the digraph *qu* before *e* and *i*. What digraph would you expect to be used for [g] before *e* and *i*? ▲

6 The [k] is a stop. Its fricative equivalent is the *jota* sound [j]. The only letter which can stand for [j] before *a, o*, or *u* is *j* as in *trabaja, ojo*, and *junio*. Before *e* or *i* the [j] may be spelled either *j* or *g* so you have to see these words to

gu (alguien)

learn to spell them. Write the spelling equivalents of the following: [arjentino], [trabajo], [pájina], [julio]. ▲

argentino, trabajo, página, julio

7 You have never seen this word: [keso]. Say it aloud in Spanish. Now write it. ▲

queso (This is Spanish for "cheese.")

8 The Spanish word for "lame" is [kojo]. It is spelled _____. ▲

cojo (Only *c* for [k] before [o]; only *j* for [j] before [o])

9 The letter *g* may stand for [g] before *a, o,* or *u,* and for [j] before *e* or *i.* Which sound does it always stand for before another consonant? ▲

[g] (*gracias, inglés*)

10 The letter *z* comes before *e* or *i* mostly in words borrowed from other languages. When Spanish words ending in *z* are made plural, *z* changes to _____. ▲

c (*luz, luces; lápiz, lápices*)

11 Antonyms: Say aloud and copy these four new antonyms; then write the other member of the pair which you have already studied in class. *adentro* (= inside; *d* stands for a fricative sound) ▲

12 *fácil* (= easy; accent mark tells you to say **fá**-*cil,* not *fá-**cil***) ▲   *afuera*

13 *tarde* (= late, tardy; you already know its noun meaning, "afternoon") ▲   *difícil*

14 *cerca* (= near; first *c* stands for [s]; the second for [k]) ▲   *temprano*

lejos

Summary

1 Words containing the italicized combinations in the chart below can be spelled by *hearing* the words if you know the rules.
2 Words containing the boxed sequences can only be spelled by having *seen* them.

You write [k]: *ca*	*co*	*cu*	*que*	*qui*
You write [g]: *ga*	*go*	*gu*	*gue*	*gui*
You write [j]: *ja*	*jo*	*ju*	je / ge	ji / gi

You write [s]: sa / za	so / zo	su / zu	se / ce / ze	si / ci / zi

Reasoning Linguistically

1 What word is missing in *We are going on _____ first Sunday after Christmas?* ▲

2 Do we have a logical sentence if we change "the" to "a"? *We are going on **a** first Sunday after Christmas.* ▲

the

no

3 Which article, "the" or "a", shows there is only one unique "first Sunday after Christmas"? ▲

4 Can we leave out "first" and still have the same meaning? *We are going on the Sunday after Christmas.* ▲   the

5 Is "Sunday" still the *first* Sunday *immediately after* Christmas? ▲   yes

6 Can we also leave out the relator "on" without really changing the meaning?   yes
We are going the Sunday after Christmas. ▲

7 Assuming that today is Wednesday, if we say, *We are going Sunday*, will this   yes
mean the *first* Sunday that comes after today? ▲

8 And if we say, *We went Sunday*, does this mean *the first* Sunday *back* from   yes
today? ▲

9 Do *Let's go there Sunday* and *Let's go there some Sunday* say the same thing? ▲   yes

10 The word "some" before "Sunday" tells us what? ▲   no

one of the many possible Sundays

11 In *Let's go there Sunday*, nothing (zero) comes before "Sunday". What does
"zero" mean in contrast with "some"? ▲

12 Spanish has no special equivalent of "some." The indefinite article is used   one unique Sunday
instead. So Spanish speakers will say, *Vamos allí _____ domingo.* ▲

13 As in "the Sunday after Christmas," Spanish uses the definite article (not   *un*
zero) to mark a unique day of the week. How will they say *Let's go Sunday?* ▲

14 How will they say, *Let's go Sundays?* ▲   *Vamos el domingo.*

15 Write the plural of *sábado.* ▲

Vamos los domingos.

16 What are the two last sounds of the names of all the other five days of the   *sábados*
week? *lunes, martes, etc.* ▲

17 Does this look like an allomorph of the plural suffix, as in *papeles*? ▲   [-es]

18 Is it logical to conclude that the Spanish speaker does not need to change   yes
those five names of the days of the week to make them plural? ▲

yes

Self-Correcting Exercises

A Translate the following sentences:

1 Let's go Wednesdays.   *Vamos los miércoles.*
2 Let's go Saturdays.   *Vamos los sábados.*
3 Let's go Fridays.   *Vamos los viernes.*
4 Let's go some Tuesday.   *Vamos un martes.*

B Try this brief experiment: The sentence *He is guggling* contains a new verb
you have never heard in English. The infinitive is "to guggle". Now, complete
these sentences using the appropriate form of this new verb:

5 He has _____. He will _____.   guggled, guggle
6 He was _____. He does not _____.   guggling, guggle

C In English you do not have to know the meaning of a verb to be able to make up the forms. The system is independent of meaning. Spanish behaves in exactly the same way. If you know what goes into the verb slots (stem and suffixes), you can generate the forms of the new verbs just as you do in English.

Here are four verbs you have never seen before: *subir* (to climb, go up), *deber* (must, ought), *entrar* (to enter), and *correr* (to run). Knowing that they are all regular in Spanish and that they belong to three different sets, write the present tense form for each infinitive in parentheses.

1	Ellos (entrar) en la clase.	entran
2	Yo (subir) la montaña.	subo
3	Luisa (deber) comer más.	debe
4	Nosotros (correr) en el campo.	corremos
5	Ella y yo (entrar) en la iglesia.	entramos
6	Nosotras no (subir) al apartamento.	subimos
7	Tú (correr) muy rápido.	corres
8	Los estudiantes (deber) estudiar más.	deben
9	¿Dónde (correr) usted?	corre
10	Ustedes (subir) rápido.	suben
11	Yo no (deber) ir al cine.	debo

Tengo hambre

Use right or left hand, or even both hands; place them over the abdominal area and either rub or pat gently. We use a similar gesture in English to mean the same thing.

New Vocabulary

luna	moon	**beber**	to drink	**cansado, -a**	tired
lección	lesson	**tener sed**	to be thirsty	**húmedo, -a**	wet, humid
gente (la)	people	**tener hambre**	to be hungry	**fácil**	easy
niño, -a	child	**correr**	to run	**rápido**	fast
empezar (ie)	to begin, start	**deber**	must, ought	**despacio**	slow
terminar	to finish, terminate	**subir**	to go up, climb	**además**	besides
				también	also, too
entrar	to go in, enter	**Vamos a . . .**	Let's . . .	**adentro**	inside
		puedo	I am able, can	**tarde**	late, tardy
				cerca (de)	near

Assignment 21

Thousands of Words for Free: Cognates

Because Spanish is a modern dialect of Latin and because English borrowed tens of thousands of words from Latin, there are a great many Spanish words which you can easily learn to recognize the first time you hear or see them.

The first five frames include many such words. Read them for meaning but *not* aloud. When you think you understand what each says, look at the answer frame.

1 Abrahán Lincoln fue asesinado por un actor llamado John Wilkes Booth. ▲

Abraham Lincoln was assassinated by an actor called John Wilkes Booth.

2 Julio César era el emperador de Roma en el año 45 antes de Cristo. ▲

Julius Caesar was the emperor of Rome in the year 45 B.C.

3 Un millonario es un hombre que tiene un millón de dólares. ▲

A millionaire is a man who has a million dollars.

4 Los Estados Unidos están divididos en cincuenta partes o estados. En España las partes o divisiones se llaman provincias. ▲

The United States is divided into fifty parts or states. In Spain the parts or divisions are called provinces.

5 Es evidente que ya tiene usted un vocabulario bastante grande en español. Usted puede leer y comprender mucho. ¿Está usted contento? ▲

It is evident that you already have a quite large vocabulary in Spanish. You can read and understand a lot. Are you content (happy) ?

You can learn to recognize thousands of cognates by yourself. However, you will learn a lot more if you know how to go about it in a scientific fashion. Here are some generalizations:

a Spanish keeps the verb suffixes of Latin: English uses only the stems. (*presentar*, present: *importar*, import)

b English also keeps only the stems of adjectives. (*contento*, content; *colombiano*, Colombian)

c The Spanish equivalents of words ending in *nd* or *nt* preserve a Latin final *e*. (*instante*, instant; *grande*, grand)

d In words like *defensivo* and *defectivo* English changes the final *o* to "e" (defensive, defective).

e The *c* of the final syllable changes to "t" for English in words like *condición* (condition) and *perfección* (perfection).

f Spanish writes *f* where English writes "ph." (*elefante*, elephant; *alfabeto*, alphabet)

g Spanish does not follow the English custom of doubling consonants in the middle of words. (*profesor*, professor; *suficiente*, sufficient)

h Spanish *ar* may become "ate" in English verbs. (*comunicar*, communicate; *concentrar*, concentrate)

i Spanish adds *idad* to many adjectives to make nouns; English adds "ity." (*real-idad*, real-ity; *inferior-idad*, inferior-ity)

j English drops the final vowel and changes *i* to "y" in words like *historia* (history) and *miseria* (misery).

k The English equivalent suffixes for Spanish *ismo* and *ista* are "ism" and "ist." (*comunismo*, communism; *comunista*, communist)

l Final *a* is replaced with "e" in words like *literatura* (literature) and *miniatura* (miniature).

6 In this and the next three frames write the English for the Spanish words given: *consultar, perfecto, evidente.* ▲

consult, perfect, evident

7 *activo, conversación, filosofía* ▲

active, conversation, philosophy

8 *posible, complicar, mentalidad* ▲

possible, complicate, mentality

9 *vocabulario, socialismo, socialista, ventura* ▲

vocabulary, socialism, socialist, venture

10 You will increase your vocabulary very rapidly by learning how Spanish builds words by adding different suffixes to the same stem. To the stem *geograf* you add *ía* for the name of the science "geography" (*geografía*), you add *ico* to make an adjective (*geográfico*), and you add *o* for the scientist (*geógrafo*). So, *geología, geológico,* and *geólogo* are translated ———. ▲

geology, geological, geologist

11 The suffix of *coleccionar* tells you it's a verb. The suffix of *colección* indicates it is a noun. What is the most logical cognate translation for *un coleccionista?* ▲

a collector

12 Many times you can figure out an English cognate which will give you the general meaning, but it will have to be replaced by another word to get the right translation. Look at the indicated word in this sentence: *Una persona que colecciona* **monedas** *se llama un coleccionista.* One English cognate of *moneda* is

_____. ▲

13 A person who collects money is not really a coin collector. So, to get the   money
right translation for *monedas* you replace the cognate "money" with _____. ▲

coins (The Spanish word for "money" is *dinero*.)

14 Here are some facts to remember. These suffixes indicate a noun: *ción, dad, ismo, ía, ura* (*perfección, realidad, comunismo, geología, literatura*). The *ista* marks a noun and a person (*socialista*) or an adjective (*una idea socialista*). The *dor* most commonly marks the doer or an adjective: *hablar* (to talk), *hablador* (talker); *un hombre hablador* (a talkative man = gossip). The *-dor* forms may have an added *a* as noun or adjective: *una persona habladora.*

You will learn much more about cognates in future Assignments. Now, a word of warning. The fact that English and Spanish do have so many recognizable cognates can be a trap. Very few share all the same meanings, and some are real demons. For example, *papa* looks like the identical cognate of

_____. ▲

papa (But *papa* means either "potato" (*una papa*) or "pope" (*un papa*) in Spanish. The Spanish equivalent of English "papa" is *papá*.)

Spelling

1 The letters *ll* and *y* stand for sounds that are alike in most Latin-American dialects. Here are all the words you have had which have *ll* in them. Say them aloud: *llamar, silla, allí, ella, ellos, ellas.* Notice that the letter *ll* can come only before a vowel *at the beginning* of a word or syllable. It is not used as the last letter of a word.

2 The *y* is used to begin a syllable (before a vowel) and to end a word (after a vowel). There are extremely few Spanish words which end in *i* after a vowel. The Spanish for these words or phrases has a *y* in them. Write the Spanish for: I am (two verbs), I go, today. ▲

yo estoy, soy, voy, hoy

3 Write the Spanish for: very, yesterday, there are, and. ▲

4 Where English uses "y" in "type," "mystery," and "symphony," Spanish   muy, ayer, hay, y
uses *i: tipo, misterio,* and *sinfonía* because Spanish never writes a *y* next to: (a) a consonant (b) a vowel. ▲

5 Spanish never writes a *v* immediately before or after another consonant in   consonant
the same syllable. You have to decide when to use a *b* or *v* only when a vowel follows. Here are some words that may give you trouble. Copy and add the missing letter: . . . *ueno,* . . . *ien,* . . . *i* . . . *ir,* . . . *entana,* . . . *einte.* ▲

bueno, bien, vivir, ventana, veinte

6 Here are all the words you have had that you must see in order to learn to

write *g* or *j* for [j]. Copy and add the missing letter: *pá . . . ina, ar . . . entino,*
relo . . . , . . . ente. ▲

página, argentino, reloj, gente

7 The letter *c* cannot stand for [s] at the end of a word or syllable or before
a, *o*, or *u*. The letter *z* rarely comes before *e* or *i*. *S* may come before all vowels.
Here are some words you have to see to spell [s] correctly. Write the Spanish
translation: five, pencil, chalk, blackboard, Brazil. ▲

cinco, lápiz, tiza, pizarra, Brasil

8 Copy and put the tilde on these words, and say them aloud: *nino, manana,*
brasileno, senorita. ▲

niño, mañana, brasileño, señorita

9 Write the Spanish for: hour, hello, until, to speak, Thursday. ▲

hora, hola, hasta, hablar, jueves

In both American and Hispanic cultures there are very common fixed expressions in
which the words are always used in the same order. Both cultures, for example, say
salt and pepper (*sal y pimienta*) rather than *pepper and salt*. This order is arbitrary and,
sometimes, a bit meaningless. Thus Americans regularly put on their *shoes and socks*
though it is obvious that the socks must be put on first.

Here are some common patterns which are just the opposite in the two cultures.

from head to foot	*de pies a cabeza*
black and white	*blanco y negro*
sooner or later	*más tarde o más temprano*
needle and thread	*hilo y aguja*
soap and water	*agua y jabón*
with hugs and kisses	*con besos y abrazos*
chicken and rice	*arroz con pollo*

Dialog II

1 Here are the phrases in which *b* and *v* stand for a stop. Say them aloud:
¡Caramba! Espera, hombre; Vamos a terminar; Bueno, yo también; Tengo mucha
hambre.

2 The *v* in these phrases stands for a fricative. Say them aloud:
Es verdad; Todavía es temprano; Pero vivo muy lejos.

3 The *d* in these phrases stands for a fricative. Say them aloud:
Es verdad; Es muy difícil estudiar; lejos de aquí; las cinco y media; todavía; no
puedo; cansado de leer; además.

4 To talk Spanish well, you run the words together. Say these aloud several
times, as fast as you can:
¡qué-ca-lo-rhace!   es-tu-dia-ra-llí;   co-me-nen-tu-casa;   va-mo-sa-terminar;
tengo-mu-chaham-bre.

5 Here is the whole dialog. Get a watch with a second hand and practice until you can say it in 20 seconds without letting speed spoil your pronunciation.

En el apartamento de Roberto

Roberto: ¡Caramba! ¡Qué calor hace!
Miguel: ¡Terrible! Creo que hace más fresco afuera.
Roberto: Es verdad, pero es muy difícil estudiar allí.
Miguel: ¡Caray! Ya son las cinco y media.
Roberto: Todavía es temprano. ¿A qué hora comen en tu casa?
Miguel: A las seis, pero vivo muy lejos de aquí.
Roberto: Espera, hombre. Vamos a terminar la lección.
Miguel: No puedo. Estoy cansado de leer.
Roberto: Bueno, yo también. Además, tengo mucha hambre.

Seasons of the Year, Ordinal Numbers, and More Antonyms

1 You have now reached the stage where your knowledge of the relationship between Spanish sounds and letters should enable you to generate the correct pronunciation of many words before you hear them in class. Here are the names of the seasons of the year with their English equivalents. The stressed syllable is indicated for the words that do not have an accent mark. Practice saying them aloud and writing them.

spring	summer	autumn	winter
*prima**ve**ra*	*ve**ra**no*	*o**to**ño*	*in**vier**no*

2 In _____ and _____, *v* stands for a stop sound; in _____, *v* stands for a fricative. ▲

verano and invierno; primavera

3 En el _____ hace mucho calor, pero en el _____ hace mucho frío. ▲

4 Octubre y noviembre son meses de _____; mayo es un mes de _____. ▲   verano, invierno

5 Here are the first four ordinal numbers. Say them aloud and copy them.   otoño, primavera

first	second	third	fourth
primero, -a	*segundo, -a*	*tercero, -a*	*cuarto, -a*

6 Does *d* in *segundo* stand for a stop or a fricative? ▲

7 Say these words aloud and note their English equivalents: stop (It follows [n].)

mentira	*morir*	*magnífico*	*descansado*	*seco*
lie (untruth)	to die	fine	rested	dry

You have already learned antonyms for all the above. In the following frames, write the word needed to complete the pair.

8 cansado ▲

9 vivir ▲

descansado

morir (related to English "mortal")

10 terrible ▲

magnífico (The cognate is "magnificent.")

11 verdad ▲

mentira

12 húmedo ▲
Check to see how much you remember.   seco
13 The names of the four seasons of the year are _____. ▲

primavera, verano, otoño, invierno

14 The first four ordinal numbers are _____. (Think of the cognates: "primer,"
"secondary," "tertiary," and "quarter.") ▲

primero, segundo, tercero, cuarto

15 The antonyms for *mentira, morir, magnífico, descansado,* and *seco* are _____. ▲

verdad, vivir, terrible, cansado, and *húmedo*

Self-Correcting Exercises

A Do this multiple substitution drill aloud.

1 Yo soy de Santiago.
    Tú . . .   Tú eres de Santiago.
2 . . . boliviano.   Tú eres boliviano.
3 Víctor . . .   Víctor es boliviano.
4 Victoria . . .   Victoria es boliviana.
5 . . . bastante bien.   Victoria está bastante bien.
6 Nosotros . . .   Nosotros estamos bastante bien.
7 . . . en Caracas.   Nosotros estamos en Caracas.
8 . . . de Caracas.   Nosotros somos de Caracas.
9 Ellos . . .   Ellos son de Caracas.
10 . . . peruanos.   Ellos son peruanos.
11 Ellas . . .   Ellas son peruanas.
12 . . . aquí hoy.   Ellas están aquí hoy.

B Say aloud the word needed to complete the pair. For additional practice
cover the left column and repeat the exercise.

1	comer	beber	**7**	siempre	nunca
2	empezar	terminar	**8**	fácil	difícil
3	poco	mucho	**9**	algo	nada
4	adentro	afuera	**10**	cerca	lejos
5	hambre	sed	**11**	temprano	tarde
6	bien	mal	**12**	nadie	alguien

New Vocabulary

estaciones (las)	seasons	**gimnasio**	gym	**tercero, -a**	third
primavera	spring	**estadio**	stadium	**cuarto, -a**	fourth
verano	summer	**mentira**	lie (untruth)	**magnífico, -a**	fine,
otoño	fall, autumn	**morir (ue)**	to die		great
invierno	winter	**primero, -a**	first	**descansado, -a**	rested
		segundo, -a	second	**seco, -a**	dry

Assignment 22

More on Cognates

There are cognates that look exactly alike (*doctor*) and many that are so different that it takes a philologist to recognize them (*buitre*, "vulture"). In between are many which hardly look alike but are recognizable if you pay attention to the context and make educated guesses.

1 Translate the last word of each of these sentences: *Hablan inglés en Inglaterra, Dublín es la capital de Irlanda.* ▲

2 You can also learn to recognize thousands of cognates when you understand what happened to Latin words as they became Spanish and English.
Compare these pairs: *estado*, state; *España*, Spain; *especial*, special. When an
English word begins with an *s* plus another consonant, the Spanish cognate
begins with _____. ▲

England; Ireland

e (As a result, when Spanish speakers try to learn English, they say *Espain, espinach,* and *estand.*)

3 Read the following: *Hoy vamos de Nueva York a Filadelfia. Hay tres maneras de ir: por automóvil, por tren y por avión. Vamos por tren y estamos en la estación central del ferrocarril.* The three ways of going from New York to Philadelphia are by automobile, _____. ▲

train, and plane (Did *avión* suggest "aviator" or "aviation"?)

4 You certainly got the meaning of *en la estación central* (the central station).
We are going by <u>train.</u> We are in the <u>central station.</u> Logic should now tell you
that *ferrocarril* translates _____. ▲

railroad (The literal meaning of *ferro-carril* is "iron road.")

5 You have already learned that an *e* in a stressed syllable in thousands of
Latin words became *ie* in Spanish. Once you know this, *sentimiento* looks more
like _____. ▲

6 English did not change *e* to *ie* when it borrowed Latin words. The English
cognate stem of *viento*, consequently, is _____. ▲

sentiment

vent (Something through which air passes to "ventilate" a building.)

7 The word for a huge fire (and Hell) in Spanish is *infierno*. In English you
spell this _____. ▲

8 "Petroleum" means "rock oil;" "petrify" means "to turn to stone." Spanish
piedra translates either _____. ▲

inferno

rock or stone (Latin *t* became Spanish *d*.)

9 The cognate *diente* probably means nothing to you all by itself. Changing
it to *dente*, however, may suggest it belongs to the same family as *dentista* and
dental. The stem of "dentist," "dentistry," and "dental" means _____. ▲

10 A stressed Latin *o* may change to *ue* in Spanish. A "portal" in English is an
entrance. The Spanish cognate you know is _____. ▲

tooth

11 What does *fuerte* suggest to you in the context "The soldiers defended *el
fuerte*"? ▲

puerta

fort (As an adjective *fuerte* can also mean "strong.")

12 What does *fuerza* suggest to you in *Habla con mucha fuerza?* ▲

force

13 When you think you understand the following, look at the translation in the answer frame: *Los Estados Unidos no es un país tropical. En unas regiones tenemos huracanes; también tenemos, en otras regiones, vientos muy fuertes y destructivos que se llaman "tornados" o "ciclones."* (Read this again before you look.) ▲

The United States is not a tropical country. In some regions we have hurricanes; we also have, in other regions, very strong and destructive winds which are called "tornados" or "cyclones."

14 *La palabra "cansado" termina en **o**, pero la palabra "cansada" termina en **a**.* The translation of *palabra* and *termina* are _____. ▲

word and ends (Think of "palaver" and "terminate.")

15 Una puerta es la entrada de una casa. La traducción de la palabra "puerta" es *door*. Un puerto es una entrada también. San Francisco y Nueva York son puertos importantes. La traducción de "puerto" no es *door*, es _____. ▲

port (*Puerto Rico* = rich port.)

16 En todos los puertos importantes siempre hay muchos barcos. El cognado inglés de "barco" es *bark*. La traducción de "barco" no es *bark*, es _____. ▲

ship (boat)

17 Cognates cannot become part of your speaking vocabulary until you can say them aloud in Spanish without a heavy accent. Three things will tend to give you an accent. First, because the words look a lot like English you may let the letters suggest English instead of Spanish sounds. Second, the Spanish cognates will not be divided into syllables in the same way as in English. Third, the stress is very often on a different syllable.

These cognates are divided into syllables and the stressed syllable is indicated. Say the English and then the Spanish: **per**-fect—*per-**fec**-to*; class—**cla**-*se*; i-**dea**—*i-**de**-a*.

18 All cognates do not have the same meanings in both languages. The word for "present" (gift) is *regalo*. What does *un vapor* suggest as its translation? ▲

a vapor

19 Let's put this in context: *Vamos a Europa en el vapor Queen Mary*. The translation of *vapor* is now _____. ▲

steamship (A standard meaning of *vapor* is "steam." Spanish just leaves off the "ship.")

20 Until you have learned a lot more Spanish, you should not try to make up Spanish words from English words borrowed from Latin. This can be *embarrassing*. Look at the italicized cognate and this statement by a woman: *Estoy embarazada*. This could be translated as _____. ▲

I am embarrassed. (Its more common meaning, however, is: "I am pregnant.")

21 Translating Spanish cognates into English can also trap you. Here's a real deceptive demon. *Estoy constipado* looks very much like "I'm constipated." Can you guess its real meaning? ▲

no (It means "My nose is plugged; I have a cold.")

Paired Words

1 Synonyms are words which have similar meanings. Words which have opposite meanings are called antonyms. The antonym of *malo* is _____. ▲

bueno

2　There are many words which are neither synonyms nor antonyms yet we regularly associate them with each other: hunger and thirst, shoes and socks, bread and butter. Learning words in pairs helps you remember them. Write the paired words for *algo, alguien, nunca.*　▲

3　Write the paired words for *fuera, fácil, tarde.*　▲

　　　　　　　　　　　　　　　　　　　　　nada, nadie, siempre
　　　　　　　　　　　　　　　　　　　dentro, difícil, temprano

4　Write the paired words for *cerca, sed, empezar.*　▲

　　　　　　　　　　　　　　　　　　　　　　lejos, hambre, terminar

5　A verb frequently associated with *comer* is _____.　▲

6　The Latin word *multo* produced two modern Spanish words: *mucho* and　　　　*beber*
muy. Which one do you use in: *Hace* _____ *viento; Tengo* _____ *hambre?*　▲

　　　　　　mucho (viento), *mucha* (hambre) (The meaning to a Spanish speaker is
　　　　　　　　　　　　　　"It makes much wind" and "I have much hunger.")

7　Translate: "It is very far." *Está* _____; and "It is very easy." *Es*
_____.　▲

　　　　　　Está muy lejos; Es muy fácil. (*Muy* combines with adverbs and adjectives.)

8　"Circle" and "circus" are cognates of the Spanish word for "near," that is,
_____.　▲

　　　　　　cerca (Circus in Latin is a "ring." Anyone in the same ring or circle with you

9　If you want to *comer* in Spanish, you must buy things at a *tienda de comestibles.*　　　is *cerca.*)
Can you guess the translation?　▲

　　　　　grocery store (Things that are edible in English may be called "comestibles.")

Phonemics and Graphemics

1　It is very hard to write about sounds without confusing people. Consequently linguists use special signs to keep things straight. They write, for example, that the Spanish phoneme /b/ has two allophones, [b] and [ƀ] which may be written by the graphemes *b* or *v*. "Grapheme" is just a technical word for
_____.　▲

　　　　　letter (*graph* = letter; *eme* = meaningful, so (#) and (+) are not graphemes.)

2　You already know that /b/ and /d/ have two allophones in Spanish, a stop and a fricative. Linguists show this by putting a bar through the letter standing for the fricative, like this [ƀ], [đ]. With these marks one can show more precisely how to say *vivir*, that is [b i ƀi r]. Spanish letters tell you what phoneme to say but not which allophone. When you say *vivir* you say [b i ƀi r]. When you say *Vamos a vivir*, you say [b a m o s a ƀi ƀi r]. [ƀi ƀi r] and [b i ƀi r] are the same word.

　　Linguists say that when two sounds are phonetically different, but do not change the meaning of a word, they belong to the same phoneme. So the two Spanish allophones [s] and [z] make up the phoneme /s/ just as [b] and [ƀ] make up the phoneme /b/. When you talk you say allophones, not phonemes, since you cannot say two or more sounds at the same time.

　　Aside from the fact that Spanish has a few phonemes that are not found in English, the biggest difference between the two languages comes from only slight changes in how allophones are made. The English phonemes /p/, /t/, and /k/ all have an aspirated or "puff" allophone but these same phonemes in Spanish do not have such an allophone.

The Spanish [t] differs from English in another way. Spanish [t] is _____. ▲

3 The phoneme /g/ is the *voiced* equivalent of /k/. The *fricative* equivalent of /k/ is the phoneme that can be written either _____. ▲

dental

4 The Spanish [l] is very different from the English [l]. Let's see if you have learned to say the Spanish sound. Say Spanish [i] and [o] several times and watch carefully what your tongue is doing. Your tongue is closer to the roof of your mouth when you say _____. ▲

j or *g* (before *i* or *e*)

5 Now say Spanish *los* and English "loss" several times and watch your tongue. Say them until you are sure you know what your tongue is doing when you make the two [l] sounds. Now look at the answer. ▲

[i]

> You have learned to say Spanish [l] if your tongue is as close to the roof of your mouth as when you say Spanish [i].

6 Here are the graphemes which signal you to make different allophones of the same phoneme: *b, v, d, n, r, s*. What tells you when *r* stands for [rr]? ▲

> The letter begins a word or follows *n, s* or *l*.

7 What tells you which allophone of /b/ or /d/ you are to say? ▲

8 After silence you always use (a) a stop (b) a fricative. ▲

What comes before.

9 Which allophone, [b] or [b̸], do you say for *b* in *también*? ▲

a stop

> the stop [b] (You will soon learn that [m] may also be written *n: tan bien* and *también* sound exactly alike.)

10 Which allophone of /d/ do you use after /n/ or /l/? ▲

11 When two letters (*ll, ch, qu, gu, ñ*) are treated as single letters they are called *dígrafos*. The English cognate is _____. ▲

the stop [d]

12 The *h* does not stand for a sound in Spanish. Do the *j* of *reloj* and the *p* of *septiembre* stand for a sound in these words? ▲

digraph

> no (You say [rreló] and [setiembre].)

Compass Directions

1 Here are the names for the points of the compass. Practice saying and writing the Spanish.

north	south	east	west
norte	*sur*	*este*	*oeste*

They end in *e* or *r* and combine, therefore, with *el: el norte, el sur, el este, el oeste.*

2 El océano Pacífico está al _____ de los Estados Unidos, y el Atlántico está al _____. ▲

3 Chile y Argentina están en el _____; Venezuela está en el _____. ▲

Read the sentences in the following frames aloud and translate the indicated word.

oeste, este
sur, norte

4 *Tejas y Nuevo Méjico están en la región* **suroeste** *de los Estados Unidos.* ▲

5 *La región de Nueva Inglaterra está en el* **noreste** *del país.* ▲

southwest
northeast

Summary

1 To English words that begin with *s* plus another consonant, Spanish adds *e* at the beginning. (*estado*, **s**tate)

2 In many Latin words an *e* in a stressed syllable became *ie* in Spanish but not in English. (*inf**ie**rno*, inf**e**rno)

3 A stressed Latin *o* may become *ue* in Spanish. (*f**ue**rte*, f**o**rt)

4 To pronounce Spanish cognates without an accent it is important to remember that the letters represent Spanish sounds, that words are divided into syllables differently in Spanish, and that the stress is very often on a different syllable than in English.

5 For Spanish [l] the tongue is as close to the roof of the mouth as for Spanish [i].

6 The names for the points of the compass in Spanish are: *norte*, *sur*, *este*, and *oeste*.

Self-Correcting Exercises

A *Reasoning Linguistically:* Answer each question and check its answer before doing the next one.

1 In the sentence "Today is the twentieth of November", the article "the" modifies what missing noun? The twentieth *what* of November?   *day*

2 Although *día* ends in *a*, does it combine with *el*, or *la*?   *el*

3 In "Today is the 20th of November" how would "the" be translated?   *el*

4 In English, ordinal numbers (second, fourth, twentieth) are used to express dates. In Spanish, with one exception, cardinal numbers (*dos*, *cuatro*, *veinte*) are used. So how would "the twentieth" be translated?   *el veinte*

5 Complete the translation of "Today is the second of October." *Hoy es* _____ *de octubre.*   *el dos*

6 The one exception is the first day of the month. Both English and Spanish use the ordinal number. Complete the translation of "Tomorrow is the first of December." *Mañana es* _____ *de diciembre.*   *el primero*

Say the Spanish equivalents of these dates:

1 the 30th of June   *el treinta de junio*
2 the first of January   *el primero de enero*
3 the fourth of July   *el cuatro de julio*
4 the 21st of February   *el veintiuno de febrero*

B Ask and answer each question several times until your performance approximates that of a native speaker.

1 ¿Cuántos meses hay en un año?   Hay doce.
2 ¿Cuántas semanas hay en un mes?   Hay cuatro.
3 ¿Cuántos días hay en una semana?   Hay siete.

4	¿Cuántas horas hay en un día?	Hay veinticuatro.
5	¿Cuántos minutos hay en una hora?	Hay sesenta.
6	¿Cuántos segundos hay en un minuto?	Hay sesenta.

C *Negative Structures:* Say aloud the Spanish equivalent.

1	It is hot.	Hace calor.
2	It is not hot.	No hace calor.
3	It is difficult to study there.	Es difícil estudiar allí.
4	It is not difficult to study there.	No es difícil estudiar allí.
5	I live very far from here.	Vivo muy lejos de aquí.
6	I don't live very far from here.	No vivo muy lejos de aquí.
7	We eat at six.	Comemos a las seis.
8	We do not eat at six.	No comemos a las seis.
9	I'm tired of reading.	Estoy cansado de leer.
10	I'm not tired of reading.	No estoy cansado de leer.
11	John always goes home.	Juan siempre va a casa.
12	John doesn't go home ever.	Juan no va a casa nunca.
13	Lola is studying something.	Lola estudia algo.
14	Lola isn't studying anything.	Lola no estudia nada.

Piensa

Place index finger of right hand over the nose so that the tip touches the center of the forehead.

New Vocabulary

norte	north	**minuto**	minute	**flaco, -a**	thin
sur	south	**sesenta**	sixty	**viejo, -a**	old
este	east	**último, -a**	last	**joven**	young
oeste	west	**pequeño, -a**	little, small	**feliz**	happy
mar	sea	**grande**	big, large	**triste**	sad
océano	ocean	**gordo, -a**	fat	**allá**	over there
desierto	desert				

Assignment 23

Two Irregular Verbs: tener *and* venir

You have already learned that a verb is regular when the stem is the same in all forms and when the morphemes of the first and second suffixes are those used by the vast majority of the verbs of the set to which it belongs. You have learned three verbs that are irregular: *estar, ser,* and *ir.* Each is irregular in a different way.

1 The verb *comer* is regular. The verb *tener* (to have) is irregular. Can you discover these facts from hearing or seeing the infinitive form? ▲

2 The verb *tener* has a regular stem *ten.* This is used to make up the form that goes with *nosotros* which is _____. ▲   no

3 The form of *tener* that goes with *yo* is *tengo.* Is this form regular? ▲   *tenemos*

no (To be regular it would have to be *teno.*)

4 The form that goes with *ustedes* is *tienen.* Is this form irregular? ▲

5 To use *tener* you have to work with three forms of the stem: **ten**-*emos,* **teng**-*o,*   yes
and **tien**-*en.* The stems *ten, teng,* and *tien,* like the two forms of the plural noun suffix, *s* and *es,* all carry the same meaning. They are *allomorphs* of the stem morpheme. When Latin became Spanish, a stressed *e* sometimes changed to

_____. ▲

6 The stress is on *tie* in *tie-nen.* The stress is not on the stem in the form that   *ie*
goes with *nosotros.* So you have _____. ▲

7 The first and second suffixes are the same as those for regular *e* verbs. Thus   *tenemos*
the *yo* form ends in _____. ▲

o (The stress, however, is on the *ten* of *tengo,* and to be consistent the form

8 The *yo*-form has the stem *teng* (*yo tengo*). The infinitive and the *nosotros*   should be *tiengo.*)
forms have the stem _____. ▲

9 All the other forms you are to learn have the stress on the stem. So the   *ten*
allomorph to be used is _____. ▲

10 To make up the form that goes with *él, ella,* and *usted,* you add *e* to the   *tien*
irregular stem allomorph _____. ▲

tien

11 To make *tiene* agree with *ellos*, *ellas*, and *ustedes*, you add the second suffix
_____. ▲

> *n* (You have now seen all the present tense forms of *tener*. Say them aloud. The stem allomorphs are indicated.)

yo **ten**go		tú **tien**es	
nosotros **ten**emos	usted		e
	ustedes		en
	él		e
	ellos	↓	en

12 You can learn the irregular *i*-verb *venir* (to come) by just learning two facts. First, the *nosotros*-form has *i*, not *e*, as the first suffix (*venimos*). Second, to get all the other present tense forms you change the *t* of the *tener* forms to *v*. So the form that goes with *yo* is _____. ▲

> *vengo* (Like *tengo*.)

13 The *venir* form that goes with *ellos*, *ellas*, and *ustedes* is _____. ▲

> *vienen* (Like *tienen*.)

14 To make *vienen* agree with *él*, *ella*, and *usted*, you drop the _____. ▲   *n*

15 To make *viene* match *tú*, you add the second suffix _____. ▲   *s*

16 The *nosotros* form of *i*-verbs differs from *e*-verbs. Write the whole form: *nosotros* _____. ▲

> *venimos*

17 You now know how to make up the forms of a special set of stem–changing *e*- and *i*-verbs. Suppose you meet a new verb in its infinitive form. Will you be able to tell whether its stem has two or more allomorphs? ▲

> no (You have to memorize the members of this set.)

Linear Movement: ir, venir, salir *and* llegar

1 Compare these sentences: (1) *Miguel viene de Venezuela.* (2) *Miguel va a Venezuela.* In terms of linear movement, *venir de* describes movement (a) away from a place (b) to a place. ▲

2 *Ir a* is associated with (a) the origin of movement (b) the destination of the mover. ▲

> away from a place

> the destination of the mover

3 In English we may say either "The train is coming!" or "The train is arriving!" What are we talking about? (a) the origin of the train (b) its getting near to its destination. ▲

> its getting near to its destination (So, in English "to come" can be associated *either* with the origin of movement *or* the arrival.)

4 When arrival at the destination is the really important part of the message neither English nor Spanish uses a verb associated with the origin of movement. Which sounds better to you? (a) The train comes to the station at six o'clock. (b) The train arrives at the station at six o'clock. ▲

> Most people prefer "arrives at."

5 Let's label a square "here" and another one "there." You pretend you are a

Spanish speaker standing at "here." This is how you see the world and linear movement.

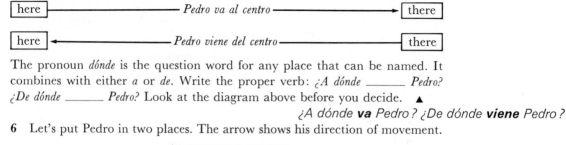

The pronoun *dónde* is the question word for any place that can be named. It combines with either *a* or *de*. Write the proper verb: ¿*A dónde* _____ *Pedro?* ¿*De dónde* _____ *Pedro?* Look at the diagram above before you decide. ▲

¿A dónde **va** Pedro? ¿De dónde **viene** Pedro?

6 Let's put Pedro in two places. The arrow shows his direction of movement.

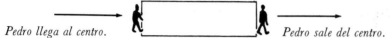

Pedro llega al centro.   *Pedro sale del centro.*

Which verb form translates "is leaving"? ▲

7 The logical opposite of *salir* is *llegar* (to arrive).   *sale*

So when you say "come" and really mean "arrive at," you will use (a) *venir* (b) *llegar* in Spanish. ▲

8 Although combinations with other relators are possible, *salir* and *venir* go   *llegar* with *de; ir* and *llegar* go with *a*. With *salir de* and *llegar a* (see illustration in 6 above), must the mover be close to the place indicated by *a* and *de?* ▲

9 *Salir* is used to describe this kind of movement.   yes

You are out in the country picnicking with some friends. One of them looks at his watch and says, "It's getting late. I have to leave now." *Salir* will not translate "to leave" in this situation. The Spanish speaker will use *ir*. Out in space he does not go from "inside" to "outside."

To learn to talk like a native speaker, you have to do more than memorize patterns and words. You have to learn to *think* like a Spanish speaker and to *see* and *organize* reality in his way.

In English a chair and a saddle are two quite different things. The Spanish speaker sees them both as something to sit on, and consequently, calls them both *silla*. In English a table and a chair are two pieces of "furniture." The Spanish speaker sees them as movable property or "movables" and says *Una mesa y una silla son muebles.* It looks as if he is saying they are "furnitures." Remember that Latin *o* often became Spanish *ue*. The cognate of *mueble* is "mobile," as in "automobile" (self–moving). So to a Spanish speaker pieces of furniture are "mobiles" (*muebles*).

Spelling Review

There are thousands of English words like *sent, cent; guild, gild; to, too, two;* or *right, rite, write,* and *wright* whose spelling must be learned word by word. This happens because modern English comes from a mixture of three different languages—Old English, Saxon, and French—and also because the language has borrowed thousands of words from many other languages (Greek, Latin, German, Spanish, Italian, Russian, *etc.*) The majority of Spanish words, in contrast, come from a single language, Latin, and the spelling system is better organized than English. As a result, learning to spell Spanish words is made much easier when you study the system instead of the spelling of individual words.

To understand the system you need to know that certain phonemes are closely related to each other and, as a result, are treated in spelling in a similar fashion. For example, there are three Spanish phonemes whose sounds are made at the same place (point of articulation) in the mouth. The back of the tongue arches up toward the roof of the mouth when you make the Spanish sounds for *c* (*nunca*), *g* (*algo*), or *j* (*lejos*). The [k] sound is an unvoiced stop. One allophone of the phoneme /g/ differs from this in only one detail. It is a voiced stop (*tengo*). The other allophone of /g/ is a voiced fricative (*amigo*), and the *jota* (*j* sound) differs from this only in the fact that it is an unvoiced fricative (*trabaja*). Sounds that are so much alike became confused as Latin became Spanish. Latin *catum* became English "cat" but Spanish *gato*.

1 The unvoiced Latin [k] sound frequently became the voiced Spanish [g] sound. Does this tell you that *c* and *g* will frequently be followed by the same letters in spelling? ▲

> yes. Here is a spelling rule whose only exception is found in foreign words. The phoneme /g/ is always spelled *g* when followed by a consonant (only *r* or *l* in the same syllable: *grande, Gloria*) or by *a, o,* or *u* (*amiga, amigo, jaguar*).

2 Translate and check your spelling: heat, cool, fourth. ▲

> *calor, fresco, cuarto* (The rule given in Frame 1 is the same for [k].

3 Translate and check your spelling: class, house, how, notebook, to believe. ▲

> *clase, casa, cómo, cuaderno, creer*

4 Translate and check your spelling: to work, I work, July. ▲

> *trabajar, trabajo, julio* (The *jota* is always written *j* before *a, o,* and *u.*)

5 What two vowels have not been mentioned so far? ▲

> *e, i* (These are signals for exceptions.)

6 Translate: what? who? ▲

> *¿qué? ¿quién?* (Before *e* and *i,* the [k] sound is spelled with the digraph *qu.*)

7 The opposite of *nadie* is _____. The translation of "Michael" is _____. ▲

> *alguien; Miguel* (Before *e* and *i* the [g] sound is spelled with the digraph *gu.*)

8 Say *mujer* (woman) and *gente* (people) aloud. The *jota* may be spelled either *j* or *g* before the vowel _____. ▲

> *e* (Also before *i.* This spelling has to be memorized.)

Reading Cognates Aloud

Understanding the nature of Spanish syllables and spelling patterns will help you read cognates aloud and add them to your active speaking vocabulary.

1 The number of single vowels in a Spanish word can determine the number of syllables. The Spanish word for "metals" is *metales*. How many syllables are there in *metales*? ▲

> three, *me-ta-les* (In contrast, "metals" has only two.)

2   Compare these two English words: *hat, hate*. The first has one vowel letter and the second has two. Both are one-syllable words. Spanish is not like English. When you see a vowel letter in a Spanish word, you must say the vowel sound (except for *u* in the digraphs *qu* and *gu*). The English word "tile" has one syllable but two vowel letters. *If* it were a Spanish word, it would have _____ syllables. ▲

> two, *ti-le* (Say it aloud.)

3   The plural of "reptile" in Spanish is *reptiles*. Count the vowels (syllables). ▲

> three (The word is divided like this: *rep-**ti**-les*. Say it aloud.)

4   In a previous assignment you learned that Spanish adds *e* to many English words that end in two consonants: *presente, grande*. Spanish also adds *a*. Write "palm" and "plant" adding *a* to each. ▲

> *palma, planta* (Say them aloud. Remember that adding a vowel also adds a syllable. The letter *o* may also be added as in *contento*.)

5   When Spanish adds a vowel to a cognate ending in two consonants, the second consonant always goes with the last syllable. Divide into syllables *planta, palma, grande*, and *contento*. ▲

> *plan-ta, pal-ma, gran-de, con-ten-to*

6   With very few exceptions, the stressed syllable in a Spanish word can be determined by looking at the last phoneme. When a word ends in a consonant other than *n* or *s* (and has no written accent mark), you stress (a) the last syllable (b) the next-to-last syllable. ▲

7   When a word ends in a vowel, *n* or *s* (and has no written accent), you stress (a) the last syllable (b) the next-to-last syllable. ▲

> the last syllable

> the next-to-last syllable.

Adjectives with One Singular Form

1   The adjectives of nationality that you have learned have four forms: *chileno, chilena, chilenos, chilenas*. A great many other Spanish adjectives behave in the same way. Copy and add the missing suffixes: *muchacho buen, muchacha buen.* ▲

> *muchacho buen**o**, muchacha buen**a*** (Any adjective that has an *o*-form also has an *a*-form.)

2   Now, make the above combinations plural. ▲

> *muchachos buen**os**, muchachas buen**as***

3   There are many Spanish adjectives which have only one singular form, for example, *importante*. These adjectives agree with their nouns only in number. Write the plural of *la idea importante*. ▲

> *las ideas importantes*

4 Write the singular of *las profesoras importantes.* ▲

la profesora importante

5 Translate "the important book" and, then, make it plural. ▲

el libro importante ; los libros importantes

Summary

1 The present indicative forms of *tener* and *venir* are: *tengo, vengo; tenemos, venimos; tiene(s, n), viene(s, n)*. The stem of each has one regular form (*ten, ven*) and two that are irregular (*teng, tien; veng, vien*). *Ten* and *ven* are used with *mos; teng* and *veng* go with the *yo*-form; and *tien* and *vien* go with the rest.

2 When many Latin words became Spanish, stressed *e* and *o* became *ie* and *ue: viento, viene, muebles, puedo.*

3 *Ir, salir, venir,* and *llegar* describe movement from (*de*) one place to (*a*) another, or linear movement.
  a *ir a* and *llegar a* are associated with the goal or destination of the movement, but *llegar* emphasizes arrival and closeness to the place indicated by *a: Ella va a la tienda. Ella llega a la tienda.*
  b *venir de* expresses movement away from a place and towards where the speaker is located: *Ellos vienen de España.*
  c *salir de* implies going from inside to outside and close proximity to the place indicated by *de.*

4 In reading cognates aloud it is helpful to know these facts:
  a In a Spanish word there are as many syllables as there are single vowel sounds: *me-ta-les.*
  b Except for the *u* in the digraphs *qu* and *gu*, all vowels in Spanish stand for a sound.
  c When Spanish adds a vowel to cognates that end in two consonants in English, the second consonant always goes with the last syllable: consonant → *consonante* → *con-so-nan-te.*
  d With very few exceptions, when Spanish words do not have an accent mark, it is possible to determine what syllable carries the stress by looking at the ending: words ending in a vowel, *n*, or *s* stress the next-to-last syllable; words ending in a consonant except *n* or *s* stress the last syllable: *cuaderno, clase, playa, hablas, trabajan; calor, papel, ciudad, reloj.* In all other cases the syllable to be stressed will have an accent mark.

5 When an adjective has two singular forms, one ending in *o* (*peruano, cansado*) and the other in *a* (*peruana, cansada*), there are two types of agreement with the noun: matching of number suffixes and matching of terminal sounds. When adjectives have only one form in the singular (*amable, importante*), they agree with their nouns in number only: *hombres amables, mujeres amables; libros importantes, ideas importantes.*

When a great many Americans and Spanish speakers meet for the first time, they have trouble establishing friendly relationships. The Spanish speaker thinks the American is cold and standoffish, and the American thinks the Spanish speaker is trying to be too intimate too soon. What neither realizes is that the two cultures have very fixed customs on how close two people should stand next to each other during a normal, relaxed conversation. When two Spanish speakers, either males or females, talk to each other they stand about 16 inches apart. For the average American this distance is common only for sweethearts or two persons discussing something very intimate or secret. In ordinary conversation Americans may stand two or three feet apart. Until the members of each culture understand this difference, each gets a wrong impression of the intentions of the other, and they have trouble trying to establish a friendly relationship.

Self-Correcting Exercises

A   Write the combinations for this visual-graphic drill.

Ejemplo: 12 = Tú eres brasileña.

1	Tú (*f*)			
2	Yo		1	tacañ- .
3	Todos los muchachos	ser	2	brasileñ- .
4	Pancho y yo		3	nuev- .
5	María		4	famos- .
6	Las señoritas			

1)	11	Tú eres tacaña.
2)	22	Yo soy brasileño (-a).
3)	33	Todos los muchachos son nuevos.
4)	44	Pancho y yo somos famosos.
5)	51	María es tacaña.
6)	62	Las señoritas son brasileñas.
7)	14	Tú eres famosa.
8)	23	Yo soy nuevo (-a).
9)	32	Todos los muchachos son brasileños.
10)	41	Pancho y yo somos tacaños.
11)	52	María es brasileña.
12)	63	Las señoritas son nuevas.

B Say aloud the word needed to complete the pair. For additional practice, cover the numbered columns and repeat the exercise.

1	pequeño	grande		**12**	siempre	nunca
2	verdad	mentira		**13**	fácil	difícil
3	feliz	triste		**14**	algo	nada
4	vivir	morir		**15**	terrible	magnífico
5	hambre	sed		**16**	cerca	lejos
6	mal	bien		**17**	temprano	tarde
7	día	noche		**18**	terminar	empezar
8	joven	viejo		**19**	poco	mucho
9	cansado	descansado		**20**	afuera	adentro
10	gordo	flaco		**21**	nadie	alguien
11	hombre	mujer		**22**	húmedo	seco

C There will be a spelling quiz in the next class. The short sentences you will be asked to write from dictation will contain the sounds studied so far including those of /g/ spelled *g* or *gu*. You will have to rely on the ear, the eye, and the rules you have learned. Here are some examples:

Aquí hace mucho calor en el verano.
Miguel viene de Argentina el jueves.
Es venezolana y habla inglés muy bien.

New Vocabulary

barco	boat	**salir**	to go out, leave	**bonito, -a**	pretty
tranvía (el)	streetcar	**venir**	to come	**feo, -a**	ugly
túnel	tunnel	**alto, -a**	tall, high	**limpio, -a**	clean
llegar	to arrive	**bajo, -a**	short, low	**sucio, -a**	dirty

"To go" and "to come": ir *versus* venir

Spanish looks at the actions of coming and going from a different point of view than English. You can only learn the cues for choosing *ir* and *venir* by understanding the *Spanish* point of view. A first step is conscious understanding of the uses and meanings of "go" and "come" in English.

In English a speaker may use his own point of view or the point of view of the person spoken to in describing his position in space. The following anecdote illustrates this. Mr. Brand phones his wife at home to tell her his car has broken down. She asks him if he is at the office. He answers, "Yes, I'm *there* now, and I'll be *here* for another hour." When he says, "Yes, I'm *there* now" he is using Mrs. Brand's point of view. When he says, "and I'll be *here* for another hour" he is using his own point of view.

Mr. Brand says, "Will you *come* to the office and pick me up?" She answers, using her husband's point of view, "I'll *come* and get you." Her son asks, "Where are you *going*?" and she answers, using her own point of view, "I'm *going* to the office to get Daddy."

1 When you are using your own point of view, where must you always be? (a) here (b) there ▲

2 When you use your own point of view, and you move from where you are (here) toward where you move (there), what verb describes your movement? (a) I'm going. (b) I'm coming. ▲

here

3 When you talk to a person who is where you are and you want to say you are departing, what do you say? (a) I'm coming. (b) I'm going. ▲

I'm going.

4 Someone knocks at your door. You are in the kitchen by the sink. You walk away from the sink, you leave the kitchen and move *toward* the door. Are you (a) going to the door? (b) coming to the door? ▲

I'm going.

5 Before you get to the door, there is another knock and a call, "Anybody home?" You say, (a) "I'm going." (b) "I'm coming." ▲

going to the door

6 Whose point of view were you using when you picked *come* instead of *go* to answer the person at the door? (a) your own (b) the person's at the door ▲

I'm coming.

the person's at the door

7 When you talk to a person in English, *go* has the meaning of "to depart" or "to leave," that is, to move away from the person to whom you are talking. *Come* has the meaning of (a) to move away from that person (b) to move toward that person. ▲

to move toward that person (So you say, "I'm coming" when someone knocks at the door.)

8 We use the point of view of the person to whom we are talking when we say, "I'm coming." We use our own point of view when we say, "I'm going." The Spanish speaker, in sharp contrast with English speakers, uses his own point of view in choosing between *ir* and *venir*. When someone knocks at his door, he says, (a) *Ya voy.* (b) *Ya vengo.* ▲

Ya voy. (Literally, "Already I go.")

9 "To come" may be translated by either *ir* or *venir*. Let's practice reading the cues for choice. "Come here!" means to move toward me, the speaker, like this:

What verb do you use? (a) *ir* (b) *venir* ▲

10 "Go!" means to move away from me, the speaker. What verb do you   *venir*
use? (a) *ir* (b) *venir* ▲

11 When you reply to the commands "Come here!" or "Go!" in Spanish, you   *ir*
use the same verb. It is (a) *voy* (b) *vengo*. ▲

> *voy* (*Voy* has two meanings. One is to move <u>toward</u> the person to whom you are speaking. The other is to move <u>away</u> from that person.)

12 Let's review. You are in the kitchen with a relative who is busy making a cake. Someone knocks at the front door. Your relative asks, "Will you go to the door?" Which verb will you use in Spanish to answer the question? ▲

13 You stop to finish a coke. The person at the door knocks again and calls out,   *ir*
"Anybody home?" You now start for the door and answer in English, (a) "I'm going." (b) "I'm coming." ▲

14 What will you say in Spanish? Remember, you have to pick your own point   I'm coming.
of view to make the right choice. (a) *Ya voy.* (b) *Ya vengo.* ▲

15 Now, let's do this all over again. You are back in the kitchen with your   *Ya voy.*
relative. Someone knocks at the front door. Your relative asks, "Will you go to the door?" You stop to finish a coke. Your relative looks at you somewhat annoyed. You get the message, and say, (a) "I'm coming." (b) "I'm going." ▲

> I'm going. (To the person in the kitchen you said, "I'm going," but to the person at the door you said, "I'm coming." Both statements describe your moving toward the door.)

16 You are on a hike in a park and everyone is sitting down on the grass resting. One person stands up and says, "Come on; come along." Does this mean, "Let's move on, depart from here"? ▲

17 Which verb will you use in Spanish? Before you answer, remember that the   yes
speaker wants them to move away from the place they are at. (a) *ir* (b) *venir* ▲

> *ir* (You translate either "Come on!" or "Come along!" with *¡Vamos!* Literally, "Let's go.")

18 We really don't care whether we are coming or going when we ask either, "Are you going with me to the store?" or, "Are you coming with me to the store?" In this situation, the Spanish speaker also uses either verb: *¿Vas conmigo a la tienda? ¿Vienes conmigo a la tienda?*

The vocabulary of a culture often influences the way people think and behave. In recent years the words *colored*, **black**, and *Negro* have created many debates in the United States which cannot be duplicated in Spanish because *negro* stands for both *Negro* and *black*, and the cognate of *colored* is *colorado*, which translates *dyed*, *red*, or *reddish*.

A/B

PEDRO ES GORDO

C/D

PEDRO ES GORDO

E/F

PEDRO ESTÁ FLACO

G/H

PEDRO ES GORDO   PEDRO ESTÁ FLACO

PEDRO ES FLACO

I/J

K/L

M

Predicate Adjectives and Our Organization of Reality

1 This part of your Assignment deals only with descriptive adjectives. A descriptive adjective in both English and Spanish may stand next to its noun: "The *big dog* is in the yard." The same adjective may come after the verb: "The dog in the yard *is big*." A predicate adjective is one which describes the subject of the sentence and comes *after* the _____. ▲

> verb (The Romans said this part of the sentence "proclaimed" something about the subject, and they used the verb *praedicare* to say this. The English word which comes from *praedicare* is "predicate.")

151

2 We will deal here only with descriptive adjectives which come *after* the verb *to be*. We use sentences like *The dog is big* to organize and describe everything in the world. Let's see how much linguistic logic there is locked up in sentences of this type. Everyone agrees that deserts have certain characteristics. Which single adjective gives the most accurate description of deserts? Deserts are _____. ▲

3 In 1925 it rained so much in the Atacama Desert in Chile that there was a great flood. Was this (a) normal (b) abnormal? ▲

dry

abnormal (From this adjective form you get the noun form "norm".)

4 What is *your norm* for a tropical jungle? (a) wet (b) dry ▲

5 What single adjective best describes your norm for ice? ▲

wet

6 *The sun is hot* and *The earth is round* are statements of natural law. *Henry is furious* is not a statement of natural law. The sentence really says that Henry has changed from the normal, that he has become furious. Which sentence is like *Your shirt is dirty?* (a) The sun is hot. (b) Henry is furious. ▲

cold

Henry is furious. (The shirt changed from clean to dirty.)

7 The norm for most people is that they are healthy. What does *María is sick* tell you? (a) It is natural for María to be sick. (b) She has changed from the normal. ▲

She has changed from the normal.

8 You have a norm for almost everything you talk about. What does this sentence talk about? *The sky is red.* (a) norm (b) deviation (change from the norm) ▲

Our color norm for the sky is blue. Red is a change or deviation from that norm.

9 There are a great many norms which we share with most of the speakers of English, but, at the same time, every person also has a large number of private or personal norms of his own. For example, Mildred White, age 10, has a brother, George, age 24. Their father is 55 years old. The father thinks that both George and Mildred *are young*, but Mildred thinks George *is old*. Do Mildred and her father have the same norms for old and young? ▲

10 Are Mildred and her father both right? ▲

no

yes (They are just describing George from different, personal points of view.)

11 You now know that the same sentence pattern ("to be" plus a predicate adjective) can be used to describe a subject in two quite different ways. *The sky is blue* states the color norm for most people. *The sky is red* gives a deviation from that norm. What does this sentence tell you? *Harvey is pale.* (a) norm (b) deviation (c) you can't tell ▲

you can't really tell (You do not know Harvey and there is nothing in the forms of the words or their arrangement to cue the meaning.)

12 However, if you have *Harvey has just seen a terrible accident. Is he pale!* There are now two things that tell you that Harvey's paleness is abnormal. First, seeing the accident *caused* Harvey to change, to turn pale. Second, _____. Before you answer, take a good look at the sentence: *Is he pale!* ▲

the word order of *Is he pale!* (And the exclamation.)

13 Now, let's see how your logic works on these sentences: *The oven is hot; The* *oven is cold.* Do both of these statements describe a change in the temperature of the oven? Think before you decide. ▲

yes (When the oven is hot, *it has been heated.* When the oven is cold, *it has*

14 We say "The door is open" and "The door is closed." Does either one of   *lost its heat.*)
these give a norm? ▲

15 There are some things for which we have no norms. We can say "Steel is   no
hard" and immediately understand that this is a standard characteristic of
steel. We really can't say which is normal for doors: being opened or closed. If
we have no norm for something, must our description always imply that there
has been a change from some previous state? ▲

16 But you have to be careful. A man buys a cup of coffee in a *café.* He tastes   yes
it, turns angrily to the waiter, and says, "This coffee is cold." Does he have a
norm for the way coffee ought to be when served? ▲

17 Does "Cement is hard" state a norm? ▲   yes

18 Does "You can go there now. *The cement is hard.*" state a norm? ▲   yes

no (It has become hard; it has changed.)

The Spanish speaker organizes the world with precisely the same kind of
logic as you do. He has norms that are just like yours, and he understands the
difference between the normal and the abnormal just the way you do. There is,
however, a great big difference between what he says and what you say. The
Spanish speaker always tells his hearer whether the predicate adjective describes
the norm or some deviation or change from his norm. He does this in a very
neat and simple way by using two verbs where you use "to be." These verbs are
ser and *estar.*

19 Look at these translations:

The sun is hot.	*El sol es caliente.*
Ice is cold.	*El hielo es frío.*
The earth is round.	*La tierra es redonda.*

To state a natural law the Spanish speaker uses the verb _____ and a predicate
adjective. ▲

20 The Spanish speaker also uses *ser* when the predicate adjective describes his   *ser*
norm for any subject. The sentence *Harvey is pale* (Frame 11) has two very
different meanings.

(1) Harvey has a light colored skin. He is normally pale.

(2) He has a dark skin. It is abnormal for him to be pale. Here are the two
Spanish translations:

| Harvey is pale. | *Harvey es pálido.* |
| | *Harvey está pálido.* |

The Spanish speaker indicates the abnormal, a change or deviation from his
norm, by using the verb _____ and a predicate adjective. ▲

estar (In English you have to figure out the meaning by logic or from **the**
context. The Spanish speaker always tells the hearer what he means.)

21 Mr. Nicanor Salcedo takes a sip of his coffee and says to his wife, *Mi café* *está frío.* Does this tell her that he normally expects his coffee to be hot?   ▲

> yes (Mr. Salcedo has a norm for good coffee. It should be hot. Being cold is a
> change from his norm.)

22 Mr. Salcedo is 84 years old. He is the oldest man in the village. Everybody in
the village says, (a) *El señor Salcedo es viejo.* (b) *El señor Salcedo está viejo.*   ▲

> 84 meets everyone's norm for old, so they say, *El señor Salcedo es viejo.*

23 Mrs. Salcedo has a reputation throughout the whole village for being a neat
and careful housekeeper. "Her house is very clean." When the villagers say this,
they use (a) *ser* (b) *estar*.   ▲

> *ser (Su casa es muy limpia.)*

24 Mr. Salcedo is a happy and cheerful man who enjoys life and has fun telling
jokes. One day he gets a letter with some terrible news in it. As he walks across
the plaza on his way home, he speaks to no one, and people say, "What's the
matter with Mr. Salcedo? He is sad!" They say, (a) *¡Es triste!* (b) *¡Está
triste!*   ▲

> *¡Está triste!* (It is not normal for Mr. Salcedo to be sad.)

25 A tourist who has just come to the village happens to see Mr. Salcedo as he
walks home thinking about that terrible news. The tourist has no norm for Mr.
Salcedo. His first impression of Mr. Salcedo is "sad." How do you think he will
describe Mr. Salcedo? (a) *Es triste.* (b) *Está triste.*   ▲

> *Es triste.* (His first impression becomes his norm for Mr. Salcedo.)

26 The villagers and the tourist do not have really different norms for a sad
and happy man. They do have very different information with which to judge
Mr. Salcedo. Is the tourist wrong when he says, *Ese señor es triste?*   ▲

> no (In terms of what the villagers know, the tourist is wrong in using *ser.*
> In terms of *his* information he is right.)

27 Spanish helps the hearer in a way that English does not. The tourist stops
to talk with a villager. The villager happens to mention that Mr. Salcedo *está
triste.* What does this immediately tell the tourist? That his first impression was
(a) right (b) wrong.   ▲

> wrong (The *estar* tells him instantly that Mr. Salcedo is not normally sad.)

28 What is normal for any individual depends entirely on *his* knowledge and
personal experience. In many of the tropical regions of South America (Colombia for example) the heavy rains turn the iron in the rocks to rust and the soil
there is red. The color norm for soil for the people of these regions is red, because wherever they go, they see red earth. In parts of Argentina where there
is less rain, the land is covered with thick, natural grass. The roots of the grass
rot and become humus, and the soil, as a result, is almost black. Mr. Martín,
from the jungles of Colombia, visits Argentina. He looks at the black soil.
The color does not fit his color norm for soil. What do you think he will say?
(a) *La tierra es negra.* (b) *La tierra está negra.*   ▲

> *La tierra está negra.* (You use *estar* to indicate that what you see does not
> fit *your* norm.)

29 Mr. Martín goes back home to his jungle knowing that there are different
colored soils. He no longer has a single color norm for soil. He wants to teach
his children about Argentina. What does he tell them? (a) *La tierra de Argentina
es negra.* (b) *La tierra de Argentina está negra.*   ▲

> One teaches norms, so he says, *La tierra de Argentina es negra.*

30 Mr. Salcedo, the old villager, never recovers from the blow of the bad news in the letter he received. His old happiness does not come back. The villagers gradually replace their old norm for him (happy) with a new norm (sad). What do they say? (a) *El señor Salcedo es triste.* (b) *El señor Salcedo está triste.* ▲

They have a new norm, so they say, *es triste.*

31 Write *ser* or *estar* as the answer to this and the next nine frames. Marta has a nice home, kind parents, and many friends. She *is happy.* ▲

32 Operating rooms in hospitals have *to be clean.* ▲   *ser*

33 You find a white glove lying in the mud. It *is dirty.* ▲   *ser*

34 Diamonds *are hard.* ▲   *estar*

35 Mr. Pimental is sixty-five and has felt fine all his life. He wakes up one morning feeling a bit stiff and not too energetic. Suddenly it dawns on him that his age is catching up with him. He explaims, *I'm old!* ▲   *ser*

36 You have washed the dishes, and you say, "All the dishes *are clean.*" ▲   *estar*

37 Gloria has the flu. She *is very sick.* ▲   *estar*

38 Fernando has just fallen down the stairs and hurt his leg. He *is lame.* ▲   *estar*

39 Panchito, the bootblack, has just been told he has won 10,000 pesos on the lottery. He shouts, "*I'm rich!*" ▲   *estar*

    estar

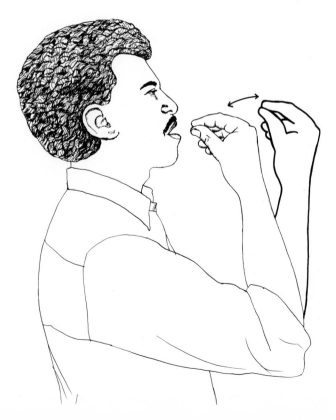

Quiero comer

Use either hand, hold hands with palm up, bring all fingers and the thumb together, tilt head slightly backward, raise hand up to within about four inches of the mouth and move hand back and forth two or three times as if cramming food into the mouth.

Summary

Ir versus *venir*

1   When the speaker and the person spoken to are at different positions in space, the English speaker (who is *here*) uses the point of view of the person spoken to in choosing between "come" and "go."

> Are you **coming here** tomorrow?
> Yes, I'm **coming there** tomorrow.

2   In Spanish, in contrast, each person uses his own point of view. The Spanish speaker, in short, believes you cannot "come" to where you are not. You have to "go" there.

> *¿**Vienes** aquí mañana?*
> *Sí, **voy** allí mañana.*

3   When both persons are at the same place and one begins to move away, this person may urge the other to come along by saying, "Come on! Let's go." Spanish uses only the equivalent of "Let's go": *¡Vamos!*

4   When both speakers are at the same place both languages use "go" (*ir*) to describe movement to somewhere else.

> **Are** you **going** to the store?   *¿**Vas** a la tienda?*

5   When one states that one person will go with the other, both languages may use either verb.

> Are you going with me?   *¿Vas conmigo?*
> Are you coming with me?   *¿Vienes conmigo?*

Predicate Adjectives

1   To state a natural law or to give your norm for anything, you use *ser* plus a predicative adjective.

> The earth is round.   *La tierra es redonda.*
> Grass is green.   *La hierba es verde.*

2   To state that the subject has changed, is deviating from the norm, you use *estar* and the adjective which describes the deviation.

> Harvey is pale. (norm)   *Harvey es pálido.*
> Is Harvey pale! (deviation)   *¡Harvey está pálido!*

3   When you meet something for the first time, and can find no evidence that a change has taken place, you state your first impression with *ser*.

> I just met Mrs. Canedo. She is very friendly. *Ella es muy amable.*

4   Two speakers of Spanish can view the same person or thing from two different points of view. What is normal for one person (*ser*) may be abnormal for the other (*estar*).

> *El señor Salcedo es triste. No, está triste.*

5 When something or someone changes, there may be no change back. When this happens you gradually get used to the change, you develop a new norm and you now use *ser*.

Self-Correcting Exercises

A Say aloud the word needed to complete the pair.

1	grande	pequeño		15	mujer	hombre
2	mentira	verdad		16	nunca	siempre
3	triste	feliz		17	difícil	fácil
4	morir	vivir		18	cruel	amable
5	feo	bonito		19	magnífico	terrible
6	bajo	alto		20	lejos	cerca
7	sed	hambre		21	tarde	temprano
8	bien	mal		22	empezar	terminar
9	noche	día		23	bien	mal (enfermo)
10	viejo	joven		24	mucho	poco
11	descansado	cansado		25	adentro	afuera
12	limpio	sucio		26	frío	calor
13	flaco	gordo		27	alguien	nadie
14	primero	último		28	húmedo	seco

B Write the combinations for this visual-graphic drill.

Ejemplo: 33 = Ellos son jóvenes.

1	Él		1	cruel.
2	Ella	ser	2	amable.
3	Ellos		3	joven.
4	Ellas			

1)	11	Él es cruel.
2)	21	Ella es cruel.
3)	31	Ellos son crueles.
4)	41	Ellas son crueles.
5)	12	Él es amable.
6)	22	Ella es amable.
7)	32	Ellos son amables.
8)	23	Ella es joven.
9)	43	Ellas son jóvenes.
10)	13	Él es joven.

New Vocabulary

ecuador	equator	**cruel**	cruel
querer (ie)	to want; love	**enfermo, -a**	sick, ill

Assignment 25

A Review of the Four Ways of Learning to Spell in Spanish

1 If you hear the word [papel], will you be able to spell it correctly? ▲

> yes (What you hear in this case tells you what to write because each phoneme in the word is always represented by the same grapheme. This is *ear spelling*.)

2 There is a city in southern Mexico whose name is pronounced [wajaca]. The Mexicans write this word *Oaxaca*. Does this spelling tell you what to say? ▲

> no (To learn to spell *Oaxaca* you have to see the word. This is *eye spelling*.)

3 The sound [k] may be spelled *c* or *qu*. Say [sinko] aloud. What tells you to write *c* for [k]? (a) what you hear (b) what you see (c) a spelling rule and what you hear. ▲

> a spelling rule and what you hear (You write [k] as *c* before *a, o,* and *u*. This is *rule spelling*.)

4 The [s] sound of [sinko] might be written either *c* or *s*. What tells you to write *cinco*? (a) rule spelling (b) ear spelling (c) eye spelling ▲

> eye spelling (You have to see *cinco* to find out that it begins with a *c*.)

5 What tells you when to write *dough* or *doe*? (a) what you hear (b) the meaning of each word ▲

> the meaning of each word (This is *meaning spelling*. You have, of course, to see each word to learn both spellings.)

6 Does the letter *h* stand for a sound in Spanish? ▲

> no (All words with *h* have to be seen before you can learn to spell them.)

7 Does *u* always stand for a sound in Spanish? ▲

> no (It is part of a digraph in **qué** and *Miguel*.)

8 Say *lunes* and *bueno* aloud. In which word does the *u* stand for [w]? ▲

> *bueno* (Pronounced [bweno]. Remember that Spanish has no letter *w* in native words and has to use *u* in its place.)

9 Do you remember the cognates "cat" and *gato*? This should remind you that [k] is the unvoiced equivalent of what voiced sound? ▲

10 A spelling rule tells you that [k] and [g] are spelled *c* and *g* before which three vowels? ▲

> [g]

11 What graphemes (letters) are used to spell [k] and [g] before *e* and *i*? ▲

> *a, o, u*
> the digraphs *qu* and *gu*

12 Say [ke] aloud. What tells you to write [ke] with or without an accent mark? (a) what you hear (b) a spelling rule (c) meaning ▲

> meaning (*Qué* has the accent mark in a question: *¿Qué es esto?*, but no accent in *El hombre que está allí*.)

13 What tells you to write "to, two, too" in English? ▲

> the meaning (Plus what you see.)

14 Will your ear tell you how to spell the subject pronoun *tú*? ▲

> no (Your ear will tell you to write *t* plus *u*, but not the accent mark. You have

to know the meaning of *tú* (the subject) and *tu* (the possessive adjective) to learn the difference.)

15 Can you write everything you can say? ▲

no (Here is the proof. You can say, "There are two . . . s in Spanish (*tú* and *tu*) and three . . . s in English (to, too, two)" but no one can write what you say in regular letters.)

16 In this and the following frames you will find a word written in phonetic script. Say the word aloud and write it in regular letters.   [tisa] ▲

tiza (You must remember what you have seen to spell *tiza* correctly.)

17 [siyas] ▲

sillas (In the dialect you are learning, *ll* stands for [y].)

18 [ola] ▲

hola (Only eye spelling tells you to write *h*.)

19 This one has two words in it: [ketal]. ▲

20 [senyor], [mwi] ▲

¿Qué tal?

señor, muy (*u* stands for [w] in speech in this word.)

21 [lwego], [¿donde?] ▲

luego, dónde (This is a question word and so it needs the accent mark on the stressed syllable.)

22 [aki] ▲

aquí ([k] is written *qu* before *i* and *e*.)

One of the major differences between the two cultures may be traced to what the people who first came to the New World had to do to make a living. The Spanish speakers found, in most areas, a sedentary Indian population which had already developed many of the traditional skills of civilization. There were farmers, craftsmen, artisans, stonecutters, miners, weavers, artists, pottery makers, etc. The Spanish speakers, as a result, not only acquired new territory in the Conquest but also a labor force large enough so that very few of the conquistadors had to do physical labor. In contrast, the Indians of the eastern United States were primarily nomadic hunters who moved to new territories as the colonists took over their lands. The early Americans, as a result, had no available work force, and they could survive only by their own work.

These different situations led to two quite different cultural attitudes. The success of the American colonies and the individual colonists depended upon hard work. No stigma, as a result, was attached to physical labor and, what was more important still, hard work could bring success to the most humble man. Thus, many of the early presidents of the United States were born in log cabins and one, the first Johnson, was illiterate at the time of his marriage and had to be taught to read and write by his wife. In contrast, Francisco Pizarro, who began life as an illiterate swineherder, became the conquerer of Peru and, as a reward for this feat, the governor of a vast territory. Success in the Latin world depended on acquiring the land and the labor of the natives, and two traditions developed as a consequence. First, the Spanish speaker gradually came to believe that manual labor or hard work was undignified and, second, the workers soon learned that hard work did not open the door to success. As a result, neither the upper nor the lower class Latin considers hard work as the stepping stone to a better life, and both find it difficult to understand the drive exhibited by the average American.

More on ser *and* estar
changed

Look at each frame below and see how fast you can spot the cues and decide whether you would use *ser* or *estar*.

1   The water in the pot *is* now *hot*. ▲

estar (It has been heated and, so, changed.)

2   The White House in Washington *is white*. ▲

ser (That's our color norm for the White House.)

3   All astronomers know that some stars *are red*. ▲

ser (There are, as a part of nature, red, and white stars.)

4   Any man who has lived 90 years *is old*. ▲

ser (90 meets our norm for old age.)

5   Charo has just gotten a new car. She *is happy*. ▲

estar (Getting the car made her happy.)

6   Somebody smashed the window. Father *is furious*. ▲

estar (The broken window caused him to become angry, a change.)

7   You can't go yet. The stoplight *is red*. ▲

estar (It always keeps changing so you have no norm for stoplights.)

8   Look at your shoes! They *are dirty!* ▲

estar (You got them dirty.)

9   Snow *is white*. ▲

ser (We would be astonished by green snow.)

10 Mr. Martel is such a nice man. He *is so kind*. ▲

ser (The speaker always sees him this way.)

11 Watch out! The floor *is slick!* ▲

estar (It's dangerous to have slippery floors. This is abnormal.)

12 I haven't seen John in weeks. Look how thin he *is now!* (What does the exclamation intonation tell you?) ▲

estar (We usually don't exclaim about what is normal.)

13 Lead *is heavy;* feathers *are light*. ▲

ser (The weight norm for both.)

14 We can't go sailing today. It's storming and the sea *is rough*. ▲

estar (The storm has caused the sea to become rough. Notice that "become" signals a change. It is sometimes the best translation of *estar*.)

15 Lincolns and Cadillacs *are expensive*. ▲

ser (Prestige cars are always expensive.)

16 That's odd. In this light your face *is green*. ▲

estar (Green is not our color norm for human skin.)

17 The pampas of Argentina *are very flat*. ▲

ser (A plain has to be fairly flat.)

18 Grown elephants *are huge*. ▲

ser (We usually think so.)

19 Pygmies *are small*. ▲

ser (It's their nature.)

20 If you got all of these correct, you *are very intelligent*. ▲

ser (You were born that way. You are also pretty smart if you got most right.)

LOS PINOS SON RECTOS

LOS PINOS SON TORCIDOS

A/B

LOS PINOS
ESTÁN
TORCIDOS

C/D

LOS PINOS
ESTÁN
RECTOS

E/F

Review of Verb Forms

1 The three sets of verbs are marked by the vowels _____. ▲

2 The set vowel of a verb tells you what morphemes to use for the (a) first (b) second suffix. ▲

a, e, i

3 In the present tense of all regular verbs, the *yo* form always ends in the morpheme _____. ▲

first

4 Aside from the *yo* form, the first suffix of *a*-verbs is always _____. ▲

o

a

161

5 The regular *e*-verbs have only two morphemes for the first suffix: _____. ▲

6 The *i*-verb forms have three morphemes for the first suffix: _____. ▲

7 The *i* always goes with the subject pronoun _____. ▲

8 The second suffix tells you something about (a) the action (b) the subject. ▲

o; e

o, e, i

nosotros (vivimos)

9 The *n* tells you the subject is either second or third person and _____. ▲

the subject

plural (*ustedes viven, ellos hablan*)

10 There are three suffixes for second person. One is zero (*usted habla*). The other two are _____. ▲

11 The *s* always goes with the subject pronoun _____. ▲

n; s

12 The *mos* tells you the subject is _____ and plural. ▲

tú

first person (*nosotros*)

13 The stem of the irregular verb *tener* has three allomorphs in the present tense: _____. ▲

14 Complete the form: *yo teng* _____ ▲

teng, ten, tien

15 Which subject pronoun goes with the stem *ten*? ▲

yo tengo

16 There are seven different subject pronouns that go with the stem *tien*. Write them down, copy *tien*, and add the matching suffixes. ▲

nosotros tenemos

tú tienes, él tiene, ella tiene, usted tiene, ustedes tienen, ellos tienen, ellas tienen

17 What verb has the same irregularities as *tener*? ▲

venir (vengo, vienes, venimos)

18 The verb *estar* has two irregularities. One is in the form that goes with *yo*: _____. The other is the stress on the (a) first suffix (b) second suffix. ▲

estoy; the stress on the first suffix

19 The two present tense forms of *estar* that do not have a written accent are _____. ▲

20 The present tense forms of what verb are like *estar*? ▲

estoy; estamos

21 Copy and fill in the forms of *ir* for: *yo* . . . , *tú* . . . , *ellos* . . . . ▲

ir

yo voy, tú vas, ellos van

22 *Ser* is one of the most irregular verbs in the Spanish language. You have to learn most forms one by one. Copy and fill in the blanks: *yo* . . . , *nosotros* . . . *mos*, *tú* . . . *s*, *ustedes* . . . *n*. ▲

yo soy, nosotros somos, tú eres, ustedes son

Review of Phonetics, Phonemics, and Graphemics

1 The phoneme /d/ has how many allophones? ▲

2 One of its allophones is a _____; the other is a _____. ▲

two

3 What tells you which allophone to say? What comes (a) before the *d* (b) after the *d*. ▲

stop; fricative

4 What do you say after silence, /n/, or /l/, the stop [d] or the fricative [đ]? ▲

before the *d*

5 The phoneme /s/ has two allophones. It is voiced before a vowel. (a) true (b) false ▲

the stop [d]

false (It may be voiced before a following voiced consonant.)

6 The graphemes *b* and *v* stand for different sounds. (a) true (b) false ▲

false (Some speakers, however, make a different sound for each.)

7 There are three digraphs which are part of the regular Spanish alphabet. They are *ñ* and _____. ▲

8 There are two other digraphs which did not get into the alphabet. They appear only before *e* and *i*. They are _____. ▲

ch; ll

qu (que); gu (Miguel)

9 Here is the English for twenty words that you have to *see* in order to learn to spell them. Write the Spanish for each and, when you are through, check your spelling word by word.

1	How?	6	How many?	11	wind	16	to live
2	Where?	7	there is	12	well	17	to drink
3	What?	8	thou art	13	difficult	18	winter
4	truth	9	Brazil	14	easy	19	immense
5	young	10	Who?	15	balcony	20	dirty ▲

1	*¿Cómo?*	6	*¿Cuántos?*	11	*viento*	16	*vivir*
2	*¿Dónde?*	7	*hay*	12	*bien*	17	*beber*
3	*¿Qué?*	8	*tú eres*	13	*difícil*	18	*invierno*
4	*verdad*	9	*Brasil*	14	*fácil*	19	*inmenso*
5	*joven*	10	*¿Quién?*	15	*balcón*	20	*sucio*

Making Choices

1 Match *yo* and *llamo* with the right object pronoun: *Yo* _____ *llamo Alberto.* ▲

2 When you address your instructor, you use (a) *tú* (b) *usted*. ▲

3 When a noun ends in a consonant, you make it plural by adding _____. ▲

4 What tells you to use *el* with *libro*? ▲

me

usted

es

the final phoneme /o/

5 You want to locate Santiago in Chile. You use the verb _____. ▲

estar (Santiago está en Chile.)

6 You want to locate *una pluma* on the table. You use the verb (a) *haber* (b) *estar* (c) *ser*. ▲

*haber (**Hay** una pluma en la mesa.)*

7 You want to say where someone is from. You use the verb _____. ▲

ser (Es de las Guayanas.)

8 You are a girl speaking for yourself and a group of girls. You use the subject pronoun _____. ▲

9 To say a person *is hot*, you use the verb _____. ▲

10 To say the weather *is hot*, you use _____. ▲

11 To change *Hace calor* to the equivalent of "It is very hot," you add (a) *muy* (b) *mucho*. ▲

nosotras

tener (Tiene calor.)

hacer (Hace calor.)

mucho (Because calor is a noun and muy is an adverb.)

12 With all clock numbers from 2 to 12 you use the verb form _____ in telling time. ▲

13 In telling time, the hour 2 can be used with two different parts of the day: *son* (But *Es la una.*) _____. ▲

14 Write the missing relator: *Vamos* _____ *cantar.* ▲

mañana ; tarde

a

Self-Correcting Exercises

Don't forget to cover the answers and check for accuracy after each response.

A Choose *ir* or *venir*.

1 You and your roommate are in your room. There's a knock at the door. Your roommate says to you: "Will you *go* to the door?"

ir

2 Before you get to the door, there is another loud knock, and you call out, "I'm *coming*!"

ir

3 Mark and Bob are studying for a test in Bob's apartment. The phone rings and Bob answers. It is Mark's wife who says: "Tell Mark to *come* home right away."

venir

4 Mark says to Bob: "Tell her I'll *come* home in about 10 minutes."

ir

5 You are away from home at school. In a letter to your family you write: "When vacation *comes*, I'm *coming* home."

venir, ir

6 Your mother gets the letter. After reading the news she says to your father, "Paul is *coming* home."

venir

7 *Come* here, Lola!

venir

8 Friends in México have invited you to visit them. You write to them: "I'll *come* down to visit you when I get out of school."

ir

9 Indian corn developed from a plant that *came* from Asia.

venir

10 Years ago many Germans *came* to America. Before they left Germany, they talked about *going* to the New World.

venir

ir

B Ask and answer these questions.

1 ¿A qué hora comen en tu residencia (dormitorio, casa)?

Comemos a las . . .

2 ¿A qué hora estudias español?

Estudio español a la(s) . . .

3 ¿Cuándo vienes a la universidad?

Vengo a la(s) . . .

4 ¿Cuándo es tu clase de inglés?

Mi clase de inglés es a la(s) . . .

5 ¿A qué hora vas al laboratorio?

Voy al laboratorio a la(s) . . .

6 ¿A qué hora trabajas?

Trabajo a la(s) . . .

7 ¿Cuándo van a ser las vacaciones?

Las vacaciones van a ser en el mes de . . .

No new vocabulary. Review your vocabulary list and study those words you have marked as problems.

Syllabication

Consonants

You do not need to know how to divide words into syllables as long as you are learning by direct imitation of speech. However, to read new words aloud without a spoken model you need this information.

1 To English cognates that end in two consonants Spanish usually adds a vowel: modern, *moderno*. There are two vowels in "modern" and two syllables. There are _____ vowels in *moderno* and _____ syllables. ▲

2 The English adjective is divided into syllables and stressed this way: *mod-ern*. Let's add the Spanish *o*. If we change nothing else, we get **mod-ern-o**. Spanish speakers would never understand this because they divide the word differently and stress a syllable which does not even exist in English. They say *mo-der-no*. Look at these words which are typical of the whole language: *to-tal, ma-lo, bue-no, vi-ven*. The first syllable ends in a _____. The second begins with a _____. ▲

three, three

vowel; consonant (A consonant between two vowels always goes with the following syllable.)

3 Copy and syllabicate these words: *pálido, feliz, pero, una, fácil.* ▲

pá-li-do, fe-liz, pe-ro, u-na, fá-cil

4 Now look at these words: *doc-tor, gor-do, tris-te, lim-pio, rec-to*. The last phoneme of the first syllable and the first phoneme of the second syllable are _____. ▲

5 In these examples when there are two consonants between two vowels, one goes with the first syllable and the other with the _____ syllable. ▲

consonants

second or next syllable

6 Copy and syllabicate these words: *Atlántico, norte, cerca, tarde.* ▲

At-lán-ti-co, nor-te, cer-ca, tar-de

7 Will the digraphs *ch* and *ll* be divided between two syllables? ▲

no (Because in Spanish each one is a letter in the alphabet and you cannot divide a letter.)

8 Copy and syllabicate these words: *mucho, pizarra, allí, señor.* ▲

mu-cho, pi-za-rra, a-llí, se-ñor

9 There is an exception to the rule on how to divide double consonants. Look what happens to these words: *ha-blar, i-gle-sia, a-le-gre, pa-dre, cen-tro*. When the second of two consonants in a row is either _____ or _____, the first goes along with it. ▲

l or *r* (The exceptions to this exception are *s* (*is-la*) and *t* (*At-lán-ti-co*).)

10 The Spanish speaker never begins a native word with *s* plus another consonant. He adds a syllable-forming *e* because, without special practice, it is difficult for him to say *s* plus another consonant in the same syllable. You may remember Spain, *España*; school, *escuela*; Spanish, *español*. Considering this fact, how will the Spanish speaker syllabicate *instante*? ▲

ins-tan-te (An *st* sequence does not bother us at all, and we syllabicate the cognate like this: in-stant.)

11 This is the way we syllabicate "con-struc-tor." How will the Spanish speaker do it? ▲

12 Syllabicate these words: *español, estado, estar.* ▲

cons-truc-tor
es-pa-ñol, es-ta-do, es-tar

In both cultures there are social rules which govern who may and may not use diminutives. People of all ages and both sexes may use the diminutives of given names to show friendliness or affection (*Pancho > Panchito, Ana > Anita, John > Johnny, Juan > Juanito*). A child or a woman may say *horsie*, but a grown male, and especially a cowboy, is not likely to use the word. This would be childish. Similarly, women may say *dearie*, but men use it less. In Latin America the diminutives are used much more frequently by women and children than by men. From the point of view of the Peninsular Spaniards, however, the Latin Americans overwork the diminutives, and there are quite a few which are not used in Spain at all; for example, *adiosito* (bye-bye) and *nadita* (hardly nothing), which are largely confined to Mexico.

Vowels

1 The letters which may stand for vowel sounds in Spanish are _____. ▲

a, e, i, o, u (*Y* is a true vowel only in the translation of "and.")

2 Spanish writes the consonant sound [w] and the vowel sound [u] with the same letter. So, if you are going to learn to read new words aloud without a model, you must learn when *u* stands for the vowel sound [u] and the consonant [w]. What does *u* stand for in these words? Say them aloud: *u-nos, su-cio, mu-cho, Ra-úl.* (a) vowel (b) consonant ▲

vowel (When the letter *u* is the only vowel letter in a syllable, it stands for the vowel sound.)

3 The spelling *cuando* stands for (a) [ku-an-do] (b) [kwan-do]. ▲

[kwan-do]

4 How many vowel sounds are there in *cuando*? (a) two (b) three ▲

two (The *u* stands for [w] and, so, there are just two vowels, [a] and [o].)

5 You pronounce *bueno* as [bwe-no]. How do you say *escuela*? (a) [es-ku-e-la] (b) [es-kwe-la] ▲

6 You have never seen this word: *cui-da-do*. Will the *u* stand for (a) [u]? (b) [w]? ▲

[es-kwe-la]

for [w] (When the letter *u* comes directly before *a, e,* or *i,* it stands for the consonant sound [w].)

7 How many vowel sounds are there in *Uruguay*? ▲

8 Divide *Uruguay* into syllables. ▲

three
U-ru-guay

9 Here's the word for "fire": *fuego*. How many vowel sounds does it have? ▲

10 Copy and syllabicate *fuego*. ▲

two

fue-go (You pronounce it [*fwe*-go].)

11 To find out how many syllables there are in a Spanish word, you count (a) the vowel letters (b) the vowel sounds. ▲

12 The cognate of "pause" is *pausa*. Spanish speakers pronounce *pausa* like [pow-sa]. But they pronounce the proper name, *Raúl*, like this [rra-úl]. What does the accent mark on the *ú* tell you? To read it aloud as [u] or as [w]. ▲

the vowel sounds

as [u] (The accent mark, then, is a spelling device to show that *u* really stands for the vowel sound [u], not the consonant [w].)

13 Let's see what this writing trick tells you about the letter *i*. Say *dí-a* and *me-dia* aloud. Do *í* in *dí-a* and *i* in *me-dia* stand for exactly the same sound? ▲

14 The accented *i* stands for the vowel sound [i]. Now say *yo* and *ya* aloud. When you say *me-dia* does it sound a lot like [me-dya]? ▲

no

15 The letter *i* has, like *u*, two jobs to do. The Spanish speaker writes *y* only at the beginning of a syllable or at the end of a word. Everywhere else he uses *i* for [y]. So he says these words like this: *media* [me-ɡ́ya], *tiene* [tye-ne], *veinte* [veyn-te], *aire* [ay-re].

yes

What does he do with *ciudad*? He divides it this way: *ciu-dad*. The *u* stands for [u], the *i* must stand for (a) the vowel [i] (b) the consonant [y]. ▲

[y] (So he says [syu-ɡ́aɡ́].)

16 Let's pull all this information together, now, so you will know the right cues for reading aloud. The letters *a*, *o*, and *e* always stand for vowel sounds. Are they always pronounced in Spanish? ▲

yes (Except when run together in rapid speech.)

17 Does what comes before or after them produce different vowel allophones? ▲

18 The letters *u* and *i* may stand for two different sounds, a vowel and another sound which is more like a consonant. (Linguists say it is sometimes a semi-vowel, a semi-consonant, or a consonant. We will say it is not a vowel.) The letters *u* and *i* always stand for the vowel sound when they have an accent mark (*ú, í*). (a) true (b) false ▲

no

true (*frí-o, dí-a, Ra-úl*)

19 The letters *u* and *i* always stand for the vowel sound when they are the only vowel letter in a syllable. (a) true (b) false ▲

true (***cin**-co, vi-**vi**-mos, **lu**-nes*)

20 When *u* has no accent mark and is immediately followed by any vowel letter, it stands for [w]. (a) true (b) false ▲

true (***cuan**-do* [kwan-do]*, **bue**-no* [bwe-no]*, **cui**-da-do* [kwi-da-do])

21 When *i* has no accent mark and is immediately followed by any vowel letter, it stands for [y]. (a) true (b) false ▲

true (*me-**dia, tie**-ne, su-**cio, ciu**-dad*)

22 In these combinations the second vowel letter always stands for a real vowel. (a) true (b) false ▲

true (This is the one you count in finding out how many syllables there are in a word.)

23 When *i* comes before *u*, the *u* stands for a vowel. When *a*, *e*, or *o* comes immediately before *u* (with no accent mark), the *u* stands for (a) a vowel (b) a sound like [w]. ▲

a sound like [w] (Remember *pausa* which is pronounced [pow-sa].)

24 When *a, e, o* comes immediately before *i* (with no accent mark), *i* stands for [i] or [y]. ▲

[y] (Compare *hay* and *ai-re*.)

25 The number of vowel sounds in a word is always the same as the number of syllables. There can, consequently, never be two vowel sounds in the same syllable. (a) true (b) false ▲

26 The English word "triumph" is divided *tri-umph*. Its Spanish cognate is *triunfo*. It has _____ pure vowel sounds. ▲

true

two (If you got it right, it's a triumph for you. The *n* and *f* must go in separate syllables, so *triun* has only one real vowel, *u*. The *i* is pronounced [y].)

Summary

To separate Spanish words into syllables you need to know these facts:

1 The number of pure vowel sounds in a word is always the same as the number of syllables. There can never be more than one pure vowel sound in a syllable.

2 All five vowel letters stand for pure vowel sounds when they do not appear immediately preceding or following another vowel: *cla-se, cu-ba-no, ti-za.*

3 The vowel letters *u* and *i* (sometimes *y*) when immediately preceding or following *a, e,* or *o,* do not stand for pure vowel sounds and should not be counted when determining the total number of syllables in a word: *Bue-nos Ai-res, San-tia-go, au-to, es-toy, Pa-ra-guay.*

4 When *ú* and *í* have an accent mark they always stand for a pure vowel sound: *Ra-úl, Ma-rí-a.*

5 A consonant between two vowels usually goes with the following syllable: *di-fí-cil, pa-sa-do ma-ña-na.*

6 Two consonants between vowels are usually separated: *nor-te, tris-te, ven-ta-na, At-lán-ti-co.*

7 *Qu* and *gu* before *e* or *i,* the digraphs *ch, ll, rr,* and usually the clusters composed of consonant plus *l* or *r* are not separated: *par-que, mos-qui-to, Mi-guel, al-guien, mu-cha-cho, a-llí, pi-za-rra, i-gle-sia, a-le-gre.*

La familia: *Vocabulary Comprehension and Writing Practice*

1 Each person in a family tree can have many different relative names. I am the "son" of my father, the "grandson" of my father's mother, the "nephew" of my aunt, and the "cousin" of my uncle's son. These relationship words are

really not names for me but for the family relationship between me and other
members of the family. You already know all these facts in English and the set
of words to describe the various relationships. The Spanish patterns are just
like English so all you need to learn is the spelling and pronunciation of the
Spanish words.

Here is the basic difference between two sets of family relationship words.
English usually tells the sex of individuals having the same relationship by
using paired words that are very different. For example:

mother   daughter   sister   aunt   niece   grandmother
father   son   brother   uncle   nephew   grandfather

English does not distinguish the sex of "cousins." In contrast, Spanish has
different paired words for *padre* and *madre* and tells the sex only by the contrast
between *o* (masculine) and *a* (feminine) in all other words. For example:

madre   hija   hermana   tía   sobrina   abuela   prima (*cousin*)
padre   hijo   hermano   tío   sobrino   abuelo   primo

Here is one other basic difference. The Spanish cognate of "parents" is
parientes, but it means "relatives." The word for "parents" is *padres*, which
looks exactly like "fathers."

Let's see, now, how well you can understand family relationships in Spanish.
Write the missing word and check your spelling: *La hija de mi padre es
mi* _____. ▲

2 Yo, Pablo, soy el _____ de mi hermana. ▲   *hermana*

3 Somos los _____ de mi padre. ▲   *hermano*

4 El hermano de mi madre o de mi padre es mi _____. ▲   *hijos*

5 La hermana de mi padre o de mi madre es mi _____. ▲   *tío*

6 Mi padre y mi madre son mis _____. ▲   *tía*

7 La madre de mi padre o madre es mi _____. ▲   *padres*

8 El padre de mi madre o de mi padre es mi _____. ▲   *abuela*

9 Los padres de mis padres son mis _____. ▲   *abuelo*

                         abuelos (Just like *muchachos*, boy and girl.)

10 Yo soy el hijo de mis _____. Yo soy el sobrino de mis _____. ▲

11 La hija de mi hermana es mi _____. ▲   *padres, tíos*

12 Los hijos de mi hermano son mis _____. ▲   *sobrina*

13 María es la hija de mis tíos. ¿Qué es? Es mi _____. ▲   *sobrinos*

14 Mi primo, Jorge, es el _____ de mis tíos. ▲   *prima*

15 El padre de Jesús y de Remigia es el señor Villarreal. Jesús y Remigia son   *hijo*
hijos del señor Villarreal. ¿Qué son también? ▲

16 Mis primos, tíos, y sobrinos son mis _____. (*Remember that deceptive cog-*   *hermanos*
nate). ▲

17 Write the Spanish equivalents for: aunt, uncle, aunt and uncle. ▲   *parientes*

18 Translate: son, daughter, children. ▲   *tía, tío, tíos*

19 One word for "priest" is *padre*. The word for "father" is *padre*. The word   *hijo, hija, hijos*
for "parents" is _____. ▲

20 Paco and Lola are my cousins. The Spanish word is _____. ▲   *padres*

21 However, Lola is my _____ in Spanish. ▲   *primos*

                                                          prima

Espera

Hold either hand, fingers up and palm out, the way a
policeman directs traffic to stop.

Self-Correcting Exercises

A   Translate orally into Spanish. Do this exercise at least twice.

I'm coming from the bank. *Vengo del banco.*

1	I'm leaving the bank.	Salgo del banco.
2	I'm going to the bank.	Voy al banco.
3	I'm arriving at the bank.	Llego al banco.
4	I'm entering the bank.	Entro en el banco.

We're going to the store. *Vamos a la tienda.*

5	We're arriving at the store.	Llegamos a la tienda.
6	We're entering the store.	Entramos en la tienda.
7	We're leaving the store.	Salimos de la tienda.
8	We're coming from the store.	Venimos de la tienda.

B   Write these clock times using Arabic numbers plus AM or PM. For additional practice cover the left column and say each time aloud.

1	La una y quince de la tarde.	1:15 PM
2	Las siete y media de la mañana.	7:30 AM

3	Las once y veinte de la noche.	11:20 PM
4	Las dos menos cuarto de la tarde.	1:45 PM
5	Las doce menos cuarto de la noche.	11:45 PM
6	Las nueve y veinticinco de la mañana.	9:25 AM
7	Las dos menos cinco de la mañana.	1:55 AM

New Vocabulary

familia	family	**hermana**	sister	**agua**	water
padre	father	**hermano**	brother	**pino**	pine tree
madre	mother	**tía**	aunt	**recto**	straight
hija	daughter	**tío**	uncle	**torcido**	crooked
hijo	son	**prima, -o**	cousin	**caliente**	hot
abuela	grandmother	**sobrina**	niece	**este, esta, esto**	this
abuelo	grandfather	**sobrino**	nephew		

Assignment 27

Word Stress and the Written Accent Mark

1   To be able to read a new word aloud you have to know three facts: (1) which sounds do and do not go together (you say *ha-blar*, not *hab-lar*), (2) how many syllables there are (you say *cuan-do*, not *cu-an-do*), and (3) which syllable is stressed (you say *o-es-te*, not *o-es-te*.)

If a word has a written accent mark, you immediately know which vowel to stress. So to say the word right you only have to be able to break it up into the right syllables. Copy and syllabicate these words, then say them aloud and underline the stressed syllable: *Asunción, último, fácil, diálogo.*   ▲

   *a-sun-**ción**, **úl**-ti-mo, **fá**-cil, **diá**-lo-go (diá is not like dí-a.)*

2   Copy and syllabicate *tienen, alumnos, popular, vienes*. Then say each aloud and underline the stressed syllable.   ▲

   ***tie**-nen, a-**lum**-nos, po-pu-**lar**, **vie**-nes*

3   When a word ends in the phoneme /s/ or /n/ (and has no written accent), the stress falls on the <u>next-to-last</u> syllable: *tie-nen, pa-pe-les*. In contrast, when a word ends in a consonant, except *n* or *s* (and has no written accent), the stress falls on the <u>last</u> syllable. Copy, syllabicate, and underline the stressed syllable: *tropical, preguntan, subir, directores.*   ▲

   *tro-pi-**cal**, pre-**gun**-tan, su-**bir**, di-rec-**to**-res*

4   The prime purpose of the written accent mark is to tell you (when you read a new word aloud) that the stressed syllable does not obey the two rules given above. Thus, when a word ending in *n* or *s* is stressed on the last syllable, it always has a written accent. Copy, syllabicate, write in the accent mark, and underline the stressed syllable: *perdon, estas, jardin, balcon.* ▲

per-**dón**, es-**tás**, jar-**dín**, bal-**cón**

5   When a word ends in a vowel, the vowel of the preceding syllable is stressed. If the final vowel is stressed, it always has a written accent mark. Copy, syllabicate, add the accent mark, and underline the stressed syllable: *Bogota, esta, aqui, alli.* ▲

Bo-go-**tá**, es-**tá**, a-**quí**, a-**llí**

6   Have you noticed that most Spanish words are stressed on either the last or the next-to-last syllable? When a word has the stress on any other syllable, it will have a written accent mark. Say these words aloud: *miercoles, rapido, ultimo, lapices.* Now copy, syllabicate them, and add the written accent. ▲

miér-co-les, **rá**-pi-do, **úl**-ti-mo, **lá**-pi-ces

7   Copy and syllabicate these words and underline the stressed syllable: *como, donde, cuantos, cuales.* ▲

co-mo, **don**-de, **cuan**-tos, **cua**-les

8   When these words are used in questions or exclamations, they always have an accent mark over the stressed vowel: *¿Có-mo? ¿Dón-de? ¿Cuán-tos? ¿Cuá-les?* Is the accent mark needed to tell you what syllable to stress? ▲

no (The accent mark now says the whole word is stressed in asking a question.)

9   When [ke] is used in exclamations, it may be stressed, and take an accent mark. Punctuate this sentence as an exclamation and write in the accent mark: *Que calor hace.* ▲

10   Here are all the words you have had which have the stress on a syllable which is *before* the last two. They must all have a written accent mark. Cover the italicized columns and think of where the accent mark goes on the syllabicated forms. Slide your cover sheet down word by word and check your accuracy.

¡Qué calor hace!

mier-co-les	*miércoles*	nu-me-ro	*número*
sa-ba-do	*sábado*	o-ce-a-no	*océano*
A-me-ri-ca	*América*	do-mes-ti-co	*doméstico*
ra-pi-do	*rápido*	zo-o-lo-gi-co	*zoológico*
dia-lo-go	*diálogo*	mag-ni-fi-co	*magnífico*
Me-xi-co	*México*	ul-ti-mo	*último*
re-pu-bli-ca	*república*	hu-me-do	*húmedo*
pa-gi-na	*página*	mu-si-ca	*música*
At-lan-ti-co	*Atlántico*	o-lim-pi-co	*olímpico*
Pa-ci-fi-co	*Pacífico*		

11   Here are all the words you have had which end in a consonant but do not have the stress on the last syllable. Cover the right column and write the Spanish equivalents. Slide your cover sheet down word for word to check your accuracy.

pencil	*lá-piz*	easy	*fá-cil*
difficult	*di-fí-cil*	tunnel	*tú-nel*

12   Here are all the words you have had that end in a vowel and are stressed on the last syllable. Cover the right column and write the Spanish equivalents.

there	*a-llí*	he is (here)	*es-tá*
here	*a-quí*	cafe	*ca-fé*

13 Here are all the words you have had which end in *n* or *s* and do have the stress on the last syllable. Cover the italicized column and say the Spanish equivalents aloud one by one.

English	*in-glés*	season	*es-ta-ción*
pardon	*per-dón*	invention	*in-ven-ción*
they are (here)	*es-tán*	television	*te-le-vi-sión*
you are (here)	*es-tás, es-tán*	garden	*jar-dín*
combination	*com-bi-na-ción*	also	*tam-bién*
lesson	*lec-ción*	country	*pa-ís*
		besides	*a-de-más*

Summary

In order to know which syllable to stress when reading aloud or where to place the accent mark when writing Spanish words, you need to know these facts:

1 When a word ends in a vowel, *s*, or *n* and has no written accent, the stress falls on the <u>next-to-last</u> syllable: *argentino, argentinos, catorce, **corren**, estudias*.

2 When a word ends in a consonant except *n* or *s* and has no written accent, the stress falls on the <u>last</u> syllable: *español, trabajar, ciudad, universidad*.

3 The main purpose of the written accent is to mark the stressed syllable in words that do not fit the above rules:
a words ending in a vowel, *n*, or *s* and having the stress on the last syllable require the accent mark: *aquí, Bogotá, están, estás*.
b words ending in a consonant except *n* or *s* and having the stress on the next-to-last syllable require an accent mark: *fácil, lápiz, mártir* (martyr).
c regardless of ending, when the stress falls anywhere else, the accent mark will be needed: *lápices, sábado, zoológico, miércoles*.

4 Words like *que, como, donde, quien, cual, cuando* require an accent mark when used in interrogative or exclamatory patterns: *¿Qué hora es?, ¡Qué tarde es!, ¿Cómo estás?, ¡Cómo estudias!*

Review *of* ser *and* estar

To choose between these two verbs you must remember two things: how they stand in contrast with each other and what cues the choice.

1 You have been taught three uses or functions of *estar*. It is used to _____ something in space: *Juan está en Granada.* ▲

2 To talk about a person's _____: *¿Cómo está usted?* ▲

3 To describe the subject with a _____ adjective: *María está triste.* ▲

4 You know that *ser, estar,* and *haber* all translate "to be." Since *ser* has more functions than either *haber* or *estar*, some of its uses do not stand in contrast

locate
health
predicate

with the other two verbs. The only one of these three verbs used to state the origin of a person or thing is _____. ▲

5 When you give the origin of a person or thing, you use *ser*, the relator _____, and a place name. ▲

ser

de (Yo soy de Argentina.)

6 When a subject noun and a predicate noun stand for the same entity, you say they are equal by using only _____. ▲

ser (The sentence *Antonio es un alumno* is very much like the formula *Antonio = alumno*.)

7 The only verb you use for adding and subtracting is _____. ▲

ser (Diez y once son veintiuno. Doce menos tres son nueve.)

8 You use two forms of the Present of *ser* in telling time. They are _____. ▲

es, son (The subject is the noun *hora* or *horas* and the forms are third person.)

9 Write this out in Spanish: It's 1:30 A.M. ▲

Es la una y media de la mañana.

10 Write out: It's 2:00 P.M. ▲

Son las dos de la tarde.

11 When you talk about the location of an entity, you must choose between *haber* and _____. ▲

12 An unmodified proper name cues the use of _____ for location. ▲   *estar*

13 When you describe the subject with a predicate adjective, you must choose between _____. ▲   *estar*

14 The sentence states your norm for the subject. You use _____. ▲   *ser* and *estar*

15 Describe Gilda as very friendly according to your experience. ▲   *ser*

Gilda es muy amable.

16 The sentence states that the subject has undergone some change. You use _____. ▲

17 Write a sentence in which you suggest with the verb chosen that something has caused Jesús to become sad. ▲   *estar*

Jesús está triste. (Remember *Jesús* is a common name in Spanish.)

18 You discover, frequently to your surprise, that something does not fit your norm or previous experience. You report this by using _____. ▲

19 Michael has thought that choosing between *ser* and *estar*, in his words, *es difícil*. He gets to this point in the Assignment and suddenly has to change his mind. He exclaims, ¡_____ *fácil!* ▲   *estar*

20 By tomorrow he gets used to this and has a new norm. He now says, _____ *fácil.* ▲   *¡Está fácil!*

21 A huge tank of chemicals catches fire at night. For hours the sky *is* brilliant white. (a) *ser* (b) *estar* ▲   *Es fácil.*

22 The sun comes up and soon the ground *is* warm. (a) *ser* (b) *estar* ▲   *estar*

estar (The sun heats up the cold ground; its temperature changes.)

23 Everybody knows that lead *is* soft. (a) *ser* (b) *estar* ▲

24 Don't touch it. Your gloves *are* dirty. (a) *ser* (b) *estar* ▲   *ser*

25 Most of the music written by de Falla *is* very Spanish. (a) *ser* (b) *estar* ▲   *estar*

ser (After all, de Falla was a Spaniard.)

Self-Correcting Exercises

A Write the combinations for this visual-graphic drill.

Ejemplo: 43 = María y Lola son populares.

1	Tú (*f*)	
2	Paco y yo	
3	Yo	ser
4	María y Lola	
5	Ustedes (*m*)	

1	baj-.
2	amable.
3	popular.
4	joven.

1)	11	Tú eres baja.
2)	22	Paco y yo somos amables.
3)	33	Yo soy popular.
4)	44	María y Lola son jóvenes.
5)	51	Ustedes son bajos.
6)	12	Tú eres amable.
7)	13	Tú eres popular.
8)	14	Tú eres joven.
9)	54	Ustedes son jóvenes.
10)	21	Paco y yo somos bajos.

B Do this drill aloud several times until you can do it quickly and with perfect pronunciation.

1	Si Pedro es de Paraguay, ¿qué es?	Es paraguayo.
2	Si Lola es de Ecuador, ¿qué es?	Es ecuatoriana.
3	Si ellos son de Brasil, ¿qué son?	Son brasileños.
4	Si ellas son de Chile, ¿qué son?	Son chilenas.
5	Si ella es de Perú, ¿qué es?	Es peruana.
6	Si ellos son de Colombia, ¿qué son?	Son colombianos.
7	Si Pablo es de Bolivia, ¿qué es?	Es boliviano.
8	Si ellas son de Uruguay, ¿qué son?	Son uruguayas.
9	Si María es de Argentina, ¿qué es?	Es argentina.
10	Si ellos son de Venezuela, ¿qué son?	Son venezolanos.

New Vocabulary

maestro, -a	teacher	**apellido**	surname	**lindo, -a**	pretty
castellano	Castilian, Spanish	**fecha**	date (calendar)	**alegre**	happy, cheerful
chico	boy; small	**contestar**	to answer		
nombre	name	**responder**	to answer, respond	**ese**	that
				aquel	that

A/B

EL JUEGA CON SU HIJO

ELLA JUEGA CON SU HIJO

C/D

EL JUEGA CON SUS HIJOS

ELLA JUEGA CON SUS HIJOS

E/F

ELLOS JUEGAN CON SU HIJO

ELLOS JUEGAN CON SUS HIJOS

G

EL PÁJARO ESTÁ EN SU NIDO

Possessive Adjectives

An adjective tells us something about whatever a noun labels. The plural suffix of the noun *dollars* tells us the number is larger than one. The adjective *ten* in *ten dollars* makes the number precise. The adjective *these* in *these dollars* tells you they are close to the speaker. The adjective *red* in *a red car* describes a feature of the car. The adjective *distant* in *a distant star* describes the space between the speaker on earth and the star.

1 If I say, *That is my book*, does *my* (a) give a characteristic of the book? (b) tell you who owns it? ▲

my tells you who owns it (However, when you say *That is my home town*, you do not own the town.)

2 Does *That is my Spanish class* say that you own the class? ▲

no (Here *my* says you belong to that group: are a member of the class.)

3 What does *That is my uncle* tell you? (a) you own him (b) you both belong to the same family and he is your father's or mother's brother ▲

you both belong to the same family, *etc.*

4 A small child says, *That's my house*. What does this tell you? (a) the house belongs to him (b) he belongs there, *i.e.*, lives there ▲

5 What does *That is my teacher* tell you? (a) the teacher belongs to you (b) you belong to the class she teaches ▲

he belongs there

you belong to the class she teaches

6 You borrow a book from the library and take it to school. Someone picks it up by mistake and starts to carry it off. You say, *That is my book*. What does *my* mean? (a) you own the book (b) you are in temporary possession of it ▲

you are in temporary possession of it

7 Someone says of a table, *Its leg is broken*. What does *its* tell you? (a) the table owns the leg (b) the leg is part of the table, that is, belongs to the table ▲

the leg is part of the table

8 The forms *my, your, his, her, our, their,* and *its* are called **possessive adjectives.** "Possession," as you have just observed, does not always mean ownership. The possessive adjectives in both English and Spanish are actually pronouns with a possessive suffix. The subject pronoun for *George* is _____. ▲

9 If we add the apostrophe *s* to *George* we get *George's* as in *That is George's hat*. So to replace *George's* we need a morpheme for *George* and another for *'s*. The possessive that replaces *George's* is _____. ▲

he

10 The subject pronoun that replaces *George and Mary* is _____. ▲

his (hi + s)

11 If you rewrite *they* as *thei*, what must you add to make the form possessive? ▲

they

12 In addition to indicating possession the form *his* tells you the possessor is (a) female (b) male ▲

r (their)

13 Rewrite *That is his hat* so that the hat belongs to a woman. ▲

male

That is *her* hat.

177

14 The possessive adjectives *his* and *her* tell us the sex of the person to which something belongs. Rewrite *That is her house* so that the house belongs to a man and a woman. ▲

That is *their* house. (*Their* does not tell you the sex of the possessor.)

15 Very young boy and girl babies look a lot alike. What do people say: (a) What is his or her name? (b) What is its name? ▲

What is its name? (When we don't know the sex of a person or animal we use the neuter adjective *its*.)

16 Do *my*, *your*, *our*, and *their* indicate the sex of the possessor? ▲

no (Only *his* and *her* indicate the sex of the possessor.)

17 The adjectives *our* and *their* tell you the possessor is (a) singular (b) plural. ▲

18 The adjectives *my*, *his*, *her*, and *its* tell you the possessor is (a) singular (b) plural. ▲

plural

19 The possessive adjective *your* is different. It may tell you the possessor is either singular or _____. ▲

singular

plural (It is like *you* which can be *you*, singular, or *you all*, plural.)

20 To learn and understand a foreign language in the easiest way, you need to discover how the foreign language differs from your own. Here is a major contrastive difference between English and Spanish. English possessive adjectives do not agree in number with their nouns. Contrast these translations:

my friend	*mi amigo*
my friends	*mis amigos*

Do *mi* and *mis* agree in number with their noun? ▲

yes (Spanish possessive adjectives, like all other Spanish adjectives, always agree in number with their nouns.)

21 Do English "my" and Spanish *mi*, *mis* mark the sex of the speaker? ▲

no (There is no need for this. The hearer usually knows who the speaker is.)

22 The forms *mi* and *mis* go with *yo*, the speaker. The *m* is the pronoun stem, the *i* indicates possession, and *s* is the plural suffix. The plural of "my" is _____. ▲

23 There are four Spanish forms that translate "our." Two are plural; two are singular, to agree with the noun in number. Look at these translations.

our

our friend	*nuestro amigo*	our friends	*nuestros amigos*
	nuestra amiga		*nuestras amigas*

The *nosotros* forms of the Spanish possessive adjectives have *o-* and *a-*forms that match the terminal phoneme of the noun.

Translate: "Our house is here." ▲

Nuestra casa está aquí.

24 Translate: Our houses are here. ▲

Nuestras casas están aquí.

25 Translate: Our books are here. ▲

Nuestros libros están aquí.

26 In speech the possessive adjective that matches the subject pronoun [tu] is [tu]. In writing it has no accent mark: *tu*. You make it plural by adding _____. ▲

s: tus (there is no *o-a* agreement.)

27 Translate: your friend; your friends (male). ▲

tu amigo; tus amigos

You now know eight possessive forms and their meanings. Here they are:

yo	mi		nosotros	nuestro		tú	tu
	mis		nosotras	nuestra			tus
				nuestros			
				nuestras			

All of the other possessive English adjectives—"your" (*usted, ustedes*), "his" (*él*), "her" (*ella*), "their" (*ellos, ellas*), and "its" (*zero*)—are translated by just two forms: the singular *su* and the plural *sus*.

Summary

1 The English possessive adjectives are: my, our, your, his, her, its and their; their Spanish equivalents are *mi, nuestro, -a, tu,* and *su.*

2 The main differences between English and Spanish possessives are:
a None of the Spanish possessives indicate the sex of the possessor; in English, only "his" and "her" indicate sex.
b "Your" and *su* do not indicate whether the possessor is singular or plural; all the others in both languages do.
c English possessives do not agree in number with their nouns (*my* book, *my* books); all Spanish possessives like all other adjectives agree in number with their nouns (*mi libro, mis libros*) and, in addition, *nuestro* and *nuestra* have to match the terminal phoneme of the noun: *nuestra casa, nuestro jardín, nuestros cuadernos, nuestras plumas.*

Self-Correcting Exercises

A With answers covered and following the models, translate these patterns aloud and check your accuracy after each response.

I believe that it's cooler outside. *Creo que hace más fresco afuera.*

1 I believe that it's hotter outside.
2 I believe that it's windier outside.
3 I believe that it's colder outside.

Creo que hace más calor afuera.
Creo que hace más viento afuera.
Creo que hace más frío afuera.

I'm tired of reading. *Estoy cansado de leer.* (Be sure to use *cansada* if you are female.)

4 I'm tired of writing.
5 I'm tired of studying.
6 I'm tired of working.
7 I'm tired of eating.

Estoy cansado de escribir.
Estoy cansado de estudiar.
Estoy cansado de trabajar.
Estoy cansado de comer.

8	I'm tired of waiting.	Estoy cansado de esperar.
9	I'm tired of singing.	Estoy cansado de cantar.

B *General Review:* In this guided conversation you assume the role of all the individuals involved and say aloud all the questions and answers.

Paco, pregúntale a Lola cuántos días hay en una semana.	¿Cuántos días hay en una semana?
Lola, contéstale.	Hay siete días en una semana.
Pregúntale cuáles son los días de la semana.	¿Cuáles son los días de la semana?
Contéstale.	Los días de la semana son lunes, martes, miércoles, jueves, viernes, sábado y domingo.
Paco, dile a Lola de dónde eres y pregúntale de dónde es ella.	Yo soy de . . . ¿De dónde eres tú?
Lola, contéstale.	Yo soy de . . .
Dile cuál es la capital de Bolivia y pregúntale cuál es la capital de Perú.	La capital de Bolivia es la Paz. ¿Cuál es la capital de Perú?
Contéstale.	La capital de Perú es Lima.
Pregúntale a la señorita dónde vive.	¿Dónde vive usted, señorita?
Contéstale que vives aquí en esta ciudad.	Vivo aquí en esta ciudad.
Pregúntale a qué hora come.	¿A qué hora comes?
Contéstale que comes a las seis y cuarto.	Como a las seis y cuarto.
Pregúntale a dónde va mañana.	¿A dónde vas mañana?
Contéstale que vas al cine.	Voy al cine.

C Read the first two sentences aloud as models, then cover the remaining 10 and continue saying aloud the first three months for each season.
1) *El primer mes de la primavera es marzo.*
2) *El segundo mes de la primavera es abril.*

1 El tercer mes de la primavera es mayo.
2 El primer mes del verano es junio.
3 El segundo mes del verano es julio.
4 El tercer mes del verano es agosto.
5 El primer mes del otoño es septiembre.
6 El segundo mes del otoño es octubre.
7 El tercer mes del otoño es noviembre.
8 El primer mes del invierno es diciembre.
9 El segundo mes del invierno es enero.
10 El tercer mes del invierno es febrero.

New Vocabulary

dinero	money	**poner**	to put	**tu**	your
pájaro	bird	**ver**	to see	**su**	your, his, her, their, its
hacer	to make, do	**jugar (ue)**	to play (a game)		
saber	to know	**mi**	my	**después**	afterwards
		nuestro, -a	our	**después de**	after

Dinero

*Use either arm, bend it at the elbow and hold
hand comfortably in front of you with palm up.
Rub thumb back and forth several times across
the tips of the middle and index fingers.*

Assignment 29

Adjectival Residuals

The answer to *Do you have some change?* may be *Yes, I have some.* In this answer
change has been deleted because it is not necessary for communication, and what
is left of the original noun phrase is the adjectival residual *some*.

In English only the demonstratives and adjectives of number or quantity
regularly become adjectival residuals:

Look at that painting!   Do you like *that*?
I need three pencils.   I'll lend you *three*.

In Spanish *any* adjective may become a residual.

1   Rewrite this sentence and leave out the noun: *El hombre está aquí.*   ▲
2   Translate the two sentences: *El hombre está aquí. Él está aquí.*   ▲

Él está aquí.
The man is here. He is here.

3   The definite article *the* cannot become an adjectival residual in English.

When we drop a noun standing for a person, we also have to drop its adjective and replace both with a _____. ▲

> pronoun (Latin *pro* means "in place of" so *pro-noun* means "in place of a noun.")

4 If you rewrite *They are going to buy the house* and drop *the house*, what will you replace *the house* with? ▲

> it (They are going to buy *it*.)

5 Now, let's look at the Spanish translation of these sentences.

They are going to buy **the house.**	*Van a comprar **la casa.***
They are going to buy **it.**	*Van a comprar**la.***

The Spanish speaker just drops the noun and keeps the article, but we have two translations of *la*: _____. ▲

6 From the Spanish speaker's point of view, *la* does not change its meaning

> the; it

when he changes *Van a comprar la casa* to *Van a comprarla*. Speakers of English get the feeling that *la* changes meaning only because we cannot use "the" as an adjectival residual and, as a result, have to use two different words to translate *la*.

Let's look at this difference in the two languages again. Translate these two sentences: *Ellos van a comprar las casas. Ellos van a comprarlas.* ▲

> They are going to buy the houses. They are going to buy them.

7 English has to replace "the houses" with "them." Spanish just drops *casas* and keeps the adjectival residual _____. ▲

8 When the subject of discourse is a thing, we have to translate *la* and *las*

> las

three different ways. Translate the indicated words: (a) *Van a comprar **la** casa.* (b) *Van a comprar **las** casas.* (c) *Van a comprar**la**.* (d) *Van a comprar**las**.* ▲

9 Now, let's see what happens when the subject of discourse is a person.

> the; the; it; them

Translate the indicated words. *Voy a ver a **la** muchacha. Voy a ver**la**.* ▲

> The first *la* is "the"; the second has to be changed in our translation to "her".
> (For the Spanish speaker, however, *la* is the same word in both sentences.)

10 Look at the article in *las muchachas*. It is made up of three parts. The plural marker is *s*. The agreement phoneme is *a*. The stem is *l*. *Los* of *los hombres* also has three parts: the stem *l*, the agreement phoneme *o*, and the plural suffix *s*. The Spanish speaker also makes *los* singular by just dropping the *s* to get

_____. ▲

11 So the Spanish speaker has two singular forms for *los*. They are _____. ▲

> *lo*

> *el* and *lo* (We say, then, that this singular stem has two allomorphs, *el* and *l*.)

12 You already know that when a morpheme has two allomorphs, you find them used in different combinations. You use *teng* with *yo* (*tengo*), but *tien* with *tú* (*tienes*). The same thing happens to *el* and *lo*. Look at these four sentences and the indicated words.

Voy a comprar *los* lápices.	Voy a comprar**los**.
Voy a comprar *el* lápiz.	Voy a comprar**lo**.

The singular of *los* before a noun object is *el*. When the noun object is dropped, the adjusted residual form is _____, not *el*. ▲

> *lo*

Practice with Cognates

Read these sentences silently. Are they true or false?

1 El animal más grande que vive en el océano es el elefante. ▲
2 Una persona que tiene tuberculosis o cáncer sufre de una enfermedad. ▲   *mentira*
3 Los cristianos creen en Jesucristo. ▲   *verdad*
4 Compramos libros en una librería, pero leemos libros en la biblioteca de la   *verdad*
universidad. ▲
5 El árbol es una planta muy pequeña. ▲   *verdad*
6 El oxígeno es un mineral. ▲   *mentira*
7 Julio César fue un emperador del imperio romano. ▲   *mentira*
8 Un gorila es un animal. Un *guerrilla* en inglés es un hombre. ▲   *verdad*
9 La física, la química y la biología son ciencias. ▲   *verdad*
10 Arlington es el nombre de un cementerio nacional que está en el estado de   *verdad*
Virginia. ▲
11 El tigre de Sudamérica es una puma. ▲   *verdad*
12 La ciudad de Washington no está en el Distrito de Columbia. ▲   *verdad*
13 Stalin fue un dictador de Rusia. ▲   *mentira*
14 San Francisco fue un santo y San Francisco es una ciudad de California. ▲   *verdad*
15 El estado más grande de los Estados Unidos es Tejas. ▲   *verdad*

          mentira (*Es Alaska.* Do not mark this wrong if you just forgot about Alaska
but understood the sentence.)

Tener *versus* "*to be*"

1 Copy and fill in the blanks with *has* or *is*: He _____ a fever. He _____
feverish. ▲

      He has a fever. He is feverish.

2 Do this again: He _____ ill. He _____ an illness. ▲

      He is ill. He has an illness.

3 Copy and fill in the command forms *have* and *be*: _____ care! _____
careful! ▲

      Have care! Be careful!

4 The parts of speech of the words that come after *to have* and *to be* tell you
which to choose. *Have* is followed by a _____. ▲
5 *Be* is followed by an _____. ▲   noun
6 In Spanish, as in English, the part of speech tells you what verb to use.   adjective
The Spanish translation of "It's wind" is *Es viento*. Spanish also uses the noun
viento to describe the weather. Translate "It's windy." ▲

      Hace viento. (Makes wind.)

7 The Spanish speaker uses the noun *calor* to describe both the weather and
people. He does not say "I am heat" for the same reason that you do not say
it. Neither do you say "I am a fever" The noun "fever" tells you to say "I
have a fever." The noun *calor* tells the Spanish speaker to say *Yo* _____ *calor*. ▲

      Yo tengo calor.

8 How will you say, "I am cold?" _____ *frío.* ▲

Tengo frío.

9 You use "have" with the noun "care" (Have care!) but "be" with the adjective "careful" (Be careful!). The Spanish speaker always uses the noun *cuidado* to say both. What verb will he choose? (a) *ser* (b) *tener* ▲

tener (And the command form : *¡Tenga cuidado!*)

10 How will you say "I am careful"? _____ *cuidado.* ▲

Tengo cuidado.

11 You translate "It is very windy" by *Hace mucho viento.* How will you say "I am very careful?" ▲

Tengo mucho cuidado.

12 We can say in English either "He has a great thirst" or "He is very thirsty." Spanish uses only the noun *sed* to say this. You will use the verb _____. ▲

13 How do you say "I am hungry?" _____ *hambre.* ▲

tener (*Tiene sed.*)

Tengo hambre.

14 What do you think *diez años* will cue the Spanish speaker to say? (a) *Es diez años.* (b) *Tiene diez años.* ▲

Tiene diez años. (He has ten years = He is ten years old.)

15 In English we use "right" as an adjective (You are right) or as a noun (You have the right). Spanish uses the noun *razón* (reason) to translate the adjective meaning. How do you say "I am right?" _____ *razón.* ▲

16 If *Tengo razón* translates "I am right," then *No tengo razón* must translate "I am _____." ▲

Tengo razón.

wrong

There are a great many teenage American boys who feel a strong emotional necessity to prove publicly that they are brave and real he-men. These young men frequently take great risks to prove this to their peers, especially to other young men. They may play the game of chicken with cars. They sometimes fight mock wars with real guns. They may even steal cars or shoplift to show off, and, often, they consider it a badge of manhood to behave in a rebellious way to their teachers and parents. However, by the time the average American reaches the age of twenty-five the emotional need to keep his manhood on constant display generally disappears.

The average Latin teenage male exhibits much of the same emotional attitudes toward manhood as his American counterpart. There is, however, a significant cultural difference. The Latin is not so much concerned with achieving manhood as he is with being identified as *muy macho* (very much a male). As a result, the Latin teenager begins to exhibit aggressive behavior toward girls considerably earlier than American youths; and, more importantly, continues to be seriously preoccupied with exhibiting his maleness after he becomes an adult. Thus one of the problems of controlling the population explosion in Latin America is the belief that having a large family is one way of proving that the man *es muy macho.* Miners have been known to test their *machismo* by playing a dangerous game of chicken. Each man holds a stick of dynamite with a six inch fuse embedded in it. The two fuses are lighted simultaneously and the man who is *el más macho* holds on to the dynamite longer than the other before throwing it away.

Summary

Adjectival Residuals

1 To avoid constant repetition of object nouns, English substitutes them with pronouns: house→it, woman→her, man→him, houses/persons→them; Spanish, however, merely omits the noun and uses whatever form of the definite article precedes it, except that *lo*, an alternate singular form of *los*, is used instead of *el*: *la casa, la mujer→la; las casas, las mujeres→las; los lápices, los hombres→los; el lápiz, el hombre→lo.* These are called adjectival residuals.

Tener **versus "to be"**

2 In patterns used to talk about someone being hot, cold, hungry, thirsty, sleepy, careful, right, and so many years old, English uses "to be" plus an adjective; Spanish uses *tener* plus a noun: *tener calor, frío, hambre, sed, sueño, cuidado, razón, años.*

Self-Correcting Exercises

A Read aloud and complete with one word.

1	La madre de mi padre es mi . . .	abuela
2	El padre de mi madre es mi . . .	abuelo
3	Los padres de mis padres son mis . . .	abuelos
4	El hermano de mi padre es mi . . .	tío
5	Los hermanos de mi padre son mis . . .	tíos
6	La hija de mi tío es mi . . .	prima
7	El hijo de mi tía es mi . . .	primo
8	La hija de mi hermano es mi . . .	sobrina
9	Los hijos de mi hermano son mis . . .	sobrinos
10	Yo soy el sobrino de mis . . .	tíos
11	Yo soy el hermano de mis . . .	hermanos
12	Yo soy el hijo de mis . . .	padres
13	Yo soy el primo de la hija de mis . . .	tíos

B This exercise will prepare you for a quiz on *ser* and *estar* in the next class session. Select the correct answer in parentheses.

1	Mi libro de geografía dice que en el Polo Norte el agua (está, es) fría.	es
2	¡Caray! El refrigerador (está, es) caliente.	está
3	Todos saben que Jorge Luis Borges (está, es) argentino.	es
4	Las iglesias importantes siempre (están, son) grandes.	son
5	Mi madre (está, es) enferma hoy.	está
6	¿De qué color (están, son) las pizarras del aula (clase)?	son
7	Yo sé que tus abuelos (están, son) muy buenos y amables.	son
8	Este chocolate (está, es) muy caliente.	está

9 El presidente del país tiene que (estar, ser) importante. ser

10 ¿No sabe Ud. que la gasolina (está, es) combustible? es

Choose *ser* or *estar* for each situation described.

11 I have the heater set for hot, but the air that is coming out *is* cool. estar

12 I've had to eat in that restaurant several times. The food *is* terrible. ser

13 Look at that new building; they say that it is forty-one stories high. It surely *is* big. ser

14 There is something wrong with your pencil sharpener. I started sharpening a brand new pencil, but now look how short it *is*. estar

15 She must have mixed the recipe wrong. The pudding should come out thick, but it *is* thin. estar

16 There's going to be a serious accident here some day; this street *is* too narrow. ser

17 When I returned from a three-week vacation, I was surprised to find that that same street *was* wide. estar

18 Michael *is* from Texas, but he *is* in Colorado. ser, estar

19 Mr. Jones *is* a lawyer. ser

New Vocabulary

cumpleaños (el)	birthday	**vecino, -a**	neighbor	**digo**	I say, tell
fiesta	party, holiday	**regalo**	gift, present	**tonto, -a**	silly, foolish
		millón	million	**hasta**	until, even
invitación	invitation	**cementerio**	cemetery	**por qué**	why
invitados	guests	**invitar**	to invite	**porque**	because
amigo, -a	friend, pal	**aceptar**	to accept	**en broma**	in jest, as a joke
chico	boy	**preguntar**	to ask (questions)		
chica	girl			**¡Claro!**	Of course!, Sure!

Assignment 30

Reading Aloud

Before you begin this section, read silently the story that follows frame 14 and be sure you understand it.

Copy and underline the stressed syllable in each of the first ten frames, check your accuracy, and, then, say them aloud at least twice.

1 es-tu-dian-tes, se-cun-da-ria, du-ran-te ▲

*es-tu-**dian**-tes, se-cun-**da**-ria, du-**ran**-te*

2 es-co-lar, a-sis-ten, es-cue-la ▲

es-co-**lar**, a-**sis**-ten, es-**cue**-la

3 ve-ra-no, in-te-li-gen-tes, a-pli-ca-dos ▲

ve-**ra**-no, in-te-li-**gen**-tes, a-pli-**ca**-dos

4 es-tu-dian, in-te-rés, quie-ren ▲

es-**tu**-dian, in-te-**rés**, **quie**-ren

5 gra-duar-se, bas-tan-te, na-cio-nal ▲

gra-**duar**-se, bas-**tan**-te, na-cio-**nal**

6 bi-ci-cle-ta, mo-to-ci-cle-ta, can-sa-dos ▲

bi-ci-**cle**-ta, mo-to-ci-**cle**-ta, can-**sa**-dos

7 pre-pa-rar, lec-cio-nes, si-guien-te ▲

pre-pa-**rar**, lec-**cio**-nes, si-**guien**-te

8 in-có-mo-do, pa-tio, a-de-más ▲

in-**có**-mo-do, **pa**-tio, a-de-**más**

9 a-gra-da-ble, di-fi-cul-tad, con-cen-trar ▲

a-gra-**da**-ble, di-fi-cul-**tad**, con-cen-**trar**

10 tiem-po, va-ca-cio-nes, mon-ta-ñas ▲

tiem-po, va-ca-**cio**-nes, mon-**ta**-ñas

11 There are two words in the story which you may not know how to read aloud. They are the adverbs *sumamente* and *solamente*. All words like these came from the Latin noun *mente* (mind) and an adjective with the /a/ phoneme of agreement.

A long time ago *Habla claramente* (He speaks clearly) actually meant *Habla con mente clara* (He speaks with a clear mind.) Today the Spanish speaker is no longer aware of this, and the *mente* has no more meaning to him than the English adverbial suffix _____ has to you. ▲

ly (clear, clearly; slow, slowly; quick, quickly)

12 The *mente* today merely says that the adjective to which it is attached describes an action (modifies a verb, not a noun). Nevertheless, the Spanish speaker still has a little memory of how these forms developed and, as a result, he stresses <u>both</u> parts as though they were still two separate words. Copy and underline the stressed syllables: *su-ma-men-te, so-la-men-te.* ▲

su-ma-**men**-te, **so**-la-**men**-te (Now, say them aloud.)

13 In Spanish, as in English, every sentence can be divided into phrases, a string of words which must be spoken together. Read this sentence aloud with a pause wherever you see a slant bar (/): *The man who / came to dinner had / a long red / beard.* Sounds kind of silly this way, doesn't it? Now, rewrite it with the pauses where they should be. ▲

The man / who came to dinner / had a long / red beard.

14 Below is the whole passage with the possible pauses marked with a slant bar (/). You do not, of course, have to pause at the bars. They show you where you may pause.

Practice reading the story aloud until you can do the whole thing without a stumble. A native can read the whole passage aloud in one minute and twenty-five seconds and sound as though he is reading slowly.

Estudios de verano

Roberto y Miguel / son estudiantes de secundaria. / Durante el año escolar /
asisten a una escuela / muy cerca de su casa. / Este año / ellos van / a la
escuela de verano. / Son alumnos inteligentes / y muy aplicados. / Estudian
en el verano / porque tienen mucho interés / en terminar pronto / sus
estudios. / Quieren graduarse / lo más pronto posible.

En su escuela / no ofrecen / cursos de verano. / Por eso / tienen que ir /
a otra escuela / bastante lejos del lugar / donde viven. / Está en el centro de
la ciudad / cerca del Banco Nacional. / Roberto va en bicicleta; / Miguel
tiene / una motocicleta muy buena. / Todos los días / los muchachos /
llegan a la casa / sumamente cansados. / Solamente / tienen clases / por
la mañana. / Por la tarde / tienen que preparar las lecciones / para el día
siguiente.

Cuando hace mucho calor / es muy incómodo / estar dentro de la casa. /
Entonces / Roberto y Miguel / salen a estudiar / al patio. / Allí hace / un
poco más fresco. / Además / el patio / es un lugar muy bonito / y agradable. / Pero los muchachos tienen dificultad / en concentrar su interés / en
sus estudios. / El verano no es tiempo / de libros y tareas escolares. / Es
tiempo / de vacaciones, / de ir a las montañas / y a la playa. / Allí están /
sus otros amigos / y compañeros de escuela. / Allí es donde / también /
ellos quieren estar.

Stem-Changing Verbs

1 The verbs *tener* and *venir* are irregular because the stem of each has more
than one allomorph. The form of *tener* that goes with *yo* is _____. ▲

> *tengo* (The stem is *teng*.)

2 The form of *venir* that is like *tengo* is _____. ▲

> *vengo* (The stem is *veng*.)

3 The stems of the *nosotros* form of *venir* and *tener* are (a) regular (b)
irregular. ▲

> regular (They are *ven* and *ten*.)

4 The Latin form of *tener* was *tenere*. When a stressed Latin *e* became Spanish,
it often changed to _____. ▲

5 The result is that the stems *ven* and *ten* sometimes changed to _____. ▲   *ie*

> *vien* and *tien* (This also happens in *fiesta* (festival), *desierto* (desert), *tienda*
> (tent), *bien* (beneficial), and in many other words.)

6 The infinitive is the form of the verb which appears in dictionaries. Can you
tell from looking at *tener* that it is irregular? ▲

> no (So bilingual dictionaries and teaching texts have to have a system to let
> you know this. Most books give a number to a model and the same number to
> all similar verbs. Some will give the infinitive and right afterwards in paren-
> theses the common stem change, for example, *tener* (*ie*).)

7 The verb *querer* (to wish, to want, or to love) is also irregular in that the *e* of the stem changes to *ie* when stressed. Which form will go with *yo*? (a) *quero* (b) *quiero* ▲

          quiero (The word ends in a vowel so the stress is on **quie**-*ro*.)

8 The infinitive form *querer* is regular because the stress is on the syllable (a) *que* (b) *rer*. ▲

        rer (The word ends in the consonant *r* and so the stress is on the last syllable.)

9 The *nosotros* form of all verb forms ends in the second suffix *mos*. Will the stress fall (a) on the stem? (b) on the first suffix? ▲

        on the first suffix (So the stem is never stressed and never irregular when the subject is *nosotros*.)

10 Write the *nosotros* form of *querer*. ▲

11 To change *quiero* to match *usted* you replace the first suffix *o* with _____. ▲   *queremos*

12 To make *quiere* agree with *ustedes* or *ellos* you add _____. ▲   *e* (*usted quiere*)

13 Write the *tú* form of *querer*. ▲   *n* (*quieren*)

14 Verbs like *tener* and *venir* have three allomorphs of the stem in the present tense. How many allomorphs of the stem does *querer* have? ▲   *tú quieres*

15 The two allomorphs of the stem *querer* are _____. ▲   two

16 The verb *pensar* translates "to think" or "to intend." Although *pensar* is an *a*-verb, it has the same stem irregularities as *querer*. The *yo* form of *querer* is *quiero*. The *yo* form of *pensar* is _____. ▲   *quer; quier*

17 To make *pienso* agree with *tú*, you change the *o* to *a* and add _____. ▲   *pienso*

18 The *nosotros* form of *pensar* (we think) is _____. ▲   *s* (*tú piensas*)

        pensamos (The stress is on *sa* so the *e* does not change to *ie*.)

19 The *ustedes* form of *pensar* is _____. ▲

        piensan (The word ends in *n*, so the stress is on *pien* and *e* changes to *ie*.)

20 There is another set of irregular verbs which had an *o* in the Latin stem. When this *o* was stressed in Spanish it changed to *ue*. The form *volver* translates "to return." What form would you use to say *They return tomorrow?* ▲

21 The *nosotros* form of this set of verbs has no irregularity in the stem. Write the *nosotros* form of *volver*. ▲   *vuelven*

     volvemos

Summary

As Latin became Spanish the stressed vowels *e* and *o* became *ie* and *ue*. These changes occurred in different types of words (*noviembre, diez, nueve, Puerto Rico*) and especially in the stem of many commonly used verbs: *tener, venir, querer, pensar, volver, poder*. As a result, stem-changing verbs have regular and irregular stem allomorphs: the regular form occurs in the *nosotros* form which is not stressed; the irregular stem occurs in all the other forms unless a third allomorph is used in the *yo* form: **queremos, quieren; pensamos, pienso; volvemos, vuelves;** but **tengo, vengo.**

In the United States a man standing on the street is not likely to pay compliments to a strange lady as she walks by. This is generally considered impolite. He may, however, whistle at her to let her know he thinks she is beautiful. Most women take this "wolf whistle" as a compliment and do not feel insulted. In the Hispanic world a man is permitted to compliment a woman he does not know with words. This is not considered impolite. There is even an idiom that describes this. It is *echar flores a una persona* (to throw flowers at a person).

Self-Correcting Exercises

A Do this drill on adjective agreement aloud two or three times.

1 Tienen una hermana bonita.
    . . . joven.   Tienen una hermana joven.
2 . . . primo . . .   Tienen un primo joven.
3 . . . primos . . .   Tienen unos primos jóvenes.
4 . . . sobrinas . . .   Tienen unas sobrinas jóvenes.
5 . . . altas.   Tienen unas sobrinas altas.
6 . . . tío . . .   Tienen un tío alto.
7 . . . bajo.   Tienen un tío bajo.

8	. . . abuela . . .	Tienen una abuela baja.
9	. . . vieja.	Tienen una abuela vieja.
10	. . . padre . . .	Tienen un padre viejo.
11	. . . flaco.	Tienen un padre flaco.
12	. . . hijas . . .	Tienen unas hijas flacas.
13	. . . amables.	Tienen unas hijas amables.
14	. . . madre . . .	Tienen una madre amable.

B Write the combinations for this visual-graphic drill on possessives.

Ejemplo: 36 = Trabajo con sus hijos.

Trabajo con

1	mi	1	hermano.
2	tu	2	sobrina.
3	su	3	tías.
4	nuestr-	4	abuelos.
		5	primas.
		6	hijos.
		7	familia.

1)	12	Trabajo con mi sobrina.
2)	14	Trabajo con mis abuelos.
3)	27	Trabajo con tu familia.
4)	25	Trabajo con tus primas.
5)	31	Trabajo con su hermano.
6)	33	Trabajo con sus tías.
7)	41	Trabajo con nuestro hermano.
8)	42	Trabajo con nuestra sobrina.
9)	43	Trabajo con nuestras tías.
10)	44	Trabajo con nuestros abuelos.
11)	34	Trabajo con sus abuelos.
12)	11	Trabajo con mi hermano.
13)	21	Trabajo con tu hermano.
14)	32	Trabajo con su sobrina.

New Vocabulary

tener calor	to be hot	**tener sueño**	to be sleepy	**poder (ue)**	to be able, can
tener frío	to be cold	**tener razón**	to be right		
tener hambre	to be hungry	**tener . . .**	to be . . .	**perro**	dog
tener sed	to be thirsty	**años**	years old	**gato**	cat
tener cuidado	to be careful	**bajar**	to go down	**enemigo**	enemy
		volver (ue)	to return, come back	**inteligente**	intelligent
				bruto, -a	dumb

Situational Discrimination

1 You already know five common verbs that translate "to be." They are *ser, estar, haber, tener,* and *hacer.*

To use *tener* (to have) the Spanish speaker has to have something. This something is labeled by a noun, the object of the verb. This noun object cues the use of *tener* to translate "to be." Here is the set of nouns that cue this choice. Memorize them.

	calor.	*I am hot.*
	frío.	*I am cold.*
	hambre.	*I am hungry.*
	sed.	*I am thirsty.*
Tengo	sueño.	*I am sleepy.*
	cuidado.	*I am careful.*
	razón.	*I am right.*
	15 años.	*I am 15 years old.*

2 When the Spanish speaker talks about the weather, he really says that something makes heat, cold, wind, *etc.* How does the Spanish speaker say, "It is windy?" ▲

3 Translate: It is hot here. Translate: What is the weather like? ▲

Hace viento.

Hace calor aquí. ¿Qué tiempo hace?

4 Translate: The weather is bad (makes bad weather). ▲

5 You use *tener* to talk of the temperature of people or living creatures (*Tengo frío*) and *hacer* to talk of air temperature (*Hace fresco*). What two verbs do you use in talking about the temperature of things (inanimate objects)? ▲

Hace mal tiempo.

6 Which verb will you use? *Los desiertos* _____ *calientes.* (a) *ser* (b) *estar* ▲

ser or *estar*

ser (The norm for deserts is hot: *Son calientes.*)

7 Which verb will you use? *¡Mamá! ¡Mi sopa* (soup) _____ *fría!* (a) *ser* (b) *estar* ▲

estar (The exclamation suggests the speaker expects soup to be normally hot.)

8 Your critical analysis of the pattern tells you when to use *tener* or *hacer.* Your analysis of reality tells you when to use *ser* or *estar.* What tells you to use *hay* in *Hay un libro en la mesa?* One fact is location (*en la mesa*); the other is the cue in the language: the use of _____. ▲

un (Remember: numbers by themselves cue *haber* for location.)

9 The cues for choice can also be found in the way the Spanish speaker organizes reality. In English someone knocks at the door and we answer, "I'm coming." The Spanish speaker sees the whole situation differently and says, _____. ▲

Ya voy, or simply *Voy.*

Stem-Changing Verbs: o > ue

1 In the last Assignment you learned a new verb *volver* in which the stressed
Latin *o* of the stem changes to _____. ▲

2 You already know the verb form *puedo* (I can). This verb is an *e* verb. The
form of *puedo* that goes with *nosotros* should logically be and is _____. ▲

      ue

         podemos (When the *o* of the stem is not stressed it does not change to *ue*.)

3 The infinitive of *puedo* and *podemos* is _____. ▲

4 The form of *poder* that goes with *tú* is _____. ▲   *poder*

5 Change *puedes* so it agrees with *usted*. ▲   *puedes*

6 Change *puede* so it agrees with *ustedes* and *ellos*. ▲   *puede*

7 The two allomorphs of the stem of the verb that translates "can" are   *pueden*

_____. ▲

8 The set of verbs in which stressed *o* changes to *ue* has to be memorized.   *pod, pued*
Here is the pattern:

yo	**pued**o
nosotros	**pod**emos
tú	**pued**es
usted, él, ella	**pued**e
ustedes, ellos, ellas	**pued**en

Excelente

*Use either hand. Bring the tips of thumb and four fingers
together, raise them to your lips, pucker your lips well and
kiss them, gently throwing the kiss forward and upward by
raising the hand and separating slightly the thumb and
fingers.*

Self-Correcting Exercises

A   Read the following dialog and write complete sentence answers to the questions.

Después de clase

Sara: ¿Qué vas a hacer el sábado?
Carmen: No sé; depende. ¿Por qué preguntas?
Sara: Porque quiero invitarte a mi fiesta de cumpleaños.
Carmen: ¡Qué bueno! ¿Quién va a estar allí?
Sara: Todos mis hermanos, mis tíos, vecinos, amigos . . . ¡Hasta el gato!
Carmen: ¡Claro! Muchos invitados, muchos regalos.
Sara: Ay, chica. No seas tonta. No te invito por eso.
Carmen: Lo digo en broma. Acepto tu invitación. Un millón de gracias.

1	Cómo se llaman las dos muchachas del diálogo?	Se llaman Sara y Carmen.
2	¿Por qué va a tener Sara una fiesta?	Porque es (va a ser) su cumpleaños.
3	¿Cuándo va a ser el cumpleaños de Sara?	Va a ser el sábado.
4	¿Quién es Carmen?	Carmen es una amiga de Sara.
5	¿Piensa ir Carmen a la fiesta?	Sí, ella piensa ir a la fiesta.
6	¿Quién va a ir a la fiesta además de Carmen?	Van a ir los hermanos, tíos, vecinos y amigos de Sara.
7	¿Acepta Carmen la invitación de su amiga?	Sí, la acepta.
8	La fiesta va a ser un domingo, ¿verdad?	No, va a ser un sábado.

B   Say aloud the word needed to complete the pair.

1	enemigo	amigo	**7**	limpio	sucio
2	perro	gato	**8**	hombre	mujer
3	bajo	alto	**9**	nadie	alguien
4	viejo	joven	**10**	bruto	inteligente
5	bajar	subir	**11**	feo	bonito
6	triste	feliz	**12**	hoy	ayer

C   Do this drill on adjectival residuals aloud. The first example gives you the model.

1	*Here is the lesson. I am going to study the lesson.* Aquí está la lección. Voy a estudiar la lección.	Voy a estudiarla.
2	Aquí están las lecciones. Voy a estudiar las lecciones.	Voy a estudiarlas.
3	Aquí están los libros. Voy a estudiar los libros.	Voy a estudiarlos.
4	Aquí está el libro. Voy a estudiar el libro.	Voy a estudiarlo.
5	Aquí está el diálogo. Voy a estudiar el diálogo.	Voy a estudiarlo.

Answer in the affirmative and omit the noun.

6	¿Sabes la fecha?	Sí, la sé.
7	¿Tienes el regalo?	Sí, lo tengo.

8	¿Pones los libros allí?	Sí, los pongo allí.
9	¿Ves las reglas?	Sí, las veo.
10	¿Haces el trabajo ahora?	Sí, lo hago.
11	¿Sabes la hora?	Sí, la sé.
12	¿Haces la tarea a las seis?	Sí, la hago a las seis.

Assignment 32

Pronunciation Review

This section is designed to help you say the dialog *Después de clase* without hesitations, with no pauses in the wrong places, with the right allophones of all phonemes, and with the intonation of natural, Spanish speech.

1 Here are all the phrases that have a /d/. Practice saying them aloud. Remember plain [d] = stop, and [d̶] = fricative.

el sábado	muchos invitados
depende	Lo digo en broma
fiesta de cumpleaños	Un millón de gracias
Todos mis hermanos	

2 The phoneme /b/, like /d/, has a stop [b] and a fricative [b] allophone. You say the stop [b] when you begin a new sentence, after a pause, and immediately after the phoneme /m/, which may be written either with the letter *m* or *n*. Here are all the phrases that have a /b/. Circle the stops and underline the fricatives.

¿Qué v as a hacer?	quiero in v itarte	¡Qué b ueno!
¿Quién v a a estar allí?	muchos in v itados	No te in v ito por eso.
Lo digo en b roma.	Acepto tu in v itación.	v ecinos ▲

¿Que vas a hacer?	quiero in(v)itarte	¡ Que bueno !
¿Quién (v)a a estar allí?	muchos in(v)itados	No te in(v)ito por eso.
Lo digo en (b)roma.	Acepto tu in(v)itación	(v)ecinos

Now practice saying the above aloud.

3 In the following words the *n* stands for [m]. Say them aloud and be sure you say [m] and, immediately after it, a stop [b]: *invitar, invitados, invito, invitación, en broma, ¿Quién va?*

4 Here are all the words with [k] in them, spelled *qu* or *c*. Say them aloud without any aspiration: *qué, porque, quiero, cumpleaños, quién, claro, chica.*

5 The letter *c* stands for [s] when it comes before _____. ▲

6 Say these words aloud: *hacer, vecinos, invitación, gracias.*

i or *e*

7 The letter *u* stands for no sound in *que*, for a vowel in *cumpleaños*, and for [ ] in *cuánto.* ▲

[w] ([kwanto])

8 When *r* is the first letter in a word, does it stand for [r] or [rr]? ▲

[rr] (Say [rregalos] aloud.)

9 These words have a single flap [r] sound. Say them aloud. Watch for the schwa too: *hacer, por, preguntas, quiero, invitar, estar, broma, gracias.*

10 Copy and put a slant bar (/) where you may pause in this sentence: *Porque quiero invitarte a mi fiesta de cumpleaños.* ▲

Porque quiero invitarte / a mi fiesta de cumpleaños.

11 When you say *por eso* the two words are run together like this: *poreso.* Divide this phrase into syllables as though it were just one word. ▲

12 The stress is now on the syllable _____. ▲

po-re-so

13 At the end of the question *¿Por qué preguntas?* the pitch (a) goes up (b) down. Before you decide, say the question aloud. ▲

re

down (In Spanish the pitch goes down at the end of questions asking for

14 The pitch also goes down in these sentences. Practice saying them this way: information.)

¡Claro! ¡Ay, chica! Un millón de gracias.

15 Here is the whole dialog. The phonemes that may give you trouble are indicated. Slant bars tell you where you may pause within a sentence. The pitch of your voice drops at the end of every sentence. Practice reading the dialog aloud several times.

Después de clase

Sara: ¿Qué **v**as a hace**r** / el sá**b**ado?
Carmen: No sé; / de**p**ende. / ¿**P**or qué preguntas?
Sara: Porque quiero in**v**itarte / a mi fiesta de cumplea**ñ**os.
Carmen: ¡Qué bueno! / ¿Quién **v**a a estar allí?
Sara: To**d**os mis hermanos, / mis tíos, / **v**ecinos, / amigos . . . / ¡Hasta el gato!
Carmen: ¡Claro! / **Mu**chos in**v**ita**d**os, / **mu**chos regalos.
Sara: ¡Ay, chica! / No seas tonta. No te **inv**ito por eso.
Carmen: Lo **d**igo e**n** **b**roma. / Acepto tu in**v**itación. / Un millón **d**e gracias.

The Done-to a

1 You have already discovered that the patterns of Spanish and English sentences are not always alike. Some of these differences can be traced to the fact that Spanish developed from Latin (a Romance language) while English is Anglo-Saxon (a Germanic language). Some differences, however, come from the fact that each language organizes the world from an entirely different cultural point of view. In English, for example, we say, *I see the blackboard* and *I see the girl.* Which word in each sentence stands for the speaker and the doer? ▲

2 I am the speaker and the one who does the seeing (the doer). Which word in *I see the blackboard* and *I see the girl* stands for the done-to (the object seen)? ▲

I

3 On the level of language, *blackboard* and *girl* are both nouns and both are the done-to in the example sentences. In actual reality, however, an inanimate entity, *blackboard,* and an animate entity *girl* do not belong to the same set.

blackboard, girl

The pattern of *I see the blackboard* and *I see the girl* tells you that the difference between *blackboard* and *girl* is not important when you make up these sentences. The Spanish speaker, however, thinks the difference should be marked. Compare:

> I see the blackboard.   *Veo la pizarra.*
> I see the girl.   *Veo a la muchacha.*

Which entity is especially marked in Spanish? (a) the thing (b) the person ▲

4 The Spanish language (like your logic) considers people and things to be members of a different set. Look at these translations:

> He knows the country well.   *Conoce el país bien.*
> He knows Ana well.   *Conoce a Ana bien.*

the person

When the done-to of a sentence is a specific person, the word that stands for it is preceded by the marker _____. ▲

5 The *a* of *Conoce a Ana bien* has no English translation. It also has no dictionary meaning in Spanish. It simply says that the done-to of the sentence is a person. Why, then, does Spanish need this *a*? Here is one good reason. The Spanish subject (the doer), unlike English, may come before or after the verb. As a result, "Pablo knows Ana well" may be translated two ways: (1) *Pablo conoce a Ana bien.* (2) *Conoce Pablo a Ana bien.* Suppose the second sentence were written *Conoce Pablo Ana bien.* Would you be able to tell which person is the doer or the done-to? ▲

a

no (So the *a Ana* tells you that Ana is the done-to; the person known by Pablo.)

6 How do you translate this sentence? *Conoce Ana a Pablo bien.* ▲

Ana knows Pablo well. (The *a Pablo* now tells you that Pablo is the done-to:

7 Because the subject (doer) and the object (done-to) can come before or after the verb in Spanish, no Spanish speaker can tell what this sentence means: *Ana conoce Pablo.* Rewrite the sentence and add *a* so that it means "Ana knows Pablo." ▲

the person known.)

Ana conoce a Pablo.

8 The cognate of "to comprehend" (to understand) is the regular *e*-verb *comprender*. The only translation of either *Los estudiantes comprenden* or *Comprenden los estudiantes* is _____. ▲

The students understand.

9 The verb form *comprenden* also takes the subject pronoun *ustedes*. How do you translate "You understand the students"? ▲

Ustedes comprenden a los estudiantes. (You need the *a* marker before *estudiantes* to show they are the done-to, not the doer. The position of the words tells you this in English.)

10 How do you translate "The students understand the lesson"? ▲

Los estudiantes comprenden la lección. ("Lesson" is not a person and you do not use the *a* marker.)

11 Which sentence needs the *a* marker in Spanish? (a) I see the book. (b) I see the school principal. ▲

I see the school principal. (*Yo veo al director de la escuela.*)

12 How do you translate "I see María"? ▲

Veo a María. (With the done-to *a* for a person.)

13 How do you translate "I see the door"? ▲

Veo la puerta. (With no *a* for a thing.)

14 Which question translates "Does Ana know my brother?" (a) *¿Conoce Ana mi hermano?* (b) *¿Conoce Ana a mi hermano?* ▲

¿Conoce Ana a mi hermano?

A/B

LLEVAN A LOS NIÑOS

LLEVAN LOS JARROS

Summary

1 Before *b* or *v*, *n* stands for [m].

2 Spanish pays more attention than English to the difference between inanimate and animate entities and, as a result has a special marker *a* for animate entities, especially people. This *a* has two prime functions. It says, first, that the done-to is a person or an animal being treated like a person, and, second, it clearly marks the difference between the doer and the done-to.

Self-Correcting Exercises

A   Write the combinations for this visual-graphic drill on adjectival residuals.

Ejemplo: 44 = Aquí están las plumas. Voy a necesitarlas pronto.

Aquí	está	1	el regalo.	1 Debo poner . . . allí.
		2	la invitación.	2 Yo . . . veo bien.
	están	3	los lápices.	3 Yo . . . pongo en la mesa.
		4	las plumas.	4 Voy a necesitar . . . pronto.
				5 Tú . . . necesitas, ¿verdad?
				6 Ellos quieren ver . . .

1) 11

2) 12

Aquí está el regalo. Debo ponerlo allí.

Aquí está el regalo. Yo lo veo bien.

3)	23	Aquí está la invitación. Yo la pongo en la mesa.
4)	24	Aquí está la invitación. Voy a necesitarla pronto.
5)	35	Aquí están los lápices. Tú los necesitas, ¿verdad?
6)	36	Aquí están los lápices. Ellos quieren verlos.
7)	41	Aquí están las plumas. Debo ponerlas allí.
8)	43	Aquí están las plumas. Yo las pongo en la mesa.
9)	42	Aquí están las plumas. Yo las veo bien.
10)	16	Aquí está el regalo. Ellos quieren verlo.

No new vocabulary. Review your vocabulary list and study all the words you have marked as problems.

Assignment 33

Review I

You are learning how to analyze, describe, and talk about language and language learning. This is only a means to an end; that is, learning how to hear, speak, read, and write Spanish.

Here is a self-test. It will tell you how you stand in the course.

1 You want to locate an entity modified by the indefinite article or a number. This cues you to use the verb _____. ▲

2 *El hombre que descubrió el Nuevo Mundo fue italiano.* He was born in _____. ▲ *haber*
Italy

3 Speakers of English often replace unstressed Spanish vowels with a special vowel sound called _____. ▲

4 To make "He eats too much" negative in English, you must say, "He does *schwa* not eat too much." Write the translation for both sentences. ▲

Él come demasiado. Él no come demasiado.

5 English /p/ has two allophones. Spanish /p/ has only one allophone. It is never _____. ▲

aspirated (made with a puff)

6 You are talking about a person. What verb do you use with these nouns: *calor, frío, hambre, sed?* ▲

7 Translate: He is nine years old. ▲ *tener*

8 In English we say, "His name is Jorge." The meaning of the Spanish is *Tiene nueve años.* "He calls himself Jorge." The Spanish is _____. ▲

9 You are describing the weather. What verb do you use with these nouns: *Se llama Jorge.* *viento, frío, calor, mal tiempo?* ▲

10 Translate: It is very windy. ▲ *hacer*

Hace mucho viento. (You use the adjective *mucho*, not the adverb *muy*.)

11 When you describe the subject with a predicate adjective in Spanish, you must choose between the verbs _____. ▲

ser and *estar*

12 The norm for the subject takes _____. Any change or deviation from the norm takes _____. ▲

norm takes *ser*; change or deviation takes *estar*

13 Look! The snow *is* pink! (a) *ser* (b) *estar* ▲

14 The second suffix of a verb gives person and number. The plural morphemes are _____. ▲

estar

15 The suffix that matches *tú* is _____. ▲

mos ; n

16 The stem of *tener* in the present tense has three allomorphs: _____. ▲

s

17 Write the form that goes with *ustedes*. ▲

teng, ten, tien

18 Where English uses the possessives *his*, *her*, *your*, *their*, and *its*, Spanish uses only two forms: _____. ▲

ustedes tienen

19 English possessive adjectives agree in number with the possessor; Spanish possessive adjectives agree in number with the noun they combine with. (a) true (b) false ▲

su ; sus

20 Write the paired word for each of the following: *sed, grande, fácil, siempre*. ▲

true

hambre, pequeño, difícil, nunca

21 When there is one consonant between two vowels, the consonant goes with the _____ vowel in syllabication. ▲

22 What usually happens when there are two consonants between two vowels? ▲

second

one goes with the first vowel; one with the second

23 One Spanish cognate of "vicinity" is _____. ▲

24 *El padre de mi madre es mi* _____. ▲

vecino

25 *La mujer* (wife) *de mi abuelo es mi* _____. ▲

abuelo

26 What verb do you use when you tell time? ▲

abuela

27 The two forms used in telling time are _____. ▲

ser

28 The Spanish speaker divides the day into: *la . . . , la . . . ,* and *la . . . .* ▲

es ; son

la mañana, la tarde, la noche

29 What greeting do you use in the morning? ▲

30 Adverbs with the suffix *mente* are not stressed like other words. Divide these into syllables and underline the two stressed syllables: *finalmente, claramente*. ▲

Buenos días.

fi-**nal**-**men**-te, **cla**-ra-**men**-te

31 A word which ends in *n* or *s* is stressed on the (a) last syllable (b) next-to-last syllable. ▲

next-to-last (Unless there is a written accent.)

32 A word which has no written accent and ends in any consonant (except *n* or *s*) is stressed on the _____ syllable. ▲

33 In what way are question words all spelled differently from other words? ▲

last

All have a written accent mark.

34 When *el* becomes an adjectival residual as the object of a verb, it is changed to _____. ▲

35 When I am taking part in a conversation, I may play four roles as subject of a verb and, so, I may have four names in Spanish. (1) When I talk, my name is _____. (2) When a close friend speaks to me, my name is _____. (3) When a stranger speaks to me, my name is _____. (4) When they talk about me (a girl), my name is _____. ▲

lo

(1) *yo*, (2) *tú*, (3) *usted*, (4) *ella*

36 Do you capitalize the names for the days of the week and the months in Spanish? ▲

37 What kind of sentences have to have a punctuation mark in front of them? ▲

no

questions and exclamations

38 You are standing at the box. Someone is moving in the direction shown by the arrow. ▭◄————————————◯ What verb describes the movement? ▲

39 To locate something on a surface, you use *haber* or *estar* and the relator _____. ▲

venir

40 Give three cues that tell you to use *estar* for location. ▲

en

Any one of these is correct: proper name, subject pronoun, definite article, demonstrative, or a possessive adjective.

41 You add the plural allomorph *es* to nouns which end in a _____. ▲

42 The sound [k] may be spelled either _____. ▲

consonant

c + a, o, u; qu + e, i

43 The letter *c* stands for [s] only before / / and / /. ▲

44 Write out: It is 9:45 A.M. ▲

/e/ and /i/

Son las diez menos quince (cuarto) de la mañana.

45 When you add or subtract numbers, you use the verb form _____. ▲

46 You address professors, strangers, and respected adults with (a) *tú* (b) *usted.* ▲

son

47 When someone knocks at your door, you answer by saying, (a) *Ya vengo* (b) *Ya voy.* ▲

usted

48 Does Spanish have a subject pronoun equivalent to "it" or its plural "they?" ▲

Ya voy.

No (You just use the verb.)

49 The opposite of *anteayer* is _____. ▲

pasado mañana (This is *el mañana,* not *la mañana.*)

50 Does *su* really mean "his, your, her, their," *etc.* to a Spanish speaker? ▲

no (It just means possessed by the person or persons being talked about.)

51 This is the last *pregunta.* The adjective which describes it is _____. ▲

última

Self-Correcting Exercises

A Write the combinations for this visual-graphic drill on adjectival residuals.

Ejemplo: 11 = Aquí está el regalo. Debo ponerlo allí.

			1	el regalo.	1 Debo poner . . . allí.
	está		2	la invitación.	2 Yo . . . veo bien.
Aquí			3	los lápices.	3 Yo . . . pongo en la mesa.
	están		4	las plumas.	4 Voy a necesitar . . . pronto.
					5 Tú . . . necesitas, ¿verdad?
					6 Ellos quieren ver . . .

1) 13

2) 14

Aquí está el regalo. Yo lo pongo en la mesa.

Aquí está el regalo. Voy a necesitarlo pronto.

3)	25	Aquí está la invitación. Tú la necesitas, ¿verdad?
4)	26	Aquí está la invitación. Ellos quieren verla.
5)	31	Aquí están los lápices. Debo ponerlos allí.
6)	32	Aquí están los lápices. Yo los veo bien.
7)	45	Aquí están las plumas. Tú las necesitas, ¿verdad?
8)	46	Aquí están las plumas. Ellos quieren verlas.
9)	12	Aquí está el regalo. Yo lo veo bien.
10)	21	Aquí está la invitación. Debo ponerla allí.

B Say this conversation aloud in Spanish three times according to the instructions. You play both roles. *J* stands for Juan or Juanita; *M* stands for Miguel. Use the familiar mode of address throughout.

J: You meet your friend Miguel, say hello to him, and ask how he is.

M: You answer, and ask him what he is going to do on Saturday.

J: You answer you don't know, and ask why he asks.

M: You tell him you plan (*pensar*) to go to the beach, and want to invite him.

J: You say you accept the invitation, tell him he is very kind, and thank him.

M: You tell him that he is welcome, and say good-by, until later.

J: You say good-by to Miguel and wave.

J: *Hola, Miguel. ¿Cómo estás?*

M: *Muy bien, gracias. ¿Qué vas a hacer el sábado?*

J: *No sé. ¿Por qué preguntas?*

M: *Pienso ir a la playa y quiero invitarte.*

J: *Acepto la invitación. Eres muy amable. Gracias.*

M: *De nada. Adiós, hasta luego.*

J: *Adiós, Miguel.*

New Vocabulary

jarro	jug	**permiso**	permission	**conocer**	to know, be
examen	test,	**llevar**	to take,		acquainted with
	examination		carry	**pedir (i)**	to ask for; to order
parientes	relatives	**mirar**	to look at	**pensar (ie)**	to think; to intend
padres	parents			**+ inf.**	

A significant difference in the two cultures can be found in the way each treats numbers and money. In the U.S. a million is 1,000,000, that is, a thousand thousands; and a billion is 1,000,000,000, that is, a thousand millions. In contrast, in Spain a *millón* is *mil millares* (a thousand thousands) but a *billón* is *un millón de millones* or 1 followed by 12 instead of 9 zeros, that is, 1,000,000,000,000. This number is a trillion in the U.S.

American dictionaries define a millionaire as a person who has at least a million dollars. The Academy dictionary defines *millonario* simply as a person who is very rich, powerful, or who has a lot of possessions and property. Since the Spanish equivalent of a billionaire would have to have a trillion dollars there is no equivalent for *billionaire*.

Assignment 34
Selective Self-Help

This Assignment is not concerned with how much you know *about* Spanish. It deals, instead, with how well you can communicate *in* Spanish, and with the forms you need in order to communicate. Do the sections which deal with problems you feel you still need to review.

Equivalents of "to be"

1 Say that the air temperature is very low. ▲

2 Describe Tula as naturally very nice. ▲

> Hace mucho frío.
> Tula es muy amable.

3 Miguel is in bed with a virus. Describe his state of health. ▲

> Miguel está enfermo.

4 Where is Asunción? / Locate a pen on the chair. ▲

> Asunción está en Paraguay. Hay una pluma en la silla.

5 Marcos was born in Lima. Give his origin. ▲

6 Write out: It is 1:45 P.M. / Write out: It is 1:25 A.M. ▲

> Marcos es de Lima.
> Son las dos menos quince (cuarto) de la tarde. Es la una y veinticinco de la

7 Locate Miranda in Quito. / Write out: 23 + 8 = 31. ▲

> mañana.
> Miranda está en Quito. Veintitrés y ocho son treinta y uno.

8 Pilar has not eaten for ten hours. Describe how she feels. ▲

9 You go to college. Say what you are. ▲

> Tiene hambre.
> Yo soy estudiante (alumno or alumna).

10 Translate: She is eleven years old. / Write out: 25 − 7 = 18. ▲

> (Ella) tiene once años. Veinticinco menos siete son dieciocho.

11 Translate: You are right. *Tú* _____. / Locate *ellas* in Caracas. ▲

> Tú tienes razón. Están en Caracas.

Regular Verbs

1 The verb set of *viven* is _____. ▲

2 So the form that goes with *nosotros* is _____. ▲

> i

3 The stem of *leer* is _____. ▲

> vivimos

4 To get the *usted* form you add _____. ▲

> le

5 And to get the *ustedes* form you add _____. ▲

> e

6 Write the *yo* form for *cantar, escribir, correr, subir, desear.* ▲

> n (ustedes leen)
> canto, escribo, corro, subo, deseo

7 Make these forms match *nosotros*: *llamo, vivo, como, llego, bebo, termino.* ▲

llamamos, vivimos, comemos, llegamos, bebemos, terminamos

8 Make these forms singular: *hablan, comen, viven, deben, esperan.* ▲

habla, come, vive, debe, espera

9 Write the infinitive for *vives, estudio, suben, deben, escribes.* ▲

vivir, estudiar, subir, deber, escribir

10 The *s* suffix tells you (a) the verb is plural (b) the subject is *tú*. ▲

11 Change to *tú* forms: *necesitar, leemos, escriben, entra, subimos.* ▲ the subject is *tú*

necesitas, lees, escribes, entras, subes

12 The subject pronouns which match the second suffix *n* are _____. ▲

13 The infinitive form of *invitado* is _____. ▲

ustedes, ellos, ellas

invitar

Irregular Verbs

1 Translate: I am sleepy. / She is thirsty. ▲

Tengo sueño. Tiene sed.

2 We are hot. / They are in La Paz. ▲

Tenemos calor. Están en la Paz.

3 I am going out. (Do not use *voy a.*) ▲

4 I make chairs. / There they come! ▲ *Salgo.*

Yo hago sillas. ¡Allí vienen!

5 I am from Lima. ▲

6 Now say a similar message with another verb: _____ *de Lima.* ▲ *Soy de Lima.*

7 *Pensar* and *empezar* each have two allomorphs of the present tense stem: *Vengo de Lima.*

_____. ▲

pens and *piens; empez* and *empiez*

8 Translate: He is beginning to talk. ▲

9 In the irregular forms of *morir* and *poder*, you change *o* to _____. ▲ *Empieza a hablar.*

10 The regular stem of these verbs appears only in the forms that go with the *ue* (*puedo, muere*)

subject pronoun_____. ▲

nosotros (*podemos, morimos*)

11 Write three different verb forms which translate "I am." ▲

12 Write the matching forms of *ser*: tú . . . , ellos . . . , nosotros . . . . ▲ *soy, estoy, tengo*

13 The regular stem of *querer* appears only in *queremos.* The stem of all other *eres, son, somos*

present tense forms is _____. ▲

quier (*quiero, quieres, etc.*)

14 The irregular stem of *volver* is _____. ▲

vuelv (Used in all forms except *volvemos.*)

15 Change *podemos* so it agrees with *ellos.* ▲

16 The irregular stem of *pedir* is _____. ▲ *pueden*

pid (Used in all forms except *pedimos.*)

17 Translate "She asks for coffee." ▲

Ella pide café.

Adjectives

1   The four forms of the definite article are _____.   ▲

2   Rewrite and delete the noun: *Voy a comprar el auto.*   ▲   *el, los, la, las*

       Voy a comprarlo. (When *el* becomes the adjectival residual, you change it to

3   The equivalent of "good" has three singular forms: _____.   ▲   *lo.*)

       bueno, buen, buena

4   Rewrite and make all words plural: *Yo tengo el lápiz blanco.*   ▲

       Nosotros tenemos los lápices blancos.

5   Translate: I want new books. / I want new pens.   ▲

       Quiero libros nuevos. Yo quiero plumas nuevas.

6   Rewrite in the plural: *Es la idea general.*   ▲

       Son las ideas generales.

7   The speaker is a woman. Translate: I am tired.   ▲

8   The speaker is a man. Translate: I am sick.   ▲   *Estoy cansada*

       Estoy enfermo

Relators

1   Translate: Why are you going? / Because I want to.   ▲

       ¿Por qué vas (va)? Porque quiero.

2   Where's she going? / Where's he from?   ▲

       ¿A dónde va ella? ¿De dónde es él?

3   Please, sir, where is the post office?   ▲

       Por favor, señor, ¿dónde está el correo?

4   María is with me. / Good-bye, until tomorrow.   ▲

       María está conmigo. Adiós, hasta mañana,

5   Father is at home.   ▲

6   Father is in the house.   ▲   *Papá está en casa.*

       Papá está en la casa.

7   They are going to work with Tom.   ▲

       Van a trabajar con Tomás.

Question Words

1   Translate: How many books do you want?   ▲

       ¿Cuántos libros quieres (quiere)? (or deseas, desea)

2   How much do they have? / How is Pilar today?   ▲

       ¿Cuánto tienen? ¿Cómo está Pilar hoy?

3   What is that? / When do we eat?   ▲

       ¿Qué es eso? ¿Cuándo comemos?

4   Which of the girls is Elena?   ▲

       ¿Cuál de las muchachas es Elena?

5 Where is he coming from? ▲
6 Where is he going to? / Who is calling? ▲

¿De dónde viene?
¿A dónde va? ¿Quién llama?

7 (Make the last sentence plural.) ▲

¿Quiénes llaman?

Pronouns

1 Translate: Somebody is coming. / Make it negative. ▲

Alguien viene. Nadie viene.

2 The abbreviation *Vds.* or *Uds.* stands for _____. ▲
3 Do they have something? / Make this negative. ▲

ustedes
¿Tienen algo? ¿No tienen nada?

4 Make this plural: *Tú tienes razón.* ▲

Ustedes tienen razón.

5 You are a woman, speaking for a group of women: We are hungry. ▲

Nosotras tenemos hambre.

6 You are a woman speaking for a group of men and women: We are very cold. ▲

Nosotros tenemos mucho frío.

7 You are talking to a very small child: Are you thirsty? ▲
8 You ask the same question of a stranger. ▲
9 Answer this question with a negative: *¿Está la casa sucia?* ▲
10 My name is Margarita. ▲

¿Tienes (tú) sed?
¿Tiene Vd. sed?
No, no está sucia.
Me llamo Margarita.

Adverbs

1 Translate: She speaks poorly. ▲
2 Here is where they live. / Elena is well, thank you. ▲

Habla mal.
Aquí es donde viven. Elena está bien, gracias.

3 The opposite of *fuera* is _____. / The opposite of *aquí* is _____. ▲
4 The opposite of *lejos* is _____. ▲
5 What are you going to do tomorrow? ▲

dentro, allí
cerca
¿Qué vas a hacer mañana?

6 Make this positive: *Nunca tiene sueño.* ▲

Siempre tiene sueño.

7 It's already late. / No, it's early. ▲

Ya es tarde. No, es temprano.

8 She is still sick. (Put the adverb first.) ▲

Todavía está enferma.

9 And, besides, it's windy. ▲

Y, además, hace viento.

10 They work too much. / Watch out! I work also. ▲

Trabajan demasiado. ¡Ojo! Yo trabajo también.

11 We are going day after tomorrow. ▲

Vamos pasado mañana.

The Done-to a

Complete the Spanish translation.

1 I see my house, but I don't see my parents. *Veo* _____, *pero no veo* _____. ▲

mi casa, a mis padres

2 She understands the lesson, but she cannot understand the professor. *Ella comprende* _____ *lección, pero no puede comprender* _____ *profesora.* ▲

3 I know the hotel, but I don't know the man who administers it. *Conozco* _____ *hotel, pero no conozco* _____ *hombre que lo administra.* ▲

la, a la

4 I look at the picture of Mary. I look at Mary. *Yo miro* _____ *fotografía de María. Yo miro* _____ *María.* ▲

el, al

5 The done-to *a* sometimes differentiates between the doer and the done-to. Rewrite the sentence *¿Conoce Martín Julia?* so it translates "Does Julia know Martin?" Do not change the word order. ▲

la, a

¿Conoce a Martín Julia?

Self-Correcting Exercises

A Write the combinations for this visual-graphic drill on stem-changing verbs.

Ejemplo: 111 = Tú quieres un papel.

1	Tú			1	un papel.
2	Lola	1	querer	2	un pájaro.
3	Ellas	2	poder ver	3	otro calendario.
4	Yo	3	pedir	4	una casa bonita.
5	Él y yo			5	un lápiz más.

1)	212	Lola quiere un pájaro.
2)	414	Yo quiero una casa bonita.
3)	511	Él y yo queremos un papel.
4)	525	Él y yo podemos ver un lápiz más.
5)	121	Tú puedes ver un papel.
6)	222	Lola puede ver un pájaro.
7)	333	Ellas piden otro calendario.
8)	431	Yo pido un papel.
9)	535	Él y yo pedimos un lápiz más.
10)	313	Ellas quieren otro calendario.
11)	124	Tú puedes ver una casa bonita.
12)	432	Yo pido un pájaro.

B Say aloud the paired opposite until you can say the entire list without hesitating.

pequeño	grande		hombre	mujer
verdad	mentira		siempre	nunca
feliz	triste		fácil	difícil
vivir	morir		amable	cruel
bonito	feo		terrible	magnífico
alto	bajo		cerca	lejos
hambre	sed		temprano	tarde
mal	bien		terminar	empezar
día	noche		enfermo	sano
joven	viejo		poco	mucho
cansado	descansado		afuera	adentro
sucio	limpio		calor	frío
gordo	flaco		nadie	alguien
último	primero		seco	húmedo

C Transform each sentence to the negative.

1 Yo voy a la playa.
2 Vamos a estudiar algo.
3 Alguien está en la oficina.
4 Sí, tengo seis libros nuevos.
5 Comemos siempre a las seis y media.

Yo no voy a la playa.
No vamos a estudiar nada.
Nadie está en la oficina.
No, no tengo seis libros nuevos.
No comemos nunca a las seis y media.
(Nunca comemos a las seis y media.)

No new vocabulary. Review your entire vocabulary list in preparation for the major test.

It is a tradition among good Catholics in the Hispanic world to give each child one name which is the name of the saint who is especially honored on the day the child is born. As a result, many men have *María* as one of their given or baptismal names (*nombre de pila*); and no one is bothered by being called *José María Sánchez*. In addition, as you already know, many men are named *Jesús* and some women even have the name *Jesusa*. Because all the saints' names are commonly used as proper names, they can have no more exclamatory punch than the English, "By George! You are right." This tradition extends to most religious words, that is, they are not used as swear words. A nun or a priest may exclaim, *¡Jesús!* or *¡Dios mío!* (My God!) with a meaning no more intense than *Good gracious* or *Good heavens*. There are two common translations of *damned*, but they come out as "condemned to eternal pain" (*condenado*) or "cursed" (*maldito* < *mal decir*). And no one uses *dios* (god) as a swear word. As a result, the Latins find the American custom of using religious names and words for swearing to be most strange and a peculiar custom. This does not mean, however, that the Spanish do not swear. Each country has developed a special set of swear words of its own.

Assignment 35/36

Getting Ready for a Test

In your next class you are going to have a major test which will cover the material specified in the list of objectives for Etapa 2 found on p. 108. If you have been doing your Assignments conscientiously and have participated actively in every class and in the laboratory, you should be well prepared for the test without having to spend long hours reviewing. The purpose of this Assignment is to identify again the areas of content that will be included in the test, to describe the techniques that will be used in evaluating the objectives, and to give you one more opportunity to practice what you will be asked to do. This practice should enable you to demonstrate how much you have learned and will minimize the possibility of making errors not related to your knowledge and abilities but to the mechanics of testing.

Do this Assignment carefully. Be sure you do *not* look at the answers *before* you have tried to think of them. If you make a mistake, study the frame carefully before continuing.

The test consists of ten parts marked **A** through **J**.

1 Part A, *Listening and Reading Comprehension* (12 points): This part consists of 12 items. You will hear a question or statement read in Spanish <u>once</u> only. On your answer sheet you will see four possible responses, and you are to circle the letter opposite the best answer. Here are two examples:

You will hear: ¿Cuál es la segunda estación del año?
You will read these four responses:

a) Es la primavera.
b) Es el otoño.

c) Es el invierno.
d) Es el verano. ▲

d (El verano es la segunda estación del año.)

2 Nuestra profesora nunca sabe la fecha.

a) ¡Claro! No tiene reloj.
b) Necesita un calendario.

c) Creo que no es inteligente.
d) No sabe los meses del año. ▲

b (is the most logical response)

3 Part B, *Present Indicative Verb Forms* (20 points): There are 20 items. First, you will *hear* only once a model sentence in Spanish: *Pedro come demasiado;* and then you will hear a cue which is a new subject for the sentence: *ustedes.* You are to write the form of *comer* that goes with *ustedes,* which is _____. ▲

4 Practice this procedure with the following examples, but remember that for the test you will be *hearing* the model and the cue. Cover the answers which appear on the right and be sure you check your answer before proceeding to the next item:

comen

Ernesto es de California. *Yo . . .*
¿Por qué está triste Nancy? *. . . tú*

soy
estás

Yo ahora no tengo sueño. *Nosotras* . . .	tenemos
Ellos vienen del dormitorio. *Yo* . . .	vengo
¿A qué hora llegas aquí? . . . *el profesor*	llega
Yo no sé la lección. *Los estudiantes* . . .	saben
Ellos juegan tenis. *Roberto y Lola* . . .	juegan
¿A qué hora salen ellos? . . . *nosotros*	salimos
Ellos corren en el campo. *Tú y yo* . . .	corremos
Yo quiero comer. *Nosotros* . . .	queremos
Yo no canto bien. *Nosotras* . . .	cantamos
Él y yo hacemos los ejercicios. *Yo* . . .	hago
¿Qué ves tú allí? . . . *yo*	veo
¿Podemos ir mañana? . . . *tú*	puedes
Pensamos ir a Perú. *Usted* . . .	piensa
¿Qué pedimos en el café? . . . *yo*	pido

5 Part C, The done-to *a* (6 points): In 6 sentences with blanks preceding the done-to (direct object) you will have to write *a* in the space provided or leave the space blank, if *a* is not needed. Would you write *a*, or leave a blank in this case? *Ellos conocen* _____ *la señora Domínguez.* ▲

6 Cover the answers on the right and practice further with these examples:

	a
Vemos _____ los abuelos todos los domingos.	a
Ella conoce muy bien _____ esa ciudad.	-
Yo llevo _____ el cuaderno a la clase de español.	-
Nosotros miramos _____ la luna todas las noches.	-
Yo conozco _____ los hijos del profesor Fernández.	a
Ellos llevan _____ su prima al cine.	a
Ellos no ven _____ el río.	-
Yo pongo _____ los papeles en la mesa de la profesora.	-
Yo pongo _____ la niña en su silla de comer.	a
Yo acepto _____ esa mujer como esposa (*wife*).	a
Yo no acepto _____ la verdad.	-

7 Part D, *ir* versus *venir* (7 points): After making sure that you understand each situation described in Spanish, you select the appropriate verb from the two given in parentheses and circle it on your answer sheet. You will have to make 7 choices in examples similar to the following:

Lola está en su casa y habla por teléfono con su amigo Tomás:

Lola: —¿A qué hora (vas, vienes) aquí a mi casa?

Tomás: —(Voy, Vengo) a las siete después de comer.

Lola: —¿Crees que debemos (ir, venir) al cine, o al juego de fútbol?

Tomás: —Creo que esta noche debemos estudiar. ¿Por qué no (vamos, venimos) al cine el viernes?

Lola: —¡Imposible! El viernes (van, vienen) mis abuelos a visitarnos y esa noche quiero estar aquí. ▲

vienes, Voy, ir, vamos, vienen

8 *Another situation:* Un niño está en el patio y su hermano está en la casa:

Niño: —¿Por qué no (vas, vienes) afuera a jugar conmigo?

Hermano: —¡Un momentito! Ahora (voy, vengo).   ▲

vienes, voy

9 Part E, *Telling Time* (8 points): On your answer sheet you will have 4 time expressions and you will have to write their Spanish equivalents in words, *not* Arabic numerals or abbreviations. For example, the Spanish equivalent of *4:15 PM* is _____.   ▲

Son las cuatro y cuarto (quince) de la tarde.

10 With the answers on the right covered, practice *writing* these examples:

1:50 AM.	Son las dos menos diez de la mañana.
12:30 PM.	Son las doce y media de la tarde.
12:50 AM.	Es la una menos diez de la mañana.
11:20 PM.	Son las once y veinte de la noche.
1:25 PM.	Es la una y veinticinco de la tarde.
11:55 AM.	Son las doce menos cinco de la mañana.

11 Part F, *Possessive Adjectives* (10 points): You will have 10 sentences with blanks indicating that possessive adjectives have been omitted. You will have to write the appropriate possessive adjective assuming that the subject (doer) is also the possessor. For example, what is the missing possessive in *Mi hermana y yo vamos al cine con* _____ *prima?*   ▲

12   Cover the answers and practice with the following: nuestra

Anita va al colegio con _____ amigas.	sus
Yo vivo con _____ padres y con _____ hermana.	mis, mi
Jorge trabaja con _____ padre en un garaje.	su
Tenemos que hablar con _____ profesores esta tarde.	nuestros
¿Por qué tú no vas a la fiesta con _____ amigas?	tus
La señorita Maldonado está ahora en _____ oficina.	su
Hugo y yo hablamos con _____ profesora.	nuestra
El perro está en _____ casa.	su
Mis tíos vienen en _____ carro.	su
¿Por qué ustedes no preparan _____ lecciones?	sus

13 Part G, *Adjectival Residuals* (8 points): In order to perform well in this part of the test you will have to remember that the adjectival residuals are the same as the forms of the definite article (*las, la, los,* and *lo* instead of *el*) and that they are attached to the end of infinitives but placed before the finite verbs that you have studied so far. On your answer sheet you will have 8 combinations of two sentences. In the blank provided you will rewrite the second sentence omitting each indicated noun and placing the appropriate residual correctly in relation to the verb. Cover the answers and practice doing that in the following items:

Aquí están los lápices. La profesora necesita los *lápices*.   La profesora los necesita.

Estas son las palabras. Vds. tienen que aprender las *palabras*.	Vds. tienen que aprenderlas.
¿Ves el edificio? Sí, yo veo el *edificio*.	Sí, yo lo veo.
¿Quieres la tiza? No, no quiero la *tiza*.	No, no la quiero.
El libro es muy interesante. ¿Quieres leer el *libro*?	¿Quieres leerlo ?
Aquí está la lección. ¿Quieres la *lección*?	¿La quieres ?
Pancho ya sabe los días de la semana. Pepe todavía tiene que aprender los *días de la semana*.	Pepe todavía tiene que aprenderlos.
¿Dónde está el doctor Ramírez? Yo deseo ver al *doctor Ramírez*.	Yo deseo verlo.
Es importante llamar por teléfono a Inés. Yo no puedo llamar por teléfono a *Inés*.	Yo no puedo llamarla por teléfono.

14 Part H, *Adjectival Agreement* (7 points): In seven examples you will have to demonstrate that you can match the right form of an adjective with a noun or pronoun. You will do it by writing the appropriate form of the indicated adjective for each blank. For example: *José es **chileno**. Ellas son* _____. ▲

15 Practice this procedure with the following examples: chilenas

Él está muy *flaco*. Sus hijas no están _____.	flacas
María Luisa es muy *gorda*. Ella tiene un amigo que no es _____.	gordo
Ella es *venezolana*. Sus hermanos también son _____.	venezolanos
Yo tengo *un* cuaderno *nuevo*. Ahora necesito _____ pluma _____.	una, nueva
Dicen que él es *viejo*. Yo sé que su señora no es _____.	vieja
Yo sé que ella no es *cruel*. Su hijo cree que todas las mujeres son _____.	crueles
El profesor está *alegre*. Las muchachas de la clase también están _____.	alegres
Mi abuelo todavía es *joven*. Tiene tres hijas que también son muy _____.	jóvenes
Mi hermana es *americana*. _____ sobrinos no son _____.	Mis, americanos

15 Part I, Translations of *to be: estar, ser, haber, hacer,* and *tener* (10 points): You will have to fill in 10 blanks in Spanish sentences with *está, es, hay, hace,* or *tiene*. Do this for the following:

En los desiertos no _____ mucha agua.	hay
¿Quién _____ en el jardín, el perro, o el gato?	está
¿A qué hora _____ la clase, a la una, o a las dos?	es
El perro quiere agua. _____ mucha sed.	Tiene
¿Quién _____ la alumna nueva?	es
En Acapulco _____ una playa muy bonita.	hay
En las ciudades del sur _____ mucho calor en el verano.	hace
Aquí _____ la pluma. ¿La necesitas?	está
Abuela no come nada y ahora _____ muy flaca.	está
Estudia por la noche y ahora _____ mucho sueño.	tiene

16 Part J, *Reading Comprehension* (12 points): The 12 items in this part of the test are of two types: completion of sentences and response to a question or statement. In both cases you will be asked to mark the letter opposite the most logical answer. Here are two practice examples:

Cuando tenemos mucha hambre, vamos . . .

a) al teatro   b) a la escuela   c) al correo   d) al café ▲

17 José está muy cansado.   d

a) No tiene hermanos.   b) Come mucho siempre.

c) Es de Asunción, Paraguay.   d) Trabaja siempre demasiado. ▲

The best way to prepare for this part of the test is by reviewing thoroughly   d
your vocabulary list.

ETAPA TRES

Performance Objectives
for Assignments 37–54/55

You will be prepared to continue your study of Spanish successfully if by Assignment 54/55 you have achieved all previous and the following objectives:

Listening and Reading Comprehension

1 Given any oral statement or question and three possible written rejoinders or responses containing structures and vocabulary practiced through Assignment 54/55, you select the most logical rejoinder or response at least eight times out of ten.

You hear: *Mi tío Marcelino llegó ayer antes de las dos de la tarde.*
You see the following and select *a* as the most logical rejoinder.
a   ¿Está aquí también nuestra tía?
b   No sé dónde tengo el cuaderno que compré ayer.
c   ¿No sabía usted que Elena está muy enferma?

Reading Comprehension

2 Given an incomplete written statement followed by three possible completions containing structures and vocabulary practiced through Assignment 54/55, you select the most appropriate completion at least eight times out of ten.

You see the following and select *c* as the most appropriate completion:
Cuando llueve mucho y yo tengo que salir para la escuela . . .
a   me compro una blusa amarilla.
b   mastico bien la comida que tengo en la boca.
c   me pongo el impermeable.

3 Given a written statement or question and three possible responses containing structures and vocabulary practiced through Assignment 54/55, you select the most logical response at least eight times out of ten.

You see the following and select *b* as the most logical response: *Según el refrán, ¿cómo es el león?*
a   Es el rey de las bestias de la selva.
b   Es fiero, pero no tanto como generalmente lo describen.
c   Siempre tiene la boca abierta, y le entran muchas moscas.

Writing and Spelling

4 You write from dictation with correct spelling five short sentences (27 words) containing any of the spelling problems practiced through Assignment 54/55 with no more than four errors.

You hear and write: *Las estrellas ya salieron.*

Vocabulary

5 You match written Spanish vocabulary words studied after Assignment 37 with their nearest English equivalents in at least eight pairs out of ten.

You see:

1	*traje*	(a)	moon
2	*luna*	(b)	Tuesday
3	*sale*	(c)	suit
		(d)	he leaves

You match *c* with 1, *a* with 2, and *d* with 3.

Morphology and Usage

6 (Evaluated following Assignment 41) For fifteen written Spanish sentences you will write the appropriate form of the Imperfect for the indicated verbs (given in the Present and followed by the infinitive in parentheses) with no more than three errors.

You see: **Llueve** (*llover*) *aquí mucho en abril.*   You write: *Llovía.*

7 (Evaluated following Assignment 47) In ten sentences twelve regular verbs are given in the infinitive. You write correctly at least nine times the appropriate conjugated form of the Preterit.

You see: *Aquella señorita* (*hablar*) *demasiado.*   You write: *habló.*

8 For ten sentences combined from a visual-graphic format with verbs given in the infinitive followed by the reflexive *se*, you write out the appropriate conjugated form in the Present and the appropriate choice and placement of the reflexive pronoun with no more than four errors out of twenty.

You see:

1	Tú	1	acostarse	a las siete.
2	Ellos	2	ir a levantarse	

1) 12
You write: *Tú vas a levantarte a las siete.*

9 The verbs in ten Spanish sentences are left in the infinitive. You write the appropriate form of the Preterit with no more than two errors.

You see: *¿Quién* (*ir*) *allí con él anoche?*   You write: *fue.*

10 In a short composition ten verbs are omitted, but the appropriate conjugated form of the Preterit and Imperfect for each verb is given in parentheses. You make the correct choice between the two forms at least eight times according to the cues from context.

You see: *Al llegar a la iglesia la primera persona que yo . . .* (*vi, veía*) *fue el cura.*   You write: *vi*

11 For ten sentences combined from a visual-graphic format with done-to nouns and pronouns indicated following the relator *a*, you write out each sentence substituting the appropriate with-verb pronoun form of the done-to and placing it appropriately within the sentence.

You see:

Ellos	1	miran	1	a ti.
	2	van a mirar	2	a sus hermanas.

1) 12
You write: *Ellos las miran.*

Assignment 37

The Purpose of Programed Assignments

Learning by programed Assignments has several advantages over group learning in a classroom. You can study and learn at the pace that is most comfortable for you. So you neither have to wait for slower learners to catch up nor be frustrated by a pace that is too rapid.

Another advantage is that learning can be broken down into small steps for easier understanding, and coverage of the content can be much more thorough. There is not enough time in the classroom to talk over all the fine points that can be taken up in a programed Assignment.

When you do an ordinary assignment, you do not find out whether you are right or wrong until your work has been checked and returned to you. When you work with programed materials, you find out immediately with each frame.

Here are some suggestions about doing your assignments properly.

1 Never "read over" a section before you are ready to study it carefully.
2 Always work with a cover sheet and always write down or think through an answer *before* you look at the answer frame.
3 When you make a mistake, go back over the frame and try to discover why.
4 Circle the number of each missed frame on your work sheet. When you have completed the section, go back to these frames and review them again.
5 Hurried learning often leads to quick forgetting. Try always to have enough time so you can do each Assignment at your most efficient learning speed.
6 If you have a vacation or a long week-end, try to do your Assignment the day before the next class. You will forget less and be better prepared.
7 Do not put off doing your Spanish Assignment until the time of the day when you are regularly tired. Do something mechanical when you are tired and save your "alert" time for real study.

One Form of the Past Tense of All Verbs: the Imperfect

Spanish, unlike English, has two sets of past tense forms, called the Preterit and the Imperfect. Each translates one or more functions of the simple English past, *e.g., He spoke Spanish.*

1 If you keep in mind the following facts, you can learn to generate all the forms of the Imperfect of *all* regular verbs by learning just two morphemes. The infinitive of the Spanish verb is made up of three morphemes: (1) the first morpheme or stem, which carries the dictionary meaning of the verb, (2) the

second morpheme or set marker vowel, *a*, *e*, or *i*, and (3) the infinitive marker, which is always _____. ▲

2 All simple verb forms in Spanish are also made up of three morphemes. In all regular verbs, the stem remains the same in all tenses. The set vowel of the infinitive is replaced by the first suffix, which indicates tense, mode, and aspect. The infinitive marker *r* is replaced by the second suffix which always indicates _____ or _____. ▲

3 Rewrite *cantamos* (we sing) with a dash between the morphemes (not the syllables). ▲

4 The stem of all regular verbs is the same in both the Present and the Imperfect. The person-number suffixes are also identical. So, what part of *cant-a-mos* must be changed to make it Imperfect? ▲

5 The first suffix of the Imperfect of all regular *a*-verbs is always *aba*. This morpheme replaces the *o* and *a* of the present tense forms. Say *aba* aloud. Which allophone of /b/ must you use? The stop [b] or the fricative [ƀ]? ▲

6 In all forms of the Imperfect the stress falls on the syllable which contains the first *a* of *aba*. So the stressed syllable of *cantaba* (*can-ta-ba*) is _____. ▲

7 When you add *mos* to this form to make it agree with *nosotros*, you must put an accent mark on the stressed syllable in writing. Copy *can-ta-ba-mos* and add the accent mark. ▲

can-tá-ba-mos (Without this mark, the stress would fall on *ba*.)

8 There are no irregular forms of *a*-verbs in the Imperfect and as a result, you now know everything you need to know to create and write the Imperfect of all the *a*-verbs in Spanish. The Imperfect is the regular back-shift of the Present. So to change the statement *Pedro trabaja en la mina* to something recalled, you change *trabaja* to _____. ▲

9 The translation of "to prepare" is *preparar*. How do you say "I prepared" or "I was preparing"? ▲

10 They were preparing. ▲

11 In the Imperfect there is only one irregular *i*-verb (*ir*) and two irregular *e*-verbs (*ver* and *ser*). All other *e*- and *i*-verbs have the *same* first suffix. It is *ía*. Change *Ellos aprenden* (They are learning) to the Imperfect (They were learning). ▲

12 Except for *ir*, *ver*, and *ser*, all of the irregular stems of the Present of *e*- and *i*-verbs are regular in the Imperfect. This means that you use the stem of the infinitive. So *Tú duermes* (from *dormir*) becomes *Tú*_____. ▲

13 The Imperfect of *vengo* becomes _____. ▲

14 The stem of *ver* is *v*, but the stem of *veo* is _____. ▲

15 The stem *ve* comes from the old infinitive *veer* and is the form used in the Imperfect. Write the Imperfect of *veo* and *vemos*. ▲

16 Although *ir* is an *i*-verb, the forms *va*, *vas*, *vamos*, and *van* are like the *a*-verb *dar*: *da*, *das*, *damos*, *dan*. This confusion appears in the Imperfect, where the *v* changes to *b* and the stem is *i*: *iba*, *ibas*. The stress in all forms is on *i*, so the *nosotros* form must be written _____. ▲

---

r

person or number.

cant-a-mos

a

the fricative

ta

trabajaba

Yo preparaba.
Ellos preparaban.

Ellos aprendían.

dormías
venía
ve

veía, veíamos

íbamos

17 The verb *ser* is irregular in almost all tenses. The stem of the Imperfect is the same as in *eres*. The first suffix of all forms is *a*. Write the Imperfect of *son*.   ▲

18 The Imperfect of *somos* requires a written accent to keep the stress on the stem. The form is _____.   ▲

eran

éramos

Summary

1 The second suffix of all Imperfect forms is the same as it is in the Present.

2 There are no irregular *a*-verb forms in the Imperfect.

3 The first suffix of all *a*-verbs in the Imperfect is *aba*. The first *a* requires an accent mark in all *nosotros* forms: *hablábamos*.

4 All regular *e*- and *i*-verbs have the same first suffix in all forms. It is *ía*.

5 There are no irregular stems in the Imperfect of these forms. The stem is the same as it is in the infinitive: *tengo > tenía, duermen > dormían, viene > venía.*

6 The Imperfect stem of *ver* is the old form *ve*, from *veer*, which appears in *veo > veía*.

7 The Imperfect stem of *ser* is the same as the stem of *eres*. The first suffix of all forms is *a*, so *eres* becomes *eras*. The *nosotros* form requires a written accent: *éramos*.

8 The Imperfect stem of *ir* is *i*, which combines with *ba: yo iba*. The *nosotros* form requires a written accent: *íbamos*.

You now have all the information needed to create the Imperfect of all the verbs in the Spanish language.

On Learning Vocabulary

With only minor exceptions, all the vocabulary you have learned so far has been presented to you in class. Moreover, each individual word has been practiced and repeated many times. The real reason for all these classroom repetitions of vocabulary words has not been to teach you the words themselves but to teach their pronunciation (the phonemic system). You are now at the stage where you can learn to pronounce words when you see them for the first time, and there is not so much need for in-class practice in saying new words. Moreover, in order to learn to read and understand Spanish well, you still have to learn several thousand new words, and there will not be enough class time to practice each new word a great many times.

In the next 15 frames, see if you can learn the meaning and the pronunciation of the 23 words presented the first time you meet them.

1 Let us imagine, for example, that you have never seen or heard the Spanish word for *island*, a piece of land surrounded by water. The first part of "island", *isla* is the Spanish word. Say *is-la* aloud in Spanish. You can now understand the meaning of *Cuba es una isla.* Translate and say aloud: Puerto Rico is an island. ▲

Puerto Rico es una isla.

2 You already know that you can learn and remember words better if you put them together in sets. An island (*isla*) is a geographic word like "peninsula," a piece of land that is almost an island. (The Latin for "island" is *insula.*) The Spanish equivalent is *península.* Translate and say aloud: Yucatán is a peninsula. ▲

Yucatán es una península.

3 The big river that separates the United States and Mexico is called *el río Grande.* The Spanish word for "river" is _____. ▲

4 A very large body of water is called an *océano* in Spanish. A small body of water which is completely surrounded by land is called *un lago* in Spanish. The English cognate of *lago* is _____. ▲

río

lake (Say *lago* aloud in Spanish.)

5 You now know three words for different kinds of bodies of water: *río, lago,* and *océano.* Keeping them together in a set will make them easier to remember. It also helps to notice that the Spanish words for "river," "lake," and "ocean" all begin with the same letter used in English. *Los ríos y los lagos* are geographic features of the earth or land. The Latin for "land" or "earth" is *terra.* The *e* of Latin *terra* is stressed in Spanish, so the Spanish word should be written (a) *terra* (b) *tierra.* ▲

tierra (Just like *tiene* or *noviembre.* Say *tierra* aloud.)

6 *Los ríos, los lagos y los océanos son partes de la tierra* (earth). The English cognate of *partes* is _____. ▲

parts (Say *partes* aloud.)

7 You already know the definition of *isla* (island). Let's see now if you can translate this: *Las islas están rodeadas de agua.* ▲

Islands are surrounded by water.

8 You also know that *el río Grande* is between the United States and Mexico. Which word in the following sentence translates "between"? *El río Grande está entre los Estados Unidos y México.* ▲

entre (The English cognate is "inter" as in "inter-collegiate.")

9 In the region of *el río Amazonas* of Brazil, there are great stretches of tropical rain forests popularly called "jungles." Which word in the following sentence translates "jungles"? *En la región del río Amazonas de Brasil hay grandes selvas tropicales.* ▲

selvas (The English cognate is "sylvan.")

10 In geographic terms the opposite of *montañas* is *llanuras.* The great expanse of flat territory between the Mississippi River and the Rocky Mountains is called *una gran llanura* in Spanish. The translation of *llanura* is _____. ▲

plain (The Pampas of Argentina are *llanuras.*)

11 Geographers talk about the earth but also about countries (*países*), the inhabitants of the countries, and their population. If you watch the cognates and use your logic, you should be able to translate this sentence: *El número de habitantes de un país es su población.* ▲

The number of inhabitants of a country is its population.

12 Say English "inhabitants," then Spanish *habitantes.* Spanish dislikes ending words in *nt,* so the singular of *habitantes* is _____. ▲

13 *Los habitantes de la tierra hablan muchas lenguas o idiomas.* Which two words above are translations of "languages?" ▲

habitante

lenguas (literally "tongues") and *idiomas* (idioms)

14 *Tierra* translates "land, earth, soil." Another word in English for "earth" as in "the earth is round," is "world." Which word in the following sentence translates "world"? *Cristóbal Colón descubrió el Nuevo Mundo en 1492.* ▲

15 Say aloud the following words and note their meanings: *luna* (moon), *tormenta* (storm), *nevar* (to snow), *mano* (hand), *sol* (sun), *niebla* (fog), *llover* (to rain), *edificio* (building), *estrellas* (stars).

mundo

16 You can learn and remember a Spanish word better if you make it a habit to associate it with a cognate in your own language. It used to be believed that too much staring at the moon could drive people crazy. Such crazy people were called "lunatics." The Spanish word for "moon" is _____. ▲

17 When there are great explosions on the surface of the sun, there are often huge sheets of flame called "solar flares." The Spanish word for "sun" is _____. ▲

luna

18 On a clear night you can always see *estrellas* in the sky. The translation of *estrellas* is _____. ▲

sol

19 It is still possible to call a raging storm or a tempest a "torment" in English. What letter do you add to "torment" to get the common Spanish word for "storm"? ▲

stars

20 The Spanish speakers named one of our western states Nevada because there was a lot of snow there. The infinitive for "to snow" is _____. ▲

a (tormenta)

21 A person who does "manual" labor works with his hands. The Spanish word for "hand" is _____. It combines with *la.* ▲

nevar

mano (*La mano* is an exception you have to memorize.)

22 A "building" in English is sometimes called an "edifice." The Spanish cognate of "edifice" translates "building." It is _____. ▲

23 Say aloud the Spanish words studied in the preceding frames which are suggested by the following cognates: lagoon, territory, inter, inhabitant, population, lingual, idiom, mundane, lunar, solar. ▲

edificio

lago, tierra, entre, habitante, población, lengua, idioma, mundo, luna, sol

24 Translate the following sentences and say the Spanish aloud: *Una isla tiene que estar rodeada de agua.* ▲

An island has to be surrounded by water.

25 En Brasil hay muchas selvas tropicales. ▲

In Brazil there are many tropical jungles.

You cannot learn to speak and understand Spanish very well until you have a large vocabulary. You need to develop a systematic and efficient way of learning and reviewing vocabulary. If you are a new student (beginning a new quarter), refer to the study procedure suggested at the end of Assignment 4, page 25.

Self-Correcting Exercises

A   Using the pictures below as reference, review your vocabulary by asking yourself and answering aloud each question (or work with a partner). Cover the answers on the right and check the accuracy of your response after each question.

1   ¿En cuál de las seis fotografías ve Vd. una tormenta?

En la fotografía B.

2 ¿Qué clase (*kind*) de edificio hay en esa foto?

Hay una casa.

3 ¿Hace poco viento?

No, hace mucho viento.

4 ¿En cuál de las fotos está nevando?

En la foto A.

5 ¿Cuántas personas hay en la foto?

Hay tres personas.

6 ¿Quiénes son?

Una madre (mujer) y dos muchachos (chicos).

7 ¿Qué tiempo hace?

Está nevando.

8 ¿En cuál de las fotos puede Vd. ver la luna?

Puedo verla en la foto E.

9 Además de la luna, ¿qué puede Vd. ver en el cielo (*sky*)?

Puedo ver las estrellas.

10 ¿Hay muchas o pocas estrellas en el cielo?

Hay muchas.

11 Los dos hombres en la foto están en un observatorio y son astrónomos. ¿Qué van a mirar ellos con el telescopio?

Van a mirar la luna y las estrellas.

12 ¿Hay luna en la foto F?

No, no hay.

13 ¿Qué tiempo hace en esa foto?

Está lloviendo. Hace mal tiempo.

14 ¿Qué hace el hombre más joven?

Toma café.

15 ¿En cuál de las fotos hay sol?

En la foto C.

16 ¿Hace viento en esa fotografía?

No, no hace viento.

17 ¿Qué tiempo hace?

Hace mucho calor.

18 ¿En cuál de las fotos hay un señor que no puede ver bien?

En la foto D.

19 ¿Por qué no puede ver bien?

Porque hay mucha niebla.

New Vocabulary

Add the following words to the vocabulary list in your notebook and study them using the procedure described on page 25 at the end of Assignment 4. If you will spend just three minutes every day doing this, you will gradually get to the point where you can review 100 familiar words in less than a minute, over 300 in the three minutes. This means you can review at least 1500 words each week. You will discover that some words seem less easy to remember than others. Make a special list of these words and spend extra time on them until they come to your mind as fast as the others.

Beginning with this Assignment, the proverbs (*refranes*) and social amenities (*fórmulas de cortesía*) will also appear in this section. Practice saying them aloud until you can say them from memory without hesitation.

isla	island	**parte (la)**	part
península	peninsula	**mano (la)**	hand
tierra	earth, land, soil	**refrán**	proverb
mundo	world	**nevar (ie)**	to snow
llanura	plain	**llover (ue)**	to rain
selva	jungle	**recordar (ue)**	to remember

río	river	**olvidar**	to forget
lago	lake	**volar (ue)**	to fly
habitantes	inhabitants	**seguir (i)**	to continue, follow
población	population	**valer**	to be worth
lengua	language, tongue	**tomar**	to take; drink
idioma (el)	language	**rodeado, -a**	surrounded
sol	sun	**cien**	one hundred
estrella	star	**entre**	between, among
tormenta	storm	**¡Salud!**	Bless you! (*health*)
niebla	fog	**¡Jesús!**	Bless you! (*Jesus*)
edificio	building	**Con permiso.**	Pardon (Excuse) me.

"Más vale pájaro en mano que cien volando."   "A bird in hand is worth two in the bush."

Assignment 38

Review of the Morphology of the Imperfect

You have to spend some more time thinking about the morphemes of the Imperfect before you reach the stage where you can talk about past events and put all your attention on the message as you produce the forms automatically.

1 The first suffix for all forms of the *a*-verb in the Imperfect is the morpheme

————. ▲

aba (There are *no* irregular *a*-verbs in the Imperfect.)

2 The stress falls on the first *a* of *aba* in all forms. This *a* takes a written accent (*ába*) only when the subject pronoun is ————. ▲

3 The person-number suffixes for the imperfect forms are the same as those of the Present. (a) true (b) false ▲

nosotros

4 Change *yo estudio* and *nosotros pensamos* to the Imperfect. ▲

true

Yo estudiaba; nosotros pensábamos

5 What letter follows the stem of all regular *e*- and *i*-verbs in the Imperfect? ▲

6 Write the Imperfect for *vengo*. ▲

í (With an accent.)

venía (The stem is always regular in the Imperfect.)

7 Write the Imperfect for *ustedes ven*. ▲

ustedes veían (The old stem of *ver* used in the Imperfect is *ve* from *veer*.)

8 Translate: They were from La Paz. ▲

Ellos eran de la Paz. (The Imperfect stem of *ser* is *er* as in *eres*.)

9 Somewhere along the way *ir* became mixed up with *a*-verb endings. As a result, "I was going" is translated by *yo* ————. ▲

iba

10 Change *iba* so it agrees with *nosotros*. ▲

íbamos (Remember the *nosotros* form always has a written accent mark.)

11 Translate: They were observing (*observar*) the girls. ▲

Ellos observaban a las muchachas.

12 Change to the Imperfect: *Hace mucho frío.* ▲

13 Change to the Imperfect: *¿Tiene usted calor?* ▲

Hacía mucho frío.

14 Translate: *¿Tenía usted calor?* ▲

¿Tenía usted calor?

15 Rewrite *Ella duerme bien* in the Imperfect. ▲

Were you hot?

16 Except for the three irregular verbs (*ser*, *ver*, and *ir*), the stem of the Imperfect is always the same as the stem of the infinitive. So the imperfect stem for *quiero* is _____. ▲

Ella dormía bien.

quer (as in *querer*)

Social Amenities (Fórmulas de cortesía)

In every society tradition prescribes that people use certain formulas when they meet each other on the street, when they interact in a social situation, when they bump into each other, *etc.* These formulas of courtesy are used to establish and maintain friendly social relationships. What they are depends on the culture, and some may seem strange to us. In Tibet, for example, people stick out their tongue as a friendly gesture of welcome.

1 What does the Spanish speaker say when he asks for permission to leave a group? ▲

Con permiso. (Literally this means "With (your) permission.")

2 Suppose a Spanish speaker bumps into someone accidentally. What does he say? (a) *Con permiso.* (b) *Perdóneme.* ▲

Perdóneme. (This is the formula that says you did not mean to be rude or impolite.)

3 There are two other common formulas that say the same thing. One is *Discúlpeme.* The infinitive is *disculpar*. If we take off the negative prefix *dis*, we can see in *culpar* (to blame) the cognate of *culprit* (doer of wrong) or *culpable* (worthy of blame). So the real meaning of *Discúlpeme* is (a) Pardon me. (b) (Please) do not blame me (for what I've done). ▲

Do not blame me. (*Dispénseme* means essentially the same thing.)

4 The three formulas that have *me* on the end are all based on *a*-verbs: *perdonar*, *disculpar*, and *dispensar*. The verb forms you use in these formulas are: *perdone*, *disculpe*, and *dispense*. Have you learned any *a*-verbs whose first suffix is *e*? ▲

5 What is *Pardon me?* (a) a question (b) a statement (c) a kind of command ▲

no

a kind of command (like *Help me*)

6 *Perdone*, *disculpe*, and *dispense* are the command forms in Spanish which are used with *usted*. To make a command form of an *a*-verb with *usted*, you change the first suffix *a* to _____. ▲

e (You add the regular plural suffix *n* for *ustedes*.)

7 The *tú* forms of the present indicative of *comprar* (to buy), *vender* (to sell), and *escribir* are _____. ▲

compras, vendes, escribes

8 To get the *tú* form of the imperative of all regular verbs, you drop the *s:* *compra, vende, escribe*. Translate *Pardon me.* ▲

Perdóname tú (But *Perdóneme usted.*)

Proverbs and Sayings

1 A foreigner never really learns to understand a strange culture until he can get the "feel" and meaning of the commonly used sayings and proverbs. Word-for-word translations usually fail to give the meaning. So a Russian understands *You can't have your cake and eat it too* when this is "translated" as *You can't take a bath with a dry hide,* and the Spanish speaker understands it as *You can't walk in the procession and ring the bell in the church steeple.*

Many people know the meaning of a saying without actually knowing the meaning of all its words. What is the meaning of "poke" in *You don't buy a pig in a poke?* ▲

2 The Spanish equivalent of *A bird in the hand is worth two in the bush* is *Bird in hand is worth one hundred flying.* Practice saying this aloud: *Más vale pájaro en mano que cien volando.*

sack or bag

3 What is the literal translation of *Quien mucho duerme, poco aprende?* ▲

Who sleeps much, learns little.

4 Practice saying these two proverbs until you can say them without hesitation. Remember that you are also learning usage of forms, phrase structure, and sentence patterns.

The Nature of Events and Getting Ready to Talk about Past Events

1 Aside from the fact that Spanish has two past tense forms—the Imperfect and the Preterit—while English has only one, both cultures analyze and organize events in the same way. Unless you have studied physics, your knowledge of the nature of events and the meaning of tense forms is probably buried in your intuition. When this knowledge is brought to the surface you will readily understand the cues for choosing the right past tense form in Spanish.

Do these three statements describe the same basic facts?
a)   He stood up and started to talk.
b)   He stood up and began to talk.
c)   He stood up and talked. ▲

2 The simple, past tense form *talked* may have the meaning of *started to* or *began to* talk. Consider, now, these three statements:
a)   He stood up and started to open the door.

yes

b)   He stood up and began to open the door.

c)   He stood up and opened the door.

Does the past tense form *opened*, like *talked*, have the meaning of *started to* or *began to* open?   ▲

3 Your intuition just told you that *to talk* and *to open* belong to two very different sets of events, and you must know the critical characteristics of each set before you can transfer this knowledge to learning Spanish. Does *He walked when he was nine months old* say that he began to walk at that age?   ▲ no

4 He is now 25 and still walking. Are *to talk* and *to walk* actions which, once begun, can be extended or kept up?   ▲ yes

5 In order to *begin* to talk, you have to talk, to say something. This logic, however, does not apply to *to close* or *to open* a door. In order to *begin* to close a door, you do not have to close it. yes

Talking takes place once it is begun. Does closing take place *before* the action is actually completed?   ▲

6 This may be confusing, but you have not *closed* the door until it is completely shut. When the door is shut, does the act of closing automatically come to an end?   ▲ no

7 You cannot keep on closing the door. You cannot, in fact, repeat the act of closing without first opening the door. yes

Try this experiment. Clap your hands once. There is no clap until your hands touch each other, and at that instant the action *takes place and ends*. To go on clapping, you must *repeat* a given series of movements.

You now have the criteria for classifying all physical events in two sets. Which of the following events cannot be extended? *to talk, to run, to sleep, to drop dead, to read*   ▲

8 All events like *to open, to close, to drop dead, to explode,* and *to enter* have two common characteristics. First, they do not actually take place until they are finished. Second, they cannot be extended. Some, of course, can be repeated. These events are like the revolution of a wheel (cycle). Each time the wheel (cycle) turns around, it starts all over again. As a result, the events of this set are called cyclic events. to drop dead

Which is the one non-cyclic event in this list? *to shoot, to strike, to hear, to collide, to split*   ▲

9 All non-cyclic events have two characteristics: they take place the instant they are initiated and they can be extended. On a wet road a car can *begin to skid* and can *keep on skidding*. Can it *begin to collide* with an on-coming car?   ▲ to hear

10 A collision either takes place and comes to an end, or it does not happen at all. Now, compare these two statements: no

At that instant both cars skidded.

At that instant both cars collided.

The past tense can be used to say that a non-cyclic event (to skid) *began* at a point in time. Can the past tense be used to say that a cyclic event *began* at some point in time?   ▲

11 Are both events in *He fell down and broke the window* cyclic?   ▲ no
yes

12 Now, consider this statement: *As he broke the window, he cut his hand.* Was the act of breaking going on when he cut his hand? ▲

13 It is now possible to write three rules about English usage:

yes

a) The simple past tense may be used to say that a cyclic event either *was in progress* or *terminated* at a point in time.

b) The simple past tense cannot be used to say that a cyclic event *began* at some point in time.

c) The simple past tense may be used to say that a non-cyclic event *was in progress* or *began* at a point in time.

Does all of this seem to indicate that you cannot get the meaning of the past tense form unless you know whether the event is cyclic or non-cyclic? ▲

14 All speakers of Spanish classify events in the same way as you do. However, there are two forms in Spanish for expressing what English must say with one. So *he talked* may be translated by *él habló* (Preterit) or *él hablaba* (Imperfect), and *he closed* by *cerraba* and *cerró*.

yes

What you have discovered in this Assignment and what you will learn in the next will give you most of the cues for using and understanding the two Spanish forms.

Summary

1 Both English and Spanish recognize that all physical events are divided into two sets. *Cyclic* events can be said to have taken place only when they terminate. A door is not closed until it is shut. A bomb either does or does not explode. Cyclic events may be repeated, but not extended. *Non-cyclic* events can be said to have taken place the instant they are initiated and they may be extended. So one "hears" the instant a sound is perceived and can keep on hearing as long as the sound persists.

2 English has only one simple past tense form. This single form is used to say that at a point in the past a non-cyclic event either began or was in progress. In contrast, the past tense also says that a cyclic event either terminated or was in progress at a point in the past. Consequently, the nature of the event and the context must cue the meaning of the form.

3 Spanish has two past tense forms: the Preterit and the Imperfect. The nature of the event and the context also cues the meaning and use of these forms.

Self-Correcting Exercises

A Review the recent vocabulary by answering the following questions and checking your responses after each one. Answer all yes-no questions in the *negative*.

1 ¿Hay mucha niebla hoy?   No, no hay mucha niebla hoy.

2 ¿En qué mes del año hay muchas tormentas?   En marzo (febrero, *etc.*) hay muchas tormentas.

3 Generalmente llueve en abril, ¿verdad?   No, generalmente no llueve en abril.
4 ¿Vemos estrellas de día o de noche?   Las vemos de noche.
5 ¿Nieva mucho aquí en el invierno?   No, no nieva mucho aquí en el invierno.
6 ¿Cómo es la luna, redonda, o cuadrada?   La luna es redonda.
7 ¿Va a haber luna esta noche?   No, no va a haber luna esta noche.
8 ¿Va a haber una tormenta mañana?   No, no va a haber una tormenta mañana.

B Repeat Exercise A in Assignment 37, page 223.

New Vocabulary

aula (el)	classroom	**dormir (ue)**	to sleep	**sin embargo**	nevertheless
observar	to observe	**redondo, -a**	round	**en (por)**	
repasar	to review	**cuadrado, -a**	square	**todas partes**	everywhere
preparar	to prepare	**según**	according to	**Perdóneme.**	Pardon
aprender	to learn	**desde ... hasta**	from ... to	**Discúlpeme.**	(Excuse)
				Dispénseme.	me.

"Quien mucho duerme, poco aprende."   "He who sleeps a lot, learns little."

Assignment 39

More on the Nature of Events

1 In your last Assignment attention was called to the fact that events are either cyclic or non-cyclic. In talking about airplanes, what kind of an event is *to take off?* ▲

cyclic (The plane cannot take off a second time until the cycle has been completed by flying and a landing.)

2 In flying an airplane, a pilot performs three separate and distinct actions: he takes off, flies, and lands. The take-off does not happen until the instant the wheels leave the runway. Similarly, the landing does not take place until the wheels touch the runway.

Is it logical to say that these two cyclic events do not actually take place until they are completed (terminated)? ▲

3 Flying is a non-cyclic event. It takes place the instant the take-off ends, that is, when the wheels leave the runway. Does flying, like taking off, have to be finished or terminated before we can say it has taken place? ▲   yes

4 Some flying takes place the instant the wheels leave the runway. Flying can be extended. It also terminates when the plane lands. Is it logical, then, to say that flying has three phases: a beginning, a middle, and an end? ▲   no

5 In linguistic terms these three phases are called *aspects*. In theory, if not in our actual perception, every event has three aspects: *initiative* (beginning),   yes *imperfective* (middle), and *terminative* (end). When the set of an event is known, the tense form tells us what aspect is being talked about. What aspect is being talked about in *The plane landed?* ▲

6 What aspect is described in *The plane was landing?* ▲

terminative (end)
imperfective (middle)

7 Both events in this sentence are cyclic: *As he was taking off, a tire blew out.* Which event was already in progress when the other happened? ▲

8 Does *As he took off, a tire blew out* say the same thing as the sentence above? ▲

taking off
yes

9 In the two sentences above, *was taking off* and *took off* both describe the middle or imperfective aspect of the event. What aspect is described in *In spite of the flat tire, he took off?* ▲

10 When English talks about a cyclic event, the progressive form (*was taking off*) always describes imperfective aspect (the middle). In contrast, in the proper context the simple past (*took off*) may describe either the imperfective aspect (middle) or the terminative aspect (end). *To fly* is a non-cyclic event. Which aspect is described in *The pilot gunned the motor and the plane flew?* ▲

terminative

11 Which aspect of *to fly* is described in *As he flew past the control tower, he waved?* ▲

12 The above sentence can be changed to *As he was flying past the control tower, he waved.* Is this a true statement? In the proper context, the English simple past tense may describe the initiative or imperfective aspect of a non-cyclic event. ▲

initiative
imperfective

13 It is important, now, to understand these facts:

yes

a) A non-cyclic event: the simple past tense may describe the *beginning* or *middle* of a non-cyclic event, but not its *end*. To state that a non-cyclic event comes to an end, you must use a helping verb such as *stopped* or *ceased*:

   He smoked (began smoking) at sixteen.
   He stopped smoking at sixty.

b) A cyclic event: the simple past tense may describe the *middle* or *end* of a cyclic event, but not its beginning. To state that a cyclic event began, you must use a helping verb such as *began* or *started*. In many cases this is not logical. *He began to break his leg* makes very little sense. In contrast, *He started to take off* may mean he got two of his six wheels off the runway.

c) When only the simple past describes the initiative aspect of a non-cyclic event, the helping verbs *to begin* or *to start* state explicitly what must be understood in the meaning:

   She picked up the microphone and *talked*.
   She picked up the microphone and *began to talk*.

d) If either kind of event is represented by an arrow, and a dot stands for any recalled point, then the above facts may be diagrammed as follows:

Recalled point	You are talking here

Initiative aspect non-cyclic event

Terminative aspect cyclic event

Imperfective aspect cyclic or non-cyclic events

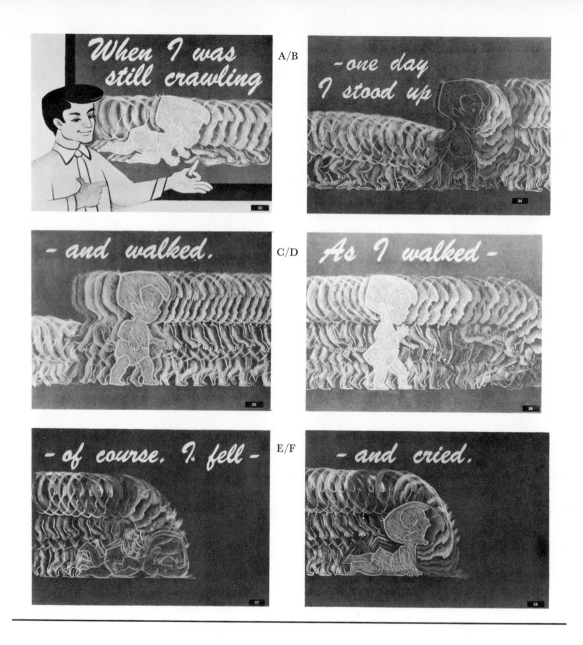

Aspect and the Order of Events

1 There are just three possible order relationships between a point in time and a whole event. The entire event may take place before or after the point, or be in progress at the point. This may be diagrammed as follows:

Moment of speaking

I talked to her.   I am talking to her.   I will talk to her.

Does *I talked to her* say that the whole event took place *before* the moment of saying the sentence?   ▲

2   You have just observed that the simple past tense may be used to say that the whole event—the beginning, the middle, and the end—took place before the moment of speaking. Can aspect be important when we talk about the entire event?   ▲

yes

3   My furnace begins to make a noise. The repair man comes to fix it. The noise is getting louder and I say, "I heard this noise about two hours ago." What aspect of *to hear* is described by *heard*?   ▲

no

The meaning is *I began to hear*. The aspect is initiative because I'm still hearing the noise.

4   It should now be obvious that the simple past tense is used to communicate a variety of messages and that you must be able to identify each in order to understand the use of the Preterit and Imperfect. Here is a summary of the crucial facts.

When we talk about a non-cyclic event (to talk, run, hear, walk, smell, etc.) we can say four different things:

a)   The *whole event took place before* the moment of speaking: I talked to her yesterday.

b)   An *event still going on began* some time *before* the moment of speaking: I heard this noise about an hour ago.

c)   The *event began at some point* in the past: And at that moment he jumped up and *ran* (began to run).

d)   The *event was going on at some point* in the past: As he *ran* (was running), he tripped.

Can an event which has length take place at a point in time which, in reality, has no length?   ▲

no (So all the past tense can say is that a non-cyclic event begins *at* a past point, *before* the moment of speaking, is going on *at* some recalled point, or that the whole event takes place *before* the moment of speaking.)

5   What the past tense can say about a cyclic event is much simpler. Since by its nature a cyclic event must terminate in order to take place, the past tense can communicate only two messages:

a)   The event is terminated *before* the moment of speaking. The point of termination may or may not be expressed:

What happened to George? He *died*.

When did he die? He *died* at one o'clock yesterday.

b)   The event was in progress (imperfective aspect) at some point in the past:

As the bomb *exploded*, this part broke away.

6   To die (*morir*) is a cyclic event. To read (*leer*) is a non-cyclic event. What aspect is described in these statements?

A la una ayer él **moría**. *A la una ayer él* **leía**.

Do you really have to think about this? At a point in the past the Imperfect always describes the _____ aspect.   ▲

imperfective (middle)

7   What is the translation of the two sentences above?   ▲

At one o'clock yesterday he *was dying*. At one o'clock yesterday he *was reading*.

Summary

1 The simple past tense in English has several functions. The meaning of this tense form is defined by the context and the nature of the event being talked about. The past tense may say that a non-cyclic event (a) began *at* some recalled point or (b) merely *before* the moment of speaking, (c) was in progress *at* some recalled point, or (d) that the whole event took place *before* the moment of speaking.

2 The past tense says that a cyclic event (a) terminated (took place) *before* the moment of speaking (the point may or may not be mentioned) or (b) was in progress (imperfective aspect) at some recalled point.

3 At a recalled point the Imperfect always describes imperfective aspect.

Practice with the Done-to a

Write *a* or Ø (nothing) after each frame number.

1 No puedes ver _____ Magdalena esta noche. ▲
2 No puedes ver _____ las montañas desde aquí.   *a*
3 Yo conozco muy bien _____ este pueblo. ▲   Ø
4 Yo conozco muy bien _____ tu tía. ▲   Ø
5 Nunca puedo olvidar _____ mi abuela. ▲   *a*
6 Nunca puedo olvidar _____ su nombre. ▲   *a*

Ø (The done-to is *nombre*, a name, not a person.)

7 ¿Quién busca _____ María? ▲
8 ¿Quién busca _____ este libro? ▲   *a*
9 Observábamos _____ los pájaros en el parque. ▲   Ø
10 Observábamos _____ las muchachas en el parque. ▲   Ø

a

Very few people are aware of the fact that there are about 250 American Indian dialects that are spoken in the United States. However, the number of people who speak an Indian language is small (about 300,000), and many Americans go all their life without ever meeting real Indians or hearing them speak in their own language. This situation is very different in Latin America. In Guatemala, Peru, and Bolivia more than half the population is Indian. Almost half the population of Ecuador is Indian, and more than 10 per cent of the population of Mexico, Venezuela, and Colombia is Indian. In Paraguay almost everyone speaks Spanish and Guarani, the local Indian language.

In Peru and Bolivia nearly half the people speak no Spanish at all, and in many other countries there are also people who speak no Spanish.

No one knows precisely how many Indian languages are spoken in Latin America. One author calculates that in South America alone there are 558 Indian languages. There are 52 in Mexico and 20 in Guatemala. Only one of all these languages has a literature. It is Guarani, the Indian language of Paraguay.

Practice with the Imperfect

With the exception of *ser*, *ir*, and *ver* the stems of all verbs in the Imperfect are regular. Consequently, when you want to backshift a form like *dicen* you have to remember the regular allomorph of the stem, *dec*, in order to make up *decían*. In addition, you must remember whether the verb is an *e-*, *i-*, or *a-*verb so you can choose between *ía* and *aba* as the first suffix. To do both of these things you must remember the infinitive form of every verb.

Below you see a present tense form for ten irregular verbs. Write the infinitive and the corresponding imperfect form.

1	yo pienso ▲	*pensar; pensaba*
2	ellos quieren ▲	*querer; querían*
3	nieva ▲	*nevar; nevaba*
4	digo ▲	*decir; decía*
5	hago ▲	*hacer; hacía*
6	vienen ▲	*venir; venían*
7	tienes ▲	*tener; tenías*
8	muere ▲	*morir; moría*
9	pueden ▲	*poder; podían*
10	empiezas ▲	*empezar; empezabas*

Self-Correcting Exercises

A   Ask and answer the following questions aloud.

1	¿Se hablan muchos, o pocos idiomas en el mundo?	Se hablan muchos.
2	¿Qué idioma hablan los habitantes de nuestro país?	Hablan el inglés.
3	Y en las tierras al sur de nuestro país, ¿qué idioma hablan?	Hablan el español.
4	¿Qué estado de la Unión Norteamericana es un grupo de islas en el océano Pacífico?	Es el estado de Hawaii.
5	¿Hay muchas selvas en Nevada?	No, no hay.
6	¿Hay llanuras en nuestro estado?	Sí, hay (No, no hay.)
7	¿Es el Amazonas un lago, o un río de Brasil?	Es un río de Brasil.

B   Write these sentences, changing the indicated verbs to the Imperfect. Remember that all stem-changing verbs have regular stems in the Imperfect.

1	Yo *pienso* comer.	Yo pensaba comer.
2	Él y yo *pensamos* comer.	Él y yo pensábamos comer.
3	Tú *piensas* estudiar.	Tú pensabas estudiar.
4	Tú *quieres* estudiar.	Tú querías estudiar.
5	Nosotros *queremos* estudiar.	Nosotros queríamos estudiar.
6	Nosotras *volvemos* a casa.	Nosotras volvíamos a casa.
7	Usted *vuelve* al aula.	Usted volvía al aula.
8	Usted *vuela* a México.	Usted volaba a México.

9 Tú *vuelas* a México.

10 Tú *empiezas* a trabajar.

11 Usted *puede* olvidar.

Tú volabas a México.

Tú empezabas a trabajar.

Usted podía olvidar.

New Vocabulary

Say the social amenity and proverb aloud several times.

Sí, cómo no.   Yes, of course (Why not?).

"Quien busca, halla." "Seek and ye shall find." (He who seeks, finds.)

Assignment 40

More on Spanish Numbers

1 It is believed that our entire numerical system came originally from people counting their fingers. Thus the word for *fingers* and the numbers from 1 to 9 is *digits*. These numbers, plus zero, make up the base for all other numbers. In *trece* you see the base of *tres*. In *treinta* (30) you also see *tre* and the form *inta* which, logically, must stand for _____. ▲

10 (Just as the "ty" of twenty, thirty, *etc.* stands for 10.)

2 Look at *cuatro* and *cuarenta*. *Cuarenta* must stand for the Arabic number

_____. ▲

3 If 31 is *treinta y uno*, then 41 should be _____. ▲   40

cuarenta y uno (After number 29 most Spanish-speaking people write all numbers as three words: *treinta y tres, cuarenta y dos, etc.*)

4 And 47 will be _____. ▲

5 Write the Arabic numbers for *cincuenta, sesenta* and *setenta*. ▲   *cuarenta y siete*

50, 60, 70 (If you were to stress *sete* in *setenta*, you would get *siete*. To distinguish between 60 and 70, remember **s-s** (*seis*) = *sesenta* and **s-t**

6 *Ochenta* and *noventa* stand for the Arabic numbers _____. ▲   (*siete*) = *setenta*.)

80, 90 (You say *noventa* with the old Latin *o* in the unstressed position.)

7 You can now recognize in writing all the tens from 10 to 90. Say them aloud so you can also hear them in speech. The stressed syllable is indicated.

10	**diez**	40	cua**ren**ta	70	se**ten**ta
20	**vein**te	50	cin**cuen**ta	80	o**chen**ta
30	**trein**ta	60	se**sen**ta	90	no**ven**ta

8 The Latin *centum* (100) gave English "cent" and two allomorphs in Spanish, *cien* and *ciento*. You already know that when you have two allomorphs you need cues that tell you which one to choose. Here is the way a Spanish speaker counts aloud: *ochenta, noventa, cien, ciento uno, ciento dos, etc.* Which allomorph is used when another number follows? ▲

ciento (Except in *cien mil*—100,000)

9 Which allomorph of the number word for 100 is used all by itself? ▲

cien

10 For the Spanish speaker, the allomorphs *cien* and *ciento* mean all by themselves "one hundred." Translate: one hundred boys. ▲

11 What are the Arabic numbers for *doscientos, trescientos,* and *cuatrocientos*? ▲

cien muchachos

12 The base word *cinco* has an allomorph in *quince*. This should tell you that *quinientos* is the number word for _____. ▲

200, 300, and 400

13 The number words for 600 and 800 are formed regularly. So you just put _____ and _____ in front of *cientos*. ▲

500

seis (seiscientos); ocho (ochocientos)

14 You already know that the *ie* of *siete* comes from a stressed Latin *e*. The stress on all hundred-words falls on the *cien* of *cientos*. How do you suppose, then, that Spanish writes the number word for 700? (a) *sietecientos* (b) *setecientos* ▲

15 By this same logic, how do you suppose Spanish writes 900? (a) *nuevecientos* (b) *novecientos* ▲

setecientos

16 Say the hundreds aloud the way you would say them in counting by hundreds. The stressed syllable is indicated: **cien, dos**cien**tos, tres**cien**tos, cuatro-**cien**tos, quin**ien**tos, seis**cien**tos, sete**cien**tos, ocho**cien**tos, nove**cien**tos.**

novecientos

17 A "cent" in English is one-hundredth of a dollar. A "mil" in English is one-thousandth of a dollar. English "cent" equals Spanish *cien* or *ciento*. The Spanish word for "one thousand" is _____. ▲

mil (Now, say it aloud in Spanish. First say *mi*, then add the *l, mil*.)

18 The Spanish speaker says *cien lagos,* for "one hundred lakes," not *un cien lagos.* If he is consistent, what will he say, (a) *mil lagos*? (b) *un mil lagos*? ▲

mil lagos (Spanish does not use the equivalent of "one" or "a" with *cien, ciento,* or *mil.*)

19 Translate: There are a thousand islands there. ▲

Hay mil islas allí.

20 All of the numbers you have learned so far are also adjectives. You say *un muchacho, treinta y una muchachas,* or *doscientas plumas.* The number *ciento,* however, never changes to agree with its noun: *ciento dos islas.* The Spanish word for 1,000,000 is not an adjective; it is, on the contrary, a noun and takes the number word *un* with it: *un millón.* As a result, the Spanish speaker can say *mil animales* (one thousand animals), but he has to say *un millón de animales* (one million of animals). Translate: The school needs 1,000,000 books. (Use the number words.) ▲

La escuela necesita un millón de libros.

21 The plural of *millón* is *millones.* Translate: 2,000,000 books. ▲

dos millones de libros

22 When you see numbers written out in Spanish, you will discover that they can be punctuated in two ways. Some countries (Puerto Rico, for example) use the English system and write 1,720,640.21 while most of the others use the European system and write 1.720.640,21. In this course this latter system will be used just to get you familiar with it.

Review of Verb Vocabulary

1 The great mountain chain of California is called the *Sierra Nevada*. The word *sierra* means "saw" (the carpenter's cutting tool). What Spanish infinitive does *nevada* come from? ▲

nevar (So *Sierra Nevada* means something like "the snow-covered saw.")

2 What Spanish infinitive is a cognate of *value*? ▲

3 The stem of "dormitory" gives you the stem of what infinitive? ▲

valer

4 Translate the indicated portion of this sentence: "Most birds have *to learn to fly*." ▲

dormir

5 The cognate *pensive* (thoughtful) suggests what infinitive in Spanish? ▲

aprender a volar

6 A *revolver* has a chamber that "revolves" and returns to its original position. What part of *revolver* is the Spanish for "to return?" ▲

pensar

7 The verb for *to ask* (to petition) is _____. ▲

volver

pedir (Another meaning is "to order" when you order something in a restaurant.)

8 The verb for *to ask* (a question) is _____. ▲

9 What Spanish verb does *mirror* make you think of? ▲

preguntar

10 The word *servant* or *serve* in English is a cognate of Spanish _____. ▲

mirar

11 A *record* is something you keep so you will remember. The translation of "to remember" is _____. ▲

servir

12 The opposite of *recordar* is _____, a cognate of "oblivion." ▲

recordar

13 Here is a sentence that is something like a *refrán* (saying). Translate it: *La persona que no quiere, no puede.* ▲

olvidar

The person who does not want (to do something), can't.

14 When you *recognize* a person, you "know" him. What verb translates this meaning of "to know?" ▲

15 Translate *Quien busca, halla* literally. ▲

conocer

16 Translate: *Yo empiezo a aprender español.* ▲

Who seeks, finds.

I am beginning to learn Spanish.

Review of the Stem of the Imperfect of Irregular Verbs

The stem-changing verbs in the Present all have regular stems in the Imperfect. This is the stem you find in the infinitive. Look at the form given below and say its infinitive aloud. Then check the answer. In order to talk you must eventually be able to make these stems changes automatically.

1	tienen	**4**	quieres	**7**	llueve	**10**	duermo	**13**	sigo
	tener		*querer*		*llover*		*dormir*		*seguir*
2	vengo	**5**	pienso	**8**	vuelvo	**11**	muere	**14**	sirven
	venir		*pensar*		*volver*		*morir*		*servir*
3	nieva	**6**	empiezo	**9**	puede	**12**	pides	**15**	digo
	nevar		*empezar*		*poder*		*pedir*		*decir*

Self-Correcting Exercises

A Ask and answer the questions aloud. Adapt the answers on the right to your own personal situation.

1	¿En qué estación del año estamos?	Estamos en otoño.
2	¿Cuál es la segunda estación del año?	Es el verano.
3	¿A qué hora llegas a la universidad?	Llego generalmente a las ocho.
4	¿Con quién vienes a la universidad?	Vengo con mi hermana.
5	¿Vienes a la universidad con una amiga?	No, no vengo con una amiga.
6	¿A qué hora vuelves a tu casa por la tarde?	Vuelvo más o menos a las cuatro.
7	¿Cuántos años tienes?	Tengo veinte años.
8	¿Tienes hermanos? ¿Cuántos?	Sí, tengo tres. Una hermana y dos hermanos.

B General Review. In this guided conversation you assume the roles of all the individuals involved, asking and answering all the questions aloud.

Paco, dile buenos días a Lola.	Buenos días, Lola.
Lola, contéstale y pregúntale qué tal.	Buenos días, Paco. ¿Qué tal ?
Paco, contéstale que muy bien y pregúntale cómo está ella.	Muy bien, gracias. Y tú, ¿cómo estás ?
Lola, contéstale.	Estoy bastante bien, gracias.
Pregúntale cuál es la capital de Argentina.	¿Cuál es la capital de Argentina ?
Contéstale que es Montevideo.	Es Montevideo.
Dile que no, que no es Montevideo, que es Buenos Aires.	No, no es Montevideo. Es Buenos Aires.
Pregúntale quién es su profesor(a) de inglés.	¿Quién es tu profesor(a) de inglés ?
Contéstale.	Es el (la) doctor(a) . . .

New Vocabulary

espacio	space, blank	**buscar**	to look for
peso	monetary unit	**hallar**	to find (discover)
peseta	monetary unit of Spain	**servir (i)**	to serve
dólar	dollar	**morir (ue)**	to die

Both American and Hispanic cultures have developed highly figurative ways of talking about human behavior. The same notion, however, may be described in surprisingly different ways. In English a person may *talk his head off;* in Spanish *he talks with his elbows* (*hablar por los codos*). Someone may *pull your leg* in English while he *pulls your hair* in Spanish (*tomarle el pelo*). *Not to know beans* becomes *no saber ni papa* (*not to know even potato*), and *to move at a snail's pace* is matched by *at the pace of a turtle* (*a paso de tortuga*).

Assignment 41

The Morphology of the Imperfect

In your next class session, you will have a written quiz on the morphemes which make up the imperfect forms of all three sets of verbs. Here is a review.

1 The three irregular verbs which have to be learned separately are _____. ▲

2 The only thing irregular about *ver* is its stem. In the Imperfect it is _____. ▲   *ser, ir, ver*

3 Which present tense form of *ser* also has the stem of the Imperfect? _____. ▲   *ve : veía*

4 The Imperfect of *eres* is _____. ▲   *tú eres*

5 The imperfect back-shift of *van* is _____. ▲   *eras*

       iban (You could, in pronunciation, put [i] in front of *va, vas,* and *van* and get the Imperfect. In writing you change the *v* to *b : iba, ibas, iban.*)

6 Aside from the three verbs just mentioned, the stem of all imperfect forms is regular. Which stem of *dormir* do you use for the Imperfect? (a) *duerm* (b) *dorm* ▲

       dorm (The stem of the Imperfect is always the same as the stem of the infinitive, except for *ir, ser,* and *ver.*)

7 The first suffix for all regular *e*- and *i*-verbs is always _____. ▲

       ía (As in *comer—comía,* and *vivir—vivía.*)

8 Is the second suffix of all verbs in the Imperfect exactly like the second suffix of the Present? ▲

       yes (Even in *ir, ser,* and *ver.*)

9 The first suffix of all *a*-verbs in the Imperfect is _____. ▲

10 Write the imperfect back-shift of *hablamos*. ▲   *aba*

11 In your quiz on the Imperfect, you will be given 15 sentences in the Present.   *hablábamos*
You will write the imperfect back-shift of the present tense form of the verb. The infinitive will be given in parentheses to remind you of what stem to use in the back-shift. Here are some practice examples: El pájaro vuela (*volar*) bien. ▲

12 Yo quiero (*querer*) ver a Rosario pronto. / Hace (*hacer*) mucho calor. ▲   *volaba*

13 ¿Van (*ir*) ustedes al teatro? (You change *v* to *b* and add what?) ▲   *quería, Hacía*

14 No pueden (*poder*) ver bien. / Nicanor nunca olvida (*olvidar*) a sus   *Iban*
amigos. ▲

15 ¿A qué hora comen (*comer*) ellos? / Yo tengo (*tener*) cinco. ▲   *podían, olvidaba*

16 Estamos (*estar*) en Montevideo. ▲   *comían, tenía*

       Estábamos

The Agreement of Number Adjectives

1 The number word *uno* is used only as the name for the Arabic number 1 or in doing math problems. When you say "one river" in Spanish, you say _____. ▲

un río (The *o* of *uno* drops before any noun that can also combine with *el* :

2 When you say "one island" in Spanish, the *o* of *uno* is replaced by _____. ▲   *el río.*)

a : *una isla* (You use *una* with any noun that also combines with *la* : *la isla*.)

3 Translate: thirty-one islands. ▲

4 Translate: forty-one lakes. ▲   *treinta y una islas*
cuarenta y un lagos

5 The *una* of *treinta y una plumas* and the *un* of *cuarenta y un libros* agree in number with *plumas* and *libros*. (a) true (b) false ▲

false (*Plumas* and *libros* are plural; *una* and *un* are singular. In these constructions, *una* and *un* are something like *treinta plumas y una pluma* or *cuarenta libros y un libro*. The *una* and *un* agree with the omitted singular form of the

6 All numbers except 1 are plural because of their meaning, so there is no   noun.)
reason for a plural suffix. The hundred-words *doscientos* through *novecientos*, however, do have a plural suffix. The number word *ochocientos* is exactly like *bolivianos*. Both have the plural suffix *s* and the *o* which matches noun forms. How do you say "Bolivian girls?" ▲

muchachas bolivianas (*A* matches *a.*)

7 How do you suppose, now, that you say "eight hundred girls?" ▲

ochocientas muchachas (*A* also matches *a.*)

8 Here is a rule of usage: the number words from 200 through 900 match *o* or *a* with nouns that also combine with *los* or *las*. Translate: the four hundred stars. ▲

las cuatrocientas estrellas

9 Here is another rule of usage: adjectives of nationality follow their nouns in Spanish; number adjectives precede their nouns. Translate: six hundred Argentine girls. ▲

seiscientas muchachas argentinas

10 The number word *uno* cannot be used in direct combination with a noun but it is used as the adjectival residual to replace *un* when the noun is omitted. For example, someone asks, *¿Tienes un lápiz?* and you answer, "Yes, I have one." The translation of this is _____. ▲

11 Translate: 100 birds. Translate: 100 islands. ▲   *Sí, tengo uno.*

cien pájaros, cien islas (The short form *cien* precedes the noun standing for the thing being counted.)

12 When another number follows 100, you use *ciento*. Translate: 110 buildings. ▲

13 The Spanish word for 1,000 is _____. ▲   *ciento diez edificios*

14 Translate: There are a thousand inhabitants on the island. ▲   *mil*

Hay mil habitantes en la isla. (This also translates, "There are *one* thousand

15 Is the word for 1,000,000 (*millón*) (a) a noun or (b) an adjective in   inhabitants.")
Spanish? ▲

16 Look at these two phrases: *un millón de estrellas; dos millones de estrellas*. We   a noun
can say in English "two million stars." The literal translation of *dos millones de estrellas* is _____. ▲

two millions of stars

Self-Correcting Exercises

A *Discrimination of Events and Aspects.* Analyze the events represented by the indicated verbs. Indicate the type of event by writing C (cyclic) or NC (non-cyclic) and the aspect by B (beginning), M (middle), and E (end). Check each correct answer in the margin before doing the next problem.

Christopher Columbus: Part II

Like other educated Europeans of the fifteenth century, Columbus *knew* **1** that the world was round. By sailing west, he *was sure* **2** that he could reach Asia and open a new route to the rich spice lands of the East. Silks, spices, and other products from these lands *cost* **3** a lot in Europe in those days. Columbus *wanted* **4** to put together an expedition. He *needed* **5** a lot of money, but King John II of Portugal refused to help him.

    Discouraged, but not beaten, Columbus and Diego *left* **6** secretly for Spain in 1484. Father and son *arrived* **7** hungry and tired at a convent called La Rábida, near the southern port of Palos. Juan Pérez, confessor of Queen Isabella, *offered* **8** them food and shelter.

    Some time later, leaving Diego at the convent school, Columbus *set out* **9** for court to see the rulers of Spain. People now *were calling* **10** him by his Spanish name, Cristóbal Colón. He was on his way to becoming the great "Admiral of the Ocean Sea."

1	NC, M
2	NC, M
3	NC, M
4	NC, M
5	NC, M
6	C, E
7	C, E
8	C, E
9	C, E
10	NC, M

B Say aloud the infinitive form of the following verbs. Remember to cover the answers.

empiezas	*empezar*	quiero	*querer*	juegan	*jugar*
vuela	*volar*	sirven	*servir*	vuelvo	*volver*
p⁀edo	*poder*	piensas	*pensar*	duermes	*dormir*
pide	*pedir*	sigo	*seguir*	recuerdo	*recordar*

New Vocabulary

héroe	hero	**tratar de** + inf.	to try to (do something)
boca	mouth	**pasar**	to happen, spend (time),
mosca	fly (insect)		pass
terminar de + inf.	to stop	**sentir (ie)**	to be sorry, regret, feel
acabar. de + inf.	to have just	**cerrado, -a**	closed
	(done something)	**nacional**	national
quedar	to remain (stay	**Lo siento mucho.**	I'm very sorry.
	behind)		(I regret it very much.)

"En boca cerrada no entran moscas."   "A closed mouth catches no flies." (Flies do not enter a closed mouth.)

Numbers from 40 to 5,000,000

cuarenta	40	doscientos	200	ochocientos	800
cincuenta	50	trescientos	300	novecientos	900
sesenta	60	cuatrocientos	400	**mil (1.000)**	1,000
setenta	70	quinientos	500	**dos mil (2.000)**	2,000
ochenta	80	seiscientos	600	**un millón (1.000.000)**	1,000,000
noventa	90	setecientos	700	**cinco millones (5.000.000)**	5,000,000

You know enough to be able to supply the missing numbers.

Assignment 42

The Preterit Forms of e- *and* i-*Verbs*

1   The first suffix of the Imperfect for all regular *e*- and *i*-verbs is _____.   ▲

2   The stem of all *e*- and *i*-verbs is always followed by *i*. This combination is   *ia*
the past tense base. The past tense bases for *comer* and *vivir* are _____.   ▲

> *comí; viví* (You have just written the Preterit forms that go with *yo*. All
> Preterit forms of all regular *e*- and *i*-verbs are built on the past tense base.)

3   *Yo escribía* says "I was writing"; *yo escribí*, in contrast, says "I wrote." To
change the imperfect form *yo comía* to the Preterit, you simply drop the mark
of imperfective aspect, the *a*. So the preterit form of *comía* is _____.   ▲

> *comí* (The past tense base *comí* and the Preterit *comí* simply state that this
> non-cyclic event either began at some point in the past or was completed
> before the moment of speaking. *Preterit* is the Latin for "gone by," past.)

4   Write the *yo* form of the Preterit of these verbs: *subir, deber, correr, escribir.*   ▲

> *subí, debí, corrí, escribí*

5   The *nosotros* form of the Imperfect of *comer* is _____.   ▲

6   From what you already know about *comía* (Imperfect) and *comí* (Preterit),   *comíamos*
the Preterit of *comíamos* should be _____.   ▲

> *comimos* (You don't need the written accent in this form because the stress
> falls normally on the *i*.)

7   All *e* and *i* Preterit *nosotros* forms are made up of the past tense base plus *mos*.
Write the Preterit *nosotros* forms for these verbs: *escribir, beber, subir, vivir.*   ▲

> *escribimos, bebimos, subimos, vivimos*

8   In all the forms of all the verbs you have learned so far, the second suffix
that goes with *tú* has always been _____.   ▲

9   In all forms of the Preterit of all verb sets, but in no other tense forms, the   *s*
second suffix that goes with *tú* is *ste*. The *ste* is added to the past tense base of
all *e*- and *i*-verbs to make up all *tú* forms. The *i* of the base has no written
accent. Change *comías* to the Preterit.   ▲

> *comiste*

10 Change *debías, corrías,* and *subías* to the *tú* form of the Preterit. ▲

debiste, corriste, subiste

11 The preterit form that combines with *usted, él,* or *ella* is made by adding *ó* to the past tense base. The accent mark is now on the *ó*, not on the *i* of the base. Change *él bebía* to the Preterit. ▲

12 Change *escribe, sube,* and *vive* to the Preterit. ▲

él bebió
escribió, subió, vivió

13 Here is the *ustedes (ellos, ellas)* form of the Preterit of *beber* (to drink): *bebieron.* To make up this form you put _____ in between the base *bebi* and the second suffix *n*. ▲

14 Copy these bases and complete them so they agree with *ustedes: comi, volvi, aprendi, escribi.* ▲

ero

comieron, volvieron, aprendieron, escribieron

15 Write the preterit form of *escribir* that goes with *nosotros.* ▲

escribimos (The *nosotros* form for all *i*-verbs is exactly the same for the Present and the Preterit. The meaning is fixed only by the context.)

Summary

You have now observed how to make up the Preterit of all regular *e-* and *i*-verbs in the whole Spanish language. Let's look at the pattern.

	comer			vivir		
yo	com	í		viv	í	
nosotros	com	i	mos	viv	i	mos
tú	com	i	ste	viv	i	ste
usted, él, ella	com	ió		viv	ió	
ustedes ellos, ellas	com	iero	n	viv	iero	n

The grand total of things you have to remember is five:

1 The stem is regular: *com, viv.*

2 There is one change in the last slot (the person-number suffixes): *s* changes to *ste.*

3 Three new first suffix forms:
  a *i (í)* for *yo, nosotros,* and *tú*
  b *ió* for *usted, él,* and *ella*
  c *iero* for *ustedes, ellos,* and *ellas*

Review of Aspect and the Nature of Events

1 In theory every event may have three aspects. In non-technical terms these three aspects may be called the _____ of the event. ▲

beginning, middle, end

2 Which of these three is also called the "imperfective" aspect? ▲

3 Every language in the world deals with aspect because knowing whether   the middle
something is still going on (imperfective) or finished is important to survival.
You need to know about aspects in order to choose between the Preterit and the
Imperfect. At any point in the past, the Imperfect always describes (a) a completed action (b) an action in progress. ▲

an action in progress

4 So the Preterit must be used to describe the beginning or the end of events.
There is nothing in the form of the Preterit that can tell you whether the form
describes the beginning or the end of an event. You must know the nature of
the event itself. How many basic kinds of events are there? ▲

5 There is one kind of an event whose essential features can be observed the   two
very instant it is begun. This type of event, moreover, can be extended (kept up)
at the will of the doer. Does *descubrir* (to discover) belong to this set? ▲

no (Columbus could discover the New World just once. He could not keep
6 Can you recognize what event is taking place the moment someone begins   on discovering it.)
to *llevar* something? ▲

7 Can the doer who is carrying something keep on doing this as long as his   yes
strength and will hold out? ▲

8 What is the technical term for events which belong to the same set as *llevar*,   yes
querer, mirar, dormir, pensar, and *observar*? ▲

9 In *He went to bed and cried* the verb *cried* says the same thing as (a) he was   non-cyclic
crying (b) he began to cry. ▲

10 When a person goes to bed, there is a certain routine that is normally   he began to cry
followed, that is, a series of steps that leads up to the end (termination) of the
event. Ignacio is brushing his teeth, taking off his shoes, removing his shirt.
These acts are steps toward going to bed. They are part of the cycle that comes
to an end when Ignacio actually climbs into bed. Once Ignacio has gotten into
bed, can the cycle be extended? ▲

11 What must Ignacio do before he can go to bed again? ▲   no

12 Does *Ignacio went to bed* tell you that the whole cycle was completed? ▲   He must get up.

13 Does *cried* in *Ignacio went to bed and cried* tell you when the crying came to   yes
an end? ▲

14 What kind of an event is *to sleep*? (a) cyclic (b) non-cyclic ▲   no
non-cyclic (Once you are asleep the action can be extended.)

15 Which is the one non-cyclic event in this group: to open, to break, to leave,
to study? ▲

16 Which is the one cyclic event in this group: to die, to read, to hear, to   to study
carry? ▲

to die (This is one cycle that cannot be repeated.)

17 Here is a short paragraph in English in which the verbs are in the past tense.
Do you still hear that noise? *I heard* (1) it at six o'clock while *we were eating.*
(2) *I got up* (3) and *went outside.* (4)
What kind of an event is *to hear*? ▲

18 What aspect is described by *heard* in the sentence above? (a) initiative (b)   non-cyclic
imperfective (c) terminative ▲

initiative (One could say, *I began to hear the noise.*)

19 What kind of an event is *to eat?* ▲

non-cyclic (The action can be extended.)

20 What aspect is described by *were eating?* ▲

imperfective (The action was in progress.)

21 What kind of an event is *to get up?* What aspect is described by *I got up?* ▲

cyclic, terminative (The whole cycle was completed at a point in the story.)

22 What kind of an event is *to go outside?* ▲

23 What aspect is described by *I went outside?* ▲   cyclic

terminative (Again the whole cycle was completed after *I got up.*)

Review of the Order of Events

1   We would all become confused if we never could tell whether an event takes place *before*, *at*, or *after* the moment of speaking. Does *He left yesterday* mean the action of leaving is (a) at the moment of speaking? (b) before the moment of speaking? ▲

before the moment of speaking

2   What order relationship is expressed by *He will do it soon:* (a) before, (b) at, or (c) after the moment of speaking? ▲

after the moment of speaking

3   There can be only three order relationships between an event and a point in time. (1) The event is anterior to (before) the point, (2) the event is simultaneous with (at) the point, and (3) the event is posterior to (after) the point. You will soon learn how verb forms and adverbs give you this information.

When the Spanish speakers came to their part of the New World, they came as conquering armies. For a long time no Spanish women came to the New World and, as a result, the soldiers who stayed often married Indian women and their children had a mixture of Spanish and Indian blood. In many countries of Latin America today the majority of the people have some Indian blood.

In contrast, when the early settlers came to the United States they brought their families with them and, as you already know, they drove the Indians off their lands. Because the Indians continued to fight the settlers until late in the 19th century there was almost no intermarriage between the two groups until the present century.

Vocabulary Review

1   The translation of "Yes, of course" is _____. The translation of "nevertheless" is *sin* _____. ▲

Sí, cómo no; embargo

2   Translate: *Está entre el sofá y el piano.* ▲

It is between the sofa and the piano.

3 The meaning of *en todas partes* is "in all parts." A good translation is

———. ▲

4 Translate: *El edificio está rodeado de gente* (people). ▲

5 Translate the boldfaced words: *Vamos **desde** aquí **hasta** allí.* ▲

everywhere

The building is surrounded by people.

from . . . to

Self-Correcting Exercises

A *Usage of Spanish Numbers:* Write the following combinations using words for the numbers, and check the correct answer after each one.

Ejemplo: 114 = Hay setenta y una pesetas allí.

		1)	71			
1	Hay	2)	900	1	estrellas	
		3)	1.400	2	habitantes	
		4)	1.000.000	3	dólares	allí.
2	Tienen	5)	600.000	4	pesetas	
		6)	3.000.000			

1)	142	Hay un millón de habitantes allí.
2)	224	Tienen novecientas pesetas allí.
3)	162	Hay tres millones de habitantes allí.
4)	161	Hay tres millones de estrellas allí.
5)	233	Tienen mil cuatrocientos dólares allí.
6)	123	Hay novecientos dólares allí.
7)	254	Tienen seiscientas mil pesetas allí.
8)	253	Tienen seiscientos mil dólares allí.
9)	213	Tienen setenta y un dólares allí.
10)	234	Tienen mil cuatrocientas pesetas allí.
11)	111	Hay setenta y una estrellas allí.
12)	141	Hay un millón de estrellas allí.

B Forms of the Imperfect and the Done-to *a*: With the answers covered, write the following combinations.

Ejemplo: 322 = Yo quiero ver a la señorita Moreno.

1	Pancho	1	recordar		1	la estrella grande.
2	Manolo y yo	2	querer ver		2	la señorita Moreno.
3	Yo	3	poder mirar	(a)	3	la terrible tormenta.
4	Tony y Elena	4	olvidar		4	el nuevo director.
5	Tú				5	mi hermana.

1)	113	Pancho recuerda la terrible tormenta.
2)	212	Manolo y yo recordamos a la señorita Moreno.
3)	424	Tony y Elena quieren ver al nuevo director.
4)	525	Tú quieres ver a mi hermana.

5)	224	Manolo y yo queremos ver al nuevo director.
6)	324	Yo quiero ver al nuevo director.
7)	141	Pancho olvida la estrella grande.
8)	415	Tony y Elena recuerdan a mi hermana.
9)	541	Tú olvidas la estrella grande.
10)	243	Manolo y yo olvidamos la terrible tormenta.
11)	331	Yo puedo mirar la estrella grande.
12)	512	Tú recuerdas a la señorita Moreno.

Assignment 43

The Preterit Forms of a-*Verbs*

1   The *nosotros* form of all regular *a*-verbs, like the *nosotros* form of all *i*-verbs, is exactly the same for the Present and the Preterit. Write the Preterit of *llegar*.   ▲

2   Change *esperábamos* to the Preterit.   ▲   *llegamos*

3   Write the *nosotros* form of the Preterit for *cantar* and *necesitar*.   ▲   *esperamos*

cantamos, necesitamos

4   To change any of these forms to the *tú* form, you replace *mos* with (a) *s* (b) *ste*.   ▲

5   Change *hablas* to the Preterit. Change *deseabas* to the Preterit.   ▲   *ste*

6   In the *i*- and *e*-verb forms, *subieron* and *comieron*, the *ie* is the set marker.   *hablaste, deseaste*
What do you logically expect will replace *ie* when you make up the preterit form of *comprar*, an *a*-verb?   ▲

a (So you get *ustedes compraron*. This is also the *ellos* form.)

7   The Preterit of *ellos hablan* is *ellos* _____.   ▲

8   There are three forms of the Preterit that have *a* right after the stem. What   *hablaron*
are they?   ▲

*nosotros compr-**a**-mos; tú compr-**a**-ste; ustedes, ellos, ellas compr-**a**-ron*

9   There is one form of the Preterit of *a*-verbs that has *é* right after the stem: *yo compré*. Write the *yo* form of *llevar*.   ▲

10   Change *yo miraba* to the Preterit.   ▲   *llevé*

11   There is one form of the Preterit which has *ó* as the first suffix. This *ó* goes   *yo miré*
with the same subject pronouns as the *ió* of *e*- and *i*-verbs. They are *usted*,

_____.   ▲

12   Change *usted observaba* to the Preterit. Write the *él* form of the Preterit of   *él; ella*
pensar.   ▲

usted observó; él pensó

13   Change these forms to the Preterit: *usted compra, él estudiaba, ella desea.*   ▲

usted compró, él estudió, ella deseó

14 Notice the difference in pronunciation. Divide these forms into syllables
and underline the stressed syllable: *(yo) canto, (usted) cantó.* ▲

> **can**-*to;* *can*-**tó** (In all regular preterit forms, the stress falls on the vowel of
> the first suffix. This stress is the only thing in speech that tells you the difference
> between *canto* (I sing) and *cantó* (he sang). You can, of course, see the
> difference in writing.)

A/B

YO ANDABA POR EL PUEBLO

CUANDO VI LOS TOROS

C/D

CORRÍ

TROPECÉ

E/F

Y CAÍ EN LA FUENTE

ESTÁBAMOS EN LA SELVA

HACÍA UN SOL BRILLANTE

APARECIÓ UNA TORMENTA

G/H

Y LLOVIÓ

EL RÍO INUNDÓ EL PUEBLO

I/J

LA TORMENTA PASÓ

BRILLÓ EL SOL

K/L

CANTARON LOS PÁJAROS

Y LA SELVA SIGUIÓ COMO ANTES

M/N

The Preterit and Imperfect in Contrast

1   The past tense base of *leer* is *leí*, which is also the *yo* form of the Preterit. What do you add to *leí* to get the Imperfect?   ▲

a (leía)

2   The Preterit and the Imperfect are not two different tenses. They are different forms of the same tense just as "is talking" and "talks" are different forms of the Present in English. Both the Preterit and the Imperfect describe past events. At a recalled point in time the Imperfect describes the _____ aspect of either cyclic or non-cyclic events.   ▲

middle (imperfective)

3   Since events, in theory, have three aspects and the Imperfect always describes only the imperfective aspect, does it follow that the Preterit must be used to talk about both initiative (beginning) and terminative (end) aspect?   ▲

4   What aspect of a cyclic event is described by the Preterit?   ▲

yes

terminative (Remember that a helping verb is needed to talk about the initiative aspect of a cyclic event.)

5   The Preterit is used to say that a cyclic event took place before the moment of speaking: *Sé que ella salió.* In *I said that she left* the event *to leave* took place before the event *said*. Translate *she left.*   ▲

ella salió (So the Preterit is used to say that a cyclic event took place before the reporting of it.)

6   Look at these two statements: *Sé que ella salió a la una. Dije que ella salió a la una.* What new information is added by *a la una?*   ▲

It tells the point in time at which the event was completed.

7   All the above facts about cyclic events may be condensed into one rule. The Preterit always says that a cyclic event terminated in the past. Is this true for non-cyclic events?   ▲

8   Because non-cyclic events can be extended, some may begin in the past and still be going on at the moment of speaking. Which event in *She loved the house the moment I showed it to her* may still be going on?   ▲

no

She loved the house (and she still does.)

9   The Preterit may say that an event still in progress began before the moment of speaking. What does *habló* tell you in *Ayer a la una el Presidente habló por televisión?*   ▲

He began to speak at one o'clock.

10   What does *habló* tell you in *Ayer el Presidente habló por televisión?*   ▲

The entire event took place yesterday.

11   The Preterit tells you only one thing about cyclic events: they took place (terminated) in the past. In contrast, the Preterit may say two things about non-cyclic events: they began at some point in the past, or the entire event took place before the moment of speaking. Only context and the logic of reality tells you whether an event began in the past, came to an end in the past or is still going on.

Here is a rule of thumb. If you are not talking about the middle (imperfective aspect) of an event, you must use the _____.   ▲

Preterit

Summary

Preterit of *a*-Verbs

You are now able to make up all the forms of all regular *a*-verbs in the whole language. Let's see what you have to remember.

yo	cant	é	
nosotros	cant	a	mos
tú	cant	a	ste
usted, él, ella	cant	ó	
ustedes, ellos, ellas	cant	aro	n

1 The stem is regular, the same as in the infinitive.

2 The first suffix has four forms: *é* for *yo*; *a* for *tú* and *nosotros*; *ó* for *usted, él,* and *ella*; *aro* for *ustedes, ellos,* and *ellas*.

3 The second suffix forms are identical to those of *e*- and *i*-verbs: zero, *mos, ste,* and *n*.

Preterit and Imperfect in Contrast

At a point in the past the Imperfect states that any event was in progress. The Preterit states that a cyclic event reached its termination and took place. In contrast, the Preterit may say either that a non-cyclic event began (and may or may not have come to an end) or that the whole event took place before the moment of speaking.

Self-Correcting Exercises

A *Present Tense Forms of Stem-changing Verbs:* Write the appropriate present tense form for each infinitive.

1 (Nevar) mucho en el invierno.   Nieva
2 Yo (querer) buscar una cometa más pequeña.   quiero
3 Ellos (jugar) siempre con los niños de allí.   juegan
4 Pepe y Alicia (seguir) a su maestro.   siguen
5 Quien mucho (dormir), poco (recordar).   duerme, recuerda
6 Si nosotros (pedir) mucho, ella (servir) poco.   pedimos, sirve
7 Las cometas (volar) muy bien cuando hace viento.   vuelan
8 ¿Qué (pensar) tú hacer esta mañana?   piensas
9 Sí, señor, siempre (llover) aquí en el mes de abril.   llueve
10 Él y yo (empezar) los estudios a las cinco.   empezamos

B *Events and Aspects:* Write *C* if the event is cyclic or *NC* if it is non-cyclic, and indicate its aspect by writing *B* for beginning, *M* for middle, and *E* for end.

Black Friday

Around 4:00 in the afternoon the neighbor's car *killed* **1** Tom, my beautiful black cat. An hour later, as we *grilled* **2** hamburgers in the patio, everyone in the family *was* **3** still very sad. Suddenly the wind *blew* **4** strongly, and we *went* **5** inside and *watched* **6** the storm.

Still thinking of poor Tom, we were finishing supper in the kitchen, when the roof *leaked* **7** and all the lights of the house *went out* **8**. I *lit* **9** a candle in the living room and didn't notice that the match *fell* **10** on Mother's favorite Persian rug. My brother *smelled* **11** the smoke and ran to put out the fire. In the excitement he *stepped* **12** on my sunglasses and they *broke* **13**.

I couldn't take it any longer, so I *went to bed* **14** and *cried* **15**.

1	C, E
2	NC, M
3	NC, M
4	NC, B
5	C, E
6	NC, B
7	NC, B
8	C, E
9	C, E
10	C, E
11	NC, B
12	C, E
13	C, E
14	C, E
15	NC, B

C   *The Done-to* a: If the done-to *a* is needed, write it. If not, leave a blank.

1	Buscamos . . . los dos continentes de América en el mapa.	-
2	Queremos conocer . . . la señora Gutiérrez.	*a*
3	Pensamos comer . . . tres bananas mañana en la cafetería.	-
4	Todos vimos . . . las estrellas anoche muy cerca de la luna.	-
5	Primero tienen que servir . . . Juan.	*a*
6	Debemos invitar . . . la nueva alumna a nuestra fiesta.	*a*

New Vocabulary

cometa (la)	kite	**fiero**	fierce
león	lion	**tan . . . como**	as much as
calle (la)	street	**Hágame** ⎫	
pintar	to paint, color	**Hazme** ⎬ **el favor de . . .**	Please.

"No es tan fiero el león como lo pintan."   "Things are not as bad as they seem." (The lion is not as fierce as they paint him.)

A great many American tourists find the long, flowing skirts of the Indian women of Latin America (and the United States) to be quaint and something typically Indian. What these people do not know is that the Indian women of the New World did not wear skirts before the Discovery. When the European women came here, the Indians began to dress like them. Since all women wore long skirts at that time, the Indians did the same thing. The difference is that the Indians have kept up the custom while the city dwellers have changed their styles to match those of Paris or New York. The "typical" Indian dress, in short, is not Indian at all. It is an inheritance of the European styles of the sixteenth and seventeenth centuries.

Assignment 44

Some Ways to Learn and Remember Words

1 One way to learn to understand the meaning of a word is to learn another word which is its opposite. The opposite of *morir* is _____. ▲

2 The opposite of *noche* is _____. ▲

vivir
día

3 When you come upon a new word, try to find out if you already have in your vocabulary an opposite which will help you remember both the word and its meaning. For example, very soon you are going to meet the verb *recibir*. It is the opposite of *dar* (to give). Now look at *recibir* and see if you know a cognate which looks like it and is the opposite of "to give." Think of the saying *It is better to give than to* _____. ▲

4 Not all words have opposites which can be used to help you remember them. There is almost no word, however, which cannot be associated with some other word which will help you learn its meaning. You know, for instance, the meaning of *hambre* and *sed*. They go together. Here is a verb which is often associated with *hambre*. It is *sufrir*. Look at this sentence: *En el mundo hay mucha gente que sufre hambre.* The translation of *sufrir* is "to _____." ▲

receive

5 You do not always have to associate a new word with another vocabulary item to learn and remember its meaning. There are other associations which are just as helpful. What made Columbus famous? *Descubrió el Nuevo Mundo.* You put Columbus together with the New World and you can hardly miss or forget the meaning of *descubrir*. It is "to _____." ▲

suffer

6 When you learn words in this way, you do not have to practice them over and over again in order to remember them. Look, now, at "discover" and *descubrir* and see if you can wring some more meaning out of them. Do both words begin with a negative prefix? ▲

discover

7 Did you ever stop to think that "dis-cover" may mean to "un-cover" something you did not know was there? Now, look at *des-cubrir* carefully. Have you discovered that the Spanish for "to cover" is _____? ▲

yes ("dis" and *des*)

8 When you really learn what *des-cubrir* means, it is not very difficult to remember its opposite, *cubrir*. In a way, you get one word for free. You can learn to get hundreds, even thousands, of words for free once you understand how to discover meaning. And you will remember them better when you make the right association. Here is another example. Christopher Columbus got the money for his *viaje* to the New World from *la reina Isabel*. Can you make an educated guess at the translation of *viaje*? ▲

cubrir

9 Now that you know the meaning of *viaje*, you should not have too much trouble with the verb form based on it. When you take a trip, you go from one place to another. The specialized word for "going on a trip" is *viajar*. The translation of *viajar* is not "to trip"; it is "to _____." ▲

voyage or trip

travel (The meaning of *viajar* in Spanish is *hacer un viaje* = to make a trip.)

10 You now know *viaje* (trip) and *viajar* (to travel). Can you make this jump?

Una persona que viaja es un viajero. What suffix do you add to "travel" to get the translation of *viajero?* ▲

er (And you get "traveler.")

11 Let's go back, now, and look at this. *Colón recibió el dinero para su viaje al Nuevo Mundo de la reina Isabel.* You know enough history to guess that the translation of *reina* is _____. ▲

12 The husband of Queen Isabella was *el rey Fernando.* Look at *reina* and *rey* carefully. Say *rey,* then *reina,* aloud. The word *rey* sounds exactly like the stem of **rei-***na.* The translation of *rey* is _____. ▲

queen

13 Kings and queens cannot *reinar* unless they have a *reino.* Which word translates "kingdom?" ▲

king

14 With this much information, you can hardly fail to figure out that *reinar* translates "to reign." It is expected, of course, that you will make some mistakes when you try to figure out the meaning of new words. You make the same kinds of mistakes in English, but you are right most of the time. You will also be right most of the time in Spanish if you learn to use your linguistic logic carefully. By making educated guesses you can learn thousands of words all by yourself and in this way you can build up enough vocabulary to become a fluent speaker of Spanish without having to spend years in class. This means that after you have mastered one language (your native English), you can be taught *how* to learn a second language and, as a result, you can learn the second language much faster than the first.

reino

Another way of building up your word vocabulary is to associate words which have a similar meaning. The verb *ir* is a cover term for the specialized verb *viajar.* When Columbus set out *de España* on his famous *viaje,* he expected to be able to *regresar a España.* One opposite of *ir* is *volver.* Does *volver* have a meaning very similar to *regresar?* ▲

yes (*Regresar* and *volver* are synonyms.)

15 Once you realize that *ir, viajar, volver,* and *regresar* belong to a set of verbs which describe movement through space, you will find it easier to remember the words. What is just as important, it will be easier for you to learn other sets of words which are associated with the movement set. Let's see how this works. You come upon, for example, this sentence: *El año pasado viajamos a Europa por avión.* The context tells you that *avión* belongs to a set of words associated with travel. You might guess that it labels a means of transportation. Now look at *avión* carefully. There are several English cognates which begin with *avi* and which are associated with a means of transportation. One cognate is _____. ▲

You might have thought of "aviation" or "aviator."

16 You do not, of course, say, "Last year we traveled to Europe by aviation." But once you have gotten this far, you know that the word for *avión* is _____. ▲

17 You already know that there is a big difference between the meaning of a word in Spanish and its translation in English. The translation of *Hace calor* is "It is hot." Its meaning in Spanish is _____. ▲

plane

18 You will remember *avión* better if you also know its real meaning. The Spanish suffix *ón* means "big." The stem *avi* appears in these cognates: aviation, aviator, aviatrix, aviculture, and aviary (the cage where birds are kept). One

Makes heat.

Spanish word for "bird" is *ave*. The original meaning of *avión* was not "plane," but _____. ▲

big bird (Aviators are sometimes called "bird men.")

19 In real life you only meet new words in life situations. The life situation— that is, the place where you are, the person you are talking to, plus the context in which you meet the new word—help make it clear to you what in general is being talked about. The subject of discourse (what is being talked about) very frequently tells you what set the new word belongs to. Thus, for example, you are in a restaurant and someone says, *No como zanahorias*. You can guess right away that *zanahorias* belongs to the set we label as _____. ▲

food

20 You are in a shop which only sells vegetables. Someone says *Esas zanahorias son muy buenas*. You can be pretty sure now that *zanahorias* belongs to the subset of food labeled _____. ▲

vegetables

21 If you watch what the person is pointing at when he says *Esas zanahorias son muy buenas*, will you immediately learn the meaning of *zanahorias*? ▲

yes (You will know at once it is the word for "carrots.")

22 The subject of discourse is Christopher Columbus and his trip to the New World: *Colón viajó por barco*. What does *barco* label? ▲

boat (The cognate is "bark.")

23 The action is *viajar*. The means of transportation is *barco*. The *viaje* is across the ocean. It is a marine voyage. The men who went with Columbus were *marineros*. Does someone have to tell you that *marineros* translates _____? ▲

sailors (The cognate "mariners" gives the Spanish meaning.)

24 Suppose you missed the meaning of *marinero*. Should you give up? Not until you have tried this trick. You learned a little while back that the action *viajar* is based on *viaje* and that the doer of the *viaje* is a *viajero*. The Spanish suffix *ero* frequently means the doer of something associated with the meaning of the stem. The stem of *marinero* is *mar*, the word for _____. ▲

sea

25 The base stem *mar* is expanded in *marinero* to the long stem *marine*. A *marinero* is a person, then, who does something associated with the sea: a doer of "marine" activities. At this point you have a much better chance of guessing the meaning of *marinero*. Let's see if you can use this procedure to guess the meaning of a word you have not had.

When Columbus came back (*regresó*) to *Palos el rey Fernando y la reina Isabel estaban en Barcelona*. It was very important that the monarchs learn at once the outcome of his trip. So Columbus immediately sent a message to them by a *mensajero*. The stem of *mensajero* is the noun *mensaje*. This is a cognate of

_____. ▲

message

26 The English name for the person who does something with a *mensaje* is, then, a _____. ▲

messenger

27 *Cuando el mensajero llegó a Barcelona, él les contó a los reyes la historia del viaje.* What can your logic do with *contó*? You know *contar* as "to count." Does it make much sense to say "he counted the history of the trip?" ▲

no

28 So you know you must find a new meaning for *contar*. You can put a prefix on count which will show you the meaning: He **re**counted the history of the trip. A more common way of saying this is _____. ▲

told or related

29 When you know the subject of discourse and the set to which a word belongs, it's often very easy to figure out a new meaning for a word you already know. The *mensajero* carried a message to Ferdinand and Isabella. What, in fact, he carried was a *carta*. Can you guess the meaning of *carta*? ▲

30 The word *carta* belongs to the same set as *periódico* and *revista*. The cognate of *periódico* is a word that stands for a publication or magazine. It is the word "periodic" plus the suffix _____. ▲

31 A *carta* is a private way of sending information. A *periódico* or a *revista* is a public and commercial way of doing the same thing. Now look at *revista*. The prefix is _____. ▲

32 One of the common meanings of the English noun *vista* is "view." A *revista* is a kind of magazine or periodical called a _____. ▲

review (*Vista* in Spanish has the same stem as *vio*, the Preterit of *ver*.)

33 *Periódicos* and *revistas* are published and bought because people want to read the *noticias*. The English cognate is *notices*. A better translation is _____. ▲

34 The meaning that you know for *poner* is "to put." You are reading about Columbus and you read that he was the first to *poner pie en la isla*. The translation *to put foot on the island* gives you the meaning. A better translation for this meaning of *poner* is "to _____." ▲

letter

al

re

news

set

Self-Correcting Exercises

A *Preterit of Regular* a-, e-, *and* i-*Verbs:* Write the combinations. Think of the meaning of each sentence.

Ejemplo: 111 = Diego salió del río.

1	Diego			1	(e)l río.
2	Diego y yo	1	salir de	2	la niebla.
3	Yo	2	volver a	3	la selva.
4	Ustedes	3	entrar en	4	(e)l lago.
5	Tú				

1)	323	Yo volví a la selva.
2)	312	Yo salí de la niebla.
3)	331	Yo entré en el río.
4)	233	Diego y yo entramos en la selva.
5)	114	Diego salió del lago.
6)	521	Tú volviste al río.
7)	411	Ustedes salieron del río.
8)	134	Diego entró en el lago.
9)	424	Ustedes volvieron al lago.
10)	513	Tú saliste de la selva.
11)	431	Ustedes entraron en el río.
12)	223	Diego y yo volvimos a la selva.

B *Present, Preterit, and Clock Time:* Ask and answer the questions aloud. Adapt the answers on the right to your personal situation.

1	¿A qué hora vuelves a casa hoy?	Vuelvo a las cinco más o menos.
2	¿A qué hora volviste a casa ayer?	Volví a las seis y media.
3	¿A qué hora vas a comer esta noche (*tonight*)?	Voy a comer a las siete.
4	¿A qué hora comiste anoche (*last night*)?	Anoche también comí a las siete.
5	¿Cuándo vas a estudiar esta noche?	Voy a estudiar después de las ocho.
6	¿Cuándo estudiaste anoche?	Anoche estudié después de comer.
7	¿A qué hora vas a mirar televisión esta noche?	Voy a mirarla a las diez.
8	¿A qué hora miraste televisión anoche?	Anoche la miré a las once.

C *Preterit versus Imperfect:* Change the indicated verbs to past tense, either the Preterit or the Imperfect. You are told whether each event is cyclic or non-cyclic and the aspect. You must discover from context what the subject of the verb is, know whether it must shift into the Preterit or the Imperfect, and then select the appropriate verb form. Remember that the middle aspect is Imperfect for both types of events, and that beginning and end are Preterit. The answer to number 1 is *cambió* because the subject is *Colón*, it is the end of a cyclic event, and the verb is *cambiar* (to change), a regular *a*-verb.

El primer viaje de Colón (segundo párrafo)

Colón *cambia* (**1,** C, E) el nombre que *tiene* (**2,** NC, M) la nueva tierra y la *llama* (**3,** C, E) Juana. *Observa* (**4,** C, E) que los indios cubanos *viven* (**5,** NC, M) en pequeños pueblos de pescadores (*fishermen*), y que *son* (**6,** NC, M) muy pobres. La tierra *es* (**7,** NC, M) extraordinariamente hermosa, un verdadero paraíso (*paradise*), pero no *tiene* (**8,** NC, M) especias (*spices*) en abundancia. Tampoco *halla* (**9,** C, E) en ninguna parte el oro (*gold*) y las ricas ciudades de los libros de Marco Polo. *Quiere* (**10,** NC, M) ver al Gran Khan, el fabuloso rey de China, porque le *trae* (*is bringing*) (**11,** C, M) una carta de los Reyes Católicos de España. Por todas estas razones, Colón no *está* (**12,** NC, M) satisfecho en tierra cubana. El propósito fundamental de su viaje *es* (**13,** NC, M) abrir una ruta nueva a las tierras de las especias. Aunque sus hombres *necesitan* (**14,** NC, M) descansar, *decide* (**15,** C, E) continuar el viaje por mar.

1	cambió
2	tenía
3	llamó
4	Observó
5	vivían
6	eran
7	era
8	tenía
9	halló
10	Quería
11	traía
12	estaba
13	era
14	necesitaban
15	decidió

D *Fórmulas de cortesía* and *Refranes:* What would you say in Spanish in the following situations?

1 Someone gives you an expensive gift.

2 Someone says *gracias* to you.

3 You want to raise the window shade to let in more light, but the professor is in the way.

4 Someone sneezes.

5 You want to ask very courteously that your instructor write something on the board.

¡Gracias!

De nada.

Con permiso, señor.

¡Salud! (¡Jesús!)

Hágame el favor de escribir . . .

6 You accidentally smear ink on somebody's white sweater.

Perdóneme. (Dispénseme.)

Which proverb would be most appropriate in the following situations?

7 You hear someone giving a very uncomplimentary description of a professor, but you know he is not nearly that bad.

No es tan fiero el león como lo pintan.

8 You know someone who always sleeps in class and consistently flunks all tests.

Quien mucho duerme, poco aprende.

9 A businessman tried to expand his business too fast and went bankrupt.

Más vale pájaro en mano que cien volando.

10 John arrived at the fair only because he finally asked somebody how to get there, but Phil just gave up and went home.

Quien busca, halla.

11 If he hadn't talked so much about it, he wouldn't be in such a predicament today.

En boca cerrada no entran moscas.

New Vocabulary

dirección	address, direction	**aparecer**	to appear	**andar**	to walk
avenida	avenue	**caer**	to fall	**tropezar (ie)**	to trip
pueblo	town, village	**brillante**	brilliant	**inundar**	to flood,
fuente (la)	fountain	**anoche**	last night		inundate
toro	bull	**esta noche**	tonight	**brillar**	to shine
esperar	to wait, hope	**cubrir**	to cover	**descubrir**	to discover
dejar	to wait, allow	**recibir**	to receive		

Assignment 45

Some Pronouns for the Doer and Done-to

You have three pronoun names when you are the speaker in English: *I* when you are the doer (I eat ice cream), *me* when you are the done-to (José bumped me), and *myself* when you are the doer and the done-to (I hurt myself). When you are the speaker for several persons, you and the group also have three names: *we* when you and the group are doers (We went to the beach), *us* when all of you are the done-to (The storm did not scare us), and *ourselves* when you and the group are both doer and done-to (We saw ourselves in the mirror).

1 When you speak for the group and something (or someone) else is the doer, the pronoun name for *you and the group* as the done-to is _____. ▲

us (They heard us; She saw us.)

2 When you are the speaker for yourself and the group and *you and the group* are both the doer and the done-to, your name as the doer is *we* and your name as the done-to is _____. ▲

3 When I am the speaker and the doer, my subject-pronoun name is _____. ▲

ourselves

4 When I am the speaker, the doer, and the done-to, my name as the done-to is _____. ▲

I (I hear music.)

5 When I am the speaker and the done-to, but someone else is the doer, my pronoun name is _____. ▲

myself (I washed myself.)

6 We may use two different pronouns to talk about Alberto, either *he* or *him*. The form *him* tells everyone that Alberto is (a) the doer (b) the done-to. ▲

me (Can you see me?)

7 *She* stands for the _____. ▲

the done-to (We don't say, "Him caught a shark.")

8 The done-to pronoun that replaces *she* is _____. ▲

doer (She grabbed the cat.)

9 Which form marks the done-to? (a) they (b) them ▲

her (The cat scratched her.)

10 The suffix *m* of *him* and *them* is the mark of the (a) doer (b) done-to. ▲

them (They see me; I see them.)

11 Which pronoun in *Can you hear me?* stands for the doer? ▲

12 Which pronoun in *Yes, I can hear you* stands for the done-to? ▲

done-to

you

you (The same pronoun *you* may stand for either the doer or the done-to. The pronoun *it* may also stand for either a doer or a done-to: I see *it*; *it* sees me.)

13 The subject of a simple sentence is the doer. The object on which the action is performed is the done-to. The pronouns *me*, *us*, *him*, *her* and *them* are (a) subject pronouns (b) object pronouns. ▲

14 The subject pronoun that replaces *her* is _____. ▲

object pronouns

15 The subject pronouns that replace *me*, *us*, *him*, and *them* are _____. ▲

she

16 Spanish, like English, has special pronoun forms for the doer (subject) and the done-to (object). The translation of *Yo te vi* is "I saw you." Look at the form *te*. What subject pronoun form has the same stem? ▲

I, we, he, they

17 *Yo te vi* translates "I saw you." The translation of *Tú me viste* is _____. ▲

tú

You saw me. (Say English "me" and Spanish *me* aloud.)

18 The doer (subject) pronoun form that matches the Spanish *me* is _____. ▲

19 Look at *Las muchachas nos vieron*. What subject (doer) pronoun begins with *nos*? Translate: *Las muchachas nos vieron*. ▲

yo

nosotros or *nosotras*; The girls saw us.

20 The normal English translation of *Ellos nos vieron* is (a) They us saw. (b) They saw us. ▲

21 In English the done-to (object) pronoun comes *after* the verb. In Spanish the object (done-to) pronoun comes _____ the verb. ▲

They saw us.

22 Translate: They see me. ▲

23 This sentence talks about *tú*. Translate: They see you. Translate: They see us. ▲

before

Ellos me ven.

Ellos te ven. Ellos nos ven.

24 Translate: *Ellos van a visitarnos.* Translate: *Ellos van a visitarme.* ▲

They are going to visit us. They are going to visit me.

25 The grammatical name for the forms *visitar* and "to visit" is _____. ▲

26 In both English and Spanish, the done-to (object) pronouns follow the
infinitive. Look at the spaces between the words in these two sentences: *Ellos
van a llamarnos.* "They are going to call us." How is Spanish different from
English? The Spanish done-to pronoun is _____. ▲

infinitive

attached to the infinitive form in writing (The same is true in speech. Say
Ellos van a llamarnos aloud.)

27 Which will you say? (a) *Él nos mira.* (b) *Él mira nos.* ▲

28 Which will you say? (a) *Yo te veo.* (b) *Yo veo te.* ▲

29 Which will you say? (a) *Voy a visitarte.* (b) *Voy a te visitar.* ▲

Él nos mira.

Yo te veo.

Voy a visitarte. (You can say *Te voy a visitar*, but for the present follow the rule
that the done-to pronoun follows and is attached to the infinitive form.)

In the United States only the very wealthy can afford to have full-time household
servants and chauffeurs. In Latin America there are more people than there are jobs
and, as a result, wages are generally very low. Many people take jobs as servants because
this gives them their food and a place to stay. Because servants are paid very little,
people with modest incomes can afford to hire them. It is not uncommon for young teen-
agers to work as servants while they are still going to school. This helps their parents
because they do not have to pay for their board, room, and clothing.

In the United States even the poor often feel that it is undignified to be a household
servant. In the Hispanic world this feeling is by no means so common.

Summary

There are three sets of pronouns in English: (1) the doer or subject pronouns, (2) the done-to pronouns used when the doer is someone else, and (3) the done-to pronouns used when the doer and done-to are the same. The three done-to Spanish pronouns you have learned in this Assignment are *me, nos, te.* They are translated by "me, us, you." In another Assignment, you will discover that the same forms are used in Spanish for "myself, ourselves, yourself."

Here is a chart of these pronouns in English:

Doer	Done-to	
	Doer and done-to are different	Doer and done-to are the same
I	me	myself
we	us	ourselves
he	him	himself
she	her	herself
they	them	themselves
you	you	yourself, yourselves
it	it	itself

The Done-to: Adjectival Residuals and Pronouns

In the previous section of this Assignment you read that the Spanish done-to pronouns *me, nos,* and *te* match the subject pronouns *yo, nosotros,* and *tú.* In this section you will learn more about how Spanish and English differ when the done-to is a noun.

   You can say, "They are going to buy the large, red house." You can also say, "They are going to buy *it.*" In the second sentence "it" takes the place of the noun, *house,* and all its modifiers (the large, red house). You previously learned that in Spanish you can say *Ellos van a comprar la casa* and that you can drop the noun *casa,* leaving *Ellos van a comprarla. La* is not a true pronoun. It is a left-over adjective (an adjectival residual) when the noun *casa* is dropped.

1   Say this sentence aloud: *Ellos van a comprar las casas.* Now say it without the noun *casas: Ellos van a comprarlas.* Translate the first sentence above.   ▲

They are going to buy the houses.

2   To get the translation of *Van a comprarlas,* you must replace "the houses" with _____.   ▲

them ("Them" is a true pronoun. It is used in place of "the houses.")

3   The translation of *Voy a leer los libros* is _____.   ▲

I'm going to read the books.

4 Complete the translation of "I'm going to read them." *Voy a* _____. ▲

> *Voy a leerlos.* (In both speech and writing, when you drop the noun in Spanish, you attach the adjectival residual to the infinitive.)

5 The word *lo* is an allomorph of *el* which must be used instead of *el* when the noun is dropped. Change *Voy a leer el libro* to the translation of "I'm going to read it." ▲

6 When you drop the noun from *comprar las casas* or *leer los libros*, the adjectival residuals are translated by _____. ▲

> *Voy a leerlo.*

7 When you drop the singular *casa* or *libro*, the adjectival residuals *la* and *lo* are translated by _____. ▲

> them

8 When you translate "to visit the girl," you must put a special marker in front of *la muchacha*. This marker of the done-to person is _____. ▲

> it

> *a (Voy a visitar **a** la muchacha.)*

9 When the Spanish speaker drops *muchacha*, he also omits the done-to *a*. The new sentence is now *Voy a* _____. ▲

10 This *la* is translated by _____. ▲

> *Voy a visitarla.*

11 These two questions talk about the same person: (1) *¿Vas a visitar a la muchacha?* (2) *Vas a visitar a María?* They can be combined into one sentence: *¿Vas a visitar a la muchacha María?* When the *a* and the two nouns (*muchacha* and *María*) are omitted, the adjectival residual is _____. ▲

> her

> *la (Sí, voy a visitarla.)*

12 *¿Vas a visitar a José?* can be answered by *Sí, voy a* _____. ▲

13 The translation of *lo* is now _____. ▲

> *visitarlo*

14 You still have to learn the done-to forms that match *usted* and *ustedes*. Can *usted* stand for either *José* or *María* when speaking to either one of them? ▲

> him

15 When you omit *a José* in *Quiero ver a José*, the done-to form is *lo: Quiero verlo.* Suppose one were to say, *Quiero ver a usted, José.* Can *lo* stand for both *usted* and *José* in *Quiero verlo* (I want to see you)? ▲

> yes

> yes (In many areas the pronoun is repeated, redundantly: *Quiero verlo a Vd., José; Quiero verla a Vd., María; Quiero verlos a Vds., José y María.* Also in some regions the *lo, la, los, las* may be replaced by *le, les.* However, this repetition is not a grammatical necessity, and either pattern may be encountered. There is no hard and fast rule for this.)

16 Rewrite, now, *Quiero ver a ustedes* (males) using the plural done-to form *los.* ▲

17 Rewrite *Quiero ver a usted* (female) using the done-to form for *usted.* ▲

> *Quiero verlos.*

> *Quiero verla.* (And *quiero verlas* for *ustedes*, females.)

18 The done-to forms have various English translations. Write the proper translation for each adjectival residual in the following frames.

You are talking about a *casa. Quiero verla.* ▲

19 You are talking about Josefina. *Quiero verla.* ▲

> it

20 You are talking to Josefina. *Quiero verla.* ▲

> her

21 You are talking about a book. *Voy a leerlo.* ▲

> you

22 You are talking about some books. *Es importante leerlos.* ▲

> it

> them

23 You are talking <u>about</u> a *muchacho. Voy a verlo.* ▲

24 You are talking <u>to</u> a man on the phone. *Voy a verlo.* ▲

25 You are talking <u>about</u> some men. *Es importante verlos.* ▲

him
you
them

Summary

1 The done-to pronouns that match *yo, nosotros,* and *tú* are *me* (me), *nos* (us), and *te* (you).

2 The done-to pronouns or residuals that match *usted, él,* and *ella* are *lo* (you, him, it) and *la* (you, her, it); those corresponding to *ustedes, ellos,* and *ellas* are *los* (you, them) and *las* (you, them).

3 All these pronouns and residuals precede conjugated verbs (*Yo **las** veo*) and follow and are attached to an infinitive (*Yo voy a ver**las***).

4 When a done-to noun marked by the done-to *a* is omitted, the *a* is deleted: *Yo veo a María.*⟶*Yo la veo.*

Self-Correcting Exercises

A *Preterit of Regular* a-, e-, *and* i-*Verbs:* Write the combinations.

Ejemplo: 423 = Ella y yo aprendimos bastante.

1	Los habitantes	1	escribir	1	todo esto.
2	El héroe	2	aprender	2	demasiado.
3	Yo	3	recordar	3	bastante.
4	Ella y yo	4	olvidar	4	mucho.
5	Tú	5	comer	5	poco.

1)	111	Los habitantes escribieron todo esto.
2)	223	El héroe aprendió bastante.
3)	345	Yo olvidé poco.
4)	132	Los habitantes recordaron demasiado.
5)	244	El héroe olvidó mucho.
6)	351	Yo comí todo esto.
7)	413	Ella y yo escribimos bastante.
8)	525	Tú aprendiste poco.
9)	312	Yo escribí demasiado.
10)	531	Tú recordaste todo esto.
11)	444	Ella y yo olvidamos mucho.
12)	512	Tú escribiste demasiado.

B *Preterit of Regular* a-, e-, *and* i-*Verbs:* After reading each sentence, decide which of the four forms given is the correct Preterit that fits the new subject, then say the new sentence aloud.

1   Los alumnos aprendieron mucho. Yo . . .   1   b
    a aprendió   **b** aprendí   **c** aprendiste   **d** aprendo
2   La cometa voló muy bien. Las cometas . . .   2   c
    a volamos   **b** vuelan   **c** volaron   **d** volé
3   Yo conocí a la nueva alumna. Él y yo . . .   3   a
    a conocimos   **b** conocemos   **c** conocen   **d** conocieron
4   Las mujeres llevaron jarros. Yo . . .   4   a
    a llevé   **b** llevo   **c** llevó   **d** llevaste
5   Usted halló el continente en el mapa. Tú . . .   5   d
    a hallé   **b** hallas   **c** halla   **d** hallaste
6   Yo pinté un león muy feroz. Ellas . . .   6   d
    a pintan   **b** pintó   **c** pintamos   **d** pintaron

C   Practice reading aloud the following selections.

Grandes noticias del siglo XVI

(Usted debe imaginar que usted es un anunciador de radio leyendo ante un micrófono las noticias del día.)

1   Valladolid, España. En este día 20 de mayo de 1506, murió en esta ciudad el gran almirante don Cristóbal Colón. Entre los años de 1492 y 1504 este gran navegante italiano hizo° cuatro viajes al Nuevo Mundo. La lista de sus descubrimientos es larga. Entre° los más importantes podemos mencionar las islas de Cuba, Santo Domingo, Jamaica, Puerto Rico, Trinidad y las Islas Vírgenes. En 1498 fue el primer europeo que vio la costa norte de América del Sur y también exploró parte de la costa de Centro América. Después del funeral su hijo Diego piensa llevar el cadáver de su famoso padre al monasterio de Santa María de las Cuevas en Sevilla.   *made* *among*

2   Darién, Panamá. En el día de hoy, 29 de septiembre de 1513, el valiente explorador español Vasco Núñez de Balboa tomó° posesión de un nuevo océano en nombre de Su Majestad, el rey de España. Cuatro días antes, desde una altura del Istmo de Panamá, el joven Balboa fue el primer hombre blanco que vio esta gran masa de agua. La llamó Mar del Sur.   *took*

3   Santiago, Cuba. Don Diego Velázquez, gobernador de esta isla, anunció hoy que la expedición de Hernán Cortés llegó a las costas de Nueva España. El día de Viernes Santo, 27 de abril de 1519, el joven capitán y sus setecientos hombres bajaron a tierra y fundaron la ciudad de Veracruz. Cuando los indios vieron a los soldados° en sus caballos,° se horrorizaron. Creen que es el ejército° invencible de Quetzalcóatl, el dios-rey de sus leyendas. Cortés destruyó sus barcos y ya se prepara para ir a ver a Moctezuma, el gran jefe° de los aztecas. La capital del imperio azteca está en el centro de un lago en el interior del país. Cortés piensa conquistar este gran imperio de los aztecas.   *soldiers/horses/* *army* *chief*

4   La Habana, Cuba. Interrumpimos este programa de música para comunicarle al público una triste noticia. El gran capitán español don Juan Ponce de León acaba de morir en esta ciudad a los 71 años de edad. La causa de su muerte fue una flecha venenosa° de un indio seminola de la Florida. Después   *poisonous arrow*

de conquistar a Puerto Rico, Ponce de León descubrió la Florida en 1513. En su
segundo viaje de exploración por las Bahamas y la costa oeste de la península,
el viejo capitán buscaba la legendaria fuente de la juventud.° El ataque de los   youth
indios fue tan feroz que la expedición volvió a La Habana en junio de 1521.

5   Sevilla, España. Y ahora tenemos una noticia sensacional para todos ustedes.
Después de un difícil viaje de tres años, la expedición de Fernando de Magallanes acaba de completar el primer viaje alrededor° del mundo. Estos valientes   around
marineros cruzaron° un estrecho muy tempestuoso en la Patagonia y navegaron   crossed
por todo el Mar del Sur. Magallanes lo llamó Océano Pacífico. Desgraciadamente,° el gran jefe portugués de la expedición murió en las Islas Filipinas   Unfortunately
antes de completar el viaje. Juan Sebastián de Elcano, uno de los oficiales que
iban con él, dirigió la última parte de esta histórica jornada.° Salieron en total   journey
239 hombres y volvieron solamente 15. Hoy, 9 de septiembre de 1522, llegaron a
Sevilla los 15 supervivientes° del primer viaje alrededor del mundo.   survivors

6   Cajamarca, Perú. Después de una larga y penosa° campaña por mar,   painful
selvas, desiertos y montañas, acaba de llegar con sus valientes hombres a esta
región, el explorador español don Francisco Pizarro. Atahualpa, el gran jefe
de los incas, le esperaba, pero indicó que no desea hablar con los visitantes
hasta el día de mañana, 16 de noviembre de 1532. Pizarro tiene informes fantásticos acerca de las ciudades que hay en este nuevo imperio de los incas. Los
indios cuentan que los templos están adornados con cantidades° enormes de   quantities
oro, plata y piedras° preciosas. Pizarro se prepara para la conquista de un   stones
imperio que es más rico que el de los aztecas.

New Vocabulary

cigarro	cigar, cigarette	**desaparecer**	to disappear	**¿Cómo?**	How's that? What did you say?
turista (el, la)	tourist	**vestir (i)**	to dress		
mono, -a	monkey	**aunque**	although	**No importa.**	It doesn't matter. It's not important.
seda	silk	**a mí**	to me		
fumar	to smoke	**a ti**	to you (*familiar*)		

"Aunque la mona se vista de seda, mona se queda."

"Clothes don't make the man." (Although the monkey dresses in silk, she remains a monkey.)

Las partes del cuerpo   The Parts of the Body

This is your first contact with these words. See if you can pronounce them
correctly and learn their meaning before you are introduced to them in class.

cabeza	head	**oreja**	ear	**nariz**	nose
pelo	hair	**frente (la)**	forehead	**diente**	tooth
cara	face	**labio**	lip	**lengua**	tongue

Assignment 46

Reading Aloud

1   You read 1506 aloud in Spanish as *mil quinientos seis*, the equivalent of "one thousand five hundred and six." Here are some dates to practice. Say them aloud until each one sounds like one long word.

1506 mil quinientos seis	1519 mil quinientos diecinueve
1492 mil cuatrocientos noventa y dos	1521 mil quinientos veintiuno
1504 mil quinientos cuatro	1522 mil quinientos veintidós
1498 mil cuatrocientos noventa y ocho	1532 mil quinientos treinta y dos
1513 mil quinientos trece	1546 mil quinientos cuarenta y seis

2   Proper names in Spanish are read aloud just like common words. Those that are spelled the same in both languages cause the most trouble because you have to learn not to project your English habits onto Spanish. You are, for example, thoroughly conditioned to read *Cuba* as if it were *Cue-ba*. The first syllable sounds like "cue." In Spanish you must say [kuba] and with a fricative [b]. Say [kyuba] and [kuba] aloud.

3   Say *Florida* aloud in English. Now say in Spanish [flo-ri-da] with the stress on *ri*. The name of the state in Spanish is *la Florida*.

4   When you say *Jamaica* in English, the syllable *mai* sounds like *may*. In Spanish it sounds like *my*. Say [ja-mai-ca] aloud.

5   When you say *Puerto Rico* in Spanish, the r of *rico* is said (a) [r] (b) [rr].   ▲

[rr]   (Say *Puerto Rico* aloud.)

6   Copy *Trinidad* and divide it into syllables.   ▲

Tri-ni-dad (Now say it aloud in Spanish. Remember there is no schwa.)

7   Say *Co-lo-ra-do* aloud in Spanish.

8   By custom most Latin Americans write *México* with an *x*. This is the old spelling. When you say the word, the *x* stands for *j*. Say [mé-ji-co].

9   Here are some names of people you should be able to read aloud without any hesitation. Say each as one long word.

Alonso del Castillo	Antonio de Mendoza	Cristóbal Colón
Andrés Dorantes	Hernando de Soto	Diego Velázquez
Francisco Pizarro	Atahualpa	

10   The following names require a little more practice. Watch the accent mark and practice each until the whole name comes out like one long word.

Hernán Cortés	Juan Sebastián de Elcano
Juan Ponce de León	Alvar Núñez Cabeza de Vaca
Fernando de Magallanes	Francisco Vázquez de Coronado
Pánfilo de Narváez	García López de Cárdenas
Vasco Núñez de Balboa	Pedro Menéndez de Avilés

11   One of the ancient gods of the Mexican Indians was *Quetzalcóatl*. This name is pronounced [ket-sal-coa-tl]. Say this aloud.

12 When you are first learning to read aloud, long words sometimes cause trouble because you cannot divide them into syllables fast enough to make them sound right. In these examples say each word slowly, syllable by syllable, then say the whole word fast. The stressed syllable is indicated.

des-cu-bri-**mien**-tos > descubrimientos
go-ber-na-**dor** > gobernador
ho-rro-ri-**za**-ron > horrorizaron
des-gra-**cia**-da-**men**-te > desgraciadamente
in-te-re-san-**tí**-si-mo > interesantísimo
nor-te-a-me-ri-**ca**-na > norteamericana
in-te-rrum-**pi**-mos > interrumpimos
le-gen-**da**-ria > legendaria
tem-pes-**tuo**-so > tempestuoso
su-per-vi-**vien**-tes > supervivientes
im-pre-sio-**nan**-te > impresionante
ci-vi-**li**-zan > civilizan

The Present and Preterit of oír (to hear)

1 The present tense stem of *oír* has three allomorphs but the suffixes are all regular. *Yo* goes with the irregular form *oigo*. The *oi* is pronounced like *hoy* (today). Say *oigo* aloud. The irregular stem is _____. ▲

2 The *nosotros* form is *oímos*. Copy and divide into syllables. ▲   *oig*
o-í-mos (Say this aloud, and remember that an accented *i* cannot be in the same syllable with another vowel.)

3 The stem of *oímos* and *oír* is regular. It is _____. ▲
o (The regular stem of a verb is what you get when you remove the two infinitive suffixes: *ir, er,* or *ar.*)

4 The stem of all the other forms is *oy*, pronounced like *hoy*. What regular first suffix do you add to *oy* to get the form that goes with *usted, él,* or *ella*? ▲
e (*Usted oye;* pronounce *oye* like *hoy-ye.*)

5 To make *oye* agree with *ustedes, ellos,* or *ellas,* you add the second suffix _____. ▲
n (*Ustedes oyen;* pronounce like *hoy-yen.*)

6 Change *oyen* so it will agree with *tú.* ▲
oyes (The *hoy* sound of *oigo* is spelled *oi* because Spanish never writes *y* immediately before a consonant in a word. The same *hoy* sound is spelled *oy* in *oye, oyes,* and *oyen* because Spanish never writes *i* between two vowels (only *í* as in *leía*).)

7 The stem of the Preterit of *oír* is regular. It is _____. ▲

8 The past tense base of *oír* is _____. ▲   *o*

9 The *yo* form is the same except that *i*, as in the preterit forms you have   *oi*
already learned, has an _____ in writing. ▲

10 You add *ste* to the past tense base to get the form that goes with _____. ▲   accent: *oí*
tú (*Tú oíste* has an accent over the *i.*)

11 The *nosotros* form of the Preterit of *i*-verbs is like the Present. So you write *nosotros* _____. ▲

12 The preterit form of *vivir* that goes with *usted* is _____. ▲

oímos

13 The first suffix of *vivió* is _____. ▲

vivió

14 Now, remember that Spanish does not write *i* between two vowels. It uses _____ instead. ▲

ió

15 So the form of *oír* that is like *vivió* is written _____. ▲

y

16 By the same rule, the form of *oír* that is like *vivieron* is written _____. ▲

oyó

oyeron (Pronounced like *hoy-yeron*.)

Summary

Here are the full conjugations:

Present				Preterit			
oig	o			o	í		
o	í	mos		o	í	mos	
oy	e	s		o	í	ste	
oy	e			o	yó		
oy	e	n		o	yero	n	

Self-Correcting Exercises

A *Done-to Pronouns and Adjectival Residuals:* Write the combinations. The items in the third column are to be replaced with the appropriate done-to pronouns or adjectival residuals and placed properly in relation to the verb.

Ejemplos: 12 = Beatriz te mira. 45 = Beatriz trata de buscarlos.

	1 mira	1 a mí.
	2 acaba de mirar	2 a ti.
Beatriz	3 busca	3 a Alfredo y a mí.
	4 trata de buscar	4 a ustedes (*f*).
		5 a los parientes.
		6 a Cristina.

1) 11   Beatriz me mira.
2) 21   Beatriz acaba de mirarme.
3) 13   Beatriz nos mira.
4) 34   Beatriz las busca.
5) 45   Beatriz trata de buscarlos.
6) 46   Beatriz trata de buscarla.
7) 16   Beatriz la mira.
8) 32   Beatriz te busca.
9) 24   Beatriz acaba de mirarlas.
10) 43   Beatriz trata de buscarnos.
11) 22   Beatriz acaba de mirarte.

B *Preterit of Regular* a-, e-, *and* i-*Verbs:* Practice answering these questions until you can do so without hesitation. Adapt the answers to your own personal situation.

1 ¿A qué hora comiste anoche?	Comí a las seis y cuarto.
2 ¿A qué hora volviste del cine anoche?	Volví a la una de la mañana.
3 ¿A qué hora volviste a la universidad esta mañana?	Volví a las siete menos cuarto.
4 Yo volví aquí esta mañana a las 10. ¿A qué hora volví yo aquí?	Vd. volvió a las diez.
5 El profesor Robles y yo volvimos aquí esta mañana a las nueve. ¿A qué hora volvimos nosotros aquí?	Vds. volvieron a las nueve.
6 Yo trabajé seis horas anoche. ¿Cuántas horas trabajé yo?	Vd. trabajó seis horas.
7 ¿Estudiaste tú mucho anoche?	Sí, yo estudié mucho.
8 ¿Miraron Vds. la televisión anoche?	No, no la miramos.

C *Stem-changing Verbs:* Referring to the three columns of information below, write the Spanish translation of the sentences.

Dorotea	(*to count*) contar (ue)	las ventanas.
Yo	(*to close*) cerrar (ie)	los libros.
David y yo	(*to move*) mover (ue)	las puertas.
Tú	(*to measure*) medir (i)	las revistas.
Ellos		

1	Dorothy counts the windows.	Dorotea cuenta las ventanas.
2	I count the books.	Yo cuento los libros.
3	David and I count the books.	David y yo contamos los libros.
4	David and I close the doors.	David y yo cerramos las puertas.
5	You close the magazines.	Vd. (Tú) cierra(s) las revistas.
6	They move the windows.	Ellos mueven las ventanas.
7	They close the windows.	Ellos cierran las ventanas.
8	David and I close the windows.	David y yo cerramos las ventanas.
9	You close the windows.	Vd. (Tú) cierra(s) las ventanas.
10	You measure the windows.	Vd. (Tú) mide(s) las ventanas.
11	David measures the books.	David mide los libros.
12	David and I measure the books.	David y yo medimos los libros.

D *Fórmulas de cortesía:* Assume both roles in this guided conversation.

A:	Please open the door.	Hágame (Hazme) el favor de abrir la puerta.
B:	Yes, of course. Make yourself at home.	Sí, cómo no. Está(s) en su (tu) casa.
A:	What did you say?	¿Cómo?
B:	(Sneezes.)	
A:	Bless you!	¡Salud! (¡Jesús!)

New Vocabulary

pie	foot (human)	**oír**	to hear	**me**	me
dedo	finger, toe	**ladrar**	to bark	**te**	you (*familiar*)
pierna	leg	**morder (ue)**	to bite	**nos**	us
brazo	arm	**contar (ue)**	to count; tell	**lo**	you, him, it
pulgar	thumb	**cerrar (ie)**	to close, shut	**la**	you, her, it
noticia	news	**abrir**	to open	**los**	you, them
periódico	newspaper	**mover (ue)**	to move	**las**	you, them
revista	magazine	**medir (i)**	to measure		

Está en su casa.   Make yourself at home.

"Perro que ladra no muerde."   "Barking dogs don't bite."

Assignment 47

Intonation

1 You have often heard people say something like this: "It's not what she said that counts, but the way she said it." The "way" in this statement deals, in part, with what is called **intonation**. One important feature of intonation is stress. What syllable is stressed in *canto*?   ▲

2 What syllable is stressed in *cantó*?   ▲   *can*

3 When we say that the *tó* of *cantó* is stressed, we mean that in speech this   *tó*
syllable is a little longer and a little louder than the unstressed syllable *can*.
Here is the word "investigation" divided into syllables: in-ves-ti-ga-tion. Say
it aloud until you are certain which syllable is longest and loudest. (Many
dictionaries say it takes the primary or main stress.) This syllable is _____.   ▲

4 There is another syllable in "investigation" which carries less stress than *ga*   *ga*
but more than any other syllable. Say *in-ves-ti-ga-tion* aloud until you can pick
out the syllable having this secondary stress. It is _____.   ▲

ves (A dictionary might show these two stresses this way: in-ves"ti-ga'tion.)

5 Here is a major difference between English and Spanish. Most long English
words have a primary and a secondary stressed syllable. In contrast, few Spanish
words have a syllable which carries a secondary stress. A few compound words
have two stresses but all simple Spanish words have only one stressed syllable.
This difference is very important in learning how to improve your Spanish
accent. All your years of training in English keep telling you (even forcing you)
to put two, and sometimes three, stresses on long words. Just out of habit you
are likely to pronounce the cognate *investigación* somewhat like English. This

sounds very strange to the Spanish speaker, so you should try to break this habit. Divide the word into syllables. ▲

6 The only stressed syllable is _____. ▲

in-ves-ti-ga-ción
ción

7 Say *ción* aloud and make the *o* sound a bit longer than the other vowels in the word. Now, let's try a backward build-up and see if you can keep any secondary stress off all the other syllables. Say aloud: **ción; gación; tigación; vestigación; investiga*ción*.**

8 In music different notes are made long or short. In speech different syllables are also made long or short. This is called **rhythm**. In English a long syllable may be two to five times longer than a short syllable. Say, in a sort of off-hand way, "We took a long walk." Now say exactly the same sentence and make it mean "a very, very *long* walk." You do this by lengthening the word _____. ▲

long (We took a long walk.)

9 A major difference between English and Spanish is to be found in the fact that Spanish long syllables are normally only about twice as long as the short syllables. Say aloud emphatically, "It's very *near*." Is *near* much longer in speech than *it's*? ▲

yes, if you said "near" emphatically

10 The translation of "It's very near" is *Está muy cerca.* When a Spanish speaker says *Está muy cerca* emphatically, the *cer* of *cerca* is only a little bit longer than the *tá* of *está*. Try saying *Está muy cerca* aloud in the Spanish way.

11 The length of syllables is closely tied to stress; stressed syllables are longer than unstressed syllables. Which language, English or Spanish, has the greatest number of long syllables? ▲

English (Your Spanish would not sound natural to a native if you put as many
long syllables in the Spanish as in the English. You would sound strangely
overemphatic.)

12 Here are two sentences in English and Spanish. The stressed syllables are indicated. Remember they are longer than the unstressed syllables.

*Ha**bla**mos de la imposibili**dad** de **ver**lo.*

We are **talk**ing of the im**pos**sibility of **see**ing **it.**

13 Another important feature of intonation is what happens when we go from sound to silence, that is, what happens when we end a sentence. The pitch can go up (↑), stay level (|), or go down (↓). Say this question aloud: *Are you going to the beach?* Say it aloud again. At the end of the question, your voice (the pitch) (a) goes up (b) goes down. ▲

If you asked the question the way you normally talk English, the pitch went

14 This type of question is called a yes-no question. Here is the Spanish for the same question: *¿Vas a la playa?* Say it aloud. Does the pitch go up as in English? ▲

up.

15 Here is a rule about **juncture** (the way sentences end). <u>The pitch rises at the end of yes-no questions in both English and Spanish.</u> Say these two sentences aloud: "Are you from Spain?" ↑ *¿Es usted de España?* ↑ Now, listen to yourself very carefully and say these two statements: "Yes, I'm from Spain." *Sí, soy de España.* At the end of each statement, the pitch (a) goes up (b) goes down. ▲

yes

goes down

16 Here is another rule about juncture: The pitch falls at the end of statements in both languages. Now, look at these questions and say them aloud: "Where are you going?" *¿A dónde vas?* Can they be answered by yes or no?   ▲

no (They are information questions.)

17 Say the information questions in Frame 16 aloud and listen to what happens to the pitch at the end of each. The pitch (a) falls (b) rises.   ▲

18 Here is a third rule about juncture: The pitch falls at the end of information

falls

questions. In all three examples given above, the terminal juncture (the direction of the voice at the end of an utterance) is the same in both languages. It is expected that you will recognize statements and automatically use the right terminal juncture in Spanish since it is the same as English. You will need, however, some practice in learning to spot yes-no and information questions, and in remembering how they end.

19 In this frame and the next one, indicate whether the given question is (a) yes-no (b) information, and indicate the terminal juncture using ↑ and ↓ . *¿Hay muchos habitantes allí?*   ▲

20 *¿Tienes tiza? ¿Cómo te llamas? ¿Cómo está usted?*   ▲

yes-no, ↑

yes-no, ↑ , information, ↓ , information, ↓

21 There is another very important feature of intonation which you control by intuition in English but which you must learn to understand consciously before you can communicate successfully in Spanish. This is **pitch**. You understand the meaning of "pitch" in "a high-pitched scream" and "a low-pitched growl." You also know something about pitch in music if you understand the difference between a high and low note or tone. Pitch deals with the number of vibrations per second of a sound wave. The greater the number of vibrations, the higher the pitch. In speech, as in music or just plain noise, there are differences in pitch.

Let's see if you can hear the difference when you talk. Say aloud, in a matter-of-fact way, "It's not George; it's Henry." Now, pretend that you were expecting George, not Henry, and say with surprise and emphatically, "It's not *George*; it's *Henry*!" Say this again with strong emphasis on the *Hen* of *Henry*. Aside from the difference in loudness, the real difference between the matter-of-fact, "It's not George; it's Henry" and the excited and emphatic, "It's not *George*; it's *Henry*!" is one of pitch. Linguists say that when you say the *Hen* of *Henry* emphatically you use the *fourth* pitch level, but when you just inform someone that "It's not George; it's Henry" you say *Hen* on the *third* pitch level. Now, here is the important difference between English and Spanish. In English speech, there are four *levels of pitch*. In contrast, there are only *three levels of pitch* in Spanish.

What does this mean in communication? Pitch adds something to the meaning of the words in a message. It says you are happy, annoyed, disgusted, excited, pleased, angry, *etc.* And here's the problem. Each language uses different pitch patterns to express these different attitudes. Say in a cheerful manner, "Good-bye. See you tomorrow." When you do this, the stressed syllables are all on pitch level "three" in English. Now, suppose you are very annoyed but feel you have to say the proper formula of courtesy. You growl,

Spanish-speaking neighborhoods or *barrios* are cities within cities. Banks, insurance companies, and stores carry on their business in Spanish. A close look at a Spanish-speaking community in the U.S. reveals open-air markets very similar to some in Puerto Rico.

Being caught between two cultures can be a source of conflict. The most influential institutions such as the schools tend to reflect the values and language of the majority Anglo culture, however, wearing traditional costumes for holidays is one way to express pride in one's cultural heritage. Will the members of minority communities dissolve in the melting pot, or can they retain their cultural identities while successfully adapting to their surroundings? Only time will tell.

It is customary to think of the United States as the great melting pot of the Americas because many people came here from England, Ireland, Sweden, Norway, Africa, Germany, Poland, Italy, China and other countries. In addition, there are a great many speakers of Spanish in the southwestern part of the country, in Florida, in New York City, and other urban areas. In contrast with the United States, there is no Spanish speaking country which has a large number of citizens who speak English. There are a few small colonies of English-speaking Mennonites in Mexico, Central America, and Bolivia. Nevertheless, Latin America is a melting pot like the United States. There are many Negroes in all the countries around the Caribbean Sea, many Germans in southern Chile and southern Brazil, Italians in Argentina, Orientals in most countries, and a considerable number of people who fled from the Turkish Empire after World War I (Syrians, Lebanese, Armenians). There are also considerable numbers of Irishmen who are descendants of the Irish who immigrated to Spain during the great potato famine of the nineteenth century. A glance through the telephone directory of any big city will reveal names like Eduardo O'Higgins, Manuela MacGregor, Rosa Kestleman, or José Stein. Contrary to the general American notion, a person who speaks only Spanish may be black, white, Indian, Oriental, or Irish; and he may very well be blond or even redheaded.

"Good-bye. See you tomorrow." The stressed syllables are now on pitch level two in English, and this pitch pattern is the way a Spanish speaker normally says a bright and cheerful *Adiós, hasta mañana.* Your English intuition will tell you that it is very wrong to say *Adiós, hasta mañana* in this way, but if you use the English pattern the Spanish speaker will get the wrong message about your attitude. He will think either that you are too emphatic, over-excited, or perhaps insincere.

Summary

1 Stress: Most Spanish words have only one stressed syllable. Many English words have both a primary and a secondary stress.

2 Rhythm: English long syllables are regularly five times the length of short syllables. Spanish long syllables are barely twice the length of short syllables.

3 Pitch: English has four pitch levels; Spanish only has three. To carry your English habits into Spanish will make your speech sound exaggerated and artificial.

4 Juncture: In Spanish, as in English, yes-no questions end with rising pitch, and information questions end with falling pitch.

Preparing for a Quiz on the Forms of the Preterit

The Preterit Forms of Regular *a*-Verbs

1 The *nosotros* forms of the Present and Preterit are exactly alike. Write this form for *hallar* (to find, discover). ▲

2 In the quiz you will be given sentences in which the verb is in the infinitive. You are to write the preterit form. For example, *Nosotros _____ (recordar) la calle muy bien.* ▲

            hallamos

3 To get the *tú* form of the Preterit of *tomamos,* you replace the *mos* with _____. ▲

            recordamos

4 Write the Preterit of *llevar. Tú _____.* ▲

        ste (tú tomaste)

5 There are two preterit forms in which *a* is the first suffix: *quedamos* and *quedaste.* This *a* also appears in the form that goes with *ustedes* and *ellos.* Write the Preterit of *quedar. Ustedes _____.* ▲

            llevaste

      quedaron (The whole second suffix is *aro.*)

6 Write the Preterit of *olvidar. Ellos _____.* ▲•

7 The suffix of the *yo* form of the Preterit of all regular *a*-verbs is _____. ▲

            olvidaron

8 Translate: I found the book. (Remember the verb you learned from Frame 1.) ▲

            é

9 Write the Preterit of *pasar. Yo _____.* ▲

      (Yo) hallé el libro

10 To make *pasé* agree with *ella,* you replace *é* with _____. ▲

            pasé

      ó (Notice, now, that two forms of the Preterit have accent marks: *pasé* and *pasó.*)

11 Write the Preterit of *entrar. Usted* _____.　▲

12 Here is another example of what you are going to see in the quiz. Write in the Preterit the form of the verb in parentheses: *Él* _____ (*quedar*) *aquí muchos meses.*　▲

entró

13 One of the common mistakes made when using the Preterit or Imperfect is to forget that the stem-changing verbs in the Present have a regular stem in the past tense forms. In this and the next four frames say the Preterit equivalent of the form you see: *duermo*　▲

quedó

dormí (The stem is the same as in the infinitive *dormir*.)

14 recuerdas, empieza　▲

15 vuelve, pienso　▲

recordaste, empezó
volvió, pensé

The Preterit Forms of the Regular *e-* and *i*-Verbs

1 The first suffix of the Imperfect of all *e-* and *i*-verbs is _____.　▲

2 The *í* of *vivía* says the tense is past and the *a* says the aspect is Imperfect. The past tense base of *vivía* is _____.　▲

ía

viví (The stem plus *i*.)

3 Change *yo vivía* to the Preterit.　▲

yo viví (You just drop the imperfective aspect marker.)

4 The *usted* form of the Preterit of *hablar* is *habló*. What do you add to the base *viví* to get the preterit form for *usted*?　▲

ó (*Usted vivió*. The accented *ó* is the mark of *usted* for the Preterit of all regular verbs.)

5 Change *vivió* so it will agree with *tú*.　▲

tú viviste (You just add *ste* to the past tense base.)

6 The Preterit of *vivimos* is _____.　▲

7 The Preterit of *comemos* is *comimos*. The Preterit of *aprendemos* is *aprendimos*. In the Preterit all regular *e*-verbs behave as though they were *i*-verbs. (a) true (b) false　▲

vivimos

8 There is a *ro* in the first suffix of the Preterit of all verb forms that agree with *ustedes* and *ellos*. The form of *hablar* that goes with *ustedes* is _____.　▲

true

9 The form of *vivir* that goes with *ustedes* is _____.　▲

10 All *e*-verbs behave just like *i*-verbs in the Preterit. So the preterit form of *correr* that goes with *ustedes* is _____.　▲

hablaron
vivieron

corrieron

The Preterit of *oír*, *leer*, and *caer*

1 *Oír, caer,* and *leer* mean _____.　▲

to hear, to fall, to read

2 Write the *nosotros* form for each in the Present.　▲

oímos, caemos, leemos

3 The present tense form *oímos* and the preterit form *oímos* are identical. To make *caemos* and *leemos* into preterit forms you must replace the first suffix *e* with _____.　▲

í (You get *caímos* and *leímos*.)

4 In the Preterit and the Imperfect all *e*-verbs have the same structure as *i*-verbs. Write the *yo* form of the Imperfect of *oír, caer,* and *leer.* ▲

5 You get the *yo* form of the Preterit of *oía, caía,* and *leía* by dropping the imperfective marker *a*. So you get _____. ▲

yo oía, caía, leía

6 The past tense base of all regular *e*- and *i*-verbs has an *i* right after the stem. This *i* has a written accent in three preterit forms: *yo oí, tú oíste, nosotros oímos.* When *i* immediately follows another vowel letter, the accent mark tells you that the sound it stands for is a syllable all by itself. Does *í* stand for a syllable all by itself in *oía, caía,* and *leía*?

oí, caí, leí

7 When *i* immediately follows another vowel, and has no accent mark, it is always part of the same syllable as the first vowel. So what do you say? (a) *o-i-go* (b) *oi-go* ▲

yes

8 The letter *i*, without an accent mark, is never used between two vowel letters. The preterit *usted* form of *oír* cannot be written *oió*. You must change the *i* to _____. ▲

oi-go

9 Write the Preterit of *caer* and *leer. Usted* _____. ▲

y (usted oyó)

10 You cannot write *oieron, caieron,* or *leieron*. You must write _____. ▲

cayó; leyó

oyeron, cayeron, leyeron

11 Change *tú oyes* to the Preterit. ▲

12 In this and the next frame change what you see to the Preterit: *ella oye, ellos oyen.* ▲

tú oíste

ella oyó, ellos oyeron

13 usted lee, ustedes caen ▲

usted leyó, ustedes cayeron

Self-Correcting Exercises

A *Done-to Pronouns and Preterit Forms:* Write the combinations. Don't do the next combination until you have checked your work against the answers given on the right. The verb form from the middle column must be in the Preterit.

Ejemplo: 314 = Julia y Pilar me oyeron.

1 Rodolfo	1 oír	1 a nosotros.
2 Yo	2 ver	2 a usted (f).
3 Julia y Pilar	3 mirar	3 a ti.
4 Tú	4 tratar de olvidar	4 a mí.
5 Toña y yo		5 a ustedes (m).

1)	111	Rodolfo nos oyó.
2)	522	Toña y yo la vimos.
3)	333	Julia y Pilar te miraron.
4)	444	Tú trataste de olvidarme.
5)	515	Toña y yo los oímos.
6)	142	Rodolfo trató de olvidarla.
7)	315	Julia y Pilar los oyeron.
8)	343	Julia y Pilar trataron de olvidarte.

9) 434   Tú me miraste.

10) 421   Tú nos viste.

B *Refranes:* Write the translation of the following proverbs and say them aloud.

1 You can't make a silk purse out of a sow's ear.

2 The lion is not as fierce as they paint him.

3 Barking dogs don't bite.

Aunque la mona se vista de seda, mona se queda.

No es tan fiero el león como lo pintan.

Perro que ladra no muerde.

New Vocabulary

viaje	trip	**besar**	to kiss	**abrazar**	to hug, embrace
viajar	to travel	**masticar**	to chew	**No se (te)**	
quebrar (ie)	to break	**oler (ue)**	to smell	**moleste(s).**	Don't bother.
molestar	to bother	**tocar**	to touch		Don't go to any
		caminar	to walk		trouble.

One very important, perhaps major, difference between the two cultures stems from the fact that speakers of English can organize and react to reality in two different ways. This is possible because, in fact, we speak *two* languages. One is Anglo-Saxon and the other is primarily Latin heavily laced with words from French and Greek. Many Latin words and expressions are considered stilted or overly ostentatious. Thus *I am enamoured of you* does not seem as sincere to some people as *I am in love with you.* Because university classes were conducted in Latin for several centuries most of the vocabulary of science, medicine, mathematics, philosophy, and related disciplines is of Latin or Greek origin. As a result, speakers of English are burdened with the necessity of learning at least two ways of saying the same thing. Thus you actually learn the meaning of *octagonal* by *translating* it into *eight-sided*, and if you want to become a doctor you must learn that an examination with a stethoscope is an *auscultation*, that is, the act of listening. Finally, because the common people have always used the Anglo-Saxon vocabulary, the upper classes could show their social superiority by rejecting common words as being vulgar. Many, as a result, have become taboo and a great deal of time, energy, and emotion has been spent on either trying to maintain the taboo or to break it.

The speakers of Spanish have much less problem with their language than we do. There are, of course, popular and erudite words, but almost all of them are Latin. The Spaniard says *Estoy enamorado de ti* because there is no other option available. The *Levante* (Levant) is not to him an exotic term for the Orient. It is, in fact, the place where *se levanta el sol.* For him the verb *auscultar* is not quite as foreign as its English equivalent because he uses a popular form of it (*escuchar*) as his regular word for *to listen*. And, finally, the Spanish do not have the problem of the four-letter words simply because they have spoken only *one* language for more than two thousand years.

The Done-to in Reflexive Constructions

1 When the doer and the done-to in a sentence are *the same*, the construction is said to be **reflexive**. The action is not done to someone or something else but is "turned back" (reflected) onto the subject.

Here is a chart of the English reflexive pronouns:

I	**my**self	he	**him**self
we	**our**selves	she	**her**self
you (singular)	**your**self	they	**them**selves
you (plural)	**your**selves	it	**it**self

Spanish is very different from English and much easier to learn. The done-to forms which match *yo*, *nosotros*, and *tú* are _____. ▲

2 These three forms are used either when the doer and the done-to are the same or different. Compare:

She washes **me**. *Ella **me** lava.*   We wash **ourselves**. *Nosotros **nos** lavamos.*
I wash **myself**. *Yo **me** lavo.*   She washes **you**. *Ella **te** lava.*
She washes **us**. *Ella **nos** lava.*

Rewrite *yo me lavo* so the doer (and the done-to) is *tú*. ▲

        me, nos, te

3 Let's go back, now, to the difference between "meaning" in Spanish and "translation" into English. What does *yo me lavo* <u>mean</u> in Spanish? (a) I me wash. (b) I wash myself. ▲

        Tú te lavas.

        I me wash. (The proper translation is "I wash myself.")

4 Spanish, unlike English, has no special form of the reflexive pronoun that matches *yo*, *nosotros*, and *tú*.

   Spanish has only one "real" reflexive pronoun. It is *se*, and it is used to match all the other subject pronouns. Look carefully at these sentences:

She washes **herself**.	*Ella **se** lava.*
He washes **himself**.	*Él **se** lava.*
You wash **yourself**.	*Usted **se** lava.*
You wash **yourselves**.	*Ustedes **se** lavan.*
They wash **themselves**.	*Ellos **se** lavan.*

All that *se* really says to a Spanish speaker is that the doer and the done-to are the same.

   What *se* says to a Spanish speaker does not, of course, tell you how to translate *se* into English. What key word in *Ella se lava* tells you to translate *se* as "herself?" ▲

        Ella (You translate *ella* as "she" and match this with "herself".)

5 Translate: *Pepe se lava.* ▲

        Pepe washes himself. (You replace *Pepe* with "He" and match "He" with "himself.")

6 What reflexive pronoun matches "we" in English? ▲

7 What single done-to pronoun matches *nosotros* in Spanish? ▲

        ourselves

        nos

8 When the doer and done-to are different, the done-to pronoun that matches *ella* is _____. ▲

9 When the doer and the done-to are the same, the done-to or reflexive pronoun that matches *ella* is _____. ▲ | *la*

10 The done-to and reflexive pronoun that matches *él, ellos, ellas, usted,* and *ustedes* is _____. ▲ | *se*

11 Suppose you have a drill which begins with the sentence *Yo me levanto temprano*. The meaning, not the translation, of *levantar* is "to raise" or "to lift up." So *Yo me levanto temprano* means "I me raise early." The most likely translation of this is _____. ▲ | *se*

12 Change *Yo me levanto* so the subject is *nosotros*. ▲

> I get up early.
> *Nosotros nos levantamos.*

13 Translate: You (*tú*) get up early. Rewrite it so the forms match *usted*. ▲

> *Tú te levantas temprano. Usted se levanta temprano.*

14 To change the above to match "you" (plural), you just add _____ to *usted* and _____ to *levanta*. ▲

> *es* to *usted* and *n* to *levanta* (The *se* remains the same.)

15 To change *Ustedes se levantan temprano* so the doer is "they" (masculine), you simply replace *ustedes* with _____. ▲

> *ellos (Ellos se levantan temprano.)*

16 Translate: He gets up early. ▲

> *Él se levanta temprano.*

Summary

Here is a chart of the English and Spanish pronouns used in reflexive constructions. You learn only four forms in Spanish.

I	myself	*yo*	*me*	he	himself	*él*	*se*
we	ourselves	*nosotros*	*nos*	she	herself	*ella*	*se*
you	yourself	*tú*	*te*	they	themselves	*ellos*	*se*
you	yourself	*usted*	*se*	it	itself	—	*se*
you	yourselves	*ustedes*	*se*				

There is no subject pronoun for "it" in Spanish. You use zero.

Review of the Uses of the Preterit and Imperfect

1 In this and the next two frames, back-shift the English verb forms to the past: It *is* July 4, 1906, and Miguel *is working* in the country. ▲

2 Carmen *is singing* when her friend *arrives*. ▲

> was; was working
> was singing; arrived

3 At that moment the dog *gets up* and *barks*. ▲

4 Here is the Spanish equivalent of the sentence in Frame 1: *Es el 4 de julio de 1906, y Miguel trabaja en el campo.* The forms *Es* and *trabaja* will not tell you whether the back-shifts are to be in the Preterit or the Imperfect. You must

> got up; barked

make a logical analysis of the situation. What aspect of *trabajar* do you see in
Miguel trabaja en el campo? (a) initiative (b) imperfective (c) terminative ▲

5 If the action is going on (imperfective), then the back-shift of *trabaja* should   imperfective
be (a) *trabajó* (b) *trabajaba.* ▲

trabajaba (So the whole sentence comes out *Era el 4 de julio de 1906, y
Miguel trabajaba en el campo.*)

6 Look at this sentence: *Carmen canta cuando su amigo llega.* Does the action
of *llegar* come to an end while the singing is going on? ▲

7 Which form do you use to say an action came to an end in the past? (a)   yes
llegaba (b) *llegó* ▲

8 If *Carmen canta* shifts to mean "Carmen was singing," then the back-shift   *llegó*
of *canta* is _____. ▲

cantaba (So the whole sentence is *Carmen cantaba cuando su amigo llegó.*)

9 Now look at *En ese momento el perro se levanta y ladra.* What aspect does *ladra*
logically describe? (a) The dog *is barking* when he gets up. (b) The dog *stops
barking* after he gets up. (c) The dog gets up and *begins to bark.* ▲

The dog gets up and begins to bark.

10 Which past tense form is used to describe the initiative aspect of an action
at some point in the past? (a) the Imperfect (b) the Preterit ▲

11 So you will change *ladra* to _____. ▲   the Preterit

12 Does the dog complete the action of getting up before he begins to bark? ▲   *ladró*

13 So you will change *se levanta* to *se* _____. ▲   yes

levantó (The Preterit states that the whole cycle of getting up was completed
or terminated before the barking began.)

14 To select the proper back shift of a verb form, you must recall all that you
know about verb forms.

    Let's see, now, just how much you have to remember to rewrite *Es la una y
María duerme* in the past tense. Is *Es (ser)* an irregular verb? ▲

15 The imperfect stem of *ser* is _____. ▲   yes

16 To this stem you add the first suffix _____. ▲   *er*

a (So you have *Era la una.* Remember, clock time is always given in the

17 Compare *duerme* and *come.* Do these forms tell you which verb is *e*-set and   Imperfect.)
which verb is *i*-set? ▲

no (You have to get this information from other forms like *dormimos* and

18 The form *duerme* has a stem change. Do any of the present tense stem   *comemos.*)
changes show up in the Preterit or Imperfect of regular *a*- and *e*-verbs? ▲

19 Is *duerme* one of the three verbs that has an irregular stem in the   no
Imperfect? ▲

no (The three are *ser, ver,* and *ir.*)

20 Does the present tense *Es la una y María duerme* say that sleeping is in progress
at one o'clock? ▲

21 Will the back-shift of *duerme,* then, be the (a) Preterit? (b) Imperfect? ▲   yes

22 The imperfect stem of *duerme* is _____. ▲   Imperfect

23 The first suffix of the Imperfect of all regular *e*- and *i*-verbs is _____. ▲   *dorm*

24 You now know everything that is needed to write the past tense back-shift   *ía*
of *Es la una y María duerme.* It is _____. ▲

Era la una y María dormía.

25 To be literate in a language you have to be able to read, write, and spell what you can hear or say. Write the Imperfect of *caen*. ▲

26 Copy *caían* and divide it into syllables. ▲

caían

ca-í-an (The accent mark over the *í* tells you it can be a syllable all by itself.)

27 Change *caían* to the Preterit. Remember what happens to plain *i* when it comes between two vowels. ▲

28 Write the Imperfect and Preterit of *oye*, the Imperfect of *ven*. ▲

cayeron

29 To get the Imperfect of *va*, you change *v* to *b* (*ba*) and add the stem

oía; oyó, veían

———. ▲

i : iba (The same thing happens to *vas, vamos,* and *van.*)

30 Write the Imperfect of *vamos*. Before you do, remember what is special about all *nosotros* forms in the Imperfect. ▲

íbamos (The special thing is the accent mark.)

31 Remember this fact and change *recordamos* to the Imperfect. ▲

32 You change only the first suffix of *eres* to get the Imperfect of *tú*

recordábamos

eres, ———. ▲

tú eras

33 To get the Preterit of *tú oyes* you must change the *y* to ——— before you add *ste*. ▲

í (tú oíste)

34 In this and the next 9 frames, decide mentally which form of the past tense seems more logical for the context.

Entraron en la casa y después (*oían, oyeron*) los animales. ▲

oyeron (And afterwards they began to hear the noise. Initiative aspect =

35 El muchacho tropezó, (*caía, cayó*) y (*lloraba, lloró*). ▲

Preterit.)

36 Después Pedro (*salía, salió*) al patio y (*veía, vio*) la luna. ▲

cayó; lloró

37 Ese día los niños (*comían, comieron*) en el momento que (*llegábamos, llegamos*). ▲

salió; vio

38 (*Era, Fue*) el 4 de octubre y (*estábamos, estuvimos*) en Santiago. ▲

comían; llegamos

39 En el invierno siempre (*hacía, hizo*) mucho frío y la gente (*tenía, tuvo*) hambre. ▲

Era; estábamos

40 Y entonces (*then*) (*olvidaba, olvidó*) su lección. ▲

hacía; tenía

41 En 1492 Colón (*hallaba, halló*) las Américas. ▲

olvidó

42 Y luego (*then*) (*entraba, entró*) en la casa y (*hablaba, habló*) con su mamá. ▲

halló

43 Y luego (*subía, subió*) al balcón mientras (*while*) nosotros (*comíamos, comimos*). ▲

entró; habló

subió; comíamos

In the United States the automobile horn is used primarily for emergencies, and, as a result, many people may drive for weeks without blowing their horn. In most of Latin America the car horn is an integral part of the driver's equipment. It is blown to announce that one is about to pass. It is used to protest against any action the driver dislikes or to complain that a policeman is not directing traffic properly. Because many of the streets in the older cities are narrow and there are many blind corners there exists an unwritten code that the person who blows his horn first has the right of way. The Latin uses his horn as the personal substitute for the rules and regulations that govern American traffic. Until the American gets used to this he often feels that city traffic is a constant turmoil of hair-raising emergencies.

Self-Correcting Exercises

A   *Intonation: Stress, Rhythm, Pitch and Juncture*

Spanish words have only one stressed syllable, whereas English words often have both primary and secondary stresses. Read aloud the English word followed by the Spanish word and compare the difference. In the English word, the primary stress is indicated by one mark, the secondary stress by two.

1   ac″-ci-den′-tal / *ac-ci-den-**tal***
2   ac-com′-mo-date″ / *a-co-mo-**dar***
3   ac-cu′-mu-la″-tive / *a-cu-mu-la-**ti**-vo*
4   ar″-bi-tra′-tion / *ar-bi-tra-**ción***

5   a″-vi-a′-tion / *a-via-**ción***
6   ben″-e-dic′-tion / *ben-di-**ción***
7   ben′-e-fac″-tor / *be-ne-fac-**tor***
8   pa″-tri-ot′-ic / *pa-**trió**-ti-co*

Note the difference between English and Spanish as you read aloud each pair of sentences. Make all Spanish syllables short and equal.

9   I heard the lion in the jungle. / *Oí el león en la selva.*
10   There were three addresses. / *Había tres direcciones.*
11   The height was tremendous. / *La altura era tremenda.*
12   Titicaca is an enormous lake. / *El Titicaca es un lago enorme.*

Decide which of the following questions are information questions and which are yes-no questions, then read them aloud with the proper intonation. Remember to use rising terminal for yes-no questions and falling terminal for information questions.

13   ¿Dónde podemos hallar el río Amazonas?   information, falling
14   ¿Cuántos habitantes hay en Brasilia?   information, falling
15   ¿Qué hora es?   information, falling
16   ¿Hace mucho calor en el patio hoy?   yes-no, rising
17   ¿Vives tú en la Avenida Revolución?   yes-no, rising
18   ¿Viste la luna anoche?   yes-no, rising

B   *Refranes:* Oral translation
¿Cómo se dice en español . . . ?

before	*antes*
before you get married	*antes que se (te) case(s)*
to bark, to bite	*ladrar, morder (ue)*
although	*aunque*
monkey, silk	*mono (mona), seda*
ferocious	*fiero (feroz)*
lion, flies	*león, moscas*
closed mouth	*boca cerrada*
to find	*hallar (encontrar)*
"Look before you leap."	*"Antes que te cases, mira lo que haces."*

C   Ask and answer aloud the following questions.

1	¿Cuántos dedos tienes en los pies?	Tengo diez dedos·
2	¿Tienes los pulgares en los pies, o en las manos?	Los tengo en las manos·
3	¿Tienes la nariz en la cara, o en la frente?	La tengo en la cara·
4	¿Qué hacemos con la cabeza?	Pensamos·
5	¿Qué hacemos con las piernas y los pies?	Caminamos y corremos·
6	¿Oímos con los ojos?	No, oímos con las orejas·
7	¿Con qué masticamos?	Masticamos con los dientes·
8	¿Qué tienes en la boca?	Tengo dientes y la lengua·
9	Abrazamos con los labios, ¿verdad?	No, abrazamos con los brazos·
10	¿Con qué olemos?	Olemos con la nariz·

New Vocabulary

altura	height		**feroz**	ferocious
molestia	bother		**encontrar (ue)**	to find, meet
dedo de la mano	finger		**casar(se)**	to get married, marry
dedo del pie	toe		**lavar(se)**	to wash
indio, -a	Indian		**ninguna**	none, no
mulato, -a	mulatto		**antes (que)**	before
mestizo, -a	person of mixed blood			

No es molestia ninguna.   It's no bother.
"Antes que te cases, mira lo que haces."   "Look before you leap." (Before you get married, look at what you are doing.)

Assignment 49

Review of Spanish Spelling

1   You have to hear and, then, see the written word for [naris] before you learn that the sound [s] in this word is spelled _____.   ▲

2   Whenever Spanish uses two or more letters for the same sound, you have to either apply a rule or *see* the word before you can learn to spell it correctly. The spelling of [naris], the singular, and of the plural [narises] is an excellent example of "eye" spelling. The singular is spelled _____.   ▲

3   But the plural is spelled *narices*. Once you see the difference between *nariz* and *narices*, you soon discover that the same thing happens in *lápiz* and *lápices*. Now you can go from "eye" spelling to "rule" spelling. Here is one rule for spelling Spanish [s]: when a word in the singular ends in the consonant *z*, you change *z* to _____ before you add the plural suffix *es*.   ▲

z

nariz

c

4 The word for one "fish" in Spanish is *pez*. Write the plural. ▲

5 The letter *c*, as just shown, can stand for the sound [s] when *c* comes right before *e*. Now write the words for "head" and "mouth." ▲

peces

6 In these words does the letter *c* stand for the sound [s] or [k]? ▲

cabeza ; boca

7 You have seen how *cabeza* and *boca* are spelled. You can now make up another rule. The letter *c* stands for the sound [k] when *c* is followed by the vowel _____. ▲

[k]

8 You can now expand your rule and say that *c* stands for [s] before *e* and for [k] before *a*. Say *cien* aloud. Does the letter *c* in *cien* stand for the sound [k] or [s]? ▲

a

9 So you can expand your rule again and say that *c* stands for [s] before *e* and _____. ▲

[s]

i (This is the complete rule on the use of *c* to stand for the sound [s].)

10 Look at what comes after *c* in *cara*, *como*, and *disculpe*. Does *c* stand for the sound [k] in all these words? ▲

11 There are only five vowels in Spanish: *i, e,* and *a, o, u*. With this knowledge you can make up the following rule. The letter *c* stands for the sound [k] before the three vowels _____. ▲

yes

12 You cannot always go from eye spelling to rule spelling. The present tense form of *ser* that goes with *nosotros* is _____. ▲

a, o, u

13 We can now say that the sound [s] may be written *s* before *o*. The word that you hear for "arm" is [braso]. How do you spell it? (a) *braso* (b) *brazo* ▲

somos

14 We can now say that the sound [s] may be written either *s* or *z* before *o*. Is it possible to make up a rule that will tell you when to write *s* or *z* before *o*? ▲

brazo

no (So the only way you can learn to spell *somos* and *brazo* is to see the two words.)

15 There are other cues which can tell you how to spell a word. Say *ciento* and *siento* aloud. Do they sound exactly alike? ▲

yes (The meaning of *ciento* (one hundred) and *siento* (I regret), once you have seen the words, tells you the way to spell each one. So you can combine eye and meaning spelling to get the correct spelling of many words.)

16 Learning to spell is made a lot easier when you find out what letters can and cannot stand next to each other in a word. Say *pie*, *pierna*, and *diente* aloud. Now say *oye* and *oyes* aloud. Do the *ie* and the *ye* sound very much alike? ▲

17 What you hear, then, is not going to tell you what to write. But this general rule will make spelling easier: Spanish never writes a *y* directly before or after a consonant in the same word. This fact, then, tells you to use *i*, not *y*, in *pie*, *diente*, and *pierna*. Spanish also writes only *i* between two vowels (*veía, caía*). When a sound like [i] as in *oigo*, comes between two vowels, it is written _____. ▲

yes

18 The dictionary of the Spanish Academy lists just eleven words that begin with *ze*. There are, in contrast, over fourteen pages of words that begin with *ce*. Does Spanish like to write *z* before *e*? ▲

y (As in *oye, oyó*.)

19 There are lots of *a*-verbs in Spanish like *tropezar* (to trip) and *comenzar* (to begin) in which *z* appears before *a*. Now the *yo* form of the Preterit of all *a*-verbs ends in the suffix _____. ▲

no

é (*hablé, fumé, cerré,* etc.)

20 From what you just learned in Frame 18, how would you expect the Spanish speaker to write the translation of "I tripped?" (a) *tropezé* (b) *tropecé* ▲

21 The *yo* form of the Preterit forces a change of letters in lots of verbs. The *c* of *buscar* stands for the sound of [k]. How will you spell the translation of "I looked for?" (a) *buscé* (b) *busqué* ▲

> *tropecé*

> *busqué* (*c* before *e* stands for [s]; [k] is spelled *qu* before *e*.)

22 Most letters stand for the same phoneme (and all its allophones) all the time. Once you have learned the exceptions, you can spell all the rest of the words by ear. So you hear [lengwa] and you write _____. ▲

> *lengua* (Spanish, except in foreign words, always writes *u* for [w].)

23 You hear [frente], [pelo], [dedo], and [mano]. Do you have to use a rule or see these words to spell them? ▲

> no (Not if you know what letter stands for each phoneme in Spanish.)

24 The accent mark in Spanish is just as much a part of spelling as the letters. Copy and divide *leía* and *oigo* into syllables. ▲

> *le-í-a; oi-go* (When [i] is the only sound in a syllable between two other vowels, it must be written *í*.)

25 Change *yo oigo* to the Imperfect. Remember the infinitive is *oír*. ▲
26 How many syllables are there in *oía*? ▲

> *yo oía*
> three (*o-í-a*)

27 In English we have many words which are spelled one way and pronounced in two different ways. We may enter a "contest" (pronounced *con'*-test), but we "con-*test*" a claim in court. Spanish, unlike English, uses the accent mark to tell people how to say certain words aloud. With minor exceptions, like *¿qué?, ¿dónde?, etc.*, the accent mark is a signal which tells the reader that the word is not stressed according to rule. When a word ends in a vowel, the stress falls (a) on the last syllable (b) on the next-to-last syllable. ▲

> on the next-to-last syllable

28 Copy and divide *hallo* into syllables. Underline the stressed syllable. ▲
29 In the Preterit of *a*-verbs, the stress falls on the first suffix: *ha-**lla**-mos, ha-**lla**-ste*. Consequently, to write "you found" and to put the stress on the final *o*, you must write (a) *usted hallo* (b) *usted halló*. ▲

> **ha**-*llo*

> *usted halló* (This tells the reader the stress does not follow the rule which says that words ending in a vowel are stressed on the next-to-the-last syllable.)

30 Words which end in *n* or *s* are also stressed on the next-to-the-last syllable. The Imperfect of *vamos* is an exception to this, so you write _____. ▲
31 The word for "lesson" ends in *n* and does not follow the general stress rules. So you must write _____. ▲

> *íbamos*

> *lección*

32 A word that ends in a consonant (except *n* or *s*) is stressed (a) on the last syllable (b) on the next-to-the-last syllable. ▲
33 The word *tunel* does not follow this rule. So it must be written _____. ▲

> on the last syllable
> *túnel*

34 The rules for stress say the stress falls either on the last or the next-to-last syllable. Will there have to be a written accent on every word in which the stress does not fall on one of these two syllables? ▲

> yes

35 Copy, divide into syllables, and write the accent mark on *ultimo* and *rapido*. ▲

> *úl-ti-mo; rá-pi-do*

36 Here are some of the words you have to see in order to spell. The letters
that may give you trouble appear in bold type.

ll**o**viendo	edifi**c**io	**v**olver	ol**v**idar	**b**oca
ne**v**ando	**h**abitante	cono**c**er	**b**uscar	**c**alle
vale	**ll**anura	**ll**evar	**h**allar	em**b**argo
volando	sel**v**a	espa**c**io	**h**éroe	**c**igarro
	po**b**la**c**ión	empe**z**ar	na**c**ional	

37 With few exceptions, when a cognate has a sound which can be written
with two letters in Spanish, the letter used will be the same as in English. So
you hear [sigarro] and you write _____. ▲

cigarro (The cognate is "cigar.")

38 Which spelling is correct for "avenue?" (a) *abenida* (b) *avenida* ▲

39 Which spelling is correct? (a) *havitante* (b) *habitante* ▲

avenida

habitante (Like "inhabitant.")

40 Which spelling is correct? (a) *difísil* (b) *difícil* ▲

difícil (Like "difficult," which has *c*, not *s*.)

41 There are many double consonants in English cognates which stand for
only one sound: profe**ss**or, co**ff**ee, cla**ss**, di**ff**erent, *etc*. Spanish writes a double
consonant only when both are actually pronounced. Write the Spanish for
"professor." ▲

42 You have reviewed the four cues for spelling: (1) meaning, (2) what you
hear, (3) what you see, (4) rules. What tells you to spell 100 as *ciento*, not
siento? ▲

profesor

43 You hear [mestiso]. What tells you to write *mestizo*? ▲

44 You hear [asta] and you write _____. ▲

meaning

what you see

hasta (Because you have always seen the word with an *h*.)

Done-to Pronouns and the Reflexive Construction

1 When the doer and the done-to in a sentence are the same, the construction
is reflexive. The doer in *Aunque la mona se vista de seda* is _____. ▲

2 The word for the done-to is the reflexive pronoun _____. ▲

la mona

3 The *se* in Spanish merely says that the done-to is the same as the doer. The
translation of *se* into English depends on who the doer is. In the proverb,
la mona is a female. So you must translate *se* as _____. ▲

se

4 A very precise or literal translation of the first part of the proverb goes like
this: "Although the monkey may dress herself in silk." Will the meaning be
changed a lot in English if *herself* is left out? ▲

herself

5 English, unlike Spanish, tends to leave out the word for the done-to when
the meaning is obvious. Who gets dressed in *He got up and dressed?* (a) he (b)
somebody else ▲

no

6 Who gets washed and shaved in *I washed and shaved?* (a) myself (b) somebody
else ▲

he

myself

7 When the doer and done-to are the same, Spanish regularly names the done-to. Translate: I get up at six. ▲

Yo me levanto a las seis. (The meaning is "I get myself up at six.")

8 In the proverb about the monkey the verb form *vista* translates "may dress." (This is a form you won't study for a few weeks. It is called the **Subjunctive**.) The translation of "The monkey dresses herself" is *La mona se viste.* The infinitive is *vestir* (a stem-changing verb in which the *e* changes to *i* in all present tense forms except the one that agrees with *nosotros*.) Translate: We dress ourselves. Translate: I dress myself. ▲

Nosotros nos vestimos. Yo me visto.

9 To change *Yo me visto* so that the doer is *tú*, you have to make three changes. First, *yo* is replaced by *tú*. Second, *me* is replaced by _____. ▲

10 You now have *Tú te*, and the verb suffixes of *visto* must be changed to _____. ▲   *te*

11 The reflexive pronoun *se* matches *ustedes, usted, él, ella, ellos*, and *ellas*.   *es (Tú te vistes.)* Translate: He dresses himself. ▲

12 Change this to: They (masculine) dress themselves. ▲   *Él se viste.*
13 Which is the more common translation of *Ellos se visten?* (a) They dress   *Ellos se visten.* themselves. (b) They dress. ▲

They dress (Except when the meaning is a contrast as in "Mother doesn't dress them anymore; they dress *themselves*.")

14 Here is another stem-changing verb which is common in reflexive constructions. It is *acostar*, the opposite of *levantar*. Translate: *Me acuesto a las nueve de la noche y me levanto a las siete de la mañana.* ▲

I go to bed at nine at night and get up at seven in the morning. (The word *costado* means the "side of a human body" and *acostarme* literally means "to put myself on my side" = to lie down on my side to sleep.)

15 The stem change in *acostar* is *o* to *ue*. Write the missing form: *Usted se* _____. ▲

16 To change *Usted se acuesta* so the doer is "you" (plural), you have to make   *acuesta* two changes: _____. ▲

Ustedes se acuestan. (You make the doer form and the verb plural.)

17 To change *Usted se acuesta* so the doer is "you" (intimate), you have to make three changes: _____. ▲

18 To change *Ustedes se acuestan* so the doer is "they" (masculine), you only   *Tú te acuestas.* have to make one change. Write the new sentence. ▲

19 In this and the next frame, write the missing done-to form. Nosotros _____   *Ellos se acuestan.* acostamos. Mis hermanos y yo _____ acostamos. ▲

20 Pedro _____ acuesta. Yo _____ acuesto. ▲   *nos, nos*
21 Here is another new verb which is commonly used in reflexive constructions.   *se, me* It is *desayunar*. The *des* is the negative prefix which is like "dis" in "disappear." The verb *ayunar* translates "to fast" or "to go hungry." So *desayunar* means "to break one's fast" or "to have _____." ▲

22 *Desayunar* is a regular *a*-verb. Write the missing form: *Yo me* _____ *a las*   breakfast *siete de la mañana. ¿A qué hora te* _____ *tú?* ▲

desayuno; desayunas

23 Translate: *¿A qué hora te desayunas tú?* The meaning of *hora* is the same as in *¿Qué hora es?* ▲

At what time do you have breakfast?

24 Change *Tú te desayunas* so that the doer is "you" (formal and singular). Remember you must make three changes. ▲

25 Make *Usted se desayuna* plural. ▲

Usted se desayuna.

Ustedes se desayunan.

26 Change *Ustedes se desayunan* so the doer is "they" (feminine). ▲

Ellas se desayunan.

Summary

When the doer and the done-to are the same, the construction is said to be reflexive. Unlike English (*He dressed* versus *He dressed himself*), Spanish consistently marks the done-to in reflexive constructions with *me*, *te*, *nos*, and *se*:

Yo me levanto.	*Vd., él, ella se* acuesta.
Nosotros nos vestimos.	*Vds., ellos, ellas se* acuestan.
Tú te llamas.	

Self-Correcting Exercises

A *Reflexive Constructions and Done-to Pronouns:* Referring to the pictures as indicated, answer the questions mentally.

A/B

In picture A:

1 Who is the doer?

2 Who is the done-to?

3 Is it a reflexive construction?

4 Why not?

5 Change *a Pepito* to a done-to pronoun and say this sentence.

mamá

Pepito

no

Because the doer and the done-to are two different people.

Mamá lo lava.

In picture B:

6 Who is the done-to and the doer?   *mamá*

7 Is it a reflexive construction?   yes

8 Why is it?   Because the doer and the done-to are the same person.

Compare *Mamá lo lava* and *Mamá se lava* and say both sentences aloud.

C/D

In picture C:

9 Who is the doer?   the nurse

10 Who is the done-to?   the boy

11 Is *Ella lo levanta* a reflexive construction?   no

In picture D:

12 Who is the doer and the done-to?   the boy

13 Is *Él se levanta* a reflexive construction?   yes

14 Why is it?   Because the doer and the done-to are the same person.

Ask and answer aloud in Spanish:

15 ¿Cómo se llama el muchacho en la foto A?   Se llama Pepito.
    ¿Quién lo lava?   Su (La) mamá lo lava.

16 ¿Quién se lava en la foto B?   La mamá se lava.
    ¿Se lava la cara, o los labios?   Se lava la cara.

17 ¿A quién levanta la señorita en la foto C?   Levanta al muchacho.
    ¿Lo levanta con los brazos, o con los pies?   Lo levanta con los brazos.

18 ¿Qué hace el muchacho en la foto D?   (Él) se levanta.
    ¿Se fracturó un brazo, o una pierna?   Se fracturó un brazo.

B *Intonation: Stress, Rhythm, Pitch and Juncture*

Spanish words have only one stressed syllable; English words have both primary
(´) and secondary (″) stresses. Read the pairs of words aloud noting the contrast.

1 i-de″-al-is´-tic / *i-de-a-**lis**-ta*   **3** nav´-i-ga″-tor / *na-ve-ga-**dor***

2 il″-le-gal´-i-ty / *i-le-ga-li-**dad***   **4** ma-ter″-i-al-is´-tic / *ma-te-ria-**lis**-ta*

5	pes''-si-mis'-tic / *pe-si-**mis**-ta*	7	e''-co-nom'-i-cal / *e-co-**nó**-mi-co*
6	can''-cel-la'-tion / *can-ce-la-**ción***	8	ed''-u-ca'-tion-al / *e-du-ca-cio-**nal***

Make all unstressed syllables short and equal when reading aloud the Spanish sentence, and compare it with the English.

9 Nevertheless, he intends to be there. / *Sin embargo, piensa estar allí.*
10 We could see stars everywhere. / *Podíamos ver estrellas por todas partes.*
11 According to John it is excellent. / *Según Juan es excelente.*
12 We intend to be here Monday. / *Pensamos estar aquí el lunes.*

Decide which questions are information questions (falling terminal) and which are yes-no questions (rising terminal), then read them aloud with the proper intonation.

13	¿Es importante todo esto?	yes-no, rising
14	¿Cuántos son cinco y nueve?	information, falling
15	¿Cuál es la capital de tu país?	information, falling
16	¿Usamos los dedos para tocar?	yes-no, rising
17	¿Quién se levantó temprano hoy?	information, falling
18	¿Te levantaste tú temprano hoy?	yes-no, rising

C *More on Reflexive Constructions:* Looking at the chart, answer the questions (1–4) mentally, and then write the appropriate done-to pronoun and form of the verb that match each subject pronoun (5–10).

	A	B	C	D	
Yo	me	levant	o		
Nosotros	nos	levant	a	mos	
Tú	te	levant	a	s	
Usted	se	levant	a		temprano.
Ustedes	se	levant	a	n	
Él	se	levant	a		
Ellos	se	levant	a	n	

1	Which column tells what the act is?	B
2	Which two columns label the doer?	D and subject pronouns
3	Which column tells when the act takes place?	C
4	Which column tells who the done-to is?	A
5	Ellos . . . temprano.	*se levantan*
6	Tú . . . temprano.	*te levantas*
7	Mi hermano y yo . . . temprano.	*nos levantamos*
8	Mi compañera de cuarto . . . temprano.	*se levanta*
9	¿Cómo . . . usted? (llamarse)	*se llama*
10	Yo . . . pasado mañana. (casarse)	*me caso*

Looking at the chart, answer the questions (11–14) mentally, and then complete the rest of the exercise in writing.

	A	B	C	D
Yo	me	acuest	o	
Nosotros	nos	acost	a	mos
Tú	te	acuest	a	s
Usted	se	↓	a	
Ustedes	se		a	n
Él	se		a	
Ellos	se	↓	a	n

temprano.

11	To what verb set does *acostar* belong?	*a*-set
12	Is it stem-changing?	*yes*
13	What is the regular stem of this verb?	*acost-*
14	What is the irregular allomorph of the stem?	*acuest-*
15	Nosotras . . . temprano.	*nos acostamos*
16	Mi abuela . . . temprano.	*se acuesta*
17	¿ . . . Vds. temprano?	*Se acuestan*
18	¿A qué hora . . . tú?	*te acuestas*
19	Yo . . . muy tarde. (dormirse)	*me duermo*
20	Nosotros . . . muy tarde. (dormirse)	*nos dormimos*

New Vocabulary

amarillo	yellow	**blanco**	white	**colores**	colors
anaranjado	orange	**negro**	black	**levantarse**	to get up, rise
rojo	red	**gris**	gray	**acostarse (ue)**	to lie down, go to bed
rosado	pink	**claro**	light, clear	**desayunar(se)**	to eat breakfast
morado	purple	**oscuro**	dark	**se**	yourself, himself,
azul	blue	**teléfono**	telephone		herself, itself,
verde	green	**bandera**	flag		yourselves,
					themselves

Many Americans driving a car in the country at night in parts of Latin America are puzzled at first to see an on-coming driver turn off his headlights for a second or two. This is a courtesy which prevents many serious accidents. Turning off the lights for a moment allows a driver to see animals or wagons in between the two cars. Since there is no law which requires a tail light on a horse or wagon, they cannot be seen against the headlights of an on-coming car. Unsuspecting American tourists often barely avoid slamming into wagons and teams of horses at sixty miles an hour.

More on the Done-to Pronouns and the Reflexive Construction

1   The done-to pronouns *me*, *nos*, and *te* match the doer pronouns _____. ▲

2   In a conversation both sets of pronouns have to be changed when you answer questions. The "yes" answer to *¿Eres tú de España?* is *Sí*, _____. ▲

yo, nosotros, tú

Sí, yo soy de España.

3   The done-to in *¿Me ves tú?* is *Me*, the speaker of the question. The person answering must say, *Sí, yo* _____ *veo.* ▲

4   Suppose someone asks, *¿A qué hora te acuestas?* Translate: I go to bed at nine. ▲

*Sí, yo **te** veo.*

Yo me acuesto a las nueve.

5   It is easy to get mixed up when you are working with several pronoun names for the same person. So let's practice this some more. Suppose you ask someone *¿Me recuerdas?* The "yes" answer will be *Sí, yo* _____ *recuerdo.* ▲

6   What will your "yes" answer be to *¿Se levanta usted temprano?* ▲

Sí, yo te recuerdo.

Sí, yo me levanto temprano.

7   When someone talks to you as a group, the done-to pronoun is *se* in the reflexive construction: *¿Se levantan ustedes temprano?* When you answer this question for the group, your doer pronoun name is _____. ▲

8   Translate: We get up early. *Nosotros* _____. ▲

nosotros

Nosotros nos levantamos temprano.

9   The "yes" answer to *¿Me conoces tú?* is *Sí*, _____. ▲

10   The no answer to *¿Me miras tú?* is _____. ▲

11   When you answer *sí* to *¿Te acuestas temprano?* you say _____. ▲

Sí, te conozco.

No, no te miro.

Sí, yo me acuesto temprano.

12   Suppose you are a male and someone reports what you just said to another person. You are being talked about; the reporter must use _____. ▲

13   The done-to pronoun that matches *él* is _____. ▲

14   The verb form *acuesto* must be changed to match *él*. Now, translate: He goes to bed early. ▲

él

se

Él se acuesta temprano.

15   To make this statement into a question, you merely put the doer pronoun after the verb and change the intonation: *¿Se acuesta él temprano?* Will the yes answer to this question be the original statement *Sí, él se acuesta temprano?* ▲

yes (In the third person, the done-to *se* remains the same in both the question

16   The Spanish verb which is a cognate of "lavatory" is _____. ▲

and the answer.)

lavar (Verbs like *lavar* always require a real or understood done-to.)

17   Remember that Spanish regularly says the word for the done-to. You say, "I'm going to wash now." What is the missing word in English? ▲

myself (So you get in Spanish *Voy a lavarme ahora.*)

18 Someone is talking to you in *usted*. What must this person do to change *Voy a lavarme* into a question? The *voy* must be changed to _____. ▲

19 The *me* is changed to _____, the done-to form that matches *usted*. ▲

va

se (So you have *¿Va usted a lavarse?*)

20 If you make the subject *ustedes*, you change *va* to _____. ▲

21 Is there a plural form of *se*? ▲

van

no (So you have *¿Van ustedes a lavarse?*)

22 You are the speaker for the group addressed as *ustedes*. Your yes answer to the question *¿Van ustedes a lavarse?* must be _____. ▲

Sí, vamos a lavarnos.

23 You are talking to a person in *tú*. Translate: Are you going to wash? ▲

24 The other person answers, *Sí,* _____. ▲

¿Vas a lavarte?

25 You are a girl. Someone reports what you just said. The report is *Ella* _____. ▲

Sí, voy a lavarme.

26 As a girl you have several pronoun names. As the speaker *and* doer your name is _____. ▲

Ella va a lavarse.

27 As the person spoken *about*, your name is _____. ▲

yo

28 As the speaker and the *done-to*, your name is _____. ▲

ella

29 As the person spoken to, you have two names in the role of the done-to. A close friend uses _____. A stranger uses _____. ▲

me

30 Translate: I wash at six. ▲

te, se

31 Fill in the blank on your answer sheet: *Ella dice que* (she washes herself) _____ *a las seis.* ▲

Me lavo a las seis.

32 Complete: *¿Es verdad que tú* _____ *a las seis?* ▲

se lava

33 Complete: *¿Es verdad que usted* _____ *a las seis?* ▲

te lavas

34 Answer the above question with *Sí, yo* _____ *a las seis.* ▲

se lava

35 When the doer and the done-to in a sentence are the same, you have a _____ construction. ▲

me lavo

reflexive

Review of Done-to Pronouns

1 One set of done-to pronouns is really made up of adjectival residuals: the forms of the definite article which are left over when the noun is dropped. The potential adjectival residual in *Voy a ver la casa* is _____. ▲

2 Translate: I'm going to see it. ▲

la

Voy a verla. (Remember: you add the residual to the end of the infinitive in

3 The done-to residual is the same in *Veo la casa*. Translate: "I see it." ▲ writing.)

La veo. (The done-to pronoun comes immediately before the finite or con-

4 The potential done-to residual in *Vamos a repasar las lecciones* is _____. ▲ jugated verb form.)

5 Translate: We are going to review them. ▲

las

6 Translate: We are reviewing them. *Nosotros* _____. ▲

Vamos a repasarlas.

Nosotros las repasamos.

7 The potential done-to residual of *Tenemos los libros* is _____. ▲

8 Translate: We have them. ▲

los

(Nosotros) los tenemos.

9 The singular form of *los* has two allomorphs. As an adjectival residual the form that replaces *el* in *Tengo el libro* is the singular of *los*. It is _____. ▲

lo (Tengo el libro; Lo tengo.)

10 The potential residual in *El profesor vive allí* is _____. ▲

11 The article *el* becomes the doer pronoun *él* (with an accent in writing) when it is the subject of the verb. The *él*, like *el*, becomes *lo* when it stands for a male done-to. So Spanish normally does not say *Vamos a ver a él*, but *Vamos a ver* _____. ▲

El

12 *Vamos a ver a ellos* is changed to *Vamos a ver* _____. ▲

lo

los (The los is the second part of el-los.)

13 What will *Vamos a ver a ella* become? *Vamos a ver* _____. ▲

la (This la is also the second part of el-la.)

14 If *ella* can stand for *María*, what will the done-to pronoun for *María* be? ▲

15 So *Vemos a María* may be changed to _____. ▲

la

16 The done-to pronoun for *mis amigos* will be _____. ▲

La vemos.

17 Translate: We see them. ▲

los

18 The done-to forms *la, las, los,* and *lo* are used when the doer and done-to are different. *Olvidé mi libro* becomes *Lo olvidé*. *Recordaron a sus amigos* becomes *Los recordaron*. *Observó a usted* (female) becomes _____. ▲

Los vemos.

19 The other done-to pronouns are *me, nos,* and *te*. *Papá busca a nosotros* becomes *Papá* _____ *busca.* ▲

La observó.

20 And *Papá busca a ti* becomes *Papá* _____ *busca.* ▲

nos

21 What will *Papá busca a él y a mí* become? *Papá* _____ *busca.* ▲

te

nos

The Preterit of Verbs Ending in -zar, -gar, *and* -car

There is nothing special about these verbs in speech. They all, however, present a problem in spelling which you already know about from writing other words. Only the *yo* form of the Preterit of regular *a*-verbs has a spelling change. All other forms are regular in their spelling.

1 The infinitive cognate of "to embrace" (hug) is *abrazar*. The first suffix of the *yo* form of the Preterit of *a*-verbs is _____. ▲

2 What letter normally replaces *z* before *e*? ▲

é

3 So *yo abrazo* becomes *yo* _____ in the Preterit. ▲

c

abracé (Since Spanish allows z before a and o, the other forms can be written abrazamos, abrazaste, abrazó, abrazaron.)

4 In *masticar* (to chew) the *c* stands for the sound [k] which is regularly written by the digraph _____ before *e* and *i*. ▲

5 So the *yo* form of the Preterit of *masticar* is written _____. ▲

qu

6 Write the *yo* form of *buscar*. Yo _____. ▲

mastiqué

busqué (All the other preterit forms of verbs like buscar and masticar have either o or a as the first vowel after the stem, so there are no spelling changes.)

7 The *g* before *e* and *i* is always pronounced like the *j* of *ojo* in Spanish. It cannot be used, then, to stand for the *g* sound of *llegar* when the first suffix is *é*.

The [g] sound is written *gu* before *e* so the *yo* form of the Preterit of *llegar* is written _____. ▲

> *llegué* (In all other preterit forms of *llegar,* the stem is followed by either *a* or *ó* so there are no spelling changes.)

8 The verb *jugar* has the same spelling changes as *llegar.* Write the preterit forms that go with *yo* and *él.* ▲

9 You have been shown that only the *yo* form of the Preterit of regular *a*-verbs has a spelling change. Eye spelling plus a rule tells you what to do. A *z* changes to _____ before *é.* Write the Preterit of *yo abrazo.* ▲

            yo jugué ; él jugó

10 The *c* before *a* changes to the digraph _____ before *é.* ▲

11 Write the Preterit of *yo busco.* ▲

12 The *g* before *a* or *o* changes to the digraph _____ before *é.* ▲

13 Write the Preterit of *yo llego.* ▲

            c, abracé
            qu
            busqué
            gu
            llegué

Self-Correcting Exercises

A *Intonation: Stress, Rhythm, Pitch and Juncture*

Spanish words have only one stressed syllable; some English words have both primary (′) and secondary (″) stresses. Read these pairs aloud and note the difference.

1 ca-pit″-u-la′-tion / *ca-pi-tu-la-**ción***
2 cat″-a-stroph′-ic / *ca-tas-**tró**-fi-co*
3 du″-pli-ca′-tion / *du-pli-ca-**ción***
4 du″-ra-bil′-i-ty / *du-ra-bi-li-**dad***

5 id″-i-o-syn′-cra-sy / *i-dio-sin-**cra**-sia*
6 il-lu′-mi-na″-tor / *i-lu-mi-na-**dor***
7 no′-men-cla″-ture / *no-men-cla-**tu**-ra*
8 no″-ti-fi-ca′-tion / *no-ti-fi-ca-**ción***

Make all unstressed syllables short and equal when saying the Spanish aloud. Note the contrast with the English.

9 Henry has a very red nose. / *Enrique tiene la nariz muy roja.*
10 They always kiss when they see each other. / *Siempre se besan cuando se ven.*
11 Don't move your head or raise your hand. / *No muevas la cabeza ni levantes la mano.*
12 Look out! That dog is very fierce! / *¡Cuidado! Ese perro es muy feroz.*

Decide whether each question is an information question (falling terminal) or a yes-no question (rising terminal), then say it aloud with the proper intonation.

13 ¿Cuál es el número de tu teléfono?
14 ¿Sabe usted el nombre de estos colores?
15 ¿Quién de ustedes es de Paraguay?
16 ¿En qué calle vives tú?
17 ¿Tienes tu libro de español aquí hoy?
18 ¿Cuándo vienes a la universidad mañana?

    information, falling
    yes-no, rising
    information, falling
    information, falling
    yes-no, rising
    information, falling

B   *Done-to Pronouns:* Write the combinations.

Ejemplo: 24 = Mamá acaba de servirte.

	1 a los invitados.
	2 a mí.
1 sirve	3 a usted y a mí.
Mamá	4 a ti.
2 acaba de servir	5 a usted (f).
	6 a mi tía.

1)	11	Mamá los sirve.
2)	12	Mamá me sirve.
3)	21	Mamá acaba de servirlos.
4)	22	Mamá acaba de servirme.
5)	13	Mamá nos sirve.
6)	23	Mamá acaba de servirnos.
7)	14	Mamá te sirve.
8)	26	Mamá acaba de servirla.
9)	15	Mamá la sirve.
10)	24	Mamá acaba de servirte.
11)	16	Mamá la sirve.
12)	25	Mamá acaba de servirla.

C   *Practice with Colors:* Ask and answer the following questions aloud. Cover the answers on the right.

1	¿Cuántos colores tiene nuestra bandera?	Tiene tres colores.
2	¿De qué color es la bandera americana?	Es blanca, azul y roja.
3	¿De qué color es la luna?	La luna es amarilla.
4	¿De qué color es la nieve?	La nieve es blanca.
5	El elefante es generalmente morado, ¿no?	No, el elefante es gris.
6	¿Tiene Vd. un lápiz rojo, o una pluma roja?	Tengo una pluma roja.
7	¿De qué color son sus ojos, verdes, o azules?	Mis ojos son negros.
8	¿Tiene usted el pelo oscuro, o claro?	Tengo el pelo muy oscuro.
9	¿Es negra la pizarra del aula donde Vd. estudia español?	No, no es negra, es verde.
10	¿Es anaranjado su libro de español?	No, no es anaranjado.

New Vocabulary

ropa	clothes	**blusa**	blouse	**calcetines**	socks
pantalones	trousers, pants	**vestido**	dress	**medias**	stockings, socks
		suéter	sweater	**dormirse (ue)**	to fall asleep
camisa	shirt	**abrigo**	overcoat, top coat	**despertarse (ie)**	to wake up
corbata	necktie			**vestirse (i)**	to get dressed
saco	coat	**impermeable**	raincoat	**de prisa**	in a hurry
traje	suit	**sombrero**	hat		
falda	skirt	**zapatos**	shoes		

Assignment 51

The Preterit of Stem-Changing i-Verbs

1 In the Present the stressed *o* of the stem sometimes changes to *ue: yo duermo*. These same verbs have two irregular forms in the Preterit: *usted (él, ella) durmió* and *ustedes (ellos, ellas) durmieron*. The *o* of the regular stem (*dormir*) changes to _____. ▲

2 The *yo* form of *dormir* in the Preterit is regular. It is _____. ▲

> *u*
>
> *dormí* (The past tense base of *dormía*.)

3 When you compare *dormí* and *durmió*, you see that the second syllable of each is stressed: *dor-mí, dur-mió*. So stress cannot be the cue to change the *o* of the stem to *u*. Instead, the cue is to be found in the first suffix. When it is just *i* as in *dormí, dormimos*, and *dormiste*, the stem is regular. When the two irregular forms are divided into their morphemes, you get: *durm-ió, durm-iero-n*. When the first suffix has *i* plus _____, the stem is irregular. ▲

> *o* or *e* (The combinations *io* and *ie* are called **diphthongs**.)

4 The verb *morir* belongs to the same class as *dormir*. The preterit form that matches *yo* is _____. ▲

5 No one can use *morí* except in a figure of speech, since one can't report one's own death. You can, however, say *Casi morí de hambre*, which means "I almost _____." ▲

> *morí*

6 Write the form of *morir* which is like *durmió*. ▲

7 Write the form of *morir* which is like *durmieron*. ▲

> died of hunger
>
> *murió*

8 The *nosotros* form of *dormir* and *morir* is regular. It is made up of the past tense base plus the second suffix _____. ▲

> *murieron*
>
> *mos* (*dormimos, morimos*)

9 Change *dormimos* and *morimos* so they match *tú*. ▲

10 There is another group of *i*-verbs which are irregular in the Present and the Preterit. These are the verbs whose stem *e* changes to *i* or *ie* in the Present: *pido, visto, siento*. The translation of *pedir*, a cognate of "petition" is _____. ▲

> *dormiste; moriste*
>
> to ask, request (Sometimes very much like "to beg.")

11 The translation of *servir*, a cognate of "servant" is _____. ▲

12 The translations of *vestir, seguir*, and *medir* are _____. ▲

> to serve
>
> to dress, to follow, to measure

13 The *i*-verbs *pedir, medir, vestir, servir*, and *seguir* change the *e* of the stem to *i* in the irregular present tense forms: *sirvo, sirves, sirve, sirven*. The Preterit of all these verbs keeps the *i* in the stem when the first suffix has a diphthong (*io* or *ie*). The *usted* form of *servir*, then, is _____. ▲

14 The first and second suffix of the *ustedes* form is *ieron*. So the stem of *servir* will be (a) *serv* (b) *sirv*. ▲

> *sirvió*

15 It is not practical to memorize every single verb which has forms in the Preterit like *servir*. It is much more economical to learn one model well and

> *sirv* (*sirvieron*)

then to learn which other verbs follow this model. *Pedir* is like *servir*, so the Preterit of *él pide* is *él* _____. ▲

16 The Preterit of *ellos sirven* is *ellos sirvieron*. So the Preterit of *ellos miden* is *ellos* _____. ▲

> *pidió*

> *midieron* (they measured)

17 Like *dormir* the *yo* form of this set of verbs is regular in the Preterit. Write the *yo* form of *servir* and *vestir*. ▲

18 Also like *dormir* the *nosotros* form is regular in the Preterit. Write the *nosotros* form of *seguir* and *pedir*. ▲

> *serví; vestí*

19 The *tú* form is also regular. Write the *tú* form of *servir* and *sentir* in the Preterit. ▲

> *seguimos; pedimos*

> *serviste; sentiste*

Summary

1 Stem-changing verbs of the *a-* and *e-*sets are regular in the Preterit (*pienso-pensé, vuelvo-volví*, etc.), but those belonging to the *i-*set have the following irregularity in the stem: *o* changes to *u*, and *e* changes to *i* in the forms having the diphthongs *ie* or *io* rather than plain *i* in the first suffix:

dormir: dormí, dormiste, dormimos but *durmió, durmieron*

pedir: pedí, pediste, pedimos but *pidió, pidieron*

2 Other verbs in this group are: *morir, medir, vestir, servir, seguir*, and *sentir*.

More Uses of the Preterit and the Imperfect

The Present usually describes what is happening while we are talking. The past tense describes the same events when we remember them. At this very instant you *are reading* this line. A second or so ago you *were reading* the sentence before this one. All present events become past events the instant they are finished and in the same way everything we say now becomes past as soon as we say it. Thus, you say, "I'm hungry," and if I do not hear you properly, I must say, "What *did* you say?" And you must answer either with a direct quote ("I said, 'I'm hungry.'") or an indirect quote ("I said I was hungry."). All of this means that all the cues of the Preterit and Imperfect won't be completely clear until you thoroughly understand the uses of the Present.

1 One of the functions of the Present in both English and Spanish is to describe what is actually going on when a statement is made. Thus the answer to *¿Qué hace Pilar ahora?* may be *Duerme*. Is Pilar sleeping at the very instant that the speaker says *Duerme*? ▲

2 The question and answer given above have been said. They are now past. To talk about them we must recall them and back-shift them into the past

> yes

tense. The question becomes *¿Qué hacía Pilar entonces?* (What was Pilar doing then?) and the answer must be (a) *Duerme.* (b) *Dormía.* ▲

3 The Present does not always describe something that is actually happening at the instant something is said. Suppose, for example, that Pilar says *Yo duermo muy bien.* Is Pilar actually sleeping when she says this? ▲

Dormía.

4 In *Yo duermo muy bien* the Present does not describe an event which is going on when the statement is made. Unless Pilar is talking in her sleep "I sleep very well" cannot describe what she is doing when she says the sentence. The statement in either language describes what Pilar (a) plans to do (b) normally does when she goes to bed. ▲

no

normally does when she goes to bed

5 Can *I eat breakfast every morning* actually describe what the speaker is doing at the moment the statement is made? ▲

No (*Now* cannot be *every morning.*)

6 Does *I eat breakfast every morning* describe what the speaker regularly does every morning? ▲

7 One of the common uses of the Present in both English and Spanish is to describe an action which is customary, habitual, or frequently repeated. You can, for example, be walking on the campus when you say, *I watch television a lot.* Now, what you customarily do at the present time may be different from what you habitually did during some time in the past. In other words, what you regularly did in the past may be in contrast with what you are accustomed to doing in the present. Let's see how words tell us these facts.

yes

What does "I *used to eat* a lot of candy" mean? (a) I still eat a lot of candy. (b) I no longer eat so much candy. ▲

I no longer eat so much candy.

8 Look at these two statements: (1) He *works* in the mine. (2) He *used to work* in the mine. The verb form *works* describes what is customary now. The phrase *used to work* describes what was customary at some time in the _____. ▲

9 A customary action, like any single event, can have a beginning, a middle, and an end. What aspect is described by "He works in the mine?" (a) initiative (b) imperfective (c) terminative ▲

past

10 If *works* in *He works in the mine* describes imperfective aspect, then we can logically say that the form *works* is the Present Imperfect. In Spanish *Él trabaja en la mina* also describes the present imperfect aspect of a customary action. Which past tense form in Spanish will say the same thing about the past? (a) *trabajaba* (b) *trabajó* ▲

imperfective

11 English, as you know, has no Imperfect and, as a result, must use *used to* or *would* to make a contrast with the Present. Spanish has a Present Imperfect (*trabaja*) and a Past Imperfect (*trabajaba*) which contrast with each other, and thus does not need a special phrase to say *used to*. This is expressed by the form of the verb. Translate: They used to eat too much. ▲

trabajaba

Ellos comían demasiado.

12 English contrasts the Present Imperfect with the "used to" construction: "I *live* in Los Angeles now; I *used to live* in Bogotá." Spanish contrasts Present

Imperfect (*vivo*) with Past Imperfect (*vivía*) and gets exactly the same meaning.
Translate: He used to talk a lot. ▲

13 English has another way of talking about customary or habitual action in   *Él hablaba mucho.*
the past. Which one of these statements describes something that happened
regularly? (a) My father laughed when I said that. (b) My father would laugh
when I said that. ▲

My father would laugh when I said that.

14 Your intuition tells you when to use *would* and *used to* to describe customary
past action. You can use this same intuition in learning to talk Spanish because
used to and *would* (as used above) are regularly translated by the Imperfect.
What you must learn is that Spanish normally lets context show this difference.
As a result, the Spanish *Cuando éramos niños íbamos a las montañas con frecuencia*
translates both of these sentences: (a) When we were children, we *used to go*
to the mountains. (b) When we were children, we *would go* to the mountains.
You will, consequently, only have troubles when you translate from Spanish
to English. Which English sentence above can be used to imply that we no
longer go to the mountains? ▲

When we were children, we used to go to the mountains.

15 There are three very different uses of the Imperfect. The Imperfect is used
to state that some action was in progress at a point in the past. Translate: At
one o'clock I was reading. ▲

16 The Imperfect is used as the back-shift of the Present to describe planned   *A la una yo leía.*
action. So *Sé que ella va pronto* becomes *Sabía que ella* _____ *pronto.* ▲

17 The Imperfect is used for customary or habitual past action. The single   *iba*
translation of "He used to talk a lot" and "He would talk a lot" is _____. ▲

18 There are three English patterns which always cue the use of the Imperfect   *Él hablaba mucho.*
in Spanish: (1) *was* or *were* plus *ing* (he was talking), (2) *would*, and
(3) _____. ▲

19 There may be just one Spanish translation for these three statements: She   used to
was singing; She used to sing; She would sing. It is _____. ▲

20 Which translation of *cantar* will you use for *Ella cantaba cuando yo entré?* ▲   *Ella cantaba.*

21 Translate *Cuando ella estaba muy triste no cantaba* so that you put emphasis   was singing
on customary action. ▲

When she was very sad, she would not sing. (If this use of "would" is not in
your dialect, you might say, "She didn't use to sing.")

22 Translate the indicated part. You want to contrast the past with the present.
Hoy ella es muy vieja y no canta bien. Cuando era joven **cantaba muy bien.** ▲

she used to sing very well

23 English uses three constructions where Spanish uses only one. The context,
however, tells the Spanish speaker what meaning is intended. Let's see, once
more, how well you can "read" the context. Look at this statement: *Cada día
antes de ir a una clase especial mi perro ladraba mucho.* What is the most logical
translation of *ladraba*? (a) was barking (b) used to (would) bark ▲

used to (would) bark "Before going to a special class, my dog used to
(would) bark a lot." The choice between "used to" and "would" depends on
your dialect.

24 You have already learned that the Preterit may describe an action that began or ended at some point in the past. What aspect is described by *corrió* in *Se levantó y corrió?* (a) initiative (b) imperfective (c) terminative ▲

initiative (He got up and began to run.)

25 What aspect is described by *sentó* in *Él llegó a la playa y se sentó?* (a) initiative (b) imperfective (c) terminative ▲

terminative (He arrived at the beach and sat down.)

26 The Present may say that the action is going on at the moment a statement about it is made. In other words, "I am seeing" the mountains when I say *Veo las montañas.* The Preterit, in contrast, may say that the action is completed before the statement is made. So "I am not looking" at the mountains when I say *Vi las montañas.* (I saw the mountains.)

At the moment of speaking, the Present says the action is going on: *Pedro cierra la puerta.* At the same moment the Preterit says the action was already completed. Translate: Pedro closed the door. ▲

Pedro cerró la puerta. (Remember the stem is regular in the Preterit.)

27 The Preterit must also stand in contrast with the Imperfect. Look at these two statements: (a) *Ayer yo leía un libro.* (b) *Ayer yo leí un libro.* Which one says that you finished reading the book yesterday? ▲

28 *Yo leo un libro* says you have started but have not finished reading the book. *Ayer yo leí un libro.* You are in the process of reading it when you make the statement. *Yo leía un libro* describes what was going on at some time in the past. Does *Yo leía un libro* say that you have finished reading it? ▲

29 At the moment of speaking, *Yo leo* says the action is in progress. *Yo leía* says the action was in progress earlier, and *yo leí* says the action is already finished. Let's see, now, whether you can read the cues that tell you when to use the Preterit and Imperfect. Which form will you use to translate *went*? "Before we got our freezer, Mother *went* to the store every day." (a) *iba* (b) *fue* ▲

no

30 Keep in mind that Mother no longer goes to the store every day. You could, then, put *used to go* in place of *went*: "Before we got our freezer, Mother *used to go* to the store every day." Which form will you use to translate this *went*? "When mother was first married, she *went* to the store every day." (a) Preterit (b) Imperfect ▲

iba

Imperfect (She customarily went to the store every day.)

31 Which form will translate *went*? "Mother *went* to the store yesterday." (a) Preterit (b) Imperfect ▲

Preterit (The action is over and done with.)

32 In this and the remaining frames you will see a present tense form which has an irregular stem. This stem, however, is regular in both the Preterit and Imperfect. Write the regular stem of *vuel—ve.* ▲

33 me acuest—o, oig—o ▲

volv

acost, o (As in *oí* and *oía.*)

34 cierr—an, muev—es ▲

35 empiez—an, conozc—o ▲

cerr, mov

36 salg—o, vuel—a ▲

empez, conoc

sal, vol

You have now studied all the rules of usage of the Preterit and Imperfect. If you want to see them all in one place, turn to your Workbook. There you will find a complete summary and more examples.

Self-Correcting Exercises

A *Silent Reading*

Read the following selection as quickly as possible. Then check your comprehension by doing the true-false problems that follow.

El idioma español: preguntas y respuestas (primera parte)

1 ¿De dónde viene el español?
Viene del latín, la lengua que hablaban en la antigua Roma.
2 ¿Es esta la misma° Roma que vemos frecuentemente en las películas,° y en programas de televisión?   *same/movies, films*
Sí, más o menos. Hay películas que presentan la vida° de la antigua Roma con   *life*
bastante exactitud; por ejemplo, *Cleopatra*, *Ben Hur* y *Los últimos días de Pompeya*.
3 Roma tenía una civilización muy avanzada, ¿verdad?
Así es. Era la civilización más avanzada del mundo en ese tiempo. Los romanos llevaron su lengua y su cultura a muchas partes de Europa, Asia y África.
4 ¿Cuándo llegaron los romanos al territorio que hoy ocupan España y Portugal?
Las legiones de Roma invadieron la Península Hispánica en el año 218 antes de Jesucristo.
5 ¿Quién vivía en la Península antes de la invasión romana?
Vivían allí varias tribus primitivas, por ejemplo, los iberos, los celtas y los vascos. Todos hablaban lenguas diferentes.
6 ¿Estuvieron mucho tiempo los romanos en la Península Hispánica?
Sí. La dominación romana duró° varios siglos. En el año 409 grupos de bárbaros   *lasted*
germánicos entraron en la Península por el norte.
7 ¿Quién invadió el territorio hispánico por el sur?
Los árabes o moros° cruzaron el estrecho de Gibraltar en el año 711. Hablaban   *Moors*
la lengua árabe.
8 Entonces podemos decir que el idioma español y la cultura española son el   *mixture*
resultado de una gran mezcla,° ¿no es cierto?
Así es. Numerosas mezclas de lenguas y culturas en diferentes momentos de la historia.

If the statement is true, write *sí*; if it is false, write *no*.

1 El idioma español viene principalmente del ruso.   *no*
2 La antigua Roma tenía una civilización muy primitiva.   *no*
3 El cine y la televisión de nuestro tiempo nos dan (*give*) una idea aproximada de la vida en la antigua Roma.   *sí*
4 Las legiones de Roma llevaron su lengua y su gran sistema de administración a la Península.   *sí*

5 Las legiones de Roma entraron en la Península Hispánica en 1492.   no

6 Nadie vivía en la Península Hispánica cuando la invadieron las legiones   no
de Roma.

7 Las tribus primitivas de la Península Hispánica hablaban lenguas diferentes.   sí

8 Las tribus germánicas entraron en la Península por el sur.   no

9 Los bárbaros germánicos llegaron a Hispania antes que los árabes.   sí

10 El idioma español es el resultado de la mezcla del latín que hablaban en   sí
España con las lenguas nativas y las lenguas de los diferentes grupos que
vinieron (*came*) a la Península en diferentes momentos de la historia.

B *General Review:* Answer these questions mentally. Adapt the suggested
answers to your own particular situation.

1 ¿Te levantaste temprano hoy?	No, me levanté muy tarde.
2 ¿Te vestiste de prisa?	Sí, me vestí muy de prisa.
3 ¿Quién te despertó esta mañana?	Me despertó mi compañero de cuarto (mi reloj despertador, radio-reloj).
4 ¿Qué hacías antes de despertarte?	Dormía profundamente.
5 Anoche a las ocho y media, ¿estudiabas, o veías la televisión?	Veía la televisión y estudiaba.
6 ¿Llovía esta mañana cuando saliste del dormitorio?	No, no llovía; estaba nevando.

C *Translation:* ¿Cómo se dice en español . . . ?

1 soup, female monkey	*sopa, mona*
2 to lose, is lost	*perder, se pierde*
3 to get dressed, to get married	*vestirse, casarse*
4 although, silk, in a hurry	*aunque, seda, de prisa*
5 "Twixt the cup and the lip there's many a slip."	*"De la mano a la boca se pierde la sopa."*

New Vocabulary

sopa	soup	**decir**	to say, tell	**perder(se) (ie)**	to lose (get lost)
pregunta	question	**sentar(se) (ie)**	to seat (sit down)	**divertirse (ie)**	to have a good time
respuesta	answer				

Que se (te) divierta(s).   Have a good time (fun).

"De la mano a la boca se pierde la sopa."   "Don't count your chickens before they're hatched."

Because there is an official separation between the state and church in the United States, the members of all religious sects must collect the money to pay the salaries of their ministers, priests, and rabbis. In contrast, in Spain the priests are treated more like public servants and get their salaries from the government.

The contradiction of skyscrapers and slums in modern cities like Caracas is the result of mass migration to urban areas as rural economies collapse. Problems of noise and congestion, which are loathed in the U.S., are accepted in under-developed areas of Latin America as welcome signs of progress.

Two nearly universal forms of entertainment are movies and dancing. We may not realize that in many parts of the world people base their ideas of North America on the exaggerated images of Hollywood. The relaxed atmosphere of the discothèque allows an intimacy which is obviously being enjoyed. Courtship traditions have changed radically; not so long ago these couples would have been strictly supervised by chaperones.

There are many types of shops in the United States which sell only one class of items: shoes, dresses, hats, lampshades, etc. It is hard, however, to find a drugstore that sells only drugs, a grocery store that sells nothing but food, or a fruit shop that sells only one kind of fruit. In the Hispanic world the shops and stalls in the markets tend to be more specialized. Drugstores tend to sell only drugs, a hat shop may sell only one type of hat, and in the public markets each stall keeper usually sells only one type of item. This is especially true in the sidewalk markets because the sales person is often the one who has produced the item being sold.

Assignment 52

The Present of decir

1 The Present of *decir* has only one completely regular form. It is *nosotros decimos*. In all the other forms the *e* of the stem changes to *i*. In the *yo* form, the [k] sound of *c* voices and becomes [g]. The suffixes are regular, so the *yo* form is _____. ▲

digo

2 The stem is *dic* in all the other forms. Write the forms that match *tú, usted, ustedes*. ▲

Tú dices; usted dice, ustedes dicen

3 *Decir* has three common translations: (1) to say, (2) to tell, and less commonly, (3) to speak. What is the translation of *dice* in *Papá dice que no tiene hambre?* ▲

4 What is the translation of *decir* in *¿No va a decir la verdad?* ▲

says

to tell (or to speak)

Spelling Review

1 You can spell a word by ear whenever each sound in it is always represented by just one letter. Can you spell [luna] by ear? ▲

2 You hear [selba] but you write _____. ▲

yes

3 You hear [kaye] but you write _____. ▲

selva

4 Say *ciento* (100) and *siento* (I feel regret) aloud. Do they sound exactly alike? ▲

calle

yes (You have to see *ciento* and *siento* and know their meaning to spell each

5 When you use spelling rules as a help, you can spell a lot more words by ear. The preterit form [mastiké] is written _____. ▲

word correctly.)

6 [k] is written *qu* before the two vowels _____. ▲

mastiqué

7 Say *lección* aloud. Which *c* stands for [k]? (a) the first (b) the second ▲

e; i

8 Here is a new spelling rule: the *c* cannot stand for [s] when it ends a syllable or comes before another consonant. Write the word for a piece of land that is entirely surrounded by water. ▲

the first

9 Transcribe in regular spelling: [akabar]. ▲

isla

10 The letter *c* always stands for the sound [k] before the three vowels _____. ▲

acabar

a, o, u (*c*alle, po*c*o, se*c*undaria)

11 What letter do you have to see in *edificio* and *espacio* before you can spell these words? ▲

c (You can write *c, s,* or *z* before *i.*)

12 There are two letters in *habitante* which you have to see before you can spell the word. They are _____. ▲

h; b

13 Since *h* can come before any vowel, you have to see every word that begins with a vowel sound before you learn how to spell it. Here are all the words you have had that begin with an *h*. For the time being, you can memorize these and remember that all other words beginning with a vowel sound have no *h*.

haber (hay)	hacer	hasta	hora	himno
habitante	hambre	hola	héroe	historia
hablar	hallar	hombre		

14 Translate: fog. ▲

> *niebla* (You never write a *v* before another consonant in Spanish.)

15 The *yo* form of the Preterit of *buscar* is _____. ▲

16 The *yo* form of the Preterit of *empezar* is _____. ▲

> *busqué*

17 The *g* has the same sound as *j* before *e* or *i*. So to keep the sound [g], the *yo* form of the Preterit of *llegar* and *jugar* must be written _____. ▲

> *empecé*

18 Which word in this set must you see before you can spell it: *cometa, perro, mundo, olvidar, aprender, lago?* ▲

> *llegué; jugué*

> *olvidar* (After a consonant Spanish may write either *b* or *v*.)

19 You hear the following. What do you write: [Yo yegué kom poka ambre.]? ▲

> *Yo llegué con poca hambre.*

The Preterit of venir *and* hacer

It is a law of language that an irregular form cannot survive unless it is used a great deal. As a result, the most irregular verbs are always the most common. This is fortunate because you will use these verbs often enough to learn their irregularities by sheer repetition.

1 The verb *venir* has two irregularities in the Present. The *yo* form is _____. ▲

2 When the stem vowel *e* is stressed in all other forms, it changes to _____. ▲

> *vengo*

> *ie (vienes, viene, vienen)*

3 The Preterit of *venir* has three irregularities: (1) The stem of all forms is *vin*. (2) The first suffix of the *yo* form is *e*. (3) The first suffix of the *usted, él,* and *ella* form is *o*. Write the *yo* form. Write the *usted* form. ▲

4 The first and second suffixes of all the other forms are regular. Write the forms that match *tú, nosotros,* and *ellos.* ▲

> *vine, vino*

> *tú viniste; nosotros vinimos, ellos vinieron*

5 The Present of *hacer* has one irregularity. The *yo* form is _____. ▲

6 The first and second suffixes of the Preterit of *hacer* are the same as for *venir*. The first suffix of the *yo* form is _____, of the *usted* form is _____. ▲

> *hago*

7 The spoken stem for all forms is [is]. Do you have to see *usted hizo* in order to know that [s] is written as *z*? ▲

> *e, o*

> yes (It could be *s*, but not *c* because *c* before *o* (*hico*) would stand for [k].)

8 In all the other forms, the stem is written *hic*. To get the *yo* form you add the irregular first suffix _____ to *hic*. ▲

> *e* (Say *yo hice* aloud.)

9 To get the *él, ella, usted* form you add *o* to _____. ▲

hiz (All other stems are spelled *hic*.)

10 The suffixes for all other forms are regular. Write the forms that match *tú*, *nosotros*, and *ellos*. ▲

hiciste, hicimos, hicieron

Present of dar, traer, and conocer

1 You already know the forms of the Present of *ir*. The form that goes with *yo* is _____. ▲

2 All the other forms take the first suffix of regular *a*-verbs. The forms that go with *usted* and *ustedes* are _____. ▲

voy

3 The present tense forms of *dar* (to give) are exactly like those for *ir*. You just put *d* in place of *v*. So the form of *dar* that goes with *yo* is _____. ▲

va; van

4 The forms that match *nosotros* and *tú* are _____. ▲

doy

5 The forms that go with *él* and *ellos* are _____. ▲

damos, das

6 The verbs *traer* (to bring, fetch) and *caer* (to fall) have just one irregularity. The *yo* forms are *traigo* and *caigo*. All other forms are regular. The forms of *traer* that go with *tú* and *nosotros* are _____. ▲

da, dan

7 The equivalent forms of *caer* are _____. ▲

traes, traemos

8 The *ustedes* form of *traer* is _____. ▲

caes, caemos

9 To make *traen* match *usted* you drop _____. ▲

traen

10 Write the *yo* form of *traer* and *caer*: _____. ▲

n

11 The *yo* form of *dar* is _____. ▲

traigo, caigo

12 *Conocer* ("to know," in the sense of "to be acquainted with") like *dar, traer*, and *caer*, has only one irregular form in the present. The *yo* form is *conozco*. The form that goes with *él* is _____. ▲

doy

conoce (The verb *traducir* (to translate) has the same irregularity as *conocer*: *traduzco*.)

The Preterit of ir, decir, and ser

1 When Latin was becoming Spanish, the forms for "to be" (*ser*) and "to go" (*ir*) became confused; as a result, the Preterit of *ser* and *ir* have exactly the same forms. The meaning, consequently, can only be determined by context. Translate: *¿A dónde fue usted ayer?* ▲

Where did you go yesterday? (The *A dónde* cues motion.)

2 Translate: *La lección fue interesante.* ▲

The lesson was interesting.

3 The plural of *fue* is *fueron*, which translates either "were" or "went." Translate: *Mis padres fueron al teatro ayer.* The cue for choice is the *a* of *al teatro*. ▲

My parents went to the theater yesterday.

4 Translate: *Mis abuelos fueron muy amables.* ▲

My grandparents were very kind (nice).

5 All the other preterit forms of *ser* and *ir* have *i* as the first suffix. The second suffix is regular. The form that matches *yo* is _____. ▲

6 Write the *tú* and *nosotros* forms. ▲

fui

7 The Preterit of *decir* has two irregularities. First, the stem for all forms is *dij*. Second, the first suffix forms are like those of *venir*. The *yo* form of *venir* is *vine*. The *yo* form of *decir* is _____. ▲

fuiste, fuimos

8 The *usted* form of *venir* is *vino*. The *usted* form of *decir* is _____. ▲

dije

9 The *tú* form of *venir* has regular suffixes. Write the *tú* form of *venir* and *decir*. ▲

dijo

10 Change *dijiste* so it matches *nosotros*. ▲

viniste, dijiste

11 The *ustedes* and *ellos* form of *venir* is *vinieron*. The *j* of the stem *dij* absorbs the *i* of the first suffix and the resulting form is _____. ▲

dijimos

dijeron

Review of Stem-Changing Verbs

1 You already know that the easiest way to learn and remember stem-changing verbs is to study them by sets. One set is made up of *a-* and *e-*verbs which have either an *e* or an *o* in the stem. When the stem is stressed, these vowels may change to _____. ▲

2 Write the present tense *yo* forms for *cerrar* and *perder*. ▲

ie; ue

3 Write the present tense *usted* forms for *acostar* and *morder*. ▲

cierro; pierdo

4 The *nosotros* forms of this set of verbs always have the stress on the first suffix, not the stem, and they are, consequently, regular. Write the present tense *nosotros* forms for *volver* and *contar*. ▲

acuesta; muerde

volvemos; contamos

5 The members of this set which you have had so far are: *e > ie: perder, despertar, cerrar, sentar, pensar, empezar, tropezar, quebrar   o > ue: recordar, acostar, contar, volver, morder, mover, jugar, encontrar*
In the Preterit of all of these verbs, the stress falls on the first suffix, not on the stem, and, as a result, all forms are regular. Write the *yo* forms for *perder* and *contar*. ▲

6 There is a set of *i*-verbs which have an *e* and an *o* in the stem which also change to *ie* and *ue*. You have had four of these verbs: *divertir, sentir, dormir,* and *morir*. Write the present tense *él* forms for all four. ▲

perdí; conté

divierte, siente, duerme, muere

7 All members of this set have a special irregularity in the *él* and *ellos* forms of the Preterit. The *e* of the stem changes to *i* and the *o* changes to *u*. Translate: They regretted (*sentir*). ▲

8 Change *sintieron* so it matches *usted* or *él*. ▲

Ellos sintieron.

9 Change *sintió* so it matches *yo*. ▲

sintió

10 To make *sentí* agree with *tú* and *nosotros* you add _____ and drop the accent mark. Translate: He slept (*dormir*). ▲

sentí

ste, mos (sentiste, sentimos); Él durmió.

11 Change *durmió* so it matches *ustedes* or *ellos*. ▲

durmieron

12 The *yo* form of the Preterit of *dormir* is regular. To make it you drop the *r* of *dormir* and stress the syllable (a) *dor* (b) *mi*. ▲

mi (So you must write this form *dormí*.)

13 Change *divierten* and *duermen* to the Preterit. ▲

divirtieron; durmieron

14 There is a set of *i*-verbs in which the *e* of the stem changes to *i*. This happens in the Present when the stem is stressed and in the Preterit when the first suffix has a diphthong (*ió* or *ie*). You have had five verbs of this set. They are: *pedir, despedir, servir, medir,* and *seguir*. Write the present tense *usted* forms for *pedir* and *servir*. ▲

15 The stem of *pide* and *sirve* is the same for their preterit forms. You just   *pide; sirve* change the suffix to _____. ▲

16 Change *pidió* and *sirvió* so they match *ustedes*. ▲   *ió* (*pidió, sirvió*)

17 In the Present of this set of verbs, only the *nosotros* forms are regular. Write   *pidieron; sirvieron* these forms for *despedir* and *seguir*. ▲

despedimos; seguimos

18 The *nosotros* forms of the Preterit are exactly the same as the Present. Write these forms for *pedir* and *servir*. ▲

pedimos; servimos (You can get the meaning only from context.)

19 The *yo, nosotros,* and *tú* forms of the Preterit are regular. To get the *yo* forms of *pedimos* and *servimos* you drop the *mos* and stress the final syllable. Write these forms. ▲

20 The present tense *yo* form of *seguir* has a spelling change. It is written   *pedí; serví* _____. ▲

21 The verbs *tener, venir,* and *decir* belong to a special set of irregular verbs.   *sigo* Their *yo* forms in the Present are _____. ▲

22 In the Present, the other forms of *tener* and *venir* are like *perder*. The *e* changes   *tengo, vengo, digo* to *ie* when the stem is stressed. Change *tenemos* and *venimos* so they match *ustedes*. ▲

tienen; vienen

Review of Reflexive Constructions

1 The done-to forms that match *yo, nosotros* and *tú* are _____. ▲

2 The done-to forms *me, nos,* and *te* are also used in reflexive constructions.   *me, nos,* and *te* Translate: I wash myself. ▲

3 Translate: We go to bed early. Translate: You (*tú*) sit down. ▲   *Yo me lavo.*
Nos acostamos temprano. Tú te sientas.

4 The reflexive pronoun and done-to form that matches *usted, ustedes, él, ella, ellos,* and *ellas* is _____. ▲

5 Translate: They have breakfast at seven o'clock. (The verb is *desayunar*.) ▲   *se*
Ellos se desayunan a las siete.

6 Rewrite the above sentence with *usted* as the subject. ▲

Usted se desayuna a las siete.

7 When the done-to pronoun is used with an infinitive it (a) comes before the infinitive (b) is attached to the end of the infinitive. ▲

is attached to the end of the infinitive

8 Copy and fill in the proper done-to pronoun. *No queremos dormir* _____ *ahora.* ▲

No queremos dormirnos ahora.

9 Translate: *No queremos dormirnos ahora.* ▲

We don't want to go to sleep now.

10 When the done-to pronoun is used with a conjugated (finite) form of the verb, it goes (a) in front of the verb (b) after the verb. ▲

11 Translate: She goes to bed late. ▲

in front of the verb
Ella se acuesta tarde.

The vast majority of the Hispanic peoples (about 97 per cent) are members of the Catholic church, which prohibits divorce. In some of the countries, divorce is illegal. As a result, when a man takes a wife (*esposa*), he is tied to her for life. Spanish speakers have a wry humor and they have made a linguistic joke out of the situation. One word for *handcuffs* is *las esposas* (= literally *the wives*).

Self-Correcting Exercises

A *Silent Reading:* After reading the following questions and answers about the Spanish language, do the comprehension exercise.

El idioma español: preguntas y respuestas (segunda parte)

1 ¿Por qué dicen que el español es una lengua romance?
Simplemente porque tiene su origen en la lengua de Roma, de los romanos. No quiere decir que el español es una lengua "romántica."
2 ¿Es el inglés una lengua romance?
No. El inglés es una lengua germánica. El portugués, el francés y el italiano son lenguas romances.
3 ¿Qué quiere decir la palabra *España*?
Hay varias interpretaciones. Algunos creen que significa "tierra de conejos."°   rabbits
Otros dicen que viene de la palabra *span* que quiere decir "llanura."
4 Otro nombre del idioma que estudiamos es *castellano*, ¿verdad?
Exactamente. El castellano era un dialecto romance que se hablaba solamente en la región de Castilla. En el siglo quince pasó a ser el idioma oficial de todas las provincias.
5 ¿Qué significa la palabra *Castilla*?
Castilla, el nombre de una de las regiones más importantes en la historia de la Península, quiere decir "tierra de castillos."°   castles
6 ¿Podemos usar los dos nombres, *castellano* y *español*, para hablar del idioma que estudiamos?

Sí, cómo no. Hoy día, sin embargo,° el nombre más apropiado es *español*.   nevertheless
En muchos países de América prefieren *castellano*.
7   ¿Qué lugar ocupa el español entre los idiomas del mundo?
Ocupa uno de los primeros lugares. Aproximadamente 500 millones de personas hablan chino; 300 millones hablan inglés y 180 millones hablan ruso. El español lo hablan más de 170 millones de personas.

Write *sí*, if the statement is true; and *no*, if it is false.

1   El español es una lengua muy "bonita" y "musical" y por eso decimos que   no
es una lengua "romance."
2   El inglés es una lengua germánica.   sí
3   El francés y el italiano son lenguas germánicas.   no
4   Cuando hablamos de lenguas "romances," la palabra *romance* se refiere   sí
a Roma.
5   Algunos investigadores asocian el origen de las palabras *español* y *España*   no
con los elefantes.
6   El idioma que estudiamos tiene dos nombres principales.   sí
7   El idioma que hablaban en Castilla se llamaba *castellano*.   sí
8   La palabra *Castilla* significa "tierra de conejos."   no
9   Entre los idiomas del mundo el español ocupa el último lugar.   no
10 El número de personas que hablan chino hoy día es insignificante.   no

B   *Fórmulas de cortesía:* Cover the answers and say the Spanish equivalent aloud. Assume that you are addressing a close friend.

Make yourself at home.	*Estás en tu casa.*
Forgive me.	*Perdóname.*
Have a good time.	*Que te diviertas.*
Don't bother.	*No te molestes.*
It's no bother.	*No es molestia ninguna.*
Please return soon.	*Hazme el favor de volver pronto.*

C   *Irregular Preterits:* Write the combinations.

Ejemplo 112: Hilda y yo nos divertimos en la playa.

1	Hilda y yo	1	divertirse en		
2	Tú	2	venir de	1	la fiesta.
3	Las monas	3	hacer esto en	2	la playa.
4	Usted	4	dormir en	3	(e)l cine.
5	Yo	5	oír la música en		

1) 111   Hilda y yo nos divertimos en la fiesta.
2) 552   Yo oí la música en la playa.
3) 452   Usted oyó la música en la playa.
4) 223   Tú viniste del cine.
5) 313   Las monas se divirtieron en el cine.

6) 432

7) 333

8) 342

9) 531

10) 441

Usted hizo esto en la playa.

Las monas hicieron esto en el cine.

Las monas durmieron en la playa.

Yo hice esto en la fiesta.

Usted durmió en la fiesta.

The population explosion in the United States has led to the creation of whole new towns and vast new suburbs. In all these new places the members of the different religious sects have built new churches. A very great many of these new churches are modernistic or even futuristic in design. In Latin America, however, the people built so many churches in the seventeenth, eighteenth, and nineteenth centuries that there has been almost no need to build new ones. In the small town of Cholula, Mexico, for example, there are over 200 churches. Almost all the churches in Latin America are old and were designed to imitate the architecture of the Middle Ages and the Renaissance. The new city suburbs, in contrast with the United States, have many modernistic homes which are often more artistically designed than those in this country. As a result, many Latins feel that even the homes of the very rich in the United States are often rather dull and uninteresting.

Assignment 53

Review of Intonation

1 English can have very long syllables when they are stressed. Say aloud very emphatically "He's a *bad* boy!" In contrast, Spanish long syllables are only about twice as long as the short syllables. To overcome your English habit of saying very long and short syllables, try to make most Spanish syllables about the same length. Say this question aloud: *¿Es una pregunta muy importante?*

2 The second important feature of intonation is stress. How many syllables are stressed in the English word "investigation?" ▲

3 How many syllables are stressed in the Spanish word *investigación?* ▲

two

one (With only minor exceptions, which you will learn later, Spanish words have only one stressed syllable.)

4 The single stress on *electricidad* falls on *dad*. Say: *e-lec-tri-ci-dad*.

5 Say "combination." Now say *combinación* with only one stressed syllable.

6 What kind of a question is "Are you ready?" (a) yes-no (b) information ▲

7 What happens to the pitch level when you say *¿Está usted listo?* At the end of the question, the pitch (a) goes up (b) goes down. ▲

yes-no

goes up (The pitch goes up at the end of yes-no questions in both English

8 What kind of a question is *¿Cuántos años tiene usted?* (a) yes-no (b) information ▲

and Spanish.)

9 At the end of an information question, the pitch (a) goes up (b) goes down. ▲

information

goes down (in both languages)

Review of the Present of Irregular Verbs

Of the thousands of verbs in the Spanish language, there are less than 500 which are irregular. Almost all of these irregular verbs, however, are very common words which have to be learned at the beginning of any Spanish course. Many students get the impression that the majority of Spanish verbs are irregular and that the language is hard to learn. This is not true. You have already met an example of most of the sets of irregular verbs, and from now on, all you have to remember is that a new verb is like one you already know. You already know, for example, the irregular forms of *cerrar*. Now you meet *perder* (to lose) and learn that it has the same irregularities as *cerrar*. This is all the new information you need to make up the forms of *perder*.

1 The *yo* form is going to be _____. ▲

pierdo (Latin *e* in Spanish sometimes changes to *ie* under stress.)

2 The *usted* form is _____. ▲

pierde

3 Change *pierde* so it matches *tú* and *ellos.* ▲

tú pierdes; ellos pierden

4 There is one form in which the stress does not fall on the stem: _____. ▲

5 This change may happen in *a-, e-,* or *i-*verbs. So the following seven verbs *perdemos* are like *cerrar* in the Present: *querer, sentir, divertir, sentar, despertar, empezar,* and *pensar.* Write the *nosotros* form for *querer, sentir,* and *sentar.* ▲

queremos, sentimos, sentamos

6 The stem of *despertar* has two *e*'s in it. Only the stressed *e* changes to *ie.* The *yo* form is _____. ▲

7 The *yo* form of *empezar* is _____. Write the *tú* form of *pensar* and *querer.* ▲ *despierto*

empiezo; tú piensas, quieres

8 The verbs *tener* and *venir* have an *e* in the stem which changes to *ie,* but they also have another irregularity. The *yo* forms of *tener* and *venir* are _____. ▲

tengo, vengo (The *e* is stressed but no change takes place.)

9 The Latin *o* when stressed in Spanish sometimes changes to *ue.* Use *contar* as the model. The *yo* and the *nosotros* forms are _____. ▲

yo cuento, nosotros contamos

10 Here are all the other verbs you have had which are like *contar* in the Present: *poder, volver, recordar, morder, morir, dormir, acostar.* Write the *nosotros* form of *poder, dormir,* and *recordar.* ▲

podemos, dormimos, recordamos

11 Write the *tú* form of *contar, morder,* and *poder.* ▲

cuentas, muerdes, puedes

12 The old infinitive of *jugar* was *jogar.* This old stem is the base for the modern present tense forms having *ue.* The *yo* form, consequently, of *jugar* is _____. ▲

juego (So you add *jugar* to the set of verbs whose forms are like *contar.*)

13 Old Latin *e* sometimes became *i* when stressed in Spanish. This happens, however, only in verbs of the *i-*set. Use *pedir* as the model. The *yo* form is _____. ▲

14 The *e* does not change to *i* in the *nosotros* form _____. ▲ *pido*

15 The *usted* and *ustedes* forms are _____. ▲ *pedimos*

16 The verbs *servir, vestir, seguir,* and *medir* belong to the same set as *pedir.* The *pide, piden* *yo* forms of *servir* and *medir* are _____. Write the *yo* form of *seguir.* ▲

17 Change *sigo* so it matches *él.* The *nosotros* form is _____. ▲ *sirvo; mido; sigo*

18 Verbs which end in a vowel plus either *cer* or *cir* have just one irregularity in *sigue; seguimos* the Present. The *yo* form of *conocer* is *conozco.* The *yo* form of *traducir* is _____. ▲

19 The verbs *hacer, traer, caer, salir,* and *saber* have only an irregular *yo* form *traduzco* in the Present. The *usted* forms are *hace, trae, cae, sale,* and *sabe.* Change these to the *yo* forms. ▲

hago, traigo, caigo, salgo, sé (The written accent over *sé* shows it is not the reflexive form *se.*)

20 Some of the most commonly used verbs have irregularities which are peculiarly their own. The *yo* forms of *estar, ir, ser,* and *dar* are _____. ▲

estoy, voy, soy, doy

21 Although *ir* is an *i-*verb, all its other present tense forms take the regular *a-*verb suffixes. The forms for *tú* and *ustedes* are _____. ▲

vas, van

22 When a verb form like *habla* or *llama* ends in a vowel, the stress falls on the first syllable. *Estar* is an exception, since the stress falls on the first suffix. You write *él* _____. ▲

23 The verb *oír* has two irregularities in the Present. The *yo* form is *oigo*. The stem of all the other forms is *oy*. Add the suffixes that go with *ustedes* and *ellos*. ▲

24 The verb *decir* has two irregularities in the Present. The *yo* form is _____. ▲

25 All the other forms are like *pedir*. Write the *tú* form of *decir*. ▲

26 The present tense stem of the *yo* form of *ver* comes from the old form *veer*. The *yo* form is _____. ▲

está

oyen

digo

dices

veo

Review of ser *and* estar *with Predicate Adjectives*

1 What is your norm for deserts? (a) wet (b) dry ▲

2 When a predicate adjective gives the norm for the subject, you use (a) *ser* (b) *estar*. ▲

dry

ser (*Los desiertos* **son** *secos.*)

3 Which verb will you use to translate "Steel is stronger than iron"? (a) *ser* (b) *estar* ▲

ser (Steel, by its nature, is normally stronger than iron.)

4 It happens, sometimes, that things change or in some way are different from the norm. Something may, for example, go wrong in the manufacturing process and a batch of steel turns out to be soft, not hard. Which verb will you use to say, "This steel *is* soft"? ▲

5 It is not normal for people to be sick. So you say a person happens to be sick with _____. ▲

estar

estar (Pedro está enfermo.)

6 Each person has private norms for many things. Your norm for the color of grass is probably green. In some places there is a grass which is red. You are surprised to see it. You exclaim, "That grass is red!" Which verb do you use? ▲

7 You have now learned that *red* can also be the norm for grass in some places. You report this fact by saying, "In that place the grass is red." Which verb do you use? ▲

estar

ser

Review of Usage: venir *versus* ir

1 English uses *to come* (1) to describe movement toward the speaker (I see him *coming* now.) and (2) to describe movement toward the first speaker when a second speaker answers a question (Are you *coming*? Yes, I'm *coming*.) Spanish, in contrast, always uses the point of view of the speaker. In other words, you cannot *come* to where you are not, you can only *go* there. So someone knocks at your door. You are in the kitchen. You call out (a) *Ya vengo.* (b) *Ya voy.* ▲

> *Ya voy.* (Literally "I am already going"; you are moving away from where you were toward the door. You are, in fact, "going" to the door.)

2   Except for the differences in usage just described, Spanish uses *ir* and *venir* very much as English uses "to go" and "to come." Which verb will you use to translate "Do you want *to come* with me to the movies?" ▲

3   Which verb will you use to translate "Do you want *to go* to the movies with me?" ▲   *venir*

4   Which verb will you use in this situation? "I can't *come* to your place today." (a) *ir* (b) *venir* ▲   *ir*

> *ir* (You move away from where you are toward the other person.)

5   You tell someone, "*Come* here right away." (a) *ir* (b) *venir* ▲

6   This person answers, "I'm coming." (a) *ir* (b) *venir* ▲   *venir*

                                                                                ir

The Preterit and the Imperfect: A Review of Usage

1   The Preterit and Imperfect have two major functions. From one point of view these forms describe events which are over or completed at the moment of speaking. *Juan se desayuna* tells what Juan is doing as the speaker says the sentence. *Juan se desayunó* tells you the action was finished before the sentence is said.

Let's look at this another way. Compare these two sentences: (1) *Mamá dice que Juan se desayuna.* (2) *Mamá dice que Juan se desayunó.* Are *dice* and *desayuna* going on at the same time? ▲

> yes (The act of speaking (*dice*) is simultaneous with the act of breakfasting

2   Are *dice* and *desayunó* going on at the same time? ▲   (*desayuna*).)

> no (The form *desayunó* says that breakfasting was finished before the act

3   This use of the Preterit is just like that of the Simple Past in English. Compare: (1) Mother says that Juan *is eating* breakfast. (2) Mother says that Juan *ate* breakfast. Translate: I know (*saber*) that she bought the hat. ▲   of speaking.)

> (*Yo*) *sé que ella compró el sombrero.*

4   Translate: Where's Carmen? She is going to the beach. ▲

> *¿Dónde está Carmen? Va a la playa.*

5   Now translate this answer: She went to the beach. ▲

6   From the point of view of the moment of speaking, the Preterit, like the   *Fue a la playa.* simple past in English, may say the action has been completed. Translate: I lost the money. ▲

> *Perdí el dinero.*

7   When a habitual or customary past action is contrasted with a different but also customary present action both English and Spanish use the Present for the present action. English employs "used to" for the contrasting past action. "He used to go to bed early, now he goes to bed late." Spanish uses the Present to translate "now he goes to bed late." *ahora se acuesta tarde.* Which form do you use to translate "He used to go to bed early?" (a) *se acostó* (b) *se acostaba* ▲

se acostaba (The "used to" construction always cues the use of the Imperfect

8 Translate: We used to live in San Diego. Now we live in San Rafael. ▲   in Spanish.)

Vivíamos en San Diego. Ahora vivimos en San Rafael. (The Past Imperfect *vivíamos* stands in contrast with the Present Imperfect *vivimos*.)

9 The major contrast between the Preterit and Imperfect shows up when you talk about events which happen at some point in the past. At a point in the past an event may begin, be going on, or come to an end. The technical terms for these three aspects are *initiative*, *imperfective*, and *terminative*. The on-going or imperfective aspect of any event is always described by the (a) Preterit (b) Imperfect. ▲

10 To state that a cyclic event was terminated at any point in the past you use   Imperfect the _____. ▲

11 What forms of the indicated infinitives will you use to make these actions   Preterit past tense? *Cuando yo **llegar** a la escuela **hacer** mucho calor.* ▲

*Cuando yo **llegué** a la escuela, **hacía** mucho calor.*

12 To say that a non-cyclic event began in the past you use the _____. ▲

13 Rewrite this in the past tense: *Él se levanta y corre.* ▲   Preterit

Él se levantó y corrió. (The real meaning is "He got up and *began* to run.")

14 Here is another way of saying all this: you use the Imperfect to talk about the middle of an event and the Preterit to describe either end. In this and the next four frames change the indicated infinitives to the proper form of the Preterit or Imperfect.

Cuando Sabino llegar a la tienda descubrir que no tener dinero. ▲

*Cuando Sabino **llegó** a la tienda **descubrió** que no **tenía** dinero.*

15 *Sabino estar triste porque querer comprar una camisa.* ▲

*Sabino **estaba** triste porque **quería** comprar una camisa.*

16 *Volver Sabino a casa pero su mamá no estar allí.* ▲

***Volvió** Sabino a casa pero su mamá no **estaba** allí.*

17 *Se quitar el sombrero y se sentar a esperar (wait for) a su mamá.* ▲

*Se **quitó** el sombrero y se **sentó** a esperar a su mamá.*

18 De repente (*suddenly*) su perro *ladrar. Haber* un señor a la puerta. ▲

*De repente su perro **ladró**. **Había** un señor a la puerta.*

19 Here is a true story to see if you can figure out when to use the Preterit or Imperfect. For each frame write *P* or *I* to indicate your choice for the indicated verbs.

In 1940 a Mexican farmer named Dionisio Pulido *was working* in his field. ▲

20 He suddenly *observed* that his plow animals *were behaving* in a strange way. ▲   I

21 He *walked up* to them, *bent over*, and *touched* the ground. ▲   P, I

22 The ground *was* very hot and as he *stood* there some smoke suddenly *came*   P, P, P *out* of the soil. ▲

23 Señor Pulido *did* not *know* what *was happening*. ▲   I, I, P

24 He *left* the field because he *was* afraid. ▲   I, I

25 In a few hours flames *shot up* from his field and huge clouds of smoke and   P, I ashes *burst* from the ground. ▲

26 Señor Pulido *did* not *understand* all this. He *did* not *know* that he *was watching*   P, P a volcano being born. ▲

I, I, I

27 The volcano soon *covered* his whole farm and in a few weeks it *grew* to be several hundred feet high. ▲

28 The whole country *was* excited, and scientists *came* from all over the world to watch the volcano grow. ▲   P, P

29 When they *arrived*, the fields for miles around *were* covered with ashes and dust. ▲   I, P

30 At that time the volcano *had* no name. Finally someone *gave* it the name it still has today. It is called Paricutín. ▲   P, I

31 There remain, now, two uses of the Imperfect which you need to remember. For some speakers of English *would* may be used as a very close equivalent of *used to*. For example, "When we were living in Chile we *would go* to the beach every day." If this form is in your dialect, you will translate "would go" as (a) *íbamos* (b) *fuimos* ▲   I, P

32 The Imperfect is used in telling time. Translate the two verbs: It was eight o'clock when we arrived at the movies. ▲   *íbamos*

Eran las ocho cuando llegamos al cine.

33 The translation of *Ella dice que va* is "She says she is going." The past tense back-shift of "She says she is going" is _____. ▲

She said she was going.

34 The back-shift of *Ella dice que va* is *Ella dijo que* (a) *fue* (b) *iba*. ▲

iba (Recalled planned action is described with the Imperfect.)

Summary

1 From the point of view of the moment of speaking, the Preterit says that the beginning or end of an event is over or completed before you say the sentence. So *Él se murió* says the event came to an end before now and *Yo lo conocí* says our acquaintanceship began before now.

2 When you are recalling some point in the past, the Preterit says either that a cyclic event terminated at that point (*Yo llegué a casa a la una*) or that a non-cyclic event began at that point (*A la una oí el ruido* (noise)).

3 At this same recalled point the Imperfect says the action was going on (*Llovía cuando llegué a casa*). The Imperfect says the same thing about either a cyclic or non-cyclic event (*Se moría cuando llegué a casa*).

4 From the point of view of the present time, the Imperfect is used to say that what once was customary or habitual stands in contrast with what is currently customary or habitual. The most common translation of this use of the Imperfect is "used to" plus the main verb: "I used to live in St. Louis but now I live in Los Angeles." *Vivía en San Luis pero ahora vivo en Los Ángeles.*

5 The Imperfect is used in telling time: *¿Qué hora era? Eran las tres.*

6 In Spanish the Simple Present is used to talk about planned future action: *Dicen que se casan en una semana.* The backshift of this use of the Present is the Imperfect: *Dijeron que se casaban en una semana.*

There is a very strong tradition in the United States that when a person dies and is buried his grave must never be disturbed. Today when one buys a lot in a modern cemetery one also pays for what is called perpetual care. This means, in theory at least, that the grave site will be kept neat, clean, and undisturbed forever. This tradition does not exist in Latin America. The members of a deceased person's family must continue to pay to take care of the grave. If the payments are not made the bones of the dead person are often dug up and someone else is buried in the grave.

Self-Correcting Exercises

A *Preterit Forms:* Write the appropriate preterit form of each infinitive.

1	El pobre viejo (morir).	*murió*
2	Yo (venir) después que ella.	*vine*
3	Ellos no (sentir) nada.	*sintieron*
4	Usted lo (hacer) también, ¿verdad?	*hizo*
5	Creo que yo me (dormir) a las nueve más o menos.	*dormí*
6	¿Cuándo se (dormir) ustedes?	*durmieron*
7	¿(Oír) ustedes el tigre en el corral?	*Oyeron*
8	No, nosotros no (oír) absolutamente nada.	*oímos*
9	¿Qué (hacer) tú ayer?	*hiciste*
10	Te digo verdaderamente que yo no (hacer) nada.	*hice*

B *Preterit versus Imperfect:* Change all the indicated verbs to the past tense, either Preterit or Imperfect. After writing each verb, check the answer on the right before doing the next one.

El oro (*gold*) de Culúa

Durante los primeros años del siglo XVI (dieciséis), miles de emigrantes españoles *vienen* **1** a organizar colonias en las islas de Santo Domingo y Cuba. Aunque *tienen* **2** tierras fértiles en abundancia y esclavos (*slaves*) indios para cultivar los campos y trabajar en las minas, muchos de los nuevos habitantes no *están* **3** contentos con ese tipo de vida (*life*). Además (*Furthermore*), el clima de las islas y los mosquitos les *molestan* **4** mucho. Por muchas razones no se *sienten* **5** satisfechos. La mayoría (*majority*) de ellos *son* **6** hombres de acción. El deseo de obtener gloria y riquezas (*riches*) y su gran espíritu aventurero *demandan* **7** otra cosa—nuevos descubrimientos, más viajes de exploración y la conquista (*conquest*) de nuevos territorios. No *pueden* **8** vivir en paz porque constantemente *oyen* **9** hablar a los indios de grandes y ricas ciudades donde *hay* **10** gran abundancia de oro, plata (*silver*) y piedras (*stones*) preciosas.

En 1517 Francisco Hernández de Córdoba, un español residente en Cuba, *hace* **11** un viaje de exploración a la península de Yucatán y *descubre* **12** las costas de México. Un año más tarde le *sigue* **13** Juan de Grijalva con una se-

1	vinieron
2	tenían
3	estaban
4	molestaban
5	sentían
6	eran
7	demandaban
8	podían
9	oían
10	había
11	hizo
12	descubrió
13	siguió
14	exploró

gunda expedición que *explora* **14** nuevas partes de la costa, pero sin poder penetrar en el interior del país. Los miembros de estas dos expediciones *ven* **15** templos magníficos de piedra y *oyen* **16** las palabras mágicas de boca de los indios: ¡Culúa, México! De la región de ese nombre dicen (decían) ellos que *vienen* **17** los objetos de oro que les *dan* **18** unas veces como regalo y otras para cambiar (*exchange*) por las cuentas (*beads*) de vidrio (*glass*) de Castilla.

Cuando Grijalva y sus expedicionarios *vuelven* **19** a Cuba con las noticias de Culúa, el gobernador Velázquez *organiza* **20** sin perder tiempo una tercera expedición capitaneada por Hernán Cortés.

15	vieron
16	oyeron
17	venían
18	daban
19	volvieron
20	organizó

C *Refranes:* ¿Cómo se dicen en español los refranes siguientes?

1 A bird in the hand is worth two in the bush.   *Más vale pájaro en mano que cien volando.*
2 He who sleeps much, learns little.   *Quien mucho duerme, poco aprende.*
3 He who seeks, finds.   *Quien busca, halla.*
4 Flies do not enter a closed mouth.   *En boca cerrada no entran moscas.*
5 The lion is not as fierce as they paint him.   *No es tan fiero el león como lo pintan.*
6 You can't make a silk purse out of a sow's ear.   *Aunque la mona se vista de seda, mona se queda.*
7 Barking dogs don't bite.   *Perro que ladra no muerde.*
8 Look before you leap.   *Antes que te cases, mira lo que haces.*
9 Twixt the cup and the lip there's many a slip.   *De la mano a la boca se pierde la sopa.*

D *Stem-Changing Verbs:* For each infinitive, say the third person singular form in the Present; then repeat the drill doing the same in the Preterit. Make note of the ones that make you hesitate and return to them for additional practice. Cover the answers.

1	encontrar	encuentra	encontró
2	despedir	despide	despidió
3	decir	dice	dijo
4	dormir	duerme	durmió
5	perder	pierde	perdió
6	divertir	divierte	divirtió
7	volar	vuela	voló
8	venir	viene	vino
9	sentar	sienta	sentó
10	morder	muerde	mordió
11	mover	mueve	movió
12	vestir	viste	vistió
13	sentir	siente	sintió
14	servir	sirve	sirvió
15	volver	vuelve	volvió
16	ir	va	fue
17	despertar	despierta	despertó
18	medir	mide	midió

19	cerrar	cierra	cerró
20	tropezar	tropieza	tropezó
21	recordar	recuerda	recordó
22	seguir	sigue	siguió
23	pensar	piensa	pensó
24	hacer	hace	hizo
25	acostar	acuesta	acostó
26	contar	cuenta	contó
27	jugar	juega	jugó
28	empezar	empieza	empezó
29	pedir	pide	pidió
30	morir	muere	murió

New Vocabulary

Dios	God	**dar**	to give	**comprar**	to buy
felicidad	happiness	**usar**	to use, wear	**vender**	to sell
tarea	homework, task	**ayudar**	to help	**traer**	to bring
		planchar	to iron	**traducir**	to translate
nube (la)	cloud	**madrugar**	to get up early	**despedirse de (i)**	to say goodby

¡Felicidades!   Congratulations!

Assignment 54/55

Getting Ready for a Test

In your next class you will have a major test. The purpose of this Assignment is to provide additional practice opportunities on the areas that will be covered and to make certain that you understand the test procedures in order to avoid making mistakes that have nothing to do with how much Spanish you actually know. Work through the Assignment carefully, use your cover sheet, and when you are finished, you will know how well prepared you are for the test. It is also suggested that you review the objectives for this Etapa on page 216.
The test consists of nine parts marked A through I.

1   Part A, *Listening and Reading Comprehension* (10 points): This part has 10 items designed to test your ability to tie what you hear with something you read. You will *hear* a statement or question once only, and on your answer sheet you will *see* three possible reactions or responses. You pick the one that is most logical and circle the letter before it. You hear, for example, *Cuando* *salimos al campo, ¿dónde nos ponemos el sombrero?* Which of the following is the most logical answer to the question?

a) Ponemos el sombrero en la mesa.

b) Lo ponemos en el río.

c) Lo ponemos en la cabeza. ▲

2 Another example: You hear *En Paraguay hablan dos lenguas, el español y una lengua india que se llama guaraní.* Which of the following is most logically associated with this statement?

a) Paraguay no es un país muy grande.

b) Sí, hay muchos indios en Paraguay.

c) Paraguay está al sur de Brasil. ▲

c

b

3 **Part B,** *Spelling Dictation* (10 points): Five short sentences similar to the ones below will be dictated, and you will be expected to write them correctly applying what you have learned about ear, eye, and rule spelling. You will hear each sentence only once. Check yourself on the following examples where *eye* and *rule* spelling problems are indicated:

La tie**rr**a es **r**edonda.

Hac**í**a un sol **br**illante.

La mona se **v**iste de seda.

Juan a**br**i**ó** la **v**entana.

La puerta est**á** ce**rr**ada.

Yo madru**gué** mucho **h**oy.

Busqué el lago **y** no lo **hallé**.

El toro es un animal feroz.

La **b**andera es **r**oja, azul **y v**erde.

4 **Part C,** *Present Tense Verb Forms and Reflexive Constructions* (20 points): This will be presented in the form of a visual-graphic drill for which you will have to write 10 combinations. Since you are already acquainted with this type of drill, in the practice that follows (after covering the answer) simply write the appropriate forms of the verb and pronoun that match the subject of the sentence.

Yo (prepararse) para el examen.

Ella y yo (pensar divertirse) en la fiesta.

Tú (necesitar acostarse) más temprano.

Mario y Estela (casarse) en junio.

Nosotros (ir a sentarse) allí.

Victoria (lavarse) el pelo.

Yo (vestirse) de seda.

Ella (desayunarse) en la cafetería.

Uds. (deber comprarse) un carro nuevo.

Ud. (ir a sentirse) bien allí.

Él (dormirse) en la clase.

Nosotros no (querer casarse).

me preparo

pensamos divertirnos

necesitas acostarte

se casan

vamos a sentarnos

se lava

me visto

se desayuna

deben comprarse

va a sentirse

se duerme

queremos casarnos

5 **Part D,** *Vocabulary Matching* (10 points): In this part of the test you will have to match 10 Spanish words with their English equivalents. You see, for example, 1) *traer* 2) *comprar* 3) *vender*. Which one of the following matches *traer*?

a) to sell b) to buy c) to sing d) to bring ▲

1) d

England has an official state church, but the constitution of the United States requires that the state be separated from all churches. The Hispanic tradition has been like that of England and the government and the Church, as a result, have worked very close together. Even today the head of state in Spain has the right to veto the appointment of high church officials. Another factor has brought the church and government closer together in the Hispanic countries. For centuries the oldest son in the family inherited all of his father's wealth. The other sons, especially of rich families, had to find some way to earn a living in a dignified way. They had little choice: army officer, government, law, teaching, and the church. And so it came about that the same families tended to supply the people who ran the government and the Church, and these two great bodies worked hand-in-hand with each other to keep each in power. With the coming of the great revolutionary movements of the nineteenth century the church regularly joined hands with the government to oppose the people.

This situation has created in the Hispanic world attitudes which are completely foreign to American Catholics. A good and very religious Hispanic Catholic may actually hate the church as an institution and also hate the priests who represent it. This attitude has sometimes resulted in actions which shock many Americans. For example, during the Spanish Civil War of 1936–39 enraged Republican soldiers killed priests who supported the Fascists. In Mexico during the 1910 Revolution a very elegant church was used as a stable by the revolutionaries.

A great many Latin men are not quite so violent in their attitude toward the church, but many middle-class people are strongly anti-clerical. Many, as a result, use the church only for the most basic rituals: baptism, marriage, and funerals. The majority of churchgoers, as a result, is made up of the rich, the poor, and women.

Prepare for this part of the test as needed by alternately covering the English and Spanish columns of the vocabulary list in your notebook. It is recommended that you review the entire list paying special attention to the words you have found troublesome and those that have been introduced in this Etapa (Assignments 37–55).

6   Part E, *Preterit Forms* (10 points): In 10 sentences you will have to write the preterit form that matches the subject of the sentence. You see, for example, *¿Qué (hacer) tú ayer?*, and in place of the infinitive in parentheses you will write

———. ▲

7 Cover the answers and practice with the following examples:	
Yo . . . (practicar) mi lección ayer.	*hiciste*
Ellos no . . . (decir) la verdad.	practiqué
Celia me . . . ; yo no la . . . . (abrazar)	dijeron
¿ . . . (Pedir) tú sopa también?	abrazó, abracé
Los estudiantes . . . (leer) en voz alta.	Pediste
¿A dónde . . . (ir) tú anoche?	leyeron
Yo . . . tenis y ellos . . . fútbol. (jugar)	fuiste
¿Qué . . . (hacer) Vds. el domingo?	jugué, jugaron
Yo . . . al presidente, pero ella no lo . . . (oír)	hicieron
	oí, oyó

Ellos . . . (abrir) las ventanas.   abrieron

Mi perro se . . . (morir) anteayer.   murió

Federico se . . . (caer) en el agua.   cayó

Yo . . . a París y ella . . . a Roma. (ir)   fui, fue

Raimundo no se . . . (despedir) antes de salir.   despidió

Yo . . . temprano; Vd. . . . tarde. (venir)   vine, vino

Yo me . . . (acostar) y me . . . (dormir), pero   acosté, dormí

el perro . . . (empezar) a ladrar y me . . . (despertar).   empezó, despertó

Ella . . . (decir) que ella . . . (hacer) la sopa.   dijo, hizo

8   **Part F,** *Preterit versus Imperfect* (10 points): In a reading about Hernán Cortés similar to the one below, you will have to make 10 choices. Two verbs are given in parentheses, one in the Preterit and the other in the Imperfect, and you will have to choose the correct one according to the meaning required by the context. Cover the answers and practice doing that with the following story. Do not write your answer until *after* you have finished reading each complete sentence; then, check each answer. It might even be more helpful to read over each whole paragraph before you begin to write your choices.

Los intérpretes de Cortés

En las playas de Guanahaní, en octubre de 1492, Colón y sus hombres (sintieron, sentían) por primera vez la necesidad de comunicarse oralmente con los nativos. En los viajes de exploración y conquista que (siguieron, seguían) al primer desembarco (*landing*), los españoles se (encontraron, encontraban) con varias tribus indias que (hablaron, hablaban) lenguas diferentes. Para resolver este serio problema, cuando (visitaron, visitaban) algún lugar nuevo, su costumbre (*custom*) era reclutar a algunos indios y enseñarles castellano con la mayor rapidez posible. En los documentos de la exploración y conquista de México encontramos los nombres de varios individuos que (sirvieron, servían) de intérpretes o traductores; por ejemplo, Julianillo, Melchorejo, Juan de Aguilar y doña Marina.

    Julianillo y Melchorejo, dos indios que el explorador Hernández de Córdoba (capturó, capturaba) en Yucatán, (aprendieron, aprendían) algo de español en Cuba y (fueron, iban) en las expediciones a México.

    En 1511, el español Juan de Aguilar (fue, iba) de Panamá a Santo Domingo cuando una fuerte tormenta (hundió, hundía) (*sank*) el barco. Diez de los pasajeros pudieron llegar a las playas de Yucatán donde varios de ellos (murieron, morían) de hambre y sed. Los otros (cayeron, caían) en manos de los indios y todos, excepto Aguilar y un compañero, fueron sacrificados en los altares de los dioses. Aguilar (vivió, vivía) como esclavo (*slave*) entre los indios por ocho años y (aprendió, aprendía) muy bien la lengua maya. Cortés lo rescató en la isla de Cozumel.

    Doña Marina, hija de un cacique (*chief*) indio, aparece también en la historia y las leyendas con los nombres Malinali, Malintzín y Malinche. Cuando la (llevaron, llevaban) de regalo con otras muchachas indias al campamento de Cortés, ella (supo, sabía) hablar varios idiomas indios. Siempre doña Marina

sintieron

siguieron
encontraron
hablaban
visitaban

sirvieron

capturó
aprendieron
fueron
iba
hundió
murieron
cayeron

vivió
aprendió

llevaron
sabía

le (explicó, explicaba) las cosas a Aguilar en maya, y él las (tradujo, traducía)   explicaba, traducía
al castellano. Estos dos intérpretes (ayudaron, ayudaban) mucho a Cortés en   ayudaron
todas sus campañas por México.

9   Part G, *Done-to Pronouns* (10 points): This will also be presented in the form
of a visual-graphic drill. You will have to write 10 combinations changing an
indicated phrase to the appropriate pronoun and placing it correctly in the
sentence. Practice this by writing the combinations for the following drill.

Ejemplos: 11 = *Pancho nos ayuda.*   41 = *Pancho va a servirnos.*

	1 ayuda	1 a nosotros.
	2 quiere ayudar	2 a ti.
Pancho	3 sirve	3 a sus amigos.
	4 va a servir	4 a Vd. (female).
		5 a Silvia y a Leonor.
		6 a mí.
		7 al profesor.

22	Pancho quiere ayudarte.
33	Pancho los sirve.
44	Pancho va a servirla.
17	Pancho lo ayuda.
36	Pancho me sirve.
25	Pancho quiere ayudarlas.
42	Pancho va a servirte.
23	Pancho quiere ayudarlos.
14	Pancho la ayuda.
31	Pancho nos sirve.

10 Part H, *Reading Comprehension, Completion* (10 points): On your answer sheet
there are 10 incomplete sentences. Each is followed by three ways of completing
it, and you are to select the most logical completion and circle the letter appearing before it. You might see, for example, *El perro de mi hermano es muy sociable.*
Nunca _____. Which of the following is the most logical completion?
a)   come vegetales.
b)   duerme en la mesa.
c)   muerde a nadie.   ▲

11 You see *Después de lavar la ropa, ella y yo* _____. Which is the most logical   c
completion?
a)   contamos los dedos.
b)   volvemos a casa.
c)   nos dormimos en la tienda.   ▲

12 You see *Antes de ponerse los zapatos, mi abuelo siempre* _____. Which is the   b
most logical completion?
a)   se pone los calcetines.
b)   plancha las camisas y los pantalones.
c)   va a la tienda a comprar ropa.   ▲

a

13 Part I, *Reading Comprehension, Response or Rejoinder* (10 points): This part consists of 10 questions or statements each followed by three possible answers or reactions. You are to pick out the best answer from the three and circle the letter before it. For example, you may see a question like this: *¿Qué quiere un hombre que tiene sed?* Which is the most logical answer?

a)   Quiere oler y masticar.

b)   Quiere hablar con el presidente.

c)   Quiere beber agua.   ▲

14 You may see *¿Cuándo usamos un impermeable?* Which is the most logical answer?

                                                                     c

a)   Cuando estamos enfermos.

b)   Cuando hace mucho frío.

c)   Cuando hay tormenta.   ▲

                                                                        c

Spend additional time studying and reviewing your notebook vocabulary list in preparation for the test.

ETAPA CUATRO

Performance Objectives
for Assignments 56–72/73

You will be prepared to continue your study of Spanish successfully if by Assignment 72/73 you have achieved all previous and the following objectives:

Listening and Reading Comprehension

1   Given any oral question and three possible written responses containing structures and vocabulary practiced through Assignment 72/73, you select the most logical response at least eight times out of ten.

You hear: *¿Has hecho la comida para esta noche?*
You see the following and select *a* as the most logical response:
a   Sí, preparé carne con papas.
b   Sí, serví té y jugo de tomate.
c   Sí, puse el agua fría en los vasos.

Reading Comprehension

2   Given any of the following types of reading problems containing vocabulary and structures practiced through Assignment 72/73, you will select the most logical alternatives at least eight times out of ten:

a   Questions followed by three possible responses
b   Incomplete statements followed by three possible completions
c   Incomplete paragraphs followed by three possible completions
d   Paragraphs followed by questions based on them and each with three possible answers

You see the following and select *c* as the most appropriate completion:
Margarita no puede ponerse el vestido rosado para ir a la fiesta porque . . .
a   no ha tenido tiempo para nadar.
b   no ha podido romperlo.
c   no ha podido encontrarlo.

Writing and Spelling

3   (Evaluated following Assignment 66) You write from dictation with correct spelling six short sentences (35 words) containing any of the spelling problems practiced through Assignment 64 with no more than five errors.

You hear and write: *No es un carro amarillo, es un autobús.*

Vocabulary

4   You match written Spanish vocabulary words studied after Assignment 56 with their nearest English equivalents for at least eight pairs out of ten.

You see:
1   *pescado*   (a)   instead of
2   *bandera*   (b)   he eats lunch

3   *almuerza*

(c)   fish
(d)   flag

You match *c* with 1, *d* with 2, and *b* with 3.

Morphology and Usage

5   (Evaluated following Assignment 60) In ten written Spanish sentences containing twelve demonstrative adjectives given in English, you write in Spanish the correct form of the demonstrative appropriate to each situation at least nine times.

You see: **Those** *casas que están allí lejos son de mi tío.*
You write: *Aquellas.*

6   You rewrite several Spanish sentences changing indicated nouns to pronouns or adjectival residuals, placing them correctly within the new sentences, and adding accent marks when necessary with no more than three errors out of a possible fifteen.

You see: *Te vendo **los libros viejos**.*
You write: *Te los vendo.*

7   In a short composition in the historical present in Spanish, ten verbs are indicated. You write correctly at least eight of them using the appropriate conjugated form of the back-shift tense, Preterit or Imperfect, according to the context that cues the choice.

You see: ***Son** las dos de la tarde. Yo **almuerzo** con mi familia cuando **llega** la terrible tormenta.*
You write: *Eran, almorzaba, llegó.*

8   In several written Spanish sentences seven irregular verbs are given in the infinitive. You write the appropriate conjugated form of the present indicative of each verb with no more than two errors.

You see: *Yo siempre (decir) la verdad.*
You write: *digo.*

9   Given five Spanish sentences written in the present tense, you rewrite each verb in the present perfect with no more than two errors out of ten.

You see: *Ellos ya vuelven.*
You write: *han vuelto.*

10   You translate four English sentences into Spanish to demonstrate your ability to use the gustar construction. At least three of the sentences must be correct.

You see: We like potatoes.
You write: *Nos gustan las papas.*

11   Given ten written Spanish sentences with the verb in the subjoined clause given in the infinitive, you write the correct form of the present subjunctive for at least eight of the infinitives.

You see: *Quiero que tú (venir) conmigo ahora.*
You write: *vengas.*

Assignment 56

A Note to the Student

You are now beginning the second half of *Communicating in Spanish, Level One*. If this is a new semester and you are a new student to *CIS*, read the information in both of the following sections. If you are a continuing student, read only the second section, which is addressed to you.

New Students to CIS

(1)   So that you have a better idea concerning these learning materials, read the Student Introduction on page v.

(2)   To be sure that your vocabulary includes what CIS students have learned, check any vocabulary at the end of each of the first 54 Assignments and make a list of all words you do not know. Study them a few minutes each day until you have learned them. This will make the remainder of the course far easier for you.

(3)   If you encounter in reviews or reading selections material that you do not know but that other students seem to understand, go to the index and find the Assignments that deal with this material. Study them on your own. Another source of help is the Workbook.

(4)   Your college may be equipped with a language laboratory and may have accompanying tapes. Use them to gain more confidence so that you can easily move through the remainder of *CIS* without difficulty.

Continuing CIS Students

The following is a reminder of aids toward success in this course:

(1)   Attend class regularly. The kind of practice provided in class cannot be obtained elsewhere.

(2)   Do all your Assignments on time and as instructed. Use a cover sheet when answers are provided, attempt each response, then check your answer immediately.

(3)   Participate in class during all choral drills and, when single students are called on to respond, you are to answer also mentally.

(4)   Read aloud in Spanish each day for three or four minutes using the best pronunciation and intonation of which you are capable. This will be very helpful toward developing oral fluency.

(5)   Keep a comprehensive vocabulary list as instructed. Study this list daily, reviewing constantly, and study most the vocabulary that you know least well.

Talking about Clothing

1 One social transaction in our culture is the buying and selling of clothing. *Vender* (to sell) and *comprar* (to buy) are regular verbs. Write the *yo* and *usted* forms of the Present of *vender*. ▲

yo vendo ; usted vende

2 Translate: *Yo compré un sombrero ayer.* ▲

I bought a hat yesterday.

3 The Present and Preterit of the *nosotros* form of *comprar* is _____. ▲

4 *Lavar* (to wash) and *planchar* (to iron or press) are also regular verbs. Translate: I washed and ironed my shirt. ▲

compramos

(Yo) lavé y planché mi camisa.

5 Can you tell, without more context, what *Planchamos las corbatas* means? ▲

no (The statement can mean "We iron" or "We iron**ed** the neckties.")

6 One meaning of *llevar* is "to carry." Another is "to wear." To avoid confusion, many Spanish speakers use *usar* for "to wear." Translate: She does not wear stockings. ▲

Ella no usa medias. (The Spanish meaning is "She does not use stockings.")

7 The most common thing we do with clothes is put them on and take them off. On *what* do we put clothes when we put them *on*? We put them (a) on the table (b) on ourselves. ▲

8 English takes it for granted that "She put the hat on" ordinarily means that she put it on her own head, that is, on herself. Spanish, in contrast, always says on whom something is put. Translate: *Yo voy a ponerme el sombrero.* ▲

on ourselves

I'm going to put on the hat. (You don't translate the *me*. English uses the reflexive "myself" only in very special constructions. Spanish uses it all the

9 The opposite of *ponerse el sombrero* is *quitarse el sombrero*. The translation of *quitar* is "to _____." ▲

time.)

10 What pronoun will you add to this sentence? *Miguel va a quitar* _____ *el sombrero.* ▲

take off

11 The translation of "I put on the hat" is *Me pongo el sombrero*. The translation of "I take off the hat" is _____. ▲

se

Me quito el sombrero.

12 Here is another difference between English and Spanish. Spanish uses the definite article where English uses the possessive adjective when it is obvious who the possessor is. So the common translation of "I put on my hat" is *Me pongo el sombrero*. Translate: "I take off my hat." ▲

Me quito el sombrero.

13 Translate, using the Present: I put on my shoes. ▲

Me pongo los zapatos.

14 When we say in English "We put on our shoes," each person puts on two shoes. How many hats does each person put on when we say, "We put on our hats?" ▲

15 In a certain sense, it is rather silly to say "We put on our hats" when each person only puts on one hat. It is just as silly, in contrast, to say "We put on

one hat each

our hat." The Spanish speaker, however, solves this problem by using the plural when two items are put on (*Nos ponemos los zapatos*), and the singular when each person puts on one item (*Nos ponemos el sombrero*). Translate: We take off our shirts.　▲

Nos quitamos la camisa.

A/B

yo

usted

C

él

Locating Things in Space: Demonstratives

1　English divides space into two areas: "here" and "there." Spanish, in contrast, divides space into three areas. The space around *yo* is *aquí*. The space around *usted* is *ahí*, and the space around *él* is *allí*. This may be diagramed like this:

yo
aquí

usted
ahí

él
allí

The space the farthest away for *yo* is _____. ▲

2   English has two demonstratives that indicate distance from the speaker: *this* combines with **here,** and *that* combines with **there.** Spanish, as you have already seen, has an area name that matches the three persons of speech: *aquí, ahí,* and *allí.* Spanish also has a demonstrative that goes along with each of these three areas. You will find the demonstrative forms that go with *libro* in these circles.

allí

| (yo aquí este) | (usted ahí ese) | (él allí aquel) |

The translation of *este* is _____. ▲

this (*este libro aquí* = this book here)

3   The closest we can come to *aquel libro* is "that book *over* there." For most practical purposes, consequently, you have to translate both *ese* and *aquel* with _____. ▲

that (But when you put "that" back into Spanish you must always choose between *ese* and *aquel*.)

4   The two demonstratives *este* and *ese* are the only two adjectives in the Spanish language which use the final *e* as a matching phoneme: *este libro, ese libro* and *esta pluma, esa pluma.* The *e* of *este* and *ese* combines with words which also combine with *el* and *un.* Translate: this hat. ▲

5   The forms *este* and *ese* cannot be made plural. The matching plurals are *estos* and *esos.* The reason why *este* and *ese* are the singular of *estos* and *esos* can be found in this question: *¿Qué es esto?* (What is this?) You use this form when you find something strange and you do not know its name. This *esto* is called the neuter form. It never agrees with a noun because it is used only to talk about something you cannot name. Translate: What is that? ▲

este sombrero

6   Although many textbooks say there are no plural neuter forms, people actually use *estos, esos,* and *aquellos* as plural neuters. Because there is a neuter form, the Spanish demonstratives have three singular forms. The three singular forms that begin with *est* end with the neuter suffix _____, the masculine demonstrative suffix _____, and the feminine suffix _____. ▲

¿Qué es eso?

o, e, a (*esto, este, esta*)

7   The plurals of *esta* and *esa* are _____. ▲
8   The plurals of *este* and *ese* are _____. ▲
9   Do the neuter forms *esto* and *eso* have a plural? ▲
10   The locative adverb that goes with *yo* and *este* is _____. ▲
11   The locative adverb that goes with *usted* and *ese* is _____. ▲

estas; esas
estos; esos
yes (*estos; esos*)
aquí
ahí

12   The demonstrative adjective that goes with *él* and *allí* is *aquel* in *aquel libro allí.* You can learn the other forms of *aquel* by using *él, ellos, ella,* and *ellas* as the models. The plural of *él* is *ellos.* The plural of *aquel* is _____. ▲

13   The plural of *aquella* is _____. ▲
14   To which stem will you add the *o* to make the neuter form that matches *esto* and *eso*? (a) *aquel* (b) *aquell* ▲

aquellos
aquellas

aquell (*¿Qué es aquello?*)

15 Which demonstrative will you put in this space? _____ *silla cerca de él.* ▲

16 _____ *animal cerca de usted.* ▲   *Aquella*

17 _____ *gato que yo tengo aquí.* ▲   *Ese*

18 The three Spanish demonstratives are also used to point out how far an   *Este*
object is away from the speaker when the actual distance is in itself not important. A Spanish speaker pointing to three books laid out in a row on a table
will say *este libro, ese libro y aquel libro.* The closest book is *este.* The one farthest
away is *aquel.* And the one in the middle distance is _____. ▲

19 The demonstratives can, like the article, become adjectival residuals. What   *ese*
is the normal way of answering *¿Vas a comprar la camisa? Sí, voy a* _____ ▲

20 Any one of the three demonstratives may replace the *la* of the above   *comprarla*
question.

$$\text{¿Vas a comprar} \left| \begin{array}{l} \text{esta} \\ \text{esa} \\ \text{aquella} \end{array} \right| \text{camisa?}$$

When the noun is dropped, the demonstrative remains as an adjectival residual,
but unlike the article this residual is not attached to the infinitive. Translate
these two sentences: *¿Vas a comprar esa camisa? Sí, voy a comprar esa.* ▲

Are you going to buy that shirt? Yes, I'm going to buy that one. (When *that*
becomes a residual in English, you may have to add the word "one.")

21 Translate the answer: Which book do you want? *This one.* ▲

Este (In most books you will see this residual written *éste.* Until 1952 the
residual demonstratives had to have an accent mark on the first vowel. This
is no longer required by the Spanish Academy, except in cases in which there
would otherwise be confusion.)

22 There are two other locative adverbs which you will encounter in your
readings and which you will learn to use later on. They are *acá* and *allá* which
have a meaning very much like *aquí* and *allí.*

Since the days of the Pilgrims it has been a firm tradition in American society that
persons who hold important public offices shall be elected to that office by the vote of
the people. This tradition is followed in many other ways. We elect by vote the chairman of committees, sometimes the director of a company or the president of a class.
We even choose the year's outstanding athletes and beauty queens by voting. In contrast, for nearly 300 years Latin America had no such tradition. Government officials
were appointed by the Spanish monarchs and church officials were appointed by the
Pope. As a result, when independence came in the first two decades of the nineteenth
century, the people had no practice in running a democracy. There have been, consequently, many dictators in Latin America and hundreds of revolutions which, in practice, have been a kind of substitute for public elections. In some countries the notion of
a change of government by free and public elections has hardly ever existed. In contrast,
the United States has never had a dictator and no public official has ever gotten into
office by revolution.

Summary

Each Spanish demonstrative has five forms. The forms that are used with nouns must agree in terminal phoneme and in number with their nouns. Here they are with their matching locative adverb:

aquí	*ahí*	*allí*
esto	eso	aquello
este	ese	aquel
esta	esa	aquella
estos	esos	aquellos
estas	esas	aquellas

Self-Correcting Exercises

A *Refranes:* Say aloud the Spanish equivalent of the following proverbs. (Memorize them if you did not do so before.)

1 A bird in the hand is worth two in the bush.   *Más vale pájaro en mano que cien volando.*
2 He who sleeps much, learns little.   *Quien mucho duerme, poco aprende.*
3 He who seeks, finds.   *Quien busca, halla.*
4 Flies do not enter a closed mouth.   *En boca cerrada no entran moscas.*
5 The lion is not as fierce as they paint him.   *No es tan fiero el león como lo pintan.*
6 You can't make a silk purse out of a sow's ear.   *Aunque la mona se vista de seda, mona se queda.*
7 Barking dogs don't bite.   *Perro que ladra no muerde.*
8 Look before you leap.   *Antes que te cases, mira lo que haces.*
9 Twixt the cup and the lip there's many a slip.   *De la mano a la boca se pierde la sopa.*

B *Vocabulary Review by Sets: Parts of the Body, Clothing, and Colors:* With the answers on the right covered, say aloud the Spanish equivalents checking the accuracy of your response after each item. Use the definite article with each noun.

1 the parts of the body   *las partes del cuerpo*
2 head, hair, forehead, face   *la cabeza, el pelo, la frente, la cara*
3 ears, eyes, nose   *las orejas, los ojos, la nariz*
4 mouth, lips, tongue, teeth   *la boca, los labios, la lengua, los dientes*
5 arms, hands, fingers, thumbs   *los brazos, las manos, los dedos, los pulgares*
6 legs, feet, toes   *las piernas, los pies, los dedos (de los pies)*

Say aloud in Spanish the name of the article of clothing generally associated with the items on the left. Use the definite article with each noun.

7 los pies y las piernas   *los zapatos, los calcetines y las medias*
8 la cabeza y la lluvia   *el sombrero y el impermeable*
9 el tiempo frío   *el suéter y el abrigo*

10	ropa de mujer	la falda, la blusa y el vestido
11	ropa de hombre (aunque también la mujer puede usarla)	los pantalones, el saco, la camisa, la corbata, el traje

Say aloud the Spanish translation.

12	black and white	*negro y blanco*
13	pink and red	*rosado y rojo (colorado)*
14	yellow and orange	*amarillo y anaranjado*
15	blue and green	*azul y verde*
16	gray and purple	*gris y morado*
17	light and dark	*claro y oscuro*

C *Reading:* Read the following selections aloud and do the multiple-choice problems at the end.

¿Sabía usted que . . .

(1)

. . . en la mayor parte de las escuelas privadas y públicas del mundo de habla española los estudiantes tienen que vestirse de uniforme? Las muchachas usan blusas, faldas, medias y zapatos idénticos. Los muchachos generalmente van a clase en pantalones de color oscuro, camisa blanca y corbata. Para las paradas y otras ocasiones especiales tienen uniformes de gala que son muy vistosos° y elegantes. En los dos tipos de uniforme llevan generalmente la insignia oficial del colegio.

showy

(2)

. . . el "Cristo de los Andes" es un símbolo de paz eterna entre Argentina y Chile? Este colosal monumento está en un lugar muy elevado de la cordillera° andina que se llama Paso de Uspallata y marca la frontera° entre los dos países. En los primeros años de nuestro siglo, argentinos y chilenos se prepararon para la guerra° a causa° de las diferencias que existían entre ellos con respecto a los límites° entre las dos naciones. En 1904 resolvieron el problema pacíficamente y decidieron usar el bronce de los cañones para hacer una enorme estatua de Cristo y ponerla en la línea divisoria entre los dos países. Al pie de esta famosa estatua aparece la siguiente inscripción: "Estas montañas se convertirán° en polvo° antes que los pueblos de Argentina y Chile rompan° la paz que a los pies de este Cristo Redentor han jurado° mantener."

mountain range
border

war/because
boundaries

will turn
dust/break
have sworn

(3)

. . . en la ciudad brasileña de Río de Janeiro también hay una estatua gigantesca del Cristo Redentor? Está en la cumbre° del monte Corcovado y desde allí podemos ver un panorama fantástico de toda la ciudad y de la bahía.

summit

(1)

1 ¿Cómo se visten los alumnos en las escuelas del mundo de habla española?
   a Se visten de negro.

1   b

   b Se visten de uniforme.

   c Se visten de seda.

2 ¿Cuándo usan uniforme de gala?   2   a

   a Cuando hay paradas.

   b Lo usan todos los días.

   c Lo usan solamente los domingos.

3 ¿Qué diferencia fundamental hay entre el vestido escolar de los Estados   3   c
Unidos y el de los países de habla española?

   a No hay absolutamente ninguna diferencia.

   b Los colores de los uniformes son más bonitos allí.

   c En la mayoría de las escuelas públicas norteamericanas los estudiantes
no usan uniformes.

4 ¿Usan uniforme los estudiantes de las universidades de América del Sur   4   c
y de España?

   a Sí, todos lo usan.

   b No, lo usan solamente los alumnos de primaria.

   c El párrafo que leímos no nos dice nada sobre la ropa que usan los
estudiantes universitarios.

(2)

5 ¿Qué hay entre Argentina y Chile?   5   b

   a Un mar y dos océanos.

   b Una alta cordillera.

   c Muchos monumentos simbólicos.

6 ¿Por qué iban a declararse en guerra los argentinos y los chilenos?   6   c

   a Porque en aquel tiempo Argentina no tenía puertos de mar.

   b Porque Chile necesitaba bronce para hacer cañones.

   c Porque existía entre ellos una gran disputa de límites.

7 ¿Está en Argentina la estatua del "Cristo de los Andes"?   7   c

   a Sí, está en territorio argentino.

   b No, está en territorio chileno.

   c Está en territorio de los dos países, en la línea que los divide.

8 ¿Qué simboliza la estatua del Paso de Uspallata?   8   b

   a El deseo (*desire*) de ir a la guerra.

   b El deseo de vivir en paz con nuestros vecinos.

   c La abundancia de cañones en dos países del sur.

(3)

9 ¿Hay otra estatua gigantesca de Cristo situada entre Brasil y Bolivia?   9   c

   a Sí, hay otra entre Brasil y Argentina.

   b El párrafo que leímos dice que hay dos.

   c Hay otra, pero está en Rio de Janeiro.

10 Si subimos al monte Corcovado, ¿podemos ver desde allí la ciudad de   10 c
Buenos Aires?

   a Sí, cómo no, en los días en que no hay niebla.

   b No, desde Corcovado podemos ver solamente la capital de Chile.

   c Eso es absurdo. Buenos Aires está demasiado lejos de allí.

D *Fórmulas de cortesía:* Say aloud and memorize if you haven't already done
so. *¿Cómo se dice en español . . . ?*

1	Pardon me (shortened form).	*Perdón.*
2	Congratulations!	*¡Felicidades!*
3	Have a good time (*tú* form).	*Que te diviertas.*
4	Don't bother (*usted* form).	*No se moleste usted.*
5	It's no bother.	*No es molestia ninguna.*
6	What did you say?	*¿Cómo?*
7	Please come with me (*usted* form).	*Hágame el favor de venir conmigo.*
8	It doesn't matter.	*No importa.*
9	Pardon me (long form).	*Perdóneme (Dispénseme.)*
10	Yes, of course.	*Sí, cómo no.*
11	We are very sorry.	*Lo sentimos mucho.*
12	Make yourself at home (*tú* form).	*Estás en tu casa.*

New Vocabulary

Review the old vocabulary from your notebook list or the lists at the end of
each Assignment. If you are a new student, refer to Assignment 4, page 25 for
suggestions on how to study vocabulary.

"A quien madruga Dios le ayuda."   "The early bird catches the worm."

Assignment 57

The Present Perfect in English and Spanish

1 In your study of the Preterit and Imperfect you learned that all events fall
into two sets: cyclic and non-cyclic. *To fall*, in the sense of *to fall down*, is a
_____ event. ▲

2 You have also learned that events have three aspects: a beginning, a middle,   cyclic
and an end. Which aspect does the form *falling* describe? (a) initiative (b) imperfective (c) terminative ▲

            imperfective (Therefore, "falling" is called the *imperfect participle*.)

3 Which aspect does *fallen* describe? (a) initiative (b) imperfective (c) terminative ▲

4 Formerly, grammars listed the opposite of "imperfective" as "perfective,"   terminative
that is, completed or finished. As a result, the form "fallen" is still called the
perfect participle. This word *perfect* appears in the name of the tense you are
studying: the **Present Perfect**. Let's see what is present in the Present Perfect.
Which form is Present? (a) has (b) had ▲

            has

5 A "fallen tree" is one that *has fallen*. The tense of *has* is Present. The form *fallen* is the perfect participle. The tense name for *has fallen* is _____. ▲

Present Perfect

6 Your intuition tells you when to use the Present Perfect in English. Let's bring this knowledge to the surface so you can use it to learn how to use the Present Perfect in Spanish. Compare these two statements: (1) The tree is falling. (2) The tree has fallen. Which one says the action has come to an end? ▲

The tree has fallen.

7 The Present Perfect, *has fallen*, stands in contrast with the Present Imperfect, *is falling*. The form *is falling* says the action is going on, is imperfect, at the moment of speaking: "Watch out! The tree is falling." The form *has fallen* says that the cylic event came to an end, was perfected, *before* the moment of speaking: "Look! The tree has fallen." Let's look more carefully at this form. It is made up, really, of two verbs. The action is actually described or defined by (a) has (b) fallen. ▲

fallen

8 The form *has* is called a "helping" or **auxiliary** verb. The tense of *has* is Present. This tells you the action, *fallen*, was completed (perfected) before the moment of speaking. "The tree had fallen" would tell you that the action was completed *before some point in the past*.

In terms of the moment of speaking there are just three things we can say about a single cyclic event: (1) it has yet to take place (*The tree will fall*), (2) it is taking place (*The tree is falling*), or (3) it is already completed (*The tree has fallen*). The Present Perfect, *has fallen*, contrasts with the Present Imperfect, *is falling*. It must also stand in contrast with the past tense. What do you say? (a) The tree has fallen yesterday. (b) The tree fell yesterday. ▲

The tree fell yesterday.

9 It is not proper to say "They have visited him last year." The Present Perfect does not combine with adverbs which stand for past intervals of time: *last year, yesterday, in 1916, etc.* The Present Perfect, then, is not a past tense. It simply says that a cyclic event is completed *before* the moment of speaking, that is, the action is not going on now. Let's see what the Present Perfect tells us when the action is non-cyclic, as in *to work*.

Which of the following sentences tells you that Peter is still working in the factory? (a) Peter worked in the factory all his life. (b) Peter has worked in the factory all his life. ▲

Peter has worked in the factory all his life.

10 When we talk about a non-cyclic event, the Present Perfect may describe an action which began in the past and is still going on in the present. Peter *began* to work in the factory a long time ago. He *has worked* there ever since.

Let's see, now, what the difference is between the simple past and the Present Perfect: "We came here, saw the beach, the mountains, and the house. We loved it." Does *We loved it* describe an event that (a) came to an end at some point in the past? (b) began at some point in the past? ▲

began at some point in the past

11 Let's add to the story above: "We came here, saw the beach, the mountains, and the house. We loved it and bought the house. Then the oil wells came and spoiled everything. Now we hate the place." The statement *We loved it* means only that the action began at some point in the past. This story, however, could have another ending: "We came here, saw the beach, the mountains, and the house. We loved it and bought the house. We *have loved* it ever since." Do we still love the house? ▲

12 Here is another example of this usage. Which sentence says that I still have confidence in Walter? (a) I believed Walter for many years. (b) I have believed Walter for many years. ▲

yes

I have believed Walter for many years. (And I see no reason not to continue believing him.)

13 Which sentence do you consider to be proper English? (a) Up to this moment we have seen ten planes. (b) Up to this moment we saw ten planes. ▲

Up to this moment we have seen ten planes. (The looking for planes is still going on, so we use the Present Perfect.)

14 Which sentence implies that we are no longer on duty as plane spotters? (a) We have seen ten planes today, captain. (b) We saw ten planes today, captain. ▲

We saw ten planes today, captain.

15 *We saw ten planes today* describes an action that came to an end at some time in the past. We are no longer looking for planes. *We have seen ten planes today*, in contrast, implies that we are still watching out for them. Here is another example of this contrast: (a) I have not seen him for a week. (b) I did not see him for a week. In which sentence does *a week* include yesterday and today? ▲

I have not seen him for a week. (The week is measured back from the moment of speaking.)

16 Which tense relates events more closely to the moment of speaking? (a) the Past (b) the Present Perfect ▲

the Present Perfect

17 Non-cyclic events may begin in the past and continue to the moment of speaking: *She has lived here since 1961.* This is not possible with a single cyclic event. So the Present Perfect says that a single cyclic event is completed *before* the moment of speaking. Someone asks, *Where's Miguel?* Are both of the following answers acceptable English? (1) He has gone out for a coke. (2) He went out for a coke. ▲

yes

18 When we are talking about a single cyclic event, the past tense, *went out*, also says the event is completed *before* the moment of speaking. May you say either *He just went out* or *He has just gone out*? ▲

yes

19 Which verb phrase is the least complex? (a) went out (b) has gone out. ▲

went out

20 When we have a choice, which form do you expect we are likely to use more often? (a) the simpler (b) the more complex ▲

the simpler

21 Spanish uses the Present Perfect to say the same things it does in English. However, when a choice between the Preterit and the Present Perfect exists, the Preterit is most frequently used. Which form will be used to translate "He went out" (He has gone out)? (a) *Salió.* (b) *Salía.* (c) *Ha salido.* ▲

Salió.

The Forms of the Present Perfect

1 The perfect participle of all regular *a*-verbs is made by replacing the infinitive *r* with *do*. So the perfect participle of *hablar*, which will translate *spoken*, is _____. ▲

hablado

2 The perfect participle of *estudiar* is _____. ▲

3 The translation of "I have spoken" is *yo he hablado*. The present tense form *he* comes from *haber*. Is it regular? ▲

> *estudiado*

> no (To be regular it should be *habo.*)

4 In writing, the *h* of *he* is all that is left of the stem of *haber*. In speech, however, the stem is lost and you say [yo e ablado]. Say this aloud. What will you add to *he* to say "we have spoken"? ▲

> *mos* (So you get *hemos hablado.*)

5 The perfect participle *hablado* stays the same in all forms: *yo he hablado, nosotros hemos hablado*. The form that goes with *usted, él,* and *ella* is *ha*. Translate: she has sung. ▲

6 Change *ella ha hablado* so the form matches *ellas*. ▲

7 Change *han hablado* so it matches *tú*. ▲

8 Translate: you (*tú*) have invited. ▲

9 Change *has invitado* so it matches *usted*. ▲

> *ella ha cantado*

> *ellas han hablado*

> *tú has hablado*

> *tú has invitado*

> *usted ha invitado*

10 The perfect participles of both *e-* and *i-*verbs are formed by adding *ido* to the stem. So the perfect participle of *tener* and *venir* is _____. ▲

> *tenido; venido*

11 There is no change in the auxiliary with *e-* and *i-*verbs. Translate: He has learned. Translate: They have served. ▲

> *Él ha aprendido. Ellos han servido.*

12 Translate: *Yo he aprendido las formas del presente perfecto en español.* ▲

> I have learned the forms of the Present Perfect in Spanish. (There are some irregular forms of the perfect participle which you will learn later.)

Summary

Present Perfect = present tense forms of *haber* + perfect participle (= stem + *ado* for *a*-verbs, and *ido* for *e-* and *i*-verbs)

Study this chart that includes all the forms:

yo	he	
nosotros	hemos	
tú	has	estudiado (aprendido, vivido)
Vd. (él, ella)	ha	
Vds. (ellos, ellas)	han	

The Spelling of Certain Forms of the Perfect Participle

1 The *i* of the perfect participle always stands as the vowel of a syllable. Consequently, it should have a written accent on it when it is preceded by *a, e,* or *o*. The perfect participle of *oír* is written _____. ▲

> *oído* (And you pronounce it o-í-do.)

2 Write the perfect participle for *creer* and *leer*, and say them aloud. ▲

> *creído; leído* (You pronounce these cre-í-do and le-í-do.)

3 Write and pronounce the perfect participle of *traer* and *caer*. ▲

> *traído; caído* (tra-í-do; ca-í-do)

4 Translate: I have heard. ▲

5 Translate: They have believed (*creer*). Translate: She has read. ▲   *Yo he oído.*

Ellos han creído. Ella ha leído.

More on Demonstratives

1 Which demonstrative does the speaker use to point out something near him? (a) *este* (b) *ese* (c) *aquel* ▲

este (Este libro que yo tengo es rojo.)

2 Which demonstrative does the speaker use to point out something near the person spoken to? ▲

3 Which demonstrative does the speaker use to point out something that is   *ese* some distance from the speaker and the person spoken to? ▲

4 Suppose I have a book in my hand and I ask you, *¿De qué color es este libro?*   *aquel* Your answer should be (a) *Este libro es rojo.* (b) *Ese libro es rojo.* ▲

Ese libro es rojo. (You do the same thing in English. Your answer to "What color is this book?" would be "That book is red.")

5 You have a book in your hand. Someone asks, *¿De qué color es ese libro?* You answer, _____ *libro es rojo.* ▲

6 Someone asks, *¿De qué color es aquel libro?* The book is at some distance from   *Este libro es rojo.* both you and the speaker. Your answer is: _____ *libro es rojo.* ▲

Aquel libro es rojo.

Self-Correcting Exercises

A *Clothing, Parts of the Body, and Reflexive Constructions:* Write the combinations. Make all the verbs past imperfect.

Ejemplo: 235 = Yo me lavaba las manos.

1 Elías y yo			1 los calcetines.
2 Yo	1	ponerse	2 el suéter.
3 Elías	2	quitarse	3 el saco.
4 Tú	3	lavarse	4 los dientes.
5 Ustedes			5 las manos.

1)	112	Elías y yo nos poníamos el suéter.
2)	522	Vds. se quitaban el suéter.
3)	134	Elías y yo nos lavábamos los dientes.
4)	434	Tú te lavabas los dientes.
5)	211	Yo me ponía los calcetines.
6)	323	Elías se quitaba el saco.
7)	535	Vds. se lavaban las manos.
8)	222	Yo me quitaba el suéter.
9)	413	Tú te ponías el saco.
10)	335	Elías se lavaba las manos.

11)   523   Vds. se quitaban el saco.
12)   311   Elías se ponía los calcetines.

B *Reading Comprehension:* After you read the following selections, do the multiple-choice problems that follow.

¿Sabía usted que . . .

(1)

. . . el lago Titicaca en la frontera entre Bolivia y Perú es el lago navegable más alto del mundo? Ocupa un área de 3.200 millas cuadradas y mide 120 millas de largo° por 40 de ancho°. Su altitud es de 12.508 pies sobre el nivel del mar° y su nombre indio significa "peña de plomo"°. Toda la región del lago que incluye 25 islas es de una importancia extraordinaria para el antropólogo por sus notables tesoros arqueológicos. Alrededor° de este gran "mar" indio se formó el imperio de los incas. Según° sus mitos° y leyendas°, los fundadores de la civilización inca (Manco Cápac y Mama Ocllo) salieron de las islas del Sol y de la Luna a buscar el lugar donde debían establecer el centro de su imperio.

Por las aguas azules del Titicaca van y vienen barcos modernos y las pintorescas balsas° de los indios. Entre el puerto peruano de Puno y el boliviano de Guaqui hay servicio regular de comercio y pasajeros. Además°, la región es también un importante centro turístico. Miles de peregrinos° de los países vecinos° vienen todos los años a la iglesia de Copacabana a celebrar fiestas religiosas en honor de la Virgen del Lago.

long/wide
sea level/boulder of lead
Around
According to/myths/legends

rafts
Besides
pilgrims
neighboring

(2)

. . . los colores de la bandera boliviana tienen un significado° especial? El rojo representa el reino° animal, el amarillo simboliza el reino mineral, y el verde es el símbolo del reino vegetal.

meaning
kingdom

(1)

1 ¿Cuál es el área del lago Titicaca?   1   a
  a Aproximadamente tres mil millas cuadradas.
  b Trescientas mil millas cuadradas.
  c Treinta mil millas cuadradas.

2 ¿Cuáles son las dimensiones del lago Titicaca?   2   c
  a Ciento veinte pies de largo por cuarenta de ancho.
  b Ciento veinte millas de alto por cuarenta de ancho.
  c Ciento veinte millas de largo por cuarenta de ancho.

3 ¿Cómo se llamaban los fundadores del imperio inca?   3   c
  a No tenían nombres.
  b Se llamaban Puno y Guaqui.
  c Se llamaban Manco Cápac y Mama Ocllo.

4 ¿Es posible ir de Bolivia a Perú por el lago Titicaca?   4   a
  a Sí, hay servicio regular de pasajeros.
  b Sí, pero solamente en balsas y canoas.
  c No, es necesario nadar o ir por tierra.

5 ¿Por qué es importante para el antropólogo la región del lago Titicaca?   5   b
  a Porque allí vivieron los aztecas.
  b Porque allí hay muchas ruinas de civilizaciones antiguas.
  c Porque los indios que viven allí hoy día no tienen pelo en la cabeza.

6 ¿Hay mucho movimiento de barcos en el lago Titicaca?   6   c
  a No, el clima no lo permite.
  b No, el lago Titicaca no es navegable.
  c Sí, hay bastante movimiento de balsas y barcos.

7 ¿Por qué van miles de peregrinos de muchos países a Copacabana?   7   b
  a Porque su propósito (*purpose*) es inspeccionar las minas.
  b Porque allí hay un santuario muy famoso.
  c Porque creen que el sol y la luna son dioses.

(2)

8 ¿Tienen algún significado especial los colores de la bandera de Bolivia?   8   b
  a Sí, son unos colores muy bonitos.
  b Sí, representan los tres reinos naturales.
  c Sí, el azul representa el color del agua del lago Titicaca.

9 ¿Qué simboliza el color amarillo en la bandera de Bolivia?   9   c
  a La abundancia de fruta en el país, por ejemplo, bananas.
  b Los animales de ese color que viven en las selvas del país.
  c El oro, la plata y otros productos minerales semejantes (*similar*).

Every culture has its own system of values in which certain things are more important than others. Ever since the Revolutionary War most Americans have had great respect for the ideals for which that war was fought: freedom, liberty, democracy, a constitutional government, *etc.* The civil rights movement of the first half of this century was a continuation of this loyalty to principles.

One of the outstanding features of the Hispanic culture is that loyalty to personalities and friends is more important than belief in abstractions and general principles. Thus, while Americans tend to be loyal to the principles of their political party, the Latins are loyal to the personality who leads that party and, as a result, treat those who oppose him as enemies. This personal loyalty, moreover, implies a favorable response when the leader achieves political power, and, as a result, "to the victor goes the spoils" is still considered proper in Hispanic culture. The frequent revolutions in the Hispanic world can be better understood when one realizes that personal loyalty to individuals is more important than loyalty to the abstract features of the system. Americans, by and large, believe in the Constitution and make amendments to it very infrequently. Latins, in contrast, frequently suspend constitutional guarantees and often rewrite their constitution to fit the personal aims and ambitions of individual leaders, the *caudillos*. No American president has been removed from office. In almost every Latin country this has happened dozens of times since their independence from Spain. Americans will continue to have trouble understanding this behavior until they realize that in the Hispanic culture loyalty to individuals is more important than maintaining an abstract system.

New Vocabulary

ponerse	to put on	**ahí**	there (*near*)	**ese, esa, eso**	that
quitarse	to take off	**allí**	there (*far*)	**esos, esas**	those
haber	to have	**este, esta, esto**	this	**aquel, aquella, aquello**	that
	(*helping*)	**estos, estas**	these	**aquellos, aquellas**	those
juntos, -as	together				

Words for Food

comida	food	**queso**	cheese	**pimienta**	pepper
bebida	drink, beverage	**huevos**	eggs	**leche (la)**	milk
ensalada	salad	**fruta**	fruit	**crema**	cream
carne (la)	meat	**pan**	bread	**azúcar**	sugar
legumbres (las)		**mantequilla**	butter	**jugo de tomate**	tomato
(vegetales)	vegetables	**sal (la)**	salt		juice
				postre	dessert

Assignment 58

Irregular Perfect Participles

1 The regular perfect participles have two suffixes. The *a* and *i* are verb set markers; the *do* is the morpheme which says the action is perfected. In the irregular perfect participles the *do* is replaced by *to* or *cho*. The stem may also have a change. The infinitive for *escrito* is _____. ▲

> *escribir* (One cognate of *escrito* is "script.")

2 In the perfect participles the *o* of the stem frequently changes under stress to *ue*. The stem of *muerto* is *muer*. The regular stem of this form is _____. ▲

3 The translation of *Él ha muerto* is _____. ▲   *mor* (As in *morir*.)

4 The infinitive for *vuelto* is _____. (What infinitive of a stem-changing verb   He has died.
do you know that begins with *vol?*) ▲

5 The preterit backshift of *pone* is *puso*. Translate: *Ella puso la mesa.* ▲   *volver*

6 Translate: *Ella ha puesto la mesa.* ▲   She set the table.
          She has set the table.

7 You know two meanings for *poner*. One is "to set" and the other is "to put." Translate: *Ella ha puesto el libro en la mesa.* ▲

> She has put the book on the table.

8 In English a "vista" is a "view." Both of these words are cognates of the perfect participle *visto*. The infinitive for *visto* is _____. ▲

> *ver*

9 The two participles *dicho* and *hecho* give you very little clue as to what their infinitives are. Nevertheless, you should be able to guess which comes from *decir* and which from *hacer*. The perfect participle of *decir* is _____.　▲

10 The perfect participle of *hacer* is _____.　▲

11 Translate: They have returned.　▲

12 Translate: I have written. Translate: She has said.　▲

dicho

hecho

Ellos han vuelto.

Yo he escrito. Ella ha dicho.

13 Translate: *¿Lo has hecho tú?* Translate: *Lo he visto.*　▲

Have you done it? I have seen it.

The most common irregular perfect participles and their corresponding infinitives and English translations are:

poner	puesto	*put, set*
romper	roto	*broken*
ver	visto	*seen*
volver	vuelto	*returned*
abrir	abierto	*opened, open*
escribir	escrito	*written*
morir	muerto	*died, dead*
decir	dicho	*said, told*
hacer	hecho	*made, done*

Gustar *and the Forms of the Involved Entity*

1 Let's begin the Program by finding out what is meant by the *involved entity*. Compare these two statements: (1) That noise annoyed me. (2) That dog bit me. On the surface both sentences seem to be alike. Each has a doer (noise, dog) and it looks like each has a done-to (me). However, your intuition tells you that the first sentence can be changed to *That noise was annoying to me.* Can you also change *That dog bit me* to *That dog was biting to me?*　▲

2 So now you know that the relationship between *annoyed* and *me* and *bit* and *me* are not the same. *That dog bit me* says the dog did something to me directly, but there is no information in the sentence which tells you what I did. In contrast, *That noise was annoying to me* really describes how I reacted to the noise. There was a stimulus (a noise) which produced a response (annoyance) and I happened to be the person who reacted to the stimulus.

no

When we say that very loud noises are annoying, we do not specify who is annoyed by loud noises. What we say is that a loud noise is a *stimulus* (a cause) which produces the *response* (reaction) of annoyance. When we specify who responds to the stimulus, we are actually stating who is involved, that is, who is reacting to loud noises. Who is the involved entity in *Juana irritates me?*　▲

me (I am the one who responds to what Juana does. I react and am involved

3 Which word stands for the stimulus in *That noise frightens me?*　▲

in some way.)

noise

4 Suppose I say, *I don't like that noise.* What am I reporting? (a) I am doing something to the noise. (b) The noise causes me to react in a negative fashion because I consider it unpleasant. ▲

> The noise stimulates my response. (It does something to *me.*)

5 I could respond in a stronger fashion and say, *That noise disgusts me.* Will this change (transformation) say just about the same thing? *That noise is disgusting to me.* ▲

> yes (So the rewording tells you I am the involved entity. I react.)

6 In the word *disgusts*, the prefix *dis* is (a) negative (b) positive. ▲

7 What does *disgusts* mean? (a) is pleasing to (b) is not pleasing to ▲   negative

8 The Spanish cognate of "to disgust" is *disgustar.* The translation of "That   is not pleasing to disgusts me" is *Eso me disgusta.* Which form, *nos* or *nosotros*, will you use to translate "That disgusts us"? ▲

> *nos (Eso nos disgusta.)*

9 In this example the person who is disgusted is *tú.* However, *tú* is the label for the person as the doer, not as the involved entity. So be careful and translate "That disgusts you." *Eso* _____ *disgusta.* ▲

10 The involved entity pronouns which match *yo, nosotros*, and *tú* are _____. ▲   *Eso te disgusta.*

> *me, nos, te* (These are the same forms as the pronouns for the done-to.)

11 The form of the involved entity pronoun which matches *usted, él*, and *ella* is *le* (you must tell from the context which person is meant). We are talking about María. Translate: That disgusts her. *Eso* _____ *disgusta.* ▲

12 Your previous experience with singular and plural forms should tell you   *Eso le disgusta.* that the plural of *le* is _____. ▲

> *les* (This is the involved entity form that matches *ustedes, ellos,* and *ellas*.)

13 Translate: That disgusts them. ▲

14 The verb *disgustar*, like "disgust," has a negative prefix. Does English have   *Eso les disgusta.* the positive equivalent of "to disgust," that is, "to gust"? ▲

15 Let's pretend for a moment that English does have a form "to gust." Now   no translate these two sentences: *Eso me disgusta. Eso me gusta.* ▲

> That disgusts me. That gusts me.

16 Spanish does have both the negative form *disgustar* and the positive opposite *gustar.* However, since English lacks the cognate of *gustar* (to gust), we have to translate the opposite of "to disgust" with "to please." In other words, instead of using a cognate of *gustar*, you must translate the meaning. The regular translation, then, of *Eso me gusta* is not "That gusts me" but _____. ▲

17 Many people who start to learn Spanish have real trouble with *gustar*   That pleases me. because one of the common translations is "to like." Let's see how to avoid this trouble. In the sentence "I eat the apples," the doer is _____. ▲

18 The done-to in the same sentence is _____. ▲   I

19 Many students become confused because the sentence *I eat the apples* seems,   the apples on the surface, to be exactly like *I like the apples.* By now you know better. Remember the notions of stimulus and response. When I say, *I like the apples*, (a) am I doing something to the apples? (b) are the apples doing something to me, that is, causing me to react? ▲

> The apples are doing something to me, that is, causing me to react.

20 The Spanish translation of "I like the apples" is *Me gustan las manzanas.* In the Spanish sentence the doer or stimulus is _____. ▲

21 The doer or stimulus, *las manzanas*, is plural and agrees with the plural verb *gustan.*

las manzanas

The same thing happens in English with "disgust." Compare:

| That **disgusts** me. | *Eso me **disgusta.*** |
| That **disgust** me. | *Esos me **disgustan.*** |

In both languages the verb agrees in number with the stimulus or doer. Spanish uses the same pattern with *gustar*. Compare: *Eso me gusta; Esos me gustan.* This agreement is lost when *gustar* is translated by "to like." Translate *Esos me gustan* using "like." ▲

22 In the English translation of *Esos me gustan*, that is, "I like them," the involved entity in Spanish (*me*) becomes the subject of the English sentence. You should now begin to understand why so many speakers of English have trouble with *gustar*. They can translate *Me disgustan esas palabras* as "Those words disgust me" because we have the cognate "disgust." They get confused when they try to translate *No me gustan esas palabras* because we do not say "Those words do not gust me." They now have to translate the meaning. One meaning is "Those words do not please me." The more common translation with *like* is _____. ▲

I like them.

I do not like those words.

23 In *Me gustan esas palabras* the plural verb form *gustan* agrees in number with the subject (stimulus) *esas palabras*. What will you put in place of *me* to get the equivalent of "We like these words"? (a) *nosotros* (b) *nos* ▲

nos (Nos gustan estas palabras. Remember this is like "Those words disgust us"—*Nos disgustan esas palabras.*)

24 Look at the following examples and think of the translations of the involved entity pronouns:

Me disgustan esas palabras.	*Me* gustan esas palabras.
Nos disgustan esas palabras.	*Nos* gustan esas palabras.
Te disgustan esas palabras.	*Te* gustan esas palabras.

There are two translations of *me, nos,* and *te*. In the first column with *disgustan* they are translated by "me, us, you." In the second column *te* is also translated by "you" (You like those words), but the translation of *me* and *nos* is changed from "me" and "us" to _____. ▲

I; we (I like those words; We like those words.)

25 Translate: *Me gusta la sopa.* ▲

I like the soup (The soup gusts me.)

26 Translate: We like the meal. ▲

Nos gusta la comida ("The meal gusts us." The meal is still the stimulus, the doer, and the subject of the sentence in Spanish. *We* are involved because we respond to the stimulus.)

27 Let's check to see whether you really understand this Spanish pattern and its English translation. Look at *Tú me gustas*. The subject of the verb *gustas* is the doer or stimulus. This subject is (a) *Tú* (b) *me*.   ▲

28 In other words *Tú* causes *me* to respond in a pleasant fashion. The meaning   *Tú* translation of *gustar* is "to like." Now, use your linguistic logic. The meaning translation of *Tú me gustas* is (a) I like you. (b) You like me.   ▲

I like you (You are pleasing to me = You cause me to respond pleasantly =

29 Let's turn this around and ask *¿Yo te gusto?* Who is the doer or stimulus?   You gust me.) (a) *Yo* (b) *te*   ▲

30 Who is the involved entity?   ▲   *Yo*

31 What is the translation of *¿Yo te gusto?* (a) Do you like me? (b) Do I like   *te* you?   ▲

Do you like me? (Do I gust you? = Am I pleasing to you?)

32 The involved entity pronoun form which matches the singular forms *usted*, *él*, and *ella* is _____.   ▲

33 Translate: She likes the beans. ("The beans gust her." The stimulus or   *le* subject more commonly comes after the verb in Spanish.)   ▲

Le gustan los frijoles.

34 The involved entity pronoun form which matches the plural forms *ustedes*, *ellos*, and *ellas* is _____.   ▲

35 Translate: They like the beans. (The beans gust them.)   ▲   *les*

Les gustan los frijoles. (You will learn later that this also translates "They like

36 Translate: They like the soup.   ▲   beans.")

Les gusta la sopa. (The soup gusts them.)

Summary

1 Here are the involved entity forms plus the matching subjects:

Eso *me* disgusta.	(yo)
Eso *nos* disgusta.	(nosotros)
Eso *te* disgusta.	(tú)
Eso *le* disgusta.	(usted, él, ella)
Eso *les* disgusta.	(ustedes, ellos, ellas)

2 Spanish has a pair of opposite verbs, *gustar* and *disgustar*. English has only the negative counterpart, "to disgust." The normal translation for *gustar* is "to like." The following contrasts occur between the "to like" construction of English and the *gustar* construction of Spanish:

   a The doer normally precedes "to like" but follows *gustar*: **I** like the book. *Me gusta **el libro.***

   b The doer of "to like" is the involved entity of *gustar*: **I** like the book. *Me gusta el libro.*

   c The done-to of "to like" is the doer of *gustar* (and, of course, *gustar* must agree with the doer in the Spanish construction): I like **the book**. *Me gusta **el libro.*** I like **the books**. *Me gustan **los libros.***

Self-Correcting Exercises

A *Fórmulas de cortesía:* Say aloud two possible responses to each situation.

1 A close friend your age says to you: —*Con permiso.*

2 Somebody sneezes.

3 You accidentally step on the toes of a stranger while in a crowded elevator.

4 Please wait.

Sí, cómo no. Tú lo tienes.

¡Jesús! ¡Salud!

¡Perdón! Perdóneme usted.

Dispénseme usted. Discúlpeme usted.

Hágame (Hazme) el favor de esperar.

Say the Spanish equivalent.

5 Congratulations!

6 Don't bother (*usted* form).

7 It's no bother.

8 Have a good time (*tú* form).

¡Felicidades!

No se moleste.

No es molestia ninguna.

Que te diviertas mucho.

B *Agreement of Demonstratives:* Write the combinations and correct them one at a time.

Ejemplo: 355 = Aquel es un suéter rojo.

1	Est-		**1**	corbatas	**1**	amarill-.
2	Es-	es	**2**	un traje	**2**	blanc- y negr-.
3	Aquel(l)-	son	**3**	vestidos	**3**	azul.
			4	una camisa	**4**	verde.
			5	un suéter	**5**	roj-.

1)	111	Estas son corbatas amarillas.
2)	222	Ese es un traje blanco y negro.
3)	333	Aquellos son vestidos azules.
4)	123	Este es un traje azul.
5)	234	Estos son vestidos verdes.
6)	345	Aquella es una camisa roja.
7)	144	Esta es una camisa verde.
8)	252	Ese es un suéter blanco y negro.
9)	312	Aquellas son corbatas blancas y negras.
10)	321	Aquel es un traje amarillo.

C *Reading Comprehension:* After reading the two selections, do the exercise.

¿Sabía usted . . .

(1)

. . . que el arroz con pollo es un plato° típico de España y muy popular en Hispanoamérica? Lo preparan generalmente en ocasiones especiales, por ejemplo, la comida de los domingos, los días de fiesta, reuniones de familia o cuando tienen invitados. Además de° los ingredientes básicos, arroz y pollo, la receta° incluye también pimienta, sal, ajo°, cebolla°, aceite de oliva, laurel, pimientos y huevo. Para darle color amarillo al arroz usan un poco de azafrán°.

dish

Besides

recipe/garlic/onion

saffron

Mucha gente le pone también pedazos° de jamón y un poco de vino° seco.   pieces/wine
La preparación de este delicioso plato requiere experiencia y mucho cuidado.
Si no se hace bien, los resultados pueden ser desastrosos. En los principales
hoteles y restaurantes sirven con frecuencia el arroz con pollo.

(2)

. . . que cuando vinieron los españoles a Ecuador, Perú y Bolivia, los incas ya
conocían el sistema de secar° las papas? Las papas secas que las amas de casa°   to dry/housewives
modernas pueden preparar casi instantáneamente no son un invento reciente.
El chuño que los indios de la región andina todavía comen en nuestros días
son papas secas. La papa o patata, como se llama en España, es originaria de
la región del lago Titicaca. Los españoles la llevaron a España en el siglo XVI
(dieciséis) para alimentar° a los animales. Como alimento humano, el uso de   to feed
la papa no se generalizó en Europa hasta cien años más tarde. Ya en el siglo
XIX (diecinueve) la papa era considerada como un alimento de primera
importancia en muchos países europeos. En 1846, por ejemplo, cuando una
epidemia destruyó la cosecha° de papas en Irlanda, más de 600.000 personas   crop
murieron de hambre.

Choose *sí*, if the statement is true; and *no*, if it is false.

(1)

1 En los países de habla española nunca comen arroz.   no
2 Algunas personas ponen pedazos de jamón en el arroz con pollo.   sí
3 En Argentina las amas de casa preparan arroz con pollo por lo menos   no
(*at least*) dos veces al día.
4 El arroz con pan es un plato típico muy común en Hispanoamérica y en   no
España.
5 En los países de habla española el arroz con pollo es un plato típico para   no
los días de invierno.
6 El azafrán es una sustancia que le da color amarillo a la comida.   sí

(2)

7 Los incas del Perú podían comer papas durante todo el año.   sí
8 En el siglo XIX (diecinueve) los irlandeses (habitantes de Irlanda) no   no
conocían las papas.
9 Los incas secaban las papas para poder comerlas durante todo el año.   sí
10 Los indios de Perú y Bolivia preparan un alimento de maíz que se llama   no
chuño.

D *Vocabulary for Food:* Ask and answer the following questions aloud. Adapt
the answers in the margin to your personal situation.

1 ¿Comiste huevos para el desayuno esta mañana?   No, no comí huevos.
2 ¿A veces (*At times*) comes huevos con queso?   Sí, a veces los como.
3 ¿Comes a veces manzanas y naranjas?   Sí, a veces las como.
4 ¿Qué bebida toma Vd. generalmente con las comidas?   Generalmente tomo leche.

Say the other word that completes the pair. Then reverse the cues.

5	pan	mantequilla	**8**	tomate	lechuga
6	crema	azúcar	**9**	jamón	huevos
7	sal	pimienta	**10**	comida	bebida

New Vocabulary

palabras	words	**bañar(se)**	to bathe (take a bath)	**a veces**	at times, sometimes

Vocabulary for Food and Eating

pollo	chicken	**frijoles**	beans	**desayuno**	breakfast
jamón	ham	**arroz (el)**	rice	**almuerzo**	lunch
pescado	fish	**manzana**	apple	**cena**	supper, dinner
papas (patatas)	potatoes	**naranja**	orange	**almorzar (ue)**	to have (eat) lunch
zanahorias	carrots	**plátano**	banana	**cenar**	to have (eat) dinner
lechuga	lettuce				

Assignment 59

More Practice with gustar

1 The forms of the involved entity pronouns which match *yo*, *tú*, and *nosotros* are _____. ▲

2 The form of the involved entity pronoun which matches *usted*, *él* and *ella* is _____. ▲

3 The plural of *le* is _____. ▲

4 The form *les* matches the subject pronouns _____. ▲

5 The positive opposite of *disgustar* is _____. ▲

6 If we had an English opposite of "to disgust," it would be "to gust." Translate: That gusts me. ▲

7 One equivalent of "That gusts me" is "That pleases me." The more common translation of *Eso me gusta* is _____. ▲

8 When I say, "I like your hat," (a) am I doing something to your hat? (b) am I reacting to your hat? ▲

9 What will be the subject of the Spanish translation of "I like your hat"? (a) *yo* (b) *su sombrero* ▲

10 Where will you put *su sombrero*? (a) before the verb (b) after the verb ▲

11 Translate: I like your hat. (Your hat gusts me.) ▲

me, te, nos

le

les

ustedes, ellos, ellas

gustar

Eso me gusta.

I like that.

I am reacting to your hat.

su sombrero

after the verb

Me gusta su sombrero.

12 Make *su sombrero* plural and rewrite the sentence. ▲

Me gustan sus sombreros.

13 Things can give you pleasure, cause you to react pleasantly. So can events or actions. Translate: *Me gusta leer.* ▲

I like to read. (Notice that the infinitive *leer* takes the singular verb form *gusta*.)

14 Translate: We like to eat. ▲

15 The form of *gustar* always agrees in number and person with the stimulus—   *Nos gusta comer.*
the doer and subject, not with the involved entity. Translate: We like the eggs. ▲

Nos gustan los huevos. (*Gustan* is plural to agree with *los huevos*.)

16 Rewrite changing the subject to *el huevo.* ▲

Nos gusta el huevo. (*Gusta* is now singular to agree with *el huevo*.)

17 Rewrite changing the involved entity to "you" (formal and plural). ▲

18 In this and the next frames translate the sentences given into Spanish: *Les gusta el huevo.*
She likes to talk. We like the meat. ▲

Le gusta hablar. Nos gusta la carne.

19 We like the mountains. I like Chile. ▲

Nos gustan las montañas. Me gusta Chile.

20 She likes the skirts. ▲

Le gustan las faldas.

21 I like you (*tú*). (You gust me.) ▲

Tú me gustas. (or *Me gustas tú.*)

22 You like me. (I gust you.) ▲

Yo te gusto.

Review of Stress and Accentuation

1 The smallest possible syllable is made up of (a) a single vowel (b) a single consonant. ▲

a single vowel (Linguists say that the nucleus of a syllable must be a vowel.)

2 You can find out the number of syllables in a word by counting the pure vowels. How many syllables are there in *contábamos*? ▲

3 When a syllable is stressed, the stress falls on the nucleus or vowel. When   four
you put a written accent on a syllable, you write it over (a) the vowel (b) the consonant. ▲

4 Write the Spanish for *sugar.* ▲   the vowel

5 When you read a strange word aloud you need rules that tell you which   *azúcar*
syllable to stress. Copy the following words, divide them into syllables, and underline the stressed syllable: *hablas, hablan.* ▲

6 When a word ends in the consonant *n* or *s* the stress falls on (a) the last   **ha**-blas; **ha**-blan
syllable (b) the next-to-last syllable. ▲

the next-to-last syllable

7 Copy, divide into syllables, and underline the stressed syllable: *papeles.* ▲

8 Copy, divide into syllables, and underline the stressed syllable: *tormenta,*   *pa-**pe**-les*
tomate. ▲

*tor-**men**-ta; to-**ma**-te*

9   When a word ends in a vowel, the stress falls on (a) the last syllable (b) the next-to-last syllable.   ▲

> the next-to-last syllable (The combined rule is: when a word ends in a vowel or *n* or *s*, the stress falls on the next-to-last syllable.)

10 Copy, divide into syllables, and underline the stressed syllable: *tenedor, animal.*   ▲

> *te-ne-**dor**; a-ni-**mal***

11 When a word ends in a consonant, except *n* or *s*, the stress falls on (a) the next-to-last syllable (b) the last syllable.   ▲

12 There are four kinds of exceptions to the two rules above. Some words that   the last syllable
end in *n* or *s* have the stress on the last syllable. Write the present tense *tú* form
of *estar* and the word for "ham."   ▲

13 When a word ends in *n* or *s* and is stressed on the last syllable, it must have   *estás; jamón*
————.   ▲

> an accent mark in writing

14 Copy these words and add the accent mark: *millon, direccion, ingles.*   ▲

> *millón, dirección, inglés*

15 Some words which end in a vowel have the stress on the last syllable. Translate: I sold (Preterit) the coffee.   ▲

> *(Yo) vendí el café.* (When a word ends in a vowel and is stressed on the last syllable, it must have a written accent mark on the final vowel.)

16 The vast majority of words have the stress on the last or next-to-last syllable.
There are, however, some exceptions which have the stress on earlier syllables.
All these must have a written accent on the stressed syllable. Write the word
for "telephone" and "bird."   ▲

17 There are some words which have only one syllable and also have a written   *teléfono; pájaro*
accent mark. The definite article *el* has no mark; the pronoun *él* has a mark.
Similarly the subject pronoun *tú* has a mark but the possessive adjective *tu*
does not. When a word having one syllable actually has two functions, the form
which can be stressed usually (a) has an accent mark (b) has no accent mark.   ▲

> has an accent mark (In *¿Dónde está él?* you stress *él*, but in *¿Dónde está el libro?* you stress *libro*, not *el*.)

18 Say the following sentence aloud: *El pueblo donde yo vivo.* Now say this
question aloud: *¿Dónde vive usted?* In which sentence did you stress *donde*, the
first or the second?   ▲

19 The stress normally falls on the *don* of *donde*. The written accent mark is   the second
used (a) to show which vowel is stressed (b) to show that the question word is
stressed.   ▲

> to show that the question word is stressed (*¿**Cómo** está usted? ¿**Qué** tiene usted?, ¿**Cuántos** años tiene usted?*)

In many American homes the children are trained to eat everything that is put on their plate. When Americans carry this custom over into the Hispanic society, they give some people the impression of being gluttons. A guest in a Hispanic home is often expected to leave a little portion of something on the plate. This is considered proper etiquette and does not insult the hostess.

Self-Correcting Exercises

A *Fórmulas de cortesía:* Say aloud the appropriate response to each situation.

1 You congratulate a friend on the occasion of
his birthday.   *¡Felicidades!*

2 A young lady walks into a room, and several
men rise to greet her, but she doesn't want them
to get up.   *No se molesten, por favor.*

3 Your sister tells you that if you don't
hurry, you will miss the bus. You answer that
you don't care.   *No importa.*

4 You express regret when your roommate
tells you that he failed a course.   *Lo siento mucho.*

B *Refranes:* Say aloud the proverb that has to do with each item on the left.

5	moscas	En boca cerrada no entran moscas.
6	perro	Perro que ladra no muerde.
7	madrugar	A quien madruga, Dios le ayuda.
8	sopa	De la mano a la boca se pierde la sopa.
9	casarse	Antes que te cases, mira lo que haces.
10	seda	Aunque la mona se vista de seda, mona se queda.

C *Present Perfect:* Write the combinations. All verbs in the second column
must be present perfect forms.

Ejemplo: 122 = Graciela ha traído estas blusas amarillas.

1	Graciela	1	ver	1	ese sombrero azul.
2	Nosotras	2	traer	2	estas blusas amarillas.
3	Graciela y tú	3	ponerse	3	aquel suéter verde.
4	Tú	4	hacer	4	aquellos zapatos grises.
5	Yo	5	quitarse		

1)	111	Graciela ha visto ese sombrero azul.
2)	222	Nosotras hemos traído estas blusas amarillas.
3)	331	Graciela y tú se han puesto ese sombrero azul.
4)	444	Tú has hecho aquellos zapatos grises.
5)	551	Yo me he quitado ese sombrero azul.
6)	533	Yo me he puesto aquel suéter verde.
7)	332	Graciela y tú se han puesto estas blusas amarillas.
8)	214	Nosotras hemos visto aquellos zapatos grises.

D *Preterit versus Imperfect:* After reading the following letter from Pilar to her
cousin Lola, imagine that you are telling somebody about its content by changing the infinitives in the exercise to the appropriate form of the Preterit or the
Imperfect.

Avenida del Sol 168
Albuquerque, Nuevo México
Enero 16 de 1974

Querida prima Lola,

El martes pasado recibí tu carta. ¡Qué bueno que vas a poder venir a visitarme en las próximas vacaciones de primavera!

El viernes, gracias a Dios, terminé mi último examen del primer semestre. Estudié muchísimo y recibí notas° excelentes en todas mis asignaturas.° Mis padres están muy contentos conmigo. — grades/subjects

El próximo° fin de semana pensamos ir a esquiar° en las montañas. Papá tiene un poco de gripe en estos días y no se siente muy bien, pero mamá y yo creemos que muy pronto va a estar completamente bien. Ya tenemos reservaciones en el hotel para el viernes y el sábado. — next/ski

¿Te dije que durante las vacaciones de Navidad pasamos tres días con tío Eugenio en Guadalajara? No te puedes imaginar cómo nos divertimos. Una noche fuimos todos a comer en un restaurante muy elegante. Papá y mamá pidieron arroz con pollo, pero yo pedí comida típica mexicana. ¡Qué platos tan deliciosos hacen en México!

Escríbeme pronto. Muchos besos y abrazos para todos.

Sabes te quiere, tu prima,

Pilar

Pilar le dijo a su prima Lola en la carta . . .

1 que el martes pasado ella (recibir) su carta. — recibió
2 que el viernes pasado, Pilar (terminar) sus exámenes de semestre. — terminó
3 que Pilar (estudiar) muchísimo para sus exámenes. — estudió
4 que sus padres (estar) muy contentos. — estaban
5 que Pilar y su familia (pensar) ir a esquiar en las montañas. — pensaban
6 que su papá (tener) un poco de gripe. — tenía
7 que él no se (sentir) bien. — sentía
8 que Pilar y su mamá (creer) que el papá (ir) a estar completamente bien muy pronto. — creían, iba
9 que Pilar y su familia (tener) reservaciones en el hotel. — tenían
10 que durante las vacaciones de Navidad Pilar y su familia (pasar) tres días en Guadalajara en casa de su tío Eugenio. — pasaron
11 que todos se (divertir) mucho en México. — divirtieron
12 que una noche todos (ir) a comer en un restaurante. — fueron
13 que los padres de Pilar pidieron arroz con pollo, pero ella (pedir) comida mexicana. — pidió

New Vocabulary

cuchara	spoon	**vaso**	glass	**carta**	letter
tenedor	fork	**mantel**	tablecloth	**gustar**	to like, be pleasing
cuchillo	knife	**servilleta**	napkin	**disgustar(se)**	to disgust (get upset)
plato	plate, dish	**trecho**	stretch	**gran**	great; big, large
taza	cup		(distance)	**mientras**	while

¿Cómo te (le) va?   How are you? How's everything?
Regular. ¿Y a ti (Vd.?)   So, so. And you?
"Del dicho al hecho hay gran trecho." More easily said than done.

Be sure you know the irregular perfect participles given on page 350. If you do not know them yet, you may wish to include them on your vocabulary list.

Most American students do not like to take an exam, and most have never stopped to think about what *to take an exam* really means. *To take* certainly does not have the same meaning as in *to take a walk*, *to take it home*, *to take a drink*, or *to take a boat to Europe.* The meaning is like that of *to take a course in English*, that is, to perform certain exercises. Spanish students, like Americans, do not like to take exams, but, unlike Americans, they have no doubts about the meaning of the verb which is the equivalent of *to take*. In addition, their standard translation makes their attitude toward exams very plain. *To take an exam* in Spanish is *sufrir un examen* (to suffer an exam).

Assignment 60

Preparing for a Quiz on the Demonstratives

1 In English just two demonstratives are used to show distances from the speaker. Spanish divides distance into three parts and has three demonstrative forms. The form that translates "this shirt" (near me) is _____. ▲

2 The English demonstratives have suffixes which indicate number. The plural of "this" and "that" are _____. ▲

3 The Spanish demonstratives also have plural forms. The plural of *esta camisa* is _____. ▲

4 The final phoneme of the singular form of the Spanish demonstrative matches the final phoneme of the noun with which it agrees. Thus the /a/ of *esta* matches the final /a/ of *camisa*. Change *esta* so it will match *sombrero*. ▲

5 The plural of *esta* is *estas*. The plural of *este* is not *estes*, but _____. ▲

6 The forms *este, estos, esta,* and *estas* point out objects near the speaker. The forms which point out something near the person spoken to are _____. ▲

7 Which of the above forms will you use to translate "What is *that* book you have in your hand"? ▲

8 You are reading a book. You say *Me gusta este libro.* A friend who is visiting you says, "I also like _____ book." What demonstrative in English goes into the blank? ▲

9 Which Spanish demonstrative will translate "that" in this context? ▲

10 You and a friend are looking at a mountain off in the distance. Your friend says, "I like that mountain." What would he say in Spanish? *Me gusta _____ montaña.* ▲

11 The form of *aquella* that matches *camino* is _____. ▲

12 The plural of *aquella* is _____. The plural of *aquel* is _____. ▲

13 The following frames have sentences like those you will see on your quiz. Translate only the words indicated: I like *those stockings* you are wearing. ▲

14 Do you see *that house* on the mountain top? ▲

15 *This skirt* that I just bought is too long. ▲

16 *That dog* of yours is very friendly. ▲

17 I can't hear *those animals* way over there. ▲

18 Will you please open *that window* near you? ▲

19 He broke *that window* up there. ▲

20 Do you like *these neckties?* ▲

21 Yes, I like *those neckties.* ▲

22 Look way over there, what are *those gauchos* doing? ▲

23 On your quiz the demonstrative will be given in English; for example, *No me gustan* (these) *camisas.* The proper form to translate "these" is _____. ▲

---

esta camisa

these; those

estas camisas

este

estos

ese, esos, esa, esas

ese

that

ese

aquella

aquel
aquellas, aquellos

esas medias
aquella casa
Esta falda
Ese perro
aquellos animales
esa ventana
aquella ventana
estas corbatas
esas corbatas
aquellos gauchos

estas

Giving Your Address in Spanish

1   In both American and Spanish culture there are special names for the
passage ways along which one travels. In English we talk of roads and highways
in the country. The Spanish equivalent of "road" is *camino*. In the old days a
camino was a path or trail along which one could *caminar* (walk). A pathway big
enough for a wagon or cart (*carreta*) was called a *carretera* and today this is the
common word for a "highway." In a town or city the common word for "street"
is _____. ▲

2   In both English and Spanish the width and elegance of a street help to   *calle*
determine whether it will be called a street, an avenue, or a boulevard. In
general, a boulevard is the most pretentious and many have center strips with
trees, grass, and flowers. The Spanish cognate of "avenue" is _____. ▲

3   English borrowed "boulevard" from the French. So did Spanish, but in   *avenida*
Spanish the word is spelled *bulevar*. Spanish also has its own word for an elegant
street like a boulevard. It is *paseo*. One of the famous streets of Mexico City is
El Paseo de la Reforma.

The Spanish word for "address" is the cognate of "direction." It is _____. ▲

4   In the following frames there are common questions used in asking about   *dirección*
an address. Translate them. *¿En qué calle vives?* ▲

On what street do you live ?

5   *¿Cuál es su dirección?* (A variation is *¿Cuál es la dirección de su casa?*) ▲

What is your address ?

6   *¿Cuál es el número de su casa?* (A variation is *¿Qué número tiene su casa?*) ▲

What is your house number ?

7   When you answer the question *¿Cuál es su dirección?*, you first give the name
of your street (*Calle Corrientes, Avenida España*), then the number of your house.
Thus, *Calle Real 28*. In writing, a comma may or may not be used between
the street name and the house number. Translate this address into Spanish:
1921 Columbia Avenue. ▲

Avenida Columbia 1921

8   When you count, the number 1921 comes out as *mil novecientos veintiuno*.
However, when you give a house number you may say either *diecinueve, veintiuno* or even *uno, nueve, dos, uno*. Using the first system above, translate: My
address is 1718 Laborde Street. ▲

Mi dirección es Calle Laborde diecisiete, dieciocho.

9   When the house number has five digits, the numbers may be given in several
ways. For example, 73945 may be said like this: 7-39-45, or 73-94-5, or even
739-45. To make learning easier for you, all such numbers will be practiced by
dividing them into two digit groups with the single odd number coming first:
5-22-43. Write this number in words. ▲

cinco, veintidós, cuarenta y tres

10   When you say what your address is, it is common but not necessary to use
the word *número* before the house number. For example, you might say, *Mi
dirección es Paseo de la Reforma número nueve, setenta y seis*. As a return address on

an envelope, you just give the street and the number in Arabic numerals. Write out the above address in this fashion. ▲

Paseo de la Reforma 976

11 Some day you may want to write to someone in the Hispanic world. When you put the return address on the envelope, remember that the letter you get back will be handled by American mailmen. Will you write your return home address (a) according to the English or (b) the Spanish system? ▲

according to the English system

12 This letter will also be handled by a Spanish-speaking mailman and he needs to know that it is supposed to go to the United States. So you will have to add to your return address the Spanish equivalent of U.S.A. One abbreviation for *Estados Unidos* in Spanish is *EE.UU.* Spanish uses two E's and two U's to show that the original words are plural. Another common abbreviation is *E.U.A.*

The Preterit of dar *and* poner

1 The early Spanish speakers used *e*-verb suffixes for the *a*-verb *dar* in the Preterit. The stem is *d* and the suffixes are the same as those for *vender*. Write the *yo* form of the Preterit of *vender* and *dar*. ▲

vendí; di (You omit the written accent in modern Spanish: *di.*)

2 The *tú* form of *vender* is *vendiste*. The *tú* form of *dar* is _____. ▲

3 The *nosotros* form of *vender* is _____. The *nosotros* form of *dar* is _____. ▲   *diste*

4 The *usted, él,* and *ella* form of *vender* is _____. ▲   *vendimos; dimos*

5 The *usted, él,* and *ella* form of *dar* is _____. ▲   *vendió*

dio (Some books still write this as *dió.* The accent mark is no longer needed.)

6 Write the *ustedes, ellos,* and *ellas* form: _____. ▲

dieron (as in *vendieron*)

7 The verb *poner* has a very irregular stem in the Preterit. It is *pus*. The suffixes of it are the same as those for *venir* or *hacer*. The *tú* suffixes are regular. Write the *tú* form: *pus* _____. ▲

8 The *nosotros* suffixes are regular. Write this form: *pus* _____. ▲   *pusiste*

9 The suffixes that match *ustedes, ellos,* and *ellas* are also regular. Add them to *pus* _____. ▲   *pusimos*

10 The suffix that matches *usted, él,* and *ella* is irregular. Write the Preterit of *venir* that matches these subjects. ▲   *pusieron*

11 Replace *vin* with *pus* and you have _____. ▲   *vino*

12 The preterit *yo* form of *venir* is *vine*. The preterit *yo* form of *poner* is _____. ▲   *puso*

puse

Summary

1 The irregular preterit stem for *poner* is *pus-*. The first and second suffixes are the same as for *venir*.

2 *Dar* would be perfectly regular in the Preterit if it were an *e-* or an *i-*verb.

Self-Correcting Exercises

A *Practice with "gustar":* Say aloud the Spanish translation and check each response carefully.

1	I like milk. *Me gusta la leche.*	*Me gusta la leche.*
2	We like milk.	*Nos gusta la leche.*
3	She likes milk.	*Le gusta la leche.*
4	They like milk.	*Les gusta la leche.*
5	You (familiar) like milk.	*Te gusta la leche.*
6	You (familiar) like beans.	*Te gustan los frijoles.*
7	He likes beans.	*Le gustan los frijoles*
8	I like beans.	*Me gustan los frijoles.*
9	We like beans.	*Nos gustan los frijoles.*
10	You (plural) like beans.	*Les gustan los frijoles.*
11	I like cheese.	*Me gusta el queso.*
12	I like potatoes.	*Me gustan las papas.*
13	We like potatoes.	*Nos gustan las papas.*
14	We like bread.	*Nos gusta el pan.*
15	She likes bread.	*Le gusta el pan.*
16	She likes eggs.	*Le gustan los huevos.*

B *Perfect Participles:* Say aloud the perfect participle of each infinitive. Cover the answers and check for accuracy after each one.

1	tener	*tenido*	**6**	traer	*traído*	**11**	venir	*venido*
2	ir	*ido*	**7**	escribir	*escrito*	**12**	hacer	*hecho*
3	poner	*puesto*	**8**	volver	*vuelto*	**13**	morir	*muerto*
4	romper	*roto*	**9**	oír	*oído*	**14**	caer	*caído*
5	ver	*visto*	**10**	decir	*dicho*	**15**	abrir	*abierto*

C *Present Perfect:* Ask and answer each question aloud. Your reply based on your own personal situation should include a present perfect form.

1 ¿Has hecho algo interesante hoy?

No, no he hecho nada interesante.

2 ¿Has roto alguna cosa?

Yo, no, pero mi amiga ha roto algo.

3 ¿Han venido muchos estudiantes aquí hoy?

Sí, han venido muchos.

4 ¿Han ido Vd. y sus amigos a algún restaurante mexicano?

Sí, hemos ido a varios.

5 ¿He llamado por teléfono yo hoy?

No, Vd. no ha llamado.

6 ¿Qué ropa se ha puesto Vd. hoy?

Hoy me he puesto . . .

7 ¿Ha vuelto Vd. a México después de las últimas vacaciones?

No, yo no he vuelto a México.

8 ¿Se ha muerto algún hombre famoso recientemente?

No, no se ha muerto nadie famoso.

9 ¿Ha visto Vd. a sus padres recientemente?

No, no los he visto.

10 ¿Ha leído Vd. el drama *La noche de la iguana?*

Sí, lo he leído y lo he visto.

D   *Fórmulas de cortesía y Refranes*

¿Cómo se dice en español . . . cuando Vd. habla con uno de sus amigos?

1	What did you say?	*¿Cómo?*
2	I said, "Don't bother."	*Dije: —No te molestes.*
3	It's no bother.	*No es molestia ninguna.*
4	I have to go to a party. Excuse me.	*Tengo que ir a una fiesta. Con permiso.*
5	Yes, of course. Have a good time.	*Sí, cómo no. Que te diviertas.*

Complete Vd. los siguientes refranes.

6	Más vale pájaro . . .	*. . . en mano que cien volando.*
7	Quien mucho duerme . . .	*. . . poco aprende.*
8	Quien busca . . .	*. . . halla.*
9	En boca cerrada . . .	*. . . no entran moscas.*
10	No es tan fiero . . .	*. . . el león como lo pintan.*
11	Del dicho . . .	*. . . al hecho hay gran trecho.*

New Vocabulary

avenida	avenue	**dirección**	address,	**acompañado, -a**	accompanied
paseo	drive		direction	**solo, -a**	alone
bulevar	boulevard	**EE.UU.**	U.S.A.	**le**	you, him, her
camino	road	**cortar**	to cut	**les**	you (plural), them
carretera	highway	**romper**	to break		

Buen provecho.   May it benefit you. May you enjoy your meal.

"Más vale estar solo que mal acompañado."   "It's better to be alone than in bad company."

Assignment 61

More on Stress and Accentuation

1   When *i* all by itself is preceded or followed by a consonant (*comida*, *mina*, *cuchillo*), it is always the nucleus of a syllable. Copy and divide the three words just given into syllables.   ▲

co-mi-da, mi-na, cu-chi-llo

2   When *i* (without an accent mark) precedes or follows *a*, the nucleus of the syllable is *a*, and *i* is part of the syllable. Divide *caigo* and *estudiar* into syllables.   ▲

3   When *i* has an accent mark (*í*), it either serves as the nucleus of a syllable   *cai-go; es-tu-diar* (*Martín*) or stands all by itself as a syllable. Copy *policía* and *caía* and divide into syllables.   ▲

po-li-cí-a; ca-í-a

4   The rules that you have just learned also describe what happens to *i* when it precedes or follows any other vowel letter. Copy *patio* and *tío* and divide into syllables.   ▲

5   How many syllables are there in either *veinte* or *diente*?   ▲

pa-tio; tí-o
two (*vein-te;-dien-te*)

6   Does *bien* have one or two syllables?   ▲

7   Copy and divide *ciudad* into syllables.   ▲

one
ciu-dad

8   Here are most of the words you have had in which *i* has an accent mark and, therefore, stands either as the syllable nucleus or as a syllable all by itself. The words are divided into syllables to show how they are pronounced. Say them aloud:

dí-a	rí-o	o-í-do	tra-í-do	le-í-do
pa-ís	tí-o	ca-í	cre-ís-te	le-í-mos
frí-o	po-li-cí-a	o-ír	ca-í-do	cre-í-mos

To this list you must add the imperfect of all regular *e-* and *i-*verbs, that is, the forms like *co-mí-a, ven-dí-as, dor-mí-an, etc.*

9   When *i* is preceded or followed by a consonant, it may also have an accent mark. This mark merely tells you what syllable to stress when you read aloud. Thus in *a-llí* and *a-quí* you stress (a) the first syllable (b) the last syllable.   ▲

10   The accent mark on *sí* has an entirely different function. It marks the difference between *sí* (yes) and *si* (if). The mark now shows a difference in meaning in writing. The two words sound exactly alike in speech.

the last syllable

Spelling Practice

1   The four ways of learning how words are spelled are: (1) by rule, (2) by hearing, (3) by seeing, and (4) by _____.   ▲

2   The sound [s] can be written *s*, *z*, or *c*. Which of these letters cannot stand for [s] when it comes directly before *a, o,* or *u*?   ▲

meaning

3   Why must you see *sopa* before you can learn how it is spelled?   ▲

c

It would sound the same if it were written *zopa*. (You will make spelling far easier to learn if you classify all spellings of [s] that use the letter *s* as ear spelling problems. This will take care of the majority of such sounds. Then you will only have to note and remember those spellings of [s] that use the letters *c, z, x,* and, occasionally, *ps*.)

4   What letter in *bebida* must you see before you can learn to spell the word correctly?   ▲

b (You would read *vevida* and *bebida* aloud in exactly the same way.)

5   Which word stands for "glass"? (a) *baso* (b) *vaso*   ▲

vaso (*Baso* sounds exactly like *vaso*, but it is the *yo* form of the verb *basar*—

6   Why must you see *cena* before you can learn to spell the word? Because the sound [s] can also be written either _____ before *e*.   ▲

"to base.")

7   There are three letters in *servilleta* which you have to see before you can learn to spell the word. They are _____.   ▲

s or *z*

sl, lv,

8 Here are all the words for food and eating which you have to see in order to learn to spell them. The letters you have to watch are indicated. Study the list to be sure you can spell each word.

sopa	**h**uevo	arro**z**	ta**z**a	**c**ena
ensalada	**b**anana	frijoles	**v**aso	almuer**z**o
sal	man**z**ana	po**ll**o	ser**vill**eta	pes**c**ado
a**z**úcar		**z**anahoria	desa**y**uno	

9 Say the translation aloud; then write the Spanish word: sugar, rice, carrot, apple, lunch, cup, dinner, egg, napkin, breakfast. ▲

azúcar, arroz, zanahoria, manzana, almuerzo, taza, cena, huevo, servilleta,

10 The sound [k] is spelled _____ before *e* or *i*. ▲   *desayuno*

11 The sound [k] is spelled _____ before *a*, *o*, *u*, and other consonants. ▲   *qu*

12 Apply the above rules for the [k] sound as you write the translations for the   *c* following words: sugar, food, cream, meat, butter, cheese, coffee, fish, knife, spoon. ▲

azúcar, comida, crema, carne, mantequilla, queso, café, pescado, cuchillo,

cuchara

Review and Self-Test of the Preterit and Imperfect

1 When you report the clock time at which some event in the past began, was going on, or came to an end, you use the (a) Imperfect (b) Preterit. ▲

2 Rewrite in the Past: *Son las doce cuando, por primera vez, vemos el avión.* ▲   Imperfect

Eran las doce cuando, por primera vez, vimos el avión.

3 In the sentence above, the phrase *por primera vez* translates "for the first time." The event labeled *ver* is (a) cyclic (b) non-cyclic. ▲

non-cyclic (The Preterit is used to describe the initiative aspect of a non-cyclic

4 Translate: *Era la una cuando llegó la tormenta y llovió.* ▲   event.)

It was one o'clock when the storm arrived and it rained. (Another possible translation is, "It was one o'clock when the storm arrived and it *began to*

5 Translate the indicated words: *It was three* in the morning when suddenly   *rain.*") *we heard* this terrible noise in the corral. ▲

Eran las tres . . . oímos

6 The verb for "to cry" is the regular *a*-verb *llorar*. Translate: I fell down and cried. "To fall down" in this context is *caerse*. ▲

7 When you fall down, you must get up before you can fall again. "To fall   *Me caí y lloré.* down" is a (a) non-cyclic (b) cyclic event. ▲

cyclic (The Preterit tells you that the whole cycle of a cyclic event was completed in the past.)

8 Is *llegar* a cyclic event?

9 Rewrite in the past tense: *Son las once de la noche cuando al fin* (finally) *llegan*   yes *a casa.* ▲

Eran las once de la noche cuando al fin llegaron a casa.

10 All non-cyclic events can have a beginning, a middle, and an end. The

Preterit can be used to say the whole action was completed at some time *before*
the moment of speaking. Translate: It rained a lot yesterday.   ▲

11 Translate: *Eran las cuatro de la tarde y llovía.*   ▲   *Llovió mucho ayer.*

It was four in the afternoon and it was raining. (The Imperfect *llovía* says that
a non-cyclic event was going on (was imperfect) at some point in the past.)

12 Translate the indicated clause: *Eran las cuatro de la tarde* **cuando llegábamos a
casa.**   ▲

when we were arriving home (The Imperfect *llegábamos* says that a cyclic
event was going on at some point in the past.)

13 Translate: When I was in Bogotá, I lost my raincoat.   ▲

Cuando estaba en Bogotá perdí mi (or *el*) *impermeable.* (Being in a place
(a non-cyclic event) was going on when a cyclic event (lost) was completed.)

14 Translate: I was sleeping when you (*tú*) returned home.   ▲

Yo dormía cuando volviste a casa.

15 Three uses of the past tense remain to be reviewed. You use the simple
Present in Spanish to describe what you are planning to do in the future.
Translate: *Mi hermana se casa en una semana.*   ▲

My sister is getting married in a week.

16 Translate: *Yo sabía que mi hermana se casaba en una semana.*   ▲

I knew that my sister was getting married in a week. (When you back-shift
planned action to the past tense, you use the Imperfect.)

17 Rewrite in the past tense: *Y luego dicen que van a comprar la casa.*   ▲

Y luego dijeron que iban a comprar la casa.

18 When we say "He used to work in the store but now he works in the bank,"
we compare what is customary now with what was customary before now.
Spanish has no commonly-used word for "used to." The same idea, however,
can be expressed by the tense form normally used to say that an action was
going on in the past. This form is the (a) Preterit (b) Imperfect.   ▲

19 Translate: He used to work in the store but now he works in the bank.   ▲   Imperfect

Él trabajaba en la tienda pero ahora trabaja en el banco.

20 "They used to be married to each other" tells you that they are no longer
married. In certain contexts *used to* clearly says that what was customary or
habitual in the past is no longer so. Is this also true for *She told me that when she
worked with him he* **would** *always* **say** *no when she asked him to do that?*   ▲

no (Because one may ask, "Does he still do it?")

21 Spanish has no commonly used special way to show the difference between
used to and *would*. As a result, there is only one translation for both of these
statements: (a) When I was a child, I *used to wake up* at 5 o'clock every morning.
(b) When I was a child, I *would wake up* at 5 o'clock every morning. The translation of the verb phrase is _____.   ▲

22 In the remaining frames you can test your knowledge.   *me despertaba*

In this sentence you want to say that one event (a non-cyclic action) was
going on when a cyclic event was terminated. Translate: Mother was ironing
the clothes when I returned from school.   ▲

Mamá planchaba la ropa cuando yo volví de la escuela.

23 You want to say that one event was completed before another event began.

Translate: We went out to the street and we saw the airplane. ▲

Salimos a la calle y vimos el avión.

24 You want to say that two events were completed before the moment of speaking. Rewrite in the Past: *Ayer me levanto temprano y trabajo diez horas.* ▲

Ayer me levanté temprano y trabajé diez horas.

25 In this sentence you give the time when a cyclic event was terminated. Translate: It was nine o'clock when I went to bed. ▲

Eran las nueve cuando me acosté.

26 This sentence describes a present customary action which contrasts with what you used to do in the past. Translate: We used to have dinner at six, now we have dinner at eight. (The verb is *cenar*.) ▲

Cenábamos a las seis, ahora cenamos a las ocho.

27 This sentence describes one action which was going on and one which was customary at the same time in the past. Translate: When he lived in the country, he would get up at five o'clock. ▲

Cuando él vivía en el campo se levantaba a las cinco.

28 Translate: I lived in San Diego four years. ▲

(Yo) viví en San Diego cuatro años.

29 It was raining when I arrived at the beach. ▲

Llovía cuando llegué a la playa.

30 I saw the word and it disgusted me. ▲

Vi la palabra y me disgustó.

31 I was a child when my father died. ▲

Yo era un niño cuando mi papá (padre) murió.

The prestige which a person has in his community in the United States can, in a rough and ready way, be measured by three criteria: (1) how much he owns, (2) the family he comes from, and (3) what he can do. Because all the Hispanic societies have had a close connection with the royalty of Spain, the importance of one's family tree continues to be the most significant factor in social prestige in the Hispanic world. Thus a person's name may be more important than his wealth or his capabilities. This emphasis on family sometimes seems incomprehensible to Americans who know farmers, carpenters, or plumbers with names which can be traced to European royalty. In contrast, the name of Cortés, the conqueror of México, had so much prestige attached to it that for nearly four centuries the Mexican government paid a pension to his direct descendants.

Summary

1 The Imperfect is used:

a To talk about past clock time.
b To say that any event, either cyclic or non-cyclic, was going on at some point in the past.
c As a back-shift of the Present to recall planned action.

d To translate either *used to* or *would* when talking about customary or habitual past actions.

2 The Preterit is used:

a To say that a whole event, either cyclic or non-cyclic, was completed *at* some point in the past or *before* the moment of speaking.
b To say that a non-cyclic event *began* either at some point in the past or *before* the moment of speaking.

Self-Correcting Exercises

A *Practice with "gustar":* Say aloud the Spanish translation.

1	I like vegetables.	Me gustan las legumbres.
2	We like vegetables.	Nos gustan las legumbres.
3	She likes vegetables.	Le gustan las legumbres.
4	They like vegetables.	Les gustan las legumbres.
5	You (familiar) like vegetables.	Te gustan las legumbres.
6	You (familiar) like to dance.	Te gusta bailar.
7	He likes to dance.	Le gusta bailar.
8	I like to dance.	Me gusta bailar.
9	We like to dance.	Nos gusta bailar.
10	You (plural) like to dance.	Les gusta bailar.
11	I like to swim.	Me gusta nadar.
12	We like to swim.	Nos gusta nadar.
13	We like coffee.	Nos gusta el café.
14	She likes coffee.	Le gusta el café.
15	She likes to dance.	Le gusta bailar.
16	They like to dance.	Les gusta bailar.
17	They like beans.	Les gustan los frijoles.

B *Present Perfect:* Change the indicated verbs to the Present Perfect. Write them and say them aloud.

Ejemplo: ¿A dónde va ella? → *¿A dónde ha ido ella?*

1	*Voy* a la tienda.	He ido
2	*Trabajan* dos horas.	Han trabajado
3	*Vemos* la televisión juntos.	Hemos visto
4	¿*Vuelves* a la oficina hoy?	Has vuelto
5	¿Quién lo *rompe*?	ha roto
6	*Leen* la carta.	Han leído
7	*Venimos* con ellos.	Hemos venido
8	No lo *hago* bien.	he hecho
9	Pero, hermano, ¿qué me *dices*?	has dicho
10	Nadie lō *sabe*.	ha sabido

C *Silent Reading:* Read through this entire selection without stopping to translate into English. The difficult words are explained. As soon as you finish, do the comprehension exercise.

El nombre de este personaje histórico es . . . (primera parte)

Este gran hombre de acción era del pequeño e° insignificante pueblo de Trujillo — and
que está en la provincia de Extremadura. De esta región de España salieron
muchos de los exploradores y conquistadores que vinieron al Nuevo Mundo.

Los expertos no han podido determinar todavía el año exacto en que nació.
Casi todos han dicho que fue entre los años de 1471 y 1478.

Los historiadores que han escrito biografías de este famoso personaje dicen
que durante su infancia vivió en la pobreza y la ignorancia. Pasó° muchos — underwent
trabajos° y mucha hambre. — hardships

Su padre era oficial de infantería y su madre una mujer del pueblo de baja
condición. No estaban casados. Dicen algunos libros que la madre abandonó a
su hijo en el portal de una iglesia cuando era muy pequeño.

Este hombre que llegó a ser gobernador de un vasto territorio en la América
del Sur y que recibió del rey el título de Marqués fue analfabeto durante toda
su vida. (La palabra "analfabeto" quiere decir que no sabía leer ni escribir.)
Cuentan° las leyendas que en vez de° asistir° a la escuela, el pobre muchachito — tell/instead of/attend
tenía que ir a los campos todos los días a cuidar° puercos.° — take care of/pigs

Cuando tenía que firmar° algún documento importante, lo hacía con una — sign
cruz. Otras veces su secretario le escribía el nombre, y él ponía la rúbrica:

Su nombre de pila (primer nombre) es igual° que la segunda parte de una — same
ciudad muy bonita en la costa norte de California. Comienza con la letra F.

¿Comprendió usted lo que leyó? Indique la respuesta escribiendo *sí* o *no* después
de cada número.

1 El hombre famoso de quien hablamos era de una ciudad española muy
populosa e importante. — no

2 Gran número de los conquistadores que vinieron a América en el siglo
XVI (dieciséis) eran de Extremadura. — sí

3 Los expertos dicen que es casi seguro (*sure*) que este hombre nació en 1267. — no

4 Una biografía es la historia de la vida (*life*) de una persona. — sí

5 La frase "pasó muchos trabajos" quiere decir que tuvo muchos problemas
y dificultades. — sí

6 Su padre era militar. — sí

7 Su madre era una señora muy rica y de una familia noble y distinguida. — no

8 La madre lo abandonó cuando era niño en el portal de un hotel muy
elegante. — no

9 La palabra "marqués" se refiere a un título de nobleza. También los
príncipes, las princesas y los condes son personas nobles. — sí

10 Las personas que saben leer y escribir las letras del alfabeto son analfabetos. — no

11 Una rúbrica no es un nombre. Llamamos rúbrica a las líneas que acompañan la firma (*signature*) de una persona. — sí

12 El nombre de pila de este hombre famoso es Antonio. — no

13 El nombre de pila de este personaje histórico es Francisco. — sí

D *Irregular Preterits:* Answer the questions aloud in any way that is logical.

1 ¿Pusiste tú la mesa para la cena anoche?

No, la puso mi madre.

2 ¿Les dio el profesor mucho trabajo en la clase ayer?

Sí, nos dio mucho trabajo.

3 ¿A dónde fueron Vd. y sus amigos anoche?

Fuimos a ver una película (*film*) europea.

4 ¿Viniste tú a la universidad ayer?

Sí, yo vine a la universidad ayer.

5 Yo no hice nada anoche. ¿Qué hice yo anoche?

Vd. no hizo nada.

6 ¿Qué te dijo tu compañera de cuarto cuando saliste del dormitorio esta mañana?

Ella me dijo adiós.

New Vocabulary

muñeca	doll	**bailar**	to dance	**nadar**	to swim
espada	sword	**arreglar**	to fix, repair	**quitar**	to take away
gritar	to shout	**llorar**	to cry, weep	**sólo**	only

Assignment 62

Review of the Present Perfect

1 The Present Perfect in Spanish has the same structure as the Present Perfect in English. In both languages there is an auxiliary (helping) verb. The auxiliary verb in English is "to have." The Spanish auxiliary is (a) *tener* (b) *haber.* ▲

2 The tense of the auxiliary verb in both languages is (a) Past (b) Present. ▲

haber

Present

3 The main verb appears in both languages in the form of the perfect participle. The perfect participle of "to look" in English is _____. ▲

4 The perfect participle of *mirar* is _____. ▲

looked

mirado

5 In speech the auxiliary verb *haber* has lost its stem in all the forms you are now learning. In writing, however, this stem is represented by *h. Haber* has two irregular forms (vowels) for the first suffix. What do you add to *h* to get the written form that matches *yo*? ▲

6 What do you add to *he* to get the regular written form that matches *nosotros*? ▲

e

7 Translate: I have looked. Translate: We have talked. ▲

mos

Yo he mirado. (Nosotros) hemos hablado.

8 The second suffix of the Present of *haber* is regular. The morpheme /s/ matches the subject _____. ▲

9 The second suffix which matches *ustedes, ellos,* and *ellas* is _____. ▲

tú

10 The first suffix that goes with *yo* and *nosotros* is *e.* In all the other forms of the Present of *haber* the irregular first suffix is _____. ▲

n

11 Translate: You (*tú*) have talked. / Change the subject to *ustedes.* ▲

a

Tú has hablado. Ustedes han hablado.

12 In all the forms of the present perfect, the perfect participle of *hablar* (*hablado*) always has the same form. To make the perfect participle of all regular *a*-verbs, you add *a* to the stem and add the perfective marker _____. ▲

13 Write the perfect participle for *llamé* and *estudió*. ▲   *do*

14 To make the perfect participle of all regular *e*- and *i*-verbs, you add _____   *llamado; estudiado* to the stem and add the perfective marker *do*. ▲

15 Write the perfect participle for *comer* and *vivieron*. ▲   *i*

16 There are a number of irregular perfect participles in Spanish which end   *comido; vivido* in either *to* or *cho*. Write the perfect participle of each infinitive: *decir, romper, poner, hacer, ver, morir, volver, escribir.* ▲

dicho, roto, puesto, hecho, visto, muerto, vuelto, escrito

17 The infinitive *ir* has no stem, so for the perfect participle you write _____. ▲

18 When you write the perfect participle of verbs like *caer, leer, traer,* and *oír,*   *ido* the stress falls on the *i* of the ending and this *i* stands as a syllable all by itself. To show this in writing, you must do what? ▲

write an accent mark over the i

19 Write the perfect participle for *caer, leer, traer,* and *oír.* ▲

caído, leído, traído, oído

20 When the construction is reflexive, the reflexive pronoun immediately precedes the auxiliary verb in Spanish. Translate: Abelardo has eaten breakfast. ▲

Abelardo se ha desayunado.

Review of Special Words

This review deals with a special class of words whose meaning generally can't be figured out from the context. You have to learn each word one by one and memorize each meaning. Translate mentally each sentence and check the translation for the indicated word.

1   *Ya* lo he visto. ▲

I have *already* seen it.

2   Comemos y *luego* estudiamos. ▲

We eat and *then* we study.

3   Pablo no ha llegado *todavía*. ▲

Pablo *still* hasn't arrived. (Or, "Pablo hasn't arrived *yet*.")

4   ¿*Por qué* dices eso? ▲

Why do you say that?

5   Lo digo *porque* es importante. ▲

I say it *because* it is important.

6   Lo hacemos *después de* cenar. ▲

We do it *after* eating dinner.

7   The opposite of the above is: Lo hacemos *antes de* cenar. ▲

We do it *before* eating dinner.

8 What comes between *antes* and *después* is expressed by *mientras*: Lo hacemos
mientras cenamos. ▲

We do it *while* we are eating dinner.

9 Colón llegó a la isla. *Entonces* descubrió que había indios allí. ▲

Colombus arrived at the island. *Then* he discovered that there were Indians

10 Nuestra casa está *entre* el río y la montaña. ▲ there.

Our house is *between* the river and the mountain.

11 There is a different meaning for *entre*: *Entre* todas las cosas que tenemos
que hacer, no hay nada importante. ▲

Among all the things we have to do, there is nothing important.

12 *Según* mi padre, no tenemos tiempo. ▲

According to my father, we don't have time.

13 Pensamos ir *desde* Buenos Aires *hasta* Córdoba. ▲

We plan to go *from* Buenos Aires *to* Córdoba.

14 Él no habla mucho, *sin embargo* sabe mucho. ▲

He does not talk a lot, *nevertheless* he knows a lot.

15 *Aunque* es muy interesante, no voy a leerlo. ▲

Although it is very interesting, I'm not going to read it.

16 No es *tan* grande *como* tú dices. ▲

It is not *as* big *as* you say.

17 Lo hacemos *a veces*. ▲

We do it *sometimes* (now and then).

18 No quiero ir. *Además* no tengo el dinero. ▲

I don't want to go. *Besides* I don't have the money.

19 No era *ni* gato *ni* león. Era un burro. ▲

It was *neither* a cat *nor* a lion. It was a burro.

20 Now reverse the procedure and go back through the above 19 frames,
covering the Spanish this time to see if you can give the Spanish equivalents of
the indicated English words.

In the United States an M.D. is regularly addressed as *doctor*, but a Ph.D. (doctor of philosophy) frequently is not addressed as *doctor* until he acquires prestige and stature in his field. In both cultures the members of the armed forces are addressed by their titles and so are high ranking officers of the government.

In the trade unions of the United States a man may become a *master* barber, plumber, or carpenter, but this title is not used in address. Its cognate, *maestro*, however, may be used in speaking to the master barber or the foreman carpenter: *Maestro, quiero que me corte el pelo.*

In all Latin countries a person licensed to practice law is a *licenciado*, and this is also a title of address: *¿Cómo está, licenciado?* No English speaker, in contrast, would say, "How are you, lawyer?" Lawyers are sometimes also addressed as *doctor*. The word *ingeniero* (engineer) is also a title.

The Latin, much more than the American, feels that if he has a prestige title it should be used in addressing him.

Self-Correcting Exercises

A *Perfect Participles:* Say aloud the perfect participle of each infinitive and notice those that require an accent mark. Check your answer immediately.

1	caer	**4**	decir	**7**	romper	**10**	mirar
	caído		*dicho*		*roto*		*mirado*
2	venir	**5**	traer	**8**	ver	**11**	poner
	venido		*traído*		*visto*		*puesto*
3	hacer	**6**	escribir	**9**	morir	**12**	ir
	hecho		*escrito*		*muerto*		*ido*

B *Present Perfect:* Write and say aloud the present perfect form of each indicated verb.

1	Ella *rompe* el reloj de Ana.	ha roto
2	Yo me *desayuno* con María Luisa.	he desayunado
3	La profesora lo *escribe* en la pizarra.	ha escrito
4	Ella y yo *leemos* la noticia en el periódico.	hemos leído
5	¿Por qué te *pones* ese saco que está roto?	has puesto
6	¿Qué *hacen* Vds. ahí?	han hecho
7	Estas noticias no me *dicen* nada.	han dicho
8	*Venimos* aquí con los otros estudiantes.	Hemos venido
9	Él me *trae* un plato de frijoles.	ha traído
10	Yo *veo* los árboles allí claramente.	he visto
11	Todas nosotras *volvemos* contentas.	hemos vuelto
12	El pobre gato se *muere*.	ha muerto

C *General Review:* Ask and answer aloud the questions.

1	Cuáles son los meses del invierno?	Los meses del invierno son diciembre, enero y febrero.
2	¿Te limpiaste los dientes esta mañana?	Sí, me limpié los dientes.
3	¿De qué color es tu pluma?	Mi pluma es azul y blanca.
4	¿Durmió Vd. ocho horas anoche?	No, yo dormí sólo seis horas.
5	¿Qué me dijiste?	Le dije que Vd. es muy amable.
6	¿Te pusiste una falda hoy?	No, me puse pantalones.
7	¿Cuándo compraste tu carro?	Lo compré el sábado.
8	¿Qué usas para poner mantequilla en el pan?	Uso un cuchillo.
9	¿Qué bebiste?	Bebí un vaso de agua.
10	¿Conoces al jefe (*chairman*) del departamento?	No, no lo conozco, pero conozco a uno de sus hijos.

D *Preterit versus Imperfect:* After reading the complete sentence in which the numbered verb appears, decide whether it should be changed to the Preterit or to the Imperfect and write it.

Un perro que ladra y sí muerde

Es cierto que el refrán español dice que un "perro que ladra no muerde." Pero también hay otro refrán que dice: "No hay regla sin excepción."

Entre (*Among*) los perros que ha tenido mi familia recuerdo a Pepito . . . un simpático (*cute*) chihuahua que *ladra* **1** mucho y, cada vez que (*whenever*) tiene (tenía) la oportunidad, también *muerde* **2**. Es (Era) el enemigo público número uno del lechero, el cartero, el basurero (*garbage man*) y de todas las personas que *vienen* **3** a nuestra casa a arreglar (*fix*) o vender algo.

Un día *viene* **4** un hombre de la compañía de teléfonos a investigar un problema que *tenemos* **5** en la extensión de mi papá. Cuando Pepito lo *ve* **6** *empieza* **7** a ladrar como un loco. Aunque es (era) un animal muy pequeño, hace (hacía) tanto ruido (*noise*) que el pobre señor del teléfono está (estaba) bastante nervioso y le *dice* **8** a mi mamá que a él no le *gustan* **9** los perros. Inmediatamente, mamá *pone* **10** a Pepito en el patio y le *da* **11** un poco de agua para calmarlo. Unos minutos más tarde, accidentalmente, mi hermanito abre (abrió) la puerta del patio. Pepito entra (entró) en la casa como una flecha (*arrow*), *va* **12** a donde está (estaba) el antipático intruso (*hated intruder*) y le *muerde* **13** una pierna. Afortunadamente, sus pequeños dientes no penetran (penetraron) el fuerte material de los pantalones.

Después de este incidente, mi mamá deja (dejó) de creer en refranes. Cada vez (*time*) que viene (venía) alguien que no es (era) de la familia a la casa, *pone* **14** a Pepito en su jaula (*cage*). Allí el furioso y feroz guardián de nuestros intereses ladra (ladraba) incansablemente hasta que se van (iban), pero no *puede* **15** salir a morderlos.

1 ladraba
2 mordía
3 venían
4 vino
5 teníamos
6 vio
7 empezó
8 dijo
9 gustaban
10 puso
11 dio
12 fue
13 mordió
14 ponía
15 podía

In this and the next Assignment you have no new words to learn. This has been done purposely, so that you will devote additional time to reviewing all the vocabulary in your notebook using the procedure suggested earlier.

Assignment 63

Review of Verb Morphology: A Self-Test

Change the infinitive to the Present:

1 Yo no *venir* aquí con mucha frecuencia. ▲
2 Si yo *salir* ahora llegaré a tiempo. ▲
3 Ella no sabe que yo lo *saber* también. ▲
4 Si yo te lo *dar*, ¿estarás satisfecha? ▲
5 Yo siempre me *poner* furioso al oír eso. ▲
6 Yo no *ver* nada aquí. ▲
7 He perdido mi dinero. ¿Qué *hacer* ahora? ▲

vengo
salgo
sé
doy
pongo
veo

8 Hay poco viento y las cometas no *volar* bien. ▲

9 Ella nunca *volver* a casa antes de las cinco. ▲

10 ¿Por qué no *dormir* Vd. bien? ▲

11 Esta cosa no *servir* para nada. ▲

12 Mi perro me *seguir* por todas partes. ▲

13 ¡Cuidado! *Empezar* a llover. ▲

hago
vuelan
vuelve
duerme
sirve
sigue
Empieza

Change the infinitive to the Imperfect:

1 Nunca supe lo que ellos *buscar*. ▲

2 Nos casamos cuando *tener* 22 años. ▲

3 Ella *medir* la tela cuando esto pasó. ▲

4 En aquel tiempo se *ver* muchos indios en este pueblo. ▲

5 Todo el mundo creía que *ser* imposible. ▲

6 Yo te dije que *ir* la semana siguiente. ▲

buscaban
teníamos
medía
veían
era
iba

Change the infinitive to the Preterit:

1 Y en aquel momento él *oír* una explosión tremenda. ▲

2 Ellos se asustaron tanto que nunca *volver* a ese lugar. ▲

3 Me dijeron que casi se *morir* ellos de miedo. ▲

4 Después de la tormenta todo *seguir* como antes. ▲

5 Ella nunca *sentir* lo que hizo. ▲

6 Él la *conocer* anoche en el baile. ▲

7 Los dos no se *mirar* durante toda la conversación. ▲

8 ¿Qué *pensar* ellas? ▲

9 Luego salí, lo *buscar* por todas partes, pero no lo encontré. ▲

10 Eran las tres de la mañana cuando yo *llegar* a casa. ▲

11 Tenía yo tanto miedo que no *empezar* a hacerlo. ▲

12 Yo se lo *pedir* varias veces pero nunca me lo dieron. ▲

13 Cuando yo era joven nunca *aprender* a nadar. ▲

oyó
volvieron
murieron
siguió
sintió
conoció
miraron
pensaron
busqué
llegué
empecé
pedí
aprendí

Change the infinitive to the Present Perfect:

1 Ellos me *escribir* que no pueden visitarnos este año. ▲

2 ¿No *volver* él todavía? ▲

3 Yo nunca lo *poner* en la mesa. ▲

4 Nosotros te *decir* muchas veces que es imposible. ▲

han escrito
ha vuelto
he puesto
hemos dicho

Self-Correcting Exercises

A *Preterit versus Imperfect:* Indicate Preterit or Imperfect for each item on the left.

1 to tell time in the past

2 to talk about an event that is completed in the past

I
P

3 to say that an event is in progress at a point of time in the past   I

4 to translate "used to"   I

5 to describe the initiative aspect of a non-cyclic event at a point of time in the past   P

6 to translate "would" when it refers to a customary act in the past   I

Change the indicated verbs to the Preterit or the Imperfect.

Sola en la casa

Cada (*each*) vez que sus padres *salen* **1** de noche y la *dejan* **2** sola en la casa, Lola *cierra* **3** todas las puertas y las ventanas. Aunque ya *tiene* **4** quince años, es (era) una muchacha muy miedosa (*easily scared*).

Son **5** las once y media de un martes por la noche y Lola está (estaba) sola en la casa. Cuando menos (*least*) lo espera (esperaba), *oye* **6** un ruido (*noise*) en el garaje.

—¿Quién está ahí?—pregunta (preguntó) Lola.

No contesta (contestó) nadie.

—¡Qué tonta soy! Debe ser el gato—piensa (pensó).

La muchacha se *sienta* **7** en el sofá a leer una revista. Otra vez (*Again*) ruidos en el garaje. Alguien quiere (quería) abrir la puerta. Lola se *levanta* **8** del sofá y *pone* **9** el televisor.

"Interrumpimos este programa para dar una noticia importante. Acaba de escapar del hospital del estado un loco . . ."

¡Qué desesperación! ¡El teléfono! ¡La policía! ¡Los vecinos! ¿Qué hacer? En el momento en que vienen (venían) todas estas ideas a la mente (*mind*) de la histérica muchacha, alguien *llama* **10** a la puerta.

—¿Quién es? —*grita* **11** desesperada.

—Abre la puerta, hija. Somos nosotros—*contesta* **12** una voz desde afuera.

Lola reconoce (reconoció) la voz de su padre y le da (dio) gracias a Dios.

1	salían
2	dejaban
3	cerraba
4	tenía
5	Eran
6	oyó
7	sentó
8	levantó
9	puso
10	llamó
11	gritó
12	contestó

B   *Reading Comprehension:* Select the letter corresponding to the answer.

1   ¿Cuál es otro refrán que significa, "Del dicho al hecho hay gran trecho"?   1   a

   a   De la mano a la boca se pierde la sopa.

   b   Más vale estar solo que mal acompañado.

   c   Antes que te cases, mira lo que haces.

2   ¿Cuál es otra expresión que significa, "Adiós"?   2   b

   a   ¿Cómo te va?

   b   Que te vaya bien.

   c   Buen provecho.

3   ¿Cómo se llama la última comida del día en muchos países de habla española?   3   c

   a   El desayuno.

   b   El almuerzo.

   c   La cena.

4   ¿Qué vale más, según el refrán, estar sola, o mal acompañada?   4   a

   a   Es mucho mejor estar sola.

    b Es mejor estar sola y también mal acompañada.

    c Más vale estar mal acompañada.

5 ¿Cuál es la primera cosa que pusiste en la mesa anoche cuando invitaste
a los distinguidos visitantes a cenar en tu casa?   5 a

    a Primero puse el mantel.

    b Primero puse leche en los vasos.

    c Primero puse zanahorias en los platos.

6 ¿Qué te gusta poner en los huevos?   6 b

    a Un poco de postre.

    b Un poco de sal y pimienta.

    c Lechuga fresca.

7 ¿Te divertiste mucho el otro día en el parque?   7 b

    a Sí, me rompí un brazo y perdí el reloj.

    b Sí, cantamos, bailamos y comimos mucho.

    c Sí, me sentí muy mal y me enfermé.

8 Yo vivo en la calle Almendro, número 43321.   8 b

    a Que te vaya muy bien, amigo.

    b Eso debe estar bastante lejos de aquí.

    c El hombre que maneja (*drives*) el autobús está muy cansado.

9 ¿Vas a cruzar (*cross*) la calle aquí?   9 a

    a Sí, voy a tener mucho cuidado.

    b Sí, el agua está muy alta en aquel río.

    c No, el gato viejo se ha muerto.

10 Dígame usted, ¿le gusta bailar con Antonio?   10 b

    a Sí, él es un niño tan pequeño que no ha aprendido a caminar todavía.

    b Sí, porque él trata de aprender todos los bailes modernos.

    c ¿Cómo le puedo contestar si no sé la fecha?

11 Ellos siempre sirven una bebida deliciosa para la cena los domingos.   11 a

    a Creo que la hacen con huevos, leche, y azúcar.

    b Este jugo de jamón está delicioso.

    c Crema, azúcar, jugo de tomate, todos se venden en aquella tienda.

12 Hombre, no te pongas esos pantalones viejos.   12 c

    a Tengo que buscar el menú para el almuerzo.

    b La bandera de su tierra nativa está a una altura de veinte pies.

    c ¿Por qué me dices eso?

C *Present Perfect:* Write and say aloud the corresponding present perfect form
of each indicated verb.

1 El pobre gato *muere.*   ha muerto

2 Sí, yo *vuelvo.*   he vuelto

3 Usted *hace* una ensalada magnífica.   ha hecho

4 Todos *decimos* que no *vemos* nada.   hemos dicho, hemos visto

5 Tú *escribes* bastante.   has escrito

6 ¿*Viven* ustedes en la calle Estancia?   Han vivido

7 ¿Quiénes *leen* las revistas?   han leído

8 No *oigo* absolutamente nada.

9 No lo *rompes* frecuentemente.

10 Él y yo no *recordamos* nada.

he oído

has roto

hemos recordado

D *Reading Comprehension:* Select the letter corresponding to the most logical completion of each statement.

1 Para el desayuno yo siempre tomo café con crema y . . .

  a zanahorias.

  b una ensalada de legumbres.

  c dos huevos.

2 Más vale estar solo que . . .

  a con una persona que vive lejos.

  b con gente de mala influencia.

  c con parientes de otro país.

3 No tengo mi traje de baño, por eso no puedo . . .

  a romper el reloj del invitado.

  b tener más hambre que Tomás.

  c nadar en el lago.

4 Los muchachos no bailan con ella porque . . .

  a es muy gorda y tiene los pies gigantescos.

  b siempre usa un vestido muy lindo en los bailes.

  c tiene solamente cinco dedos en cada mano.

5 Pancho me dijo que no se divirtió en el baile el sábado pasado porque . . .

  a se cayó y se rompió los pantalones.

  b tenía que bailar con una muchacha muy bonita.

  c sirvieron solamente los postres que a él le gustaban.

6 Páseme usted la crema.

  a Me gusta mucho el azúcar.

  b No me gusta el café negro.

  c Me gusta la leche caliente.

1 c

2 b

3 c

4 a

5 a

6 b

Review past vocabulary lists concentrating on the words that have caused you problems (which you have probably marked in your notebook vocabulary list).

Assignment 64

The Doer, the Done-to, and the Involved Entity

1 Who is the doer in *Marcos fixed the car for María?* ▲

2 The done-to in this same sentence is _____. ▲

Marcos

the car

3 María is the interested party, the involved entity. She may be just the person who was driving the car, or she may be its owner. It is important to observe that there can be *three* entities in a sentence. In *Pablo gave Alonso a present* the three entities are _____. ▲

Pablo, Alonso, present

4 Which one is the involved entity? ▲

Alonso (Pablo is the doer, the present is the done-to, and Alonso is the receiver

5 Let's change "Pablo gave Alonso a present" to "Pablo gave him a present."   of the present.)
The involved entity form that matches *él* is _____. ▲

le (Remember that *Le gusta la carne* means "The meat gusts him.")

6 The word for "present" (a gift) is *regalo*. So the translation of "Pablo gave him a present" is: *Pablo* _____ *dio un regalo*. ▲

7 The verb *quitar* translates the opposite of *dar*, that is, "to take away." Com-   *le*
pare these two sentences: (1) *Pablo le dio un regalo.* (2) *Pablo le quitó un regalo.*
Pablo is the doer in both sentences. The done-to in both sentences is _____. ▲

un regalo (And the third entity (*le*) is the involved entity in both sentences.)

8 Because the *le* can match *usted*, *él*, or *ella*, Spanish often clarifies statements like this by mentioning the involved entity twice. When this happens, the name of the involved entity is always preceded by the relator *a*. For example: (1) *Pablo le da un regalo a Alonso.* (2) *Pablo le quita un regalo a Alonso.* The *a* which marks the involved entity in Spanish has many English translations. Translate the first sentence above. ▲

Pablo gives a present to Alonso.

9 When the action in English is "to give," the third or involved entity is marked by the relator _____. ▲

10 Read Frame 7 again and translate: *Pablo le quita un regalo a Alonso.* ▲   to
Pablo takes a present away from Alonso.

11 When the action in English is "to take away," the third or involved entity is marked by the relator _____. ▲

12 We are talking about Manuela. Translate: *Mamá le plancha la ropa.* ▲   from
Mother irons the clothes **for** her. (The full Spanish sentence is: *Mamá le plancha la ropa a Manuela.*)

13 You know that the English translation of a Spanish word may be very different from the meaning of the Spanish word. Give the translation of the *a* for each of the following sentences: (a) *Pablo le da un regalo a Alonso.* (b) *Pablo le quita un regalo a Alonso.* (c) *Mamá le plancha la ropa a Manuela.* ▲

(a) to, (b) from, (c) for (The function of *a* in all three sentences is to mark or point out the involved entity. English gives the facts twice: once with the verb and again with the relator that comes before the involved entity. In Spanish you must figure out the nature of involvement by analyzing the

14 Consider these two sentences: (1) Pedro stole the money from me. (2) Pedro   action.)
stole my money. Spanish can translate both of the sentences with just one sentence: *Pedro me robó el dinero.* The doer is _____. ▲

15 The done-to is _____. ▲   *Pedro*

16 The money belonged to _____. ▲   *el dinero*

me (It also was taken away from me.)

A/B

C/D

E

Expressions with vez

1 We can count events when they are labeled by a noun, for example, "The whale gave him *two bumps*." This statement can be transformed (changed) to: "The whale bumped him two _____." ▲

2 Spanish is very much like English when it counts events. There is, however, no equivalent for "once, twice, thrice." Spanish always says "one time, two

times

times, three times," *etc.* "Time" in this sense is translated as *vez*. The translation
of *Tú lo hiciste una vez* is _____. ▲

> You did it once (one time).

3 Translate: I saw him four times. ▲

> *(Yo) lo vi cuatro veces.*

4 The translation of "many" as in "many shirts" is _____. ▲

5 Translate: I have done it many times (often, frequently). ▲

> *muchas*
> *Lo he hecho muchas veces.*

6 The opposite of *muchas veces* is *pocas veces*. Translate: *pocas veces.* ▲

> few times (infrequently)

7 One translation of *a* is "at." The literal translation of *a veces* is "at times."
Do these two statements say about the same thing? (1) At times he does not
know what to do. (2) Sometimes he does not know what to do. ▲

> yes (Both of the above sentences may be translated into Spanish by: *A veces*
> *no sabe qué hacer.*)

8 Translate: *Lo he hecho una vez. Ahora voy a hacerlo otra vez.* ▲

> I have done it once. Now I am going to do it another time (again).

9 Translate: *¿Qué vas a hacer esta vez?* ▲

> What are you going to do this time? (You may use *esta, esa,* or *aquella*
> with *vez.*)

10 The literal translation of *a la vez* is "at the time." We can say, "I was going
in at the time that Pedro was coming out." To state very clearly that both
actions were simultaneous, we usually add a word between "at the" and "time."
This word is _____. ▲

> same (So the best equivalent of *a la vez* is "at the same time.")

11 The English idiom "once in a while" is translated into Spanish by this
idiom: *de vez en cuando*. The literal (word for word) translation of *de vez en
cuando* is _____. ▲

> from time in when (You cannot, obviously, get the meaning of the phrase
> from its word for word translation, so you must learn the meaning of the whole
> phrase: "from time to time" or "once in a while.")

12 Here is another idiom that uses *vez: en vez de*. The literal translation is "in
time of." Try to figure out its meaning from context. Someone says, *Pablo no
puede hacerlo hoy*. Then asks the question, *¿Puede usted hacerlo en vez de él?* The
translation "Can you do it in time for him?" makes no sense. What should the
translation be? ▲

> Can you do it instead of him? (in place of him)

13 The literal translation of the idiom *de una vez* is "of one time." This tells you
nothing, so you must learn that the phrase means "once and for all." Translate:
Quiero decirle a usted de una vez que no es verdad. ▲

> I want to tell you once and for all that it is not true.

14 Translate: *¿Quién va en vez de Juan?* ▲

> Who is going instead of Juan?

15 Translate: *Yo lo hago de vez en cuando.* ▲

> I do it from time to time (once in a while).

16 Translate: *¿Cuántas veces lo hiciste tú?* ▲

> How many times did you do it?

17 Suppose the answer to *¿Cuántas veces lo hiciste tú?* is *Ninguna vez*. What Spanish negative word may be used to replace *ninguna vez?* ▲

nunca (So you will translate *ninguna vez* as "never.")

Certain people in the United States have been struggling with the problem of who is a Black. The question, you should notice, is never "Who is white?" because from the first, popular opinion considered anyone with any black ancestry to be a Black.

In Latin America there were never any laws prohibiting marriage between the Spanish and the Indians and there are, as a result, millions of people who have Indian ancestry. The Latins, nevertheless, are preoccupied with who is and who is not an Indian. Strange as it may seem, in Latin America a person who has an absolutely pure Indian ancestry may not be an Indian at all. In Bolivia a pure Indian may be classified as white when he acquires a certain level of education and economic status. The same is true for Mexico where the shift may be accomplished by shifting from Indian costume to store-bought clothes. One Mexican once jokingly defined the difference between Indian and white by saying, "Anyone who wears shoes is *not* an Indian."

Self-Correcting Exercises

A *Silent Reading:* Read this selection as fast as you can, understanding as much as possible *without* being concerned about direct translation. Then do the comprehension exercise.

Los trece de la fama (segunda parte)

I

Además de Almagro que iba y venía a buscar las cosas necesarias para continuar los viajes de exploración, Pizarro tenía un tercer socio que se llamaba Hernando de Luque. Era un sacerdote° muy respetado que tenía gran influencia con el gobernador de Panamá, Pedrarias Dávila. Su responsabilidad principal era conseguir° dinero para el proyecto. Al Padre Luque le llamaban "el loco Luque" porque muchos creían que el proyecto era absurdo y no podía tener éxito.

priest

get

II

Cuando Almagro regresó a Panamá, Dávila, "el tigre de Darién", ya no estaba allí. El nuevo gobernador era un hombre llamado Ríos y el Padre Luque no lo conocía muy bien. La tarea° de conseguir hombres y provisiones para Pizarro era cada vez más difícil. Además, Almagro no sabía que dentro de un regalo que él le había° traído a la señora Ríos, uno de los hombres de la Isla del Gallo puso una carta en que acusaba a Pizarro de ser muy cruel y tiránico. Parte de la carta estaba escrita en verso y decía así:

task

had

"Pues, señor Gobernador,	(Watch out, Governor,
mírelo bien por entero;	look into this matter thoroughly;
que allá va el recogedor,	the one going to see you is the recruiter,
y acá queda el carnicero."	the one remaining here is the butcher.)

Muchas personas sabían los versos de memoria y los cantaban por las calles. Salir a explorar con Almagro y Pizarro significaba ir a una muerte segura. El Gobernador Ríos dio órdenes de salir inmediatamente a recoger° a Pizarro y a los supervivientes° de la Isla del Gallo.

pick up
survivors

III

La mayoría° de los supervivientes querían volver a sus casas. Estaban enfermos, cansados y disgustados. Pizarro, sin embargo, seguía firme en su propósito° de continuar hacia° el sur. Cuando se preparaban para subir a los barcos, Pizarro sacó° su espada,° hizo una raya° en la arena° y miró a sus hombres diciendo:

majority
purpose
toward
took out/sword/line/
sand

"Compañeros y amigos: por aquí se va al Perú a obtener fama y riquezas; y por aquí se regresa a Panamá a ser pobres y al olvido.° Los que° quieran acompañarme, crucen esta raya."

to be forgotten
Those who

Pizarro cruzó la línea inmediatamente. Después de unos segundos de terrible indecisión, cruzaron la raya trece valientes más. Meses más tarde, "los trece de la fama" formaron el núcleo de una nueva expedición que descubrió el Perú y conquistó el imperio de los incas. La historia no ha olvidado sus nombres. Aquí están:

Pedro Alcón
Alonso Briceño
Pedro de Candia
Antón de Carrión
Francisco de Cuéllar
García de Jerez
Juan de la Torre

Alonso de Molina
Martín de Paz
Cristóbal de Peralta
Nicolás de Rivera
Bartolomé Ruiz
Domingo de Soria Luce

I

1 Pizarro, Almagro y Luque eran . . .
   a enemigos.
   b socios.
   c hombres muy ricos.

2 La responsabilidad principal de Almagro era . . .
   a llevarle a Pizarro las cosas que necesitaba.
   b pedirle dinero al rey de España.
   c hablar con los amigos ricos del Padre Luque.

3 La responsabilidad principal del Padre Luque era obtener fondos para la expedición porque . . .
   a era un soldado magnífico.
   b era un hombre muy influyente.
   c creía que la expedición era un proyecto absurdo.

1 b

2 a

3 b

II

4 Cuando Almagro regresó a Panamá, "el tigre de Darién" . . .   4 c
   a lo decapitó en el momento.
   b recibió un regalo que le gustó mucho.
   c ya no era gobernador de aquella provincia.

5 La carta que acusaba a Pizarro de ser un carnicero y un tirano vino de . . .   5 a
   a la Isla del Gallo.
   b un continente.
   c Panamá.

6 La carta que llegó escondida (*hidden*) en el regalo para la esposa (*wife*)
del gobernador . . .   6 b
   a ayudó mucho a Pizarro y a sus socios.
   b convenció a la gente de Panamá de que Pizarro llevaba a sus hombres a
morir.
   c fue escrita por un espía (*spy*) del Gobernador Pedrarias Dávila.

III

7 Cuando los barcos del Gobernador Ríos llegaron a la Isla del Gallo,
Pizarro . . .   7 c
   a decidió obedecer la orden y volver a Panamá.
   b forzó a todos sus hombres a continuar con él hacia el sur.
   c habló con sus hombres y les dio la oportunidad de seguir con él o
volver a sus casas.

8 Pizarro hizo una línea en la arena con su . . .   8 b
   a cuchillo.
   b espada.
   c pie.

9 La lectura (*reading*) dice que trece hombres . . .   9 c
   a regresaron a Panamá.
   b estaban disgustados y subieron a los barcos.
   c decidieron quedarse con su líder Pizarro.

10 Los cronistas (*historians*) que escribieron la historia de la conquista del
Perú . . . los nombres de "los trece de la fama".   10 b
   a olvidaron
   b recordaron
   c perdieron

B *Review of Weather:* Answer the questions aloud. Adapt the suggested responses, if necessary.

¿Qué tiempo hace hoy afuera?	Está nevando.
¿Qué tiempo hace aquí en el verano?	Hace calor y llueve bastante.
¿Qué tiempo hace aquí en el invierno?	Hace frío y nieva demasiado.
¿En qué meses llueve mucho?	En abril, julio y agosto.
¿En qué mes hace más viento?	Generalmente en marzo.
¿Dónde nieva, en la playa, o en las montañas?	Nieva en los dos lugares.

¿Qué ropa nos ponemos cuando llueve?   Nos ponemos un impermeable.
¿Está lloviendo o nevando ahora?   No está lloviendo ni nevando.
¿Qué ropa nos ponemos cuando hace mucho frío?   Nos ponemos abrigos y suéter.
¿Cuál es el mes de más calor en esta parte de nuestro país?   Julio es el mes de más calor.
Cuando es invierno en los Estados Unidos, ¿qué estación es en Argentina?

                                        Es verano.

New Vocabulary

autobús	bus	**cruz (la)**	cross
camión	truck	**cruzar**	to cross
taxi (el)	taxi	**doblar**	to turn, fold
tren	train	**manejar**	to drive
ferrocarril	railroad	**derecho, -a**	right
avión	airplane	**izquierdo, -a**	left
aeropuerto	airport	**otro, -a**	other, another
puente	bridge	**Que te (le, les) vaya bien.**	May all go well with you. (Good-by.)

Expressions with vez

una vez	once, one time
dos (tres, cuatro, etc.) veces	twice (three, four times)
muchas veces	many times, often
a veces	at times
pocas veces	a few times, infrequently
otra vez	again, another time
esta vez	this time
a la vez	at the same time
de vez en cuando	once in a while, from time to time
en vez de	instead of
de una vez	once and for all
ninguna vez	never

"Vísteme despacio que estoy de prisa."   "Haste makes waste."

Assignment 65

The Forms and Positions of Object Pronouns

1   You have learned that there are three different patterns in which there is a pronoun that does not stand for the doer or subject of a sentence. The three forms *me*, *nos*, and *te* are the same in all patterns. They may all stand for the done-to:

$$\text{El perro} \left|\begin{array}{c} \text{me} \\ \text{nos} \\ \text{te} \end{array}\right| \text{mordió.}$$

All three may be used in a reflexive construction:

(1) Yo *me* desperté temprano.

(2) Nosotros *nos* despertamos temprano.

(3) Tú *te* despertaste temprano.

All three may also be used to stand for the involved entity:

$$\text{Ella} \left|\begin{array}{c} \text{me} \\ \text{nos} \\ \text{te} \end{array}\right| \text{dio el libro.}$$

There are two possible translations of *Ella me dio el libro*. One is "She gave me the book." The other is "She gave the book _____." ▲

to me (The "to me" construction proves that *me* is the involved entity.)

2 The pronoun *usted* can stand for either a male or a female. It must, consequently, have two matching done-to forms. They are _____. ▲

3 The plurals of these forms that match *ustedes* are _____. ▲   *lo ; la*

4 The done-to forms that match *él* and *ella* are _____. ▲   *los ; las*

5 The done-to forms that match *ellos* and *ellas* are _____. ▲   *lo ; la*

los ; las (These are actually the last half of *el-los* and *el-las*.)

6 When you have a reflexive construction in which the doer and done-to are the same, there is only one done-to pronoun to match *usted, ustedes, él, ellos,* and *ella, ellas*. It is _____. ▲

7 Write the missing pronoun: *Ellas _____ sentaron aquí.* ▲   *se*

8 Write the missing pronoun: *Ustedes _____ sentaron aquí.* ▲   *se*

9 The single reflexive pronoun that matches *usted, ustedes, él, ellos,* and *ella, ellas* is _____. ▲   *se*

10 The involved entity pronoun that matches *usted, él,* and *ella* ends in the suffix *e*. We are talking about *ella*. Translate: She likes the house. ▲   *se*

11 The plural of *le* is _____. ▲   *Le gusta la casa.*

12 Translate: They like the house. ▲   *les*

Les gusta la casa (Remember: "The house gusts them" = The house is pleasing to them.)

13 The three subject pronouns which match *les* are _____. ▲

14 Write the missing involved entity pronoun: *Voy a dar _____ el libro a*   *ustedes, ellos, ellas*
ustedes. ▲

*Voy a dar**les** el libro a ustedes.*

15 Here are two new facts about object pronouns. If we substitute *lo* for *el libro* in *Voy a darles el libro a ustedes*, we should get *Voy a darleslo a ustedes*. However, whenever this happens the *les* is changed to the allomorph *se* and you get *Voy a darselo a ustedes*. Look at *darselo* as if it were a single word. According to the rules of accentuation the stress should fall on (a) *dar* (b) *se* (c) *lo*. ▲

16 But in actual speech the stress falls on *dar* in *darselo*. Rewrite *darselo* and   *se*
add the accent mark. ▲

17 Here are two more important facts. First, as you have just seen, the object   *dárselo*
pronouns are attached to the end of an infinitive in both speech and writing.

Second, which pronoun comes first in *dárselo*? (a) the involved entity pronoun
(b) the done-to pronoun ▲

the involved entity pronoun *se*

18 This sequence is like English: "I am going to give you it." The doer is "I";
the done-to is "it"; the involved entity is "you". The involved entity pronoun,
as in Spanish, comes before the done-to pronoun and both follow the infinitive
"to give." Now compare these two translations: "I give him it." ("I give it to
him" in some dialects.) *Se lo doy.* In English the two object pronouns follow a
finite or conjugated verb form also. In Spanish the two object pronouns _____.
a finite verb form. ▲

come before (precede)

19 When there are two object pronouns together, both *le* and *les* are changed
to _____. ▲

20 Rewrite *Voy a darles la mesa* with *mesa* omitted. You do not write *Voy a*
dárlesla, you write _____. ▲

se

21 Rewrite *Di la casa a Manuela* and use an object pronoun for both *la casa*
and *Manuela*. ▲

Voy a dársela.

22 Do the same with *Voy a dar la casa a Manuela.* ▲

Se la di.

23 Rewrite *Va a quitar la muñeca a Linda* using two object pronouns. ▲

Voy a dársela.

24 The subject of discourse is Melinda. She is the involved entity. Translate: I
wrote her a letter. ▲

Va a quitársela.

(Yo) le escribí una carta.

25 The doer in the above sentence is *yo*. The done-to is _____. ▲

una carta (So the third or involved entity is *le* = Melinda.)

26 One can omit *una carta* and simply say *Le escribí.* The translation of this
is _____. ▲

27 This frame tests whether you have really learned the difference between
the involved entity and the done-to. The translation of "I wrote her" is *Le escribí*
(I wrote *to* her). Now, be careful. The translation of "I saw her" does not equal
"I saw *to* her," so it must be _____. ▲

I wrote her.

(Yo) la vi.

Reading Comprehension

1 In this and the next nine frames, read the Spanish and then translate the
indicated word.
Pablo *rompió* su vaso. ▲

2 Voy a *arreglar*te el saco en un minuto. ▲

broke

3 *Quítese* el sombrero. ▲

to fix

4 Todos los días *almuerzo* a las doce. ▲

Take off

5 El señor se levantó de la mesa y me dijo, —*Buen provecho*. ▲

I have lunch
(May you) enjoy your meal.

6 ¿Quieres una *taza* de café? ▲

7 Va a haber una tormenta. Hay muchas *nubes* negras. ▲

cup

8 Por favor, *tráiga*me más pan. ▲

clouds
bring

9 Ya es tarde y tengo que *despedirme*. ▲

10 El muchacho tiene muchas dificultades. Voy a *ayudar*le. ▲   say good-bye

help

11 In this and the next ten frames you will see a statement in Spanish. If the statement is true, write *sí* on your answer sheet. If it is false, write *no*.

El coche, el autobús, el camión y el taxi son, en realidad, diferentes clases de automóviles. ▲

12 En la ciudad hay caminos y en el campo hay calles y avenidas. ▲   *sí*

13 En las regiones frías del Polo Norte viven muchos monos. ▲   *no*

14 En general las muchachas usan calcetines y los muchachos usan medias. ▲   *no*

15 El café, la leche y el jugo de tomate son bebidas. ▲   *no*

16 Podemos cruzar un océano en un barco o en un avión. ▲   *sí*

17 Muchos profesores se duermen muchas veces en la clase. ▲   *sí*

18 Hay muchas montañas muy grandes en el estado de Montana. ▲   *no*

19 Los frijoles, la naranja, el arroz y el plátano son carnes. ▲   *sí*

20 El Dios de los cristianos se llama Buda. ▲   *no*

21 Cuando nos despedimos de un amigo decimos, —Buenos días. ▲   *no*

                                            no

Summary

1 The forms *me*, *nos*, and *te* may stand for the done-to, the involved entity, and may be used in a reflexive construction.

2 The forms *lo*, *la*, *los*, and *las* may stand for the done-to. In a reflexive construction the done-to pronoun is *se*. The involved entity pronouns are *le* and *les*.

3 When there are two object pronouns together, the involved entity pronoun comes first and both *le* and *les* are changed to *se*.

4 The object pronouns are placed before conjugated verbs but are attached to the end of an infinitive.

Self-Correcting Exercises

A *Involved Entity Pronouns:* Write the combinations and say them aloud as you check them against the correct answer on the right.

Ejemplo: 11 = *Dolores va a decirme la verdad.*

		1	a mí.
1	Dolores va a decir la verdad	2	a ustedes.
2	Mi hermano quita la regla	3	a ti.
3	Mamá quiere comprar zapatos	4	a nosotros.
		5	a ella.

1) 21   Mi hermano me quita la regla.

2) 35   Mamá quiere comprarle zapatos.

3) 33   Mamá quiere comprarte zapatos.

4)	12	Dolores va a decirles la verdad.
5)	25	Mi hermano le quita la regla.
6)	32	Mamá quiere comprarles zapatos.
7)	13	Dolores va a decirte la verdad.
8)	34	Mamá quiere comprarnos zapatos·
9)	23	Mi hermano te quita la regla.
10)	14	Dolores va a decirnos la verdad.
11)	24	Mi hermano nos quita la regla.
12)	31	Mamá quiere comprarme zapatos.

B *General Review:* In this guided conversation, assume both roles and say aloud both questions and replies (or work with a partner, if one is available). Generate the Spanish patterns—don't just read them.

A: You ask your friend if he is going to make a trip (*hacer un viaje*) this summer.

A: ¿Vas a hacer un viaje este verano?

B: He answers yes, that he likes to travel a lot.

B: Sí, me gusta mucho viajar.

A: You ask him where he plans to go.

A: ¿A dónde piensas ir?

B: He says that he intends to go to the mountains this time.

B: Pienso ir a las montañas esta vez.

A: You ask him where he went the last time.

A: ¿A dónde fuiste la última vez?

B: He says that he went to Santiago by (*por*) plane.

B: Fui a Santiago por avión.

A: You ask if he had a good time.

A: ¿Te divertiste mucho?

B: He answers yes, that he had a very good time.

B: Sí, me divertí mucho.

A: Then you tell him that you like to travel by train and that you do not like to go by plane.

A: A mí me gusta viajar por tren. No me gusta ir por avión.

B: He says that he is going to the mountains by train.

B: Yo voy a las montañas por tren.

A: You ask him if he is going to write you a letter.

A: ¿Vas a escribirme una carta?

B: He says yes, of course, and asks what your address is.

B: Sí, cómo no. ¿Cuál es tu dirección?

A: You tell him.

A: Mi dirección es . . . (Calle San Francisco, 579)

The American male takes it for granted that he is a male and he does not feel insecure doing some things that by tradition are usually done by women. The American frequently likes to cook, often does not object to doing the dishes, and carries groceries to the car without giving the matter a second thought. Spanish speakers, in contrast, are *muy macho* (very much a male), and many of them believe it is undignified to do anything that is woman's work. Those who believe this will not carry a baby on the street or even a grocery bag. Many would not ever think of doing the dishes or sweeping the floors. There is, consequently, a sharp contrast between what a man and a woman may do in the Hispanic world.

New Vocabulary

Add these words to your notebook list.

cielo	sky, heaven	**gusto**	pleasure,	**mismo, -a**	same
flor (la)	flower		taste	**propio, -a**	own, proper
hoja	leaf	**mediodía**	noon	**único, -a**	only, unique
árbol	tree	**medianoche**	midnight	**desgraciado, -a**	unfortunate
piedra	stone, rock	**presentar**	to introduce	**tanto, -a**	so much
arena	sand		(a person)	**igualmente**	likewise,
vida	life	**dejar**	to stop,		equally
dolor	pain, ache		leave, allow	**para**	for, in order
éxito	success	**lleno, -a**	full		to
		vacío, -a	empty	**por**	by, through

A: **Quiero presentarte(le) a . . .**   I want to introduce you to . . .
B: **Mucho (Tanto) gusto.**   Pleased to meet you (Much pleasure.)
C: **Igualmente. Gracias.**   The same here. Thanks.

"No dejes para mañana lo que puedas hacer hoy."   "Don't leave for tomorrow what you can do today."

Assignment 66

Commands with usted *and* ustedes: *the Imperative Mode*

1   Which sentence is a command? (a) John closes the door, (b) John, close the door!   ▲

John, close the door!

2   You have just seen that we can talk about closing the door in two different ways: "John closes the door" and "John, close the door!" Here is another way: "I insist that he close the door."

The Roman word for "way" (meaning a "way" of doing something) was *modus*. The English form of this is *mode*. Look at these sentences: (1) His way of talking is strange. (2) His mode of talking is strange. Do both sentences say essentially the same thing?   ▲

yes

3   What mode of speaking is this? *Comb your hair! Brush your teeth! Shine your shoes!* (a) the statement mode (b) the command mode   ▲

the command mode

4   The commander-in-chief of the Roman armies was the *imperator*. The adjective "imperative" comes from this word. What linguists call the *imperative mode* is a technical way of saying the (a) statement mode (b) command mode.   ▲

command mode

5   To change the statement *He is quiet* into the question *Is he quiet?*, you change only the word order and the intonation. There is no change in the verb. Do we use the same mode for either statements or questions?   ▲

6   The Latin infinitive *indicare* means "to declare," "to make known," or "to state." So the technical term *indicative mode* is just another way of saying the "statement mode." In which sentence is the indicated verb in the indicative mode? (a) I insist that he *is* quiet. (b) I insist that he *be* quiet.   ▲

yes

I insist that he is quiet. (The statement is: *He is quiet.*)

7   Now look at the verb forms in these sentences: (a) He *talks* Spanish. (indicative mode) (b) *Talk* Spanish! (imperative mode) Are the verb forms the same in the indicative and imperative mode?   ▲

8   Look at the verb forms in these sentences: (a) *¿Habla usted español?* (b) *¡Hable usted español!* Spanish, like English, has one form of the verb for the indicative and another for the imperative. Notice that the imperative is used here in talking to the second person (*usted, ustedes*) only. There are special forms for *tú* which you will learn later. Which sentence above is in the imperative?   ▲

no

¡Hable usted español!

9   In the present indicative the first suffix of all regular *a*-verbs is either *o* (for *yo*) or *a* for all other subjects. In the imperative mode the first suffix is changed to *e*. Write the imperative for *comprar:* _____ *usted.*   ▲

Compre (The subject pronoun regularly follows the verb in the imperative.)

10   Write the imperative for *bailar:* _____ *ustedes.*   ▲

11   Regular *a*-verbs use the *e*-verb suffix to make up the imperative forms: *hable, hablen, compre, compren, etc.* Spanish is very systematic about this. Hence regular *e*-verbs reverse the process and use the _____ verb suffix to make up the imperative mode.   ▲

Bailen

12   Write the imperative forms of *comer* that match *usted* and *ustedes.*   ▲

13   The imperative forms of *i*-verbs are made in the same way as *e*-verbs. Write the imperative forms of *vivir* that match *usted* and *ustedes.*   ▲

a

coma; coman

14   Write the *ustedes* form of the imperative of *subir* and *beber.*   ▲

15   With the exception of a few highly irregular verbs, the imperative of irregular verbs uses the same stem as the *yo* form of the present indicative. Thus the stem of *tengo* is used to form *tenga*, and *tengan*. Write the two imperative forms of *venir.*   ▲

viva; vivan

suban; beban

16   The *yo* form of the Present of *hacer* and *decir* is _____.   ▲

17   Write the singular and plural imperative forms of *hacer* and *decir.*   ▲

venga; vengan

hago; digo

haga, hagan; diga, digan

18   Write the imperative *usted* form for *cerrar* and *contar.*   ▲

19   Write the imperative *ustedes* form for *salir* and *poner.*   ▲

20   Write the imperative *usted* form for *dormir.*   ▲

21   Translate: *¡Vaya usted a la pizarra!*   ▲

cierre; cuente

salgan; pongan

duerma

Go to the blackboard.

22   The imperative *vaya* has the *v* stem of *voy* and the first suffix *a* but the rest of the form is very irregular. You have to memorize *vaya* as a special class. The *ustedes* form, however, takes the regular second suffix. This form, then, is _____.   ▲

vayan ustedes

23 The imperative of *ser*, like *vaya*, uses the *s* of *soy* but adds *ea*. The *usted* form is *sea*. The *ustedes* form is _____. ▲

           sean

24 In spite of the fact that *estoy* and *doy* are irregular, the imperative forms of *estar* and *dar* are made up like all regular *a*-verbs. To change the indicative *está* and *están* to the imperative, you simply replace the first suffix *a* with _____. ▲

         e (And you get *esté* and *estén.*)

25 Change *dan* and *da* to the imperative. ▲

    den ; dé (Though it makes no difference in speech, *dé* is written with an accent

26 A change in spelling takes place when the stem of an *a*-verb ends in *z*.   mark.) Write the *ustedes* form of the imperative for *almorzar* and *empezar*. ▲

27 The *yo* form of the present indicative of *traducir* is _____. ▲

        almuerce ; empiece

28 The imperative forms are _____. ▲

             traduzco

        traduzca ; traduzcan

29 The imperative of *juego* has a spelling change for *g*. Write the form for *usted*. ▲

30 Write the imperative for *buscar:* _____ *usted.* ▲

           juegue

31 The *yo* form of the present indicative of *seguir* is _____. ▲

           busque

32 Translate using *usted*: Follow the road until the bridge. ▲

            sigo

    Siga usted el camino hasta el puente.

33 Translate using *ustedes*: Go to the board and write your name. ▲

    Vayan a la pizarra y escriban el nombre.

34 Translate using *usted*: Carry (*llevar*) the meat to the table. ▲

        Lleve la carne a la mesa.

35 Translate using *usted*: Put the bread here. ▲

36 English and Spanish do not make up negative imperatives in the same way.   *Ponga el pan aquí.* Rewrite "Close the door!" and make the sentence negative. ▲

        Do not close the door.

37 The negative imperative in English requires the helping form "do" plus the negative "not." Spanish, as usual, simply negates the verb with *no*. Compare: *Cierre usted la ventana; No cierre usted la ventana.* Translate using *usted*: Do not iron that blouse. ▲

        No planche usted esa blusa.

38 To be very polite and formal you should use the subject pronouns *usted* or *ustedes* with the imperative. It is not, however, improper to drop the subject pronoun: *No tome ese café. Está frío.*

39 In English we say, "If the shoe fits, wear it." The Spanish equivalent is *Si le viene el saco, póngaselo.* In both languages, do the object pronouns precede or follow the verb in the imperative? ▲

           follow

40 Take another look at *póngaselo*. In writing, as in speech, the object pronouns are attached to the verb and the whole unit is treated like a single word. In speech you must put the stress on the same syllable of the verb as when it is spoken by itself. In writing you must put an accent mark on the *o* of *pon: póngaselo*. Translate using *usted*: "Buy it!" (We are talking about *carne*.) ▲

    Cómprela. (There must be an accent mark on *cóm* to show where the stress

41 We are talking about *crema*. Translate: "Bring me it." (Before you do, say   falls.) the *yo* form of the present indicative of *traer*.) ▲

         Tráigamela.

42 Look at these translations: (1) "Tell me it." *Dígamelo.* (2) "Don't tell me it."
No me lo diga. In English the object pronouns follow the verb in both example
sentences. When the command is negative in Spanish, the object pronouns
come _____ the verb.   ▲

before (And in writing they are written as separate words. In speech, however,
you really say *Nomelodiga*.)

43 Translate using *usted*: Set the table.   ▲
44 Now rewrite the sentence and leave out *mesa*.   ▲   *Ponga la mesa.*
45 Make the same command negative.   ▲   *Póngala.*
46 Translate, using *beber* and the *ustedes* form: Drink the milk.   ▲   *No la ponga.*
47 Rewrite this command and leave out *leche*.   ▲   *Beban la leche.*
48 Now make the above command negative.   ▲   *Bébanla.*
49 Translate using *usted*: Buy me it (*el carro*).   ▲   *No la beban.*
50 Translate using *usted*: Sell me it (*la casa*).   ▲   *Cómpremelo.*
51 Translate using *usted*: Give him it (*el sombrero*).   ▲   *Véndamela.*

Déselo.

Getting Ready for a Dictation Quiz

In your next class you will write six sentences from dictation. Your instructor
will read each sentence *only once*. The emphasis will be on words dealing with
travel and streets.

1   What do you put in front of *carril* to get the word for "railroad"?   ▲
2   Do you have to see *ferrocarril* to learn to spell it?   ▲   *ferro*
3   Do you have to see *veces* to learn to spell it?   ▲   *no*
4   Excluding the *s* of the plural suffix, what two letters in *veces* could be replaced   *yes*
with other letters without changing what you would read aloud?   ▲

v: and *c* (You might write *bezes*.)

5   Copy these words and add the written accent mark: *autobus, camion, avion,*
direccion.   ▲

autobús, camión, avión, dirección

6   Say the following aloud in Spanish and then write the sentence with regular
spelling: [El taksi está serka del banko.]   ▲

El taxi está cerca del banco.

7   Write the cognate of "direction."   ▲
8   Why must there be an accent mark on *dirección*?   ▲   *dirección*

It ends in *n* and is stressed on the last syllable.

9   You hear [pwente]. What do you write?   ▲
10 You hear [krusan]. What do you write?   ▲   *puente*
11 The cognate of "boulevard" is _____.   ▲   *cruzan*
12 The cognate of "car" is _____.   ▲   *bulevar*
13 Is this word spelled correctly? *abenida.*   ▲   *carro*

no (Remember that most cognates are spelled like English: "avenue." So you
use *v*: *avenida*.)

14 There are three words in Spanish that stand for elegant streets: *avenida,*
bulevar, and _____. ▲

15 The word for "to travel" is _____. ▲   *paseo*

16 The word for "to drive" (a car) is _____. ▲   *viajar*

17 The noun that comes from *caminar* is _____. ▲   *manejar*

18 When a road is big and broad, it is called *una* _____. ▲   *camino*

       carretera (Check your spelling.)

19 Translate "bus" and "truck." ▲

       autobús, camión

Summary

1 To make up the first suffix for the imperative forms, regular *a*-verbs use *e;*
e- and *i*-verbs use *a* for the first suffix.

2 The stem of the imperative of irregular verbs is the same as the *yo* form
of the present indicative, when this form ends in *o*. (An exception would be a
highly irregular verb like *ir*, in which this form is *voy*.)

3 Object pronouns follow and are attached to the verb in affirmative commands. They precede the verb when the command is negative.

Self-Correcting Exercises

A *Irregular Preterits:* Write the *usted* form of each infinitive in the Preterit,
say it aloud, and then check your response.

1	decir	*dijo*		**7**	ir	*fue*
2	dormir	*durmió*		**8**	vestir	*vistió*
3	pedir	*pidió*		**9**	sentir	*sintió*
4	venir	*vino*		**10**	hacer	*hizo*
5	poner	*puso*		**11**	dar	*dio*
6	morir	*murió*		**12**	despedir	*despidió*

Ask and answer the questions aloud.

13 ¿Te pusiste un suéter esta mañana?   No, no me puse un suéter.

14 ¿Viniste a la universidad solo(a)?   No, vine con mi vecina.

15 ¿Durmió Vd. bien anoche?   Sí, dormí perfectamente.

16 Yo fui al cine el sábado. ¿A dónde fui yo el
sábado?   Vd. fue al cine.

17 ¿Vine yo rápido, o despacio?   Vd. vino muy rápido.

18 ¿Le dijiste algo en español a la profesora?   No, no le dije nada.

19 ¿Qué hiciste ayer después de cenar?   Leí el periódico y vi un programa de televisión.

20 ¿Le diste el dinero a tu sobrina?   Sí, le di cincuenta centavos.

21 Ayer fue el cumpleaños de María Dolores,
y yo le di un regalo. ¿Qué le di yo ayer a María
Dolores?   Vd. le dio un regalo.

B *General Review:* Select the letter that corresponds to the Spanish equivalent
of the items on the left.

1	he drives	(*a*)	camión			1	f
2	he turns	(*b*)	según			2	p
3	highway	(*c*)	puente			3	i
4	never	(*d*)	zanahoria			4	q
5	bridge	(*e*)	otra vez			5	c
6	truck	(*f*)	maneja			6	a
7	he crosses	(*g*)	se despidió			7	r
8	again	(*h*)	camino			8	e
9	instead of	(*i*)	carretera			9	o
10	doll	(*j*)	pescado			10	n
11	he swims	(*k*)	se divirtió			11	m
12	fish	(*l*)	tenedor			12	j
13	he said good-by	(*m*)	nada			13	g
14	according to	(*n*)	muñeca			14	b
		(*o*)	en vez de				
		(*p*)	dobla				
		(*q*)	ninguna vez				
		(*r*)	cruza				

C *Involved Entity Pronouns:* As you write the combinations given below, keep
in mind that the prepositional phrase in the second column must be changed
into the appropriate with-verb involved entity pronoun and placed properly
in the sentence.

Ejemplo: 12 = ***Nos** los ha roto*.

1	Los ha roto	1	a mí.
2	Va a arreglarlo	2	a Pancho y a mí.
3	Antonio las quita	3	a Enriqueta.
4	Lo han hecho	4	a ti.
		5	a sus compañeros.

1)	11	Me los ha roto.
2)	22	Va a arreglárnoslo.
3)	33	Antonio se las quita.
4)	44	Te lo han hecho.
5)	15	Se los ha roto.
6)	21	Va a arreglármelo.
7)	32	Antonio nos las quita.
8)	43	Se lo han hecho.
9)	14	Te los ha roto.
10)	45	Se lo han hecho.

New Vocabulary

lástima	pity	**reír (i)**	to laugh
dudar	to doubt	**sonreír (i)**	to smile
saltar	to jump	**conseguir (i)**	to get, obtain
parecer	to seem		

¡Qué lástima!   What a pity!

¡Qué formidable!   How wonderful!

"Si le viene el saco, póngaselo."   "If the shoe fits, wear it."

Assignment 67

The Subjunctive Mode

Whenever a new category of verbs is dealt with, two basic learning problems confront you as the learner: (1) verb morphology (the way in which the verb forms differ from already known forms) and (2) usage (the meaning of and kinds of situations in which the verb forms are used). The following frames are intended to instruct you in how to form most of the present subjunctive, and how to use it in one instance. Precisely, you should learn that

a   when a sentence has two clauses (parts) connected by *que* (*that*), and the subject of the first clause tries to influence the behavior of the subject of the second clause (introduced by *que*), the verb form of the second clause is in the subjunctive.

b   the stem for all present subjunctive forms is the same as the stem for the *yo* form in the present indicative (except when this form does not end in *o* and in the case of some stem-changing verbs). The first suffix for all *a*-verbs is *e* and for all *e*- and *i*-verbs is *a*; the second suffix for all verbs is regular (the same as for the present indicative).

The Subjunctive for Influencing Behavior

1   Although there is considerable use of the present subjunctive in English, it frequently goes unnoticed because all of its forms are identical to the infinitive. There is a reason why the indicated verb in one of the following sentences stands out more obviously as a subjunctive form. Can you tell which one it is?

   a   He insists that they *go* also. (they go)
   b   He insists that they *give* us more time. (they give)
   c   He insists that they *be* here tomorrow. (they be)   ▲

c He insists that they *be* here tomorrow.

2 In sentences *a* and *b* the subjunctive form is identical to the indicative. In fact, without more context it is impossible to know whether they are subjunctive or indicative (which will probably be obvious to you only if you take the time to read this part of your Assignment twice). However, since *are* is the usual present form that goes with *they*, it is easy to recognize *be* as subjunctive in sentence *c*. Notice that *be* is also the command form: *Be quiet!* Which one of the indicated verbs in the following sentences is easiest to spot as subjunctive?

 a I demand that you *do* this now. (you do)
 b I demand that she *do* this now. (she do)
 c I demand that they *do* this now. (they do) ▲

> b I demand that she *do* this now. (*Do* contrasts with *does*, which is the present indicative form that matches *she*. In the other two cases, the subjunctive and indicative forms are identical.)

3 In which of the following sentences is the subject of the first clause trying to influence the behavior of the subject of the second clause?

 a Her mother insists that she study more.
 b Her mother insists that she studies more. ▲

> a Her mother insists that she study more. (The subjunctive is *study*, not *studies*.)

4 In which sentence is the subject of the first clause merely reporting insistently what the subject of the second clause regularly does?

 a Mother insists that he practices daily.
 b Mother insists that he practice daily. ▲

> a Mother insists that he practices daily. (In the second sentence the subjunctive is used because "Mother" influences "his" behavior.)

5 Fill in the correct form of the verb *to be* in the following sentences:

 a I request that she _____ my secretary.
 b I know that she _____ my secretary. ▲

> I request that she *be* my secretary (influencing); I know that she *is* my secretary (no influencing).

6 One use of the subjunctive in Spanish is like that of all the above subjunctive examples in English. Notice that in all instances the two requirements for the subjunctive are present: (1) that there be two clauses connected by *that* (*que* in Spanish), and (2) that the subject of the first clause try to influence the subject of the second (subjoined = subjunctive) clause. (Did you notice that 1 and 2 above were both "subjoined" clauses connected by "that" to the rest of the sentence, and that the subjunctive was used in both, *be* and *try*?)

Morphology of the Present Subjunctive

1 In CIS you have already learned about two modes, the indicative and the imperative. The subjunctive mode, in some respects, is like the imperative mode. In fact, the *usted-* and *ustedes*-imperative are borrowed subjunctive forms. So you have two ways of approaching present subjunctive morphology. The first is simply to take the imperative *usted* form of any verb and add the appropriate second suffix (zero, *-s*, *-n*, *-mos*). (You will need a little more information

about stem-changing verbs.) See if you can do this with *venir*. Do you remember
the *usted* imperative? Give the *nosotros, tú* and *ellos* present subjunctive forms. ▲

vengamos, vengas, vengan

2 If you have not yet learned the forms of the imperative sufficiently well to
use them as mental "anchors" for the subjunctive, you can follow the second
procedure, which has two steps. With minor exceptions to be mentioned later,
use the stem allomorph that matches *yo* in the present indicative. For *a*-verbs
use *e* for the first suffix; for *e*- and *i*-verbs use *a*. The second suffixes are regular
as in the present indicative.

Let's try it with the verb *salir*. The stem of the *yo* form is *salg-* (*salgo*). To it we
add the first suffix *a* (since it is an *i*-verb) and the usual second suffixes: *salga,
salgamos, salgas, salgan*. Let's see if you can do the same with the verb *hacer*.
Give the present subjunctive forms that match *tú, ustedes, yo,* and *nosotros*. ▲

hagas, hagan, haga, hagamos

3 Give the same forms for *ver*. ▲

veas, vean, vea, veamos

4 Now try it with an *a*-verb. Give the same forms for *cenar*. ▲

cenes, cenen, cene, cenemos

5 You know six verbs that have a *yo* form in the present indicative that does
not end in *o* (*voy, soy, estoy, doy, sé, he*). In all these verbs there is a special irregularity in the present subjunctive. You may remember some of these from
your work with the imperative. *Ir* and *ser* are irregular because of the subjunctive stems, *vay-* and *se-*. Give the *tú* and *nosotros* forms for each. ▲

vayas, vayamos, seas; seamos

6 *Saber* and *haber* also have irregular stems, *sep-* and *hay-*. Give the *yo* and *ellos*
forms for each. ▲

sepa, sepan; haya, hayan

7 *Dar* is regular except that the form *dé* must be written with the accent to
differentiate it from the relator *de*. Write the *yo* and *nosotros* forms. ▲

8 *Estar* is irregular only because it retains the stress on the first suffix through- | *dé, demos*
out, requiring the written accent for all forms except *estemos*. Give the *tú* and
ustedes forms. ▲

9 Remember that the subjunctive verb is always in the subjoined clause | *estés, estén*
(after *que*). Fill in the appropriate form of the present subjunctive for the
following three sentences:

Pido que ustedes _____ (ir) con nosotros.

Demandan que él y yo _____ (salir) pronto.

Quiere que tú _____ (ser) presidente algún día. ▲

vayan, salgamos, seas

10 Translate the following sentences:

They ask (*pedir*) that she sing also.

I demand that you (*tú*) tell the truth. ▲

Piden que ella cante también. Demando que digas la verdad.

11 What is a more common way in English of saying *They ask that she sing
also*?

They ask her to sing also.

12 Spanish does not use this construction (except with a very few verbs that you will learn later). It is easier to first convert the English construction to the one that matches the Spanish, and then to translate. Give the Spanish-matching English construction of *She asks me to come.*

She asks that I come.

13 Now give the Spanish equivalent. ▲

Ella pide que yo venga.

14 Use the above two-step process to give the Spanish for *He wants me to work tomorrow.*

First, you convert the pattern to *He wants that I work tomorrow;* then you translate it; *Quiere que yo trabaje mañana.*

15 Do the same for "They beg (*rogar* (*ue*)) him to clean the room." ▲

They beg that he clean the room. *Ruegan que él limpie el cuarto.*

16 The rules for positioning with-verb pronouns are the same for the subjunctive as for the indicative. The translation of *He knows it* is *Él lo sabe.* Translate *I demand that he know it.* ▲

Demando que él lo sepa.

17 Fill in the blanks: *Desean que yo* _____ (*levantarse*) *temprano.* ▲
18 No permiten que nosotros _____ (traerlo).
19 Quiero que tú _____ (leérmelo). ▲

me levante
lo traigamos
me lo leas

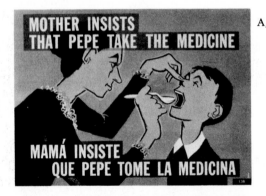

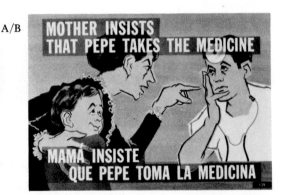

A/B

MOTHER INSISTS THAT PEPE TAKE THE MEDICINE

MAMÁ INSISTE QUE PEPE TOME LA MEDICINA

MOTHER INSISTS THAT PEPE TAKES THE MEDICINE

MAMÁ INSISTE QUE PEPE TOMA LA MEDICINA

C/D

QUIERE QUE SE CASE CON ÉL

PIDE QUE SE CASE CON ÉL

E/F

Summary

1 You must use the subjunctive after *que* when action in the non-*que* clause aims toward influencing the action in the *que* clause.

2 You can usually form the subjunctive by attaching *e* for *a*-verbs and *a* for *e*- and *i*-verbs, plus the usual second suffixes to the stem used with *yo* in the present indicative. ▲

3 Six common exceptions to 2:

ser: *sea, etc.*
ir: *vaya, etc.*
dar: *dé, demos, des, den*

saber: *sepa, etc.*
haber: *haya, etc.*
estar: *esté, estemos, estés, estén*

4 English constructions such as *I want you to do it* are converted into two clauses connected by *that* (*I want that you do it*) in order to be directly translatable into Spanish.

5 The position of with-verb pronouns in subjunctive clauses is the same as in indicative clauses, as in *Yo sé que él lo hace, Yo demando que él lo haga.*

Changing Nouns to Pronouns

1 Rewrite in English "María gave Henry the books" and replace "Henry" with a pronoun. ▲

María gave him the books.

2 Transform: *María dio los libros a Juan* so it translates: "María gave him the books." ▲

María le dio los libros.

3 Transform: *María le dio los libros* and replace *María* with a pronoun. ▲

Ella le dio los libros.

4 You can say the above sentence and omit the noun *libros*. The residual *los* must come before the verb. Is it correct to say: *Ella le los dio?* ▲

no

5   When the involved entity is *le* or *les* and there is another object pronoun (*lo*, *la*, *las*, or *los*), you must change the *le* or *les* to_____ .   ▲

se (So you say *Ella se los dio.*)

6   In this and the next ten frames, rewrite each sentence and change the italicized words to pronouns or adjectival residuals.   ▲
La niña llevó *la camisa* a su abuela.

Ella la llevó a su abuela.

7   *El señor López* visitó *a sus sobrinos* ayer.   ▲
8   *Mamá* vendió *la casa a su hermano.*   ▲
9   ¿Quieres plancharme *la corbata?*   ▲

Él los visitó ayer.
Ella se la vendió.
¿Quieres planchármela?

10   Te traigo *la leche.*   ▲
11   *Eduardo* va a quitarse *el sombrero.*   ▲
12   *Papá y mamá* van a comprarnos *la ropa.*   ▲

Te la traigo.
Él va a quitárselo.
Ellos van a comprárnosla.

13   *Elena* ve *a los muchachos.*   ▲
14   Yo lavo *las cucharas.*   ▲
15   *Juan* vendió *las bananas a los muchachos.*   ▲

Ella los ve.
Yo las lavo.
Él se las vendió.

The Verbs reír *and* sonreír

1   The verbs *reír* and *sonreír* present a special problem. First, they are conjugated like *pedir*. Second, the *e* and *i* are always in different syllables, so when they are <u>side by side</u> the *i* must have a written accent mark (í). Let's see, now, if you can use *pedir* as a model and from this get the right form and spelling of *reír* and *sonreír*. Write the forms of these two verbs that match *pido*. (The *e* of the stem changes to *i*.)   ▲
2   Write the forms that are like *pedimos.*   ▲

río; sonrío
reímos; sonreímos

3   The perfect participle of *pedir* is *pedido*. To write the perfect participles of *reír* and *sonreír* you just replace the final *r* with the suffix _____.   ▲

do (reído, sonreído)

4   Write the forms that are like *pedías*, *pedí*, and *pediste.*   ▲

reías, sonreías, reí, sonreí; reíste, sonreíste

5   Write the forms that are like *pidió.*   ▲

rió; sonrió (This is one of the few cases where the Spanish spelling system does not tell you what to say. You say *ri-ó* and *son-ri-ó*. Originally *rió* had two *i*'s, *ri-ió*, and the first one was part of a different syllable. Today the two *i*'s are fused, but the word still has two syllables in speech.)

Self-Correcting Exercises

A   *Pronouns and Adjectival Residuals:* In this exercise you are to delete each italicized noun and to rewrite each sentence either by replacing the deleted noun with a pronoun or by keeping the adjectival residual and placing it properly in relation to the verb.

Ejemplos: *El profesor* nos explica *las lecciones.* (**É**l nos las explica.)
          Juanita quiere darme *el regalo.* (Ella quiere dármelo.)

1 *María* me trae *las noticias.*	Ella me las trae.
2 Yo doy *la nueva revista* a *Beatriz.*	Yo se la doy.
3 *Papá* quiere leer *el periódico.*	Él quiere leerlo.
4 *Mamá* sirve *las papas* a *papá.*	Ella se las sirve.
5 *Enrique y Ana* van a ponerse *el impermeable.*	Ellos van a ponérselo.

B *Fórmulas de cortesía:* Say aloud the Spanish translation.

1 God bless you (following a sneeze).	Salud. Jesús.
2 I'm sorry.	Lo siento.
3 What did you say?	¿Cómo?
4 It doesn't matter.	No importa.
5 Don't bother (*usted*).	No se moleste usted.
6 It's no bother.	No es molestia ninguna.
7 Have a good time (*tú*).	Que te diviertas.
8 What a pity!	¡Qué lástima!
9 Congratulations!	¡Felicidades!
10 How wonderful!	¡Qué formidable!

C *Refranes:* Say aloud the proverb which is appropriate to the following situations.

1 She talks so much that she accidentally let out an important secret that should not have been revealed.	En boca cerrada no entran moscas.
2 He is always saying that he is going to do all kinds of wonderful things, but I've never seen him perform.	Del dicho al hecho hay gran trecho. De la mano a la boca se pierde la sopa.
3 If you had done it yesterday instead of putting it off, we wouldn't be having all this trouble.	No dejes para mañana lo que puedas hacer hoy.
4 You wouldn't have gotten stuck with a lemon, if you had tried out that car before buying it so hastily.	Antes que te cases, mira lo que haces.
5 I know it is very urgent and we are quickly running out of time, but I will not ruin everything by hurrying.	Vísteme despacio que estoy de prisa.

D *Reading Comprehension:* Read through the following selection without stopping to translate. Can you guess the name of the animal being described?

¿Cuál es el nombre de este animal?

El nombre del animal que usted tiene que identificar en los siguientes párrafos comienza con la primera letra del alfabeto. Incluye varias especies de mamíferos° que habitan en la América del Sur y también en algunas partes de Norte América. Son muy buenos amigos de los agricultores porque su comida preferida consiste casi exclusivamente de larvas, insectos y gusanos.° Su tamaño varía de región a región. En las selvas de Brasil y Paraguay podemos encontrar una especie de tamaño gigante y en las zonas arenosas de Argentina existe un tipo miniatura que mide solamente varias pulgadas° y tiene ojos pequeñísimos, casi invisibles.

    Todos los animales que pertenecen° a esta familia tienen una característica en común: su cuerpo está casi enteramente cubierto por un tipo de armadura° de hueso° dividida en secciones movibles que les sirven de protección. Otra característica muy interesante de todo el grupo es que cada vez que la hembra° tiene hijos son todos del mismo sexo. Nacen en grupos de cuatro a seis y cada vez son todos hembras o machos.° Esto no pasa, por ejemplo, con los gatos. Cuando una gata tiene gatitos, algunos son hembras y otros son machos.

    Cuando son atacados por algún enemigo, estos animales corren tan rápidamente que es casi imposible verles las patas. (La palabra "pata" significa lo mismo que pierna, pero en español se usa pata para los animales. Por ejemplo, una persona tiene dos piernas, pero un caballo tiene cuatro patas.) Como ya dijimos, los animales de que hablamos corren muy rápidamente a buscar protección en las cuevas° subterráneas donde viven. Si están lejos de ellas cuando los atacan, pueden hacer otra cueva nueva con una rapidez fantástica. Cuando no tienen tiempo suficiente para hacer esto antes de llegar el enemigo, se enroscan° dentro de su armadura como verdaderas pelotas o bolas. Entonces sus enemigos no pueden hacerles nada. La dura° cubierta° que les dio la naturaleza° los protege e° impide que otros animales los muerdan.

    El nombre que los soldados españoles le dieron a esta familia de animales viene de la palabra *armado* que quiere decir llevar armas o estar vestido con una armadura de metal. ¿Ha visto o leído usted algo sobre estos animales? ¿Hay armad . . . en el parque zoológico de la ciudad o región donde usted vive?

    See top of page 408 for the answer.

(glosses, right margin:)
mammals
worms
inches
belong
armor
bone
female
males
caves
curl up
hard/cover/nature
and

It is quite customary in the United States for married couples or sweethearts to greet each other after a long absence with a hug. In the Hispanic world after similar absences, men often greet each other with a big hug called *un abrazo* (embrace). It is also common for men friends to end a letter with *Con un abrazo* (With a hug). It is considered quite proper for grown men to hug each other. In Russia men friends sometimes hold hands when they go for a walk together. If you react negatively to these customs, the sociologist says you are suffering from "cultural shock." This means you are not ready to accept the notion that behavior patterns that are taboo in our society may be very acceptable in another culture.

New Vocabulary

bolsa (**cartera**)	purse, bag	**simpático, -a**	nice, cute, charming
bolsillo	pocket	**antipático, -a**	obnoxious, unpleasant
oro	gold	**sin**	without
plata	silver	**a propósito**	by the way
película	movie, film	**por lo menos**	at least
equivocado, -a	mistaken		

Assignment 68

The Subjunctive and Indicative in Contrast

Understanding of the information on the subjunctive in Assignment 67 will increase the usefulness of this Assignment. Check the Summary (page 403).

There are three modes: (a) the imperative (used to tell someone to do something: *Salga usted de aquí*), (b) the indicative (used when there is only one doer in the sentence, with minor exceptions), and (c) the subjunctive. When a sentence contains a main and a dependent verb, each with a different doer (subject), you have to choose between indicative and subjunctive in the dependent clause.

You have learned that the subjunctive (sub-joined) is used in the dependent clause (after "that" or *que*) when the event in the main clause attempts to influence the event in the dependent clause. The following frames help you to learn these three facts about dependent clauses:

(1)   When a statement is made about what someone does, with no intent to influence his behavior, the indicative is used.

(2)   When a command is reported, the subjunctive is used.

(3)   When a statement is reported, the indicative is used.

Influencing versus Awareness

1   There are two English patterns in which one doer tries to influence (cause) the behavior of another. One pattern (like Spanish) has two clauses and the linking word *that*: "He demands *that* she pay the bill." The other pattern has two doers and two verbs, but the second verb and its subject are treated as a noun phrase. In the following examples the indicated phrase is the object of *want.*

I want *an apple.*

I want *to eat an apple.*

I want *him to eat an apple.*

Let's transform the last sentence to use the connector word *that* and a subjoined clause. What mode will you use in English to fill the blank? "It is my

The answer to *¿Cual es el nombre de este animal?* (page 406) is *armadillo*.

wish that he _____ an apple." (a) indicative: eats (b) subjunctive: eat ▲

> subjunctive: eat (This contrast may not be in your dialect. If so, you may learn it in both English and Spanish.)

2 My saying that "I want" is an attempt to get him to eat an apple. However, before you are ready to put "I want him to eat an apple" into Spanish, you must change the pattern to "I want that he eat an apple." Translate this pattern. ▲

> *Quiero que él coma una manzana.*

3 One can influence the actions or behavior of another person in three ways:

(1) By direct command: *Lea la lección.* This is a very strong and often impolite way of causing the other person to act.

(2) A softer and more pleasant way of getting the same result is to request that someone do something or to say that you want them to do something: *Pido que lea la lección. Quiero que lea la lección.*

(3) A third and more impersonal way to get the same results is to say that it is important or necessary to do something. Translate using *usted*: It is necessary that you read the lesson. ▲

> *Es necesario que lea la lección.*

4 The cognate of "important" is *importante*. Translate the indicated verb, using *tú*: "It is important that you *be* here at eight o'clock." (The *be* in English is subjunctive.) ▲

5 Here are the verbs you have had that are used to influence the action of the doer of the subjoined (dependent) clause. Note that "influence" may be restated as "cause, prevent, or permit."

estés

dejar (to let, allow)	*desear* (to desire)
pedir (to ask, request)	*impedir* (to prevent)
querer (to wish, want)	*permitir* (to permit)

Why is *permitir* a verb of influencing? Because the person who "permits" also has the authority to deny that permit, so he controls someone's behavior. Translate the indicated verb: "He prevents her from *going out*." (He prevents that she *go out*.) ▲

6 Which of the following sentences is an example of influencing?

salga

(a) *Es buena idea que te pongas el abrigo.* (b) *Veo que te pones el abrigo.* ▲

> (a) *Es buena idea que te pongas el abrigo.* (Sentence *b* is merely a statement— in this case an observation—about what someone does.)

7 Fill in "subjunctive" or "indicative": When a comment is made concerning an event and with no intention by the doer to influence that event, the _____ is used in the dependent clause. ▲

8 Following are some verbs you have had that are <u>not used to influence</u>, but merely to <u>talk about or indicate awareness of</u> events. All may be followed by a clause that begins with *que*.

indicative

ver (to see)	*observar* (to observe)	*recordar* (to remember)
saber (to know)	*informar* (to inform)	*responder* (to answer, reply)

oír (to hear)   *contestar* (to answer)   *relatar* (to tell, relate)

contar (to tell)   *leer* (to read)   *parecer* (to seem)

Fill in the blanks with the appropriate form of the infinitive:

Sabemos que ellas _____ (tocar) el violín.

Mamá pide que los niños no _____ (gritar) más.

Veo que mi perro _____ (saltar) más que otros perros.   ▲

tocan, griten, salta

Subjunctive versus Indicative in Reporting

1   There are many verbs used to report what someone says or how he says it. Suppose Miguel says, "Juan is coming." You do not hear this precisely. So you ask Pablo, "What is he saying?" Pablo answers, "He is saying that Juan is coming." Here is an important rule: <u>When a report verb is used to report a statement that was originally in the indicative, the verb of the subjoined clause remains in the indicative.</u> Let's see how this conversation goes in Spanish:

Miguel: *Ahí viene Juan.*

You ask Pablo: *¿Qué dice Miguel?*

Pablo answers: *Dice que ahí viene Juan.*

In which pair of sentences is "insists" (*insiste*) a report verb which says "She says emphatically"?

(1)   Mother insists that Pepe takes the medicine.

Mamá insiste que Pepe toma la medicina.

(2)   Mother insists that Pepe take the medicine.

Mamá insiste que Pepe tome la medicina.   ▲

in pair (1) which uses the indicative in both languages; (In pair (2) the base
meaning of the subjoined clause is the imperative, "Take the medicine"—

2   The verb *insistir*, like its English cognate, has two meanings: (1) to say   *Tome la medicina.*) insistently or emphatically, and (2) to demand. When the meaning is "to demand," the subjoined verb is in the (a) indicative (b) subjunctive.   ▲

3   Verbs of reporting can also be used to report what was originally said in the   <div align="right">subjunctive</div> imperative. Here is how this happens in a real conversation:

Pepe to Carlos: *Cierre la ventana.*

Juan to Ana: *¿Qué dice Pepe?*

Ana: *Dice que Carlos cierre la ventana.*

Which of the following sentences reports an original command? (a) *Dice que viene.* (b) *Dice que venga.*   ▲

Dice que venga. (In direct quotes this would be *Dice, —¡Venga!*)

4   Here is another important rule: <u>When a report verb is used to report an original command, the subjoined (dependent) verb is in the subjunctive.</u> The verb *gritar* translates "to shout." Which of the following sentences reports an original command? (a) *Grita que sube al balcón.* (b) *Grita que suba al balcón.*   ▲

Grita que suba al balcón. (The original, shouted command was *¡Suba al
balcón!*)

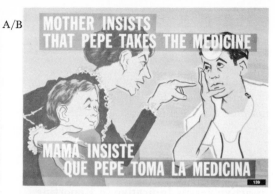

A/B

C/D

E/F

G

Summary

The following apply to the verb form in the subjoined clause:

1 The choice of mode is $\dfrac{\text{subjunctive}}{\text{indicative}}$ in reporting $\dfrac{\text{a command.}}{\text{a statement.}}$

2 The choice of mode is $\dfrac{\text{subjunctive}}{\text{indicative}}$ when the doer in the main clause $\dfrac{\text{attempts to influence}}{\text{expresses awareness of}}$ an event.

Review of the Preterit and the Imperfect: Morphology and Usage

1 The first suffix of the Imperfect of all *a*-verbs is _____. ▲

2 Write the *nosotros* forms of *mandar* and *esperar*. ▲
aba
mandábamos; esperábamos (Did you remember the accents?)

3 The first suffix of the Imperfect of all regular *e*- and *i*-verbs is _____. ▲
ía (The *i* has an accent mark in all forms.)

4 Write the *yo* form of the Imperfect of *dormir*. ▲

5 The *yo* form of the Imperfect of all regular verbs (*a*, *e*, and *i*) may be treated *dormía* as the base on which to build all the other forms. To get the *nosotros* form of *insistía*, you simply add the second suffix _____. ▲

6 Write the *tú* form of the Imperfect of *saltar* and *impedir*. ▲
mos

7 There are only three verbs which are irregular in the Imperfect. The first *saltabas; impedías* and second suffixes of *ver* are regular. The stem, however, is not *v* but _____. ▲

8 The Imperfect of *ser* is highly irregular. The stem is *er*. The first suffix which *ve: veía* you add to this is _____. ▲

9 To change *era* to the *nosotros* form you add *mos* and _____. ▲
a
a written accent (*éramos*)

10 A long time ago the Spanish gave *a*-verb suffixes to the Imperfect of *ir*. Write the *tú* form of *ir*. ▲

11 The preterit and imperfect forms of all regular *e*- and *i*-verbs have an *i* right *ibas* after the stem. Change *él permitía* to the Preterit. _____ ▲

12 Write the preterit form that goes with the pronoun given: *usted* (insistir); *él permitió* *ellos* (nacer). ▲

13 The *nosotros* form of the Preterit of all *a*-verbs is the same as the present *insistió; nacieron* indicative. Write this form for *mandar*, *viajar*, and *presentar*. ▲
mandamos, viajamos, presentamos

14 Write the preterit form that goes with the pronoun given: *yo* (manejar); *nosotros* (dudar); *usted* (dejar); *ustedes* (gritar); *él* (tocar); *ellos* (relatar); *ella* (informar); *ellas* (mandar); *tú* (quemar). ▲
manejé; dudamos; dejó; gritaron; tocó; relataron; informó; mandaron; quemaste

15 Here is a list of all the verbs you know which have some irregularity in the Preterit.

Can you say the *él* form of the Preterit of each?

impedir	dar	oír	seguir	venir
impidió	*dio*	*oyó*	*siguió*	*vino*
poner	medir	pedir	ser	reír
puso	*midió*	*pidió*	*fue*	*rió*
despedir	decir	sentir	morir	sonreír
despidió	*dijo*	*sintió*	*murió*	*sonrió*
dormir	servir	hacer	ir	conseguir
durmió	*sirvió*	*hizo*	*fue*	*consiguió*

16 Most of the people who travel by plane today used to travel by railroad. What do you use to translate *used to travel?* (a) Preterit (b) Imperfect ▲

17 Translate: I used to live in San Diego. ▲   Imperfect

Yo vivía en San Diego. (The Imperfect is used to talk about a past customary action which contrasts with what is customary today.)

18 The Imperfect is also used to describe an action which was customary during some specified period in the past. Whether you say one or the other of the following sentences in English depends on your dialect. As a result, both of them have the same Spanish translation.

When we were in Buenos Aires we *used to go* to the beach every day.

When we were in Buenos Aires we *would go* to the beach every day.

The translation of both indicated phrases is _____. ▲

19 In English a planned future action is expressed by the present progressive: *íbamos* "They *are getting married* tomorrow." In Spanish you say the same thing with the _____ present tense form. ▲

simple (*Ellos se casan mañana.*)

20 When you recall a planned future action, the simple present *casan* is backshifted to _____. ▲

casaban (*Me dijeron que ellos se casaban mañana.*)

21 Translate the above sentence. ▲

They told me that they were getting married tomorrow.

22 All events are divided into two sets: cyclic and non-cyclic. At any point in the past, the Imperfect always describes the _____ aspect of either a cyclic or a non-cyclic event. ▲

23 *Morir* is a cyclic event. Write the form that shows the event was in progress   imperfective at the time given: *A la una ayer él (morir).* ▲

24 *Dormir* is a non-cyclic event. Write the form which would replace *morir* and   *moría* say the action was in progress. ▲

A la una ayer él dormía.

25 The English phrase *was (were)* plus the *-ing* of the main verb always cues the use of the _____. ▲

26 The simple past tense forms in English do not cue the choice between   Imperfect Preterit and Imperfect. You have to decide what the message is. What is the

most logical message in *He talked a lot* below? "Do you remember Roberto?"
"I sure do. *He talked a lot.*" (a) *Habló mucho.* (b) *Hablaba mucho.* ▲

> *Hablaba mucho.* (This describes his customary behavior, the only logical meaning for the context given.)

27 At a point in the past the Imperfect describes the same aspect of any event. In contrast, what the Preterit tells you depends on whether the event is cyclic or non-cyclic. Since a cyclic event does not, in fact, take place until it is completed (terminated), the Preterit always describes which aspect of this set of events? (a) beginning (b) middle (c) end ▲

28 The Preterit always says the same thing about a cyclic event regardless of whether the event takes place <u>at</u> a specific point in the past or merely <u>before</u> the present moment of speaking. So the meaning of *cerré* in *Ya la cerré* and *La cerré a la una esta mañana* is the same. Translate these two statements. ▲

end

> I already closed it. I closed it at one this morning.

29 At a point in the past the Preterit describes which aspect of a non-cyclic event? ▲

30 Translate *ran* as used in "He jumped up and ran." ▲

beginning

31 The Preterit may also say that an entire non-cyclic event took place before the moment of speaking. Translate *ran* as used in "I'm tired. I ran too much." ▲

corrió

32 In this and the remaining frames you will see a sentence in the Present. Consider the context and then change the indicated verbs to either the Preterit or Imperfect.

corrí

Mi mamá *tiene* 20 años cuando yo *nazco.* ▲

33 *Compran* la casa en 1956 y la *venden* en 1959. ▲

tenía ; nací
compraron ; vendieron

34 *Son* las diez cuando *oigo* por primera vez que el perro *ladra.* ▲

35 Yo *sé* muy bien cuántos dedos *tengo.* ▲

Eran, oí, ladraba

36 La primera isla que Colón *ve* no *es* muy grande. ▲

sabía ; tenía

37 *Voy* a la ventana, la *abro,* y les *digo* adiós. ▲

vio, era
Fui, abrí, dije

Spelling Review

1 The *meaning* of many words is the only cue to how they are spelled. Thus the spoken word [ola] may stand for either the equivalent of "wave" (an ocean wave) or the greeting "hello." In writing, however, each meaning has a different spelling: *ola* and *hola.* Which spelling stands for "hello"? ▲

2 The spoken word [se] also has several meanings and functions. It also has two spellings: *se* and *sé.* Which spelling stands for "I know"? ▲

hola

3 You can spell many thousands of Spanish words *by ear* because every sound (phoneme) in them is *always* represented by the same letter (grapheme): *a, ch, d, e, f, l, ñ, o, p, t, u.* Can you trust your ear in spelling the spoken word [plata]? ▲

sé

4 You can almost always spell the [k] sound correctly *by rule.* When [k] is followed by [a], [o], or [u] it is always written *c* (*casa, cosa, cuchillo*). In contrast,

yes

when [k] is followed by [e] or [i], as in [keso] or [kiero], it is almost always spelled with the digraph _____.   ▲

> *qu: queso, quiero* (The only exceptions are a few foreign words like *kimono, kodak, kerosina*, and the words of the metric system: *kilo, kilogramo, kiló-metro.*)

5 Before [e] and [i] the letter *c* stands for the sound _____ in all dialects except Castilian.   ▲

6 The sound [g], as in *pagar*, is always written *g* except before [e] and [i] when it must be spelled with the digraph _____.   ▲

> [s] (*cena, cien*)

> *gu* (As in the Preterit *yo pagué, yo seguí,* and the Imperative *¡Pague usted!*)

7 The *jota* sound [x], as in *trabajo*, is always spelled *j* before [a], [o], and [u]. Before [e] and [i], in contrast, it may be spelled either *j* or *g*. Thus the word for "horseman" is *jinete* and the word for "people" is _____.   ▲

8 The sound [i] may stand for the Spanish equivalent of "and". When it does, you spell this word _____.   ▲

> *gente*

9 When it precedes or follows another vowel, but is not in the same syllable with the other vowel, [i] must have a written accent mark. Translate "day" and "country" (nation).   ▲

> *y*

> *día (dí-a) ; país (pa-ís)*

10 When the [i] sound follows another vowel, is in the same syllable, and is the last phoneme in the word, it is spelled *y*. Translate "very" and "there is" (as in "There is a man at the door.").   ▲

> *muy; hay*

Self-Correcting Exercises

A *Vocabulary Review:* Read each question aloud; then answer in three words or less.

1 ¿Usamos la mano derecha, o la izquierda para saludar la bandera?

> la derecha

2 ¿Dónde guardan las mujeres el dinero?

> en su bolsa (cartera)

3 ¿Qué usan los hombres en vez de bolsa?

> los bolsillos

4 ¿Cuánto tiempo dura esta clase?

> cincuenta minutos

5 ¿Cuál es el verbo que nombra la acción de llegar a este mundo por primera vez?

> nacer

6 Una persona que dice que el idioma oficial de Argentina es el chino está equivocada, ¿verdad?

> sí

7 En el otoño y en el invierno, en las regiones frías, ¿qué pierden los árboles?

> las hojas

8 La palabra "antónimo" significa lo opuesto, lo contrario. ¿Cuál es el antónimo de lleno?

> vacío

B *Involved Entity Pronouns:* Write the combinations. Each phrase in the second column is to be converted to an involved entity pronoun.

Ejemplo: 11 = Me los ha dado.

1	Los ha dado	1	a mí.
2	Va a decirlo	2	a Pancho y a mí.
3	Quiere cantarla	3	a Enriqueta.
4	Las traduce	4	a ti.
		5	a sus compañeros.

1)	25	Va a decírselo.
2)	32	Quiere cantárnosla.
3)	12	Nos los ha dado.
4)	45	Se las traduce.
5)	21	Va a decírmelo.
6)	44	Te las traduce.
7)	43	Se las traduce.
8)	13	Se los ha dado.
9)	31	Quiere cantármela.
10)	14	Te los ha dado.
11)	23	Va a decírselo.
12)	35	Quiere cantársela.

C *Reading Comprehension:* Try to read the following selection in five minutes. Can you guess the name of the animal being described?

¿Cómo se llama este animal?

El animal que usted tiene que identificar en esta selección vive principalmente en Perú y en las regiones altas y montañosas de Bolivia y el norte de Argentina. Algunas de las especies de esta familia del reino animal pueden hallarse también en Chile, la región de Patagonia y en Tierra del Fuego. Es muy apreciado por su lana° y por los servicios que le ha rendido° al hombre de los Andes durante muchos siglos como bestia de carga.° Los incas comían su carne y muchos de sus descendientes todavía hoy día la comen también. En 1528, cuando Pizarro fue a España a pedirle ayuda a Carlos V (quinto) para terminar la conquista del Perú, llevó en su barco varios de estos animales que los españoles llamaban "camellos u ovejas° de los Andes". En España causaron gran sensación porque los europeos no conocían estos animales de América.

Pertenecen° a la familia del camello, pero no tienen joroba.° Además tienen las orejas más largas y sus patas° son más cortas que las del camello. Su piel° puede tener uno o más colores. Los hay blancos, negros, grises y de color castaño.° Son animales muy útiles porque pueden caminar con gran facilidad por lugares montañosos donde no existen carreteras o caminos buenos. Además, no demandan comida y agua en abundancia. Pueden pasar hasta cinco días sin beber. Pueden llevar cargas° de casi cien libras° y caminar grandes distancias. Sin embargo, su temperamento puede causar problemas. Por ejemplo, si la carga que les han puesto es excesiva, se echan° en el suelo° y es casi imposible obligarlos a levantarse. Si alguien insiste en que caminen más rápido o si los obligan a trabajar demasiadas horas en un día, se declaran en huelga° y no se mueven. Podemos decir que estos animales son bestias brutas, pero es evidente que saben mucho y tienen gran inteligencia.

Glosses: wool/rendered; beast of burden; sheep; They belong/hump; legs/fur; chestnut; loads/pounds; throw/ground; strike

La naturaleza les ha dado una manera muy peculiar y un poco cómica para defenderse de sus enemigos. Si alguien los molesta o los sorprende, le escupen° en la cara con una puntería° formidable. El resultado del ataque es terrible porque el olor° de su saliva es muy desagradable. La costumbre° de escupir a sus enemigos es común a todos los animales que pertenecen a esta familia que incluye también el guanaco, la vicuña y la alpaca.

    spit
aim
smell/custom

El guanaco y la vicuña viven en estado salvaje.° La lana de la alpaca y de la vicuña es muy fina y suave como la seda. Se vende a precios muy altos. En el tiempo de los incas la lana de la vicuña se reservaba para los vestidos de la familia real.° En nuestros días un abrigo o un traje hecho de esta lana cuesta mucho dinero. La vicuña no es un animal doméstico y es necesario matarla° para quitarle su lana.

wild

royal
kill

Si todavía no sabe usted cuál es el nombre del cuarto animal de esta familia, vuelva a leer el título de esta selección. Una de las formas del verbo "llamar" es idéntica a su nombre, pero recuerde que no se pronuncia de la misma manera en español y en inglés.

See top of page 418 for the answer.

New Vocabulary

pareja	couple (*people*)	**quemar**	to burn	**permitir**	to permit
costumbre (la)	custom	**relatar**	to tell, relate	**prohibir**	to prohibit
fuego	fire	**notar**	to note, notice	**impedir (i)**	to prevent
mandar	to order, command	**informar**	to inform, report	**ancho, -a**	wide
		nacer	to be born	**estrecho, -a**	narrow
demandar	to demand	**asistir**	to attend	**diario, -a**	daily
durar	to last	**insistir**	to insist	**hacia**	toward

Assignment 69

The Forms of the Subjunctive of Stem-Changing Verbs

1 The *a*- and *e*-verbs which have *e* or *ie* in their stems which you have learned so far are *perder, sentar, despertar, cerrar, empezar,* and *querer*. These verbs have the <u>same</u> irregular stems in both the indicative and the subjunctive. Write the subjunctive of *pierdo*. ▲

2 Write the subjunctive of *perdemos*. ▲

3 Write the subjunctive of *despiertan*. ▲

pierda
perdamos
despierten

4 When you write the subjunctive of *empiezan*, you have to change *z* to *c* before
e just as in the plural of *lápiz*. The form, then, is _____. ▲

> *empiecen* (This *c* appears in all present subjunctive forms of this verb.)

5 The present indicative of the *nosotros* form of *querer* is _____. ▲

6 The subjunctive that matches this form is _____. ▲   *queremos*

7 Change *queramos* so it matches *usted*. ▲   *queramos*

8 So far you have learned just two verbs which have *e*, *ie*, and *i* in the stem.   *quiera*
These verbs are *sentir* and *divertir*. In this set of verbs the *ie* of the indicative
appears in the same forms of the subjunctive but the *e* of the *nosotros* form
changes to *i* in the subjunctive. Write the subjunctive of *sientes*. ▲

> *sientas* (Notice that this looks exactly like the indicative of *sentar: tú te*

9 Write the subjunctive of *sentimos*. Remember there are two changes. ▲   *sientas*.)

> *sintamos* (This irregular *i* appears only in the *nosotros* form.)

10 The verb *dormir*, like *sentir*, has three allomorphs of the stem: *o* in *dormir*,
dormimos; *ue* in *duermo*, *duermes*, *duerme*, and *duermen*, and *u* in the *nosotros* form
of the subjunctive. The *ue* appears in the same subjunctive forms as in the
indicative. Write the subjunctive forms that match *duermo* and *duermes*. ▲

11 Write the subjunctive form that matches *dormimos*. ▲   *duerma, duermas*

> *durmamos* (There are two changes: *o* to *u*, and *i* to *a*.)

12 The present indicative stem of verbs like *pedir*, *despedir*, *impedir*, *medir* and
servir has two allomorphs. One has *e* (*servir* and *servimos*) and the rest have *i* in
the stem in all forms. Write the subjunctive form that matches *servimos*. ▲

> *sirvamos* (There are two changes: *e* to *i*, and *i* to *a*.)

13 The verb *morir* belongs to the same set as *dormir*. The subjunctive *yo* form
of *morir* is _____. ▲

14 The subjunctive form that matches *morimos* is _____. ▲

> *muera*
> *muramos*

More Spelling Review

1 The sound [rr] is written *rr* only between _____. ▲

> vowels (*cierra, pizarra*.)

2 At the beginning of a word the sound [rr] is *always* spelled _____. ▲

> *r: ropa, rojo, recordar* (You may hear [rr] for emphasis before a consonant
> within a word, [puerrta] for *puerta*, or at the end of a word, as in [marr] for

3 The phoneme /b/ may be written with two different letters. They are   *mar*.)
_____. ▲

4 There is no rule which can tell you when to write *b* or *v* before a vowel or   *b; v*
after another consonant. Cognates, however, almost always take the same
letter as English. Translate: inhabitant. ▲

5 There is one spelling rule which will help you choose between *b* and *v*.   *habitante*
Write the translation for "to speak" and "hat." ▲

> *hablar; sombrero* (Spanish writes only *b* before another consonant.)

6 The phoneme /m/ is spelled *m* before vowels. As syllable final before *v* or *b*

El animal que se ha descrito en la página 416 es la llama.

it may be spelled either *n* or *m*. Which do you use in *i . . . vierno* and *ta . . .*
bién? ▲

7 In all dialects except·Castilian, the phoneme /s/ may be represented by *s*   *invierno; también*
and two other letters. They are _____. ▲

8 Can *c* stand for [s] before [a], [o], or [u]? ▲   *c; z (cena, pizarra)*

9 The letter *c* cannot be used to represent [s] before another consonant or   *no*
at the end of words. It may stand for [s] only before the vowels _____. ▲

10 Excepting *c*, *qu*, and *g*, the letter *z* rarely stands for [s] before another con-   *e; i*
sonant. It represents [s] before any vowel and as word final. However, *z* is so
rare before [e] that when the plural suffix *es* is added to a noun ending in *z*,
such as *lápiz*, the *z* is replaced by _____. ▲

c (So lápiz becomes lápices.)

11 This same change takes place when the stem of an *a*-verb ends in *z*. Write
the *yo* form of the Preterit of *cruzar* and *abrazar*. ▲

crucé; abracé

Self-Correcting Exercises

A *Usage of Verb Forms:* In this exercise you will have the opportunity to put
into practice almost everything you have been learning about various types of
verbs and how they are used. In order to change each infinitive given in parentheses to the form that fits the situation, you will have to *understand* what you
are reading. It is the meaning and the context that will tell you whether to use
present, present perfect, preterit, imperfect, indicative or subjunctive forms.
Therefore, before making your choice, you *must* read the complete sentence.
In some cases, it might even be better to read quickly the whole paragraph.

Hablar por los codos (primera parte)

La frase "hablar por los codos (*elbows*)" quiere decir en español "hablar   1   pueden
demasiado, hablar constantemente." En todos los países del mundo hay hom-   2   conozco
bres, mujeres y niños que *poder* **1** tener este defecto. Las personas que hablan   3   voy
hasta por los codos generalmente no comprenden que sus interminables cuentos   4   empieza
molestan mucho a sus amigos y familiares (*relatives*).   5   leído

Yo *conocer* **2** a una muchacha que habla por los codos. Es una verdadera   6   dicho
cotorra (*parrot*). Se llama Lisa y es hermana de Diana Robles, una de mis   7   ha visto
compañeras de clase. Cada vez que yo *ir* **3** a casa de mi amiga, su hermanita   8   salgo
empezar **4** a conversar y no sabe nunca cuándo acabar. Me habla de libros que
ha *leer* **5**, de chistes (*jokes*) que le han *decir* **6** sus amigos y, sobre todo (*above all*),
le gusta hablar de los programas de televisión y de las películas que ella *haber*
ver **7**. Es algo insoportable y generalmente yo *salir* **8** de allí con dolor de cabeza
y de muy mal humor.

El jueves pasado, por ejemplo, yo *ir* **9** a casa de Diana a estudiar geometría con ella porque al siguiente día *tener* **10** un examen importante. Lisa *venir* **11** a abrirme la puerta. En el momento que me *ver* **12** dijo con entusiasmo:

—Hola, Norma. ¿Qué tal? ¿Has visto la película *Los hijos del sol*? Yo la *ver* **13** anoche con mamá. ¿Quieres que (yo) te la *contar* **14**? Es fantástica. Los incas del Perú y los soldados españoles . . .

—Perdón, Lisa, pero vengo a estudiar geometría con tu hermana y ya es un poco tarde. Nosotras *tener* **15** examen mañana y es muy importante que . . .

—¡Qué bonitas las montañas de los Andes! Diana está en su cuarto (*room*). ¿Quieres que yo la *llamar* **16**? ¡Diana, Diana! Aquí está tu amiga Norma. Dice que *venir* **17** a estudiar contigo.

—Voy, Norma. Lisa, dile a Norma que *entrar* **18** y que *sentarse* **19**.

Mientras yo *esperar* **20** a Diana, Lisa siguió hablando de la película y no me permitió decir ni una palabra. ¡Qué muchachita, Dios mío! ¡Habla hasta por los codos!

9	fui
10	teníamos
11	vino
12	vio
13	vi
14	cuente
15	tenemos
16	llame
17	viene
18	entre
19	se siente
20	esperaba

B *Reflexive Constructions:* Ask and answer the questions aloud. Compare your answers with those on the right which are merely suggestions.

1 ¿Te desayunas todas las mañanas?

A veces no me desayuno porque no tengo tiempo.

2 ¿Cerca de quién te sientas en la clase de español?

Me siento cerca de un joven alto que se llama Guillermo y le dicen Bill.

3 Yo me dormí anoche a las once. ¿A qué hora me dormí yo?

Ud. se durmió a las once.

4 ¿A qué hora se despertó ella esta mañana?

Ella se despertó a las seis y media.

5 ¿Te bañas todos los días, o un día sí y un día no?

Me baño todos los días antes del desayuno.

6 ¿Te pusiste un suéter antes de salir afuera hoy?

No, no me lo puse porque no lo necesitaba.

7 ¿De qué color te gusta vestirte?

Me gusta vestirme de morado y amarillo.

8 ¿Piensas divertirte mucho en la fiesta el sábado que viene?

Eso depende. Si hay buena música para bailar me voy a divertir mucho.

9 ¿Por qué te levantaste y te fuiste de la clase hoy?

Me levanté y me fui de la clase porque tenía que ir al dentista.

10 ¿Por qué te acostaste tan temprano anoche?

Porque tenía mucho sueño.

New Vocabulary

This is the last vocabulary you will have until after the next major test. It is important that you begin to review your entire vocabulary list in preparation for the test.

caballo	horse	**esconder**	to hide	**caro, -a**	expensive
sangre (la)	blood	**coger**	to take hold of, catch	**barato, -a**	cheap
		escoger	to choose	**gratis**	free (of charge)

In most of the United States when a person becomes very ill he goes to see a doctor and when he is seriously ill, he goes to a hospital. In many rural areas of Latin America there are neither doctors nor hospitals and, as a result, when a person becomes sick he goes to see the *curandero*. A *curandero* has no formal education or training in medicine and is sometimes very much like a witch doctor. Occasionally a *curandero* discovers from experience real cures for certain diseases and modern drug companies will often send out expeditions to find out what *curanderos* use for medicine. The ancient Indian *curanderos* discovered that digitalis is good for heart trouble and that quinine will cure malaria and reduce fevers. Most of their "prescriptions," however, are useless, but the patient often feels better and even gets well simply because of the attention paid to him.

Assignment 70

Review of Pronouns

1   With a few minor exceptions, you have studied and practiced using all the pronouns in Spanish. The twenty-two forms are divided into five sets. The prime set is made up of those which stand for the doer or the subject of a verb. In English there are seven: "I, we, you, they, he, she, it." Spanish has no subject pronoun for "it." You simply use the verb without a pronoun. You are talking about a pen. Translate: It is on the table.   ▲

Está en la mesa.

2 "We" and "they" must be translated by two forms each, one for males (or males and females together), the other for females. These forms are _____. ▲

nosotros, nosotras; ellos, ellas

3 "You" has three subject pronoun equivalents. When you talk to an intimate friend the form is _____. ▲

tú

4 In Spain the plural of *tú* is *vosotros*. In the rest of the Hispanic world the plural of *tú* is _____. ▲

ustedes

5 When you talk to a stranger, the Spanish equivalent of the subject pronoun "you" is _____. ▲

usted

6 In English the subject pronoun normally precedes the conjugated verb in a statement (*They are here.*) and follows it in a question (*Are they here? Does he want to go?*). In Spanish the subject pronoun may precede or follow the verb in either a statement or a question. Since either position is possible, you will probably find it easier to use your English pattern until you have spoken Spanish for a long time. You are talking about some boys. Translate: Are they here? ▲

¿Están ellos aquí?

7 When a statement sentence in English has only one verb, the subject almost always has to be expressed. When the suffix of the Spanish verb defines the subject, or when the context makes it clear who the subject is, the subject pronoun can almost always be omitted. As a result the simple, unemphatic statement "I am cold" will usually be translated as _____. ▲

Tengo frío.

8 The four remaining sets of pronouns are made up of forms which match the subject pronouns. With two exceptions, the forms which follow a relator in Spanish are the same as the subject pronouns. Thus one says *de él* or *con nosotros*. The two exceptions are the forms that match *yo* and *tú*. These forms are _____. ▲

mí; ti (¡Démelo a mí! No te lo dio a ti.)

9 The subject pronouns and those used as objects of relators may be used in utterances which do not have a verb. Thus the answer to *¿Quién va a hacerlo?* may be simply *Yo* or *Nosotros*. Similarly the answer to *¿A quién va a dar el dinero?* may be *A mí* or *A ella*. The three remaining sets of pronouns cannot be used in an utterance which has no verb. These pronouns, consequently, are called **with-verb pronouns**. They either immediately precede or are attached to the end of a verb form.

The done-to pronouns which match *yo*, *nosotros*, and *tú* are _____. ▲

me, nos, te

10 The three forms, *me, nos,* and *te*, are also used in reflexive constructions and to mark the involved entity. Translate: I sat down there. ▲

Me senté ahí.

11 Translate: We went to bed. ▲

Nos acostamos.

12 Which pronoun stands for the involved entity in *Ella me dio el libro?* ▲

me

13 There is just one reflexive pronoun to match *usted, ustedes, él, ellos, ella* and *ellas*. Translate: He got up. ▲

Él se levantó.

14 Change the subject to *ustedes* and rewrite the sentence. ▲

Ustedes se levantaron.

15 There are three forms of the involved entity pronoun which match *usted, ustedes, él, ellos, ella* and *ellas*. The singular form *le* matches _____. ▲

usted, él, ella

16 The plural form which matches *ustedes, ellos,* and *ellas* is _____. ▲

les

17 The third form replaces either *le* or *les* when there are two with-verb pronouns in the same sentence. Rewrite *Voy a darles los zapatos* with the adjectival residual for *zapatos* and the other necessary change. ▲

Voy a dárselos. (The *se* always comes before the other pronoun.)

18 Rewrite the above sentence so it translates "I give them to them." ▲

Se los doy. (The pronouns precede a conjugated verb in a statement or

19 There are four forms of the done-to pronouns which match *usted*, *ustedes*,   question.)
él, ellos, and *ellas*. The form *lo* matches two subject pronouns: *él* and _____. ▲

20 The form *la* matches *usted* and _____. ▲   *usted*

21 The subject pronouns that match *los* are _____. ▲   *ella*

22 The done-to pronoun that matches *ustedes* and *ellas* is _____. ▲   *ustedes; ellos*

23 You are talking about girls. Translate: I see them. ▲   *las*

24 When you are talking about things, the done-to pronouns are actually   *Las veo.*
adjectival residuals. Rewrite *Voy a comprar la casa* with *casa* omitted. ▲

Voy a comprarla. (You attach the residual to the infinitive in writing.)

25 Rewrite the above sentence so it says "I buy it." ▲

26 You are talking about *una camisa*. Translate: Give me it (*usted*). ▲   *La compro.*

Démela. (In affirmative commands the with-verb pronouns are attached to the end of the verb in speech and writing.)

27 Change *Démela* into a negative command. ▲

No me la dé. (In negative commands the pronouns precede the verb and in writing are treated as separate words. In speech, of course, you say *Nomeladé.*)

28 Here is a chart of all the pronouns you are learning. When the twenty-two forms are properly categorized there is not too much to learn. You will learn more about the "Object of Relators" in future lessons.

Subject of the Verb	Object of Relators (with-relator forms)	With-verb Pronouns		
		Reflexive Constructions (Done-to or involved entity forms)	Involved Entity	Done-to Forms (Non-reflexive constructions)
yo	mí	←————— me —————→		
nosotros nosotras		←———— nos ————→		
tú	ti	←———— te ————→		
usted él ella ustedes ellos ellas		se	le se les	lo, la los, las

Orthographic Changes in Subjunctive Forms

1 Rewrite *busco* and *mastica* in the subjunctive. ▲
2 Rewrite *llega* and *madrugo* in the subjunctive. ▲   *busque; mastique*
3 Rewrite *almuerzo, cruzan, empiezas,* and *tropieza* in the subjunctive. ▲   *llegue; madrugue*

almuerce, crucen, empieces, tropiece (You change the final *z* of the stem to *c*
when you add an *e*-suffix.)

4 The sound [g] is written with the digraph *gu* in *seguir* because it precedes *i*.
The *yo* form of the present indicative ends in *o*. So you write this form with a
plain _____. ▲

5 Since *seguir* is an *i*-verb, the first suffix in the present subjunctive is _____. ▲   *g (sigo)*

a (So *sigo* becomes *siga* which is the base for all present subjunctive forms.)

Self-Correcting Exercises

A *Subjunctive versus Indicative:* Write each combination, make sure you did it
right, and then say it aloud.

Ejemplo: 111 = Mandan que él y yo nos sentemos aquí.

1	Mandan		1	él y yo	1	sentarse aquí.
2	Ven		2	tú	2	volver pronto.
3	Esperan	que	3	yo	3	sentirlo.
4	Oyen		4	ustedes	4	dormir más.
5	Es necesario		5	Chela	5	servirla.

1)	554	Es necesario que Chela duerma más.
2)	253	Ven que Chela lo siente.
3)	353	Esperan que Chela lo sienta.
4)	125	Mandan que tú la sirvas.
5)	215	Ven que él y yo la servimos.
6)	512	Es necesario que él y yo volvamos pronto.
7)	114	Mandan que él y yo durmamos más.
8)	214	Ven que él y yo dormimos más.
9)	535	Es necesario que yo la sirva.
10)	322	Esperan que tú vuelvas pronto.
11)	131	Mandan que yo me siente aquí.
12)	231	Ven que yo me siento aquí.
13)	521	Es necesario que tú te sientes aquí.
14)	542	Es necesario que Uds. vuelvan pronto.
15)	211	Ven que él y yo nos sentamos aquí.
16)	141	Mandan que Uds. se sienten aquí.

B *Usage of Verb Forms:* Read each complete paragraph before you start writing
the answers. Context provides the cues for selecting the appropriate form of
each indicated infinitive.

¡Gracias a Dios que hoy es viernes! (primera parte)

Vivian Rodríguez Mena es una estudiante graduada que estudia y enseña (*teach*) en una universidad del estado. Es una joven bonita, inteligente y muy simpática que se especializa en español y francés. Sus estudiantes, a la vez que aprenden la lengua, se *divertir* **1** mucho también.

En una de las clases de primer año que la señorita Rodríguez Mena enseña, los alumnos *haber* **2** aprendido de memoria varios refranes en español. A ellos les *gustar* **3** mucho estos refranes porque les parecen interesantes y fáciles. Además su instructora les ha *decir* **4** muchas veces que las personas de habla española los *usar* **5** frecuentemente en la conversación ordinaria. Según ella, estos viejos refranes revelan modos muy diferentes de pensar y de organizar la realidad, y ayudan a comprender y apreciar mejor la cultura hispánica.

Aunque los alumnos de la señorita Rodríguez sólo han estudiado español por un semestre, ya muchos de ellos *empezar* **6** a comunicarse en esta lengua con bastante facilidad. Ellos *saber* **7** todos los refranes perfectamente bien y han descubierto que, cambiando (*changing*) el orden de algunas de las palabras, ellos *poder* **8** obtener resultados humorísticos o ideas completamente contrarias a la intención original del refrán. También dos jóvenes, Tomás y Paco, que son un poco bromistas (*jokers*), han *observar* **9** que en los días de examen, cuando solamente quedan pocos minutos de la hora de clase, su maestra usa ese tiempo para practicar los refranes.

Un viernes por la tarde, después del examen semanal, cuando todos los estudiantes *estar* **10** cansados de trabajar, Tomás y Paco *decidir* **11** divertirse un poco en la clase. Ellos *conocer* **12** muy bien a la profesora. Tiene tan buen sentido del humor y es tan amable y simpática que ellos estaban seguros (*sure*) que no se *ir* **13** a ofender si bromeaban (*joked*) un poco después del examen.

—Bueno, señores. ¡Silencio, por favor! Todavía (nosotros) *tener* **14** unos minutos de clase y quiero que ustedes me *decir* **15** algunos refranes.

Tomás *mirar* **16** a Paco y los dos pícaros (*rascals*) *sonreír* **17** maliciosamente (*naughtily*). Su plan iba a tener éxito. Sin sospechar (*suspecting*) nada, la profesora siguió hablando.

—En español tenemos un refrán que menciona algo de las personas que duermen mucho. A ver, ¿quién lo *recordar* **18**?

Inmediatamente, Paco *levantar* **19** la mano y respondió:

—Quien poco duerme, mucho aprende.

—Bueno, es más o menos la misma idea, Paco, pero tú *haber cambiar* **20** el orden de las palabras.

—Es que anoche yo *dormir* **21** solamente cuatro horas en vez de ocho porque hoy nosotros *tener* **22** examen y . . .

(Continúa en la próxima lección.)

1	divierten
2	han
3	gustan
4	dicho
5	usan
6	empiezan
7	saben
8	pueden
9	observado
10	estaban
11	decidieron
12	conocían
13	iba
14	tenemos
15	digan
16	miró
17	sonrieron
18	recuerda
19	levantó
20	has cambiado
21	dormí
22	teníamos

C *Reading Aloud:* It is important to read aloud in Spanish with a reasonable degree of speed. You will acquire the necessary proficiency in this skill, if you make it a habit to devote two or three minutes of your pre-class preparation each day to the reading aloud of portions of the reading selections corresponding to the current lesson. Here is a passage of 66 words. If you can read it with good pronunciation in 30 seconds, you have acquired good speed.

Cuando Cortés les dice a sus hombres que siente grandes deseos de empezar la marcha al interior de México, sus partidarios aplauden la idea. Los amigos del gobernador Velázquez, sin embargo, le dicen que ellos van a volver a Cuba. Para resolver el problema, Cortés da órdenes de destruir los barcos. No los quema, como dice la leyenda; los hunde en las aguas del Golfo.

Assignment 71

Review of the Forms of the Subjunctive

1   To get the present subjunctive forms of all regular *a*-verbs you replace the present indicative first suffix (*o* or *a*) with _____.   ▲

2   Write the form that should replace the infinitive: *Nuestro profesor quiere que nosotros* _____ (*hablar*) *español en la clase.*   ▲

3   To get the subjunctive form of regular *e*- and *i*-verbs, the morphemes of the present indicative first suffix are all replaced by _____.   ▲

4   Write the form that should replace the infinitive in this and the next frame. *Es necesario que usted* _____ (*vender*) *la casa.*   ▲

5   *Las piedras enormes impiden que él* _____ (*subir*) *la montaña.*   ▲

6   In many irregular verbs the *yo* form of the present indicative provides the irregular stem for the imperative and subjunctive forms. Write the *tú* form for each of the following: *tengo, pongo, salgo, vengo, traduzco, traigo, digo, oigo, conozco, hago, caigo.*   ▲

7   The *e*- and *i*-verbs are more likely to be irregular than the *a*-verbs. Only *e*- and *i*-verbs have irregular *yo* forms like *digo, oigo, traigo.* This tells you that the first suffix of the subjunctive is going to be *a: diga, oiga, traiga.* Only *e*- or *i*-verbs have the extra [k] = *c* in the *yo* form: *traduzco* (*traducir*), *conozco* (*conocer*). This also helps you remember that the first suffix of the subjunctive is going to be _____.   ▲

8   When an *a*-verb in the *yo* form of the present indicative has an irregular first suffix this is replaced by the regular *e* in the subjunctive. So *doy* and *estoy* become _____ (with written accent marks).   ▲

9   As Latin, Old German, and Arabic became Spanish the people had trouble keeping separate the voiced [b] and its unvoiced counterpart [p]. One often replaced the other: thus the same Germanic stem gave *robar* and *ropa*, which come from the same Germanic word. With this knowledge you can understand a little better why the *yo* form of the present subjunctive of *saber* is _____.   ▲

e

hablemos

a

venda
suba

tengas, pongas, salgas, vengas, traduzcas, traigas, digas, oigas, conozcas, hagas, caigas

a

dé; esté

sepa

10 The base form of the irregular forms of the subjunctive which you have just studied derives from the *yo* form of the present indicative. To get all the other forms you simply add the regular second suffixes to the base form. Make *vaya* agree with *ellos*. ▲

11 Make *tenga* agree with *nosotros*. ▲

vayan

12 Make *salga* agree with *tú*. ▲

tengamos

13 The base forms like *venga*, *oiga*, and *traduzca* agree with three different subject pronouns. These pronouns are _____. ▲

salgas

14 When the last phoneme of the stem of an *e*-verb is the *jota* sound, it may be spelled *g* or *j*. When it is spelled *g*, as in *coger* or *escoger*, the *yo* form of the present indicative cannot be spelled with *g* because *g* before /o/, /a/, and /u/ stands for the phoneme /g/, not for /x/. Consequently, in writing the *g* must be replaced by _____. ▲

yo, usted, él

15 Write the *yo* form of the present subjunctive of *coger* and *escoger*. ▲

j

16 Say aloud the present subjunctive form that matches the subject given: *nosotros* (esconder), *él* (nacer), *ellos* (quemar), *usted* (tocar), *ellos* (parecer), *tú* (dudar), *ustedes* (saltar), *ella* (gritar), *yo* (sonreír), *tú* (buscar). ▲

coja, escoja

escondamos, nazca, quemen, toque, parezcan, dudes, salten, grite, sonría, busques

17 There is a set of irregular *e*- and *a*-verbs which have an *e* or an *o* in the stem which change to *ie* or *ue* in the present indicative when stressed. The *a*-verbs are: *cerrar, almorzar, sentar, despertar, acostar, contar, jugar* (< *jogar*), *recordar, empezar,* and *pensar*. The *e*-verbs are: *perder, morder, mover, poder, volver,* and *querer*. All these verbs have the same stems in both the indicative and subjunctive. Write the *usted* form of the subjunctive of *cerrar, contar, perder,* and *volver*. ▲

cierre, cuente, pierda, vuelva

18 Now change these to the *nosotros* form of the subjunctive. ▲

cerremos, contemos, perdamos, volvamos

19 The verbs *pedir, servir, vestir, medir,* and *despedir* belong to a set which has an irregular *i* when the stem is stressed. Write the *yo* and the *nosotros* forms of *pedir* in the present indicative. ▲

20 The verbs of this set have *i* in all the stems of the subjunctive. Change *sirvo* and *servimos* to the subjunctive. ▲

pido; pedimos

21 The verbs *dormir* and *morir* belong to a set which has two allomorphs of the stem in the present indicative: *duerm* and *dorm*, *muer* and *mor*. Write the present indicative *nosotros* forms of these verbs. ▲

sirva; sirvamos

dormimos; morimos (All the other subjects take the *duerm* or *muer* stem.)

22 The stems *duerm* and *muer* appear with the same subjects in the subjunctive. Add the suffixes that go with *ustedes* and *ellos*. ▲

23 There is a special change in the *nosotros* form of the subjunctive stem. The *o* of *dorm* and *mor* is replaced by *u*. Write the *nosotros* forms of the subjunctive that match *dormimos* and *morimos*. ▲

duerman; mueran

durmamos; muramos

24 There is a set of *i*-verbs which have a stressed *e*-stem which changes to *ie* in the indicative: *sentir, divertir*. The stem of the subjunctive is the same as the indicative with one exception: the *e* of *sentimos* and *divertimos* changes to _____ in the subjunctive. ▲

i (sintamos, divirtamos)

25 You have had six verbs which have a special irregular *yo* form in the present indicative and, also, a special irregular base in the present subjunctive. Say the subjunctive equivalent of the *yo* form that is given: *sé, soy, estoy, doy, voy.* ▲

sepa, sea, esté, dé, vaya

26 The subjunctive equivalent of *hay* is _____. ▲

27 Let's review, now, the three ways one can influence the action of another *haya* person. The most direct way is a command. Write a command in which you tell somebody (*usted*) to close the door. ▲

28 You can influence the behavior of others by expressing your desire, wish, *Cierre la puerta.* or hope. The verb for "to hope" is *esperar*. Write a sentence in which you express your hope that another person (*tú*) comes with you to the beach. ▲

Espero que vengas conmigo a la playa.

29 The third way to influence the behavior of another person is to talk about how necessary or important the action is. Translate: It is very important that you (*ustedes*) get up early. ▲

Es muy importante que se levanten temprano.

Review of Usage of the Subjunctive

1 The verbs which we use in trying to get other people to do something describe in a general way how much influence we feel we can exert on the other person. Arrange the following from the one that exerts the most influence down to the one that exerts the least influence: (1) I order you to go. (2) It is important for you to go. (3) I hope that you go. (4) I want you to go. (5) I insist that you go. ▲

They would probably be ordered this way: 1, 5, 4, 3, 2 (I order you to go. I insist that you go. I want you to go. I hope that you go. It is important for

2 Spanish, like English, has two sentence patterns which are used to say that you to go.) one person is trying to influence the action of another. The one which is like "Let him go" (*Déjelo ir*) is restricted to a very few verbs. The other which is exactly like "I ask that he be here at six" (*Yo pido que él esté aquí a las seis*) may be used with all verbs which describe an attempt to influence the action of another person. In this pattern the subjoined (dependent) verb is always in the subjunctive mode. Here is all you need to know to use this pattern correctly:

(1) One entity, the subject of the main verb, attempts to influence the action of another entity, the subject of the dependent verb.

(2) Spanish (with very few exceptions) uses two clauses and two conjugated verbs. In other words, "I will not permit him to go" is transformed into "I will not permit that he go." In this pattern the verb in the clause introduced by *that* is in the subjunctive mode.

(3) The two clauses are joined together with the connector word *que* (that).

3 Rewrite "I want him to be here at six" so it is like the standard Spanish pattern. ▲

I want that he be here at six.

4 Now, translate the above pattern into Spanish. ▲

Quiero que él esté aquí a las seis.

5   Transform this sentence into the Spanish pattern: It is necessary for him to be here at six.   ▲

It is necessary that he be here at six.

6   Write the missing form of *estar: Es necesario que él _____ aquí a las seis.*   ▲

7   In "It is important that he read well" the dependent verb is in the sub-   *esté*
junctive. Supply the missing form of *leer: Es importante que él _____ bien.*   ▲

8   The verbs which describe the way someone says something (shout, scream,   *lea*
whisper, *etc.*) do not provide a cue that tells you whether the dependent verb is in the indicative or the subjunctive. The cue is to be found in what the person actually says. Let's see how this works in English. The sentence *He shouts, "She is coming"* can be transformed into *He shouts that she is coming*. This transformation is called the transformation of indirect discourse.

He shouts, "Come!" cannot be transformed into *He shouts that she is coming*. Can you give the most common correct transformation?   ▲

He shouts for her to come.

9   The difference between *He shouts that she is coming* and *He shouts for her to come* depends upon the mode used in the original quote. The indicative "She is coming" remains in the indicative in indirect discourse. The imperative "Come!" requires a different transform (*for her to come*).

The Spanish transformations of indirect discourse are much easier. When the direct quote is in the indicative, *Grita, —¡Ella viene!*, you simply add the connector *que* and you get *Grita que ella viene*. When the direct quote is in the imperative, *Grita, —¡Venga!*, you insert the connector *que* and replace the imperative with the subjunctive: *Grita que venga*. In this example there is no change because *venga*, the imperative for *usted*, is used as the subjunctive with *usted*, *él*, or *ella*. Suppose, however, the direct quote is *vengan ustedes* and is directed at us. What form will you use to complete this sentence? *Grita que nosotros _____.*   ▲

vengamos (The translation is "He shouts for us to come.")

10   Let's put into practice what you have just reviewed. Translate: The teacher (male) says that Margarita studies a lot.   ▲

El profesor dice que Margarita estudia mucho.

11   Translate: "The teacher insists that I study more." (The meaning is "requires.")   ▲

El profesor insiste que yo estudie más.

12   Translate: "The director shouts to us to stand up." Remember that what he shouts is *¡Levántense!*   ▲

El director grita que nos levantemos.

13   Transform the following into indirect discourse, using a main and a dependent clause pattern: *Pablo dice, —María no está aquí.*   ▲

Pablo dice que María no está aquí.

14   Transform "He asks us to go up the mountain" into the Spanish pattern.   ▲

He asks that we go up the mountain.

15   Now translate the above transformation.   ▲

Pide que subamos la montaña.

(If you missed any of the last six frames, you should review the section on the subjunctive in Assignments 67 and 68.)

Self-Correcting Exercises

A *Subjunctive versus Indicative:* Write the combinations.

Ejemplo: 222 = *Desea que usted vaya a Quito.*

					1	estar en Chile.
1	Lee		1	tú	2	ir a Quito.
2	Desea		2	usted	3	saber todas las reglas.
3	Impide	que	3	él y yo	4	darle oro al rey.
4	Sabe		4	ustedes	5	tocar en la orquesta.
5	Deja		5	yo	6	llegar hasta la costa.
					7	cruzar el Mar Caribe.

1) 111   Lee que tú estás en Chile.
2) 212   Desea que tú vayas a Quito.
3) 333   Impide que él y yo sepamos todas las reglas.
4) 444   Sabe que ustedes le dan oro al rey.
5) 555   Deja que yo toque en la orquesta.
6) 211   Desea que tú estés en Chile.
7) 224   Desea que usted le dé oro al rey.
8) 345   Impide que ustedes toquen en la orquesta.
9) 546   Deja que ustedes lleguen hasta la costa.
10) 257   Desea que yo cruce el mar Caribe.
11) 135   Lee que él y yo tocamos en la orquesta.
12) 452   Sabe que yo voy a Quito.

B *Usage of Verb Forms:* Write the appropriate verb form of each infinitive in parentheses.

¡Gracias a Dios que hoy es viernes! (segunda parte)

—Está bien, Paco. Yo *saber* **1** que eres muy trabajador y que te gusta mucho exagerar. Bueno, a ver, otro refrán. Ese que *empezar* **2** así: No dejes para mañana . . .

Esta vez Tomás *levantarse* **3** del pupitre y contestó en voz alta:

—No dejes para mañana lo que puedas hacer *pasado* mañana.

Toda la clase empezó a reír. Con la cara un poco seria, la maestra *decir* **4**:

—¡Incorrecto! Creo que Paco y tú hablan en broma.

—Señorita, yo sé por experiencia que a veces es mejor esperar . . .

—Sí, sí. Ya sé lo que vas a decir, pero eso no es verdad. Bueno, nos queda tiempo para uno más. Cuando una persona *perder* **5** una cosa y la busca por todas partes . . .

Paco no permite que la profesora *terminar* **6** la frase y la interrumpe.

—Yo sé ese refrán, señorita. ¿Quiere que se lo diga?

—No, gracias, Paco. Tampoco quiero que *contestar* **7** tú, Tomás. Lola, tú lo sabes, ¿verdad?

Lola generalmente es una alumna muy seria, pero en ese momento *decidir* **8** continuar la broma.

1   sé
2   empieza
3   se levantó
4   dijo
5   pierde
6   termine
7   contestes
8   decidió

—Sí, cómo no, profesora. Yo lo sé muy bien. Ese refrán dice: Quien busca, muchas veces *no* halla. Esta mañana yo *perder* **9** mi cartera (bolsa), la *buscar* **10** por todas partes y no la *encontrar* **11**.

—La señorita Rodríguez Mena *comprender* **12** entonces que sus estudiantes bromeaban con ella. La comprensiva (*understanding*) maestra *sonreírse* **13**, *cerrar* **14** su libro, lo *poner* **15** en la mesa y *sentarse* **16**. No estaba ofendida con sus alumnos. Sabían tan bien los refranes que no era necesario practicarlos más. *Ser* **17** casi las tres y media del último período de clase. Antes de salir de la clase, Tomás, Paco y Lola le *pedir* **18** perdón a la maestra. ¡Gracias a Dios que era viernes!

9	perdí
10	busqué
11	encontré
12	comprendió
13	se sonrió
14	cerró
15	puso
16	se sentó
17	Eran
18	pidieron

Among the superstitious people of the United States, Friday is considered to be an unlucky day, and Friday the thirteenth is the unluckiest day of all. In the Hispanic world the unlucky day of the week is Tuesday. Superstitious people feel that one should not undertake major enterprises on Tuesday. This belief is expressed in a well known saying, *En martes, ni te cases ni te embarques.* The translation is *On Tuesday don't get married or start a trip.*

Assignment 72/73

Preparing for a Major Test

In your next class session you will have a major test. This Assignment, like others you have had before tests, is designed to give you additional practice on the topics that will be covered and to tell you what to expect so you will not make mistakes which have nothing to do with how much Spanish you actually know. Use your cover sheet and take all the time you need to go through this program carefully. It is also recommended that you review the objectives for Etapa 4 on page 332.

The test consists of nine parts marked A through I.

1 **Part A,** *Listening and Reading Comprehension:* This part is worth 10 points and tests your listening *and* reading comprehension. You will *hear* a statement or question only once. On your answer sheet you will *see* three statements or questions. You pick the one most logically associated with what you hear and circle the letter before it.

You hear, for example: *En las selvas del río Amazonas hay muchos tigres.* You see:
a) ¿Quién te ha dicho eso?
b) Yo tengo tres perros en mi casa.
c) Su abuelo está en Montevideo. ▲
2 Here is another example: *Tu hermana hizo la ensalada.*
a) Está exquisita, pero la sopa está muy caliente.

b)   Está deliciosa, pero estoy muy gordo y no como postres.

c)   Está muy buena, pero ya no puedo comer más.   ▲

3   **Part B,** *Vocabulary Matching:* This part is also worth 10 points. You will see two columns of words, one in Spanish and one in English, and you are to match those that translate each other. For example, match the following:

1	sale	(a)	left
2	hoja	(b)	he leaves
		(c)	leaf ▲

c

1 b, 2 c

By reviewing the vocabulary list in your notebook you will not only be preparing yourself for this part of the test but for all the other parts as well. Pay special attention to the words you have identified as problems and to all the new words that have been introduced in Etapa 4 (Assignments 56–73).

4   **Part C,** *Pronouns, Adjectival Residuals, and Their Syntactic Position:* This part is worth 15 points: You can make two kinds of mistakes: choosing the wrong pronoun, and putting it in the wrong position in relation to the verb. In the following practice items, rewrite each sentence, either deleting the indicated parts or changing them to pronouns or adjectival residuals, and placing them correctly in relation to the verb. You will also be expected to know whether an accent mark is needed or not.

Josefina ha perdido *la bolsa.*	Ella **la** ha perdido.
No me has traído *el café.*	No me **lo** has traído.
Vamos a dar *las flores a María.*	Vamos a dár**selas**.
Dé *el dinero a Pepe.*	**Déselo**.
Le escondió *la bolsa a la pobre muchacha.*	**Se la** escondió.
María y Elena nacieron el tres de julio.	**Ellas** nacieron el tres de julio.
Paco se quemó *el dedo pequeño de la mano derecha.*	**Él** se **lo** quemó.
Debemos buscar *a las niñas* por todas partes.	Debemos buscar**las** por todas partes.
No nos sirva *la ensalada* ahora.	No nos **la** sirva ahora.
Voy a arreglar *la muñeca a Ana.*	Voy a arreglár**sela**.

5   **Part D,** *Morphology and Use of the Preterit and the Imperfect:* This is worth 20 points. You can make three kinds of mistakes: you can make the wrong choice between the Preterit and the Imperfect, you can pick the wrong form of either, and you can misspell it. In the test you will have a story in the Present. You are to change the indicated verbs to the Preterit or the Imperfect as in this and the following sentences:

En ese momento Hilario se *levanta* y *canta.*	se levantó y cantó
Es una costumbre. *Tengo* que estar en casa cuando los niños *vuelven* de la escuela.	Era, Tenía, volvían
Yo *estoy* en casa cuando *vuelves* a la una.	estaba, volviste
Esta mañana temprano yo *salgo* a la calle y *veo* el coche.	salí, vi
Es la una de la mañana cuando ellos *ven* por primera vez la ciudad.	Era, vieron

6   Continue the tense-shift of the indicated present tense verbs in the following paragraph. Do one verb at a time and then check your answer.

Cuando el avión *aterriza* **1** (*lands*) en Nueva York y *vemos* **2** a nuestro padre en el aeropuerto, mi hermano y yo *sentimos* **3** una profunda emoción; pero nos *sorprende* **4** mucho que mamá no *está* **5** allí con él. Más tarde *sabemos* **6** que ellos *tienen* **7** muchos problemas y que ya no *viven* **8** juntos. Cuando *vamos* **9** en el taxi para el hotel, papá nos *dice* **10** confidencialmente que ellos se *van* **11** a divorciar.

1	aterrizó
2	vimos
3	sentimos
4	sorprendió
5	estaba
6	supimos
7	tenían
8	vivían
9	íbamos
10	dijo
11	iban

7　**Part E,** *Present Indicative Forms of Irregular Verbs:* This part is worth 7 points. You can make two types of mistakes: choosing a form that does not match the subject, and writing it incorrectly. On your answer sheet you will see sentences with one or more infinitives in parentheses and you will write the form that should replace the infinitive. For example: *Yo lo* (*hacer*) *cuando me lo* (*pedir*) *ellos.* The correct forms are _____.　▲

8　Practice this procedure with the following sentences:

Yo (saber) que ellos (tener) mucho dinero en el banco.

Si tú lo (querer), yo te lo (poder) traer.

Yo (traer) muchos regalos para todos.

Nosotros no (poder) hacerlo cuando ellos (estar) aquí.

Yo (oír) el pájaro. ¿Lo (oír) tú?

Yo no (seguir) el ejemplo de mi padre.

> hago, piden
> sé, tienen
> quieres, puedo
> traigo
> podemos, están
> oigo, oyes
> sigo

9　**Part F,** *Present Perfect Forms:* 10 points. You can make two types of mistakes: you may pick the wrong form of the auxiliary verb (*haber*) or a wrong form of the perfect participle. You must be especially careful with the verbs which have an irregular perfect participle. On the answer sheet you will see sentences with indicated verbs in the simple present which you are to change to the present perfect form. In *Ella toca el piano*, the present perfect of *toca* is _____.　▲

10 Continue practicing with the following:

Vendemos los edificios.

Ellos no nos *escriben* con mucha frecuencia.

Tú no *rompes* las muñecas.

¿*Va* Vd. a la playa muchas veces?

Me *dan* los cheques, y yo los *pongo* en el banco.

¿*Ves* a Fernando hoy? ¿Por qué él no *vuelve* a la clase?

Ellos me *dicen* que la expedición *descubre* un nuevo territorio.

Nos *reímos* mucho con los payasos.

¿Por qué no *resuelves* mi problema?

> ha tocado
> Hemos vendido
> han escrito
> has roto
> Ha ido
> han dado, he puesto
> Has visto, ha vuelto
> han dicho, ha descubierto
> hemos reído
> has resuelto

11　**Part G,** *Gustar:* For this part you will be asked to write the translation of four short English sentences worth two points each for a total of 8 points. For example, the Spanish equivalent of *I like salads* is _____.　▲

Me gustan las ensaladas.

12 Translate the following sentences:

We like to travel.

She likes animals.

They like tennis.

Do you like Mexican food, sir?

Do you like blondes, Tom?

Nos gusta viajar.

Le gustan los animales.

Les gusta el tenis.

¿Le gusta la comida mexicana, señor?

¿Te gustan las rubias, Tomás?

13 **Part H,** *Present Subjunctive Forms:* In 10 Spanish sentences, infinitives are given in parentheses in the subjoined clause. You are to write the appropriate present subjunctive form of each infinitive. Each correct form is worth one point. For example, in *Yo quiero que tú (estudiar) conmigo esta tarde, estudiar* should be replaced with _____. ▲

14 Practice the above in these sentences:

Yo quiero que tú me (ayudar) a hacer la comida.

No es necesario que yo (cubrir) las plantas del jardín esta noche porque no va a hacer frío.

No me gusta que Tonito (romper) sus libros.

Dile a tu vecino que (cerrar) todas las ventanas.

¿Por qué no quieres que nosotros (ir) contigo?

Prohiben que los estudiantes (traer) perros a la clase.

Insisto en que Vd. (comer) un poco más de postre.

estudies

.ayudes

cubra

rompa

cierre

vayamos

traigan

coma

15 **Part I,** *Reading Comprehension:* This last part is worth 10 points and consists of statements or questions each followed by three possible responses or completions. You will select the most logical of these three choices and circle the letter before it. For example:

En mi vida he visto a nadie que sepa más que mi tío Guillermo.

a) ¿Ha vivido él muchos años en las selvas de Brasil?

b) No tiene mucho pelo en la cabeza y le gusta tocar el violín.

c) Pues eso no me sorprende porque sé que es un profesor muy distinguido. ▲

16 Here is another example:

Mi padre nació en 1918 en el estado de la Florida.

a) Yo nunca he visitado esa parte del país.

b) Su padre debe ser un hombre muy inteligente.

c) Parece que en un momento va a llover. ▲

c

17 In some cases you will be expected to answer questions or complete statements which are related to a short paragraph. For example:

En muchos de los países de habla española es costumbre tomar café con leche para el desayuno. Para preparar esta bebida, generalmente ponen leche caliente en una taza. Después le ponen un poco de café negro muy concentrado y azúcar. Así es que podemos decir que . . .

a) en el mundo de habla española el café con leche se toma generalmente frío.

b) el café con leche se toma siempre a las cinco de la tarde.

c) para preparar café con leche necesitamos más leche que café. ▲

a

c

/

ETAPA CINCO

Performance Objectives
for Assignments 74–90

You will be prepared to continue your study of Spanish successfully if by Assignment 90 you have achieved all previous and the following objectives:

Reading Comprehension

1 Given in Spanish a written statement or question and three possible written responses containing structures and vocabulary practiced through Assignment 90, you select the most logical response at least eight times out of ten.

You see the following and select *b* as the most logical response:

No sé por qué Alberto ha hecho tantas cosas malas recientemente.
a   Puede ser que Elena sea su novia ahora.
b   Dime con quién andas, y te diré quién eres.
c   Sin duda es porque pasa tanto tiempo en la iglesia.

2 Given three paragraphs written in Spanish, based on structures and vocabulary practiced through Assignment 90 and containing ten vocabulary words new to you, you write correctly the English meaning of at least eight of these words as the result of your understanding the context in which they are found.

You see: Ya he pintado las cuatro paredes de mi cuarto. Ahora tengo que pintar el techo. Yo no soy ningún gigante y necesito una escalera para alcanzar el techo.
Escriban en inglés el significado de las palabras siguientes:
1) techo   2) escalera   3) gigante

You write: 1) ceiling,   2) ladder,   3) giant

Morphology, Usage, and Vocabulary

3 (Evaluated following Assignment 78) Given ten written sentences in Spanish, each with a verb left in the infinitive and some of these with object pronouns, you give the *tú* command forms for each and place accompanying object pronouns correctly in relation to the verb with no more than three errors out of fifteen.

You see: *No (darle) la leche al niño.*
You write: *le des.*

4 (Evaluated following Assignment 84) Given fourteen written sentences in Spanish and with the verbs in the subjoined clauses left in the infinitive, you write the correct conjugated form of the present subjunctive or indicative, depending upon rules of usage, with no more than five errors out of thirty.

You see: *Ojalá que tú (ir) también.*
You write: *vayas.*

5 Fifteen words in English used to express comparisons appear in ten otherwise Spanish sentences.

You translate correctly into Spanish at least twelve of them according to the context in which they are found.

You see: *Este libro es el* **most** *interesante* **in** *toda la biblioteca.*
You write: *más, de.*

6   Given several sentences written in Spanish with nine verbs left in the infinitive, you write the appropriate conjugated form of the Future with no more than two errors.

You see: *Mañana Olga y yo (tener) que ir al banco.*
You write: *tendremos.*

7   In five sentences written in Spanish you transform the indicated verb from the Present to the present progressive and from the Imperfect to the imperfect progressive with no more than two errors in the form of estar or the imperfect participle.

You see: *Cuando llegué, todos los alumnos* **cantaban**.
You write: *estaban cantando.*

8   Given a paragraph written in Spanish with ten verbs in subjoined clauses left in the infinitive, you write the correct conjugated form of the present subjunctive or indicative depending upon rules of usage with no more than four errors out of twenty.

You see: Creo que todo el mundo (1 saber) ya que Enriqueta y yo nos (2 casar) dentro de poco. Quiero que tú me (3 acompañar) a la iglesia.

You write: 1 sabe, 2 casamos, 3 acompañes.

9   Given several written English sentences with certain words indicated and followed by the Spanish translation with blanks for the indicated words, you write in the blanks the appropriate Spanish translation with no more than five errors out of a possible 26. Included are the following problems: the conjunctions *e* and *u*, diminutives, the *-ería* suffix, *tal* for "such a", *al* + infinitive for "upon . . .", the *-mente* suffix, *vamos a* for "let's", ordinal numbers, and recent miscellaneous vocabulary.

You see: Elena **and** Irma are in the **shoestore**. Elena says, "**Let's buy** new shoes."
Elena . . . Irma están en la . . .   Elena dice: . . . zapatos nuevos.

You write: *e, zapatería, Vamos a comprar.*

Affirmative and Negative Command Forms with tú

1 Write the command forms which match *ustedes* for *comprar, vender,* and *insistir.* ▲

compren, vendan, insistan (The subjunctive forms are the same.)

2 Change the above subjunctive forms so they will match *tú.* ▲

compres, vendas, insistas

3 Spanish uses the *tú* form of the subjunctive as a command form <u>only when the command is negative</u>. Translate: Do not come tomorrow. ▲

No vengas mañana. (The *tú* is commonly omitted.)

4 When the command form with *tú* is affirmative, the form is the same as the regular third person singular of the indicative. Which form is the command form in this proverb? *Antes que te cases, mira lo que haces.* ▲

mira (This form does not have the *s*-suffix that normally goes with *tú.*)

5 *Mira* is also an indicative mode form which can combine with three different subject pronouns: _____. ▲

usted, él, ella

6 Write the affirmative *tú* command forms for *dar, esconder,* and *permitir.* ▲

da, esconde, permite

7 Whatever irregularity appears in the third person present indicative remains the same in the *tú* form of the affirmative command. Write the *tú* command forms for *cerrar, perder,* and *contar.* ▲

cierra, pierde, cuenta

8 Nine verbs have special irregular forms. Only eight are in common use. Four of these simply use the stem of the infinitive as the command form. Write the stems for *tener, venir, poner,* and *salir.* ▲

ten, ven, pon, sal (These are the *tú* command forms.)

9 Translate: "Put (*tú*) the pencil on the table." ▲

Pon el lápiz en la mesa.

10 Rewrite the above sentence and make it negative. ▲

No pongas el lápiz en la mesa.

11 Change *No salgas por la ventana* to an affirmative command. ▲

12 Change to the affirmative: *No vengas aquí ahora.* ▲   *Sal por la ventana.*

13 There are four forms which just have to be memorized: *haz (hacer), sé (ser),*   *Ven aquí ahora.*
ve (ir), and *di (decir).* Write the affirmative form of these negative commands:
no tengas, no vengas, no pongas, no salgas, no hagas, no digas, no seas, no vayas. ▲

ten, ven, pon, sal, haz, di, sé, ve

14 An object pronoun is attached to the end of the verb in an affirmative command. It immediately precedes the verb in a negative command. Rewrite *Escríbala en la pizarra,* and change the verb so it agrees with *tú.* ▲

Escríbela en la pizarra.

15 Rewrite the above sentence and make it negative. ▲

No la escribas en la pizarra.

16 Translate using *usted* and *levantarse*: Get up! ▲
17 Rewrite the above command using *tú*. ▲
18 Rewrite the above and make the command negative. ▲

¡Levántese usted!
¡Levántate tú!
¡No te levantes!

Summary

1 Negative command forms with *tú* are the same as the subjunctive forms.

2 Affirmative command forms with *tú* are the same as the third person singular forms of the indicative including irregularities (except for *tener* (ten), *venir* (ven), *poner* (pon), *salir* (sal), *hacer* (haz), *ser* (sé), *ir* (ve), and *decir* (di)).

3 Object pronouns follow and are attached to affirmative commands, and they precede the verb when the command is negative.

More Spelling Review

1 Of the twenty-three phonemes that you have learned, there are nine which are represented by two or more graphemes. These may be divided into two sets. The first set is composed of three phonemes which you can learn to spell by rule.

/g/ | *gu* before *e* and *i*: *pague, seguir*
/g/ | *g* in all other combinations: *hago, grande, gusta*

/k/ | *qu* before *e* and *i*: *toqué, quitar*
/k/ | *c* in all other combinations: *clase, como, cuatro*

/rr/ | *rr* between two vowels: *cerrar, carretera, perro*
/rr/ | *r* at the beginning of words, and after /s/, /n/, and /l/: *romper, recto, Israel, Enrique, alrededor*

The second set is composed of six phonemes whose spelling you can learn only by seeing the words in which they are used.

The phoneme /s/ is commonly spelled in three different ways: _____. ▲

s, c, z (Before a consonant it may also be *x*: [estra] = *extra*.)

2 The phoneme /m/ may be spelled _____. ▲
3 The /y/ may be spelled _____. ▲ •
4 The /x/, the *jota*, may be spelled _____. ▲
5 The /i/ may be spelled _____. ▲
6 The /b/ may be spelled _____. ▲

m or *n*
y or *ll*
j or *g*
i or *y*
b or *v*

7 The letter *x* when occurring between vowels usually stands for the sound [ks] or [gs]: *examen, éxito*. However, when it precedes another consonant it more frequently stands for the sound [s], although a few natives pronounce it [ks] or [gs]: *excelente, explicar*. Occasionally *x* stands for the *jota* [x]: *México*;

and in some words of Indian origin it may stand for [s] at the beginning of a word: *Xochimilco*. Spanish has a phoneme /w/. When you hear [w], you write ———. ▲

u (So [kwando] is written *cuando*.)

8 The letter *q* is used only in the digraph ———. ▲

9 There are two letters in the Spanish alphabet which are digraphs: ———. ▲ *qu*

ch; ll (The phoneme /rr/ is not considered to be a separate letter by the Spanish Academy Dictionary.)

10 When an English cognate has a *ph* in it, you usually write ——— in the Spanish equivalent. ▲

11 English has a great many words like "appetite" and "ladder" which have *f* the same consonant used twice. In speech, however, you hear only one sound for *pp* and *dd*. Say and write the Spanish for "professor." ▲

profesor (Spanish usually pronounces a sound for each double letter: *lección* [leksión].)

Irregular Forms of the Preterit

1 The two verbs *ser* and *ir* have the same forms in the Preterit. Write the forms that match *yo, tú, nosotros, usted*, and *ustedes*. ▲

yo fui, tú fuiste, nosotros fuimos, usted fue, ustedes fueron

2 In the Preterit *dar* takes all the suffixes of an *e-* or *i-*verb. Write the forms that match *yo, tú, él, nosotros*, and *ustedes*. ▲

yo di, tú diste, él dio, nosotros dimos, ustedes dieron (Note, however, that *di* and *dio* may be written without the accent mark.)

3 Write the preterit stem of *venir, hacer*, and *poner*. ▲

4 The suffix that matches *yo* is ———. ▲ *vin, hic, pus*

e: yo vine, hice, puse

5 The suffix that matches *usted, él* and *ella* is ———. ▲

o: usted vino, hizo, puso

6 Write the Preterit for "you (*tú*) came, we made, they put." ▲

tú viniste, nosotros hicimos, ellos pusieron (These suffixes are regular.)

7 The three verbs *estar, tener*, and *andar* have a similar irregularity in their preterit stems: *estuv, tuv*, and *anduv*. The suffixes are the same as those for *venir, hacer*, or *poner*. Copy the stems and add the suffix that goes with *yo*. ▲

estuve, tuve, anduve

8 Rewrite the forms so they agree with *usted*. ▲

estuvo, tuvo, anduvo

9 The rest of the forms take the regular suffixes for *e-* and *i-*verbs. Rewrite the forms and make them agree with *ellos*. ▲

estuvieron, tuvieron, anduvieron

10 There are three more verbs that also have irregular stems in the Preterit and use the same first suffixes in the *yo* and *usted* forms: *poder > pud, saber > sup*, and *querer > quis*. Copy these stems and add the suffix that matches *yo*. ▲

yo pude, supe, quise

11 Rewrite the forms and make them agree with *usted* (*él, ella*). ▲

usted pudo, supo, quiso

12 Rewrite the forms so they match *nosotros*. ▲

pudimos, supimos, quisimos

13 When the stem of an irregular Preterit ends with *j* the *i* of *iero* is dropped. Rewrite *dije* ("I said" from *decir*) so it matches *ustedes*. ▲

14 The verb *traer* has the irregular stem *traj*. Write the form that matches *ellos*. ▲

dijeron

15 Change this form so it matches *yo* and *usted*. ▲

trajeron

16 All the verbs in the language which end with *ducir*, like *traducir*, were made up by adding a prefix to the verb *ducir* which has disappeared from the language but which meant "to lead." So *traducir* (to translate) comes from *tras* (across) and *ducir* (to lead) and, so, used to mean "to lead across"—"to translate." The preterit stem of all these compounds based on *ducir* is *duj*, and the first suffix has the same irregularities as *decir*. So the *yo* form of *traducir* is _____. ▲

yo traje ; usted trajo

17 Change this form so it matches *ustedes*. ▲

traduje

18 The verbs *tener, estar, andar, saber, poder,* and *querer* describe a state (*estar*), a potential (*poder*), or an event which is non-cyclic. What aspect of a non-cyclic event is indicated by the Preterit? (a) beginning (b) middle (c) end ▲

tradujeron

19 Translate: *En ese momento él supo que era verdad.* ▲

beginning

At that moment he knew that it was true. (The meaning of *supo* is "began to know." It is common, however, to translate *supo* with a different English verb: "At that moment he *learned* that it was true.")

20 Translate: *Ayer tuve una carta* (letter) *de mi amigo.* ▲

Yesterday I had a letter from my friend.

21 Does this definitely mean that you *don't* have the letter today? ▲

no (So *tuve*, like *supo*, is often translated by another verb: "Yesterday I *got* (received) a letter from my friend.")

22 *Yo quise hacerlo* means to the Spanish speaker "I began to want to do it," and *Yo no quise hacerlo* means "I did not begin to want to do it." The best literal English equivalent of this negative statement is "I did not want to do it." The most common translation is the more emphatic "I refused to do it."

More on Cognates

Until the late Middle Ages all of the courses in the universities of Western Europe were conducted in Latin and all educated people, as a consequence, could speak both their native language (English, French, German, Spanish, *etc.*) and Latin. The educated speakers of English, as a result, borrowed many thousands of words from Latin which gradually became part of our modern English vocabulary, and, of course, cognates of their Spanish equivalents. These cognates today tend to differ from each other in three general ways.

1 First, Spanish has no native words which *end* with "ic," "ty," or "ry." So, when an English cognate ends with "ic" the Spanish equivalent is very likely to end with *ico*. Moreover, Spanish is like English in that it does not put the stress on the *i* of this suffix but on the first vowel that comes before it. As a result, in writing this vowel must have an accent mark. Write the Spanish equivalents of: pacific, tragic, economic. ▲

pacífico, trágico, económico

2   The English word-forming suffix "ty" is frequently matched in Spanish by *dad*. Write the Spanish equivalents of: university, curiosity, electricity, formality. ▲

universidad, curiosidad, electricidad, formalidad

3   In the Spanish writing system a *y* can never precede or follow a consonant as in "type" or "history" in English. All Spanish cognates, as a result, will have an *i* in place of the English *y* (*tipo, historia*). One common Spanish equivalent of "ry" is *rio*. Write the Spanish for: voluntary, secretary, contrary. ▲

voluntario, secretario, contrario

4   There are three things you must learn about cognates. First, you cannot be certain that every Latin word in the English language will have an equivalent cognate in Spanish. Many of the old Latin words have disappeared from Spanish. Second, you cannot predict with certainty that an English word-forming suffix will always be matched by a given suffix in Spanish, and, third, you must be aware of the fact that cognates do not always have the same meaning in both languages. Thus in Spanish *propaganda* regularly translates "advertising," *Estoy constipado* may mean not "I'm constipated" but "I have a cold in the head," and *Ella está embarazada* does not translate "She is embarrassed" but "She is pregnant."

In the beginning of this section it was said that cognates tend to differ in three general ways. First, the form of a suffix may be changed in a predictable way. Thus English "ic" is matched by Spanish *ico*. English "ous," as in "precious," has as its equivalent *oso* (*precioso*). Second, an English suffix is matched by an entirely different form: "ty" is replaced by *dad* ("reality"—*realidad*). The third difference appears in the spelling of cognates. The *t* of a suffix when followed by *i* as in "tion" or "tious" (condition, superstitious) appears as a _____ in Spanish. ▲

c (condición, supersticioso)

5   English "th" is matched by *t* in Spanish: *autor*; "ss" becomes *s: imposible;* and "ph" becomes _____. ▲

f (Also, the spelling of an English cognate cues the choice of the right letter in Spanish: **s**uperficial, **v**isual, **b**eneficial, **h**onorable.)

6   Linguistics divides all cognates into three categories. **Identical cognates** have the same form and meaning in both languages: *motor, fatal, probable.* **Non-identical cognates** may have different forms or spellings but the same meaning: "generous"—*generoso*. **Deceptive cognates** are look-alikes which have different and very contrasting meanings in the two languages: *propaganda*.

There are a great many non-identical cognates which do not look much like each other but whose meaning you can learn to guess if you learn to look at their stems. Thus, for example, "mortuary" (funeral home) and "mortal" (a mortal wound) both have the stem *mor* which is the stem of *morir* in Spanish.

Let's see if you can figure out the meaning of this word: *carnicería*. The suffix *cería* says the word stands for a shop or store. In English there are "carnivorous" animals. Does the stem *carni* look like a noun you already know? What is sold in a *carnicería*? ▲

meat—*carne* (Carnivorous animals are meat-eaters.)

Self-Correcting Exercises

A *Subjunctive versus Indicative:* You must watch out for three things: choice between indicative and subjunctive, selecting the appropriate verb ending, and spelling the verb form correctly.

1 Es necesario que los caballos (estar) en este corral.	estén
2 Los bomberos (*firemen*) mandan que ellos (saltar).	salten
3 Yo recuerdo que tú (saber) más de esto que yo.	sabes
4 Quiero que ustedes (llegar) más temprano mañana.	lleguen
5 Los abuelos no permiten que los niños (tocar) el piano.	toquen
6 Ellos impiden que yo (oír) la verdad.	oiga
7 Desean que yo (esconder) el oro.	esconda
8 Contestan que ella (doblar) en esta calle.	dobla
9 No quiero que nosotros (almorzar) hasta las doce.	almorcemos
10 Desean que él y yo lo (pedir).	pidamos
11 Leo que los soldados (*soldiers*) ya (estar) en la isla.	están
12 Dejan que nosotros lo (hacer).	hagamos

B *Reading Comprehension:* Read through the following selection without stopping to translate, and do the comprehension exercise following it.

La Carretera Panamericana (primera parte)

Al oír° el nombre "carretera Panamericana," muchas personas piensan en una larga carretera intercontinental que va por la costa del Pacífico desde Alaska hasta Tierra del Fuego. Esto no es exactamente la verdad. En primer lugar, ninguna de las numerosas carreteras que hay al norte del Río Grande en Estados Unidos y Canadá es considerada oficialmente como parte de la Carretera Panamericana o Interamericana. En segundo lugar, al hablar° de la Carretera Panamericana, es necesario recordar que ese nombre no se refiere exclusivamente a una sola vía de comunicación sino° a todo el sistema de caminos que conecta a las capitales de México, Centro y Sur América. Incluye también oficialmente algunas carreteras en los países del Caribe: Cuba, Haití, la República Dominicana y el territorio de la isla de Puerto Rico.

El sistema interamericano de carreteras comienza en varios puntos de la frontera° entre Estados Unidos y México. En la capital mexicana las diferentes rutas se unen° para seguir después en dirección sur hacia° la América Central y terminar en un pequeño pueblo panameño que se llama Chepo. Al llegar° a Chepo, el viajero que desea continuar su viaje por tierra en los países de América

Upon hearing

when speaking

but

border
unite/towards
Upon arriving

del Sur tiene que transportar su carro por barco a uno de los puertos de Colombia o Venezuela. La parte de la carretera que va a comunicar a Panamá con Colombia todavía está en construcción. Va a costar millones de dólares porque es necesario cruzar el territorio de Darién, 425 millas de impenetrable selva tropical donde llueve torrencialmente y es muy difícil construir caminos y mantenerlos en buena condición. En América del Sur la Carretera Panamericana continúa por más de 13.000 millas de caminos pavimentados y más de 6.000 millas sin pavimentar pero transitables en todas las estaciones del año.

    Los requisitos° para viajar por la Carretera Panamericana varían según el país y el número de días que el viajero va a pasar allí. En general, es buena idea llevar los siguientes documentos: un pasaporte oficial o tarjeta° de turista, certificados de nacimiento° y de vacuna,° varias fotografías recientes y documentos especiales para el automóvil y para manejar.

       requirements

       card
birth/vaccination

Comprehension exercise: Select the letter corresponding to the answer.

1 ¿Qué carretera californiana es parte oficial de la Carretera Panamericana?
    a La carretera que pasa por el centro de Sacramento, la capital del estado.
    b En California no hay ninguna. Está en el estado de Nuevo México.
    c El gobierno de Estados Unidos no ha decidido oficialmente porque hay varias que se unen al sistema panamericano.

       1 c

2 ¿Qué es oficialmente la Carretera Panamericana?
    a Es una sola carretera muy larga que va por la costa del Pacífico hasta Chile.
    b Es un sistema de caminos y carreteras que conectan a las principales capitales de las Américas.
    c Es un sistema de carreteras que comunica a Canadá con los Estados Unidos.

       2 b

3 ¿Qué países panamericanos son islas o parte de una isla?
    a Cuba, Haití y la República Dominicana.
    b Panamá y Guatemala.
    c Colombia, Venezuela y Puerto Rico.

       3 a

4 ¿Dónde comienza la Carretera Panamericana?
    a Comienza en la frontera entre Estados Unidos y Canadá.
    b Comienza en un pueblo de Panamá que se llama Chepo.
    c Comienza en la línea que separa a México de Estados Unidos.

       4 c

5 ¿Es posible ir directamente por tierra en automóvil desde Ciudad México hasta Santiago, Chile?
    a La selva tropical de Darién no lo permite porque esa parte de la carretera todavía está en construcción.
    b Es posible, pero es mucho más fácil ir directamente en ferrocarril.
    c En la región de Darién es muy difícil el transporte porque allí hay muchos desiertos.

       5 a

6 ¿En qué país está el pueblo de Chepo?
    a En Guatemala.
    b En Colombia.

       6 c

   c En Panamá.

7 ¿Por qué no hay carreteras en la región de Darién?   7 c

   a Porque no son necesarias.

   b Porque allí hay muchos animales feroces.

   c Porque en la selva tropical llueve mucho y es difícil y costoso construir caminos y mantenerlos.

8 ¿Cuántas millas de caminos pavimentados hay aproximadamente en la   8 c
Carretera Panamericana de América del Sur?

   a 2.000 millas.

   b Más de 80.000 millas.

   c Más de 13.000 millas.

9 ¿Qué documentos se necesitan para viajar por la Carretera Panamericana?   9 b

   a Las notas de la escuela y un certificado de la policía.

   b Depende del país y del número de días que la persona se quede en el país.

   c Depende de la estación del año y de la temperatura.

10 ¿Cuál de las frases siguientes es verdad?   10 c
Los caminos que forman el sistema de la Carretera Panamericana . . .

   a están pavimentados en su totalidad.

   b fueron completamente terminados en 1950.

   c están interrumpidos en parte por una selva tropical.

C *Cognates and Spelling:* Write the Spanish equivalent and check immediately to see if you did it right; then say each Spanish word aloud.

1	futility	*futilidad*	**7**	hospitality	*hospitalidad*
2	inferiority	*inferioridad*	**8**	individuality	*individualidad*
3	locality	*localidad*	**9**	integrity	*integridad*
4	generality	*generalidad*	**10**	humanity	*humanidad*
5	impossibility	*imposibilidad*	**11**	identity	*identidad*
6	maternity	*maternidad*	**12**	intensity	*intensidad*

Americans usually have only three meals a day: breakfast, lunch, and dinner. For most people lunch is at noon and dinner is around six o'clock in the evening. A great many Spanish speakers, in contrast, regularly have four meals a day: breakfast, lunch, *merienda*, and dinner. The reason for the fourth meal (*merienda*) is that dinner is served very late in the evening (sometimes as late as 10 o'clock) and the *merienda* is something like an after-school snack or our five o'clock tea. The Spanish breakfast and *merienda* are light meals. Their lunch and dinner are both heavy meals. The American custom of having just a sandwich for lunch seems strange to the Spanish speaker, and only restaurants that cater to tourists normally have sandwiches on their menus.

    The heavy noon meal makes people sleepy, and this helps explain the Spanish habit of taking a *siesta*. And, of course, having an afternoon nap explains why so many people stay up later at night than most Americans.

New Vocabulary

Add these new words to your notebook list and study them for a minute or two on four occasions before your next class. You will be expected to know them for your next class.

cuarto	room	**escalera**	stairway	**sofá (el)**	sofa
sala	living-room	**arriba**	upstairs	**cama**	bed
comedor	dining-room	**abajo**	downstairs	**espejo**	mirror
cocina	kitchen	**muebles**	furniture	**lámpara**	lamp
baño (cuarto de)	bathroom	**sillón**	arm chair	**escritorio**	desk
cuarto de dormir	bedroom				

ojalá (que) . . .   I wish, God grant, would that
(Requires a verb in the subjunctive.)
"Haz bien y no mires a quién."   "Do good no matter for whom."

Assignment 75

E *and* u *for* y *and* o

1 Since two repetitions of the same vowel tend to fuse into one sound, you will not hear the "and" (*y*) in *Habla español y inglés*. There can be a lot of confusion in communication if one cannot hear the "and" in speech. Spanish solves this problem by changing *y* to *e* before words that begin with *i* or *hi*. You neither say nor write *madre y hijo* but, instead, *madre e hijo*. Say the following aloud: *españoles e indios, venir e ir, tiendas e iglesias, otoño e invierno*. Translate: rivers and islands. ▲

2 The *y* does not change to *e* when the following word begins with [hie] or with [y] because these beginning sounds are not pure vowels and, as a result, the "and" sound does not fuse with them. You say and write *píldoras y hierbas* (pills and herbs). Translate: he and I. ▲

3 For the same reasons the conjunction *o* (or) changes to *u* (in both speech and writing) before words beginning with *o* or *ho*. Translate: woman or man. ▲

4 Translate: silver or gold; fire or water; tree or leaf. ▲

ríos e islas

él y yo

mujer u hombre

plata u oro ; fuego o agua ; árbol u hoja

The Adverbial Suffix mente

1 In English many adjectives may be changed into adverbs by adding the suffix "ly." So "clear" becomes "clearly" in "He spoke clearly." The Spanish equivalent of "ly" is *mente: Habló claramente*. Today the *mente* of *claramente* (clear mind) is simply an adverbial suffix which is added to an adjective. Is it likely that *clara* has a companion form *claro*?   ▲

2   "The mind" is *la mente*. Why, then, does the Spanish speaker say *claramente* instead of *claromente*?   ▲

yes

> Because *clara* still agrees with the *mente* just the way it did when *mente* was still a noun (*la mente > la clara mente*) and not just an adverbial suffix.

3   When an adjective has only one form you simply add *mente* to it to get the adverbial form. Translate: easily; sadly.   ▲

fácilmente ; tristemente

4   All *mente* forms were originally two words. In terms of word stress, the *mente* forms are not treated as <u>one</u> word which has only <u>one</u> stressed syllable. They are spoken as though they were <u>two</u> words with <u>two</u> stressed syllables: one for the adjective and one for the suffix. Divide *clara* and *mente* into syllables and underline the stressed syllable of each.   ▲

5   Say the following aloud and be careful to stress the indicated syllables: *fácilmente, tristemente, alegremente, magníficamente*.

cla-ra ; **men**-te

6   Adjectives like *normal, formal,* and *mortal* have the stress on the last syllable in Spanish; when *mente* is added to them, there are <u>two</u> stressed syllables in a row. This is so rare in English that there is no standard English word which has two sequential strong stresses. Consequently, your speech intuition will object to your saying *for-**mal-men**-te* and you will, if you are not very careful, change the Spanish to *for-mal-**men**-te*. Practice saying the following aloud: *nor-**mal-men**-te, mor-**tal-men**-te, for-**mal-men**-te*.

Review of the Subjunctive

1   *María plancha la ropa* is a statement which describes either what María customarily does or what she is actually doing when the statement is made. This simple statement may be incorporated into a more complex statement in such a way that *planchar* becomes a subjoined verb. What form will you use in *Veo que María* _____ *la ropa*?   ▲

2   When the verb of the main clause describes some type of observation—see, hear, observe, notice, *etc.*—the verb of the subjoined clause is always in the (a) indicative (b) subjunctive mode.   ▲

plancha

indicative

3   When the verb of the main clause is used to report what someone else is doing, the verb of the subjoined clause is always in the (a) indicative (b) subjunctive mode.   ▲

indicative

4   Look at this statement: *Pepe grita que María viene*. Is Pepe shouting at María?   ▲

no (He is shouting the information to someone else.)

5   What does Pepe actually shout?   ▲

6   Pepe is not shouting at María. María, in fact, may be a thousand miles away and Pepe has just gotten a letter saying that she is coming. Can Pepe's shouting be what is causing María's action?   ▲

¡María viene!

no

7 Is *gritar* a verb of reporting? ▲

yes (*Gritar* simply describes the way something is said, that is, "to say very loudly.")

8 Look at this sentence: *Pepe le grita a María que venga.* At whom is Pepe shouting? ▲

9 What does Pepe actually shout to María? ▲

at María

10 Is *¡Venga!* a command form? ▲

¡Venga!

11 Is Pepe trying to influence María's action? ▲

yes

12 When the verb of the main clause is used to report a command directed at another person the verb of the subjoined clause is always in the (a) indicative (b) subjunctive mode. ▲

yes

13 All of the following are verbs of reporting: *informar, gritar, decir, responder, contestar, escribir.* Which one of them cannot logically be used to report a command? ▲

subjunctive

14 The verb *mandar* means "to command" or "to send." When it means "to command" must the verb of the subjoined clause be in the subjunctive or the indicative? ▲

informar

15 *Insistir* has two meanings: "to state emphatically" and "to demand emphatically." Which meaning requires the subjunctive in the subjoined verb? ▲

subjunctive

to demand emphatically (*Insisto que tú lo hagas.*)

16 The action of a person may be influenced in three ways: (1) it may be caused, (2) it may be permitted, or (3) it may be prevented. All of these ways of influencing another person require the subjunctive in the subjoined verb. Here are the verbs you have had that belong to this set:

esperar	impedir	dejar	invitar
mandar	permitir	pedir	hacer
insistir	conseguir	querer	desear

Self-Correcting Exercises

A *Cognates and Spelling:* Write the Spanish equivalent of each word, check to see if you did it right after each one, and then say it aloud.

1	nationality	*nacionalidad*		**6**	revolutionary	*revolucionario*
2	voluntary	*voluntario*		**7**	reality	*realidad*
3	personality	*personalidad*		**8**	salary	*salario*
4	reactionary	*reaccionario*		**9**	sincerity	*sinceridad*
5	popularity	*popularidad*		**10**	secretary	*secretario*

B *Reading Comprehension:* You now know enough Spanish to be able to read the following selection quite fast without stopping to translate. Do the comprehension exercise at the end.

La Carretera Panamericana (segunda parte)

La idea de construir un gran camino intercontinental para unir° física y espiritualmente a los países de América tiene una vieja y larga historia. En el siglo XVI (dieciséis), después de las conquistas de México y Perú, el emperador

unite

Carlos V (quinto) de España dio órdenes de construir un "camino real" para comunicar a la ciudad de México con los nuevos territorios del sur. En los últimos años del siglo XIX (diecinueve) los gobiernos de varias naciones americanas se interesaron mucho en la construcción de un gran ferrocarril interamericano. Al aparecer el automóvil como uno de los medios° principales de transporte en el siglo XX (veinte), la idea del ferrocarril intercontinental fue abandonada. En 1923, en Santiago, Chile, los delegados a la Quinta Conferencia Panamericana recomendaron la construcción de una carretera panamericana. Han pasado más de 400 años y el proyecto de unir a las Américas por carretera todavía no ha sido terminado en su totalidad. Queda el gran problema de completar el camino por la selva de Darién.

Desde 1927, sin embargo, aventureros de varios países han hecho viajes a pie, a caballo y en auto por el territorio de América. Uno de ellos tardó° nueve años en llegar a Nueva York y otros murieron por el camino. El deportista° argentino Miguel Divo, en su viaje desde Buenos Aires a Nueva York, tuvo que comer carne de mono en varias ocasiones para no morirse de hambre. En junio de 1939, Richard Tewkesbury, un maestro de Carolina del Norte cruzó a pie el territorio de Darién. Quería demostrar° que era posible viajar por esa selva tropical y que los indios que vivían allí no eran caníbales.

En nuestros días, el viaje en automóvil por Centro América es una experiencia educacional inolvidable. No presenta tantos problemas y dificultades como en los primeros años, pero es muy necesario que el turista ordinario se prepare bien antes de salir. Aunque las carreteras están pavimentadas casi totalmente, suben a grandes alturas y hay curvas peligrosas° en varias secciones. En los meses de mucha lluvia (de junio a octubre) es difícil y costoso° mantener los caminos en buena condición.

El paisaje° centroamericano es verdaderamente espectacular. Las carreteras principales pasan por lugares muy interesantes: pueblos y mercados° indios, ruinas de civilizaciones desaparecidas, ciudades coloniales, volcanes activos, lagos de agua azul y grandes plantaciones de café, bananas y caña de azúcar. Entre el Río Grande y Panamá hay siete capitales que ofrecen muchas atracciones al visitante: Ciudad México, Ciudad de Guatemala, San Salvador en El Salvador, Tegucigalpa en Honduras, Managua en Nicaragua, San José en Costa Rica y, finalmente, Panamá. ¡Buen viaje y que se diviertan mucho!

Comprehension exercise: Select the letter corresponding to the answer.

1 ¿Quién dio órdenes de construir un "camino real" entre Ciudad México y la América del Sur en el siglo XVI (dieciséis)?

    a Los delegados a la Quinta Conferencia Panamericana que se celebró en Santiago, Chile.

    b El rey de España.

    c El inventor del automóvil.

2 ¿Qué recomendaron los delegados a la Quinta Conferencia Panamericana en Santiago, Chile?

    a La construcción de un ferrocarril interamericano.

    b La construcción de una carretera intercontinental.

----

means

took
sportsman

show

dangerous
costly

landscape
markets

1 b

2 b

c   La construcción de un camino por la selva de Darién.

3 ¿En qué año empezaron los viajes intercontinentales por auto?   3 a
   a   1927.
   b   1840.
   c   1959.

4 ¿Qué hizo el deportista argentino Miguel Divo?   4 b
   a   Hizo un viaje muy diverti do(*fun*) por la selva del Amazonas.
   b   Hizo un viaje largo y difícil desde Buenos Aires hasta Nueva York.
   c   Se murió de hambre en la selva de Darién.

5 ¿Qué hizo un profesor norteamericano en 1939?   5 c
   a   Cruzó la selva de Darién a caballo.
   b   Cruzó la selva de Darién en automóvil.
   c   Caminó de un extremo a otro de la selva de Darién.

6 ¿Por qué es necesario que los turistas que viajan por Centro América   6 c
vayan bien preparados?
   a   Porque las carreteras no están pavimentadas.
   b   Porque el paisaje es verdaderamente espectacular.
   c   Porque en partes de la carretera puede haber problemas cuando llueve.

7 ¿En qué meses del año es mejor viajar por la América Central?   7 c
   a   De junio a octubre.
   b   En los meses de mucha lluvia.
   c   De noviembre a mayo.

8 ¿Cuál es el nombre de la capital de Honduras?   8 a
   a   Tegucigalpa.
   b   Managua.
   c   San Salvador.

9 ¿Cuál es la capital de Costa Rica?   9 c
   a   San Salvador.
   b   Managua.
   c   San José.

10 ¿Qué es San Salvador?   10 c
   a   Es el nombre de una carretera.
   b   Es el nombre de una plantación.
   c   Es el nombre de una ciudad.

C   *Commands with* tú *and* usted: Say aloud the affirmative and negative familiar commands for each infinitive.

1	tener	*ten, no tengas*		5	salir	*sal, no salgas*
2	venir	*ven, no vengas*		6	ir	*ve, no vayas*
3	ser	*sé, no seas*		7	hacer	*haz, no hagas*
4	poner	*pon, no pongas*		8	decir	*di, no digas*

D   *Irregular Preterit Forms in Inverted Order Statements:* Write the combinations, placing the subject pronoun after the verb as in the example.

Ejemplo: 43 = No tuvieron que hacerlo ellos.

1	No querer		1	nosotros.
2	Poder		2	yo.
3	Saber	hacerlo	3	ellos.
4	No tener que		4	tú.
5	Estar allí para		5	ella.

1) 11

2) 22

3) 33

4) 44

5) 55

6) 51

7) 12

8) 23

9) 34

10) 45

No quisimos hacerlo nosotros.

Pude hacerlo yo.

Supieron hacerlo ellos.

No tuviste que hacerlo tú.

Estuvo allí para hacerlo ella.

Estuvimos allí para hacerlo nosotros.

No quise hacerlo yo.

Pudieron hacerlo ellos.

Supiste hacerlo tú.

No tuvo que hacerlo ella.

New Vocabulary

dejar de	to stop, quit (doing something)	**de veras**	really
salir bien	to do (come out) well	**¿Qué pasó?**	What happened?
salir mal	to do (come out) poorly	**No le hace.**	It doesn't matter.

Assignment 76

Review of Done-to and Involved Entity Pronouns

1 All events may be divided into two great sets. One set is composed of actions which cannot take place unless something or someone is acted upon. You have to "love" something or someone. You cannot "carry" unless you have something to carry, and you cannot "make" unless you produce or create something. The verbs which stand for the actions of this set are called **transitives** (from *transire*—to cross over) because the action of the doer is performed on the done-to. Does *traer* (to bring) belong to this set? ▲

2 Which word stands for the done-to in *¿Quién va a traer la fruta?* ▲

3 You already know that there are many patterns in which there are a doer, a done-to, and, in addition, a third or involved entity. So the above sentence may be extended to *¿Quién va a traer la fruta a mamá?* When common focus has been established this sentence can be transformed by omitting *fruta*. Rewrite the sentence with this deletion. ▲

yes

fruta

¿Quién va a traerla a mamá?

4 The original sentence (*¿Quién va a traer la fruta a mamá?*) can also be transformed by replacing *a mamá* with an involved entity pronoun. In this case the pronoun would be _____. ▲

5 Where do you put *le*? ▲

le

immediately after and attached to *traer* (*traerle*)

6 Transform *¿Quién va a traer la fruta a mamá?* so that it translates "Who is going to bring her it (it to her)?" ▲

¿Quién va a traérsela ? (*Le* is changed to its allomorph *se* and is placed before

7 Translate this answer to the above question: "I am bringing her it (it to her)." ▲

la.)

Yo se la traigo. (The object pronouns are now written as two words and are placed before the verb.)

8 When you have a done-to and an involved entity pronoun in a pattern, the involved entity pronoun comes first. Transform "Bring it to me" so you have the literal equivalent of the Spanish pattern in English. ▲

9 Translate the sentence using the *usted* command form of the verb. (Use *lo* for "it.") ▲

Bring me it.

10 Rewrite the sentence and make it negative. ▲

Tráigamelo.

No me lo traiga. (The object pronouns are placed *between* the negative adverb and the verb.)

11 The statement *Va a traérmela* may be transformed to *Me la va a traer.* (a) true (b) false ▲

12 The done-to and involved entity pronouns which match *yo*, *tú*, and *nosotros* have the same forms. They are _____. ▲

true

13 Since *usted* may be either male or female, the done-to pronoun which matches *usted* has two forms. They are _____. ▲

me, te, nos

14 These two forms also match two other subject pronouns. They are _____. ▲

lo ; la

15 The subject pronouns which match the done-to forms *los* and *las* are _____. ▲

él ; ella

16 The involved entity pronoun that matches *usted*, *él*, and *ella* has two allomorphs. They are _____. ▲

ustedes, ellos, ellas

17 The involved entity pronoun that matches *ustedes*, *ellos*, and *ellas* also has two allomorphs. They are _____. ▲

le ; se

18 When the involved entity is indicated by a noun, this noun must be preceded by the relator *a*, as in the English pattern: "I gave the money *to* Raquel." In a pattern of this type Spanish usually requires the involved entity pronoun also. Translate the above sentence. ▲

les ; se

(Yo) le di el dinero a Raquel.

19 Rewrite and use pronouns for both nouns. ▲

20 When a done-to entity is moved from one person to another it may in actuality move in two possible directions. Write the missing relator: He gave the money _____ Hilario. ▲

(Yo) se lo di.

21 Write the missing relator: He stole the money _____ Hilario. ▲

to

from (The meaning of *gave* and *stole* told you when to use *to* and *from.* We do not really need two different relators to send these messages.)

22 The missing relator in "I washed the car _____ Jorge" is _____. ▲

for

23 You can use two possible relators in "I bought the car _____ Jorge" to show the direction of movement of the done-to entity. They are _____. ▲

24 When the Spanish speaker uses *le* and also a noun to label the involved entity there is only <u>one relator</u> that may be used before the noun. Translate: "Jorge gave the money to Hilario." Remember to use *le*. ▲

from; for

*Jorge le dio el dinero **a** Hilario.*

25 Translate "He stole (*robar*) the money from Hilario." Use *le*. ▲

*Él le robó el dinero **a** Hilario.*

26 Keep going and translate: He bought the car from Hilario. ▲

*Él le compró el carro **a** Hilario.*

27 Now, translate: "He bought the car for Hilario." ▲

*Él le compró el carro **a** Hilario.* (This sentence all by itself does not tell you which meaning to give it. The meaning can only be determined by context. When this fails, the Spanish speaker drops the *le* and translates "for" with *para: Él compró el carro para Hilario.*)

28 In English, as in Spanish, you do not need to have the relator to get the meaning. The fact that Spanish uses *a* where English uses "to," "from," and "for" should not be confusing to you after you get used to looking to the verb and the nature of the event for the meaning. Let's practice this.

A small child has gotten hold of a bottle (*una botella*) of poisonous material. The mother says to an older brother, *¡Quítasela a ella!* Translate using an English relator. ▲

Take it away *from* her!

29 Two boys on a street corner are selling flowers. You come up and say that you are interested in buying some of the flowers. The two boys are competitors. One says to you, *¡Cómpremelas a mí!* Translate using an English relator. ▲

30 A girl and her mother go into a store. The girl sees a blouse that she likes very much. She says to her mother, *¡Cómpramela, mamá!* Translate using an English relator. ▲

Buy them *from* me!

Buy it *for* me, Mother!

31 In this and the next five frames rewrite the sentence by using pronouns for all nouns. *Mamá va a dar el carro a Pepe.* (Use two pronouns for *Pepe*.) ▲

Ella va a dárselo a él.

32 María leyó el libro a su hermano. (Use two pronouns for *hermano*.) ▲

33 Por favor, pláncheme la camisa. ▲

Ella se lo leyó a él.
Por favor, plánchemela.

34 No me cuente esa historia. ▲

35 ¿Vas a traernos el café? ▲

No me la cuente.
¿Vas a traérnoslo?

In the restaurants of the Hispanic world, one almost always finds on the tables bottles with vinegar and oil. Americans are upset because there is almost never any catsup, mustard, pepper, jams or jellies on the table. Catsup and mustard are not a part of the regular Latin diet, nor are hamburgers and hotdogs. There are millions of Latins who do not know that catsup and mustard even exist.

Expressions of Emotion

1 There are three ways that we can talk about the psychological states or reactions of a person. First, we can say that something causes or produces a reaction, as in "That surprises me." The Spanish speaker can say this in the same way. Translate the sentence. Use *eso*. The verb is *sorprender*. ▲

2 Similarly we can say "That makes me mad." Translate this. The verb is *enojar*. ▲

Eso me sorprende.

3 If something surprises me or makes me mad, you can say this about me. "He is surprised." "He is mad." Since my psychological state has been changed, which verb will you use? (a) *ser* (b) *estar* ▲

Eso me enoja.

4 Translate: He is surprised. ▲

estar

5 The use of *estar* in these sentences tells the Spanish speaker that a change has taken place in the subject. Very few people are normally always surprised or angry. So one of the things that we commonly say about the psychology of a person is that it changes. A person *becomes* angry, furious, jealous, *etc.*

Él está sorprendido.

In both English and Spanish there is a difference between saying "She made him jealous" and "He became jealous of her." Which sentence implies that the reaction may have been without real cause? ▲

He became jealous of her.

6 When the Spanish speaker wants to talk about these self-generated reactions he uses a reflexive construction. Compare these two statements and their translations:

Eso me enojó.	That made me mad.
Me enojé de eso.	I got mad at that.

The second Spanish sentence literally says "I angered myself (because) of that." The responsibility for this change is in me.

Joaquín and Miguel heard a news broadcast which predicted rain. Joaquín wanted to go to the beach. Miguel wanted rain for his dried-out hay fields. On hearing the news report, *Joaquín se enojó y Miguel se alegró.* What Joaquín and Miguel wanted personally, not the news report, is responsible for their different reactions. Where Spanish uses a reflexive construction to say this, English uses "to become" or "to get." Do these two sentences say the same thing? (1) *Joaquín se enoja.* (2) *Joaquín se pone enojado.* ▲

7 In both English and Spanish there are many psychological or emotional changes which cannot be described by a verb. We do not say "I furioused at that" or "I jealoused at her." These changes have to be described by a helping verb and an adjective. English uses "to become" or "to get" and Spanish uses _____ in the reflexive. ▲

yes

8 Translate: He becomes furious (*ponerse furioso*). ▲

poner

9 *Ponerse* and "to become" or "to get" may also be used to describe a change in a person's physical state. Translate: He became fat. ▲

Él se pone furioso.

10 Write the missing relator: He became tired _____ working so hard. ▲

Él se puso gordo.

You may have used either "from" or "of."

11 Write the missing relator: He became jealous _____ his wife. ▲

of

12 Write the missing relator: He became angry _____ his wife. ▲

13 The Spanish speaker uses *de* to translate "from," "of," and "at" in the same way that he uses *a* to translate "to," "from," and "for" in the case of the involved entity. Translate: *Él se enojó de eso.* ▲

at, or with

He became angry at that.

14 When verbs like *alegrarse*, *enojarse*, or *sorprenderse* are in the Present, they do not describe a change in process but, rather, a state that has been achieved. To translate these forms you use the equivalent English adjective and "to be." Translate: *Me alegro de que Vd. está aquí.* Notice that English has no equivalent for *de*. ▲

I am happy that you are here.

Self-Correcting Exercises

A   *Refranes:* Say aloud the Spanish equivalent of each proverb.

1	He who sleeps much learns little.	*Quien mucho duerme poco aprende.*
2	Flies do not enter a closed mouth.	*En boca cerrada no entran moscas.*
3	A barking dog does not bite.	*Perro que ladra no muerde.*
4	The lion is not as fierce as they paint him.	*No es tan fiero el león como lo pintan.*
5	He who seeks, finds.	*Quien busca halla.*
6	'Twixt the cup and the lip there's many a slip.	*De la mano a la boca se pierde la sopa.*
7	From the word to the act there is a great gap.	*Del dicho al hecho hay gran trecho.*
8	Practice makes perfect.	*El ejercicio hace maestro.*

B   *Reading Comprehension:* You can read this selection and understand its meaning without stopping to pronounce the long unfamiliar words in it. Do the comprehension exercise at the end.

Centroamérica y su historia (tercera parte)

La entrada de Hernán Cortés en Tenochtitlán y la fundación de la ciudad de Panamá tuvieron lugar en el mismo año de 1519. Casi inmediatamente por el norte y por el sur, por tierra y por agua empezaron los viajes de exploración y conquista al territorio centroamericano.

Casi al mismo tiempo, en 1524, estaban en Centroamérica cuatro expediciones diferentes. Por el norte, Pedro de Alvarado, uno de los capitanes de Cortés, invadió el territorio que ocupan hoy El Salvador y Guatemala. Alvarado le hizo la guerra° a los indios cakchiqueles y quichés, descendientes de los antiguos mayas. De la isla de Santo Domingo, la primera colonia española fundada en América, vino Gil González Ávila. En su expedición vinieron las primeras mujeres españolas a Centroamérica. González Ávila también trajo el primer grupo de negros africanos. Por el mar, desde Veracruz, México, Cristóbal de Olid, otro de los capitanes de Cortés, vino a conquistar el territorio de Honduras. De Panamá, Francisco Hernández de Córdoba llevó otra expedición a Nicaragua y fundó las ciudades de Granada y León.

Muchos de los miembros de estas cuatro expediciones se quedaron en América Central a vivir principalmente de la agricultura. En los años que siguieron, los

war

españoles de México empezaron a interesarse en los territorios del norte, hoy ocupados por los estados de California, Arizona y Nuevo México. Los españoles residentes en Panamá concentraron casi toda su atención en el Perú que prometía entonces extraordinarias riquezas.

Las guerras, la costumbre de secuestrar° a los indios para venderlos como esclavos° y las epidemias de viruela° y otras enfermedades contagiosas redujeron considerablemente la población india de Centroamérica. Los indios que quedaban no querían trabajar en el campo y los españoles tuvieron que importar negros africanos.

Así comenzó la mezcla° de razas que produjo el gran número de mestizos, mulatos y zambos que viven hoy día en América Central. Los mestizos son los descendientes de español e india; mulatos, los de blanco y negra; y zambos, los de negro e india. Los hijos de blancos que han nacido en América se llaman criollos. Los indios que han adoptado el traje y las costumbres de los blancos reciben en muchas partes el nombre de ladinos.

kidnap
slaves/smallpox

mixture

Comprehension exercise: Select the letter corresponding to the answer.

1 ¿En qué año entró Hernán Cortés en Tenochtitlán, la capital de los aztecas?

    a En el año de mil seiscientos veinticuatro.
    b En el año de mil quinientos diecinueve.
    c En el año de mil cuatrocientos noventa y dos.

2 ¿Qué hizo Pedro de Alvarado en 1524?
    a Fue a la isla de Santo Domingo.
    b Invadió el territorio de Panamá.
    c Invadió el territorio de Guatemala y El Salvador.

3 ¿De dónde vinieron las primeras mujeres blancas que trajeron los españoles a la América Central?
    a Vinieron de Ciudad México.
    b Vinieron de Santo Domingo.
    c Vinieron de Panamá.

4 ¿Cómo se llamaba el conquistador español que trajo a los primeros negros africanos a Centroamérica?
    a Se llamaba Pedro de Alvarado.
    b Se llamaba Francisco Hernández de Córdoba.
    c Se llamaba Gil González Ávila.

5 ¿Cómo se llamaba el capitán de Cortés que fue por mar desde Veracruz a Honduras?
    a Cristóbal de Olid.
    b Pedro de Alvarado.
    c Gil González Ávila.

6 Después de las primeras expediciones a Centroamérica, los españoles que residían en Panamá preferían ir a Perú. ¿Por qué?
    a Los indios de Centroamérica eran demasiado crueles.
    b Creían que en Perú no había grandes problemas con los indios.
    c Creían que en Perú iban a encontrar mucho oro y plata.

1	b
2	c
3	b
4	c
5	a
6	c

7 ¿Qué es la viruela?   7 b
  a Un nombre que le dan a los esclavos.
  b Una enfermedad contagiosa.
  c Un lugar en la costa de Nicaragua.

8 Los españoles tuvieron que importar negros africanos a Centroamérica.   8 a
¿Por qué?
  a No tenían indios suficientes para trabajar los campos.
  b A los indios les gustaba mucho trabajar en los campos.
  c En España había millones de negros que querían venir a América.

9 ¿Qué nombre le dieron a los descendientes de un hombre blanco y de   9 a
una mujer de raza negra?
  a Mulatos.
  b Ladinos.
  c Zambos.

10 ¿Cómo le llaman en algunas partes de Centroamérica a los indios que han   10 b
adoptado el traje y las costumbres del hombre blanco?
  a Zambos.
  b Ladinos.
  c Mestizos.

C   E *for* y, u *for* o, *and the Suffix -ly:*

Say each pair of words, joining them with **y** or **e** according to the initial sound
of the second word.

1	venir . . . ir	*(e)*		**7**	Perú . . . Ecuador	*(y)*
2	señor . . . señorita	*(y)*		**8**	África . . . India	*(e)*
3	padre . . . hijo	*(e)*		**9**	lámpara . . . espejo	*(y)*
4	verano . . . invierno	*(e)*		**10**	él . . . ella	*(y)*
5	sillones . . . sofá	*(y)*		**11**	playa . . . iglesia	*(e)*
6	español . . . inglés	*(e)*		**12**	adentro . . . afuera	*(y)*

Say each pair of words, joining them with **o** or **u** according to the initial sound
of the second word.

13	agosto . . . octubre	*(u)*		**19**	Atlántico . . . Pacífico	*(o)*
14	unos . . . otros	*(u)*		**20**	viejo . . . joven	*(o)*
15	mar . . . océano	*(u)*		**21**	rápido . . . despacio	*(o)*
16	gordo . . . flaco	*(o)*		**22**	este . . . oeste	*(u)*
17	verano . . . otoño	*(u)*		**23**	primero . . . último	*(o)*
18	verdad . . . mentira	*(o)*		**24**	Ana . . . Hortensia	*(u)*

Say aloud the adjectives in the first column, and then convert them orally to
adverbs by adding *-mente* and making any other necessary changes.

1	normal	*normalmente*		**5**	oral	*oralmente*
2	noble	*noblemente*		**6**	posible	*posiblemente*
3	cómodo	*cómodamente*		**7**	seco	*secamente*
4	primero	*primeramente*		**8**	frío	*fríamente*

9	total	*totalmente*	**11**	fácil	*fácilmente*
10	inmediato	*inmediatamente*	**12**	perfecto	*perfectamente*

D *Subjunctive versus Indicative:* After reading each complete sentence, decide whether the verb in parentheses should be indicative or subjunctive and write the correct form.

1 El director del laboratorio demanda que los estudiantes (llegar) a tiempo a sus prácticas.

lleguen

2 El periódico de hoy informa que varios grupos estudiantiles (estar) muy disgustados porque la administración no ha permitido que ellos (participar) en los planes.

están
participen

3 El profesor quiere que nosotros (ir) directamente al laboratorio y nos (sentar) para empezar inmediatamente nuestros proyectos.

vayamos
sentemos

4 Hoy yo sé que (ir) a llegar tarde porque me levanté a las ocho en vez de a las siete.

voy

5 Yo no quiero que todo el mundo (notar) que yo (estar) un poco nerviosa.

note, estoy

6 Me despierto, miro el reloj en el escritorio junto a mi cama y veo que ya (ser) muy tarde; es necesario que yo me (vestir) de prisa.

es, vista

7 ¿Tienes un calendario? Yo digo que hoy (ser) martes, pero ella insiste en que hoy (ser) lunes.

es
es

8 Ellos no quieren que la policía (castigar (*to punish*)) a esos estudiantes porque están seguros (*sure*) que ellos no (haber) hecho nada malo.

castigue
han

E *Preterit versus Imperfect:* Back-shift the indicated verbs to the Preterit or the Imperfect according to context. Write and say aloud each form.

En la unión está la fuerza

En los meses que *siguen* **1** a la proclamación de la independencia centroamericana, Agustín de Iturbide *invita* **2** a los centroamericanos a unirse al imperio que él *piensa* **3** formar en México. Cuando El Salvador, la más pequeña de las provincias, *sabe* **4** la noticia, no *quiere* **5** aceptar de ninguna manera. Iturbide entonces *manda* **6** a sus tropas a la frontera para forzarlos si *es* **7** necesario.

La situación *es* (era) tan crítica en ese momento que los salvadoreños *nombran* **8** una comisión para ir a Washington con el plan de pedir la unión a los Estados Unidos de Norte América. Dicha comisión no *tiene* **9** tiempo suficiente para presentar el plan al gobierno norteamericano. Las tropas mexicanas *invaden* (invadieron) el territorio y *capturan* **10** la ciudad de San Salvador, la capital salvadoreña.

Entre los años de 1821 y 1838 aproximadamente las provincias centroamericanas se *unen* **11** para formar una sola nación bajo el nombre de Provincias Unidas del Centro de América. Este plan, desgraciadamente, no *tiene* **12** éxito. Desde esa fecha las repúblicas de América Central han intentado la unión varias veces, pero siempre sin éxito. La idea, sin embargo, no ha muerto por completo. En periódicos centroamericanos aparece con frecuencia la frase: "América Central es un sólo país." Los habitantes de Centroamérica se dan cuenta (*realize*) que según dice el refrán: "En la unión está la fuerza."

1	siguieron
2	invitó
3	pensaba
4	supo
5	quiso
6	mandó
7	era
8	nombraron
9	tuvo
10	capturaron
11	unieron
12	tuvo

New Vocabulary

esclavo	slave	**ponerse celoso**	to become (get) jealous
ratón	mouse	**tener miedo**	to be afraid
proteger	to protect	**tener prisa**	to be in a hurry
temer	to fear	**tener suerte**	to be lucky
enojarse	to become (get) angry	**tener mala pata**	to be unlucky
alegrarse	to become (get) happy	**tener la culpa**	to be to blame
sorprenderse	to become surprised	**tener éxito**	to be successful
ponerse serio	to become (get) serious	**tener catarro**	to have a cold
ponerse furioso	to become (get) furious	**tener ganas de**	to be eager, feel like (doing something)

Assignment 77

The Subjunctive in Stimulus-Response Situations

You have studied the use of the subjunctive in two basic patterns:

(1)   The main verb reports (and sometimes describes the way in which someone gives) a command. Someone shouts, "Run," and this is reported in indirect discourse as *Grita que corra*, or "He shouts for him to run."

(2)   The main verb describes the manner in which its subject attempts to influence the action of the subject of the subjoined verb. *Quiero que corras*. "I want you to run."

The purpose of the first part of this assignment is to introduce you to a third, but related use of the subjunctive: the subjoined verb is in the subjunctive when it is the stimulus (cause) that brings about the psychological or emotional response stated in the man verb.

1   There are three ways to categorize influencing: permit, prevent, cause. Which is expressed in each of the following?
(a)   Pido que no lleguen hasta más tarde.
(b)   Dejan que nosotros lo hagamos también.
(c)   El policía impide que sigan adelante.   ▲

(a) cause, (b) permit, (c) prevent

2   Influence can be brought to bear on someone in several ways:
(1)   by physical force: *Impide que pase*.
(2)   by using words which describe a way of getting someone to do something: *Manda que se vayan*.
(3)   by stating one's desire, hope, or wish: *Quiero que me acompañes*. To which category does the following belong? *Es necesario que vayas a la izquierda*.   ▲

(2) (This is a less direct way of using words to influence behavior.)

3 To which category does this belong? *Esperamos que no llueva mañana.* ▲

(3) (This states our hope, "We hope that it doesn't rain tomorrow.")

4 In all cases of influencing it can be said that there is a type of cause-and-effect relationship between the influencer and the influenced. The cause is whatever influence is brought to bear, and the effect is the response that is made to that influence: *Es muy importante* (cause) *que este niño coma mejor* (effect, hopefully). A cause-and-effect relationship is also possible in situations where an emotional response results. Which is the cause and which is the effect in the following? *Todos estamos tristes porque el profesor está enfermo hoy.* ▲

cause = *profesor está enfermo;* effect = *estamos tristes*

5 Because this type of situation deals with psychological or emotional responses, it seems simpler to use the psychologist's terms, stimulus and response, rather than cause and effect. In the above sentence the stimulus (cause) is the instructor being ill and the response (effect) is our being sad. Delete the connecting word (*porque*) and see if you can make two simple sentences out of it. ▲

Todos estamos tristes. El profesor está enfermo hoy.

6 This shows that there are two independent clauses in the original sentence. There is no dependent or subjoined clause. One requirement for the subjunctive is that it be in a subjoined clause. If we reword the above sentence so that there is a subjoined clause, the verb in that clause must be in the subjunctive. Let's try to do this. Change *porque* to *de que.* Now write out the new sentence. ▲

Estamos tristes de que el profesor esté enfermo hoy. (Did you remember the subjunctive?)

7 Let's construct another such statement. The stimulus is the fact that today is Saturday, and the response is that we are glad. Put all this information into one sentence in English containing a subjoined clause. ▲

We are glad that today is Saturday.

8 Now translate it. You will also need a *de* before the *que* in this sentence. ▲

Estamos alegres de que hoy sea sábado.

9 The relator *de* normally is used with the following kinds of verbs that express a psychological or emotional response: reflexive verbs (*enojarse, ponerse triste, etc.*), verbs made up of *estar* + an adjective (*estar alegre, etc.*) or verbs made up of *tener* + a noun (*tener miedo, etc.*). Which of the following may use *de* in the blank?

(a) Le sorprende _____ que tengan tantos animales allí.

(b) Se pone alegre _____ que su hermana venga.

(c) Sienten _____ que no haya suficiente tiempo para hacer eso.

(d) Estamos contentas _____ que ellos estén equivocados. ▲

(b) and (d) (Did you understand that (a) is not reflexive?)

10 Fill in the blanks in the following sentences with ∅ or *de* and the appropriate verb form.

Nos sorprende _____ que ellas ya lo _____ (saber).

Están furiosas _____ que ellos todavía no _____ (haber) llegado.

Me enojo _____ que tú no _____ (querer) esconderlo aquí. ▲

∅, *sepan; de, hayan; de, quieras* (Native speakers sometimes leave out *de.*)

11 You are learning always to use the subjunctive in the subjoined clause in stimulus-response situations. Some native speakers occasionally will prefer the indicative where you put the subjunctive. Some feel that there is a slight difference in the meaning of what is said according to the mode of the subjoined verb. This is discussed in Level Two. For now, always use the subjunctive. Compare the following two sentences:

(a) El profesor pide que sus alumnos salgan bien en el examen.

(b) El profesor se alegra de que sus alumnos salgan bien en el examen.

In sentence (a) the cause is in the main clause. In sentence (b) is the cause (stimulus) in the main or subjoined clause? ▲

> subjoined (The cause or stimulus can be in either clause depending upon how the speaker wishes to state the sentence. The important thing to remember is that the subjunctive is to be used in the subjoined clause regardless of whether it states the cause, effect, stimulus, or response.)

12 The verb *sentir* has two meanings, "to regret" and "to feel." Which meaning would require the subjunctive in a subjoined clause? ▲

> to regret (This is a psychological response. "To feel" means "to be aware of" or "to sense.")

13 Fill in the correct verb form:

Busco el perro. Siento que _____ (estar) en la cocina.

Ya enterramos (*buried*) el perro. Siento que se _____ (haber) muerto. ▲

> está (I sense that he is in the kitchen); *haya* (I regret that he has died.)

14 The verb *temer* (to fear) has two common meanings in both English and Spanish. One is to be afraid of something (Many people fear death) or to be afraid that something may happen (He fears that the dog may bite him). The other meaning is "to conclude regretfully" or "to suspect" (I fear he is lost).

You have red blotches all over your skin and a high temperature. You go to your doctor. He examines you and says, "I'm sorry, *but I fear you have measles.*" Translate the indicated clause. The word for "measles" is *sarampión.* ▲

> *Lo siento,* **pero temo que Vd. tiene sarampión.** ("To conclude," however regretfully, is a logical decision, not an emotional response, so you use the indicative in the subjoined clause.)

15 Translate: "Margarita fears that the dog may bite her." The verb for "to bite" is the stem-changing *morder.* ▲

> *Margarita teme que el perro la muerda.* (She reacts psychologically, and you use the subjunctive to describe her fear.)

16 In this and most of the remaining frames you will see an infinitive in parentheses in the subjoined clause. Look at the cues carefully and then write the proper mode of the verb.

Estás muy nerviosa, hija. ¿Temes que (volver) la policía? ▲

17 Sé que Vd. no (recordar) qué día es hoy. ▲

> *vuelva*

> recuerda (*Saber* reports knowledge and does not cue the subjunctive.)

18 Ella se enoja de que tú no le (hablar). ▲

19 Why does *se enoja* cue the use of the subjunctive? ▲

> *hables*
> emotional response

20 No me digas más, hijo, ya sé bastante, y temo que ya me (haber) dicho demasiado. ▲

21 Which meaning of *temo* cued the indicative? ▲

> *has*
> I conclude regretfully, or I suspect

22 ¡Ay, hijo! Siento mucho que (estar) enfermo.　▲
23 The meaning of *siento* is _____.　▲　　　　　　　　　　　　*estés*

        I regret (An emotional reaction and, so, the subjunctive.)

24 Me sorprendo mucho de que tú (haber) dicho eso.　▲
25 He oído que tú (ir) a Honduras.　▲　　　　　　　　　　　　*hayas*

     vas (*Oír* reports how I got the information and, so, the indicative.)

26 Micaela se pone triste de que su padre se (haber) ido.　▲
27 Ella no sabe que él (volver) muy pronto.　▲　　　　　　　　*haya*

                 vuelve

ELLA SIENTE QUE SE VA

A/B

ELLA SIENTE QUE SE VAYA

C

ELLA SIENTE QUE SE HAYA IDO

The Equivalents of "Let's"

1　The most common meaning of "Let us go" is "Permit us to go." In contrast, the only common meaning of "Let's go" is that of a proposal or suggestion that we go. There are three Spanish patterns which are best translated into English by "Let's." The one most widely used is composed of *Vamos a* plus the infinitive which stands for the proposed action. Translate: Let's eat.　▲

Vamos a comer.

2 Only the situation and intonation can tell you when *vamos a* is the equivalent of "Let's" or "We are going." *Vamos a leer* can mean either "We are going to read" or "Let's read."

There is a form of the verb, which is exactly like the subjunctive, which has the fancy name of **hortatory imperative**: the imperative which one member of the *nosotros* group uses to exhort (urge) the other members to do something. Translate "Let's eat" (*comer*) and use this form. It matches *nosotros*. ▲

¡Comamos! (This usage is common, but not as common as *Vamos a comer.*)

3 When one person asks another what they should do, the question may have the subjunctive in the subjoined verb. For example:

¿Qué quieres que hagamos?

¿Qué propones (propose) *que hagamos?*

¿Qué aconsejas (advise) *que hagamos?*

The person who answers questions like these frequently does not repeat the main verb. He just uses *que* and replaces the subjoined verb with the same mode of the verb used in the question. For example:

Eduardo: *¿Qué quieres que hagamos?*

Micaela: *Que vayamos al cine.*

Micaela's reply can be translated as "That we go to the movies." This is rather stiff and stilted, and the more common equivalent is "Let's go to the movies." Translate the second sentence of the following dialog. The verb is *cenar*.

Jorge: What do you propose that we do tonight?

Manuela: Let's have dinner in a café. ▲

Que cenemos en un café.

Indirect Commands

An indirect command is spoken to an intermediary who then conveys the message to another person. Mrs. Pereda comes into her husband's study to inform him that the mechanic has come with his car. She asks *¿Qué quieres que haga?* Mr. Pereda does not use a complete sentence in his reply. Instead he begins with the *que* of the subjoined clause and changes the verb so it says what he wants done: *Que lo ponga en el garaje.* (Have him put it in the garage.) The intermediary, Mrs. Pereda, now has two choices when she goes out to speak to the mechanic. She may convert the indirect command into a direct command (*Póngalo, por favor, en el garaje.*) or she may restore the main verb of her original question and say, *Quiere que lo ponga en el garaje.*

1 In this and the next three frames translate the sentence.

Have Enrique open the door. ▲

Que abra la puerta Enrique. (The name of the doer usually follows the verb.)

2 Have Pablo come here. ▲

Que venga aquí Pablo.

3 Have Manuelita iron the clothes. ▲

Que planche la ropa Manuelita.

4 Have her wait (*esperar*). ▲

Que espere ella.

Have Rosa iron it.

Diminutives

In both English and Spanish a diminutive is a word having a special suffix which may carry three kinds of information:

1 reduction of size: kitchenette (*cocinita*), dinette (*comedorcito*)

2 young age: kiddy (*niñito*), sonny (*hijito*), birdie (*pajarito*)

3 intimate relationship or an attitude of friendliness and affection: dearie (*queridito*), Johnny (*Juanito*), horsie (*caballito*)

In Spanish, however, there are more diminutive suffixes (about 19) which are regularly added not only to nouns but also to adjectives and to some adverbs. The most commonly used diminutive suffixes are: *ito, cito* (or *ecito*) and *ico*. All three have a matching form ending in *a*, and *ito* is the most widely used of all.

You will be expected to recognize all three suffixes in words, but will be asked to generate only the *ito* diminutives which are formed according to these basic rules:

1 If the noun ends in a vowel (*Ana, Pedro, Pepe, casa, carro*), the final vowel is dropped and *ito* is added if the noun stands for a male or combines with *el* (*Pedrito, Pepito, carrito*); *ita* is added if the noun stands for a female or combines with *la* (*Anita, casita*).

2 If the noun ends in a consonant, *ito* or *ita* is just added to it.

1 Write and say aloud the diminutives of: *espejo, estrella, Pancho, Teresa, Lupe, costumbre, garaje.* ▲

> *espejito, estrellita, Panchito, Teresita, Lupita, costumbrita, garajito*

2 Translate the following diminutives that use varied suffixes: *viejita, pianito, florecita, jovencito, gatico, perrito, dientecito.* ▲

> little old lady, small piano, little flower, youngster, kitty, small dog, little tooth

3 Write and say aloud the diminutives of: *animal, Luis, azul, negra, momento, papel, ahora, adiós, Raquel, fácil, inglés.* ▲

> *animalito, Luisito, azulito, negrita, momentito, papelito, ahorita, adiosito,*

> *Raquelita, facilito, inglesito* (Note that the accent mark is not needed when the additional syllables change the stress pattern of the words.)

4   The same rules of spelling that govern the Spanish language as a whole will have to be applied as you write and say aloud the diminutives of these words: *barco, muñeca, lago, amiga, nariz, cabeza, lápiz.* ▲

> *barquito, muñequita, laguito, amiguita, naricita, cabecita, lapicito*

In some contexts the diminutive may carry pejorative overtones of contempt, belittlement, or poor quality: *doctorcito* (insignificant, two-bit doctor), *periodiquito* (second rate newspaper), *etc.*

The rules that determine which diminutive suffix may be added to a given word are complicated and at times quite arbitrary. For this reason, many diminutives will have to be learned as new vocabulary words.

A/B

PACO Y SU NIETO, PAQUITO, TRABAJAN EN EL OLIVAR

PAQUITO, ¿QUÉ HACES TÚ AHÍ?

Summary

Subjunctive

(1)   When the main verb describes a psychological or emotional response to a stimulus which is described by the subjoined verb, use the subjunctive mode for the subjoined verb. *Me alegro de que tú **sepas** tocar la guitarra.*

(2)   The verbs in these situations that take the relator *de* include those that use *estar*, *tener*, or a reflexive construction. Natives sometimes omit the *de*.

"Let's"

There are three ways to translate "let's" as in "Let's eat."

1   *Vamos a* + infinitive (the most common way): *Vamos a comer.*

2   The *nosotros* form of the present subjunctive: *Comamos.*

3   Same as 2, but preceded by *que: Que comamos.*

Self-Correcting Exercises

A *Commands with* tú: Write the *tú* command for the infinitives in parentheses.

1 Pancho, (ser) buen hermano y (venir) conmigo al cine esta noche.   sé, ven
2 Bien, (preguntarle) a mamá si te permite ir conmigo.   pregúntale
3 No quiero. (Ir) tú a preguntárselo porque ella siempre se enoja mucho
conmigo.   Ve
4 Bueno, no (salir) del cuarto hasta que yo te diga.   salgas
5 Mamá te da permiso. (Vestirte) pronto y (traerme) el suéter.   Vístete, tráeme
6 Hombre, no (ponerte) ese saco, (ponerte) el otro.   te pongas, ponte
7 No (decirme) siempre qué ropa debo usar.   me digas
8 Perdón. No quería ofenderte. Pero (darte) prisa, que ya es tarde.   date
9 (Decirme) el nombre de la película que vamos a ver.   Dime
10 Solamente sé que tú no la has visto. (Pedirle) el carro y vamos. No quiero
llegar tarde.   Pídele

B *Subjunctive versus Indicative:* After reading each sentence, decide whether the form of the verb in parentheses should be indicative or subjunctive, then write it.

1 No queremos que ellos se (enojar).   enojen
2 Mamá pide que yo (mover) los muebles en este cuarto.   mueva
3 ¿Recuerdas que yo siempre (tener) miedo cuando hay una tormenta?   tengo
4 Deseamos que los niños se (bañar) antes de ir.   bañen
5 Nos informan que tú siempre (tener) mala pata cuando esto ocurre.   tienes
6 No permitimos que ustedes se (poner) furiosos.   pongan
7 Observo que Paquito (tener) catarro.   tiene
8 Es importante que ellos (mandar) que los otros no (asistir) a esa clase hoy.   manden, asistan
9 Espero que al llegar, nosotros (ver) que Elena ya (saber) manejar.   veamos, sabe
10 Es necesario que nosotras (dormir) un poco más.   durmamos
11 Me mandan que yo lo (masticar) bien.   mastique

C E *and* u *for* y *and* o, *the Suffix* -mente, *and* al *plus infinitive:* Write the Spanish translation of the words and phrases in English; then say the entire Spanish sentence.

1 (*Upon leaving*) de la casa, la muchacha caminó (*happily*) a su trabajo.   1 Al salir (irse),
2 Pancho (*and*) Enrique van al cine (*or*) a la playa.   felizmente
3 Observamos que (*upon buying*) la camisa, María (*and*) Inés perdieron   (alegremente)
la bolsa.   2   y, o
4 —En verano (*or*) otoño el tiempo es igual,—dijo el viejo (*sadly*).   3   al comprar, e
5 (*Upon reading*) la historia otra vez, no supe si fue la primera (*or*) la última   4   u, tristemente
oportunidad que perdieron.   5   Al leer, o
6 ¿Es hoy (*possibly*) el día en que Aníbal (*and*) Hilario van a salir bien (*or*)   6   posiblemente,
mal en sus experimentos?   e, o
7 (*Upon asking me*) si quería plata (*or*) oro, trató de indicar que la diferencia   7 Al preguntarme,
no importaba.   u

D *Refranes:* Say the Spanish translation of each proverb aloud.

1 It is better to be alone than in poor company.

Más vale estar solo que mal acompañado.

2 Haste makes waste.

Vísteme despacio que estoy de prisa.

3 Don't leave for tomorrow what you can do today.

No dejes para mañana lo que puedas hacer hoy.

4 Do good no matter for whom.

Haz bien y no mires a quién.

5 Practice makes perfect.

El ejercicio hace maestro.

6 A chip off the old block.

De tal palo, tal astilla.

7 Like father, like son.

De tal padre, tal hijo.

New Vocabulary

esposo, marido	husband	**bisabuela**	great-grandmother
esposa, mujer	wife	**palo**	stick
suegro	father-in-law	**astilla**	splinter
suegra	mother-in-law	**pesadilla**	nightmare
cuñado	brother-in-law	**sueño**	dream
cuñada	sister-in-law	**soñar (ue)**	to dream
nieto	grandson	**calentar (ie)**	to heat, warm up
nieta	granddaughter	**irse**	to go away, leave
bisabuelo	great-grandfather	**tal**	such (a)

"De tal palo, tal astilla."   A chip off the old block.

Assignment 78

The Subjunctive in Situations of Uncertainty and Disbelief

The subjunctive is used in the subjoined clause: (1) when reporting a command, (2) when attempting to influence someone's behavior, and (3) when describing the stimulus that causes a psychological or emotional response.

The purpose of the following is to introduce you to a fourth use of the subjunctive in a subjoined clause. It is used when, in the main clause, uncertainty or disbelief is expressed toward the content of the subjoined clause.

1 In relation to anything that we do not know there can exist two different mental attitudes. We can express an attitude of certainty or belief if the evidence so warrants, or we can express an attitude of uncertainty or disbelief. For want of better labels we will call the attitude of certainty or belief "positive" and the attitude of uncertainty or disbelief "negative." Common verbs and expressions with their antonymous counterparts may be categorized under these two labels in the following manner:

Positive	Negative
to believe (*creer*)	not to believe (*no creer*)
not to doubt (*no dudar*)	to doubt (*dudar*)
to be certain (*estar cierto*)	not to be certain (*no estar cierto*)
to be sure (*estar seguro*)	not to be sure (*no estar seguro*)

Change the following two English sentences from the positive category to the negative:

  It is certain that milk is good for adults.
  They do not doubt that children are foolish. ▲

> It is not certain that milk is good for adults. They doubt that children are
2   Now look at the verbs in the subjoined clauses. Are they the same or differ-   foolish.
ent in both the positive and negative instances? ▲
3   In which mode are they, indicative or subjunctive? ▲   same
> indicative (All forms would be *be* if they were subjunctive.)
4   Spanish differs from English in that the subjunctive is used regularly in the subjoined clause that follows expressions of uncertainty or disbelief (the negative category). Spanish and English are alike in that the indicative is used following expressions of certainty or belief (the positive category). With this information, see if you can change these sentences in Spanish from the positive to the negative category:

  Es cierto que la leche es buena para los adultos.
  Ellos no dudan que los niños son tontos. ▲

> *No es cierto que la leche sea buena para los adultos. Ellos dudan que los niños sean tontos.* (Both now require the subjunctive.)

5   Write the appropriate form of the indicated verbs in this and the following three frames:

  Todos creen que *haber* treinta y un días en enero.
  No estoy segura de que él me *querer*. ▲

> *hay* (positive category); *quiera* (negative category)

6   No es cierto que el león *ser* más feroz que el tigre.
Dudamos que los alumnos *comprender* todo esto. ▲

> *sea, comprendan* (both from the negative category)

7   No hay duda de que *pasar* con rapidez el año académico.
Estamos seguros de que ella *estar* equivocada. ▲

> *pasa, está* (both from the positive category)

8   Can you work with the following expressions not listed in categories in frame 1 above?

  No es probable que Gregorio *tener* más años que su tía.
  Es verdad que todo el mundo *soñar* (*ue*) cada noche. ▲

> *tenga* (negative category), *sueña* (positive category) (If your answers were

correct for these two, you have demonstrated a grasp of the principle rather than merely the ability to refer to a table to find answers.)

9 Although we ask you at present to follow the rule given in frame 4, you will find many instances when a native speaker seems to violate it. Remember that rules are provided principally as a means for you to gradually acquire the same "feel" for the language that the native has. The "feel" that he is working with has to do with his attitude concerning certainty or belief, not the need to follow arbitrary rules. So, if he does tend to believe something to be a fact, yet does not want to express as much surety as would result from the use of the indicative in the subjoined clause, he may shift to the subjunctive: *Creo* (positive category) *que ellos tengan razón*. Which translation of this is probably closer to what he is saying?

I believe that they may be right.

I believe that they are right. ▲

I believe that they may be right. (The Spanish speaker can produce these nuances by shifting modes. English must resort to helping words.)

10 When people are conversing they might have different attitudes of certainty or belief toward something. Each person will normally express his attitude in normal statements, but the choice of mode within a question can be based on various subtleties underlying the intent of the question. Opinions can be influenced by the choice of mode in a question. For example, suppose that a school superintendent exercises a high degree of influence over members of the school board. He feels that teachers should have an increase in salary, but he has reason to believe that the school board members feel that teachers already are overpaid. In bringing up the subject for discussion with one school board member, it is likely that his chances of getting an affirmative response are greater if he expresses his own opinion within the question that he asks. Which question would you logically expect him to ask? (Note: *merecer* = to deserve.)

¿No cree usted que los profesores merezcan un aumento de salario?

¿No cree usted que los profesores merecen un aumento de salario? ▲

¿No cree usted que los profesores **merecen** un aumento de salario? (He is expressing his belief by using the indicative (*merecen*). He would be expressing some doubt about the matter if he had chosen the subjunctive.)

11 You can probably see several uses that choice of mode could have in interrogative statements depending upon social relationships, desire to influence, desire to please, desire to be totally honest, etc. So the choice of mode for the subjoined clause of questions dealing with certainty, uncertainty, belief, or disbelief is left up to you as the speaker. However, in all declarative statements (non-questions), use the subjunctive in subjoined clauses following expressions of uncertainty or disbelief. Choose the appropriate form for the following indicated verbs:

Creo que mi amigo Raúl *tener* catarro.

¿Crees tú que él *ir* a estar en clase mañana?

Yo dudo que él *salir* de casa en ocho días. ▲

tiene (positive category), *va* or *vaya* (speaker's option), *salga* (negative category)

A/B

CREE QUE VUELA — 149

DUDA QUE VUELE — 150

C/D

ESPERA QUE VUELE — 151

ES IMPOSIBLE QUE VUELE — 152

E/F

HAY UN ELEFANTE EN EL JARDÍN — 155

NO SABE QUE HAY UN ELEFANTE ALLÍ — 156

G/H

DICE QUE HAY UN ELEFANTE EN EL JARDÍN — 157

PAPÁ NO CREE QUE HAYA UNO ALLÍ — 158

470

I/J

Summary

In declarative sentences the indicative is used in subjoined clauses following expressions of certainty or belief; the subjunctive is used following expressions of uncertainty or disbelief. However, in questions the choice of mode is optional, depending upon the intent of the speaker.

Review of the Subjunctive

The following is a diagnostic test to aid you in understanding how well you handle the subjunctive. Write the appropriate form of each indicated verb. Put a check by each problem that you miss.

1 Es importante que él lo *saber*. ▲

2 Ellos creen que usted no *fumar*. ▲

sepa

3 Demandan que nosotros *tener* cuidado de aquí en adelante. ▲

fuma

4 Es muy dudoso que ella ya *haber* llegado. ▲

tengamos

5 Antes de salir mi compañero de cuarto siempre me dice que yo *arreglar* mis cosas. ▲

haya

6 El muchacho grita que *llover* ahora mismo. ▲

arregle

7 He oído que el Sr. Méndez me *buscar*. ▲

llueve

8 Tienen miedo de que él no *llegar* a tiempo. ▲

busca

9 Ella está cierta de que sus hijos *poder* hacerlo. ▲

llegue

10 Hemos observado que nuestro perro *ladrar* bastante. ▲

pueden

11 No creen que el elefante *medir* veinte pies. ▲

ladra

12 Nos cuentan que el niño *acostarse* muy tarde cada noche. ▲

mida

13 A Pancho le molesta que Elena *abrazar* a sus amigos. ▲

se acuesta

14 Mamá grita que tú y yo le *traer* bebidas de la tienda, si no es inconveniente, porque ella no puede salir de la casa hoy. ▲

abrace

Here are the rules that govern the use of the subjunctive or the indicative in the above subjoined clauses. Opposite each rule are the numbers of the test items to which that rule applies. From the checks that you made for incorrect responses you can see where you need more practice. Of course, an error may be a problem of incorrect morphology or spelling.

traigamos

(1)   The subjunctive is used to report commands. (5, 14)

(2)   The indicative is used to report indicative statements. (7, 12)

(3)   The subjunctive is used in cases of attempted influence. (1, 3)

(4)   The indicative is used when one expresses awareness of an event and there is no attempt to influence. (7, 10)

(5)   The subjunctive is used in stimulus-response statements. (8, 13)

(6)   The subjunctive is used when uncertainty or disbelief is expressed. (4, 11)

(7)   The indicative is used when certainty or belief is expressed. (2, 9)

Getting Ready for a Quiz on Commands with tú

1   The imperative mode forms that go with *usted* or *ustedes* came from the subjunctive and have the same form in either affirmative or negative commands. Rewrite *Dígamelo Vd.* and make it negative.   ▲

No me lo diga Vd.

2   The imperative mode forms that go with *tú* have two forms. The negative forms are like the subjunctive. To make *No me lo diga* match *tú* you simply add _____ to *diga*.   ▲

3   Translate, using the *tú* form: "Don't talk to me!"   ▲

s (No me lo digas.)

4   Translate, using *la*: "Don't hide it!" (The infinitive is *esconder*.)   ▲

¡No me hables!

5   With the exception of eight common irregular verbs, the affirmative command forms for *tú* are exactly the same as the _____ person singular forms of the present indicative.   ▲

¡No la escondas!

6   Write the affirmative *tú* command forms of *hablar*, *escribir*, and *vender*.   ▲

third

habla, escribe, vende

7   Translate: "Kiss me." The infinitive is *besar*. Remember the accent mark.   ▲

8   Translate: Write it. (*lo*)   ▲

Bésame.

9   If there is an irregularity in the third person form of the present indicative this same irregularity appears in the affirmative command with *tú*. Translate: "Come back soon." (*volver*)   ▲

Escríbelo.

10   Translate: "Think it (over) well." (*lo*)   ▲

Vuelve pronto.

11   There are four irregular verbs which use the infinitive stem for the affirmative imperative. Change these negative sentences to the affirmative: *No tengas cuidado. No vengas ahora. No la pongas allí. No salgas ahora.*   ▲

Piénsalo bien.

Ten cuidado. Ven ahora. Ponla allí. Sal ahora.

12   The affirmative command form of *ser* looks and sounds exactly like the *yo* form of the present indicative of *saber*. It is _____.   ▲

13   Change the negative to the affirmative. There is a radical change in the verb form. *No lo hagas. No me lo digas. No vayas.*   ▲

sé

Hazlo. Dímelo. Ve.

Self-Correcting Exercises

A   *Subjunctive versus Indicative:* Write the appropriate subjunctive or indicative form of the infinitive in parentheses.

1   Es necesario que ellos (llegar) aquí antes de las seis.

1   lleguen

2 Yo sé que Tomás y Elías también (ser) miembros de nuestro club.

3 Elena teme que su hija no (salir) bien en su examen de geografía.

4 ¿Por qué desean ustedes que yo me (alegrar) de que ellos (venir) a visitarnos?

5 Hemos observado que papá siempre se (enojar) de que sus nietos (decir) palabras feas.

6 He oído decir que Horacio se (poner) celoso de que tú y yo (tener) tanta suerte con las muchachas.

7 Nos escriben que Pancho (ir) a estar aquí dentro de dos días.

8 ¿Es verdad que tú (estar) sorprendida de que Alicia (haber) salido tan mal en el examen?

9 Veo que ustedes (comprender) que yo no (ser) tan malo como me pintan.

10 Mis padres me piden que Pascual, Petra y yo (dejar) de asistir a las reuniones del club.

2	son
3	salga
4	alegre, vengan
5	enoja, digan
6	pone, tengamos
7	va
8	estás, haya
9	comprenden, soy
10	dejemos

B *Diminutives:* Say aloud the diminutive form of each noun.

1	abuelo	*abuelito*	**7**	cuñado	*cuñadito*
2	abuela	*abuelita*	**8**	cuñada	*cuñadita*
3	Adela	*Adelita*	**9**	hermano	*hermanito*
4	catarro	*catarrito*	**10**	hermana	*hermanita*
5	Pepe	*Pepito*	**11**	esposa	*esposita*
6	Andrés	*Andresito*	**12**	esposo	*esposito*

C *Reading Comprehension:* Meaning from Context

In the following paragraphs you will find several words that are completely new. Since not all of them are cognates, the only clue to their meaning will be in the context or situation in which they are used. Cover the answers on the right and write the English of the words listed after each paragraph.

La otra noche en el baile, cuando Manuel vio que su amiga Elena bailaba con Antonio, se puso muy celoso y no le gustó. Manuel y Elena eran más que amigos. Eran novios. Ellos pensaban casarse después de la graduación. Aquel mismo día, Manuel había pasado casi toda la tarde en las tiendas. Sabía el tamaño del cuarto dedo de la mano izquierda de su novia y buscaba un anillo de oro para ella.

Escriban en inglés el significado de las palabras siguientes:

1 novios   sweethearts

2 tamaño   size

3 anillo   ring

Déjame contarte lo que me pasó en una tienda la otra noche. Iba a ser el cumpleaños de mi hermano Edmundo y yo lo invité a ir a la Casa de Música a escoger el regalo que yo quería comprarle. A mi hermano le gusta mucho la música y tiene una colección fantástica de discos. Después de oír varios discos,

Edmundo escogió uno que le gustaba mucho y me dio las gracias. Cuando fui a pagar no encontraba mi dinero. Registré todos mis bolsillos, pero no tenía ni un centavo. Edmundo tuvo que prestarme diez dólares para pagar por su propio regalo.

4	discos	records
5	Registré	I searched
6	prestarme	lend me

El baño de nuestra casa nueva es muy moderno. Cuando queremos agua fría, abrimos una llave que tiene una *F*; la otra llave está marcada con la letra *C* y es para el agua caliente. Tenemos un lavabo de porcelana blanca. Cuando tenemos las manos muy sucias, llenamos el lavabo de agua y usamos jabón para limpiarlas bien. Hay jabón de diferentes colores con un perfume muy agradable.

7	llave	faucet, tap
8	lavabo	sink
9	jabón	soap

D Vamos a *for "Let's"*: Say aloud the Spanish equivalent of each sentence.

1	Let's work in the kitchen.	*Vamos a trabajar en la cocina.*
2	Let's look for gold and silver.	*Vamos a buscar oro y plata.*
3	Let's organize a party.	*Vamos a organizar una fiesta.*
4	Let's dance in the classroom.	*Vamos a bailar en el aula (la clase).*
5	Let's have a good time all day.	*Vamos a divertirnos todo el día.*
6	Let's bark like a dog.	*Vamos a ladrar como un perro.*

E *Preterit versus Imperfect:* Write the appropriate preterit or imperfect form of each indicated infinitive.

La motocicleta de Daniel

(Arriving home on a visit to his family, David meets his younger brother Daniel and they are talking in the driveway of their home.)

David: Hola, Daniel. ¿Y esa motocicleta? Yo no *saber* **1** que tú *tener* **2** una moto. ¿Es nueva?

Daniel: No, no es nueva. Se la *comprar* **3** a mi amigo Frank la semana pasada. Él *necesitar* **4** una más grande para repartir (*deliver*) los periódicos y me la *vender* **5** por ochenta dólares.

David: Me sorprende que mamá te permita . . .

Daniel: Sí, cómo no. Ya tengo licencia para manejar. Hoy *ir* **6** a la escuela en la moto por primera vez. Pero probablemente sea la primera y última vez.

David: ¿Por qué dices eso, hombre? Veo que estás un poco preocupado. ¿Qué te *pasar* **7**?

Daniel: Estoy más que preocupado. ¡Estoy disgustado y furioso!

1	*sabía*
2	*tenías*
3	*compré*
4	*necesitaba*
5	*vendió*
6	*fui*
7	*pasó*

David:	Cuéntame que te pasa. *¿Recibir* **8** alguna mala noticia, o es que *tener* **9** algún problema serio por el camino?	8 *Recibiste* 9 *tuviste*
Daniel:	Esta mañana yo *ir* **10** muy contento en mi motocicleta por la avenida Central, sin molestar a nadie, cuando un policía me *detener* **11** al llegar a la calle Veinte.	10 *iba* 11 *detuvo* 12 *hice*
David:	¿Por qué? Bueno, es que tú no tienes mucha experiencia y es probable que . . .	13 *preguntó* 14 *tenía*
Daniel:	Yo estoy seguro que no *hacer* **12** nada malo. El policía me *preguntar* **13** que cuántos años yo *tener* **14** y que a dónde yo *ir* **15** con tanta prisa.	15 *iba* 16 *dijiste*
David:	Y tú, ¿qué le *decir* **16**?	17 *puse*
Daniel:	Yo me *poner* **17** un poco nervioso y le *decir* **18** que no había hecho nada malo. Entonces él me *pedir* **19** la licencia de manejar y me *decir* **20** que yo *estar* **21** muy joven para andar en motocicleta y que *deber* **22** tener mucho cuidado.	18 *dije* 19 *pidió* 20 *dijo* 21 *estaba* 22 *debía*
David:	Pues, no debes enojarte por eso, hombre. Creo que el policía lo *hacer* **23** para protegerte. Hoy día anda mucha gente irresponsable por las calles y ocurren muchos accidentes.	23 *hizo* 24 *ocurrió*
Daniel:	Es cierto. Pero yo tengo 15 años y sé manejar muy bien. Además no soy ningún irresponsable.	
David:	No le hace, Daniel. Es muy importante que manejes con cuidado.	
Daniel:	Oye, hazme un favor. No le digas nada a mamá. Ya sabes como es ella.	
David:	Está bien, hombre. Vamos para adentro y trata de olvidar lo que *ocurrir* **24**.	

New Vocabulary

preocuparse	to worry	**sexto, -a**	sixth	**por fin**	finally, at last
mejorarse	to get better, improve	**séptimo, -a**	seventh		
		octavo, -a	eighth	**ya no**	no longer
echar de menos	to miss	**por supuesto**	of course		
estar seguro, -a de	to be sure of	**de repente**	suddenly	**Nos vemos.**	See you later.
quinto, -a	fifth	**¡Claro!**	Of course!		

Assignment 79

Possession with de

1 In English there are five different ways of talking about the relationship called possession: (1) Robert's keys, (2) his keys, (3) the car keys, (4) the keys to the car, (5) the keys of the car. Spanish has only two ways of expressing possession. Like English it may use a possessive pronoun form as an adjective. So "his keys" becomes *sus llaves*. In contrast with English, when the possessor and the object possessed are both labeled by nouns, the relationship of possession can only be expressed by the relator *de*. So "Robert's keys" must be translated as *las llaves de Roberto*. And there is only one translation for "the car keys," "the keys to the car," and "the keys of the car." This translation has the same pattern as *las llaves de Roberto*. You simply replace *Roberto* with

————. ▲

el carro or *el coche*

2   Here is an important point to remember. You can say "It is Robert's key," but you do not say "It is a Robert's key." You say, instead, either "It is a key of Robert's" or "It is one of Robert's keys." All this means that in "It is Robert's key" the key is a unique entity and in Spanish you must use the definite article with the word for "key." Translate: It is Robert's key. ▲

Es la llave de Roberto.

3   In English you may say either "She saw a friend of Robert" or "She saw a friend of Robert's." Spanish has no *'s* construction and, as a result, both sentences are translated exactly alike. Translate the sentence. (The friend is female.) ▲

Ella vio a una amiga de Roberto.

4   You must be very careful in translating certain constructions with the apostrophe plus *s* (*'s*). The plural of "It's a child's shoe" is "They are children's shoes." The plural of "It's the child's shoe" is "They are the children's shoes." Of these four sentences, which two describe something made to be worn by a child or children? Think of your choice, then look at the answer frame. ▲

It's a child's shoe; They are children's shoes.

5   In the two sentences above the *'s* does not indicate possession. The forms "child's" and "children's" describe or classify "shoe" and "shoes." In the Spanish translation of these two sentences the word for "child" or "children" is usually singular and is never modified by an article or any other limiting adjective.

  It's a child's shoe.   *Es un zapato de niño.*
  They are children's shoes.   *Son zapatos de niño.*

Because of this special usage you must remember this rule: a construction with *de* plus a common noun can only indicate possession when the noun is modified by a limiting adjective (an article, a number, a demonstrative, or a possessive). Rewrite "It's the child's shoe" and use the *of* construction in English. ▲

It's a (the) shoe of the child.

6   This is the pattern you must use in Spanish. Write the translation. ▲

Es un (el) zapato del niño.

7   "They are the children's shoes" may be transformed to "They are the shoes of the children." Translate this last sentence. ▲

Son los zapatos de los niños.

8   Here is something which you do in English which may help you understand why the Spanish speaker only uses the *de* construction to show the possessive relationship between two nouns. Do you say "the mountain's foot" or "the house's key"? ▲

no (In English we rarely use the *'s* with a noun standing for an inanimate entity. We much prefer a construction with a relator word. We regularly say "Harold's foot," not "the foot of Harold," or "Harold's keys," but we can only say "the foot of the mountain." Spanish uses this pattern all the time, that is, when talking about either animate or inanimate entities.)

A/B

UNA PINTURA DE GOYA

UNA PINTURA DE GOYA

C/D

UNA PINTURA DEL MUSEO

UNA PINTURA DEL MUSEO

E/F

ESTAS SON LAS LLAVES DE LA CASA

LAS CATARATAS DEL IGUAZU SON LAS MÁS FAMOSAS DE SUD AMÉRICA

G/H

LA LINDA MUJER DE DON FELIPE

LOS BLANCOS CABELLOS DE DON HUGO

I

LA ENORME ESTATUA DEL CRISTO DE LOS ANDES

Summary

1 Both English and Spanish use possessive adjectives to show ownership or belonging: his keys⟶*sus llaves, etc.*

2 The other four ways of showing possession in English are reduced in Spanish to one pattern which uses the relator *de* and remains the same for both animate and inanimate entities:

    Robert's keys⟶ *las llaves de Roberto*
    the car keys⟶*las llaves del carro*
    the keys to the car⟶*las llaves del carro*
    the keys of the car ⟶*las llaves del carro*

3 The pattern composed of noun + *de* + unmodified common noun does not show possession, but rather it describes or indicates which type of entity is under consideration:

    los zapatos de niño   children's shoes
    las llaves de casa   house keys

Ordinal Numbers

1 A "quartet" is a group of singers made up of four people. The Spanish ordinal number cognate of "quart" is _____. ▲

cuarto (All Spanish ordinals end in *o* or *a*.)

2 A "quintet" is a group of five singers. The Spanish stem for "fifth" is *quint*. The word is _____. ▲

3 The Spanish stem for "sixth" is *sext*. The word is _____. ▲

quinto

4 *Séptimo* translates "seventh." For some reason, a grouping of seven musical instruments or seven singers is uncommon. "Octets," however, are quite common. You see the same stem in "octagon," a polygon which has eight angles and sides, and in "octave," a scale of eight musical tones. In the printing business eight pages cut from one sheet form an *octavo*. Say this word aloud in Spanish. This is the Spanish word for _____. ▲

sexto

5 "November" and "December" were once the months bearing the numbers nine and ten. These words became *noveno* and *décimo*. Say the Spanish for these ordinals: fifth, sixth, seventh, eighth, ninth, tenth. ▲

eighth

quinto, sexto, séptimo, octavo, noveno, décimo

"Let's" and Indirect Commands

1 Who is the subject of *let* in "Let us go now, please"? (a) the speaker of the sentence (b) the person spoken to ▲

the person spoken to (The meaning of *let* is "permit" or "allow.")

2 When you say, "Let's go now," the sentence has the meaning of "I propose that *we* go now." When you translate "let's" the subject of the verb will be _____. ▲

nosotros (It is, however, very rarely said in this construction.)

3 There are two ways of translating "Let's eat." They are *comamos* and _____. ▲

4 The pattern of the indirect command is that of a subjoined clause that is introduced by *que* and with the verb in the (a) indicative (b) subjunctive. ▲

Vamos a comer.

5 Write an indirect command using *Inés* and the proper form of *venir*. ▲

subjunctive

6 The best translation of *Que venga Inés* is _____. ▲

Que venga Inés.
Have Ines come.

More Practice with Diminutives

1 A child comes running to his mother with a banged elbow. She says, *Did you hurt your little elbow?* The meaning of *little* in such a situation has nothing to do with size. It reveals, rather, the attitude of the mother toward the hurt child. This attitude is one of (a) sympathy (b) endearment ▲

sympathy (A diminutive in Spanish may also reveal this same attitude.)

2 In "He bored me with all his little questions and little details" the meaning
of *little* is (a) small (b) insignificant or trivial. ▲

insignificant or trivial (A Spanish diminutive may also have this meaning.)

3 In "Bless your dear, little heart" the words *dear* and *little* reveal an emotional
response in the speaker. This response is one of (a) insignificance (b) sympathy
(c) tenderness. ▲

tenderness (A Spanish diminutive may also have this meaning. The word
translation of "little" (*pequeño*) would not.)

4 In English the adjectives "sweet," "dear," and "nice" are frequently used
along with "little": my dear little mother, a nice little old man, a sweet little
girl. These phrases reveal an emotional response of mild pleasantness or a kindly
attitude. The best Spanish equivalents are the diminutives: *madrecita, un
viejecito,* and the diminutive of *niña* which is _____. ▲

5 "I see through your little trick" means that the speaker is being (a) friendly   *niñita*
(b) slightly ironical. ▲

slightly ironical (A Spanish diminutive may also have this meaning.)

6 Which of the following requests is the least demanding? (a) May I have
something to eat? (b) May I have a little something to eat? ▲

May I have a little something to eat? (In Spanish *un poquito de comer* also
makes the request more modest than *algo de comer.*)

7 When a woman exclaims, "What a darling hat!" she probably means that
the hat is (a) becoming to the person wearing it (b) pretty. ▲

8 A man may flatter his wife by saying to her, "How's my pretty wife to-   pretty
night?" A Spanish speaker could do the same with *mi mujercita*. Translate the
sentence, "I like your pretty eyes." (You use the diminutive of *ojos* to translate
"pretty.") ▲

Me gustan tus ojitos. (Did you use *tus?* Flattery of this kind requires an
intimacy that demands the familiar form of the possessive pronoun.)

9 So far you have learned only the diminutive suffix *ito*, the most frequently
used suffix. It is added directly to nouns which have two or more syllables and
end in a (a) vowel (b) consonant. ▲

10 Translate: "little Miguel" or "Mickey," and "small table cloth." ▲   consonant
Miguelito; mantelito

11 What told you to add *ito* instead of *ita*? Think about the answer, then
check it. ▲

Nouns that stand for a male or which match *un* or *el* must take *ito*. Those that
stand for a female or match *una* and *la* take *ita*.

12 When a word ends in a vowel you must _____ the final vowel before you
add the suffix. ▲

13 Translate: "a tiny joke." (The noun is *broma*.) ▲   delete or drop

14 When you drop the final vowel and have an *i* as the last phoneme of the   *una bromita*
stem, what will happen? Will Rosario become (a) *Rosariito* or (b) *Rosarito*? ▲

Rosarito (The two *i*'s fuse into one in speech and writing.)

15 Remember what happens to *g, c,* and *z* before *e* and *i*, and write the diminutive for *Olga, chica,* and *cabeza*. ▲

Olguita; chiquita; cabecita (The spelling changes to *gu, qu,* and *c.*)

Self-Correcting Exercises

A *Reading Comprehension:* After reading the selection, do the comprehension exercise.

Las islas del Caribe

Entre Florida y la costa de Venezuela hay una larga cadena° de islas que   chain
aparecen en el mapa en forma de curva y separan al mar Caribe del océano
Atlántico. Es el gran archipiélago (grupo de islas) de las Antillas, una enorme
cordillera° de montañas volcánicas que desde tiempos muy remotos ha estado   range
sumergida en las aguas del mar. Este archipiélago incluye aproximadamente
7.000 islas de tamaños muy diferentes. Los tres grupos principales son las
Bahamas, las Antillas Mayores (o Grandes Antillas), y las Antillas Menores
(o Pequeñas Antillas).

    Las Antillas Mayores son Cuba, Santo Domingo (o Hispaniola), Puerto Rico
y Jamaica. Cuba es la más grande de todas. Dos naciones independientes,
Haití y la República Dominicana, ocupan el territorio de la isla de Santo
Domingo. La capital de Haití es Puerto Príncipe. Se llama en francés Port-
au-Prince. La ciudad de Santo Domingo que se llamó por un tiempo Ciudad
Trujillo es la capital dominicana. Puerto Rico dejó de ser posesión española
en 1898 después de la Guerra Hispano-Norteamericana y es hoy un estado
libre asociado a los Estados Unidos. Jamaica obtuvo su independencia de
Inglaterra en 1962 y es miembro de la Comunidad Británica de Naciones.
En las Antillas Menores solamente Trinidad y Tobago tienen gobierno independiente. Las demás islas del grupo son colonias francesas, inglesas u ho-
landesas. En 1917 los Estados Unidos le compró a Dinamarca sus posesiones
en las Islas Vírgenes por 25 millones de dólares.

    Al describir las islas del Caribe en su diario y cartas, Cristóbal Colón las
comparó muchas veces con el paraíso° terrenal.° El turista moderno que   paradise/earthly
vuela o navega hoy día por las Antillas encuentra muchas cosas que le hacen
pensar que el gran descubridor tenía razón. El clima es siempre cálido° y el   warm
paisaje° no puede ser más hermoso: playas blancas y doradas° bañadas por   landscape/golden
un mar azul y verde; gran abundancia de árboles, flores y frutas tropicales;
campos de color verde esmeralda cubiertos por abundante vegetación tropical.
No hay duda que estas tierras son de veras un paraíso tropical. Sin embargo,
desde los tiempos de Colón hasta el presente, la vida en este jardín tropical
ha sido dura y difícil para la mayoría de los habitantes. Han tenido y tienen
todavía problemas muy serios: ataques de piratas, esclavitud,° exceso de po-   slavery
blación, conflictos políticos y raciales, un porcentaje muy alto de analfabetos,°   illiterates
mucha pobreza, y áreas que sufren periódicamente los efectos desastrosos de
las erupciones volcánicas y las tormentas tropicales llamadas en esa región
ciclones o huracanes.

    Del total de 20 millones de habitantes la mayoría son negros o mestizos.
Hay algunos grupos de orientales, principalmente de la India, y una minoría
de europeos blancos. El antillano por lo general es un tipo alegre y simpático.

A pesar de° sus muchos problemas trata constantemente de mejorar sus condiciones de vida. Sus bailes y su música han circulado con mucho éxito por todas las grandes capitales del mundo. ¿Quién no ha oído en los Estados Unidos, por ejemplo, la música calipso de Trinidad o la música afro-cubana? Bailes como la rumba, el mambo, el cha-cha-chá y el merengue han sido y siguen siendo muy populares en los Estados Unidos.   In spite of

Write *sí* when the following statements are true, *no* when they are false.

Párrafo 1

1 La palabra "archipiélago" es un nombre geográfico que se le da a un grupo de islas.   sí
2 En el archipiélago de las Antillas hay millones de islas.   no

Párrafo 2

3 La capital de la República Dominicana es la Habana.   no
4 El Estado Libre Asociado de Puerto Rico es una posesión española.   no
5 Los Estados Unidos, Francia, Inglaterra y Holanda tienen islas en la región del Caribe.   sí

Párrafo 3

6 En una de las cartas que escribió Cristóbal Colón, el gran descubridor menciona que en una isla antillana encontró a dos indios que se llamaban Adán y Eva.   no
7 En algunas islas del Caribe hay actividad volcánica.   sí

Párrafo 4

8 Los habitantes de las Antillas son generalmente personas muy antipáticas y de temperamento muy triste.   no
9 A los antillanos no les gusta cantar ni bailar.   no
10 La música y los bailes antillanos no son muy conocidos fuera de la región del Caribe.   no

B *Subjunctive versus Indicative:* Write the appropriate form of the indicative or the subjunctive.

Este ejercicio es un diálogo entre Pedrito y su compañero de quinto grado, Juanito. Van a pasar el fin de semana juntos. Ya son más de las diez de la noche. Los dos muchachitos están acostados, pero no tienen sueño. Hablan de fantasmas (*ghosts*) mientras el perrito Spooks duerme a los pies de la cama de Pedrito.

Juanito no cree en fantasmas

1 —Oye, Pedrito, ¿por qué es que tu mamá no permite que tú y yo (ver) la película de Frankenstein que van a poner en el canal 13 a medianoche?   veamos

2 —Porque dice que esas películas no (ser) buenas para mí. Que me dan pesadillas (*nightmares*). Además ella demanda que yo (dormir) por lo menos ocho horas todas las noches.   son
duerma

3 —¡Caramba! Si sé eso, me quedo en mi casa. A mi mamá no le importa que yo (ver) películas de monstruos y de vampiros.   vea

4 —Siento mucho que (nosotros) no (poder) verla, Juanito. Mi mamá es muy estricta. Dudo mucho que ella (cambiar) de opinión.   podamos / cambie

5 —¡Qué mala pata! Y yo que creí que nos íbamos a divertir mucho este fin de semana. ¡Qué aburrido! (*boring*)

6 —Oye, Juanito, ¿tú crees en los fantasmas y en los vampiros?

7 —Yo creo que los fantasmas en realidad no (existir). Los vampiros, sí. Son unos pájaros negros con cara de ratón que chupan (*suck*) la sangre de las personas. ¿Por qué me preguntas?   existen

8 —¿Tú has visto una casa vieja abandonada que hay en la Calle Séptima? Me dijo una señora que vive cerca de allí que en esa casa ocurrió un crimen terrible.

9 —Sí, sí, ya sé. Mucha gente cree que en la casa (haber) un fantasma y que (salir) siempre a medianoche.   hay, / sale

10 —La señora dice que ella lo (haber) visto y lo (haber) oído varias veces. No te rías que no es juego.   ha, ha

11 —Me sorprende mucho que tú (creer) esas cosas. Son cuentos de la gente. Estoy seguro que no (ser) verdad lo que dicen.   creas / es

12 —Pues, ojalá que tú (tener) razón y que yo (estar) equivocado (*mistaken*).   tengas, esté

13 —Oye, Pedrito, ¡tengo una idea! ¿Por qué no vamos tú y yo a investigar la situación? Tengo muchas ganas de encontrarme cara a cara con un fantasma.

14 —¿A la casa del fantasma? ¿Pero tú estás loco? Mi mamá no va a querer que nosotros (salir) a esta hora de la noche.   salgamos

15 —Mira, chico. Ella está en la sala viendo televisión con tu hermana. No es necesario que tú le (pedir) permiso. Podemos escaparnos por la ventana sin hacer ruido.   pidas

16 —No sé, Juanito. Yo tengo un poco de miedo. Y si mi mamá nota que tú y yo no (estar) en el cuarto, seguramente que ella (ir) a llamar en seguida a la policía.   estamos, va

(The second part of this narration will be presented in class as a listening comprehension activity to give you the opportunity to hear diminutives and children talking in Spanish.)

C *General Review:* Write the translation. The word "little" indicates that you are to use the diminutive.

1 Have Johnny do it.   *Que lo haga Juanito.*
2 Let's visit my grandchildren.   *Vamos a visitar a mis nietos.*
3 Let's visit my sister-in-law.   *Vamos a visitar a mi cuñada.*

4 Have my little (dear) husband cook the fish.	*Que mi maridito cocine el pescado.*
5 Have the little children come.	*Que vengan los niñitos.*
6 Have Annie be to blame.	*Que tenga la culpa Anita.*
7 Let's study more.	*Vamos a estudiar más.*

New Vocabulary

escoba	broom	**pensamiento**	thought
piso	floor	**corazón**	heart
alfombra	rug, carpet	**bien**	good
pared	wall	**mal**	evil, bad
cuadro	picture	**barrer**	to sweep
techo	roof, ceiling	**encender la luz**	to turn on the light
llave (la)	key; faucet	**apagar la luz**	to turn off the light
edad	age	**abrir la llave**	to turn on the faucet
ruido	noise	**dulce**	sweet
peligro	danger	**amargo**	bitter

Assignment 80

Subjunctive in Adjectival Clauses of Non-experience

You have studied how the subjunctive is used in the subjoined clause when: (1) reporting a command, (2) attempting to influence someone's behavior, (3) describing the stimulus that causes a psychological or emotional response, and (4) following expressions of uncertainty or disbelief in declarative sentences.

You will now be introduced to the use of the subjunctive in a subjoined (adjectival) clause that describes an entity whose existence has not yet been experienced or is not yet accepted by the speaker or doer of the main clause.

1 An adjective is a word that modifies (describes, points out, limits, *etc.*) a noun or pronoun. An adjectival clause is a subjoined clause that functions as an adjective. What part of the following sentence is the adjectival clause? My sister is a person who is very neat and tidy. ▲

who is very neat and tidy (This modifies *person*.)

2 The common connecting words for these clauses in English are *who*, *that* and *which*. From past experience with subjoined clauses in Spanish, see if you can guess what single connecting word translates all three English words. ▲

3 From a linguistic point of view, sentences containing adjectival clauses are actually two sentences combined into one. By using the connecting word see

que

if you can make one sentence out of these two: *Tengo un radio. No funciona.* ▲

Tengo un radio que no funciona.

4 Try combining these two sentences: *Tengo un perro. Ladra mucho.* ▲

Tengo un perro que ladra mucho.

5 In both of the above sentences I have had experience with the entities modified by the adjectival clause, i.e., the radio (I know that it doesn't work) and the dog (I know that it barks a lot).

Because I have had experience with them, I use the indicative in the subjoined (adjectival) clause. In contrast, if the entity has not been experienced, the subjunctive is used. Translate this sentence: "I am looking for a dog that does not bark." ▲

Busco un perro que no ladre. (Subjunctive is used because I have not yet experienced this dog.)

6 Translate "I want a dog that does not bark." ▲

Quiero un perro que no ladre.

7 When I find the dog I am seeking I have had at least enough experience to know that it doesn't bark. Use *hallar* and translate "I have found a dog that does not bark." ▲

He hallado un perro que no ladra.

8 You need not have personal experience with something or someone to believe that it exists. You can learn from a reliable source. Even though you have never been to Patagonia you can believe that it exists because others have had experience with it. Translate: *Hay una parte de Sudamérica que* **is called** *Patagonia.* ▲

Hay una parte de Sudamérica que **se llama** *Patagonia.*

9 Translate: *No hay ninguna parte de los Estados Unidos que* **is called** *Patagonia.* ▲

No hay ninguna parte de los Estados Unidos que **se llame** *Patagonia.*

10 You have been told that in a certain village there is a man who makes very fine shoes. You go to the village and say to a native, "I am looking for the man who makes shoes." Do you believe there is a man there who makes shoes? ▲

yes (Or you wouldn't have bothered to go there.)

11 Translate the indicated clause: I'm looking for the man *who makes shoes.* ▲

12 On the way back your car breaks down. You walk to a farmer's house and   *que hace zapatos.*
say to him, "I'm looking for a man who knows how to repair cars." Do you know if any such man is in this area? ▲

13 What form of *saber* will you use in your translation of the above statement?   no
(a) *sepa* (b) *sabe* ▲

14 You are in a strange part of town looking for a man who you know lives   *sepa*
nearby. Someone notices your hesitation and asks if he can help. You say, "I am looking for a man. He lives near here. His name is Martínez." The transformation of the first two sentences is "I am looking for a man *who lives near here.*" Translate the adjectival clause. ▲

que vive cerca de aquí. (When you have a particular person or thing in mind the verb of the adjectival clause is in the indicative mode.)

15 In this and the remaining frames write the form of the indicated infinitive which is cued by the context.

Conozco a un doctor que *poder* ayudarte. ▲

16 Yo no conozco a ningún hombre que *poder* hacerlo. ▲   *puede*

17 Tengo un amigo que *hablar* japonés. ▲   *pueda*

18 Manolo busca una esposa que *ser* rica. ▲   *habla*

19 Hay una clase de perro que no *ladrar*. ▲   *sea*

20 ¿Vamos a un café donde (ellos) *servir* tacos? (You don't have one in mind.   *ladra*
Remember that *servir* has a stem change.) ▲

21 ¿Vamos a una tienda donde *vender* camisas modernas? Yo sé donde está. ▲   *sirvan*

22 ¿No hay ningún vestido que te *gustar*? ▲   *venden*

23 Quiero el libro que *estar* en la mesa. ▲   *guste*

24 Vd. necesita un profesor que *saber* geología. ▲   *está*

25 Creo que no hay nadie que se lo *permitir*. ▲   *sepa*

       permita

A/B

HA HALLADO ZAPATOS QUE LE GUSTAN

¿NO HAY ZAPATOS QUE LE GUSTEN?

C/D

HA COLECCIONADO MARIPOSAS QUE TIENEN ALAS ROJAS

BUSCA MARIPOSAS QUE TENGAN ALAS AZULES

Summary

1 The indicative is used in adjectival clauses that modify entities experienced by the doer or speaker, or when he believes that they have been experienced by others.

2 The subjunctive is used in adjectival clauses when the modified entity has not been experienced by the doer or speaker and he is not yet convinced of its existence.

Learning New Vocabulary

The purpose of this Program is to teach you a study procedure which research in learning theory has shown to be effective. If you follow instructions carefully and concentrate on what you are doing, you will learn seventeen new words in just fourteen minutes of work. Here is what you are to do first. You are to study the new words in five short periods. You will need to check yourself with a watch. Here is the division of time:

     Period 1: 4 minutes
     Period 2: 4 minutes
     Period 3: 2 minutes
     Period 4: 2 minutes
     Period 5: 2 minutes

You begin with period 1 and work for four minutes. Then you go do something else, anything you like, for at least fifteen to twenty minutes, but forget about Spanish. When this time is up, study the vocabulary again for four minutes only. Then do something else for fifteen to twenty minutes and, then, study for just *two minutes*, and, once again, forget about Spanish for fifteen to twenty minutes, and again study for just *two minutes*. At this time you will have studied for two four-minute and two two-minute periods. It is important, now, to do something else for *one whole hour*. When this hour is up, study the vocabulary again for just *two minutes*.

For each study period you will work with the same seventeen words. However, they will be arranged in a different order each time. This is to prevent you from developing what is called a chain-memory pattern in which you remember a word because it is always preceded or followed by the same words.

You will see the English and the Spanish words side by side. Which one comes first will be changed for each period. Here are the steps to follow:

Period 1:

(1) Look over the whole list of words and see if you can think of an English cognate which will help you remember some of the Spanish words. You will see, for example, *guerra*. You know the diminutive form of this word because it has been borrowed from Spanish and is now a standard English word. It is "guerrilla," the name for soldiers who fight in small groups with hit and run techniques. Do not use more than one minute doing this.

(2) Go back and go over the list twice again. Look at the English and say the Spanish aloud. Pay close attention to any special spelling. For example, you will say [pas] but see *paz*. Do not spend more than one minute doing this.

(3) Cover the column of English words, look at each Spanish word and try to recall its English equivalent. If you cannot do this for each word in two seconds, slide your cover sheet down and look at the English word. Then say both aloud.

(4) Reverse the process. Cover the Spanish column and look at each English word and, then, say the Spanish equivalent out loud. Do steps 3 and 4 just as many times as you can in two minutes.

Periods 2, 3, 4, and 5:
For each period do steps 3 and 4 above just as many times as you can. Here are the words you are to learn.

Period 1

peace	**paz**	bloody	**sangriento**
battle	**batalla**	he kills	**mata**
war	**guerra**	he suffers	**sufre**
soldier	**soldado**	he fights	**pelea**
officer	**oficial**	he struggles	**lucha**
chief	**jefe**	he wounds	**hiere**
sailor	**marinero**	he shoots	**tira**
army	**ejército**	he overcomes	**vence**
enemy	**enemigo**		

Period 2

oficial	officer	**batalla**	battle
tira	he shoots	**ejército**	army
hiere	he wounds	**sangriento**	bloody
pelea	he fights	**mata**	he kills
marinero	sailor	**jefe**	chief
vence	he overcomes	**soldado**	soldier
paz	peace	**enemigo**	enemy
lucha	he struggles	**sufre**	he suffers
guerra	war		

Period 3

battle	**batalla**	bloody	**sangriento**
soldier	**soldado**	he wounds	**hiere**
peace	**paz**	he struggles	**lucha**
sailor	**marinero**	he kills	**mata**
enemy	**enemigo**	army	**ejército**
officer	**oficial**	he suffers	**sufre**
he overcomes	**vence**	war	**guerra**
chief	**jefe**	he fights	**pelea**
he shoots	**tira**		

Period 4

sufre	he suffers	**ejército**	army
mata	he kills	**marinero**	sailor
vence	he overcomes	**jefe**	chief
pelea	he fights	**oficial**	officer
tira	he shoots	**soldado**	soldier
hiere	he wounds	**guerra**	war

lucha	he struggles	**batalla**	battle
sangriento	bloody	**paz**	peace
enemigo	enemy		

Period 5

bloody	**sangriento**	he shoots	**tira**
he suffers	**sufre**	officer	**oficial**
enemy	**enemigo**	he wounds	**hiere**
he kills	**mata**	soldier	**soldado**
army	**ejército**	he struggles	**lucha**
he overcomes	**vence**	peace	**paz**
sailor	**marinero**	battle	**batalla**
he fights	**pelea**	war	**guerra**
chief	**jefe**		

If you have done this exercise properly, you have learned a powerful technique for studying many other subjects in which you have to memorize a great deal of material. Research has demonstrated that short periods of spaced learning are much more effective than a single long period doing the same thing. This procedure is especially effective in memorizing a piece on a musical instrument.

Don't forget to add these words to your vocabulary list.

Self-Correcting Exercises

A *Preterit versus Imperfect:* Write the appropriate form of the Preterit or the Imperfect for each numbered verb.

Daniel va al colegio en motocicleta

Son **1** las siete de la mañana. El despertador (*alarm clock*) *empieza* (empezó) a sonar y Daniel se *despierta* **2**. Se *levanta* (levantó), *va* **3** al baño a lavarse y se *viste* **4** sin prisa. Antes de ir a la cocina a desayunar, Daniel *hace* **5** su cama y *pone* **6** las cosas en su lugar. Es un muchacho muy ordenado (*orderly*) y le gusta tener todo en orden. Después del desayuno se *despide* (despidió) de sus padres y *sale* **7** para la escuela.

Es (Era) un bonito día de otoño. ¡Qué fresco tan agradable! Aunque *hace* **8** sol, cuando Daniel *ve* (vio) las nubes negras en el cielo, *piensa* (pensó) que por la tarde *va* **9** a llover. Por la Avenida Central carros y camiones *van* (iban) y *vienen* (venían) en todas direcciones. ¡Qué bueno *es* (era) tener motocicleta propia! El muchacho *viaja* (viajaba) feliz y contento hacia la escuela.

La luz del tráfico en la Calle Veinte *está* **10** roja, pero Daniel no la *ve* **11** y *sigue* **12** adelante (*forward*). ¡Qué bueno *es* (era) ir al colegio en motocicleta propia! De repente *nota* (notó) en el espejo que un carro negro y blanco le *sigue* **13**. Se *pone* (puso) un poco nervioso, pero no le *da* (dio) importancia y *continúa* (continuó). De repente *oye* (oyó) el ruido de una sirena y se *da* **14** cuenta (*realizes*) de que el señor de uniforme azul oscuro *quiere* **15** hablar con él. ¡Qué mala suerte!

1	Eran
2	despertó
3	fue
4	vistió
5	hizo
6	puso
7	salió
8	hacía
9	iba
10	estaba
11	vio
12	siguió
13	seguía
14	dio
15	quería

It is well known that each culture has its own favorite foods and dishes. Although Americans eat pizza, hot dogs, and Chinese food, the traditional dishes are meat, potatoes, apple pie, chicken, turkey, hamburger, bread, butter, *etc.* In Spain, the use of butter in cooking is quite uncommon. They much prefer olive oil. In Cuba the traditional meat for Christmas dinner is pork. In many parts of the Hispanic world, kids (young goats) are considered a delicacy. In tropical countries the natives eat monkeys. Corn is not a staple in the Peninsular diet; it is replaced by rice or potatoes. Rice, corn, beans, and potatoes are common in most of Latin America. The tortillas of Mexico are made from corn flour.

What each group considers a delicacy is often surprising to the other. Ice cream and Coca Cola are found in every country, but many people drink their cokes *de tiempo* (at air temperature). Cokes and cookies are so foreign in some places that there are no words for them in Spanish. A favorite dessert is like a rich custard called *flan*, something for which we have no word. The same is true for *paella*, a dish made of rice and different meats and fish. In Mexico there is a rather large worm which grows on the *maguey* plant. These worms are harvested, fried crisp, and are sold by street vendors as a special delicacy. The vendors stand on street corners with the worms in a small paper bag tied with a loop of string attached to each finger. They hawk their wares by calling out *gusanillos* (the diminutive of *gusanos* (worms)).

When most Americans think of Spanish food they are usually thinking of the extremely hot, spicy food of Mexico. This is not typical for the rest of the Hispanic world.

B *General Review:* Translate the following sentences. The word "little" indicates that you are to use the diminutive.

1	Have little Adela see them.	*Que Adelita los vea.*
2	Let's help your father-in-law.	*Vamos a ayudar a tu suegro.*
3	Have Rosie iron it.	*Que lo planche Rosita.*
4	Have it last a hundred years.	*Que dure cien años.*
5	Let's turn on the little lamp.	*Vamos a encender la lamparita.*
6	Let's get better soon.	*Vamos a mejorarnos pronto.*
7	Let's not get mad.	*No vamos a enojarnos.*

C *Subjunctive versus Indicative:* Write the combinations.

Ejemplo: 132 = Es necesario que tú lo creas.

1	Es necesario		1	yo	1	poner la mesa así.
2	Cuentan		2	ella y yo	2	creerlo.
3	Se han enojado de	que	3	tú	3	seguir ese camino.
4	Está segura de		4	los muchachos	4	querer usarlo.
5	Duda mucho		5	usted	5	ir allí.

1)	111	Es necesario que yo ponga la mesa así.
2)	222	Cuentan que ella y yo lo creemos.
3)	333	Se han enojado de que tú sigas ese camino.
4)	444	Está segura de que los muchachos quieren usarlo.
5)	555	Duda mucho que usted vaya allí.
6)	123	Es necesario que ella y yo sigamos ese camino.
7)	234	Cuentan que tú quieres usarlo.
8)	345	Se han enojado de que los muchachos vayan allí.
9)	512	Duda mucho que yo lo crea.
10)	451	Está segura de que usted pone la mesa así.

New Vocabulary

bosque	forest, woods	**mezcla**	mixture
culebra	snake	**trozo**	piece; excerpt
caballero	gentleman, knight	**preciso**	necessary; precise
alma	soul	**próximo, -a**	next
espíritu (el)	spirit	**resistir**	to stand (endure)
mayoría	majority		

"No hay mal que dure cien años ni cuerpo que lo resista."

"Every cloud has a silver lining." (There is no evil that can last 100 years, nor a body that can stand it.)

See also the "war vocabulary" on p. 488.

Learning New Words from Context

1 You are probably now at a stage in learning Spanish that makes it possible for you to determine the meaning of more than 10,000 words the instant you see them in context. With the proper kind of practice you should be able to double this number of words in the next few months. How many new words you actually learn will depend a lot on how well you use the knowledge you already have. You know, for example, that the English cognates of Spanish verb forms do not have the same suffixes. Consequently, you look <u>only</u> at the stem of the Spanish verb to see if an English cognate will help you make an educated guess at its meaning. What is the cognate of *armar* as used in *armar a los soldados*? ▲

2 When you are trying to guess the meaning of a word from context it is often useful to pretend the word is not there at all. There is just a blank space which you need to fill. You now ask yourself a number of questions of the kind you would ask in playing the game of twenty questions. For example: "What, in general, is being talked about?" This eliminates a great many words which do not have to be considered at all.

to arm

You are, for example, reading about *una guerra* and *las armas que tienen los soldados*. The subject of discourse in this immediate context is weapons, the cover word for the one whose meaning you are trying to guess. It is not logical, under these conditions, to think of "toothpick" or "cream puffs."

Your context deals with *guerra*, *soldados*, and *armas*. You have guessed that the cover term for the word you are trying to figure out is "weapon." What is the translation of *bomba* and *granada*? ▲

3 Let's see, now, how well your logic works.

bomb; grenade

La señora Cernuda va a preparar la comida. Quiere hacer una ensalada de frutas y va a la tienda a comprarlas. Compra manzanas, naranjas y tres granadas.

Does she buy three hand grenades? ▲

4 In the context above the Spanish cover word for *granada* also stands for *manzanas* and *naranjas*. It is _____. ▲

no

5 You now know the definition of *granada* for this context: *La granada es una fruta*. You must, at this point, ask yourself this question. Do I need to know anything more about *granada* to understand what I am reading? You know that Mrs. Cernuda is going to make a fruit salad with three kinds of fruit: apples, oranges, and *granadas*. Is it important that you know anything more? The chances are it is not and you should go on reading. However, you feel insecure, so you look up *granada* and find it is a "pomegranate."

fruta

Having found out that a *granada* is a pomegranate and that a pomegranate is a fruit, what do you know that you didn't know before? ▲

Very little. You now know that *granada* and "pomegranate" both stand for the same thing, a fruit.

6 Let's see, now, what you would do in a comparable situation in English. You are reading a novel in which the main character is a woodsman who is working for a lumber company. The scene is a forest in the southeastern United States. It is early morning and Mark is working in a tall stand of loblolly. What is a "loblolly"? ▲

7 Would you look the word up if you had never seen it before? ▲
a tree

probably not (You only need to know more than "tree" if the plot hinges on the fact that it's a pine.)

8 Let's go back to frame 2. There you met *bomba* and figured out it stood for "bomb." You are now conditioned to believe that other words built on the stem "bomb" should have something to do with bomb. This can be deceptive. Let's see if you can guess the meaning of *bomba* and *bombero* in a different context. There are a lot of other new words. Guess at them and keep reading.

Ya tú sabes que mi familia vive ahora en el campo. Aunque nuestro rancho está bastante cerca de la ciudad, tiene solamente agua de pozo (*well*). Anteayer, cuando mis padres volvían de su trabajo, se horrorizaron al ver que nuestra casa se quemaba. Mi papá corrió a la casa de un vecino a telefonear a la estación de incendios. Después salió a la calle a esperar la llegada de los bomberos. En pocos minutos se oyó la sirena del camión de bomba que tiene un gran tanque de agua. Sin perder tiempo los bomberos saltaron del camión con la manguera y corrieron a apagar el fuego. Recibieron una gran sorpresa al ver que el agua no salía de la manguera. Un bombero había olvidado abrir la llave de la bomba que hace que el agua salga por la manguera.

You should not need any help with *bomberos*. They are _____. ▲

9 *Bomba* in this context may give you some trouble. There are several obvious
firemen
cues to consider: (1) a special kind of fire truck for an area that has no water hydrant (*camión de bomba*), one with *un tanque de agua*, (2) to everyone's surprise no water comes out the *manguera*, (3) a fireman had forgotten to do something, (4) what you turn on on a fire truck to make water come out the *manguera*. The answer is the _____. ▲

10 Reread the Spanish paragraph in frame 8 and pay special attention to
pump (*bomba*)
incendios, llegada, sirena, fuego, and *manguera.* When you are finished, write the translation of these words. ▲

fire, arrival, siren, fire, hose

11 Let's go back now and bring to the surface all the steps you should have taken to get the meaning of these words.

The first and most important step was to keep reading until you knew what was being talked about: the subject of discourse. The key words in this case were *casa* and *quemar*. Papa now runs to telephone someone. Your logic eliminates Aunt Minnie and the rector of the church. When your house is on fire you telephone the . . . . You hardly have to look at the words to know their meaning. (fire station)

Papa runs to the street to wait for something. The ice cream man? No. And in addition you know that *llegar* translates "to arrive." If your logic is working well the *la* in front of *llegada* says: change "arrive" into a noun, and you get "arrival."

So Papa is now awaiting the arrival of *los bomberos*. At this point you only have vague cues as to the meaning of *bomberos*. Your logic, however, should reduce the choice to what is going to come from the fire station, either firemen or fire trucks. You now keep reading until you come to *saltaron*. The *bomberos* arrive and jump down from the truck. *Bomberos* have to be men; you have eliminated fire trucks, and you know they are firemen.

The *bomberos* jump from the truck and run to *apagar el fuego*. Your logic should tell you that firemen come to a house that is burning to put out the fire.

When firemen fight a fire they usually use water. Your experience tells you that they carry hoses on their truck. You now put *agua, no salía*, and *de la manguera* together and conclude that about the only thing that the water must not be coming out of is a hose.

The water does not come out of the hose, and you are now up to *bomba*. You could not get the meaning of *bomba* when it was used in *oyó la sirena del camión de bomba*. There is nothing in this context which can serve as a cue to its meaning. So, if you follow instructions, you keep on reading. You have, at this point, accumulated a lot of cues: fire truck, firemen, water, hose, and you know that *abrir la llave* translates "to turn the water on." There is a *camión de bomba*, the water does not come out the hose. This means there is no pressure. There is something on the *camión de bomba* that needs to be turned on to force the water out through the nozzle of the hose. You now have enough information to guess "pump."

It is highly unlikely that you did everything described above or that if you did, that you were consciously aware of everything you did do. However, you now have a model procedure which you can follow consciously, and if you use it carefully your ability to guess the meaning of new words will improve dramatically. Read the following passage and then write the translation of *mundial*.

Los soldados y marineros de los Estados Unidos han peleado en muchas guerras y han luchado contra los enemigos del país en muchas partes del mundo. Pelearon en la guerra de Independencia de 1776, en la Guerra Civil, en la primera guerra *mundial* de 1918 y también en la segunda guerra *mundial*. ▲

Mundial is the adjective derived from *mundo* = "world."

12 Read the following and write the translation of *herida* and *bala*: *Mi padre peleó en la primera guerra mundial dos años, pero en todo este tiempo solamente sufrió una* **herida** *pequeña. La* **bala** *de un rifle pasó por su oreja.* ▲

13 Translate: *firma, tratado.*   wound; bullet

Cuando se termina una guerra los representantes de los dos países enemigos van a una conferencia de paz. Después de hablar mucho preparan un documento especial que se llama el *tratado* de paz. Al fin un representante de cada país saca su pluma y *firma* el *tratado*. ▲

14 Translate: *grados.*   signs; treaty

En el ejército hay muchos *grados*. Un soldado puede ser un soldado de fila, un sargento, un capitán, un mayor, o un coronel o general. Cada soldado tiene un *grado*. ▲

rank

15 Translate *asesino* with a word which is not its cognate.
Cuando un soldado pelea contra el enemigo y mata a muchos de ellos, es un
héroe. Si una persona que no está en el ejército mata a otra persona no es un
héroe, es un *asesino*. ▲

16 Translate: *rendirse*.   murderer
Cuando un ejército ha perdido muchos soldados y ya no puede continuar la
guerra está vencido y tiene que *rendirse*. ▲

to surrender

In most American stores everything for sale has the price marked on it. Except during sales, this price is fixed and the customer does not argue over it. In the large stores and supermarkets of Latin America the prices are also fixed. However, in small shops and the market place, the prices are rarely fixed. The buyer must haggle with the seller. The seller usually begins by setting a price according to what he thinks the customer can afford. After that, the bargaining becomes a kind of a game of wits and patience to see who gives up first. Many American tourists do not understand the unwritten rules of this game and, as a result, they often settle for a price that may be many times higher than a native would pay for the same article. One knowledgeable tourist once bought an ashtray from an Indian craftsman for 50 cents. His friend happily paid two dollars for the same article.

The word for this bargaining process is *regateo*. The verb is *regatear*.

Making Comparisons

1 When two or more entities are compared in terms of their qualities or attributes only two conclusions are possible: they are alike or different. In both English and Spanish the simple form of an adjective is used to compare two entities which are alike. You must, of course, use comparative words to do this. Write the missing words: This book is _____ long _____ that one. ▲

2 The translation of the above sentence is *Este libro es tan largo como ese*. Both   as; as
languages make statements of this kind negative by negating the verb. Translate "This book is not as long as that one." ▲

*Este libro **no** es tan largo como ese.*

3 In both languages the degree of the attribute of an entity or a set of entities may be increased by modifying the simple form of the adjective with an adverb. "This book is very (exceedingly, extremely, excessively, tremendously) long." Translate: This book is very long. ▲

Este libro es muy largo.

4 When an adjective has an opposite, two entities may be compared by using both of the paired words in either language:

This book is long.   That book is short.
Este libro es largo.   *Ese libro es corto.*

In English this same comparison may be made by deleting (omitting) the second sentence and by adding a comparative suffix to "long." This suffix is _____. ▲

er (This book is longer.)

5   There is a second kind of transformation of these two sentences. You add "er" to "long," you delete "is short," replace "book" with "one," and tie the two parts of the original two sentences together with a comparative conjunction. Can you follow instructions and do this transformation?   ▲

This book is longer than that one.

6   Adding "er" to some English adjectives produces an odd or clumsy form. You do not say "tremendouser," "interestinger," or "beautifuler." What adverb do you use with "tremendous," "interesting," and "beautiful" to make a comparison?   ▲

7   Spanish makes a comparative statement by doing the same thing. Translate: She is more beautiful.   ▲

more

Ella es más linda (or *bonita*).

8   One way of stating the opposite of "She is more beautiful" is to make the sentence negative: "She is not more beautiful," *No es más linda.* Another way, in both languages, is to use the opposite of "more" and *más.* Rewrite the Spanish sentence above and make this change.   ▲

9   When two entities are compared and both are mentioned, there are three ways of expressing this information:

Ella es menos linda.

    (1)   Margarita is beautiful. Pepita is more beautiful.
    (2)   Margarita is beautiful, *but* Pepita is more beautiful.
    (3)   Pepita is more beautiful *than* Margarita.

You already know how to translate the first two examples. You get the third by using *que* for "than." Translate the sentence.   ▲

Pepita es más linda que Margarita.

10   The degree of an English adjective can be increased another step by replacing the comparative suffix "er" with the superlative suffix: long, longer, long _____.   ▲

11   The same effect can be achieved by modifying the "er" form with an adverb: "This is much (even, still) longer." The same modifiers may be used with "more": "It is much more interesting." An alternate way is to change "more" to its superlative form _____.   ▲

longest

most (It is the most interesting one.)

12   The superlative of "less" is _____.   ▲

least (It is the least interesting one.)

13   Spanish, like English, may modify *más* with another adverb. Translate: This movie (*película*) is much more interesting.   ▲

Esta película es mucho más interesante.

14   Spanish, unlike English, has no superlative suffix which can be added to an adjective. The following two phrases are translated by the same phrase in Spanish:

    The more industrious boys | *Los muchachos más industriosos*
    The most industrious boys |

The Spanish speaker is, of course, well aware of the fact that there can be a degree of comparison higher than the comparative. He shows this awareness, for example, by using *mucho* as a modifier of *más*: *Este libro es mucho más interesante.* Although there are times when it is impossible to tell whether the meaning is comparative or superlative, the difference is very frequently indicated by contexts. Write the missing adverbs:

The Spanish author, Pereda, wrote many books. There is one of these books which is _____ interesting than all the others. In my opinion *Peñas Arriba* is his _____ interesting book. ▲

more; most (The Spanish speaker uses *más* in both cases.)

15 Remember that some English adjectives are translated by nouns. "I am hungry" becomes _____. ▲

16 "I am hungrier" has to be transformed to "I have more hunger." Translate the sentence. ▲

Tengo hambre.

17 Translate: I am thirstier than you. (*Vd.*) ▲

Tengo más hambre.
Tengo más sed que Vd.

18 In English one may say, "He is the biggest member *of* the family" or "He is the oldest *in* the family." Spanish more regularly uses *de* to translate both these relators. Translate: "He is the most friendly (*amable*) person in my family." (Have you noticed that when *más* is used the adjective follows the noun in Spanish?) ▲

Él es la persona más amable de mi familia.

A/B

C/D

E/F

EL AVIÓN ES UNA
INVENCIÓN MÁS MODERNA

EL SATÉLITE ES
LA INVENCIÓN MÁS MODERNA

G

PEPE TIENE MÁS MONOS QUE PACO

Practice with the Forms of the Subjunctive

1   To get the forms of the present subjunctive of *a*-verbs, you replace all the indicative allomorphs of the first suffix with the single morpheme _____.   ▲

2   Transform *cocino* and *cocinamos* into the subjunctive.   ▲   *e*

3   Write the subjunctive for *saca*.   ▲   *cocine, cocinemos*

4   Write the subjunctive for *llegan*.   ▲   *saque*

5   Write the *yo* form of the subjunctive of *empezar*.   ▲   *lleguen*

6   To get the present subjunctive forms of *e*- and *i*-verbs, you replace all the   *empiece*
indicative allomorphs of the first suffix with the single morpheme _____.   ▲

7   Write the subjunctive for *tememos*, *escribimos*, and *vivo*.   ▲   *a*

temamos, escribamos, viva

8   If there is an irregularity in the form or spelling of the *yo* form of the present
indicative which ends in *o*, this is retained in the present subjunctive. Very
irregular verbs may have a special form. Write the indicative and subjunctive
yo forms of *seguir* and *proteger*.   ▲

sigo, siga ; protejo, proteja

9   In this and the remaining frames, write the *yo* form of the subjunctive of
the given infinitives.

   ir, enojar, escoger, coger, conseguir, tocar, reír, conocer   ▲

vaya, enoje, escoja, coja, consiga, toque, ría, conozca

10 cruzar, viajar, perder, dormir, divertir, sentar, despertar, abrazar ▲
cruce, viaje, pierda, duerma, divierta, siente, despierte, abrace

11 tocar, oír, cerrar, contar, vestir, jugar, sentir, buscar ▲
toque, oiga, cierre, cuente, vista, juegue, sienta, busque

12 recordar, empezar, pedir, parecer, poder, volver, querer, decir ▲
recuerde, empiece, pida, parezca, pueda, vuelva, quiera, diga

13 ser, saber, poner, hacer, salir, venir, tener, morir, haber, estar ▲
sea, sepa, ponga, haga, salga, venga, tenga, muera, haya, esté

Self-Correcting Exercises

A *Silent Reading:* After reading the selection, do the comprehension exercise.

"El Grito de Dolores"

También México tiene su Campana de la Libertad. Está en el Palacio Nacional en la capital. Es la campana de la iglesia de un pueblecito del estado de Guanajuato que se llama Dolores. En la madrugada del 16 de septiembre de 1810, el sonido de esta campana despertó a los indios y campesinos° de la región. Era domingo y ellos no sabían que esta vez la campana no los llamaba a los servicios religiosos. Los llamaba a libertar a su patria° mexicana. El hombre que tocaba la campana tan urgentemente era el cura° del pueblo. Se llamaba don Miguel Hidalgo y Costilla, "padre de la independencia de México." Las acciones de este hombre en esa gloriosa mañana pasaron a las páginas de la historia de América con el nombre de "Grito de Dolores."

En 1808 los ejércitos de Napoleón Bonaparte invadieron a España. El pueblo español pasaba por momentos muy difíciles y su situación política era crítica y sumamente° complicada. En las colonias españolas de América existía gran confusión y nadie sabía de un día para otro qué iba a pasar. Grupos de patriotas criollos en varias partes del continente declaraban que había llegado por fin la hora de la libertad. En el pueblo de Dolores, el padre Hidalgo y un grupo de sus amigos y vecinos organizaron una conspiración contra el gobierno colonial de México. Desgraciadamente, en el grupo había un hombre cobarde° y traidor que los denunció. La noche del 15 de septiembre, sin estar completamente preparados para empezar la lucha, fue necesario entrar en acción antes de tiempo.

El padre Hidalgo y su pequeña tropa salieron del pueblo gritando: "¡Viva la Virgen de Guadalupe! ¡Viva América! ¡Muera el mal gobierno!" El viejo sacerdote° de sesenta años iba montado en un caballo a la cabeza del grupo. Sus vecinos le seguían a pie armados con palos, piedras y machetes (cuchillos grandes). En los otros ranchos y pueblos de la región miles de hombres se unieron al grupo. Aunque pudieron vencer a las tropas españolas en varias batallas importantes, el equipo y la disciplina del ejército enemigo eran muy superiores. Después de varios meses de luchas sangrientas, Hidalgo y sus jefes principales tuvieron que huir° hacia el norte. En la ciudad de Chihuahua fueron capturados y fusilados. A Hidalgo le quitaron sus vestidos de sacerdote y le cortaron la cabeza.

(marginal glosses)
farmers
homeland
priest
extremely
coward
priest
flee

La lucha por la independencia de México continuó en el sur bajo la dirección de otro gran héroe. Se llamaba José María Morelos y era también sacerdote y gran admirador de Hidalgo. Gracias al sacrificio de estos dos curas y de otros patriotas que les siguieron, México llegó a ser una nación libre e independiente. En su honor, todos los años los mexicanos celebran el 16 de septiembre con grandes fiestas y actos patrióticos. El presidente de México toca la Campana de la Libertad y da el famoso "Grito de Dolores."

Write *sí* or *no* to each of the following statements, according to whether the statement is true or false.

1	En esta lectura, Dolores es el nombre de un pueblito mexicano.	sí
2	El héroe mexicano Miguel Hidalgo era gobernador del estado de Guana-juato.	no
3	La invasión napoleónica de España causó muchos problemas en las colonias españolas de América.	sí
4	Los indios que asistían a la iglesia del padre Hidalgo le dijeron al comandante español que su cura se iba a rebelar contra el gobierno colonial.	no
5	Las palabras "cura" y "sacerdote" tienen el mismo significado.	sí
6	Cuando dio el "Grito de Dolores", Hidalgo era un hombre muy joven.	no
7	Los hombres que siguieron al padre Hidalgo la mañana del 16 de septiembre eran soldados profesionales, muy bien armados con armas de guerra y muy disciplinados.	no
8	Las tropas del padre Hidalgo ganaron (*won*) varias batallas.	sí
9	El apellido del general español que peleó contra Hidalgo era Morelos.	no
10	La muerte del "Padre de la Patria Mexicana" en Chihuahua fue horrible y muy sangrienta.	sí

B *Subjunctive versus Indicative:* Decide whether the subjoined verb should be Indicative or Subjunctive and write the appropriate form.

1	—Oye, Abelardo, ¿sabes dónde puedo conseguir un almanaque escrito en español que (tener) informes sobre los países latinoamericanos?	tenga
2	—No sé, profesor. ¿Busca usted uno que (relatar) lo que pasó en las diferentes batallas y guerras . . . ?	relate
3	—No, no. Tengo un libro de referencia que (dar) toda clase de datos históricos y que (explicar) algo de la geografía, el gobierno, la religión y las costumbres de cada país.	da explica
4	—Pues, yo creo, profesor, que (ser) preciso que usted (ir) a una librería (tienda) donde venden libros en español.	es, vaya
5	El profesor le hace todas estas preguntas a su alumno porque él sospecha que Abelardo (tener) su copia del *Almanaque Mundial*, pero no quiere que el muchacho lo (saber).	tiene, sepa
6	Abelardo sabe que el profesor (tener) una copia del *Almanaque Mundial* porque lo ha visto muchas veces en su oficina y está sorprendido de que el profesor le (hacer) esas preguntas.	tiene haga
7	A Abelardo también le molesta mucho que el profesor (pensar) mal de sus alumnos.	piense

8   El profesor es muy estricto y no quiere que sus estudiantes (usar) sus libros   usen
sin pedirle permiso.

9   El profesor sigue pensando que Abelardo (saber) algo del *Almanaque*, pero   sabe
no quiere decírselo.

10   En ese momento, una alumna entró en la oficina con el almanaque del
profesor en la mano y le dijo: —No me (regañar (*scold*)), profesor, pero olvidé   regañe
devolverle (*return*) el libro que usted me prestó (*lent*) la semana pasada.

New Vocabulary

pañuelo	handkerchief	**velocímetro**	speedometer	**peor**	worse, worst
gallina	hen	**poner huevos**	to lay eggs	**mayor**	older, oldest
raíz (la)	root	**hondo, -a**	deep	**menor**	younger, youngest
cuadra	block (city)	**mejor**	better, best		(minor)

Words related to entertainment

diversiones	amusements, entertainment
divertir(se)	to amuse (have a good time)
pasear (ir de paseo)	to go for a walk
pasear en coche	to go for a ride in a car, drive
ir de caza (cazar)	to go hunting (hunt)
ir de pesca (pescar)	to go fishing (fish)
ir a un juego de pelota	to go to a ball game
ir de excursión	to go camping, on a picnic
esquiar (en (sobre) la nieve, en (sobre) el agua)	to ski (on the snow, to waterski)
patinar (en (sobre) el hielo, en ruedas)	to skate (on ice, to roller skate)
nadar en una piscina	to swim in a pool
bañarse en el mar (la playa)	to bathe in the ocean (at the beach)
montar a caballo	to ride horseback

"Dime con quién andas, y te diré quién eres."

"We are known by the company we keep." (Tell me with whom you go around, and I'll tell you who you are.)

Assignment 82

More on Comparisons

1   Write the comparative and superlative of "fast."   ▲

faster; fastest (Spanish has no suffix equivalent of "er" and "est.")

2   Spanish has just four irregular forms which have a fossil suffix ("*or*") which
is used in making comparisons. All four of these words have stems which are
completely different from the base of their matching positive forms. In this

they are like some English adjectives. The comparative and superlative forms that go with "good" are _____.   ▲

3   The Spanish word that translates both of these is _____.   ▲   better; best
4   The positive form that goes with *mejor* is _____.   ▲   *mejor*
5   The adverb which matches *bueno*, as used, for example, in the answer to   *bueno*
¿Cómo estás?, is _____.   ▲

   bien (The comparative form of *bien* is also *mejor: Habla mejor que yo.*)

6   The forms that translate "bad, worse, worst" are _____ and *peor*.   ▲
7   The adverbial form of *malo* is the same as the adjective minus the matching   *malo*
suffixes. It is _____.   ▲

   mal (The comparative form of *mal* is also *peor: Habla peor que yo.*)

8   In both English and Spanish the words for age and size are used almost interchangeably in talking about children. We may say, for example, that Mrs. Jones has six children and that the smallest (youngest) is Pearl.

   Spanish goes farther than English in confusing size and age. The standard word for "younger" and "youngest" is *menor*, but this same word may be used in place of *más pequeño* (smaller). To avoid unnecessary confusion, you will be asked in this course to use *menor* when talking of the age of people and *más pequeño* for size. The opposite of *más pequeño* is *más* _____.   ▲

9   Spanish may use *mayor* as the equivalent of *más grande* when talking of the   *grande*
size of a person. It also uses *mayor* to translate "older" and "oldest." Following the above decision, you are to use *más grande* for the size of people and *mayor* for age.

   The adjective *grande* also translates "great." When we talk about a great social problem, we are concerned with neither physical size nor age. Either *más grande* or *mayor* may be used. Thus, one translation for "My problems are smaller" is *Mis problemas son menores.* The other is _____.   ▲

   Mis problemas son más pequeños. (Also, *Mis problemas son menos grandes.*)

The Future

1   The compound form *hemos vendido* has two stems: _____.   ▲

   h; vend (In speech the stem of *haber* is lost.)

2   The *e* of *hemos* marks the tense, which is _____.   ▲
3   The *hemos* is Present. The participle *vendido* is perfect. When you put those   Present
two descriptive labels together you get the name of the compound *hemos vendido.*
It is _____.   ▲
4   At the moment of speaking you can say that an action is going on (*Vendemos*   present perfect
nuestra casa) or that the action has been completed (*Hemos vendido nuestra casa*).
You can also say that the action is anticipated, that is, predictable, but has not yet taken place: *Venderemos nuestra casa.* (We will sell our house.)

   Venderemos ends in the same two suffixes as *hemos* and *vendemos.* In *venderemos* the form to which the tense marker *e* and the subject suffix *mos* are attached is exactly like the form of the verb called the _____.   ▲

   infinitive

5 Historically the base form of *venderemos* is the infinitive and the *emos* is *hemos* with the useless *h* deleted. In fact, in Old Spanish, this form was written as two words: *vender hemos*. The future forms of *vender* are composed of the infinitive *vender* plus the first and second suffixes of the Present of *haber*. The stem *h* is not there in speech and is dropped in writing.

You have now to learn just one fact to be able to make up *all* the forms of the Future of *all* the regular verbs in the Spanish language. In all future forms the stress falls on the first suffix. When this does not happen according to rules of stress, this suffix must have an accent mark in writing.

In this and the next four frames you will find a form of the Present Perfect of *vender*. Write the matching future form of the verb.

Yo he vendido la casa. ▲

> *venderé* (According to rule the stress should fall on the second *e* (*vend**e**re*), so the accent mark is required to put the stress on the last *e*: *vend**e**ré*. The stress is kept on the first suffix of the auxiliary verb: *vender-hé* > *venderé*.)

6 Tú has vendido la casa. ▲
7 Usted ha vendido la casa. ▲   *venderás*
8 Ellos han vendido la casa. ▲   *venderá*
9 Nosotros hemos vendido la casa. ▲   *venderán*

> *venderemos* (This is the only form *not* requiring an accent mark.)

10 Copy the infinitives given and add the suffixes that match the subject:
tú te (bañar), ella (cocinar), nosotros (ir), ellos (proteger), usted (permitir). ▲

> *bañarás, cocinará, iremos, protegerán, permitirá*

11 Only eleven verbs are irregular in the Future. The first and second suffixes are *always* regular. There are two *i*-verbs and three *e*-verbs which replace the set vowel with *d* to get the future stem. Write the Future for the forms given:
yo (poner), ellos (salir), usted (tener), el carro (valer), el día (venir). ▲

> *pondré, saldrán, tendrá, valdrá, vendrá*

12 Four of the *e*-verbs that you already know simply drop the set vowel in the future stem. Write the future of the forms given: *hay (haber), yo (poder), tú (querer), nosotros (saber).* ▲

> *habrá, podré, querrás, sabremos*

13 There are two future forms which are based on ancient infinitive forms:
dir (decir) and *har (hacer)*. Write the *ellos* forms of the Future of these verbs. ▲   *dirán ; harán*

14 In this and the next eight frames, write the future form that corresponds to the one given. The second sentence in each frame is a response to the first. The irregular forms are marked by *.

¿Lo han leído ustedes? No, pero lo _____. ▲
15 ¿Lo escribiste? No, pero lo _____. ▲   *leeremos*
16 ¿Salían los niños? No, pero _____.* ▲   *escribiré*
17 ¿Se alegró ella? No, pero se _____. ▲   *saldrán*
18 ¿Vino el carpintero? No, pero _____.* ▲   *alegrará*
19 ¿Han visto ustedes esta película? No, pero la _____. ▲   *vendrá*
20 ¿Lo sabía ella? No, pero lo _____.* ▲   *veremos*
21 ¿Pediste agua? No, pero la _____. ▲   *sabrá*
22 ¿Ha escogido ella la más linda? No, pero la _____. ▲   *pediré*

     escogerá

 A/B

C/D

E/F

G

Summary

1   The future forms of all regular verbs are composed of the infinitive plus the first and second suffixes of the Present of *haber*.

2   In all future forms the stress falls on the first suffix.

3   Eleven verbs are irregular in the Future: *poner, salir, tener, valer, venir, haber, poder, querer, saber, decir,* and *hacer*.

Review of the Subjunctive

In your last Assignment you reviewed the forms of the present tense of the subjunctive mode. This part of your Assignment is a review of the cues which tell you when to use the subjunctive. In the five uses that you have studied, the subjunctive appears only in subjoined clauses. Of these five uses only one is like the English subjunctive (influencing). In four of the five uses you must choose between the subjunctive and the indicative. In one use (stimulus-response situations) normally only the subjunctive is used, so you do not have to worry about an indicative alternative.

The following generalizations apply to the verb in the subjoined clause.

The choice of mode is:

1a   subjunctive ——————— command.
1b   indicative ——— in reporting a ——— statement.

2a   subjunctive ——— attempts to influence ———
         when the main   an event.
2b   indicative ——— clause subject ——— expresses awareness of ———

3   subjunctive in a psychological stimulus-response situation.

4a   subjunctive ——————— uncertainty or disbelief.
         in declarative sentences
4b   indicative ——— after expressions of ——— certainty or belief.

5a   subjunctive ——— a non-experienced ———
         to describe   entity.
5b   indicative ——— an experienced ———

Your competence in using the subjunctive is essentially the consequence of your ability to recognize the appropriate cues. In the following several frames read the cues, decide whether indicative or subjunctive would be used in a subjoined clause, then refer to the above categories and indicate the number (and letter except for 3) of the generalization that applies.

1   Todos creemos que . . .   ▲

indicative, 4b

2 Estamos muy alegres de que . . . ▲

3 Tenemos ganas de hallar un caballo que . . . ▲ subjunctive, 3

4 Según la ley es necesario que . . . ▲ subjunctive, 5a

5 El director nos dice que . . . ▲ subjunctive, 2a

subjunctive or indicative, 1a or 1b

6 No hay nadie aquí que . . . ▲

7 Ellos se han enojado de que . . . ▲ subjunctive, 5a

8 Aunque no me lo crees, es muy dudoso que . . . ▲ subjunctive, 3

9 Quiero que hables con mi amigo, un señor que . . . ▲ subjunctive, 4a

10 Pues, es evidente que las circunstancias demandan que . . . ▲ indicative, 5b

11 Sí, pero yo estoy seguro de que . . . ▲ subjunctive, 2a

12 Algún día yo quiero conocer una mujer que . . . ▲ indicative, 4b

13 Muy pronto vas a ver que . . . ▲ subjunctive, 5a

14 It is very important, now, to remember that the cues which tell you to choose indicative, 2b
between the indicative and subjunctive can be verbalized in many different
ways. *Estoy muy cierto* cues the indicative just as well as *creo*. *María tiene miedo de*,
María teme, and *María tiene temor* (fear) *de* all cue the _____ mode in the subjoined clause. ▲

15 Write the proper form of the indicated infinitives in this and the next six subjunctive
frames.

No existe la posibilidad de que *haber* un hombre que *tener* trescientos años. ▲

16 Ella sabe que usted *tener* un amigo que *escribir* novelas. ▲ *haya; tenga*

17 Se pone enojada de que no la *invitar* (Vd.) a visitarlo. ▲ *tiene; escribe*

18 Yo siento, en realidad, yo lamento mucho que no *haber* nadie que *querer* *invite*
ayudarte. ▲

19 Yo creo que algún día los astrónomos *ir* a descubrir un planeta que *tener* *haya; quiera*
vida. ▲

20 Hombre, es importante que tú *creer* que ella *poder* hacerlo. ▲ *van; tenga*

21 Hijo, yo siento mucho que tu nueva esposa *hacer* que tú *poner* a los niños en *creas, puede*
ese colegio. ▲

haga, pongas

Self-Correcting Exercises

A *Subjunctive versus Indicative:* Write the appropriate present subjunctive or
indicative form of each infinitive in parentheses.

1 ¿Sabes que esta tarde los miembros de la expedición (ir) a salir en canoas van
hacia el interior de la selva? Ellos quieren hacer un estudio de las tribus primitivas que (vivir) allí. viven

2 Yo pienso mucho en los jóvenes que (morir) en la guerra y no quiero que mueren
mis compañeros (ir) a pelear. vayan

3 Ella teme que algún día tú (tener) que participar en alguna batalla. tengas

4 Creo que esa nación (necesitar) un jefe de gobierno que (saber) com- necesita, sepa
prender mejor los problemas sociales y económicos del pueblo.

5 Dicen que las guerrillas (pelear) ferozmente y que el ejército no (ser) tan pelean, es
fuerte y poderoso como nosotros creemos.

6 Me han dicho que en esos ríos (haber) pirañas, unos peces feroces que (poder) devorar a cualquier (*any*) animal grande.

7 Estoy segura de que la lucha (ir) a ser muy sangrienta.

8 Me alegro mucho de que tú no (haber) tenido que matar a nadie.

9 Tú sabes que a mí no me (gustar) la violencia.

10 Sí, yo sé que tú no deseas que las personas inocentes (sufrir).

11 Yo estoy segura de que no (existir) ningún problema en el mundo que no se (poder) resolver sin ejércitos y batallas.

12 Yo tengo mis dudas. Ojalá que (ser) verdad lo que tú dices.

13 Esperamos que todos los prisioneros de guerra (volver) pronto a sus respectivos países.

14 Ojalá que no (morir) mucha gente en ese conflicto.

	hay
	pueden
	va
	hayas
	gusta
	sufran
	existe
	pueda
	sea
	vuelvan
	muera

B *Preterit versus Imperfect:* After reading what each character says, decide whether the situation calls for the Preterit or the Imperfect. Then write the correct form.

Conversación entre Oscar y su mamá

Mamá: Veo que esta mañana (tú) *recibir* **1** carta de tu primo Danielito.

Oscar: ¡Te he dicho que no le llames Danielito! Recuerda que cuando tú y yo *estar* **2** en su casa la última vez, él nos *decir* **3** que no le *gustar* **4** que tú le llames siempre Danielito.

Mamá: Está bien, hijo. ¿Qué cuenta Daniel en la carta?

Oscar: Dice que (él) le *comprar* **5** una motocicleta muy buena a un amigo.

Mamá: ¿Y no te dice que el primer día que la llevó al colegio (él) *tener* **6** un problema con la policía? Anoche yo *hablar* **7** con tus tíos por teléfono y ellos me *decir* **8** que *estar* **9** muy disgustados con el problema de la motocicleta y que no le *ir* **10** a dejar que la lleve al colegio por un mes.

Oscar: Sí, ya sé. Daniel me lo contó todo en la carta. El pobre Daniel no tuvo la culpa de lo que *pasar* **11**.

Mamá: ¿Cómo es eso? Tu tía me dijo que él *ir* **12** por la Avenida Central cuando le detuvo un policía porque pasó una luz que *estar* **13** roja. ¿Vas a decirme que la culpa es de tus tíos? ¿Del policía?

Oscar: Mira, mamá. La luz cambió en el momento en que él pasaba y Daniel no *poder* **14** parar (*to stop*) porque *haber* **15** mucho tráfico.

Mamá: Cuando el policía le *pedir* **16** la licencia, Daniel no la *llevar* **17** en la cartera. Dime quién tiene la culpa de eso.

Oscar: Es que la *haber* **18** olvidado en los pantalones que se había quitado la noche anterior. Esas cosas le pasan a todo el mundo.

Mamá: ¿Sabes cuánto *tener* **19** que pagar sus padres? ¡Diez dólares! Daniel *gastar* (*to spend*) **20** todo su dinero en la motocicleta y en el momento de pagar la multa (*fine*) él no *tener* **21** ni un centavo.

Oscar: Pues yo sigo creyendo que un mes sin montar motocicleta es demasiado. Dice Daniel que *ir* **22** a venderla y que ahora él *pensar* **23** empezar a ahorrar (*to save*) dinero para comprarse un carro.

Mamá: Pues, no creo que esa sea una solución muy buena. Me parece que eso es "salir de Guatemala para entrar en Guatepeor" (*From bad to worse*). Espero que sus padres no se lo permitan.

1	recibiste
2	estuvimos
3	dijo
4	gustaba
5	compró
6	tuvo
7	hablé
8	dijeron
9	estaban
10	iban
11	pasó
12	iba
13	estaba
14	pudo
15	había
16	pidió
17	llevaba
18	había
19	tuvieron
20	gastó
21	tenía
22	iba
23	pensaba

C *Fórmulas de cortesía:* Think of a logical response for each of the following expressions that might be said to you by a native speaker of Spanish.

1	No te molestes.	No es molestia ninguna.
2	Con permiso.	Usted lo tiene. *Or* Sí, cómo no.
3	Quiero presentarle al señor Fulano.	Mucho gusto.
4	Buen provecho.	Gracias.
5	¿Cómo te va?	Bien . . . , gracias.

¿Cómo se dice en español . . . ?

6	Same here.	Igualmente.
7	Congratulations!	¡ Felicidades !
8	What did you say?	¿Cómo ?
9	What a pity!	¡ Qué lástima !
10	How wonderful!	¡ Qué formidable !

New Vocabulary

quehaceres de la casa	household chores		**mercado**	market
cuidar a los niños	to take care of the children		**mariposa**	butterfly
sacudir los muebles	to dust the furniture		**ala**	wing
recoger las cosas	to pick up things		**sino**	but
tender (ie) la ropa	to hang clothes up (to dry)		**Sr.**	Mr.
colgar (ue) la ropa	to hang clothes up (in a closet)		**Sra.**	Mrs.
satélite	satellite		**Srta.**	Miss
sabio, -a	wise			

Assignment 83

Comparison of Equality

1 Compare these four sentences:

*Nueva York es **más** famosa **que** Londres.*   New York is **more** famous **than** London.

*Nueva York es **tan** famosa **como** Londres.*   New York is **as** famous **as** London.

*Manuela es **menos** interesante **que** Pepita.*   Manuela is **less** interesting **than** Pepita.

*Manuela es **tan** interesante **como** Pepita.*   Manuela is **as** interesting **as** Pepita.

Translate: He is as tall as she. ▲

Él es tan alto como ella.

2 The same words in both languages are used when two events are compared.
Translate the indicated words: She walks **more** rapidly **than** he. ▲

Ella camina (anda) **más** *rápidamente* **que** *él.*

3 Rewrite the indicated words to show equality. ▲

Ella camina **tan** *rápidamente* **como** *él.*

4 When English makes a comparison of inequality and uses the suffix "er,"
this suffix is dropped and replaced by "as" in a comparison of equality: (1) I
am tired**er than** you. (2) I am **as** tired **as** you. Translate the indicated words. ▲

Estoy **más** *cansado* **que** *usted :* *Estoy* **tan** *cansado* **como** *usted.*

5 The Spanish equivalent of "as much" is *tanto*. Translate: I work as much
as you. ▲

Trabajo tanto como usted (tú).

6 A comparison may be made between the quantity or number of an entity
which one person has, produces, writes, *etc.*, and the quantity or number that
another person has, produces, *etc.*

Inequality: I have **more** money **than** you. (*usted*)

Equality: I have **as much** money **as** you.

Spanish uses the same words in these cases as above. Translate the indicated
words in these two sentences. ▲

Tengo **más** *dinero* **que** *usted;* *Tengo* **tanto** *dinero* **como** *usted.*

7 In the above usage *tanto* is treated as an adjective. How will you translate
"as much" when you translate "I have as much sand as you" (*tú*)? Remember:
"sand" is **la** *arena*. ▲

Tengo **tanta** *arena como tú.*

8 The form *menos*, when used as an adjective, does not match its noun either
in terms of the final phoneme or number. Translate: I have **less** sand **than**
you. ▲

Tengo **menos** *arena* **que** *tú.*

9 When the noun in a comparison stands for a measure entity (money, sand,
butter, *etc.*) English uses "more" or "less" in comparisons of inequality and
"as much" in comparisons of equality. When the noun stands for a count
entity, "much" is frequently replaced by "many." Compare:

I have as **much** butter as you.

I have as **many** books as you.

In many cases only "many" may be used. Spanish, in contrast, uses only the
singular of *tanto* with a measure entity and the plural with count entities.
Translate the indicated words: I read *more* books *than* you; I read *as many*
books *as* you. ▲

Leo **más** *libros* **que** *tú;* *Leo* **tantos** *libros* **como** *tú.*

10 In this and the next four frames translate the indicated words.
There are *more* nails (*clavos*) in this box *than* in that one. ▲

11 There should be *as many* nails in this box *as* that one. ▲ | *más ; que*
12 She is *as* thin *as* Pilar. ▲ | *tantos ; como*
13 Does she have *as much* money *as* he? ▲ | *tan ; como*
14 I work *less than* you. ▲ | *tanto ; como*

menos que

15 When any form of *tanto* is used as an adjective the noun may be deleted (once it has been mentioned) and the forms of *tanto* become an adjectival residual:

> Speaker 1: *¿Tiene Genoveva tantas hermanas como yo?*
> Speaker 2: *Sí, tiene _____ como tú.* ▲

tantas

Hints for Listening and Reading Comprehension

1 Find out as quickly as possible *what* is being talked about: the subject of discourse. This helps you establish a chain of associations which makes it easier to remember more of the facts. Knowing the subject of discourse, in addition, is frequently the only way of defining ambiguous or unknown words. Compare:

(1) The subject of discourse is horses: Margaret has just bought a bay.
(2) The subject of discourse is sailing: Margaret fell into the bay.

In which sentence does "bay" stand for a color? ▲

Margaret has just bought a bay.

2 Listen for all the key words which are closely linked to what is being talked about. Look for the key words in this passage.

En el año mil novecientos treinta y seis la Guerra Civil de España empezó.
Los miembros de la Falange, un partido político, querían destruir la República.

Is *año* a key word? ▲

no (*En 1936* contains all the really meaningful information of the first phrase.)

3 Try to hang on to the key words as though they were in a telegram. Copy the following and leave out everything not needed to get the basic message.

La hija del Sr. Figueroa se puso enferma anoche y tuvieron que llevarla al hospital. La pobre gritaba cuando entró el médico en su cuarto. ▲

You should have something like this: *Hija Figueroa enferma anoche, llevarla hospital, Gritaba entró médico.*

4 Identify the key concepts: who, what, when, where, how, and why. Read this passage.

Miguel quería ser marinero. Le fascinaba la vida de los marineros. Viajan por todo el mundo. Visitan ciudades lejanas y misteriosas como Hong Kong, Singapur y Manila. Llegan a conocer países que para muchos existen solamente en los libros de geografía.

Why did Miguel want to be a sailor? ▲

5 You are certain to miss something more important if you stop to concentrate on the meaning of a new word. Keep listening for everything you *can* understand and don't worry about the words you miss. Here is a passage with a lot of new words. Read it twice, and see how much more meaning you pick up on the second reading.

Según las teorías de la estrategia militar, un ejército que está en batalla siempre tiene que mantener la capacidad de defenderse. También, por supuesto, y mucho más importante, tiene que estar preparado para montar

to travel

un ataque cuando se presenta el momento propicio para atacar al enemigo. El general que no entiende estas reglas fundamentales de la guerra, que olvida que la teoría es la base de la práctica, nunca va a salir triunfante de la batalla. En la historia de las guerras se puede observar que la estrategia militar muchas veces ha ganado más batallas que los soldados. Es mucho más importante saber pelear. En muchas batallas un ejército pequeño puede vencer a un ejército grande si el general sabe más del arte de la guerra que el general enemigo.

Now, let's see if you can answer *sí* or *no* to these sentences.
El ejército que no puede defenderse va a vencer. ▲

6 ¿Vencerá el general que no sabe mucho de la estrategia militar? ▲   *no*

7 Es mejor muchas veces saber más del arte de la guerra que tener un ejército grande. ▲   *no*

8 Un ejército no puede vencer al enemigo si no puede montar un ataque. ▲   *sí*

9 Los generales aprenden las reglas fundamentales de la guerra en los libros de estrategia. ▲   *sí*

10 Hay una diferencia entre saber la teoría y saber aplicarla. ▲   *sí*

                                                                      sí

Practice with the Forms and Uses of the Future

1 The base or stem of the Future of all regular verbs is the _____ of the verb. ▲

2 The first and second suffix of all future forms (either regular or irregular) are exactly the same as those of the _____ of the auxiliary verb *haber*. ▲   infinitive

3 In speech the stress falls on the syllable which contains the vowel of the _____ suffix. ▲   present indicative

4 In writing this vowel has an accent mark in all forms except the one whose second suffix is _____. ▲   first

5 In this and the next nine frames you will see the Present Perfect of a verb in a sentence. Read the sentence aloud and then say it in the Future: *He ido a un juego de pelota.* ▲   *mos*

6 Hemos paseado muchas veces por el parque. ▲   *Iré*

7 Ellos han esquiado en las montañas. ▲   *Pasearemos*

8 ¿Has patinado sobre el hielo? ▲   *esquiarán*

9 No, he patinado en ruedas. ▲   *Patinarás*

10 Él ha nadado en esta piscina. ▲   *patinaré*

11 ¡Vd. no ha montado a caballo nunca! ▲   *nadará*

12 Vds. han esquiado sobre el agua. ▲   *montará*

13 No me he bañado en la playa nunca. ▲   *esquiarán*

14 Han ido de excursión a la selva. ▲   *bañaré*

15 In order to speak and write Spanish well you must be able to instantly change any verb form into the Future. In this and the next frame you will see a subject and a verb form which has an irregularity either in form or spelling. Write the future equivalent: *tú te sientas; ellos se van; yo crucé.* ▲   *Irán*

sentarás; irán; cruzaré

16 no rías; ustedes consiguieron; no escoges   ▲

reirás; conseguirán; escogerás

17 The old infinitive of *decir* and *hacer* used in the Future are _____.   ▲

18 In this and the next two frames say aloud the form of the Future that *dir; har*
corresponds to the form given: *había*   ▲

habrá (You delete the class vowel of *haber* > *habr.*)

19 pusiste   ▲

pondrás (You replace the class vowel with *d*: *poner* > *pondr.*)

20 puedo; salgamos; quería; tuvieron; supiste; vale; vino   ▲

podré; saldremos; querrá (or *querré*); *tendrán; sabrás; valdrá; vendrá*

Practice with Comparisons

In this part you are going to see in each frame a Spanish sentence with two
omissions. In the first space there will be a math symbol.

+   means a comparison of inequality (superiority).

−   means a comparison of inequality (inferiority).

=   means a comparison of equality.

Say each sentence aloud and fill in the missing words.

1 Un caballo puede correr + rápidamente _____ un hombre.   ▲

2 El Salvador es − grande _____ México.   ▲   *más; que*

3 Yo duermo = _____ Vd.   ▲   *menos; que*

4 ¿Tiene Guatemala = ciudades _____ Panamá?   ▲   *tanto como*

5 Las montañas de México son + altas _____ las de California.   ▲   *tantas; como*

6 Los negros son = inteligentes _____ los blancos.   ▲   *más; que*

7 Hay + indios en Bolivia _____ blancos.   ▲   *tan; como*

8 Lope de Vega escribió = libros _____ Shakespeare.   ▲   *más; que*

9 No hay un español que tenga = dinero _____ Rockefeller.   ▲   *tantos; como*

10 La gente pobre de Sud América tiene − dinero _____ los pobres de los   *tanto; como*
Estados Unidos.   ▲

11 No hay = arena en esta playa _____ en aquella.   ▲   *menos; que*

12 Los colombianos hablan español = bien _____ los españoles.   ▲   *tanta; como*

13 La gente del campo, los campesinos, trabajan = horas cada día _____   *tan; como*
los trabajadores de las ciudades.   ▲

14 Si Vd. no ha cometido ningún error en este ejercicio, ya sabe = _____ un   *tantas; como*
español sobre cómo hacer comparaciones en español.   ▲

tanto como

When a Spanish speaker joins a group of people at a table in a café or at a party, he
shakes hands with each individual and greets each one personally. He also shakes
hands with everyone when he leaves the group. Because of this many Spanish speakers
consider Americans impolite because they often just say "Hello" or "Good-bye" to a
group and do not always shake everyone's hand.

Self-Correcting Exercises

A *Vocabulary Review:* Match the two columns.

1	*rueda*	**a**	broom	1	d
2	*jefe*	**b**	camping	2	p
3	*pesca*	**c**	handkerchief	3	j
4	*escoba*	**d**	wheel	4	a
5	*raíz*	**e**	ball	5	k
6	*pañuelo*	**f**	heart	6	c
7	*pesadilla*	**g**	hunting	7	o
8	*de excursión*	**h**	ice	8	b
9	*pelota*	**i**	danger	9	e
10	*trozo*	**j**	fishing	10	n
11	*hielo*	**k**	root	11	h
12	*cuadro*	**l**	picture	12	l
13	*corazón*	**m**	army	13	f
14	*peligro*	**n**	piece	14	i
		o	nightmare		
		p	chief, boss		

B *Refranes:* Say aloud the Spanish equivalent of each proverb.

1	You are known by the company you keep.	*Dime con quién andas, y te diré quién eres.*
2	A chip off the old block.	*De tal palo, tal astilla.*
3	Practice makes perfect.	*El ejercicio hace maestro.*
4	Do good no matter for whom.	*Haz bien y no mires a quién.*
5	If the shoe fits, wear it.	*Si le viene el saco, póngaselo.*
6	Listen, or your tongue will make you deaf.	*Escucha, o tu lengua te hará sordo.*

C *Future:* Write the combinations using the future form of the verb.

Ejemplo: 131 = Yo lo sabré la próxima semana.

1	Yo	1	salir	1	la próxima semana.
2	Tú y yo	2	venir	2	inmediatamente.
3	Vds.	3	saberlo	3	a las diez menos cuarto.
4	Tú	4	ir de pesca	4	por fin.
5	Ud.	5	hacer las camas	5	muy temprano por la mañana.

1)	225	Tú y yo vendremos muy temprano por la mañana.
2)	524	Ud. vendrá por fin.
3)	232	Tú y yo lo sabremos inmediatamente.
4)	145	Yo iré de pesca muy temprano por la mañana.
5)	552	Ud. hará las camas inmediatamente.
6)	111	Yo saldré la próxima semana.
7)	151	Yo haré las camas la próxima semana.
8)	333	Uds. lo sabrán a las diez menos cuarto.
9)	544	Ud. irá de pesca por fin.

10)	413	Tú saldrás a las diez menos cuarto.
11)	252	Tú y yo haremos las camas inmediatamente.
12)	321	Uds. vendrán la próxima semana.
13)	445	Tú irás de pesca muy temprano por la mañana.
14)	212	Tú y yo saldremos inmediatamente.
15)	431	Tú lo sabrás la próxima semana.

D *Future:* Ask and answer these questions aloud. The suggested answers on the right should be changed to fit your own personal situation.

1 ¿A qué hora saldrás del trabajo hoy?

Creo que saldré a las nueve.

2 ¿Te levantarás temprano, o tarde el sábado?

Creo que me levantaré tarde.

3 ¿Comerán tú y tu familia en la cafetería, o en un restaurante?

Comeremos en un restaurante.

4 ¿Vendrá alguien a visitarle esta semana?

Creo que no vendrá nadie.

5 ¿Tendrás mucha responsabilidad en el nuevo trabajo?

Sí, tendré una responsabilidad tremenda, pero ganaré buen sueldo (*salary*).

6 ¿Cuándo comprarán Uds. una alfombra nueva para su cuarto?

Nosotros no compraremos ninguna alfombra por largo tiempo.

7 ¿Crees que habrá paz, o guerra en los próximos años?

Yo soy muy optimista. Creo que habrá paz. Por lo menos así lo espero.

8 ¿Cuándo será el próximo juego de pelota?

Será pronto, pero a mí no me interesan los juegos de pelota.

9 ¿Sabe Ud. de memoria un refrán que usa el futuro de "decir"?

Sí lo sé. Es "Dime con quién andas, y te diré quién eres."

10 ¿Recuerda Ud. un refrán que usa el futuro del verbo "hacer"?

Sí, lo recuerdo. Es "Escucha, o tu lengua te hará sordo."

New Vocabulary

un rato	a while	**regar (ie) las flores**	to water the flowers
placer	pleasure	**sacar la basura**	to take out the trash (garbage)
oveja	sheep	**hacer los mandados**	to run errands
pastor	shepherd	**hacer las compras**	to do the shopping
agradable	pleasant, agreeable	**escuchar**	to listen
sordo, -a	deaf	**tan . . . como**	as . . . as
cortar la hierba	to mow the lawn	**tanto . . . como**	as much . . . as

Adverbial conjunctions:

cuando	when	**para que**	
mientras (que)	while	**de manera que**	
después (de) que	after	**de modo que**	so that, in order that
antes (de) que	before	**con tal (de) que**	provided that
hasta que	until	**sin que**	without
tan pronto como		**a menos que**	unless
en cuanto	as soon as	**siempre que**	whenever
luego que			

—**Mil gracias por todo. Pasamos un rato muy agradable.**
—**Ha sido un placer.**

"**Escucha, o tu lengua te hará sordo.**"

—Thanks a lot for everything. We had a very pleasant time.
—It has been a pleasure.

"Listen, or your tongue will make you deaf."

Assignment 84

Getting Ready for a Quiz on the Subjunctive

In your next class session you are to be given a quiz that provides two kinds of information concerning your knowledge about the present subjunctive: (1) whether you know the morphology and (2) whether you know when to use it. The following frames review usage and give you practice in both usage and morphology. In each problem you are to write the appropriate form of the indicated infinitive. The quiz consists of similar problems, except that in some of them you are given constructions involving with-verb pronouns for you to place. This is not evaluated on the quiz.

1 You have studied five uses of the subjunctive. (1) The subject of the main verb or the speaker of an impersonal clause (*Es importante*) attempts to influence the action of the subject of the subjoined verb:
Jesús no permitirá que su esposa *fumar* cigarrillos. ▲

2 Yo observo que ella *haber* conseguido el oro. ▲

3 Ella no quiere que nosotros *casarse*. ▲

4 (2) Either the indicative or the subjunctive may be used in an adjectival clause. The choice depends on whether the speaker or the doer can or cannot call to mind something which can be described by the clause:
No hay hombre que *tener* tres brazos. ▲

5 Tengo una cuñada que *cantar* muy bien. ▲

6 (3) In indirect discourse when repeating a command, the subjunctive is used; in repeating indicative forms, the indicative is used:
Me grita que la casa *quemarse*. ▲

7 —No te vayas, hombre.
—¿Qué me dices?
—Te digo que no *irse*. ▲

8 (4) You are to use the subjunctive when, in the opinion of the subject or speaker of the main clause, there is some doubt or unlikelihood that the action of the subjoined clause has taken place, is going on, or will happen:
He believes that it will rain.   Él cree que *llover*. ▲

9 Pero nosotros dudamos que *llover*. ▲

10 (5) In a stimulus-response situation, one action (the stimulus) produces the reaction (response) of some other entity. You are to use the subjunctive in the subjoined clause:

fume
ha
nos casemos

tenga
canta

se quema

te vayas

lloverá
llueva

Me alegro de que ella *haber* olvidado los huevos.   ▲
11 Ella se pone celosa de que él *hablar* con otras chicas.   ▲
12 Los soldados temen que el enemigo *matarlos*.   ▲

haya
hable
los mate

The Subjunctive in Adverbial Clauses of Order Relationship

The sixth use of the subjunctive presented below will not appear on the quiz. However, you will soon see how it will improve your understanding of the subjunctive as a whole because of its logical extension of what you have already learned.

There are three common ways of answering the questions *¿Cuándo lo hacen ellos?* and *¿Cuándo lo harán ellos?* (1) By giving the point in clock time at which the action is initiated or terminated: *A las dos.* (2) By stating the interval of time during which the action takes place: *Por la tarde, El sábado, En el verano, etc.* (3) By setting the action in an order relationship to another event. This Assignment is concerned with what happens when the third alternative is used.

1   Since time may be diagrammed as a straight line and all events can be plotted on this line, there are only three possible order relationships between two events:

(1) The two events may be simultaneous in part or in whole: They do it *when* we are sleeping. (2) One event happens *before* the other: They do it *before* we sleep. (3) One event happens *after* the other: They do it *after* we sleep.

Do these three examples answer the question that asks about (a) habitual or customary behavior (*¿Cuándo lo hacen?*) or (b) behavior yet to occur (*¿Cuándo lo harán?*)?   ▲

habitual or customary behavior

2   Is the behavior spoken of in these examples experienced already or not yet experienced by the speaker?   ▲

3   Here are the Spanish translations of the three examples: experienced already

(1)   Lo hacen cuando dormimos.
(2)   Lo hacen antes de que durmamos.
(3)   Lo hacen después de que dormimos.

Spanish, like English, uses the indicative in the adverbial clause for behavior that has already been experienced except after one adverbial connecting phrase, which requires the subjunctive. Which of these adverbial connectors is that one? *cuando, antes de que, después de que*   ▲

antes de que (Occasionally you may hear a native speaker follow this with the indicative, but you always are to use the subjunctive, whether or not the behavior has been experienced.)

4   From what you already know about experience and non-experience, which mode—indicative or subjunctive—would you guess to be used in adverbial clauses containing behavior that has not yet been experienced?   ▲

You, no doubt, said the subjunctive, and you are correct. Now let's see how

5   Copy only the following sentence that talks about behavior that has <u>not</u> yet   this works.
been experienced and change the indicated infinitive to thé appropriate form.

Ella me ayuda cuando *estar* descansada.

Ella me ayudará cuando *estar* descansada.   ▲

Ella me ayudará cuando esté descansada. (She will help me when she is rested. For this particular event her being rested has not yet occurred, so it could not have been experienced.)

6   You are learning two rules, and one of them has two parts. Let's see how
well you can apply them. Change the indicated infinitives to the appropriate
verb forms.

Ellos se desayunan antes de que *llegar* la leche.

El soldado siempre dispara cuando *ver* al enemigo.

Saldremos de aquí tan pronto como el doctor nos *dar* permiso.   ▲

llegue (Whether or not the behavior has been experienced, the subjunctive is always used after *antes de que*) ; *ve* (indicative for customary behavior, experienced) ; *dé* (subjunctive for behavior not yet experienced)

7   You are learning several adverbial connectors. Here is some useful information about them.

(1)   *Hasta, siempre* (whenever), *luego, antes de* and *después de* always take *que*.

(2)   *Cuando, en cuanto, tan pronto como*, and *mientras* do not take *que*.

So you won't be surprised when you run into them, you should know that *antes*
and *después* may be used without the *de* and *mientras* may sometimes be used
with *que*.

Because there are only three ordinal relationships but several adverbial connectors, some of these connectors must be different ways of saying the same
thing. Intuitively in English you already know that this is so. Let's see you
apply what you already know to Spanish. Make the first clause of this sentence
negative and substitute a different adverbial connector so that it still conveys
the same message.

Los niños saldrán después de que su mamá les dé permiso.   ▲

Los niños no saldrán hasta que (or *antes de que*) *su mamá les dé permiso.*

8   Do the same by making this first clause affirmative.

La señora no preparará la comida hasta que vengan los invitados.   ▲

La señora preparará la comida cuando (luego que, tan pronto como, en cuanto, or *después de que) vengan los invitados.*

9   In this and the remaining frames translate only the indicated words: She
regularly becomes jealous *when he looks* at Josefina.   ▲

10   He will become furious *when he hears* this.   ▲   *cuando mira*

11   The dog begins to bark *as soon as he sees* me.   ▲   *cuando oiga*

tan pronto como (en cuanto, luego que), ve

12   I will not send more *until they pay* me.   ▲

13   We always do it *while she is* here.   ▲   *hasta que, paguen*

14   Will he do it *while she sweeps* the room?   ▲   ▲   *mientras, está*

15   I will use the subjunctive *whenever it is* necessary.   ▲   ▲   *mientras, barra*

siempre que sea

A/B

C/D

CUANDO VIAJA, SIEMPRE LLEVA SÓLO DOS CARTERAS

SIGA ESPIÁNDOMELO. UN DÍA, CUANDO VIAJE, LLEVARÁ LA CAJA

E/F

HIJO, JUÉGALA DONDE QUEDA

PAPÁ, AHORA JUÉGALA TÚ DONDE QUEDE

G/H

NO TRABAJAN HASTA QUE SE PONE CLARO EL CIELO

NO TRABAJARÁN HASTA QUE SE PONGA CLARO EL CIELO

I/J

HA COLECCIONADO MARIPOSAS
QUE TIENEN ALAS ROJAS

BUSCA MARIPOSAS
QUE TENGAN ALAS AZULES

Summary

1 *Antes* and *después* may take *de* and must take *que*.

2 *Hasta*, *luego*, and *siempre* require *que*.

3 *Cuando*, *en cuanto*, *mientras*, and *tan pronto como* are used alone.

4 When the two events are recalled, you use the indicative for both verbs, except after *antes* (*de*) *que*.

5 When the two events are anticipated, the verb in the adverbial clause is in the present subjunctive. The main verb may be in the Future or in any form that indicates anticipation, for example: *Vamos a hacerlo tan pronto como ellos lleguen* or *Se casan luego que encuentren un apartamento.*

Learning New Vocabulary

This part of your assignment deals with the set of words for materials, both natural and manufactured, and is intended to help you improve your study habits. There are 12 words you have met before and 15 new ones.

1 Read the following passage and try to identify the meaning of each indicated word immediately on seeing it.

There are two precious *metales* which are used in coins. The most precious is *oro*; the other is *plata*. The very abundant *metal* used to make heavy cooking pots and frying pans is *hierro*. The *hierro* is a rather soft metal, but when it is refined and processed properly it turns into an extremely hard *metal* called *acero*. The cans in which fruit comes are made of thin sheets of *acero* which is covered with *lata*.

If you missed a word, don't worry. Go on to frame 2 and try to guess the meaning of the indicated words.

2 A house is built of many *materiales*. The building code usually requires that the foundation be made of *cemento*. The word *cemento* has two meanings. It may stand for the powdery *material* which is mixed with water, *arena*, and crushed *piedra* to make concrete or *cemento*. Once the foundation of a house is laid the builder nails together the frame. The frame is usually made of *madera* and the most commonly used *madera* is *pino*. Once the frame is completed the outside walls may be faced with small blocks of baked clay called *ladrillos*. They are held together with a mortar which is also made with *cemento*. In the old days, and infrequently now, these *ladrillos* were made of a special kind of clay called *adobe*. When the structural part of the house is finished, the windows are set in. The frames of the windows are made either of *metal* or of *madera*. The part you see through is always made of *cristal*. The inside walls may be painted or covered with *papel*. The curtains in the bathroom and kitchen are often made of *plástico*, but the ones in the living room are usually made of *tela*. One of the most commonly used *materiales* in making *tela* comes from a *planta* which is widely grown in the South. The white fibers of this plant, the plant itself, and the *tela* made of the fibers are all called *algodón*.

The doors of most houses are made of *madera*. To keep them from bumping into the walls door-stops are installed. A door-stop is a round piece of *hierro* with a screw on one end and a small, button-like cap on the other to keep the *hierro* from marking up the door. This cap may be made of a *plástico* or of the same *material* used in automobile tires, that is, *goma*.

Go on to frame 3.

3 There are many useful *materiales* which come from *animales*. Every *animal* is completely covered with a protective layer of *piel*. This *piel* may have hairs all over it. When the *piel* of a cow is removed and tanned, it becomes the *cuero* of which shoes and belts are made. The flesh of the cow goes to the store as meat and the skeleton, which is made of *hueso*, is ground up to be used in dog food or as fertilizer. The *piel* of some *animales* is not covered with hairs. The *piel* of a sheep, for example, is covered with *lana* which is used to make sweaters and the *tela* for warm clothing. There is another very fine and expensive *tela* which is made of the tiny threads of material produced by an Oriental worm. This *tela* is *seda*. When *seda* is shipped from the Orient it is often packed in boxes made of a very thick paper called *cartón*.

Below are all the words whose meaning you were supposed to guess from context. Cover the English column and check to see whether you guessed them all correctly. If you missed a word, copy both the Spanish and the English, then say them aloud. Then cover the Spanish and see if you can say each matching word aloud.

metal	metal	*cristal*	glass
oro	gold	*papel*	paper
plata	silver	*plástico*	plastic
hierro	iron	*tela*	cloth
acero	steel	*planta*	plant
lata	tin	*algodón*	cotton
material	material	*goma*	rubber
cemento	cement	*piel (la)*	skin (hide)
arena	sand	*cuero*	leather
piedra	stone	*hueso*	bone

madera	wood	*lana*	wool
pino	pine	*seda*	silk
ladrillo	brick	*cartón*	cardboard
adobe	adobe		

Go do anything you like now for fifteen minutes. Then come back and do frame 4.

4 Here are all the words you should now be able to recognize on sight. You have seen them before, but have not had much practice with them. Check them and say them aloud.

<u>metal</u>	<u>material</u>		<u>planta</u>	<u>animal</u>	<u>tela</u>
oro	piedra	cristal	pino		seda
plata	arena	plástico			lana
	adobe	papel			algodón
	cemento				

Go through the following sentences rapidly. See if you can immediately get the meaning of the indicated words. If you cannot recall the meaning of a word just keep going.

Locomotives used to be called iron horses because they were made of *hierro*.

The metal, *hierro*, is too soft to be used in the frame and body of a car. They are made of *acero*.

People think that a tin can is made of tin. Actually what is called a tin can is made of a thin sheet of *acero* which is coated with *lata*.

The *material* inside the bark of a tree is called *madera*.

One of the most common conifers, or cone-bearing trees, is the *pino*.

When clay is pressed into small blocks and baked in a furnace you get *ladrillos*.

The pages of this book are made of *papel*. Its covers are made of thick *cartón* which is covered with *tela*.

Expensive wine glasses are made of fine *cristal*.

In many parts of Latin America people live in *adobe* houses.

When you get a sunburn your *piel* turns red.

Motorcycle policemen wear boots made of *cuero*.

George fell down and broke a *hueso* in his leg.

A rubber band is made of *goma*.

A worm produces the material for the very fine *tela* called *seda*.

Sheep provide the material for the *tela* called *lana*. (The oil that comes from the *lana* of sheep is called *lano*lin.)

A cotton sheet is made of *algodón*.

Go back to frame 4 and study the list for two minutes; after that, do whatever you want to for fifteen minutes and then come back and start with frame 5.

5 By now you have partially learned most of the words. Cover the English column below with your cover sheet, look at the Spanish word, say the Spanish word aloud, and think of its English equivalent; then slide the cover sheet down to see if you remembered the right English word. When you have gone through the whole list, reverse the process. Go over them several more times. Keep this up for *three minutes*.

metales	metals	*tela*	cloth
plata	silver	*plástico*	plastic
oro	gold	*animal*	animal
hierro	iron	*piel (la)*	skin (pelt)
acero	steel	*cuero*	leather
lata	tin	*hueso*	bone
madera	wood	*seda*	silk
pino	pine	*lana*	wool
piedra	stone (rock)	*planta*	plant
arena	sand	*papel*	paper
ladrillo	brick	*cartón*	cardboard
adobe	adobe	*goma*	rubber
cemento	cement	*algodón*	cotton
cristal	glass (crystal)		

Now do whatever you want for a *whole hour*, then come back and do frame 6.

6 Work on this frame for *just* three minutes. When you are through you should have learned most of the words. Cover each column above alternately and say the matching word aloud. Remember to spend more time on those that need the most practice, and don't forget to add all the words to your list.

There live in the United States some members of a group of about 500,000 Spanish speaking people whose ancestors have not been citizens of a Spanish speaking country since 1492. In that year Ferdinand and Isabella ordered all the Jews in Spain to either become Catholics or leave the country. Thousands of Jews left, but they took with them their language (Spanish) and their Spanish customs and rituals which have been preserved to this day. These people do not speak modern Spanish. They talk like the Spaniard of the fifteenth century. There is no *usted* in their language, only *tú*, because *vuestra merced* had not become *usted* in 1492. They sing songs (ballads) which have not been heard in a Spanish speaking country in nearly 400 years. They write their Spanish with Hebrew letters, and they are called the Sephardim because in Hebrew the name for Spain is *Sepharad*.

Self-Correcting Exercises

A *Comparisons:* Figure out the answers mentally, and then check them.

1 Ella patina (*better than*) yo, pero ella esquía sobre el agua (*worse than*) yo.   mejor que, peor que

2 ¿Quién es (*older*), tú o ella?   mayor

3 Pues, ella es (*younger than*) yo.   menor que

4 Esquía con el (*greatest*) cuidado posible.   mayor

5 No tengo (*as many*) gallinas (*as*) ellos.   tantas, como

6 Ella tiene (*less*) talento (*than*) yo.   menos, que

7 Ellos no montan a caballo (*as much as*) nosotros.   tanto como

8 Yo sé patinar en ruedas (*as*) rápidamente (*as*) Jorge.   tan, como

9   Don José no tenía la (*least*) idea de lo que iba a ocurrir.   menor
10 Nosotros hacemos (*more*) viajes de excursión (*than*) nuestros vecinos.   más, que
11 Yo voy de caza (*as many*) veces cada año (*as*) Tomasito.   tantas, como
12 No hay (*as many*) marineros en la marina (*as*) soldados en el ejército.   tantos, como

B *Vocabulary Matching:* Match the words mentally and check after each one.

1	*quehacer*	**a**	desk	1	p
2	*suerte*	**b**	sheep	2	g
3	*escritorio*	**c**	he waters	3	a
4	*marinero*	**d**	he hangs	4	l
5	*por supuesto*	**e**	splinter	5	o
6	*oveja*	**f**	trash	6	b
7	*basura*	**g**	luck	7	f
8	*cuadra*	**h**	he fights	8	n
9	*cuelga*	**i**	skates	9	d
10	*pelea*	**j**	jealous	10	h
11	*riega*	**k**	he shoots	11	c
12	*rueda*	**l**	sailor	12	m
13	*astilla*	**m**	wheel	13	e
14	*celoso*	**n**	block	14	j
		o	of course		
		p	chore		

C *Future Forms of Regular Verbs:* Write the appropriate form of the Future for each infinitive in parentheses.

1 Creo que nosotros (ir) al cine la próxima semana.   iremos
2 Pues si van, Miguel (estar) allí y Vds. (ver) a Matilde también.   estará, verán
3 Yo (estudiar) mucho esta noche y mañana y, si Vds. me permiten, yo   estudiaré, iré
(ir) también.
4 Si estudias así, sin duda tú (ir) también.   irás
5 ¿Quién (sacar) la basura mañana?   sacará
6 No me mires a mí, porque yo (preguntar) quién (regar) la hierba. preguntaré, regará
7 Pues les digo que nadie (patinar) en el garaje hasta después de ter-   patinará
minar todos los quehaceres de la casa.

D *Refranes: ¿Cómo se dice en español . . . ?*

1 Listen, or your tongue will make you deaf.   *Escucha, o tu lengua te hará sordo.*
2 You are known by the company you keep.   *Dime con quién andas, y te diré quién eres.*
3 Every cloud has a silver lining.   *No hay mal que dure cien años, ni cuerpo que*
                                                                        lo resista.
4 A chip off the old block.   *De tal palo, tal astilla.*
5 Like mother, like daughter.   *De tal madre, tal hija.*
6 Practice makes perfect.   *El ejercicio hace maestro.*
7 Before making an important decision, sleep   *Antes que resuelvas nada, consúltalo con la*
on it.   *almohada.*

New Vocabulary

hierro	iron	**plástico**	plastic	**algodón**	cotton
acero	steel	**piel (la)**	skin, fur (pelt)	**cartón**	cardboard
lata	tin	**cuero**	leather	**goma**	rubber
madera	wood	**hueso**	bone	**almohada**	pillow
ladrillo	brick	**tela**	cloth	**consultar**	to consult
cemento	cement	**lana**	wool	**resolver (ue)**	to solve, resolve
cristal	glass (crystal)				

"Antes que resuelvas nada, consúltalo con la almohada."

"Before making an important decision, sleep on it." (Before you resolve anything, consult with the pillow.)

Assignment 85

Hacer *in Expressions of Time*

1   Let's pretend that we are talking about a time interval of one week which begins with Sunday, September 14 and ends on Saturday, September 20. The day on which we are talking is Saturday, September 20. The subject of discourse is two people and the interval of time of their being in Santa Fe.

Does "They arrived in Santa Fe on Sunday" permit you to calculate that the time between their arrival and the moment of speaking is one week?   ▲

2   Does "They have been in Santa Fe since Sunday" mean that they arrived on Sunday, they are still there, and the time between their arrival and the moment of speaking is one week?   ▲

yes

3   Does "They have been in Santa Fe for a week" permit you to conclude that they arrived on Sunday and that they are still there?   ▲

yes

4   Does "They arrived in Santa Fe a week ago" likewise permit you to conclude that they arrived on Sunday and that they are still there?   ▲

yes

5   The first two sentences above deal with a date and both have the same pattern in Spanish as in English: *Ellos llegaron a Santa Fe el domingo. Ellos han estado en Santa Fe desde el domingo.*

yes

The second two sentences deal with an interval of time. To get one translation of the third sentence you simply replace *desde el domingo* with _____.   ▲

por una semana (Ellos han estado en Santa Fe por una semana.)

6   Spanish has no literal equivalent of "ago." In its place Spanish adds up the time between the aspect of the past event being talked about and the moment of speaking. The dictionary of the Spanish Academy uses the following sentence to exemplify one meaning of *hacer: Nueve y cuatro hacen trece.* The literal translation of this is _____.   ▲

Nine and four make thirteen.

7   The meaning of both *hacen* and "make" is "_____ up to."   ▲

add

8 When the Spanish speaker "adds up" the time between a past event and the moment of speaking, he uses two clauses: one for the addition and one for the event being talked about. Translate: They arrived in Santa Fe. ▲

9 Now translate: It makes a week. ▲

Ellos llegaron a Santa Fe.
Hace una semana.

10 These two statements can be combined in one sentence in two ways. First, if you begin with the event clause, you simply add the measurement clause to the end and you get *Ellos llegaron a Santa Fe hace una semana.* Second, if you begin with *Hace una semana*, you must treat the event clause as a subjoined clause and introduce it with the standard connector word _____. ▲

11 Is one of the pieces of information that can be deduced from "They have been in Santa Fe for a week" the fact that *están en Santa Fe?* ▲

que

12 Spanish, unlike English, can add up the time from the beginning of an on-going event and the moment of speaking and get the meaning: It makes a week that they are in Santa Fe. Translate this literally. ▲

yes

Hace una semana que ellos están en Santa Fe.

13 Now translate the above into standard English. ▲

They have been in Santa Fe for a week.

14 When you studied the Preterit and Imperfect you learned that at a point in the past a cyclic event can terminate, a non-cyclic event can begin, and either event can be in the Imperfect. If one measures the interval between this past point and the moment of speaking, the information may be diagramed in this fashion:

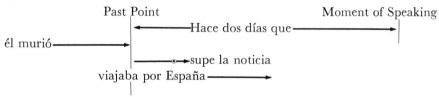

The translation of *Hace dos días que* for all three statements is _____. ▲

15 Here, now, are some facts you have to remember. When the tense of the event clause is past in English and the interval of time between the event and the moment of speaking is given, English requires the use of "ago": He left two days ago.

two days ago.

In contrast, when the tense of the event clause is present perfect and the interval of time measures either the initiation or termination of the event, English requires "for" plus the time interval: *I have known her for two years. I have not seen her for three months.* Spanish must translate all patterns having "ago" with the *hace . . . que* construction. Translate: He left two days ago. (*irse*) ▲

Hace dos días que él se fué.

16 When the present perfect is used in English, Spanish has two options when the event clause is positive. It may use the same pattern as English. Translate: I have known her for two years. ▲

La he conocido por dos años.

17 The same information can be expressed by saying *la conozco* and the *hacer* construction, which is by far the more common way of stating this concept. Write this translation. ▲

Hace dos años que la conozco.

18 When the tense is present perfect and the event verb is negated, Spanish has three options. First, the same pattern may be used. Translate: I have not seen her for three months.　▲

> *No la he visto por tres meses.* (This is less frequent.)

19 Second, the *por tres meses* can be replaced with the *hace . . . que* construction. Write this pattern.　▲

> *Hace tres meses que no la he visto.*

20 Third, the present perfect can be replaced with the simple Present and you get *Hace tres meses que no la* _____.　▲

> *veo*

21 English has a variety of ways of sending the same message: (1) Amado arrived nine days ago. (2) It has been nine days since Amado arrived. (3) It is nine days since Amado arrived. (4) Nine days have passed since Amado arrived. Spanish will normally translate all four of these sentences in the same way. Do this.　▲

> *Hace nueve días que Amado llegó.*

22 When you want to ask a question which gets the above answer, you ask in English "how long": How long has Amado been here? How long ago did Amado arrive here? Spanish translates "How long" by "How much time does it make that . . . " Translate: How much time does it make that he is here?　▲

> *¿Cuánto tiempo hace que él está aquí?*

23 Now translate the above sentence into standard English.　▲

> How long has he been here?

24 The answer might be *Él ha estado aquí por un mes* or _____.　▲

> *Hace un mes que él está aquí.*

25 In this and the next four frames translate the indicated words: I cut the grass *ten days ago*.　▲

26 *It has been two months since* you watered it.　▲　　　*Hace diez días que*

27 I have not skied *for a year*.　▲　　　*Hace dos meses que*

28 The gentleman was in the living room *a minute ago*.　▲　　　*Hace un año que*

29 This store has sold this cloth *for years*.　▲　　　*Hace un minuto que*

> *Hace años que*

A/B

Hace una hora que empezó a pintar.

Practice with the Forms of the Future

1 There are, as you already know, eleven verbs in Spanish which have an irregular future stem. Of these, the following five replace the class vowel with *d*: *poner, salir, tener, valer, venir*. In this and the next four frames, write the Future of the indicated infinitive.

Yo no *poner* los ladrillos en la piscina. ▲

2 Ellos *salir* de la oficina a las cinco. ▲   *pondré*

3 ¿*Tener* tú tiempo mañana? ▲   *saldrán*

4 Esta casa no *valer* más de mil pesos en diez años. ▲   *Tendrás*

5 ¿Cuándo *venir* el día en que haya paz en todo el mundo? ▲   *valdrá*

6 There are four verbs which drop the class vowel in the future stem: *haber,*   *vendrá*
poder, querer, saber. In this and the next three frames write the Future of the indicated infinitive.

Tenemos que anticipar que llegará el día en que él *querer* cinco dólares cada semana. ▲

7 Yo estoy seguro de que *haber* más gente mañana. ▲   *querrá*

8 No sé cuándo yo *poder* hacerlo, señor. ▲   *habrá*

9 Mis padres no *saber* la noticia hasta mañana. ▲   *podré*

10 Centuries ago the infinitives of *decir* and *hacer* were *dir* and *har*. These   *sabrán*
ancient infinitives still survive as the stem of the Future. Write the *yo* and the
nosotros forms for each. ▲

yo diré, nosotros diremos : yo haré, nosotros haremos

11 Write the Future of the forms given: *trajeron; estuviste; anduve; tuvo; vinieron* ▲

traerán ; estarás ; andaré ; tendrá ; vendrán

In the United States there is still some antisemitism, but Jews have always been allowed to have their own schools and synagogues. When Ferdinand and Isabella expelled the Jews from Spain in 1492, all synagogues were either closed or converted to churches, and no Jewish religious ceremonies could be performed in Spanish territory. This ban was not officially lifted until 1968, when the government permitted the building of the first new synagogues since the fourteenth century. The number of non-Catholic permanent residents in Spain is still not very high.

Summary

1 When an action begun in the past is still in progress at the moment of speaking, the present perfect and *por*, or the Present and *hacer* are used to measure the elapsed time (*Manuel ha vivido aquí por un mes. Hace un mes que Manuel vive aquí.*).

2 When the tense of the measured event is Past, the Present of *hacer* is used with either the Preterit or Imperfect. (*Hace un año que se fueron. Se fueron hace un año. Hace una hora que estaba aquí. Estaba aquí hace una hora.*)

Self-Correcting Exercises

A *Subjunctive versus Indicative with Events of Experience and Non-experience:* Write the combinations and check them one by one.

Ejemplo: 122 = Lo haré después que ella salga.

1	Lo haré	1	siempre que			
2	Lo hago	2	después (de) que		1	escribirnos.
3	Dirán eso	3	en cuanto	ella	2	salir.
4	Dicen eso	4	antes (de) que		3	tenerlo.
5	Vendrá	5	mientras (que)			
6	Viene					

1)	113	Lo haré siempre que ella lo tenga.
2)	213	Lo hago siempre que ella lo tiene.
3)	322	Dirán eso después que ella salga.
4)	422	Dicen eso después que ella sale.
5)	531	Vendrá en cuanto ella nos escriba.
6)	631	Viene en cuanto ella nos escribe.
7)	252	Lo hago mientras que ella sale.
8)	342	Dirán eso antes que ella salga.
9)	141	Lo haré antes que ella nos escriba.
10)	432	Dicen eso en cuanto ella sale.
11)	553	Vendrá mientras ella lo tenga.
12)	642	Viene antes de que ella salga.

B *Subjunctive versus Indicative:* Write the appropriate form of the verb that fits the context.

1 No creo que esta camisa (ser) de lana; creo que (deber) ser de algodón. — *sea, debe*

2 Nos mandan que (tener) cuidado y que no (romper) el cristal. — *tengamos, rompamos*

3 Me enojo mucho de que él siempre (cortar) la hierba antes de que yo (recoger) las hojas. — *corte, recoja*

4 Lo haremos tan pronto como ellos nos (dar) permiso. — *den*

5 Dudamos que ellos (estar) en ese ejército. — *estén*

6 Quiere que nosotros lo (conocer) tan pronto como él (llegar). — *conozcamos, llegue*

7 Sabemos que mamá no permitirá que los niños (sacar) el perro hasta que su papá les (dar) permiso. — *saquen, dé*

8 Siempre llegamos aquí cuando ellos (salir). — *salen*

9 Saldremos de aquí luego que ellos (llegar). — *lleguen*

C *Future:* Do not write the appropriate future verb form until after you have read and understood the meaning of each sentence.

1 Creo que el sábado (ser) el día que hemos esperado. — *será*

2 Todos nuestros parientes (llegar); también (estar) aquí mis primos que están en el ejército. — *llegarán, estarán*

3 Nosotros (tener) una fiesta y (servir) un gran banquete.

tendremos, serviremos

4 (Haber) tíos, abuelos, primos, hermanos y cuñados, y todos (poder) comer cuanto nos guste.

Habrá, podremos

5 Mamá no (saber) cuántos (venir) hasta que lleguen.

sabrá, vendrán

6 Cuando ella lo sepa, me (decir) el número exacto y yo (poner) la mesa.

dirá, pondré

7 (Valer) más tener todo bien preparado lo más pronto posible, por eso nosotros (hacer) todos los mandados de antemano (*before hand*).

Valdrá, haremos

8 Yo (querer) ir al cine después de comer, pero no sé si mis primos (poder) acompañarme.

querré, podrán

D *Silent Reading:* Read as fast as possible.

El hombre que se casó con una mujer muy fiera (segunda parte)

La discusión entre los padres de Catalina y Perico duró varias horas. El resultado fue que el domingo siguiente la boda° de los dos jóvenes era anunciada en la iglesia del pueblo.

wedding

Catalina no quería casarse. Llegó el día de la boda y fue necesario llevarla a la iglesia contra su voluntad.° Los criados que la llevaron sufrieron toda clase de golpes,° mordidas° y arañazos.° Después de la ceremonia, Perico tomó° a su mujer por la cintura,° la puso sobre el hombro° izquierdo y empezó a caminar en dirección a la casa donde iban a vivir. Los padres y parientes de los novios y el resto de los invitados los seguían por la calle. Con los puños,° las uñas,° los dientes y la punta de los zapatos, Catalina trataba de escaparse, pero no podía. Perico era mucho más fuerte que ella.

will
blows/bites/scratches/
took
waist/shoulder
fists/nails

Cuando llegaron a la casa, Perico se despidió de toda la gente, entró en la casa con su esposa y cerró todas las puertas con llave. Los gritos y los insultos de Catalina se oían desde fuera. Al irse para sus casas, los amigos y parientes del novio° estaban seguros que a la mañana siguiente iban a encontrarlo muerto o, por lo menos, gravemente herido.

groom

Como era costumbre en aquel tiempo los familiares° de los novios les habían preparado un gran banquete. Catalina y Perico se sentaron a la mesa en silencio. Perico empezó a mirar por el cuarto, vio un perro que dormía en una esquina° y le gritó de repente:

relatives

corner

—Perro, tráenos agua para lavarnos las manos.

El perro levantó las orejas y abrió los ojos, pero no se movió. Perico se puso furioso y repitió la orden en voz más alta:

—Perro, te dije que nos traigas agua para las manos.

Viendo que el animal no le obedecía, Perico se levantó con la espada° en la mano y corrió detrás° de él por todo el cuarto. El perro trató de escaparse, pero no pudo. Furioso porque el animal no le había obedecido, Perico le cortó la cabeza y le hizo pedazos con la espada. Catalina observó la escena sin decir ni una sola palabra. Estaba muy sorprendida de la conducta de su marido. Perico volvió a la mesa, se sentó, miró a su mujer y tampoco dijo nada.

sword
behind

(El resto de este cuento será presentado en clase oralmente.)

Most Americans consider the bullfight to be a national sport in the Hispanic world. This impression, however, is created primarily by just two countries, Spain and Mexico, although bullfights are also staged regularly in Colombia and Peru, and occasionally in other countries.

What most Americans do not know is that soccer attracts more attention than bullfighting and that cockfights, which are illegal in the United States, are very popular.

New Vocabulary

ayuntamiento	city hall	**estación de gasolina**	gas station (garage)
estación de policía	police station	**botica (droguería,**	drug store
cárcel (la)	jail	**farmacia)**	
biblioteca	library	**carnicería**	butcher shop (meat
museo	museum		market)
estadio	stadium	**lechería**	dairy (milk store)
fábrica (factoría)	factory	**panadería**	bakery
casa de apartamentos	apartment house	**dulcería**	candy store (sweet shop)
rascacielos (el)	skyscraper	**zapatería**	shoe store
supermercado	supermarket	**peluquería**	barber (beauty) shop
almacén	department store	**lavandería**	laundry
garaje	garage	**librería**	book store

¿En qué puedo servirle? (¿Qué se le ofrece?)   What can I do for you? (May I help you? May I be of service?)

Assignment 86

Review of the Subjunctive

1 The common spelling problems you encounter in writing the forms of the subjunctive all stem from the fact that   (1) some phonemes may be written with two different letters before *a, o, e,* or *i*   (2) *a* replaces the suffixes *o, e,* and *i* of the present indicative of *e-* and *i*-verbs in the subjunctive, and   (3) *e* replaces the *o* and *a* suffixes of *a*-verbs. The letter *c* may stand for [s] only before /e/ and /i/. Write the *yo* form of the present indicative and subjunctive of *convencer.* ▲

> *convenzo, convenza* (Change *c* to *z* before *o* or *a* to retain the [s] sound.)

2 The letter *g* stands for the *jota* sound <u>only before</u> /e/ and /i/. Write the *yo* form of *escoger* in the present indicative, subjunctive, and Preterit. ▲

> *escojo, escoja, escogí* (The *jota* sound must be written *j* before /a/, /o/, and /u/.)

To start its industries, an underdeveloped country usually depends on the investment of outside capital. Such economic influence also engenders political influence. This Ford plant supplies work and goods for Venezuelans, in a co-operative venture with the United States.

The mechanization of agriculture is a recent development in many Latin American countries. Since most countries lack the industry to produce tractors, they must obtain them from the United States or Europe. This Cuban farm probably got theirs from eastern Europe.

3 The *c* stands for [k] before /a/, /o/, and /u/. Write the *yo* form of *sacar* in the present indicative, subjunctive, and Preterit. ▲

saco, saque, saqué (You write [k] as *qu* before /i/ and /e/.)

4 The letter *g* stands for *jota* before /e/ or /i/. When you want to write the sound of /g/, as in *gato*, before /e/ or /i/, you must use _____. ▲

5 Write the *yo* form of *seguir* in the present indicative, subjunctive, and Preterit. ▲

gu

6 There are three allomorphs for the stems of both *sentir* and *dormir*. Can you give all of them? (Only two are used in the present subjunctive.) ▲

sigo, siga, seguí

sent, sient, sint; dorm, duerm, durm

7 Give both the *tú* and *nosotros* present subjunctive forms of *pedir*, *sentir*, and *dormir*. ▲

pidas, pidamos; sientas, sintamos; duermas, durmamos

8 Give the *usted* present subjunctive form of the following irregular verbs: *ir*, *haber*, *estar*, *ser*, *dar*, and *saber*. ▲

vaya, haya, esté, sea, dé, sepa

9 The use of the subjunctive with which you have had the least practice is the one that you learned last, the subjunctive in adverbial clauses of order relationships.

What are you asking about when you say: *¿Se cae Vd. cuando esquía?* (a) What has happened up to now. (b) What is going on now. (c) What is being anticipated. ▲

What has happened up to now, that is, the habitual or customary. (A single instance would be reported as *¿Se cayó Vd. cuando esquió?*)

10 For the present, the contrast between recall and anticipation deals only with the difference between what is habitual or customary (recall) and the anticipation of either a pair of single events or a statement of what is to be customary. The order words or phrases which have been presented to you are *antes, cuando, después, en cuanto, hasta, luego, mientras, siempre,* and *tan pronto como*. It is an arbitrary convention that six of these must be followed by *que*. What are the four that do not require the *que*? ▲

cuando, en cuanto, mientras, tan pronto como.

11 After which adverbial connector do most Spanish speakers use the subjunctive for both recall and anticipation? ▲

12 In this and the next nine frames write the appropriate indicative or subjunctive form of the infinitive in parentheses.

antes (de) que

Le doy el dinero siempre que ella lo *necesitar*. ▲

13 Continuaré dándole dinero siempre que ella lo _____ (necesitar). ▲

necesita

14 La niña se echa a llorar tan pronto como _____ (ver) el perro. ▲

necesite

15 Lo compraré luego que ellos me _____ (dar) permiso. ▲

ve

16 No llegaremos a casa antes que _____ (empezar) la tormenta. ▲

den

17 No olvides tomar tu medicina después que _____ (comer). ▲

empiece

18 El sábado mientras tu papá _____ (estar) jugando golf, limpiaré su oficina. ▲

comas

19 Prepararé la comida en cuanto él se _____ (despertar). ▲

esté

despierte

20 Él siempre dice eso cuando yo se lo _____ (preguntar). ▲

21 No trabajaré más hasta que ellos me _____ (pagar). ▲

pregunto
paguen

A/B

Grita de manera que salte.

No puede escapar sin que salte.

C/D

Grita para que ellos sepan que él salta.

Le daré una naranja con tal de que me permita pasar.

E/F

Corre de modo que vuele la cometa.

La cometa no volará a menos que alguien la arregle.

More on the Subjunctive

1 Just as Spanish uses the subjunctive in the dependent clause when there is a verbal attempt to influence behavior, so also is the subjunctive used when non-speech actions attempt to influence behavior.

There are many non-speech actions whose purpose is to cause an action to take place (You push something to make it fall over), to prevent something from happening (You lock the door so that burglars can't get in), or to permit something to happen (You open the door so that the dog may go out). Give the appropriate form of the indicated infinitive:

Te llevaré allí para que (tú) *poder* nadar. ▲

2 You have been learning to use adverbial conjunctions that deal with clauses of order relationships. The following conjunctions connect clauses having a cause and effect relationship with the independent clause:

puedas

para que			*con tal (de) que*	provided that
de manera que	so that, in order that		*sin que*	without
de modo que			*a menos que*	unless

How many of these six conjunctions use *que*? ▲

3 The fundamental logic behind the following two sentences is the same. Read them carefully and translate the indicated connectors:

all six

(1) You have to turn on the faucet *so (that)* the water can come out.

(2) The water does not come out *unless* you turn on the faucet. ▲

para que, a menos que

4 Indicate whether "turn on the faucet" is in the first or second clause of the two above sentences: (1) _____ clause, (2) _____ clause. ▲

(1) first clause, (2) second clause

5 As in dealing with stimulus-response situations, it does not matter whether the cause (stimulus) or effect (response) is in the main or subjoined clause. The important thing to remember is that the subjunctive must always be used in the _____ clause. ▲

6 Give the appropriate form of the indicated infinitives:

subjoined

Tú *tener* que abrir la llave para que *salir* el agua.

El agua no *salir* a menos que tú *abrir* la llave. ▲

tienes, salga; sale, abras

7 The translation of *provided that* is *con tal que*. Miguel wants some money. His mother says, "I'll give you the money *provided that* you clean your room." What must Miguel do to *cause* his mother to give him the money? ▲

8 Translate the sentence given in quotes above. ▲

clean his room.

Te daré el dinero con tal que limpies tu cuarto.

9 Some actions can be done in a manner which is not effective, that is, they fail to cause, or prevent another action. When Spanish focuses attention on the *manner* or *way* an action is done *so that* something else does or does not happen, *para* is replaced by either *de manera* or *de modo*. Translate (using *Vd.*):

Do it so that (in such a way that) they can see it. (*lo*) ▲

Hágalo de manera (de modo) que puedan verlo.

The Present Progressive

1 The Present is frequently used to talk about an event which may or may not be going on at the moment of speaking. *Flight 271 arrives at 9:30 P.M. Mother always cleans the house before guests arrive.* This happens in both English and Spanish and, as a result, both languages need a way to say very clearly that an event is *in progress* at the moment the verb labeling it is spoken. This is one of the functions of the *present progressive.* Change "The plane has departed" so the new sentence describes the action in progress. ▲

The plane is departing.

2 The auxiliary verb in "The plane is departing" is _____. ▲

is or *to be* (In Spanish this verb is *estar.*)

3 From the point of view of morphology the present progressive should be called the present imperfect. The "-ing" forms in English are the imperfect participles when used in the progressive construction. The mark of the regular perfect participle in Spanish is the suffix *do.* The imperfect participle of all regular *a*-verbs is made by inserting an *n* between the class vowel *a* and the *do*: *hablando.* Translate: Catalina is cutting the grass! ▲

¡Catalina está cortando la hierba!

4 The imperfective suffix *-ndo* is used with all verbs. When it is added to the infinitive base of an *e*-verb, the stressed *e* that precedes the *ndo* suffix becomes *ie.* Write the imperfect participle of *ofrecer, resolver,* and *barrer.* ▲

ofreciendo, resolviendo, barriendo

5 The imperfect participle of all *i*-verbs is made in the same way as *e*-verbs. The class vowel *i* becomes *ie.* Write the imperfect participle of *sufrir, permitir,* and *salir.* ▲

sufriendo, permitiendo, saliendo (The letter *i* is replaced by *y* in the imperfect participle of *ir: yendo.*)

6 In spelling, the unstressed *i* between two vowels is replaced by *y.* Write the imperfect participle of *leer, oír,* and *caer.* ▲

leyendo, oyendo, cayendo

7 Since the stress does not fall on the stem of the imperfect participle, there is no reason to change the *e* and *o* of irregular *a-* and *e*-verbs (*tiene, sienta, vuelve,* etc.) to *ie* and *ue.* You use the infinitive stem for the participle. (One exception is *poder = pudiendo.*) Write the imperfect participle of the verbs given above. ▲

teniendo, sentando, volviendo

8 Write the *Vd.* form of the Preterit for *dormir, reír* and *sentir.* ▲

9 Write the *nosotros* form of these same verbs in the present subjunctive. ▲   *durmió, rió, sintió*

durmamos, riamos, sintamos

10 Any verb in which the *o* of the stem changes to *u* or the *e* to *i* in the Preterit or present subjunctive also has the same irregular stem in the imperfect participle. Change *durmió, rió* and *sintió* to the imperfect participle. ▲

durmiendo, riendo, sintiendo

11 Translate: I am hanging up my hat. (The verb is *colgar.*) ▲

Estoy colgando mi sombrero.

Summary

More on the Subjunctive

The subjunctive is used after the following conjunctions to express a cause and effect relationship: *para que, de modo que, de manera que, con tal (de) que, a menos que, sin que.* For example: *No lo haré sin que tú me ayudes.*

The Present Progressive

1 The imperfect participle of all regular verbs is made by inserting *n* between the class vowel and the perfect participle *do: habla-do, habla-***n***do.*

2 The set suffixes *e* and *i* change to *ie: temer* > *temiendo, vivir* > *viviendo.*

3 Unaccented *i* becomes *y* between two vowels: *leer* > *leyendo.*

4 When the *o* of a stem changes to *u* or the *e* to *i* in a form of the Preterit or present subjunctive, the stem of the imperfect participle has the same irregularity: *servir* > *sirvió* > *sirviendo, morir* > *muramos* > *muriendo.* Otherwise the imperfect participle uses the stem of the infinitive.

How Words Are Formed, and Vocabulary Practice

1 In *baker, bakes,* and *bakery,* the stem is *bake.* The verb *bakes,* however, belongs to a set of forms which take person, number, tense, and aspect suffixes: *they bake, he bakes, she baked, they are baking.* Is the action the same in all these words regardless of the suffix used? ▲

2 Linguists say that these words are created by *inflection,* that is, by adding a suffix which does not create a form having an entirely new meaning. When you make *cake* plural by adding *s* (*cakes*), do you change the meaning of the stem? ▲

yes

3 When you add the suffix *-r* or *-ry* to *bake,* do you get an entirely new word? ▲

no

yes (baker, bakery)

4 The words *baker* and *bakery* come from or are *derived* from *bake.* These forms, consequently, are said to be created by *derivation.* There are thousands of derived forms in both English and Spanish which were created by just one person who needed a new word to describe something. Alexander Graham Bell, for example, invented not only the telephone but the word for it. The scientist who discovered the antibiotic oxytetracycline invented its name, and the drug company that first marketed it created the trade name *terramycin* (= earth mold). Derived forms like these are frozen at the instant of creation, that is, the speakers of the language may use them but can change them only by inflection. Thus you may say he *telephones, telephoned,* or is *telephoning.* In contrast, there are in both languages a great many base words or stems which any speaker of the language may use to derive a new one, sometimes one which he has never used before in his whole life. Thus I have the privilege, if I want to be funny, of saying, "I'm not going to the *bakery*, I'm going to the *cakery*." Non-natives rarely acquire the feel for language which permits one to play this kind of linguistic game, but you cannot learn to use Spanish for communication until you understand how the native creates *baker* and *bakery* from *bake*. In both English and Spanish the base form of a derived noun may be another noun, a verb, or an adjective. What does *lavandería* come from? (a) *lavar* (b) *lavando* ▲

5   The word *dulcería* comes from a noun which came from the adjective   *lavando*

_____. ▲

dulce (*El azúcar es dulce.*)

6   You can see *pan* in *panadería* just as you can see *flor* in *florería*. Is *panadería* directly derived from *pan*? ▲

no (It comes from the verb *panadear* = to make bread.)

7   So really a *panadería* to the Spaniard is not a *bakery*, it is a _____. (Can you make up this word in English? You won't find it in any dictionary.) ▲

8   The suffix which says that someone does something with the object labeled   *breadery*
by the stem is *ero*. What one actually does, however, depends on the object labeled by the stem. Thus a *zapatero* makes *zapatos* (or repairs them). What does a *lechero* do? ▲

He *sells* milk (or delivers it).

9   In English a shoe factory is a place where shoes are made, a shoe shop is where they are repaired, and a shoe store is where they are sold. A shoemaker may work in a shoe factory or a shoe shop. The Spanish speaker does not make a distinction between factory, shop, and store. As a result, a *panadería* may be the place where bread is made or the store in which it is sold, and a *zapatero* may be a shoemaker, a shoe repairer, or a shoe _____. ▲

seller (dealer, salesman)

10   At the present time you do not know enough Spanish to be able to figure out what all derived words come from. You know, for example, that the stem of *peluquero* and *peluquería* must be _____. ▲

11   Can you figure out the meaning of *peluqu-* the way you can get the meaning   *peluqu-*
of the stem of *mueblería?* ▲

no (Don't worry about this. Even some natives may not know that the original base word of *peluquería* is *peluca* (wig) or that a *peluquero* may be a wig maker.)

12   At the same time you do not yet know enough Spanish to be able to make up forms like *zapatero* and *zapatería* all on your own. Nevertheless, you need to learn to understand these forms and to be able to make them when you are told that they exist.

When a word ends in a consonant, you simply add *-ero*, or *-ería*. Write the words for "garden-er," and "flower shop." ▲

jardinero (from *jardín*, accent mark drops), *florería*

13   When a word ends in a vowel, the vowel is deleted before adding the suffixes. Change *libro* and *dulce* to "book store" and "candy store." ▲

14   In English you add "-er" to "ranch" to get "rancher." Change *rancho* to   *librería, dulcería*
"rancher." ▲

ranchero

The majority of Americans are conditioned to believe that the things we make or build are going to have to be replaced in a given length of time. A skyscraper, for example, has a predictable life of about 100 years. Most cars are junked before they are 10 years old. The great superhighways of today frequently replaced roads less than 50 years old. In many cities large areas of homes are continuously being torn down in order to build modern dwellings and many people believe that a house is old when it is 50 years old.

The Hispanic world has a quite different attitude. Cars are frequently driven for as long as 20 years. There are train engines in regular use that are over 100 years old. In Spain there are roads, bridges, and even a few buildings still in use which were built by the Romans nearly two thousand years ago. In the New World some of the homes built by the conquistadores in the sixteenth century are still being lived in, and in all of the old cities there are large sections with cobblestone pavement and, often, streets so narrow that a modern car cannot be driven through them. The ancient past is ever present in the Hispanic world and the people feel no need to replace something which still fulfills its original purpose. People still go to church in the same building where Columbus prayed before he set out to discover the New World.

15 Write the imperative of *saca*, then change *vaca* (cow) to "cowboy." ▲

16 A soldier is a warrior. Translate this last word. Its base is the word for *war*. ▲

saque, vaquero

17 Make *caballo* into a gentleman. ▲

guerra > guerrero

18 What does a *relojero* make, sell, or repair? ▲

caballero

19 Where does the *relojero* do all these things? *En una* _____. ▲

relojes

20 What is made in a *cuchillería*? ▲

relojería

21 You need to understand that not all words ending in the suffix *-ero* have the meaning of doer. Translate the indicated words: *Mamá, no hay flores en el* **florero** *ni sal en el* **salero**. ▲

cuchillos

vase (flower container), salt shaker (salt cellar) (Here *-ero* changes the base word into one standing for the container in which the referent of the base word is kept.)

22 The suffix *-ero* may also be used to create adjectives. Translate: *Pedrito es un muchacho aventurero.* ▲

Pete is an adventurous boy.

23 Here is a strange case of coincidence in the development of words. In classical Latin the noun *apotheca* stood for a warehouse. This meaning survives in modern Spanish *bodega*, a cellar for strong wine. German changed *apotheca* to *Bude* with the meaning of *shop*, old French made it *botica* which became in modern French *boutique* (a shop or its merchandise). English has borrowed *boutique* and given it the meaning of a specialty shop which sells very fancy ladies' clothes and accessories. Both English and Spanish, by some rare coincidence, have given the word essentially the same meaning in one instance: An apothecary is a druggist, while the word for drugstore in Spanish is _____. ▲

botica

24 Since the Spanish gave *apotheca* (warehouse) a special meaning, it was necessary to find another word with this meaning. They solved this problem by borrowing *almacén* from Arabic. Today *almacén* still stands for warehouse, but it is also used to translate _____. ▲

25 When a person is jailed, he is "in-carcer-ated." The cognate of *carcer* is _____. ▲

department store

26 A bibliography is a list of titles of books or articles. The Spanish cognate of "library" is *librería* which is a bookstore, not a library. The Spanish word for "library" is the cognate of *bibliography* or _____. ▲

cárcel

27 The word "merchant" is an obvious cognate of *mercado* which came from *mercatus* whose modern English form is "market." Both languages use the Latin prefix _____ to get the word for a huge store. ▲

biblioteca

super (supermarket, *supermercado*)

28 English regularly uses one noun to describe another (gas station, police station, apartment house). Spanish does this very rarely, and when it does, the descriptive noun follows (*el hombre masa* = the mass man). To make the common equivalent of "gas station" you translate both words literally, put "gasoline" in second place, and tie the two together with the relator _____. ▲

de (*estación de gasolina*)

29 You have to add two letters to "apartment" to get the Spanish _____. ▲

30 Almost all Spanish nouns are derived from the accusative (done-to) case of the Latin noun. The suffix for this case was *um* for many words. The *m* dis-

apart**amento**

appeared and the *u* changed to *o*. In this way the Latin *museum*, which we use unchanged, became Spanish _____. ▲

31 Similarly Latin *stadium* became _____. ▲   *museo*

      estadio (Remember Spanish speakers refuse to say *s* plus another consonant at the beginning of words; they add an *e*: special > *especial*.)

32 The Romans borrowed from the Greeks their word for a sleeping-chamber and changed it to *coemeterium*. This changed to *cemeterium* which became modern Spanish _____ (cemetery). ▲

33 The noun cognate of "to fabricate" is _____. ▲   *cementerio*

      fábrica factory (The verb is *fabricar.*)

34 Spanish could spell "garage" as in English, but the standard spelling is _____. ▲

35 The verb for "to scrape" is *rascar*. To get "skyscraper", you translate "it   *garaje* scrapes skies" and make it one word. ▲

36 A *puerta* is a door or entrance way. *Un puerto* is a much bigger entrance way   *rascacielos* for ships or a _____. ▲

      port (So the island of *Puerto Rico* got its name from its fine harbor.)

37 The noun *aire* has an adjectival form _____ which is added to *puerto* to get "airport." ▲

38 There is an obsolete verb *ayuntar* which means "to get together." The "get-   *aero* (*aeropuerto*) together place" (town hall) of the city fathers in Spanish is an _____. ▲

      ayuntamiento

Self-Correcting Exercises

A *Future:* Change each infinitive in parentheses to the appropriate future form.

1 El próximo sábado un grupo de mis amigos y yo (ir) de excursión al rancho de la familia Duarte en las montañas.

2 Los muchachos del grupo (comprar) refrescos (*soft drinks*) y perros calientes; mis amigas y yo (hacer) ensalada de papa y algún postre.

3 Esta noche Bárbara Duarte (llamar) por teléfono al rancho y le (decir) a su tío que ponga varios melones en el agua fría del río para que estén fríos cuando nosotros lleguemos.

4 Bárbara cree que nosotros (tener) oportunidad de montar a caballo y que, si su tío no está muy ocupado, ese día él (poder) enseñarnos (*show*) las vacas (*cows*) y toros importados que tiene en su rancho.

5 No sé si Dorotea y Ester (querer) ir con nosotros.

6 Tampoco sé si ellas (saber) que la excursión va a ser este fin de semana.

7 Bárbara y yo (preparar) toda la comida y la (poner) en una nevera (*ice box*).

1   iremos
2   comprarán, haremos
3   llamará, dirá
4   tendremos, podrá
5   querrán
6   sabrán
7   prepararemos, pondremos

8   Yo le (informar) a los muchachos que no es necesario que compren hielo seco para los refrescos.

9   Al llegar al rancho, Bárbara los (llevar) al agua del río y cuando sea hora de comer (estar) tan fríos como los melones.

10   Al tío de Bárbara le gustan mucho las fiestas, y estamos seguros que él se (divertir) tanto como nosotros.

8	informaré
9	llevará, estarán
10	divertirá

B   Hacer *with Expressions of Time:* Say aloud the Spanish translation.
Ejemplo: It has been raining for ten minutes. *Hace diez minutos que llueve.*

1 It has been snowing for ten minutes.	*Hace diez minutos que nieva.*
2 I've been working for ten minutes.	*Hace diez minutos que trabajo.*
3 I've been working for a week.	*Hace una semana que trabajo.*
4 I've been here for two weeks.	*Hace dos semanas que estoy aquí.*
5 I've been here for three years.	*Hace tres años que estoy aquí.*
6 I've lived here for ten years.	*Hace diez años que vivo aquí.*

Ejemplo: It rained ten minutes ago. *Hace diez minutos que llovió.*

7 It snowed ten minutes ago.	*Hace diez minutos que nevó·*
8 I arrived ten minutes ago.	*Hace diez minutos que llegué.*
9 I watered the flowers an hour ago.	*Hace una hora que regué las flores.*
10 I cut the grass two weeks ago.	*Hace dos semanas que corté la hierba.*
11 I cut the grass a long time ago.	*Hace mucho tiempo que corté la hierba.*
12 I did the shopping three days ago.	*Hace tres días que hice las compras.*
13 I did the shopping a week ago.	*Hace una semana que hice las compras.*
14 I was there a year ago.	*Hace un año que estuve allí.*
15 I was there a long time ago.	*Hace mucho tiempo que estuve allí.*

C   *Subjunctive versus Indicative:* After figuring out the meaning of each sentence, write the appropriate present indicative or subjunctive verb form.

1   En las montañas conocí a un señor bastante viejo que (ser) pastor de ovejas.

2   Un lobo mató a su perro en una pelea muy feroz y sangrienta y ahora necesita otro perro que (saber) cuidar ovejas.

3   Las ovejas no temen que los perros las (morder), pero tienen miedo de que los lobos las (atacar).

4   Las ovejas no tienen hambre porque están en un lugar donde (haber) mucha hierba.

5   El pastor se alegra mucho de que (haber) tanta hierba este año porque no es necesario que él (caminar) grandes distancias con su rebaño (*flock*).

6   El pastor regresará a su rancho tan pronto como (llegar) el invierno.

7   Piensa quedarse en las montañas un mes más, a menos que (empezar) a nevar.

8   Muchas de las ovejas llevan campanas (*bells*) para que el pastor (oír) dónde están.

es
sepa
muerdan
ataquen
hay
haya
camine
llegue
empiece
oiga

9 En el futuro, cuando yo (poder), pienso volver a las montañas a visitar   pueda
a mi amigo.

10 Ojalá que el viejo pastor (tener) mucha suerte y que los lobos no (salir)   tenga, salgan
del bosque a atacar a sus ovejas.

D *Refranes:* Say the Spanish equivalent aloud.

1	Like father, like son.	*De tal padre, tal hijo.*
2	A chip off the old block.	*De tal palo, tal astilla.*
3	Practice makes perfect.	*El ejercicio hace maestro.*
4	Do good no matter for whom.	*Haz bien y no mires a quién.*
5	If the shoe fits, put it on.	*Si le viene el saco, póngaselo.*

6 Don't leave for tomorrow what you can do   *No dejes para mañana lo que puedas hacer*
today.   *hoy.*
7 Nothing ventured, nothing gained.   *Quien no se aventura no pasa la mar.*

New Vocabulary

ofrecer	to offer	**—¿Se puede?**	—May I come in?
morirse de hambre	to starve to death	**—Adelante (Pase).**	—Come on in.

"Quien no se aventura no pasa la mar."   "Nothing ventured, nothing gained." (He who does
not venture does not get across the sea.)

Assignment 87

More on the Progressive

1 English has three common uses of the progressive. Which sentence says that
the action going on, is in progress, at the moment of speaking? (a) He kisses her
good night. (b) He is kissing her good night. ▲

He is kissing her good night.

2 English uses the simple present to talk about a scheduled future action: *The
plane leaves at nine o'clock each night.* When one talks about a single, planned
future action one uses the present progressive: *We are having dinner at nine
tonight.* Does Spanish use the progressive in this case? ▲

no (Spanish uses the simple present for both scheduled and unscheduled
but planned future action: *Cenamos a las nueve esta noche; El avión sale
a las nueve.*)

3 Both English and Spanish use the simple present to describe what is customary or habitual. When you want to know what a person's regular occupation is, what do you ask? (a) What are you doing to earn a living? (b) What do
you do to earn a living? ▲

What do you do to earn a living? (*¿Qué hace Vd. para ganarse la vida?*)

4 Both languages use the progressive to ask about something that is not habitual but which is happening at the present time. For example:
Mr. Cárdenas has worked for years as the manager of a store. The store is burned down during a riot. The owner has yet to rebuild it. A friend asks Mr. Cárdenas: (a) What do you do to earn a living? (b) What are you doing to earn a living? ▲

What are you doing to earn a living? *(¿Qué está haciendo para ganarse la vida?)*

5 A prime function of the progressive in both languages is to focus attention on what is going on at the moment of speaking.
    Tito is a house painter. It is lunch time and he is sitting in the patio eating. Someone asks, *¿Qué hace Tito?* May you answer, *Está pintando la casa?* ▲

no (He is not actually painting at the moment.)

6 May you answer, *Está almorzando?* ▲

yes

7 Both English and Spanish use the simple present to state universal laws (The earth revolves around the sun.) or to describe what is customary, habitual, or frequently repeated (The Maya Indians live in Yucatán.). Since many customary events are intermittent, the event described by the simple present does not have to be in progress at the moment of speaking. Thus the sky may be absolutely clear when someone tells a stranger that it rains here a lot. In principle, then, the progressive contrasts with the simple present in two ways: (1) the action is temporary and may or may not be going on at the moment of speaking; (2) the action is in progress at the very moment it is mentioned. What do you say? (a) Right now we are studying worms in our biology class. (b) Right now we study worms in our biology class. ▲

Right now we are studying worms in our biology class.

8 Spanish, unlike English, may use almost any verb in the simple present to describe an event that is in progress at the moment of speaking. It is, for example, perfectly normal to say, *¡Oiga! Llueve.* Translate this. ▲

Listen! It is raining. (English does not say, *Listen! It rains.*)

9 Because both the Present and the progressive in Spanish may regularly be used to describe an event in progress, Spanish uses the progressive much less frequently than English. Since Spanish has a choice, the use of the progressive puts more stress on the notion that the action is either temporary or is actually in progress at the moment of speaking.
    Pepito is in the kitchen. There is a sudden crash of breaking glass. Mother jumps up with a start and says: (a) *¡Dios mío, hijito! ¿Qué haces?* (b) *¡Dios mío hijito! ¿Qué estás haciendo?* ▲

¿Qué estás haciendo?

10 In both languages there are some verbs which only rarely or never are used in the progressive. Would you say, "I am loving my grandmother"? ▲

Not as a simple statement.

11 Spanish does not normally use *estando, yendo,* or *viniendo* with *estar* in the progressive. As a result, until you become much more sophisticated in your use of Spanish, you are always to translate "he is going" or "she is coming" as _____. ▲

él va; ella viene

12 In reality many actions that are going on may or may not be halted temporarily. Both languages, as a result, may use verbs like "to keep on," "to continue" (*seguir, continuar*) to say either the action goes on without interruption (And he just keeps on working) or that after an interruption the doer picks up where he left off (After lunch he kept on working).
Fill in the missing part with the Preterit of *seguir* and the imperfect participle of *trabajar: Después de almorzar él* _____ . ▲

13 When you use a helping verb and an infinitive, you may say either *Vamos*   *siguió trabajando*
a hacerlo mañana or *Lo vamos a hacer mañana*. The same patterns are possible when the progressive is used.

   Divide *sacudiendo* and *colgando* into syllables and underline the stressed syllable. ▲

*sa-cu-**dien**-do, col-**gan**-do*

14 If you add an object pronoun, say *los*, to the end of these forms, you have added another syllable, and in writing what must you add to keep the stress on *dien* and *gan*? ▲

accent mark (*Estoy sacudiéndolos; Estoy colgándolos.*)

15 With the exception of the imperative, the *estar* progressive may be used in all tenses and all modes. Translate: I shall be working when he arrives. ▲

Estaré trabajando cuando él llegue.

16 Translate the indicated words in both sentences: *I will sleep* when you (*tú*) leave. *I will be sleeping* when you leave. ▲

Dormiré *cuando tú te vayas.* **Estaré durmiendo** *cuando tú te vayas.*

17 Both the Preterit and the Imperfect of *estar* may be used to form the past progressive. However, you will not be asked for some time to use the construction with the Preterit. Translate the indicated words: *He was working* (temporarily) in the drugstore when they got married. ▲

Él estaba trabajando.

18 You must, however, choose between the Preterit or Imperfect of *seguir* or *continuar* when they are combined with an imperfect participle. Write the proper form of *seguir: Me miró un momento y luego* _____ *trabajando.* ▲

siguió (The meaning is "after a short interruption, he began working again —he continued working." The initiative aspect requires the Preterit of *seguir*.)

19 What aspect of *seguir* will you use in this example? (*Joaquín* is a calm, professional soldier. Nothing disturbs him.) *El enemigo atacaba por todas partes. Tiraba bombas y granadas. Había soldados heridos en todas las trincheras, pero Joaquín* _____ *tirando sin temor.* ▲

seguía (There was no interruption of the action of *tirando*.)

20 Write the imperfect participle of the forms given: *murieron, sintamos, siguió, leyó, pidieron, pude.* ▲

muriendo, sintiendo, siguiendo, leyendo, pidiendo, pudiendo.

21 In this and the next frame, delete the object noun and rewrite the sentence.
Estoy escribiendo la carta. ▲

Estoy escribiéndola.

22 Estaban mirando las montañas. ▲

Estaban mirándolas.

PANCHO TRABAJA EN LA MINA

A/B

TRABAJA EN LA MINA
ESTÁ TRABAJANDO EN LA MINA

ESTÁ SENTÁNDOSE

C/D

SIGA ESPIÁNDOMELO. UN DÍA,
CUANDO VIAJE, LLEVARÁ LA CAJA

LLEVANDO PAN...
EL CHICO QUE LLEVABA PAN...

E/F

...EL CHICO, SE CAYÓ
...SE CAYÓ

ESTÁ (DES)TAPÁNDOLO

G/H

ESTÁ (DES)CUBRIÉNDOLO

545

Learning New Vocabulary: Health and Medical Terms

You are going to meet sixteen new words in this Assignment. If you follow instructions carefully, you will have them all memorized in a total of just fourteen to sixteen minutes of actual work. There are four parts or steps which are to be done with time in between each. Do not do the whole Program in one sitting. Remember that research has provided evidence that several short learning efforts are more efficient than one long period of study.

Part 1: Contact with the New Words

1 You now know enough Spanish and have had enough practice in figuring out the meaning of new words that you should be able to understand the italicized words in the passage below almost immediately. If you don't understand the meaning of one, don't worry, and read on. You will have three more chances to learn each word.

Hace más de dos semanas que Manolo Durán está *gravemente* enfermo. No está en un hospital, pero su *médico* viene a visitarle cada día. Manolo está tan *enfermo* que el médico insiste que tenga dos *enfermeras*. Una *enfermera* lo cuida de día y la otra de noche. Cada día el médico le pone una *inyección* de *medicina* antibiótica y las *enfermeras* le dan tres *píldoras* cada cuatro horas. Su mamá ha tenido que ir a la botica con la *receta* que escribió el médico para obtener las píldoras. Manolo sufre mucho con problemas de respiración, es decir, le es difícil *respirar*; y cuando *respira*, el aire entra y sale de sus *pulmones* con bastante ruido. Cuando el aire sale de sus *pulmones* y pasa por la *garganta* y por la boca parece que pasa por agua y hace un ruido bastante raro. Si no se mejora pronto el *médico* cree que será necesario llevarlo al hospital y ponerlo en un *pulmón* de hierro para que *respire* mejor. Antes de enfermarse, Manolo era un muchacho muy fuerte y muy activo. Le gustaba mucho cazar, pescar y esquiar en el mar, pero ahora está tan *débil* que casi no puede levantar la cabeza. Todas las noches la temperatura le sube a 104. Para reducir esta *fiebre* el médico le ha dado otra *receta*. Esta *medicina* es un líquido y es muy *fuerte*. La *enfermera* saca la *medicina* de la botella con un gotero (cuentagotas) y le da solamente tres *gotas* en un vaso de agua cada tres horas. ¡Pobre Manolito! Tiene dolor en todo el cuerpo. La luz le molesta tanto que durante el día la *enfermera* le pone una *venda* de tela sobre los ojos para que él esté más cómodo. Sólo puede tomar líquidos porque la comida sólida no le pasa por la *garganta*. Sus *pulmones* no reciben bastante oxígeno porque no puede respirar bien, y allí está con los ojos *vendados*, con una *fiebre* de 104 grados, y mañana es el primer día de clases.

Here is the list of the words in the order in which they appeared in the above story. Cover the English column and check to see whether you were able to get the correct translation from the context. If you miss more than four, reverse the process and go through the list again.

gravemente	gravely (seriously)	*respirar*	to breathe
médico	doctor	*pulmón*	lung

enfermo	sick	*garganta*	throat
enfermera	nurse	*débil*	weak
inyección	injection (shot)	*fiebre (la)*	fever
medicina	medicine	*fuerte*	strong
píldoras	pills	*gota*	drop
receta	prescription	*venda*	bandage
		vendado	bandaged

Do whatever you like for the next ten to fifteen minutes, and, then, go on to Part 2.

Part 2: Rapid Review

In each frame below you will find one or more italicized Spanish words. Think of the English translation, then check the answer. If you miss a word write both the English and the Spanish on your answer sheet, and say both aloud. Remember that writing and saying a word help you remember it.

1 When you are sick your *médico* writes a *receta* for *medicina*. ▲

doctor, prescription, medicine

2 Aspirin comes in the form of a *píldora*. ▲

3 When a *medicina* is a liquid, you may take it by the spoonful. Some *medicinas*   pill
are so *fuertes* you measure them out with an eyedropper *gota* by *gota*. ▲

medicine, medicines, strong, drop, drop

4 When you gargle you are trying to kill germs in your *garganta*. ▲

5 A *zapatero* does something with shoes. An *enfermera* takes care of people who   throat
are *enfermos*. ▲

shoemaker, nurse, sick

6 When a person who is *fuerte* and healthy becomes ill, he usually loses his
fuerza and soon is very *débil*. ▲

strong, strength, weak (feeble)

7 It is common for *médicos* to give liquid *medicina* with a needle, that is, by
inyección. ▲

doctors, medicine, injection

8 The great air sacks in our chests are our *pulmones*. ▲

9 One way of saying that a person has a high temperature is to say that he   lungs
has a *fiebre*. ▲

10 If your *pulmones* are congested you cannot *respirar* well. ▲   fever
11 When you cut your finger you have to *vendar* it with a *venda* to stop the   lungs, breathe
bleeding. ▲

to bandage, a bandage

12 Lola is very ill—perhaps worse. *Está grave.* ▲

She is seriously (dangerously) ill.

For the next fifteen to twenty minutes do whatever you wish, then go on to Part 3.

Part 3: Matching English and Spanish

Spend *only three minutes* on this activity. First, cover the English column, look at each Spanish word, think of the English, then slide your cover sheet down to check. Then, reverse the process, cover the Spanish column, look at the English word, and, then, *say* the Spanish word *aloud*. Do this as many times as you can in three minutes.

médico	doctor	*receta*	prescription
enfermera	nurse (female)	*venda*	(a) bandage
medicina	medicine	*vendar*	to bandage
fiebre (la)	fever	*garganta*	throat
pulmón	lung	*débil*	weak
inyección	injection	*fuerte*	strong
gota	drop	*grave*	seriously ill
píldora	pill	*respirar*	to breathe

Now do whatever you like for *at least one hour.*

Part 4: Matching English and Spanish

Repeat the activity described in Part 3, but use the list below. Concentrate more this time on going from English to Spanish. Don't forget to say each Spanish word aloud. Spend *only three minutes* on this activity.

respirar	to breathe	*médico*	doctor
pulmón	lung	*enfermera*	nurse
vendar	to bandage .	*fiebre (la)*	fever
venda	(a) bandage	*gota*	drop
medicina	medicine	*garganta*	throat
receta	prescription	*débil*	weak
inyección	injection (shot)	*fuerte*	strong
píldora	pill	*grave*	seriously ill

Don't forget to add these words to your vocabulary list.

Self-Correcting Exercises

A *Fórmulas de cortesía:* ¿Cómo se dice en español . . . ?

1	Congratulations!	*¡Felicidades!*
2	Have a good time. (*usted*)	*Que se divierta.*
3	What did you say?	*¿Cómo?*
4	Don't bother. (*usted*)	*No se moleste.*
5	It's no bother.	*No es molestia ninguna.*
6	Make yourself at home. (*usted*)	*Está en su casa.*
7	We are very sorry.	*Lo sentimos mucho.*
8	May I come in?	*¿Se puede?*
9	Come on in.	*Adelante (Pase).*

B *Subjunctive versus Indicative:* Decide mentally whether the Subjunctive (S) or the Indicative (I) would be used for the indicated subjoined verbs if the following sentences were to be translated into Spanish.

1	When we *go* to Panama next week, we want to visit the famous canal.	**1**	S
2	There is no bird in Central America that *is* more beautiful than the *quetzal.*	**2**	S

3 Everybody knows that there *are* many volcanoes in Central America.

4 I want you to *visit* my uncle Pedro in Tegucigalpa.

5 Ruben insists that it *rains* a lot in Central America at this time of the year.

6 In San José, Costa Rica, three evenings a week, while the band *plays*, young men and women walk in opposite directions around the park.

7 I do not believe that the letter *is* from your uncle in Guatemala.

8 There are still a few sections of the Pan American Highway that *are* not paved.

9 I believe that an American dollar *is worth* approximately twelve Mexican pesos.

10 I am so glad that you *are going* to San Juan, Puerto Rico!

11 I am sure that Pepita no longer *lives* on Bolívar Street.

12 I will write to my friend in Santo Domingo so that he *will meet* you at the airport.

13 The guide will not let us go into the cathedral unless we *wear* dresses instead of shorts.

14 My father knows a man in El Salvador who *owns* a coffee plantation.

15 My neighbors are moving to Nicaragua and are looking for somebody who *will teach* them Spanish four nights a week.

16 My geography teacher always asks me to *talk* to the class about my experiences in Honduras.

17 I hear that your brother *works* for the government in Costa Rica.

18 As soon as we *arrive* in Managua next Sunday, I'll call your grandmother.

19 Whenever my aunt *comes* to visit us from Mexico, we try to practice our Spanish with her.

20 I doubt very much that we *will have* another volcanic eruption this year.

3	I
4	S
5	I
6	I
7	S
8	I
9	I
10	S
11	I
12	S
13	S
14	I
15	S
16	S
17	I
18	S
19	I
20	S

C Hacer *with Expressions of Time:* Translate and say the Spanish aloud.

1 She went to the airport an hour ago.

Hace una hora que fue al aeropuerto.

2 They have been at the city hall for forty minutes.

Hace cuarenta minutos que están en el ayuntamiento.

3 We have been swimming for half an hour.

Hace media hora que nadamos.

4 I sold it three months ago.

Hace tres meses que lo vendí.

5 They have been working at the candy store for a year.

Hace un año que trabajan en la dulcería.

6 They began to work there a year ago.

Empezaron a trabajar allí hace un año.

7 I began to like avocados (*aguacates*) three years ago.

Hace tres años que empezaron a gustarme los aguacates.

8 I have liked avocadoes for three years.

Hace tres años que me gustan los aguacates.

D *Present Progressive:* Say aloud the present progressive equivalent of each verb.

1 muere   está muriendo

2 duerme   está durmiendo

3 oye   está oyendo

4 escojo   estoy escogiendo

5	pongo	estoy poniendo
6	pedimos	estamos pidiendo
7	llueve	está lloviendo
8	nieva	está nevando
9	trabajo	estoy trabajando
10	me enojo	estoy enojándome (me estoy enojando)
11	sentimos	estamos sintiendo
12	tememos	estamos temiendo
13	mejoramos	estamos mejorando
14	lees	estás leyendo

Write answers to the following questions using the present progressive of the infinitive given in parentheses.

15	Dime, ¿qué está haciendo el niño? (dormir)	Está durmiendo.
16	¿Sabes qué están haciendo los otros niños? (jugar en la arena)	Están jugando en la arena.
17	Hombre, ¿qué estás haciendo? (regar la hierba)	Estoy regando la hierba.
18	Y Vd., señor, ¿qué está haciendo? (oír el radio)	Estoy oyendo el radio.
19	¿Qué está haciendo Miguel? (pedir una ensalada)	Está pidiendo una ensalada.
20	¿Qué estoy haciendo yo? (leer las noticias)	Está(s) leyendo las noticias.
21	¿Qué están haciendo Vds.? (divertir al niño)	Estamos divirtiendo al niño.
22	¿Qué están haciendo ellas? (cocinar en la cocina)	Están cocinando en la cocina.

E *Commands with* tú: Say aloud both the affirmative and negative familiar commands for each infinitive.

1	tener	*ten, no tengas*		5	salir	*sal, no salgas*
2	venir	*ven, no vengas*		6	ir	*ve, no vayas*
3	ser	*sé, no seas*		7	hacer	*haz, no hagas*
4	poner	*pon, no pongas*		8	decir	*di, no digas*

New Vocabulary

Add the health and medical terms on page 548 to your list and study them.

Assignment 88

Some Uses of the Relators por and para

In the diagram that follows, a small circle ○ represents a person, an arrow represents an action, and the other geometric forms represent shaped space, that is, a building, a street, a city, *etc.*

1 When one moves through space in a linear fashion (*ir, andar, correr, viajar,* *etc.*) there are three possible relationships between the person moving and shaped space. There is, first, the point or place of departure. Second, there is the space that is passed through as one moves, and, third, there may be a destination. These three relationships may be diagrammed as follows.

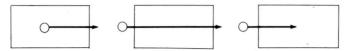

The cover verb *ir* may stand for any linear movement. However, when the movement is away from (= leaving) a point or place of departure you must add a special modifying word. Write the missing word: *Pablo _____ fue hace una hora.* ▲

> *se* (*Ir* means to move in a general way, but *irse* means to move away from the point or place where movement begins.)

2 The meaning of *se* can also be expressed by a relator. Write the missing word: *Pablo se fue _____ aquí hace un momento.* ▲

3 The verb *ir*, without *se*, describes movement *through* space, or movement *to* a destination. Write the missing relator: *Hace dos días que Miguel fue _____ las montañas.* ▲

de

4 You now know that *de* is associated with departure (movement away *from*) and that *a* is associated with arrival (reaching a destination). English may use two relators to establish this last relationship. Write the missing words: We arrived _____ the airport at nine o'clock. We went _____ the airport at nine o'clock. ▲

a

5 What relator does Spanish use for both of these statements? ▲

at, to

6 No matter what word you use in English to show the relationship of a moving object and shaped space, if the idea is one of movement in relation to shaped space without any reference to the point of departure or a destination, Spanish almost always uses *por*. So you translate "He was walking *down* the street" as *Andaba _____ la calle*, and "He was passing *through* the town" as *Pasaba _____ el pueblo*, and "He was running *along* the bank of the river" as *Corría _____ la orilla del río.* ▲

a

7 Write the missing relators: *El ranchero salió _____ la ciudad, pasó _____ el campo, y una hora más tarde llegó _____ su pueblo.* ▲

por, por, por

8 Which one of these two sentences clearly says that Roberto reached his destination? (a) Roberto went to Albuquerque last week. (b) Roberto left for Albuquerque last week. ▲

de, por, a

> Roberto went to Albuquerque last week.

9 Here is the translation of the two sentences above. Which one translates sentence (b) above? (a) *Roberto se fue para Albuquerque la semana pasada.* (b) *Roberto fue a Albuquerque le semana pasada.* ▲

> *Roberto **se** fue **para** Albuquerque la semana pasada.* (***Para*** means to pass *through* space *before* arriving *at* a destination. *Va **a** Albuquerque* leaves out the notion of passage through space.)

10 You can also make this distinction in English in certain patterns. Translate these two sentences: *Miguel se va para San Francisco. Miguel va a San Francisco.* ▲

> Miguel is leaving for San Francisco. Miguel is going to San Francisco.

11 English, however, has no way of showing this difference in meaning when the verb describing movement does not also clearly mean departure. So how will you translate these two sentences? (1) *Pepe va para San Pablo.* (2) *Pepe va a San Pablo.* ▲

Pepe is going to San Pablo.

12 Translate mentally the following pairs of sentences.• (1) *Micaela llegó a las montañas anoche.* (2) *Micaela llegó a las nueve anoche.* Do English and Spanish use the same relator for both space and time? ▲

13 Spanish also uses *por* for space and time. English uses two relators. Translate *por* in: (1) *Jorge camina por el parque todos los días.* (2) *Jorge camina por una hora todos los días.* ▲

yes

14 The relator *para* indicates ultimate destination. Who ultimately gets the book in this sentence? *Me han mandado un libro para Josefa.* ▲

through, for

15 Spanish uses *para* to establish a relationship between an event and a point of time (time destination). Translate *para* in: *Tenemos que llegar allí para las cinco y media.* ▲

Josefa

16 Spanish also uses *para* to establish a relationship between an event and an interval of time. Translate *para* in: *Aquí tengo su lección para mañana.* ▲

by

for (The meaning is "the lesson you are to study for tomorrow.")

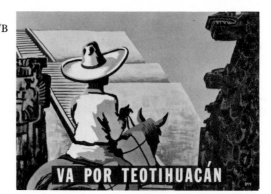

A/B

C/D

Review of hacer *to Measure Elapsed Time*

1   You can make two kinds of statements about an event and the moment of speaking. First, you can say how long an event in progress has been going on. When you use an interval of time to say this, English has only one pattern: He has lived here for a year. Spanish, in contrast, has two options. One is just like the English: *Él ha vivido aquí por un año.* In the other you use the Present of *vivir* and the *hacer* construction. Write this version and put *hacer* first.   ▲

Hace un año que él vive aquí.

2   Rewrite the above and delete *que*.   ▲

Él vive aquí hace un año.

3   Second, you can measure the time between the three possible aspects of past events and the moment of speaking. *Casarse* is a cyclic event which terminated at a point in the past. The time between this past point and the moment of speaking adds up to ten years. Translate: We got married ten years ago. (Put *hacer* first.)   ▲

Hace diez años que nos casamos.

4   *Vivir* is a non-cyclic event which can be Imperfect at some past point. Use the pattern without *que* and translate: He was living here ten years ago.   ▲

Él vivía aquí hace diez años.

5   *Oír* is a non-cyclic event which can begin at some past point. The following statement says that I began to hear the noise at a point in the past, but I do not hear it now. Write the proper form of *oír* and translate the sentence: *Hace una hora que _____ el ruido.*   ▲

oí (I heard the noise an hour ago.)

6   This statement says that I began to hear the noise at a point in the past *and* I am still hearing it now. Write the proper form of *oír* and translate the sentence: *Hace una hora que _____ el ruido.*   ▲

oigo (I have heard the noise for an hour.)

7   This statement says that at a point in the past the noise was going on and I was hearing it. Write the proper form of *oír* and translate the sentence: *Hace una hora que _____ el ruido.*   ▲

oía (I was hearing the noise an hour ago.)

8   When the present perfect describes an event which has not happened for some time, there are two possible Spanish translations. Write both of them for "I have not seen her for several months."   ▲

No la he visto por varios meses. Hace varios meses que no la veo.

Practice in Reading Aloud

1   Say these words aloud. Remember that the *jota* is a fricative version of [k].

recoger	enojar	dejar	coger	jugar
mejorar	escoger	manejar	viajar	vigilar

2   A single *r* at the beginning of a word stands for [rr]. Say these words aloud.

rancho	recibir	redondo	regresar	rojo	rosa

rápido	recordar	regalo	reina	ropa	romper
razón	recta	regla	río	roto	revista

3 The only place [rr] is written *rr* is between vowels. Say these words aloud.

arreglas	carretera	cerrar	correo	ferrocarril	pizarra
arroz	carro	cigarro	correr	perro	tierra

4 In simple declarative statements, the pitch goes down at the end in both English and Spanish. Read these statements aloud. *Yo comí la naranja. Subió al camión. Hace mucho calor.*

5 Say the following aloud and run the sounds together as indicated:

Los abuelos van a la tienda.

Mis amigos se irán en abril.

El director es tan amable.

6 Say the following aloud and fuse the indicated vowels:

tanta arena	ese estudiante	mi hijo
mucho oro	agua amarilla	tu última oportunidad

7 Say this sentence aloud: *Viene de ver a Dolores.* There is only one stop sound in the whole sentence. The letter for it is _____. ▲

V (in *Viene*)

8 Say the following aloud. The first sound of the second word in each phrase is a stop.

un dedo	tan dudoso	mil dificultades	salen demasiado
del desierto	el día	tan disgustado	al dormir

9 Here are some suggestions for practice:

(1) Read the passage below through once silently to find out what is being talked about. Then read it aloud twice.

(2) Pick out each noun and say it aloud as a citation form (i.e. by itself). Then say it with the word which precedes and follows it. Check to see if there is a change of an allophone. You will say, for example, *biólogos* with a stop [b], but *los biólogos* with a fricative.

(3) Say each verb by itself, then say it syllable by syllable, and as a whole word. When you say it syllable by syllable, watch for changes of allophones.

(4) Read the passage aloud at a normal rate and, then, a second time just as fast as you can. At normal speed the following passage can be read in about fifty-five seconds.

Nadie sabe exactamente cuándo ni de dónde vino el hombre al Nuevo Mundo. El análisis del carbono de los huesos encontrados por los antropólogos indica que había hombres en el oeste de los Estados Unidos hace más de quince mil años. Estos hombres vinieron, sin duda, de la parte de la tierra que es hoy Rusia.

Los biólogos que han estudiado la historia del maíz° han demostrado que barcos de las islas del Pacífico vinieron a Perú hace miles de años. Estos expertos saben que el maíz moderno es un híbrido° de dos plantas, una americana y otra asiática.

corn

crossbreed

Las leyendas de los indios mayas de Yucatán y también muchos aspectos de su religión parecen indicar que los hombres blancos llegaron a México por casualidad.° El dios más importante de los antiguos mayas era, según una leyenda, un hombre blanco.

chance

Summary

1 *Por* is used to describe any movement which is related neither to a point of departure nor a destination in space or time.

2 *Para* is used to establish a relationship between an event and ultimate destination in space or time.

In the United States it is often said that "time is money." A great many Americans feel that time should not be wasted and that things should get done as soon as possible and, moreover, with as much dispatch as possible. This attitude produces a style of life very different from that in the Hispanic world.

Almost all human affairs in the Hispanic culture are conducted with more ceremony than in America. Introductions and farewells are more elaborate. The Spanish speaker very frequently uses more words to say the same thing as an American. Ordinary meals are frequently like dinner parties in America. The signatures to formal letters are often elaborate and, by American standard, stilted and over-done. There are more rituals to be observed in almost all social situations. For the American who is not accustomed to all this the Latin seems to lack directness and, often, normal behavior is interpreted as a sign of insincerity. The Latin appears to be putting things off.

How to Get Meaning from Stems and from Context

1 You will be able to learn and remember the meaning of a huge number of new words once you understand that the fundamental meaning of a word is carried by its stem. Moreover, when the word is a cognate, the stems are very frequently the same in both English and Spanish. The suffixes are usually different in shape, but usually carry the same information. Compare "celebr-ity" and *celebr-idad*; "celebr-ate" and *celebr-ar*.

2 Once these suffixes are identified and their function is understood, it should not be necessary to look up words like *preparación*, *preparar*, *dedicación*, *imitar*, and *multiplicación*. Write the English equivalents of the preceding five words. ▲

preparation, to prepare, dedication, to imitate, multiplication

3 Both English and Spanish borrowed many words from Latin. The stems are frequently the same. Those that were made into verbs in Spanish frequently became *a*-verbs. The infinitive of a very large number of cognates that have the suffix *-ación* can be formed by simply replacing *-ción* with *-r*. Write the infinitive forms of *revelación*, *explicación*, *consideración*, *condensación*, and *preocupación*. ▲

revelar, explicar, considerar, condensar, preocupar

4 In English you know intuitively how to manipulate the various suffixes that can be added to a given stem (celebrate, celebration, celebrity, celebrated, etc.). You need to learn to do the same just as automatically in Spanish. Practice doing that in this and the next three frames. Knowing that the Spanish cognate of "education" is *educación*, write the translation of *to educate*, *educated* (female), *educating*, and *I educated* (preterit form). ▲

educar, educada, educando, eduqué

5 Transform *admiración* into the infinitive form, the *nosotros* form of the Imperfect, the *ellos* form of the Preterit, and the perfect participle form. ▲

admirar, admirábamos, admiraron, admirado

6 Translate *intensidad, eliminaciones, educadores, elevación, elevar,* and *indicar.* ▲

intensity, eliminations, educators, elevation, to elevate, to indicate

7 Translate *leche condensada, elevador, devaluación del dólar, exploración lunar, negociaciones de paz, aire acondicionado.* ▲

condensed milk, elevator, devaluation of the dollar, lunar exploration, peace negotiations, air conditioning.

8 Here is a passage which has a lot of new words which you have never heard or seen before. In the next several frames you will be given the steps you can go through to figure out the meaning of all of them. Read the passage first.

Hermenegildo está en el puerto de Buenos Aires. Allí ve barcos de *vela* que no se mueven porque no hay viento. También ve los barcos de *vapor* que van a Europa cargados de carne. Uno de estos grandes *buques de vapor* se *acerca* al *muelle* para *descargar* las cosas que trae de Europa. Cerca del lugar donde Hermenegildo está sentado hay otro *vapor* que *echa* un poquito de *humo* por sus dos *chimeneas.* Está *atado* al *muelle* cerca de un *montón* de carne *helada.* Un grupo de *trabajadores* va a *cargar* la carne en el *vapor.* Son los *estibadores* que *cargan* y *descargan* los barcos en los *muelles.*

The first thing you do when you come to a new passage is to find out who or what is being talked about. What tells you that *Hermenegildo* is a person and a male? ▲

The verb *ver* suggests a person, and the final *o* of Hermenegildo says male. Spanish first names for men, except in cases like José María, do not end in *a*. This is a name inherited from the Visigoths who conquered Spain in the fourth century.

9 The next thing to find out is the locale or location of the action. Where is Hermenegildo? ▲

At the port or harbor of Buenos Aires (*Puerto* is port or harbor; *puerta* is door.)

10 Is Hermenegildo (a) an observer of or (b) an active participant in what is going on? ▲

11 What does Hermenegildo see first? ▲   an observer

12 Are there two kinds of them? ▲   ships

13 Does one kind of ship carry meat to Europe? ▲   yes

14 You now have a lot of useful information about the physical situation (a harbor, two kinds of ships, one hauls meat to Europe) which, in combination with context, should help you figure out the meaning of the unknown words. What kind of a ship cannot move without wind? Translate: *vela.* ▲   yes

15 Now look at *vapor.* It is the stem of the English verb "to _____." ▲   sail

16 What kind of a ship vaporizes something so it can move under its own power? Translate: *buque de vapor.* ▲   vaporize

17 What adverb do you see in the verb *acerca*? ▲   steamship

18 Can you add "ing" to "near" and get a verb form? ▲   *cerca*

19 So *acercar* means literally "to near." A better translation would be _____. ▲   yes

to approach, to come up to

20 What is the stem of *cargados* and *cargar*? ▲

21 What English word associated with ships that haul stuff looks like *carg*-? ▲
carg

22 You can *cargar* and *descargar* a ship in Spanish. Translate these words. ▲
cargo
load, unload (cargo)

23 A ship approaches the *muelle* in the harbor to unload cargo. There is also meat on the *muelle* ready to be loaded on another ship. A *muelle* is a _____. ▲

24 A steamship makes steam by turning water into steam. This requires a fire (except in nuclear ships). What is associated with fire that looks something like *yo fumo?* You may have to go back to frame 8 and read the fifth sentence. ▲
dock or wharf

smoke (Latin *f* sometimes becomes *h* in Spanish.)

25 Now associate smoke with the stem of *chimeneas* and this should suggest the English cognate _____. ▲

26 A chimney on a ship is called a _____. ▲
chimney
smoke stack or funnel

27 You should now be ready to give some meaning to *echa* in *un vapor que echa un poquito de humo por sus dos chimeneas.* ▲
The general idea is "sending up." Other verbs are possible.

28 The ship is stationary; it is ready to be loaded with meat. It is next to the dock. Now, guess the meaning of *atado* in *Está atado al muelle.* ▲

29 Look at the stem of the noun *montón*. Does this stem appear in *montaña?* ▲
tied up

30 What is a *montón de carne?* ▲
yes
A stack, a huge pile, a "mount" of meat.

31 The stem of *helada* is _____. ▲

32 When you get a stem like this and it suggests nothing, remember what often happens to a stressed *e* in Spanish. It changes to _____. ▲
hel

33 What word do you know that looks like *hiel*-? (If your association processes are working right, you should now be thinking of *patinar*.) ▲
ie

34 What is *hielo?* Water which has been _____ into a solid. ▲
hielo

35 The verb *helar* translates _____. ▲
frozen

36 The *or* on the end of a word based on a verb says "doer." Translate *trabajadores*, and go back and read the last sentence in frame 8. ▲
to freeze

37 The stem of *estibadores* is the verb form *estiba*. When you are looking for a cognate of a word that begins with *e* plus *s* and another consonant, what do you do? ▲
workers

38 You now have *stiba* from *estibar*. The *a* is a verbal suffix which does not appear in English. So you are down to *stib*. Remember that Spanish often mixes up *b* and *v* in writing. So, now, think of *stiv* and the special name given to men who load ships. The word is _____. ▲
Drop the *e*.

stevedore (= longshoreman) If *stevedore* was not a part of your vocabulary, you could not, of course, have guessed it. The context, nevertheless, tells you it means "men who load ships." Unless there is a major reason for knowing the English word you should not look up a word whose meaning is clear to you.

Now go back and read through the Spanish passage again in frame 8.

Americans, by and large, are slaves to the clock and to unwritten social rules which are tied to the clock. It is expected that you come to class on time. If you don't, you may get a tardy mark. Conductors get annoyed if people come late to concerts. You must get to the doctor's office at the appointed hour or you may miss your turn or upset his schedule. Every effort is made to be certain that trains, buses, and planes leave on time. One must check out of hotels and motels at a certain time of day or pay an extra day's rent. People buy things on a time payment plan. And, in addition, there is an unmentioned but general agreement that the importance of the person with whom you have an appointment determines how much you arrive *ahead of time* to keep the appointment. Because we are afraid of being *late*, we give ourselves more time in proportion to the importance of the person we are to meet. The more insecure a person is, the earlier he arrives. Many people go to the airport an hour before their plane is to leave.

The Latins are much more nonchalant about arriving on time. Millions of them do not even own a watch or clock and many live a life which is almost totally unregulated by clocks.

Guests may arrive for dinner an hour late and no one expects an apology. Teachers are frequently late for classes. Knowledgeable people call the railroad station or airport before going to meet arrivals because trains and planes are often behind schedule.

The following anecdote clearly reveals the difference in attitude toward punctuality. A North American living in a Latin country had a date to go to the theater with a man and his wife. Because of heavy traffic there was a delay, and upon arriving *five* minutes late he found the couple gone. On next meeting they explained their action in this manner, "We are so accustomed to having you arrive *ahead of time*, we just assumed that you couldn't make it. So we left."

Self-Correcting Exercises

A *Silent Reading*

Grandes hombres de las Américas: Simón Bolívar (primera parte)

Padre de cinco países

Al mencionar la palabra *Libertador*, todo latinoamericano sabe que estamos hablando de Simón Bolívar, el gran héroe venezolano que dedicó toda su vida y su fortuna a la causa de la independencia de varios países de América del Sur. En los primeros treinta años del siglo XIX (diecinueve), este gran patriota fue el líder de los movimientos revolucionarios en los territorios que ocupan hoy día las repúblicas de Venezuela, Colombia, Ecuador, Perú y Bolivia. La unidad monetaria de dos países (el boliviano de Bolivia y el bolívar de Venezuela) y un gran número de instituciones, edificios, parques, calles y ciudades se llaman hoy día Bolívar en honor a este gran apóstol de la libertad.

Primer amor° de su vida   love

Simón Bolívar, cuarto y último hijo de Juan Vicente Bolívar y de María de la Concepción Palacios, nació en Caracas, el 24 de julio de 1783. Sus padres eran muy ricos y pertenecían a la aristocracia colonial. Murieron cuando Simón era muy joven y le dejaron una fortuna de varios millones de pesos que incluía también minas, tierras y cientos de esclavos. Bolívar tenía dieciséis años cuando sus parientes lo mandaron a España a completar su educación. En Madrid conoció a María Teresa Rodríguez del Toro, hija de un amigo de su familia, e inmediatamente se enamoró° de ella. A los diecisiete años de edad, Simón quiere casarse, pero los familiares de la muchacha insisten en que están demasiado jóvenes para el matrimonio.

fell in love

Viudo° a los veinte años

Widower

Después de un viaje de dos años a París, Simón regresó a la capital española y se casó con María Teresa. Perdió el interés en sus proyectos de estudio y decidió volver a su hacienda en Venezuela. La felicidad de los jóvenes esposos no duró mucho tiempo. En menos de un año, María Teresa cayó gravemente enferma y murió víctima de la fiebre amarilla. Esta gran tragedia personal cambió el curso de la vida del futuro *Libertador*. Juró° no volverse a casar y, deseando olvidar su gran pena,° salió otra vez para Europa. Primero fue a Madrid y después a Francia.

He swore
grief

Juramento° en Roma

Oath

En la primavera de 1803, en compañía de Simón Rodríguez, su gran maestro y amigo, Bolívar hizo un viaje a pie desde París hasta Roma. En la histórica capital de Italia, una tarde de agosto, maestro y alumno salieron a pasear por la ciudad y subieron al monte Aventino, una de las siete colinas° que rodean a Roma. Allí recordaron a los héroes de la historia y hablaron de los muchos problemas que Venezuela sufría en aquel tiempo. En un momento solemne de gran emoción, Bolívar le hizo a su maestro la siguiente promesa:

hills

"Juro° delante de usted, juro por el Dios de mis padres, juro por ellos, juro por mi honor y juro por la Patria que no daré descanso° a mi brazo ni reposo a mi alma hasta que haya roto las cadenas° que nos oprimen por voluntad° del poder español."

I swear
rest
chains/will

After the number corresponding to each statement, write *sí* if it is true and *no* if it is false.

1   Bolívar libertó a solamente un país latinoamericano.
2   Las guerras de independencia en América del Sur tuvieron lugar durante la segunda parte del siglo diecinueve.
3   Simón era el menor de los cuatro hijos de la familia Bolívar.
4   Los padres de Bolívar eran millonarios.
5   Los familiares de María Teresa insisten en que se case con Simón inmediatamente.
6   Los planes de estudio de Bolívar en España fueron interrumpidos por Cupido (dios del amor).
7   Simón y María Teresa tuvieron varios hijos.
8   María Teresa se murió porque no le gustaba vivir en Venezuela.
9   Bolívar y su maestro tenían el mismo nombre de pila.
10   El monte donde Bolívar hizo su famoso juramento está en París.

1	no
2	no
3	sí
4	sí
5	no
6	sí
7	no
8	no
9	sí
10	no

B   *New Verbs from Cognates:* Ask and answer the following questions adapting the answers in the margin to your personal situation.

1   ¿Crees que es mejor meditar en una iglesia, o en las montañas?

Creo que es mejor meditar cerca del mar.

2   ¿Es posible abreviar la palabra "usted"?

La abreviamos así: Ud. o Vd.

3   ¿Qué evapora el agua, el calor, o el frío?

La evapora el calor.

4   El profesor anticipa las preguntas de los alumnos, ¿verdad?

Sí, las anticipa siempre.

5   ¿Quién determina cuándo van a ser los exámenes en esta clase?

Eso lo determina el profesor.

6   ¿Con quién te imaginas que Lola vaya al cine el sábado?

No puedo imaginármelo.

7   ¿Cómo transportan a los soldados cuando tienen que cruzar el mar?

Los transportan por barco o por avión.

8   ¿Nos obliga el gobierno federal a pagar impuestos (*taxes*) todos los años?

Sí, nos obliga. Generalmente en el mes de abril.

C   Hacer *with Expressions of Time:* Translate and say the Spanish aloud.

1   I called the doctor two hours ago.

Hace dos horas que llamé al médico.

2   He has been sick for years.

Hace años que está enfermo.

3   I took the yellow pill ten minutes ago.

Hace diez minutos que tomé la píldora amarilla.

4   He has been breathing better for a while (*un rato*).

Hace un rato que respira mejor.

5   The nurse has not come to see me for an hour.

Hace una hora que la enfermera no viene a verme.

Assignment 89

Use of Post-relator Pronouns

1   In English the pronoun form that is bound to a verb or to a relator is the same: (1) Give *me* it. (2) Give it to *me*. The English forms are: *me, us, you, her, him, them, it*. Which two forms may also be used as subject of a verb?   ▲

you, it

2   In Spanish seven of the nine subject pronouns are used unchanged when they follow a relator: *nosotros (nosotras), usted, ustedes, él, ella, ellos,* and *ellas*. Does Spanish have a subject pronoun form equivalent to "it" or "they" when these forms stand for inanimate entities?   ▲

no (*¿De qué color es tu medicina? Es verde. ¿Dónde están las pelotas? Están allí.* All of the third person forms, however, may be used for inanimate entities after a relator.)

3 You have just two new forms to learn: those that match *yo* (*mí*) and *tú* (*ti*). *Ti* has no accent mark because there is no other form like it, while *mí* has a mark to make it contrast with the possessive pronoun _____. ▲

                                mi

4 Is it all right to stress the indicated forms in these utterances? (1) *Who* has it? *I* have it. (2) You got it from *whom*? (3) That's *my* book! (4) I see *him*, but I can't see *her*. ▲

yes (In English a pronoun in any form may be stressed for emphasis.)

5 The spelling contrast between *tú* (subject case) and *tu* (possessive case) tells you that the possessive case forms (a) are (b) are not stressed in Spanish. ▲

are not stressed (*¡Tú lo sabes! Me gusta tu piscina.*)

6 Here, now, is an important difference between the English and Spanish use of the pronoun forms. Is it all right to say this in English? "Whom did you see? Him or her?" ▲

yes (The done-to forms in English are free forms, that is, they can stand alone

7 Is it all right to say this in English? "Who sent it? He or she?" ▲   in an utterance.)

yes (The doer forms are also free forms.)

8 Which pair sounds better in English? (a) To whom did you send it? To him or to her? (b) To whom did you send it? Him or her? ▲

To whom did you send it? To him or to her?

9 Is it possible, however, to say this? "From whom did you get it? Now, tell me! Him or her?" ▲

yes (Although it is considered more elegant to use the relator (to him, from her) in the answers above, the relator may be omitted in ordinary speech.)

10 In Spanish, as in English, the doer pronouns may be used as free forms. Translate: Who arrived? He or she? ▲

¿Quién llegó? ¿Él o ella?

11 In contrast, with the exception of the question words, a pronoun in any other function is a bound form. This means that it <u>must</u> be accompanied in speech by either a verb or by a relator. The with-verb pronouns *me, nos, te, se, le, lo, la, les, los,* and *las* are used <u>only</u> with a verb: *Me lo dieron: Quiero verlas.* You now have enough information to translate the answer to this question: *¿A quién vio usted?* Him or her? ▲

¿A él o a ella? (You just replace the *quién* of *a quién* with the post-relator form. This is like the English in this pattern: *From whom* did he get it? Not

12 Your English intuition tells you when you can use a pronoun all by itself. *from me.*)
The difference between English and Spanish lies in the fact that Spanish *always repeats* the relator with either a name or a pronoun. What you are going to have to do in speaking Spanish is to break yourself of the habit of answering with just a name or a pronoun. In this and the next four frames translate the English answer.

¿De quién recibiste el telegrama? Mary. ▲

13 *¿A quién mandó Vd. la carta?* Her. ▲   *De María.*

14 *¿Para quién compraste las rosas?* You (familiar singular). ▲   *A ella.*

15 *¿Con quién fue Vd. al cine?* Them. ▲   *Para ti.*

16 *¿A quién mirabas?* John. ▲   *Con ellos.*

17 The two post-relator pronouns which have a special form are _____ and *A Juan.*
_____. ▲

mí, ti (After *con* these have another form: *conmigo, contigo.*)

18 There are many ordinary speech situations in which you have to respond to a statement which contains no relator. Someone, for example, says: "That pleases her a lot." May you respond with, "Me too?" ▲

19 The statements above may be transformed to these: "That is very pleasing　　　　　yes to her. To me, too." There is just one Spanish translation for "To me too" and "Me too." It is _____. ▲

20 Translate "With whom did he talk? Me." *¿Con quién habló él?* _____. ▲　　　*A mí también.*

21 Someone says: *A nadie le gustan las culebras* very emphatically. You reply　　　　*Conmigo.* with the translation of "*I* like snakes." You will use two pronouns for "I" to be emphatic. ▲

A mí me gustan las culebras.

22 If you wanted to be very emphatic in English, which pattern would you use? (a) Give *me* it! Not *her*! (b) Give it to *me*! Not to *her*! ▲

Give it to *me*! Not to *her*!

23 The Spanish speaker uses the same pattern for emphasis or contrast, but with a difference. He says, "Give me it to me!" Translate this literally. ▲

24 Say the following aloud in an angry and emphatic fashion: Give it to *me*!　　　*¡Démelo a mí!* Right *now*!

　You intuitively used pitch level four for both of the stressed words. This would be hysterical in Spanish. Say the English without emphasis, and, then, the Spanish in <u>exactly</u> the same way: Give it to me. *Démelo a mí.* Remember that Spanish also gets a lot of contrast or emphasis from using the stem *m* twice: *¡Démelo a **mí**!*

25 Translate: I gave him the money. ▲

26 You may use two syntactic patterns to make this statement emphatic:　　　*Le di el dinero.* *A él le di el dinero. Le di el dinero a él.* Say "I gave him it" without being empha-

---

The United States has been characterized as an extremely mobile society. There are highways and roads that lead just about everywhere, and every day thousands of people use cars, buses, trains and planes to move about. Communications media are also very highly developed, and the gradual result of all this is a breakdown in regional loyalties and differences.

In many parts of Latin America, however, communications are not so highly developed and transportation is still a major problem. This is in part due to local geography and climate, and many millions of people rarely if ever travel very far from their homes. The frequent result of this is a strong sense of regional identification; historically, this in part explains the formation of so many small countries, each with their fixed prejudices against people of other regions. There are often great differences in customs, social mores and even dialects. In fact, linguists have discovered areas where people on opposite sides of the same town exhibit noticeable differences in speech. An expression exists in Spanish, *la patria chica*, "the little home-country," which defines the area in which one is born and to which one owes the greatest emotional attachment. This expression in Spanish is more like "home is where your heart is" than is the contrasting English expression "home is where you hang your hat."

tic. Now say *Se lo di a él* in the same way. What does this intonation tell the Spanish speaker? ▲

27 You are talking to a friend about someone who is always trying to borrow something from you. This is very annoying to you. Today he wanted a dollar and pestered you a lot. Your friend asks you what you did. You are tired and disgusted and reply in a flat and tired tone: "Oh, I gave it to him." Use this same tone and say, *Se lo di.* Does this tell the Spanish speaker you are tired and disgusted? ▲

> You are emphatic.

> no (This is the normal Spanish intonation for a simple, declarative state-ment.)

Review of Comparisons

1 In both languages there are three kinds of comparison: equality, inferiority, and _____. ▲

2 In English a comparison of equality is made with "as . . . as." In Spanish the second "as" is _____. ▲

> superiority

3 The first "as" can be translated by a short or a long form of the same word: _____ and _____. ▲

> *como*

4 You use *tan* when the comparison is made with (a) a noun (b) an adjec-tive. ▲

> *tan, tanto*

5 Translate the indicated words: This war is *as* bloody *as* that one. ▲

> an adjective

6 When two actions are said to be equal, you use the long form _____. ▲

> *tan . . . como*

7 Translate: I admire (*admirar*) him as much as you (*Vds.*). ▲

> *tanto*
> *Lo admiro tanto como Vds.*

8 When a noun is the key word in a comparison of equality, you must make *tanto* agree with it. When the noun stands for a measure entity, the form of *tanto* is *always* (a) singular (b) plural. ▲

9 Translate the indicated words: There is *as much sand* here as there. ▲

> singular
> *tanta arena*

10 When you use "much" in English you are talking about a measure entity. When you use "many," the noun that follows is always (a) singular (b) plural. ▲

> plural

When the Spaniards took over the New World, they did not totally destroy the Indian civilization. There are still many villages which are completely Indian and some in which the people do not speak Spanish. As a result, folk traditions, customs, and art have survived. The silversmiths of Mexico and Peru are famous for their craftsmanship, and each country that has a large Indian population produces its own special artifacts: pottery, blankets, leatherwork, *etc.* In the past, these home industries produced articles primarily for local use. With the growth of tourism, new markets opened up and modi-fications in designs began to develop. Today many craftsmen produce imitation handi-craft articles which sell almost exclusively to tourists. In the areas where there are ruins of ancient Indian civilizations, the craftsmen make copies of original art objects which are sometimes sold to the unsuspecting tourist as originals.

11 Translate the indicated words: I have seen *as many battles* as you. ▲

12 A comparison of inequality is cued in English by the adverbs "more," "less," or the suffix -_____. ▲

tantas batallas

13 The "than" in these comparisons is translated in Spanish by _____. ▲

-er

14 Translate: She is taller than I. ▲

que

Ella es más alta que yo.

15 In this and the next five frames you will find all the key information needed to construct a comparative statement. Supply the missing words and write the Spanish sentence.

Inferiority, Present: *Ella tener dinero yo.* ▲

Ella tiene menos dinero que yo.

16 Superiority, Present: *Mi cuñado tener años Vd.* ▲

Mi cuñado tiene más años que Vd.

17 Equality, Imperfect: *Mi nieto tener frío yo.* ▲

Mi nieto tenía tanto frío como yo.

18 Equality, Preterit: *Mi abuelo trabajar yo.* ▲

Mi abuelo trabajó tanto como yo.

19 Equality, Future: *Yo traer flores ellos.* ▲

Yo traeré tantas flores como ellos.

20 Superiority, Future: *Él aprender español tú.* ▲

Él aprenderá más español que tú.

Summary

1 Only two subject pronouns have different forms after a relator: *yo = mí, tú = ti.*

2 These two have another special form: *conmigo, contigo.* These post-relator pronouns are bound forms.

Self-Correcting Exercises

A *Silent Reading*

Grandes hombres de las Américas: Simón Bolívar (segunda parte)

Conspirador y soldado

En Italia, Bolívar se despidió de su maestro y, después de visitar varias ciudades en el este de los Estados Unidos, regresó a su patria.° Los triunfos de Napoleón en Europa y las intrigantes ideas que había aprendido de su maestro torturaban su mente° con sueños de gloria y grandes propósitos para el futuro de su patria y de toda la América. Al llegar a Caracas se unió a varias de las organizaciones secretas que conspiraban contra la dominación española. España había caído en manos francesas y el movimiento revolucionario de las colonias americanas estaba en marcha desde el Río Orinoco hasta el Río de la Plata. El 5 de julio de 1811 un grupo de ciudadanos° de Caracas proclamó oficialmente la independencia de las Provincias Unidas de Venezuela.

homeland

mind

citizens

La catástrofe de 1812

Pero la nueva república tenía más adversarios que amigos. Parecía que hasta° ————— even
los elementos se oponían a la causa revolucionaria. El 27 de marzo de 1812 un
fuerte terremoto° sacudió a Caracas en el momento en que los habitantes de la ————— earthquake
ciudad llenaban las iglesias asistiendo a las ceremonias religiosas del Jueves
Santo. Casi todos los edificios fueron destruidos y más de diez mil personas
murieron entre las ruinas. Cuando empezaron los temblores,° Bolívar estaba ————— tremors
durmiendo la siesta. Salió corriendo a la calle y se encontró con personas que
iban diciendo que el terremoto era un castigo° que Dios mandaba a los vene- ————— punishment
zolanos por rebelarse contra la autoridad divina del rey español Fernando VII
(séptimo). Cuenta la historia que en aquel momento de pánico, sobre las ruinas
del templo de San Jacinto, Bolívar pronunció delante de la multitud estas
famosas palabras: "Si la Naturaleza° se opone a la Independencia, lucharemos ————— Nature
contra° ella y haremos que nos obedezca.°" ————— against/obey

Fin de la Primera República

El gobierno español mandó una poderosa expedición a pelear contra los patriotas. Bolívar fue ascendido a coronel y luchó valientemente contra las fuerzas
enemigas. Pero las tropas rebeldes fueron vencidas, y la primera república cayó
víctima de la superioridad del enemigo, la indiferencia de gran parte de la
población y los conflictos y divisiones que existían entre los líderes republicanos.
Con un pasaporte que le consiguió un amigo español, Bolívar pudo escapar a
la isla de Curazao. De allí pasó a Cartagena en el territorio de Nueva Granada
que es hoy Colombia.

Peligro de invasión

Una de las primeras cosas que hizo Bolívar en Cartagena fue publicar un
documento explicando las causas del fracaso° de la primera república vene- ————— failure
zolana. Con sus ideas políticas y su total devoción a la causa de la libertad,
Bolívar conquistó la admiración y la simpatía de sus vecinos de Nueva Granada.
Fue nombrado jefe de las operaciones militares y comenzó a organizar la
invasión de Venezuela. El juramento° hecho en Roma no fue en vano. Bolívar ————— oath
lo recordará por el resto de su vida.

Comprehension Exercise: Write the letter that corresponds to the best answer.

1 ¿Qué hizo Bolívar al regresar de Europa?   1   c
   a Visitó a Jorge Washington.
   b Se casó con una muchacha criolla.
   c Empezó a trabajar por la independencia.
2 Los venezolanos celebran su independencia el cinco de julio, . . . que los   2   b
norteamericanos de Estados Unidos.
   a el mismo día
   b un día después
   c un día antes

3 ¿Qué ocurrió en Caracas el 27 de marzo de 1812?   3   c
   a   Un eclipse de sol.
   b   Una erupción volcánica.
   c   Un terremoto.

4 La gran catástrofe ocurrió mientras que los habitantes de la ciudad . . .   4   b
   a   dormían la siesta.
   b   estaban en las iglesias.
   c   se desayunaban.

5 ¿Qué estaba haciendo Bolívar cuando la tierra empezó a temblar (*shake*)?   5   c
   a   Estaba bañándose.
   b   Estaba vistiéndose.
   c   Estaba durmiendo.

6 ¿Cuántas personas murieron en la catástrofe?   6   b
   a   Más de 1.000.000.
   b   Más de 10.000.
   c   Más de 1.000.

7 Había gente en la calle que decía que el terremoto . . .   7   a
   a   era el castigo de Dios.
   b   indicaba el apoyo (*support*) de Dios.
   c   ayudaba mucho a los revolucionarios.

8 ¿Qué hizo Bolívar después que fracasó la primera república?   8   a
   a   Se fue del país.
   b   Se fue al campo.
   c   Se fue a Europa.

9 Nueva Granada es el nombre antiguo de . . .   9   b
   a   Venezuela.
   b   Colombia.
   c   Ecuador.

10 En Nueva Granada, Bolívar se preparó para . . .   10   b
   a   libertar a Perú.
   b   invadir a su patria.
   c   invadir a Ecuador.

B   *Present and Imperfect Progressive:* Write out the combinations using the present progressive following *Notan* and the imperfect progressive after *Notaron.*

Ejemplo: 112 = Notan que Vd. está leyendo una revista.

				Vd.			dormirse.
1	Notan		1	Vd.	1	dormirse.
		que	2	tú	2	leer una revista.
			3	ella y yo	3	tender la ropa.
2	Notaron		4	yo	4	sacudir las muebles.
			5	Vds.	5	dárselo al niño.

1)   111   Notan que Vd. se está durmiendo (está durmiéndose).
2)   212   Notaron que Vd. estaba leyendo una revista.
3)   222   Notaron que tú estabas leyendo una revista.

4)	145	Notan que yo se lo estoy dando (estoy dándoselo) al niño.
5)	123	Notan que tú estás tendiendo la ropa.
6)	225	Notaron que tú se lo estabas dando (estabas dándoselo) al niño.
7)	234	Notaron que ella y yo estábamos sacudiendo los muebles.
8)	151	Notan que Vds. se están durmiendo (están durmiéndose).
9)	134	Notan que ella y yo estamos sacudiendo los muebles.
10)	255	Notaron que Vds. se lo estaban dando (estaban dándoselo) al niño.

C *Subjunctive versus Indicative:* Write the appropriate form of each infinitive in parentheses twice: the first time, make the first verb present indicative; the second time, make it Future. In some cases this will influence the choice between indicative or subjunctive in the subjoined verb.

1 Él (vestirse) tan pronto como su esposa (llamarlo).

se viste . . . lo llama; se vestirá . . . lo llame

2 Él y yo (regar) el jardín sin que ella (decírnoslo).

regamos . . . nos lo diga; regaremos . . . nos lo diga

3 La hija (sacudir) los muebles mientras que su tía (planchar) la ropa.

sacude . . . plancha; sacudirá . . . planche

4 Yo (enojarse) de que ellos no (hacerlo).

me enojo . . . lo hagan; me enojaré . . . lo hagan

5 Tú (hacer) la cama antes de que (llegar) la enfermera.

haces . . . llegue; harás . . . llegue

6 Ellos (decirnos) que (saberlo) para mañana.

nos dicen . . . lo sepamos; nos dirán . . . lo sepamos

(Note: In the last sentence the second verb could be future indicative in both cases, depending upon whether a command or a future event is reported.)

D Por *versus* para: Decide mentally whether *por* or *para* would be used for the items in parentheses, if these sentences were translated into Spanish.

1	(For) several days we did nothing except get ready (for) the trip.	*Por, para*
2	Finally, the time to depart arrived, and we left (for) the airport.	*para*
3	While going (through) the tunnel, we had a flat tire.	*por*
4	We had to stop (in order) to fix it, but we did not miss our plane.	*para*
5	We had to be at the airport (by) 5:00, and we got there at 5:15.	*para*
6	The plane left (for) Caracas at 5:45.	*para*
7	We were in the air (for) six hours.	*por*
8	Going (through) the city where Simón Bolívar was born was an exciting experience.	*por*
9	I will remember it (for) a long time.	*por*
10	Soon it was time to head back (for) home.	*para*
11	(In order) to see all the places of interest in Caracas, one needs more time.	*Para*
12	I had to be back at work (by) Monday.	*para*

E *General Review:* Rewrite each entire sentence, replacing the indicated parts with those in parentheses and making any other changes that may be necessary.

1 Yo *sé* que *mañana* todos los *niños* estarán allí. (dudo, pasado mañana, niñas)

Yo dudo que pasado mañana todas las niñas estén allí.

2 *Dijeron* que la *enfermera* olvidó darle la *medicina* al *enfermo*. (Dicen, médico, píldoras, señora)

Dicen que el médico olvidó darle las píldoras a la señora.

3 *Quieren* que *yo* esté allí para *el 10 de abril*. (Demandan, nosotros, diez días)

Demandan que nosotros estemos allí por diez días.

4 *Siempre* lo hacemos mientras que *ellos* se desayunan. (Mañana, tú)

Mañana lo haremos (hacemos) mientras que tú te desayunes.

5 *Todos los sábados* tan pronto como mi esposa plancha nuestra *ropa*, ella quiere que *nosotros* la colguemos en nuestro *cuarto*. (Mañana, pantalones, tú, cuartos)

Mañana tan pronto como mi esposa planche nuestros pantalones, ella querrá que tú los cuelgues en nuestros cuartos.

6 Dime *tú* con quién andas y te diré quién eres. (usted)

Dígame usted con quién anda y le diré quién es.

Assignment 90

Getting Ready for a Major Test

In your next class you are going to have another major test. It will cover the material specified in the list of objectives for Etapa 5 found on page 436. If you have been doing your Assignments conscientiously and have participated actively in every class and in the laboratory, you should be well prepared for the test without having to spend many hours reviewing. This Assignment, like all previous pre-test Assignments, is designed to identify again for you the areas of content that will be included in the test, to describe the techniques that will be used in evaluating the objectives, and to give you one more opportunity to practice what you will be asked to do.

Do this Assignment carefully. Be sure you do <u>not</u> look at the answers <u>before</u> you have tried to think of them. If you make a mistake, study the frame carefully before continuing.

The test consists of seven parts marked A through G and totals 100 points.

1 **Part A,** *Making Comparisons* (15 points): There are 10 Spanish sentences containing one or more items in English. Write the Spanish equivalent of the English parts which are indicated in parentheses. For example, *Félix tiene* (as many) *camisas* (as) *Santiago*. The correct Spanish equivalents are _____. ▲

tantas, como (Félix tiene tantas camisas como Santiago.)

2 Cover the answers on the right and practice with the following examples keeping in mind that when used with a noun, *tanto* must match it in terminal phoneme and number: *tantas camisas, tantos trajes, tanto calor, tanta humedad*. The short form of *tanto* is *tan* and it is used when the comparison is made with an adjective or an adverb: *tan simpática, tan temprano*.

El metro tiene (*more*) pulgadas (*than*) la yarda.   más, que
Los oficiales son (*as*) crueles (*as*) los soldados.   tan, como
Dicen que hay (*as many*) culebras aquí (*as*) allá.   tantas, como
No hay (*as much*) basura esta semana (*as*) la anterior.   tanta, como
¿Quién es (*older*), tú, o Paco?   mayor
Manuel es (*younger than*) yo.   menor que
Ella no toma (*as much*) leche (*as*) tú.   tanta, como
En el bosque, es (*worse*) encontrar una víbora (*than*) una rata.   peor, que
¿Quién es el alumno (*most*) inteligente (*in*) esta sección?   más, de
Sé que el profesor nuevo es el (*least*) amable (*in*) el departamento. menos, de(l)
¿Tienen los Gómez (*as much*) dinero (*as*) los Ortiz?   tanto, como
No sé, pero las dos familias tienen (*less*) capital (*than*) yo.   menos, que
Febrero no tiene (*as many*) días (*as*) enero.   tantos, como

3 Part B, *The Forms of the Future* (9 points): You are to write the appropriate
future form for nine infinitives appearing in parentheses in Spanish sentences.
Both regular and irregular verbs are included. For example, in *Yo* (*tener*) *que*
ir a la biblioteca, tener is replaced with _____. ▲

4 As you practice with the following examples, remember that: (1) for all   *tendré*
regular verbs the whole infinitive is the future stem, (2) the first and second
suffixes are identical to those of the present tense of *haber* but are all spelled
with an accent except for the *mos*-form, (3) there are very few verbs with irregularities in the Future, and they always occur in the stem.

Este fin de semana yo (descansar), (comer), (dormir) y   descansaré, comeré
  me (divertir).   dormiré, divertiré
Ella te lo (poner) en la escalera porque tú (salir) antes   pondrá
  que nos levantemos.   saldrás
¿(Venir) ustedes conmigo?   Vendrán
¿(Haber) un hotel bueno en este pueblo?   Habrá
Ya tú (ver) que ellos lo (hacer) muy bien.   verás, harán
Ellos no (decir) nada y nosotras no lo (saber).   dirán, sabremos
¿Cuánto (valer) esta guitarra? ¿(Poder) tú comprármela   valdrá, Podrás
  para mi cumpleaños?

5 Part C, *Present and Imperfect Progressive Forms* (10 points): Before practicing
for this part of the test, here is a brief review of what you have to know: Which
participle, the perfect or the imperfect, is used in progressive verb forms? ▲
6 The imperfect participle is formed by adding *ando* to the infinitive stem of   imperfect
a-verbs and *iendo* for *e*- and *i*-verbs. The imperfect participles of *ayudar, temer,*
and *sufrir* are _____. ▲

                                ayudando, temiendo, sufriendo

7 Spanish may write *í* between two vowels as in *leía*, but not plain *i* without
the accent. As a result, you do not write *leiendo* (from *leer*); you write _____. ▲
8 If an *i*-verb has an irregular stem in the *él* form of the Preterit, the same stem   *leyendo*
will be used in the imperfect participle. Write the participle for *durmió, sintió,*
murió, pidió, and *consiguió.* ▲

        durmiendo, sintiendo, muriendo, pidiendo, consiguiendo

9 Change the following into the present progressive: *Ellos estar cantar.* ▲

Ellos están cantando.

10 To back-shift the above you change *están* to _____ and the second verb remains the same. ▲

estaban (*Estaban cantando* is the imperfect progressive.)

11 In this part of the test there are five Spanish sentences in which the verbs are in the simple present or past imperfect. If the verb is in the simple present, you change it to the present progressive; if it is in the past imperfect, you change it to the imperfect progressive. You can make three kinds of mistakes: (1) using the wrong person, number, or tense of *estar*, (2) using the wrong stem or suffix of the imperfect participle, (3) or an error in spelling. In the following sentences write the present or imperfect progressive transform of the indicated verbs.

Quemaban los libros en la plaza central.	Estaban quemando
No me gusta oír eso cuando *como*.	estoy comiendo
Caen insectos en la comida.	Están cayendo
¿Duermes mejor ahora?	Estás durmiendo
La madre *vestía* a Juanito.	estaba vistiendo
Ella y yo *pensamos* cancelar nuestro viaje.	estamos pensando

12 Part D, *Subjunctive versus Indicative* (20 points): There will be a story in Spanish with ten verbs in the infinitive. You are to decide whether to use the indicative or the subjunctive and then write the corresponding form of each infinitive. You can make two mistakes by either selecting (1) the wrong mode or (2) the wrong form or tense of the verb. Cover the answers on the right and do this practice paragraph:

Pilar es una joven muy bonita que (tener **1**) muchos amigos. Es tan popular entre los jóvenes que su madre cree que ella se (ir **2**) a casar muy pronto. Ella quiere que Pilar se (casar **3**) con un hombre bien educado y que (tener **4**) dinero y buena posición. La opinión de Pilar, sin embargo, es muy diferente a la de su madre. Pilar busca un hombre que (haber **5**) estudiado alguna carrera, pero no le importa que él no (ser **6**) rico. Ella cree que (ser **7**) más importante que él se (dedicar **8**) a una profesión interesante. Debe ser un trabajo que a él le (gustar **9**) y le (dar **10**) satisfacción.

tiene
va
case, tenga

haya
sea, es
dedique
guste, dé

13 Part E, *Vocabulary and Structure: Fill in Translation* (26 points): This part covers general vocabulary, ordinal numbers, the conjunctions *e* and *u*, the diminutives, the noun-forming suffix *-ería*, the adverbial suffix *-mente*, and the constructions *al* plus infinitive, *vamos a* for "let's", and *tal* for "such a". You will be asked to translate into Spanish the indicated parts of several sentences. In the following practice sentences, complete the Spanish translation by writing what goes into each blank. *Upon sweeping the rug*, she discovered that there was a *snake* under the sofa.

_____, ella descubrió que había una _____ debajo del sofá. ▲

Al barrer la alfombra, culebra (serpiente, víbora)

14 I've already done the exercises in the *first* chapter and in the *second* also, but I have not finished the *third* chapter. I'm on the *third* page.

Yo he hecho los ejercicios en el _____ cápitulo y también en el _____, pero todavía no he terminado el _____ capítulo. Estoy en la _____ página. ▲

primer, segundo, tercer, tercera

15 *Upon crossing* the street, seven *or* eight policemen ran to arrest me.

_____ la calle, siete _____ ocho policías corrieron a arrestarme. ▲

16 *Tommy* has grown so much that he doesn't fit in his *little bed. Let's* buy him another one *immediately.*

Al cruzar, u

_____ ha crecido tanto que no cabe en su _____. _____ comprarle otra

_____. ▲

Tomasito, camita, Vamos a, inmediatamente

17 Near his store there is a *butcher shop*, a *shoe store*, and a *skyscraper*.

Cerca de su tienda hay una _____, una _____ y un _____. ▲

carnicería, zapatería, rascacielos

18 Ramona *and* Irma told me: *"We're glad. Have a good time."*

Ramona _____ Irma me dijeron: —_____. _____. ▲

e, Nos alegramos mucho *or* ¡ Cuánto nos alegramos !, Que (te) se divierta(s).

19 Why don't you invite the *little Spaniard to go for a walk* with us?

¿Por qué no invitas al _____ a _____ con nosotros? ▲

españolito, ir a pasear

20 *Upon entering* I *generally* say: *"May I come in?"*

_____ yo digo _____: —¿_____? ▲

Al entrar, generalmente, ¿Se puede ?

21 *First and* last time that I do *such a* thing.

_____ _____ última vez que yo hago _____ cosa. ▲

Primera, y, tal

22 Part F, *Reading Comprehension* (10 points): In ten excerpts from dialogs you are to circle the letter in front of the most logical response for the second speaker. Indicate your answer by letter in the following two examples:

Una madre muy enojada le dice a su hija:

—¿Cuántas veces tengo que decirte, muchacha, que el piso de la cocina está muy sucio? ¡Quiero que lo barras inmediatamente! Y después, plánchame esta ropa y cuélgala en mi cuarto.

La hija busca una excusa para no hacerlo y replica:

(a) —Pero, mamá, ¿no ves que hace mucho viento?

(b) —No seas impaciente, mamá. Solamente me lo has dicho diez veces.

(c) —Ay, mamá. Tengo tanto que estudiar para mañana. ▲

(c) (Homework is often used as an excuse for getting out of doing household chores.)

23 Un alumno habla con un profesor:

—Mi hermano Roberto quiere que Ud. sepa que no ha venido a clase porque está en el hospital. Le operaron anteayer de apendicitis.

El profesor contesta:

(a) —Dile que se mejore.

(b) —Dile que venga a bailar esta noche.

(c) —Dile que nos alegramos mucho. ▲

(a) (—*Dile que se mejore.*)

24 Part G, *Reading Comprehension: Meaning from Context* (10 points): This part tests your ability to establish the meaning of an unknown word by observing the speech situation, the subject of discourse, and the verbal context. You do this all the time in English. For example, you immediately know which "root" stands for a part of a plant in "That hog roots in the earth for roots." You can do the same with *pesca* in *El hombre que pesca tiene que ir de pesca.* You will never really learn to use Spanish like a native until you are sufficiently sure of yourself to be willing to make educated guesses and, of course, to be prepared to be wrong once in a while.

Here is a story similar to the one you will have in the test. The title of it is: *Mi hermanito Jaime es un genio que tiene muy mal genio.* How many times does the word *genio* appear in the title? ▲

25 Obviously *genio* and "genius" are cognates, but you suspect after reading the title that *genio* has another meaning which must be quite different from "genius." You don't let this bother you for the moment and you begin the reading of the first paragraph:

twice

> El psicólogo de la escuela dice que mi hermano Jaime es un genio. Le ha dado varios exámenes para medir su inteligencia y los resultados han sido fantásticos. Su cociente intelectual (*IQ*) pasa de 150.

Is the meaning of *genio* in the paragraph you just read the same as in the first part of the title? ▲

yes (It is "genius" in both cases.)

26 So far in the reading, no clues have occurred to help you with the meaning of *tiene mal genio*. You must be patient and not give up when you discover that the next paragraph will not be of any help either. Instead, another characteristic of Jaime is presented in the second paragraph with a completely new word: *haragán*.

> Este genio que se llama Jaime y yo vivimos en el mismo cuarto. Yo sé por experiencia que vivir con un genio no es fácil. En primer lugar, Jaime es muy haragán. No hace absolutamente nada. No hace la cama, no recoge sus cosas, no le gusta barrer ni limpiar el cuarto. No hay muchacho en el mundo que sea tan haragán como mi hermano Jaime.

The English translation of *haragán* is _____. ▲

27 Still no clues have occurred to help you with the meaning of *tiene muy mal genio*, so you continue reading.

lazy

> En segundo lugar, mi hermano Jaime que es tan inteligente y tan haragán, tiene un genio terrible. Por nada se pone furioso. Y cuando está enojado, se pone tan violento que es necesario que yo me vaya del cuarto. Grita como un loco, rompe cosas, me insulta y si no tengo cuidado, un día de estos puede atacarme. Mis padres saben que Jaime es un genio y que tiene un genio terrible. Siempre me indican que tenga paciencia porque yo soy mayor que él.

The translation of *genio* in *tiene mal genio* and *tiene un genio terrible* is not "genius" but _____. ▲

28 After reading about Jaime you have learned that the Spanish word for "lazy" is _____, and that the Spanish word *genio* can be translated as the cognate _____ or as _____, depending on the context. ▲

temper

haragán; genius, temper

29 Now do the following reading selection without guidance applying all the hints given in the story about Jaime. There are enough clues in the selection to enable you to guess the meaning of the new words listed at the end of each paragraph. Remember to cover the answers on the right.

El ratón y la rata

El ratón y la rata son dos animales que pertenecen a la misma familia. Tienen dos dientes incisivos arriba y otros dos abajo. Estos dientes están adaptados para roer. Por esa razón estos animales reciben el nombre de roedores. Los dientes de los roedores son tan fuertes que con ellos pueden roer madera y metales blandos (*soft*) como el plomo (*lead*). El ratón y la rata se originaron en Asia, pero han seguido al hombre a casi todos los países y regiones del mundo. Primero fueron a Europa y de allí vinieron al Nuevo Mundo en los barcos de los descubridores.

Traduzcan al inglés:

ratón

roer

roedor

mouse

to gnaw

rodent

Hay varias especies de ratas, pero las más importantes son la rata negra y la rata común. La rata común es más grande que la rata negra y se ha adaptado a vivir en todas partes. La hembra pare (*gives birth*) de cinco a diez veces al año y cada vez tiene de ocho a veinte hijos que empiezan a reproducirse cuando tienen solamente cuatro meses de edad. Se reproducen tan rápidamente y causan tanta destrucción que es necesario exterminarlos. Son animales muy peligrosos porque pueden propagar enfermedades infecciosas como la peste bubónica o peste negra, la triquinosis y el tifus. No todas las especies de ratas son enemigas del hombre. La rata blanca o albina es muy usada como animal de laboratorio en las investigaciones de medicina, nutrición, genética, biología general y sicología experimental.

hembra

peligroso

peste

female

dangerous

plague

El ratón no es tan grande como la rata y es menos repulsivo. Le gusta comer granos y frutas, pero su alimento preferido (favorito) es el queso.

alimento

food

ETAPA SEIS

Performance Objectives
for Assignments 91–109/110

You will be prepared to continue your study of Spanish successfully if by Assignment 109/110 you have achieved all previous and the following objectives:

Listening Comprehension

1 After hearing twice a selection in Spanish based on vocabulary and structures practiced through Assignment 109/110, you answer correctly in one or two words at least nine of twelve questions (which you hear only once) based on the content of these paragraphs.

You hear twice: José Martí sabe que los veteranos que pelearon en los campos de Cuba desean ofrecer sus vidas a la gran causa.
You hear once: ¿Qué es lo que quieren ofrecer los veteranos a la gran causa?
You write: sus vidas.

Reading Comprehension

2 After reading five paragraphs in Spanish based on vocabulary and structures practiced through Assignment 109/110, you answer correctly in one or two words at least nine of twelve questions based on the content of these paragraphs.

You see: Carmen y Pepe querían que su primer hijo naciera en tierra cubana.
¿En qué país querían Carmen y Pepe que naciera su hijo?
You write: en Cuba.

Vocabulary

3 You match written Spanish words practiced after Assignment 89 with their nearest English equivalents at least ten times out of twelve.

You see:

1 *aceite*	(a)	he deserves
2 *merece*	(b)	it happens
3 *desarrollo*	(c)	development
	(d)	oil

You match *d* with 1, *a* with 2, and *c* with 3.

Morphology and Usage

4 (Evaluated following Assignment 96) Given in Spanish in a visual-graphic format twelve infinitive phrases with several alternate subjects and introduced by a clause that requires the subjunctive, you write the indicated sentences changing the infinitives to the past subjunctive with no more than three errors out of twelve.

You see:

No creía que	1	Vd.	1	decirlo así.
	2	tú	2	dormir bien.

1) 21

You write: *No creía que tú lo dijeras así.*

5 (Evaluated following Assignment 102) Given a written selection in Spanish with twelve verbs left in the infinitive you write the appropriate conjugated form of each infinitive with correct choice of mode, tense, person and number according to the meaning conveyed by context with no more than three errors out of twelve.

You see: Yo (ir) mañana si tú me acompañas. Pero María me dijo que no quería que Tomás (quedar) en casa solo.
You write: iré, quedara.

6 Given five sentences written in English in the pattern "What a generous person!", you translate them into Spanish with no more than two errors.

You see: What pretty flowers!
You write: *¡Qué flores tan (más) lindas (bonitas, hermosas)!*

7 In two paragraphs written in Spanish there are thirteen nouns preceded by a blank. You write the appropriate definite or indefinite article or "zero" for each blank with no more than three errors.

You see: *Ya es . . . una de la tarde, y todavía no ha llegado . . . señor Guevara.*
You write: *la, el.*

8 Given several sentences written in Spanish with eleven verbs left in the infinitive, you write the appropriate conjugated form of the present or past indicative or subjunctive for at least eight of the infinitives.

You see: Era muy importante que Pedro y Pablo me (ayudar) anoche, porque ellos no (poder) ayudarme mañana.
You write: ayudaran, pueden.

9 Five different forms of the perfect indicative appear in English in five otherwise Spanish sentences. You translate at least four of them correctly into Spanish.

You see: *Mi amigo ya **will have arrived** para cuando tú me llames.*
You write: *habrá llegado.*

10 Given four sentences containing a noun with blanks on either side followed in parentheses by the singular *o*-form of an adjective and an indication as to whether the noun represents one unique, one of many, some, or all of the entities labeled, you write the noun and adjective with correct syntax and agreement with no more than two out of eight possible errors.

You see: *Ellos me trajeron los . . . perros . . . (pequeño, some)*
You write: *perros pequeños.*

11 Several phrases in English (cueing probability, limiting adjectives, and the reciprocal reflexive) appear in ten otherwise Spanish sentences. You translate them into Spanish with no more than two errors out of ten.

You see: *Nosotros **will see each other** mañana sin duda.*   You write: *nos veremos (vemos).*

Assignment 91

Some Uses of the Relator de

1 Your vocabulary is made up of words whose meaning you know (horse, car, aspirin, sell, *etc.*) and other words which you know when to use but whose meaning you do not really know. You really don't know, for example, the meaning of "up" in "Don't give *up* the ship" or "to run *up* a bill" or "to sew *up* a convention."

You have been conditioned to reject "He works night" as an acceptable sentence. Your intuition tells you that a relator word is missing, and your experience with this English pattern says that this word should be _____. ▲

> at; He works *at* night. (But, "He sleeps *by* day." The choice of the relators *at* and *by* is conditioned by a purely arbitrary convention (a choice that seems to have no logical basis) of the English language.)

2 Is it proper to say this? He fights *at* the night. ▲

> no (When you use *the* with *night* you are arbitrarily required to replace *at* with *during*.)

3 What relator does convention demand in this sentence? "Many people go to church _____ Sunday." ▲

> on

4 What relator does convention demand in this sentence? "I'll do it the first thing _____ the morning." ▲

> in (The relators *at, by, on, in,* and *during* all perform the same function, that is, they establish a relationship between an event (work, sleep, *etc.*) and an interval of time (night, day, Sunday, the morning, *etc.*) The event either takes place *within* the interval of time or takes place *throughout* the interval of time.)

Here are some important facts about language which will make it much easier to learn how and when to use the Spanish relators. (1) There may be no logical explanation for why a given relator is used to perform a specific function. Choice frequently depends on arbitrary convention. (2) When two or more relators perform the same function, the choice does not depend on the nature of the relationship but on the syntactic pattern (combination of words). (3) The meaning of a relator is in reality the nature of the relationship existing between: two entities, an event and an entity, two events, *etc.* (4) You frequently cannot get the meaning of a relator from its translation because you have no conscious understanding of the meaning of the word used to translate it. (5) There are so many factors governing the choice of relators that you cannot duplicate your native learning processes in the classroom. There is simply not enough time for your intuition to figure out the cues for choice. You must, consequently, consciously learn the rules that govern choices. (6) The only meaningful point of departure in learning to use a relator is the nature of the relationship being described.

There are only twenty-one commonly used relators in the Spanish language. Fifteen of them perform so few functions that their meaning can be learned like that of any other word. For example, *sin* means "without" whether it combines with a noun (*sin dinero*) or an infinitive (*sin comer*). In contrast, there are six relators (*a, con, de, en, para,* and *por*) which are used to indicate relationships between so many different sets of entities and events, that their meanings and functions can only be learned by analyzing the logical relationship between the set which precedes and the set that follows the relator in each specific syntactic pattern.

The rest of this section deals with some of the patterns in which *de* is used.

5 The sentence *Yo soy de Cuba* may be translated word for word into English: "I am from Cuba." The most common meaning is "I was born in Cuba." Keep in mind now that the function and meaning of *de* is determined by the sets which precede and follow it. Does *Yo soy del Banco Nacional* mean that I was born in the National Bank? ▲

6 What relationship exists between *Yo* and *el Banco Nacional?* ▲   no

I am an employee of the bank or its representative.

7 The statement *Esta silla es de España* gives the place where the chair was

———. ▲

made or manufactured

8 What is the relationship between *El jacarandá* (a flowering tree) and *Brasil* in *El jacarandá es de Brasil?* ▲

The jacaranda is a tree *native* to Brazil.

9 What is the relationship between *letter* (a written message) and *Honduras* in *Esta carta es de Honduras?* ▲

The letter was mailed in Honduras.

10 What is the relationship between *piedra* (the building material) and *Italia* in *La piedra de este edificio es de Italia?* ▲

The stone was taken from a quarry in Italy.

11 In each of the examples cited above, the meaning is determined by the nature of the relationship which exists between the subject and shaped space. All of the examples (with the exception of *Yo soy del Banco Nacional*), however, have one thing in common: they all give the place where the subject originates, that is, the place from which it moved to where it now is. Here, then, is a generalization which will tell you all that a native knows intuitively about one function of *de*. Anything that can move or be moved through space (a person, animal, wind, sound, bullet, *etc.*) has a place or point of origin or departure. However you express this, you will use *de* before the word for the place or point of origin or departure.

English does not always require a relator word before the place of departure. Spanish does. Complete the translation: He left the bank an hour ago. *Hace una hora que él salió* ———. ▲

12 In the following sentence there are two possible relationships between   *del banco*
dinero and *Miguel.* One is origin; the other is ownership. English must use two sentences to say this. Write them: *Este dinero es de Miguel.* ▲

This money is *from Miguel.* This is *Miguel's* money.

13 Is origin a logical possibility in this question? *¿Es esta la casa del señor Montenegro?* ▲

no (You can make two different translations, both of which say the same thing: Is this the home of Mr. Montenegro? Is this Mr. Montenegro's home?)

14 In the phrase "a brick house" English uses a noun (brick) to modify another noun (house). Spanish almost never uses this pattern. It uses, instead, the relator *de*. Translate: a brick house (a house of bricks). ▲

una casa de ladrillos

15 The descriptive noun comes first in English. It always follows *de* in Spanish. Translate: *ladrillos de casa.* ▲

16 Translate: *los ladrillos de la casa.* ▲   house bricks

the bricks of the house (when the noun following *de* is modified, the *de* indicates possession or a component part as in "the roof of the house."

17 In both English and Spanish a noun standing for a unit of measurement cannot modify directly the noun standing for the entity being measured. You do not say "an amount money"; you say "an amount _____ money." ▲

18 The word for amount is *cantidad*. Translate: an amount of money. ▲   of

una cantidad de dinero

19 You may say in Spanish *Tiene poco dinero* (He has little money). However, you cannot translate "He has a little money" word for word. When you say *un poco* the word *poco* becomes a noun like *cantidad*. So the translation of "He has a little money" must be _____. ▲

Tiene un poco de dinero.

20 A container may be a unit of measurement. Translate: a cup of sugar. ▲

21 Read the following sentence and consider what logical relationship exists   *una taza de azúcar* between *libro* and *Guerra Civil*. Then translate *de: La semana pasada leí un libro de la Guerra Civil.* ▲

22 Translate: They were talking about Julia. ▲   about

23 The relationship between *hablar* and *Julia* is the subject of discourse: what   *Hablaban de Julia.* is being talked "about." The relationship between *libro* and *Guerra Civil* is the same: what the book talks about or its content. Does "the story *of* his life" show the same relationship? ▲

yes (So English uses either "about" or "of" with the same function. Spanish, however, is more consistent. It uses *de* for all similar patterns: *la historia de su vida.*)

The Morphology of the Past Subjunctive

1 Look carefully at the four indicated forms in these models:
Sé que ellos *pierden* el dinero.   Siento que ellos *pierdan* el dinero.
Sabía que ellos *perdieron* el dinero.   Sentía que ellos *perdieran* el dinero.
The only difference between the preterit indicative (*perdieron*) and the past subjunctive (*perdieran*) is the contrast between _____ and _____. ▲

2 All the forms of the past subjunctive of both regular and irregular verbs are   *o, a* built on the preterit stem, and, in addition, any irregularity in either form or spelling which appears in the third person plural of the preterit indicative will also appear in all forms of the past subjunctive. The Preterit of *dicen* and *andan* is _____. ▲

dijeron, anduvieron

3 Rewrite the following in the past tense: *Papá insiste que ellos digan la verdad.* ▲

Papá insistió (insistía) que ellos dijeran la verdad.

4 The subjunctive equivalent of *hablaron* is _____. ▲

5 The stem (*habl*) and the first suffix (*ara*) of the third person plural make the   *hablaran* base form for *all* the other past subjunctive forms. The second suffix is the same form used in either the present indicative or the present subjunctive. So to get the past of *tú hables*, you use the base form *hablara* and add _____. ▲

6 In all the tenses and modes of all verbs the forms that match *yo, usted, él,*   *s (tú hablaras)* and *ella* have no second suffix. As a result, the past subjunctive form of *hablar* that goes with *all* these subjects must be _____. ▲

hablara (Mi familia insistía que yo hablara español.)

7 The past subjunctive of all *nosotros* forms of *a*-verbs has the stress on the same vowel as the Imperfect. So when you add *mos* to *hablara* you write and say

_____. ▲

habláramos (Also vendiéramos and viviéramos).

8 Write the Preterit and the past subjunctive of *ellos van.* ▲

9 Rewrite in the past: *Yo quiero que Vds. vayan conmigo.* ▲   *ellos fueron, fueran*

Yo quería que Vds. fueran conmigo.

10 In this frame you will see the present subjunctive of verbs in the third person plural. Write the matching form of the Preterit and the form of the past subjunctive indicated by the pronoun given.

compren: nosotros	tengan: usted	lean: ellos
puedan: tú	digan: él	vayan: ella
sepan: yo	mueran: tú	traigan: nosotros
quieran: nosotros	sigan: ustedes	▲

compraron, compráramos; pudieron, pudieras; supieron, supiera; quisieron, quisiéramos; tuvieron, tuviera; dijeron, dijera; murieron, murieras; siguieron, siguieran; leyeron, leyeran; fueron, fuera; trajeron,

11 The past subjunctive is usually a simple back-shift of the present subjunctive.   *trajéramos* In this and the remaining frames, rewrite the sentence in the past. In parentheses you are told whether to make the first verb Preterit or Imperfect. You use the same mode as the one given in the model to be backshifted.

Grita (Pret.) que vienen.   ▲

12 Grita (Pret.) que vengan. ▲   *Gritó que venían.*

13 Es (Imp.) importante que lo sepan. ▲   *Gritó que vinieran.*

Era importante que lo supieran.

14 Manda (Pret.) que vayamos. ▲

Mandó que fuéramos.

15 Sé (Imp.) que Vd. lo hace (Imp.) todos los días. ▲

Sabía que Vd. lo hacía todos los días.

16 Es (Imp.) necesario que ella esté aquí. ▲

Era necesario que ella estuviera aquí.

17 Dice (Pret.) que tú tienes el dinero. ▲

Dijo que tú tenías el dinero.

18 Permite (Imp.) que pasen. (The action is habitual.) ▲

Permitía que pasaran.

19 Demanda (Pret.) que le den el carro. ▲

Demandó que le dieran el carro.

20 Temen (Imp.) que muera el bisabuelo. ▲

Temían que muriera el bisabuelo.

Summary

1 English uses word order and <u>no</u> relator to say "a stone house." Spanish uses *de: una casa **de** piedra.*

2 English uses no relator in "He left the bank an hour ago." Spanish uses *de* to show departure from: *Salió **del** banco.*

3 English uses "from" to indicate origin, place or point of departure. Spanish uses *de.*

4 English uses "of" or " 's" to indicate possession. Spanish uses *de.*

5 English uses "of" to show that one thing is a part of another. Spanish uses *de.*

6 English uses either "about" or "of" to indicate the theme, content, subject matter of a speech, a book, a story, *etc.* Spanish usually uses *de.*

7 *All* past subjunctive forms of *all* verbs use the third person plural preterit stem, including any irregularity in form or spelling.

8 The second suffixes (*s, mos, n, Ø*) are the same as in the present indicative.

9 The past subjunctive is usually a simple backshift of the present subjunctive.

Self-Correcting Exercises

A *Silent Reading:* Meaning from Context

There are enough clues in the following paragraphs to permit you to guess the meaning of the new words.

La otra noche después del cine mis amigas y yo fuimos a ver los escaparates de las tiendas. Yo buscaba un par de zapatillas. Dentro de la casa, siempre me quito los zapatos y me pongo zapatillas porque son más cómodas. En el escaparate de una zapatería vi unas zapatillas que creo son del mismo color de mi pijama. No las pude ver bien porque la luz era mala, y el vidrio del escaparate estaba bastante sucio. Es ridículo que los cristales del escaparate de una de las zapaterías más importantes de la ciudad estén tan sucios.

¿Qué otra palabra en español significa lo mismo que *cristal*?

vidrio

Escriban en inglés el significado de las palabras siguientes:

1 escaparate

store window

2 zapatillas

slippers

Mi tío es carpintero. Hace muebles muy bonitos y trabaja en la construcción de casas y edificios. El otro día estaba cortando un pedazo de madera con un serrucho y se lastimó un dedo. Salió mucha sangre, pero no fue nada serio. La enfermera le puso una venda. Todavía él tiene cinco dedos en cada mano.

3	serrucho	hand saw
4	lastimó	hurt

Después de escribir una carta la ponemos dentro de un sobre y la cerramos. En el sobre ponemos la dirección de la persona a quien escribimos. En la esquina izquierda del sobre es buena idea poner siempre el nombre y la dirección de la persona que ha escrito la carta. En la esquina derecha del sobre ponemos el sello o estampilla. Si queremos que la carta llegue rápidamente, ponemos un sello aéreo. Si no podemos ir al correo, podemos depositar las cartas en un buzón. En las esquinas de las calles principales hay buzones para cartas. En los Estados Unidos los buzones están pintados de rojo y azul.

5	sobre	envelope
6	esquina	corner
7	sello	stamp
8	buzón	mail deposit box

B Por *versus* para: The meaning of the sentence determines whether you will select *por* or *para* for each blank.

1 ¿Cuántos de ustedes han terminado ya la tarea . . . mañana? — para
2 Para llegar al gimnasio no es necesario que Uds. pasen . . . el campo de fútbol. — por
3 Para preparar ese plato tan delicioso, es necesario cocinar los ingredientes . . . ocho horas. — por
4 Mis padres van a comprar muebles nuevos . . . el comedor. — para
5 Paco y Lola van a comprar la comida . . . la fiesta. — para
6 La profesora quiere que terminemos los mapas . . . el viernes. — para
7 El avión . . . Las Vegas sale a las tres menos diez. — para
8 Para llegar al lago donde pensamos pescar, es necesario pasar . . . un bosque. — por

C *With-relator Pronouns:* Read the part of the sentence given in Spanish and use that to decide how the English portions should be translated.

1 ¿Con quién trabajas hoy, *with her or with me*? — con ella o conmigo
2 Trabajo *with you*. — contigo
3 ¿A quién estás mirando? *At you*. — A ti.
4 ¿A quién le gusta estudiar? *I do*. — A mí.
5 Solamente veo a Pepe y *you*, *plural*. — a ustedes
6 ¿A quiénes les dieron la medicina? *To us*. — A nosotros.
7 No la vi *her* pero lo vi *him*. (*Emphasize the contrast.*) — a ella, a él

New Vocabulary

echar(se) a perder	to spoil	**dar patadas (bofetadas)**	to kick (slap)
echarse a reír (llorar)	to burst out laughing (crying)	**dar golpes**	to hit
echar miradas	to glance at, throw glances	**dar mucha lata**	to annoy, bother
		dar la mano	to shake hands
echar la casa por la ventana	to throw a lively party	**dar las cinco (seis, etc.)**	to strike five (six, etc.)
echar de menos	to miss	**vejez (la)**	old age
		juventud	youth

¡Cuánto me alegro! **Me alegro mucho.**	I'm very glad.	**¡Qué bueno!**	Great! Fine!
		No tenga pena.	Don't be embarrassed.

"Si juventud supiera y vejez pudiera."   "Youth is wasted on the young."
(If youth knew how and old age were able.)

Assignment 92

Review of the Subjunctive and Indicative in Subjoined Clauses

Select the appropriate present indicative or subjunctive form of the indicated infinitives:

1 Me alegro de que la enfermera me *haber* vendado el dedo lastimado. ▲
haya (stimulus-response = subjunctive)

2 Noto que el pobre enfermo *estar* respirando mejor. ▲
está (observation of behavior = indicative)

3 Es importante que nuestro grupo se *organizar* lo más pronto posible. ▲
organice (influencing behavior = subjunctive)

4 Creo que ellos siempre *comer* juntos de noche. ▲
comen (belief = indicative)

5 Van a escaparse tan pronto como se *terminar* la batalla. ▲
termine (non-experienced event = subjunctive)

6 Tenemos un ejército que *poder* vencer al enemigo. ▲
puede (experienced entity = indicative)

7 Todos dicen que Manolo *haber* ido de pesca. ▲
ha (reporting an indicative statement = indicative)

8 Vds. ven aquí veinte gallinas que *poner* huevos verdes. ▲
ponen (experienced entity = indicative)

9 Más vale que tú *ir* por este camino para que no te *caer* en algún precipicio. ▲
vayas (influencing behavior = subjunctive), *caigas* (cause and effect = subjunctive)

10 Te digo que (tú) lo *hacer* ahora mismo o vas a perder el derecho de hacerlo. ▲

      hagas (reporting a command = subjunctive)

11 Se preocupan mucho de que la suegra todavía no *haber* llegado. ▲

      haya (stimulus-response = subjunctive)

12 El juez duda que yo *tener* la culpa. ▲

      tenga (doubt = subjunctive)

13 Ellos van de excursión siempre que (ellos) *tener* ganas de hacerlo. ▲

      tienen (experienced event = indicative)

14 En este pequeño país no hay ningún bosque que *tener* culebras peligrosas. ▲

      tenga (non-experienced entity = subjunctive)

15 Vamos a investigarlo de manera que no lo *saber* mis parientes. ▲

      sepan (cause and effect = subjunctive)

16 Yo quemaré la basura mañana mientras ustedes *cortar* la hierba. ▲

      corten (non-experienced event = subjunctive)

Now go back to the beginning of this section and back-shift appropriately all verbs. Back-shift the Present to the Imperfect even though a preterit form might also be acceptable. Check your efforts with the answers given below.

(1)	alegraba, hubiera	(9)	valía, fueras, cayeras
(2)	Notaba, estaba	(10)	decía, hicieras, ibas
(3)	Era, organizara	(11)	preocupaban, hubiera
(4)	Creía, comían	(12)	dudaba, tuviera
(5)	Iban, terminara	(13)	iban, tenían
(6)	Teníamos, podía	(14)	había, tuviera
(7)	Decían, había	(15)	Íbamos, supieran
(8)	veían, ponían	(16)	quemaría, cortaran

Practice with por *and* para

Select *por* or *para* for each blank.

1 Dionisio Pulido no podía dormir. Sacó su reloj del bolsillo y descubrió que ya iban _____ las dos de la mañana. ▲

2 Creyó, _____ un momento, que el reloj andaba mal, pero al mirar ▲

      para

3 la luna _____ la tela de su mosquitero (*mosquito net*), observó que ya era muy tarde. ▲

      por

4 Se puso muy enojado. Le molestaba el ruido de los monos que saltaban de árbol en árbol _____ la selva. ▲

      por

5 Le molestaba también el zumbido (*hum*) constante de los miles de mosquitos que trataban de penetrar el mosquitero _____ picarle (*bite*). ▲

      por

6 Puso el reloj en su bolsillo y al hacerlo tocó el rifle que tenía a su lado (*side*) en la hamaca (*hammock*). Era un rifle automático y al tocarlo olvidó los monos y los mosquitos y empezó otra vez a pensar en los planes que tenía preparados _____ el día siguiente. ▲

      para

      para

7 Sabía todos los detalles de memoria. Una hora antes de salir el sol, sus tropas iban a salir de la selva _____ las montañas. ▲

8 Tenían que pasar de noche _____ los campos que estaban entre la selva y las montañas. ▲

      para

9 Era muy importante que nadie viera las mulas y las cajas de municiones que llevaban _____ los soldados revolucionarios. ▲

      por

10 ¡Qué alegras se iban a poner ellos al recibir las armas nuevas! _____ seis meses se habían defendido con sus armas anticuadas. ▲

      para

11 Dionisio los vio en su imaginación y dejó de estar enojado. Pronto iba a ser un héroe _____ todo el territorio. ▲

      Por

12 Y con este feliz pensamiento se durmió precisamente en el momento en que un mosquito enorme entró _____ un agujero (*hole*) del mosquitero y le picó (*bit*) en la nariz. ▲

      por

      por

Review of Idioms with echar *and* dar

The word "idiom" belongs to the same family of words as "idiot," "idiotic," "idiosyncrasy," and "idiolect." In other words, an idiom is a peculiar way of saying something. Often the individual words in an idiom make no sense at all, but the whole expression is meaningful. You know, for example, when to use "nevertheless" and "notwithstanding" but you cannot get their meaning or function from an analysis of "never the less" or "not with standing." In a similar fashion the Spanish speaker knows that when you say, "I miss him," he says *Lo echo de menos*. The Spanish speaker, however, can make no sense out of *echar de menos* because the literal meaning of *echar* is "to throw," and "to throw of minus" does not come out as "to miss." What the modern Spanish speaker does not know is that *echar* in this idiom is a corruption of *hallar* (to find) and, as a result, *hallarlo de menos* originally meant something like "to find him minus"—subtracted from his usual place. You will be less frustrated in learning some idioms if, like the native, you simply learn to use them without worrying about how the words can mean what they say.

    In each of the following frames you will see an idiom in context and, then, the literal meaning. Think of the best translation and then check, the answer.

1 La cocinera *echó a perder* la sopa. (threw to lose) ▲

2 El niño se cayó y *se echó a* llorar. (threw himself to) ▲

      spoiled

began to, burst out (The meaning is *to begin something suddenly*.)

3 Anoche *echamos la casa por la ventana.* (We threw the house out the window.) ▲

We had a real party; we threw a party.

4 Ella siempre *me echa miradas.* (throws me looks) ▲

5 El niño le *dio una patada* al perro. (gave a paw blow) ▲

6 No me *da golpes.* (give blows) ▲

7 Ella siempre *me da mucha lata.* (gives me a lot of bother) ▲

8 *Dale la mano al* señor, hijo. (give the hand to) ▲

9 En un momento el reloj *dará las nueve.* (will give the nine) ▲

      throws me glances

      kicked

      hit

      annoys, bothers

      shake hands with

      will strike nine

Self-Correcting Exercises

A *With-relator Pronouns:* Write translations for the answers to the following questions.
Who likes chocolate? *¿A quién le gusta el chocolate?*

1	I do.	*A mí.*
2	You (plural) do.	*A Vds.*
3	He does.	*A él.*
4	They (all girls) do.	*A ellas.*

With whom is Daniel going to the movies tonight? *¿Con quién va Daniel al cine esta noche?*

5	With you (familiar singular).	*Contigo*
6	With them.	*Con ellos.*
7	With me.	*Conmigo.*
8	With her.	*Con ella.*

B *Fórmulas de cortesía:* ¿Cómo se dice en español . . . ?

Use la expresión *Tenga Ud. la bondad de* . . . en las siguientes frases:

1	Please write your name.	*Tenga Ud. la bondad de escribir su nombre.*
2	Please tell me what time it is.	*Tenga Ud. la bondad de decirme qué hora es.*
3	Please sit down.	*Tenga Ud. la bondad de sentarse.*
4	Please wait.	*Tenga Ud. la bondad de esperar.*
5	Please write it on the board.	*Tenga Ud. la bondad de escribirlo en la pizarra.*

Imagínese que está hablando con una persona mayor a quien debe tratar de usted para el grupo siguiente:

6	Don't worry.	*No tenga pena.*
7	Have a good time.	*Que se divierta.*
8	Make yourself at home.	*Está en su casa.*
9	How are you? (How is everything going?)	*¿Cómo le va?*
10	Not very well, and you?	*No muy bien. ¿Y a Ud.?*

C *Some Uses of* de: Translate the English and say your answer aloud.

1	a little milk	*un poco de leche*
2	a little money	*un poco de dinero*
3	the money from Mexico	*el dinero de México*
4	the lamp from Mexico	*la lámpara de México*
5	Paco's lamp	*la lámpara de Paco*
6	Paco's watch	*el reloj de Paco*
7	the gold watch	*el reloj de oro*
8	the silver watch	*el reloj de plata*
9	Lola's book	*el libro de Lola*
10	the book from Chile	*el libro de Chile*

11	the book about Chile	*el libro de Chile*
12	the book of animals	*el libro de (los) animales*
13	the wooden animals	*los animales de madera*
14	the animals of glass	*los animales de cristal*

D Por *versus* para: Select *por* or *para* for each blank.

1 Hemos viajado en este país . . . más de seis meses.   por

2 Es necesario que estemos en El Salvador . . . el 10 de octubre.   para

3 Esta vez no pensamos pasar . . . la ciudad de Guatemala.   por

4 Si alguien pregunta por nosotros, dígale que nos fuimos . . . los Estados Unidos.   para

5 Los reporteros de varios periódicos nos han molestado . . . mucho tiempo.   por

6 Queremos viajar . . . la Carretera Panamericana en paz.   por

7 Deseamos visitar los puntos de interés que hay . . . el camino.   por

8 También queremos comprar algunos regalos . . . nuestra familia.   para

E *Silent Reading:* Try to read this selection in four minutes and then answer the questions at the end orally.

La piñata

En muchas partes del mundo de habla española es costumbre romper una piñata en las fiestas de niños. La piñata es en realidad una simple olla de barro° decorada con papel de colores y llena de dulces° y de juguetes.° Algunas personas también ponen en las piñatas dinero (monedas) o frutas como naranjas y manzanas. Hay piñatas muy artísticas construidas en forma de animales como burros, toros y pájaros. Otras veces las piñatas tienen forma de avión o de barco. Es más divertido hacer la piñata en la casa, pero en México, por ejemplo, hay tiendas que venden piñatas de todos los tamaños, formas y colores a precios° muy razonables.

 Cuando van a una fiesta, los niños se ponen su mejor ropa. A sus madres les gusta que vayan muy elegantes y limpios. La piñata es siempre la parte más emocionante° de la fiesta. La cuelgan generalmente del techo o de un árbol. Cuando llega el momento de romperla, todos los niños forman un círculo. Con los ojos cubiertos por una venda,° cada niño le da golpes a la piñata con un palo. Es muy cómico y divertido verlos dando golpes al aire. No es fácil romper la piñata. Generalmente un adulto por medio de° una cuerda° sube y baja la piñata cambiándola de posición constantemente. No permite que nadie la rompa hasta que todos los niños hayan tenido la oportunidad de darle por lo menos tres golpes cada uno.

 Cuando por fin permiten que alguien rompa la piñata, los dulces y los juguetes caen por el piso y los niños los recogen. A veces hay pequeñas peleas, y la fiesta termina entre risas° y lágrimas.° Los niños chiquitos no pueden competir con los más grandes y se echan a llorar. Es preciso tener mucho cuidado para evitar accidentes. Con los ojos cubiertos es tan fácil romper la cabeza de alguien como romper la piñata. El niño que rompe la piñata recibe un premio.° El niño que rompe una cabeza recibe . . .

clay pot

candies/toys

prices

thrilling

blindfold

by means of/rope

laughs/tears

prize

1 ¿Con qué rompen los niños la piñata?   La rompen con un palo.

2 ¿Puede ver el niño que le da golpes a la
piñata?   No, no puede ver porque tiene los ojos tapados.

3 ¿Es fácil romper una piñata?   No, no es muy fácil.

4 Traduzcan al español las palabras siguientes:
candies, toys, rope, laughs, tears, prize.   dulces, juguetes, cuerda, risas, lágrimas, premio

New Vocabulary

bondad	kindness, goodness
darse una caída	to fall down
dar a la calle (al jardín)	to face the street (the garden)
dar en el clavo	to hit the nail on the head (be right)
dar de comer (beber)	to feed (water, give drink to)
dar que hacer	to cause a lot of work (be a lot of trouble)

Tenga la bondad de ayudarme.   Please help me. (Have the kindness of . . .)

Assignment 93

More on the Past Subjunctive

1 In a recent assignment you learned the morphology of the past subjunctive. It is important to understand that any subjunctive mode form in Spanish is also a **tense** form. With minor exceptions, this is not true of English. Compare the indicated forms in both languages:

I **had demanded** that she **go** home.   *Yo **había demandado** que ella **fuera** a casa.*

I **demanded** that she **go** home.   *Yo **demandé** que ella **fuera** a casa.*

I **have demanded** that she **go** home.   *Yo **he demandado** que ella **vaya** a casa.*

I **demand** that she **go** home.   *Yo **demando** que ella **vaya** a casa.*

I **shall demand** that she **go** home.   *Yo **demandaré** que ella **vaya** a casa.*

When you are talking about causing, permitting, or preventing the action of the subject of the subjoined verb, the past subjunctive is used when the influencing verb is in the past tense. In contrast, the present subjunctive is used when the influencing verb has a present tense form in it. Write the proper form of the indicated infinitive:

Mi mamá siempre insistía que yo *beber* leche. ▲

2 Yo quiero que tú *beber* tu leche también. ▲   *bebiera*

3 El general ha mandado que los soldados *atacar*. ▲   *bebas*

4 El señor no permitió que nosotros *entrar*. ▲   *ataquen*

                                                                           entráramos

5 In "I wanted him to sell the house" the dependent form "to sell" provides no tense cue. The tense of the subjunctive, consequently, is cued only by the tense of "wanted." Write the form of *vender: Yo quería que él (vender) la casa.* ▲

6 When the main clause describes an emotional reaction (*alegrarse, enojarse, etc.*) or a judgment (*dudar, no creer, no es cierto, etc.*) the tense of the subjunctive is cued only by the facts of the situation. Thus you may doubt that he went, that he has gone, that he is going, or that he will go. In addition to its use of the subjunctive in these patterns, Spanish differs from English in another important way. The present subjunctive is used for:

vendiera

(1) an action in progress:
    I doubt that he is doing it right now.   *Dudo que lo haga ahora mismo.*
(2) for planned future action:
    I doubt that he is leaving tomorrow.   *Dudo que se vaya mañana.*
(3) where English uses the future tense:
    I doubt that they will get married soon.   *Dudo que se casen pronto.*

This means that Spanish has only one form for the present <u>and</u> future subjunctive. The difference in meaning must be supplied by context or the universe of discourse. Translate the indicated verb: I am glad that she *went* to Spain. ▲

fuera

7 I am not sure that he *will be* here tomorrow. ▲

esté

8 It is impossible that they *have heard* us. ▲

9 Write the proper form for all the indicated infinitives, then check the answers.

hayan oído

Me alegro mucho, Elena, de que tú (1) *haber* podido visitarnos hoy.
Yo también, al recibir tu carta temía que no (2) *haber* tiempo para la visita.
Sé que tú (3) *haber* estado muy ocupada con los exámenes.
¡Tanto trabajo! Yo creía, a veces, que (4) *ir* a volverme loca.
Pero, Elena, no había nadie que (5) *dudar* que no (6) *salir* tú bien en los exámenes. ▲

       (1) *hayas* (2) *hubiera* (3) *has* (4) *iba* (5) *dudara* (6) *salieras*

In both English and Spanish there are common adjectives which are also used as last or surnames. Some are the same, *Brown* (*Moreno*), *White* (*Blanco*), but many do not match. Spanish does not generally use *Black* or *Green*, while English does not use Rojo (red), Rubio (blond), Bello (beautiful), Caro (expensive) or Calvo (bald).

Most American girls called *Dolores* probably do not know that the word comes from Our Lady of Sorrows (*Nuestra Señora de los Dolores*) and the majority of *Lindas* are probably unaware of the adjectival meaning "pretty." In Spanish there are many first names which would sound extremely strange in English. Boys, for example, may be named *Severo* (severe), *Modesto* (modest), *Justo* (just), *Cándido* (candid), or *Amado* (loving). Girls may be called *Dulce* (sweet), *Pura* (pure), *Clara* (clear), *Bárbara* (barbaric), *Blanca* (white), *Celeste* (heavenly), or *Modesta* and *Cándida*. When an adjective has two forms (*Modesto, Modesta*), the form ending in *o* is a boy's name; the form ending in *a* is a girl's name. The name, like a common adjective, agrees with the sex of the person bearing it. Diminutives may also be used as a first name: *Blanquita* (from *blanca*).

Vocabulary for Occupations

Before doing this section, study the New Vocabulary for a few minutes.

1 English, unlike Spanish, frequently makes up a label for what a person does by using a noun to modify "man." These combinations may be run together in speech and writing (fireman, postman, mailman, laundryman) or they may be kept separate in writing (business man, garbage man, army man). English may also derive labels of this kind by adding a suffix-indicating doer to a noun or a verb stem. Thus "bombard" produces "bombardier," "import" gives "importer," and "write" becomes "writer."

At first glance the word "engineer" looks like "engine" plus the derivational suffix *-er*. The word, however, is not based on "engine" but on the stem of "ingenious" because "engineer" once meant an "ingenious" contriver of tricks and mechanical devices. The Spanish equivalent of "engineer," as a result, has the stem of "ingeni-ous." Add the Spanish doer suffix to this and you get

————. ▲

ingeniero (= an ingenious doer).

2 The verb *bombear* translates "to pump." Before fire hydrants became common, fire engines had their own pumps (*bombas*) to force water out of fire hoses. Spanish speakers, as a result, called firemen "pumpers" or "pumpmen." So when you add the doer suffix to the stem "bomb" you get ————. ▲

bombero (which still translates "pumper," "pumpman," or "fireman")

3 The word for "chin," "beard," or "whiskers" is *barba*. So a person who makes his living working on chins and beards is a ————. ▲

barbero (Have you noticed that you drop the final *a* before adding *-ero*?)

4 The word for "letter" is *carta*, and the man who delivers it is not a "mailman," but a "letter-man." The word for this man is ————. ▲

cartero

5 Spanish, like English, has a few words borrowed from the Greek which begin with the sound [s] which may be written *ps* or *s*. These words differ in spelling from English in two ways. First, because Spanish never writes *y* between two consonants, the *psy* becomes *psi*. Second, except for the *ps*, Spanish writes what it says. Is the *ch* of "psychology" pronounced like the (a) *ch* of "chocolate" or the (b) *c* of "college"? ▲

6 Write the Spanish equivalent of "psycho." ▲

the *c* of "college"

7 In Greek *logos* meant "word" or "talk," and so "psychology" means "talk about psyche." When the name of a science is based on *logos* (biology, mineralogy, psychology), the scientist is an *-ist* in English and *-o* in Spanish. Translate: psychologist. ▲

psico (or *sico*)

psicólogo (The stress in all words of this type is on *-ólogo*. So you need an accent mark.)

8 The "curate" of a parish is a man who takes care of the souls of the parishioners. A "minister" may be the servant of a government (foreign minister) or the servant of a church group. The Spanish cognates of "curate" (priest) and "minister" are ————. ▲

cura, ministro

9 A man engaged in "commerce" may be a business man or a "merchant." The cognate of "commerce" is *comercio* and the equivalent of the suffix "-ant"

is *ante*. If you add this to the stem of *comercio* you get the form _____, the
equivalent of "business man" or "merchant." ▲

> *comerciante* (This time you drop the final *-o* of *comercio*, as in *comerci-al*.)

10 Change *basura* to the name of the man who collects it. ▲

11 The cognate of "judge" is _____. ▲

> *basurero*

> *juez* (What you hear does not tell you to write *z*.)

12 The act of pleading a case before a *juez* is *abogar*. The lawyer who does this
is an _____. ▲

13 The final *e* of "police" is not pronounced. What do you add to *polic* to get

> *abogado*

the Spanish cognate? ▲

14 Say aloud the occupational nouns related to *jardín, cocina, pescar,* and *banco.* ▲

> *-ía (policía)*

> *jardinero, cocinero, pescador, banquero*

15 *Política, mecánica,* and *música* translate *politics, mechanics,* and *music.* By
changing the final *a* to *o* you get the equivalents of *politician, mechanic,* and
musician which in Spanish are _____. ▲

> *político, mecánico, músico*

16 The cognates of *astronaut, carpenter, scientist,* and *secretary* are _____. ▲

> *astronauta, carpintero, científico, secretario*

17 A *conserje* is a _____. ▲

> janitor or custodian

Self-Correcting Exercises

A Por *versus* para: Choose *por* or *para* for the blanks.

1 El enemigo va a atacar . . . la derecha.

> por

2 Los tanques y los camiones vinieron . . . aquel camino.

> por

3 Esos soldados no están listos . . . el ataque.

> para

4 Necesitan armas . . . pelear contra el enemigo.

> para

5 Ojalá que las nuevas tropas estén aquí . . . mediodía.

> para

6 Uno de los oficiales habló con el general . . . más de veinte minutos.

> por

7 Es necesario que nos vayamos inmediatamente . . . el campamento que
está a veinte millas de aquí.

> para

8 Creo que podemos escapar . . . esa ventana.

> por

9 ¿Tienes suficiente energía . . . correr?

> para

B *Reading Comprehension and* Fórmulas de cortesía: Write the most appropriate
social amenity for the parts in English.

Imagínate que . . .

. . . estás en el edificio de Humanidades de la universidad. Son las cinco y
media de la tarde y necesitas hacer una llamada telefónica a tu casa para que
alguien venga a recogerte. La única oficina que hay abierta en el edificio es la
de la Sra. Ríos, tu profesora de español. Llegas a la puerta de la oficina y dices:
—(*May I come in?*)

> —¿Se puede?

La Sra. Ríos contesta:

—(*Yes, of course. Come on in. May I help you?*)   —Sí, cómo no. Adelante. (Pase.)
                                             —¿Qué se le ofrece? (¿En qué puedo servirle?)

Tú le explicas el problema y le pides que te deje usar su teléfono. La Sra. Ríos
contesta muy amablemente que ella se va para su casa en ese momento. Su
marido está esperándola abajo en el coche y ellos pueden llevarte a tu casa que
está muy cerca de donde ellos viven. Tú le dices:

—(*Great! But it will be a lot of trouble.*)   —¡Qué bueno! Pero será mucha molestia.
—(*It's no bother at all. Let's go.*)   —No es molestia ninguna. Vamos.

En el coche la Sra. Ríos te dice:
—(*I want to introduce you to my husband.*)   —Quiero presentarle a mi esposo (marido).
—(*It's a pleasure, sir.*)   —Mucho gusto, señor.

El Sr. Ríos contesta:
—(*The pleasure is mine.*)   —El gusto es mío.

Por el camino la Sra. Ríos le explica a su marido que tú eres uno (una) de sus
mejores estudiantes de español y que piensas ir a México el próximo semestre a
perfeccionar tu español. Al llegar a tu casa, antes de bajar del coche, le dices
al Sr. Ríos:

—(*It has been a pleasure to meet you, Mr. Ríos.*)   —Ha sido un placer conocerlo, Sr. Ríos.
—(*The same here. Have a good time in Mexico.*)   —Igualmente. Que se divierta mucho en
                                           México.

—(*You thank Mrs. Ríos profusely . . .*)   —Mil (Un millón de) gracias por todo, señora
                                           Ríos. Adiós.

C *Vocabulary Review:* Complete the translation and say the whole Spanish
sentence aloud.

1 (*Upon seeing the skyscraper*), me dijo que tenía ciento dos   Al ver el rascacielos
pisos.
2 (*I feel like going camping*) con unos amigos este fin de   Tengo ganas de ir de excursión
semana.
3 Sí, señora, tomé (*the pills three days ago*).   las píldoras hace tres días.
4 Elena (*and*) Inés siempre (*spoil*) las fiestas.   e, echan a perder
5 Buscamos (*a little brick house*).   una casita de ladrillo.
6 Ten cuidado. (*The little donkey kicks.*)   El burrito da patadas.
7 Este es su (*seventh*) día en la (*jail*).   séptimo, cárcel.
8 El reloj del ayuntamiento (*has struck five*). Es hora de (*feed*)   ha dado las cinco, dar de comer
a los animales.
9 Cuando mi mamá termina (*the household chores*), se sienta a   los quehaceres de la casa
mirar la televisión.
10 Estoy segura de que mi (*uncle is to blame*).   tío tiene la culpa.

D *With-relator Pronouns:* Translate the English responses. Cover the answer
in parentheses under each sentence until you are ready to check it.

1 ¿A quién le dan mucha lata los niños? —*Me and him also.*

(A mí y a él también.)

2 Ella te echa muchas miradas, ¿verdad? —*Not at me.* —*Nor at me either.*

(A mí no. (Ni) a mí tampoco.)

3 El sábado van a echar la casa por la ventana. ¿Quieres ir conmigo? —*Not with you, with him.*

(Contigo no, con él.)

4 ¿A quién le gusta patinar? —*She does and so do I.*

(A ella y a mí también.)

5 ¿A quién le gusta lavar los platos? —*I don't and neither do they.*

(A mí no, (ni) a ellos tampoco.)

6 ¿Para quién es esta carta? —*It's not for us.*

(No es para nosotros.)

7 ¿Quieres dármela a mí? —*Not to you, to her.*

(A ti no, a ella.)

New Vocabulary

cartero	postman	**secretario**	secretary	**cura**	priest
basurero	trash man	**banquero**	banker	**ministro**	minister
jardinero	gardener	**barba**	beard	**sicólogo**	psychologist
cocinero	cook	**tampoco**	neither,	**(psicólogo)**	
barbero	barber		either	**policía**	policeman
carpintero	carpenter	**rogar (ue)**	to beg,	**político**	politician
bombero	fireman		plead	**astronauta**	astronaut
pescador	fisherman	**comerciante**	business	**científico**	scientist
mecánico	mechanic		man	**ingeniero**	engineer
conserje	janitor	**abogado**	lawyer	**músico**	musician
	(custodian)	**juez**	judge		

Assignment 94

The Meanings and Functions of sino and pero

1 You already know that there is often a great difference between the meaning of a word in Spanish and its translation in English. The word *sino* is an interesting example of this difference. It is actually a combination of *si* (if) and *no* (not), and may still be used with this original meaning:

To whom ought I to give it *if not* to my mother?
*¿A quién debo dárselo **si no** a mi mamá?*

However, the two most common uses of *sino* today make it the equivalent of "except" or "but." The question above can be recast as a statement:

I shall give it to no one *if not* to my mother.
*No se lo daré a nadie **sino** a mi madre.*

A more modern translation of the Spanish is either "I shall give it to no one *except* my mother" or "I shall give it to no one *but* my mother."

With the exception of its meaning of "if not", *sino* can be used <u>only</u> when whatever follows it replaces a previous negative. This can happen only in a special syntactic pattern, that is, in precisely the same pattern that cues the use of "not . . . but" in English. To transform "It is white, not black" into the "not . . . but" pattern you must change the positions of "white" and "not black." Write the transformation. ▲

It is not black, but white.

2 Translate the above sentence. ("It" stands for *tiza*.) ▲

No es negra, sino blanca.

3 To transform *Él es mi tío, no es mi padre* into the *no . . . sino* pattern you put the negative clause first after *Él*, then connect the affirmative clause by deleting *es* and using *sino*. Do this. ▲

Él no es mi padre, sino mi tío.

4 In "It is white, not black" one adjective replaces another. In "It is Carlos, not Antonio" one noun replaces another. Transform the last sentence into the "not . . . but" pattern and translate it. ▲

It is not Antonio, but Carlos. *No es Antonio, sino Carlos.*

5 In this sentence an adverb replaces another adverb:

He put it in front, not behind.
*Él lo puso **enfrente, no detrás.***

Transform this into the *sino* pattern: (1) use *no* to negate the verb, instead of *detrás*, (2) reverse the positions of the indicated adverbs, and (3) add *sino*. ▲

Él no lo puso detrás, sino enfrente.

6 In these sentences an infinitive replaces an infinitive: *No quiero jugar. Quiero comer.* Write the *sino* pattern. ▲

No quiero jugar, sino comer.

7 In these sentences a conjugated verb replaces a conjugated verb: *No quiero que te vayas. Quiero que te quedes.* Write the *sino* pattern. ▲

No quiero que te vayas, sino que te quedes.

8 In this sentence one *porque* is replaced by another: *Ella me gusta **porque es amable, no porque es linda.*** To get the *sino* transform you reverse the position of the indicated clauses and add *sino*. Do this. ▲

Ella me gusta no porque es linda, sino porque es amable.

9 Translate: *Hablé no soló con el hijo, sino también con el padre.* ▲

I spoke not only with the son but also with the father.

10 It is most important, now, for you to be aware of these facts: (1) The *sino* pattern, like the "not . . . but" pattern, requires a negative word in the first part of the sentence.   (2) The contradiction is always between the same parts of speech.   (3) The contradiction is also between members of the same set, that is, black, a color, replaces white, another color. Which two of these conditions are not fulfilled in this sentence? "This book is interesting, but old." ▲

11 So you now use *pero: Este libro es interesante, pero es viejo.* The verb is usually repeated after *pero.* In this and the remaining frames decide whether to use *sino* or *pero.*

He is not funny, but he thinks he is. ▲

12 Not this one but that one. ▲	*pero*
13 It was Matilda who did it, but I don't care. ▲	*sino*
14 It was not Matilda who did it, but I don't care. ▲	*pero*
15 It was not Matilda, but Leonor, who did it. ▲	*pero*
16 The house does not have six but only four rooms. ▲	*sino*
17 The problem is not one of religion but of politics. ▲	*sino*
18 Both are sensitive but not quick to react. ▲	*sino*
19 There was no one home, but a light was burning. ▲	*pero*
20 They run, skip, and jump, but almost never walk. ▲	*pero*
21 Nobody ate but Elena. ▲	*pero*
22 I buy them not for their colors but for their warmth. ▲	*sino*
23 I don't want you to be sad but happy. ▲	*sino*
24 Money may make you rich, but not happy. ▲	*sino*
25 What's wrong? You don't do anything but cry. ▲	*pero*
	sino

Some Useful Expressions

In this part of the Assignment you are to learn fourteen new expressions all of which begin with the relator *a.* There is no fixed translation for *a,* so you must try to see what it means to the Spanish speaker. The key to the meaning of each expression is not *a,* but the word that follows. You will learn more and forget less if you follow the procedure outlined below.

Part 1: Learning the Meaning

1 An interval of time, like an event, has a beginning, a middle, and an end. All time intervals, in addition, are made up of smaller intervals. As a result, one can locate an event in time in several ways. One may say "at the beginning of October," "in the middle of October," or "at the end of October." One may also say "early in October," "about the middle of October," or "late in October." Or one may say "toward the first of October," "toward the middle of October," or "toward the end of October." All of these statements locate an event in a somewhat vague fashion, something like "in the first few *days* of October" or "during the last *days* of the month." Spanish has one set of expressions which can translate all these notions by saying "at the first days of a month," "at the middle days of the month," or "at the last days of the month." The word "days," however, is not said, and the notion is expressed by the plural of the word for beginning, middle, and end: *a principios de octubre, a mediados de octubre, a fines de octubre.*

2 The demonstrative *eso* may be used to point out something in space or a vague interval of time. If one says *Llegó más o menos a la una de la mañana,* the interval of time during which he arrived includes the point labeled *la una.* English can say this with "He arrived *about* one o'clock in the morning." Spanish gets precisely the same meaning with *Llegó **a eso de** la una de la mañana.*

3 In English you arrive at school either "early," "late," or "on time." In Spanish you arrive either *temprano, tarde,* or *a tiempo.* Spanish uses *a* with *tiempo* in the same way it uses *a* with *Llegó a la una, Llegó a tiempo* (He arrived *on time.*).

4 Spanish can make nouns out of perfect participles by changing the final *o* to *a.* So an "entrance" is *entrada,* an "exit" is *salida.* The perfect participle of *ver* is *visto.* The noun *vista* may translate "view," "sight," or "glance." So the translation of "At first sight (glance) it appears enormous but, in reality, it is quite small" is ***A primera vista** parece enorme pero, en realidad, es bastante pequeño.*

5 The cognate of *causa* is "cause." Translate the indicated phrase: *Ella no pudo visitarnos **a causa de** estar enferma.* ▲

because of, on account of

6 The second sentence contradicts the first: (1) *Mañana iremos a la playa **con tal** que no llueva.* (2) *No, **al contrario**, iremos **a pesar de** que llueva.*
A free translation of both sentences is: (1) Tomorrow we'll go to the beach *provided* it does not rain. (2) No, *on the contrary,* we'll go *in spite of* the rain.

7 *Vamos a ver* translates either "We are going to see" or "Let's see." In ordinary speech when one wants to say "Let's see," the *vamos* is frequently deleted. So *A ver* also says "Let's see."

8 You can guess the meaning of this expression. *No tenía carro y, por eso, tuve que ir allí **a pie**.* ▲

9 When you stand on the sidewalk and look at a house, it has a front, a back, and two sides, the right and the left. In the diagram below you are standing at the spot marked "X." The four sentences locate a tree, marked by a circle, from your point of view.

on foot

El árbol está *detrás de* la casa.

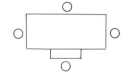

El árbol está *al lado izquierdo de* la casa.

El árbol está *al lado derecho de* la casa.

El árbol está *en frente de* la casa.

X

Another translation of *al lado de* is "next to." *Al lado de nuestra casa hay una tienda.* The literal meaning of *lado* is "side."

10 "Appear" and "apparent" have similar meanings: The child is, *apparently,* very tired. *El niño está, **al parecer**, muy cansado.*

11 Remember *a principios de octubre* translates "at the beginning of October."

Translate the indicated phrase: *Yo fui a España después de estudiar el español solamente tres meses. **Al principio** no entendí mucho.* ▲

at first

Part 2: Review

Spend just three minutes on this part. Here are the steps.

1 Cover everything but the first line below. Look at the Spanish expression and say it aloud. Then look at the English translation. Then slide your cover sheet down to the next line and do the same thing.

2 Cover the English column and see if you can remember the translation of each expression.

3 Cover the Spanish column and see if you can remember the Spanish equivalent of each expression.

a principios de julio	early in July (at the beginning of July)
a mediados de agosto	about the middle of August
a fines de septiembre	late in (toward the end of) September
al principio	at first
a eso de la una	at about one o'clock
a tiempo	on time
a primera vista	at first glance (sight)
a causa de	on account of (because of)
al parecer	apparently
a pesar de	in spite of
(vamos) a ver	let's see
(ir) a pie	(to go) on foot
al contrario	on the contrary
al lado de	next to (at the side of)

Now do whatever you want for fifteen minutes. Then go on to Part 3, which you should be able to do in less than three minutes.

Part 3: Review

Go through the following frames and think of the translation of the indicated expression. Check the answer. If you make a mistake, copy the Spanish expression and its translation.

1 Hacía un sol brillante y al salir del teatro *al principio* casi no podíamos ver. ▲

2 La iglesia está *al lado* del parque. ▲

3 No insistió en que fuéramos, *al contrario*, lo prohibió. ▲

4 Casi todos los alumnos van a la escuela *a pie*. ▲

5 *A ver*, hijito, ¿qué tienes en la mano? ▲

6 *A pesar de* estar herido, el soldado siguió tirando al enemigo. ▲

7 No hay nadie, *al parecer*, que sepa hacerlo. ▲

8 *A causa de* tener tantos años no podrá ayudarnos. ▲

at first
next to
on the contrary
on foot
Let's see
In spite of
apparently
Because of (on account of)

9 No verás, *a primera vista*, que el cristal está roto. ▲

at first glance (sight)

10 Tienes que llegar a clase *a tiempo*. ▲
11 Me acosté anoche *a eso de* las diez. ▲

on time

12 Mi bisabuelo se murió *a fines del* verano. ▲

at about

late in, toward the end of, at the end of

13 Se casaron *a mediados del* mes. ▲
14 *A principios del* invierno no llueve aquí. ▲

about the middle of

At the beginning (In the early part of)

15 Now go back to Part 2, cover the Spanish and see how many of the expressions you can say aloud. Then do whatever you want for an hour, then go on to Part 4.

When a person does not know the name of a shoemaker or a carpenter, it is socially acceptable in English culture to address him as Mr. Carpenter or Mr. Shoemaker. It is this custom which accounts for the fact that *mason, baker, cook,* and many more words like them may be found in both the dictionary and the telephone directory. In the Hispanic world it is also proper to address a man as *Sr. carpintero,* but the translations of the above English name words (*carpintero, zapatero, albañil, panadero, cocinero*) are not used as proper names as frequently as in English. The phonemic structure of Spanish words, however, makes it possible to do something in Spanish which is impossible in English. When it is customary for only men to follow a given trade or occupation, words like *carpintera* and *zapatera* translate as *the wife of the carpenter, the wife of the shoemaker.* The use of these forms, once universal, is today largely restricted to small towns in the rural areas.

Part 4: Final Review

Since all these expressions begin with *a*, the key word or words to be memorized follow. Half of them also have *de* after the key word. In the following frames the key word is first given in English. Then there is a Spanish sentence with a blank for the key word (or words). Write the Spanish equivalent.

1 (side) No hay una casa al _____ de la nuestra. ▲
2 (contrary) Ella no es española; al _____, es colombiana. ▲

lado

3 (foot) Desde aquí en adelante no hay carretera. Tendremos que ir a

contrario

_____. ▲

4 (see) A _____ la mano, chiquita. ▲

pie

5 (spite) Voy a hacerlo a _____ de lo que digan. ▲

ver

6 (apparently) Ellos no lo supieron, al _____. ▲

pesar

7 (because) No vinieron a _____ de la lluvia. ▲

parecer

8 (first sight) A _____ parece ser una mesa, pero es una montaña. ▲

causa

9 (time) Si no llegas a _____ mañana, no encontrarás asiento (*seat*). ▲

primera vista

10 (about) Volvimos a casa a _____ de las tres de la mañana. ▲

tiempo

eso

11 (first) Llovía tanto que no la vi al _____. ▲	
12 (late) Recuerdo que la conocí a _____ de octubre. ▲	*principio*
13 (middle) Te visitaré a _____ de marzo. ▲	*fines*
14 (early) Siempre tiene dinero a _____ del mes. ▲	*mediados*
	principios

If you really want to be prepared, find time to go over Part 2 for two minutes twice before going to class. Don't forget to add these expressions to your vocabulary study list.

Self-Correcting Exercises

A   *Subjunctive versus Indicative:* On the basis of meaning, decide whether to write the indicative or the subjunctive form of each numbered infinitive.

Mis padres quieren que yo sea médico

Mi padre y mi abuelo son médicos y quieren que yo *seguir* **1** la tradición de la familia y *estudiar* **2** también medicina. Ellos creen que yo *tener* **3** aptitud para esa carrera (*career*), pero yo dudo que (ellos) *tener* **4** razón. Ellos me dicen que *ser* **5** muy importante que yo *escoger* **6** una carrera de prestigio. Desean que yo *vivir* **7** cómodamente después que (yo) *terminar* **8** mis estudios. Pero, en mi opinión, hay otras cosas en la vida que *ser* **9** tan importantes como el prestigio y el dinero. Yo pienso mucho en todo esto y cuando *llegar* **10** el momento apropiado, sabré decidir.

Me molesta que otras personas me *indicar* **11** constantemente qué carrera es más importante para mí. Les he dicho varias veces que no pienso decidir definitivamente hasta que (yo) *haber* **12** terminado mi segundo año en la universidad. Todas las noches mientras nosotros *comer* **13** mis padres mencionan el tema (*topic*) de mi educación. No hay nada que me *molestar* **14** más que eso. Sigo repitiendo que tan pronto como yo *saber* **15** cuál es mi verdadera vocación, se lo diré.

1	siga
2	estudie
3	tengo
4	tengan
5	es
6	escoja
7	viva
8	termine
9	son
10	llegue
11	indiquen
12	haya
13	comemos
14	moleste
15	sepa

B   *Reading Comprehension:* Select the most logical rejoinder.

1   Ese muchacho va a darse una buena caída si no tiene mucho cuidado.   1   b
   a   Es cierto; va a echar la casa por la ventana.
   b   Se cae tantas veces cada día que, de veras, no le molesta nada.
   c   Sí, llegará a ser un buen ingeniero algún día.

2   Si juventud supiera y vejez pudiera.   2   b
   a   La juventud vale más que la vejez.
   b   Sí, pero los jóvenes no saben, y los viejos no pueden.
   c   La vejez vale más que la juventud.

3   Mi señora tiene tres almohadas en su cama.   3   a
   a   Le gusta pasar mucho tiempo acostada, leyendo libros de misterio.
   b   Allí es donde prepara los vegetales para la cena cada día.

    c No tiene en qué acostarse en su cuarto de dormir.

4 Nuestra sala da a la calle en vez de al patio.   4 b

    a La niña es la que da de comer al perro.

    b De esta manera sabemos casi todo lo que ocurre delante de la casa.

    c Por eso en la clase de matemáticas siempre damos en el clavo.

5 Los alumnos que estudian menos dan más que hacer a los maestros.   5 c

    a El ejercicio hace maestro.

    b La gallina le dio una patada bastante fuerte al gato.

    c Afortunadamente no soy yo uno de ellos.

6 Por fin llegaron al pequeño pueblo. Pero comenzaron a echar mucho de   6 b
menos al resto de la familia.

    a Están seguros de que ya abrieron la llave.

    b No me sorprende mucho que piensen volver a casa dentro de muy poco.

    c Me parece que es una mezcla de almas y espíritus del otro mundo.

C *Present and Past Subjunctive:* Write the combinations.

Ejemplos: 121 = Llegó antes de que nos durmiéramos nosotros.
          221 = Llegará antes de que nos durmamos nosotros.

			1	traérselo	1	nosotros.
1	Llegó		2	dormirse	2	los otros.
		antes de que	3	poder decirlo	3	Vd.
2	Llegará		4	hacerlo	4	yo.
			5	llegar	5	tú.

1)	144	Llegó antes de que lo hiciera yo.
2)	244	Llegará antes de que lo haga yo.
3)	112	Llegó antes de que se lo trajeran los otros.
4)	233	Llegará antes de que pueda decirlo Vd.
5)	155	Llegó antes de que llegaras tú.
6)	255	Llegará antes de que llegues tú.
7)	131	Llegó antes de que pudiéramos decirlo nosotros.
8)	213	Llegará antes de que se lo traiga Vd.
9)	124	Llegó antes de que me durmiera yo.
10)	232	Llegará antes de que puedan decirlo los otros.
11)	151	Llegó antes de que llegáramos nosotros.
12)	243	Llegará antes de que lo haga Vd.

New Vocabulary

See the Expressions on page 598.

"La oportunidad la pintan calva y con un solo pelo."	"Opportunity knocks only once." (They paint opportunity as bald, and with only one hair.)

Assignment 95

More Useful Expressions, and Vocabulary Review

Review of Expressions with *a*

This section reviews the fixed expressions with *a* introduced in the previous Assignment. Write and say aloud the translation of the English expression.

1 Mi familia llegó a la Ciudad de México *at the beginning of* diciembre. ▲

2 Tendremos que correr si vamos a llegar *on time.* ▲

3 Te verá esta noche *at about* las nueve. ▲

4 Me voy a El Salvador *toward the end of* el mes próximo. ▲

5 *At first glance* ella parece ser muy linda. ▲

6 Siempre lo hacíamos *about the middle of* el verano. ▲

7 Pizarro, *apparently*, no sabía leer ni escribir. ▲

8 Lo haré *in spite of* lo que Vd. diga. ▲

9 La única manera de llegar allí es ir *on foot.* ▲

10 Hay un museo *next to* la iglesia. ▲

11 No voy a venderlo, *on the contrary*, voy a comprarlo. ▲

12 Al entrar en la selva tenía yo, *at first*, mucho miedo. ▲

13 *Let's see.* ¿Quién tiene el número uno? ▲

14 ¿Vas a quedarte en casa solamente *because of* la lluvia? ▲

a principios de
a tiempo
a eso de
a fines de
A primera vista
a mediados de
al parecer
a pesar de
a pie
al lado de
al contrario
al principio
A ver
a causa de

New Expressions

At first glance most of the expressions you are going to meet in this section are going to seem to be meaningless. Their English translations, moreover, provide almost no cues to the meaning of the individual words. This happens because each language organizes reality in a way which is peculiarly its own. You will, however, be less frustrated about the meaning of the Spanish phrases once you realize that you do not, in fact, always know the meaning of the individual words in their English translations. For example, it is a hot and sticky day and there is nothing interesting going on. So someone asks, "Do you want to go swimming?" And you answer, "Of course." You know what this phrase means. You could replace it with "Naturally," but you really don't know what "course" means. Similarly, you know what "anyway" means in "I don't care what you say. I'm going to do it anyway." You really don't know, however, what "way" means. Many Spanish speakers, just like you, do not know the meaning of the individual words in their translations of these expressions. They simply know, for example, that when you say, "I'm going to do it anyway," they will say, *Voy a hacerlo de todos modos.* You must, in view of this situation, learn to match whole expressions without trying to figure out how it is possible for the words to mean what they say.

Study the following in this way for two minutes.

ahora mismo	right now
cuanto antes	as soon as possible
de vez en cuando	from time to time
de nuevo	again
de pronto	all of a sudden
desde luego	of course
de todos modos	anyway
darse cuenta de	to realize

The following expressions are made up of words whose meaning is more apparent. The translation in parentheses is what they mean to a Spanish speaker. The second translation is their normal English equivalent. Study them for one minute.

como de costumbre	(as of custom)	usually, as usual
con razón	(with reason)	no wonder; rightly
de buena gana	(of good desire)	willingly
de mala gana	(of bad desire)	unwillingly
dejar caer	(to let fall)	to drop
dentro de poco	(inside of a little)	in a short time.

Go back over all the above expressions once. Say the Spanish aloud. Then do whatever you want for fifteen or twenty minutes. Then do the first Review which follows. Keep in mind that your purpose in doing this is memorization. Some students do it mechanically and learn nothing.

Review

In each frame below you will see an indicated expression. Think of the English equivalent, then check the answer. If you make a mistake, just keep going.

1 No puedo hacerlo *ahora mismo*. Estoy ocupado. ▲	right now
2 ¿Iremos *como de costumbre* al cine el sábado? ▲	as usual
3 *Con razón* lo hizo. Hoy es el veinte y cuatro. ▲	No wonder
4 Tengo mucha prisa. Hágalo *cuanto antes*. ▲	as soon as possible
5 ¿Qué dijo ella cuando *se dio cuenta de* que tengo un tigre en el garaje? ▲	realized
6 Se lo pedí y él lo hizo *de buena gana*. ▲	willingly
7 Te escribiré *de vez en cuando*. ▲	from time to time
8 Bésame *de nuevo*. ▲	again
9 No sé por qué, pero *de pronto* se puso muy enojado. ▲	all of a sudden
10 ¿Qué tiene Martín? Lo hace todo *de mala gana*. ▲	unwillingly
11 —¿Quieres ir conmigo? —*Desde luego*. ▲	Of course.
12 Sabe que fumar es malo pero sigue fumando *de todos modos*. ▲	anyway
13 Espere un momento. Estaré listo *dentro de poco*. ▲	in a short time
14 Si lo *deja caer* en la alfombra no se romperá. ▲	drop

15 Go back to Part 2 and study the list of expressions for just two minutes. Do what you wish for a half hour, then do the last Review section.

Review

Step 1: Cover the English column below and see if you now remember the equivalent of each Spanish expression.

Step 2: Reverse the process, and continue switching back and forth until you can think of each expression instantly.

de todos modos	anyway	*dentro de poco*	in a short time
desde luego	of course	*cuanto antes*	as soon as possible
de pronto	all of a sudden	*con razón*	no wonder, rightly
de nuevo	again	*de buena gana*	willingly
ahora mismo	right now	*de mala gana*	unwillingly
dejar caer	to drop	*de vez en cuando*	from time to time
como de costumbre	as usual	*darse cuenta de*	to realize

Add these to your study list.

Self-Correcting Exercises

A *Subjunctive versus Indicative:* After reading each sentence, select the appropriate form of the Indicative or Subjunctive for each infinitive.

Problemas domésticos

Marido: Oye, Josefina, ¿sabes dónde *estar* **1** la criada (*maid*)? Necesito que (ella) me *planchar* **2** esta camisa inmediatamente.

Esposa: La mandé a la tienda a comprar unas cosas.

Marido: Pero, mujer, ¿no te dije que quería que ella me *planchar* **3** esta camisa antes que (ella) *salir* **4** a hacer los mandados?

Esposa: No te pongas furioso, Roberto. Estoy segura que ella *volver* **5** dentro de unos minutos.

Marido: Ya son las diez menos cuarto y el jefe (*boss*) va a venir a recogerme a las diez. No voy a estar listo cuando él *llegar* **6** y hoy tenemos una junta (*meeting*) muy importante.

Esposa: ¡Cálmate, hombre! Ten paciencia. En cuanto Juana *regresar* **7** de las tiendas, (ella) te *planchar* **8** la camisa.

Marido: Mi opinión es que Juana no *ser* **9** muy buena criada. Siempre que ella *ir* **10** al mercado, en vez de volver inmediatamente, le gusta demasiado hablar con el carnicero, el panadero y . . .

Esposa: No seas injusto, Roberto. Juana habla mucho, pero no hay criada más trabajadora que ella. En realidad, tú sabes muy bien que los quehaceres de esta casa *ser* **11** tantos que necesitamos por lo menos dos criadas más: una que *cuidar* **12** a los niños y otra que *limpiar* **13** la casa. En casa de mi madre siempre ha habido tres o más criadas.

Marido: Mira, Josefina, cuando yo *ser* **14** presidente de la compañía donde trabajo, tú *poder* **15** tener tantas criadas como tu madre. Por el momento, es importante que (tú) *recordar* **16** que yo *ser* **17** un simple

1	está
2	planche
3	planchara
4	saliera
5	volverá
6	llegue
7	regrese
8	planchará
9	es
10	va
11	son
12	cuide
13	limpie
14	sea
15	podrás
16	recuerdes
17	soy

empleado. Y si alguien no me plancha inmediatamente esta camisa, cuando *venir* **18** el jefe no seré nada.

Esposa: Alguien está a la puerta. Creo que *ser* **19** Juana. (Que) Dios quiera que *ser* **20** ella, porque yo no sé planchar.

Marido: Ojalá que (tú) *tener* **21** razón. Que Dios te *oír* **22**. Porque si en vez de ser Juana, es el jefe . . .

Esposa: ¡Ay, Dios mío! No es Juana.

18 venga
19 es
20 sea
21 tengas
22 oiga

B *Useful Expressions:* Cover the answers in the margin, translate mentally the appropriate expression, and check your response.

1 Tengo una cita con el sicólogo *early* in mayo.

a principios de

2 Juan está *next to* Jorge y los dos vienen *on foot*.

al lado de, a pie

3 No recuerdo si tenemos que investigarlo *about the middle of* junio o *late in* esta semana.

a mediados de

a fines de

4 *Apparently, at first sight* él no supo lo que pasó.

Al parecer, a primera vista

5 *On the contrary* esto ocurrió *at first*.

Al contrario, al principio

6 *Let's see* si Jorge llega *on time* esta vez.

A ver, a tiempo

7 Tendremos que salir *at about* las seis *on account of* (e)l nuevo horario (*schedule*) del tren.

a eso de, a causa de

8 Él no vino *in spite of* lo que le dijo Tomás.

a pesar de

C *Refranes:* Say aloud the proverb(s) that fits each situation.

1 María Dolores tiene la mala costumbre de hablar demasiado. Algún día, a causa de eso, ella va a tener problemas.

"En boca cerrada no entran moscas" or "Escucha, o tu lengua te hará sorda."

2 Panchito trabaja en el garaje de su abuelo. No hay muchacho más trabajador e industrioso que él. Pero a veces no hace muy bien las cosas porque es demasiado joven y no ha tenido mucha experiencia. El abuelo de Panchito ha sido mecánico por 30 años. Sabe mucho de automóviles, pero está un poco débil, y hay muchas cosas que ya él no puede hacer.

"Si juventud supiera y vejez pudiera."

3 Say aloud the Spanish equivalent of "Opportunity knocks only once."

"La oportunidad la pintan calva y con un solo pelo."

D *General Review:* Rewrite each sentence replacing the indicated parts with the items in parentheses and making whatever changes are necessary.

1 Mis *padres* quieren que yo vaya de *pesca* con ellos. (padre, -ía, excursión)

Mi padre quería que yo fuera de excursión con él.

2 *Algún día Juan José* llegará a ser bombero porque le gusta *apagar fuegos*. (Pronto, yo, cortar pelo)

Pronto yo llegaré a ser barbero porque me gusta cortar pelo.

3 *Tendremos* que regar la hierba para *las seis y media* cada *día*.   (Nos mandan, treinta minutos, tres días)

Nos mandan que reguemos la hierba por treinta minutos cada tres días.

4 Dice que está dándole *golpes* a la *máquina* para que *funcione mejor*.   (de comer, gato, no morirse)

Dice que está dándole de comer al gato para que no se muera.

E *Silent Reading:* Read as fast as you can without stopping to translate and answer the question at the end.

Si quieres saber quién soy, lee.

No soy un personaje histórico sino ficticio, pero el autor que me creó, conoció a muchos muchachos como yo en los días de su juventud cuando vivió en un pueblo de Misuri a mediados del siglo diecinueve. Los lugares, personas y costumbres que él describe y las aventuras que narra tienen una relación muy íntima con sus experiencias personales.

   Yo no recuerdo a mi padre. Mi mamá murió cuando yo estaba muy chiquito. Después de su muerte, mi hermano, mejor dicho, mi medio hermano y yo fuimos a vivir con mi tía Polly y su hija María. Hacía varios años que el marido de mi tía se había muerto y ella era una viuda° bastante amable, pero demasiado estricta. A mí, sobre todo, ella me daba mucha lata.   **widow**

   Cuando el escritor que me creó, comienza la narración de mis aventuras, estoy viviendo en San Petersburgo, un pueblito situado en las márgenes° del río más grande de los Estados Unidos. El río es la atracción principal para los muchachos del pueblo. Allí nadamos, pescamos, paseamos en bote y jugamos a los piratas.   **banks**

   Yo no soy el niño modelo del pueblo. Al contrario, mucha gente cree que soy malo, desobediente, un poco estúpido y muy travieso.° Mi tía Polly nunca está satisfecha con mi conducta y siempre está diciendo que yo la hago sufrir mucho. Yo estoy convencido de que ella no me comprende.   **mischievous**

   La siguiente lista menciona varias cosas que no puedo tolerar: trabajar, ir a la escuela, ser puntual, ir a la escuela dominical° y aprender de memoria versos de la Biblia, acostarme y levantarme temprano, lavarme y bañarme, ponerme ropa limpia, jugar con los niños buenos del pueblo y hacerle mandados a mi tía.   **Sunday**

   Para que obtengan una idea correcta de mi carácter y mi personalidad mencionaré también las cosas que más me gusta hacer: pelear con mis compañeros y con mi hermano que es menor que yo, molestar a mi maestro y a mis compañeros de clase, escaparme de la escuela por las tardes para ir al río (sobre todo en los días de calor), coleccionar animales vivos y muertos y jugar con ellos en la escuela y en la iglesia, escaparme de noche por la ventana de mi cuarto y salir de excursión con mi compañero de aventuras, el hijo de un borracho° a quien toda la gente decente detesta.   **drunkard**

   Olvidaba mencionar que una de mis preocupaciones principales es hacerme amigo de todas las muchachas bonitas que vienen a nuestro pueblo. Soy muy joven, pero ya he tenido varias amiguitas. Estoy loco por Rebeca, una linda y

graciosa° muchachita de pelo amarillo y ojos azules que es hija del juez   cute
Thatcher.

Si todavía no has adivinado° quién soy, te diré que en la novela del gran   guess
escritor norteamericano Mark Twain, donde aparezco como personaje principal, me llaman Tom cuando soy bueno, pero cuando soy malo me llaman
Tomás. Mis aventuras han sido filmadas para el cine y la televisión.

¿Cómo se llama este personaje?   Tom Sawyer

New Vocabulary

en fin	in short	**después de todo**	after all
en seguida	at once, immediately	**echar una carta al correo**	to mail a letter
en lugar de	in place (instead) of	**rey**	king
en todo caso	in any event	**reina**	queen
en punto	on the dot, sharp	**entrada**	entrance
en cuanto a	in regard to, as for	**salida**	exit
en la actualidad	nowadays, at the	**calvo, -a**	bald
	present time	**sino**	but
el mes (año) que viene	next month (year)		

See also the "Useful Expressions" on page 604.

Assignment 96

Getting Ready for a Quiz on the Morphology of the Past Subjunctive

1   In the quiz in the next class session you will see something like this: *Era
preciso que yo **llevar** el dinero al banco* and you will write _____.   ▲
2   The first suffix for all regular *a*-verbs is _____.   ▲   *llevara*
          ara (ára when the subject is *nosotros)*
3   There are three forms of the first suffix of the past subjunctive for all *e*- and
i-verbs and for irregular *a*-verbs. The regular form is *iera*. The two irregular
forms are _____ and _____.   ▲
          era, yera (Remember that if you aren't sure of what the form is to be, the
          ellos form of the Preterit provides all the cues.)
4   When the Preterit has a *y* after the stem (*leyó, leyeron*), the subjunctive suffix
is _____.   ▲
5   When the first suffix of the Preterit is *ero* (fu-*ero*-n), the subjunctive suffix is   *yera*
_____.   ▲

          era

6 For each of the six infinitives write the *ustedes* form of the Preterit, then
rewrite the form to make it past subjunctive and the form used with *nosotros*.
navegar, indicar, cubrir, sufrir, ofrecer, resolver ▲

> *navegaron, navegáramos; indicaron, indicáramos; cubriéramos; sufrieron, sufriéramos; ofrecieron, ofreciéramos; resolvieron, resolviéramos*

7 For each of the infinitives given, think of the *ellos* form of the Preterit, then
write the matching form of the past subjunctive. All of these verbs are irregular
either in form or spelling.
ser, querer, poner, andar, leer, dormir ▲

> *fueran, quisieran, pusieran, anduvieran, leyeran, durmieran*

8 Continue as above but write the *tú* form. The verbs are still irregular.
tener, decir, ir, hacer, poder, estar ▲

> *tuvieras, dijeras, fueras, hicieras, pudieras, estuvieras*

9 Now write the *yo* form. The verbs are still irregular.
traer, dar, venir, saber, pedir, sentir ▲

> *trajera, dijera, viniera, supiera, pidiera, sintiera*

10 The past subjunctive is simply a backshift of the present subjunctive. In
this frame you will see a present subjunctive form. Say and then write the
matching form of the past subjunctive. If you make a mistake, say the *ellos*
form of the Preterit and then change this to the subjunctive. One change,
o > a, gives you the base for all forms, both regular and irregular.
yo hable, tú vivas, él coma, ustedes imiten, ellos sean, yo ofrezca, él tenga, ellas
recojan, tú sufras, usted saque ▲

> *hablara, vivieras, comiera, imitaran, fueran, ofreciera, tuviera, recogieran, sufrieras, sacara*

11 When the *usted* or *él* form of the Preterit has an irregular stem, that stem
will be used in <u>all</u> forms of the past subjunctive. Write the matching form of the
past subjunctive.
él fue, usted pidió, él durmió, usted supo, él tradujo, usted tuvo, ella vino,
usted hizo, él anduvo ▲

> *fuera, pidiera, durmiera, supiera, tradujera, tuviera, viniera, hiciera, anduviera*

The Future of the Past: The Conditional

1 Although it is customary to talk about the present perfect, the Present, and
the Future as different tenses, you already know that they are, in fact, different
forms of the present tense. The diagram below shows the order relationship
between the event *saber* and the event *perder*. English uses different forms, but
it organizes the relationship between two events in precisely the same way as
Spanish.

	Sé	
que lo **hemos** perdido	que lo **perdemos**	que lo **perderemos**
that we **have** lost it	that we **are** losing it	that we **will** lose it
	I **know**	

Backshift "I know that we are losing it" so that the tense forms are past. ▲

I knew that we *were* losing it.

2 Translate the above sentence. Use the simple Imperfect of *perder*. ▲

Yo sabía que lo perdíamos.

3 Backshift "I know that we have lost it." ▲

I knew that we *had* lost it.

4 Is the "had" of "had lost" the past tense of "have"? ▲

5 Backshift "I know that we will lose it." ▲

yes

I knew that we *would* lose it.

6 Is the "would" of "would lose" the past tense of "will"? ▲

7 The diagram below shows how the past tense forms describe exactly the same order relationship between two events as the present tense forms.

yes

	I know	
that we *have* lost it	that we *are* losing it	that we *will* lose it
that we *had* lost it	that we *were* losing it	that we *would* lose it
	I knew	

If we say that "we have lost" is Present Perfect, then it is logical to say that "we had lost" is _____ Perfect. ▲

8 In "I know that we will lose it" and *Yo sé que lo perderemos* the "will" and *hemos* are Present, but the event "lose" (*perder*) is yet to happen. In other words, the tense form is Present (will, *hemos*) but the event being talked about (lose, *perder*) is Future. Does the order relationship between "I know" and "will lose" change when the original statement is backshifted to: I *knew* that we *would* lose it? ▲

Past

9 At the moment of "I knew" the event "lose" had yet to happen. It was, at that moment, in the future. So we can say that "would lose" is to "knew" precisely what "will lose" is to "know"—or that "would lose" is the future of the past. This form is erroneously called the Conditional because of its use in statements in which one act can happen only if a given condition is fulfilled. For example: If he *were* here, he *would help* us. You will not learn this use of the Conditional until later. You now have to learn just two facts in order to be able to make up all the forms of the Spanish Past Perfect and the Conditional. The imperfect backshift of *perdemos* is made by replacing the first suffix *e* with

no

_____. ▲

10 The same operation on *perderemos* gives you the form of the Conditional:

ía

_____. ▲

11 Translate "I knew that we would lose it." ▲

perderíamos

Sabía que lo perderíamos.

12 The base form of the Future, either regular or irregular, is also the base form of the Conditional. To get all forms you replace the first suffix of the Future with *ía*. So *irá* becomes _____ and *haré* becomes _____. ▲

13 Translate: "He said that he would write us." ▲

iría ; haría

Dijo que nos escribiría.

14 Backshift *Él sabe que lo compraremos.* Notice that you replace the *e* of *sabe* and the *e* of *compraremos* with the same suffix. ▲

*Él sab**ía** que lo comprar**ía**mos.*

15 *Haber* is an *e*-verb and, as a result, the first suffix of the Imperfect is
_____. ▲

16 You make up the Future by dropping the stem of *haber* and adding the   *ía*
remainder to the infinitive *comprar(h)emos.* You get the Conditional by the same
procedure, *comprar(hab)íamos > compraríamos.* So all verbs, *a, e,* and *i,* have *ía*
as the first suffix after the infinitive. Write the backshifts of: *ella vivirá, tú
comerás, yo hablaré.* ▲

ella viviría, tú comerías, yo hablaría

17 The stem of the Imperfect of *haber* is *hab.* The first suffix is *ía* and the second
suffixes are the same as in the Present. So now you know how to make all the
forms of the past perfect indicative. Backshift the following: *yo he visto, tú has
dicho, nosotros hemos regado.* ▲

yo había visto, tú habías dicho, nosotros habíamos regado

18 The diagram below shows that the Present and the Past establish exactly
the same order relationships between two events (*saber* and *perder*).

Sé

que lo hemos perdido	que lo perdemos	que lo perderemos
que lo habíamos perdido	que lo perdíamos	que lo perderíamos

Sabía

Backshift *Él dice que lo ha escrito.* (Use *dijo.*) ▲

Él dijo que lo había escrito.

19 Backshift *Él dice que lo escribe.* (Use *dijo.*) ▲

Él dijo que lo escribía.

20 Backshift *Él dice que lo escribirá.* (Use *dijo.*) ▲

Él dijo que lo escribiría.

21 The Conditional, like the Future, has no matching form of the subjunctive.
You use the present subjunctive to replace the future indicative and the past
subjunctive to replace the Conditional. Backshift these two statements: (1) *Sé
que lo venderá pronto.* (2) *Dudo que lo venda pronto.* ▲

Sabía que lo vendería pronto. Dudaba que lo vendiera pronto.

22 Look at the forms given below. Say the corresponding backshift for each
form, then check the answer.

1	ha gritado *había gritado*	4	hemos puesto *habíamos puesto*	7	cruzaré *cruzaría*
2	saltarás *saltarías*	5	han escogido *habían escogido*	8	he tocado *había tocado*
3	haremos *haríamos*	6	quemarán *quemarían*		

Notice that *he tocado,* because of the irregular form *he,* tells you the subject is *yo.*
You will have to learn to add the *yo* to *había tocado* when the context does not
make it plain who the subject is: *yo había tocado, Vd. había tocado,* etc.

Summary

1 The base form of the Future, either regular or irregular, is also the base form of the Conditional.

2 The first suffix for *all* verbs is *ía*.

3 The so-called Conditional is the future of the past.

Self-Correcting Exercises

A *Subjunctive versus Indicative:* Write the combinations.

Ejemplo: 14 = ¿Lo harán con tal que tú madrugues?

1	¿Lo harán con tal que tú	1	leer esos libros?
2	¿Hay aquí alguna persona que	2	comer vegetales?
3	¿Pidieron que tú y yo	3	venir temprano?
4	¿Se alegraba de que Vd.	4	madrugar?
5	¿Supieron que Vds.		

1)	11	¿Lo harán con tal que tú leas esos libros ?
2)	42	¿Se alegraba de que Vd. comiera vegetales ?
3)	22	¿Hay aquí alguna persona que coma vegetales ?
4)	13	¿Lo harán con tal que tú vengas temprano ?
5)	33	¿Pidieron que tú y yo viniéramos temprano ?
6)	24	¿Hay aquí alguna persona que madrugue ?
7)	44	¿Se alegraba de que Vd. madrugara ?
8)	31	¿Pidieron que tú y yo leyéramos esos libros ?
9)	51	¿Supieron que Vds. leyeron esos libros ?
10)	52	¿Supieron que Vds. comieron vegetales ?

B *Silent Reading:* Read as fast as you can and answer the question at the end.

Si quieres saber quién soy, lee.

No soy un personaje imaginario sino real. Estoy casi seguro que todos Uds. han leído algo de mi vida y han visto mi fotografía en los libros de historia.

Nací en la ciudad de Boston. Mi padre era inglés y tuvo 17 hijos. Yo fui el décimoquinto hijo de la familia. Aunque su negocio de velas° no era muy productivo, mi padre insistió siempre en que todos sus hijos obtuvieran una buena educación. A mí me mandó a la escuela cuando yo tenía ocho años porque él quería que yo estudiara para ministro de la iglesia.   °candles

Yo no quería ser ministro sino marinero. Me fascinaban los barcos y el mar. Al cabo de dos años de estudios tuve que dejar la escuela por razones económicas. Para evitar° que yo me escapara en algún barco, mi padre me puso a trabajar de aprendiz° en la imprenta° de uno de mis hermanos. Él era mayor que yo y allí aprendí mucho. Pero mi hermano y yo éramos como el perro y el   °avoid   °apprentice/print shop gato. Siempre estábamos peleando. A los 17 años me fui para Filadelfia a buscar fortuna.

En Filadelfia conocí a Débora, la mujer que iba a ser mi esposa. Mis negocios de imprenta prosperaron rápidamente. Mi periódico y mi almanaque, donde apareció mi famosa colección de refranes, eran leídos por todo el territorio colonial.

A los 42 años ya tenía buen capital y decidí retirarme de los negocios y dedicar mi vida a varias actividades cívicas. Fundé la primera biblioteca circulante y una academia; ayudé a organizar el primer hospital y a reformar y mejorar el servicio de correos, policía y bomberos.

No recibí una educación formal, pero leí muchos libros. En una ocasión, dejé de comer carne y me hice vegetariano de manera que pudiera tener más dinero para comprar libros. Aprendí a leer en español, francés, italiano, latín y alemán. También aprendí a tocar varios instrumentos musicales.

Las ciencias me interesaron mucho durante toda la vida. Hice estudios e investigaciones de navegación, física, fisiología y geología. De todos mis experimentos el más conocido es el de la cometa. En 1752, durante una tormenta, elevé un objeto metálico hasta las nubes con una cometa y pude demostrar que los rayos° y la electricidad son la misma cosa. Este experimento me dio la idea para la invención del pararrayos.° También inventé los lentes bifocales y un tipo de sillón.   *lightning* / *lightning rod*

En los últimos años de mi vida tuve el privilegio de participar activamente en la política de mi país. A mediados del siglo XVIII (dieciocho) estuve varios años en Inglaterra y en Francia trabajando a favor de la independencia de las colonias inglesas en América.

Durante mis 84 años de vida obtuve grandes éxitos como inventor, diplomático, publicista, editor, autor, científico, filósofo y humorista. Tuve el honor de firmar varios documentos históricos, entre ellos la Declaración de Independencia y la Constitución de los Estados Unidos de América.

El nombre de pila de este famoso hombre es Benjamín, ¿cuál es su apellido?   *Franklin*

C Sino *versus* pero: After reading each complete sentence, select *sino* or *pero* for the blank.

1 No estamos listos para empezar . . . para terminar la lección.   sino

2 No, hombre, no tengo hambre . . . mucha sed.   sino

3 Sí, señor, ella fue la primera alumna que lo hizo, . . . Paco fue el último.   pero

4 En cuanto a la nueva alumna, no es muy bonita . . . sí es bastante inteligente.   pero

5 No estaremos aquí el mes que viene . . . en dos meses más.   sino

6 No lo hacemos de buena gana, . . . lo hacemos bien.   pero

7 Desde luego que está muy cansado, . . . estará de vuelta para empezar de nuevo dentro de poco.   pero

8 Como de costumbre Enriqueta no llega temprano . . . tarde.   sino

9 Sí, el número de científicos es grande hoy, . . . será bastante pequeño mañana.   pero

10 Ese caballo no es grande, fuerte y negro, . . . pequeño, débil y blanco.   sino

New Vocabulary

regalar	to give presents	**hoy (en) día**	nowadays
parecerse a	to look like (resemble)	**mientras tanto**	meanwhile
llevar a cabo	to carry out (finish)	**a menudo**	often
estar de vuelta	to be back	**más bien**	rather
hacer falta	to need, lack	**junto a**	next to
	(Used like **gustar**.)	**¡Eso es!**	That's right (it)!

"A caballo regalado no se le mira el diente."   "Don't look a gift horse in the mouth."

During the colonial period in the United States lotteries were very commonly used as a substitute for taxation and to raise money for public purposes. Most people do not know, for example, that profits from lotteries were used to finance universities which have now become famous such as Harvard, Columbia, and Dartmouth. After the Revolutionary War lotteries were common in all states, but fraud, forgeries, and corruption brought them to an end in 1892. Recently some states have made them legal again.

Every Hispanic country has a national lottery and millions of people regularly buy a ticket for each drawing. To play the lottery (*jugar a la lotería*) is part of the way of life in the Hispanic world. For the poor it makes the dream of riches have substance. All other types of gambling are also legal in the Hispanic world. The lottery itself was invented by the Romans.

Assignment 97

Tense Backshifts

1 The simple Present in Spanish has three common functions: a) It describes a habitual or customary repetition of an event, that is, what the doer has regularly done up to now and, as a result, what may be expected of him in the future: *Juan siempre se va temprano.* Juan always leaves early. b) It states that the event is in process at the moment of speaking: *Juan se va.* Juan is leaving. c) It describes a planned future action: *Juan se va mañana.* Juan is leaving tomorrow. Does the Present in any of these functions describe the beginning or end of a single event? ▲

2 The Preterit states that an event either began or came to an end at some point in the past. Can the Preterit, as a result, be used as a backshift of any of the examples given above? ▲

no

3 The Imperfect describes what was habitual at some time in the past, what was happening at some recalled point or what was planned for the future. Write the backshift of *Juan siempre se va temprano.* ▲

no

Juan siempre se iba temprano.

4 Suppose you say today, "I know that Juan is leaving tomorrow," and a week from now you recall what you said. Write this backshift in English. ▲

I knew that Juan was leaving the next day. ("Tomorrow" cannot be the day after some past day, so you have to replace it with "the next day" or "the following day.")

5 The translation of "the next day" is *el día siguiente.* Write the backshift of *Sé que Juan se va mañana.* ▲

Sabía que Juan se iba el día siguiente.

6 In both English and Spanish the verbs of reporting (say, tell, inform, write, hear, *etc.*) do not follow the standard rules of usage. For example, a friend asks you if you would like to go to Europe. You reply that you must ask your boss. After asking him you say, "He _____ I may go." May you fill the blank with either "says" or "said"? ▲

7 Do both "says" and "said" describe a single event completed in the past? ▲

yes

8 Which aspect, the Preterit or the Imperfect, describes a single event completed in the past? ▲

yes

9 Write the backshift of *Él dice que puedo ir* as used in the above context. ▲

Preterit

Él dijo que puedo (podía) ir.

10 The form "say" may also describe a habitual or repeated event as in "They always say that I cannot do it." Write the backshift of this in Spanish. ▲

Ellos siempre decían que no podía (puedo) hacerlo.

11 Does "I hear" in "I hear that she is sick" describe an action that is going on at the moment of speaking? ▲

12 If you backshift "I hear that she is sick," what will you use in Spanish for "I hear"? (a) Preterit (b) Imperfect. ▲

no

Preterit (Because "I hear" is really a substitute for "I heard," an action completed before the moment of speaking.)

13 Backshift *¿Sabes que lo venderán pronto?*   ▲

¿Sabías que lo venderían pronto?

14 Backshift *Me han dicho que no irán.*   ▲

Me habían dicho que no irían.

15 Backshift *Me escribe que desea visitarnos.* (In this context *escribe* describes an action already completed.)   ▲

Me escribió que deseaba visitarnos.

Infinitives after Relators

1 You can talk about a verb in two ways. First, you can talk about it as a linguistic form. When you do this you use the infinitive as the cover term for all its possible forms: *to be* is an irregular verb. The Spanish infinitive is used in the same way: **Ser** *es un verbo irregular.*

Second, you can talk about what the verb stands for in reality: Swimming is fun. Does "It is fun to swim" say the same thing?   ▲

2 In English you may use two forms of a verb to label the reality for which it   yes
stands: the imperfect participle (*swimming*) or the infinitive (*to swim*). Which sentence is standard English? (a) Most people wash their hands *before to eat*. (b) Most people wash their hands *before eating*.   ▲

Most people wash their hands *before eating*.

3 Which sentence is standard English? (a) I am tired *of to read*. (b) I am tired *of reading*.   ▲

I am tired *of reading*.

4 Your intuition tells you to use the participle (*-ing*) form of a verb after a relator (*of*, *before*) in English. Do these two sentences say the same thing? (1) Work makes me tired. (2) Working makes me tired.   ▲

5 "Work" and "working" both perform the function of what part of   yes
speech?   ▲

6 In English there are two forms of the verb which can be used as nouns.   noun
Here is the proof:

I like *dogs*.   I like *to talk* with you.   I like *talking* with you.

In Spanish, in contrast with English, there is (with one minor exception) only one form of the verb which can function as a noun, and, as a result, there is only one translation for the last two sentences above: *Me gusta* _____ *con usted.*   ▲

7 Translate: I am tired of reading. (A male is speaking.)   ▲   *hablar*

Estoy cansado de leer.

8 Translate the English phrase in: *Me lavo las manos* before eating.   ▲

9 Translate: I want an apple. I want to work.   ▲   *antes de comer*

Quiero una manzana. Quiero trabajar.

10 To make *Lo haré después de la cena* translate "I'll do it after eating supper," you replace *la cena* with _____.   ▲

11 Translate: We can't do it (*lo*) without studying.   ▲   *cenar*

No podemos hacerlo sin estudiar.

12 Translate the italicized phrases: *After eating*, will you (*tú*) have time *for reading your lesson?* ▲

Después de comer, ¿tendrás tiempo para leer tu lección?

More Review of the Subjunctive

The subjunctive is normally used in the subjoined clause under the following conditions:

a When stating events or describing entities that have not yet been experienced: *No lo haremos hasta que nos den permiso. Necesito conseguir un camión que quepa en el garaje.*

b When doubt or uncertainty is expressed about the veracity of the content of the subjoined clause: *Ellos no están seguros de que la hierba crezca bien por aquí.*

c When there is a potential cause and effect relationship between the two clauses, either

psychological: *Me enojé de que ya lo supieran.*

physical: *Cerré la puerta para que no entraran.*

or an attempt to influence behavior: *No quieren que lo castiguemos.*

d When reporting a command: *Le gritó que no saliera todavía.*

1 For this and the next six frames write the appropriate form of the infinitives in parentheses:

Antes de llegar a casa ayer nosotros (comprar) esta revista. ▲

2 Compraremos la revista antes de que Vd. (volver) a casa. ▲

3 Es cierto que ella (querer) ir con nosotros. ▲

4 Pues, yo dudo que su mamá le (permitir) ir. ▲

5 Era imposible que él (llegar) tan temprano. ▲

6 ¿Cree Vd. que (llover) mañana? ▲

7 Yo dudo que (ir) a llover. ▲

compramos

vuelva

quiere

permita

llegara

lloverá (llueva)

vaya

8 There exists in modern Spanish an archaic (old) future subjunctive which is so rarely used that you will have to learn the forms only if you wish to read Old Spanish. For all practical purposes, consequently, it is proper to say that the present and future subjunctive have the same forms. There is, as a result, only one translation for both of these sentences. Write it: (1) I am afraid that she is sick. (2) I am afraid that she will be sick. ▲

Temo que ella esté enferma.

9 Spanish never had a subjunctive which replaced the conditional indicative, and, as a result, the past subjunctive has functions similar to those of the present subjunctive. It replaces the Preterit, the Imperfect, and the Conditional. Write the Spanish backshift of the sentences given above. ▲

Temía que ella estuviera enferma.

In the remaining frames, write the backshift of the indicated portion of each sentence.

10 Ellos *creen* que Vd. *es* el director. ▲

creían, era

11 *Sabemos* que ellas lo *han* hecho. ▲

12 *Parece* que *va* a llover. ▲

13 *Demandan* (a single action) que los *pague* en seguida. ▲

14 *Dice* (a single action) que no *es* así. ▲

15 *Es* posible que lo *tengan*. ▲

16 *Es* cierto que lo *tienen*. ▲

17 Él me *escribe* (a completed action) que nos *visitará* en una semana. ▲

18 *Dudo* que nos *visite* tan temprano. ▲

19 *Quiere* saber cuándo *llegaremos*. ▲

20 Le dije que *tendré* cuarenta años el año que *viene*. ▲

21 *Es* importante investigar quién lo *ha* escrito. ▲

Sabíamos, habían
Parecía, iba
Demandaron, pagara

Dijo, era
Era, tuvieran
Era, tenían
escribió, visitaría
Dudaba, visitara
Quería, llegaríamos
tendría, venía
Era, había

Self-Correcting Exercises

A   *Subjunctive versus Indicative:* After reading each sentence, rewrite it, making the changes indicated. Cover the answers below each sentence.

1   Todos creen que la tienda del Sr. Aragón tiene los precios más bajos del pueblo.   (*Change this sentence to say that everyone doubts that Mr. Aragón's store has the highest prices in the city.*)

(Todos dudan que la tienda del Sr. Aragón tenga los precios más altos de la ciudad.)

2   Hay tres personas aquí que saben patinar.   (*Change this sentence to say that there is no one here who knows how to ice skate.*)

(No hay nadie aquí que sepa patinar en (sobre) el hielo.)

3   El inspector llegará hoy cuando el reloj dé las siete y antes de que tú riegues el jardín.   (*Change the time to yesterday at nine.*)

(El inspector llegó ayer cuando el reloj dio las nueve y antes de que tú regaras el jardín.)

4   Yo no quería que toda la familia fuera de excursión.   (*Shift this sentence forward to the present.*)

(Yo no quiero que toda la familia vaya de excursión.)

5   Creo que lo hacen diariamente (*daily*).   (*Make this sentence negative and express real lack of belief by your choice of the mode in the subjoined verb.*)

(No creo que lo hagan diariamente.)

B   *Review of Useful Expressions:* Cover the answers in the margin and translate mentally the appropriate expression. Check after each sentence to see if your choice is right.

1   *We shall be back early in* marzo, si nos es posible.

Estaremos de vuelta a principios de

2 *On the contrary* nosotros nos iremos *about the middle of* junio.

Al contrario, a mediados de

3 *That's right.* Es muy importante *to carry out* su plan.

Eso es, llevar a cabo

4 *Meanwhile* él y yo vamos a visitarlo *often.*

Mientras tanto, a menudo

5 *No wonder.* Él no *mailed the letter.*

Con razón, echó la carta al correo

6 *Nowadays* algunos jóvenes no van al ejército *willingly.*

Hoy (en) día, de buena gana

7 *In any event,* yo *rather* prefiero el banco que está *next to* la florería.

En todo caso, más bien, junto a

8 Pancho siempre llega *on time,* o por lo menos *at about* las nueve.

a tiempo, a eso de

9 *At the present time, instead of* dar más dinero a los enfermos, prefiero que se lo den a los pobres.

En la actualidad, en lugar de

10 Esta camisa *looks like* la camisa que él *let drop* en el agua ayer.

se parece a, dejó caer

11 *Of course* debemos ir allá *from time to time* para ver si *he needs* algo.

Desde luego, de vez en cuando, le hace falta

C *Conditional:* Backshift each sentence aloud. You will have to change *dice* to *dijo* and the second verb from the Future to the Conditional.

1	Dice que lo llevará a cabo.	Dijo que lo llevaría a cabo.
2	Dice que valdrá más mañana.	Dijo que valdría más mañana.
3	Dice que tú lo dirás también.	Dijo que tú lo dirías también.
4	Dice que habrá un caballo allí.	Dijo que habría un caballo allí.
5	Dice que no tendrán pan allí.	Dijo que no tendrían pan allí.
6	Dice que Elena y Juan irán con nosotros.	Dijo que Elena y Juan irían con nosotros.
7	Dice que pronto estarán de vuelta.	Dijo que pronto estarían de vuelta.
8	Dice que viviremos en Chicago.	Dijo que viviríamos en Chicago.
9	Dice que se acostará dentro de poco.	Dijo que se acostaría dentro de poco.
10	Dice que se despedirán pronto.	Dijo que se despedirían pronto.

D Sino *versus* pero: Choose *sino* or *pero* for the blanks.

1 No eran políticos, . . . les gustaba hablar mucho.

pero

2 El carpintero lo arregló, . . . el conserje lo rompió de nuevo.

pero

3 Fue una cosa muy negativa y difícil de comprender, . . . parecía que al joven eso no le importaba nada.

pero

4 Los niñitos ya no me dan mucha lata, . . . antes me molestaban muchísimo.

pero

5 Aquellos animales no son burros, . . . mulas y caballos.

sino

6 No, hombre, no son mis hijos . . . mis primos.

sino

7 . . . , ¿por qué me dices eso?

Pero

8 Te equivocaste. No fue el abogado . . . el juez quien lo dijo.

sino

9 No trates de convencerme de que ella no se echó a llorar . . . a reír.

sino

10 La enfermera no me dio gotas de medicina según la recomendación del médico . . . tres píldoras, y me mandó que las masticara.

sino

E *General Review:* Rewrite each sentence, replacing the indicated parts with the items in parentheses and making all other necessary changes. Then say the new sentence aloud.

1 Dime *tú* si *crees* que va Alicia o *Norma.* (Vd., dudar, Ofelia)

Dígame Vd. si duda que vaya Alicia u Ofelia.

2 Ven *tú* con*migo* a la florería para comprar *flores.* (Vd., ella, dulces)

Venga Vd. con ella a la dulcería para comprar dulces.

3 *Junio* es el sexto mes del año y el primer mes de verano. (Agosto)

Agosto es el octavo mes del año y el tercer mes de verano.

4 María *quiere* que todos visitemos *Managua,* capital de Nicaragua, antes de que llegue el *invierno.* (quería, San José, primavera)

María quería que todos visitáramos San José, capital de Costa Rica, antes de que llegara la primavera.

New Vocabulary

pedir prestado, -a	to borrow	**por lo pronto**	for the time being
poner en marcha	to get going, start	**por lo general**	in general, generally
por lo tanto	therefore	**por regla general**	as a general rule
por consiguiente	consequently	**por aquí**	this way
por si acaso	just in case	**rara vez**	seldom

The titles of address which you have learned (*señor, señora, señorita*) are used, like their English equivalents, with last names. They may also be used in speaking to anyone who is old enough to be addressed with a formal title and in addressing a person of any social class. In contrast, Spanish has two titles, *don* and *doña*, which are used only with first names and which originated as class titles, that is, were used only as titles of respect for the nobility. These titles are no longer reserved for just the nobility, but unlike the other titles of address, they still indicate either a difference of social class or a high degree of deference or respect. Thus, a person of a higher social class does not normally use *don* or *doña* in speaking to a person of lower class.

These titles, like *tú* and *usted*, permit a kind of inter-personal reaction which is impossible in English. They are used when two people are too intimate to interact on a last-name basis, but not intimate enough to be on a first-name basis. In general, however, only one of the two people in a conversation uses *don* or *doña* in addressing the other. Thus, a highly respected scholar may be addressed as *don Felipe* by his colleagues. Similarly, the owner of a ranch may address all his employees as *tú*, calling them by their first names, while they, in turn, use *don* and his first name, and *usted*.

One cannot get a deep understanding of Hispanic culture until one is thoroughly aware of the fact that the use of *tú, usted, don* and *doña* establish very special social relationships between people. English approaches this kind of relationship only in very special cases. For example, the nurses in a clinic may address a doctor with whom they are very friendly as "Doctor Jim."

Shortened Adjectival Forms

1 Using a language for communication is rule-governed behavior. But it is possible to learn a language without learning the rules consciously. Here is an example of an English rule of behavior which you follow very well but which you never learned consciously. Someone says, "I have an apple. Shall I get you _____?" (a) an (b) one ▲

> one (The rule is: when a noun is deleted, the article "an" is replaced by the number "one.")

2 Spanish has a similar rule which you could eventually learn unconsciously. In the statement *Yo tengo un libro pero él tiene dos*, the noun *libros* is deleted in the second part. The sentence can be transformed to *Él tiene dos libros pero yo tengo* _____ (one). ▲

> *uno* (Here is your Spanish rule. The word for "one" in Spanish has three allomorphs: *un, uno,* and *una*. The short form *un*, like "a" or "an" in English, is used only when an *o*-noun follows in the same phrase. When the noun is deleted, *un* is replaced by *uno: Yo tengo uno; él tiene dos*. The long form *una* remains unchanged when the noun is deleted: *Él tiene dos plumas pero yo tengo una*.)

3 Spanish has three more very commonly used adjectives which also have three allomorphs: *algún, alguno, alguna; ningún, ninguno, ninguna; buen, bueno, buena*. You need three rules to use these forms correctly. (1) When these adjectives follow their noun, you use the matching long form: *Es un hombre bueno. Es una mujer buena*. (2) When the adjective precedes its noun, you use the long *a* form and the shortened *o* form: *Es un buen hombre. Es una buena mujer*. (3) When the noun is deleted, you use only the long forms: *Ella es muy buena. Él es muy* _____. ▲

> *bueno*

4 Rewrite the Spanish question *¿Hay algún hombre que pueda hacerlo?* and make it a negative statement. ▲

> *No hay ningún hombre que pueda hacerlo.*

5 The three common adjectives *primero, tercero,* and *malo* also have shortened forms which behave exactly like *alguno, ninguno,* and *bueno*. What form, *mal, malo, mala*, will you use in *Hace tiempo muy* _____ *allí?* ▲

6 What form will you use in *Hace muy* _____ *tiempo hoy?* ▲

> *malo*
> *mal*

7 The adjective *grande* needs to be treated as a special case. As Latin was becoming Spanish it was often shortened to *grand* and, then, because Spanish does not like words which end with two consonants, it was further shortened to *gran*. The result is that modern Spanish has two forms: *grande* and the shortened form *gran*. Since neither *grande* nor *gran* has a matching terminal phoneme, the shortened form is used before all nouns: *una gran señora*, a great lady; *un gran señor*, a great gentleman. The adjective *grande* has two common meanings to the Spanish speaker: one is "great" (fine, wonderful, *etc.*) and the other is "big" or "large." The form *gran* never has the meaning of "large." The translation of "a large man" must be _____. ▲

> *un señor (hombre) grande*

8 Five of these shortened forms are used whenever they are followed by a noun in the same phrase. They are *un, algún, ningún, primer,* and *tercer.* Three shortened forms, however, are used only when they come directly before the following noun. These are *buen, mal,* and *gran.* Translate: a good and great man. ▲

> *un bueno y gran señor* (You will not get much practice with this form for some time, so don't worry about it.)

9 Translate: the third great man. ▲

> *el tercer gran señor*

Review of sino *and* pero

1 Because both *sino* and *pero* are translated by "but," you must find the cues for choice in the context. The two statements "It is not red" and "It is white" can be transformed into one: "It is not red *but* white." The Spanish translation is _____. ▲

> *No es rojo* **sino** *blanco.* (There is a negative word in the first part of the sentence and the two adjectives belong to the same set.)

2 The two statements "He has no money" and "He has friends" may also be joined by "but": "He has no money but he has friends." You can also say *Él no tiene dinero* and *Tiene amigos* and, then, join them together with (a) *pero* (b) *sino.* ▲

> pero (*Él no tiene dinero,* **pero** *tiene amigos. Dinero* and *amigos* do not belong to the same set.)

3 Will you use *sino* or *pero* to translate this sentence? "She is happy but tired." ▲

> pero (There is no negative in the first part and "tired" does not replace "happy." It adds information. You could say "She is happy and tired.")

4 In the sentences of the remaining frames will you use *sino* or *pero* to translate the sentence?
Si observas con cuidado verás que no es un tigre _____ un león. ▲

5 No lo hago para molestarte _____ para ayudarte. ▲   *sino*

6 Es una persona muy amable, _____ siempre habla demasiado. ▲   *sino*

7 Dice que no vendrá a las ocho _____ a las nueve. ▲   *pero*

8 ¡_____ me has dicho que lo harías! ▲   *sino*

> *Pero*

Locating Things in Space

1 In both English and Spanish things may be located in relation to something else by using the relators "above," "below," "under," "in," "on," or "behind" or by using a relator phrase. The opposite of "behind" is "in front of" because "front" comes from the French for "forehead." So something that was "on the forehead of" came to mean "in front of." The Spanish word for "forehead" is *frente,* and Spanish also has the relator phrase *en frente de* which means "in front of and *facing*." (*En* and *frente* have combined into one word.) Can *enfrente de* be used to translate "The lamp is in front of the door"? ▲

> no (Because lamps do not face a door.)

2 The *anteroom* of a building is at the front of the building. From the Latin *de in ante*, Old Spanish got *denante* which eventually changed to *delante*. Add *de* to this and you can translate "The tree is in front of the house." ▲

> *El árbol está delante de la casa.*

3 The opposite of *ante* is *tras*. So the translation of *detrás de* in *El árbol está detrás de la casa* is _____. ▲

4 The following diagram represents a house with a front porch, and the dot   behind is a tree. Rewrite the last sentence above so it describes the positional relationship between tree and house. ▲

> *El árbol está al lado de la casa.*

5 This square represents *el patio*. Rewrite the above sentence to show this location of the tree. ▲

> *El árbol está en el patio.*

6 In English you may say "This will be on the exam" or "in the exam." Spanish has only one word for both "in" and "on." It is _____. ▲

> en (Most of the time the context makes the meaning clear.)

7 The word "supervisor" is made up of *super* and *visor*. *Super* means "over." The suffix *-or* of *visor* says "doer." The stem *vis* is the same stem that you see in the Spanish perfect participle *visto*, from *ver*. When you "translate" *super-visor* into common English words you get _____. ▲

8 When Latin became Spanish, *super* became *sobre*. Translate *El avión está*   over-seer *sobre nuestra casa ahora mismo.* ▲

> The plane is over our house right now.

9 The opposite of *sobre* is *debajo de*. Say where the cat (male) is. ▲

> *El gato está debajo de la mesa.*

ESTÁ SOBRE LA PAJARERA

A/B

ESTÁ DEBAJO DE LA PAJARERA

C/D

ESTÁ EN LA PAJARERA

ESTÁ EN LA PAJARERA

E/F

ESTÁ DETRÁS DE LA PAJARERA

ESTÁ DELANTE DE LA PAJARERA

Self-Correcting Exercises

A *General Review:* Rewrite each sentence, making the indicated changes. Cover the answer under each sentence until you are ready to check it.

1 *Yo hablaré con él cuando llegue.* Back-shift this sentence, introducing it with *Dije que . . .*

(*Dije que yo hablaría con él cuando llegara.*)
2 Now take the original sentence above and change it to say that you actually did speak to him when he arrived.

(*Yo hablé con él cuando llegó.*)
3 You hear someone say the following. *Te pido que no me traigas más manzanas.* You are to make the same request of this person, except that you want to put it in the affirmative, not the negative. Also, this person is someone whom you would address with *usted*, even though the other person addresses him with *tú*.

(*Le pido que me traiga más manzanas.*)
4 He didn't quite hear you and asks you to repeat it. You could leave what you say in the same tense as before, but you decide to back-shift it. What do you say now?

(*Le pedí que me trajera más manzanas.*)

5 *Tendré los otros papeles para mañana.* You want to back-shift this and introduce it by saying *Quería decir que* . . . Also, since the subject of *quería* becomes ambiguous, you had better insert it.

(*Yo quería decir que tendría los otros papeles para mañana.*)

B *Infinitives after Relators:* Cover the answers on the right while you translate mentally the English portions of the sentences. Check each item before moving on to the next one.

1 *Before arriving* se detuvieron en un café.	*Antes de llegar*
2 Fue a Lima *instead of going* a Ecuador.	*en vez (lugar) de ir*
3 El problema *of selling* el coche no le permite dormir.	*de vender*
4 *As for leaving* a tiempo, eso es imposible.	*En cuanto a salir*
5 No me dijo nada *after talking* con el Sr. Gómez.	*después de hablar*
6 *Besides giving me* su teléfono, me dio su dirección.	*Además de darme*
7 *Without saying* una palabra más, se fue.	*Sin decir*
8 *Upon paying* la cuenta notó que había olvidado su recibo (*receipt*).	*Al pagar*
9 *In spite of* la mala noticia, seguía sonriendo.	*A pesar de*

C *Conditional:* Write the combinations.

Ejemplo: 112 = Dijo que tú podrías regarlo.

1	Dijo		1	tú	1	tenerlo pronto.
2	Pensaba		2	él y yo	2	poder regarlo.
3	Creía	que	3	Vds.	3	saber cantarlo.
4	Recordaba		4	yo	4	poner la mesa.
5	Olvidó		5	Vd.	5	sacar la basura.

1)	111	Dijo que tú lo tendrías pronto.
2)	123	Dijo que él y yo sabríamos cantarlo.
3)	222	Pensaba que él y yo podríamos regarlo.
4)	234	Pensaba que Vds. pondrían la mesa.
5)	333	Creía que Vds. sabrían cantarlo.
6)	345	Creía que yo sacaría la basura.
7)	444	Recordaba que yo pondría la mesa.
8)	451	Recordaba que Vd. lo tendría pronto.
9)	555	Olvidó que Vd. sacaría la basura.
10)	512	Olvidó que tú podrías regarlo.

D *Silent Reading:* Read without stopping to translate into English.

Grandes hombres de las Américas: Simón Bolívar (quinta parte)

Ayacucho: fin del imperio español en Suramérica

Entre los años de 1821 y 1826, Bolívar y su primer general Antonio José Sucre libertaron el territorio que es hoy Ecuador, completaron la campaña por la independencia de Perú iniciada por José de San Martín y fundaron una nueva nación que recibió el nombre de Bolivia en honor a su fundador. La batalla de Ayacucho en Perú, el 9 de diciembre de 1824, marca el fin del imperio español en América del Sur. En esta memorable batalla combatieron venezolanos, colombianos, ecuatorianos, peruanos y argentinos. El gran héroe de Ayacucho fue el general Sucre, "brazo derecho" de Bolívar y uno de sus más fieles° amigos.

loyal

"Padre y Libertador del Perú"

Después de la victoria de Ayacucho, el Congreso peruano confirió en Bolívar el título de "Padre y Libertador del Perú" y lo eligió Presidente de la Nación por el resto de su vida. Para expresar su gratitud los peruanos también le dieron un millón de pesos para sus oficiales y soldados y otro millón para él. Bolívar se ofendió con el regalo y no lo aceptó diciendo: "Yo he venido al Perú a buscar gloria y no dinero . . ." El gobierno insistió en que aceptara el dinero y lo usara para obras de caridad.° En la antigua ciudad de Cuzco un comité de damas° le ofreció una corona° de perlas y diamantes. Bolívar en seguida dio órdenes de que se la mandaran al general Sucre diciendo: " . . . él es el héroe de Ayacucho y el verdadero libertador de esta tierra."

charity
ladies/crown

Un regalo de la familia de Jorge Washington

La familia de Jorge Washington reconoció el mérito de Bolívar y le demostró su admiración mandándole varios objetos de gran valor sentimental: la medalla que le había regalado a Washington la ciudad de Williamsburg, una de sus cartas originales, un mechón° de su pelo y un retrato° en miniatura. Bolívar era gran admirador del primer presidente de los Estados Unidos y apreció mucho este regalo que el marqués de Lafayette le mandó de Mount Vernon.

lock/portrait

"Yo temo más la paz que la guerra"

Después de completar la liberación del Perú, Bolívar decidió empezar cuanto antes la organización y unificación política y social de todo el continente. En el Congreso de Panamá intentó formar una liga de naciones americanas, pero su plan no tuvo éxito. Intrigas, conspiraciones, diferencias de opinión y las ambiciones personales empezaron a dividir y a separar a los pueblos hermanos que él tanto deseaba consolidar en una gran confederación. Sus enemigos le acusaban de ser un tirano ambicioso y traidor. Diariamente los periódicos publicaban insultos y ataques contra él. Con razón Bolívar le había escrito años antes a un amigo: "Estamos sobre un volcán listo para hacer explosión. Yo temo más la paz que la guerra."

"Hemos arado° en el mar"

plowed

A fines de septiembre del año 1828, un grupo de conspiradores asaltó el Palacio de Gobierno en Bogotá con el propósito de asesinar a Bolívar. Varios de los centinelas murieron en el ataque. Bolívar intentó defenderse, pero sus amigos insistieron en que se escapara por una ventana. Así lo hizo y pudo salvar° su vida. Pero la situación política en la Gran Colombia iba de mal en peor. Enfermo de tuberculosis y totalmente desilusionado, Bolívar decidió renunciar° de la presidencia y retirarse a la vida privada. Sus últimas palabras ante el Congreso son una expresión elocuente de su estado espiritual: "Los que° hemos trabajado en América por su libertad e independencia hemos arado° en el mar y edificado sobre arena. No hay buena fe° en América, ni entre los hombres ni entre las naciones. Los tratados° son papeles; las constituciones, libros; las elecciones, combates; la libertad, anarquía; y la vida, un tormento . . . "

save

resign
We who
plowed
faith
treaties

Comprehension exercise: Select the letter corresponding to the correct answer.

1 Antonio José Sucre fue . . .
  a uno de los principales enemigos de Bolívar.
  b el general español que venció en Mount Vernon.
  c un gran general y amigo de Bolívar.

2 El héroe de la batalla de Ayacucho no fue Bolívar sino . . .
  a José de San Martín.
  b Antonio José Sucre.
  c Francisco de Miranda.

3 ¿Quién le ofreció a Bolívar un millón de pesos?
  a Un grupo de damas de Cuzco.
  b La familia de Jorge Washington.
  c El gobierno de Perú.

4 ¿Qué hizo Bolívar con la corona de piedras preciosas?
  a Se la puso en la cabeza.
  b Se la dio a los pobres.
  c Se la mandó a su amigo.

5 ¿Por qué no aceptó Bolívar el regalo que le mandaron de Mount Vernon?
  a No valía mucho.
  b Era enemigo de los norteamericanos.
  c No es verdad que no lo aceptó.

6 Después que terminaron las guerras de independencia, Bolívar . . .
  a volvió a España a vivir.
  b tenía muchos enemigos.
  c fue muy cruel con la gente.

7 En 1828 unos asesinos atacaron el Palacio Presidencial de Bogotá y . . .
  a mataron a Bolívar.
  b mataron a varios.
  c mataron al Presidente del Congreso.

8 Bolívar quería retirarse de la vida pública porque . . .
  a era muy ambicioso.
  b tenía mucho dinero y quería divertirse.
  c estaba enfermo y desencantado.

1 c

2 b

3 c

4 c

5 c

6 b

7 b

8 c

New Vocabulary

ir de compras	to go shopping	**llover a cántaros**	to pour (rain pitchforks, cats and dogs)
entregar	to give, hand over		
portarse bien (mal)	to behave (misbehave)	**Claro que sí (no).**	Of course (not).
enterarse de	to find out	**¡Ay!**	Ouch! Oh! (Often not translatable.)
avisarle a alguien	to let someone know (notify someone)	**¡Auxilio! ¡Socorro!**	Help! Help!
estar de acuerdo	to agree (be in agreement)	**¡Qué barbaridad!**	How terrible!
		¡Basta!	Enough!
tomarle el pelo a alguien	to tease someone (pull his leg)	**¡Qué casualidad!**	What a coincidence!
		¡Qué sé yo!	How should I know!
		¡Cállate! (callarse)	Shut up! Be quiet!

"A mal tiempo, buena cara."   "Smile in the face of adversity."

Assignment 99

Review of the Forms of the Conditional

1 With the exception of just twelve verbs all forms of the Conditional can be made by remembering three simple facts. The base to which the first suffix is added is not the stem but the whole _____. ▲

2 The first suffix for all verbs and all forms is _____. ▲   infinitive

3 The second suffix is the same as for all tenses (except the Preterit). What   *ía*
second suffix goes with *ustedes*, *ellos*, and *ellas*? ▲

4 The Conditional is the backshift of the Future. Write the backshift of *Él*   *n*
dice (Preterit) *que irá.* ▲

In the next three frames you will see the infinitive of verbs which change to   *Él dijo que iría.*
become the base for the Future and the Conditional. Write the future <u>and</u>
conditional forms that go with *él* or *usted*.

5 poder, querer, saber ▲
     podrá, podría;   querrá, querría;   sabrá, sabría (The class vowel e drops

6 Something different happens to *venir, poner, tener, valer.* ▲   from the infinitive.)
     vendrá, vendría;   pondrá, pondría;   tendrá, tendría;   valdrá, valdría (The
                                                        class vowel is replaced by *d.*)

7 decir, hacer ▲
     dirá, diría;   hará, haría   (*c* and *e* are deleted from each infinitive)

In the remaining frames, change the infinitive to the Conditional.

8 De pronto me di cuenta que nosotros no (llegar) a tiempo. ▲

                                                        llegaríamos

9   Te dije que tú no (poder) ir de compras hasta mañana.   ▲
10   Ellos me prometieron que (venir) en seguida.   ▲
11   Yo sabía que ellos no se (enterar) de eso al día siguiente.   ▲
12   Yo estaba seguro que él lo (tener) en el banco.   ▲

podrías
vendrían
enterarían
tendría

Review of the Imperative Forms that Match tú

1   There are two forms of the imperative that go with *tú*. One of these forms is the same as the present subjunctive: *Quiero que vayas tú*. You may use this form (*vayas*) as an imperative only when the command is (a) positive (b) negative.   ▲

negative (*No vayas.*)

2   When the command is positive and the verb is regular, the imperative form that goes with *tú* is exactly like a different person form of the present indicative. This form cannot have an overt person-number suffix as in *hablo, hablan,* or *hablamos,* nor can it be *hablas.* So the positive imperative of *hablar* that goes with *tú* must be _____.   ▲

3   Write the positive *tú* imperative for *escribir* and *vender*.   ▲

habla

4   If the third person singular of the Present has an irregularity, this same irregularity appears in the *tú* imperative. Write the positive *tú* imperative of *volver* and *sentar*.   ▲

escribe, vende

5   You have learned eight verbs which have a highly irregular and shortened form of the positive imperative. Say aloud the negative and positive imperative of each: *decir, hacer, ir, poner, salir, ser, tener, venir.*   ▲

vuelve, sienta

no digas, di;   no hagas, haz;   no vayas, ve;   no pongas, pon;   no salgas, sal;   no seas, sé;   no tengas, ten;   no vengas, ven

An Infinitive Phrase for an Adverbial Clause

1   Do these two sentences send essentially the same message? (1) *Cada día cuando volvemos a casa comemos algo.* (2) *Cada día después de volver a casa comemos algo.*   ▲

2   The opposite of *después* is _____.   ▲

yes

antes (So you could say *Antes de volver a casa comemos algo.*)

3   An event may be set in an order relation to another event or to a point in clock time. So you may say *Comemos **antes** de las siete* or *Comemos **después** de las siete.* What relator will you use for the third possible relationship between eating and *las siete?*   ▲

*Comemos **a** las siete.*

4   *Comemos antes de las siete* is like *Comemos antes de volver a casa. Comemos después de las siete* is like *Comemos después de volver a casa.* Write the third sentence that is like *Comemos a las siete.*   ▲

You may have either *Al volver a casa comemos* or *Comemos al volver a casa.*

The Conjunctive Forms y, e, o, *and* u

1   The cues for choice between *y* and *e* and between *o* and *u* are (a) the sound that precedes (b) the sound that follows. ▲

the sound that follows

2   The conjunction *y* is pronounced [i] and is hard to hear if you say the following fast: *español y inglés.* So you change [i] to [e] when the following word begins with [i]. This sound may be written *i* or _____. ▲

hi (español e historia)

3   By the same logic you change *o* to *u* before _____ and _____. ▲

o, ho (dinero u oro; mujer u hombre)

The Adverbial Suffix

1   The Spanish equivalent of *-ly* comes from the word for "mind": *la mente.* The adjective for "slow" is *lento.* What do you change when you combine it with *mente*? ▲

2   When the adjective has only one form in the singular there is no change.   *o to a: lentamente*
Translate: equally (*igual*) ▲

3   When you say these Spanish adverbs aloud do you stress (a) one syllable   *igualmente*
(b) two syllables? ▲

*two syllables (You put the regular stress on the original adjective and another on **men**-te. If the adjective has a written accent, you keep it: rápidamente.)*

Equivalents of "Let's"

1   The full statement *Vamos a ver* is a shortened form of the imperative *Vayamos a ver* and translates "Let's see." The shortened form of *Vamos a ver* is _____. ▲

2   The English "let's" is used when you propose that something be done, for   *A ver*
example, "Let's go," "Let's eat." While *A ver* is very common, the *vamos a* construction is used with most other verbs. Translate: Let's write today. ▲

Vamos a escribir hoy.

Diminutives

1   The diminutive suffixes in Spanish carry essentially the same information as those in English. When they are added to a noun standing for a thing that has size they function like an adjective and indicate _____. ▲

smallness (So a small house is a casita.)

2   When they are added to nouns standing for people, they may refer to size or _____. ▲

age (niño > niñito)

3   A diminutive may also indicate sympathy, tenderness, friendliness, triviality, or degree of acquaintanceship. Will the actual meaning be shown by (a) the suffix alone (b) the suffix plus context?   ▲

the suffix plus context

4   Diminutive suffixes may be added to nouns, adjectives, and, sometimes, adverbs: *casa > casita, blanco > blanquito, ahora > ahorita.* The three most commonly used suffixes are -*cito*, -*ecito*, and _____.   ▲

5   When a word ends in a vowel you drop this vowel before adding the suffix. So *Juana* becomes _____.   ▲

-ito

Juanita

Ordinal Numbers

1   Ordinal numbers are adjectives which give the place or order relationship of an entity in a sequence. The two in Spanish which may have a shortened form are _____.   ▲

primero, tercero (*primer, tercer*)

2   Say the Spanish ordinal for the number given: *dos, cuatro, cinco, seis, siete, ocho, nueve, diez.*   ▲

segundo, cuarto, quinto, sexto, séptimo, octavo, noveno, décimo

3   You have never seen *duodécimo.* If you think of the meaning of *duo* in English, you can guess that *duodécimo* means _____.   ▲

twelfth (*duo* = 2, *décimo* = 10; 10 + 2 = 12th.)

4   And that the meaning of *decimosexto* is _____.   ▲

sixteenth

Vocabulary: New Words and Expressions, and Review

In frames 1 through 9, ten new words and expressions are introduced. Before doing these frames, study the list of new vocabulary at the end of this assignment for a couple of minutes.

1   The adjective *rubio* is related to *rubí* (ruby) which is a red gem stone, and *rubio*, as a result, is only an approximation of "blond." It means in Spanish a clear red color like gold. Similarly, *moreno* is not a neat translation of "brunet" (brown-haired); the color is darker and closer to black in Spanish. The adjective *pelirrojo* is made up of *pelo* (hair) and *rojo* and means "red hair." In English "hair" is replaced by _____ in, "She is a red _____."   ▲

head

2   The nouns *novio* and *novia* come from Latin *novus*, the same word that gave Spanish the adjective *nuevo.* One meaning, consequently, of *novios* is "newlyweds" in which you also see the word "new." Another meaning is "sweethearts" (about to be married, engaged). The word *enamorados* is also used to describe people in (*en*) love (*amor*). Give the Spanish for "bride" and "groom."   ▲

novia, novio

3 In English legend the heart is where emotions and memories are stored. We say "to learn by heart." Spanish associates this with "memory" and you must *aprender de* _____. ▲

4 And when you "know it by heart," you must say *yo lo* _____. ▲

memoria

5 The verb *valer* is a cognate of "value" and is often translated as "to be   *sé de memoria* worth." The noun *pena* is a cognate of "pain." The meaning of *valer la pena* is "to be worth the pain." The translation is _____. ▲

to be worth the effort (trouble, while)

6 The verb *apurar* comes from *a* and *puro* and one of its meanings is "to carry to extremes." In terms of movement through space, if you push yourself to extremes you are _____. ▲

7 *¡Cuidado!* translates _____. ▲

hurrying

8 When you want to say "be careful *with*" something, you add _____. ▲

Be careful !

9 English says "there's nothing like." Spanish deletes "nothing" and makes   *con* the verb negative. The result is _____. ▲

No hay como (estar en el campo en esta estación del año.)

10 In this and the remaining frames, write the translation of the indicated part of each sentence. *I'll be back* in an hour. ▲

11 *Nowadays* there are many young people who do not know that. ▲   *Estaré de vuelta*

Hoy día (En la actualidad)

12 That's right! ▲

13 Put it *next to* the table. ▲   *¡Eso es!*

14 What *do you need?* (= What is lacking to you?) ▲   *junto a*

15 It's important *to carry out* that project. ▲   *le hace falta*

16 He is not stupid. I would say, *rather*, that he doesn't work enough. ▲   *llevar a cabo*

17 Ella no sabe *after all* que estuvimos allí. ▲   *más bien*

18 Cuando vaya al centro hágame el favor de *mail this letter.* ▲   *después de todo*

echar esta carta al correo.

19 No puedo hacerlo este mes pero lo haré *next month.* ▲

el mes que viene (or *el mes próximo*)

20 No me han dicho nada *in regards to* sus planes. ▲

21 Prefiero esta corbata *instead of* esa. ▲   *en cuanto a*

22 No te preocupes. Estaré allí a las diez *on the dot.* ▲   *en lugar de*

23 Doctor, mi esposa está enferma. ¿Puede Vd. venir *immediately?* ▲   *en punto*

24 No sé qué hacer pero *in any case (event)* tendremos que hacer algo. ▲   *en seguida*

25 Y esto, *in short*, es todo lo que voy a decirles. ▲   *en todo caso*

26 Es importante *enterarnos de* lo que hace ella allí. ▲   *en fin*

27 Cuando llueve mucho decimos que *llueve a cántaros.* ▲   (for us) to find out

It pours, rains pitchforks (cats and dogs) (The meaning of *cántaros* is "large

28 Cuando vamos de tienda a tienda para comprar cosas decimos que *vamos de*   jugs.") *compras.* ▲

we are going shopping.

29 Si ella no sabe que estamos esperándola, alguien tiene que *avisarle.* ▲

let her know (The cognate of *avisar* is "advise.")

30 Quiero que lleves esta carta a tu abuela y que se la *entregues* sin abrirla. ▲

hand (it to her), give

31 A Juan le gusta *tomarle el pelo* a María. ▲

32 Su mamá le dio una bofetada porque no *se portaba* bien. ▲

to tease
behave (was not behaving)

33 No me preguntes a mí dónde está él. *¿Qué sé yo?* ▲

How should I know?

Self-Correcting Exercises

A Sino *versus* pero: Select *sino* or *pero* for the blanks.

1 Lástima que hoy día no usemos caballos . . . automóviles para ir al centro a hacer las compras. sino

2 Yo sé que no es la costumbre en la actualidad, . . . a mí también me gusta mucho montar a caballo. pero

3 Rara vez vemos familias que tengan caballos, . . . todo el mundo tiene gatos y perros. pero

4 A mí me gustan mucho los perros, . . . los gatos no me gustan nada. pero

5 Al contrario, yo prefiero los gatos. En mi casa no tenemos perros . . . gatos. Tú no has visto mi nuevo gato siamés, ¿verdad? sino

6 No, no lo he visto. Iba a pasar por tu casa ayer por la mañana, . . . tuve que ir al banco. pero

7 Te esperé por más de una hora, . . . tú no tuviste la cortesía de llamarme. pero

8 Quise llamarte, . . . no pude. Estuve hablando largo rato con el banquero, el padre de Anita. pero

9 Te equivocas. No es el padre de Anita . . . de Gladys. sino

10 ¿La chica de ojos azules se llama Gladys? Creí que su nombre era Anita, . . . creo que tú tienes razón. pero

11 Los ojos de Gladys no son azules . . . verdes. ¿Estás ciego *(blind)*? sino

12 No es que esté ciego . . . que a primera vista parecían azules. sino

13 Siento decírtelo, . . . Gladys usa lentes de contacto. pero

14 ¡No me digas! . . . no importa. Es bonita y eso basta. Pero

15 Eso es. Pero creo que no te interesa el color de sus ojos . . . el dinero de su padre, el banquero. sino

B *Shortened Adjectival Forms:* Decide whether to use the long or short form of the adjective in parentheses, then check your answer and read the entire sentence aloud.

1 El toro más (grande) está en el (tercero) corral. grande, tercer

2 No hay (ninguno) lápices mejores que los (grande) que tienen allí. ningunos, grandes

3 Cuando (alguno) amigo va a Europa, le decimos: (Bueno) viaje. algún, Buen

4 Las (primero) flores (grande) salieron el (tercero) día del mes. primeras, grandes, tercer

5 Con (uno) (malo) amigo como tú, no necesito enemigos. un, mal

6 Es un edificio muy (grande) y muy (bueno). grande, bueno

7 ¿Le has oído decir (malo) palabras (alguno) vez? malas, alguna

8 (Ninguno) (grande) hombre puede dejar pasar una oportunidad tan (bueno) como esta. Ningún, gran
buena

C *General Review:* Follow the directions given to rewrite each sentence. Cover the answer in parentheses under each sentence until you are ready to check it.

1 *Tengo ganas de comer algunas de las deliciosas manzanas que veo en aquel árbol.* Change this sentence to report what you were doing rather than what you are doing, and change *feel like eating* to *wanted to buy, delicious apples* to *beautiful hats,* and *tree* to *store.*

(Quería comprar algunos de los bonitos sombreros que vi en aquella tienda.)
2 *Después de que yo recoja (recoger) los documentos, tendré que entregárselos al jefe de policía.* Change *después de que* to *después de* and omit *documentos.* Then, instead of delivering them to the chief of police, you want to say that you will have to mail them.

(Después de recogerlos, tendré que echarlos al correo.)
3 *No es la primera vez que el médico le pide a la enfermera que me dé la medicina.* Backshift this sentence and make it the *sixth* rather than the *first* time.

(No fue (era) la sexta vez que el médico le pidió (pedía) a la enfermera que me diera la medicina.)
4 *Conchita no es bonita y joven, pero es muy buena secretaria.* Change the second clause so that it merely corrects the first part of the sentence.

(Conchita no es bonita y joven, sino fea y vieja.)

D *Verb Review:* The context will give you the cues you will need to determine the proper tense-mode and person-number form of the verbs in parentheses.

Aventuras de Jorge y Gerardo

Jorge y Gerardo son dos jóvenes que yo *conocer* **1** muy bien y sus familias viven en mi barrio (*neighborhood*). Hace varios meses ellos *terminar* **2** sus estudios de tercer año en la universidad. Los dos son muy industriosos y quieren seguir estudiando, pero después de tres años de trabajo continuo, al llegar junio, Jorge y Gerardo se *sentir* **3** ya completamente agotados (*exhausted*). Por consiguiente, los dos amigos decidieron que *ser* **4** una idea magnífica organizar una expedición a las selvas tropicales de Venezuela y Brasil.

Durante los meses del pasado verano, mis amigos *pasar* **5** muchas horas en la biblioteca haciendo investigaciones sobre el territorio que ellos *ir* **6** a explorar. Jorge es un fotógrafo excelente y tiene un equipo completo de cámaras para fotografiar la expedición. Creo que ellos *poder* **7** hacer buen dinero vendiendo sus fotografías y películas al regresar.

La última vez que yo *hablar* **8** con Jorge y Gerardo, ellos me *decir* **9** que *salir* **10** para Panamá a mediados del mes pasado. Era muy urgente que ellos *empezar* **11** el viaje por la selva antes de la estación de las lluvias.

Nadie ha recibido noticias de los dos aventureros recientemente. Según el itinerario del viaje que ellos *dejar* **12** para sus familias, a principios de la semana que viene si Dios quiere, ellos estarán

1	conozco
2	terminaron
3	sentían
4	sería
5	pasaron
6	iban
7	podrán
8	hablé
9	dijeron
10	saldrían (salían)
11	empezaran
12	dejaron

navegando por el río Amazonas. Ojalá que no *tener* **13** ningún problema. En la última carta que escribieron, ellos rogaban a sus familiares que no se *preocupar* **14** por ellos. Mencionaban que (ellos) no se morirían de hambre porque, en sus propias palabras, "la carne de mono es mejor que el pollo y los huevos de cocodrilo son deliciosos."

Antes de que Jorge y Gerardo *salir* **15** para Suramérica, un día yo *discutir* **16** con ellos su proyecto. Me sorprendió que (ellos) me *decir* **17** que a ellos no les *importar* **18** tener que comer serpientes e insectos. Gerardo dijo, —Otras personas que han *hacer* **19** viajes por la selva amazónica *haber* **20** tenido que hacer exactamente la misma cosa.

13	tengan
14	preocuparan
15	salieran
16	discutí
17	dijeran
18	importaría (importaba)
19	hecho
20	han

E *Conditional:* Write the appropriate conditional form of each verb in parentheses. Then check each answer and read the sentence aloud.

1 Me dijeron que ellos no (poder) hacérnoslo para el próximo sábado, pero que (ellos) nos lo (hacer) el mes que viene.
2 Ella me recordó que a mediados del mes que viene, mi abuela (venir) a verme y (ella) me (decir) todo lo que pasó.
3 El jefe nos informó que durante el mes de agosto mi hermano mayor (cortar) la hierba, mi hermano menor (sacar) la basura y mi hermana y yo (tender) la ropa después de que Sofía la lavara.
4 Te dije que tú (tener) que apurarte y que (tú) (deber) entregarle el dinero al jardinero.
5 Recordé que él nos dijo que (ser) más de las cinco de la tarde y que (estar) lloviendo a cántaros antes que pudiéramos irnos de aquí.
6 Dijo que si nos portábamos mal ella nos (dar) muchos golpes y que nosotros no (ir) al cine en tres meses.
7 Me di cuenta de que tú (querer) poner la mesa, pero pensé que la cocinera ya la (haber) puesto.

1	podrían, harían
2	vendría, diría
3	cortaría, sacaría, tenderíamos
4	tendrías, deberías
5	serían, estaría
6	daría, iríamos
7	querrías, habría

New Vocabulary

rubio, -a	blond(e)	**No hay como...**	There's nothing like...
moreno, -a	brunet(te), dark	**¡Cuidado!**	Be careful!
pelirrojo, -a	redhead	**enfrente de**	in front of (facing), opposite
novio, -a	sweetheart, fiancé(e), groom (bride)	**delante de**	in front of
apurar(se)	to hurry up	**detrás de**	behind
aprender (saber) de memoria	to learn (know) by heart	**debajo de**	under(neath)
valer la pena	to be worth the effort (trouble)	**sobre**	on, over

"En tierra de ciegos, el tuerto es rey."   "In the land of the blind, the one-eyed (man) is king."

The Hispanic world is not a single, unified society. When a Latin American goes to Spain, he identifies himself as *un americano*, and when he travels around his own hemisphere he is a *chileno* or *mexicano* or *boliviano*. The dialect that he speaks (even many of the words he uses) almost always defines him as a foreigner when he is in another Hispanic country, and often when he is merely in another province of his own country. In Spain, which is roughly 63,000 square miles smaller than Texas, five different languages are spoken: Galician, a dialect of Portuguese; Basque, a language so unique that no source for it has yet been confirmed; Catalan, a language derived from Old French; Romany, the language of the gypsies; and Castilian, Leonese, Navarrese, and Andalusian, all dialects of Spanish.

In the Hispanic world, as in the United States, many people have to learn a *lingua franca*, that is, a second language which everyone understands, and even when one grows up speaking only Spanish, it may be necessary to learn another dialect in order to be successful in the world of culture, government, or business. Thus in Spain the prestige dialect is Castilian. The natives of Buenos Aires and Montevideo must learn to talk general Latin American just as Southerners or New Englanders in the United States must learn general American if they want to work in radio, television, or the theater.

What you are learning is general American Spanish. You may, some day, become so fluent that you can pass as a native, but you will never be accepted as a native of any place where you happen to be speaking. You may be taken for a native, but you will always be from some place else.

Assignment 100

Review of Comparisons

1 The Spanish equivalents of "good" and "better" are _____. ▲

2 Three other Spanish adjectives have a special form for the comparative. The positive or non-comparative form of *mayor* is either *grande* or *viejo*. The similar forms for *menor* and *peor* are _____. ▲

      bueno, mejor

      pequeño (joven), malo

3 With the exception of the four adjectives given above, Spanish has no suffixes which are like *-er* and *-est*. In addition, both *-er* and *-est* are translated in the same way. So the Spanish equivalent of "taller" and "tallest" is _____. ▲

4 The opposite of this is _____. ▲

5 There are just four adverbs in Spanish which have a special comparative form. Translate the English adverb: *Él hace mucho; yo hago* _____ (more). ▲

      más alto

      menos alto

6 *Él hace poco; yo hago* _____ (less). ▲

7 *Él lo hace bien; yo lo hago* _____ (better). ▲

8 *Él lo hace mal; yo lo hago* _____ (worse). ▲

9 When the attributes of two entities are compared, you may say they are equal or unequal. With the exceptions just noted, these comparisons are made

      más

      menos

      mejor

      peor

with just three words which are equivalent to the mathematical symbols for plus, minus, and equals: *más alto, menos alto*, and _____ *alto* (as tall). ▲

10 When two entities are compared in a sentence the connector word that goes with *más* and *menos* is _____. (*Él es más alto* _____ *yo; Él es menos alto* _____ *yo.*) ▲

    tan

11 When the comparison is one of equality, you use *tan* and the connector word _____. (*Él es tan alto* _____ *yo.*) ▲

    que

12 The same three secondary modifiers (*más, menos* and *tan*) and the same two connector words are used with adverbs: *Él corre* **más** *rápido* **que** *yo. Él corre* **menos** *rápido* **que** *yo. Él corre* **tan** *rápido* _____ *yo.* ▲

    como

13 The modifier *tan* is a shortened form which cannot stand alone. Write the missing form: *Él corre* **más** *que yo. Él corre* **menos** *que yo. Él corre* _____ *como yo.* ▲

    como

14 When *tanto* is used in comparing entities, it functions as an adjective. Write the missing forms: *Él tiene* **más** *libros* **que** *yo. Él tiene* **menos** *libros* **que** *yo. Él tiene* _____ *libros* _____ *yo. Él tiene* _____ *dinero* _____ *yo.* ▲

    tanto

    Él tiene **tantos** *libros* **como** *yo ; Él tiene* **tanto** *dinero* **como** *yo.*

15 The translations of *tantos* and *tanto* are _____. ▲

    as many (books), as much (money)

Review of the Forms and Function of the Future and Conditional

1 To make the Future of all regular and irregular verbs you add the first and second suffixes of the Present of the auxiliary verb _____ to either the regular infinitive or to a modified form of the infinitive. ▲

2 So to get "we shall eat," you add _____ to *comer.* ▲

    haber

    emos (This is *hemos* with the *h* deleted.)

3 To change either *comeremos* or *comerá* to the Conditional, you replace the suffixes *e* and *á* with the first suffix of the _____ of *haber.* ▲

4 This suffix for all forms is _____. ▲

    Imperfect

5 Backshift *iremos* to the Conditional. ▲

    ía

6 There are in all of Spanish just twelve verbs which have an irregular base for the Future and Conditional. You have studied eleven of them. Change the regular infinitive into the form used in these two tenses:

    iríamos

haber, poder, querer, saber, poner, salir, tener, valer, venir, decir, hacer. ▲

    habr, podr, querr, sabr, pondr, saldr, tendr, valdr, vendr, dir, har

7 In English the present progressive is used to talk about a planned future action: *I am leaving tomorrow.* In contrast, you may use either "shall" or "will" to predict or anticipate a future event: *I shall (will) go tomorrow.* Does Spanish translate both forms (shall and will) the same way? ▲

    yes (*Me iré mañana.* But Spanish does not use the progressive for planned future action, only the simple Present: *Me voy mañana.*)

8 The past tense of "will" is _____. ▲

    would

9 Write the backshift of "I know that he will go." ▲

I knew that he would go.

10 Translate both sentences given above. ▲

(Yo) Sé que él irá; (Yo) Sabía que él iría.

Hacer *to Measure Elapsed Time*

Translate the sentences.

1 She has been here for a week. (Two different translations.) ▲

Hace una semana que ella está aquí; Ella ha estado aquí por una semana.

2 She arrived a week ago. ▲

Hace una semana que ella llegó.

3 I have not seen her for ten years. (Two different translations.) ▲

No la he visto por diez años; Hace diez años que no la veo.

Review of the Present and Imperfect Progressive

1 Spanish, like English, uses the simple form for the norm and the progressive for what is happening right at the moment of speaking. The difference between the two languages stems from the fact that the simple Spanish form can also be used for something that is going on at the moment of speaking. So one may ask, *¿Qué haces, chiquita?* to get the answer, *Estoy tocando el piano.* Spanish, as a result, uses the progressive much less than English; it is used to stress the fact of on-goingness at the very moment of speaking. The phone rings. My secretary answers. It's for me. I ask, "Who's calling?" What do I say in Spanish? (a) *¿Quién llama?* (b) *¿Quién está llamando?* ▲

¿Quién llama? (The caller is actually doing nothing when I ask the question.)

2 Since the progressive, except for future planned action, does the same thing in English as in Spanish, your basic learning problem is to discover when to use the simple form where English uses the progressive.

You come to a friend's house and find him sitting at the table, pen and paper in front of him. He gets up, greets you, and you ask, "To whom are you writing?" What do you say in Spanish? (a) *¿A quién escribes?* (b) *¿A quién estás escribiendo?* ▲

¿A quién escribes? (Remember: he is standing up when you ask him and is *not* writing at that moment.)

3 To form the progressive you use *estar* and the imperfect participle. The imperfect participle of all *a*-verbs is formed by adding _____ to the stem. ▲

ando (comprando, cantando)

4 The participle of all *e*- and *i*-verbs is formed by adding [yendo] to the stem. This may be spelled either *yendo* or _____. ▲

iendo

5 Write the imperfect participle for *escribir* and *leer*. ▲

escribiendo, leyendo

Por *versus* para

Translate the italicized word in each sentence using *por* or *para*.

1　Will it be ready *by* ten o'clock?　▲

　　　　　　　　　　　　　　　　　　　　para (destination in time)

2　We were there *for* a week.　▲

　　　　　　　　　　　　　　　　　　　　por (length of time)

3　I shall do it *for* tomorrow.　▲

　　　　　　　　　　　　　　　　　　　　para (destination in time)

4　I have a book *for* you.　▲

　　　　　　　　　　　　　　　　　　　　para (figurative destination)

5　They were walking *through* the park.　▲

　　　　　　　　　　　　　　　　　　　　por (movement through space)

6　They were going *to* the town.　▲

　　　　　　　　　　　　　　　　　　　　para (ultimate destination)

7　We drove *by* the store.　▲

　　　　　　　　　　　　　　　　　　　　por (movement through space)

8　They were walking *along* the street.　▲

　　　　　　　　　　　　　　　　　　　　por (movement through space)

Practice in Reading Aloud

1　Copy *lentamente*, divide it into syllables, and underline the stressed syllables.　▲

　　　　　　len-*ta*-**men**-*te* (When you add *mente* to an adjective both parts retain their

2　Say *mortalmente* aloud and listen for the two stressed syllables.　▲　　　　original stress.)

　　　　　　*mor***tal***men*te (Speakers of English dislike saying two stressed syllables next to each other. This is common in Spanish.)

3　*José María*, a common name for a male in Spanish, is said as just one word, like "Rosemary" in English. Will there be two stressed syllables when you say *José María?*　▲

　　　　　　　　　　　　　　　　　　　　no (You say [josemaría].)

4　When a word ends in a consonant, except _____ or _____, you stress the last vowel (syllable).　▲

5　Say aloud: *casualidad, general, lugar, pescador, navegar, cristal.*　　　　　*n, s*

6　When a word ends in *n* or *s*, and is stressed on the last syllable, it must have an _____ in writing.　▲

7　Say aloud: *almacén, razón, autobús, dirección.*　　　　　accent mark

8　When a word ends in a vowel or *n* or *s*, it is stressed on the _____ syllable.　▲

9　Say aloud: *consiguiente, prestado, acuerdo, menudo, clases, demandan.*　　　next-to-last

10　If a word is not stressed on the last or next-to-last syllable it will always have a written accent over the stressed _____.　▲

11　Say aloud: *político, sicólogo, médico, perdóneme, magnífico.*　　　　　vowel

12　In normal speech all the words in a phrase are run together in Spanish. (a) true (b) false　▲

　　　　　　　　　　　　　　　　　　　　true

13 Read this passage aloud. The bars indicate where you may pause. Remember what allophone you should say after the pause.

En los países hispánicos / la mayoría de la gente / deja de trabajar / a eso de las cinco / de la tarde / para tomar té o chocolate / y algo dulce de comer. Esta comida es la merienda. Normalmente / no se sirve la cena / hasta las nueve o las diez / de la noche. A veces, / especialmente en España, / no sirven la cena / hasta las once / de la noche.

Vocabulary Review: A Home Quiz

Write the Spanish equivalent of the indicated parts, check your spelling and, when necessary, the punctuation. There are twenty frames. If you take off one point per spelling error and five if you miss the whole frame, you can give yourself a grade. Any grade below 80 means you need to make a list of the missed words and study them.

1	I'll have to *borrow* the money. ▲	
2	*Start it* (tú). (Get it going.) ▲	pedir prestado
3	We'll have to go out *this way*. ▲	Ponlo en marcha.
4	They must know, *of course*, that we don't have much time. ▲	por aquí
		por supuesto
		(desde luego)
5	Bring your gun *just in case*. ▲	por si acaso
6	Imagine seeing you here! *What a coincidence!* ▲	¡Qué casualidad!
7	Spanish speakers, *as a general rule*, have dinner later than we do. ▲	por regla general
8	Why is he shouting, "*Help!*"? ▲	¡Auxilio!
9	I'm going to keep it *for the time being*. ▲	por lo pronto
10	Look, all the windows are broken! *How awful!* (terrible) ▲	¡Qué barbaridad!
11	They have not paid the rent and, *consequently*, they'll have to move. ▲	por consiguiente
12	I can't stand all this noise. *Be quiet!* (tú) ▲	¡Cállate!
13	People, *in general*, want to be friends with their neighbors. ▲	por lo general
14	Do you think we should sell it? *Of course not!* ▲	¡Claro que no!
15	How do you say *ouch* in Spanish? ▲	¡Ay!
16	Then, we'll go next week. *Agreed?* ▲	¿De acuerdo?
17	They have done a lot for us and, *therefore*, deserve more respect. ▲	por lo tanto
18	Would you like a raise? *Of course!* ▲	¡Claro que sí!
19	They *rarely* do this. ▲	rara vez
20	*Enough!* I'm going home. ▲	¡Basta!

Self-Correcting Exercises

A *General Review:* Rewrite each sentence, substituting the items in parentheses for the italicized parts. Make all other necessary changes. Cover the answer in parentheses under each sentence until you are ready to check it; then read the new sentence aloud.

1 Yo *sé* que mi hijo *mayor* llegará a ser sicólogo porque le gusta mucho *estudiar los problemas de la mente humana.* (querer, menor, leer libros de viajes fantásticos a otros planetas)

(Yo quiero que mi hijo menor llegue a ser astronauta porque le gusta mucho leer libros de viajes fantásticos a otros planetas.)

2 *Yo dudo* que el *quinto* señor de esta *lista* sea el *mejor mecánico* de aquel *garaje.* (Me parece, tercero, grupo, bueno, ingeniero, fábrica)

(Me parece que el tercer señor de este grupo es el buen ingeniero de aquella fábrica.)

3 Nos *piden* que compremos nueve o *diez* libras (*pounds*) de carne, cuando salgamos a las *tiendas.* (pidieron, once, mercado)

(Nos pidieron que compráramos nueve u once libras de carne, cuando saliéramos al mercado.)

4 *Dice* que esto es de *acero,* un metal muy fuerte. (Dijo, algodón)

(Dijo que esto era de algodón, una tela muy fuerte.)

5 *Creen* que *Tomás* es *más* alto que *Juanito,* su hermano. (No creen, Hilda, tan, Juanita)

(No creen que Hilda sea tan alta como Juanita, su hermana.)

B *Infinitives after Relators, and Shortened Adjectives:* Copy the Spanish sentence, filling the blanks with the translation of the parts in parentheses. Then read the Spanish sentence aloud. Cover the answers below each sentence.

1 *Keep on walking down* (*Third*) *Avenue* (*until arriving*) *at the* (*first*) *park.*
Sigue caminando por la ... Avenida ... al ... parque.

(tercera, hasta llegar, primer)

2 *That country has* (*a bad*) *government.*
Ese país tiene ... gobierno.

(un mal)

3 *With such a* (*bad*) *government,* (*in order to solve*) *their* (*great*) *problems, they need* (*a great*) *leader.*
Con un gobierno tan ... , ... sus ... problemas, necesitan ... líder.

(malo, para resolver, grandes, un gran)

4 (*No*) *pupil in this class has had a cold* (*after taking*) *those pills.*
... alumno de esta clase ha tenido catarro ... esas píldoras.

(Ningún, después de tomar)

5 (*Some*) *of the pills they gave me* (*at the moment of leaving*) *are to be taken* (*before having breakfast*).
... de las píldoras que me dieron ... son para tomar ....

(Algunas, al momento de salir, antes de desayunar)

C *Vocabulary: Review of Expressions.* Cover the answers in the margin, translate mentally each English expression, and then check the correct response.

1 Los perros de este lugar *bother* (*pester*) *me a lot.*

me dan mucha lata

2 ¿El niño le *slapped* a la niña? *No wonder*, ella siempre le está *kicking* a él.

dio una bofetada, Con razón, dando patadas

3 Vamos al banco a *borrow money.*

pedir dinero prestado

4 Y él, *as usual*, lo hizo *unwillingly.*

como de costumbre, de mala gana

5 ¡Vas a *fall*, muchacho! Después no quiero oírte gritar, *help, help!*

darte una caída (*caer*) *¡auxilio, socorro!*

6 *Nowadays* ellos siempre *are back late in* junio.

Hoy (*en*) *día, están de vuelta, a fines de*

7 *After all*, es mejor que tú *mail the letter next week.*

Después de todo, eches la carta al correo, la semana que viene

8 *Behave yourselves*, niñitos, o no pueden *go shopping* conmigo.

Pórtense bien, ir de compras

New Vocabulary

jabón	soap	**patillas**	sideburns	**crecer**	to grow
cepillo	brush	**lluvia**	rain (the)	**ciego, -a**	blind
uña	nail (finger or toe)	**afeitar(se)**	to shave	**tuerto, -a**	one-eyed

"Lo barato es caro."   "You get what you pay for."
(That which is cheap is expensive.)

From the point of view of how much each country produces in national wealth each year, the countries of Latin America are classified among the developing countries of the world. The United States produces per person more than $3,000 of products each year. In contrast there is no Latin American country whose gross national product per person exceeds $1,000 and there are only three (Argentina, Uruguay, and Venezuela) which produce more than $500 per person. Spain, like its former colonies, produces considerably less than its European neighbors. Tiny Switzerland produces almost four times the wealth per year that Spain does.

One cannot really understand the differences in the two cultures without understanding that the Spanish-speaking countries do not create enough wealth to enjoy the same standard of living as the United States. In the wealthier U.S. states many people on public relief have a much better yearly income than many people who work for a living in Latin America. In the United States a person is considered to be officially poor if he makes less than $3,000 a year. In the Hispanic world there are many professional people whose income is no larger than this amount.

Assignment 101

Review of Pronouns

1 The pronoun which stands for the speaker in English has five allomorphs: I, *m*e, *m*y, *m*ine, *m*yself. The pronoun which stands for the speaker in Spanish has six written forms. You have learned five of these. When the speaker is also the doer the form is _____. ▲

2 In all other cases the speaker is labeled, as in English, by the stem _____ plus a suffix. ▲

yo

3 When the speaker is the done-to or the involved entity, the suffix added to *m* is, like English, _____. ▲

m

*e (Tú **me** viste allí. Dé**me**lo. (**Me** levanto temprano.* Spanish has no special form like "myself" for the reflexive done-to.)

4 The post-relator form of *yo* and the possessive form sound alike [mi]. The first is written _____, the second _____. ▲

5 The possessive pronoun functions as an adjective and agrees in number with its noun. As a result, it may have two forms: *mi* and _____. ▲

mí, mi

mis (mi libro, mis libros)

6 The Spanish equivalent of old English "thou" has the same stem in all its forms. It is _____. ▲

7 To get the subject form you add the suffix _____. ▲

t

ú (The written accent only tells you that *tú* can be stressed.)

8 The singular possessive form sounds exactly like *tú* in speech, but because it cannot be stressed, it is written _____, and the plural is _____. ▲

9 The form for the done-to and the involved entity is _____. ▲

tu, tus

10 The form that follows a relator is _____. ▲

te

ti (Since *ti* cannot be confused with *tu*, the stressed *ti* has no accent mark.)

11 The translation of "we" used to be two words that meant something like "we others": *nos otros*. When the speaker is a girl speaking for a group of girls, the modern form is _____. ▲

12 The possessive form that matches *nosotros* has four forms. They are _____. ▲

nosotras

nuestro (libro), nuestros (libros), nuestra (casa), nuestras (casas)

13 The form that stands for the done-to and the involved entity is _____. ▲

nos (Él nos levanta, nosotros nos levantamos.)

14 Which form follows a relator? (a) *nosotros* (b) *nos* ▲

15 The pronouns *usted, ustedes, él, ellos,* and *ella, ellas* have the same form as subject of a verb or object of a relator. When the doer is someone else, the stem of the done-to form for all these pronouns is _____. ▲

nosotros

16 The first suffix shows sex and, so, may be either _____ or _____. ▲

l

17 The second suffix indicates plurality: _____. ▲

o, a

18 The stem *l* is also used for all the involved entity forms. When the form is singular you add _____, and to make this plural, you add _____. ▲

los, las

e, s (le, les)

19 When the involved entity form is immediately followed by a done-to pronoun, both *le* and *les* are changed to a single form _____. ▲

20 The one reflexive form for *usted, ustedes, él, ellos,* and *ella, ellas* is _____. ▲

21 To make this a possessive, you replace the suffix *e* with _____. ▲

22 The forms *mí* and *ti* cannot be used after *con.* You use _____. ▲

23 Are there Spanish equivalents for the subject pronouns "it" and "they" when these stand for entities which either have no sex or whose sex is unknown? ▲

se

se

u (su, sus)

conmigo, contigo

no (You maintain common focus only by the number of the verb form: *¿Dónde está la ciudad? Está en Panamá.*)

24 Here is a chart of all the forms you have just reviewed. Study it until you see the overall patterns clearly. Note that *me, te,* and *nos* have three functions.

Subject (doer)	Post-relator	Done-to (but not doer)	Involved entity	Reflexive (Done-to and doer)	Possessive
yo tú	mí-migo ti-tigo	←———— me ————→ ←———— te ————→			mi, mis tu, tus
nosotros, -as		←———— nos ————→			nuestro, -a, -os, -as
usted él ella ustedes ellos ellas		l o a s	l-e / l-es \ se	se	su, sus

Practice with Pronouns

Think of the Spanish equivalent of the indicated words.

1 *I* bought *myself* a new hat. ▲

2 I hurt *myself* when I fell down. ▲

3 She will give *you* the book. (Three ways) ▲

4 She will give *you it (lo).* (Two ways) ▲

5 We *will wash ourselves* first. ▲

6 They *got up.* ▲

7 *He* hit *himself* on *his* head. ▲

8 Give *him* the money. ▲

9 *Give him it (Vd.).* ▲

yo, me

me

te, le, les

Te lo; Se lo

nos lavaremos

se levantaron

Él, se, su (la)

le

Déselo.

10 To whom shall I send it? *To me.* ▲

11 From whom did he get it? *From you?* (With three different pronouns.) ▲   *A mí*
                                                                        ¿De ti? ¿De usted? ¿De ustedes?

12 Marlena is over there. Can you see *her?* ▲

13 That's *her* home. ▲   *la*
                                                                                                          su

Position of Pronouns

1 When the verb form is a simple indicative or subjunctive, a done-to or involved entity form always comes _____ the verb. ▲
                                            before (*Te dará eso. Quiero que te dé eso.*)

2 An object pronoun follows and is _____ to an infinitive in writing. ▲
                                            attached (*Es importante mandarlo hoy.*)

3 May a subject pronoun come between the auxiliary *haber* and the perfect participle in Spanish? (Has he gone?) ▲

4 When an imperative (command) is affirmative, the object pronouns _____   no (*¿Ha ido él?*) it and are _____ to it in writing. ▲
                                            follow, attached (*¡Pregúnteselo!* But, *¡No se lo pregunte!*)

5 When the verb is in the progressive, the object pronouns may precede or follow the whole form. Translate "I am washing them" (las ventanas). ▲
                                            Estoy lavándolas or *Las estoy lavando.*

6 When two pronouns precede or follow a verb, which comes first? (a) done-to (b) involved entity ▲
                                            involved entity (*Me lo quitarán.*)

Review of The Subjunctive

Morphology

There are only four tenses in Spanish which have a subjunctive form of their own: the Present, the present perfect, the Past, and the past perfect. You have yet to study the past perfect. Do this section carefully to find out whether you need to review the morphology more.

1 Write the *ellos* form of the present subjunctive of *comer, vivir,* and *vender.* ▲
                    coman, vivan, vendan (The first suffix of all forms of the present subjunctive of all *e-* and *i-*verbs is *a.*)

2 Write the *nosotros* form of *pintar, limitar,* and *cultivar.* ▲
                    pintemos, limitemos, cultivemos (The first suffix of all forms of the present subjunctive of all *a-*verbs is *e.*)

3 Write the *yo* form of the present indicative and subjunctive of *tener, hacer, salir, decir,* and *ir.* ▲
                    tengo, tenga; hago, haga; salgo, salga; digo, diga; voy, vaya (When a verb has an irregular *yo* form in the present indicative ending in *o,* this form always serves as the base for *all* the forms of the present subjunctive.)

4 The subjunctive equivalents of *siento* (*sentir*) and *duermes* are _____. ▲

> *sienta, duermas* (When the *e* or *o* of an infinitive of an *i*-verb changes to *ie* or *ue*
> in the present indicative, the same stem is used in the subjunctive.)

5 Something special, however, happens to *sentimos* and *dormimos*. They become

_____. ▲

> *sintamos, durmamos*

6 Write the *Vd.* form of the present subjunctive of *cerrar*, *volar*, *perder*, and *volver*. ▲

> *cierre, vuele, pierda, vuelva* (When the *e* or *o* of an infinitive of an *a*- or *e*-verb
> changes to *ie* or *ue* in the indicative, the subjunctive has the same change in

7 Write the *yo* form (indicative) and the *nosotros* form (subjunctive) of the   the same forms.)
Present of *servir*. ▲

> *sirvo, sirvamos* (In this class of *i*-verbs, the *e* of the infinitive stem changes to *i*
> when the first suffix is *o, a,* or *e*. So all present subjunctive forms have *i* in the

8 Write the *yo* form of the present indicative and subjunctive of *conocer*. ▲   stem.)

9 To change *ellos han dicho* to the subjunctive, you replace *han* with _____. ▲   *conozco, conozca*

10 Give the present subjunctive *yo* form for *ser, ir, estar, dar,* and *saber*. ▲   *hayan*

> *sea, vaya, esté, dé, sepa*

11 You have learned one transformation which will give you the base for all
forms of the past subjunctive. To get the subjunctive of *compraron, leyeron,* or
pusieron you change the *o* of the first suffix to _____. ▲

12 Any irregularity which appears in the *ustedes* and *ellos* form of the preterit   *a*
stem or first suffix will also appear in all forms of the past subjunctive of that
verb. Write the *yo* form of the past subjunctive of *volver, saber,* and *dar*. ▲

> *(volvieron) volviera, (supieron) supiera, (dieron) diera*

13 What must you add to these forms to make the spelling correct? (1) *obser-
varamos* (2) *ofrecieramos* ▲

> An accent mark: *observáramos, ofreciéramos*

Usage

1 With a very few minor exceptions the subjunctive is only used in a _____
clause. ▲

> subjoined (dependent)

2 Since the indicative may also be used in subjoined clauses, there must be a
second factor which is needed to cue the use of the subjunctive. This second
factor is often the relationship between the event of the main and the event of
the subjoined clause. Which mode will you use for the indicated verb in these
three sentences? (1) I know that he *is* rich. (2) She told me that they *live* nearby.
(3) I see that you *have grown* a lot. ▲

> indicative (Stating your knowledge, reporting facts, or observing actions cue
> the use of the indicative.)

3 What is the relationship between the two events in this statement? I'll *turn
down* the radio so (that) we *can hear* each other. ▲

> Turning down the radio *permits* us to hear better.

4 Translate: so that we can hear. ▲

> *para que podamos oír*

5 Which mode will you use for the subjoined verb? Will you close the door so the cat *can't get out?* ▲

6 The opposite of the above is "Will you open the door so the cat can go out?" When one event permits or prevents another, the verb of the subjoined clause is in the subjunctive. Will you use the subjunctive in these transforms of the above statements? (1) The cat can't get out unless you open the door. (2) The cat will go out provided you open the door. ▲

subjunctive

7 When one person attempts to influence the action of another *in any way*, the subjoined verb is in the subjunctive. Translate: It is important that you be here tomorrow. (Use *tú*) ▲

yes

Es importante que estés aquí mañana.

8 One event can cause a physical action to take place. Push it so that it will fall this way. One event may cause an emotional reaction. Translate the indicated verbs: *I'm sorry* that she *has lost* her purse. ▲

Siento, haya perdido

9 We can talk about reality in three different ways. First, we can report what has been observed and say, for example, *El gato está en la cocina.* Second, we can consider certain evidence and conclude that something is or is not so. For example, I hear some noise and say, *Creo que el gato está en la cocina.* Third, we can speculate, with no real evidence, that something may be so. Thus, since there are billions of planets in the universe, there exists the probability that some may have life such as we have here on earth: "It is possible that there is another planet which has human life."

The qualifying clause "It is possible" makes the subjoined clause acceptable as a speculation. All qualifying clauses fall into one of two sets. One set indicates that the speaker accepts the qualified statement either as true, possible, or probable. The other set indicates that the speaker rejects the qualified statement and, in fact, proposes that its negative is correct. The first set of qualifiers cues the indicative in the subjoined clause; the second set cues the use of the subjunctive. In the next four frames translate mentally the indicated verbs.

10 All Christians believe that *there is* a God. ▲ ▲

hay

11 An atheist does not believe that *there is* a god. ▲ ▲

haya

12 Many people are doubtful that *there is* a devil. ▲

haya

13 It is impossible that *there is* any life on the sun. ▲

haya

14 You are doubtful about the notion that Mars can sustain any form of life. You ask this question: Do you believe that it *is* possible that *there is* life on Mars? You want to emphasize your doubt. How do you translate "is" and "there is"? ▲

sea, haya

15 Translate the indicated verb: "Astronomers are searching for another planet which *has* human life." ▲

tenga

16 When an adjectival clause describes an entity which has not been experienced and about which you cannot make a statement of fact, the verb of the descriptive clause is in the subjunctive. What form of *poder* will you use in this sentence? *No hay gatos que _____ hablar inglés.* ▲

puedan

17 Which sentence requires the subjunctive? (1) He wants to marry the girl who *is* rich. (2) He wants to marry a girl who *is* rich. ▲

> The article "the" in sentence (1) maintains common focus on a known girl, so you use the indicative. You have no experience of "a girl" (= any girl) in (2), so you use the subjunctive.

18 In which sentence will you use the subjunctive? (1) We stay home when it rains. (2) We will stay home when it rains. ▲

> (2) *Nos quedaremos en casa cuando llueva.*

19 Which sentence takes the subjunctive? (1) We do it after they leave. (2) We will do it after they leave. ▲

> (2) *Lo haremos después que se vayan.* (When two events are set in an order relationship to each other by words like *antes, cuando,* and *después* and both events are anticipated, you use the Future in the main clause and the subjunctive in the adverbial clause.)

20 After *Ojalá* or *Ojalá que*, the verb must be _____. *Ojalá que ellos (están, estén) bien.* ▲

> subjunctive, estén

Self-Correcting Exercises

A *General Review:* Follow the instructions given for each problem. Cover the answer in parentheses under each sentence until you are ready to check it.

1 The teacher is checking your address and says, *Tú vives en la Quinta Avenida, ¿verdad?* You reply that you don't live on Fifth Avenue but on Third Avenue.

(*Yo no vivo en la Quinta Avenida sino en la Tercera.*)

2 One of your neighbors asks you, *¿Quieres ir de caza con nosotros el sábado que viene?* You answer negatively explaining that you don't like to kill animals and that you have to work next Saturday.

(*No, no me gusta matar animales y tengo que trabajar el sábado que viene*).

3 You tell one of your classmates that you are glad she (he) is going to the dance with you.

(*Me alegro que vayas al baile conmigo.*)

4 Your friend tells you as he looks out the window at the rain, *¡Qué mal tiempo hace hoy! ¿Verdad?* You like the rain very much and so must disagree. Tell him that you do not agree, that you like the rain and that you would like (Use the Conditional) for it to rain more often.

(*No estoy de acuerdo. Me gusta la lluvia. Me gustaría que lloviera más a menudo.*)

5 A classmate has just said to you, *El primer semestre termina a mediados de este mes.* You contradict him by saying that you are sure it ends at the beginning of next month.

(*No, estoy seguro(a) que termina a principios del mes que viene.*)

In the U.S., since the invention of the internal combustion engine and until recently when it became a fashion particularly among young people, back packs were usually used only by boy scouts, hikers or campers. Similarly, pack animals have been seldom used except by forest rangers or explorers going into the back country where there are no roads.

In Latin America pack animals are still a standard way of transporting goods even in areas where there are roads. The two most common pack animals are, however, the burro and, in the Andes, and especially Peru, the llama. A large llama can carry about 100 pounds. The llamas object to being overloaded and when, in their opinion, they feel overloaded they will spit in their driver's face. Sometimes they lie down and refuse to get up until the load is reduced.

Indian women carry jugs and small loads on their heads. The men frequently work as packers. In addition to back straps, they use a sling which passes over the forehead. With this arrangement a strong and trained packer can carry enormous loads, much more than a burro or a llama.

B *Silent Reading:* Read the following quickly, without mental translation—as if you were reading English.

Grandes hombres de las Américas: José de San Martín (segunda parte)

El regimiento de Granaderos a Caballo

Cuando José de San Martín llega a Buenos Aires en 1812, hace dos años que Argentina es libre, pero su independencia está amenazado° por los españoles y los portugueses. La grave situación demanda que el coronel San Martín organice cuanto antes una escuela para oficiales y soldados. A esta escuela militar asisten no solamente los hijos de los ricos sino también indios de Yapeyú y gauchos de las pampas. En pocos meses San Martín tiene a su disposición un regimiento modelo que él llama Granaderos a Caballo.° Pertenecer a este regimiento es un alto honor para la juventud argentina. Los Granaderos a Caballo obtienen su primera victoria en la batalla de San Lorenzo donde San Martín estuvo a punto de perder la vida.

   threatened

   Mounted Grenadiers

Matrimonio con "Remeditos"

A los cinco meses de estar de vuelta en Buenos Aires, San Martín se casa con doña María de los Remedios Escalada. El novio tiene 34 años y la novia tiene solamente 15. Las muchas obligaciones militares impiden que San Martín pase mucho tiempo en compañía de su "Remeditos" como él llama a su joven esposa. Es necesario que él vaya a reorganizar las tropas del Ejército del Norte y ella se queda en Buenos Aires en casa de sus padres. Es la primera de muchas separaciones que la buena esposa sufrirá con resignación por el resto de su vida.

El gran secreto

Después de pasar algún tiempo reorganizando el Ejército del Norte, San Martín llega a la conclusión de que sería imposible vencer a los españoles en las montañosas regiones del norte. Se da cuenta al mismo tiempo de que Argentina no podrá mantener su independencia mientras Chile y Perú estén dominados por el enemigo. Concibe entonces un plan grandioso: cruzará la cordillera de los Andes para libertar a Chile y seguirá por mar a Lima para atacar allí a los españoles. San Martín sabe que este difícil y costoso proyecto no será aceptado en Buenos Aires y decide mantenerlo en secreto hasta que llegue el momento oportuno para entrar en acción. Por algún tiempo ha estado muy enfermo del estómago y ha tenido problemas serios de respiración. Su cuerpo y su espíritu requieren calma y reposo en el campo. Las autoridades le permiten que se retire a una hacienda cerca de Mendoza, una ciudad a los pies de los Andes. Su esposa Remedios viene de Buenos Aires a cuidarlo y más tarde San Martín consigue que el gobierno lo nombre gobernador de Cuyo, el territorio que está a las puertas de Chile.

El Ejército de los Andes

En Mendoza nace Mercedes, hija única de los esposos San Martín. Ella será quien cuidará a su padre en la vejez y lo confortará en la tristeza de su exilio en Europa. Durante tres años el nuevo gobernador y su esposa movilizan a todos los habitantes de la región para organizar un gran ejército de liberación. De Chile viene el líder revolucionario Bernardo O'Higgins buscando refugio con sus soldados y todos se ponen al servicio de San Martín. Los ricos contribuyen a la causa con dinero y esclavos; los agricultores traen comida y animales; los pobres ofrecen su trabajo; las mujeres entregan sus joyas y cosen los uniformes para los soldados. Doña Remedios y sus amigas bordan° la bandera que el ejército llevará a Lima. El ex-fraile° Luis Beltrán, un verdadero genio mecánico, dirige la producción de materiales guerreros. El ingeniero Álvarez Condarco hace un viaje a Santiago con el pretexto de llevarle un mensaje al gobernador español y vuelve con mapas del territorio que tienen que cruzar. Los indios que admiran al líder moreno ayudan distribuyendo noticias falsas sobre los posibles puntos de ataque. No hay nadie en la región que no participe de algún modo al éxito del gran proyecto. Para fines de enero de 1817 todo está listo para iniciar la marcha. A San Martín no le preocupa la oposición que puedan hacerle sus enemigos; lo que no le deja dormir son los inmensos montes que sus miles de hombres y animales tendrán que atravesar para llegar a Chile.

°embroider
°priest

Lectura adicional: Pensamientos de San Martín

Las naciones americanas deben unirse si quieren ser respetadas.

Para los hombres de coraje se han hecho las empresas grandes.

Serás lo que debes ser o no eres nada.

La educación es la llave maestra que abre las puertas de la abundancia y hace felices a los pueblos. Yo deseo que todos se eduquen en los sagrados derechos° que forman la conciencia de los hombres libres.

sacred rights

Entre los papeles que dejó San Martín hay una lista de máximas o reglas de conducta que él preparó para su hija Mercedes. Esta lista nos da una buena idea de las cualidades femeninas que se consideraban importantes en aquel tiempo. San Martín deseaba que su hija . . .

1 fuera bondadosa y compasiva con todo el mundo, inclusive con los animales.

2 amara° la verdad y odiara° la mentira.

love/hate

3 fuera sociable pero que mostrara siempre respeto.

4 ayudara a los pobres.

5 respetara la propiedad ajena (de otros).

6 supiera guardar secretos.

7 aprendiera a respetar todas las religiones.

8 fuera dulce y amable con los criados, pobres y viejos.

9 hablara poco y solamente lo necesario.

10 se portara bien en la mesa.

11 estuviera siempre limpia y vistiera bien, pero sin preocuparse demasiado por el lujo.°

luxury

C *Vocabulary Review:* Copy the Spanish sentence filling the blanks with the Spanish equivalent of the parts in parentheses; then read the completed Spanish sentence aloud.

1 *(Upon) leaving the (bakery), the (baker) (handed) the money to his (wife).*
. . . salir de la . . . , el . . . le . . . el dinero a su . . . .

(Al, panadería, panadero, entregó, esposa (mujer))
2 *In our house the (bathroom) is (upstairs).*
En nuestra casa el . . . está . . . .

((cuarto de) baño, arriba)
3 *(In spite of (the fact)) that the ((male) nurse) was very careful, he (ruined) the (shot).*
. . . que el . . . tuvo mucho cuidado, él . . . la . . . .

(A pesar de, enfermero, echó a perder, inyección)
4 *When I was at the (drugstore), the druggist said: ("Cheaply) bought, (expensive) in the end."*
Cuando estuve en la . . . , el boticario dijo: "Lo . . . es . . . ."

(botica (droguería, farmacia), barato, caro)
5 *She (gave me) a terrible (look) and (hit me) with a shoe, but she didn't break any (bone).*

Ella . . . terrible y . . . con un zapato, pero no me rompió ningún . . . .

(me echó una mirada, me dio un golpe, hueso)
6 *I (learned (found out)) that (at present) very few women paint their toe (nails).*
Yo . . . que . . . muy pocas mujeres se pintan las . . . de los pies.

(me enteré, en la actualidad, uñas)

Assignment 102

Review of the Preterit and Imperfect

Morphology

1 In the forms of the Preterit there is one second suffix which is different from all the other tense forms. This second suffix _____ goes with the subject pronoun _____. ▲

2 The first suffix of the Imperfect of all regular *e-* and *i-*verbs is _____. ▲ | *ste, tú*

3 The first suffix of the Imperfect of all regular *a-*verbs is _____. ▲ | *ía*

4 In both the Preterit and Imperfect of all *e-* and *i-*verbs, the first phoneme that follows the stem is _____. ▲ | *aba*

5 So you can change *yo vendía* to the Preterit simply by _____. ▲ | /i/

dropping the final *a: vendí.*

6 To the Preterit base *vendi* you add _____ and _____ to get the *tú* and *nosotros* forms. ▲

ste, mos (vendiste, vendimos)

7 The *Vd.* and *Vds.* forms of the Preterit of *vender* are _____. ▲

8 The *nosotros* form of the Preterit of *a-*verbs is exactly like the _____ indicative. ▲ | *vendió, vendieron*

present (So *compramos* translates "we are buying" and "we bought.")

9 There are two other forms of the Preterit which have *a* immediately after the stem. For *comprar*, they are _____. ▲

compraste, compraron

10 The only difference between the present indicative *compro* or the present subjunctive *compre* and the *Vd.* and *yo* forms of the Preterit (*Vd. compró, yo compré*) is a change in stress shown by the _____ in writing. ▲

11 Write the *él* form of *leer*. ▲ | accent mark

leyó (Unstressed *i* becomes *y* between two vowels.)

12 Write the *yo* form of the Preterit of *tener, poner, venir,* and *traer*. They are all irregular. ▲

tuve, puse, vine, traje

13 The *ella* form of the Preterit of *sentir* is _____. ▲

sintió

Usage

Read through this summary of the rules for usage and refer to it, if necessary, as you complete the frames below. The Imperfect is used   (a) to talk about past clock time   (b) to say that any event or state, either cyclic or noncyclic, was going on at some point in the past   (c) as a back-shift of the Present to recall planned action   (d) to translate either *used to* or *would* when talking about customary or habitual past actions.

The Preterit is used   (a) to say that a whole event, either cyclic or non-cyclic, was completed *before* the moment of speaking   (b) to say that a non-cyclic event *began* either at some point in the past or *before* the moment of speaking (c) to say that a cyclic event was completed either *at* some point in the past or *before* the moment of speaking.

In the following narration most of the verbs are in the infinitive. Decide whether to use the Preterit or the Imperfect, then write the proper form.

1 Yo fui a México por primera vez cuando *tener* diecinueve años. ▲

2 *Cruzar* el Río Grande por el puente que conecta a Brownsville, Texas, con la ciudad mexicana de Matamoros. ▲   *tenía*

3 En los Estados Unidos en aquel tiempo la venta de bebidas alcohólicas *estar* prohibida y, por eso, *haber* muchas tabernas en Matamoros y mucha gente *vivir* del turismo. ▲   *Crucé*

4 Yo *tomar* un autobús y *ir* a la plaza central. ▲

estaba, había, vivía

5 Yo no *saber* entonces ni una palabra de español, pero muy pronto me *dar* cuenta de que mucha gente *hablar* inglés. ▲   *tomé, fui*

6 Después de pasear por la ciudad por varias horas, *volver* a la frontera donde un guardia me *pedir* el pasaporte. ▲   *sabía, di, hablaba*

7 Le *decir* que no *tener* pasaporte. ▲

volví, pidió

8 Él me *preguntar* de dónde *ser*. ▲

dije, tenía

9 Le *dar* el nombre de la ciudad donde *nacer*. ▲

preguntó, era

10 Es una ciudad pequeña que está en un estado del norte del país. Cuando el inspector *oír* el nombre de mi pueblo natal, él se *sonreír*. (Both verbs are irregular.) ▲   *di, nací*

11 ¡Qué pequeño es el mundo! Me *contar* que él *conocer* muy bien el lugar y que *pensar* ir allí a pescar para sus próximas vacaciones. ▲   *oyó, sonrió*

contó, conocía, pensaba

12 Entonces él me *hacer* varias preguntas y *permitir* que yo pasara la frontera. ▲

hizo, permitió

Getting Ready for a Quiz on Verbs

The quiz you will have in the next class is designed to find out whether you can discover from context what tense, mode, aspect, and person suffix should be used to replace a given infinitive. In a selection in Spanish you will be asked to change 12 infinitives to the form that fits the context. Practice doing this in the following frames.

1 Ya eran las dos de la mañana. (*Llover*) torrencialmente y todavía nuestros padres no (*estar*) de vuelta en casa. Al oír un ruido en el garaje, mis hermanitos (*tener*) mucho miedo. ▲

Llovía, estaban, tuvieron

2 Los niños (*estar*) durmiendo, y cuando el ruido los (*despertar*), ellos (*venir*) corriendo a la sala donde yo estaba viendo la televisión. ▲

estaban, despertó, vinieron

3 Ellos querían que yo (*llamar*) a la policía, pero les dije que no (*ser*) necesario. Para convencerlos yo los (*llevar*) al garaje. ▲

4 Yo (*encender*) la luz del garaje y mis hermanitos (*ver*) que allí no (*haber*)   *llamara, era, llevé* nadie. Después de unos minutos ellos se (*dormir*) otra vez en la alfombra. ▲

encendí, vieron, había, durmieron

5 En realidad yo no quería que ellos se (*alarmar*), pero por la ventana yo (*ver*) la sombra (*shadow*) de alguien y poco después (*sentir*) el motor de un carro que se alejaba rápidamente. ▲

6 Cuando mis padres vuelvan de su fiesta, yo les (*decir*) inmediatamente todo   *alarmaran, vi, sentí* lo que pasó para que ellos (*reportar*) el incidente, si ellos (*querer*). ▲

diré, reporten, quieren

7 ¡Espero que ellos (*venir*) pronto! Ojalá que el ladrón (*thief*) no (*decidir*) volver antes que ellos (*estar*) de vuelta. Ahora yo también (*tener*) un poco de miedo. ▲

vengan, decida, estén, tengo

8 Cuando él y yo (*ir*) a la playa el sábado que viene, nos (*divertir*) mucho. Siempre que nosotros vamos a la playa nos (*divertir*) mucho. ▲

vayamos, divertiremos, divertimos

Self-Correcting Exercises

A *General Review:* Rewrite each sentence, replacing the indicated parts with those in parentheses and making all other necessary changes. Cover the answer in parentheses under each sentence until you are ready to check it.

1 *Podremos* comprar o *conseguir* de otro *modo* lo que *ellos* necesitan.   (Tener que, obtener, manera, Juanita)

(Tendremos que comprar u obtener de otra manera lo que Juanita necesita.)
2 *Es probable* que *Vds.* tengan *más* ovejas que ellos.   (Era importante, Vd., tanto)

(Era importante que Vd. tuviera tantas ovejas como ellos.)
3 *Ve* a la *casa* y no *regreses hasta* que *sepas* portarte mejor.   (Salir, jardín, volver, antes de, decidir)

(Sal al (del) jardín y no vuelvas antes de que decidas portarte mejor.)
4 La *semana* que viene *ella irá* con *nosotros* a San José y *pescará*.   (mes, tú, poder ir, mí, cazar)

(El mes que viene tú podrás ir conmigo a San José y cazarás.)

5 *Paco prometió* que lo *haría* mañana.   (Vds., decir, saber)

(Vds. dijeron que lo sabrían mañana.)

6 A él no *le parece verde* sino *azul*.   (me, gustar, viejo, nuevo)

(A mí no me gusta viejo sino nuevo.)

B *Silent Reading, Meaning from Context:* Some of the words in the following selection are new to you. Pay close attention to the context and see if you can guess their meaning.

El pelo de la cara

En español hay tres palabras que se usan con mucha frecuencia para referirse al pelo que crece en la cara de los hombres: barba (pelo que crece debajo de la boca), bigote (pelo que cubre el labio superior) y patillas (pelo que crece a los lados de la cara).

Las mujeres, con excepción de algunos casos anormales que vemos en los circos, generalmente no tienen pelo notable en la cara. A los quince años más o menos el pelo empieza a crecer en la cara masculina y los muchachos tienen que empezar a afeitarse. Al principio se afeitan una o dos veces por semana, pero más tarde es necesario que lo hagan más a menudo. A menos que deseen ser barbudos como Fidel Castro u otros personajes de la historia famosos por su barba.

Para afeitarse los hombres usan una brocha, jabón o crema de afeitar y una navaja o una maquinilla. La navaja es una especie de cuchillo que se usaba mucho en el pasado para afeitarse en la casa. Aunque todavía hay hombres que prefieren afeitarse con este instrumento, hoy día las navajas son usadas principalmente en las barberías. En la casa el hombre moderno usa una gran variedad de maquinillas o maquinitas de afeitar. Algunas son eléctricas y otras tienen finas hojas o cuchillas de acero que cortan por los dos lados. Cuando estas hojas han sido usadas varias veces, es necesario poner una hoja nueva en la maquinilla. Es mucho más cómodo y rápido afeitarse con una maquinilla eléctrica porque puede hacerse sin jabón, crema y agua. Solamente se necesita un poco de loción antes o después de afeitarse. Aunque tampoco es absolutamente necesario usar lociones.

Con una maquinilla eléctrica es posible afeitarse en autos, trenes, aviones y en casi todos los lugares. Hoy día también hay maquinillas de afeitar eléctricas para las damas, pero ellas generalmente no las usan para la cara sino para las piernas. La maquinilla de afeitar es uno de los instrumentos más útiles y prácticos que se han inventado.

Escriban el equivalente inglés de las siguientes palabras:

1 barba   beard (chin)
2 bigote   mustache

3	patillas	sideburns
4	afeitarse	to shave
5	barbudos	bearded
6	brocha de afeitar	shaving brush
7	navaja de afeitar	straight razor
8	maquinilla de afeitar	(electric) razor
9	damas	ladies
10	hojas o cuchillas de afeitar	razor blades

C *Verb Review, Pre-quiz Practice:* You must read each complete sentence before deciding on the correct form of the verb.

1 Cuando la señora de San Martín se enteró que su esposo (*estar*) enfermo y se (*sentir*) muy mal, ella (*salir*) de Buenos Aires y (*ir*) a Mendoza a cuidarlo. — estaba, sentía, salió, fue

2 Durante tres años San Martín (*ser*) gobernador de la región de Cuyo y todo ese tiempo su esposa (*estar*) allí con él. — fue, estuvo

3 Mercedes, la única hija de los esposos San Martín (*nacer*) en la ciudad de Mendoza. — nació

4 En el futuro, cuando Mercedes (*ser*) mujer, ella cuidará a su padre en Francia y (*tener*) dos hijas que (*hacer*) muy feliz al general San Martín. — sea, tendrá, harán

5 Antes de salir para Chile con su gran ejército de los Andes, San Martín insistió en que su esposa e hija (*volver*) a Buenos Aires. — volvieran

6 Él sabía que allí ellas (*poder*) vivir más cómodamente y que los familiares las (*ayudar*) en caso de que tuvieran algún problema. — podrían, ayudarían

7 Cuando pasaron los Andes ningún soldado (*morir*), pero miles de caballos y mulas (*caer*) muertos en el camino. — murió, cayeron

8 En Chile los españoles (*tener*) un ejército poderoso (*powerful*), pero ellos (*esperar*) que San Martín los (*atacar*) por un lugar diferente. — tenían, esperaban, atacara

9 Las tropas de San Martín (*sorprender*) a los españoles y los vencieron en la batalla de Chacabuco. — sorprendieron

10 Los chilenos querían que San Martín (*ser*) su presidente, pero él no (*buscar*) gloria personal y no aceptó tan alto honor. — fuera, buscaba

New Vocabulary

cumplir	to fulfill, complete years of age		**agradecer**	to thank, be grateful (for)
doler (ue)	to ache, hurt, pain		**merecer**	to deserve
meter (en)	to put (into)		**obedecer**	to obey
suceder	to happen		**desobedecer**	to disobey
toser	to cough		**pertenecer**	to belong
bendecir (i)	to bless		**reconocer**	to recognize
maldecir (i)	to curse		**envolver (ue)**	to wrap
predecir (i)	to predict		**devolver (ue)**	to return (something)

Assignment 103

General Review

Post-relator Pronouns

1 In speech the morpheme /mi/ has two functions. It may indicate possession: *mi libro*. The second function is to replace *yo* after a relator. When this /mi/ is the only label for *yo* in the utterance it may or may not be emphatic: *Hablan de mí*. When it is the second label for *yo*, *Démelo a mí*, it is emphatic. The reason that *mí* has an accent mark in writing is just to show that it can be _____ in speech. ▲

2 Which form, *yo, me, mí, mi*, can be used as a complete utterance? Someone asks, for example, *¿Quién vive aquí?* You may answer _____. ▲

stressed

3 The form *mi* must be followed by a _____. ▲

Yo

noun (The label for something you possess.)

4 The form *me* must either precede or follow a _____ ▲

verb (*Déme la cuchara. No me dé el tenedor.*)

5 The form *mí* cannot be the subject or object of a verb, so it is used only after a _____. ▲

relator (*Me lo quitaron a mí.*)

6 Someone asks, *¿A quién se lo dieron?* May you answer with just *A mí?* ▲

yes (Any relator plus *mí* may be used as a complete utterance.)

7 *Mí* is changed to _____ after *con*. ▲

8 Which form is used with a relator: *tú, te, ti, tu?* ▲

migo

ti (*A **ti** no te importa eso.*)

9 The *ti* changes to _____ after *con*. ▲

10 Suppose you want to say *Tengo el libro de* _____. May you fill the missing slot with any one of these forms? *él, ella, ellos, ellas, usted, ustedes* ▲

tigo

11 Is there a special form of *nosotros* to be used after a relator? ▲

yes

no (Up to now you have learned that only *yo* and *tú* have special forms that follow a relator.)

Function of the Relator *de*

Go back to Assignment 91, p. 578, and read again the section on the relator *de*.

Sino versus *pero*

In each of the frames below decide whether to use *sino* or *pero*.

1 *But* you can't do that! ▲
2 He's not rich *but* poor. ▲
3 I asked for two *but* he gave me six. ▲
4 They're not coming *but* I don't care. ▲

Pero
sino
pero
pero

5 I'll work this afternoon, *but* not tonight. ▲

6 They are not brown *but* black. ▲   *pero*

7 He's not crying *but* laughing. ▲   *sino*

8 Not five *but* six. ▲   *sino*

9 Five *but* not six. ▲   *sino*

10 No one knows it *but* you. ▲   *pero*

                                                                                                   sino

Relators plus Verb Forms

Translate the indicated phrases.

1 I just came *from swimming*. ▲

2 *After going to bed* I remembered that I had not locked the door. ▲   *de nadar*

                                                                                 Después de acostarme

3 This stuff is good *for washing* oily clothes. ▲

4 I'll do it *before going* shopping. ▲   *para lavar*

5 I'm tired *of reading*. ▲   *antes de ir*

          de leer (All relators must be followed by the infinitive form of the verb.)

Shortened Forms of Adjectives

Translate the indicated words.

1 I want *a book* and *a magazine*. ▲

2 I have two dogs. I'll give you *one*. ▲   *un libro, una revista*

3 He's a *great* man. ▲   *uno*

4 We are having *bad weather*. ▲   *gran*

5 *The first day* of the month. ▲   *mal tiempo*

6 He's a *good friend* of mine. ▲   *El primer día*

7 *Someday* I'll find it. ▲   *buen amigo*

8 This is *the third* boy I've seen today with measles. ▲   *Algún día*

9 I do not see *any man* there. ▲   *el tercer*

10 I do not see *any*. ▲   *ningún hombre*

11 He's *a large man*. ▲   *ninguno*

12 He's the second one and I'm *the third*. ▲   *un hombre grande*

13 That is not *good* for you. ▲   *el tercero (la tercera)*

                                                                                                  bueno

The Location of One Thing Relative to Another

1 When one object is in contact with either a horizontal or a vertical surface,
you say this in Spanish with the relator _____. ▲

                                             *en (La mosca está **en** la mesa, **en** la ventana.)*

2 When something is above (but not in contact with) a surface you use
_____. ▲

                                                                                                 sobre

3   The opposite of *sobre* is the phrase _____.   ▲
4   *At the side of* is _____.   ▲
5   *Next to* is _____.   ▲
6   *In front of*, but not facing, is _____.   ▲
7   The opposite of *delante de* is _____.   ▲

debajo de
al lado de
junto a
delante de
detrás de

Use of the Articles with Count and Measure Entities

Most of the entities which exist in the real world belong to one or the other of two sets. The members of one set can be counted, so they are called *count entities* (house, man, book, class, door, *etc.*). The members of the other set can be measured, so they are called *measure entities* (water, sugar, dust, mud, wine, heat, *etc.*). This is important to know because we do not treat the members of these two sets the same way linguistically in either English or Spanish.

Most nouns standing for count entities have two forms, a singular and a plural: *cup, cups*. Most nouns standing for measure entities have only one form: *coffee*. This looks like a singular form but it is actually numerically neutral because it does not combine with any number adjective.

When you call a person's attention to count entities you must indicate whether you are talking about one or more than one. You can do this by using the plural form of the noun without an article: *Look! There are **flies** on the table.* When you change this statement to make *flies* singular, you must add the indefinite article: *Look! There is **a** fly on the table.* You do not say *There is fly on the table.* When you call a person's attention to measure entities you simply use the noun all by itself: *Look! There is **dust** on the table.* The verb form is singular because the noun *dust* looks like a singular form.

Both English and Spanish treat count and measure entities in essentially the same way. Compare:

Look! There are **flies** on the table.	*¡Mire! Hay **moscas** en la mesa.*
Look! There is **a fly** on the table.	*¡Mire! Hay **una mosca** en la mesa.*
Look! There is **dust** on the table.	*¡Mire! Hay **polvo** en la mesa.*

1   We cannot talk about count entities and communicate successfully until we tell our listener three things. First, we must label what we are talking about (the subject of discourse); second, we must say how many we are talking about; and, third, we must inform our hearer whether we share or do not share some common experience or knowledge of the subject of discourse. The subject of discourse in *The world is round* is _____.   ▲
2   The number of worlds being talked about is _____.   ▲
3   When I say *The world is round*, am I talking about an entity of which both you and I have common experience and knowledge?   ▲
4   There is just one word in *The world is round* which tells you I am talking about an entity of which you and I have common experience and knowledge. That word is _____.   ▲

world
one

yes

The

5   Which sentence will tell my wife that the man being talked about is the one who delivers mail to our house? (a) There goes **a** mailman. (b) There goes **the** mailman.   ▲

There goes the mailman.

6   In both *The world is round* and *There goes the mailman* the subject of discourse (world, mailman) is a unique entity. The world is unique because there is only one in our solar system. The mailman is unique because there is only one who regularly delivers mail to our house. When we initiate a conversation, one function of the definite article in both English and Spanish is to tell the hearer to focus his attention on an entity which, according to our shared experience and knowledge, is unique. When the hearer succeeds in focusing his attention on this entity, it is said that we are in common focus; that is, our attention is directed to the same entity. There are, of course, many entities in the world of which we have no shared experience or knowledge.

Suppose you and I have just met. Which sentence may I use to start a conversation with you? (a) I bought **a** car today. (b) I bought **the** car today.   ▲

I bought a car today.

7   When we initiate a conversation one function of the indefinite article, in both English and Spanish, is to tell the hearer to focus his attention on one entity of the set labeled by the noun which marks the subject of discourse. Suppose, now, that I have just said to you *I bought a car today*, and I want to say something more about it. Which sentence will I use? (a) The car cost $4,700.00. (b) A car cost $4,700.00.   ▲

The car cost $4,700.00.

8   One function of the definite article, in both English and Spanish, is to tell the hearer to keep his attention focused on the entity previously defined as the subject of discourse. This is called maintaining common focus. In which pair of sentences is common focus maintained? (a) I saw a man. A man was swimming nearby. (b) I saw a man. The man was swimming nearby.   ▲

I saw a man. The man was swimming nearby. (The first two sentences talk about two different men. The second pair talks about only one.)

9   When one talks about count entities one can initiate a conversation by talking about some of them. This can be done in two ways. One is to just use the plural noun: I saw men running down the street. (*Vi hombres corriendo por la calle.*) Or one may add a word like "some": I saw some men running down the street. (*Vi unos hombres corriendo por la calle.*) Suppose, now, you want to maintain common focus on these men. Write the missing article: _____ men were chasing a cow.   ▲

The (In both languages the definite article is used to maintain common focus on either a single or a plural entity.)

10   There are times when one wishes to talk about all the entities labeled by a given noun. English can say either *The horse is a valuable work animal* or *Horses are valuable work animals*. Spanish has no equivalent of the second sentence because Spanish requires the definite article, either singular (*el caballo*) or plural (*los caballos*) when the noun stands for <u>all</u> the entities it may label. Suppose, then, you like all horses. How will you translate "I like horses"?   ▲

Me gustan los caballos.

11 You now have to learn just two facts to be able to use the articles in Spanish. First, English does not always use the definite article when talking about a unique entity. We say, for example, "I'll see you Monday" or "Mr. Churchill was a famous man." Since Monday and Mr. Churchill are unique entities Spanish requires the use of the definite article: *Te veré el lunes. El señor Churchill era un hombre famoso.*

Second, as shown in frame 10, when Spanish talks about all the entities a noun may label, it uses the definite article. So you translate "Man is mortal" or "Men are mortal" by *El hombre es mortal* and *Los hombres son mortales.* With only a few minor exceptions, all other uses of the articles with count entities are just like English.

12 When you talk about count entities you may talk about all, some, one of many, or one unique. Since measure entities cannot combine with number words they are not compatible with the concepts of one of many or one unique. As a result, when you initiate common focus, you can talk only about all or some. So you may say:

I like milk (all milk).   *Me gusta la leche.*

I need milk (some milk).   *Necesito leche.*

The modified noun (*la leche*) indicates all; the unmodified noun (*leche*) stands for some. When you want to maintain common focus on a previously mentioned measure entity you use the definite article just as you do with count entities. Translate: Did you (*tú*) buy milk? Yes, the milk is on the table. ▲

¿Compraste leche? Sí, la leche está en la mesa

The Each-Other Construction

1 There is one set of events which normally do not take place unless two people perform the same action on each other. *They kissed and made up* automatically means they kissed each other. *They shook hands* and *They embraced* belong to the same set. When we talk about events of this set is there any need to add *each other* to the sentence? ▲

No (Saying *They embraced **each other** and made up* adds no new information.)

2 There is another set of events which one can perform on oneself, on somebody else, or which two people can do to each other. For example: (1) He hurt himself. (2) He hurt her. (3) They hurt each other. Which sentence has a reflexive construction? ▲

3 The Spanish translation of this is *Él se lastimó.* Make this sentence plural. ▲

He hurt himself.

Ellos se lastimaron.

4 This sentence has two meanings in Spanish. One meaning is that each person hurt himself. The other meaning is that they hurt each other. In most cases either the verbal context or the life situation (universe of discourse) makes the meaning clear. What is its meaning in *They got into a fight **y se lastimaron?*** ▲

They hurt each other.

5 What is its meaning in *They both tripped over the rope **y se lastimaron?*** ▲

They hurt themselves.

6   There are times in Spanish when neither the verbal context nor the universe of discourse clarifies the meaning. Two barbers, for example, *se afeitan*. To make the meaning clear you have to add more context or change the statement. What is the meaning of *Se afeitan uno a otro?*   ▲

They shave each other.

7   When several people are doing the same thing to each other you clarify the meaning by making *uno a otro* plural. The verb "to hit" is *golpear*. Translate *Se golpearon unos a otros.*   ▲

They hit each other. (Now you have the same kind of ambiguity or confusion in English. You cannot tell whether *They hit each other* means two people hit each other or many people hit each other. Each language has its own peculiar ambiguities. You just have to learn to live with them or to find some other way of sending the message.)

A/B

SE MIRAN   SE MIRAN

Summary

1   Spanish treats count and measure entities linguistically in essentially the same way as English.

2   Count entities have a plural form; measure entities do not.

3   To initiate common focus on count entities the plural form of the noun is used without an article; the singular form requires the indefinite article.

4   To initiate common focus on measure entities the noun does not require an article.

5   The definite article is used to say that the subject of discourse is unique, to say that the noun stands for *all* the entities it may label, and to maintain common focus on a previously defined entity.

Self-Correcting Exercises

A *Position of Limiting Adjectives:* Translate the following sentences mentally and check your answers one at a time.

1	I shall have five other pencils.	*Tendré otros cinco lápices.*
2	I shall have five other pens.	*Tendré otras cinco plumas.*
3	I shall have two other pens.	*Tendré otras dos plumas.*
4	I shall have two other notebooks.	*Tendré otros dos cuadernos.*
5	I shall have four other notebooks.	*Tendré otros cuatro cuadernos.*
6	I shall have four other rulers.	*Tendré otras cuatro reglas.*
7	I shall have three other rulers.	*Tendré otras tres reglas.*
8	I shall have three other books.	*Tendré otros tres libros.*
9	I shall have seven other books.	*Tendré otros siete libros.*
10	I read three more books than he. (past)	*Leí tres libros más que él.*
11	I read three more lessons than he.	*Leí tres lecciones más que él.*
12	I read two fewer (less) lessons than he.	*Leí dos lecciones menos que él.*
13	I read one more novel than he.	*Leí una novela más que él.*
14	I read five fewer (less) novels than he.	*Leí cinco novelas menos que él.*
15	I read four more letters than he.	*Leí cuatro cartas más que él.*
16	I did four more exercises than he.	*Hice cuatro ejercicios más que él.*
17	I did one less exercise than he.	*Hice un ejercicio menos que él.*

B *Subjunctive versus Indicative:* Write the following combinations and check your work carefully.

1	Sabe que				
2	Lo harán cuando	1	tú	1	dormir.
3	Quiere que	2	Vds.	2	volver.
4	Se enoja de que	3	yo	3	acompañarlos.
5	Lo dice mientras	4	tú y yo	4	seguir hablando.
6	No permite que	5	Vd.	5	ver la televisión.
7	No van sin que				

1)	111	Sabe que tú duermes.
2)	612	No permite que tú vuelvas.
3)	222	Lo harán cuando Vds. vuelvan.
4)	723	No van sin que Vds. los acompañen.
5)	333	Quiere que yo los acompañe.
6)	134	Sabe que yo sigo hablando.
7)	444	Se enoja de que tú y yo sigamos hablando.
8)	245	Lo harán cuando tú y yo veamos la televisión.
9)	555	Lo dice mientras Vd. ve la televisión.
10)	351	Quiere que Vd. duerma.
11)	413	Se enoja de que tú los acompañes.
12)	724	No van sin que Vds. sigan hablando.

New Vocabulary

enloquecerse	to become crazy	**oscurecer**	to grow dark
envejecerse	to become old	**atardecer**	to become dusk
entristecerse	to become sad	**amanecer**	to dawn
enriquecerse	to become rich	**anochecer**	to become night
enfurecerse	to become furious		

Assignment 104

The Future of Probability

1 One function of the future tense in both English and Spanish is to say that an anticipated state or event will take place at some point in the future. Translate: They will be home tomorrow. ▲

Ellos estarán en casa mañana. (Both *estarán* and *mañana* refer to future time.)

2 A second function in both languages is to indicate that something is probably so at the moment of speaking. The basic idea can be expressed in several ways. For example: "They are probably home now." *Están probablemente en casa ahora.* In these examples the tense is Present and the idea of probability is expressed by the adverb. Another way is to use "must" (*deber*). Translate: They must be home now. ▲

Ellos deben estar en casa ahora.

3 The third way is to use the Future of the main verb and combine it with an adverb indicating present time. This illogical combination, future plus present, becomes the signal that the speaker is not positive. Thus "They are home now" is a statement of fact while "They will be home now" is more like "I'm pretty sure they will be home now." Spanish does the same thing: *Casi estoy seguro que estarán en casa ahora.* Translate: They will be home now. ▲

Ellos estarán en casa ahora.

4 The notion of uncertainty can be expressed by "wonder." There used to be a popular American song whose Spanish translation of the title is *¿Quién estará besándola ahora?* What was the English title? ▲

"I Wonder Who's Kissing Her Now"

5 Someone asks "Where's the cat?" Translate the answers: "He's probably in the patio." and "He must be in the patio." ▲

Está probablemente en el patio. Debe estar en el patio.

6 Now say the same thing using the future tense. ▲

Estará en el patio.

7 Both English and Spanish also use the future perfect to express the same notions of uncertainty or probability. Rewrite *Ya lo ha leído probablemente* and say the same thing without using the adverb *probablemente*. ▲

Ya lo habrá leído.

¿QUÉ HACE AQUEL HOMBRE?

ESTARÁ BUSCANDO HUEVOS DE CÓNDOR

A/B

ÉSE DEBE COMER MUY POCO

DEBE PRACTICAR MÁS QUE NADIE

C/D

Probability in the Past

1 The standard back-shift of the Future is the Conditional. English, like Spanish, uses the Future to express probability. Some English speakers also use the Conditional to do this. All Spanish speakers use the Conditional in this way. The translation of *En 1960 ella tenía veinte años*, is _____. ▲

> In 1960 she was twenty years old.

2 The common translation of *En 1960 ella tendría veinte años* is _____. ▲

> In 1960 she was probably twenty years old.

3 Translate: It was probably two o'clock when I arrived. ▲

> *Serían las dos cuando yo llegué.*

4 Write the back-shift of *Ya amanece y los animales tendrán hambre.* ▲

> *Ya amanecía y los animales tendrían hambre.*

5 Write the back-shift of *Estará triste porque llueve tanto.* ▲

> *Estaría triste porque llovía tanto.*

6 Translate: It is very cold and the children must be cold. ▲

> *Hace mucho frío y los niños tendrán frío.*

7 Translate: I said it was very cold and that the children must have been cold. ▲

> *Dije que hacía mucho frío y que los niños tendrían frío.*

A/B

C/D

E

More on the Articles

1 Before you can talk about what you observe in reality you must know whether an entity is either countable or measurable. Decide whether the nouns given stand for a count or measure entity, checking the answer under each one.

mantequilla	país	hierba
measure	*count*	*measure*

arroz	montaña	sal
measure	*count*	*measure*
libro	azúcar	pino (= tree)
count	*measure*	*count*
agua		
measure		

2 Communication is possible only if the speaker and hearer focus their attention on the same entity. When this happens, it is said that they are in common focus. There are two types of common focus. When in the experience and shared knowledge, the entity to be talked about is unique, common focus may be initiated in both English and Spanish by the use of the _____ article. ▲

3 English divides those entities which are considered to be unique into two   definite
sets: those which do not require the definite article to initiate common focus and those which do. *They believe sinners don't go to* **heaven**. *The astronauts went to* **the moon**. With the exception of the months of the year, Spanish consistently uses the definite article with nouns standing for unique entities to initiate common focus. Sunday is a unique day of the week. Translate: I'm going to San Diego Sunday. ▲

> *Voy a San Diego el domingo.* (English may use the definite article with the days of the week when something special makes a given day especially unique: *The Sunday we got married. . . .*)

4 All streets in a given town are unique. How does Spanish say "We live on Fourth Street"? (a) *Vivimos en Calle Cuarta.* (b) *Vivimos en la Calle Cuarta.* ▲

> *Vivimos en la Calle Cuarta.*

5 In English when we use the titles *Mr., Miss,* or *Mrs.* the absence of the definite article says that the person being talked about is that unique person known by both the speaker and hearer. Translate "A Mr. Maldonado phoned" and "Mr. Maldonado phoned." (The verb is *telefonear.*) ▲

> *Un señor Maldonado telefoneó. El señor Maldonado telefoneó.*

6 The definite article is *not* used with these titles in Spanish when you speak directly to a person. Can you think of a logical reason for this? ▲

> When you are speaking <u>to</u> a person there is no need to say that he or she is

7 In frame 2 it was said that there are two types of common focus. You   unique.
establish one by signaling the hearer that the entity is unique in your and his shared experience and knowledge. When this is not so you must tell the hearer (in the case of count entities) to put his attention on a given number of the members of the set labeled by the noun to be used in initiating common focus. There are just two adjectives that can logically be used to complete this sentence: My brother fell down and broke _____ leg. ▲

8 You go into a strange store and say to a clerk: I want to buy _____ shirt.   Either *his* or *a*
Will you use *the* or *a*? ▲

9 Translate the above sentence. ▲   a

> *Quiero comprar una camisa.*

10 Once you have established common focus on an entity, it is necessary in both English and Spanish to have a cue which tells the hearer to keep his attention on this entity. This is called maintaining common focus and the cue used in both languages is the _____ article. ▲

11 Think of which article you would use if you were to translate the following story into Spanish—definite or indefinite.

I met _____ man today downtown ▲

12 who was carrying _____ small box. ▲

13 _____ man seemed very nervous, ▲

14 and he held onto _____ box very tightly. ▲

15 All of a sudden _____ man jumped out of an alley ▲

16 and grabbed _____ box. ▲

17 In the above story both English and Spanish use the same articles. Will English use an article in this sentence? _____ rich and _____ poor have different problems. ▲

definite

indefinite
indefinite
definite
definite
indefinite
definite

yes (*The* implies that the sentence is talking about all the rich and all the poor.)

18 In this and the next two frames write the missing Spanish article.

No me gustan _____ vegetales. ▲

19 _____ habitantes de Argentina hablan español. ▲

20 ¿Son _____ hombres más fuertes que _____ mujeres? ▲

21 Translate the above sentence. ▲

los

Los

los, las

Are men stronger than women ?

22 Linguists consider *some* to be a special kind of indefinite article which is frequently used to initiate common focus on measure entities. We frequently say, for example, *I want some milk*. Spanish has no equivalent for this *some*. The same information is conveyed by the unmodified noun: *Quiero leche*. Translate: I need some money. ▲

Necesito dinero.

The Communication Process

1 You have now reached a point in learning how to send messages where knowing a lot more about the communication process will make future learning easier, faster, and more meaningful. Linguists consider a language to be a code, something like the Morse code used in sending telegrams. When you send a telegram, you make up a message and the telegrapher turns it into dots and dashes, that is, he encodes it. At the other end another telegrapher turns the dots and dashes back into words, that is, he _____ the message. ▲

2 There are three similar steps in the process of communication by means of speech or writing. A speaker, for example, can observe a ▢ without saying a word. This act of observation is part of what is called his precoding activity. To send a message about what is observed the speaker must encode it, that is, use a _____ for ▢ . ▲

decodes

word (In Spanish, he will use *caja*.)

3 The sounds that are made in speaking travel through space, just as electrical impulses travel along a wire in sending a telegram. These sounds strike the ear of the listener and are converted into meaningful symbols which are decoded to get the message. The entire process may be diagrammed as follows.

Speaker   Listener

Precoding   *Encoding*   *Hearing*   *Decoding*

[caja] ～～～～→ [caja]

Observation of

If the listener decodes correctly, does he focus his attention on the same reality as the speaker? ▲

4 The spoken word [caja] is made up of physical sound waves. So we are dealing with two kinds or levels of reality: one is the physical and touchable

and the other is the physical and hearable [caja]. The semanticists or specialists in the meanings of words call   the "referent" of the spoken "symbol" [caja]. When we say that *caja* is a noun, are we talking about the physical entity   ? ▲

yes

no (We are talking about its grammatical form and its combinatory potential (possible combinations) in a syntactic pattern. "Noun" is the label for the grammatical set to which the word *caja* belongs.)

5 "Noun" is also a word, that is, it belongs to a set which is larger than the set it labels. When we talk about language for communication and the processes of encoding and decoding messages, we can operate at different levels. The speaker observes the referent   and encodes this as [caja] which the grammarian classifies as *noun* which, in turn, is classified as a *word*. We have, in fact, two sets of words: one set is composed of symbols which have referents in the real world and the other set is made up of the words which are used to classify and describe these symbols.

In the classical grammars and traditional teaching texts the rules for usage were written with the words of the second set. Here is an example which is a true statement: *There is a set of nouns in Spanish which cannot be made plural.*

A native child learning Spanish does not learn a rule of this type. He begins instead with the reality on which the rule is based. He operates only on two levels: what he observes in reality and how he encodes messages. He discovers, from observation, that real entities fall into two sets: those he can count and those he can measure. Thus if he sees   , he will encode a message containing the Spanish number symbol _____. ▲

6 And he has been trained by everything he has heard that if he encodes *tres*, he must add the morpheme _____ to *caja*. ▲

tres

/s/ (So he will automatically say *tres cajas*.)

7 What kind of precoding activities must go on before he can encode a message? He must decide whether □ is an entity or an event if □ is

going to be the subject of discourse. He must also decide whether □ is a

count or a measure entity. If he does not know the symbol for □ , can he

discover it all by himself? ▲

> no (He can invent his own label or use a cover term like *cosa*, but somebody
> has to tell him the right word or he has to hear someone use it while he is
> looking at it.)

8 Let us suppose, now, that he knows the word *caja* and he wants to encode

a message. Must he observe □ and decide that it is one, not two or more? ▲

9 Up to this point there has been nothing in the precoding activity that can   yes
legitimately be considered under the heading of grammar or linguistics. The
speaker, however, cannot begin the encoding process without being aware of
certain rules of usage. By arbitrary convention Spanish requires him to select

the form *caja*, not *cajas*, for □ . Why? ▲

> Because he is going to encode the fact that he is talking about *one*.

10 If □ is going to be the subject of discourse, the speaker must decide

what message he wants to encode. Suppose, for example, he decides he wants
to say *esta caja*, not *esa caja* or *aquella caja*. Where does he get the cue for selecting

esta? (a) from the language (b) from the position of □ in reality. ▲

> from the position of □ in reality (It is near him.)

11 Where does the speaker get the cue to select *esta* instead of *este*? (a) from
reality (b) from the language conventions ▲

> from the language conventions (By arbitrary convention, the terminal
> phoneme of *esta* matches the terminal phoneme of *caja*.)

12 You have now observed that you cannot learn how to communicate in a
foreign language from formal grammar rules alone simply because they do not
describe all of the precoding activities which must take place before a message
can be encoded. You have also observed that you must look for cues for choice
in two places: in the conventions of the language and in the _____ the speaker
wants to talk about. ▲

13 Except for a few people born with physical or mental defects, everyone   reality
learns to use a language for communication and, moreover, does this without
being formally taught and at a very early age. This learning process for many
young children appears to be so effortless, so natural, and so free from mental
stress and strain, that few people realize that using a language for thinking
and communication is the most complicated operation that man performs. This
may seem to be an exaggeration, but it is a fact that without language the trip
to the moon would have been impossible. Without language and writing, the
knowledge needed for this accomplishment could not have been accumulated
and passed on from generation to generation, the engineers and astronauts

could not have been trained, and the computer languages needed to plan and monitor the flight could not have been invented. While the flight to the moon was a fantastic accomplishment, it may be said without hesitation that man will never do anything more spectacular than learning how to talk and write.

Language is so complex, so flexible, and so capable of change that no one ever learns enough of it to become a complete master of all its potentials. Think of this. What are the probabilities that the above sentence has ever been said or written before? (a) one in a thousand (b) one in a million (c) practically zero ▲

14 One of the truly amazing things about all of us is our ability to generate sentences which neither we nor anyone else has ever said before, and in addition, for our listeners to decode these novel sentences instantaneously, and often without any special effort.

practically zero

It takes time and effort to learn <u>consciously</u> everything that goes on in the precoding, encoding, and decoding process. But when you know what you are trying to learn, both you and your instructor can discover <u>when</u> you have learned it.

For a very long time the *siesta*, or afternoon nap or rest period, has been a special feature of Hispanic culture, especially in the hotter countries and during the summer. This custom, however, is gradually disappearing. Very few young people take the siesta. In many places, however, the shops still close down between one and four, and as a result, remain open late in the evening. There are other remnants of the custom. In general it is still not considered proper to make social calls during the siesta hours. Many social functions still begin late in the evening, especially formal dinners, and many people still believe that there should be a rest period of some kind during the hot part of the day. Thus in Southern Spain the siesta is considered as something necessary to maintain good health.

Self-Correcting Exercises

A *Subjunctive versus Indicative:* Write the combinations and correct your work carefully.

Ejemplo: 112 = Cree que tú vuelves.

1	Cree que				
2	Vendrá tan pronto como	1	tú	1	dormir.
3	Esperan que	2	Vds.	2	volver.
4	Se sorprende de que	3	yo	3	irse.
5	Lo demanda siempre que	4	tú y yo	4	seguir hablando.
6	Prohiben que	5	Vd.	5	ver la televisión.
7	No lo hace a menos que				

1)	111	Cree que tú duermes.
2)	612	Prohiben que tú vuelvas.
3)	222	Vendrá tan pronto como Vds. vuelvan.
4)	723	No lo hace a menos que Vds. se vayan.
5)	333	Esperan que yo me vaya.
6)	134	Cree que yo sigo hablando.
7)	444	Se sorprende de que tú y yo sigamos hablando.
8)	245	Vendrá tan pronto como tú y yo veamos la televisión.
9)	554	Lo demanda siempre que Vd. sigue hablando.
10)	351	Esperan que Vd. duerma.
11)	413	Se sorprende de que tú te vayas.
12)	524	Lo demanda siempre que Vds. siguen hablando.

B *General Review:* Rewrite the following sentences, substituting the words in parentheses for the indicated parts. Make all other necessary changes. Cover the answer in parentheses under each sentence until you are ready to check it.

1 *Dice* que *María* viene con *nosotros* mañana.   (Dijo, tú, mí)

(Dijo que tú venías conmigo mañana.)

2 *Piensa* que todos somos del mismo *lugar*.   (Pensaba, ciudad)

(Pensaba que todos éramos de la misma ciudad.)

3 *Quiero* comprar dos camisas *más* que no tengan botones.   (Haber, otro)

(He comprado otras dos camisas que no tienen botones.)

4 *Ya tenemos otras* dos píldoras que son más fuertes.   (Todavía, buscar, más)

(Todavía buscamos dos píldoras más que sean más fuertes.)

5 *Cree* que *ellos* van a enfurecerse a causa de la llegada de nuestra *tía*.   (Creía, nosotros, abuelo)

(Creía que nosotros íbamos a enfurecernos a causa de la llegada de nuestro abuelo.)

C *Silent Reading:* Read as rapidly as you can and do the comprehension exercise at the end.

El día de las elecciones

Cada cuatro años, el primer martes que sigue al primer lunes de noviembre son las elecciones presidenciales en los Estados Unidos. Son las cinco de la tarde, y los miembros de una familia norteamericana hablan de los eventos del día.

Hijo: ¿Ya fuiste a votar, papá?
Padre: Todavía no, hijo. Voy a esperar hasta que oscurezca. A esta hora vota toda la gente que vuelve del trabajo, y no me gusta tener que esperar en las colas.°   lines (tails)
Hijo: Pues si no te apuras, no vas a poder votar. A las siete cierran.

Padre: Ya lo sé, hijo. No te preocupes que llegaré a tiempo. ¿Ya votó tu mamá?

Hijo: Sí, ella fue una de las primeras. Pero tuvo que esperar casi dos horas.

Padre: ¿Por qué fue eso? ¿Qué sucedió?

Hijo: Una de las máquinas de votar no funcionaba. Dijo mamá que las personas que tenían prisa para ir a sus trabajos se enfurecieron.

Padre: Esas máquinas me enloquecen. Prefiero los métodos de votar que usábamos antes. Eran menos rápidos pero más seguros y tenían la ventaja de no costar tanto.

Hijo: No creo que hables en serio, papá. No te enfurezcas, pero acaban de anunciar en la televisión que los computadores electrónicos predicen la victoria total del partido demócrata.

Padre: Yo no creo en las predicciones absurdas de esas máquinas infernales y las maldigo. Es ridículo que sin terminar la votación en todo el territorio nacional . . .

Hijo: ¡Cálmate, viejo! A mí también me parece mal que hagan eso porque podría afectar el resultado final.

Padre: A pesar de lo que digan los comentaristas de televisión y los computadores, yo sigo creyendo que el próximo presidente de nuestro país va a ser republicano.

Hijo: Creo que tu candidato va a necesitar tu voto para ganar.° Ya está   win
anocheciendo y no te queda mucho tiempo para ir a votar.

Padre: ¡Tienes razón! Dile a tu madre cuando venga que volveré dentro de media hora más o menos.

Hijo: Está bien. Ojalá que la máquina de votar no te cause ningún problema serio.

Contesten escribiendo *sí* o *no:*

1 Las elecciones presidenciales en los Estados Unidos se celebran todos los   no
años el tercer martes de septiembre.

2 Los norteamericanos eligen a su presidente cada cuatro años.   sí

3 Al empezar el diálogo ya todos los miembros de la familia han votado.   no

4 Al padre le gusta votar al anochecer porque a esa hora no va mucha gente.   sí

5 La madre y el padre votaron al mismo tiempo.   no

6 Los computadores electrónicos predijeron que iban a ganar los republi-   no
canos.

7 El padre cree que los demócratas no van a ganar.   sí

8 El padre se enfureció porque su hijo no quería ir a votar.   no

Lectura adicional: El tema del día

Sentado frente a la televisión, hace varias horas que Marcos está viendo los resultados de la elecciones. Su hermana Victoria no puede dormir con el ruido° del televisor.   noise

V: ¿No crees que ya es hora de acostarte y de apagar el televisor? Pronto va a amanecer y con tanto ruido no he podido cerrar los ojos en toda la noche.

M: Bajaré un poco el volumen para que no te moleste, pero no pienso irme a la cama sin saber quién va a ser el nuevo presidente.

V: ¿Por qué tanto interés? Tú no eres político y, de todos modos, tú no votaste en esta elección porque tienes solamente 17 años.

M: No me lo recuerdes que me enfurezco. Espero que el nuevo presidente cambie esa ley tan absurda que no me permitió votar hoy.

V: ¿Sabes de qué hablamos en mi clase de español?

M: Me imagino que de elecciones. Nadie ha hablado de otro tema° en todo el día.   topic

V: La profesora nos dijo que en Honduras las mujeres casadas pueden votar a los 18 años, pero las solteras° tienen que esperar hasta los 21.   single

M: En ese caso te sugiero que salgas inmediatamente para Honduras y te cases con un hondureño. ¿Por qué no me dejas ver los resultados en paz?

V: ¡Ay, chico! ¡Qué pesado° eres! ¡Ojalá pierda tu candidato!   annoying

M: Cállate que van a dar unos resultados muy importantes . . .

9   Victoria no ha podido dormir pensando en el resultado de la elección.   no

10   Marcos votó por primera vez en su vida.   no

11   Marcos apagó el televisor para que su hermana pudiera dormir.   no

12   Marcos dijo que bajaría el volumen del televisor pero no lo iba a apagar.   sí

New Vocabulary

satisfacer	to satisfy	**reunir(se)**	to meet, gather (reunite)
prometer	to promise	**aburrir(se)**	to bore (get bored)
encogerse	to shrink	**escupir**	to spit
mentir (ie)	to lie (not to tell the truth)	**huir**	to flee

Assignment 105

Allomorphs of the Articles

1   In general, the terminal phoneme of an adjective matches the terminal phoneme of the noun with which it combines. However, as Latin became Spanish a few exceptions developed. For example, when *illam acuam* (that water) became *illa acua* the stressed *a* of *acua* absorbed the unstressed *a* of *illa* and the people heard only *ill acua*. When this finally became Spanish the *ill* became *el* and the unvoiced *c* of *acua* became voiced and changed to *g* and, so, today you say *el agua*. The phonetic change of *illa* to *el* means that Spanish now has two allomorphs of the definite article which combine with *a*-nouns: *el* and *la*. The general rule is that if the noun ends in /a/ you use the definite article form *la*. The exception is that when a noun of this class *begins* with a *stressed* [a] written either *a* or *ha*, you use the allomorph *el*. *Agua*, however, is still an *a*-noun. What will you say? (a) *el agua frío* (b) *el agua fría*   ▲

     el agua fría (The phonetic change of Latin *illa* to *el* had no affect on the other adjectives that match *agua*.)

2 This change, moreover, could not happen when there was an adjective in between Latin *illa* and *acua*. So, what will you say today? (a) *el buena agua* (b) *la buena agua* ▲

3 This change, in addition, only happened when *illa* came <u>directly before</u> nouns, that is, not before adjectives or verbs. So one does not say *el alta mujer*, one says _____ *alta mujer*. ▲

la buena agua

4 The noun *arma* translates "weapon." The translation of "the weapon" is _____. ▲

la

el arma (The plural is *las armas*.)

5 The final *a* of *una* was also absorbed when the first *a* of the following noun was stressed, so how do you say "a weapon"? ▲

un arma (Other examples are *un hambre, un alma*.)

A/B

C/D

The Position of Limiting Adjectives

1 Limiting adjectives deal with number, quantity, possession, or location in space (demonstratives). Descriptive adjectives tell us something about the nature of the entity or event labeled by the noun. Translate: the two men ▲

los dos hombres

2 In both English and Spanish the definite article precedes any number above one, and both come before the noun. In both languages there are two common words which are used to increase or decrease a given number: "more" (*más*) and "less" (*menos*). In English you may say either "I want one more hour to do this" or "I want one hour more to do this." What must you say in Spanish? (a) *una más hora* (b) *una hora más* ▲

3 What cues you to put both *más* and *menos* after the noun in Spanish? You regularly say *Tengo más hermanos* or *Tengo menos hermanos*, but you must also say *Tengo dos hermanos más* or *Tengo dos hermanos menos*. The *más* and the *menos* follow the noun when it is preceded by a _____. ▲

una hora más

4 What do you say in English? (a) I saw other two soldiers (b) I saw two other soldiers. ▲

number

I saw two other soldiers (The adjective *other* follows the number in English.)

5 What must you say in Spanish? (a) *Vi a dos otros soldados.* (b) *Vi a otros dos soldados.* ▲

Vi a otros dos soldados. (The *otros* precedes the number in Spanish.)

6 In English you may say *one other book* or *another book*. Spanish does not use *otro* in combination with *un* or *una*. So if "another" means "one more," you say _____. ▲

un libro más (In contrast, if "another" means a "different" one, you simply say *otro libro*.)

Review of the Articles

Each frame has a sentence in English with a noun italicized. On your answer sheet indicate *count* (*c*) or *measure* (*m*), and write ∅ for *no article* or give the article that would be used in Spanish.

1 We'll need some *sand* to do this right. ▲

2 Some people object to bearing *arms*. ▲

m, ∅

3 The man is not carrying a *weapon*. ▲

c, ∅

4 I'm going to the store to buy *eggs*. ▲

c, *un*

5 The *eggs* I bought are rotten. ▲

c, ∅

6 They just discovered *oil* there. ▲

c, *los*

7 The *oil* (*petróleo*) is very good. ▲

m, ∅

8 She needs *oxygen* (*oxígeno*). ▲

m, *el*

9 Be careful. The *coffee* is hot. ▲

m, ∅

10 Do you like *rice*? ▲

m, *el*

m, *el* (to show totality)

11 The *rice* we had for dinner was very good. ▲

m, *el* (to maintain common focus)

12 She hates *snakes* (*culebras*). ▲

c, *las* (to show totality)

13 The *sun* is always hot. ▲

c (one unique; count for astronomers), *el* (Because it is unique in our system.)

14 You have *egg* on your chin. ▲

m, ∅

15 I need some *salt*. ▲

16 Where's the *salt*? ▲   m, ∅

17 There are *dogs* in the patio. ▲   m, *la*

18 The *dog* is man's best friend. ▲   c, ∅

c, *el* (to show totality)

19 Mother, where's *Mr.* Cuervo? ▲

c, *el* (to show one unique for the two persons talking)

20 I'll see you *Monday*. ▲

c, *el* (to show a unique Monday)

More on the Communication Process

The purpose of this section is to call to your attention most of the things a native must do to generate and send the following, very simple exclamation: *¡Mamá! ¡El gato está en el piano!* The speaker is José, age ten.

1 The family has just bought an extremely expensive grand piano. José observes the family cat on the piano and is astonished. José's astonishment is his precoding reaction to the stimuli *cat with claws on shiny, new piano*. Does he encode his astonishment by using a high or low pitch level? ▲

2 Will mother decode the use of high pitch level as meaning the statement is   high about something unusual or urgent? ▲

3 What other information has José encoded with his shout "*¡Mamá!*"? ▲   yes

He wants her attention. (So she will be certain to hear the rest of what he is

4 The language permits José to choose between *mamá* and *madre*. Does either   going to say.) the language or a grammar rule tell him which to say? ▲

5 Which is more formal, *mamá* or *madre*? ▲   no

6 Has José been conditioned to use formal words in a relaxed, home   *madre* situation? ▲

7 Would there be a higher probability of his choosing *madre* if he were testi-   no fying in court? ▲

8 Do you suppose that José has learned a rule that tells him to stress the *a*   yes of *está*? ▲

You probably answered "no," but the fact is that José has learned intuitively that *estar* does not follow the standard stress patterns in the Present. He has been conditioned to say *está*, not *esta*. So he "knows" this rule.

9 What José perceives in reality (cat on piano) and what he says are simultaneous. Is this the cue that tells him to use the present tense? ▲

10 Why does José use the indicative mode? ▲   yes

Because he has discovered intuitively what you have learned consciously: the indicative is used to make a statement when there is no subjoined clause.

11 José needs two cues to encode *está* in the singular form. One cue comes from reality and the other comes from the arbitrary conventions of the language. What is the cue that comes from reality? ▲

12 What is the cue that comes from the language? ▲   *one* cat

When the subject is singular, the verb is singular.

13 José needs <u>four</u> cues in order to pick *estar*, not some other verb. Three come from reality and one comes from the language. Choose the three that come from reality: (1) Is cat an entity or event? ▲

14 (2) Does saying *el gato* (the cat) indicate that José considers the cat to be a   entity
unique entity in the household? ▲

15 (3) Is he locating the cat? ▲   yes

> yes (The cue that comes from the language is: given these three conditions, use *estar* to encode the message. This is a rule you have not learned up to now.)

16 José still must have two more cues before he is ready to encode his message. Does he want to talk *to* the cat or *about* the cat? ▲

17 When you talk *about* an entity, the language requires a _____ person form   about
of the verb. ▲

> third (If you count up all the cues that José needs just to encode *está* correctly, you will discover that there are twelve. Six come from reality and what José wants to do, and six come from the conventions of the language.)

18 Let's go on now with the tasks that José must perform in order to encode the rest of his message. He needs several facts just to pick *el*. On the level of language convention, he must observe that *gato* ends in the phoneme *o*, and this tells him to pick the form of the definite article that ends in the phoneme _____. ▲

19 Reality, <u>one</u> cat, tells him to pick the singular form *gato* and convention   /l/
demands that the determiner (*el*) must be in the _____ form also. ▲

20 He needs to know that since the family has only one cat, he can use *el gato*.   singular
Is this like saying *nuestro gato?* ▲

> yes (He must also deal with the same kinds of facts to pick the *el* that goes

21 Remember, now, that José observes the location of the cat. He must encode   with "piano.")
this information twice: once with the verb (*está*) and once with a _____. ▲

22 There are two factors which tell him what relator to select. One is the actual   relator
positional relationship between the cat and the piano and the other is the number of relators available that can describe this relationship. There are three that might fit the situation: *sobre*, *encima de*, and *en*. *Sobre* is slightly ambiguous since it may mean "above but not in contact with," *encima* contains the redundant *cima*, and also requires a following *de*, so the clearest and most economical choice is _____. ▲

23 Up until now nothing has been said about the fact that *¡El gato está en el*   *en*
piano! has a syntactic pattern. There are six words in the utterance, and if they were arranged in all of their possible sequences, there would be 720 different sentences. Somewhere along the way José has learned that he cannot encode a message with the words in random order. In short, his intuition has become aware of phrase structure rules which tell him that in Spanish the article must come _____ the noun. ▲

> before (You have not been taught this fact as a rule in this course because you do this automatically in English and so you do the same thing automatically in Spanish, that is, you project your English habits onto Spanish. There are literally hundreds of such rules which José had to learn from scratch which you can transfer to Spanish without being aware of what is happening. This is one reason you can learn Spanish faster than the native child. If, however, you

were a speaker of Haitian French, you would have to learn the rule about the position of the article in Spanish because in that language it follows the noun.)

24 Have you been taught that a locative relator precedes the noun which stands for the entity on which or in which another entity is located?   ▲

no (There has been no need to tell you this because you do this intuitively in English. This pre-position accounts for the traditional label *preposition*.)

25 José is aware that the message he wants to encode has three key or head words. They are _____.   ▲

gato, está, and *piano*

26 This means that there can be only three phrases in the sentence and, as a result, only six possible sequences of these phrases:

1	*El gato está en el piano.*	The cat is on the piano.
2	*El gato en el piano está.*	The cat on the piano is.
3	*Está el gato en el piano.*	Is the cat on the piano.
4	*Está en el piano el gato.*	Is on the piano the cat.
5	*En el piano el gato está.*	On the piano the cat is.
6	*En el piano está el gato.*	On the piano is the cat.

Your intuition immediately tells you that some of the English patterns are not acceptable in normal speech. Look at 2 and 5. Can the verb be last in English?   ▲

no (Yet you can use either pattern if you add something: *The cat on the piano is mine. On the piano the cat is more interesting.*)

27 Does your intuition like the English patterns 4 and 6?   ▲

28 It should now be apparent that you have a sentence-analyzing mechanism   probably not
in your head which inhibits the generation of certain patterns and rejects them as incorrect when they are generated by a foreigner. In fact, of the six possible English sequences, you are really comfortable with only two: the statement pattern (*The cat is on the piano.*) and the question pattern (*Is the cat on the piano?*)

To a sophisticated speaker of Spanish all six of the sequences are possible. There is, however, an order of preference and frequency of usage plus a difference between speech and literary style. Most natives, for example, would probably accept *En el piano el gato está* only in poetry and *El gato en el piano está* only in literary style or in an astonished response question. In other words, Spanish, like English, tends to reject the patterns in which the verb comes last. Can you think of any logical reason for this?   ▲

no (It is an arbitrary convention. The pattern is extremely common in German and was also common in Latin.)

29 Let's go back now to José and the priorities he had in mind <u>before</u> he encoded his exclamation: *¡Mamá! ¡El gato está en el piano!* Was his first priority to get his mother's attention?   ▲

30 What did he consider to be his prime subject of discourse? (a) the piano   yes
(b) the location of the cat   ▲

the location of the cat

31 In view of this fact, is it likely that he would pick out either of the four patterns in which *el piano* is mentioned before *el gato*?   ▲

no (Under stress conditions one normally mentions high priority things first. This rules out four of the possible sequences: 2, 4, 5, and 6.)

32 So in terms of effective communication José had just two choices: *¡El gato está en el piano!* and *¡Está el gato en el piano!* Which pattern would he use for a question? ▲

the second (So now you know why he probably picked the first one.)

33 Nothing has been said so far about the intonation pattern José used nor about the fact that he had to use eleven of the 23 Spanish phonemes to say just seven words. It is important, now, to stress the fact that, ignoring phonemics and the intonation pattern, José had to react to about thirty cues to encode his message and that he probably did all of this <u>and</u> uttered his exclamation in about two seconds. Could he have processed all this information consciously in that length of time? ▲

no (Now you know that you will not be able to use Spanish for communication until the rules you have been learning consciously become a part of your intuition where they can be used at something like computer speeds.)

34 Who had to perform more operations and work harder: José to encode his message or his mother to decode it? ▲

35 To decode José's message his mother had to get the following information: I want your attention (*¡Mamá!*). Excitement (Pitch level three). Subject of discourse ("family cat" and "piano" marked by *el*). Locative relationship between cat and piano, indicated by _____. ▲

José

36 You have observed in this program an application of an analytical technique called *task analysis*, that is, a detailed description of most of the things that José had to know and do, and in what order, just to encode a very short and simple message. You should also have discovered that you have learned to do many more things in Spanish than you may have suspected and that you already know how to deal effectively with tremendously complex linguistic problems in that language. You now *know consciously* what José *knew intuitively*. Which kind of knowledge will help you more in all other studies in which you have to use words to learn or to solve problems? ▲

está en

conscious knowledge (There is convincing evidence that students who learn a foreign language the way you are doing show improvement in learning.)

Learning New Vocabulary

In this section you are introduced to 14 new verbs. Study them following the steps outlined, and see how many you can remember for the next class.

Step 1: Think of the answer for each frame.

1 The *unidos* in *los Estados Unidos* is the perfect participle of *unir*. The translation of *unir* is: to _____. ▲

2 The two most common ways of cooking eggs (*huevos*) are *hervirlos* or *freírlos*. Which verb form looks most like "to fry"? ▲

unite

3 An educated guess should tell you the translation of *hervir* is: to _____. ▲

freír

4 One opposite of *llegar* is *partir*. One meaning of *partir* is: to _____. ▲

boil

leave (The English cognate is *to depart*.)

5 When you make a mistake in Spanish your instructor *tiene que corregirlo*. The cognate of *corregir* is: to _____. ▲

6 What happens to ice when you put it out in the hot sun? *Se derrite*. The infinitive *derretir* translates: to _____. ▲

correct

7 A person who is all mixed up is said to be *confundida*. The cognate of *confundir* is: to _____. ▲

melt

8 If a boat fills with water it will *hundir*. The translation of *hundir* is: to _____. ▲

confound, confuse

9 When someone gives you directions on how to get somewhere he *está dirigiéndole*. The cognate of *dirigir* is: to _____. ▲

sink

direct (Another meaning is *to guide*.)

10 What do you do from the end of a pool's springboard? *Se zambulle en el agua*. The meaning is _____. ▲

You dive into the water. (When the construction is not reflexive *zambullir* can have the meaning of "to duck" somebody in the water.)

11 A person who makes a dress must *saber coser; coser* = _____. ▲

12 This package is too big. It won't *caber* in the trunk of the car; *caber* = _____. ▲

to sew

to fit (The meaning always deals with the space for something.)

13 When a person dies, his estate *se reparte* among his relatives; *repartir* = _____. ▲

to divide up (In some contexts it means *to hand out*.)

14 When you can't solve a problem you often ask that someone *sugerir* a solution; *sugerir* = _____. ▲

15 Here is the complete list of verbs you have just studied along with their most common English translations. Copy them on your study list and spend two minutes studying them.

to suggest

unir	to unite	*hundir*	to sink
hervir (ie)	to boil	*dirigir*	to direct (guide)
freír (i)	to fry	*zambullir(se)*	to dive (to duck)
partir	to leave (depart)	*coser*	to sew
corregir (i)	to correct	*caber*	to fit (in something)
derretir (i)	to melt	*repartir*	to divide up, to hand out
confundir	to confuse	*sugerir (ie)*	to suggest

Now go do whatever you wish for 10 minutes, then go on to Step 2.

Step 2: Review

In the frames below you will see first the Spanish of the 14 verbs you just studied. Say the verb aloud and then think of the English translation. Next you will see the English. Say the Spanish equivalent aloud and, then, check the answer. Remember that research has shown that many short periods of study, called spaced learning, makes learning things to be memorized much easier. Try to work rapidly.

1 *partir* ▲

to leave (to depart)

2	*hundir* ▲	
3	*sugerir* ▲	
4	*repartir* ▲	

to sink

to suggest

to divide up (to hand out)

5	*unir* ▲	
6	*corregir* ▲	
7	*derretir* ▲	

to unite

to correct

to melt (Associate this with what happens to ice.)

8 *dirigir* ▲

9 *hervir* ▲

10 *caber* ▲

11 *confundir* ▲

12 *zambullirse* ▲

13 *freír* ▲

14 *coser* ▲

15 to dive ▲

16 to boil ▲

17 to direct ▲

18 to confuse ▲

19 to leave (depart) ▲

20 to suggest ▲

21 to fit (in something) ▲

22 to sew ▲

23 to correct ▲

24 to divide up (hand out) ▲

25 to unite ▲

26 to fry ▲

27 to sink ▲

28 to melt ▲

to direct (guide)

to boil

to fit

to confuse

to dive

to fry

to sew

zambullirse

hervir

dirigir

confundir

partir

sugerir

caber

coser

corregir

repartir

unir

freír

hundir

derretir

Now take a 15-minute rest and then go on to Step 3.

Step 3: Review

Below you will find the verbs you are learning in two columns. Cover the English, look at the Spanish and see if you can remember the English translation. Then cover the Spanish, look at the English and say the Spanish equivalent aloud. Repeat this process two more times. If you now miss a word copy the Spanish and the English.

derretir	to melt	*caber*	to fit
hundir	to sink	*sugerir*	to suggest
freír	to fry	*partir*	to leave (depart)
unir	to unite	*confundir*	to confuse
repartir	to divide up	*dirigir*	to direct
corregir	to correct	*hervir*	to boil
coser	to sew	*zambullirse*	to dive

Step 4: Review

Go back to Step 3, cover the Spanish columns and see whether you can now remember the translation of all the 14 verbs. If you have been concentrating properly you should now know them all.

The manufacturers of breakfast cereals in the United States spend a lot of money suggesting that fruit mixed with cereal makes a delicious breakfast. Many Americans put slices of banana in their cereal or eat banana with sugar and cream. This would horrify most Cubans who firmly believe that eating bananas with milk or cream will make one sick.

The bananas that you eat are not tree-ripened. When the stalks are taken from the trees the bananas are a deep green. They "ripen" to their yellow color in the warehouse.

In the tropical countries of Latin America there is a common type of banana plant called plantain which is rarely seen in the United States. This banana is more angular than the one you are accustomed to and, when ripe, it is a yellowish green. This is a staple item of diet for many people. In contrast with American custom, this banana is not eaten raw. It is usually fried or cooked.

Self-Correcting Exercises

A *General Practice:* Rewrite each sentence, substituting the items in parentheses for the italicized parts. Cover the answer in parentheses under each sentence until you are ready to check it.

1 *Dice* que el *muchacho* mira *a la señorita otras* dos veces.   (Dijo, muchachos, unos a otros, más)

(Dijo que los muchachos se miraron unos a otros dos veces más.)

2 A *mí* no me gusta *comer carne* porque no quiero que *nadie* mate *a los animales.* (él, las guerras, los hombres, unos a otros)

(A él no le gustan las guerras porque no quiere que los hombres se maten unos a otros.)

3 *Sabemos* que *tú* traes *los perros calientes* cuando vamos *de excursión.*   (No queremos, ellos, Marta, al campo la semana que viene)

(No queremos que ellos traigan a Marta cuando vayamos al campo la semana que viene.)

4 *Pancho* dijo que tenía un *tigre* en el *corral.*   (Ellos, gasolina, garaje)

(Ellos dijeron que tenían gasolina en el garaje.)

B *Position of Limiting Adjectives:* Rewrite the original sentences in Spanish, making the necessary changes to match the English. Keep the covered answer in parentheses after each sentence until you are ready to correct your work.

1 Este río tiene más puentes que el otro. *This river has two more bridges than the other.*

(Este río tiene dos puentes más que el otro.)

2 Ella tiene seis rosas; tiene más flores que yo. *She has six other roses; she has four more flowers than I.*

(Ella tiene otras seis rosas; tiene cuatro flores más que yo.)

3 José plantó dos pinos; ha plantado menos árboles que yo. *Joe planted two other pine trees; he has planted three less trees than I.*

(José plantó otros dos pinos; ha plantado tres árboles menos que yo.)

4 Ana recibió más muñecas que María. *Ana received one more doll than Mary.*

(Ana recibió una muñeca más que María.)

5 Chicago tiene menos aeropuertos que Nueva York. *Chicago has one less airport than New York.*

(Chicago tiene un aeropuerto menos que Nueva York.)

C *Expressions of Probability:* Change each of the following sentences to a statement of probability using the Future or the Conditional. The meaning of each sentence is to remain the same. Cover the answer on the right, change the sentence mentally, then check to see if you are right. Remember that the Future is used to state a conjecture in the present, and the Conditional is used to state it in the past.

1 Ahora deben ser las 9:00 de la mañana.   Ahora serán las 9:00 de la mañana.

2 En este momento deben estar en las cata-   En este momento estarán en las cataratas del
ratas del Niágara.   Niágara.

3 Yo le dije al policía que el accidente ocurrió probablemente a eso de las 5:30.

Yo le dije al policía que el accidente ocurriría a eso de las 5:30.

4 Debe ser demasiado tarde para llamarlos por teléfono.

Será demasiado tarde para llamarlos por teléfono.

5 Yo le dije a ese señor que el jefe probablemente estaba en su oficina a esa hora.

Yo le dije a ese señor·que el jefe estaría en su oficina a esa hora.

6 Estoy casi segura que ya ellos deben saberlo.

Estoy casi segura que ya ellos lo sabrán.

7 Probablemente eran sus nietos y no sus hijos.

Serían sus nietos y no sus hijos.

8 A esta hora del día Eduardo debe estar en la oficina.

A esta hora del día Eduardo estará en la oficina.

9 Probablemente fue Ernesto quien vino a verme.

Sería Ernesto quien vino a verme.

10 Me dijo que los vecinos ya debían pertenecer a ese club.

Me dijo que los vecinos ya pertenecerían a ese club.

D *Vocabulary and Reciprocal Reflexive:* You are to translate mentally the English in the following sentences. Verb forms may have to be conjugated. Check your answer in the margin, but keep it covered until you have worked the problem.

1 Existe tanta hostilidad entre los dos grupos que a menudo ellos *curse each other*.

se maldicen

2 Dime, mamá, ¿por qué es que yo *grow* tan despacio?

crezco

3 Me preocupa mucho, hijita, que tú *lie* tanto.

mientas

4 Para *satisfy* a su maestra todos los alumnos han *promised* que no *will fight with each other*.

satisfacer, prometido
se pelearán

5 Yo nunca *disobey* a mis padres.

desobedezco

6 Mi ambición es *to become rich* y *belong* a los mejores clubs y sociedades.

enriquecerme, pertenecer

7 Los *wines* que hacen en ese país no le *satisfy*.

vinos, satisfacen

8 Muchos animales en la selva se comen *each other*.

unos a otros

9 Yo te *will be grateful* que me des una aspirina porque me *ache* mucho la cabeza.

agradeceré, duele

10 No me gusta *predict*, pero creo que Uds. *will become bored* viendo esa película.

predecir, se aburrirán

11 Después de batallar *against each other* cientos de soldados *fled*.

unos contra otros, huyeron

12 Yo soy tu madre y no *deserve* que me trates de ese modo.

merezco

13 No puedo hacer ese postre sin *wheat flour and honey*, además para la otra receta (*recipe*) voy a necesitar *oil and lard*.

harina de trigo y miel
aceite y manteca

14 Ya verás que no va a *happen* nada hasta el *dawn*.

suceder, amanecer

New Vocabulary

aceite	oil	**vino**	wine	**trigo**	wheat
manteca	lard	**miel (la)**	honey	**harina**	flour

See also the list of verbs on p. 681.

Assignment 106

The Position of Descriptive Adjectives

In English some descriptive words precede the noun and some follow it. However, the vast majority of descriptive words precede the noun. You say *a tall girl*, *the long cars*, or *a red book*. In contrast, in Spanish one finds descriptive adjectives before or after the noun with almost the same frequency. Up until the present time linguists have not been able to discover rules which can explain precisely why all descriptive adjectives happen to be where they are in a given sentence. This section, consequently, deals only with a part of what is known. In all other cases you will have to learn where to put a descriptive adjective by imitation.

1 You have learned that a noun can stand for all the entities it labels, for some of them, any one of them, or for one that is unique. So *los libros* can stand for all the books in the world. Is it logical to suppose that the adjective *españoles* can describe <u>all</u> the books in the world? ▲

no (*Los libros españoles* means something like "those books which are Spanish.")

2 When adjective position in a given sentence is the *only* thing that tells the hearer whether the speaker is talking about some or all of the entities labeled by the noun, then the adjective follows the noun in Spanish to indicate *some*.

So what will you say? (a) *los viejos hombres del mundo* (b) *los hombres viejos del mundo* ▲

los hombres viejos del mundo. (Only some men in the world are old.)

3 A man never gets appointed to the Supreme Court until he has had many years of experience as a lawyer and, usually, as a judge in a lower court. So it turns out that from one point of view *all* the members of the Supreme Court are old. How will you say this with adjective position? (a) *los viejos hombres de la Corte Suprema* (b) *los hombres viejos de la Corte Suprema.* ▲

los viejos hombres de la Corte Suprema.

4 There can, however, be another point of view. Some justices are in their fifties, others are in their seventies or eighties. If fifty-five is young, then some are old. The differences in these two points of view can be shown in English by "The men of the Supreme Court are old" and "The men of the Supreme Court who are old." The second meaning in Spanish would be shown by placing *viejos* before or after *hombres* in *los _____ hombres _____ de la Corte Suprema.* ▲

after (*los hombres viejos de la Corte Suprema*)

5 All of Bolivia is in the high mountains. So from the point of view of sea level one may say *Todas las montañas de Bolivia son altas.* To convey the same message you will say (a) *las montañas altas de Bolivia* (b) *las altas montañas de Bolivia.* ▲

las altas montañas de Bolivia

6 There are many times when we are clearly aware that some of the entities labeled by a noun have one characteristic while others have a different characteristic. When we talk about this contrast in English, we stress the descriptive adjective: I'm not concerned with *healthy* people, I'm worried about *sick* people. Where will you put these two adjectives in Spanish? (a) before *la gente* (b) after *la gente*. ▲

> after *la gente* (Spanish uses the post-position of the adjective to do what English accomplishes with stress. So you will normally say *la gente sana* and *la gente enferma* with no extra stress on the two adjectives.)

7 There are many adjectives which can almost never describe all of the entities labeled by a noun. *All* animals are not domesticated. *All* dogs are not black. *All* plants are not poisonous. When it is logically obvious that the adjective cannot describe all the entities labeled by the noun, then the adjective follows the noun.

So where will you put *domésticos*, *negros*, and *venenosas* when you translate "domesticated animals," "black dogs," and "poisonous plants"? Before or after the noun? ▲

8 You already know that some entities are unique by nature (*el sol*, *la luna*,   after
el mundo) or that some are made unique by custom or law. If the post-position of a descriptive adjective can indicate some (not all) what will the post-position indicate when the noun labels only one entity? (a) a unique (b) one of many ▲

9 How do you suppose, then, a young man will begin a letter to his *novia*?   one of many
(a) *Mi novia querida* (b) *Mi querida novia* ▲

10 There is just one Statue of Liberty in New York. It is very big. Is it   *Mi querida novia*
unique? ▲

11 How will you say "the enormous Statue of Liberty"? (a) *la estatua enorme*   yes
de la libertad (b) *la enorme Estatua de la Libertad* ▲

> *la enorme Estatua de la Libertad.* (With the definite article the pre-position of the adjective indicates one unique.)

12 What will this sentence tell you? *¿Conoces al hijo rico de la señora Sosa?* Does Mrs. Sosa have (a) only one son (b) more than one son? ▲

> more than one son (The post-position of the adjective indicates one of many.)

You were told that linguists still do not know how to explain the position of descriptive adjectives in all sentences. There are some adjectives, for example, which have two meanings and position is used to indicate which meaning the speaker is using. So *un pobre hombre* means "a poor (to be pitied) man" while *un hombre pobre* means "a poor (without money) man." The total list of adjectives of this set has yet to be compiled and you must, for the present, learn them from experience.

When an adjective is modified by *un* (*una*) or any other number word, many descriptive adjectives may either precede or follow the noun: *Es una buena persona*, *Es una persona buena*. The reason for this has yet to be discovered. However, on a frequency basis the descriptive adjective follows more frequently than it precedes the noun. Consequently, as a practical solution to this problem put the descriptive adjective in post-position until you learn differently.

A/B

C/D

E/F

G/H

687

I/J

K/L

M

Additional Perfects

1 In the present perfect the stem of *haber* (*hab-*) has disappeared in the speech of the dialect you are learning. In writing, it survives as the letter _____. ▲

h (él ha hablado, nosotros hemos partido)

2 The imperfect backshift of *hay* is _____. ▲

había

3 The Imperfect of *haber* keeps the stem and takes the regular imperfect suffixes. These forms are used to make up the past perfect, the backshift of the present perfect. Translate: José had eaten. ▲

José había comido.

4 Change *Ya hemos sugerido* to past perfect. ▲

Ya habíamos sugerido.

5 The stem of *haber* for the future perfect is *habr-* (like *saber, sabr-*). How would you say "You (*Tú*) will have slept" in Spanish? ▲

6 Change *Hemos leído* to the future perfect. ▲

Habrás dormido.

7 Do the same for *Ellos han prometido*. ▲

Habremos leído.

Ellos habrán prometido.

8 And for *Él ha salido* (He has gone out.). ▲

9 The translation of *Él habrá salido* is _____. ▲

Él habrá salido.

He will have gone out.

10 The conditional perfect in both English and Spanish is the backshift of the future perfect. A better name would be the *past future perfect*. Write the *English* backshift of *I know that at one o'clock he will have left.* ▲

I knew that at one o'clock he would have left.

11 If you know the future perfect there is just one thing to be done to make the conditional perfect of *all* verbs. Replace the first suffix that follows *habr-* with *ía*. Write the backshift of *Yo sé que a la una él habrá partido.* ▲

Yo sabía que a la una él habría partido.

12 The backshift of *Habremos metido* is _____. ▲

13 And that of *Ellos habrán huido* is _____. ▲

Habríamos metido.

14 You have now been shown how to form the four perfect tenses that there *Ellos habrían huido.* are in Spanish. They are the present perfect with its backshift the past perfect (sometimes called the Pluperfect) and the future perfect whose backshift is the misnamed conditional perfect. Write these four forms of *prometer* and make them agree with *ustedes*. ▲

ustedes han prometido, habían prometido, habrán prometido, habrían prometido

Summary

1 The position of some descriptive adjectives gives additional information.

2 When an entity is one unique, the descriptive adjective precedes the noun.

3 When it is the speaker's intention to say that *all* the entities that the noun can stand for have the same characteristic, the adjective precedes the noun.

4 When it is the speaker's intention to say that *only one* or *some* of the entities that the noun can stand for have the characteristic mentioned, the adjective follows the noun.

5 There does not exist at present a set of rules which can explain the position of *all* descriptive adjectives in *all* patterns.

Self-Correcting Exercises

A *General Review:* Rewrite each sentence, substituting the items in parentheses for the indicated parts. Cover the answer in parentheses under each sentence until you are ready to check it.

1 Pásame el *pan* y la *sal*, por favor, *Hortensia*. (miel, agua, Srta. Gómez)

(Páseme Vd. la miel y el agua, por favor, Srta. Gómez.)
2 *¿Hay* una *cuchara*, un *tenedor* y un *cuchillo* en la mesa? (Has puesto, mantel, cucharas, aceite)

(¿Has puesto un mantel, cucharas y aceite en la mesa?)
3 Cuando *recibieron* el *telegrama* con la *mala* noticia, *madre e hija* se miraron una a otra llenas de *tristeza*. (llegó, carta, buenas, todos los alumnos de la clase, alegría)

(Cuando llegó la carta con las buenas noticias, todos los alumnos de la clase se miraron unos a otros llenos de alegría.)
4 Pilar y *Ana* no *desean* que el *señor* les arregle sus *muñecas* sino que él *se las devuelva*. (Isabel, merecen, mamá, ropa, es muy buena y lo hará)

(Pilar e Isabel no merecen que la mamá les arregle su ropa, pero ella es muy buena y lo hará.)
5 *No, no* creo que la tercera *lección* sea *tan difícil* como la *segunda*. (Sí, sí, ejercicio, más, fácil, primero)

(Sí, sí creo que el tercer ejercicio es más fácil que el primero.)

B *Use of Articles:* Write the combinations and correct your work.

Ejemplo: 21 = *Nos gusta la miel.*

1	Allí está(n)	1	miel.
2	Nos gusta(n) ?	2	arma nueva.
3	Aquí hay	3	muebles modernos.
		4	luna.
		5	señor Baca.

1)	11	Allí está la miel.
2)	23	Nos gustan los muebles modernos.
3)	22	Nos gusta el arma nueva.
4)	24	Nos gusta la luna.
5)	33	Aquí hay muebles modernos.
6)	25	Nos gusta el señor Baca.
7)	12	Allí está el arma nueva.
8)	31	Aquí hay miel.
9)	13	Allí están los muebles modernos.
10)	32	Aquí hay un arma nueva.
11)	14	Allí está la luna.

12)	34	Aquí hay una luna.
13)	15	Allí está el señor Baca.
14)	35	Aquí hay un señor Baca.
15)	21	Nos gusta la miel.

C *Use of the Articles:* Write the form of the article that fits each blank. If none is needed, write Ø (for nothing).

1 . . .católicos y . . . mayoría de . . . protestantes generalmente van a sus iglesias . . . domingos.

Los, la, los, los

2 . . . judíos o hebreos (*Jews*) por lo general van al templo o sinagoga . . . sábados, pero en todas . . . religiones celebran festividades religiosas que pueden caer en cualquier (*any*) día de . . . semana.

Los, los, las, la

3 Yo tengo . . . amigo que está muy interesado en . . . religión; no solamente . . . religión a la cual él pertenece sino todas . . . religiones.

un, la, la, las

4 Él ha visitado . . . templos e iglesias de diferentes denominaciones y ha asistido a . . . servicios religiosos de diferentes clases con el propósito de observar las diferentes maneras de adorar a Dios y estudiar las ideas que otras personas tienen sobre . . . cielo, . . . infierno (*hell*), . . . naturaleza, . . . alma y otras doctrinas religiosas.

Ø, Ø, el, el, la, el

5 . . . domingo pasado, . . . reverendo Sánchez, . . . ministro protestante de esta ciudad, lo invitó a visitar su iglesia que está en . . . Avenida Colombia.

El, el, un (el *if only one in the city*), la

6 . . . padre Soto, pastor de la iglesia de Nuestra Señora de Guadalupe, lo ha invitado a . . . misa (*mass*) de las 10:00 de la mañana . . . domingo que viene.

El, la, el

7 Mi amigo ya ha ido varias veces a la sinagoga y ha tenido discusiones muy interesantes con . . . Dr. Espinosa, rabino (*rabbi*) de . . . congregación.

el, la

The people of every nation view their own history with a highly prejudiced and privately patriotic point of view. Americans take pride in the charge of Roosevelt's Rough Riders up San Juan hill in the Spanish-American War. Most school children learn to "Remember the Alamo," and the marching Marines sing of their exploits "from the Halls of Montezuma to the shores of Tripoli." From the Hispanic point of view this American patriotism is a constant reminder of historic disaster. Mexico lost a huge portion of its lands to the U.S. in the war which began with the Alamo, and the Marine song only reminds them that American armed forces once occupied down-town Mexico City. In the Spanish-American War Spain lost the last remnants of her once mighty empire (Cuba, Puerto Rico, and the Philippine Islands). The Hispanic school children, consequently, see history in a very different way and, as a result, it often shocks Americans when they discover that they are thoroughly disliked by many Latins. In the vocabulary of the Latin the words *yanqui*, *yanquismo*, *yanquilandia*, and *gringo* are all insulting terms which have about the same emotional punch as *Yankee* for some people who live in the Deep South.

New Vocabulary

consejo	advice	**pecar**	to sin
castigo	punishment	**desarrollar**	to develop
pecado	sin	**semejante**	similar
desarrollo	development	**contra**	against
semejanza	similarity	**como**	like, as
aconsejar	to advise	**excepto**	except (for)
castigar	to punish		

Assignment 107

More Practice on Perfect Verb Forms

1 Both English and Spanish have the same number of perfect verb forms. This number is _____. ▲

2 A perfect verb form is always made up of two parts. The first part is the auxiliary (helping) verb which carries the suffixes indicating tense, mode, person, and number. The auxiliary in English is to _____; in Spanish it is _____. ▲

four

3 The second part of each perfect form in both languages says that the action either begins or is finished before some point in time or before some other event. This part is the _____ participle. ▲

to have, *haber*

4 Write the missing suffixes for the Present Perfect:

    yo h _____ *visto*   *(él, ella) usted h* _____ *visto*
    nosotros h _____ *visto*   *(ellos, ellas) ustedes h* _____ *visto*
    tú h _____ *visto* ▲

perfect

*yo **he** visto, (él, ella) usted **ha** visto, nosotros **hemos** visto, (ellos, ellas)*
*ustedes **han** visto, tú **has** visto*

5 Change *yo he pedido* to the future perfect. ▲

6 To change this form so it matches *él, ella,* and *usted* you replace *é* with _____. ▲

yo habré pedido

á (él, ella, usted habrá pedido)

7 There is just one form of the future perfect which has no accent mark in writing. It is the form that matches *nosotros.* Translate: We will have ordered. ▲

(nosotros) habremos pedido

8 The backshifts of the present perfect and the future perfect are the past perfect and the conditional perfect. To get all the forms of the conditional perfect you simply replace <u>all</u> the first suffixes of the future perfect with _____. ▲

9 Backshift *nosotros habremos pedido.* ▲

ía
nosotros habríamos pedido

10 Translate the above. ▲

we would have ordered

11 To get the backshift of the present perfect you use the regular stem of *haber*, _____ and the first suffix, _____. ▲

12 Backshift *ellos han vendido.* ▲

hab, ía (había)
ellos habían vendido

13 The perfect participle of all regular *a*-verbs is made by adding _____ to the stem. ▲

14 The perfect participle of all regular *e*- and *i*-verbs is made by adding _____ to the stem. ▲

-ado

15 There is, however, no way of efficiently systematizing the learning of the irregular forms of perfect participles. These have to be memorized. In the remaining frames write the perfect participle of each verb: *poner.* ▲

-ido

puesto (Also used with all forms which add a prefix to *poner: componer,*

16 satisfacer (The *facer* is an old form of *hacer.*) ▲

oponer, suponer.)

17 devolver, resolver (like *volver*) ▲

satisfecho

18 predecir (like *decir*), bendecir (not like *decir*) ▲

devuelto, resuelto

predicho, bendecido (There is another form, *bendito.*)

19 cubrir (like *abrir*), morir, romper ▲

cubierto, muerto, roto

20 ver, ir, escribir, abrir ▲

visto, ido, escrito, abierto

Review of Expressions of Probability

1 There are three common ways of expressing probability, conjecture, or wonderment by using (1) the adverb *probablemente* or its equivalent, (2) the helping verb *deber*, and (3) the Future or Conditional plus an incompatible point in time. Rewrite the italicized portion of each sentence using either the Future or Conditional of probability.
Ya son las cinco. A esta hora el señor Comabella *debe estar* en casa. ▲

2 En aquel año ella *tenía probablemente* treinta años. ▲

estará

3 No tengo mi reloj, pero *deben ser* las tres. ▲

tendría

4 Él lo *supo probablemente* antes que ella. ▲

serán

5 No hay luz en la casa. *Deben estar* durmiendo. ▲

sabría
Estarán

The Reciprocal Reflexive

1 In the standard or systemic reflexive the doer (subject) and the done-to (object) are the same. In other words, the subject performs the action upon itself: *yo me lavo, tú te afeitas, él se levanta, etc.* When the subject is singular and the done-to is singular, the reflexive construction <u>cannot</u> be reciprocal. There are two conditions which must be fulfilled before a reflexive construction can be reciprocal: (1) the subject must be plural and (2) the event must be of a kind which at least two entities can perform on each other. Can "they went to sleep" be reciprocal? ▲

2 Can "they committed suicide" be reciprocal? ▲   no

3 Can the events labelled by *ver* or *confundir* be reciprocal? ▲   no

4 Translate: "They embraced (*abrazarse*) and kissed (*besarse*)." They = male   yes
and female. ▲

Ellos se abrazaron y se besaron.

5 Which sentence describes a reciprocal action? (a) They hurt themselves.
(b) They hurt each other. ▲

They hurt each other.

6 Both of these sentences have the same translation in Spanish: *Ellos se lastimaron*. The meaning, then, can be established only by verbal context or the universe of discourse (the situation). The verb *pelear* translates "to fight." Do you normally fight with yourself? ▲

no (It takes two to fight, just as it takes two to tango.)

7 Translate: *Y luego ellos se pelearon y se lastimaron.* ▲

And then they fought and hurt each other.

8 When neither logic, the verbal context, nor the situation clarifies the meaning one must add either *uno a otro* or *unos a otros* to mark the each-other construction. Is this special mark necessary in *Llovía tanto que no podían verse*? ▲

no (You cannot see yourself except in something that reflects your image. So the meaning has to be *they could not see each other*.)

9 Translate the English in the following: *Cuando ellos están juntos **they always bore each other**. The verb is *aburrirse*. ▲

10 *No podemos ser amigos si **we insult each other**.* ▲

siempre se aburren
nosotros nos insultamos

11 *Van a aprender más si ellos **correct each other** uno a otro.* ▲

se corrigen (One can correct oneself so the *uno a otro* is needed to make the action reciprocal.)

Self-Correcting Exercises

A *Position of Adjectives:* Notice the difference between English and Spanish phrase patterns in the following:

What a pretty flower!   *¡Qué flor tan (más) linda!*

Now write the translations of these English sentences:

1 What a large horse!		*¡Qué caballo tan (más) grande!*
2 What a bad pencil!		*¡Qué lápiz tan (más) malo!*
3 What a good lesson!		*¡Qué lección tan (más) buena!*
4 What expensive purses!		*¡Qué carteras (bolsas) tan (más) caras!*
5 What excellent food!		*¡Qué comida tan (más) excelente!*
6 What kind children!		*¡Qué niños tan (más) amables!*
7 What red blood!		*¡Qué sangre tan (más) roja!*

After reading each of the following sentences, answer mentally with *one unique*, *one of many*, *all*, or *some*, according to whether the adjective precedes what it modifies (*one* or *all*) or follows it (*one of many* or *some*).

8	Su tío calvo se lo prometió.	one of many
9	Mi celoso hermano no quiso acompañarme.	one unique
10	Me gustan los buenos platos que sirven en este restorán.	all
11	Mis hermanas mayores van con nosotros.	some
12	Las señoras furiosas no dejaban pasar a las otras.	some
13	Comen solamente las manzanas dulces.	some
14	Estas simpáticas muchachas servirán la comida.	all
15	Su simpático hijo nos explicó lo que sucedió.	one unique
16	No me gustan esas dulces bebidas que ellos sirven siempre.	all
17	Los altos árboles de mi patio no dan fruta.	all
18	Dame el vaso vacío.	one of many
19	Compré el vestido barato.	one of many
20	El caro traje de la novia era blanco.	one unique
21	Sus amables nietos vinieron a traerle regalos.	all

B *Expressions of Probability and Reciprocal Reflexive:* Rewrite the indicated portion of the sentence, replacing it with the Future or Conditional of probability, whichever is appropriate.

1	Yo me imagino que ella ya *debe conocer* a nuestro hijo.	conocerá
2	*Probablemente* en aquel momento *estaban* escribiendo la famosa carta.	estarían
3	En la actualidad los estudiantes *probablemente respetan* más a sus profesores, ¿verdad?	respetarán
4	Ellos *probablemente hablaron* con tu tío Ramón en Madrid, ¿verdad?	hablarían
5	Ahora creo que tú ya *debes comprender* mejor por qué hice eso.	comprenderás

Translate orally the English part of each sentence:

6	Estoy seguro de que ellos ya *know each other*.	se conocen
7	Mi amiga y yo *write to each other* muy a menudo.	nos escribimos
8	Cuando yo vivía con esa familia, noté que tenían muchos problemas porque no *respect each other*.	se respetan
9	Sonia y Roberto tienen problemas. Hace varios meses que ellos no *speak to each other*.	se hablan
10	Ellos decidieron divorciarse. Han llegado a la conclusión de que ellos no *understand each other*.	se comprenden

C *Silent Reading:* Read each paragraph as rapidly as you can and, before going on to the next one, answer the comprehension questions.

Grandes hombres de las Américas: José Martí (Segunda parte)

En el colegio de San Pablo que dirigía el señor Mendive, José Martí se sentía completamente feliz y participaba con entusiasmo en las discusiones y actividades políticas que tanto le interesaban. En su casa, sin embargo, la situación

era muy distinta (diferente). Con su familia él se sentía incómodo y completamente fuera de su elemento, como un pez° fuera del agua. Su padre trabajaba   fish
entonces de policía y su situación económica era bastante difícil. Los conflictos
y problemas entre padre e hijo eran cada vez más notables y serios. Don
Mariano no era mal padre y Pepe lo sabía, pero al mismo tiempo el joven
criollo se daba cuenta de que las diferencias de opinión que existían entre ellos
no tenían solución. El viejo español no comprendía las aspiraciones e ideales de
su único hijo. Veía con malos ojos (le molestaba) que el muchacho hablara mal
de España y que escribiera versos. Creía que ya tenía bastante educación y que
Pepe debería empezar a trabajar para contribuir a los gastos° de la familia.   expenses
Tampoco Pepe era mal hijo. Él no odiaba° a España ni a los españoles sino al   hated
gobierno español que impedía que Cuba fuera libre. Cuando su maestro Rafael
Mendive fue puesto en prisión, Pepe sufrió una gran crisis, pero no dejó de
seguir trabajando y hablando en favor de la independencia. Su padre le amenazaba° con castigos severos. Su madre y sus hermanas le aconsejaban llenas de   threatened
buenas intenciones y le rogaban que tuviera mucho cuidado, pero el joven
idealista no les prestaba atención.

Antes de leer el próximo párrafo, conteste las preguntas siguientes con
una o dos palabras:

1   ¿Dónde prefería pasar el tiempo Martí, en el colegio, o en su casa?   colegio
2   ¿Le gustaba a don Mariano que su hijo fuera poeta?   no
3   ¿Quería don Mariano que Pepe siguiera estudiando, o que trabajara?   que trabajara
4   ¿A quién odiaba Pepe, a los españoles, o a su sistema de gobierno en   gobierno
Cuba?

Una noche un grupo de soldados españoles fueron al cuarto de Fermín
Valdés, un amigo íntimo de Pepe, y encontraron allí una carta en que los dos
amigos acusaban a uno de sus compañeros de colegio y lo insultaban por
haber ingresado° como oficial en las tropas españolas. Pepe y Fermín fueron   joined
detenidos inmediatamente y los llevaron ante los tribunales de justicia. Pepe
acababa de cumplir 17 años. La sentencia del juez fue muy severa: seis años de
prisión y trabajos forzados en las canteras.° Pepe que no había sido nunca un   stone quarries
muchacho fuerte ni saludable° se enfermó en la cárcel y sufrió mucho viendo los   healthy
horribles castigos y torturas que recibían los prisioneros políticos. Los golpes
de una pesada° cadena° de hierro que le pusieron en los pies y a la cintura° le   heavy/chain/waist
causaron un tumor canceroso que le hizo sufrir mucho durante el resto de
su vida.

5   ¿Qué encontraron los soldados españoles en el cuarto de Fermín, el   carta
amigo de Pepe?
6   ¿Qué edad tenía José cuando lo metieron en la cárcel?   17 años
7   ¿Cómo trataron a Martí en la cárcel, muy bien, o muy mal?   muy mal
8   ¿Qué problema serio tuvo Martí toda su vida como resultado de los
golpes de las cadenas de hierro que le pusieron en la cárcel?   tumor

Después de varios meses de prisión, por influencia de unos amigos de su
padre, las autoridades españolas perdonaron a José, pero no le permitieron

que siguiera viviendo en Cuba y lo deportaron a España. Al salir de la cárcel, José Martí, el prisionero número 113, pidió que le entregaran las horribles cadenas que había usado. Con el hierro de una de estas cadenas, Pepe mandó que le hicieran un anillo° que él usó por el resto de sus días. Se sentía orgulloso° de haber estado en la cárcel por defender la libertad de su patria.

  ring/proud

9 ¿Cón qué hicieron el anillo que José usó en el dedo toda su vida?

10 ¿Le importaba a José que la gente supiera que él había estado en la cárcel?

  hierro de las cadenas

  no

D *Future Perfect and Conditional Perfect:* Write the combinations. *Dice* cues the Future Perfect and *dijo* cues the Conditional Perfect.

Ejemplos: 135 = *Dice que para esa fecha yo lo habré devuelto.*
          235 = *Dijo que para esa fecha yo lo habría devuelto.*

			1	Vd.	1	romperlo.
1	Dice		2	ellas	2	abrirlo.
		que para esa fecha	3	yo	3	decírselo.
2	Dijo		4	nosotros	4	entregárselo.
			5	tú	5	devolverlo.

1) 111   Dice que para esa fecha Vd. lo habrá roto.
2) 154   Dice que para esa fecha tú se lo habrás entregado.
3) 222   Dijo que para esa fecha ellas lo habrían abierto.
4) 243   Dijo que para esa fecha nosotros se lo habríamos dicho.
5) 145   Dice que para esa fecha nosotros lo habremos devuelto.
6) 211   Dijo que para esa fecha Vd. lo habría roto.
7) 122   Dice que para esa fecha ellas lo habrán abierto.
8) 233   Dijo que para esa fecha yo se lo habría dicho.
9) 144   Dice que para esa fecha nosotros se lo habremos entregado.
10) 255   Dijo que para esa fecha tú lo habrías devuelto.
11) 134   Dice que para esa fecha yo se lo habré entregado.
12) 253   Dijo que para esa fecha tú se lo habrías dicho.

Assignment 108

Review of the Preterit and Imperfect

1 What is the proper way to think about the Preterit and the Imperfect? (a) They are two different tenses. (b) They are two forms of the same tense. ▲
        They are two forms of the same tense (So you can say that the past tense in Spanish has two forms.).

2 When a tense has two forms, these forms can provide more information about the past event you are talking about than when there is only one form. Which form of *saber—sabía* or *supe*—will you use to translate this sentence:

When I heard the roar of the water, then I *knew* we were in trouble. ▲

3 Does *supe* say that knowing began at that moment? ▲   *supe*

4 Which form of *saber*—*sabía* or *supe*—will you use to translate this sentence?   yes

Before I heard the roar of the water, I already *knew* we were in trouble. ▲

5 Does *sabía* say that knowing was going on when you first heard the roar of   *sabía*
the water? ▲

6 What kind of an event is *saber*? (a) cyclic (b) non-cyclic ▲   yes

7 Which aspect of *saber* does *supe* describe? (a) beginning (b) middle   non-cyclic
(c) end ▲

8 Which aspect does *sabía* describe? ▲   beginning

9 To be able to use and understand the Preterit and the Imperfect, you have   middle
to know these basic facts: (1) All events belong to one of two sets: cyclic or
non-cyclic. (2) All events (in theory) have three aspects: beginning, middle,
and end. (3) The middle or imperfect aspect of any event is always described
by which form of the past tense? ▲

10 (4) If the middle of either a cyclic or non-cyclic event is always described   Imperfect
by the Imperfect, then (5) the Preterit must have at least two functions. At a
point in the past it describes the _____ aspect of a non-cyclic event. ▲

11 When the event is cyclic the Preterit describes the _____ aspect. ▲   initiative

12 What kind of an event is *conocer*? ▲   terminative

13 Which sentence describes the beginning of my acquaintance with Roberto?   non-cyclic
(a) *En 1961 yo conocí a Roberto.* (b) *En 1961 yo conocía a Roberto.* ▲

En 1961 yo conocí a Roberto.

14 You now need to observe that non-cyclic events are divided into two subsets. One subset of these events can begin in the past and continue on into the
present. The second subset may begin and end in the past. Do these two
sentences supply you with essentially the same information? *Hace cinco años que
conocí a Roberto. Hace cinco años que conozco a Roberto.* ▲

yes (The first sentence places emphasis on the beginning of our acquaintance
while the second stresses the continuation of the relationship.)

15 Do these two sentences supply you with essentially the same information?
Hace cinco años que hablé con Roberto. Hace cinco años que hablo con Roberto. ▲

16 Does the first sentence above say the equivalent of *Hace cinco años que no*   no
hablo con Roberto? ▲

17 The difference, then, between the two subsets of non-cyclic events is this: yes
(1) one subset of events can begin in the past and continue into the present:
conocer, querer, saber, etc., (2) the other subset may begin and end in the past:
hablar, dormir, etc. The Preterit, consequently, may describe the beginning of
one subset or, in the case of the second subset above, the entire event. When
this happens the Preterit simply tells you that the whole event took place some-
time before the present moment of speaking, for example, *Sí, nos divertimos
mucho.* Does this, all by itself, tell you when in the past we had a good time? ▲

18 The simple present tense frequently describes what happens regularly, cus-   no
tomarily, habitually: *Él va a la oficina todos los días a las ocho.* Suppose, now,
you want to say that this custom was also true five years ago. What would you

say? (a) *Él fue a la oficina todos los días a las ocho.* (b) *Él iba a la oficina todos los días a las ocho.* ▲

Él iba a la oficina todos los días a las ocho.

19 The Imperfect is used to say that something was customary or habitual during some period in the past: *Cuando yo era niño íbamos a la playa con frecuencia.* It should be quite logical, then, that the Imperfect will also be used to contrast with the Present when what once was a custom contrasts with what is now a different custom: *Las muchachas modernas usan faldas muy cortas; sus madres, al contrario, usaban faldas muy largas.* Translate *usaban.* ▲

wore (or *used to wear*)

20 In English you use the present progressive to describe planned future action: *They said that they are leaving in a week.* What tense form do you use to say the same thing in Spanish? ▲

the simple present (*Dijeron que salen en una semana.*)

21 If you backshift the above Spanish sentence, you keep the *dijeron* and change *salen* to _____. ▲

salían (The Imperfect is used to recall planned future action.)

22 Translate only the italicized forms.
He suddenly jumped up and *ran.* ▲

23 In those days they *worked* ten hours per day. ▲   *corrió*

24 I don't remember when he *died.* ▲   *trabajaban*

25 They told me they *were selling* their house the next day. ▲   *murió*

26 At that time I *did not know* the answer. ▲   *vendían*

27 I *met* (*conocer*) him a year ago. ▲   *no sabía*

28 I *talked* with him yesterday. ▲   *conocí*

29 The dog *bit* me four times. ▲   *hablé*

30 And then I *knew* she was right. ▲   *mordió*

31 I *was* there when it happened. ▲   *supe*

estaba

The gun has played a very different role in the history of the Hispanic world and the United States and there are variations in the development of the vocabulary of the two languages. In Latin America, excepting the periods of conquest and independence movements, guns played a fairly minor role and most people never even owned one. In contrast, during the settling of most of the United States the possession and use of firearms was widespread. As a consequence, there are in American English many "gun" words which have no equivalent in Spanish. When something goes wrong in a shop the boss sends for a "troubleshooter." If he is a very important person, he is a "big shot," but if he fails, he is a "dud." If he is honest, he is a "straight shooter" who sometimes tells the workers that they need to "raise their sights." If the troubleshooter is very successful, the company buys his suggestions "lock, stock and barrel." You could probably think of many other examples of this type of "gun" vocabulary if you tried. It would probably be almost impossible for a Spanish speaker to come up with even one.

Review of the Uses of the Subjunctive

1 With very few exceptions, the subjunctive mode cannot be used unless there is a main and a _____ clause. ▲

subjoined (Some books call this the dependent or subordinate clause.)

2 There is a set of verbs which are used to describe how a person says something (*decir, gritar, murmurar, etc.*). These verbs may be followed by a direct quote. This original statement may be in the indicative or the imperative: *Grita, —¡Lo hace! Grita, —¡Hágalo!* To transform these into indirect discourse you insert a *que* between the two parts. Rewrite the two sentences and make any other changes necessary. The subject of *hacer* is *ella.* ▲

Grita que ella lo hace. Grita que ella lo haga.

3 The purpose of the imperative mode (*¡Hágalo!*) is (a) to report what someone is doing (b) to get someone to do something. ▲

to get someone to do something

4 One can influence the action of another in three fundamental ways. One may (1) cause the action to take place, (2) prevent it, or (3) permit it. Which of these applies to this situation? *Papá, ¿puedo comprar este dulce? Sí, hijita, cómpralo.* ▲

5 We can report this situation by saying *El papá permite que la hija lo _____.* ▲   permission

6 Which of the ways of influencing described in Frame 4 applies to this situation? *Hay una tormenta tremenda. Llueve mucho. Los niños van a salir a jugar. Papá dice, —No salgan ahora.* ▲   compre

7 The basic information is also contained in these two transforms: prevention
Papá no permite que ellos _____. Papá prohibe que ellos _____. ▲

8 Which way of influencing applies to this situation? *Los niños están haciendo mucho ruido y papá quiere leer. El ruido, al fin, lo enfurece y grita, —Salgan ahora mismo y déjenme en paz.* ▲   *salgan*

9 This can be reported as *Papá manda que ellos _____.* ▲   cause

10 In all the above examples causing, permitting, and preventing are done   *salgan*
with words. The same kinds of influence can be exerted by physical actions. Which kind of influence applies to this situation? *¿Para qué abriste la puerta? Abrí la puerta para que saliera el gato.* ▲

permission (I opened the door to let the cat go out.)

11 The opposite of this is prevention. Complete the sentence. *Cerré la puerta para que _____.* ▲

12 The third alternative is revealed by this situation.   *no saliera el gato.*
Abrí la puerta y el gato no salió. ¿Qué hago ahora?
Hay que darle un golpe para que _____ ▲

13 The basic facts presented in the previous sentences can be reformulated in   *salga*
many different ways. The information in the last sentence above may be recast as follows: *El gato no saldrá a menos que le _____ un golpe.* ▲

14 If there is a main and a subjoined clause *and* one entity attempts to cause,   *dé*
prevent, or permit the action of another, then the verb of the subjoined clause is in the _____ mode. ▲

subjunctive

15 Events may be classified in three sets: verbal, physical, and psychological. Thus *enfurecerse* is a psychological reaction to some stimulus. Many psychological reactions are caused unintentionally by what one does. From the point of view of the use of the subjunctive the difference between intending and not intending is not relevant. When an action causes a reaction, the subjoined clause is in the subjunctive. Fill in the proper form of *volver: Su esposa se enfureció de que él _____ a casa muy tarde.* ▲

volviera

16 Another difference between the use of the indicative and subjunctive depends on the fact that a statement can be modified to reveal our judgment about whether it is a fact, not a fact, or whether it is possible, probable, *etc.* What, for example, would be the reaction of most people to the question *¿Hay hombres en el sol?* (a) *Hay hombres en el sol.* (b) *No hay hombres en el sol.* ▲

No hay hombres en el sol.

17 In these examples, the facts are clear and there can be no reason for debate: *No hay hombres en el sol.* There are, however, many situations in which judgments must be made on insufficient evidence and, as a result, when a base sentence is modified the range may be from positive to negative with all kinds of variations in between. These variations may be shown in two ways. First, by the modifying clause: *I know, I'm positive, I'm sure, I'm pretty sure, I believe, I doubt, It's possible, It's probable, It's impossible, etc.* Second, the same variations may be reinforced or be restricted by the use of the indicative or subjunctive in the modified clause. When the modifying clause leans toward the acceptance of the basic sentence as a fact, the indicative is used. For example:

(1) *María está en Montevideo.*
(2) *Sé que María está en Montevideo.*
(3) *Estoy seguro de que María está en Montevideo.*
(4) *Creo que María está en Montevideo.*

In contrast, when the modifying clause leans towards the rejection of the basic sentence as a fact, the subjunctive is used. For example:

(1) *No estoy seguro de que María esté en Montevideo.*
(2) *No creo que María esté en Montevideo.*
(3) *Dudo que María esté en Montevideo.*
(4) *Es imposible que María esté en Montevideo.*

This neat matching of judgment and mode breaks down with modifiers like *Es posible* or *Es probable.* Both are ambiguous and, as a result, the way the speaker leans in his judgment has to be indicated by the mode of the modified clause. Which pair of sentences indicates greater acceptance of the statement *María está en Montevideo?*

a { *Es posible que María está en Montevideo.*
      { *Es probable que María está en Montevideo.*

b { *Es posible que María esté en Montevideo.*
      { *Es probable que María esté en Montevideo.* ▲

a (Until you have had much more experience with Spanish you should follow the patterns described above. No native will consider what you say to be wrong.)

18 A third contrast between the indicative and subjunctive deals with a different kind of modification. In this pattern the first clause makes a statement about some entity and the second clause describes a characteristic of that entity. When the speaker knows the entity mentioned in the first clause or has a definite entity in mind, the mode of the descriptive clause is _____. ▲

19 Which sentence will take the indicative? (a) *Hay un hombre aquí que **saber** reparar relojes.* (b) *No hay un hombre aquí que **saber** reparar relojes.* ▲

> indicative

> *Hay un hombre aquí que **sabe** reparar relojes.*

20 When the speaker has no knowledge or experience of the entity mentioned in the first clause, the mode of the verb in the descriptive clause is subjunctive. Which sentence requires the subjunctive? (a) *Necesito un libro que **dar** más información.* (b) *Necesito el libro que **dar** más información.* ▲

> *Necesito un libro que **dé** más información.* (The *el* of the second sentence maintains common focus on *un libro* previously mentioned and, consequently, known to the speaker.)

21 There remains, now, one more contrast between the indicative and the subjunctive which you have studied. This deals with the order relationship between two events and whether you are recalling or anticipating them. Change the underlined infinitive into the mode to be used: *Discutimos nuestros planes para el día siguiente después que los niños se **acostar**.* ▲

22 Do the same for this sentence: *Discutiremos nuestros planes para mañana después que los niños se **acostar**.* ▲

> acuestan

> acuesten

23 The three most common words to describe the order relationship between two events are *antes*, *cuando*, and *después*. Which one of these almost always requires the subjunctive in the subjoined clause? ▲

> *antes* (This is an illogical exception to the general pattern.)

24 The rules for the use of the indicative and subjunctive are independent of the tense of the verb used. Transform these two sentences into indirect discourse, that is, join the two parts with *que* to get an indirect quote. Make the other necessary changes. *Gritó,—¡Lo hace! Gritó,—¡Hágalo!* ▲

> *Gritó que lo hacía. Gritó que lo hiciera.*

25 In this and the remaining frames rewrite the verbs in the past tense. *Papá no permite que ellos salgan.* (You are talking about a single instance, not habitual action.) ▲

> *Papá no **permitió** que ellos **salieran.***

26 *Cierro la puerta para que no salga el gato.* (You are talking about habitual action.) ▲

> ***Cerraba** la puerta para que no **saliera** el gato.*

27 *El gato no saldrá a menos que le dé un golpe.* ▲

> *El gato no **saldría** a menos que le **diera** un golpe.*

28 *Estoy seguro de que María está en Montevideo.* ▲

> ***Estaba** seguro de que María **estaba** en Montevideo.*

29 *Es imposible que María esté en Montevideo.* ▲

> ***Era** imposible que María **estuviera** en Montevideo.*

30 *Necesito un libro que dé más información.* ▲

> ***Necesitaba** un libro que **diera** más información.*

Self-Correcting Exercises

A *Subjunctive versus Indicative:* Write the appropriate forms of the infinitives in parentheses:

1 Cuando Mariano Martí (*ir*) a trabajar en un pueblo del interior de Cuba, llevó a su hijo Pepe con él para que lo (*acompañar*) y lo (*ayudar*) en su nuevo trabajo.

fue, acompañara, ayudara

2 Doña Leonor, su esposa, se había quedado en la casa que la familia (*tener*) en La Habana.

tenía

3 A la madre de Pepe no le gustó mucho que su hijo se (*ir*) para el campo.

fuera

4 Pero desde el primer momento a Pepe le gustó mucho el campo. Tan pronto como don Mariano (*terminar*) su trabajo todos los días él (*salir*) con su hijo a pasear a caballo y los domingos lo llevaba a las peleas de gallos (*cock fights*).

terminaba, salía

5 En el Museo Nacional de Cuba hay una carta que José le (*escribir*) a su mamá cuando él (*tener*) solamente nueve años de edad.

escribió, tenía

6 En la carta Pepe le decía a su mamá que (*estar*) muy contento y que no se (*preocupar*) por él.

estaba, preocupara

7 También le contaba entusiasmado a su madre que unos amigos del papá le (*haber*) regalado un caballo y un gallo fino (*fighting cock*).

habían

8 Pepe quería que su caballo (*comer*) mucho maíz y mucha hierba para que (*engordar*) mucho.

comiera, engordara

9 Aunque era verdad que Pepe se (*divertir*) mucho, también era cierto que él (*trabajar*) muy duro (*hard*).

divertía, trabajaba

10 Aunque todavía Pepe (*ser*) muy joven, estaba muy adelantado en la escuela, y su padre le pedía que (*copiar*) sus documentos y (*escribir*) algunas cartas.

era, copiara, escribiera

11 El padre de José tuvo problemas con sus superiores y perdió su puesto. Si esto no (*haber*) ocurrido, se habrían quedado allí más tiempo.

hubiera

12 Padre e hijo tuvieron que regresar a La Habana en el otoño, y en seguida Pepe ingresó en un colegio que (*llamarse*) "San Pablo." Su director, don Rafael Mendive, trató siempre a Martí como si (*ser*) su propio hijo.

se llamaba, fuera

B *General Practice:* Position of Adjectives, Future and Conditional of Probability, and Reciprocal Reflexives

Using the adjective and the information given in parentheses, decide mentally whether the adjective should come before, or after the indicated noun.

1 La ... *alumna* ... no vino a clase hoy. (alto, *one of many*)

alumna alta

2 Ayer vi a tus ... *profesores* ... (simpático, *all*)

simpáticos profesores

3 La ... *niña* ... me miró y se sonrió. (rubio, *one unique*)

rubia niña

4 Los ... *tigres* ... de estas montañas atacan a nuestros animales. (feroz, *all*)

feroces tigres

Indicate probability in the Present or in the Past by translating the English with the Future or the Conditional.

5 Si no me equivoco, en este momento ellos *are probably having a good time.*   estarán divirtiéndose (se divertirán)

6 Al contestar tan difíciles preguntas, él *probably lied*, ¿verdad?   mentiría

7 Mi hermana dice que la niña de Eva *must be* ahora cuatro años, pero. no está segura.   tendrá

8 *It was probably* la una más o menos cuando eso sucedió.   Sería

Translate the English:

9 Allí había *ten more men* ayer.   diez hombres más

10 Todos iban a *help each other* para poder terminarlo más pronto.   ayudarse

11 Sí, señores, nosotros ya *know each other*.   nos conocemos

12 Y ¿dónde han metido los *two other forks*?   otros dos tenedores

C *Perfect Tenses:* Shift these sentences to the corresponding perfect tense. After correcting your answer, say the new sentence aloud.

1 Él lo compone.	Él lo ha compuesto.
2 Él lo componía.	Él lo había compuesto.
3 Él se oponía.	Él se había opuesto.
4 Él se opone.	Él se ha opuesto.
5 Él lo repone.	Él lo ha repuesto.
6 Él lo reponía.	Él lo había repuesto.
7 Él lo pospondrá.	Él lo habrá pospuesto.
8 Él lo pospondría.	Él lo habría pospuesto.
9 Él lo supondría.	Él lo habría supuesto.
10 Él lo supondrá.	Él lo habrá supuesto.
11 Él lo propondrá.	Él lo habrá propuesto.
12 Él lo propondría.	Él lo habría propuesto.

D *General Review:* Rewrite each sentence, substituting the words in parentheses for the indicated parts and making all other required changes. Cover the answer in parentheses under each sentence until you are ready to check it.

1 *Dice* que *tú* has recibido *otras* dos cartas de la *señora* Martínez. (Dijo, nosotros, más, señor)

(Dijo que nosotros habíamos recibido dos cartas más del señor Martínez.)

2 *Tú* eres de Nueva York donde hay *edificios muy grandes*. (Ella, en, la Estatua de la Libertad)

(Ella está en Nueva York donde está la Estatua de la Libertad.)

3 Me inform*an* que la *clase* va a ser *a las diez y media*. (-aban, alumnos nuevos, en el primer edificio)

(Me informaban que los alumnos nuevos iban a estar en el primer edificio.)

4 ¿Hay *bastante* azúcar en esa *taza* roja?   (el, vaso)

(¿Está el azúcar en ese vaso rojo?)

5 Es importante que tú *agradezcas* los *favores* que te han *hecho*.   (dirigir, actividades, asignar)

(Es importante que tú dirijas las actividades que te han asignado.)

You were just told that English has four pitch levels while Spanish has only three. Let's see what bearing this has on inter-cultural communication and also, on what you still have to learn.

The vast majority of speakers of both English and Spanish do not know that the two languages have a different number of pitch levels and most teachers, as a result, teach the opposite language with the pitch levels of their own language. Here are two examples of what happens when this is not understood.

A Latin American who married an American girl lived in this country several years before he discovered why his wife insisted that he always got up grouchy. For years he protested, saying that he almost always awoke feeling very cheerful. His wife refused to believe him, and this misunderstanding was not resolved until he discovered that he always said *Good morning* with only the two pitch levels of Spanish, those used in English when you are grouchy or annoyed.

A very beautiful, talented, and highly cultured young woman from a Latin country found a job in the United States in an exclusive jewelry shop as a salesgirl. Although she knew how to deal with people most graciously in her own culture and spoke English quite fluently, she was, to the confusion of everyone, an immediate failure and had to give up the job. The explanation was eventually found in the fact that she spoke English only with the normal pitch levels of Spanish, and the customers all thought her bored and totally indifferent to their needs.

Unless you are careful, you are going to speak Spanish with the three pitch levels of English. Spanish speakers will believe that you are "pushy," over-emphatic, domineering, rude, or peculiar.

Assignment 109/110

Preparing for a Major Test

You have been studying CIS long enough to know that there are two kinds of tests. The short ones are diagnostic to let you and your instructor find out how well you are learning new materials and, of course, what corrective procedures must be adopted if you are not progressing properly. In contrast, the major tests are designed to find out whether you are reaching the objectives of the course and whether you have learned enough to be able to continue your study of Spanish with some satisfactory degree of success.

The forthcoming major test will evaluate the objectives for Etapa 6 found on page 576. It will consist of eight parts marked A through H and totaling

100 points. This Assignment explains all the techniques that will be used in testing and gives you practice on what you will be asked to do.

1   Part A, *Listening Comprehension* (12 points): You will hear a short passage in Spanish about a portion of the life of the Cuban patriot, José Martí. Listen the first time to get the general outline of the story and to pin-point any word whose meaning is not immediately clear. The second time around concentrate on the facts and details, the message. Keep in mind that it is impossible to test your listening comprehension without automatically testing your memory of what has been said. After listening to the passage twice, you will hear questions which can be answered with either one word or a very short phrase. You will hear each question only once. Part of what this test is designed to find out is if you can understand what you hear *the first time* you hear it.

The following selection which also deals with the life of José Martí is similar to the one that will be used in the test. Answer the questions mentally after each paragraph.

José Martí regresa a Cuba

José Martí y Carmen Zayas Bazán se casaron en México. Después de la boda se fueron a vivir en la ciudad de Guatemala, pero no se quedaron mucho tiempo allí. Iba a nacer su primer hijo y se fueron para Cuba porque ellos querían que naciera en tierra cubana.

¿En qué país se casó José Martí?   México
¿Dónde se establecieron Carmen y José después de la boda?   Guatemala
¿Dónde querían ellos que naciera su primer hijo?   Cuba

De vuelta en La Habana, Pepe consiguió en seguida trabajo en las oficinas de un abogado y dio clases en un colegio de la capital. La "Guerra de los Diez Años" había terminado y todavía Cuba no era libre. Muchos cubanos estaban desilusionados, pero Martí continuaba sus actividades revolucionarias sin descansar. Cada vez que él tenía la oportunidad, expresaba públicamente sus ideas sin miedo y continuaba conspirando en secreto contra el régimen español.

¿Cómo se llama en español la capital de Cuba?   La Habana
¿Es verdad, o mentira que Martí estaba desilusionado porque no podía con-
seguir trabajo?   mentira
¿Es verdad, o mentira que Martí continuó trabajando por la independencia de
Cuba?   verdad

Un día que Martí, su esposa y un amigo estaban almorzando en casa oyeron de repente que alguien llamaba con mucha insistencia a la puerta. Carmen fue en seguida a ver quién era y volvió al comedor muy preocupada. Un hombre insistía urgentemente en ver a José. Ella creía que era un agente secreto de la policía.

¿Qué hacía Martí cuando llegó a su casa el agente?   almorzaba
¿Quién fue a la puerta, José, o Carmen?   Carmen

Con la servilleta todavía en la mano, Martí se levantó de la mesa, corrió a su cuarto a recoger algún dinero y le pidió a su esposa que le trajera una tacita de café. Carmen se lo trajo y después de tomarlo con mucha prisa, se despidió y salió con el señor para la estación de policía. Hacía días que las autoridades militares observaban todos los movimientos de Martí sin que él lo supiera. Creían que era un loco, pero un loco peligroso, y lo llevaron a la cárcel. Esta vez no estuvo mucho tiempo en prisión. Los jueces ordenaron su inmediata deportación a España. Nuevamente Martí tuvo que abandonar a su querida Cuba.

¿Para qué fue Martí a su cuarto, para buscar dinero, o ropa?   dinero
¿Qué le pidió Martí a su esposa?   café
¿Estuvo Martí en la cárcel mucho, o poco tiempo esta vez?   poco
¿A qué país fue deportado Martí?   España

2   Part B, *Position of Adjectives* (5 points): For this part of the test you are to write a complete exclamatory sentence which will be the Spanish equivalent of the English pattern *What (a) + adjective + noun!* If you can translate the following sentence, chances are you will do well in this part: *What a pretty moon!* ▲

> *¡Qué luna tan bonita!* (Do not mark this frame wrong until after you look at the next three frames.)

3   What other word might replace *tan?* ▲

> *más* (These two modifiers are free variants in this pattern.)

4   Are there other adjectives that might replace *bonita?* ▲

> yes (You might have, for example, used *linda.*)

5   In *¡Qué luna tan bonita!* the terminal phoneme of *bonita* matches the terminal phoneme of _____. ▲

6   *Luna* and *bonita* also agree in number. Both are _____. ▲   *luna*

7   Translate: What tall trees! ▲   singular

> *¡Qué árboles tan altos!*

8   The matching phonemes of *árboles* and *altos* are _____ and _____. You match what precedes the plural suffixes. ▲

9   The matching plural suffixes are _____ and _____. ▲   *l* and *o*

10   The regular translation of *¡Qué árboles tan altos!* is "What tall trees!" The   *es* and *s* literal translation is _____. ▲

> What trees so tall! (In exclamations as in comparisons with *tan* or *más*, the adjectival phrase follows the noun.)

11   Translate the following exclamatory sentences using *tan* with the first four and *más* with the rest. Make sure the adjective agrees with the noun.

What rare butterflies!   ¡Qué mariposas tan raras!
What ferocious animals!   ¡Qué animales tan feroces!
What a dry year!   ¡Qué año tan seco!
What industrious women!   ¡Qué mujeres tan industriosas!
What a pretty girl!   ¡Qué chica (muchacha) más linda!
What a bad fall!   ¡Qué caída más mala!

What a modern city!	¡ Qué ciudad más moderna !
What interesting machines!	¡ Qué máquinas más interesantes !
What difficult tests!	¡ Qué exámenes más difíciles !
What a useful invention!	¡ Qué invención más útil !

12 Part C, *Vocabulary Matching* (12 points): In two columns on your answer sheet you will see twelve Spanish words and fourteen English words (two extras that have no Spanish equivalent in the twelve given). You are to write the letter that precedes the English word in the space provided in parentheses. For example, you see this:

1 casa (   )

(a) thing
(b) marries
(c) can

What letter do you write in the space given? ▲

b (While *casa* may translate "house" or "home", the only logical choice above is the translation of *casa* as a verb form of *casar*, to marry.)

13 Practice doing the above with the following exercise:

1	miente	(a)	*it grows*	1	e
2	aceite	(b)	*it is growing light*	2	h
3	semejante	(c)	*sin*	3	m
4	merece	(d)	*it happens*	4	j
5	pecado	(e)	*he lies*	5	c
6	hierve	(f)	*honey*	6	o
7	amanece	(g)	*she is blessing*	7	b
8	une	(h)	*oil*	8	l
9	crece	(i)	*he returns (gives back)*	9	a
10	maldice	(j)	*she deserves*	10	p
11	devuelve	(k)	*he bores*	11	i
12	desarrollo	(l)	*he unites*	12	n
13	miel	(m)	*similar*	13	f
14	sucede	(n)	*development*	14	d
		(o)	*she boils*		
		(p)	*he is cursing*		

14   Part D, Use of Articles (13 points): In this part there will be several sentences in Spanish with numbered blanks. You must decide (1) whether an article is needed to complete the sentence, (2) whether no article is needed, (3) if one is needed, whether it should be the definite or indefinite article, and (4) what form must be used to match the noun.
What will you do in this case? (Watch the cues.) _____ *casa de María está en el campo.* ▲

La (The locative *en el campo* plus *está* cues the use of the definite article.)

15 *Voy a la tienda para comprar* _____ *harina.* (You are initiating common focus.) ▲

No article (*Harina* stands for a measure entity and the indefinite article, a number word, cannot be used to initiate common focus. If you use *la harina*, you have already talked about *harina*.)

16 *Veo que* _____ *luna está cubierta de nubes.* ▲

la (Since *luna* is unique, you need the definite article.)

17 Write the appropriate forms of the article or Ø (zero) when none is needed:

No nos gustan . . . exámenes difíciles.   los

. . . señor Franklin descubrió . . . electricidad.   El, la

. . . mujeres viven más que . . . hombres.   Las, los

En . . . avenida Miramar hay . . . sinagoga donde celebran . . . ceremonias   la, una
religiosas todos . . . sábados.   Ø, los

¿Viste a . . . presidente Cárdenas en . . . Ayuntamiento?   el (al), el

Por favor, . . . señorita, . . . niños quieren . . . leche.   Ø, los, Ø

Yo prefiero . . . taza de café.   una

. . . español, . . . francés y . . . italiano son . . . lenguas romances.   El, el, el, Ø

Después de . . . clase de . . . español tenemos que buscar . . . tienda donde   la, Ø
vendan . . . hielo seco. También necesito comprar . . . huevos, . . . mante-   una, Ø
quilla y . . . escoba.   Ø, Ø, una

¿Dónde está . . . teléfono? Necesito . . . médico urgentemente.   el, un

18 Part E, *Subjunctive versus Indicative* (22 points): There will be several Spanish
sentences on your answer sheet, with blanks followed by an infinitive in parentheses. You have to do three things: (1) select the right mode, indicative or
subjunctive, (2) choose the tense form that matches the context, and (3) make
the form agree with the subject. Do this here and in the next two frames.

   En 1947 mi abuelo _____ *(tener) ochenta años pero no permitía que nadie* _____
(decir) que ya era viejo. ▲

19 *Te prometo que yo lo* _____ *(hacer) tan pronto como ellas nos* _____ *(visitar).* ▲   *tenía, dijera*

haré, visiten (You can only promise to do something in the future, which cues
haré, and the adverbial clause must then be in the present subjunctive.)

20 _____ (Ser) importante hoy día que muchas personas _____ (saber)
hablar más de una lengua. ▲

21 Continue practicing the above in the following story.   Es, sepan

Martí en Nueva York

   Deportado por segunda vez a España, José Martí sufría mucho en
Madrid. Sabía que su esposa e hijo (estar) bien en Cuba viviendo con sus   estaban,
suegros, pero le entristecía que Carmen no (ser) feliz y que no le (escribir). fuera, escribiera

   Martí dudaba mucho que el gobierno español (cambiar) su injusta   cambiara,
política hacia Cuba y se dio cuenta de que allí él no (poder) hacer nada   podía
por la independencia de su país.

   Muchos de los cubanos que (haber) luchado sin éxito durante tantos   habían
años en las guerras por la independencia cubana estaban viviendo en
Nueva York, México, Centroamérica y en las diferentes islas del Caribe.

   Era muy necesario e importante que él se (reunir) con ellos para unirlos   reuniera,
y organizar una nueva revolución que (tener) éxito.   tuviera

   El 3 de enero de 1880, Martí llegó a Nueva York. Era preciso que él
(aprender) inglés lo más rápido posible para poder trabajar.   aprendiera

   Los quince años que Martí (pasar) en Nueva York fueron los más pro-   pasó
ductivos de toda su vida: pronuncia grandes discursos, escribe miles de

páginas en prosa y verso, traduce libros y da clases de español en una escuela secundaria por las noches.

Aunque hay muchos clubs y asociaciones que se (interesar) en libertar a Cuba, están muy desorganizados y necesitan que alguien los (unir) y los (dirigir).

Desde Cayo Hueso (*Key West*) hasta Nueva York, Martí visita a los diferentes grupos revolucionarios y pide que los cubanos se (sacrificar) y (contribuir) dinero para la revolución.

Poco a poco la mayoría de ellos reconocen que Martí (ser) un hombre honrado y sincero, y empiezan a llamarle "Maestro."

Martí también viaja por México, Centroamérica y Santo Domingo. En estos países viven algunos veteranos que ya (haber) peleado en los campos de Cuba.

Estos viejos soldados esperan impacientemente que (llegar) el momento de volver a Cuba.

Martí sabe que todos (desear) ofrecer sus vidas a la gran causa, pero es muy importante que no (haber) divisiones entre ellos y que todos los grupos (atacar) al enemigo al mismo tiempo.

> interesan,
> una,
> dirija
>
> sacrifiquen,
> contribuyan
> es
>
> han
>
> llegue
>
> desean,
> haya,
> ataquen

22 Part F, *Perfect Verb Forms* (10 points): This part of the test is designed to discover whether you can make simple translations from English to Spanish in the Present Perfect, the Past Perfect, the Future Perfect, and the Conditional Perfect. You need to know two things: (1) the various forms of *haber* in the Present, the Imperfect, the Future and the Conditional, and (2) the perfect participles for all the Spanish verbs that you have studied until now. Remember that some of the perfect participles are irregular. On the test there will be five sentences in Spanish each containing a verb phrase in English. You translate the English to Spanish. For example: *El policía creyó que yo* (would have seen) *el accidente porque me vio cruzando la calle.* ▲

23 Practice with these additional examples:

Eugenio y yo ya (have put) el dinero en el banco.
En su país él (had been) director de un colegio por muchos años.
¿Crees tú que ellos (would have gone) con nosotras?
El mundo científico opina que tú (have discovered) una técnica sensacional.
Para esa fecha ya nosotros (will have done) el resto del trabajo.
Los músicos de la orquesta no (had heard) la nueva sinfonía.
Nosotros se lo (would have told), pero tú lo prohibiste.
Tú no (had returned) de España todavía.
¿Por qué Vds. no nos (have fixed) el televisor?
¿Cómo puedes pensar que yo no te (would have protected)?

> *habría visto*
>
> hemos puesto
> había sido
> habrían ido
> has descubierto
> habremos hecho
> habían oído
> habríamos dicho
> habías vuelto
> han arreglado
> habría protegido

24 Part G, *General Evaluation* (14 points): This part of the exam deals with four separate problems: (1) the position of descriptive adjectives, (2) the two ways of expressing probability, (3) the reflexive construction in which two persons are doing the same thing to each other, and (4) special problems of word order when you translate *other*, *more*, and *less*.

In the first section you will see four Spanish sentences each with a blank preceding and following a noun. In parentheses immediately following each sentence there will be a Spanish descriptive adjective and either the word *all*, *some*, *one of many*, or one *unique*. With this information you decide where to put the descriptive adjective. For example: *Allí viene la _____ hija _____ de don José.* (*linda*, one of many) ▲

Allí viene la hija *linda* de don José.

25 In the second section there are four Spanish sentences with *probably* plus an English verb. You are to translate the English with a single verb form. For example: *Yo me imagino que ellos* (probably are) *en casa ahora.* ▲

estarán (This is the future of *probability* which is not logically compatible with *ahora*.)

26 The third section of this part has six sentences with one part in English. For example: *Voy a comprar* (two other) *libros.* ▲

otros dos (Spanish reverses the word order.)

27 *Quiere* (two more hours) *para terminarlo.* ▲

dos horas más (Spanish puts the translation of *more* after the noun.)

28 *He trabajado* (three weeks less) *que ustedes.* ▲

tres semanas menos (Here Spanish and English are alike.)

29 The last three sentences have a reflexive each-other construction. Translate the English part of this sentence: *Nosotros* (see each other) *con frecuencia.* ▲

nos vemos

30 The following sentences contain additional practice of all the above problems.

A toda mi familia le gusta la . . . fruta . . . de mis árboles.   (exquisito, *all*)

exquisita fruta

José y su novia (*fight with each other*) constantemente.

se pelean

Necesito comprar (*three other*) árboles frutales para mi patio.

otros tres

El policía cree que el accidente (*probably occurred*) más o menos a las cinco ayer.

ocurriría

Cuando la profesora anunció el examen, los alumnos (*looked at each other*) sin decir nada.

se miraron

Es casi mediodía. Creo que (*we probably are*) cerca de Panamá.

estaremos

Las . . . rosas . . . tienen mucho perfume. (rojo, *some*)

rosas rojas

Me parece que ella (*probably has*) cien (*less dollars*) than I.

tendrá, dólares menos

(*It's probably three*) ahora, pero no estoy seguro.

Serán las tres

Tu reloj (*was probably*) atrasado, ¿no crees?

estaría

(*There probably were*) mucha gente allí, ¿verdad?

Habría

Voy a servirles mi . . . postre . . . esta noche. (exquisito, *one unique*)

exquisito postre

31 Part H, *Reading Comprehension* (12 points): This last part of the exam continues with the biography of José Martí. There are three separate paragraphs and after each, four questions in Spanish which can be answered in one to four words. Read each paragraph carefully, then read the questions and answer those you know immediately. Skip any question you have doubts about. When you have answered the ones you are sure about, reread the passage to get the answer to any you skipped. Practice with the following paragraph:

Hace casi treinta años que yo visité México por primera vez. Ya hablaba español pero nunca había vivido en un país de habla española y lo que ya sabía de la cultura hispánica lo había aprendido de libros o de las conferencias de mis profesores en la universidad. Al llegar a la frontera casi inmediatamente me di cuenta de que no sabía en realidad mucho de las costumbres de los mexicanos. Nadie me había hablado de la moneda (*money*), por ejemplo, y no sabía cambiar las millas inglesas a kilómetros.

¿Cuantos años hace que yo visité México por primera vez? ▲

29 *¿De dónde había aprendido yo algo de la cultura hispánica?* ▲   *treinta*

30 *¿De qué no me había hablado nadie?* ▲   *libros, conferencias*

     la moneda

31 You now know what the exam is going to be about. So the best thing to do is relax and make sure you have a good night's sleep. You'll do much better if you are not tense and tired.

Ejercicios

Ejercicio 1 Unaspirated [p], Dental [t], and Vowels: Reading Aloud

1	a, e, i, o, u	5	tuta, tute, tuti, tuto, tutu
2	pa, pe, pi, po, pu	6	pata, pate, pati, pato, patu
3	popa, pope, popi, popo, popu	7	tepa, tepe, tepi, tepo, tepu
4	ta, te, ti, to, tu		

Ejercicio 2 Dialog One: Reading Aloud

Tomás y Luisa

1 T: ¡Hola, Luisa! ¿Qué tal?
2 L: Bastante bien. Y tú, ¿cómo estás?
3 T: Estoy muy bien, gracias.
4 L: ¿A dónde vas, Tomás? ¿A clase?
5 T: No, voy a la oficina.
6 L: Bueno, adiós. Hasta luego.
7 T: Adiós, Luisa. Hasta pronto.

Ejercicio 3 Reading Aloud

1	libro	7	pluma	13	regla
2	cuaderno	8	silla	14	luz
3	lápiz	9	mesa	15	tiza
4	reloj	10	ventana	16	muchacho
5	papel	11	puerta	17	muchacha
6	pupitre	12	pizarra		

Ejercicio 4 Unaspirated [p], Dental [t], and Vowels: Reading Aloud

1 a, e, i, o, u
2 tapa, tepe, pate, poti, tupo
3 fama, mafo, tufi, fatima, pitafo
4 tomate, pimopa, pamote, motepu, tipapu
5 impotu, patufa, atumi, empo, amo
6 pupitre, papel, pluma, puerta, lápiz
7 El papel está en el pupitre de Pepe.

Ejercicio 5 Numbers 0–20: Addition

5 + 5 = 10	2 + 7 = 9	3 + 13 = 16	10 + 8 = 18
4 + 6 = 10	8 + 8 = 16	5 + 15 = 20	
8 + 5 = 13	1 + 11 = 12	10 + 6 = 16	

Ejercicio 6   Stop [d] and Fricative [d̶]:   Reading Aloud

1	da/ida	**4**	esdi/endi	**7**	arde/alde	**10**	du/ud
2	de/ide	**5**	esdo/endo	**8**	ardi/aldi	**11**	do/od
3	di/idi	**6**	esdu/endu	**9**	ardo/aldo	**12**	di/id

Ejercicio 7   Numbers 0–20:   Addition and Subtraction

$$4 + 2 = 6 \qquad 12 + 6 = 18$$
$$4 - 2 = 2 \qquad 12 - 6 = 6$$
$$10 + 5 = 15 \qquad 19 + 1 = 20$$
$$10 - 5 = 5 \qquad 19 - 1 = 18$$
$$14 + 4 = 18 \qquad 13 + 3 = 16$$
$$14 - 4 = 10 \qquad 13 - 3 = 10$$

Ejercicio 8   Stop [b] and Fricative [b̶]:   Reading Aloud

1	va/iba	**6**	bien/Estoy bien.
2	be/ive	**7**	bien/Muy bien.
3	vi/ibi	**8**	ventana/una ventana
4	bo/ivo	**9**	ventana/la ventana
5	vu/ibu	**10**	veinte/las veinte ventanas

Ejercicio 9   Stop [b] and Fricative [b̶]:   Reading Aloud

1	ba/iba	**6**	bien/estoy bien	**10**	las veinte ventanas/veinte
2	be/ibe	**7**	bien/muy bien	**11**	Buenos días./Dígale buenos días.
3	bi/ibi	**8**	ventana/una ventana	**12**	Es un buen día./Es una buena ventana.
4	bo/ibo	**9**	ventana/la ventana	**13**	Es un buen libro./Es una buena pluma.
5	bu/ibu			**14**	Están bien./Está bien.

Ejercicio 10   Noun and Verb Agreement

Your instructor will give you four numbers corresponding to different items from each column. Write the sentence that corresponds to each number combination making all the necessary agreements.

Ejemplo: 2314 = La señora trabaja aquí.

1	El	1	muchach-	1	trabaj-	1	en la clase.
2	La	2	alumn-	2	estudi-	2	en la universidad.
3	Los	3	señor-	3	habl-	3	allí.
4	Las	4	profesor-			4	aquí.

Ejercicio 11   Reading Aloud

Always remember to use the pronunciation that you have been learning. It is easy to forget and let your English habits interfere.

En la oficina del Centro Internacional

(**1**) En la oficina del Centro Internacional hay dos estudiantes: un muchacho y una muchacha. (**2**) El muchacho se llama David y es de Santiago de Chile. (**3**) Él habla español y desea estudiar inglés. (**4**) La señorita se llama Luisa y es de San Antonio. (**5**) Ella habla un poquito de español y trabaja en la oficina del Centro. (**6**) Luisa estudia español en la clase de la doctora Navarro que es una profesora muy buena. (**7**) David tiene que hablar con el señor Moreno, el director de actividades del Centro. (**8**) El señor Moreno es de California y él habla inglés y español perfectamente. (**9**) Él estudia en la Escuela de Medicina y es un hombre muy amable. (**10**) David y Luisa conversan en español; ellos necesitan hablar con el señor Moreno.

Ejercicio 12   [r] and [rr]:   Reading Aloud

1	puerta/tres	**7**	rosa/zorra	**13**	ere/erre
2	árbol/Brasil	**8**	roca/corra	**14**	era/erra
3	Vargas/gracias	**9**	rana/narra	**15**	pero/perro
4	tarde/grande	**10**	ropa/porra	**16**	pera/perra
5	martes/frío	**11**	roba/borra	**17**	caro/carro
6	miércoles/creo	**12**	rabo/barro	**18**	fiero/fierro

Ejercicio 13   Reading Cues for Stop and Fricative /d/ and /b/

Number a column from 1 to 22. Write *f* (fricative) or *s* (stop) after each number to identify the sound represented by *d*, *b*, or *v*.

　　　　　　　　1　　　　　　　　　　　　　2　　　3

En la oficina del Centro Internacional hay dos estudiantes: un muchacho y

　　　　　　　　　　　　　4　　5　　　6

una muchacha. El muchacho se llama David y es de Santiago de Chile. Él

　　7　　　　　　8　　　　9　　　　　　　　　　　　　　　　　10

habla español y desea estudiar inglés. La señorita se llama Luisa y es de San

　　　　　　　　　　　　　　　11

Antonio. Ella habla un poquito de español y trabaja en la oficina del Centro.

　　　　　　　　　　　　　12　　　　　　　13

Luisa estudia español en la clase de la doctora Navarro que es una profesora

　　　14　　　15　　　　　　　　　　　　　　　　　　16　　17　　18

muy buena. David tiene que hablar con el señor Moreno, el director de actividades del Centro. El señor Moreno estudia en la Escuela de Medicina y es un

19   20   21   22

hombre muy amable. David y Luisa conversan en español; ellos necesitan hablar
con el señor Moreno.

Ejercicio 14   Present Indicative of *a*-Verbs, and *ser, haber,*
and *estar*

A/B

C/D

Ejercicio 15   [r] and [rr]:   Reading Aloud

1 coro/corro	5 ida/ira	11 árbol/Brasil
2 cero/cerro	6 todo/toro	12 Vargas/gracias
3 caro/carro	7 cero/cedo	13 tarde/grande
4 foro/forro	8 cara/cada	14 martes/frío
	9 vado/varo	
	10 mido/miro	

Ejercicio 16   General Review: Reading Aloud

Don't forget to use your new Spanish habits; forget your old English ones.

1   Hay treinta pupitres y tres pizarras en la clase.
2   Una señorita amable dice perdón y gracias.

3 Hoy es viernes y anteayer fue miércoles.
4 Deseo hablar con la profesora y con el director.
5 El nuevo alumno tiene un libro muy bueno.
6 ¿De dónde son ustedes? ¿De Bolivia?
7 Margarita, dile buenos días a Roberto.

Ejercicio 17 *p, d, b, r, rr*, and Vowels: Reading Aloud

Remember what you have learned about the pronunciation of the sounds represented by *p, d, b, r, rr* and the vowels.

1 Hoy es miércoles y hace mucho viento.
2 Pancho va a trabajar en la mina hoy.
3 La mina donde trabaja Pancho es bastante nueva.
4 Él va a la oficina antes de ir a trabajar.
5 El director de la mina está allí en una silla.
6 Los dos señores hablan en español un rato (*a while*).
7 Pancho le pregunta dónde va a trabajar hoy.
8 El director le contesta que debe preguntarle al señor Romero.
9 Pancho pregunta dónde está ese señor.
10 El director no contesta nada; va a la puerta.
11 Pancho y el director van a donde está Pedro Romero.
12 Pancho es boliviano y su señora es paraguaya.
13 Los dos viven en La Paz, capital de Bolivia.
14 La señora de Pancho se llama Dolores y le dicen (*call her*) Lola.

Ejercicio 18   *Ser* and Adjectives of Nationality

Write out the combinations as your instructor gives them. Be sure to use the correct form of *ser*. Make all adjectives of nationality agree with the subject; when you use *Yo* the adjective will end in *a* if you are female, and in *o* if you are male.

Ejemplo: 32 = Enrique y tú son argentinos.

1 Paco		1	bolivian-
2 Él y yo		2	argentin-
3 Enrique y tú		3	chilen-
4 Yo	ser	4	uruguay-
5 María y Alicia		5	ecuatorian-
6 Tú (*f*)		6	venezolan-

Ejercicio 19   *Ser* versus *estar*

The phrases in the third column will cue you to choosing correctly between *ser* or *estar*. Note the problem of adjectival agreement in the last two items. Write the combinations that your instructor will give you.

1	María	1	bastante bien.
2	Pepe y tú	2	aquí hoy.
3	Yo	3	en la oficina.
4	Ustedes	4	de Bolivia.
5	Tú	5	chilen-.
6	Pancho y yo	6	peruan-.

estar
ser

Ejercicio 20   [r], [rr], and the Allophones of /d/ and /b/

In the following sentences, circle the numbered instances of [r] and of the stop sounds: underline the numbered instances of [rr] and of the fricative sounds.

```
1          2         3    4                    5
D o n a l d o   R o d r í g u e z   t r a b a j a   e n
6       7       8                  9          10
B o l i v i a.   V o y   a l l í   u n   b u e n   d í a   c o n
       11              12   13                          14
M a r í a   H e r r e r a.   Y o   t e n g o   u n a   r e g l a
15                          16                 17
b u e n a   y   u n   c u a d e r n o   g r a n d e.
```

Ejercicio 21   Vocabulary Matching

Number a column from 1 to 10. After each number write the letter that corresponds to the translation of each Spanish word.

1	espera	(a)	*day before yesterday*
2	noche	(b)	*book*
3	lápiz	(c)	*today*
4	silla	(d)	*with*
5	hoy	(e)	*wait*
6	viernes	(f)	*needs*
7	semana	(g)	*Friday*
8	necesita	(h)	*night*
9	con	(i)	*pencil*
10	anteayer	(j)	*Thursday*
		(k)	*chair*
		(l)	*week*

Ejercicio 22   [s] and [k]:   Reading Aloud

pico	casa	lección	zanco	zanja	luces
tico	caza	que	acción	ceja	cinco
choque	cola	kimono	quema	celda	catorce
zorro	corra	café	coche	ciclo	lápices
zafo		kilo	queda	cigarro	pez
				zinc	

Ejercicio 23   [g] and [j]:   Reading Aloud

gafo	gajes	gente	giras	gitano	giga
gelatina	gigote	giba	goce	gordo	Gil
gleba	globo	glosa	grapa	gratis	gusano
graba	grado	guija	coge	lago	agosto
tragamos	guerra	garaje	gancho	cogimos	gas

Ejercicio 24   [j] and [g]:   Reading Aloud

lugar	gaucho	imagen	Regina	vigilante	gigante
mujer	página	lenguaje	diálogo	graduación	Guadalajara
iglesia	ejercicio	anglosajón	magnífico	Ginebra	pregunta
tigres	gracias	alguien	virgen	Juan José	agosto
elegante	guerrilla	garaje	gaucho	guardacostas	gasolina

Ejercicio 25   [y] and [ñ]:   Reading Aloud

calla	hiena	ya	hierba	hay	doña	joya
valle	llena	yeso	yerba	rey	soñar	llover
allí	hiante	yuca	hierro	muy	uña	hielo
pollo	llanta	yodo	yerro	hoy	señal	guayaba

Ejercicio 26   Cognates: Reading Aloud

ma-**má**	ca-**nal**	**pam**-pa	na-**tal**	ma-**ní**-a	San-ta **Fe**
gas	he-mis-**fe**-rio	pa-**pa**-ya	fi-**nal**	Ma-**ni**-la	Ma-**drid**
ba-**na**-na	pa-**pá**	**at**-las	Ma-**til**-de	**mi**-ca	a-**pa**-che
con-ti-**nen**-te	al-**pa**-ca	**San**-ta	**Chi**-na	ti-**tán**	**ba**-se
al-**fal**-fa	Pa-na-**má**	fa-**tal**	chic	la-**tín**	ar-ma-**di**-llo

Ejercicio 27   General Review: Reading Aloud

1 Creo que alguien está a la puerta de la casa.
2 Todos los veranos vamos a la playa por la mañana.
3 Venimos de Santiago de Chile y vamos a una ciudad de Alaska.
4 Los pobres niños tienen sed y están muy cansados.
5 Aquí en las montañas hace mucho calor en el mes de julio.
6 Mamá dice que el vicepresidente del club tiene un problema mental.
7 Yo creo que cuando hace fresco estudio más fácilmente.
8 Hoy es jueves, el treinta y uno del mes de octubre.
9 Hoy es un día magnífico y vamos al parque nacional.
10 La última estación del año es el invierno; viene después del otoño.
11 El tigre de las Américas es el jaguar o puma.
12 Lima no es una ciudad muy grande, pero es bastante vieja.

Ejercicio 28 Cognates: Reading Aloud

del-ta	so-**fá**	**so**-lo	do-mi-**nó**	ko-**dak**
den-**tal**	ho-**tel**	**al**-to	ca-**si**-no	ki-**ló**-me-tro
sen-ti-men-**tal**	ki-**mo**-no	so-**na**-ta	**pin**-to	lo-**cal**
man-do-**li**-na	re-pu-bli-**ca**-no	**pe**-so	**si**-lo	al-co-**hol**
ha-lo	ca-li-**có**	to-**tal**	**co**-ma	cho-co-**la**-te
di-**plo**-ma	con-ti-nen-**tal**	pos-**tal**	pro-fe-**sión**	con-**trol**

Ejercicio 29 Cognates: Reading Aloud

fun-da-men-**tal**	ca-**fé**	**tan**-que	Don Qui-**jo**-te	**jun**-ta	ca-**ñón**
mo-nu-men-**tal**	**Con**-go	**di**-que	an-ge-li-**cal**	**án**-gel	me-**lón**
sul-**tán**	bi-fo-**cal**	qui-**ni**-na	**Gé**-ne-sis	Jor-**dán**	co-rres-pon-**der**
hos-pi-**tal**	**che**-que	**ki**-lo	Jo-**sé**	**Mé**-ji-co	di-vi-**dir**
me-**nú**	mos-**qui**-to	**San**-cho	Je-**sús**	gen-**ti**-les	Es-**pa**-ña

Ejercicio 30 *Ser* versus *estar*

This exercise covers all uses of *ser* and *estar* learned so far. Write the correct form of the verb plus the cue for choosing it. Select your cue from the following:

a) origin
b) equation
c) location
d) health
e) telling time
f) adjective of nationality

1 ¿Dónde . . . el papel?
2 Francisco y Gloria . . . de Paraguay.
3 Entonces ellos . . . paraguayos, ¿verdad?
4 Sí, pero ahora ellos . . . en Panamá.
5 Yo . . . muy bien, gracias.
6 Este . . . un lápiz muy bueno.
7 ¿Qué hora . . . ?
8 . . . exactamente las tres y cuarto.
9 Yo . . . de Perú.
10 ¿De dónde . . . tú?
11 Yo tengo que . . . en la universidad mañana a las siete.
12 Nosotros . . . argentinos, de la capital.

Ejercicio 31 Cognates: Reading Aloud

an-ces-**tral**	prin-ci-**pal**	for-**mal**	ho-ri-zon-**tal**	pa-ra-**sol**
á-re-a	cri-mi-**nal**	**fór**-mu-la	mor-**tal**	plu-**ral**
crá-ter	cul-tu-**ral**	**hé**-ro-es	o-**ral**	ser-**món**
flo-**ti**-lla	chin-**chi**-lla	Za-**pa**-ta	fez	zinc
mo-**der**-no	**lla**-ma	Zu-**lú**	cris-**tal**	mo-**ral**
mi-**llón**	Sal-**ti**-llo	zig-**zag**	dis-**tan**-cia	co-**ral**

Ejercicio 32 *Ser* and *estar* with Predicate Adjectives

A/B

HACE FRÍO

EL AGUA ES FRÍA

C/D

SU CAFÉ PRONTO ESTÁ FRÍO

HACE CALOR

E/F

ESTA AGUA ES CALIENTE

ESTA AGUA ESTÁ CALIENTE

Ejercicio 33 *Ir* versus *venir*

Choose between the two forms in parentheses.
1   Mañana después de clase mis amigos y yo (venimos, vamos) a las montañas.
2   Yo creo que ellos (vienen, van) aquí a las dos y cuarto.
3   Cuando alguien me llama y yo estoy ocupado contesto: —(Vengo, Voy) en un momentito.

4 El presidente de México (viene, va) aquí a nuestro país en mayo.

5 A la puerta del cine yo le pregunto a Susana: —¿Deseas (venir, ir) a este cine otra vez el domingo por la noche?

6 Dos estudiantes hablan en una playa. Uno de ellos dice: —Cuando hace mucho calor, mis amigos y yo siempre (vamos, venimos) a esta playa.

7 Dos compañeros de clase hablan por teléfono. Uno de ellos pregunta: —¿No deseas (venir, ir) aquí a mi casa a estudiar conmigo? El otro contesta: —Sí, (voy, vengo) en una hora.

Ejercicio 34   Reading Aloud

See if you can sound like a native as you read this dialog with a classmate.

Nombres y apellidos

Lola: Tomás, la secretaria del director quiere saber cuál es tu apellido.

Tomás: Mi apellido es Martínez Sarmiento.

Lola: ¿Cómo? ¿Son necesarios dos apellidos?

Tomás: Sí, es la costumbre (*custom*) de mi país. Martínez por parte de padre (*on my father's side*) y Sarmiento por parte de madre.

Lola: Entonces tu nombre completo es Tomás Martínez Sarmiento, ¿verdad?

Tomás: No, Lola, es Tomás Juan Martínez Sarmiento.

Lola: ¡Caramba! ¡Qué largo (*long*) y complicado es tu nombre!

Tomás: Largo, sí; complicado, no. Es muy fácil.

Lola: Explícamelo (*Explain it to me*), por favor.

Tomás: Tomás es por mi tío, el hermano de mi papá.

Lola: ¿Y por qué Juan? ¿Por tu abuelo?

Tomás: No, chica. Juan es por mi santo.

Lola: ¡Tu santo! No comprendo (*understand*).

Tomás: En el calendario el 24 de junio es el día de San Juan.

Lola: ¿Y qué tiene que ver eso (*what does that have to do*) con tu nombre?

Tomás: Eso es muy importante: Yo nací (*was born*) el 24 de junio, día de San Juan. Por eso me llamo Juan.

Lola: Ya comprendo. Te llamas Tomás, por tu tío; Juan, por el santo del día; y . . .

Tomás: ¡Exacto! Martínez es el apellido de la familia de mi papá y Sarmiento el de la familia de mi mamá.

Lola: ¡Tomás Juan Martínez Sarmiento! ¡Dios mío! (*Good heavens!*) ¿Cómo le explico todo esto a la secretaria?

Tomás: No hay problema. Ustedes pueden usar solamente Tomás Martínez. El nombre completo es para los documentos principalmente.

Ejercicio 35   *Ir* versus *venir*

Choose between the two verbs in parentheses.

1 En la clase de español una alumna le dice a la profesora: —Mi compañera de cuarto quiere (venir, ir) a visitar esta clase mañana.

2 El decano (*dean*) le dice a su secretaria: —Teresa, cancele todos mis planes para mañana. Tengo que (ir, venir) a una reunión muy importante fuera de la ciudad.

3 Juana y Luisa están en casa de Margarita. Margarita dice: —El domingo voy a tener una fiesta aquí. ¿(Van, Vienen) ustedes a mi fiesta? Juana dice: —Sí, cómo no. Yo pienso (venir, ir). Luisa responde que el domingo ella tiene que (ir, venir) a casa de su familia.

4 Es viernes. Luisa y Roberto están en la universidad. Luisa pregunta: —Roberto, (vas, vienes) a la fiesta en casa de Margarita el domingo?
Roberto contesta: Sí, (voy, vengo), ¿y tú?

5 Alguien llama a la puerta. La señora Alarcón contesta: —¡(Voy, Vengo)!

6 Víctor le dice a su compañero de cuarto: —Aquí en el dormitorio es muy difícil estudiar. ¿Por qué no (vamos, venimos) a la biblioteca (*library*)?

7 Usted está en casa. Por teléfono un compañero de clase le pregunta: —¿Vienes a la universidad mañana?
Usted responde: —No, mañana no (voy, vengo).

Ejercicio 36   Cognates: Reading Aloud

doc-**tor**	co-**lor**	re-du-**ci**-ble	re-**al**	ca-pi-**tán**	es-**ti**-lo
hu-**mor**	**tu**-na	te-**rror**	pla-**ne**-ta	ru-**mor**	prin-**ce**-sa
po-**lar**	pro-**du**-ce	po-pu-**lar**	**pu**-ma	re-flec-**tor**	rec-**tor**
mo-**tor**	tu-**tor**	ho-**rror**	**rum**-ba	**mú**-si-ca	

Ejercicio 37   *Ser* versus *estar*

Choose between the two verbs in parentheses, and be ready to explain the reason for your choice.

1 Pancho y Enrique (están, son) en las montañas.
2 La pobre Elena (está, es) muy cansada de trabajar.
3 Pancho (está, es) de Caracas; (está, es) venezolano, pero ahora (está, es) en España.
4 ¿Cuántos (están, son) diez y tres?
5 María dice que (está, es) bien hoy.
6 Yo quiero (estar, ser) en las montañas para las vacaciones.
7 ¡Caray! Ya (es, está) la una y media.
8 Yo quiero (estar, ser) profesor de español.
9 Este (es, está) mi hermano José. El (es, está) en primer año.
10 ¡Caray! La alumna gorda de nuestra clase de inglés ahora (es, está) muy flaca. Yo creo que ella (es, está) enferma.

Ejercicio 38   Cognates: Reading Aloud

Ben-ja-**mín**	va-**por**	**vi**-rus	Ba-**bel**	glo-**bal**
am-bu-**lan**-te	ma-**rim**-ba	vul-**gar**	ha-bi-**ta**-ble	i-ma-gi-**na**-ble
ver-ti-**cal**	in-ven-**tor**	ab-**do**-men	ho-no-**ra**-ble	com-bus-**ti**-ble

de-tes-**ta**-ble	i-ne-vi-**ta**-ble	u-ni-ver-**sal**	li-be-**ral**	au-to-**mó**-vil
sa-**li**-va	se-pa-**ra**-ble	na-**val**	pro-**ba**-ble	**lar**-va
ri-**val**	in-vi-**si**-ble	mi-se-**ra**-ble	vi-ce **ver**-sa	ob-ser-**va**-ble

Ejercicio 39   Cognates: Reading Aloud

propaganda	hindú	indisputable	indispensable	occidental
agenda	don	cóndor	góndola	melodrama
indivisible	abdomen	drama	adobe	idea
candor	tilde	fundamental	radical	pedestal
torpedo	incidental	guerrilla	permanente	organizable
armadillo	ideal	matador	mortal	liberal
cardinal	accidental	medicinal	Congo	magnate
Júpiter	jade	pagoda	cargo	regular

Ejercicio 40   Reading Aloud

Estudios de verano

1   Es el mes de julio y hace un calor terrible en toda la ciudad.

2   Son más o menos las tres de la tarde y es sábado.

3   Roberto y Miguel, dos estudiantes universitarios, estudian sus lecciones en el patio de la casa de apartamentos donde viven.

4   En su apartamento no hay aire acondicionado y ellos salen a estudiar afuera.

5   Roberto y Miguel van a empezar el cuarto año de su carrera universitaria en septiembre.

6   Están en la escuela de verano porque saben que no van a poder completar los requisitos de graduación durante el año académico.

7   Los dos jóvenes tienen mucho interés en graduarse lo más pronto posible y empezar a trabajar.

8   Están cansados de estudiar y además ellos no tienen suficiente dinero para volver a la universidad un año más.

9   El lugar donde viven los dos estudiantes está bastante lejos de la universidad.

10   Ellos no tienen carro, pero en realidad no lo necesitan.

11   Roberto tiene una motocicleta magnífica y su amigo Miguel va a sus clases en bicicleta.

12   Cuando quieren llegar más rápido a la universidad, los dos amigos van en la moto.

13   Cuando hace mal tiempo, una vecina muy amable que vive en el apartamento número seis los lleva en su auto hasta la universidad.

14   Miguel tiene que estar en la universidad muy temprano porque su primera clase es a las siete de la mañana.

15   Roberto generalmente va más tarde porque su primera clase no empieza hasta las nueve y media.

16   Miguel estudia historia y literatura; todos los días tiene que leer muchas páginas en sus libros de texto.

17 Roberto también estudia dos cursos, uno de matemáticas y otro (*another*) de física; todos los días tiene que resolver problemas difíciles.

18 A las doce más o menos los dos jóvenes comen algo en una cafetería y vuelven a su apartamento a preparar sus lecciones para el día siguiente.

19 Miguel y Roberto son estudiosos y aplicados, pero los cursos de verano son demasiado concentrados y requieren muchas horas de estudio.

20 Cuando ellos están muy cansados, ellos piensan en las dos semanas de vacaciones que van a tener en agosto.

21 Van a ser unas vacaciones muy cortas (*short*) y todavía no saben si van a ir a las montañas o a la playa.

22 No van a tener mucho tiempo porque el semestre de otoño empieza en los primeros días de septiembre.

23 Roberto y Miguel piensan estudiar mucho durante su último año en la universidad.

24 Necesitan acumular treinta créditos más para graduarse y no quieren estudiar más durante el verano.

Ejercicio 41   Family Vocabulary: Reading Comprehension

Write the missing word. The first sentence gives the clue.

Ejemplo: Juan es el hijo de mi padre. Juan es mi . . . (hermano)

1 María es la hija de mi tía. Es mi . . .

2 Mi padre tiene dos hijos; mi . . . José y yo.

3 Mis abuelos tienen, además de mi padre, siete hijas. Por eso, yo tengo siete . . .

4 Mi hermana tiene una hija, María Luisa. Es mi . . .

5 Juan Ramón Sánchez es el hermano de mi mamá. Es mi . . .

6 La madre de mi padre es mi . . .

7 ¿Qué soy yo? Yo soy . . . de mis padres.

8 Cada persona tiene dos padres y cuatro . . .

Ejercicio 42   *Ir* versus *venir*

Choose between the two verbs in parentheses.

1 El director le dice al profesor Molina, —Señor Molina, (venga, vaya) usted aquí inmediatamente.

2 El señor Molina responde, —(Vengo, Voy) inmediatamente.

3 Hablo con un amigo en la clase, —¿Sabes, Pancho, que Juan y yo (venimos, vamos) al cine esta noche después de estudiar?

4 Pancho responde, —¡Qué bueno! ¿Me permiten ustedes (venir, ir) también?

5 María y yo hablamos por teléfono. Ella está en casa y quiere invitarme a una fiesta allí el sábado. Dice, —¿Quieres (venir, ir) a una fiesta aquí el sábado?

6 Yo le contesto, —Sí, quiero (venir, ir), pero no puedo porque mis padres, (vienen, van) aquí para pasar dos días de vacaciones conmigo.

Ejercicio 43   Cognates: Reading Aloud

Norma	Nina	propaganda	musical	confeti
álbum	famoso	angora	Mesa Verde	poncho
económico	federal	angular	San Francisco	final
sentimental	experimental	taxi	Jamaica	extra
solo	explicable	máximum	audible	cigarrillo
sultán	exportable	inflexible	plausible	aire

Ejercicio 44   Translations of "To Be"

HACE FRÍO

A/B

ESTA AGUA ESTÁ CALIENTE

C

HAY UN ELEFANTE EN EL JARDÍN

Ejercicio 45   Possessive Adjectives

Complete the following sentences. The subject of the sentence is the possessor.

Ejemplo: Ella tiene . . . libro. (The answer is *su*.)

1 Yo tengo . . . lecciones.
2 Nosotros trabajamos con . . . sobrinas.
3 María está aquí con . . . abuelos.
4 María y yo tenemos . . . plumas nuevas.
5 Tú vas al cine esta noche con . . . hermana, ¿verdad?

6 Ustedes deben tener . . . libros también.

7 Yo voy allí con . . . tío.

8 José tiene que hablar con . . . hermanos.

9 Pablo y yo tenemos que trabajar con . . . prima.

10 Tú vas a hablar con . . . profesor, ¿verdad?

Ejercicio 46 *Ir* versus *venir*

Choose between the two verbs in parentheses.

1 En la residencia de estudiantes Héctor y su compañero de cuarto hablan de (ir, venir) a su casa para las vacaciones.

2 En la casa de Hugo, su madre le dice a una amiga: —Mi hijo (va, viene) el viernes a pasar aquí las vacaciones.

3 Yo tengo que (venir, ir) al banco esta tarde. ¿Quieres acompañarme?

4 Pepe y Carlos viven en las montañas. Cuando me escriben, ellos siempre me preguntan: —¿Cuándo (vienes, vas) aquí a pasar unos días con nosotros? Yo siempre les contesto que no puedo (venir, ir) allí hasta los días de vacaciones.

5 Jorge llama por teléfono a una amiga que vive lejos de la universidad y le dice: —El viernes (vengo, voy) a verte. La amiga le contesta: —¿No puedes (venir, ir) el sábado? El viernes no voy a estar aquí.

6 Ellos nunca (vienen, van) a visitarme aquí en Chicago. Está demasiado lejos de donde ellos viven.

Ejercicio 47 Silent Reading and Response

Tampa: ciudad americana y española

La ciudad norteamericana de Tampa es un centro comercial muy importante en el estado de la Florida. Está situada en la costa oeste de la península. Turistas de todos los estados de la Unión van a Tampa porque allí hace muy buen tiempo en todas las estaciones del año. La región tiene un clima ideal, ni° mucho calor, ni° mucho frío. *neither / nor*

Tampa es un puerto de mar muy importante. Allí hay mucho movimiento de barcos que van y vienen del Canal de Panamá y también de otros puertos del mundo°. La bahía° de Tampa tiene mucha importancia en la historia del Golfo de México. *world/bay*

En los siglos° XVI (dieciséis) y XVII (diecisiete) la bahía de Tampa fue un lugar favorito para los piratas de muchas naciones. Uno de estos piratas famosos de la historia es el capitán español José Gasparilla. En su honor, todos los años en el mes de febrero, la ciudad celebra una gran fiesta que se llama el carnaval de Gasparilla. *centuries*

Estamos en el siglo veinte, pero Tampa no olvida° los primeros años de su interesante historia, los días románticos de las visitas de los piratas a la ciudad. Hay otras ciudades en los Estados Unidos que conservan la tradición española del pasado. Por ejemplo°, la conservan en Santa Fe, Nuevo México, en Santa Bárbara, California, y en varias más. En todas estas ciudades hoy día° viven muchas personas y familias enteras que hablan español. *does not forget / for example / nowadays*

Ejercicio 48 Cognates: Reading Aloud

feudal	demanda	cuota	sugestión	materia
neutral	gradual	acumular	gramatical	suposición
bestial	radio	suficiente	anual	continental
trío	tuberculosis	variable	usual	
televisión	salmón	superior	universal	
violín	superficial	tornado	repórter	

Ejercicio 49 Paired Words

Match the following words.

1	subir		(a)	*nunca*
2	morir		(b)	*hombre*
3	gato		(c)	*noche*
4	caliente		(d)	*bajar*
5	día		(e)	*frío*
6	mujer		(f)	*perro*
7	amigo		(g)	*descansado*
8	mentira		(h)	*nada*
9	siempre		(i)	*vivir*
10	algo		(j)	*alguien*
			(k)	*verdad*
			(l)	*enemigo*

Ejercicio 50 Translations of "To Be": *haber, hacer, estar, tener, ser*

First decide which of these five verbs should be used to fill the blank, then select the correct form of the verb you choose and write it.

Ejemplo: Los gauchos . . . en Nueva York, pero . . . de Argentina. (están, son)

1 ¡Caray, hombre! . . . mucho calor esta mañana.
2 Pancho . . . de Ecuador, y ahora . . . en la ciudad de Quito.
3 ¿Qué hora . . . ? . . . las cinco y media.
4 Elena dice que . . . mucha hambre.
5 ¿Cuántos lápices . . . en la mesa?
6 Juan . . . muy enfermo hoy.
7 Hoy en el desierto . . . mal tiempo y todo . . . muy húmedo.
8 Dos y cuatro . . . seis.
9 Esa muchacha nueva que se llama Lola . . . muy bonita.
10 . . . un alumno nuevo en la escuela hoy.

Ejercicio 51   Adjectival Agreement

Complete the sentences with the correct form of the adjective indicated in the model.

Ejemplo: *La mujer está* **contenta**. *Pancho está* . . . (*contento*)

1   Paco es muy *tonto*. Lola es muy . . .
2   Mi padre es *joven*. Mis abuelos son . . .
3   Este es *el nuevo* alumno. Estas son . . . alumnas.
4   Los muchachos son *felices*. Yo soy . . .
5   Yo estoy *cansado*. Ellos están . . .
6   *Mi* primo está *alegre*. . . . primas están . . .
7   *Todas las* señoritas son *venezolanas*. . . . señores son . . .
8   Ella es *una* chica muy *gorda*. Él es . . . chico muy . . .

Ejercicio 52   Possessive Adjectives

Complete the following sentences. The subject of the sentence is the possessor.

1   Las señoritas van al cine con . . . amigas.
2   Yo estudio en casa con . . . hermano Horacio.
3   Pancho trabaja en la mina con . . . padre.
4   Nosotros tenemos que hablar con . . . profesores.
5   Tú debes ir a la fiesta también con . . . sobrinas.
6   El profesor de inglés habla con . . . alumnos.
7   Ella y yo vamos a estudiar con . . . amigas, Carmen y Sara.
8   Yo necesito ir a la tienda con . . . primos.
9   El tigre no sale de . . . corral.

Ejercicio 53   *Ir* versus *venir*

Choose between the two verbs in parentheses.

1   Creo que ellos nunca (vienen, van) aquí a Santa Mónica porque está muy lejos de donde ellos viven.
2   Carmen, ¿por qué no (vienes, vas) a comer aquí conmigo esta tarde?
3   Si mañana hace buen tiempo, pensamos (venir, ir) a la playa. Tenemos unos amigos que tienen una casa muy buena allí.
4   Estamos muy cansados de trabajar. Necesitamos (ir, venir) dos o tres días a las montañas.
5   La secretaria del dentista llama a un paciente y dice: —¿Cuándo puede Vd. (venir, ir) a la oficina a ver al doctor?
6   Oye, ¿quieres acompañarme? Tengo que (venir, ir) un momento al correo.
7   Yo no puedo (ir, venir) con mi amiga al cine esta noche porque tengo mucho que estudiar.
8   Fernando habla por teléfono con su familia y dice: —¡Una operación de emergencia! Bueno, (vengo, voy) inmediatamente.

Ejercicio 54   The Done-to *a*

Write *a* only for the blanks that need it.

1 Pepe, ¿conoces . . . la muchacha nueva?
2 Nosotros conocemos . . . esa novela de Hemingway muy bien.
3 ¿Por qué miran ellos . . . las montañas a esta hora todos los días?
4 Yo no voy a contestar . . . la carta (*letter*).
5 Yo no quiero mirar . . . Rosa porque es muy tímida.
6 ¿Ven Vds. . . . los barcos en la distancia?
7 Creemos que ellos hacen . . . el trabajo bastante bien.
8 ¿Van a invitar . . . los argentinos también?

Ejercicio 55   Reading Comprehension

Choose the letter corresponding to the most logical completion of each sentence.

1 Aquí en Estados Unidos el día de la Independencia es . . .
  a el catorce de febrero.
  b el veintidós de febrero.
  c el primero de abril.
  d el cuatro de julio.

2 La unidad de tiempo que consiste de doce meses es . . .
  a el año.
  b el semestre.
  c el mes.
  d el año académico.

3 El mes que tiene treinta y un días, es un mes de primavera y es también el tercer mes del año, es . . .
  a marzo.
  b julio.
  c agosto.
  d noviembre.

4 Mi hermano tiene un hijo que se llama Juanito y una hija, Lolita. El niño tiene tres años y la niña tiene siete meses. Juanito y Lolita son mis . . .
  a sobrinos.
  b abuelos.
  c hermanos.
  d tíos.

5 Si la madre se llama Gertrudis Montes y el nombre del padre es Eugenio Iglesias, el apellido completo de sus hijos es . . .
  a Eugenio Gertrudis.
  b Montes y nada más.
  c Iglesias Montes.
  d Montes, si son mujeres; Eugenio, si son hombres.

Choose the letter corresponding to the most logical reaction to each of the following:

6 En los países que están al sur del ecuador, hace mucho frío en el mes de julio.
   a Porque allí hay muchos gatos y perros.
   b Porque allí las estaciones del año no corresponden a nuestras estaciones.
   c Porque la gente no quiere tener calor.
   d Porque allí nunca hay verano.

7 Mi amigo insiste que las Guayanas están en el norte de México.
   a La verdad es que están en África.
   b Él no tiene razón.
   c El mapa indica que son montañas.
   d Mi amigo tiene cuidado.

8 ¿Sabes cuál es la fecha de hoy?
   a Si voy afuera, pronto voy a saberlo.
   b Sí, y a esta hora siempre tengo sueño.
   c El cuatro de julio es una fecha histórica.
   d No sé, pero en mi mesa hay un calendario.

9 Es sábado y hace un calor terrible.
   a Sí, estamos en medio del invierno.
   b ¿Por qué no vamos a la playa?
   c Vamos donde hace más calor.
   d Sí, hasta el gato tiene frío.

10 Mi hermano dice que los elefantes comen a los niños chiquitos.
   a Los elefantes viven en el mar Caribe.
   b Lo dice en broma.
   c En África no hay elefantes.
   d En el jardín hay muchas flores.

Ejercicio 56   Adjectival Residuals

Rewrite the second sentence, omitting the noun.

Ejemplo: Yo veo la iglesia. Pancho también ve la iglesia. (Pancho también la ve.)

1 Este es el libro. Pero no puedo leer el libro.
2 Aquí está la tiza. Pongo la tiza allí.
3 ¿Tienes los diálogos? Quiero leer los diálogos.
4 Roberto tiene el regalo. Voy a ver el regalo mañana.
5 Yo no tengo la hora. Él tiene la hora.
6 Esta es la pluma de que hablas. Él necesita la pluma.
7 ¿Quién tiene las invitaciones? Sara tiene las invitaciones.
8 Aquí está el ejercicio. Debo escribir el ejercicio.
9 ¿Cuáles son las lecciones? Ellos saben las lecciones.

Ejercicio 57   Guided Conversation

Following the English outline, perform this dialog in Spanish with a partner. Go through it twice, reversing roles.

1   You meet a friend on the campus in the morning hours and exchange greetings.
2   You ask your friend how his sister is.
3   He answers that she is not too well.
4   You ask him if he is going to Spanish class now.
5   He answers no, that it is Thursday and there is no Spanish class.
6   You answer that he is right, that there isn't. You ask where he is going.
7   He answers that he is going to the store, and in the afternoon (*por la tarde*) he is going to the country.
8   You ask him if he is going to visit relatives (*parientes*).
9   He says no, that he has a friend that lives in the country.
10   You excuse yourself and say that you have to go to work.
11   You both say good-by until Monday (*hasta el lunes*).

Ejercicio 58   Stem-Changing Verbs

Write the combinations that your instructor will give you.

Ejemplo: 112 = Yo duermo demasiado.

1	Yo			1	mucho.
2	Tú y yo	1	dormir (ue)	2	demasiado.
3	Tú	2	servir (i)	3	a las seis.
4	Él	3	empezar (ie)	4	por la noche.
5	Ellos				

Ejercicio 59   The Done-to *a*

Decide whether or not the done-to *a* is needed in the blank.

1   Nosotros tenemos . . . un cuaderno y . . . seis libros.
2   Pronto vas a olvidar . . . las dos señoritas.
3   ¿Quién puede recordar . . . el nombre del libro?
4   Vamos a mirar . . . la televisión esta noche, porque podemos ver . . . la famosa actriz Dolores del Río.
5   ¿Conoce usted . . . la señorita Álvarez?
6   Yo conozco . . . este lugar muy bien.
7   Tenemos que invitar . . . Maruja.
8   Yo miraba . . . los nuevos lápices.

Ejercicio 60   Silent Reading and Response

Your instructor will give you the necessary instructions.

Un poco de geografía

1 Un continente es una gran extensión de tierra rodeada de mar.
2 Una isla también es una porción de tierra rodeada de agua por todas partes.
3 En el caso de una península, la tierra está rodeada de agua excepto en una parte.
4 La diferencia fundamental entre isla y continente es de tamaño (*size*).
5 Las islas siempre son mucho más pequeñas.
6 Hay siete grandes continentes en nuestro globo.
7 Sus nombres son los siguientes: África, América del Norte, América del Sur, Antártica, Asia, Australia y Europa.

Un problema de vocabulario

1 Para los habitantes que ocupan el territorio que está al norte del Río Grande, la palabra "América" significa comúnmente "Estados Unidos", y "americano" es el adjetivo de nacionalidad que ellos usan generalmente para identificar a las nativas de los 50 estados de la Unión.
2 Este es un concepto o criterio demasiado exclusivista que sorprende y molesta a nuestros vecinos del sur, y ellos no lo aceptan.
3 Los habitantes de los países que están al sur del Río Grande consideran que ellos también viven en "América" y son "americanos."
4 Este problema de vocabulario causa confusiones innecesarias que debemos eliminar.
5 Desde el punto de vista geográfico, "América" es el nombre del inmenso territorio que se extiende desde Alaska y las regiones árticas hasta Tierra del Fuego.
6 En este enorme territorio que incluye dos continentes y es parte del hemisferio occidental viven millones de personas de diferentes razas, idiomas y culturas, y todos ellos son "americanos."

Ejercicio 61   Cyclic versus Non-cyclic Events

In the following story, decide whether each indicated verb represents a cyclic (C) or a non-cyclic (NC) event.

The Little Old Lady and the Supermarket Crook

(Someone is reporting what happened at the supermarket while waiting to be checked out.)
The man waiting in line ahead of me suddenly *took out* **1** a gun from his pocket. He *pointed* **2** it at Mrs. Jones, the clerk. She got terribly frightened and *shook* **3** like a leaf.

Mr. Smith, the manager, *came* **4** to rescue her. The thief *hit* **5** him on the head with his gun. Mr. Smith *fell* **6** to the floor and *moaned* **7**. Mrs. Jones *opened* **8** the cash register.

I was so scared, I didn't know how to act. A little old lady, however, hiding behind me, *grabbed* **9** a big ripe tomato and *threw* **10** it at the thief with all her might.

It was a direct hit between the eyes and made a big red splash! The crook *fainted* **11**. Everyone *laughed* **12**. Minutes later the police *took* him *away* **13**.

Ejercicio 62 The Done-to *a*

If the done-to *a* is needed, write it; if it is not needed, leave the blank.

1 Debes llamar . . . Elena por teléfono.
2 Tenemos que estudiar . . . estas dos páginas.
3 Yo quiero conocer bien . . . esta ciudad; voy a vivir aquí.
4 Observábamos . . . los cuatro muchachos en el parque.
5 Vamos a buscar . . . la nueva alumna.
6 Puedo olvidar . . . la escuela, pero nunca puedo olvidar . . . los alumnos.
7 Ellos siempre sirven . . . las señoritas primero.
8 Paco y Roberto miraban . . . la casa pero no veían . . . María.

Ejercicio 63 Discrimination of Events and Aspects

Write C or NC for cyclic or non-cyclic, and B, M, or E for beginning, middle, or end.

Has This Ever Happened to You?

(Larry, one of your classmates, is explaining why he was late for class this morning.)

Before going to bed last night, I *set* **1** the alarm. At 7:00 this morning, it *rang* **2** all right, but I *turned* it *off* **3**! I *was* so *tired* **4** that I *fell asleep* **5** again. Suddenly I *felt* **6** the sun shining on my eyes. I *jumped out* **7** of bed and *rushed* **8** as much as I could. It was 8:25 already! As I *ran* **9** on my way to class, I *remembered* **10** that I had left my books in my room, and I had to go back for them. As I *entered* **11** the classroom, I saw that the students *were taking* **12** a test.

Ejercicio 64 Forms of the Imperfect

Write the imperfect form of all the indicated verbs.

1 Vd. *quiere* estar allí mañana.
2 Todos los alumnos *empiezan* la lección.
3 No *es* posible hacerlo.
4 ¿Qué *buscas*?

5 Ella siempre *pide* un favor.
6 Este pájaro ya no *vuela*.
7 ¿Qué *piensan* hacer?
8 Pizarro *conoce* bien a Atahualpa.
9 *Trabajamos* mucho todos los días.
10 Tú *sabes* esto, ¿verdad?
11 Nunca *llueve* allí.
12 María *sigue* con sus amigas.

Ejercicio 65 Discrimination of Events and Aspects

Indicate the type of event (cyclic or non-cyclic) by C or NC, and then indicate its aspect (beginning, middle, or end) by B, M, or E.

Christopher Columbus (Part 1)

It is generally believed that Columbus *was born* **1** in Genoa, Italy, around 1451. When they *baptized* **2** him, his parents gave him the name *Cristoforo* after the patron saint of sailors and travelers. Since they *lived* **3** in an important seaport, he had the chance to learn a great deal about boats and the sea. Throughout the entire city in those days there *circulated* **4** fabulous stories about strange lands beyond the sea.

He was poor and his life was hard, so in 1476 he *left* **5** his hometown on a ship bound for England. As they *sailed* **6** off the coast of Portugal, they were attacked by pirates. The boat *sank* **7** and many *drowned* **8**, but Columbus *swam* **9** and *reached* **10** the shore safely.

Years later in Portugal Columbus *married* **11** the daughter of a retired sea captain who had worked for Prince Henry the Navigator. Shortly after giving birth to their only son, Diego, his wife Felipa *died* **12**.

Ejercicio 66 Silent Reading

Go through the following selection at your normal reading speed without stopping to translate into English. As soon as you finish, write the answers of the comprehension exercise that follows the reading. You have a limited time to go through the entire operation.

Una noticia sensacional

Cuando un astronauta de la Tierra pone pie° en la luna, lo sabemos inmediatamente. Hoy día es muy fácil y cómodo recibir° en nuestra casa las noticias° que vienen de todas partes del mundo. Podemos oírlas° por radio, verlas por televisión y leerlas en periódicos° y revistas°. El telégrafo, los superaviones°, los cohetes° y los satélites permiten la comunicación rápida entre los lugares más remotos del universo.

¡Qué diferente era la situación en el siglo quince! En octubre de 1492, Cristóbal Colón y 87 marineros° españoles bajan de sus tres barcos y ponen pie en las playas de una pequeña isla del grupo de las Bahamas. Siguen su viaje°

sets foot
to receive/news
hear
newspapers/maga-
zines/jet planes
rockets

sailors
trip

de una isla a otra y ponen la bandera° de España y una cruz° en las tierras que   flag/cross
hallan. Colón y sus hombres toman posesión de las nuevas tierras en nombre
de su rey° Fernando y de su reina° Isabel. El descubrimiento° de estos territorios   King/Queen/discovery
es, sin duda alguna°, la noticia más sensacional del momento. España y el resto   without any doubt
de Europa, sin embargo, tienen que esperar casi seis meses para recibirla.

    La sensacional noticia del descubrimiento llega a Europa por carta°. El viaje   by letter
de regreso° a España fue muy difícil. Las tormentas y el mal tiempo de invierno   return trip
en el Atlántico obligan a Colón a buscar refugio en Lisboa. Antes de salir de
allí, Colón le da la carta a un mensajero°. Viajando° probablemente en mula,   messenger/Traveling
el mensajero la lleva a Barcelona, en la costa este de España, donde están los
reyes, Fernando e Isabel.

    La carta de Colón cuenta° cosas muy interesantes acerca de los indios, las   tells
plantas, los animales y los minerales de las Indias. Colón creía que las islas de
Cuba y Santo Domingo eran en realidad parte de Japón y de India. Después de
tres viajes más, el 21 de mayo de 1506, Colón muere en España. Muere sin
saber nunca que había descubierto° un mundo nuevo que hoy llamamos   had discovered
América.

Comprehension Exercise: Choose the letter that corresponds to the best completion of each statement.

1 Hoy día podemos ver las noticias en nuestra casa porque tenemos . . .
    a teléfono.   **b** telégrafo.   **c** televisión.

2 También podemos leer las noticias en nuestra casa porque tenemos . . .
    a periódicos.   **b** cohetes.   **c** barcos.

3 Los marineros trabajan generalmente en . . .
    a superaviones.   **b** revistas.   **c** barcos.

4 En el siglo quince en Europa no tenían . . .
    a barcos.   **b** radios.   **c** cruces.

5 Los hombres que iban con Colón de isla en isla por las Antillas eran principalmente . . .
    a portugueses.   **b** ingleses.   **c** españoles.

6 La gente de Europa recibe la noticia del descubrimiento de Colón . . .
    a inmediatamente.   **b** después de seis meses.
           c después de seis años.

7 La noticia del descubrimiento de América va a Europa por . . .
    a carta.   **b** radio.   **c** televisión.

8 Colón creía que Cuba y Santo Domingo eran parte de . . .
    a África.   **b** un mundo nuevo.   **c** India y Japón.

9 Colón murió en España . . .
    a el 12 de octubre de 1492.   **b** el 14 de marzo de 1496.
           c el 21 de mayo de 1506.

Ejercicio 67   Silent Reading

Read again the selection in Ejercicio 66 and write the answers to the following multiple choice problems.

1 ¿De dónde vienen las noticias que recibimos en nuestras casas?
   a Vienen de los barcos de Colón.
   b Vienen de todas partes del mundo.
   c Vienen de una isla en las Bahamas.

2 ¿Por qué es fácil hoy día oír, ver y leer las noticias en la casa?
   a Porque vivimos en un planeta.
   b Porque tenemos radio, televisión y periódico.
   c Porque estamos en el siglo diecinueve.

3 ¿Dónde está la primera isla que descubrió Colón?
   a En el océano Pacífico.
   b En el mar Mediterráneo.
   c En el grupo de las Bahamas.

4 ¿Qué bandera ponía Colón en las tierras que descubría?
   a Ponía la bandera española.
   b Ponía la bandera italiana.
   c Ponía la bandera americana.

5 ¿Cuál fue la noticia más sensacional del siglo quince?
   a Fue el descubrimiento de la luna.
   b Fue el descubrimiento del telégrafo.
   c Fue el descubrimiento de América.

6 ¿Cómo fue el viaje de regreso a España?
   a Fue magnífico.
   b Fue cómodo.
   c Fue terrible.

7 ¿Qué animales usaban en España en el siglo quince para viajar de un lugar a otro?
   a Usaban elefantes.
   b Usaban mulas y burros.
   c Usaban tigres.

8 ¿Cuántos viajes en total hizo (*made*) Colón al Nuevo Mundo?
   a Hizo cuatro viajes.
   b Hizo tres viajes.
   c Hizo solamente un viaje.

Ejercicio 68   Discrimination of Events and Aspects

First, categorize the event as cyclic or non-cyclic (C or NC) and then indicate its aspect (B, M, or E).

Christopher Columbus (Part 3)

Upon his arrival in Court, Colón *discussed* **1** his expedition with King Ferdinand and Queen Isabella of Spain. They *were fighting* **2** against the Moors at this time. The Queen in particular *wanted* **3** to help him, but the war *was costing* **4** them a great deal of money.

   The Moors finally *surrendered* **5** in Granada, on January 2, 1492. Colón *returned* **6** to the royal castle, but this time his plan was turned down by the court experts. In despair, as he *rode* **7** away from Granada on a mule, perhaps on his way to France, a messenger from the Queen *stopped* **8** him on a bridge. Her Majesty had changed her mind and *was ready* **9** to sell her jewels in order to raise money for the voyage.

Colón *got* **10** his money, about $14,000, and the Queen's jewels did not have to be sold. The agreement papers *were signed* **11** and *sealed* **12** in April. On Friday, August 3, 1492, at 8:00 A.M., Cristóbal Colón and 87 reluctant men *sailed* **13** in three ships from Palos into history.

Ejercicio 69   Discrimination of Events and Aspects

Mark each event as NC or C and its aspect as B, M, or E.

My Dog Doesn't Know the Days of the Week

(One of your classmates has a dog named Taco that wakes her up every morning in time to go to class. She is reporting to you what Taco did last Saturday morning.)

It was 7:00 in the morning, and I *was* fast *asleep* **1** in my bed. My dog, Taco, *came* **2** into my bedroom and *jumped* **3** on my bed. His loud barking *woke* me *up* **4**. I *glared* **5** at him, and he *got off* **6** the bed. He still *growled* **7** and *barked* **8** at me furiously and wouldn't leave the room. Finally, I *got out* **9** of bed and *chased* **10** him. I *closed* **11** the door and *went back* **12** to my warm bed. As I *lay* **13** there unable to go back to sleep, Taco *whined* **14** outside the door.

I finally *understood* **15** that my poor Taco doesn't know the days of the week.

Ejercicio 70   Numbers and Adjectival Agreement

When necessary, change the adjectives in parentheses to match the nouns.

1 Puedo contar (doscientos veintiuno) estrellas ahora.
2 Tenemos (veintiuno) ríos en (nuestro) estado.
3 Hay muy (poco) niebla hoy.
4 (El) boca de (el) señorita no está (cerrado).
5 (El) maestros (chileno) están cerca del lago.
6 Es (un) mosca muy (bonito).
7 En (su) escuela hay (cuatrocientos cincuenta y uno) alumnos.

Ejercicio 71   Listening and Reading Comprehension

Your instructor will read a question or a statement *twice*. From the three choices given below, you are to select the most appropriate answer or rejoinder by writing the letter that corresponds to it.

1 **a** Es un insecto que corre por las montañas.
   b Es un insecto que vuela.
   c Es un insecto que tiene una boca enorme.

2 a Empiezan generalmente en mayo o junio.
   b Empiezan en el siglo doce.
   c Terminan generalmente en junio.

3 a Un período de tiempo de mil años.
   b Una estación del año muy fría.
   c Un período de tiempo de cien años.

4 a El descubrimiento de los Estados Unidos.
   b La independencia de los Estados Unidos.
   c La independencia de las colonias españolas en América.

5 a Hablaba con un amigo de mi familia.
   b Hablaba en portugués.
   c Hablaba con el descubridor del Océano Pacífico.

6 a Quien busca, halla.
   b ¡Salud!
   c Lo siento mucho.

7 a ¡Qué mal tiempo hace!
   b ¡Qué mala memoria tienes!
   c Sí, cómo no.

8 a Hay mucha niebla. Yo no voy.
   b Es mejor ir cuando está nevando.
   c En el desierto hace mucho calor.

9 a Si quieres, puedes comer algo.
   b En el refrigerador hay agua fría.
   c Aquí tienes el agua caliente.

10 a ¡Caramba! No sabía que tú tenías tanto dinero.
   b ¡Caramba! No sabía que tú conocías a José.
   c ¡Caramba! No sabía que tenías una amiga millonaria.

Ejercicio 72   Preterit versus Imperfect

It is important that you understand what you read well enough to choose correctly between the two verb forms given in parentheses. Remember that the Imperfect is used for middle aspect, and the Preterit is used for beginning and end aspects.

El primer viaje° de Colón (primer párrafo)   trip

En los últimos meses del año 1492, Colón (**1** descubrió, descubría) varias islas pequeñas en la región de las Antillas. En la primera de estas islas, (**2** capturó, capturaba) a varios de los nativos y los (**3** llevó, llevaba) a sus barcos.°   boats Para continuar sus exploraciones él (**4** necesitó, necesitaba) guías°   guides y estos nativos (**5** pudieron, podían) ayudarle mucho. Mientras° Colón (**6** viajó,   While viajaba) de un lugar a otro, los indios que le (**7** acompañaron, acompañaban), le (**8** hablaron, hablaban) constantemente de una tierra grande y rica que estaba al sur. Al°   Whenever hablar de esta tierra la (**9** llamaron, llamaban) siempre Cuba. (**10** Pasaron, Pasaban) dos semanas y en la mañana del domingo, 28 de octubre, Colón y sus acompañantes (**11** desembarcaron, desembarcaban) en la costa norte de Cuba. Inmediatamente el Almirante° (**12** pensó, pensaba) que por fin ya estaba sobre el territorio del continente que él (**13** buscó, buscaba).

Admiral

Ejercicio 73   Discrimination of Events and Aspects

Write C for cyclic, NC for non-cyclic and B, M, or E for aspect.

Babysitter's Nightmare

(A girl in your class is reporting what happened to her a few nights ago on her first babysitting job with the neighbor's 18 month old son.)

When I *wasn't looking* **1**, the baby *picked up* **2** something brown that he *found* **3** on the floor and *swallowed* **4** it. I wasn't sure what it was, but immediately I thought of a pill, and I *worried* **5**.

When the baby's parents *returned* **6**, they didn't want to take any chances, so they *put* **7** him in the car, and we all rushed to the hospital. By the time we *arrived* **8** in the emergency room, I *was scared* **9** to death.

During the examination, however, the baby *seemed* **10** to be all right. The doctor *tickled* **11** him, and he *smiled* **12** happily. I *was crying* **13**.

We found out later that he had swallowed a chocolate covered peanut.

Ejercicio 74   Silent Reading

After reading this selection silently, and trying not to stop to translate into English, do the comprehension exercise in writing.

Las cartas de Colón

Además de sus interesantes diarios de viaje,° sabemos que Colón escribió varias cartas a los reyes de España, a su hermano Bartolomé, a su hijo Diego y a otras personas importantes. Estos documentos históricos están escritos° en español antiguo° y son difíciles de comprender para los alumnos que empiezan a estudiar el idioma. Los párrafos° que siguen son un resumen° en español moderno de las primeras impresiones que recibió Colón de la gente y la naturaleza° del Nuevo Mundo.

"Me parece° que esta gente es muy pobre. Hombres y mujeres andan desnudos.° Tienen cuerpos° hermosos° y muy buenas caras.° Sus ojos son grandes y muy hermosos. Son muy tímidos y creen que venimos del cielo.° Cuando nos ven, tienen miedo° y corren para la selva, porque creen que los vamos a comer. Poco a poco° pierden° el miedo y nos hacemos amigos. Son muy inocentes y muy buenos y amables con nosotros. Vienen a nuestros barcos nadando° o en sus canoas. Nos traen agua, pescado,° papagayos,° algodón° y muchas cosas de comer y de beber. No tienen muchos animales domésticos, solamente una

trip diaries

written
old
paragraphs/summary

nature
It seems to me
naked/bodies/
beautiful/faces
heaven
fear
Little by little/they lose
swimming
fish/parrots/cotton

clase de perros que no ladran.° Hablan una lengua muy dulce° y tienen cos- **bark/sweet**
tumbres° muy buenas. Creo que en el mundo no hay mejor gente. No hallamos **customs**
monstruos en estas islas, pero nos dicen por señas° que cerca de aquí viven **sign language**
hombres feroces con un solo ojo y cara de perro. Dicen que esos hombres
terribles comen a la gente y beben su sangre,° pero yo no lo creo. Los llaman **blood**
caníbales.

"La tierra de todas estas islas es muy fértil. En las costas hay puertos de mar
que no tienen comparación con otros que yo conozco. Hay ríos muy bonitos y
grandes que son una maravilla.° Hay también sierras y montañas muy altas que **marvel**
parecen° llegar al cielo. Los árboles° son verdes° como los de España en pri- **seem/trees/green**
mavera y no pierden las hojas° en noviembre. Hay varias clases de palmas y **leaves**
también pinos. Por el cielo° vuelan bandadas° de pájaros de colores brillantes **sky/flocks**
que oscurecen el sol y cantan dulcemente. También hay miel° muy dulce, **honey**
muchas flores lindas y frutas deliciosas. Dicen que hay minas de oro y plata° **silver**
cerca de aquí . . . ¡Es la tierra más hermosa que ojos humanos han visto!"° **have seen**

Comprehension Exercise: Select the item that best completes each statement.
Indicate your choice by letter.

1   Cristóbal Colón escribió su diario y sus cartas . . .
   a   en español moderno.
   b   en español antiguo.
   c   en italiano.
2   Colón dice en sus cartas que los indios . . .
   a   tenían el cuerpo desnudo.
   b   usaban sombrero y suéter.
   c   tenían el cuerpo torcido.
3   Los indios creían que los españoles . . .
   a   venían de España.
   b   venían de otro planeta.
   c   venían del cielo.
4   Colón dice que los indios de las Antillas tenían . . .
   a   barcos de motor.
   b   canoas.
   c   automóviles convertibles.
5   Los indios le traían a Colón . . .
   a   toros y elefantes.
   b   muchos perros y gatos.
   c   papagayos, algodón y otras cosas.
6   Los perros que tenían los indios . . .
   a   no ladraban.
   b   no comían nada.
   c   no bebían agua.
7   Colón dice que la tierra de las islas que descubrió era . . .
   a   muy mala.
   b   un desierto.
   c   muy fértil.

8 Colón dice que los árboles . . .
- **a** eran muy feos.
- **b** no perdían las hojas en noviembre.
- **c** eran de muchos colores.

Ejercicio 75   Preterit versus Imperfect

Select one of the two forms in parentheses according to the meaning of the context.

El primer viaje de Colón (tercer párrafo)

Colón y sus marineros (**1** volvieron, volvían) a sus barcos y (**2** navegaron, navegaban) de nuevo en dirección a la isla que llamamos hoy día Santo Domingo. Después de varias semanas de navegación (**3** llegaron, llegaban) a la costa norte de la isla. El aspecto general de esta nueva tierra les (**4** recordó, recordaba) inmediatamente a España. Por esta razón la (**5** llamaron, llamaban) *La Española*. Era el 25 de diciembre, día de Navidad.° Colón (**6** paró, paraba)° allí los barcos y (**7** bajó, bajaba) a tierra. Los indios del lugar (**8** parecieron, parecían) muy amables y el Almirante° (**9** vio, veía) que muchos de ellos (**10** usaron, usaban) adornos de oro y plata en diferentes partes del cuerpo. El lugar (**11** pareció, parecía) ideal para la construcción de un fuerte.

Christmas/stopped

Admiral

Change the indicated verbs to the past tense. Choose either the Preterit or the Imperfect according to the meaning within the paragraph and using the added information in parentheses.

(cuarto párrafo)

A poca distancia de la costa dominicana el barco principal de la expedición se *encalla*° (**12** C, E) una noche en un banco de arena.° Con gran disgusto Colón *abandona* (**13** C, E) a la *Santa María* y *usa* (**14** C, E) muchos de sus materiales en la construcción del fuerte° *La Navidad*. *Llega* (**15** C, E) el mes de enero y el Almirante° ya *está* (**16** NC, M) muy cansado de tanto explorar. *Tiene* (**17** NC, M) grandes deseos de volver a España con la sensacional noticia de sus descubrimientos. En el fuerte *La Navidad deja*° (**18** C, E) a un pequeño grupo de sus hombres y *sale* (**19** C, E) para España en la *Niña*. Después de muchos problemas y tormentas terribles de invierno, el primer viaje a las Indias *termina* (**20** C, E) en Palos, el 15 de marzo de 1493. *Son* (**21** NC, M) más o menos las doce del día cuando Colón y sus marineros *entran* (**22** C, E) en el puerto.°

goes aground/sand

fort

Admiral

leaves

port

Ejercicio 76   Preterit versus Imperfect

Select one of the two forms in parentheses according to the meaning of the context.

El primer viaje de Colón (párrafo cinco)

Cuando los residentes de Palos (**1** vieron, veían) que una de las tres carabelas°

ships

de Colón venía en dirección al muelle,° se (**2** alegraron, alegraban) muchísimo. (**3** Tocaron, Tocaban) las campanas de la iglesia y (**4** corrieron, corrían) al muelle a recibirlo. Alegres y felices, después de una larga ausencia de seis meses y medio, los marineros (**5** bajaron, bajaban) rápidamente del barco. Al pisar tierra española, muchos de ellos (**6** lloraron, lloraban) de felicidad, mientras toda la gente del pueblo (**7** miró, miraba) el impresionante espectáculo con gran emoción y curiosidad. Mientras Colón y sus hombres (**8** caminaron, caminaban)° por la calle en dirección a la iglesia para darle gracias a Dios, todos los habitantes del pueblo (**9** gritaron, gritaban),° locos de alegría, y (**10** aplaudieron, aplaudían) con entusiasmo. (**11** Desearon, Deseaban) saludar° y abrazar a los primeros hombres que el 12 de octubre de 1492 (**12** pisaron, pisaban) la tierra de las Antillas.

dock

walked

shouted
greet

Ejercicio 77   Pre-test Practice: Preterit Substitution

Write the correct preterit form of all the infinitives in parentheses.

1 Yo (cerrar) la puerta y (salir).
2 Los leones no me (mirar), gracias a Dios.
3 Primero nosotros (ver) la noticia, y entonces ellos (escribir) el párrafo.
4 Tú no me (olvidar) nunca, ¿verdad?
5 El perro (morder) el nuevo cuaderno.
6 Sí, Jorge y yo (cerrar) esa ventana.
7 Tú (medir) todos los jarros y yo los (llevar) a la tienda.
8 El pobre turista no (llegar).

Ejercicio 78   Preterit versus Imperfect

Change the indicated verbs to the past tense. Choose either the Preterit or the Imperfect according to the meaning within the paragraph and using the added information in parentheses.

El primer viaje de Colón (párrafo seis)

Sin perder mucho tiempo con sus amigos en Palos, el grupo de Colón *sale* (**1** C, E) por tierra para Barcelona. Allí *están* (**2** NC, M) entonces los Reyes Católicos. Miles de personas los *esperan* (**3** NC, M) ansiosos° en las calles de la ciudad. Todos *miran* (**4** NC, M) a los indios con asombro.° Por primera vez *ven* (**5** NC, B) los papagayos° y otros regalos extraños° de las nuevas tierras que los indios *llevan* (**6** NC, M) para los reyes. Cuando *aparece* (**7** C, E) Colón en la puerta del enorme salón real,° la reina Isabel y el rey Fernando se *emocionan*° (**8** NC, B). Rodeado de sus compañeros y del pequeño grupo de nativos, el Almirante° se *sienta* (**9** C, E) ante los reyes y les *cuenta* (**10** NC, B) las maravillosas aventuras de su viaje. Nadie se *imagina* (**11** NC, M) en aquel momento que las nuevas tierras de que *habla* (**12** NC, M) el descubridor no *son* (**13** NC, M) realmente parte de las Indias sino° un mundo nuevo.

anxiously
astonishment
parrots/strange

royal hall/became
excited
Admiral

but

Ejercicio 79   Done-to Pronouns

Answer each question affirmatively using a done-to pronoun.

Ejemplo: ¿Mordió a la niña?   Sí, la mordió.

1   ¿Conoces a Beatriz?
2   ¿Conoces a Fernando?
3   ¿Quieres conocer a Luisa y a Manuela?
4   ¿Quieres conocer a estos muchachos?
5   ¿Quieres invitarme a la fiesta?
6   ¿Puedo invitarte a la fiesta?
7   ¿Puedo invitarlos a ustedes a la fiesta?

Ejercicio 80   Intonation

Match the items in the column on the right with the appropriate words in the column on the left.

1	Rhythm	(a)	*going up and down in speech as in singing*
2	Terminal	(b)	*only three pitch levels*
3	Spanish	(c)	*the voice goes up at the end*
4	Pitch	(d)	*the voice goes down at the end*
5	Information questions	(e)	*the degree of loudness of a syllable in speech*
6	English	(f)	*four pitch levels*
7	Stress	(g)	*the variation in length of syllables in speech*
8	Yes-no question	(h)	*the direction of the voice at the end of an utterance*

Ejercicio 81   Preterit versus Imperfect

Select one of the two forms in parentheses according to the meaning of the context.

La serpiente que quería aprender inglés

(La siguiente narración no es un cuento.° Es una historia verdadera que ocurrió   fiction
en una escuela secundaria del estado de Arizona. Esta es la primera parte. En
la próxima clase ustedes van a leer la segunda parte de esta historia.)

Estábamos en la clase de inglés. El segundo timbre° (**1** sonó, sonaba),° como   bell/rang
siempre a las 2:30, pero varios de los estudiantes (**2** hablaron, hablaban) en
voz alta y no lo (**3** oyeron, oían). La señora Willoughby, nuestra profesora,
(**4** esperó, esperaba) impaciente, con una cara muy seria, para empezar la
lección. Por fin, se (**5** sentaron, sentaban) todos y (**6** empezamos, empezábamos)
a leer un cuento sobre las aventuras de un famoso detective inglés en que aparece
una víbora.°   snake

Todos (**7** leímos, leíamos) en silencio acerca de la víbora, mientras la profesora (**8** escribió, escribía) en la pizarra. De repente, mi amiga Ester, sentada°   seated

cerca de la puerta abierta, se (**9** levantó, levantaba) y (**10** gritó, gritaba) como una loca. Yo me preocupé muchísimo. De pronto todos (**11** vimos, veíamos) horrorizados que una enorme serpiente se (**12** movió, movía) sigilosa y descaradamente° en dirección a la mesa de la profesora . . .

silently and im-
pertinently

(Continúa en la próxima lección.)

Ejercicio 82   Silent Reading

Read the following selection without stopping to translate mentally into English. See if you can figure out what proverb Alfredo is going to say at the end.

Hay un refrán español que dice . . .

(Lea usted la siguiente conversación entre Alfredo y su padre. Al fin° de la selección usted tiene que decidir cuál es el refrán que Alfredo va a decir.)

end

Alfredo: Hola, papá, ¿qué tal?

Padre: Bastante cansado, hijo. ¿Ya llegó el periódico?

Alfredo: Sí, acaba de llegar. Aquí está. ¿Cómo andan las cosas por la oficina?

Padre: Bastante bien, hijo, pero en esta época° del año siempre tenemos muchísimo trabajo. Estoy muy cansado y con dolor° de cabeza.

time
ache

Alfredo: Si quieres, te traigo una aspirina.

Padre: No, gracias, hijo. Eres muy amable, pero no voy a necesitar ninguna medicina. Voy a sentarme en mi silla favorita a leer el periódico con calma y pronto me voy a sentir mejor.

Alfredo: Oye, papá. No quiero molestarte, pero quería pedirte un favor.

Padre: ¡Cómo no, hijo! ¿Qué deseas?

Alfredo: ¿Puedes prestarme° cincuenta dólares?

lend

Padre: ¿Cómo? Hazme el favor de repetir la pregunta. Creo que no te oí bien. ¿Cinco dólares, dices?

Alfredo: Cinco no, papá, cincuenta. Tengo que comprar unas botas° especiales que necesito para las excursiones a las montañas.

boots

Padre: ¿Cómo? ¿Cincuenta dólares para un par de botas? ¡Ay! ¿Dónde están las aspirinas?

Alfredo: No te excites, papá. Es que este semestre tengo un curso de alpinismo° y además° soy miembro del Club de Alpinistas de la universidad.

mountain climbing
besides

Padre: Cincuenta dólares es demasiado. Con un par de zapatos fuertes o botas ordinarias que ya tienes puedes caminar muy bien por las montañas.

Alfredo: Mira, papá. No es una simple cuestión de caminar en las montañas. Los aficionados al alpinismo suben o escalan montañas altas como el monte Everest, Aconcagua y Matterhorn. Y para eso es necesario tener un equipo especial.

Padre: Entonces las botas son solamente° una pequeña parte del costoso° equipo que vas a necesitar, ¿no? Mira, Alfredo, cuando tu madre y yo estábamos en la universidad . . .

only/costly

Alfredo: Sí, sí. Ya sé muy bien qué vas a decirme. Cuando ustedes eran jóvenes, iban a las montañas gratis° o les costaba muy poco. Te olvidas que hoy día las cosas son muy diferentes.

free of charge

Padre: En mis tiempos de estudiante nos considerábamos muy afortunados y felices con . . .

Alfredo: ¡El sermón de siempre que ya sé de memoria! Los tiempos cambian, viejo, pero tú no cambias. Solamente° el viaje que pensamos hacer a México nos va a costar doscientos dólares por persona.

Just

Padre: ¿Qué dices? ¡Doscientos nada más, eh! ¡Caramba! Muy económico . . . ¡Ay, mi cabeza . . . ! Las aspirinas, por favor, ¡pronto!

Alfredo: Perdón. Nunca creí que el anuncio de mi viaje a México te iba a afectar tanto. Lo siento.

Padre: Tú estás loco, Alfredo. Crees que eres hijo de millonario.

Alfredo: No es necesario ser millonario. Todos mis compañeros del club van a ir. Es parte del curso. Pensamos subir a Popocatépetl.

Padre: ¿Popo . . . qué? No entiendo. ¿Y por qué no escalan las montañas altas que tenemos cerca de aquí?

Alfredo: Popocatépetl es uno de los volcanes extintos más bonitos y famosos de México y de todo el mundo. En las montañas de nuestro estado vamos a practicar los fines de semana.

Padre: Pues no veo por qué ustedes tienen que ir tan lejos. Cuesta° demasiado.

It costs

Alfredo: La excursión a Popo va a ser algo muy especial, la culminación del curso y de todas las actividades del club. Para eso tenemos que esperar hasta las vacaciones de Navidad° porque necesitamos dos semanas.

Christmas

Padre: Y después de México, ¿a dónde van a ir? ¿A los Andes, los Alpes, o las Himalayas? Si crees que yo te voy a dar el dinero . . .

Alfredo: Yo calculo que con $500 voy a tener suficiente para los gastos° de todo el semestre.

expenses

Padre: ¡Caray! ¿Y crees que eso es poco? Empezaste con $50 y, como buen alpinista, ya subiste a $500. No quiero saber más. Si insistes en practicar un deporte° tan caro° vas a tener que hacerlo con tu propio° dinero. Yo bastante hago con pagar° los gastos de tu educación.

sport/expensive/own
pay

Alfredo: Estas experiencias son una parte muy esencial de mi educación.

Padre: Pues si las consideras tan importantes, con el dinero que ganas° trabajando en el garaje los sábados, puedes . . .

earn

Alfredo: Olvidé decirte que no voy a trabajar más allí. Este sábado va a ser mi último día. Me pagan solamente uno setenta y cinco la hora, y yo quiero ganar más.

Padre: Piensa, Alfredo. Más vale algo que nada. El trabajo del garaje es algo seguro° y hoy día no hay mucha abundancia de trabajos. El estado deplorable de la economía de nuestro país . . .

sure

Alfredo: Es un salario miserable. Hay muchos trabajos que pagan más.

Padre: Bueno, hijo. Tú eres quien tiene que hacer esa decisión. Te deseo mucha suerte. En español hay un refrán que dice . . .

Alfredo: Sí, sí. Ya lo sé. El refrán español dice . . .

Ejercicio 83   Intonation

Decide which are information questions and which are yes-no questions and prepare to read them aloud with the proper rising or falling intonation.

1 ¿Qué tiempo hace hoy afuera?
2 Tú tienes mucha hambre, ¿verdad?
3 ¿Es la Pampa argentina una llanura?
4 ¿Ladra el perro que muerde?
5 ¿Quién en esta clase no tiene tres pulgares?
6 ¿Cuántos habitantes tiene Montevideo?

Ejercicio 84   Preterit versus Imperfect

Select the correct form from the two in parentheses and write it.

La serpiente que queria aprender inglés (segunda parte)

La señora Willoughby, nuestra profesora de inglés, es bastante gorda. Pesa (*She weighs*) cerca de 200 libras (*pounds*). Cuando ella (**1** vio, veía) que la serpiente venía hacia ella, se (**2** subió, subía) a su mesa con la rapidez de un relámpago (*bolt of lightning*). Libros, flores y papeles (**3** cayeron, caían) por el suelo (*floor*). ¡Qué tragedia! Ahora, Ester no era la única muchacha de la clase que (**4** gritó, gritaba) histéricamente. Sin poder controlarse un momento más, los muchachos (**5** rompieron, rompían) a reír (*burst into laughter*). ¡Qué escándalo, Dios mío!

Al llegar a la mesa donde estaba subida la profesora, la serpiente (**6** levantó, levantaba) la cabeza, (**7** sacó, sacaba) (*stuck out*) la lengua insolentemente y (**8** miró, miraba) con interés a la pobre señora Willoughby. Yo me (**9** alarmé, alarmaba) (*became alarmed*) muchísimo. Con sus pequeños ojos que (**10** brillaron, brillaban) como dos diamantes, el terrible animal la (**11** miró, miraba) fijamente. ¡Qué horror!

En medio de todo el escándalo, (**12** entró, entraba) en la clase el profesor de biología y dijo sorprendido: —¡Cleopatra! Pero, ¿qué haces tú aquí fuera de tu jaula (*cage*)?

Con mucho cuidado, pero sin miedo (*fear*) ninguno, el buen señor (**13** cogió, cogía) (*caught*) a Cleopatra con la mano por la parte posterior de la cabeza y la (**14** llevó, llevaba) para su laboratorio. ¡Cleopatra (**15** deseó, deseaba) aprender inglés, señora Willoughby!

Ejercicio 85   Intonation and Reading Aloud

1 ¿De qué color es tu cuaderno?
2 Tienes los ojos azules, ¿verdad?
3 ¿De dónde eres tú?
4 ¿Hay tres colores en nuestra bandera?
5 ¿Cree usted que esto es mucha molestia?
6 ¿Quién acaba de cerrar la puerta?
7 ¿Quién se desayuna a las seis?
8 ¿Te desayunas tú a las seis?
9 ¿Por qué no te sientas aquí?

Ejercicio 86   Done-to Pronouns and Reflexive Constructions

Your instructor will give you the combinations which you are to write one at a time. Column three tells you which pronoun to use, and if you think the construction is reflexive, indicate it with R.

Ejemplo: *212 = Tú te acuestas. (R)*

1 Yo	1 acostar (ue)	1 a mí.
2 Tú	2 despertar (ie)	2 a ti.
3 El niño	3 servir (i)	3 al niño.
4 Las niñas	4 acabar de mirar	4 a las niñas.
5 Nosotros		5 a nosotros.

Ejercicio 87   Done-to Pronouns

Write the combinations that your instructor will give you.

Ejemplo: *11 = Pablo me abraza.*

		1 a mí.
	1 abraza	2 a ti.
Pablo		3 a usted y a mí.
	2 va a abrazar	4 a Mónica.
		5 a mis primos.
		6 a usted (*m*).

Ejercicio 88   Intonation and Reading Aloud

1 ¿Saben ustedes usar el diccionario?
2 ¿Existe la posibilidad de ir a Ecuador?
3 ¿En qué parte del país hay más oportunidad para trabajos de oficina?
4 ¡Qué barbaridad! ¿Quién cambió el tema de la conversación?
5 ¿Es obligatorio el servicio militar en tu país?

Ejercicio 89   Preterit of Stem-Changing Verbs

A/B

LA MAMÁ DUERME AL NIÑO

SE DUERME EL NIÑO

Ejercicio 90   Intonation and Reading Aloud

1   ¿Fue una ceremonia muy bonita?
2   ¿Perdió la posición por su incapacidad?
3   ¿Crees que es desagradable la música?
4   ¿Por qué hablas de esa imposibilidad?
5   ¿Es difícil esta pronunciación?
6   ¿Comprendes la terminación de esta frase?

Ejercicio 91   Preterit versus Imperfect

After reading the complete sentence, indicate whether the Spanish equivalent for each indicated verb will be expressed in the Preterit (P) or in the Imperfect (I).

My First Experience on Skis

Although I *was* **1** only seven at the time, I will never forget my first experience on skis. One Friday afternoon on the way home from work, Dad *heard* **2** the news about the season's first snowfall over the car radio. He ran into the house and *ordered* **3** everyone to get ready for the trip to the ski area in the northern part of the state. My father *loved* **4** winter sports more than any other human being I know, and he *was* **5** terribly excited.

We left in such a hurry that Dad *forgot* **6** to make reservations at the lodge where we *were going* **7** to spend the night. Fortunately, the season *was* barely *getting started* **8** and *we were able* **9** to get rooms without difficulty. We were all exhausted when we arrived at the lodge, so everyone *went* **10** to bed without delay. We were going to need a good rest before morning.

After eating a hearty breakfast, the entire family headed for the snow. The weather was beautiful and skiing conditions perfect. Everyone already *knew* **11** how to ski well except me. Dad *stayed* **12** in the children's area to give me the first lessons. After several hours of patient tutoring and much encouragement from my father, I began to hold my own on the snow, so he *left* **13** me alone in the beginner's area.

It wasn't very long before the inevitable had to happen. I *fell* **14** down and couldn't get on my feet again. When my older brother came to my rescue, my left leg *hurt* **15** terribly. Fortunately, it *did* not *break* **16**.

After many more experiences of this type and many more trips to the mountains, I, too, became an expert on the slopes.

Ejercicio 92   Listening and Silent Reading

From the three responses given below choose the one that best corresponds to the question or statement which you will hear once. Indicate your answer by letter.

1   **a**   Siempre me levanto muy cansado.

    b Me levanto casi siempre a las seis.

    c Me levanto siempre de mal humor.

2 **a** Pues, vas a tener una cara muy sucia.

    b Ella se lava los dientes cada mañana.

    c Mamá me lava la ropa los lunes.

3 **a** Sigue el número doscientos setenta.

    b Sigue el número trescientos sesenta y nueve.

    c Sigue el número doscientos ochenta.

4 **a** Pasa el Río Grande.

    b Pasa el Magdalena.

    c Pasa el Amazonas.

5 **a** Tenemos que masticarlo mejor.

    b Entonces ustedes están bastante lejos del parque.

    c Creo que ustedes deben ponerse los sombreros nuevos.

6 **a** La pobre tiene una cara muy fea.

    b Tiene unas piernas gigantescas.

    c Tiene los brazos largos como las monas.

Ejercicio 93   Preterit Forms and Their Spelling

Write the preterit form of each infinitive in parentheses.

1 ¿Qué (hacer) tú anoche? ¿(Estudiar) tus lecciones para hoy?

2 Ellos (salir) de allí a las cinco y (llegar) aquí a las seis.

3 Primero yo (buscar) mi cuaderno y después yo (empezar) el trabajo.

4 ¿A qué hora (venir) tú anteayer?

5 Usted (aceptar) las cartas que ella me (regalar).

6 Yo me (levantar) a las siete y cuarto y (jugar) con mis hermanos.

7 Todos ellos se (divertir) y entonces se (dormir).

Ejercicio 94   Intonation: Word Linkage and Reading Aloud

1 Le habla al profesor.

2 Va a haber mucha gente.

3 Yo no oigo bien.

4 Yo oigo bien.

5 Él lee el periódico.

6 Mi hijo se llama Ángel.

7 Mi idioma favorito es el ruso.

8 Tu última clase es la mejor.

9 Mi hija se llama Amelia.

10 Su uniforme es muy raro.

Ejercicio 95   *Ser* versus *estar*

Choose between *ser* and *estar*, for each blank, and make the verb Imperfect.

1 Antes de venir a América Cristóbal Colón sabía que la tierra . . . redonda.

2 Cuando nos llamaron por teléfono del aeropuerto, mi madre y yo no . . . en casa.

3 Cuando tu padre y yo ... soldados, no había guerra (*war*).
4 Todo el mundo sabía que la serpiente no ... venenosa (*poisonous*).
5 Los vikingos ... del norte de Europa.
6 ¡Qué bonita ... Anita anoche con su traje largo antes de ir a la fiesta!
7 ¡Qué fría ... la noche cuando salimos a cantar villancicos (*carols*) de Navidad (*Christmas*).
8 Pedimos chocolate caliente en el café porque hacía mucho frío, pero cuando lo sirvieron ... frío.
9 En ese tiempo Pancho ... el mejor amigo que yo tenía.

Ejercicio 96   Irregular Preterits

Your instructor will give you the combinations one at a time. All verbs in the middle column must be Preterit.

Ejemplo: *111 = Tú llegaste a las nueve.*

1	Tú	1	llegar	1	a las nueve.
2	Usted y yo	2	venir	2	en diciembre.
3	Claudia	3	hacerlo	3	durante el otoño.
4	Yo	4	caerse	4	en la primavera.
5	Tú y Jorge	5	pedirlo	5	durante el invierno.

Ejercicio 97   Preterit versus Imperfect

Read each complete sentence in the story, and change each indicated verb form from the Present to the past tense. The meaning will tell you which past tense form to use, the Preterit or the Imperfect.

Hernán Cortés: un muchacho problema

El hombre que va (iba) a ser en 1519 la figura central de la invasión y conquista de México no es (fue) en sus primeros años de vida° un niño modelo. Hoy día lo llamaríamos° un joven problema. Primero por razones de salud y más tarde por su conducta, desde el momento en que *ve* 1 la primera luz del día, Hernán Cortés le *causa* 2 muchos dolores° de cabeza a su familia.

Nace° 3 en el año de 1485 en un pequeño pueblo° español de la región de Extremadura que se *llama* 4 Medellín. Sus padres, Martín Cortés Monroy y Catalina Pizarro Altamirano, *son* 5 de familia noble, pero no rica. Cuando su hijo *tiene* 6 catorce años lo *mandan°* 7 a estudiar para abogado° en la ciudad de Salamanca donde *hay* 8 una famosa universidad que todavía existe en nuestros días. Después de dos años el inquieto muchacho se *cansa* 9 de estudiar y *vuelve* 10 a la casa de sus padres.

Por toda la provincia donde *vive* 11, se *oyen°* 12 noticias y rumores exagerados de los viajes al Nuevo Mundo. El joven Hernán o Hernando *empieza* 13 a imaginar grandes aventuras. *Hace* 14 planes para buscar trabajo de marinero en alguna de las expediciones que *salen* 15 de Sevilla frecuentemente para las Indias. *Quiere* 16 buscar fortuna y fama en las nuevas tierras.

life
would call
aches
He is born/town
send/lawyer
there are heard

Por fin,° a los diecinueve años, *viene* **17** a la isla de Santo Domingo a vivir   At last
de la agricultura y de las minas. Dos años más tarde *sale* **18** a colonizar la isla
de Cuba con Diego Velázquez, el futuro gobernador de la isla. Durante varios
años *sirve* **19** a su amigo don Diego de secretario y también en capacidad de
alcalde° de Santiago, la capital de la isla. En 1518 el gobernador Velázquez   mayor
nombra **20** a Cortés jefe° de la tercera expedición a la tierra llamada por los   chief
indios Culúa o México.

Ejercicio 98   Reading Comprehension

Read the following sentences and select the most logical completion for each.

1 Los colores de la bandera de los Estados Unidos son . . .
   a azul, verde y blanco.
   b blanco, azul y rojo.
   c blanco, rosado y azul.
2 Después de lavar nuestra ropa, generalmente mi mamá . . .
   a la plancha.
   b la vende.
   c la compra.
3 Nos ponemos los calcetines . . .
   a en las orejas.
   b en los pies.
   c en los brazos.
4 Yo tengo la costumbre de leer las noticias del mundo . . .
   a antes de despertarme en la mañana.
   b en el periódico que viene todos los días.
   c en las cartas que me escribe mi sobrina de cinco años.
5 Cada día, después de levantarme, lavarme y vestirme . . .
   a me desayuno.
   b me acuesto.
   c me duermo.

Ejercicio 99   Preterit of Irregular Verbs

Select and copy from the alternatives given the appropriate preterit form of
the verbs in parentheses.

1 Los niños (hacer) una pequeña casa para el pájaro. (hacen, hacían, hicieron, hacíamos)
2 El pobre pájaro (morir). (murió, moría, muere, morí)
3 Yo (oír) decir que el nuevo director (venir) ayer. (oí, oía, oye, oigo; venía, viene, vine, vino)
4 Cuando yo (llegar), yo (comenzar) a buscarlo por todas partes. (llegó, llegué, llego, llegaba; comenzaba, comienzo, comencé, comenzó)
5 Pancho me (decir) que ellos (ir) al centro. (dije, dijo, digo, decía; fueron, iban, fuimos, íbamos)

6 Ella es la señorita que nos (servir). (sirvió, sirve, servía, serví)

7 El señor del suéter azul (tropezar) y (caer) en la fuente. (tropecé, tropieza, tropezó, tropezaba; caía, cayeron, caigo, cayó)

Ejercicio 100 Preterit versus Imperfect

Change all indicated verbs to the Preterit or the Imperfect.

Los periodistas de Moctezuma

Cuando leemos los viejos documentos que nos *dejan*° **1** varios de los partici- — leave
pantes en la conquista de México, es muy interesante notar los métodos aztecas
para la transmisión de las noticias del día. El emperador Moctezuma no *va* **2**
nunca a la costa para conferenciar con Cortés. La capital de su imperio, Tenochtitlán, *está* **3** en el interior del país a una distancia considerable del mar.
Sin embargo, mientras Cortés y sus hombres *exploran* **4** las diferentes regiones
del Golfo de México, en el palacio real° de la capital, Moctezuma y sus caciques° — royal/chiefs
no solamente *oyen* **5** las noticias que *traen* **6** diariamente° sus mensajeros,° — daily/messengers
sino que° también las *ven* **7** con sus propios° ojos. Bernal Díaz del Castillo, el — but/own
soldado cronista de las tres expediciones a México, nos cuenta° en su *Historia* — tells
verdadera de la conquista de la Nueva España que él *ve* **8** a pintores indios haciendo
dibujos° de los barcos, el vestido de los españoles, sus armas, sus caballos y — drawings
hasta el perro de uno de los marineros.

Los mensajeros de Moctezuma que hoy llamaríamos° "periodistas" o "re- — would call
porteros" *ven* **9** y *pintan* **10** acontecimientos° de gran importancia para su señor — happenings
Moctezuma y para la historia de América. Por ejemplo, la destrucción de los
ídolos en los templos mayas de la costa, los pactos y alianzas que Cortés *hace* **11**
con varias de las tribus, la fundación de la ciudad de Veracruz y la división que
existe **12** en aquel momento entre los soldados del campamento español.

Cuando Cortés les *dice* **13** a sus hombres que *siente* **14** grandes deseos de
empezar la marcha al interior de México, sus partidarios° *aplauden* **15** la idea. — followers
Los amigos del gobernador Velázquez, sin embargo, le *dicen* **16** que ellos *van* **17**
a volver a Cuba. Para resolver el problema, Cortés da (dio) órdenes de destruir
los barcos. No los quema° (quemó), como dice la leyenda; los hunde° (hundió) — burns/sinks
en las aguas del Golfo.

Cuando Cortés *llega* **18** a la capital meses más tarde, Moctezuma *sabe* **19**
todas las cosas que ocurren (ocurrieron) en la costa. Las había visto° en las — had seen
pinturas que *hacen* **20** sus magníficos reporteros.

Ejercicio 101 Listening and Reading Comprehension

One of the three responses given below is a logical reaction to a question or
statement that you will hear *once*. Indicate your choice by letter.

1 **a** Tiene cinco en cada mano y en cada pie, veinte en total.
   b No tiene dedos porque es un profesor de biología.
   c Tiene catorce dedos y dos pulgares.

2   **a**   Vuela como un pájaro.
     b   Tropieza y cae en la fuente.
     c   Anuncia a la gente que no muerde.

3   **a**   Muerde a la gente mala, pero no a la buena.
     b   No muerde a nadie.
     c   Hace un viaje por mar.

4   **a**   La tenemos en medio de la cara.
     b   No tenemos nariz; en lugar de la nariz, usamos los dientes.
     c   No tenemos nariz porque hace tanto calor.

5   **a**   Era cierto, pero los perdimos en el cine.
     b   No, no es cierto, porque no andamos mucho estos días.
     c   Sí, señor, yo creo que usted tiene razón.

6   **a**   Son blancas y muy secas.
     b   Nunca hay nubes durante una tormenta.
     c   Son negras y oscuras.

7   **a**   Que una persona plancha la ropa inmediatamente después de lavarla.
     b   Que alguien pasa unos momentos muy agradables.
     c   Significa comer por la mañana después de despertarse.

Ejercicio 102   Vocabulary Matching

Match each Spanish word with its English equivalent.

1	ayudar	(a)	*to measure*
2	divertirse	(b)	*to say good-by*
3	ponerse	(c)	*raincoat*
4	despedirse	(d)	*feet*
5	impermeable	(e)	*to help*
6	bandera	(f)	*to have a good time*
7	molestia	(g)	*bother*
8	altura	(h)	*to put on (clothing)*
9	pueblo	(i)	*town*
10	tropezar	(j)	*flag*
11	cerrar	(k)	*to trip*
12	medir	(l)	*height*
		(m)	*to close*

Ejercicio 103   Present of Irregular Verbs in Reflexive Constructions

Write the combinations that your instructor will give you one at a time and correct your work by the work on the board. Several steps are involved:
(1)   select the form of the verb that goes with the doer.
(2)   select the appropriate done-to pronoun.
(3)   decide whether the pronoun should be placed before or after the verb.

Ejemplo: *55 = Tú y yo nos vestimos en casa.*

1 Yo	1 sentarse	
2 Los niños	2 ir a acostarse	
3 Tú	3 dormirse	en casa.
4 Pepe	4 venir a desayunarse	
5 Tú y yo	5 vestirse	

Ejercicio 104   Done-to Pronouns

Write the combinations that your instructor will give you.

Ejemplo: *24 = Mamá acaba de servirte.*

Mamá	1 sirve	1 a los invitados.
		2 a mí.
		3 a usted y a mí.
	2 acaba de servir	4 a ti.
		5 a usted (*f*).
		6 a mi tía.

Ejercicio 105   Reading Comprehension

After reading each problem, indicate your choice by letter. The choices are responses or rejoinders (not completions) to the first sentence.

1 Pero, hombre, no te molestes con todo esto.
   a Te digo que no es ninguna molestia.
   b Hay pantalones en la mesa y calcetines en la silla.
   c Espera. Tengo que ponerme el abrigo.

2 ¿Cuándo es una buena idea planchar la ropa?
   a Después de venderla.
   b Después de lavarla y secarla.
   c Mientras uno se divierte en una fiesta.

3 ¿Quién fue el primero en despertarse?
   a Luisa no llegó anoche hasta las doce.
   b No sé, pero Miguel se desayunó antes que los otros.
   c No había luna anoche.

4 "Antes que te cases, mira lo que haces."
   a ¿Te vas a casar muy pronto?
   b Es una buena idea casarse en junio.
   c Es tarde para decir eso porque el pobre muchacho se casó anteayer.

5 ¿Qué vestido vas a ponerte para ir al banco?
   a Ese que tiene un lugar especial para los pies.
   b Mi camisa nueva está muy sucia.
   c Uno que tiene los colores, verde, amarillo y negro.

6 ¿Cuál de las siguientes frases es verdad?
   a La cabeza está conectada a la mano.

b El pie está conectado a la pierna.
c La nariz está conectada al brazo.

Ejercicio 106   Intonation, Word Linkage: Reading Aloud

1 Esa alumna le habla a Toni.
2 ¿Qué va a hacer ese señor?
3 No olvidan su nombre.
4 Lo olvidan fácilmente.
5 Yo dije eso también.
6 Ese ejemplo es fácil.
7 Mi interés es viajar.
8 Yo fui inmediatamente.
9 ¡Qué lindo es tu Uruguay!
10 Tu humor no ofende.

11 Va a darnos la certificación.
12 La acomodación resultó bien.
13 El grupo occidental no tiene instituciones importantes.
14 No oí el otro oratorio.
15 Hay una nube extraordinaria allí.
16 ¿Le dijiste eso a tu última amiga?
17 Mi independencia desapareció.
18 No te molestes, mi hijo.
19 Su uniforme está sucio.
20 ¿Cuál es tu universidad?

Ejercicio 107   Present of Irregular Verbs

Write the appropriate form of the Present for each infinitive given in parentheses.

1 Yo me (despertar) generalmente a las siete de la mañana.
2 Yo me lavo la cara y me (vestir) antes del desayuno.
3 Son las siete y media cuando yo (salir) para la universidad.
4 Mi hermana (decir) que yo no (saber) hablar francés muy bien.
5 Yo (oír) bien, pero tengo los ojos malos y no (ver) muy bien.
6 Ahora yo (estar) en casa de José, pero dentro de unos minutos él y yo (ir) para el dormitorio.
7 Yo le (decir) que Enrique (venir) a verme todas las tardes, pero no es verdad.
8 Después del banquete ella y yo nos (despedir) de todos nuestros amigos.
9 Mi familia y yo (empezar) nuestras vacaciones el sábado.
10 Yo no (conocer) a todos los estudiantes de esta clase y por eso (*because of that*) yo (poner) sus nombres y apellidos en este cuaderno.

Ejercicio 108   *Venir* versus *ir*

Choose the verb that fits the situation described in each sentence.

1 El verano pasado mi hermano mayor (fue, vino) a estudiar español en la universidad de Guadalajara.
2 Mis abuelos (fueron, vinieron) de México a pasar un mes de vacaciones en los Estados Unidos con nosotros.
3 Cristóbal Colón (fue, vino) a América cuatro veces.

4 De la isla de Santo Domingo, Colón (fue, vino) a la costa norte de América del Sur.

5 Cuando yo (fui, vine) a Europa con mis padres, vi muchos lugares de gran interés histórico.

6 Los Peregrinos del Mayflower que fundaron nuestro país (fueron, vinieron) a Nueva Inglaterra en 1620.

7 Adela y yo no (fuimos, vinimos) a la fiesta en casa de Margarita porque ella vive muy lejos de aquí.

8 Estoy aquí en el dormitorio porque no (fui, vine) a mis clases hoy.

9 Lola y Cristina están en la playa. Cristina le pregunta a Lola, —¿(Fuiste, Viniste) aquí ayer?

10 En la clase de inglés Ernesto le pregunta a un amigo, —¿(Fuiste, Viniste) al cine el sábado por la noche?

Ejercicio 109   Guided Conversation

Select a partner and perform twice the following dialog in Spanish. Change roles the second time.

1 You tell your roommate that you are going downtown.
2 He (She) asks you why (*por qué*) you are going downtown.
3 You answer that you are going to buy new shoes.
4 He (She) says that he (she) wants to go with you (*contigo*).
5 You say that you are going to the show afterwards (*después*).
6 He (She) says, fine, that he (she) also wants to go.
7 You ask him (her) if he (she) has money.
8 He (She) answers, yes, a little, enough to go (*para ir*) to the show.
9 You say that you have to find your sweater.
10 He (She) says that you don't need it. It is not cold.

Ejercicio 110   Intonation and Linkage: Reading Aloud

When you read Spanish, the spaces between words on the page do not tell you to pause. Read the sentences below, linking words into groups the way Spanish speakers do.

1 Voy a hacer un viaje a Argentina.
2 Una carta a Alicia llegó ayer.
3 Su elefante es grande.
4 Duda hay, si no lo cree él.
5 Ella usa una blusa azul.
6 El rey encuentra a la reina.
7 Regresó a ese hotel.
8 Si ese alumno va, también voy yo.
9 Yo toqué el diente inferior.
10 Toda esta comida es buena.
11 Sin embargo Ofelia le ayuda.
12 Esto es para ojos, no es para orejas.
13 La carne está en el plato.
14 Recibí y abrí esa carta ayer.
15 La nube es aquella allí.
16 Enrique está en su auto.

Ejercicio 111   Present of Irregular Verbs

Write the appropriate present tense form of each infinitive in parentheses.

1 Los sábados en mi casa generalmente nosotros nos (despertar) temprano porque todos (tener) que trabajar.
2 Hoy mis padres (ir) a trabajar solamente hasta la una.
3 Esta noche yo (pensar) salir a divertirme un poco.
4 Mi madre siempre nos (servir) un buen desayuno.
5 Yo (ver) que ya son las ocho menos diez y yo (saber) que no debo llegar tarde a mi trabajo.
6 Yo (recordar) que Margarita (querer) hablar conmigo por teléfono a las diez.
7 Mi amiga me (decir) que ella lo (sentir) mucho, pero que ella no (poder) acompañarme esta noche.
8 En mi trabajo yo (poner) gasolina en los carros.
9 ¿(Ser) verdad que "quien mucho (dormir) poco aprende"?
10 Yo (seguir) en la estación de gasolina; mi amigo y yo no (poder) conseguir (*get*) otro tipo de trabajo.

Ejercicio 112   General Review

A/B

C/D

E/F

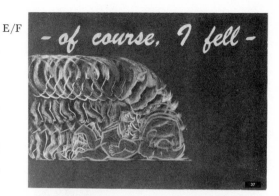

G/H

I

Ejercicio 113   General Review

Work with a partner and take turns asking and answering the following questions.

¿Cuál es la fecha de hoy?

¿A qué hora te levantaste esta mañana?

¿Te desayunaste?

¿Viniste a la universidad con un amigo?

¿Fuiste al cine anoche?

¿De qué color son los pantalones de . . . (nombre de un muchacho de su clase)?

¿De qué color es la blusa de . . . (nombre de una muchacha de su clase)?

Ejercicio 114   Present Perfect

Write the combinations that your instructor will give you one at a time and correct your work by the example on the board. Change the first infinitive in the second column to the Present Perfect.

Ejemplo: 55 = Esos señores se han levantado temprano.

1	Yo	1	traer zanahorias.
2	Pepe y yo	2	creer en Dios.
3	Usted	3	tratar de hacerlo.
4	Tú	4	dormirse.
5	Esos señores	5	levantarse temprano.

Ejercicio 115   Demonstratives

Translate the demonstratives in parentheses into Spanish.

1   (*This*) comida está deliciosa.

2   ¿De quién son (*these*) blusas?

3   (*That*) suéter que usted usa es muy lindo.

4   Vamos por (*this*) camino.

5   ¡Qué amarillos son (*those*) plátanos allí!

6   (*Those*) manzanas que tú tienes deben ser muy buenas.

7   ¿No quieres traerme (*that*) periódico que está allí cerca de la ventana?

8   Todavía no he visto (*that*) revista que tienes.

9   Es muy fácil leer (*those*) palabras allí en la pizarra.

10   (*Those*) zapatos nuevos que ustedes tienen son muy feos.

Ejercicio 116   Demonstratives

Translate the demonstratives in parentheses into Spanish.

1   Aquí en (*this*) casa grande vivo yo con mis padres; ahí en (*that*) apartamento detrás del garaje viven mis abuelos; y allí en (*that*) edificio alto que puedes ver en la distancia tienen su apartamento mis tíos.

2   ¿Por qué no lees tú (*this*) libro que tengo aquí, y yo leo (*that*) novela corta que tienes en tu bolsillo (*pocket*).

3   (*Those*) corbatas que tienes en la mano son muy finas.

4   (*These*) papeles que tengo aquí en mi mesa son muy importantes.

5   (*Those*) aviones que vuelan allá muy lejos por las nubes van muy rápido.

6   (*Those*) huevos que comes no tienen sal.

7   (*Those*) montañas allá muy lejos en el horizonte que casi no podemos ver son los Andes.

Ejercicio 117 *Gustar* with Involved Entity Pronouns

Write the combinations that your instructor will give you.

Ejemplo: 12 = *A Cristina le gusta el postre.*

1	A Cristina	1	las legumbres.
2	A mí	2	el postre.
3	A ti	gusta(n)	3 los huevos.
4	A Alfredo y a mí	4	el queso.
5	A ustedes	5	la crema y el azúcar.

Ejercicio 118 Stress and Accentuation: Reading Aloud

1	llevo/llevó	**11**	despertar
2	estudio/estudió	**12**	azúcar
3	madrugó/madrugo	**13**	hablan
4	trabajo/trabajó	**14**	jamón
5	desayunó/desayuno	**15**	gramática
6	encuentro/encontró	**16**	café
7	durmió/duermo	**17**	dispénseme
8	pierdo/perdió	**18**	francés
9	despidió/despido	**19**	árboles
10	siento/sintió	**20**	despide

Ejercicio 119 Street Addresses: Reading Aloud

1	2	3	4	5
Mi dirección es	Paseo	Vista del Mar		52243.
	Avenida	Juárez	número	6532.
Vivo en el (la)	Calle	Tucumán		986.
	Bulevar	Revolución		1659.

Ejercicio 120 Listening and Response

A/B

SUBE AL BALCÓN

LA GENTE ENTRA

AQUI VENDEN ESPADAS

C/D

RASGA EL VESTIDO

SE CORTA EL PELO

E/F

VD. VA A LA LUNA

VD. DEBE COMER MENOS

G/H

EMPIEZA A PINTAR

DICE QUE VIENE

I/J

¿CÓMO LE GUSTAN LOS HUEVOS?

Ejercicio 121   General Review

Work with a partner. Ask and answer the following questions.

¿A qué hora te despertaste esta mañana?
¿Comiste mucho para el desayuno?
¿Cuándo llegaste a la universidad?
¿Qué día es hoy?
¿Qué tiempo hace ahora?
¿Cuántos dedos tienes en los pies?
¿De qué color es la camisa de . . . (nombre de un muchacho en su clase)?
¿De qué color es el vestido de . . . (nombre de una muchacha en su clase)?
¿Quién llegó tarde a clase hoy?

Ejercicio 122   Stress and Accentuation: Reading Aloud

platico/platicó	glándula	personal	carga
atrevió/atrevo	legítimo	automóvil	aptitud
asustó/asusto	obstáculo	solicitar	cuartel
gozo/gozó	celeste	carácter	colocarlo

Ejercicio 123   Stress and Accentuation: Reading Aloud

continúo	enviado	Eduardo	Almeida	Hilario
continuo	seguías	Díaz	Ignacio	Mariano
continuó	siguió	Manuel	Antonio	Bandeira
estudia	sigue	Aguilar	Álvarez	Manuel
envía	seguido	Bautista	Ariosto	Nicanor

Ejercicio 124   Pronunciation (Vowels, *g*, *j*) and Stress:
Reading Aloud

Alemán	Angulo	Inés	Onís
Leopoldo	Asensio	Insúa	Unamuno
Alonso	Escalante	Molina	Uziel
Gabino	Espina	Ochoa	Guadalupe
Angelina	Ángel	Gumersinda	Brígida
Domingo	Magdalena	Jorge	Genoveva
Guido	Gertrudis	Gil	Gilberto

Ejercicio 125   Pronunciation (/b/, /k/, /s/) and Stress:
Reading Aloud

Cáceres	Campillo	Cánovas	Cansinos
Celestina	Céspedes	Cuervo	Encina

Quintana	Quirós	Quintero	Sabuco
Vicente	Macías	Lucena	Quiqui
Balbuena	Álvarez	Belmonte	Baena
Eusebio	Benavente	Valencia	Blasco
Viana	Cantabria	Navas	Vega

Ejercicio 126   Silent Reading

Read without stopping to translate; then do the comprehension exercise by answering *sí* or *no* to each question.

Los trece de la fama (primera parte)

I

Los primeros viajes de exploración que hizo Francisco Pizarro con su socio° Diego de Almagro fueron un verdadero fracaso.° Exploraron la costa de Tierra Firme, nombre que le daban entonces al continente suramericano, y llegaron hasta° la costa del Ecuador. Sin embargo, en vez del fabuloso país que esperaban descubrir, los dos viejos capitanes y sus hombres encontraron un "infierno° verde" de impenetrable vegetación tropical. Estaba lleno° de animales feroces y de insectos venenosos° que producían fiebre° y enfermedades mortales. Los pocos grupos de indios que vivían en la costa colombiana eran pobres y no tenían una civilización avanzada.

partner
failure

up to
hell
full
poisonous/fever

II

Era entonces la estación de las lluvias, la peor° época° del año para viajar por aquellas regiones. Ni los barcos, ya viejos y en mala condición, ni los expedicionarios podían soportar° las lluvias torrenciales, los vientos y las frecuentes tempestades° en el mar. La costa no les ofrecía protección adecuada porque, en vez de buenas playas, encontraron ciénagas° pestilentes donde la humedad era insoportable° y el calor sofocante. Hambrientos,° enfermos y a veces casi desnudos,° los hombres de Pizarro apenas° tenían la energía necesaria para defenderse contra los ataques de los indios. Murieron en gran número y en una ocasión Pizarro recibió heridas° graves que le pusieron a la puerta de la muerte. Almagro fue herido° por una flecha° que le hizo perder el ojo izquierdo.°

worst/time

stand
storms
swamps
unbearable/Hungry
naked/hardly

wounds
wounded/arrow/left

III

Cerca de la costa ecuatoriana, en la pequeña y desolada Isla del Gallo, Pizarro decidió mandar° a su socio a Panamá. Necesitaban urgentemente más hombres, armas y provisiones. Pizarro conocía demasiado bien al gobernador Pedrarias Dávila y no quería ir a verlo en persona. No olvidaba que pocos años antes, el "tigre de Darién" (así llamaban a Dávila) había° decapitado a Balboa, el descubridor del Mar del Sur.

send

had

I

1 El primer viaje de exploración de Pizarro por la costa oeste de América del Sur fue un verdadero éxito.

2 Cuando uno o más hombres forman una *soci*edad o a*soci*ación para trabajar juntos y participar en los mismos proyectos, decimos que esos individuos son *socios*.

3 La primera expedición de Pizarro llegó hasta la costa norte de Chile.

4 El "infierno verde" es un nombre que le damos algunas veces a la selva tropical.

5 Los primeros grupos de indios que encontraron los hombres de Pizarro en las costas colombianas vivían en grandes ciudades.

II

6 El mal tiempo afectó mucho a los expedicionarios y a los barcos en que navegaban.

7 Muchos de los expedicionarios murieron de frío.

8 En la costa colombiana Pizarro y sus tropas hallaron playas de arena (*sand*) muy blanca y fina.

III

9 Almagro volvió a Panamá a buscar soldados, rifles, municiones y comida.

10 El gobernador Pedrarias Dávila era tan cruel que le llamaban "el tigre de Darién".

Ejercicio 127 Pronunciation (*ch, d, h*) and Stress: Reading Aloud

Menéndez	Amadís de Gaula	Chocano	Calderón
Díaz	Chacón	Galdós	Delgado
Ledesma	Dámaso	Madoz de Chole	Landa
Hilda	Machado	Abrahán	Hernando
Hilario	Hortensia	Humberto	Homero
Heriberto	Haydée	Hidalgo	Hernández
Huerta	Coahuila	Cahuenga	Atahualpa

Ejercicio 128 Pronunciation (*j, g*) and Stress: Reading Aloud

Gabriel	Eugenia	Gloria	Julia
Juanita	Greta	Ángela	Agustina
Jacobo	Jesusita	Jaime	José
Javier	Benjamín	Quijote	Jorge

Ejercício 129   General Review

A/B

CORRE RÁPIDO

HAY QUE MOVER MUCHA TIERRA

C/D

TOMA UN AVIÓN A BOGOTÁ

¡AH, TÚ CONOCES A CHUCHO!

E/F

¿CÓMO LE GUSTAN LOS HUEVOS?

SALE DEL COCHE

Ejercicio 130   The Involved Entity and Done-to Pronouns

In writing the combinations that your instructor will give you, keep in mind that you have to change the prepositional phrase in the second column into its corresponding with-verb involved entity pronoun and then place it properly in the sentence.

Ejemplo: 21 = *Este señor va a dármelos.*

1	2
1 Manuel la escribe	1 a mí.
2 Este señor va a darlos	2 a él.
3 Elena las trae	3 a ellas.
	4 a nosotros.
	5 a ti.

Ejercicio 131 Pronunciation (*l*) and Stress: Reading Aloud

Adolfo	Alberto	Anselmo	Isabel
Calvino	Manuel	Gabriel	Aníbal
Marcela	Matilde	Leticia	Leandro
Casals	Iglesias	Milán	Salcedo

Ejercicio 132 Pronunciation (*ll, y, ñ*) and Stress: Reading Aloud

Guillermo	Llampillas	Toñica	Toña
Yolanda	Hazañas	Mariquilla	Goyita
Yáñez	Núñez	Villalobos	Yanguas
Valle-Inclán	Llorente	Muñoz	Villaespesa

Ejercicio 133 Pronunciation (*p, qu, r*) and Stress: Reading Aloud

Guadalupe	Pelayo	Gaspar	Cipriano
Ezequiel	Penélope	Esperanza	Queta
Leopoldina	Pereda	Pérez	Padilla
Abelardo	Adriana	Alejandro	Páez
Bernarda	Brígida	Carlitos	Arnaldo
Darío	Ester	Everardo	Humberto
Quintero	Quirós	Salafranca	Urabayan

Ejercicio 134 Pronouns and Adjectival Residuals

Write the following sentences using pronouns or adjectival residuals for the indicated words. Place them properly in relation to the verb.

1 *Mamá* nos preparó *una comida magnífica.*
2 *Roberto* rompió *el coche* a *Eugenio.*
3 ¿No quieres traducirme *esta frase*?
4 Vamos a encontrar *los aviones* allí.
5 *El pobre muchacho* perdió *su cometa.*
6 Tienen que buscar *las invitaciones.*

Ejercicio 135 Preterit versus Imperfect

Translate the English.

1 Cuando yo (*was*) niño, yo siempre (*used to cross*) la calle aquí.
2 Pancho siempre (*would travel*) con nosotros durante el verano.
3 (*I didn't use to like*) las zanahorias.
4 Eduardo (*opened*) la puerta y me (*said*) —Buenas tardes.
5 Ella (*was dancing*) cuando su hermano se (*fell*).
6 Cuando nosotros (*lived*) en San Joaquín, (*we would go to bed*) más temprano que ahora.
7 Ellos (*sat down*) y (*read*) el periódico.

Ejercicio 136 Pronunciation (*rr*) and Stress: Reading Aloud

Raquel	Rogelio	Arriaza	Ruperto
Carranza	Enriqueta	Rodrigo	Socorro
Rosario	Rosaura	Israel	Arrieta
Ramiro	Enríquez	Ferreras	Rivero

Ejercicio 137 Present Subjunctive Forms of Stem-Changing Verbs and Reflexive Constructions

Write the appropriate form of the subjunctive and the appropriate reflexive pronoun for each verb in parentheses.

Ejemplo: La profesora quiere que nosotros (sentarse).   (= nos sentemos)

1 Ella nos dice que (acostarse) a las nueve.
2 Ellos mandan que tú (sentarse) aquí.
3 Es necesario que yo (despertarse) temprano mañana.
4 No quieren que ustedes (morderse) la lengua.
5 Es necesario que esos hermanos (quererse).
6 Él impide que ellos (acostarse).
7 Mandamos que ustedes no (moverse).
8 Permiten que él y yo (sentarse) con ellos.
9 No quiero que tú (morderse) el dedo.

Ejercicio 138 Preterit versus Imperfect and Pronouns

Translate the English in parentheses.

A young child is telling you what happened last week when his aunt Elisa took him to an amusement park.

1 La semana pasada mi tía Elisa (*took me*) a un parque de diversiones.

2 En el lugar donde venden dulces (*candy*) (*I asked her for*) diez centavos para comprar chicle (*chewing gum*).

3 Mi tía (*said to me*) que ella no (*had*) dinero para esas cosas y que los dentistas dicen que el chicle no es bueno para los dientes.

4 Unos minutos después (*I told her*) que (*I wanted*) una manzana acaramelada (*candied*).

5 Ella (*answered me*) que las manzanas acarameladas tienen demasiado azúcar.

6 En ese momento (*I saw*) a mi abuelo que (*he was coming*) en dirección a donde nosotros (*were*).

7 Yo (*explained to him*) a mi abuelo el problema del chicle y de la manzana.

8 Mi abuelo inmediatamente (*explained to her*) a su hija que todos los médicos recomiendan las manzanas para la salud y dicen que debemos comer por lo menos una cada día.

9 —Elisa,— dijo mi querido abuelo, —tú has olvidado que cuando tú (*were*) chiquita y tu madre y yo (*would take you*) a las ferias, (*you used to like*) mucho las manzanas acarameladas.

10 Entonces mi abuelo (*gave me*) un dólar y yo (*bought*) tres manzanas rojas y deliciosas: una para mí, otra para mi abuelo y la tercera para mi tía.

11 Mi abuelo (*smiled*) y mi tía Elisa, aunque un poco enojada (*annoyed*), me dio un abrazo y un beso.

Ejercicio 139   Present Subjunctive Forms

Write the appropriate present subjunctive form for each infinitive in parentheses.

1 Nos permiten que (hacerlo).
2 Es importante que ellos (venir) lo más pronto posible.
3 La profesora quiere que ellos (saber) esto para mañana.
4 Ella impide que yo (servirla).
5 Es necesario que tú (acostarse) pronto porque es muy tarde.
6 No desean que tú (ir) al hospital.
7 Pedimos que ellos (traernos) zanahorias.
8 No quieren que tú y yo (sentirlo) tanto.
9 ¿Insistes que yo (ponerlas) allí?

Ejercicio 140   Pronunciation (*t, z, s, c*) and Stress: Reading Aloud

Trinidad	Toribio	Arturo	Ernestina
Beatriz	Clarita	Clotilde	Violeta
Teresita	Teodoro	Timoteo	Téllez
Montoro	Ortiz	Trueba	Tartarín de Tarascón
Atotonilco	Tintoreto	Eloísa	Francisca
Gustavo	Horacio	Lázaro	Tatiana
Moisés	Susita	Zacarías	Zúñiga
Zayas	Suárez	Sáez	Rodríguez

Ejercicio 141　General Review:　Guided Conversation

Working with a partner, go through the outlined conversation twice.

You tell your friend that it seems to you that it is going to rain today.
He answers that he likes the rain.
You ask him if he knows that couple over there.
He answers that he knows the boy, that his name is David, and that he believes that the girl's name is Claudia and that she is Mary's cousin.
You tell him that he is mistaken, that Mary's cousin has not been in the university this week, and that she went to Buenos Aires with her parents.
He says that he did not know that and asks how they made the trip.
You answer that they went by plane.
You excuse yourself and say that you have to go to class and that today you have a test.
He says he hopes (*Ojalá*) that your test does not last long and says goodby (may it go well with you).

Ejercicio 142　Pronouns and Adjectival Residuals

Rewrite each sentence changing all indicated nouns to pronouns or using adjectival residuals. Are there any accent marks required?

1　*María* va a manejar *el coche.*
2　*Juan y yo* vamos con *Pancho.*
3　¿Vas a presentar *la carta* a *los invitados?*
4　Crucen ustedes *la calle* aquí.
5　Quiero que ellos den *el caballo* a *los niños.*
6　Señor, deje usted a *sus hijas* aquí.
7　*María y Claudia* llevan *la planta* a *sus amigos.*
8　No me traiga *los zapatos.*

Ejercicio 143　Pronunciation and Stress:　Reading Aloud

Miguel José (Junípero) Serra
Domingo Faustino Sarmiento Albarracín
Santiago Ramón y Cajal
Juan Zorrilla de San Martín

Victoria de los Ángeles
Gertrudis Gómez de Avellaneda
Federico García Lorca
Gabriel de la Concepción Valdés

Ejercicio 144　Pronouns and Adjectival Residuals

Rewrite each sentence using pronouns or adjectival residuals for the indicated parts.

1　*Los piratas* me escondieron *los caballos.*
2　Debemos dar *la tarea* a *esos alumnos.*
3　Presente usted *este regalo* a *la reina.*

4 Quiero que ustedes dejen *el carro*.
5 *El fuego* quemó *el edificio*.
6 Papá va a leerle *la revista* a *Elena*.
7 Crucen ustedes *el puente*.
8 Él usa *los pantalones azules*.
9 No me traiga usted *esas medias*.

Ejercicio 145   Present of Irregular Verbs

Write the appropriate present tense form of each infinitive in parentheses.

1 Todos los días yo (venir) aquí y (seguir) con mis estudios.
2 Ahora yo (ver) que ellos no me (oír).
3 El maestro (volver) aquí si yo se lo (pedir).
4 Yo lo (hacer) cada día después de que Uds. (empezar) a comer.
5 Yo no (poner) dinero en el banco porque yo no (poder).
6 Yo (pensar) que ellos no lo (haber) hecho todavía.
7 Yo no (saber) a qué hora tú (tener) que salir.

Ejercicio 146   Present Subjunctive Forms

Write the appropriate present subjunctive form of the verbs in parentheses.

1 Nos permiten que (decirlo).
2 Es importante que ellos (hacerlo) lo más pronto posible.
3 Dígales a los alumnos que ellos (venir) mañana también.
4 Ella impide que yo (salir) ahora.
5 Es necesario que tú (levantarse) ahora porque es muy tarde.
6 ¿Insistes que yo (ponerlas) aquí?
7 No quieren que tú y yo (ir) hasta más tarde.
8 Pedimos que ellas (traernos) papas y frijoles.

Ejercicio 147   Listening and Reading Comprehension

Select the most appropriate response to the question or statement which you will hear only once.

1 a Sí, es roja, pero no es una fruta; es un vegetal.
   b Sí, pero también hay manzanas amarillas.
   c Sí, es una fruta roja y también cuadrada.

2 a Creo que fue mi hermana o mi mamá.
   b Creo que María López de Castillo estaba allí.
   c Si no lo planchan, voy a plancharlo yo.

3 a Eso lo dudo. ¿Quién te lo dijo?
   b El burro es un animal muy común en México.
   c Pues, no olvides ponerte el abrigo porque hace mucho frío allí.

4 **a** No, no pueden aceptar el regalo hasta más tarde.
  b No, hombre, acaban de terminarla.
  c Sí, Pancho la escondió y no pueden hallarla.

5 **a** Margarita va a salir con Miguel el próximo sábado.
  b Sí, pero lo importante ahora es preguntar quién sabe arreglarlo.
  c Yo no sé quién lo hizo ayer, pero tú debes hacer tu propio trabajo esta noche, porque mañana tenemos examen.

6 **a** No, solamente voy a comer pan y ponerle un poco de mantequilla.
  b Sí, solamente tengo tenedor y cuchara.
  c Sí, voy a despedirme de ti y de Cuchi si ya no me necesitan.

7 **a** En esta parte de la ciudad es necesario tomar un taxi.
  b Sí, señor. Vaya usted a la playa y allí puede divertirse bastante.
  c Sí, cómo no. Más vale estar solo que mal acompañado.

Ejercicio 148   Preterit versus Imperfect

The following reading is written in the historical present. When you back-shift the events, represented by the italicized verbs, to the past, you will have to decide which go to the Preterit and which go to the Imperfect.

Centroamérica y su historia (primera parte)

Han pasado muchos años desde que° las "ciudades perdidas" de los mayas *son* (fueron) descubiertas en las selvas tropicales de México y Centroamérica. Sin embargo, todavía en nuestros días, no sabemos exactamente de dónde, cómo y en qué fecha *vienen* **1** al territorio centroamericano las tribus indias que *construyen* **2** tan famosas pirámides y misteriosos templos.   *since*

Los expertos de varias naciones que han excavado y estudiado las ruinas mayas creen que el desarrollo° de varias civilizaciones indias *empieza* **3** aproximadamente diez mil años antes de Jesucristo. De todas estas civilizaciones, la más avanzada *es* (fue) la de los mayas. Cuando Colón *llega* **4** al Nuevo Mundo, los grandes centros de la cultura maya *están* **5** ya en ruinas y cubiertos en gran parte por la vegetación tropical. Los descendientes de la tribu original *viven* **6** entonces en pequeñas comunidades del territorio que ocupan hoy la península de Yucatán y varias repúblicas centroamericanas.   *development*

La opinión de muchas autoridades es que el período clásico de la civilización maya se *extiende* **7** desde el año 300 hasta el año 900 más o menos de la era cristiana. Por razones que los investigadores no han podido interpretar de manera satisfactoria, en el siglo diez aproximadamente, los mayas *abandonan* **8** sus grandes ciudades centroamericanas y su cultura *comienza* **9** a decaer.°   *decay*

Las investigaciones científicas han revelado que los mayas *inventan* **10** un sistema bastante avanzado de escritura° jeroglífica. Cientos de años antes de llegar Cortés a las costas de México, ya esta gente extraordinaria *tiene* **11** un excelente calendario y *sabe* **12** mucho de matemáticas, astronomía, arquitectura, arte y religión. Los mayas *viven* **13** principalmente de la agricultura. El maíz *es* **14** el producto más importante en su vida. Para divertirse, a los mayas les *gusta* **15** mucho cantar, bailar y jugar a la pelota.°   *writing*   *ball*

Ejercicio 149   Vocabulary Matching

1	*it burns*	(a)	muñeca
2	*pocket*	(b)	ayuda
3	*he fixes*	(c)	falda
4	*truck*	(d)	morado
5	*bridge*	(e)	quema
6	*doll*	(f)	a veces
7	*he helps*	(g)	según
8	*sometimes*	(h)	camión
9	*knife*	(i)	bolsillo
10	*skirt*	(j)	cuerpo
11	*purple*	(k)	arregla
12	*according to*	(l)	cuadrado
		(m)	cuchillo
		(n)	puente

Ejercicio 150   Present Perfect Forms

Rewrite the following sentences, changing each indicated verb to the Present Perfect.

1   Yo *leo* dos páginas hoy.
2   ¿*Vienes* tú aquí muchas veces?
3   ¿*Oye* usted lo que ha pasado?
4   Ellos lo *dicen* también.
5   *Vemos* los nuevos árboles.
6   ¿A qué hora *vuelven*?
7   Sí, yo lo *rompo*.

Ejercicio 151   Reading Comprehension

Select the best response to each question or statement. Indicate your answer by letter.

1   Antes que te cases, mira lo que haces.
    a   Sí, es importante pensar antes de llegar a una decisión.
    b   Conchita se casó el año pasado.
    c   Tienen dos hijos y van a traerlos aquí mañana.
2   Siempre guarda su dinero en el bolsillo izquierdo, pero los pantalones nuevos que compró no tienen bolsillos. ¿Qué puede hacer ahora?
    a   Debe estudiar más para causar buena impresión a sus profesores.
    b   Podemos sugerirle que lo ponga en el bolsillo del saco.
    c   Pues, podemos decirle que aunque la mona se vista de seda, mona se queda.
3   La última vez que lo operaron, notaron que tenía sangre verde. Los médicos están seguros de que no es un habitante de nuestro planeta. ¿Qué opina usted?

a Lo único que puedo decir es que si Jorge no nos acompaña mañana va a tener que quedarse aquí solo.

b Antes de expresar mi opinión, quiero estudiar con cuidado todos los informes de la clínica. Eso va a llevar mucho tiempo, pero no me gusta llegar a conclusiones rápidas.

c En realidad, no sé pensar. Si se casan dentro de dos semanas no van a poder tener vacaciones. Es el problema más complicado del planeta.

4 En aquel tiempo el ferrocarril pasaba por el pueblo y los trenes iban y venían llenos de pasajeros, pero vinieron varios años de grandes tormentas y casi todos los habitantes del valle decidieron abandonar la región y buscar un clima mejor. Quedaron las casas vacías y las calles desiertas.

a Hay tanta gente en los pueblos del valle que una compañía de transporte va a construir dos escuelas públicas y un hotel de veinte pisos para los turistas.

b El pueblo está desierto porque lobos, tigres y otros animales feroces empezaron a bajar de las montañas porque a los niños les gustaba mucho darles de comer.

c Esa es una de las razones que dio el presidente de la compañía de ferrocarriles cuando anunció que el servicio de trenes entre San Miguel y Hermosillo no podía continuar en el futuro.

Ejercicio 152   Present Indicative of Stem-Changing Verbs; *al* plus Infinitive

Write the combinations your instructor will give you.

Ejemplo: 152 = *Ella siempre se viste para hacerlo al volver.*

1	Ella		1	tener que			1	*arriving.*
2	Yo		2	poder			2	*returning.*
3	Tú	siempre	3	querer	hacerlo	upon	3	*leaving.*
4	Ustedes		4	recordar			4	*entering.*
5	Usted y yo		5	vestirse para			5	*coming.*

Ejercicio 153   Subjunctive versus Indicative

Write the appropriate indicative or subjunctive form for each infinitive.

1 Quiero que tú lo (buscar).
2 Ellos nos informan que (ser) las dos y media de la tarde.
3 Me contesta que él (ir) a estar aquí más tarde.
4 No impida usted que ellos lo (hacer).
5 Me piden que yo (permitir) que tú (venir) también.
6 Es muy necesario que usted (empezar) ahora.
7 Desean que él y yo (estar) aquí, pero que ella no nos (oír).
8 Es necesario que nosotros (dormir) ahora.
9 Deje usted que nosotros nos (divertir).
10 No queremos que ellos (llegar) hasta mañana.

Ejercicio 154   Pronunciation and Stress: Reading Aloud

Bernal Díaz del Castillo
Miguel Hidalgo y Costilla
Eugenio María de Hostos
Sor Juana Inés de la Cruz

José Victorino Lastarria
Ángel Valbuena Prat
Julio Jiménez Rueda
Juan Pablo Francisco del Rosario Sánchez

Ejercicio 155   Preterit versus Imperfect

Write the appropriate preterit or imperfect form of each infinitive.

1 Cuando yo (ser) niño, siempre me (gustar) mucho oír el cuento de "Los tres osos."

2 Es la historia de una niñita que un día se (separar) de sus padres y se (perder) en el bosque.

3 Después de caminar mucho tiempo por el bosque, ella (llegar) a una casa donde (vivir) tres osos.

4 Los osos no (estar) en casa en aquel momento y la niña (abrir) la puerta y (entrar).

5 Ella (tener) mucha hambre y se (alegrar) mucho cuando (ver) que (haber) comida en una mesa.

6 Inmediatamente la niña (empezar) a comer la comida del plato pequeño que no (estar) demasiado caliente.

7 Después de comer ella se (sentar) en una silla que (ser) demasiado pequeña para ella, y la silla se (romper).

8 (Ser) aproximadamente las cinco de la tarde, y la niña (estar) cansada y (tener) mucho sueño.

9 En uno de los cuartos de dormir ella (encontrar) una cama.

10 La niña se (acostar) en la cama. La cama (ser) tan cómoda que ella se (dormir) inmediatamente.

11 Cuando los tres osos (venir) a casa, ellos (hallar) a la niña dormida en la cama. La muchachita se (despertar) y . . . *etc. etc.*

12 Cuando el profesor de español nos dijo que nosotros (ir) a escuchar este cuento en la clase, yo me (sorprender) mucho y (recordar) los días felices de mi infancia.

Ejercicio 156   Preterit versus Imperfect

Change the indicated verbs to the Past. Some will require a preterit form; others the Imperfect.

Centroamérica y su historia (segunda parte)

Los primeros hombres europeos que *visitan* **1** el territorio que es hoy Centro-américa *vienen* **2** en la cuarta y última expedición de Cristóbal Colón al Nuevo Mundo. En sus tres viajes anteriores, Colón había° descubierto gran número de islas en el Caribe y la costa norte de Sur América. El gran Almirante, sin

had

embargo, todavía no *está* (estaba) satisfecho. *Es* **3** el año de 1502 y el viejo descubridor *sigue* **4** firme en su propósito de buscar una ruta nueva a China y Japón.

El 14 de agosto Colón *pone* **5** pie en el territorio que ocupa hoy la república de Honduras. Como° él *hace* **6** siempre al descubrir una nueva tierra, *toma* **7** posesión de la región en nombre del rey de España. En aquella parte de la costa, Colón *observa* **8** que el mar *tiene* **9** grandes "honduras."° De ahí viene el nombre que más tarde le *dan* **10** a esa región de Centroamérica, Honduras.

As

depths

Después de descubrir el territorio hondureño, la expedición *sigue* (siguió) adelante° por la costa y *llega* **11** a un lugar donde Colón y sus marineros *son* (fueron) recibidos por un grupo de indios que *llevan* **12** muchos adornos° de oro. Al verlos, todos *creen* **13** que *están* **14** en una tierra muy rica. Aunque° no *es* (era) verdad que aquellos indios *tienen* (tenían) grandes cantidades° de oro y plata, el nombre "costa rica" *queda* **15** en la historia. El país que años más tarde se *va* (iba) a organizar en aquella región se llama todavía hoy Costa Rica.

forward
decorations
Although
quantities

Al volver a España, Colón *muere* **16** y no *sabe* **17** nunca que en la costa opuesta *está* (estaba) la ruta que *busca* **18**, el gran océano Pacífico que años más tarde *va* (iba) a ser descubierto por Vasco Núñez de Balboa.

Ejercicio 157   Subjunctive versus Indicative

After reading each complete sentence, decide whether each blank should be filled with a subjunctive or an indicative form of the infinitive in parentheses.

1   Ojalá que mañana nosotros (poder) dormir hasta muy tarde.
2   No, señores, yo quiero que ustedes se (levantar) temprano.
3   Sí, yo estoy de acuerdo (*in agreement*) con eso. Es muy importante que todos nosotros (estar) preparados y que (ir) con el jefe.
4   Pero, ¿no ven ustedes que ya (ser) muy tarde?
5   De veras que es tarde. Es una lástima. Es muy necesario que tú y los otros (hacer) exactamente lo que yo les he dicho.
6   Pero, hombre, permite que yo me (quedar) aquí hasta las siete.
7   No te permito eso. ¿No recuerdas que mañana yo (tener) que salir con los otros también?
8   Deseamos que Pancho no (tener) dificultades y que (volver) a estar con nosotros dentro de doce horas.
9   Ojalá que todo (salir) como tú lo deseas.
10 Te digo, amigo, que Pancho (ir) a estar aquí a la hora que he indicado.

Ejercicio 158   Commands with *tú*

Change the infinitives to the appropriate *tú* command form and place any with-verb pronoun properly in relation to the verb.

1   No (ir) con ella, por favor.
2   (Despertarte), hombre, y (levantarte). Ya es tarde.
3   (Tener) tu libro aquí mañana también.

4 (Venir) aquí con ella, pero no (volver) con ella.
5 (Ir) allí y (hacer) esto inmediatamente.
6 No (salir) sin el permiso de mamá.
7 No (ponerte) esa camisa; no me gusta.
8 No (acostarte) hasta más tarde.
9 (Ponerlo) allí, por favor.
10 No (irte) hombre; (decirme) todo lo que pasó.

Ejercicio 159   Guided Conversation

Perform the following dialog with a partner. Do it twice, changing roles the second time.

A: Be a good pal (*compañero*) and come with me to the restaurant.
B: Fine. I want to talk with you. But I don't have any money.
A: I can buy you a cup of coffee, if you wish.
B: I don't like coffee. May I order (*pedir*) something else (*otra cosa*)?
A: Sure. You can eat something also.
B: No, thanks. I'm not hungry. Are we going in your red car?
A: It's not red. I have a blue car. Look, it's over there.
B: Why don't we walk? The place is not far.

Ejercicio 160   Pronouns and Adjectival Residuals

Delete the noun and keep the adjectival residuals or replace the noun phrase with a pronoun and rewrite the entire sentence, placing the pronouns or adjectival residuals in their proper position.

1 He traído *las flores* a *mi novia* (sweetheart).
2 *Mi primo* dejó de escribir *cartas* a *mi amiga*.
3 *Juanita* tiene que subir *la escalera*.
4 *Horacio e Hilario* tienen *el bolsillo* lleno de tomates.
5 Le hemos comprado a *Anita el sofá azul*.
6 Al entrar en la sala vimos *todos los muebles*.
7 *Mamá* piensa cocinar *papas y zanahorias*.
8 Pancho, tráeme *ese espejo*, por favor.

Ejercicio 161   Preterit Forms

Write the appropriate preterit form of each infinitive in parentheses.

1 Anteanoche, como era viernes y al día siguiente no teníamos que levantarnos temprano, mi compañera y yo (dar) una pequeña fiesta en nuestro apartamento. Comimos, bebimos y vimos una película de horror en la televisión a medianoche.
2 Después que la película (terminar), nuestros amigos se fueron; mi compañera se (poner) la payama y al caer en la cama se (dormir) inmediatamente sin problema.

3 Yo, sin embargo, no me (dormir) hasta muy tarde y (tener) un sueño (*dream*) terrible.

4 Esa noche yo (soñar (*to dream*)) que estaba en una cueva gigantesca que había al pie de una montaña.

5 ¡Qué lugar tan oscuro! Yo (abrir) los ojos, pero no (ver) a nadie.

6 De pronto (*suddenly*), yo (oír) una voz muy suave (*soft*) que me llamaba diciendo: —Ven, Luisa. Ven conmigo. Dame la mano y no tengas miedo.

7 Inmediatamente yo (querer) gritar, pero no (poder).

8 También yo (tratar) de correr, pero mis piernas y mis pies no se movían.

9 ¡Qué sensación tan horrible! Quería gritar y correr, pero no podía. Entonces yo (sentir) la voz de mi compañera que me llamaba.

10 Ella (poner) su mano en mi frente (*forehead*) y en ese momento me (despertar).

11 Estaba tan nerviosa que yo (tener) que tomar una pastilla (*pill*) para los nervios.

12 Cuando yo les (contar) la pesadilla (*nightmare*), mis amigos se (reír) mucho. No sé si fue que comí y bebí demasiado o que la película de monstruos me impresionó, pero nunca más me voy a quedar viendo televisión hasta las dos de la mañana.

Ejercicio 162   Commands with *tú*

Write the *tú* command form of each verb given in parentheses.

1 (Decirme) la verdad, hombre.
2 No (hacerlo) ahora.
3 (Venir) conmigo a la sala.
4 (Despertarte) pronto y vamos.
5 No (ponerte) ese traje, que no me gusta.
6 (Salir) mañana en vez de hoy.
7 ¡(Estarte) quieto, niño!
8 (Irte) y (traerme) el espejo.
9 (Hacerlo) pronto y (ponerlo) en el escritorio.

Ejercicio 163   *E* and *u* for *y* and *o*, the Suffix *mente*, and *al* plus Infinitive

Write the translation of the English words and phrases.

1 (*Upon reading*) el anuncio no pudieron decidir si debían quedarse en un motel (*or*) hotel.

2 Manuel (*and*) Ignacio no sabían si estaban en el mes de septiembre (*or*) octubre.

3 (*Furiously*) (*and*) con palabras feas el conquistador insultó a los esclavos.

4 (*Finally*), quiero decirles que (*upon finding*) el tesoro perdido, voy a darles un poco de oro (*or*) plata.

5 Inés, Isabel (*and*) Eva saben hacerlo (*rapidly*).

6 ¿Recuerdas (*or*) olvidas que tenemos que doblar a la derecha (*and*) a la izquierda más tarde?

7 Dijo (*sadly*) que no sabía si ella estaba en el hospital (*or*) en casa ahora.

8 (*Upon finishing*) este curso (*possibly*) van a saber hablar español (*and*) inglés.

Ejercicio 164   Expressions of Emotion

		serio	alegrarse
temer	ponerse	celoso	enojarse
		furioso	sorprenderse

A/B

C/D

E/F

G/H

COMPRÓ UN SOMBRERO PARA SU MUJER

LA LINDA MUJER DE DON FELIPE

Ejercicio 165   Indirect Commands

Your instructor will give you the necessary instructions.

Que se levante.	Que vaya a la pizarra.
Que escriba en la pizarra.	Que abra la puerta.
Que levante la mano.	Que cierre la puerta.
Que diga un refrán.	Que presente a Lola a la clase.

Ejercicio 166   Subjunctive versus Indicative

Write the appropriate indicative or subjunctive form of the infinitive in parentheses.

1 Mi tía nos acaba de informar que mi primo Raúl y yo (tener) un bisabuelo
en Europa.

2 Ella cree que nuestro bisabuelo (tener) noventa y cinco años.

3 Mi papá duda que él (ser) tan viejo.

4 Acabamos de recibir la noticia de que él (venir) a visitarnos en la primavera.

5 Mamá no cree que un señor tan viejo (poder) hacer el viaje solo y no le
gusta la idea de que él (viajar) sin alguien joven de la familia para acom-
pañarlo.

6 Mi tía dice que él no (ir) a tener problemas porque es la sexta vez que él
va a salir de Europa solo.

7 Papá quiere que él (venir) en abril y que se (quedar) con nosotros hasta
junio.

8 Raúl y yo nos alegramos mucho de que el bisabuelo nos (visitar) porque
queremos hacerle muchas preguntas sobre Europa.

9 Mi primo y yo pensamos ir a Europa en las vacaciones, pero la familia no
quiere que nosotros (hacer) el viaje solos.

10 Dicen que Raúl y yo (ser) un poco descuidados (*careless*) y temen que
nosotros (encontrar) dificultades.

11 Si el bisabuelo nos acompaña, ellos van a permitir que nosotros (ir) a
Europa.

Ejercicio 167   General Review

Rewrite each sentence entirely, replacing the italicized words with those in parentheses.

1 *Mis* primas Elena y *Rosa* son *inteligentes* y *están en* el *tercer* año de secundaria en una *escuela* privada. (Nuestro, Isabel, chileno, acabar de terminar, cuarto, colegio)

2 *Yo creo* que *mañana* es el *santo* de *José.* (Tú y yo, no creer, pasado mañana, cumpleaños, el señor Sánchez)

3 Ya *nosotros* sabemos que *tú* leíste siete o *nueve libros* la *semana* pasada. (yo, Rosita, ocho, novelas, mes)

4 La *profesora* no *quiere* que Tomás y *Paco* digan que las *muchachas* salieron mal en *los* exámenes. (señor Nieto, saber, Enrique, Lola, el)

Ejercicio 168   Diminutives, Let's, and Indirect Commands

Translate the following sentences.

1 Let's buy the little house.
2 No, have him buy it.
3 Have little Daniel come.
4 Have them work.
5 Have little Inés do it.
6 Let's get up.

Ejercicio 169   Subjunctive versus Indicative

Write the appropriate indicative or subjunctive form of each infinitive.

1 No me gusta que esa niña (salir) sola a la calle.
2 Me preocupa que ellos (venir) en avión cuando hay tormenta.
3 Sí, Pedrito, veo que todas tus cosas (estar) en orden.
4 Yo no creo que la alfombra gris (cubrir) todo el piso de la sala.
5 Estamos completamente seguros de que no (haber) peligro.
6 Mira qué sucio está el piso. No hay duda que ella no lo (haber) barrido hoy.
7 Ellos dudan mucho que el director lo (saber).
8 ¡Qué lástima que tú no (poder) estar aquí para la fiesta!
9 ¡Qué amargo está este café! Si no tenemos azúcar en casa insisto en que tú (ir) a la tienda a comprar más.
10 Es imposible que el camión (cruzar) ese puente en medio de la tormenta. Hay mucho peligro.

Ejercicio 170   General Review

Rewrite each sentence entirely, replacing the indicated words with those in parentheses.

1 Nuestro *cuñado* es el hermano de mi esposa; es un señor muy *simpático*. (nieta, gordo) (¡Ojo!)

2 *Por fin saben* que las *alumnas estudiosas salen* con *notas buenas.* (Por supuesto, tener miedo de, leones, fiero, saltar, la boca, abierto)

3 Las *legumbres* más comunes de la *cena* son papas, frijoles y tomates. (muebles, sala)

4 *Ojalá* que *esos alumnos, Manuel* y *Rafael, dejen de fumar muy pronto.* (Nosotros notamos, aquel, muchachitas, María, Inés, haber empezado, correr, de repente)

Ejercicio 171   Preterit versus Imperfect

After reading what Daniel and Frank say to each other, decide whether the verb should be Preterit or Imperfect, and write the appropriate form.

Daniel va a la universidad a pie

In front of the Student Union Building Daniel talks to his friend Frank, who sold him a motorcycle.

Frank: Hola, Daniel. ¿Por qué (venir **1**) a pie? ¿Y tu motocicleta?

Daniel: La (dejar **2**) en casa. Ayer (tener **3**) un problema con la policía y me suspendieron la licencia de manejar.

Frank: ¡No me digas! Cuéntame qué (pasar **4**).

Daniel: Cuando yo (venir **5**) por la Avenida Central, al llegar a la Calle Veinte, no (ver **6**) la luz roja, y un policía me (parar **7**).

Frank: Y tú ¿qué le (decir **8**)?

Daniel: ¿Qué le (ir **9**) a decir? Yo no me (dar **10**) cuenta (*realized*) que la luz había cambiado. El policía pidió la licencia. La (buscar **11**) en todos los bolsillos pero no la (tener **12**). Desgraciadamente, estaba en la cartera en los pantalones que me quité la noche anterior.

Frank: ¡Caramba! De veras que eso es tener mala pata. ¿Es tu primera violación de tráfico?

Daniel: No, hombre. El mes pasado (tener **13**) varios otros problemas. Ahora por el resto del mes voy a tener que venir a la universidad a pie.

Frank: ¡Cuánto lo siento! Pero, no te preocupes. Esas cosas le pasan a todo el mundo (*everybody*). Oye, ¿me (traer **14**) el dinero que todavía me debes (*owe*)?

Daniel: Mira, chico, la semana pasada no (poder **15**) trabajar y no tengo ni un centavo. ¿Puedes esperar hasta la semana que viene?

Frank: Sí, cómo no. No tengo prisa.

Ejercicio 172   Subjunctive versus Indicative

After reading each complete sentence, stop and decide—without writing anything down—whether the verb should be indicative or subjunctive, and what its correct spelling should be. Then before going on to the next problem, check the correct answer given in the margin.

1 En el patio de mi casa hay muchos árboles que (tener) fruta; ahora busco árboles que (dar) flores.

2 Yo conozco a un señor que (haber) conocido a personas que (venir) de otros planetas, y ahora él busca a alguien que (ir) con él a Venus.

3 Cuando ella (salir) sola de noche tiene mucho miedo de que alguien la (atacar).

4 Las madres y las abuelas siempre les dicen a ellos que (tener) mucho cuidado y que no se (ir) lejos de la casa.

5 Siempre hay niños pícaros (*rascal*) que no (obedecer) a los mayores y que no creen que (haber) peligro en irse a jugar lejos.

6 Ella no me deja ir a Las Vegas porque teme que yo (jugar) a la ruleta y (perder) mucho dinero.

7 Insiste en que ellos (volver) al laboratorio y que (practicar) más la lección de pronunciación.

8 Esos filósofos creen en realidad que Dios no (existir).

9 ¿Estás seguro que no hay ningún médico que (poder) curarla?

10 Me sorprende mucho que esos arquitectos no (haber) empezado el proyecto.

11 Yo temo que (llegar) el día del examen y que él nos pida que (traducir) partes del drama.

12 Es muy importante que ella no (saber) que su hijo (estar) en la cárcel.

13 El naturalista ve con interés que una enorme serpiente (bajar) silenciosamente de un árbol y (comenzar) a devorar a un conejo.

14 El profesor Franco dice que (ser) muy necesario que nosotros (hacer) todos los ejercicios para el jueves y que (leer) la primera parte del capítulo trece.

1	tienen / den
2	ha / vienen, vaya
3	sale / ataque
4	tengan / vayan
5	obedecen / haya
6	juegue / pierda
7	vuelvan / practiquen
8	existe
9	pueda
10	hayan
11	llegue / traduzcamos
12	sepa, está
13	baja, comienza
14	es / hagamos, leamos

Ejercicio 173   General Review: Guided Conversation

Working with a partner, go through this conversation twice so that you will have the opportunity to play both roles.

You meet a friend after an afternoon class and greet him.
He responds.
You ask him how he is.
He answers that he has a cold and does not feel very well.
You tell him that you are sorry.
He says that it was very cold last night.
You ask him if he slept near a window.
He says that he slept near a small window (use the diminutive), that he does not have a bed, and that he sleeps on the floor.
You ask why.
He says that he is going to buy a new bed because the old one was not comfortable.
You tell him that you hope that he finds one that he likes.
He says thanks, and that he will see you (*Nos vemos*) soon.
You say may all go well with him. (*Que te vaya bien.*)

Ejercicio 174 Silent Reading: Meaning from Context

After reading each of the following short passages, answer the questions.

1 Mira, Rita, ese niñito que está sentado al lado° de tu hijo tiene mucho | *side*
catarro. Necesita que alguien le limpie la nariz. Yo creo que él no tiene pañuelo.
Cuando los niños tienen catarro las mamás tienen la obligación de ponerles un
pañuelo en el bolsillo y deben insistir en que lo usen. ¿Crees tú que su mamá
se enoje si yo le limpio la nariz con mi pañuelo?

¿Cómo se dice *pañuelo* en inglés?

2 Me gusta mucho visitar a mis tíos porque en su rancho tienen muchos
animales. Los vegetales, frutas y huevos que ellos sirven son siempre frescos. La
última vez que estuve con ellos recibí una gran sorpresa porque no me sirvieron
huevos para el desayuno. Mi tía explicó que antes tenían muchas gallinas, pero
decidieron matarlas todas porque comían mucho y ponían muy pocos huevos.
Mi tío que hace versos muy malos me dijo:

> Si no pone huevos la gallina,
> Termina en mi sopa en la cocina.

¿Qué es una *gallina*?
¿Qué significa *poner huevos* en inglés?

3 —No manejes tan rápido, Carlos. El velocímetro indica que vamos a 120.

—No te preocupes, mujer. No son millas, son kilómetros. ¿Sabes cuántos
kilómetros hay en una milla?

—No es necesario que sepa eso para darme cuenta° de que vamos a una | *realize*
velocidad excesiva.

—Vamos a 75 millas aproximadamente. En una milla hay diez cuadras.

—¿Cuadras dijiste? Yo siempre he creído que una cuadra es la distancia
entre dos calles.

—Tienes razón. El problema es que todas las cuadras no son del mismo
tamaño.

—¡Cuadras, kilómetros o millas! ¡No le hace! El velocímetro ya pasa de 120
y demando que vayas más despacio. ¿Me oíste?

¿Cómo se dice en inglés *velocímetro*? ¿Y *cuadra*?

4 La última tormenta que tuvimos fue terrible. Solamente dos árboles que
tienen las raíces muy hondas pudieron resistir la fuerza tremenda del viento.

¿Cómo se dice en inglés *raíces*? ¿Y *hondo*?

Ejercicio 175 Subjunctive versus Indicative

After reading each complete sentence, decide whether the verb in parentheses
should be indicative or subjunctive and then write the correct form.

1 Después de trabajar en la ciudad muchos años, Marta y León, unos amigos de mi padre, compraron un rancho. Ellos creen que la vida del campo (ser) mucho mejor que la de la ciudad.

2 León está convencido de que en poco tiempo él (ir) a hacer mucho dinero vendiendo pollos y huevos.

3 Pero las gallinas que (tener) León comen mucho y casi nunca ponen huevos.

4 Marta quiere que su marido (matar) las gallinas o que las (vender) en el mercado.

5 Ella sabe muy bien que (poder) comprarle huevos frescos a los vecinos.

6 Un día vino a visitar a León uno de sus vecinos, un señor viejo que (haber) pasado toda su vida en el campo.

7 León le explica que sus gallinas (estar) muy gordas, pero que no (producir) huevos y su señora demanda que él las (llevar) al mercado° o que él las (comer).   market

8 El viejo campesino le pregunta cuántos gallos° él (tener) y León contesta   roosters que no tiene ninguno y que él no (necesitar) gallos.

9 El viejo se sorprende de que León le (decir) eso y no sabe qué pensar de su vecino.

10 Al día siguiente el viejo vuelve con tres gallos y le dice a León que los (poner) en el gallinero.°   chicken house

11 Varios días más tarde León ve que (haber) varias docenas de huevos en los nidos.°   nests

12 Corre a la casa y le dice a su señora que (ir) a recoger° los huevos.   gather

13 Marta no sabe lo que (haber) pasado y no cree que las gallinas (haber) puesto tantos huevos.

14 Con sus propios ojos la mujer ve que su marido (decir) la verdad y los dos (estar) muy contentos.

15 León le cuenta a su esposa todo lo que pasó y los dos se ríen como dos tontos. Ahora todas las mañanas los gallos los despiertan cantando quiquiriquí.°   cock-a-doodle-doo Marta quiere que León le (traer) a las gallinas por lo menos dos gallos más.

Ejercicio 176   General Review

Rewrite each sentence replacing the indicated words with those in parentheses.

1 *Quiero* que Ana e *Isabel nos* acompañen al *cine esta noche.* (Recordar, Marta, te, playa, mañana)

2 *Busco* un *amigo* que *quiera* ir a *pasear conmigo* en el *bosque.* (Tener, prima, deber, montar a caballo, contigo, selva)

3 *Ellos* están seguros de que su cuñada es aquella señora, *Elena Gutiérrez.* (Panchita, Juan Gómez.)

4 *Algún día* iremos a ver la *séptima* maravilla (*wonder*) del mundo. (Esta mañana a las diez, quinto)

Ejercicio 177   Guided Conversation

With a partner, do twice the following guided conversation and change roles the second time.

You tell your friend that John wants to eat in the cafeteria.
Your friend answers, "Let's eat there with him."
You say that you do not like the food there.
He answers, "All right, let John eat alone in the cafeteria."
You ask if this is the first or second time that he has eaten there.
Your friend answers that it is the seventh time.
Then you ask where you and he are going to eat.
He answers that he wants you and him to eat in a new cafe that is near.
You answer, "All right, but let's hurry (*apurarnos*) because I am very hungry."
   (Use the appropriate gesture.)

Ejercicio 178   Silent Reading: Vocabulary from Context

After reading each of the following paragraphs, answer the question.

1   Ya he pintado las cuatro paredes de mi cuarto. Ahora tengo que pintar el techo. Yo no soy ningún gigante y necesito una escalera para alcanzar el techo. Soy el más bajo de toda la familia. Solamente mido cinco pies y dos pulgadas. El techo del cuarto está a ocho pies de altura y sin escalera no puedo alcanzarlo.

¿Cómo se dice en inglés *techo*? *escalera, alcanzar, gigante, pulgadas*

2   Para trabajar en el jardín y mantenerlo limpio y bonito necesitamos diferentes tipos de herramientas. Yo solamente tengo una cortadora para cortar la hierba y un rastrillo que uso principalmente para recoger las hojas que caen de los árboles. Después de recoger las hojas, las echo en la basura.

¿Cómo se dice en inglés *herramientas*? *cortadora, rastrillo, echar*

3   Yo tengo un hermano que es mecánico y sabe los nombres de todas las partes de un automóvil. Él insiste en que yo las aprenda. El cristal que nos sirve de protección contra el viento y permite que el chofer (persona que maneja) vea la carretera se llama parabrisas. Los automóviles tienen generalmente cuatro ruedas y cada rueda tiene una llanta. Las llantas son de goma y están llenas de aire a una presión que nos permite viajar cómodamente. Las ventanas de un coche o de un avión se llaman generalmente ventanillas. El lugar donde nos sentamos en un coche no se llama silla sino (*but*) asiento.

¿Cómo se dice en inglés *parabrisas*? *rueda, llanta, goma, ventanilla, asiento*

Ejercicio 179   Pre-quiz Practice: Subjunctive versus Indicative

After reading each complete sentence, decide between indicative and subjunctive and then write the appropriate verb form. A young boy is speaking.

1   Yo tengo una hermanita que (tener) nueve años.
2   Ella y yo ayudamos siempre a mi mamá con los quehaceres de la casa. Pero no hay duda que yo (trabajar) mucho más que mi hermana.

3 Es verdad que ella (ser) menor que yo, pero yo soy hombre y creo que muchas de las tareas que mamá pide que yo (hacer) son en realidad trabajo de mujer.

4 Mamá exige (demanda) que yo (sacar) la basura y que (ir) a hacer los mandados a la tienda.

5 Algunas veces ella me manda que (hacer) las camas, (colgar) la ropa y (lavar) los platos.

6 Cuando le digo a mi hermanita que ella me (ayudar) con las tareas del jardín, en seguida (*right away*) ella me dice que ese (ser) un trabajo para hombres.

7 La única cosa que ella (hacer) en el jardín es regar de vez en cuando las flores.

8 Mamá demanda que yo (cortar) la hierba y que (recoger) las hojas secas que (haber) caído de los árboles.

9 En un tiempo tuvimos gallinas. ¡Cuánto me alegro que ya no (tener) esos animales!

10 —Tomás,— me decía mamá constantemente —quiero que (tú) (recoger) los huevos. Tomás, es muy importante que (tú) (dar) de comer y de beber a las gallinas.

11 ¡Qué pesadilla, Dios mío! Dudo mucho que otros muchachos de mi edad (tener) tantas tareas domésticas como yo.

Ejercicio 180   Comparisons of Equality

1 Ella lee	. . . *as much*	. . . *as* Ángela.
2 Ella tiene	. . . *as much* comida	. . . *as* Ángela.
3 Ella tiene	. . . *as many* pañuelos	. . . *as* Ángela.
4 Ella tiene	. . . *as much* dinero	. . . *as* Ángela.
5 Ella tiene	. . . *as many* muñecas	. . . *as* Ángela.
6 Ella es	. . . *as* bonita	. . . *as* Ángela.
7 Ella habla	. . . *as* bien	. . . *as* Ángela.

tan(*to, -a, -os, -as*) . . . *como*

A/B

C/D

ELLA NO ANDA TAN RÁPIDO COMO ÉL

ÉL NO ESTÁ TAN CANSADO COMO ELLA

Ejercicio 181 Comparisons

Figure out the answer to each problem mentally without writing the answers.

1 Ella patina (*better than*) yo, pero ella esquía sobre el agua (*worse than*) yo.
2 ¿Quién es (*older*), tú o ella?
3 Pues, ella es (*younger than*) yo.
4 Esquía con el (*greatest*) cuidado posible.
5 No tengo (*as many*) gallinas (*as*) ellos.
6 Ella tiene (*less*) talento (*than*) yo.
7 Ellos no montan a caballo (*as much as*) nosotros.
8 Yo sé patinar en ruedas (*as*) rápidamente (*as*) Jorge.
9 Don José no tenía la (*least*) idea de lo que iba a ocurrir.
10 Nosotros hacemos (*more*) viajes de excursión (*than*) nuestros vecinos.
11 No hay (*as many*) marineros en la marina (*as*) soldados en el ejército.

Ejercicio 182 Preterit versus Imperfect

Your teacher will read the following dialog aloud while you follow it in your text. As soon as you can figure out the answer, raise your hand.

Conversación por teléfono entre dos señoras

Margarita: ¿Diana? Te habla Margarita.
Diana: ¿Qué hay Margarita? ¿Cómo estás? ¿Y la familia?
Margarita: Todos bien. Oye, ayer (ver 1) a tu marido en la tienda y me (decir 2) que tú no te (sentir 3) bien. ¿Qué te pasa?
Diana: No sé, chica. Me he sentido tan mal esta semana. Primero creí que (ser 4) un simple dolor de cabeza, pero ahora tengo miedo de que sea un tumor.
Margarita: ¡No digas eso, mujer! Espero que no sea nada malo. ¿No has ido al médico?
Diana: Sí, ayer (ir 5) a consultarme con un especialista muy bueno que mi suegra me (recomendar 6).
Margarita: Mira, yo no soy doctora, pero sé muy bien que tú trabajas de-

masiado. ¿Por qué no le dices a tus hijos que te ayuden con los quehaceres de la casa?

Diana: Ellos me ayudan bastante. Esta mañana, por ejemplo, Josefina (hacer 7) todas las camas, (barrer 8) la casa y (lavar 9) los platos del desayuno antes de irse para el colegio.

Margarita: Y Pepe, ¿no ayuda?

Diana: Sí, cómo no. Él está muy joven todavía, pero hace lo que puede. Esta mañana él (sacar 10) la basura y me (regar 11) el jardín. Además cuando su padre no está aquí siempre me hace los mandados y corta la hierba.

Margarita: Pero cuando tú te quedas sola en la casa, ¿quién te cuida al bebito?

Diana: Él es muy bueno y no me da mucho trabajo. Esta mañana, por ejemplo, él (dormir 12) casi dos horas. Mientras él (dormir 13), mi vecina Julia (venir 14) a traerme un postre para la comida.

Margarita: ¡Qué amable! Oye, yo (conocer 15) a Julia la última vez que (estar 16) en tu casa, ¿verdad?

Diana: Creo que no. La mujer que tú (conocer 17) ese día aquí se llama Teresa. Julia (estar 18) de vacaciones cuando tú (venir 19) a visitarme.

Margarita: Bueno, Diana, es mejor que colguemos (*hang up*) porque ya es hora de ir a recoger a los niños en el colegio. ¡Que te mejores muy pronto y llámame si necesitas algo!

Diana: Gracias. Eres muy amable. Adiós.

Ejercicio 183 Silent Reading

Read the following selection as quickly as you can.

El joven que se casó con una mujer muy fiera (primera parte)

This very old story from Persia was used in medieval times with the serious intention of advising young men who might be considering marriage to quick-tempered, bossy women. This modernized version comes from *El Conde Lucanor*, a collection of 51 stories written by don Juan Manuel in Spain in the fourteenth century. If you have seen a stage, film, or television version of the musical *Kiss Me Kate* or Shakespeare's *The Taming of the Shrew*, you will notice how closely their plot resembles this story.

Había una vez dos jóvenes que se llamaban Catalina y Perico. Vivían en el mismo pueblo y sus padres eran muy amigos. Todos los habitantes del pueblo conocían a Catalina y a Perico y sabían que su personalidad era tan diferente como la noche y el día.

Ella era de familia rica y noble, consentida,° desobediente, de carácter muy dominador y temperamento violento. Él era de familia pobre y humilde,° industrioso, obediente y de muy buen carácter e intachable° conducta. Aunque Catalina era una muchacha muy bonita, tenía tan mal genio° que los jóvenes de toda la región la temían. Su padre estaba muy preocupado porque nadie

spoiled
humble
spotless
temper

quería casarse con ella. Perico, sin embargo,° no creía que era tan fiero el león como lo pintaban. La belleza° de Catalina le fascinaba, y la posición social de su noble y rica familia le ofrecía una magnífica oportunidad de mejorar sus condiciones de vida y llegar a ser algo en el futuro.

nevertheless
beauty

Un día Perico le dijo a su padre:

—Estoy muy disgustado, padre. Trabajo diariamente de sol a sol,° pero somos tan pobres que es imposible progresar. Hay dos soluciones para mi problema: irme del pueblo a buscar fortuna o casarme con Catalina, la hija de tu amigo rico.

from sunrise to sunset

—¿Casarte con Catalina? —contestó el padre. —¡Qué locura! ¿Pero no sabes que esa muchacha es una fiera?° Todo el pueblo conoce su mal genio. Su propio padre me ha dicho que no sabe qué va a hacer con ella. Precisamente ayer se puso furiosa con uno de sus criados° y lo atacó con un palo. Y todo fue porque el criado no hizo inmediatamente lo que ella quería.

wild beast

servants

—Yo sé que todo el mundo cree—replicó Perico—que Catalina es un diablo° y que no hay hombre en el mundo que pueda controlarla. Pero yo no le tengo miedo a ninguna mujer. Le demostraré desde el primer día que yo voy a ser el jefe de la casa y demandaré que ella me obedezca. Quiero que vaya usted inmediatamente a casa de su amigo a pedirle la mano de su hija en matrimonio. Si usted no lo hace, me voy de aquí para siempre.

devil

Al ver que su hijo estaba decidido a irse de la casa, el padre de Perico se puso su mejor traje y fue a pedir la mano de Catalina para su hijo. El padre de Catalina se alegró mucho al oír que Perico quería casarse con su hija, pero después de pensarlo un poco le dijo a su amigo:

—Esa hija mía es un demonio y va a acabarme la vida. Es cierto que tengo muchas ganas de que se case y se vaya de esta casa, pero no puedo permitir que el hijo de uno de mis mejores amigos sea la víctima. Deja que tu hijo se vaya del pueblo a buscar fortuna. Más vale que Perico esté lejos o muerto que casado con una muchacha tan fiera como Catalina. Por favor, buen amigo, no me pidas que firme la sentencia de muerte de un joven tan bueno como tu hijo. No hay duda que el hombre que se case con mi hija se expone a perder la vida.

Ejercicio 184   Comparisons

LA CASA FUE DESTRUIDA

A/B

CORRÍ

C/D

EL RÍO INUNDÓ EL PUEBLO

NO TRABAJARÁN HASTA QUE SE PONGA CLARO EL CIELO

E/F

PEPE TIENE MÁS DE DOS MONOS

PACO NO TIENE MÁS QUE DOS MONOS

G/H

CORRE RÁPIDO

Ejercicio 185   Guided Conversation

Go through the following dialog in Spanish twice with a partner. Change roles the second time.

A: What do you have to do this afternoon?
B: I have to clean my apartment.
A: I work more than you.
B: I don't believe it. You do not work as much as I.
A: This afternoon I have to take care of three children.

B: What children?
A: My little (use diminutive) nephews and niece.
B: You are right. I work less than you.

Ejercicio 186   Comparisons

Write a sentence with each of the items in the third column. Each of these items cues you to the choice you must make in the first, second, and fifth columns.

1	2	3	4	5
		sangrienta		
		pastores		
Hemos visto (a)	tan(t-)	Ø (nothing)	como	la guerra civil.
La batalla fue		nieve		ellos.
Patinamos sobre el hielo		amarga		
		piscinas		

Ejercicio 187   Subjunctive versus Indicative

After figuring out the meaning of each sentence, write the appropriate indicative or subjunctive verb form.

1 Abelardo, quiero que tú me (acompañar) a la estación de policía.
2 Anoche tuve un accidente cuando regresaba del cine, y la ley (*law*) demanda que yo (hacer) un informe completo de todo lo que pasó antes de 24 horas.
3 Pero antes de que (tú y yo) (ir), es preciso que yo (completar) este cuestionario que me dio un señor que (trabajar) en el Departamento de Vehículos.
4 ¡Caray! ¿No hay ningún lápiz en esta casa que no (estar) roto?
5 Pero, hombre, ¿no sabes que no permiten que (tú) (usar) lápiz para contestar esas preguntas?
6 ¿Cómo? No creo que (tú) (ir) a decirme que (yo) (escribir) con tiza.
7 Mira, chico, déjate de bromas (*stop joking*). Tú sabes muy bien que (ser) importante llenar estos cuestionarios con pluma.
8 ¡A buena hora me lo dices! Hace varios minutos que yo (estar) escribiendo con lápiz y no me dijiste nada.
9 Todo el mundo sabe que los cuestionarios oficiales (tener) que llenarse con tinta (*ink*).
10 Está bien. Borraré (*I will erase*) todo lo que he escrito. No quiero que ellos me (echar) en la cárcel.

Ejercicio 188   Subjunctive versus Indicative with Events of Experience and Non-experience

Write the appropriate subjunctive or indicative form of each infinitive.

1 Todas las tardes, en cuanto Pepe (terminar) sus clases en la universidad, va a tomar café y a conversar con sus amigos.

2   Esta tarde él no podrá hacerlo porque tan pronto como (llegar) a su casa tendrá que regar el jardín y cortar la hierba.

3   Si no termina estos quehaceres antes que su esposa (venir) del laboratorio, él va a tener un gran problema con ella.

4   Generalmente mientras su señora (preparar) la comida, Pepe se sienta en un sillón a leer el periódico, pero si ella está cansada Pepe es el que cocina.

5   Siempre que el padre de Pepe (ir) a cenar con ellos, ella le hace un postre especial.

6   Él irá a visitarlos la semana próxima cuando él (volver) de un viaje a California.

7   Cada vez que él (viajar) a algún lugar, les trae un buen regalo.

8   Esta noche Pepe y su esposa no podrán ver televisión hasta que ellos (hacer) todas las tareas para el día siguiente.

9   Pepe le dice a su mujer que no importa porque no hay ningún programa bueno y además ellos van a tener mucho sueño cuando (terminar) todos sus estudios.

Ejercicio 189   Present and Imperfect Progressive

Write the answer to each question using the appropriate progressive form of the cued answer given in parentheses.

1   ¿Qué estabas haciendo cuando te llamé por teléfono ayer?   (regar la hierba)
2   ¿Y qué estaba haciendo tu hermana?   (vestirse para salir)
3   ¿Qué crees que estoy haciendo yo ahora?   (prepararse para un examen)
4   ¿Qué estaban haciendo los niños?   (leer libros de cuentos)
5   ¿Qué estaba haciendo yo entonces?   (ver la televisión)
6   Y Paquito, ¿qué estaba haciendo?   (dormir)
7   Y mi esposa, ¿qué estaba haciendo?   (servir la comida)

Ejercicio 190   *Hacer* with Expressions of Time

Translate the following sentences.

1   She has been seriously ill for six months.
2   I have been weak for a year.
3   He has had a fever for an hour.
4   Twenty minutes ago the nurse brought me the drops for my (the) nose.
5   The doctor put the bandage on that wound several days ago.

Ejercicio 191   Guided Conversation

Work with a partner; go through the following dialog twice in Spanish, changing roles the second time.

A: Where are you going?
B: To the drug store to buy pills.

A: Are you ill?

B: They are for my neighbor. She has been ill for a long (*mucho*) time.

A: They told me that she was in the hospital.

B: Now she is at home. She has a tumor (cognate) on the left lung and doesn't breathe very well.

A: What a pity! I am very sorry.

B: It is necessary for her to take (that she take) many medicines.

A: I hope (*Ojala*) that she gets better soon.

Ejercicio 192   *Hacer* with Expressions of Time

Translate the following sentences.

1 He went to the doctor four days ago.
2 He has been there for three days.
3 It has been warm here for two weeks.
4 I got up two hours ago.
5 We bought the medicine a month ago.
6 She has been working here for three years.
7 They arrived ten minutes ago.

Ejercicio 193   With-relator Pronouns

Read the part of the sentence given in Spanish and use that to decide how to translate the English portions given in parentheses.

1 —*¿A quién ves, a él, o a ella?*— . . . (her).
2 "Who likes to swim?" "I like to swim." —*¿A quién le gusta nadar?* — . . . (I) *me gusta nadar.*
3 —*¿Cómo te va?* —*Bien, gracias, ¿y* . . . (you)?
4 —*¿Con quién ha hablado?*— . . . (with me).
5 *Quiero ir* . . . (with her) *al teatro y* . . . (without him).
6 *Espérame, hombre, que yo voy* . . . (with you).
7 *Ayúdame a mí y también* . . . (him).

Ejercicio 194   Subjunctive versus Indicative

Write the present indicative or subjunctive of each verb in parentheses.

1 Hace dos semanas que Hugo (estar) en el hospital.
2 Sus amigos sienten mucho que Hugo (estar) tan enfermo y esperan que él se (mejorar) muy pronto.
3 Pero, en realidad, Hugo no está tan mal. En el quinto piso donde está su cuarto, hay enfermeras que (ser) jóvenes, bonitas, muy amables que lo (cuidar) muy bien.
4 Todas las mañanas, cuando su médico (venir) a visitarlo, Hugo no le permite que él le (poner) las inyecciones.

5   Prefiere que una enfermera rubia (*blonde*) de ojos azules lo (hacer).

6   Dice Hugo que ella (saber) poner inyecciones mejor que nadie y que (ella) (ser) la mejor enfermera del mundo.

7   En el cuarto de Hugo no hay teléfono. Él le pide a la supervisora que lo (cambiar) para otro cuarto donde (haber) teléfono.

8   Todos los cuartos del quinto piso que (tener) teléfono están ocupados.

9   Hugo no quiere irse a otro piso porque teme que las enfermeras no (ser) tan bonitas ni tan amables como en el quinto piso.

Ejercicio 195   Future

Write the appropriate form of the Future for each infinitive in parentheses.

1   Mañana mis primos (venir) aquí, y después nosotros (ir) a la playa.

2   Pues si van, Miguel (estar) allí y Uds. (ver) a Matilde también.

3   Yo (terminar) de estudiar mañana y, si Uds. quieren, yo (poder) acompañarlos pasado mañana.

4   ¿Nos (acompañar) tú al aeropuerto?

5   ¿Quién (sacar) la basura mañana?

6   Ella (decir) que Uds. y yo lo (hacer) si es necesario.

7   Ellos (regar) la hierba y las flores si yo se lo pido.

Ejercicio 196   Present and Imperfect Progressive

Change all the indicated verbs in the Present to the present progressive and all the verbs in the Imperfect to the past (imperfect) progressive.

1   Mi prima *lee* una novela y *come* dulces a la vez.

2   Mientras los niños *dormían*, nosotros *echábamos* la casa por la ventana.

3   *Se enojan* mucho.

4   ¿*Piden* muchas cosas, pero no *compran* nada?

5   *Resuelves* tus problemas después de consultar con la almohada.

6   *Estudiábamos* en mi cuarto.

7   María *barría* el piso y Alicia *tendía* la ropa.

8   *Me lo sirven* ahora.

Ejercicio 197   Vocabulary and Structure Review

Translate the English words into Spanish.

1   (*Upon arriving at the flower shop*), Enrique (*and*) Hilario decidieron comprar flores (*for*) sus novias.

2   Mi (*sister-in-law*) siempre (*has bad luck*).

3   Yo voy a (*turn on the light*) después de (*sweeping the floor*). (*Remember to use the infinitive after relators.*)

4   Pancho me dio (*a little book about*) cuentos de misterio.

5   Yo fui al (*supermarket three hours ago*) para comprar una caja de chocolates (*for my sister and brother*).

6 Nunca he visto (*such a snake*).

7 *The granddaughter is older than the aunt.*

8 *I don't like to dust the furniture.*

9 La niña (*has a cold*), y (*the grandmother is to blame*).

10 Pusiste (*so much*) sal en la ensalada que ahora (*they don't like it*).

Ejercicio 198   With-relator Pronouns

After studying the model below, write translations for the various answers to the questions.

Model: Who likes these vegetables? *¿A quién le gustan estas legumbres?*
I don't. *A mí no.*
Me neither. *A mí tampoco.*
I do. *A mí sí.*
I do too. *A mí también.*

Who likes to play the violin? *¿A quiénes les gusta tocar el violín?*
We don't. . . .
We don't either. . . .
But we do. *Pero* . . . .
And we do too. *Y* . . . .

With whom is Daniel going to the movies? *¿Con quién va Daniel al cine?*
Not with me. . .
Nor with me either. *Ni* . . . .
With us. . . .
With me also. . . .

Ejercicio 199   Reading Comprehension and *Fórmulas de cortesía*

Select for the blanks the most appropriate social amenity.

Imagínate que . . .

In this and future exercises under this title, a situation will be described in Spanish and you are asked to pretend that you are one of the participating characters. At appropriate places, you will be asked to write what you would say if the dialog were taking place in real life.

Imagínate que . . . hace tres años que estudias español. Eres uno de los mejores alumnos (o alumnas) en la clase de la profesora Ríos. Vas a completar todos los requisitos de graduación en enero y te han ofrecido un excelente trabajo en una compañía de aviones para los meses de verano. Este trabajo requiere que hables español. Ya lo hablas bastante bien, pero quieres perfeccionarte asistiendo a un curso especial en la universidad de Guadalajara, México. Necesitas que tu profesora te escriba una carta de recomendación.

Son las 4:30 de la tarde y ya han terminado todas tus clases. El ómnibus que te lleva todos los días a tu casa va a salir en diez minutos. Si pierdes (*miss*) el ómnibus no habrá otro hasta las 6:00. Es urgente que vayas a hablar con la señora Ríos hoy. No lo puedes dejar para mañana.

Al llegar a la puerta de su oficina encuentras a la señora Ríos muy ocupada hablando con el jefe (*chairman*) del departamento. Eres una persona respetuosa y un poco tímida. Sabes que no debes entrar en la oficina sin permiso e interrumpir la conversación. Esperas a la puerta. Miras tu reloj. El tiempo vuela y temes que el ómnibus se vaya. Ellos no notan que alguien está a la puerta. Por fin, decides interrumpir muy cortésmente (*politely*) diciendo:

Usted: . . .

Profesora: Adelante. ¿Qué se te ofrece? Perdone un momento, señor.

Usted: (*Tell Professor Ríos to pardon you for bothering her.*) . . . Quiero pedirle un favor.

Profesora: ¡Cómo no! ¿En qué puedo servirte?

Usted: Quiero ir a México a estudiar y necesito que usted me dé una carta de recomendación.

Profesora: ¡Cuánto me alegro que vayas a México! ¿Para cuándo necesitas la carta?

Usted: Tiene que estar en Guadalajara para el día 15. Aquí está la dirección.

Profesora: Muy bien. Esta misma noche la mando por correo aéreo.

Usted: (*Thank her and excuse yourself.*) . . . Tengo mucha prisa. Ya se va el ómnibus. Hasta mañana.

Ejercicio 200 *Por* versus *para*

After reading each complete sentence, write whether its meaning requires *por* or *para* for the blank.

1   Es importante que lleguemos allá . . . las diez de la mañana.
2   Le diremos que nos preparen la ropa . . . el miércoles.
3   Cuando vayamos a cazar, cerraremos la oficina . . . tres días.
4   Hazme el favor de pasar . . . el correo y recoger mi correspondencia.
5   La semana que viene es el santo de mi novia, y este regalo que acabo de comprar es . . . ella.
6   Quiero mandárselo inmediatamente . . . correo aéreo.
7   Si no sale hoy, dudo que el regalo llegue a su casa . . . el día de su santo.

Ejercicio 201 Preterit versus Imperfect

After reading each complete sentence, decide whether the verb should be Preterit or Imperfect. Then write the appropriate form.

Peleas entre hermanos

El miércoles pasado, unos amigos de mis padres (querer 1) ir a un concierto y me (pedir 2) que cuidara a sus dos hijos por tres horas. David es el mayor y tiene nueve años. Frank tiene dos años menos que su hermano. A nadie le gusta cuidar a estos muchachitos porque son como el perro y el gato. Se pelean constantemente.

Después que los padres se (ir 3) para el concierto, mientras los dos muchachitos (estar 4) viendo un programa de televisión, yo (leer 5) mi lección de historia para el día siguiente. De repente, (yo) (oír 6) gritos y ruidos en la sala. (Yo) (correr 7) a ver qué (pasar 8).

—¿Qué te pasa, Frank? ¿Por qué lloras?

—David me (dar 9) una bofetada. Se lo voy a decir a mi mamá.

—¿Por qué (tú) (hacer 10) eso, David? Los buenos hermanos no se dan golpes. ¿No ves que él es más pequeño que tú?

—Será más pequeño que yo, pero da patadas como un mulo.

Por el resto del tiempo que (yo) (estar 11) con ellos, hasta que los padres (volver 12) del concierto, yo (tener 13) que separarlos varias veces. Cada vez que el programa cambiaba, si David (poner 14) un canal nuevo, Frank insistía en que pusiera otro diferente. Esos muchachos me (dar 15) tanta lata que yo no (poder 16) terminar mi lección de historia. Aunque me ofrezcan cinco dólares por hora, no volveré a cuidar a esos muchachos a menos que sus padres compren un segundo televisor.

Ejercicio 202   General Review

Rewrite each entire sentence, replacing the indicated words with those in parentheses and making any other necessary changes.

1 Es *verdad* que todos *llegarán* allí para *las diez de la mañana*.   (importante, estar, tres semanas)

2 ¿Qué estás *haciendo, Pancho*?   (leer, doctor Sánchez)

3 Hace un *año* que no *vemos a la Srta.* López.   (semana, hablar, con, Sr.)

4 ¿*Vas* a *estudiar* con *ella*, o con *nosotros*?   (Pensar, trabajar, mí, él)

5 *Con placer* lo *haré* cuando vengan.   (Siempre, hago)

Ejercicio 203   Subjunctive versus Indicative

Write first the appropriate indicative or subjunctive form of the verb in parentheses; then backshift both the main and the subjoined verbs.

Ejemplo: Es necesario que ellas (venir) temprano.   (vengan; Era, vinieran)

1 Es muy importante que (tú) (ir) a la botica.

2 El médico quiere que el niño (tomar) la medicina tres veces al día.

3 Yo no creo que él se (mejorar) con esas píldoras.

4 Tu padre quiere que (nosotros) (buscar) otro médico que (tener) más experiencia.

5 Mi amiga dice que ella (conocer) a un médico que (ser) especialista de niños.

6 Voy a esperar hasta que tu padre (volver) esta noche.

7 Quiero que tú (hacer) eso tan pronto como (tú) (salir) de la escuela.

Ejercicio 204 Por versus para

Select *por* or *para* for each blank.

1 Mi tía trabajó . . . ocho horas y no puede ir a ver a su marido que hace tiempo está en el hospital.

2 Le pidió a mi mamá que fuera a visitarlo hoy . . . unos minutos.

3 Pero mi mamá tiene que ir a una junta (*meeting*) y no podrá estar allí . . . las 3:00.

4 Esta mañana ella llamó a una florería . . . que le mandaran unas flores.

5 Antes de salir . . . Nueva York, mis primos también lo visitaron.

6 Esta tarde voy a ir a la droguería a comprar una tarjeta (*card*) . . . mi pobre tío.

7 Ojalá que él se mejore y no tenga que quedarse en el hospital . . . mucho tiempo.

8 Hoy llegaron dos cartas . . . él.

9 Para ir al hospital más rápidamente es mejor ir . . . la Avenida Central.

Ejercicio 205 Translation and Tense-shift

A/B

C/D

E/F

DUDA QUE VUELE
150

¿NO HAY ZAPATOS QUE LE GUSTEN?
176

G/H

BUSCA MARIPOSAS
QUE TENGAN ALAS AZULES
178

CARLOTA ROGÓ QUE NO FUSILARAN
A MAXIMILIANO
179

I/J

COLÓN TEMÍA QUE SE SUBLEVARAN...
180

PERO MANDÓ
QUE SIGUIERAN ADELANTE
181

K/L

CORONADO BUSCABA UNA CIUDAD
QUE TUVIERA CALLES DE ORO
182

MOCTEZUMA SUPO DE CORTÉS ANTES
DE QUE LLEGARA A TENOCHTITLÁN
183

Ejercicio 206   Reading Comprehension and *Refranes*

Write the most appropriate proverb for each situation.

1   Hace tres semanas que trabajo en una tienda. Estoy en un departamento donde trabajan cuatro personas: el supervisor y tres estudiantes de universidad. El jefe me dijo ayer que yo soy el mejor trabajador del grupo. A él le van a dar un puesto° más importante en otro departamento y ayer me dijo que él quiere que yo sea el nuevo supervisor del grupo. El sueldo° es excelente y la oportunidad no puede ser mejor. Pero la responsabilidad es muy grande y creo que no aceptaré la oferta. Yo soy un poco tímido.

2   Ya tengo dieciocho años y estoy en el primer año de universidad. Mis notas no son muy buenas. No me gusta estudiar y tengo muchos problemas. Estoy locamente enamorada° de un soldado. Él tiene dos años más que yo. Acaba de escribirme diciendo que quiere que me case con él dentro de un mes. Pienso contestarle inmediatamente y decirle que acepto.

3   Mi padre es comerciante.° Tiene la mejor tienda de ropa en el centro de la ciudad. Ha trabajado mucho toda su vida. Vino de Europa a este país hace treinta y cinco años. Tenía trece años cuando llegó a Nueva York y nunca tuvo la oportunidad de asistir mucho a la escuela. Su gran deseo° es que yo estudie para alguna profesión importante como médico, abogado o ingeniero. Mi abuelo materno también fue comerciante, y él insiste en que yo siga la tradición familiar. A mí me gusta mucho el mundo de los negocios.° Algún día quiero ser el presidente de una gran corporación.

position
salary

in love

businessman

desire

business

Ejercicio 207   Subjunctive versus Indicative

After reading each complete sentence, write the appropriate indicative or subjunctive form of the infinitive in parentheses.

Conversación entre madre e hija

Madre: Mira, hija, esta tarde tan pronto como (tú) (llegar **1**) de la universidad es muy importante que (tú) (empezar **2**) a preparar la comida.

Hija: Está bien, mamá. ¿Qué quieres que (yo) (hacer **3**)?

Madre: Prepara la carne que (estar **4**) en el refrigerador y una ensalada que no (tener **5**) mucho tomate. Tú sabes que a tu padre no le (gustar **6**) el tomate.

Hija: Papá me dijo que él (querer **7**) que yo le (hacer **8**) el postre nuevo que yo (aprender **9**) a hacer ayer.

Madre: No, hija. Es mucha lata hacer postres. Además el médico ha prohibido que tu padre (comer **10**) postres.

Hija: ¿Qué le digo a papá cuando (venir **11**) esta tarde?

Madre: Dile que pienso estar en el hospital con tu abuela hasta que (terminar **12**) las horas de visita.

Hija: ¿Comemos antes que tú (volver **13**), o te esperamos?

Madre: Es mejor que (Uds.) no me (esperar **14**). Tu padre siempre tiene mucha hambre cuando (él) (venir **15**) del trabajo. Además quiero pasar por la zapatería. Necesito comprar un par de zapatos.

Hija: ¿Qué clase de zapatos?

Madre: Unos zapatos que (ser **16**) baratos y que me (durar **17**) por mucho tiempo. Son para usarlos todos los días.

Hija: Ojalá que (tú) los (encontrar **18**). No te preocupes. Haré todo lo que me dices.

Ejercicio 208   *Sino* versus *Pero* and General Review

PEDRO ES GORDO

A/B

ESTÁBAMOS EN LA SELVA

C/D

HACE FRÍO

TIENEN FRÍO

E/F

VD. DEBE COMER MENOS

VA A SENTARSE

HAY UN TIGRE EN EL CORRAL

G/H

LOS SOLDADOS LLEVAN ARMA

EL PRISIONERO VA A LA CÁRCEL

I/J

LA REINA...

CORRE RÁPIDO

K/L

NO ES UNA CALAVERA...

M

SINO UN DULCE

Ejercicio 209   With-relator Pronouns

Translate the answers which appear in parentheses.

1 *¿A quiénes de ustedes les gustan las zanahorias?*
— . . . (I don't.)
— . . . (I don't either.)
—*Pero,* . . . (I do).
—*Y* . . . (I do too).

2 —*¿De quién te despediste?* —*De* . . . (you—singular familiar) *y de* . . . (them).

3 —*¿Con quién están estudiando los hermanos Trujillo?* — . . . (With me and with her.)

4 —*Este saco es para ti, ¿verdad, José?* —*No, no es para* . . . (me), *es para* . . . (you—plural).

Ejercicio 210   Guided Conversation

Work with a partner; go through the following dialog twice in Spanish, changing roles the second time.

A: Say (*Oye*), Paco, have you seen my friend Alfonso?
B: Who is Alfonso? The Mexican who is in our English class?
A: Yes, he came from Mexico three days ago.
B: Don't get angry, but your friend is a bit strange (*raro*).
A: Strange? Why do you say that?
B: When I introduced him to the girls in the class, he burst out laughing and began to shake (*darles*) hands (with them). I think he is a little crazy!
A: Don't say that, man. It's that he misses his country and has many problems with (*el*) English.
B: I don't think his problems are with (*el*) English. I think he needs to consult with a psychologist.
A: You don't understand, Paco. In Mexico it is correct to shake hands with (*a*) the girls
B: I didn't know that.
A: Well, you know it now. I won't permit you to say (that you say) that my friend Alfonso needs a psychologist.

Ejercicio 211   Subjunctive versus Indicative

After reading each complete sentence, select the appropriate indicative or subjunctive form of the verb in parentheses.

Conversación entre compañeros de clase

—Esta tarde en cuanto (tú) (salir **1**) de tu última clase, quiero que me (esperar **2**) en el primer piso al pie de la escalera. Necesito que me (acompañar **3**) a la oficina del consejero.° Quiero consultar con él para que me (hacer **4**) un cambio en el horario.°

counselor

schedule

—¿Cómo es eso? ¿Vas a cambiar tu horario otra vez? ¿No me dijiste ayer que ya él (haber **5**) aprobado todas tus clases para el segundo semestre?

—Sí, pero anoche cuando (estudiar **6**) la lista de los cursos que yo (escoger **7**), cambié de idea. Cuatro cursos los martes y jueves va a ser demasiado. Además varios profesores del departamento de música me rogaron que (continuar **8**) en la banda.

—Pues, creo que ellos (tener **9**) mucha razón. Hace cinco años que tocas la trompeta en la banda y es importante que (seguir **10**) con la música. No hay nadie en tu sección que (ser **11**) mejor músico que tú. Eres nuestro principal solista de trompeta y te echaremos mucho de menos.

—Eres muy amable, pero va a ser mi último semestre aquí y voy a estar muy ocupado. Además, ahora hay otras cosas que me (interesar **12**) más que tocar en la banda.

—No me digas que también tú (haber **13**) decidido no tocar en la banda de baile que Luis y yo vamos a organizar cuando (empezar **14**) las vacaciones.

—Eso tendré que pensarlo un poco más.

—No olvides lo que dice el refrán . . .

—Sí, ya sé. Antes que (resolver **15**) nada, consúltalo con . . . ¡tus amigos! Bueno, nos vemos a las tres.

Ejercicio 212   General Review

Rewrite the following sentences, replacing italicized items with the words in parentheses and making all the necessary changes.

1 *Es* imposible que ellos quieran estudiar para abogados porque no les gusta *hablar delante de mucha gente*. (Era, ver sangre)

2 Juanito *quería* que *sus* abuelos vinieran *de vez en cuando* para que su *mamá* estuviera contenta. (sabe, nuestra, a fines de este mes, nietos)

3 *Búsqueme* una *criada* que sepa *cocinar* y cuide bien a los *niños*. (Tengo, criado, manejar, jardín)

4 *Estoy seguro* de que todos *ellos* tienen la culpa de haber *roto* las *ventanas*. (No era posible, nosotros, dejar caer, basura)

Ejercicio 213   Guided Conversation

Go through the following dialog in Spanish twice with your partner, changing roles the second time.

A: Say, are you going hunting this week-end?
B: No, I don't like to hunt.
A: I don't either, but I like to fish.
B: I do, too. I'm (a) good fisherman.
A: I'm better than you are!
B: I doubt it (*lo*). Why don't we go to the lake this week-end?
A: Good idea! But first I have to wash my truck.
B: I'll help you.

A: No, I won't permit you to do that.
B: I want to help you, please.
A: O.K. Come back in a little while.

Ejercicio 214   General Review

Rewrite the following sentences, replacing the indicated parts and making all the necessary changes.

1 *Ha estado* aquí *cinco* veces de manera que es la quinta vez que *lo ha hecho*. (Venir, siete, decírmelo)
2 *Pon* las *cucharas* en la mesa y *ve* a la *cocina*. (Dejar, tenedores, venir, comedor)
3 *El perrito y el gatito jugarán* con Alicia y *Silvia esta noche*. (La niñita, hacerlo, Inesita, pasado mañana)
4 *Yo tengo* una *prima* que *tiene más años* que *yo*. (Nosotros, buscar, ingeniero, ser mayor, ellos)

Ejercicio 215   Past Subjunctive

Write the combinations which your teacher will dictate. All subjoined verbs should be past subjunctive.

Ejemplo: 112 = *Era preciso que yo echara una carta al correo.*

1 Era preciso que	1 yo	1 andar allí.
2 Dudaban que	2 tú	2 echar una carta al correo.
3 Se sorprendieron de que	3 tú y yo	3 darse cuenta de eso.
4 Lo trajeron antes de que	4 Vd.	4 hacerlo de buena gana.
	5 Vds.	5 decirlo todo.

Ejercicio 216   *Sino* versus *pero* and General Review

A/B

JUAN ES ALTO

C/D

VAN PARA LAS DOS

MARÍA ESTÁ EN LA CORRIDA

E/F

ÉL VA A LA TIENDA POR SU MAMÁ

G/H

HAY QUE CORTAR UNA BUENA PARTE DE LA PLANTA

I/J

LLEVA UN AVIÓN A BOGOTÁ

Ejercicio 217 Preterit versus Imperfect

The context will determine whether the past tense form that fits in each blank will be Preterit or Imperfect.

Lamentaciones de Larry

Hace varios meses, le dije un día a mi padre:

—Papá, no quiero que le pagues cientos de dólares a un pintor profesional para que nos pinte la casa por fuera. Yo puedo hacerlo.

Mi papá (tomar **1**) mi oferta en serio y desde ese día no me ha dejado en paz:

—Larry, ¿cuándo vas a pintar la casa? Larry, recuerda que (tú) me (prometer **2**) el mes pasado que (tú) (ir **3**) a pintar la casa antes que terminen las vacaciones. Larry, ¿ya (tú) (comprar **4**) la pintura? Larry, ya va a empezar a nevar y . . .

¡Qué lata! Por fin, para que no me lo recordara más, el sábado pasado, (yo) (comprar **5**) varios galones de pintura, varias brochas de pintar y (yo) (volver **6**) a casa con todo el equipo que se (necesitar **7**) para comenzar el gran proyecto.

Después de pasar todo el sábado y la mayor parte del domingo subido en techos y escaleras, he llegado a una conclusión: el arquitecto que (hacer **8**) los planos de nuestra casa, o (estar **9**) loco en aquel momento, o su misión es complicar la vida de los pintores no profesionales como yo. Han pasado tres días desde que (yo) (terminar **10**) de pintar el exterior de nuestra casa y todavía me duelen° los brazos, las piernas, en fin, todos los huesos de mi pobre esqueleto. Hace tres días que no puedo caminar derecho.°

    ache
    straight

Y como si todo eso no fuera suficiente, ayer mi madre le (decir **11**) a mi padre que no le (gustar **12**) los colores de la pintura que yo (escoger **13**) . . . que la casa (estar **14**) más fea que nunca . . . que yo (dejar **15**) caer gotas de pintura negra en sus geranios y petunias . . . y que (ella) (querer **16**) que alguien pintara la casa otra vez. Ese alguien no voy a ser yo. A la tierna° edad de 19 años, ha terminado definitivamente mi corta carrera de pintor.

    tender

Ejercicio 218 Subjunctive versus Indicative

Read each sentence and the instructions on how to restructure it. Then write the new sentence.

1 *El señor buscaba una mariposa que tuviera alas azules.*
Change this to say that he found one. In order to do this, you must:
  a replace *buscar* with another verb, either *hallar* or *encontrar,*
  b change the Imperfect to the Preterit, and
  c change *tuviera* to *tenía.*

2 *Mamá, como siempre, no pondrá la mesa hasta que lleguen nuestros familiares.*
Change this so it merely describes what mother habitually does. To do this you must:
  a delete *como siempre,* and
  b change both verbs to the present indicative.

3 *Yo siempre tengo que lavar la ropa antes de que la planche Rosa.*
Backshift the sentence. You should need no further instructions.
4 *El niño sabía que no vendrían sus amiguitos.*
Say that the boy doubted this. Use the subjunctive in your answer.

Ejercicio 219   *Sino* versus *pero*

Choose for the blanks either *sino* or *pero*.

1 Este señor no es joven como yo pensaba, . . . bastante viejo.
2 Yo no soy rico como tú crees, . . . soy muy generoso.
3 Ella no es alta y bonita, . . . tampoco es baja y fea.
4 Estos sicólogos no trabajan de día . . . de noche.
5 Don Felipe no es ministro . . . cura.
6 No queremos salir . . . llegar antes de la hora del almuerzo.
7 Ese animal no es un gato, . . . le gusta mucho el pescado.
8 En cuanto a mi señora, te diré que ha mejorado, . . . es necesario que siga tomando la medicina.
9 Esta no es la última . . . la primera vez que nos ha faltado algo que decir.
10 Es verdad que la oficina del director no está cerca de nuestra clase, . . . no puedo decir tampoco que queda muy lejos.

Ejercicio 220   General Review

Rewrite each sentence, replacing the italicized parts and making all the necessary changes.

1 A mí *me* gustan las *camisas* de *algodón.* (te, ropa, lana)
2 *Los muchachos estarán* en Chicago por *dos semanas* más o menos. (Ella y yo, llegar, las cinco y media)
3 *Dicen* que están *comiendo* mucho porque la *comida* es tan *buena.* (Dijeron, sufrir, batallas, terrible)
4 *La cocina y el comedor* están *abajo*; *tú* tendrás que bajar la escalera para verlos. (Mi cuarto de dormir, arriba, Vd.)
5 La farmacia es el lugar donde *compramos medicinas.* (ponen a los muertos)

Ejercicio 221   Subjunctive versus Indicative

After reading each complete sentence, decide whether the infinitive should be changed to the present or past of the indicative or the subjunctive.

1 Hoy día es muy importante que una persona (saber) manejar un carro.
2 Querían que nosotros (estar) de vuelta para las seis.
3 No es coincidencia que padre e hijo se (parecer) mucho.
4 Pare (*Stop*) Vd. el coche en la próxima esquina para que yo (echar) esta carta al correo.
5 Me alegro de que nadie lo (llevar) a cabo el año pasado. (*¡Ojo!*)
6 No pudieron encontrar ningún indio que (hablar) español.

7 Micaela se enojó muchísimo de que su mamá me (pedir) que la (ayudar) con los platos.

8 Nos hace falta un cuchillo especial que (cortar) la carne más dura.

9 Seguiremos trabajando mientras que ella nos (necesitar).

10 Ojalá que te (ir) bien, amigo.

Ejercicio 222   Subjunctive versus Indicative

1 Iremos al pueblo después de que el Sr. Moreno nos (traer) el periódico.

2 Después de levantarnos vimos que el sol (brillar) mucho.

3 No queríamos que ellos (oír) el discurso del abogado.

4 Cada vez que pasaba por aquella casa, el muchacho temía que el perro lo (morder).

5 No permite que los niños (tocar) el piano nuevo.

6 Nos quedábamos allí para que Luisa no (llorar) al ver al hijo del juez.

7 Mis amigos se alegran mucho de que yo, por fin, lo (haber) hecho.

8 Espero que Elías me (invitar) a su fiesta de cumpleaños.

9 Ella dudaba que yo (decir) aquellas palabras.

10 Era muy importante que nadie (salir) antes de dar las cuatro.

Ejercicio 223   Silent Reading

Read the following selection the way you read English. Do not stop to translate.

Grandes Hombres de América: Simón Bolívar   (cuarta parte)

Jefe Supremo y Presidente de la República

Después de su exilio° en las islas del Caribe, ayudado por el generoso presidente de Haití, Simón Bolívar llevó varias expediciones a las costas venezolanas con el propósito de completar la lucha por la independencia de su patria. Los diferentes grupos revolucionarios lo proclamaron Jefe Supremo de las operaciones militares. También recibió entonces la ayuda de un grupo de veteranos ingleses e irlandeses° que instruyeron a sus soldados en tácticas modernas de combate. Al organizarse la nueva república, Bolívar fue nombrado presidente de la nación.   `exile`   `Irish`

El paso° de los Andes   `crossing`

Pero Bolívar no pensaba solamente en la libertad de Venezuela sino que quería también libertar las colonias españolas al otro lado de la gigantesca cordillera de los Andes. Mientras que sus hermanos de Nueva Granada (Colombia), Ecuador y Perú sufrieran la opresión de los españoles, el brazo del Libertador no podía descansar. A fines de mayo de 1819, Bolívar organizó un ejército de 3.000 hombres y se puso en marcha de nuevo. Era el principio de la estación de las lluvias. El sofocante calor de las llanuras era insoportable. Una gran parte del territorio que tenían que cruzar estaba inundado.° Durante muchos días   `flooded`

los soldados marcharon con el agua a la cintura.° Al llegar a las grandes ele- ⟶ waist
vaciones a miles de pies sobre el nivel° del mar, ya no tenían comida. Los ⟶ level
soldados iban medio desnudos° y les hacía mucha falta ropa que fuera adecuada ⟶ naked
para el clima de aquella región glacial. El frío era tan intenso que penetraba
hasta los huesos y era muy difícil mantenerse en pie. No pudiendo resistir el
frío, el hambre y la fatiga, cientos de hombres murieron por el camino.

La batalla de Boyacá

A pesar de tantos obstáculos las tropas siguieron adelante al lado de su gran
líder y cruzaron con éxito los Andes, una de las más difíciles barreras naturales
del mundo. A principios de agosto entraron en combate contra sus enemigos
españoles y los vencieron definitivamente en la famosa batalla de Boyacá. A la
cabeza de su victorioso ejército, Bolívar entró triunfalmente en Bogotá después
de una gloriosa campaña que duró 75 días y le aseguró° un puesto° de honor ⟶ insured/place
entre los héroes de la historia universal.

Presidente de la Gran Colombia

Después de libertar a Nueva Granada, Bolívar regresó a Venezuela y le pidió
al Congreso que autorizara la creación de una gran república que incluyera el
actual territorio de Venezuela, Colombia y Ecuador. Se daba cuenta de que
al separarse de España, los pueblos libertados tendrían grandes problemas.
Para resolver estos problemas sería muy necesario que estuvieran unidos.
El Congreso no sólo autorizó la creación de la Gran Colombia sino que también
nombró a Bolívar su presidente.

La batalla de Carabobo

Dentro del territorio venezolano quedaban todavía algunas regiones dominadas
por los españoles. Ayudado por los llaneros (hombres de las llanuras) y por
una legión británica, el ejército de Bolívar venció a los españoles en la famosa
batalla de Carabobo el 24 de junio de 1821. Esta victoria puso fin al dominio
español en territorio venezolano.

Comprehension exercise: Choose the letter that corresponds to the correct
answer.

1 Los oficiales que entrenaron (*trained*) a los soldados de Bolívar en las tácticas
modernas de guerra eran de . . .

    a Haití.

    b Inglaterra e Irlanda.

    c Argentina y Perú.

2 ¿Durante qué parte del año empezó Bolívar su histórica marcha a través
de (*across*) los Andes?

    a En los meses de seca.

    b En el tiempo de las lluvias.

    c En el tiempo de fresco.

3 ¿Qué les hacía mucha falta a los soldados de Bolívar cuando iban por las
grandes elevaciones de los Andes?

    a   Agua y hambre.

    b   Frío y lluvia.

    c   Ropa y comida.

4 Al cruzar los Andes, muchos de los soldados de Bolívar . . .

    a   abandonaron a su jefe.

    b   se murieron de hambre y frío.

    c   se perdieron en la selva.

5 La batalla que decidió la independencia de Nueva Granada (Colombia) fue la batalla de . . .

    a   Boyacá.

    b   los Andes.

    c   Haití.

6 Después de obtener la independencia de Colombia, Bolívar . . .

    a   decidió que no iba a pelear más.

    b   vivió en Bogotá por el resto de su vida.

    c   volvió a Venezuela y siguió luchando por la causa de libertad.

7 Bolívar creía que, al separarse de España, los nuevos países de América iban a tener muchos problemas y era muy importante que todos . . .

    a   se separaran.

    b   se unificaran.

    c   tuvieran un rey.

Ejercicio 224   *Sino* versus *pero*

Select *sino* or *pero* for each blank.

1 Sí, hay diferencia entre la culebra y la víbora. Aquella no era culebra . . . víbora.

2 Estoy segura de que puedes explicarme la diferencia, . . . no te molestes porque a mí eso no me importa nada.

3 . . . , señora, tenga paciencia con nosotros.

4 Yo no le iba a pedir prestado su carro . . . su bicicleta.

5 La actitud de Rodolfo es por lo general muy negativa, . . . a veces él trata de cooperar.

6 No deben hacer su viaje a principios de esta semana . . . a fines de este mes.

7 Sí, señor, lo hizo de muy buena gana, . . . como de costumbre se fue sin despedirse.

8 No es que ellos no sepan hacerlo . . . más bien que no tienen ganas de hacerlo.

Ejercicio 225   General Review

Rewrite each sentence, replacing each indicated part with the word or phrase in parentheses. Other changes may also be required.

1 *Antes de que* lo resuelva *él*, quiero *tratar de investigar*lo. (Antes de, yo, saber, analizar)

2 *Después de que* termine de leer *Pancho*, tendré que estudiar todo *esto*. (Después de, yo, mis lecciones)
3 *Contestan* que *Vd.* estará en el *banco* para *las diez* y media mañana. (Contestaron, tú, playa, tres horas)
4 *Ella* no es alta e *inteligente* como su *prima* pero es *joven* y *fuerte*. (Ellos, gordo, primos, bajo, flaco)

Ejercicio 226   Guided Conversation

Work with a partner; do the dialog twice in Spanish. Change roles the second time.

A: I want you to go to the show (*cine*) with me tonight.
B: I'm sorry, but my parents don't permit me to go to the movies on Thursdays.
A: Really? I think that you don't want to accept my invitation.
B: Why don't you invite me for (*para*) Friday night (*por la noche*)?
A: Today is not Thursday but Friday! Don't you remember we had a test this morning?
B: I remember it. But tomorrow we're having another one.
A: What? Impossible! I thought today was Friday!
B: Look at the calendar and you'll see.
A: It's not necessary. You're right. I invite you for Friday.
B: I accept your invitation. I feel like seeing a good movie (*película*).

Ejercicio 227   General Review

Rewrite each sentence, replacing the italicized portions and making all other required changes.

1 El *primer* marido de Matilde no *va de compras* pero *irá al banco más tarde*. (tercero, estar en la capital, en un pueblo muy cerca)
2 Los *padres querían* que los niños se portaran *bien*. (mamá, notar, mal)
3 Ellos *dicen* que lo tendrán listo para el *viaje a* Cuzco. (decían, celebración en)
4 *Tengo* que llevar mis *zapatos* a la zapatería para que el zapatero me los *arregle*. (Tenía, ropa, lave)
5 A *ella* le gusta que los niños estén *allí jugando* con ella. (mí, en la sala, escribir)
6 Venga *Vd.* conmigo a *Santo Domingo*, capital de la República Dominicana. (tú, Managua)

Ejercicio 228   Shortened Adjectival Forms

Cover the answers in the margin, decide what form of the adjective given in parentheses should be used, and then check your answer.

1 (Alguno) de los miembros de nuestro club están en el (primero) cuarto a la derecha.   Algunos, primer

2 Llegaron (uno) (bueno) amigos que yo no había visto desde el (tercero) día de este mes.

3 (Ninguno) perro ha quedado vivo con la excepción de (uno) que debe pertenecer a (alguno) familia pobre.

4 Va a ser un (grande) banquete, pero yo no tengo (ninguno) ganas de comer.

5 Yo tengo (uno) amigo muy (bueno) que siempre tiene muy (malo) suerte.

6 (Alguno) de las noticias que he recibido este mes fueron (bueno) y otras fueron (malo).

7 La (tercero) persona en esta fila pronto va a ser la (primero).

8 A (malo) tiempo, (bueno) cara.

unos, buenos
tercer

Ningún, uno
alguna

gran, ningunas

un, bueno, mala

Algunas, buenas
malas

tercera, primera

mal, buena

Ejercicio 229   Conditional

(All the numbered verbs in this selection require the Conditional.)

Queremos ir de caza, pero . . .

Rubén, mi vecino, y yo le dijimos a nuestras esposas que a fines de noviembre él y yo (ir **1**) de caza a las montañas. Mi mujer no se opuso a nuestro proyecto, pero Clara, la señora de Rubén, se excitó mucho con la noticia. Enseguida explicó que un viaje a las montañas en esta época° del año (ser **2**) muy peligroso, y que ella (preferir **3**) que nos quedáramos en casa. Dijo que ella se (preocupar **4**) mucho sabiendo que nosotros (estar **5**) en peligro de ser atacados por algún animal salvaje y que (hacer **6**) tanto frío que seguramente nosotros nos (enfermar **7**) de catarro o algo peor. Insistió con mucha determinación que ella no (dar **8**) su consentimiento para el viaje. Rubén le explicó que nosotros (tener **9**) mucho cuidado, que nos (vestir **10**) con ropa adecuada y que (llevar **11**) todo el equipo necesario para resolver cualquier° problema que se presentara. Con todo el equipo listo para salir el viernes que viene, a Rubén y a mí no nos (gustar **12**) tener que cancelar nuestros planes.

time

any

Ejercicio 230   Infinitives Following Relators, and Shortened Adjectives

Translate the indicated words.

1 *Before entering* the *great* hall, he introduced me to the *good* gentleman of the house.

. . . *en la . . . sala, me presentó al . . . caballero de la casa.*

2 *Upon meeting* your *third* sister-in-law, I became tired of your relatives.

. . . *a tu . . . cuñada, me cansé de tus parientes.*

3 *In spite of dreaming* often, I've never had *any bad* nightmares.

. . . *a menudo, nunca he tenido . . . . . . pesadilla.*

4 If *some* friend calls me, don't say anything to *any* of my relatives *without consulting* me *first*.

Si . . . amigo me llama, no le digas nada a . . . de mis parientes . . . conmigo . . . .

5 *After returning* from work, the *first* piece of furniture I saw was *a big* armchair which had arrived during the day.

. . . del trabajo, el . . . mueble que vi fue . . . sillón que había llegado durante el día.

Ejercicio 231   Verb Review

Read each complete sentence, before deciding on the correct tense, mode, person and number of each verb in parentheses. If you have time, do the *Práctica adicional*.

Los últimos días de Bolívar

En 1830, después de 20 años de guerras y problemas, Simón Bolívar se sentía totalmente fatigado y (estar **1**) gravemente enfermo. Tenía 47 años de edad, pero (parecer **2**) un viejo de 60. A principios de mayo salió de Bogotá para no volver más. Los amigos que lo acompañaban se daban cuenta de que si no encontraban pronto un médico que lo (atender **3**), Bolívar se (morir **4**) de tuberculosis. No podían llevarlo a su país de nacimiento° porque el gobierno venezolano acusaba a Bolívar de ser un traidor y prohibía que (él) (poner **5**) pie en el territorio de Venezuela. La situación no podía ser más triste y trágica para el líder de la independencia suramericana.

birth

En estos momentos tan difíciles, un español de muy buen corazón le (ofrecer **6**) a Bolívar su casa de campo en Santa Marta, una ciudad en la costa colombiana del Atlántico. Cuando viajaba en dirección a Santa Marta, Bolívar (recibir **7**) una carta de Bogotá con muy malas noticias. Un grupo de conspiradores había (asesinar **8**) brutalmente a su gran amigo el general Sucre. Esta trágica noticia fue un golpe mortal para el Libertador.

A principios de diciembre, al llegar a Santa Marta, Bolívar (tener **9**) una fiebre muy alta. Un médico francés del pueblo (venir **10**) a atenderlo. Al verlo tan débil y grave, el doctor no quiere que él (ir **11**) a la casa del español porque está fuera de la ciudad. Bolívar le dice que él (necesitar **12**) el aire fresco del campo e insiste en que sus amigos lo (llevar **13**) en una silla de mano. Con el aire de campo y las medicinas, al principio el enfermo (mejorar **14**) un poco, pero ya era demasiado tarde. Después de varios días de agonía, el 17 de diciembre de 1830 (llegar **15**) el momento final.

Práctica adicional

A la una en punto de la tarde de ese día, Simón Bolívar (dejar **16**) de respirar y le entregó su alma a Dios. El médico francés le (cerrar **17**) los ojos, y su criado de muchos años se echó a llorar. Uno de los oficiales que acompañó a su jefe hasta el último momento (salir **18**) a buscar una de sus camisas porque había notado que la camisa de Bolívar (estar **19**) vieja y rota. El hombre más grande que ha (producir **20**) la América española murió en la miseria en casa de un español.

Ejercicio 232   Infinitives Following Relators, and
Shortened Adjectives

Translate the indicated words.

1 *Some* day we'll be able to visit *some* of my relatives in Spain.
. . . *día podremos visitar a . . . de mis parientes en España.*

2 *Instead of studying* the *third* chapter, I studied the *third* section.
. . . *el . . . capítulo, yo estudié la . . . sección.*

3 *Without hurrying*, we will not arrive on time *to see* the *first* movie, and the second one is very *bad*.
. . . , *no llegaremos a tiempo para . . . la . . . película y la segunda es muy . . .*

4 *After finishing* my homework, I saw *a great* movie on television.
. . . *mi tarea, vi . . . . . . película en televisión.*

5 *None* of our relatives gave us *any* money.
. . . *de nuestros parientes nos dio . . . dinero.*

6 *In spite of it being bad* weather they went shopping and found several *good* things at a very *good* price.
. . . *un tiempo muy . . . , fueron de compras y encontraron varias cosas . . . a muy . . . precio.*

Ejercicio 233   General Review

Follow the instructions given for each problem.

1 Your brother says, *Me siento enfermo esta mañana y quiero que tú saques la basura.* You have evidence that he really is not sick. So you tell him that you don't believe him, and that you insist that he take out the trash.

2 *Hoy es jueves y es preciso que lavemos y planchemos ropa todo el día.* You reply that it is not Thursday but Wednesday, and that it is not necessary for you (plural) to do any work today.

3 *Creo que Berta va para San Miguel.* You respond that you know that Bertha is going through the country outside the city, but that you doubt that she is going to San Miguel.

4 *No tengo ganas de echar esta carta al correo.* You respond to your little brother that you told him to mail it yesterday, and that he better do it now just as soon as possible.

5 You say, *Nos veremos la semana que viene.* Your friend asks you, *¿Qué me dijiste?* Answer his question in indirect discourse.

Ejercicio 234   General Review

Rewrite each sentence replacing the italicized items as indicated and making all other required changes.

1 *Ve* con *tu* tío a la zapatería a comprar *zapatos*. (Venir, mi, pan)

2 *Acuéstate* ahora, hijito, y *duérmete en seguida*. (No acostarse, no dormirse, hasta más tarde)

3 Miguel y *yo* no recordamos bien si la *fecha* fue *enero* o *febrero*. (Inés, mes, septiembre, octubre)

4 *Miguel* ha *hablado* muy *clara*mente. (Use diminutive of *Miguel*, leer, *rápido*)

5 Estamos en *abril*, el cuarto mes del año, y hace un *tiempo muy agradable* porque ya empezó la primavera. (octubre, poco de frío)

6 *Creo* que el *muchacho* rubio tiene *más* fiebre que tú. (Dudo, muchacha, tanto)

Ejercicio 235   Guided Conversation

Work with a partner and do the following dialog twice in Spanish. Change roles the second time. This dialog is written for two men. Women should make appropriate changes.

A: Say (*Oye*), did I tell you that I have a girl friend (sweetheart)?

B: Only one? You always have at least two or three.

A: Don't exaggerate! (*¡No exageres!*) This is the nicest (*simpática*) girl that I've met.

B: You've told me that 50,000 times!

A: This girl is a blonde and has a brunette sister. Do you want to meet them?

B: I already know them. Their father is bald, right?

A: I think so. How come (*¿Cómo es que . . .*) you know that?

B: A year ago that blonde and I were sweethearts. When I found out that her father was bald, I dropped (*dejar*) her.

A: I don't understand. Why did you do that?

B: Because the biology (cognate) teacher said one day in class that the children of bald parents . . .

A: Be quiet! Don't be ridiculous (*ridículo*)!

Ejercicio 236   General Review

Rewrite each sentence, replacing the italicized words and making all other required changes.

1 Ramona tiene *tantos* cepillos como su hermana *Marina*. (más, José)

2 *Creo* que todos *mis compañeros* estudian tanto *tiempo* como yo. (No creo, señoritas, industriosamente)

3 Me *dicen* que Elena tiene cuatro años y Felipe tres, de manera que *Elena* es mayor que *Felipe*. (dijeron, Felipe, Elena)

4 Casi todas las *enfermeras pidieron* que los *médicos* no les dieran tanto *trabajo* cada *día*. (médicos, saber, enfermeras, ayuda, hora)

5 Su nuevo *novio* no es *alto* pero es *inteligente*. (novia, bonito, feo)

6 *Ellos* querían que *los acompañáramos*. (Tú, te, decirlo todo)

Ejercicio 237   Silent Reading

See how much of the following selection you can read in seven minutes.

Grandes Hombres de América: José de San Martín
(primera parte)

"Libertador del Sur"

Mientras Simón Bolívar luchaba por la independencia de Venezuela, Colombia y Ecuador, en los territorios del sur otro gran líder llamado José de San Martín dedicaba todas sus energías y gran talento militar a mantener la independencia argentina, libertar a Chile y preparar un ataque por mar a Perú, el centro más fuerte e importante del imperio español en Sudamérica. La vida de este heroico Libertador del Sur ha quedado en la historia como un ejemplo extraordinario de coraje, generosidad, modestia, disciplina y devoción total al ideal de la libertad y la democracia.

El "indio" de Yapeyú

José Francisco de San Martín, el menor de los cinco hijos de Juan de San Martín y su esposa Gregoria Matorras, vino al mundo el 25 de febrero de 1778 en Yapeyú, un oscuro y remoto rincón° de la selva tropical americana. Este pequeño pueblo indio estaba situado en el lado argentino del río Uruguay cerca de la frontera con Brasil. Durante la vida de San Martín, cuando sus enemigos políticos querían insultarlo, lo hacían llamándole "indio." San Martín no consideraba este nombre como un insulto, pero en realidad no era indio sino criollo; es decir, blanco nacido en las colonias americanas de padres españoles. Es cierto que, a primera vista, San Martín daba la impresión de ser indio porque era muy moreno y tenía el pelo y los ojos muy negros. También es verdad que durante los primeros tres años de su vida el niño José Francisco vivió entre los indios guaraníes hasta que su padre dejó su puesto de gobernador militar de Yapeyú para volver a Buenos Aires y educar allí a sus hijos. corner

Cadete del ejército español a los once años

En Buenos Aires, es muy probable que José Francisco aprendiera a leer y escribir e iniciara sus estudios de doctrina cristiana, historia sagrada° y gramática, las asignaturas° principales en las escuelas de aquel tiempo. Cuando tenía siete años, sus padres decidieron regresar a su tierra natal.° Al llegar a España, los hijos mayores de la familia San Martín, siguiendo el ejemplo del padre, entraron en el ejército español. José Francisco fue a Madrid a continuar su educación en el Seminario de Nobles. Durante los cuatro años que él estuvo en este aristocrático colegio, el joven criollo se distinguió por su fantástica memoria, su aplicación y su facilidad para las matemáticas. La falta de dinero impidió que José siguiera estudiando y a los once años fue aceptado como cadete en un regimiento de caballería del ejército español. A esta temprana edad San Martín empezó a luchar contra los enemigos de España en África, Portugal

sacred
subjects
of birth

y Francia. Tenía solamente 17 años cuando fue ascendido a teniente° y en 1808 recibió una medalla de oro por su heroísmo en la batalla de Bailén, la gran victoria de las tropas españolas contra los ejércitos napoleónicos.

La voz del destino lo llama

En 1811, después de veinte años de participar con distinción en varias guerras, José de San Martín era teniente coronel del ejército y tenía un brillante porvenir (futuro) en España. Al enterarse de que la independencia argentina estaba en peligro, hizo una decisión memorable: abandonaría la patria de sus padres y pondría su talento y experiencia militar al servicio de su verdadera patria y del resto de América. Con un pasaporte falso que le consiguió un amigo escocés,° el coronel San Martín salió para Londres, la capital de Inglaterra, y allí se embarcó con otros patriotas criollos para Buenos Aires. Llegó sin fortuna y sin fama. Al principio los argentinos sospecharon de él y creyeron que era un espía al servicio del rey de España. Pero antes de terminar su primer año de residencia en Buenos Aires, el joven criollo demostró su patriotismo y su lealtad° venciendo a los invasores españoles en la batalla de San Lorenzo, su primera victoria en tierra americana.

(Esta sección es para los alumnos que leen muy rápidamente o para ser usada al final de la lección.)

Frases sanmartinianas

Debo seguir al destino que me llama.
Mi ejército viene decidido a morir o a ser libre.
El tiempo de la opresión y de la fuerza ha pasado. Yo vengo a poner término a esa época (tiempo) de dolor y humillación.
Por América, por su independencia y felicidad sacrificaría mil vidas.
Cada gota de sangre que se vierte° en luchas políticas me llega al corazón.
Lo que no me deja dormir, no es la oposición que puedan hacerme los enemigos, sino el atravesar° estos inmensos montes (los Andes).

lieutenant

Scottish

loyalty

is spilled

crossing

Ejercicio 238   General Review

VD. VA A LA LUNA

A/B

ESTARÁ BUSCANDO HUEVOS DE CÓNDOR

C/D · VD. DEBERÍA COMER MENOS · LA LAVA HABRÁ CUBIERTO EL PUEBLO

E/F · APRENDE A JUGAR · ¿QUÉ VAN A HACER VDS.?

G/H · DICE QUE VIENE · DICE QUE HAY UN ELEFANTE EN EL JARDÍN

Ejercicio 239   Interview

You and your partner are to use only Spanish to get information from each other about the topics listed below. You will be asked to pass on the information obtained to someone else in the class.

1 Su asignatura (*subject*) favorita (explicando por qué).
2 Cosas que le gusta hacer los sábados por la noche.
3 Sus planes para el próximo verano.

4 Su diversión favorita.

5 Las cosas que más le molestan en casa (o en el dormitorio).

Ejercicio 240 Verb Review

After reading each complete sentence, write the appropriate form of each infinitive. The context cues you to the selection of the correct mode and tense.

1 José de San Martín, el libertador de Argentina, Chile y Perú, (nacer 1) el 25 de febrero de 1778, en Yapeyú, Argentina, una antigua misión guaraní que (estar 2) cerca de la frontera brasileña. Este pequeño pueblo indio fue destruido más tarde por los portugueses.

2 Cuando José (tener 3) tres años, su padre (dejar 4) su puesto de gobernador militar de la región y todos (ir 5) a vivir en Buenos Aires.

3 Allí José (aprender 6) a leer y escribir y (seguir 7) el programa de cursos que las escuelas (enseñar 8) en aquellos tiempos.

4 Los padres de San Martín se (quedar 9) en Buenos Aires cuatro años solamente y en 1785 ellos (volver 10) a España, su tierra natal.

5 Al llegar a España, Juan de San Martín quería que su hijo se (educar 11) en el Colegio de Nobles de Madrid.

6 José (estar 12) en ese prestigioso colegio solamente cuatro años.

7 Sus padres no (ser 13) ricos y su modesta situación económica impidió que José (seguir 14) estudiando.

8 Al dejar el colegio, el joven José piensa que la carrera militar (ser 15) una carrera honorable.

9 Es una época (*time*) de invasiones y revoluciones, y cree que es importante que él (servir 16) a la patria de sus padres.

10 Después de 20 años de servicio militar dentro y fuera de España, San Martín hace una decisión importante. Sabe que los pueblos de América (estar luchar 17) por su independencia y necesitan líderes como él que (poder 18) dar instrucción militar a la juventud.

11 Él era criollo y quería que América (ser 19) libre e independiente.

12 La voz del destino lo llamaba. Volvería a Buenos Aires y allí él (organizar 20) un gran ejército de liberación.

Ejercicio 241 Subjunctive versus Indicative

After reading each complete sentence, you will have enough information to choose between present and past indicative or subjunctive.

1 En 1812 los patriotas argentinos quieren que San Martín (organizar **1**) una escuela militar que (educar **2**) a la juventud del país y los prepare para servir en el ejército tan pronto como (ser **3**) posible.

2 San Martín empezó a organizar la escuela en seguida y pidió que las autoridades (traer **4**) a Buenos Aires jóvenes que (querer **5**) defender a su patria cuando sus enemigos la (atacar **6**).

3 Los argentinos temen que los españoles y portugueses los (atacar **7**), pero saben que San Martín y sus Granaderos a Caballo (ser **8**) muy valientes (*brave*) y los vencerán.

4 Una noche en un baile San Martín conoció a una muchacha que (ser **9**) muy joven y bonita y le propuso que se (casar **10**) con él.

5 Poco tiempo después de la boda (*wedding*) fue necesario que San Martín (hacer **11**) un largo viaje al norte del país y su esposa tuvo que quedarse en la casa que sus padres (tener **12**) en Buenos Aires.

6 Después de estudiar la situación de las tropas revolucionarias del norte, San Martín cree que no (ser **13**) buena idea atacar a los españoles en las montañas y duda mucho que ellos (poder **14**) vencerlos allí.

7 En aquel tiempo San Martín no se sentía bien y se daba cuenta de que su cuerpo enfermo (necesitar **15**) la calma y el reposo del campo.

8 Le pidió permiso a sus superiores para que (ellos) le (permitir **16**) retirarse a Mendoza, una ciudad que (estar **17**) a los pies de los Andes.

9 El enfermo espera que cuando su esposa (venir **18**) de Buenos Aires a cuidarle, él se pondrá bien.

Ejercicio 242   Review of Pronouns

Rewrite each sentence with pronouns or adjectival residuals.

1 *El jefe de la tribu de indios* quiere traernos las frutas.
2 Quiero que tú le des *el jabón y el cepillo* a *Tomasita*.
3 Le gusta que *su hija* sea más alta que *Tomás y David*.
4 Entrégame *esas cartas*.
5 *Los carpinteros* nos construyen la casa.
6 No le des *las píldoras* a *Samuel*.

Ejercicio 243   Conversation

Work with a partner; carry on a five-minute discussion on the topics listed below. Everything both of you say must be in Spanish.

El próximo examen.
Los otros alumnos de la clase.
Por qué (no) me gustan los refranes españoles.
El peor día de la semana.
Lo que hago los domingos por regla general.

Ejercicio 244   General Review

Rewrite each sentence, replacing the italicized words and making all other required changes.

1 *Dicen* que vendrán antes que el sol se ponga. (Dijeron)
2 *Algunos* de sus *tíos* son *calvos*, pero *no* son feos. (Ninguna muchacha, grupo, bonita, tampoco)

3   A *mí* me gusta mucho ir con*tigo* a los *bailes*. (ti, mí, cine)
4   *Creo* que debemos *ir* para el pueblo que está *lejos*. (No creo, pasar, cerca)
5   *Ellos* están *trabajando más* que *nosotros*. (Tú, dormir, tanto, yo)
6   *Dime* qué debo hacer y *lo haré*. (No decir, te, escuchar)

Ejercicio 245   Use of the Articles

Write the form of the definite or indefinite article that fits into each blank. If no article is used, indicate this by writing the symbol Ø.

Carmita perdida en el parque

1   . . . domingo pasado, caminando por . . . Parque Balboa, mi amiga y yo encontramos a . . . niñita que parecía estar separada de sus padres.
2   . . . niñita lloraba amargamente y estaba muy asustada (*frightened*).
3   —¿Qué te pasa, . . . muchachita? —le preguntó mi amiga.
4   . . . muchachita siguió llorando sin contestar. Entonces . . . policía vino a ver qué pasaba.
5   —Yo soy . . . sargento O'Higgins—dijo . . . oficial. —¿En qué puedo servirles?
6   —Esta niña está perdida, . . . sargento O'Higgins. No sabemos quién es.
7   . . . sargento O'Higgins ya iba a llevarla para la estación de policía que está en . . . Quinta Avenida cuando . . . señora vino a donde estábamos y reconoció en seguida a . . . niña diciéndole: —¡Carmita! ¿Qué haces sola por aquí? ¿Qué pasa, . . . señor oficial?
8   —¿Es usted . . . madre de esta niña?
9   —No, señor, pero la conozco. Se llama Carmita y es la hija de una de mis amigas, . . . señora Campos. Carmita no entiende inglés.
10   Al reconocer a . . . amiga de su madre, . . . niña dejó de llorar y se sonrió.
11   —Ven conmigo, Carmita. Vamos a buscar a tu mamá. Ella estará muy preocupada pensando que te habrá pasado algo malo. ¡Qué nerviosa estás! ¿Quieres . . . agua?
12   Carmita respondió: —Tengo mucha hambre. Cómprame . . . perro caliente, . . . papas fritas y . . . refresco (*soft drink*) de naranja. Y diles que no me gusta . . . mostaza (*mustard*).

Ejercicio 246   Position of Limiting Adjectives

Rewrite each sentence, changing it to match the English given in parentheses.

1   *Paco me dio tres cepillos.* (Paco gave me three other brushes.)
2   *Ella tiene más caballos que él.* (She has three more horses than he.)
3   *Vd. tiene menos pieles que yo.* (You have five less furs (skins) than I.)
4   *Compró diez ovejas ayer.* (He bought ten other sheep yesterday.)
5   *Recibieron dos espejos y ocho lámparas. Ahora tienen más muebles que yo.* (They received two other mirrors and eight other lamps. Now they have five more (pieces of) furniture than I.)
6   *Juan vio menos culebras que yo.* (John saw six fewer snakes than I.)

Ejercicio 247 *Meter, poner, quitar,* and *sacar*

LA METE EN LA MALETA

A/B

LA PONE EN LA MALETA

C/D

LA QUITA DE LA MALETA

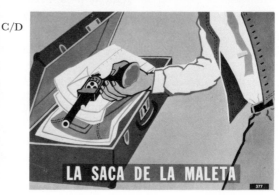
LA SACA DE LA MALETA

Ejercicio 248 Use of the Articles

1 It is the fourth day of this month.
Es . . . de este mes.

It is the fourth of this month.
Es . . . de este mes.

2 It is the fourth Monday of this month.
Es . . . de este mes.

It is Monday of this week.
Es . . . de esta semana.

3 He lives on the boulevard.
Vive . . . bulevar.

He lives on Pico Boulevard.
Vive . . . bulevar Pico.

After reading each complete sentence, write the form of the article that would fit in each blank. If no article is needed, write Ø (zero).

1 . . . sábado pasado fui a una fiesta en . . . Calle Broadway y allí conocí a . . . muchacho de Inglaterra.

2 . . . fiesta estuvo fantástica y me sorprendió mucho que . . . muchacho inglés dijera que a él no le gustaban . . . fiestas.

3 Yo le pregunté que si él tenía . . . discos (*records*) de música popular.

4 Me contestó que a él no le gustaba . . . música popular y que prefería . . . música clásica.

5 Me dijo también que . . . viernes que viene habrá . . . concierto en . . . Auditorio Municipal que está en . . . Avenida de la Independencia.

6 No quiero ofenderlo, pero voy a tener que decirle que no iré a . . . concierto con él porque yo me aburro mucho y a veces me duermo en . . . conciertos de música clásica.

Ejercicio 249 Subjunctive versus Indicative

After reading each complete sentence, write the appropriate form of the infinitive given in parentheses. Watch carefully the choice of tense as well as mode.

1 El doctor espera que yo (toser) menos esta noche.
2 Impedían que él y yo (cumplir) con nuestro deber (*duty*).
3 Les dan el papel para que ellos (envolver) el paquete.
4 Notamos que, después de lavarla, esa tela se (encoger).
5 En algunas partes de México los niños llevan a sus animales a la iglesia para que el señor cura los (bendecir).
6 Llamaré a la policía a menos que Ud. me (devolver) el dinero.
7 En aquel tiempo había una ley (*law*) que prohibía que las personas (escupir) en la calle.
8 Me casaré contigo cuando tú (cumplir) veinte años.
9 Todos los días cuando (oscurecer) salimos a dar un paseo.
10 Siempre me levanto antes que (salir) el sol, es decir, antes de que (amanecer).

Ejercicio 250 Guided Conversation

Work with a partner and go through the following conversation in Spanish twice. The second time through, reverse roles.

A: Do you still have a cold?
B: I'm much better. I plan to return to class tomorrow.
A: What a pity that you weren't in our biology class today.
B: Why? Did the instructor take one of his horrible snakes to (the) class?
A: It wasn't the instructor but one of the students.
B: I'm glad I didn't go!
A: On the contrary, it was very interesting.
B: Interesting for you because you like animals.
A: It's a huge snake. He has three more and he's going to take them to (the) class tomorrow.
B: I'm glad to know it. Tell the professor that I still have a cold!

Ejercicio 251 Position of Limiting Adjectives

Rewrite each Spanish sentence, changing it to conform with the English.

1 *Visité a tres cuñadas.* (I visited three other sisters-in-law.)
2 *Pepe tiene cuatro tías y quince primos; tiene más parientes que yo.* (Pepe has four

other aunts and fifteen other cousins; he has twenty more relatives than I.)

3 *Aquella gallina pone menos huevos cada semana que esta.* (That hen lays three less eggs each week than this one.)

4 *El enemigo tenía más soldados que nosotros.* (They had a thousand more soldiers than we.)

5 *Debes barrer los otros cuartos.* (You ought to sweep five other rooms.)

Ejercicio 252   Subjunctive versus Indicative

A/B

C/D

E/F

G/H

GRITA QUE SALTE — ES NECESARIO QUE SALTE

I/J

GRITA QUE SALTA — QUIERE QUE SE CASE CON EL

K/L

PIDE QUE SE CASE CON ÉL — IMPIDE QUE PASE

M/N

PERMITE QUE PASE — ESPERA QUE SE CASE

E117

ESPERA QUE SE CASARÁ

Ejercicio 253   Use of the Articles

Write the appropriate form of the article or Ø (zero) if none is needed.

A la hora del almuerzo

—Oye, Lola, ¿vamos a almorzar en . . . cafetería?

—Sí, pero espérame . . . momento, Paco. Primero tengo que pasar por . . . biblioteca a devolver . . . libro.

—¿Cómo se llama . . . libro que tienes que devolver?

—Se llama *Viajes de Gulliver*. Me lo recomendó . . . señora Ponce . . . semestre pasado.

—Ah, sí. . . . profesor de inglés nos habló de ese libro . . . viernes. ¿Te gustó?

—Sí, mucho. . . . héroe del libro visita . . . lugares muy extraños.° Primero va a . . . tierra habitada por . . . pigmeos y después visita . . . país donde todos . . . habitantes son . . . gigantes.

—¡Qué ridículo! A mí no me gustan . . . novelas.

—Mira, es mejor que tú vayas para . . . cafetería que ya es tarde. Cómprame . . . leche y . . . refresco° que tengo mucha sed. ¿Necesitas . . . dinero?

—No, yo tengo. Después me lo pagas.° Apúrate. Te espero en . . . puerta que da a . . . Calle Doce.

strange

soft drink

pay

Ejercicio 254   Sentence Restructuring

Follow the instructions given after each sentence.

1 *¿Qué hora es?* Answer this question by saying that it is probably three thirty, and express the idea of probability in your choice of verb form.

2 Your friend tells you, *Nuestros amigos ya estarán allí.* You don't hear him too well and ask, *¿Qué me dijiste?* What does he answer?

3 Your name is Paco. Jorge asks you and Jaime, —*Paco y Jaime, ¿quién les ayuda a ustedes con la tarea?* Answer him by saying that you help each other, stressing the "each other" part of the sentence.

4 Your brother says, *Ahora tengo otras tres horas de tarea.* Tell him that he has two more hours of homework than you.

5 A friend asks, —*¿Qué tal estás?* Answer that you feel worse than yesterday.

Ejercicio 255 Position of Adjectives

G/H

I/J

TRABAJA EN LA MINA
ESTÁ TRABAJANDO EN LA MINA

FUE ASUSTADA POR EL PERRO

LA GENTE SE ENTRA

RASGA EL VESTIDO

Ejercicio 256   Silent Reading

After reading each paragraph as rapidly as you can, write the answers to the comprehension items before going on with the next one.

Grandes hombres de las Américas: José Martí   (primera parte)

En el grupo de los grandes libertadores de Hispanoamérica—Bolívar, San Martín, Hidalgo, O'Higgins y Morelos—es necesario incluir el nombre del gran héroe nacional de Cuba, José Martí. Para el año de 1824 los principales territorios latinoamericanos ya se habían separado de España. Solamente la isla de Cuba quedaba en manos de los españoles. Cuba fue la última colonia española en América y no obtuvo su independencia hasta 1902. El alma del movimiento revolucionario cubano fue José Martí. Con razón los cubanos hablan de él llamándole Maestro o Apóstol. El resto de los latinoamericanos también lo admiran como gran poeta, escritor, orador y pensador.

(Antes de continuar la lectura del siguiente párrafo, conteste en español las siguientes preguntas con una o dos palabras:)

1   ¿Cuál era la nacionalidad de José Martí?
2   ¿A qué país pertenecía Cuba antes de 1902?

José Martí Pérez nació en la ciudad de La Habana, el 28 de enero de 1853, en una modesta y limpia casita de la calle Paula marcada con el número 102. Fue bautizado con el nombre de José Julián, pero sus amigos y familiares le llamaban Pepe. Su padre, Mariano Martí, había venido a Cuba de Valencia, España, con un regimiento del ejército español. Su madre, Leonor Pérez, era también española, nacida en las Islas Canarias. No eran ricos y casi toda su vida vivieron modestamente.

3 ¿En qué ciudad nació el Apóstol de la independencia cubana?
4 Su verdadero nombre era José Julián, pero familiarmente ¿cómo le llamaban?
5 ¿Cuál era el apellido materno (de la madre) de este gran hombre?

Después de aprender sus primeras letras en una escuelita municipal de su barrio,° Pepe asistió al colegio de don Rafael María de Mendive, distinguido educador cubano, gran amigo de la libertad y enemigo de los tiranos. Este gran maestro tuvo una gran influencia en la vida del inteligente muchacho y fue como un segundo padre para él. El colegio del señor Mendive estaba en el Paseo del Prado, una de las calles más anchas° y bonitas de la capital cubana. Allí se reunían en aquel tiempo los jóvenes y patriotas que deseaban que Cuba fuera cubana y no española.

neighborhood

wide

6 ¿Por qué fue importante el señor Mendive en la vida de José Martí?
7 ¿Cuál es el nombre de una de las calles más hermosas de La Habana donde estuvo en un tiempo el colegio donde estudió Martí?

Cuando empezó la primera guerra de independencia que iba a durar diez años, José Martí era un adolescente de 15 años. Cuando las noticias de la rebelión en la región oriental de la isla llegaron al colegio del Paseo del Prado, hubo muchos aplausos y manifestaciones de alegría. Tanto el director Mendive como sus discípulos (alumnos) creían que la guerra era justa y necesaria, y que Cuba tenía derecho° a ser un país libre e independiente. En periódicos y revistas que circulaban clandestinamente (secretamente), Pepe y otros estudiantes publicaban versos y artículos defendiendo la libertad cubana y condenando los abusos y la tiranía del gobierno español.

right

8 ¿Cuántos años duró la primera guerra de independencia cubana?
9 Cuando escribían para los periódicos y revistas, ¿a quién atacaban Martí y sus compañeros?

Ejercicio 257   Expressions of Probability

Rewrite each sentence replacing the indicated expression of probability with the future or conditional of probability.

1 Creo que en este momento mis amigos *deben estar* buscándome por toda la casa.
2 Ahora *probablemente* lo *cuida* su abuela, ¿verdad?

3 Al ver a su padre *probablemente* lo *abrazó*.

4 Cuando tú los dejabas solos en casa *probablemente* se *peleaban*, ¿verdad? Todos los niños hacen eso.

5 Tu hermano *debe estar* en este momento en el aeropuerto despidiéndolos.

Ejercicio 258   Position of Adjectives

A/B

C/D

E/F

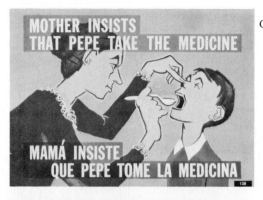

MOTHER INSISTS THAT PEPE TAKE THE MEDICINE

MAMÁ INSISTE QUE PEPE TOME LA MEDICINA

G/H

HAY UN ELEFANTE EN EL JARDÍN

I/J

NO TRABAJAN HASTA QUE SE PONE CLARO EL CIELO

HA HALLADO ZAPATOS QUE LE GUSTAN

Ejercicio 259   Reciprocal Reflexive

Translate the indicated parts to Spanish.

1 Durante una hora *we looked for each other.*
2 Las dos viejitas *take care of each other.*
3 Cuando se reunieron después de tantos años de ausencia, los dos hermanos *embraced each other.*
4 El día que tú dejaste a tus niños aquí, ellos *did not fight with each other.*
5 Los vi en al aeropuerto en el momento en que ellos *were saying good-by to each other.*

Ejercicio 260   Subjunctive versus Indicative

Write the appropriate form of the infinitives in parentheses.

1 Al mencionar los héroes de la independencia de Hispanoamérica, es importante que tú (incluir) el nombre de José Martí.
2 Martí fue un hombre extraordinario que (dar) su vida por la libertad de Cuba.
3 El padre de José Martí tenía 34 años cuando (llegar) a la isla de Cuba.

4 Era un militar que no (ganar) (*earn*) mucho dinero, pero toda su vida trabajó mucho para que su familia (tener) todo lo necesario.

5 El día que su primer hijo (nacer) fue muy feliz para él.

6 Cuando Martí (ser) niño, vivió en una casa de la calle Paula que (tener) un patio en el centro.

7 Cuando Martí (tener) cuatro años, su padre lo llevó a Valencia, España, para que los abuelos lo (conocer).

8 Después de tres años de residencia en España, el padre de Martí creyó que (ser) mejor que ellos (volver) a Cuba.

9 No quería seguir en el ejército y buscó un trabajo que le (permitir) ganar mejor sueldo (salario).

10 Por fin un día le dieron un trabajo de policía y lo mandaron a un pueblo de campo que no (estar) muy lejos de La Habana.

11 Insistió en que su hijo mayor (ir) con él y que su esposa e hijas se (quedar) viviendo en la capital.

12 Necesitaba a alguien que lo (ayudar) con el trabajo de oficina.

Ejercicio 261   Position of Adjectives

Your instructor will give you the necessary instructions.

1	perro (one unique)	pequeño
2	libro (one of many)	rojo
3	primas (all of them)	bonito
4	amigos (some)	simpático
		estudioso

Mi(s) . . . está(n) aquí.

Ejercicio 262   Use of the Articles

Write the form of the article that fits each blank or Ø (zero).

1 Cuando . . . capitán Mariano Martí fue a trabajar en . . . pueblo del interior de Cuba, llevó a su hijo Pepe con él para que lo acompañara y lo ayudara en su nuevo trabajo.

2 . . . madre de José Martí, . . . señora Leonor Pérez de Martí, había quedado en La Habana en su casa que estaba en . . . calle Industria.

3 Desde . . . primer momento, a Pepe le gustó mucho . . . campo.

4 En . . . Museo Nacional de Cuba hay . . . carta que José le escribió a su madre . . . 23 de octubre de 1862 cuando tenía solamente 9 años de edad.

5 José le decía a su mamá en . . . carta que estaba muy bien y muy contento porque tenía . . . animales, y a él le gustaban mucho . . . animales.

6 Le contaba entusiasmado a su mamá que tenía . . . caballo y . . . gallo fino.°   fighting cock

7 Aunque era verdad que se divertía mucho, también era cierto que . . . hijo de doña Leonor estaba trabajando muy duro.°   hard

8 Todos . . . días, desde . . . mañana hasta . . . tarde, . . . muchacho pasaba

largas horas en la oficina de su padre copiando . . . papeles y escribiendo . . .
cartas.

9 Desgraciadamente . . . padre de José tuvo . . . problemas con sus superiores
y perdió su puesto.°   job

10 Padre e hijo regresaron a La Habana en . . . otoño, y José ingresó° en . . .   entered
escuela que estaba en . . . Paseo del Prado.

11 . . . colegio se llamaba "San Pablo" y su director, . . . profesor Mendive,
era . . . persona muy amable que llegó a querer° a Martí como a un hijo.   love

---

Ejercicio 263   Sentence Restructuring

Follow the instructions given for each sentence.

1 Your brother tells you, —*Tengo otras dos cucharas aquí.* Tell him that he
has two more spoons than you.

2 You say, —*Vamos al banco a la una.* Your friend doesn't quite hear you and
asks, —*¿Qué dijiste?* Answer him.

3 In response to the question, —*Y entonces, ¿qué hicieron?*, you answer that
they insulted (*insultar*) each other (and clarify the reflexive pronoun) and
left (*irse*).

4 Tell your friend that you want him to return the book to you tomorrow.

5 Give his answer in Spanish: "Why? I have two fewer books than Mr.
López."

Ejercicio 264   Preterit versus Imperfect

Write the appropriate forms of the infinitive in parentheses.

José Martí en España   (primera parte)

José Martí (estar **1**) en una cárcel cubana por un período de siete meses.
Amigos de influencia que tenía su padre (conseguir **2**) que le perdonaran
la sentencia bajo la condición de que se fuera para España. Al momento de
partir, José y su padre (abrazarse **3**). Su madre y sus hermanas lo (besar **4**)
y le (dar **5**) el poco dinero que (tener **6**).

Durante el largo viaje por mar, Martí pensó mucho en los problemas de Cuba
y en su vida futura. En Madrid le (esperar **7**) días muy amargos y difíciles.
El joven de 18 años (saber **8**) que echaría mucho de menos a su familia y
a Cuba. Tenía muy poco dinero y le (doler **9**) todo el cuerpo a causa de los
golpes y castigos que había recibido en la prisión.

En Madrid, para no morirse de hambre, Martí (empezar **10**) a dar clases
a los hijos de una familia cubana. En su tiempo libre iba a los cafés y (visitar **11**)
los museos y las bibliotecas. También (asistir **12**) a la universidad todos los
días porque (querer **13**) estudiar para abogado. Por las noches en su cuarto,
Martí (pensar **14**) y (escribir **15**) algunas veces hasta el amanecer. En sus
versos y artículos para las revistas y los periódicos, Cuba (estar **16**) siempre

presente. Con su brillante pluma la (defender **17**) y (demandar **18**) urgentemente su libertad.

Ejercicio 265 Position of Adjectives

Copy the indicated noun and place the appropriate form of the adjective (in
parentheses) either before or after the noun to indicate that the entity is one
unique, one of many, all, or some.

1 Acabo de hablar con el . . . *caballero*. . . . (*distinguido*, one unique)
2 Llévele Ud. esto a la . . . *niña* . . . . (*débil*, one of many)
3 Los . . . *alumnos* . . . recibieron un castigo después de la clase. (*desobediente*,
some)
4 Los . . . *profesores* . . . se reunieron en la biblioteca después que terminaron
las clases. (*cansado*, all)

Ejercicio 266 Future and Conditional of Probability

Indicate probability by translating the English with the Future or the Conditional.

1 ¿Mamá? *She is probably* afuera colgando la ropa.
2 Dijo que ellos *probably returned* el jueves pasado de su viaje a Madrid.
3 Creemos que ella *is probably* muy preocupada con lo que ocurrió.
4 Él *probably didn't have* suficiente dinero para el viaje, ¿no crees?

Ejercicio 267 Position of Limiting Adjectives, and the Reciprocal Reflexive

Translate the English.

1 Ellos nos entregaron *twelve dollars less* que la última vez.
2 Necesito *four other lemons* para la limonada.
3 Los estudiantes siempre *used to look at each other* cuando el profesor empe-
zaba a contar cuentos.
4 Ellos *knew each other* desde que eran muy pequeños.

Ejercicio 268 Silent Reading

José Martí en México

Después de obtener los títulos° de abogado y doctor en filosofía en España,   degrees
José Martí decidió irse para México a reunirse con su familia. Antes de partir,
su amigo Fermín Valdés insistió en que José fuera con él a pasar unos días en
París. En un puerto francés los dos amigos se dijeron adiós y Fermín, como
había hecho varias otras veces, le dio dinero a Martí para el viaje. José no quería
aceptarlo, pero Fermín se lo metió en el bolsillo antes de subir al barco.

1 ¿Cuántas carreras (*careers*) terminó Martí en sus estudios en España?
2 ¿En qué ciudad francesa pasaron José y Fermín algunos días juntos?
3 ¿Qué metió Fermín en el bolsillo de José antes de que él subiera al barco?

El largo viaje por mar terminó en el puerto de Veracruz situado en el golfo de México. Allí Martí tomó un tren que subiendo por las altas montañas de la Sierra Madre lo llevó a la capital azteca. En la estación de ferrocarril de la ciudad de México José y su padre se abrazaron después de una separación de varios años. Al ver que su padre vestía de negro, José se alarmó pensando que alguien de la familia había muerto. Su padre entonces tuvo que darle la triste noticia de que acababan de enterrar° a Ana, una de sus hermanas. Al día siguiente José fue al cementerio a poner flores en la tumba de su hermana favorita.

bury

4 ¿Cómo viajó Martí desde la costa hasta la ciudad de México?
5 Al verse por primera vez después de varios años de separación, ¿qué hicieron Martí y su padre?
6 En muchos países de habla española es costumbre vestirse de negro cuando se muere un familiar. ¿Quién había muerto en la familia Martí?

A Martí no le gustaba mucho la profesión de abogado y decidió dedicarse a escribir para varios periódicos y revistas. Se hizo amigo de políticos, poetas, periodistas y pintores. Muy pronto empezó a adquirir fama y popularidad por su gran talento como escritor y orador.° Por razones políticas tuvo que irse para Guatemala donde trabajó algún tiempo de profesor. Volvió a México para casarse con Carmen Zayas Bazán, una linda cubana a quien Martí había conocido en un baile. Después de la boda° los jóvenes esposos establecieron su hogar° en la ciudad de Guatemala.

speaker

wedding
home

7 Después de pasar algún tiempo viviendo en México, ¿a qué país centroamericano fue?
8 ¿En qué país se casó?
9 ¿Cuál era el apellido de su esposa?
10 ¿De qué país era la esposa de Martí?

Ejercicio 269   Use of the Articles

Write the appropriate form of the article that fits each blank or Ø when none is needed.

1 Yo generalmente ayudo a mi señora con . . . quehaceres de la casa sin protestar, pero una de . . . cosas que no me gusta hacer es ir a . . . tienda a hacer compras.
2 Ayer por . . . tarde a eso de . . . 4:00 después que salí de . . . trabajo, ella no se sentía bien.
3 Tenía . . . fuerte dolor de cabeza y me pidió que fuera a comprarle varias cosas que necesitaba para . . . comida.
4 —He hecho una lista—me dijo—de todo lo que quiero que me compres

para que no olvides nada. Aquí está . . . dinero que vas a necesitar. Es . . . billete° de veinte dólares.

bill

5 Sin mirar . . . lista, la puse en . . . bolsillo izquierdo de . . . camisa y metí . . . billete de $20 en mi cartera.

6 Fui a . . . garaje, saqué . . . bicicleta y salí para el supermercado que está en . . . calle Lincoln cerca de . . . parque Central.

7 Ya estaba dentro de . . . supermercado cuando me di cuenta de que la lista no estaba en . . . bolsillo donde la había puesto.

8 Le pregunté a . . . empleado dónde había . . . teléfono público para llamar a mi mujer, pero . . . línea estaba ocupada y no pude comunicarme con ella.

9 Entonces empecé a imaginar qué cosas ella podría necesitar para la comida. Terminé comprando . . . lechuga, . . . tomates, . . . docena de huevos, . . . helado° de fresa° y . . . carne.

ice cream/strawberry

10 Cuando volví a casa, ella me estaba esperando en . . . cocina porque ya eran casi . . . cinco y quería empezar a preparar . . . comida.

11 Puse . . . paquete° con las cosas que había comprado en . . . mesa de la cocina y fui a . . . sala a ver . . . programa de televisión.

package

Ejercicio 270   Forms of the Perfect

Translate the English parts.

1 Las niñas *have played* a menudo con Tomasito.
2 Me dijeron que ellos *would have slept* dos horas más.
3 Creo que para las doce él ya *will have arrived*.
4 El agua no salió porque yo no *had opened* la llave.
5 Alguien *had closed* la puerta.
6 Mi hijo todavía no me *has written*.
7 Cuando él llegó, ella ya se *had died*.
8 *I would have returned*, pero no me avisaron.
9 Para mañana a mediodía ya tú lo *will have done*.
10 Creo que ellos no lo *would have broken*.

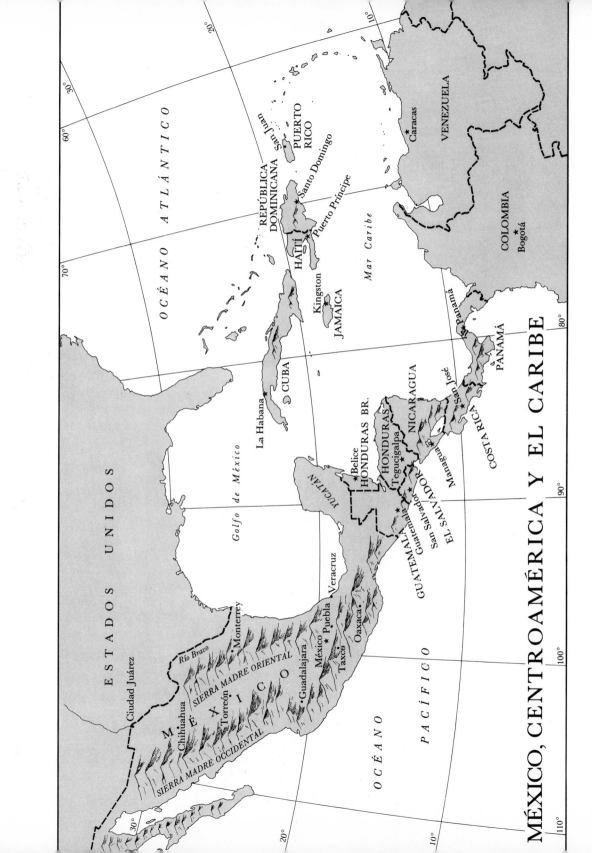

MÉXICO, CENTROAMÉRICA Y EL CARIBE

SUD AMÉRICA

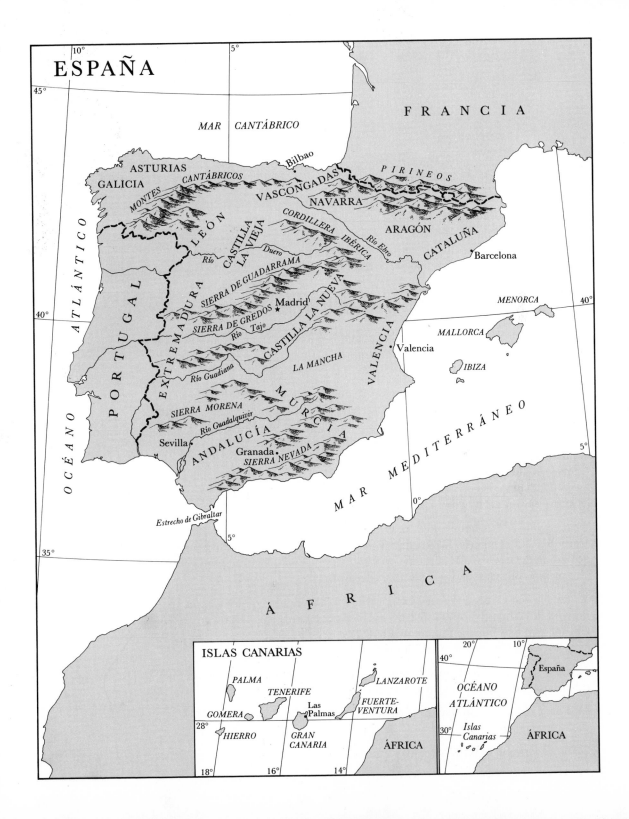

Spanish-English Vocabulary

Most nouns ending in *-n, -o, -r, -s, -e,* and *-l* and those that stand for males combine with *el;* most nouns ending in *-a, -d, -ción (-sión, xión, -tión), -umbre, -sis, -itis* and those labeling females combine with *la,* so the agreement of articles with nouns has not been indicated except in the following cases:

a) to mark exceptions to the rules: *mano* (*la*), *día* (*el*), *flor* (*la*), *sangre* (*la*), *miel* (*la*), *etc.*

b) to indicate that in most cases when both forms of the article combine with the same noun there is a difference in meaning: *cometa* (*el,* comet; *la,* kite); *policía* (*el,* policeman; *la,* police force), *etc.*

Nouns and adjectives having two forms, one ending in *-a* and the other in *-o* are arranged as follows: the *a*-form is given first and is followed by the suffix *-o* to indicate the alternate form: *gorda, -o; alumna, -o.* Adjectives not ending in *-o* that have an alternate *a*-form are indicated as follows: *español, -a; inglés, -a, etc.*

You should be able to spell any Spanish word that you hear spoken unless it belongs to the category of "eye-spelling" or "meaning-spelling" words. The letters that you need to see in order to spell are indicated as follows:

1) The sound [s] is represented in writing by various letters or letter combinations. Since the majority are spelled with the letter *s,* when this sound is represented by the letter *s,* it is not indicated. In this way you only need to memorize the spelling of this sound when it is spelled with *c, x, z,* or *ps.*

2) All *b*'s and *v*'s are indicated except when followed immediately by another consonant. When [b] is followed by another consonant, it is always spelled *b.* But these sounds may be represented by *b* or *v* in all other cases, and it is necessary for you to memorize which letter is used in each word.

3) All *h*'s are indicated since this letter represents no sound. So also are any other letters that represent no sound, such as the *j* in *reloj.*

4) The [j] (jota) sound may be spelled either *g* or *j* before *i* or *e.* Therefore, all such instances are indicated.

5) Since *ll, y* and *hi* plus vowel may represent the same sound, they are always indicated.

6) Words that bear a written accent mark, the function of which is to distinguish meaning rather than to mark the stressed syllable in speech, fall into the "eye-spelling" as well as the "meaning-spelling" category. The vowel over which the accent is written is indicated; e.g., m**í**, d**ó**nde, s**ó**lo.

7) All *n*'s and *m*'s preceding bilabials (*m, p, v, b*) are indicated since they are both pronounced [m] in such combinations; e.g., i*n*mediatamente, ta*m*bién, i*n*vierno.

A

a at, by, from, on, to
a causa de because of
a eso de at about (clock time)
a fines de toward the end of
a la vez at the same time
a mediados de around the middle of
a menos que unless
a menudo often
a pesar de in spite of
a pie on foot
a primera vista at first sight
a principios de early in, toward the beginning of
a propósito by the way
a tiempo on time
a veces sometimes
a ver let's see
abajo below, underneath; downstairs
abierta, -o open, opened
abogado lawyer
abrazar to hug, embrace
abreviar to abbreviate
abrigo overcoat, top coat
abril April
abrir to open
abrir la llave to turn on the faucet or tap
abuela grandmother
abuelo grandfather
abuelos grandparents, grandfathers
aburrir(se) to bore (tire), get bored

acabar to finish, complete, end
acabar de to have just (+ verb)
acaso perhaps, maybe
aceite oil
aceptar to accept
acercar(se) to approach
acero steel
acompañar to accompany, join
aconsejar to advise
acontecimiento happening, event
acostar (ue) to put to bed
acostarse (ue) to go to bed
acostumbrarse to become accustomed
acuerdo agreement
¡Adelante! Come in!
además besides, moreover
adentro inside
adiós good-by
administrar to administrate
admirar to admire
adondequiera anywhere
aeropuerto airport
afeitar(se) to shave
afuera outside
agosto August
agradable pleasant
agradecer to thank
agua water
ahí there
ahora now
ahora mismo right now
ahorrar to save (money)
al (a + el) to the
al aire libre in the open air
al contrario to the contrary
al lado de next to, to the side of

al parecer apparently
al principio at first, at the beginning
ala wing
alcanzar to reach
alegrarse to become happy
alegre glad, cheerful, happy
alejarse to move (go) away
alfombra rug, carpet
algo something
algodón cotton
alguien someone, somebody
allá (over) there
allí there
alma soul
almacén department store
almohada pillow
almorzar (ue) to eat lunch
almuerzo lunch
alquilar to rent
alta, -o tall, high; loud
altura height
alumna, -o pupil, student
amable kind
amanecer to dawn
amanecer (el) dawn, daybreak
amarga, -o bitter
amarilla, -o yellow
ambiente environment, atmosphere
americana, -o American
amiga, -o friend
amistad friendship
amputar to amputate
anaranjada, -o orange-colored
ancha, -o wide
andar to walk, go

anoche last night
anochecer to become night
anochecer (el) nightfall
anteayer day before yesterday
anteojos (los) (eye) glasses
antes (de que) before
anticipar to anticipate
antipática, -o unpleasant, disagreeable
año year
año que viene next year
apagar la luz to turn off the light
aparecer to appear
apartamento apartment
apellido surname, last name
apenas hardly
apostar (ue) to bet
aprender to learn
aprender de memoria to learn by heart
apurar(se) to hurry
aquel, aquella that
aquellas, -os those
aquello that
aquí here
árbol tree
ardua, -o hard
arena sand
argentina, -o Argentinian
arreglar to fix, repair; to arrange
arriba upstairs; up, above
arroz (el) rice
asamblea assembly
así so, thus, like that
asiento seat
asistir to attend
asociar to associate
astilla splinter
astronauta (el) astronaut
atardecer to become evening (dusk)
atardecer (el) dusk, evening
aula classroom
aunque although, even though
ausente absent
autobús bus
automóvil car
auxilio help
avenida avenue

aventurarse to take a chance (risk)
averiguar to find out, ascertain
avión airplane
avisarle a alguien to let someone know
¡Ay! Oh!, Ouch!
ayer yesterday
ayudar to help
ayuntamiento city hall
azúcar sugar
azul blue

B

bailar to dance
baile dance
bajar to come down, lower
baja, -o short, low
balcón balcony
banco bank; bench
bandera flag, banner
banquero banker
banquete banquet
bañar to bathe
bañarse to take a bath
bañarse en la playa to bathe at the beach
baño bath
barata, -o cheap, inexpensive
barba beard; chin
barbaridad barbarity; outrage
barbero barber
barco boat, ship
barrer to sweep
basta (it is) enough
bastante enough; fairly, pretty
basura garbage, trash
basurero trash collector
batalla battle
batea washing trough
bautizo baptism
beber to drink
bebida drink, beverage
bella, -o beautiful
belleza beauty
bendecir to bless
besar to kiss
biblioteca library

bicicleta bicycle
bien well, fine
bien (el) good, righteousness
bigote mustache
bisabuela great-grandmother
bisabuelo great-grandfather
bisabuelos great-grandparents, ancestors
blanca, -o white
blanda, -o soft
blusa blouse
boca mouth
boda wedding
bofetada slap
bola ball
boliviana, -o Bolivian
bolsa bag, purse
bolsillo pocket
bombero fireman
bondad goodness
bonita, -o pretty, beautiful
bosque woods, forest
botica drugstore
brasileña, -o Brazilian
brazo arm
brillante shining, brilliant
brillar to shine
broma joke, fun
bruta, -o dumb
buen good
buena, -o good
bulevar boulevard
burlarse de to make fun of
burro donkey, burro
buscar to look for

C

caballero gentleman, horseman
caballo horse
caber to fit (in space)
cabeza head
cada each, every
caer(se) to fall (down)
café coffee; restaurant
cafetería cafeteria
caída fall
calcetines socks
calendario calendar

calentar (ie) to heat
caliente hot
calor heat
calva, -o bald
callarse to become quiet
¡Cállate! Shut up! Be quiet!
calle (la) street
cama bed
cambiar to change
caminar to walk
camino road, way
camión truck
camisa shirt
campo field; country
cansada, -o tired
cantar to sing
cántaro large jug
capaz capable
cara (la) face
cara, -o expensive
¡Caramba! Gosh!, Confound it! Wow!
¡Caray! variant of ¡Caramba!
cárcel (la) jail
carne (la) meat; flesh
carnicería meat market
carpintero carpenter
carretera highway
carro car
carta letter
cartel poster
cartero mailman
cartón cardboard
casa house, home
casa de apartamentos apartment house
casada, -o married
casar(se) to marry, get married
castellana, -o Castilian, Spanish
castigar to punish
castigo punishment
casualidad coincidence
catarro cold (illness)
catorce fourteen
causa cause
caza hunt
cazar to hunt
celebrar to celebrate
celosa, -o jealous
cementerio cemetery

cemento cement
cena supper, dinner
cenar to eat supper
centro center, downtown
cepillo brush
cerca (de) near
cero zero
cerrar (ie) to close
cesta basket
ciega, -o blind
cielo sky, heaven; ceiling
científico scientist
cien(to) hundred
cigarro cigarette, cigar
cinco five
cincuenta fifty
cine movies
circulación traffic
circular to circulate
ciudad city
civilizar to civilize
clara, -o light; clear
¡Claro! Of course!
claro que no of course not
claro que sí of course
clase (la) class, classroom; kind
clavo nail
cobarde (el) coward
cobrar to collect; charge
cocina kitchen
cocinar to cook
cocinera, -o cook
coche car
codo elbow
coger to catch; to take
colgar (ue) to hang
colgar (ue) la ropa to hang the clothes
colombiana, -o Colombian
comedor dining room
comenzar (ie) to begin
comer to eat
comerciante businessman
cometa kite; (el) comet
comida food, dinner
como like, as
cómo what, how
como de costumbre as usual
cómoda, -o comfortable
compañera, -o companion

compensar to compensate
complicada, -o complicated
componer to compose
compra purchase
comprar to buy
comprender to understand
común common
comunicar to communicate
con with
con razón no wonder; rightly
con tal (de) que provided that
concentrar to concentrate
concierto concert
conejo rabbit
conferencia lecture
confirmar to confirm
confundir to confuse
conmigo with me
conocer to know, be acquainted with
conocida, -o acquaintance; known
conseguir (i) to get
consejo advice
conserje janitor, custodian
considerar to consider
construir to build
consultar to consult
contar (ue) to tell; to count
contestar to answer
continuar to continue
contra against
cooperar to cooperate
corazón heart
corbata necktie
corregir (i) to correct
correo post office; mail
correr to run (on foot)
corta, -o short
cortadora lawnmower
cortar to cut
cortar la hierba to mow the lawn
cortesía courtesy, politeness
corteza bark
cosa thing
coser to sew
costar (ue) to cost
costumbre custom
crear to create
crecer to grow (in size)
creer to believe

crema cream
cristal glass
cruz (la) cross
cruzar to cross
cuaderno notebook, workbook
cuadra (city) block
cuadrada, -o square
cuadro picture
cuál which, what
cuando when
cuándo when
cuánta, -o how much
cuántas, -os how many
cuanto antes as soon as possible
cuarenta forty
cuarta, -o fourth
cuarto room; quarter
cuarto de baño bathroom
cuarto de dormir bedroom
cuatro four
cuatrocientas, -os four hundred
cubrir to cover
cuchara spoon
cuchillo knife
cuerda, -o sane
cuero leather
cuerpo body
cuidado care; careful
cuidado con be careful with
cuidar to take care of, care for
cuidar a los niños to take care
  of the children
culebra snake
culpa blame
cultivar to cultivate
cumpleaños (el) birthday
cumplir to fulfill
cuna cradle
cuñada sister-in-law
cuñado brother-in-law
cura (el) priest

Ch

chica, -o small; girl, boy
chilena, -o Chilean
chiste joke

D

dar to give

dar a la calle (al jardín) to
  face the street (garden)
dar de beber to give a drink
dar de comer to feed
dar en el clavo to hit the nail
  on the head (be right)
dar golpes to hit
dar las cinco (seis) to strike
  five (six) (o'clock)
dar la mano to shake hands
dar mucha lata to annoy, bother
dar que hacer to give trouble
dar una bofetada to slap
dar una patada to kick
darse cuenta de to realize
darse una caída to fall
de of, from, about, by
de acuerdo agreed, in agreement
de buena gana willingly
de compras shopping
de mala gana unwillingly
de manera que so that
de memoria from memory,
  by heart
de modo que so that
de nada You're welcome.
de nuevo again
de prisa in a hurry
de pronto all of a sudden
de repente suddenly
de todos modos anyway
de una vez once and for all
de veras really
de vez en cuando from time
  to time
debajo de under, underneath
deber ought, must
débil weak
décima, -o tenth
decir to say, tell, speak
declarar to declare
decorar to decorate
dedicar to dedicate
dedo finger; toe
dejar to let, permit; to leave
dejar caer to drop
dejar de to stop, cease
del (de + el) of the
delante de in front of
demandar to demand, require

demasiada, -o too much
demasiadas, -os too many
demasiado too much, too
dentro de inside (of)
dentro de poco in a short while
derecha, -o right; straight
derretir (i) to melt
desaparecer to disappear
desarrollar to develop
desarrollo development
desayunar(se) to eat breakfast
desayuno breakfast
descansada, -o rested
descomponer to decompose; to go
  out of order, break
desconocida, -o unknown; stranger
descubrimiento discovery
descubrir to discover
desde from
desde luego of course, certainly
desde que since
desear to desire, wish, want
desgraciada, -o unfortunate
desierto desert
desobedecer to disobey
desocupada, -o unoccupied, va-
  cant
despacio slowly
despedir (i) to send off, dismiss
despedirse (i) de to say
  goodby to
despertar(se) (ie) to wake up,
  awaken
despierta, -o awake
después (de que) after, after-
  ward, later
después de todo after all
destapar to uncover, take the
  top off
determinar to determine
detrás (de) behind
devolver (ue) to return (something)
diálogo dialog
diaria, -o daily
diario diary; newspaper
día (el) day
dicho said, told; saying
diciembre December

diecinueve nineteen, nineteenth
dieciocho eighteen, eighteenth
dieciséis sixteen, sixteenth
diecisiete seventeen, seventeenth
diente tooth
diez ten
diferente different
difícil difficult
dificultad difficulty
dinero money
Dios God
dirección address; direction
director, -a principal, director
dirigir to direct
disculpar to excuse, pardon
discurso speech
diseño design
disgustada, -o disgusted, displeased
disgustar(se) to get upset; to disgust
disminuir to diminish
dispensar to excuse, pardon
dispuesta, -o (a) ready (to)
diversión amusement, entertainment
divertirse (ie) to have a good time
doblar to turn (a corner)
doce twelve
dólar dollar
doler (ue) to ache, pain
dolor ache, pain
domingo Sunday
donde where
dónde where
dormida, -o asleep
dormir (ue) to sleep
dormirse (ue) to go to sleep
dos two
doscientas, -os two hundred
droguería drug store
duda doubt
dudar to doubt
dulce sweet; candy
dulcería candy store
duplicar to duplicate
dura, -o hard
durante during
durar to last

E

e and
ecuador equator
ecuatoriana, -o Ecuadorian
echar to throw
echarse a llorar to burst out crying
echar a perder to spoil
echarse a reír to burst out laughing
echar de menos to miss
echar la casa por la ventana to throw a lively party
echar miradas to glance, throw glances
echar una carta al correo to mail a letter
edad age
edificio building
EE.UU. U.S.A.
ejemplo example
ejercicio exercise
ejército army
el the
él he, him
elefante elephant
elevar to elevate
eliminar to eliminate
ella she, her
ellas they, them
ellos they, them
empezar (ie) to begin
en in, on, at, into
en cuanto as soon as
en cuanto a as for, in regards to
en fin in short
en la actualidad at present
en lugar de instead of, in place of
en punto on the dot, sharp
en rodillas on one's knees
en seguida immediately
en todo caso in any event (case)
en vez de instead of
encender (ie) la luz to turn on the light
encima de on top of
encoger(se) to shrink
encontrar (ue) to find; to meet
enemiga, -o enemy

enero January
enferma, -o sick, ill
enfermera, -o nurse
enfrente (de) opposite, in front and facing
enfurecerse to become furious
enloquecerse to become crazy
enojar to anger
enojarse to become angry
enriquecerse to become rich
ensalada salad
ensayar to practice, rehearse
ensayo rehearsal, practice
entender (ie) to understand
enterarse de to find out
entierro burial
entonces then
entrada entrance, admission
entrar to come in, enter
entre among, between
entregar to give, hand
entretanto meanwhile
entristecerse to become sad
envejecerse to become old
envolver (ue) to wrap (up)
equivocada, -o mistaken
esa, ese that
escalera stairs, stairway, ladder
esas, esos those
esclava, -o slave
escoba broom
escoger to choose, select, pick out
esconder to hide
escribir to write
escrita, -o written
escritorio desk
escuela school
escupir to spit
eso that
eso es that's it, that's right
espacio space, blank
espada sword
España Spain
español Spanish
español, -a Spanish, Spaniard
espejo mirror
¡Espera! Wait
esperar to wait (for); hope
espíritu (el) spirit
esposa wife

esposo husband

esquiar to ski

esquiar sobre el agua to water ski

esquiar sobre la nieve to snow ski

esta this

esta noche tonight

estación season; station

estación de gasolina gasoline station

estación de policía police station

estadio stadium

estado state

Estados Unidos (E.U., EE.UU.) United States (U.S.)

estar to be

estar de acuerdo to agree (be in agreement)

estar de vuelta to be back (returned

estar segura, -o to be sure

estas, -os these

este this; (el) east

esto this

estrecha, -o narrow

estrecho strait

estrella star

estudiante student

estudiar to study

estudios studies

evaporar to evaporate

exacta, -o exact

exagerar to exaggerate

examen examination

excelente excellent

excepto except

exclamar to exclaim

éxito success

explicar to explain

exponer to expose

F

fábrica factory

fácil easy

falda skirt

falta lack; fault

familia family

famosa, -o famous

farmacia pharmacy, drugstore

febrero February

fecha date (calendar)

felicidad happiness

¡Felicidades! Congratulations!

fea, -o ugly

feliz happy

feroz fierce, ferocious

ferrocarril railroad (track)

fiebre (la) fever

fiera, -o fierce, wild

fiesta party; holiday

fin end

firmar to sign

flaca, -o thin, skinny

flor (la) flower

florería flower shop

formar to form

foto(grafía) photo(graph), picture

francés, -a French

frase (la) phrase; sentence

frecuencia frequency

frecuente frequent

freír (i) to fry

frente (la) forehead

fresca, -o fresh, cool

fría, -o cold

frijol bean

frío (el) cold

fruta fruit

fuego fire

fuente (la) fountain

fuera de outside of

fuerte strong

fumar to smoke

funeral funeral

furiosa, -o furious

G

gallina hen, chicken

ganadería cattle

ganar to earn

garaje garage

garganta throat

gasolina gasoline

gastar to spend

gata, -o cat

gente (la) people

geografía geography

gesto gesture

gigante giant

gimnasio gym(nasium)

golpe blow, hit

gorda, -o fat

gota drop

goma rubber

gracias thanks

gran great

grande big, large

gratis free (of charge)

grave seriously ill

gris gray

gritar to shout

guerra war

gustar to be pleasing; to like

gusto pleasure

H

haber to have

habitante inhabitant

hacer to do, make; to be

hacer falta to lack, need

hacer las compras to do the shopping

hacer los mandados to run errands

hacer . . . que ago, for (with expressions of time)

hacia to, toward

hallar to find, discover

hambre hunger

harina flour

hasta until; even

hasta que until

hay is, are, there is (are)

hecha, -o done; made

hecho (el) fact

hemisferio hemisphere

herir (ie) to wound

hermana sister

hermano brother

hermanos brothers, brother(s) and sister(s)

héroe hero

hervir (ie) to boil

hielo ice

hierba grass

hierro iron

*h*ija daughter
*h*ijo son
*h*ijos sons; children
*h*ilo thread
*h*imno hymn
*h*istoria history; story
*h*oja sheet (of paper); leaf
*h*ola hi, hello
*h*ombre man
*h*onda, -o deep
*h*onrada, -o honest
*h*ora hour, time
*h*oy today
*h*oy día nowadays
*h*uelga strike
*h*ueso bone
*h*uevo egg
*h*uir to flee
*h*úmeda, -o humid
*h*umilde humble
*h*undir to sink

I

idioma (el) language
iglesia church
igual equal, same
igualmente same to you; equally
ilustrar to illustrate
ima*g*inar to imagine
imitar to imitate
im*p*edir to prevent, impede
im*p*ermeable raincoat
im*p*oner to impose
importar to matter, be important
incómoda, -o uncomfortable
independen*c*ia independence
india, -o Indian
indicar to indicate
indí*g*ena native
informar to inform
in*g*eniero engineer
inglés, -a English
inigualable incomparable
injusta, -o unjust
in*m*ediatamente immediately
insistir to insist
inspirar to inspire
instalar to install

inteli*g*ente intelligent
interés interest
interesante interesting
intérprete interpreter, translator
inundar to flood
inútil useless
in*v*estigar to investigate
in*v*ierno winter
in*v*itación invitation
in*v*itada, -o guest
in*v*itar to invite
in*y*ec*c*ión shot, injection
ir to go
ir a pasear to take a walk
ir a pasear en coche to take a ride
ir a un juego de pelota to go to a ball game
ir de ca*z*a to go hunting
ir de co*m*pras to go shopping
ir de e*x*cursión to go camping
ir de pesca to go fishing
irse to leave, go away
isla island
italiana, -o Italian
i*z*quierda, -o left

J

ja*b*ón soap
jamón ham
jardín garden
jardinero gardener
*j*efe chief, boss
¡Jesús! Bless you!
joven young; young person
juego game
jue*v*es Thursday
jue*z* judge
jugar (ue) to play (a game)
jugo juice
julio July
junio June
junta meeting
junta, -o together, united
junto a next to
justa, -o just, right
ju*v*entud youth

L

la the, her, you, it
la*b*io lip
lado side
ladrar to bark
ladri*ll*o brick
lago lake
lágrima tear
lá*m*para lamp
lana wool
lápi*z* (el) pencil
larga, -o long
las the, them, you
lástima shame, pity
lata bother, annoyance; tin, can
latinoamericana, -o Latin American
la*v*adora washing machine
la*v*andería laundry shop
la*v*ar(se) to wash
le him, you; to him, her, you, it
lec*c*ión lesson
leche (la) milk
lechería dairy
lechuga lettuce
leer to read
legumbre vegetable
lejos (de) far, far away (from)
lengua tongue; language
león lion
les to them, you
letrero sign, poster
le*v*antar(se) to get up; to raise
li*b*erar to liberate
librería bookstore
libro book
liebre (la) hare, rabbit
li*g*era, -o light
limitar to limit
limón lemon
li*m*piar to clean
li*m*pia, -o clean
linda, -o pretty, beautiful
lista list, roll, roster
lista, -o ready
lo the, it, him, you
loca, -o crazy
lograr to succeed in

los   the; them, you
luchar   to struggle
luego   then; later
luego que   as soon as
lugar   place
luna   moon
lunes   Monday
luz (la)   light

Ll

llamar   to call; to knock
llamarse   to be called, named
llanta   tire
llanura   plain, flat land
llave (la)   key; faucet, tap
llegar   to arrive
llena, -o   full
llevar   to carry, take; to wear
llevar a cabo   to carry out, complete
llorar   to cry, weep
llover (ue)   to rain
llover (ue) a cántaros   to rain pitchforks, cats and dogs
lluvia   rain

M

madera   wood
madre (la)   mother
madrugar   to get up early
madura, -o   mature, ripe
maestra, -o   teacher
magnífica, -o   great, wonderful
mal   bad, badly, evil
mal (el)   evil
mala, -o   bad; sick, ill
maldecir   to curse
mamá   mother, mom
mandar   to order; to send
manejar   to drive
manera   manner, way
manifestación   demonstration
mano (la)   hand
manteca   lard
mantel   tablecloth
mantequilla   butter

manzana   apple
mañana (la)   morning; (el) tomorrow
mapa (el)   map
mar   sea
marido   husband
marinero   sailor
mariposa   butterfly
martes   Tuesday
marzo   March
más   more, most
más bien   rather
masticar   to chew
matar   to kill
mayo   May
mayor   older, oldest; larger, largest
mayoría   majority
me   me, to me
mecánico   mechanic
media, -o   half
medianoche (la)   midnight
medias   socks, hose
medicina   medicine
médico   doctor
mediodía (el)   noon
medir (i)   to measure
meditar   to meditate
mejor   better, best
mejorarse   to get better
memoria   memory
menor   younger (-est); minor
menos   minus, less
mentir (ie)   to lie
mentira   lie
mercado   market
merecer   to deserve
mes   month
mes que viene   next month
mesa   table
mestizo   half-breed
meter   to put (in, into)
mezcla   mixture
mi   my
mí   me
miedo   fear
miel (la)   honey
mientras   while
mientras que   while

mientras tanto   meanwhile
miércoles   Wednesday
mil   thousand
millón   million
mina   mine (iron, gold, etc.)
ministro   minister
minuto   minute
mirada   glance
mirar   to look (at)
misa   Mass
misma, -o   same
mitin   meeting
moda   fashion
molestar(se)   to bother
molestia   bother, trouble
momento   moment, minute
mona, -o   monkey
moneda   coin, change
montaña   mountain
montar a caballo   to ride horseback
morada, -o   purple
morder (ue)   to bite
morena, -o   brunet(te), dark
morir (ue)   to die
morir (ue) de hambre   to die of hunger, starve to death
mosca   fly
mostrar (ue)   to show
motocicleta   motorcycle
mover (ue)   to move
mucha, -o   much, many, a lot
muchacha   girl
muchacho   boy
muchachos   boys, boy(s) and girl(s)
muchísima, -o   a great deal, very much
mueble   piece of furniture
muebles   furniture
mueblería   furniture store
mujer (la)   woman; wife
multiplicar   to multiply
mundo   world
muñeca   doll; wrist
museo   museum
música   music
músico   musician
muy   very

N

nacer to be born
nación nation
nacional national
nada nothing, anything
nadar to swim
nadar en una piscina to swim in a pool
nadie nobody, no one, anybody
naranja orange
nariz (la) nose
navegar to navigate
necesaria, -o necessary
necesitar to need
negra, -o black; Negro
nerviosa, -o nervous
nevar (ie) to snow
ni . . . ni neither, nor
nido nest
niebla fog
nieta granddaughter
nieto grandson
nieve (la) snow
ningún none, any, no
ninguna, -o none, any, no
niña girl
niño boy
niños children, boy(s) and girl(s)
no no, not
no hay como there's nothing like
no le hace it doesn't matter
noche (la) night
nombre name
norte (el) north
nos us, to us, ourselves
nos vemos I'll be seeing you, see you later
nosotras, -os we, us
notar to note, notice
noticia news
novecientas, -os nine hundred
novena, -o ninth
noventa ninety
novia sweetheart; bride
noviembre November
novio sweetheart; groom
nube (la) cloud
nuestra, -o our, ours
nueva, -o new

nueve nine
número number
nunca never

O

o or
obedecer to obey
obligar to obligate, oblige
observar to observe
océano ocean
ochenta eighty
ocho eight
ochocientas, -os eight hundred
octava, -o eighth
octubre October
ocupar to occupy
oeste west
oficial officer
oficina office
ofrecer to offer
oído (inner) ear; hearing
oír to hear
ojala (que) I wish, may God grant, would that
ojo eye
¡Ojo! Look out!, Be careful!
oler (ue) to smell
olvidar(se) to forget
once eleven
operar to operate
oponer to oppose
oreja (outer) ear
organizar to organize
orgullosa, -o proud
oro gold
oscura, -o dark, obscure
oscurecer to grow dark
otoño fall, autumn
otra, -o other, another
oveja sheep

P

padre father; priest
padres parents, fathers
pagar to pay
página page
país country, nation

paisaje landscape
pájaro bird
palabra word
palo stick
pan bread
panadería bakery
pantalones (los) pants, trousers
pañuelo handkerchief
papa potato
papá father, dad
papel paper
para to, for, toward, in order to
para que in order that, so that
parada, -o standing
paraguaya, -o Paraguayan
parecer to seem, appear (to be)
parecerse a to look like
pared wall
pareja couple, pair
pariente relative
parque park
parte (la) part
partir to leave, depart
pasada, -o past
pasado mañana day after tomorrow
pasar to pass, enter; to spend (time); happen
pasear to go for a walk (drive, ride)
paseo drive (Elm Drive)
pastor shepherd
pata paw, foot, leg (of an animal)
patada kick
patillas (las) sideburns
patinar to skate
patinar en ruedas to roller skate
patinar sobre el hielo to ice skate
paz (la) peace
pecado sin
pecar to sin
pedir (i) to order, request, ask for
pedir (i) prestada, -o to borrow
pelear to fight
película film, movie
peligro danger
pelirroja, -o redhead
pelo hair
pelota ball

peluquería barber shop

pena trouble, embarrassment, shame

penetrar to penetrate

pensamiento thought

pensar (ie) to think; to intend, plan

peor worse, worst

pequeña, -o little, small

perder (ie) to lose; to miss; to spoil

perdón pardon

¡Perdón! Pardon me!, Excuse me!

perdonar to pardon

perezosa, -o lazy

¡Perfecto! Perfect!, Fine!, That's it!

periódico newspaper

periodista reporter

permiso permission, permit

permitir to permit, allow

pero but

perro dog

persona person

pertenecer to belong (to)

peruana, -o Peruvian

pesada, -o heavy

pesadilla nightmare

pescado (caught) fish

pescador fisherman

pescar to fish

peseta monetary unit of Spain

peso peso (monetary unit)

pez (el) (live) fish

pie foot

piedra stone

piel (la) skin, pelt

¡Piensa! Think!

pierna leg

pijama (payama) pajamas

píldora pill

pimienta pepper

pino pine

pintar to paint, color

piscina (swimming) pool

piso floor

pizarra blackboard

placer pleasure

plancha iron

planchar to iron

plástico plastic

plata silver

plátano banana

plato plate; dish

playa beach

pluma pen, feather

población population

pobre poor

poca, -o little, few, a little

poder (ue) to be able, can, may

poder power

poderosa, -o powerful

policía (la) police

policía (el) policeman

político politician

Polo Norte North Pole

pollo chicken

poner to place, put; to set; to turn on

poner en marcha to get going, start

poner huevos to lay eggs

ponerse to put on, become

ponerse celosa, -o to become jealous

ponerse furiosa, -o to become furious

ponerse seria, -o to become serious

poquito a little bit

por through, by, per, for, in behalf of; across; on account of

por aquí this way

por consiguiente consequently

por eso because of that, therefore

Por favor. Please.

por fin finally

por lo general generally

por lo menos at least

por lo pronto for the time being

por lo tanto therefore

por qué why

por regla general as a general rule

por si acaso just in case

por supuesto of course

porque because

portarse bien to behave well

portarse mal to misbehave

portugués, -a Portuguese

posponer to postpone

postre dessert

practicar to practice

precisa, -o necessary

predecir to predict

pregunta question

preguntar to ask (questions)

preocuparse to worry

preparar to prepare

presentar to present, introduce

presente present

preservar to preserve

prestar to lend

prima, -o cousin

primavera spring (season)

primer first

primera, -o first

primos cousins

principal main

principio beginning

prisa hurry, haste

privada, -o private

problema (el) problem

profesor, -a teacher, professor

programa (el) program

prohibir to prohibit, forbid

prometer to promise

pronto soon, fast

pronunciar to pronounce

propia, -o own, one's own

proponer to propose

propósito purpose

proteger to protect

provecho profit, good, benefit

próxima, -o next

prueba proof

psicólogo psychologist

pública, -o public

publicar to publish

pueblo people; town, village

puente bridge

puerta door

puerto (sea, river) port

puesta, -o put

puesto job, position

pulgada inch

pulgar thumb

pulmón lung

pupitre (pupil's) desk

Q

que   what, that, which, who
qué   what, how
¡Qué barbaridad!   How terrible!
¡Qué casualidad!   What a coincidence!
¿Qué pasó?   What happened!
¿Qué sé yo?   How should I know!
quebrar (ie)   to break
quedarse   to remain, stay
quehacer (el)   chore
quehaceres de casa   household chores
quemar   to burn
querer (ie)   to want, wish; to love
queso   cheese
quien   who, whom
quién   who, whom
quince   fifteen, fifteenth
quinientas, -os   five hundred
quinta, -o   fifth
quitar(se)   to take off; to take away

R

raíz (la)   root
rancho   ranch, farm
rápida, -o   fast, quick, rapid
rápidamente   rapidly, fast, quickly
rara vez   seldom
rascacielo(s)   skyscraper
rastrillo   rake
rato   while
ratón   mouse
razón (la)   reason
receta   prescription; recipe
recibir   to receive, get
recoger   to gather, pick up
recoger las cosas   to pick up things
recomendar (ie)   to recommend
reconocer   to recognize
recordar (ue)   to remember, recall
recta, -o   straight
redonda, -o   round
refrán   proverb, saying

regalar   to give presents
regalo   gift, present
regañar   to scold
regar (ie)   to water, irrigate
regar (ie) las flores   to water the flowers
regatear   to bargain
regla   ruler, rule
regresar   to return, come back
regular   fair; regular
reina   queen
reír(se)   to laugh
relatar   to tell, relate
reloj (el)   clock, watch
repartir   to share, distribute
repasar   to review
repetir (i)   to repeat
reponer   to replace
representar   to represent
rescatar   to rescue
resistir   to endure, resist
resolver (ue)   to solve; to resolve
respirar   to breathe
responder   to answer, respond
respuesta   answer
resto   rest, remainder
reunión (la)   meeting
reunir(se)   to meet
revelar   to reveal
revista   magazine
rey   king
rica, -o   rich
río   river
riqueza   wealth, riches
rodear   to surround
rogar (ue)   to beg, plead
roja, -o   red
romper   to break
ropa   clothes
rosa   rose
rosada, -o   pink
rosario   rosary
rubia, -o   blond(e)
rueda   wheel
ruido   noise

S

sábado   Saturday
saber   to know

saber de memoria   to know by heart
sabia, -o   wise
sacar   to take out
sacar la basura   to take out the trash (garbage)
saco   coat
sacudir   to shake; to dust
sacudir los muebles   to dust the furniture
sal (la)   salt
sala   living room, room
salario   salary, wages
salida   exit; departure
salir   to leave, go out
salir bien   to come out well
salir mal   to come out poorly
saltar   to jump
salud   health
¡Salud!   Bless you!
san   saint (San Patricio)
sangre (la)   blood
sangrienta, -o   bloody
santa, -o   saint, holy
santo   saint's day
satélite   satellite
satisfacer   to satisfy
satisfecha, -o   satisfied
se   self; to him, her, them, you
¿Se puede?   May I come in?
seca, -o   dry
secretaria, -o   secretary
secundaria, -o   secondary
sed   thirst
seda   silk
seguir (i)   to continue; to follow
según   according to
segunda, -o   second
segura, -o   sure
seis   six
seiscientas, -os   six hundred
selva   jungle
semana   week
semejante   similar
semejanza   similarity
semestre   semester
sencilla, -o   simple
sentada, -o   seated
sentar (ie)   to seat
sentarse (ie)   to sit down

sentir (ie) to feel; to regret, be sorry
señor Mr., sir, man, gentleman
señora Mrs., lady, wife
señorita Miss, young lady
separar to separate
septiembre September
séptima, -o seventh
ser to be
ser (el) being
seria, -o serious
servilleta napkin
servir (i) to serve; to help
sesenta sixty
setecientas, -os seven hundred
setenta seventy
sexta, -o sixth
si if, whether
sí yes
sicólogo psychologist
siempre always
siempre que whenever
siesta nap
siete seven
siglo century
significar to mean, signify
siguiente following
silla chair
sillón armchair
simpática, -o nice, cute, pleasant
sin without
sin embargo nevertheless
sin que without
sino but
sistema (el) system
sobre on, over; about
sobrina niece
sobrino nephew
sobrinos nephews, niece(s) and nephew(s)
¡Socorro! Help!
sofá (el) sofa, couch, divan
sol sun
sola, -o alone, single
solamente only
soldado soldier
sólo only
soltera, -o unmarried, single
sombrero hat
sonreír (i) to smile

soñar (ue) to dream
sopa soup
sorda, -o deaf
sorprender to surprise
sorprenderse to become surprised
Sr. (Sra., Srta.) Mr. (Mrs., Miss)
su his, her, its, their, your
suave soft
subir to climb, go up
suceder to happen
sucia, -o dirty
sud south
suegra mother-in-law
suegro father-in-law
sueño sleep; dream
suerte (la) luck
suéter sweater
sufrir to suffer
sugerir (ie) to suggest
sumamente exceedingly
suntuosa, -o sumptuous
superficie (la) area, surface
supermercado supermarket
suponer to suppose
sur south

T

tabaco tobacco; cigar
tacaña, -o stingy, tightwad
tal such, such a
tal vez perhaps
también also, too
tampoco neither, either
tan so, as
tan . . . como as . . . as
tanta, -o . . . como as much (many) . . . as
tanto como as much as
tan pronto como as soon as
tapar to cover, cap
tarde (la) afternoon, evening
tarde late
tarea task, homework
taza cup
te you, to you, yourself
té tea
techo roof
tela cloth

teléfono telephone
temer to fear
temprano early
tender (ie) to hang
tender (ie) la ropa to hang the clothes (to dry)
tenedor fork
tener to have, possess
tener . . . años to be . . . years old
tener calor to be hot
tener catarro to have a cold
tener éxito to be successful
tener frío to be cold
tener ganas de to feel like
tener hambre to be hungry
tener la culpa to be to blame
tener mala pata to have bad luck
tener miedo to be afraid
tener prisa to be in a hurry
tener que to have to
tener razón to be right
tener sed to be thirsty
tener sueño to be sleepy
tener suerte to be lucky
tenga la bondad de please
teñir (i) to dye
tercer third
tercera, -o third
terminar to finish, terminate, end
terminar de to finish (stop) (doing something)
tertulia tertulia (a social gathering)
ti you
tía aunt
tiempo time; weather
tienda store, tent
tierra earth, land, dirt
tigre tiger; cougar, mountain lion
tío uncle
tíos uncles, aunt(s) and uncle(s)
tipo type, kind
tirar to shoot; to throw
título title
tiza chalk
tocar to touch; to play (musical instrument)
toda, -o all, every
todavía still, yet

todo everything

todo el mundo everybody; all the world

tomar to take; to drink; to eat

tomar el pelo to tease, pull someone's leg

tomate tomato

tonta, -o foolish, silly; fool

torcida, -o crooked, twisted

tormenta storm

toro bull

torre (la) tower

toser to cough

total total

trabajar to work

trabajo job, work

tradición tradition

traducir to translate

traer to bring

traje suit

trampa trap

transformar to transform

transportar to transport

tranvía (el) streetcar

trascurso course (of time)

tratar (de) to try

trece thirteen, thirteenth

trecho stretch, space, gap

treinta thirty

tremenda, -o tremendous

tren train

tres three

trescientas, -os three hundred

trigo wheat

triste sad

tropezar (ie) to trip, stumble

trozo piece

tu your

tú you

tuerta, -o one-eyed

túnel tunnel

U

u or

Ud. = usted you

Uds. = ustedes you

última, -o last, final

un a, an, one

una, -o a, an, one

única, -o only, unique; only one

unir to unite

universidad university

uña nail (of the finger or toe)

uruguaya, -o Uruguayan

usar to use; to wear

usted you

útil useful

V

vacaciones vacation

vacía, -o empty

valer to be worth

valer la pena to be worth the effort

valiente brave, valiant

vamos a let's

variar to vary

varias, -os various, several

vaso glass

vecina, -o neighbor

vegetal vegetable

veinte twenty, twentieth

veintiún twenty-one

veintiuna, -o twenty-one

veinticinco twenty-five

veinticuatro twenty-four

veintidós twenty-two

veintinueve twenty-nine

veintiocho twenty-eight

veintiséis twenty-six

veintisiete twenty-seven

veintitrés twenty-three

vejez (la) old age

velocidad speed, velocity

velocímetro speedometer

velorio wake

vencer to overcome, conquer

venda bandage

vendar to bandage

vender to sell

venezolana, -o Venezuelan

venir to come

ventana window

ventanilla car window

ver to see

verano summer

verdad truth

¿Verdad? Isn't it true?, Right?

verdadera, -o true, real

verde green, unripe

vestido dress; clothes

vestir (i) (se) to dress, get dressed

vez (la) time, repetition

viajar to travel

viaje trip

víbora snake, viper

vida life

vieja, -o old

viento wind

viernes Friday

vino wine

violenta, -o violent

virgen (la) virgin

virrey (el) viceroy

visita visit

visitar to visit

vivir to live

vocabulario vocabulary

volar (ue) to fly

voluntad will (power)

volver (ue) to return

volver (ue) a to (do something) again

voz (la) voice

vuelta, -o returned

Y

y and

ya already

ya no no longer

ya que since

yo I

Z

zambullirse to dive

zanahoria carrot

zapatería shoe store

zapato shoe

zoológico zoo

Index

Each entry is followed by the numbers of the Assignments in which it occurs. To find the **page number** of an Assignment, refer to the Table of Contents on pp. ix–xiii. Most entries are first presented in the Assignments. A few entries, presented initially in class, are practiced intensively in succeeding classes, both alone and in combination with other exercises. They are also reinforced as an integral part of subsequent Assignments.

Most irregular **verb forms** are listed by infinitive. To find regular verb forms and irregular verb forms that fall into sets, look under the name of a particular tense. For example, under *estar* you would find references for the present indicative and preterit forms (which are irregular), as well as uses of *estar* which contrast with other translations of "to be." Since the imperfect forms of *estar* are regular you would look under "imperfect, forms of regular verbs."

To find information on an **individual letter or sound,** refer to "pronunciation" and "spelling."

A

Y se va

Moderato

El cla - vel que tú me dis - te el dí - a de la A - sun - ción,

no fue cla - vel si - no cla - vo que cla - vó mi co - ra - zón.

Coro:

Y se va, y se va por el me - dio de las o - las

y las o - las me res - pon - den, ya tu a - mor no vuel - ve más.

Y se va

El clavel que tú me diste
el día de la Asunción,
no fue clavel sino clavo
que clavó mi corazón.

Coro:
Y se va, y se va
por el medio de las olas
y las olas me responden,
ya tu amor no vuelve más.

El clavel para ser doble
No ha de ser de dos colores.
La mujer para ser fiel
no ha de amar dos corazones.

Si me pierdo que me busquen
bajo el sol de Andalucía,
donde nacen las morenas,
y donde la sal se cría.

She's Going Away

The carnation that you gave me
on the Day of the Assumption
was not a carnation (*clavel*) but a nail (*clavo*)
that you drove (*clavó*) into my heart.

Coro:
And she's going away, and she's going away
over the waves,
and the waves answer me,
your love will never more return.

The carnation in order to be double
must not be of two colors.
Woman in order to be faithful
must not love two hearts.

If I should get lost, let them seek me
under the sun of Andalucía,
where brunettes are born,
and charm abounds.

Las mañanitas

Es - tas son las ma - ña - ni - tas que can - ta - ba el rey Da - vid,

Ins - pi - ra - das y bo - ni - tas, te las can - ta - mos a ti.

Des - pier - ta, mi bien, des - pier - ta, mi - ra que ya a - ma - ne - ció,

Ya los pa - ja - ri - tos can - tan, la lu - na ya se me - tió.

Las mañanitas

Estas son las mañanitas
que cantaba el rey David,
Inspiradas y bonitas,
te las cantamos a ti.

Coro:
Despierta, mi bien, despierta,
mira que ya amaneció,
Ya los pajaritos cantan,
la luna ya se metió.

Estas son las mañanitas
que cantaba el rey David,
Hoy por ser día de tu santo
te las cantamos a ti.

¡Qué bonitas mañanitas
con su cielo de zafir,
Con su sol resplandeciente
que nos alegra el vivir!

Mañanitas mexicanas
que nos causan frenesí,
Mañanitas de mi tierra,
no hay otras que sean así.

The Mañanitas

These are the *mañanitas*
that King David sang,
Inspired and beautiful,
we sing them to you.

Coro:
Awake, my love, awake,
notice that it is already daylight,
Already the little birds are singing,
and the moon has set.

These are the *mañanitas*
that King David sang,
Because today is your Saint's Day,
we sing them to you.

What beautiful *mañanitas*
with their sky of sapphire,
With their shining sun
that makes us glad to be alive!

Mexican *mañanitas*
that excite us,
Mañanitas of my land,
there are no others like them.

Arrorró mi niño

A - rro - rró mi   ni - ño,   a - rro - rró mi sol,

a - rro - rró pe - da - zo   de mi co - ra - zón.

Arrorró mi niño

Arrorró mi niño,
arrorró mi sol,
arrorró pedazo
de mi corazón.

Este niño lindo
ya quiere dormir.
Hágale la cuna
de rosa y jazmín.

Esta leche linda
que le traigo aquí
es para este niño
que se va a dormir.

Arrorró My Child

Arrorró my child,
arrorró my sun (light of my life)
arrorró dear
heart (piece of my heart).

This pretty child
no longer wants to sleep.
Fix the cradle for him
with roses and jasmine.

This nice milk
that I bring here for him
is for this child
who is going to fall asleep.

Photo Acknowledgements

p. ii   Owen Franken, Stock/Boston   Caracas, Venezuela
pp. xiv-1   Owen Franken, Stock/Boston   Caracas, Venezuela
p. 67   Owen Franken, Stock/Boston   Santiago, Chile
pp. 106–107   Owen Franken, Stock/Boston   Santiago, Chile
p. 146   Owen Franken, Stock/Boston   Santiago, Chile
p. 190   Owen Franken, Stock/Boston   Caracas, Venezuela
pp. 214–215   Shari G. Kessler   Cartageña, Colombia
p. 261   Owen Franken, Stock/Boston   Caracas, Venezuela
p. 274 top   Peter Jarvis   Boston, Mass.
p. 274 bot   Editorial Photocolor Archives   New York, N.Y.
facing p. 274 top   © Charles Harbutt, Magnum Photos   California
facing p. 274 bot   © Charles Harbutt, Magnum Photos   New York, N.Y.
facing p. 275 top   Owen Franken, Stock/Boston   Venezuela
facing p. 275 bot   Owen Franken, Stock/Boston   Santiago, Chile
p. 275   Peter Jarvis   Cartageña, Colombia
p. 306 top   Owen Franken, Stock/Boston   Caracas, Venezuela
p. 306 bot   Owen Franken, Stock/Boston   Caracas, Venezuela
facing p. 306 top   Owen Franken, Stock/Boston   Venezuela
facing p. 306 bot   Owen Franken, Stock/Boston   Viña del Mar, Chile
facing p. 307 top   Owen Franken, Stock/Boston   Palmer, Puerto Rico
facing p. 307 bot   Owen Franken, Stock/Boston   Bolivia
p. 307   Owen Franken, Stock/Boston   Bolivia
p. 315   Owen Franken, Stock/Boston   Cuzco, Peru
pp. 330–331   Owen Franken, Stock/Boston   Caracas, Venezuela
p. 361   Lynn McLaren   Honduras
p. 420   Shari G. Kessler   Saquisili, Ecuador
pp. 434–435   Lynn McLaren   Honduras
p. 490 top   Owen Franken, Stock/Boston   Caracas, Venezuela
p. 490 bot   Paul Conklin   San Lorenzo, Peru
p. 530   Transocean Press   Argentina
facing p. 530 top   Eric Simmons, Stock/Boston   Lima, Peru
facing p. 530 bot   Transocean Press   Argentina
facing p. 531 top   Transocean Press   Argentina
facing p. 531 bot   © Howard Harrison   Havana, Cuba
p. 538   John Running, Stock/Boston   Mexico
facing p. 562 top   Owen Franken, Stock/Boston   near Cuzco, Peru
facing p. 562 bot   Shari G. Kessler   Huila, Colombia
facing p. 563 top   Jacques Jangoux   Suriqui Island, Bolivia
facing p. 563 bot lt   Josef Muench   Antigua, Guatemala
facing p. 563 bot rt   Owen Franken, Stock/Boston   Pisaq, Peru
pp. 574–575   Owen Franken, Stock/Boston   Caracas, Venezuela
p. 613   Owen Franken, Stock/Boston   Venezuela
p. 648   Shari G. Kessler   Quito, Ecuador
p. 682   Cornell Capa, Magnum Photos   Honduras